This is a Pornographic Picture

Brad Farwell

This is a Pornographic Picture

AWMA

Published by Another White Male Artist, Brooklyn NY.

www.bradfarwell.com

Paperback Edition, August 2012

ISBN 978-0-9882093-0-5

This book records every bit (either a zero or a one) of a small pornographic JPEG found on the Internet in 2009.

11111111

11011000 11111111 11100001 00110100 00011100 01000101 01111000 01101001 01100110 00000000
00000000 01001001 01001001 00101010 00000000 00001000 00000000 00000000 00000000 00010101
00000000 00001111 00000001 00000010 00000000 00001010 00000000 00000000 00000000 00001010
00000001 00000000 00000000 00010000 00000001 00000010 00000000 00001000 00000000 00000000
00000000 00010100 00000001 00000000 00000000 00010010 00000001 00000011 00000000 00000001
00000000 00000000 00000000 00000001 00000000 00000000 00000000 00011010 00000001 00000101
00000000 00000001 00000000 00000000 00000000 00011100 00000001 00000000 00000000 00011011
00000001 00000101 00000000 00000001 00000000 00000000 00000000 00100100 00000001 00000000
00000000 00101000 00000001 00000011 00000000 00000001 00000000 00000000 00000000 00000010
00000000 00000000 00000000 00110001 00000001 00000010 00000000 00001010 00000000 00000000
00000000 00101100 00000001 00000000 00000000 00110010 00000001 00000010 00000000 00010100
00000000 00000000 00000000 00110110 00000001 00000000 00000000 00010011 00000010 00000011
00000000 00000001 00000000 00000000 00000000 00000010 00000000 00000000 00000000 01101001
10000111 00000100 00000000 00000001 00000000 00000000 00000000 00100010 00000010 00000000
00000000 00000001 10100100 00000011 00000000 00000001 00000000 00000000 00000000 00000000
00000000 00000000 00000000 00000010 10100100 00000011 00000000 00000001 00000000 00000000
00000000 00000000 00000000 00000000 00000000 00000011 10100100 00000011 00000000 00000001
00000000 00000000 00000000 00000000 00000000 00000000 00000000 00000100 10100100 00000101
00000000 00000001 00000000 00000000 00000000 01001010 00000001 00000000 00000000 00000101
10100100 00000011 00000000 00000001 00000000 00000000 00000000 00100011 00000000 00000000
00000000 00000110 10100100 00000011 00000000 00000001 00000000 00000000 00000000 00000000
00000000 00000000 00000000 00000111 10100100 00000011 00000000 00000001 00000000 00000000
00000000 00000001 00000000 00000000 00000000 00001000 10100100 00000011 00000000 00000001
00000000 00000000 00000000 00000000 00000000 00000000 00000000 00001001 10100100 00000011
00000000 00000001 00000000 00000000 00000000 00000000 00000000 00000000 00000000 00001010
10100100 00000011 00000000 00000001 00000000 00000000 00000000 00000000 00000000 00000000
00000000 10100101 11000100 00000111 00000000 11010000 00000000 00000000 00000000 01010010
00000001 00000000 00000000 11110000 00011001 00000000 00000000 01010000 01100001 01101110
01100001 01110011 01101111 01101110 01101001 01100011 00000000 01000100 01001101 01000011
00101101 01000110 01011000 00111000 00000000 01001000 00000000 00000000 00000000 00000001
00000000 00000000 00000000 01001000 00000000 00000000 00000000 00000001 00000000 00000000
00000000 01010110 01100101 01110010 00101110 00110001 00101110 00110000 00100000 00100000
00000000 00110010 00110000 00110000 00110110 00111010 00110000 00110010 00111010 00110010
00110111 00100000 00110000 00110000 00111010 00110010 00110111 00111010 00110000 00110011
00000000 00000000 00000000 00000000 00000000 00001010 00000000 00000000 00000000 01010000
01110010 01101001 01101110 01110100 01001001 01001101 00000000 00110000 00110010 00110101
00110000 00000000 00000000 00001110 00000000 00000001 00000000 00010110 00000000 00010110
00000000 00000010 00000000 00000000 00000000 00000000 00000000 00000011 00000000 01100100
00000000 00000000 00000000 00000111 00000000 00000000 00000000 00000000 00000000 00001000
00000000 00000000 00000000 00000000 00000000 00001001 00000000 00000000 00000000 00000000
00000000 00001010 00000000 00000000 00000000 00000000 00000000 00001011 00000000 10101100
00000000 00000000 00000000 00001100 00000000 00000000 00000000 00000000 00000000 00001101
00000000 00000000 00000000 00000000 00000000 00001110 00000000 11000100 00000000 00000000
00000000 00000000 00000001 00000101 00000000 00000000 00000000 00000001 00000001 00000001
00000000 00000000 00000000 00010000 00000001 10000000 00000000 00000000 00000000 00001001
00010001 00000000 00000000 00010000 00100111 00000000 00000000 00001011 00001111 00000000
00000000 00010000 00100111 00000000 00000000 10010111 00000101 00000000 00000000 00010000
00100111 00000000 00000000 10110000 00001000 00000000 00000000 00010000 00100111 00000000
00000000 00000001 00011100 00000000 00000000 00010000 00100111 00000000 00000000 01011110
00000010 00000000 00000000 00010000 00100111 00000000 00000000 10001011 00000000 00000000
00000000 00010000 00100111 00000000 00000000 11001011 00000011 00000000 00000000 00010000
00100111 00000000 00000000 11100101 00011011 00000000 00000000 00010000 00100111 00000000
00000000 00000000 00000000 00000000 00000000 00000000 00000000 00000000 00000000 00000000
00000000 00000000 00000000 00000000 00000000 00000000 00000000 00000000 00000000 00000000
00000000 00000000 00000000 00000000 00000000 00000000 00000000 00000000 00000000 00000000
00000000 00000000 00000000 00000000 00000000 00000000 00000000 00010111 00000000 10011010
10000010 00000101 00000000 00000001 00000000 00000000 00000000 00111100 00000011 00000000
00000000 10011101 10000010 00000101 00000000 00000001 00000000 00000000 00000000 01000100
00000011 00000000 00000000 00100010 10001000 00000011 00000000 00000001 00000000 00000000
00000000 00000010 00000000 00000100 00000000 00100111 10001000 00000011 00000000 00000001
00000000 00000000 00000000 11001000 00000000 00000100 00000100 00000000 10010000 00000111
00000000 00000100 00000000 00000000 00000000 00110000 00110010 00110010 00110000 00000011
10010000 00000010 00000000 00010100 00000000 00000000 00000000 01001100 00000011 00000000
00000000 00000100 10010000 00000010 00000000 00010100 00000000 00000000 00000000 01100000
00000011 00000000 00000000 00000001 10010001 00000111 00000000 00000100 00000000 00000000
00000000 00000001 00000010 00000011 00000000 00000010 10010001 00000101 00000000 00000001
00000000 00000000 00000000 01110100 00000011 00000000 00000000 00000100 10010010 00001010
00000000 00000001 00000000 00000000 00000000 01111100 00000011 00000000 00000000 00000101
10010010 00000101 00000000 00000001 00000000 00000000 00000000 10000100 00000011 00000000
00000000 00000111 10010010 00000011 00000000 00000001 00000000 00000000 00000000 00000101
00000000 01001011 00000001 00001000 10010010 00000011 00000000 00000001 00000000 00000000
00000000 00000000 00000000 00000011 00000000 00001001 10010010 00000011 00000000 00000001
00000000 00000000 00000000 00010000 00000000 01110100 01010101 00001010 10010010 00000101

00000000 00000001 00000000 00000000 00000000 10001100 00000011 00000000 00000000 01111100
10010010 00000111 00000000 01011100 00010110 00000000 00000000 10010100 00000011 00000000
00000000 00000000 10100000 00000111 00000000 00000100 00000000 00000000 00000000 00110000
00110001 00110000 00110000 00000001 10100000 00000011 00000000 00000001 00000000 00000000
00000000 00000001 00000000 00000000 00000000 00000010 10100000 00000100 00000000 00000001
00000000 00000000 00000000 00000000 00001000 00000000 00000000 00000011 10100000 00000100
00000000 00000001 00000000 00000000 00000000 00000000 00000110 00000000 00000000 00010111
10100010 00000011 00000000 00000001 00000000 00000000 00000000 00000010 00000000 00000000
00001010 00000000 10100011 00000111 00000000 00000001 00000000 00000000 00000000 00000011
00000000 00000001 00000000 00000001 10100011 00000111 00000000 00000001 00000000 00000000
00000000 00000001 00010000 00000111 00000000 00000000 00000000 00000000 00000000 00001010
00000000 00000000 00000000 01010000 00000000 00000000 00000000 00011100 00000000 00000000
00000000 00001010 00000000 00000000 00000000 00110010 00110000 00110000 00110110 00111010
00110000 00110010 00111010 00110010 00110111 00100000 00110000 00110000 00111010 00110010
00110111 00111010 00110000 00110011 00000000 00110010 00110000 00110000 00110110 00111010
00110000 00110010 00111010 00110010 00110111 00100000 00110000 00110000 00111010 00110010
00110111 00111010 00110000 00110011 00000000 00000100 00000000 00000000 00000000 00000001
00000000 00000000 00000000 00000000 00000000 00000000 00000000 01100100 00000000 00000000
00000000 00011110 00000000 00000000 00000000 00001010 00000000 00000000 00000000 00111010
00000000 00000000 00000000 00001010 00000000 00000000 00000000 01010000 01100001 01101110
01100001 01110011 01101111 01101110 01101001 01100011 00000000 00000000 00000000 00011100
00000000 00000001 00000000 00000011 00000000 00000001 00000000 00000000 00000000 00000010
00000000 00000000 00000000 00000010 00000000 00000111 00000000 00000100 00000000 00000000
00000000 00000000 00000001 00000000 00000101 00000011 00000000 00000011 00000000 00000001
00000000 00000000 00000000 00000001 00000000 00000000 00000000 00000111 00000000 00000011
00000000 00000001 00000000 00000000 00000000 00000001 00000000 00000000 00000000 00001111
00000000 00000001 00000000 00000010 00000000 00000000 00000000 00010000 00000000 00000000
00000000 00011010 00000000 00000011 00000000 00000001 00000000 00000000 00000000 00000010
00000000 00000000 00000000 00011100 00000000 00000011 00000000 00000001 00000000 00000000
00000000 00000010 00000000 00000000 00000000 00011111 00000000 00000011 00000000 00000001
00000000 00000000 00000000 00000001 00000000 00000000 00000000 00100000 00000000 00000011
00000000 00000001 00000000 00000000 00000000 00000010 00000000 00000000 00000000 00100001
00000000 00000111 00000000 11011010 00010100 00000000 00000000 11110110 00000100 00000000
00000000 00100010 00000000 00000011 00000000 00000001 00000000 00000000 00000000 00000000
00000000 00000000 00000000 00100011 00000000 00000011 00000000 00000001 00000000 00000000
00000000 00000000 00000000 00000000 00000000 00100100 00000000 00000011 00000000 00000001
00000000 00000000 00000000 00000000 00000000 00000000 00000000 00100101 00000000 00000111
00000000 00010000 00000000 00000000 00000000 11010000 00011001 00000000 00000000 00100110
00000000 00000111 00000000 00000100 00000000 00000000 00000000 00110000 00110001 00110000
00110011 00100111 00000000 00000011 00000000 00000001 00000000 00000000 00000000 00000000
00000000 00000000 00000000 00101000 00000000 00000011 00000000 00000001 00000000 00000000
00000000 00000001 00000000 00000000 00000000 00101001 00000000 00000100 00000000 00000001
00000000 00000000 00000000 01110110 01001101 00000001 00000000 00101010 00000000 00000011
00000000 00000001 00000000 00000000 00000000 00000000 00000000 00000000 00000000 00101011
00000000 00000100 00000000 00000001 00000000 00000000 00000000 00000000 00000000 00000000
00000000 00101100 00000000 00000011 00000000 00000001 00000000 00000000 00000000 00000000
00000000 00000000 00000000 00101101 00000000 00000011 00000000 00000001 00000000 00000000
00000000 00000000 00000000 00000000 00000000 00101110 00000000 00000011 00000000 00000001
00000000 00000000 00000000 00000010 00000000 00000000 00000000 00101111 00000000 00000011
00000000 00000001 00000000 00000000 00000000 00000001 00000000 00000000 00000000 00110000
00000000 00000011 00000000 00000001 00000000 00000000 00000000 00000001 00000000 00000000
00000000 00110001 00000000 00000011 00000000 00000001 00000000 00000000 00000000 00000001
00000000 00000000 00000000 00110010 00000000 00000011 00000000 00000001 00000000 00000000
00000000 00000000 00000000 00000000 00000000 00110011 00000000 00000010 00000000 00010100
00000000 00000000 00000000 11100000 00011001 00000000 00000000 01000100 01010110 00000001
00000010 01000101 01010000 00000000 00000000 11110000 00111111 01000100 01000010 01001000
00000011 11110000 00111111 01000001 01000110 10010010 00000000 01100000 01000111 00100000
10000000 01100010 01000111 00010001 00000001 01100100 01000111 00010000 00000000 01100110
01000111 00000000 00000000 01001110 01000111 01110100 00000000 01110010 01000111 00000111
00000000 01110100 01000111 00000010 00000000 01111010 01000111 00000010 00000000 01111100
01000111 11111000 11111111 01111110 01000111 00000000 00000000 01000000 01000111 01111011
00000010 01000010 01000111 10100110 01000000 01001100 01000111 11010000 00000111 01011100
01000111 01010110 00000000 01110110 01000111 10000000 00000000 01111000 01000111 00000000
00000000 01010010 01000111 00010001 00000001 01010110 01000111 00010100 00000000 01010100
01000111 00111100 00000000 01101100 01000111 01110001 00000001 01110000 01000111 00011110
00000000 01101110 01000111 01000110 00000000 01011000 01000111 00000000 00000000 10011110
01000111 01010000 00000000 10011100 01000111 11001000 00000000 10001100 01000111 00000000
00000000 10001110 01000111 00000001 00000000 10001010 01000111 10100110 01000000 10010000
01000111 00000001 00000000 10010010 01000111 00000001 00000000 10010100 01000111 00000000
00000000 10010110 01000111 00000000 00000000 10011000 01000111 10001100 00001000 10011010
01000111 00000000 00000000 11111010 01000111 00000010 01010100 11110000 00111111 01010011
01010100 01001010 00000000 10100100 01000110 00000000 00000000 10100110 01000110 00000000
00000000 10101000 01000110 00000000 00000000 10101010 01000110 00000000 00000000 10101100

01000110 00000000 00000000 11111000 01000111 00000000 00000000 10101110 01000110 00000000
00000000 10110000 01000110 00000000 00000000 10110110 01000110 00000000 00000000 10111000
01000110 00000000 00000000 10111010 01000110 00000000 00000000 11110100 01000111 00000000
00000000 11110110 01000111 00000000 00000000 10110010 01000110 00000000 00000000 10110100
01000110 00000000 00000000 10110000 01000100 00000000 00000000 10110010 01000100 00000000
00000000 11110000 00111111 01000001 01000101 11001010 00000000 00111100 01000101 00001000
00000000 00010100 01000101 00110100 00000001 11101010 01000110 01000000 00000001 00101000
01000101 11100000 00000001 00101100 01000101 11100000 00000001 00100100 01000101 10010010
00000001 00010000 01000101 00110110 00000010 00010010 01000101 00011110 00000010 00100000
01000101 11110111 00000001 00110110 01000101 10110110 00000001 00100010 01000101 11010000
00000001 00111010 01000101 00000001 00000000 00111011 01000101 00000001 00000000 00100110
01000101 00001011 00000000 11000000 01000110 00000000 00000000 00101010 01000101 01111100
00000000 11001000 01011001 10000000 00000001 11000110 01011001 01111100 00000001 00101110
01000101 00000000 00000000 00110000 01000101 00000000 00000000 00110010 01000101 00000000
00000000 01000000 01000101 00000000 00000000 01000001 01000101 00000000 00000000 01000010
01000101 00000000 00000000 11001110 01011001 00000000 00000000 11010000 01011001 00000000
00000000 11010010 01011001 00000000 00000000 01000011 01000101 00000000 00000000 00111110
01000101 00000100 00000000 00011100 01000101 01110001 00000011 01000100 01000101 10110110
00000010 00100010 01001010 00110111 00000001 11000000 01011001 00000001 00000000 11000001
01011001 00000001 00000000 11101000 01000110 11110010 00100100 11001100 01000110 00000000
00000000 11010100 01000110 00000000 00000001 11001110 01000110 00000000 00000000 11010000
01000110 00000000 00000000 11010110 01000110 00000000 00000000 01010000 01011000 00000000
00000000 11011010 01000110 00000000 00000000 11000101 01011001 00000010 00000000 11101111
01000110 00000001 00000000 11010100 01011001 00000000 00000000 11010110 01011001 01110110
00101100 11011000 01011001 00000000 00100110 11011010 01011001 11100001 00001011 11101110
01000110 00000000 00000000 11110000 00111111 01010111 01000010 00001110 00000001 00000000
01000100 00001000 00000001 00000010 01000100 01011101 00000010 01011100 01000100 00010001
00000001 00000100 01000100 10010010 00000000 00000110 01000100 10000000 00000000 00010010
01000101 00011110 00000010 00011010 01000100 10000100 00000000 01011110 01000100 00010000
00000000 01011111 01000100 00000110 00000000 00010010 01000100 10010010 00000000 00010100
01000100 10000000 00000000 00010110 01000100 10111000 00000001 00011000 01000100 00101101
00000001 11001100 01000100 00010100 00000001 11001110 01000100 11100000 00000001 11010000
01000100 10000110 00000001 11010010 01000100 00010110 00000001 11011100 01000100 11100011
00000001 11011110 01000100 00001101 00000001 10110100 01000100 00000000 00000101 10110110
01000100 00000000 00000000 00110000 01000100 01100100 00000000 00111000 01000100 01101100
00000000 00110010 01000100 01101100 00000000 00111010 01000100 10001111 00000000 00110100
01000100 00001000 00000000 00111100 01000100 00101000 00000000 00110110 01000100 00011110
00000000 00111110 01000100 00110000 00000000 01001100 01000100 01101100 00000000 01001110
01000100 00000110 00000000 11000000 01000100 01101100 00000000 11000010 01000100 00000110
00000000 11101010 01000100 00000000 00000000 10000000 01000101 00010000 00000000 10000010
01000101 00110110 00000000 10000011 01000101 00000011 00000000 10000100 01000101 00000000
00000000 10000110 01000101 00000000 00000000 10000111 01000101 00000000 00000000 10001000
01000101 00000000 00000000 10001010 01000101 00000000 00000000 10001011 01000101 00000000
00000000 10001100 01000101 00000000 00000000 10001110 01000101 10011101 00000000 10001111
01000101 10000001 00000000 10010000 01000101 00000000 00000000 10010010 01000101 00000000
00000000 10010011 01000101 00000000 00000000 01010010 01000100 10010010 00000000 01010100
01000100 10000000 00000000 01010110 01000100 10010010 00000000 01011000 01000100 10000000
00000000 11010100 01000100 10010010 00000000 11010110 01000100 10000000 00000000 11011000
01000100 10010010 00000000 11011010 01000100 10000000 00000000 11010100 01011101 00000000
00000000 11110000 01000100 00000000 00000000 11110010 01000100 00000000 00000000 11110100
01000100 00000000 00000000 11110110 01000100 00000000 00000000 11111000 01000100 00000000
00000000 11111010 01000100 00000000 00000000 11111100 01000100 00000000 00000000 11111110
01000100 00000000 00000000 11110000 00111111 01011001 01000011 01100110 00000000 11001100
01000101 01010000 00000000 01100000 01000101 00000011 00000000 01100010 01000101 00000000
00000000 01100100 01000101 00001000 00000000 01100110 01000101 00001000 00000000 01101000
01000101 00001100 00000000 01101010 01000101 00001000 00000000 01101100 01000101 00000111
00000000 01101110 01000101 00000101 00000000 01110000 01000101 00000010 00000000 01110010
01000101 00000001 00000000 01110100 01000101 00000000 00000000 01110110 01000101 00001011
00000000 01111000 01000101 00001011 00000000 01111010 01000101 00001011 00000000 01111100
01000101 00001011 00000000 11010000 01000101 00000001 00000000 11010010 01000101 00000000
00000000 11010100 01000101 00000000 00000000 11010110 01000101 00001000 00000000 11110000
01000101 00000011 00000000 11110010 01000101 00000011 00000000 11110100 01000101 00000000
00000000 11001110 01000101 00000000 00000000 11110000 00111111 01000011 01001101 00001010
00000000 11111100 01000101 00001001 11110000 11110000 00111111 01001001 01010011 00011110
00000000 10010100 01000110 01011110 00000011 10010110 01000110 01101110 00000011 10011000
01000110 11100101 00000011 10011010 01000110 11100101 00000011 01100000 01000110 00001001
00000010 01100010 01000110 11111101 00000001 00000000 00000000 00000000 00000000 00000000
00000000 00000000 00000000 00000000 00000000 00000000 00000000 00000000 00000000 00000000
00000000 00000000 00000000 00000000 00000000 00000000 00000000 00000000 00000000 00000000
00000000 00000000 00000000 00000000 00000000 00000000 00000000 00000000 00000000 00000000
00000000 00000000 00000000 00000000 00000000 00000000 00000000 00000000 00000000 00000000
00000000 00000000 00000000 00000000 00000000 00000000 00000000 00000000 00000000 00000000
00000000 00000000 00000000 00000000 00000000 00000000 00000000 00000000 00000000 00000000

00000000 00000000 00000000 00000000 00000000 00000000 00000000 00000000 00000000 00000000
00000000 00000000 00000000 00000000 00000000 00000000 00000000 00000000 00000000 00000000
00000000 00000000 00000000 00000000 00000000 00000000 00000000 00000000 00000000 00000000
00000000 00000000 00000000 00000000 00000000 00000000 00000000 00000000 00000000 00000000
00000000 00000000 00000000 00000000 00000000 00000000 00000000 00000000 00000000 00000000
00000000 00000000 00000000 00000000 00000000 00000000 00000000 00000000 00000000 00000000
00000000 00000000 00000000 00000000 00000000 00000000 00000000 00000000 00000000 00000000
00000000 00000000 00000000 00000000 00000000 00000000 00000000 00000000 00000000 00000000
00000000 00000000 00000000 00000000 00000000 00000000 00000000 00000000 00000000 00000000
00000000 00000000 00000000 00000000 00000000 00000000 00000000 00000000 00000000 00000000
00000000 00000000 00000000 00000000 00000000 00000000 00000000 00000000 00000000 00000000
00000000 00000000 00000000 00000000 00000000 00000000 00000000 00000000 00000000 00000000
00000000 00000000 00000000 00000000 00000000 00000000 00000000 00000000 00000000 00000000
00000000 00000000 00000000 00000000 00000000 00000000 00000000 00000000 00000000 00000000
00000000 00000000 00000000 00000000 00000000 00000000 00000000 00000000 00000000 00000000
00000000 00000000 00000000 00000000 00000000 00000000 00000000 00000000 00000000 00000000
00000000 00000000 00000000 00000000 00000000 00000000 00000000 00000000 00000000 00000000
00000000 00000000 00000000 00000000 00000000 00000000 00000000 00000000 00000000 00000000
00000000 00000000 00000000 00000000 00000000 00000000 00000000 00000000 00000000 00000000
00000000 00000000 00000000 00000000 00000000 00000000 00000000 00000000 00000000 00000000
00000000 00000000 00000000 00000000 00000000 00000000 00000000 00000000 00000000 00000000
00000000 01000001 01000101 01000010 01001101 11101101 00000001 00010000 00000010 11010111
00000010 01010110 00000010 00010101 00000010 01010010 00000010 00010100 00000010 00001011
00000001 10010101 00000000 10011011 00000000 10000111 00000000 10111100 00000000 11111100
00000000 11000110 00000001 11100100 00000010 11000010 00000010 10011010 00000010 01011010
00000010 00100000 00000010 11000100 00000001 11100000 00000000 10001011 00000000 10110001
00000000 11011001 00000000 10101011 00000001 00000100 00000010 11010011 00000010 10111000
00000010 10010010 00000010 01011100 00000010 00100110 00000010 11110010 00000001 10001010
00000001 10111110 00000000 11000000 00000000 11101110 00000000 10111010 00000010 11000110
00000010 10110000 00000010 01001111 00000010 00101010 00000010 01010011 00000010 00011111
00000010 11101100 00000001 10110010 00000001 00100101 00000001 11010111 00000000 11010001
00000000 10011010 00000010 01100110 00000010 01101011 00000001 10101000 00000001 01101001
00000000 01011110 00000001 00010001 00000010 11011001 00000001 01010010 00000001 10100010
00000000 10011001 00000000 10100011 00000000 01100111 00000010 01111001 00000010 11001000
00000001 01101111 00000001 10100111 00000000 10111100 00000000 11101000 00000001 10101110
00000001 00010000 00000001 01010101 00000000 01100010 00000000 10111010 00000000 00100010
00000010 00101101 00000010 11110101 00000001 10111010 00000001 00000101 00000001 01111010
00000000 00100001 00000001 00111100 00000001 10001110 00000000 01011110 00000000 01110010
00000000 10000100 00000000 01101110 00000001 11100111 00000001 00001110 00000010 01001110
00000001 10001110 00000001 01000110 00000001 11101110 00000000 01110001 00000000 01101101
00000000 01011011 00000000 01001000 00000000 00111110 00000000 01111100 00000000 10001000
00000000 01001111 00000001 01000110 00000001 11101110 00000000 00011000 00000001 11010010
00000000 11101101 00000000 10101010 00000000 10001000 00000000 01011100 00000000 01111101
00000000 10101011 00000000 01110000 00000000 00000100 00000001 00000000 00000001 10010110
00000000 11011000 00000000 00100001 00000001 11100010 00000000 00100001 00000001 00010100
00000001 00100010 00000001 11110000 00000000 10000110 00000001 10101010 00000001 00000101
00000001 01110101 00000000 11010001 00000000 00110100 00000001 00111110 00000001 00011101
00000001 11110011 00000000 00000100 00000001 11110001 00000000 01101111 00000000 11001000
00000000 11010010 00000000 10000111 00000000 01001100 00000000 11010101 00000000 11101000
00000000 11010010 00000000 10110110 00000000 10011111 00000000 11000110 00000000 11011011
00000000 01011110 00000000 01010000 01010010 01010011 01010100 11111010 00011110 10100001
00100000 01010101 00101101 01000111 00100101 00110101 00100001 00111000 00100101 01011100
00100001 11001110 00010000 01011011 00001001 11000000 00001001 01110110 00001000 11000110
00001011 11001010 00001111 00101010 00011100 01001010 00101110 00110010 00101100 10111101
00101001 11001000 00100101 11111100 00100001 01101100 00011100 00001001 00001110 10111100
00001000 00001111 00001011 10011101 00001101 10000000 00011010 00000001 00100000 00110011
00101101 01110011 00101011 00011111 00101001 10101110 00100101 01110011 00100010 00010000
00011111 10101100 00011000 11101000 00001011 11100010 00001011 11101110 00001110 10011011
00101011 11111010 00101011 11110101 00100111 11000110 00100001 10010101 00011111 11011000
00100100 11110101 00100001 11011110 00011110 01010000 00011011 01111110 00010010 10101101
00001101 00110101 00001101 10011000 00101001 01000011 00101001 10011001 00010101 01101010
00011110 10000111 00000111 11001001 00010011 00011010 00100001 10010101 00011101 01101111
00010101 01001000 00001010 10010110 00001001 01000011 00001010 10011001 00100110 11000100
00100111 11010001 00100001 11111011 00010101 01110011 00001010 01110100 00001010 00111110
00011110 00000000 00011011 01000010 00010001 01101001 00000101 00111011 00000110 10010011
00001011 00100000 00100010 11101011 00100010 10011011 00011111 10010011 00011110 11010011
00010001 01100011 00000111 11010100 00010010 00000111 00010100 00000101 00001001 11101110
00000101 00100100 00000111 01001000 00001000 11111000 00010110 10011101 00011110 01000001
00100001 10111110 00010100 11000001 00011000 11111011 00010011 10101111 00010001 00011101
00000111 11011101 00000110 10111100 00000101 10100111 00000100 11100011 00000011 11011100
00000111 10001000 00001000 00001100 00010101 10111110 00010100 01001110 00010000 00100111
00010010 01011110 00001100 10100000 00001110 01111100 00001010 10000000 00001000 11100000
00000101 10110011 00000111 10101100 00001010 11011101 00000110 11101001 00001111 01010011

00010000 01010110 00001001 11010101 00001101 11110110 00010001 00101110 00001110 11111001
00010001 01000111 00010001 00101101 00010010 11011100 00001110 01111100 00011000 11001010
00011010 00111010 00010001 10010010 00000111 10110011 00001100 00010101 00010011 00001010
00010100 11101010 00010001 01000110 00001111 01011100 00010000 00101100 00001111 00101100
00000111 10011110 00001100 01010010 00001101 10010000 00001000 11000110 00000100 00100100
00001101 10100101 00001110 00110011 00001101 10010011 00001011 11110101 00001001 01111101
00001100 11000010 00001101 00000000 00000110 00000111 00011111 11010001 00100000 01100111
00101101 01100011 00100101 01001110 00100001 01000011 00100101 01100111 00100001 11000100
00010000 01011010 00001001 11010101 00001001 01111001 00001000 11010011 00001011 11100111
00001111 01001011 00011100 01111000 00101110 01101111 00101100 11111000 00101001 00010000
00100110 01010001 00100010 10001011 00011100 00011111 00001110 11010010 00001000 00110000
00001011 10110010 00001101 10001001 00011010 00011010 00100000 01101001 00101101 10110111
00101011 01110101 00101001 00011011 00100110 11001000 00100010 01011001 00011111 11010011
00011000 11111001 00001011 00000011 00001100 11111011 00001110 10111101 00101011 00010111
00101100 00110110 00101000 00011110 00100010 00001101 00100000 10111000 00100101 10011001
00100010 00101100 00011111 01101011 00011011 01111101 00010010 10101001 00001101 00111010
00001101 10111101 00101001 01101001 00101001 10100100 00010101 10101011 00011110 11010100
00000111 00110000 00010101 00000111 00100011 00001110 00011110 10001101 00010101 01001100
00001010 10011011 00001001 00111010 00001010 10110110 00100110 00000000 00101000 00001010
00100010 01010010 00010110 01111101 00001011 01111011 00001100 11011111 00100000 10100000
00011011 01101000 00010001 01101101 00000101 01000110 00000110 10110111 00001011 00111011
00100010 00011000 00100011 11011111 00011111 10101111 00011110 10011110 00010010 11101110
00001000 11000100 00010011 01101110 00010100 00000110 00001001 11111110 00000101 00100101
00000111 01000101 00001000 00000111 00010111 10011010 00011110 01100000 00100001 00001011
00010101 01011110 00011001 01101110 00010101 01010010 00010001 00110111 00000111 11101001
00000110 11000000 00000101 10101111 00000100 11101000 00000011 11011010 00000111 10001101
00001000 00011000 00010101 11001001 00010100 00001010 00010000 00101000 00010010 10010111
00001100 11111011 00001110 10001100 00001010 10010100 00001000 11100100 00000101 10110000
00000111 10110000 00001010 11110111 00000110 00001111 00010000 01011010 00010000 01111010
00001001 00010011 00001110 00111001 00010010 01101100 00001110 00110001 00010010 01101000
00010001 00110011 00010010 11100110 00001110 10001101 00011000 11011001 00011010 00101111
00010001 10010011 00000111 11100100 00001100 00111000 00010011 00101000 00010100 00001100
00010010 01010101 00001111 01110001 00010000 01000101 00001111 00111000 00000111 10100001
00001100 01011110 00001101 10010111 00001000 11010001 00000100 01000101 00001101 11010000
00001110 01010101 00001101 10101001 00001011 00001100 00001010 10000110 00001100 11001110
00001101 00001100 00000110 00000000 00000000 00000000 00000000 11110000 00000000 11110000
00000001 11110000 00000000 11110000 00000001 11110000 00000000 11000000 00000001 00010000
00000000 00000000 00000000 00000000 00000000 00000000 00000000 00011010 00000000 00000000
00000000 00000000 00000000 11110000 00000000 11110000 00000000 11110000 00000000 11110000
00000000 11110000 00000000 00000000 00000000 00000000 00000000 00000000 00000000 00000000
00000000 00000000 00000000 00010100 00000000 00000000 00000000 00000000 00000000 00000000
00000000 00000000 00000000 00000000 00000000 00000000 00000000 00000000 00000000 00000000
00000000 00000000 00000000 00000000 00000000 00000000 00000000 00000000 00000000 00000000
00000000 00000000 00000000 00000000 00000000 00000000 00000000 00000000 00000000 00000000
00000000 00000000 00000000 00000000 00000000 00000000 00000000 00000000 00000000 00000000
00000000 00000000 00000000 00000000 00000000 00000000 00000000 00000000 00000000 00000000
00000000 00000000 00000000 00000000 00000000 00000000 00000000 00000000 00000000 00000000
00000000 00000000 00000000 00000000 00000000 00000000 00000000 01000110 01000011 01000011
01010110 00000110 00000000 00000001 00000000 10100110 01000000 10100110 01000000 00000000
00000000 00000000 00000000 00000000 00000000 00000000 00000000 00000000 00000000 00000000
00000000 00000000 00000000 00000000 00000000 00000000 00000000 10000011 01000100 01110000
00111101 11000100 01000000 11001100 01000000 11001001 01000000 11001001 01000000 11001000
01000000 11001001 01000000 11001000 01000000 00000000 00000000 00000000 00000000 00000000
00000000 00000000 00000000 00000000 00000000 00000000 00000000 01000100 00111110 10101111
00000001 00001000 00000000 00000101 00000000 00011010 00000000 00100010 00000000 00000000
00000000 00000000 00000000 00000000 00000000 00000000 00000000 10100000 00000101 00000100
00000000 00000100 00000000 00011100 00000000 00100100 00000000 00000000 00000000 00000000
00000000 00000000 00000000 00000000 00000000 00000000 00000000 00000000 00000000 00000000
00000000 00000000 00000000 00000000 00000000 00000000 00000000 00000000 00000000 00000000
00000000 00000000 00000000 01000100 00111111 10101110 00000001 00001000 00000000 00000101
00000000 00011010 00000000 00100010 00000000 00000000 00000000 00000000 00000000 00000000
00000000 00000000 00000000 00010101 00000110 00000100 00000000 00000100 00000000 00011100
00000000 00100100 00000000 00000000 00000000 00000000 00000000 00000000 00000000 00000000
00000000 00000000 00000000 00000000 00000000 00000000 00000000 00000000 00000000 00000000
00000000 00000000 00000000 00000000 00000000 00000000 00000000 00000000 00000000 01000100
01000000 00001111 00000010 00001000 00000000 00000101 00000000 00011010 00000000 00100010
00000000 00000000 00000000 00000000 00000000 00000000 00000000 00000000 00000000 11000001
00000110 00000100 00000000 00000100 00000000 00011100 00000000 00100100 00000000 00000000
00000000 00000000 00000000 00000000 00000000 00000000 00000000 00000000 00000000 00000000
00000000 00000000 00000000 00000000 00000000 00000000 00000000 00000000 00000000 00000000
00000000 00000000 00000000 00000000 00000000 01000100 01000001 01111011 00000010 00001000
00000000 00000101 00000000 00011010 00000000 00100010 00000000 00000000 00000000 00000000
00000000 00000000 00000000 00000000 00000000 11111101 00000110 00000100 00000000 00000100

00000000 00011100 00000000 00100100 00000000 00000000 00000000 00000000 00000000 00000000
00000000 00000000 00000000 00000000 00000000 00000000 00000000 00000000 00000000 00000000
00000000 00000000 00000000 00000000 00000000 00000000 00000000 00000000 00000000 00000000
00000000 01000100 01000010 11011110 00000001 00001000 00000000 00000101 00000000 00011010
00000000 00100010 00000000 00000000 00000000 00000000 00000000 00000000 00000000 00000000
00000000 01111010 00000110 00000100 00000000 00000100 00000000 00011100 00000000 00100100
00000000 00000000 00000000 00000000 00000000 00000000 00000000 00000000 00000000 00000000
00000000 00000000 00000000 00000000 00000000 00000000 00000000 00000000 00000000 00000000
00000000 00000000 00000000 00000000 00000000 00000000 00000000 01000100 01000011 10101101
00000001 00001000 00000000 00000101 00000000 00011010 00000000 00100010 00000000 00000000
00000000 00000000 00000000 00000000 00000000 00000000 00000000 10111000 00000101 00000100
00000000 00000100 00000000 00011100 00000000 00100100 00000000 00000000 00000000 00000000
00000000 00000000 00000000 00000000 00000000 00000000 00000000 00000000 00000000 00000000
00000000 00000000 00000000 00000000 00000000 00000000 00000000 00000000 00000000 00000000
00000000 00000000 00000000 11001010 01000011 11010010 00000001 00001000 00000000 00000101
00000000 00011010 00000000 00100010 00000000 00000000 00000000 00000000 00000000 00000000
00000000 00000000 00000000 11101001 00000011 00000100 00000000 00000100 00000000 00011100
00000000 00100100 00000000 00000000 00000000 00000000 00000000 00000000 00000000 00000000
00000000 00000000 00000000 00000000 00000000 00000000 00000000 00000000 00000000 00000000
00000000 00000000 00000000 00000000 00000000 00000000 00000000 00000000 00000000 11001010
01000100 11010100 00000001 00001000 00000000 00000101 00000000 00011010 00000000 00100010
00000000 00000000 00000000 00000000 00000000 00000000 00000000 00000000 00000000 10101101
00000100 00000100 00000000 00000100 00000000 00011100 00000000 00100100 00000000 00000000
00000000 00000000 00000000 00000000 00000000 00000000 00000000 00000000 00000000 00000000
00000000 00000000 00000000 00000000 00000000 00000000 00000000 00000000 00000000 00000000
00000000 00000000 00000000 00000000 00000000 10000011 01000100 11001010 00000001 00001000
00000000 00000101 00000000 00011010 00000000 00100010 00000000 00000000 00000000 00000000
00000000 00000000 00000000 00000000 00000000 01001010 00000101 00000100 00000000 00000100
00000000 00011100 00000000 00100100 00000000 00000000 00000000 00000000 00000000 00000000
00000000 00000000 00000000 00000000 00000000 00000000 00000000 00000000 00000000 00000000
00000000 00000000 00000000 00000000 00000000 00000000 00000000 00000000 00000000 00000000
00000000 10000011 01000011 11000010 00000001 00001000 00000000 00000101 00000000 00011010
00000000 00100010 00000000 00000000 00000000 00000000 00000000 00000000 00000000 00000000
00000000 11111100 00000101 00000100 00000000 00000100 00000000 00011100 00000000 00100100
00000000 00000000 00000000 00000000 00000000 00000000 00000000 00000000 00000000 00000000
00000000 00000000 00000000 00000000 00000000 00000000 00000000 00000000 00000000 00000000
00000000 00000000 00000000 00000000 00000000 00000000 00000000 10000011 01000010 11001001
00000001 00001000 00000000 00000101 00000000 00011010 00000000 00100010 00000000 00000000
00000000 00000000 00000000 00000000 00000000 00000000 00000000 01000111 00000110 00000100
00000000 00000100 00000000 00011100 00000000 00100100 00000000 00000000 00000000 00000000
00000000 00000000 00000000 00000000 00000000 00000000 00000000 00000000 00000000 00000000
00000000 00000000 00000000 00000000 00000000 00000000 00000000 00000000 00000000 00000000
00000000 00000000 00000000 10000011 01000001 11011100 00000001 00001000 00000000 00000101
00000000 00011010 00000000 00100010 00000000 00000000 00000000 00000000 00000000 00000000
00000000 00000000 00000000 00100010 00000111 00000100 00000000 00000100 00000000 00011100
00000000 00100100 00000000 00000000 00000000 00000000 00000000 00000000 00000000 00000000
00000000 00000000 00000000 00000000 00000000 00000000 00000000 00000000 00000000 00000000
00000000 00000000 00000000 00000000 00000000 00000000 00000000 00000000 00000000 10000011
01000000 10011110 00000010 00001000 00000000 00000101 00000000 00011010 00000000 00100010
00000000 00000000 00000000 00000000 00000000 00000000 00000000 00000000 00000000 01100010
00001000 00000100 00000000 00000100 00000000 00011100 00000000 00100100 00000000 00000000
00000000 00000000 00000000 00000000 00000000 00000000 00000000 00000000 00000000 00000000
00000000 00000000 00000000 00000000 00000000 00000000 00000000 00000000 00000000 00000000
00000000 00000000 00000000 00000000 00000000 10000011 00111111 00101100 00000010 00001000
00000000 00000101 00000000 00011010 00000000 00100010 00000000 00000000 00000000 00000000
00000000 00000000 00000000 00000000 00000000 00010111 00000111 00000100 00000000 00000100
00000000 00011100 00000000 00100100 00000000 00000000 00000000 00000000 00000000 00000000
00000000 00000000 00000000 00000000 00000000 00000000 00000000 00000000 00000000 00000000
00000000 00000000 00000000 00000000 00000000 00000000 00000000 00000000 00000000 00000000
00000000 10000011 00111110 11000110 00000001 00001000 00000000 00000101 00000000 00011010
00000000 00100010 00000000 00000000 00000000 00000000 00000000 00000000 00000000 00000000
00000000 11100100 00000101 00000100 00000000 00000100 00000000 00011100 00000000 00100100
00000000 00000000 00000000 00000000 00000000 00000000 00000000 00000000 00000000 00000000
00000000 00000000 00000000 00000000 00000000 00000000 00000000 00000000 00000000 00000000
00000000 00000000 00000000 00000000 00000000 00000000 00000000 10000011 00111101 00010000
00000001 00010110 00000000 00010110 00000000 00001000 00000000 00001111 00000000 00000000
00000000 00000000 00000000 00000000 00000000 00000000 00000000 11100010 00000001 00011111
00000000 00001111 00000000 00001001 00000000 00001010 00000000 00000000 00000000 00000000
00000000 00000000 00000000 00000000 00000000 00000000 00000000 00000000 00000000 00000000
00000000 00000000 00000000 00000000 00000000 00000000 00000000 00000000 00000000 00000000
00000000 00000000 00000000 00000011 00111101 11100110 00000000 00000110 00000000 00001011
00000000 00000111 00000000 00010100 00000000 00000000 00000000 00000000 00000000 00000000
00000000 00000000 00000000 01011001 00000000 00000111 00000000 00000000 00000000 00000101

```
00000000 00001100 00000000 00000000 00000000 00000000 00000000 00000000 00000000 00000000
00000000 00000000 00000000 00000000 00000000 00000000 00000000 00000000 00000000 00000000
00000000 00000000 00000000 00000000 00000000 00000000 00000000 00000000 00000000 00000000
00000000 00000000 00000000 00000000 00000000 00000000 00000000 00000000 00000000 00000000
00000000 00000000 00000000 00000000 00000000 00000000 00000000 00000000 00000000 00000000
00000000 00000000 00000000 00000000 00000000 00000000 00000000 00000000 00000000 00000000
00000000 00000000 00000000 00000000 00000000 00000000 00000000 00000000 00000000 00000000
00000000 00000000 00000000 00000000 00000000 00000000 00000000 00000000 00000000 00000000
00000000 00000000 00000000 00000000 00000000 00000000 00000000 00000000 00000000 00000000
00000000 00000000 00000000 00000000 00000000 00000000 00000000 00000000 00000000 00000000
00000000 00000000 00000000 00000000 00000000 00000000 00000000 00000000 00000000 00000000
00000000 00000000 00000000 00000000 00000000 00000000 00000000 00000000 00000000 00000000
00000000 00000000 00000000 00000000 00000000 00000000 00000000 00000000 00000000 00000000
00000000 00000000 00000000 00000000 00000000 00000000 00000000 00000000 00000000 00000000
00000000 00000000 00000000 00000000 00000000 00000000 00000000 00000000 00000000 00000000
00000000 00000000 00000000 00000000 00000000 00000000 00000000 00000000 00000000 00000000
00000000 00000000 00000000 00000000 00000000 00000000 00000000 00000000 00000000 00000000
00000000 00000000 00000000 00000000 00000000 00000000 00000000 00000000 00000000 00000000
00000000 00000000 00000000 00000000 00000000 00000000 00000000 00000000 00000000 00000000
00000000 00000000 00000000 00000000 00000000 00000000 00000000 00000000 00000000 00000000
00000000 00000000 00000000 00000000 00000000 00000000 00000000 00000000 00000000 00000000
00000000 00000000 00000000 00000000 00000000 00000000 00000000 00000000 00000000 00000000
00000000 00000000 00000000 00000000 00000000 00000000 00000000 00000000 00000000 00000000
00000000 00000000 00000000 00000000 00000000 00000000 00000000 00000000 00000000 00000000
00000000 00000000 00000000 00000000 00000000 00000000 00000000 00000000 00000000 00000000
00000000 00000000 00000000 00000000 00000000 00000000 00000000 00000000 00000000 00000000
00000000 00000000 00000000 00000000 00000000 00000000 00000000 00000000 00000000 00000000
00000000 00000000 00000000 00000000 00000000 00000000 00000000 00000000 00000000 00000000
00000000 00000000 00000000 00000000 00000000 00000000 00000000 00000000 00000000 00000000
00000000 00000000 00000000 00000000 00000000 00000000 00000000 00000000 00000000 00000000
00000000 00000000 00000000 00000000 00000000 00000000 00000000 00000000 00000000 00000000
00000000 00000000 00000000 00000000 00000000 00000000 00000000 00000000 00000000 00000000
00000000 00000000 00000000 00000000 00000000 00000000 00000000 00000000 00000000 00000000
00000000 00000000 00000000 00000000 00000000 00000000 00000000 00000000 00000000 00000000
00000000 00000000 00000000 00000000 00000000 00000000 00000000 00000000 00000000 00000000
00000000 00000000 00000000 00000000 00000000 00000000 00000000 00000000 00000000 00000000
00000000 00000000 00000000 00000000 00000000 00000000 00000000 00000000 00000000 00000000
00000000 00000000 00000000 00000000 00000000 00000000 00000000 00000000 00000000 00000000
00000000 00000000 00000000 00000000 00000000 00000000 00000000 00000000 00000000 00000000
00000000 00000000 00000000 00000000 00000000 00000000 00000000 00000000 00000000 00000000
00000000 00000000 00000000 00000000 00000000 00000000 00000000 00000000 00000000 00000000
00000000 00000000 00000000 00000000 00000000 00000000 00000000 00000000 00000000 00000000
00000000 00000000 00000000 00000000 00000000 00000000 00000000 00000000 00000000 00000000
00000000 00000000 00000000 00000000 00000000 00000000 00000000 00000000 00000000 00000000
00000000 00000000 00000000 00000000 00000000 00000000 00000000 00000000 00000000 00000000
00000000 00000000 00000000 00000000 00000000 00000000 00000000 00000000 00000000 00000000
00000000 00000000 00000000 00000000 00000000 00000000 00000000 00000000 00000000 00000000
00000000 00000000 00000000 00000000 00000000 00000000 00000000 00000000 00000000 00000000
00000000 00000000 00000000 00000000 00000000 00000000 00000000 00000000 00000000 00000000
00000000 00000000 00000000 00000000 00000000 00000000 00000000 00000000 00000000 00000000
00000000 00000000 00000000 00000000 00000000 00000000 00000000 00000000 00000000 00000000
00000000 00000000 00000000 00000000 00000000 00000000 00000000 00000000 00000000 00000000
00000000 00000000 00000000 00000000 00000000 00000000 00000000 00000000 00000000 00000000
00000000 00000000 00000000 00000000 00000000 00000000 00000000 00000000 00000000 00000000
00000000 00000000 00000000 00000000 00000000 00000000 00000000 00000000 00000000 00000000
00000000 00000000 00000000 00000000 00000000 00000000 00000000 00000000 00000000 00000000
00000000 00000000 00000000 00000000 00000000 00000000 00000000 00000000 00000000 00000000
00000000 00000000 00000000 00000000 00000000 00000000 00000000 00000000 00000000 00000000
00000000 00000000 00000000 00000000 00000000 00000000 00000000 00000000 00000000 00000000
00000000 00000000 00000000 00000000 00000000 00000000 00000000 00000000 00000000 00000000
00000000 00000000 00000000 00000000 00000000 00000000 00000000 00000000 00000000 00000000
00000000 00000000 00000000 00000000 00000000 00000000 00000000 00000000 00000000 00000000
00000000 00000000 00000000 00000000 00000000 00000000 00000000 00000000 00000000 00000000
00000000 00000000 00000000 00000000 00000000 00000000 00000000 00000000 00000000 00000000
00000000 00000000 00000000 00000000 00000000 00000000 00000000 00000000 00000000 00000000
00000000 00000000 00000000 00000000 00000000 00000000 00000000 00000000 00000000 00000000
00000000 00000000 00000000 00000000 00000000 00000000 00000000 00000000 00000000 00000000
00000000 00000000 00000000 00000000 00000000 00000000 00000000 00000000 00000000 00000000
00000000 00000000 00000000 00000000 00000000 00000000 00000000 00000000 00000000 00000000
00000000 00000000 00000000 00000000 00000000 00000000 00000000 00000000 00000000 00000000
00000000 00000000 00000000 00000000 00000000 00000000 00000000 00000000 00000000 00000000
00000000 00000000 00000000 00000000 00000000 00000000 00000000 00000000 00000000 00000000
00000000 00000000 00000000 00000000 00000000 00000000 00000000 00000000 00000000 00000000
00000000 00000000 00000000 00000000 00000000 00000000 00000000 00000000 00000000 00000000
```

00000000 00000000 00000000 00000000 00000000 00000000 00000000 00000000 00000000 00000000
00000000 00000000 00000000 00000000 00000000 00000000 00000000 00000000 00000000 00000000
00000000 00000000 00000000 00000000 00000000 00000000 00000000 00000000 00000000 00000000
00000000 00000000 00000000 00000000 00000000 00000000 00000000 00000000 00000000 00000000
00000000 00000000 00000000 00000000 00000000 00000000 00000000 00000000 00000000 00000000
00000000 00000000 00000000 00000000 00000000 00000000 00000000 00000000 00000000 00000000
00000000 00000000 00000000 00000000 00000000 00000000 00000000 00000000 00000000 00000000
00000000 00000000 00000000 00000000 00000000 00000000 00000000 00000000 00000000 00000000
00000000 00000000 00000000 00000000 00000000 00000000 00000000 00000000 00000000 00000000
00000000 00000000 00000000 00000000 00000000 00000000 00000000 00000000 00000000 00000000
00000000 00000000 00000000 00000000 00000000 00000000 00000000 00000000 00000000 00000000
00000000 00000000 00000000 00000000 00000000 00000000 00000000 00000000 00000000 00000000
00000000 00000000 00000000 00000000 00000000 00000000 00000000 00000000 00000000 00000000
00000000 00000000 00000000 00000000 00000000 00000000 00000000 00000000 00000000 00000000
00000000 00000000 00000000 00000000 00000000 00000000 00000000 00000000 00000000 00000000
00000000 00000000 00000000 00000000 00000000 00000000 00000000 00000000 00000000 00000000
00000000 00000000 00000000 00000000 00000000 00000000 00000000 00000000 00000000 00000000
00000000 00000000 00000000 00000000 00000000 00000000 00000000 00000000 00000000 00000000
00000000 00000000 00000000 00000000 00000000 00000000 00000000 00000000 00000000 00000000
00000000 00000000 00000000 00000000 00000000 00000000 00000000 00000000 00000000 00000000
00000000 00000000 00000000 00000000 00000000 00000000 00000000 00000000 00000000 00000000
00000000 00000000 00000000 00000000 00000000 00000000 00000000 00000000 00000000 00000000
00000000 00000000 00000000 00000000 00000000 00000000 00000000 00000000 00000000 00000000
00000000 00000000 00000000 00000000 00000000 00000000 00000000 00000000 00000000 00000000
00000000 00000000 00000000 00000000 00000000 00000000 00000000 00000000 00000000 00000000
00000000 00000000 00000000 00000000 00000000 00000000 00000000 00000000 00000000 00000000
00000000 00000000 00000000 00000000 00000000 00000000 00000000 00000000 00000000 00000000
00000000 00000000 00000000 00000000 00000000 00000000 00000000 00000000 00000000 00000000
00000000 00000000 00000000 00000000 00000000 00000000 00000000 00000000 00000000 00000000
00000000 00000000 00000000 00000000 00000000 00000000 00000000 00000000 00000000 00000000
00000000 00000000 00000000 00000000 00000000 00000000 00000000 00000000 00000000 00000000
00000000 00000000 00000000 00000000 00000000 00000000 00000000 00000000 00000000 00000000
00000000 00000000 00000000 00000000 00000000 00000000 00000000 00000000 00000000 00000000
00000000 00000000 00000000 00000000 00000000 00000000 00000000 00000000 00000000 00000000
00000000 00000000 00000000 00000000 00000000 00000000 00000000 00000000 00000000 00000000
00000000 00000000 00000000 00000000 00000000 00000000 00000000 00000000 00000000 00000000
00000000 00000000 00000000 00000000 00000000 00000000 00000000 00000000 00000000 00000000
00000000 00000000 00000000 00000000 00000000 00000000 00000000 00000000 00000000 00000000
00000000 00000000 00000000 00000000 00000000 00000000 00000000 00000000 00000000 00000000
00000000 00000000 00000000 00000000 00000000 00000000 00000000 00000000 00000000 00000000
00000000 00000000 00000000 00000000 00000000 00000000 00000000 00000000 00000000 00000000
00000000 00000000 00000000 00000000 00000000 00000000 00000000 00000000 00000000 00000000
00000000 00000000 00000000 00000000 00000000 00000000 00000000 00000000 00000000 00000000
00000000 00000000 00000000 00000000 00000000 00000000 00000000 00000000 00000000 00000000
00000000 00000000 00000000 00000000 00000000 00000000 00000000 00000000 00000000 00000000
00000000 00000000 00000000 00000000 00000000 00000000 00000000 00000000 00000000 00000000
00000000 00000000 00000000 00000000 00000000 00000000 00000000 00000000 00000000 00000000
00000000 00000000 00000000 00000000 00000000 00000000 00000000 00000000 00000000 00000000
00000000 00000000 00000000 00000000 00000000 00000000 00000000 00000000 00000000 00000000
00000000 00000000 00000000 00000000 00000000 00000000 00000000 00000000 00000000 00000000
00000000 00000000 00000000 00000000 00000000 00000000 00000000 00000000 00000000 00000000
00000000 00000000 00000000 00000000 00000000 00000000 00000000 00000000 00000000 00000000
00000000 00000000 00000000 00000000 00000000 00000000 00000000 00000000 00000000 00000000
00000000 00000000 00000000 00000000 00000000 00000000 00000000 00000000 00000000 00000000
00000000 00000000 00000000 00000000 00000000 00000000 00000000 00000000 00000000 00000000
00000000 00000000 00000000 00000000 00000000 00000000 00000000 00000000 00000000 00000000
00000000 00000000 00000000 00000000 00000000 00000000 00000000 00000000 00000000 00000000
00000000 00000000 00000000 00000000 00000000 00000000 00000000 00000000 00000000 00000000
00000000 00000000 00000000 00000000 00000000 00000000 00000000 00000000 00000000 00000000
00000000 00000000 00000000 00000000 00000000 00000000 00000000 00000000 00000000 00000000
00000000 00000000 00000000 00000000 00000000 00000000 00000000 00000000 00000000 00000000
00000000 00000000 00000000 00000000 00000000 00000000 00000000 00000000 00000000 00000000
00000000 00000000 00000000 00000000 00000000 00000000 00000000 00000000 00000000 00000000
00000000 00000000 00000000 00000000 00000000 00000000 00000000 00000000 00000000 00000000
00000000 00000000 00000000 00000000 00000000 00000000 00000000 00000000 00000000 00000000
00000000 00000000 00000000 00000000 00000000 00000000 00000000 00000000 00000000 00000000
00000000 00000000 00000000 00000000 00000000 00000000 00000000 00000000 00000000 00000000
00000000 00000000 00000000 00000000 00000000 00000000 00000000 00000000 00000000 00000000
00000000 00000000 00000000 00000000 00000000 00000000 00000000 00000000 00000000 00000000
00000000 00000000 00000000 00000000 00000000 00000000 00000000 00000000 00000000 00000000

```
00000000 00000000 00000000 00000000 00000000 00000000 00000000 00000000 00000000 00000000
00000000 00000000 00000000 00000000 00000000 00000000 00000000 00000000 00000000 00000000
00000000 00000000 00000000 00000000 00000000 00000000 00000000 00000000 00000000 00000000
00000000 00000000 00000000 00000000 00000000 00000000 00000000 00000000 00000000 00000000
00000000 00000000 00000000 00000000 00000000 00000000 00000000 00000000 00000000 00000000
00000000 00000000 00000000 00000000 00000000 00000000 00000000 00000000 00000000 00000000
00000000 00000000 00000000 00000000 00000000 00000000 00000000 00000000 00000000 00000000
00000000 00000000 00000000 00000000 00000000 00000000 00000000 00000000 00000000 00000000
00000000 00000000 00000000 00000000 00000000 00000000 00000000 00000000 00000000 00000000
00000000 00000000 00000000 00000000 00000000 00000000 00000000 00000000 00000000 00000000
00000000 00000000 00000000 00000000 00000000 00000000 00000000 00000000 00000000 00000000
00000000 00000000 00000000 00000000 00000000 00000000 00000000 00000000 00000000 00000000
00000000 00000000 00000000 00000000 00000000 00000000 00000000 00000000 00000000 00000000
00000000 00000000 00000000 00000000 00000000 00000000 00000000 00000000 00000000 00000000
00000000 00000000 00000000 00000000 00000000 00000000 00000000 00000000 00000000 00000000
00000000 00000000 00000000 00000000 00000000 00000000 00000000 00000000 00000000 00000000
00000000 00000000 00000000 00000000 00000000 00000000 00000000 00000000 00000000 00000000
00000000 00000000 00000000 00000000 00000000 00000000 00000000 00000000 00000000 00000000
00000000 00000000 00000000 00000000 00000000 00000000 00000000 00000000 00000000 00000000
00000000 00000000 00000000 00000000 00000000 00000000 00000000 00000000 00000000 00000000
00000000 00000000 00000000 00000000 00000000 00000000 00000000 00000000 00000000 00000000
00000000 00000000 00000000 00000000 00000000 00000000 00000000 00000000 00000000 00000000
00000000 00000000 00000000 00000000 00000000 00000000 00000000 00000000 00000000 00000000
00000000 00000000 00000000 00000000 00000000 00000000 00000000 00000000 00000000 00000000
00000000 00000000 00000000 00000000 00000000 00000000 00000000 00000000 00000000 00000000
00000000 00000000 00000000 00000000 00000000 00000000 00000000 00000000 00000000 00000000
00000000 00000000 00000000 00000000 00000000 00000000 00000000 00000000 00000000 00000000
00000000 00000000 00000000 00000000 00000000 00000000 00000000 00000000 00000000 00000000
00000000 00000000 00000000 00000000 00000000 00000000 00000000 00000000 00000000 00000000
00000000 00000000 00000000 00000000 00000000 00000000 00000000 00000000 00000000 00000000
00000000 00000000 00000000 00000000 00000000 00000000 00000000 00000000 00000000 00000000
00000000 00000000 00000000 00000000 00000000 00000000 00000000 00000000 00000000 00000000
00000000 00000000 00000000 00000000 00000000 00000000 00000000 00000000 00000000 00000000
00000000 00000000 00000000 00000000 00000000 00000000 00000000 00000000 00000000 00000000
00000000 00000000 00000000 00000000 00000000 00000000 00000000 00000000 00000000 00000000
00000000 00000000 00000000 00000000 00000000 00000000 00000000 00000000 00000000 00000000
00000000 00000000 00000000 00000000 00000000 00000000 00000000 00000000 00000000 00000000
00000000 00000000 00000000 00000000 00000000 00000000 00000000 00000000 00000000 00000000
00000000 00000000 00000000 00000000 00000000 00000000 00000000 00000000 00000000 00000000
00000000 00000000 00000000 00000000 00000000 00000000 00000000 00000000 00000000 00000000
00000000 00000000 00000000 00000000 00000000 00000000 00000000 00000000 00000000 00000000
00000000 00000000 00000000 00000000 00000000 00000000 00000000 00000000 00000000 00000000
00000000 00000000 00000000 00000000 00000000 00000000 00000000 01010111 01000010 01000011
01011010 00000100 00000100 00000100 00000100 00000100 00000100 00000100 00000100 00000100
00000100 00000100 00000100 00000100 00000100 00000100 00000100 00000100 00000100 00000100
00000100 00000100 00000100 00000100 00000100 00000100 00000100 00000100 00000100 00000100
00000100 00000100 00000100 00000100 00000100 00000100 00000100 00000100 00000100 00000100
00000100 00000100 00000100 00000100 00000100 00000100 00000000 00000100 00000100 00000100
00000100 00000100 00000100 00000100 00000100 00000100 00000100 00000100 00000100 00000100
00000100 00000100 00000100 00000100 00000100 00000000 00000100 00000100 00000100 00000100
00000000 00000100 00000100 00000100 00000100 00000100 00000100 00000100 00000100 00000100
00000100 00000100 00000100 00000000 00000100 00000100 00000000 00000100 00000100 00000100
00000100 00000100 00000100 00000100 00000100 00000100 00000100 00000100 00000100 00000100
00000100 00000100 00000100 00000100 00000100 00000100 00000100 00000100 00000100 00000100
00000100 00000100 00000100 00000100 00000100 00000100 00000100 00000100 00000100 00000100
00000100 00000100 00000100 00000100 00000100 00000100 00000100 00000100 00000100 00000100
00000100 00000100 00000100 00000100 00000100 00000100 00000100 00000100 00000100 00000100
00000011 00000000 00000000 01001011 00000001 00000000 00000000 00000000 00010000 01101000
00110000 00000000 01001000 00000110 00010000 00000011 00000000 00000001 00000000 00000000
00000000 00000000 00000000 00000000 00000000 00000000 00000000 01110100 01010101 00000010
01010100 00000000 00000000 00001100 00000000 00000000 00000000 00000000 00000000 11110100
01010101 00000010 01010100 00000001 00000000 00000000 00000000 00010010 00000000 00000000
00010000 00000000 00000001 00000000 00000000 00000000 00000000 00000000 00000000 00000001
00000000 00000000 00000000 00000000 10000000 11001000 00011010 00000100 00000000 00000000
00000000 00000001 00000001 00000000 00010101 00000000 00000000 00000000 00000000 00011000
10100101 00000011 01010100 00000000 00000000 00000000 00000000 00010011 00001010 00000000
00000000 10000000 00000111 00000000 00000000 00000000 00000000 01110000 00000000 00000000
00000000 00000000 01000000 00000000 01010000 00000110 00010000 00011100 00000000 00000010
00000000 00000000 00001010 00000000 00000000 10000000 00000111 00000000 00000000 00010001
00000000 00000000 00000000 00000001 00000000 00000000 00000000 00000000 00000011 00000000
00000000 00000000 01000000 00000110 00010000 00000111 00000000 00000110 00000000 00000101
01110000 00000000 00000000 10000000 01110011 00000010 01010100 00000000 00000000 00000000
00000000 00000111 00000000 00000110 00000000 00000101 01110000 00000000 00000000 10100000
```

01110011 00000010 01010100 00000000 00000000 00000000 00000000 00000111 00000000 00000110
00000000 00000101 01110000 00000000 00000000 11000000 01110011 00000010 01010100 00000000
00000000 00000000 00000000 00000000 00000000 00100000 00110000 01101000 00000011 00000000
00000000 01001011 00000001 00000000 00000000 00000000 00000000 00000000 00000000 00000000
00000000 00000000 00000000 11111100 00000000 01000110 00110000 00111001 00110000 00110101
00110000 00110110 00110000 00111000 00110000 00110011 00110101 00110110 00000000 01001001
01101101 00111001 00111001 00111001 00111001 00111010 00111001 00111001 00111010 00111001
00111001 00100000 00110000 00110000 00111010 00110000 00110000 00111010 00110000 00110000
00000000 00001000 00000000 00000011 00000001 00000011 00000000 00000001 00000000 00000000
00000000 00000110 00000000 10100000 01110011 00010010 00000001 00000011 00000000 00000001
00000000 00000000 00000000 00000001 00000000 00000101 01110000 00011010 00000001 00000101
00000000 00000001 00000000 00000000 00000000 01010110 00011010 00000000 00000000 00011011
00000001 00000101 00000000 00000001 00000000 00000000 00000000 01011110 00011010 00000000
00000000 00101000 00000001 00000011 00000000 00000001 00000000 00000000 00000000 00000010
00000000 00111001 00110000 00000001 00000010 00000100 00000000 00000001 00000000 00000000
00000000 01100110 00011010 00000000 00000000 00000010 00000010 00000100 00000000 00000001
00000000 00000000 00000000 10101110 00011001 00000000 00000000 00010011 00000010 00000011
00000000 00000001 00000000 00000000 00000000 00000010 00000000 00000000 00000000 00000000
00000000 00000000 00000000 01001000 00000000 00000000 00000000 00000001 00000000 00000000
00000000 01001000 00000000 00000000 00000000 00000001 00000000 00000000 00000000 11111111
11011000 11111111 11011011 00000000 10000100 00000000 00000100 00000100 00000100 00000100
00000100 00000100 00000100 00000100 00000100 00000100 00001000 00000100 00000100 00001000
00001000 00001011 00001000 00001000 00001000 00001000 00001000 00001111 00001011 00001011
00001000 00001011 00010011 00001111 00010011 00010011 00010011 00001111 00010011 00010011
00010111 00010111 00011110 00011010 00010111 00010111 00011010 00010111 00010111 00010011
00011010 00100010 00011010 00011010 00011110 00011110 00100010 00100010 00100010 00010011
00011010 00100110 00100110 00100110 00100010 00100110 00011110 00100010 00100010 00100010
00000001 00000100 00001000 00001000 00001000 00001000 00001000 00001111 00001000 00001000
00001111 00100010 00010111 00010011 00010111 00100010 00100010 00100010 00100010 00100010
00100010 00100010 00100010 00100010 00100010 00100010 00100010 00100010 00100010 00100010
00100010 00100010 00100010 00100010 00100010 00100010 00100010 00100010 00100010 00100010
00100010 00100010 00100010 00100010 00100010 00100010 00100010 00100010 00100010 00100010
00100010 00100010 00100010 00100010 00100010 00100010 00100010 00100010 00100010 00100010
00100010 00100010 00100010 00100010 00100010 11111111 11000000 00000000 00010001 00001000
00000000 01111000 00000000 10100000 00000011 00000001 00100001 00000000 00000010 00010001
00000001 00000011 00010001 00000001 11111111 11000100 00000001 10100010 00000000 00000000
00000001 00000101 00000001 00000001 00000001 00000001 00000001 00000001 00000000 00000000
00000000 00000000 00000000 00000000 00000000 00000000 00000001 00000010 00000011 00000100
00000101 00000110 00000111 00001000 00001001 00001010 00001011 00010000 00000000 00000010
00000001 00000011 00000011 00000010 00000100 00000011 00000101 00000101 00000100 00000100
00000000 00000000 00000001 01111101 00000001 00000010 00000011 00000000 00000100 00010001
00000101 00010010 00100001 00110001 01000001 00000110 00010011 01010001 01100001 00000111
00100010 01110001 00010100 00110010 10000001 10010001 10100001 00001000 00100011 01000010
10110001 11000001 00010101 01010010 11010001 11110000 00100100 00110011 01100010 01110010
10000010 00001001 00001010 00010110 00010111 00011000 00011001 00011010 00100101 00100110
00100111 00101000 00101001 00101010 00110100 00110101 00110110 00110111 00111000 00111001
00111010 01000011 01000100 01000101 01000110 01000111 01001000 01001001 01001010 01010011
01010100 01010101 01010110 01010111 01011000 01011001 01011010 01100011 01100100 01100101
01100110 01100111 01101000 01101001 01101010 01110011 01110100 01110101 01110110 01110111
01111000 01111001 01111010 10000011 10000100 10000101 10000110 10000111 10001000 10001001
10001010 10010010 10010011 10010100 10010101 10010110 10010111 10011000 10011001 10011010
10100010 10100011 10100100 10100101 10100110 10100111 10101000 10101001 10101010 10110010
10110011 10110100 10110101 10110110 10110111 10111000 10111001 10111010 11000010 11000011
11000100 11000101 11000110 11000111 11001000 11001001 11001010 11010010 11010011 11010100
11010101 11010110 11010111 11011000 11011001 11011010 11100001 11100010 11100011 11100100
11100101 11100110 11100111 11101000 11101001 11101010 11110001 11110010 11110011 11110100
11110101 11110110 11110111 11111000 11111001 11111010 00000001 00000000 00000011 00000001
00000001 00000001 00000001 00000001 00000001 00000001 00000001 00000001 00000000 00000000
00000000 00000000 00000000 00000000 00000001 00000010 00000011 00000100 00000101 00000110
00000111 00001000 00001001 00001010 00001011 00010001 00000000 00000010 00000001 00000010
00000100 00000100 00000011 00000100 00000111 00000101 00000100 00000100 00000000 00000001
00000010 01110111 00000000 00000001 00000010 00000011 00010001 00000100 00000101 00100001
00110001 00000110 00010010 01000001 01010001 00000111 01100001 01110001 00010011 00100010
00110010 10000001 00001000 00010100 01000010 10010001 10100001 10110001 11000001 00001001
00100011 00110011 01010010 11110000 00010101 01100010 01110010 11010001 00001010 00010110
00100100 00110100 11100001 00100101 11110001 00010111 00011000 00011001 00011010 00100110
00100111 00101000 00101001 00101010 00110101 00110110 00110111 00111000 00111001 00111010
01000011 01000100 01000101 01000110 01000111 01001000 01001001 01001010 01010011 01010100
01010101 01010110 01010111 01011000 01011001 01011010 01100011 01100100 01100101 01100110
01100111 01101000 01101001 01101010 01110011 01110100 01110101 01110110 01110111 01111000
01111001 01111010 10000010 10000011 10000100 10000101 10000110 10000111 10001000 10001001
10001010 10010010 10010011 10010100 10010101 10010110 10010111 10011000 10011001 10011010
10100010 10100011 10100100 10100101 10100110 10100111 10101000 10101001 10101010 10110010

10110011 10110100 10110101 10110110 10110111 10111000 10111001 10111010 11000010 11000011
11000100 11000101 11000110 11000111 11001000 11001001 11001010 11010010 11010011 11010100
11010101 11010110 11010111 11011000 11011001 11011010 11100010 11100011 11100100 11100101
11100110 11100111 11101000 11101001 11101010 11110010 11110011 11110100 11110101 11110110
11110111 11111000 11111001 11111010 11111111 11011010 00000000 00001100 00000011 00000001
00000000 00000010 00010001 00000011 00010001 00000000 00111111 00000000 10000111 11000011
00011010 00111110 10111101 10100100 10111101 11000101 11000101 11001011 01011011 01011110
01001100 11101000 10111001 00010001 01001100 10100100 10110001 11100111 10111001 11000111
10110101 01101001 11101011 11010110 00111110 00100000 11010111 11110100 11001111 10110010
11000011 01100011 11100110 10100011 00000101 11011010 01111110 11010011 00011001 00001110
00111101 01000001 11011111 11101001 01011111 00000111 01011001 01001101 11001110 11101011
01101101 00001111 01100010 10001100 11101000 11000110 00001001 01001111 11100010 01010111
00110001 01110100 01001101 00000111 11000111 00110110 10110111 10011110 00100110 10111000
00111010 00110011 11000101 00110101 11001100 00110001 11000101 01101110 00111100 11111000
01011011 00100000 00111000 11000010 01100111 01111111 01010000 10000100 10001100 10011110
11001010 00111011 11100000 01010111 00100101 10101011 11111000 01011011 11000100 01110110
00111010 10101111 10001000 00101111 01110100 11111101 00001010 11101010 01011011 01011001
00100011 01011011 01111011 01111000 01100010 00111001 01010110 01000011 00011001 01010110
00101101 10001100 11100100 01111011 01110000 01111001 11100011 00010101 11101000 11000101
01000001 00111001 01011001 11111100 01011011 11111101 11001001 01111110 01001000 11110010
11101110 11011101 10101111 11010000 11100100 11111100 00110101 11100000 00101111 00011100
11000111 01111111 00001110 10101011 01101111 10100111 00110101 10010100 11110001 01001100
00110011 11110110 10100100 01110100 00100111 00111100 10010110 11101001 10010011 11111000
01111010 11010111 10101010 11111000 10110110 01011101 01001010 00001001 00101101 10100001
10001010 00100111 00000101 10010100 10011001 00011000 11000110 01111110 01100011 10010001
11000000 00011101 10111011 01110011 11011110 10111001 10110001 00010010 10001011 10011100
01111001 00110101 11111110 10111111 11100001 11001110 11001010 00101101 00111111 01110110
01111101 11111111 00000000 10101111 11010000 11001001 10111010 10111001 10110101 10110101
10000110 00001001 01011010 01110001 00011001 00111111 00101011 10110000 00111101 01000001
00011101 01110001 11011100 11100111 00000011 10111101 01110011 00011111 01101111 10001011
01010010 11010110 00110100 01011011 00011011 00110000 10110011 00001111 10110111 01000011
00101100 10001100 10101110 00001111 01000110 00000011 10101111 11010011 10110101 01000101
00101000 11001001 10110101 01100100 01110100 01001110 01011010 10110110 01111101 00010011
00100001 11001111 11010010 10101010 00111101 00100110 11001111 00101000 10101001 00111100
01110000 11011100 11000011 00101101 10111101 11001100 01000010 01111011 01110111 00011011
01011001 00011000 01100100 00010001 01011111 00110001 01111000 11000111 11000011 10011010
10000111 10000111 00110101 01010011 01111000 10001100 01101110 00101101 10100101 10010100
11001011 00000100 11111000 11101000 11011001 11001110 11010011 11101000 01000111 11100100
01111011 01110111 00000011 10100110 10001100 10101101 00111101 01000100 11110110 00110011
11100001 10111110 10111001 10110101 01100100 10111011 10000001 00001101 11011101 10010101
11011011 00010000 11001011 11010100 11000101 00100001 00100111 00101010 00111110 10111100
10011100 01110111 11001111 11100011 01001011 00011101 11100010 11011011 01011101 10100101
11100101 10101010 10010001 10110100 11111100 11001000 11011100 01100100 00010001 11001000
00111111 10101111 11100101 01010011 11101100 10010010 10010111 00110100 01110110 11011001
11111111 00000000 01011110 10000111 10110111 01000010 01001101 11111011 10110010 11101011
11111010 10011011 01111010 10100010 11101001 10111010 10101110 10011011 00101101 11010111
10010001 00011011 10001101 10100100 10000111 01100101 00000001 10010100 11100000 01100111
11110001 11000000 11000111 11100000 00101011 11001100 00110101 10001101 00100110 00011011
00100101 01011011 10001011 01110111 00111011 01001111 01010100 00111100 11100011 11110001
10101110 10001000 01010100 10011100 01100110 10100011 11010001 11101000 01110001 00111010
01001010 11010010 01001111 01110100 01101111 01101000 11011010 10100000 11010110 01010001
01101100 10101111 01001000 01101101 01001001 00010111 11110111 01101110 01111010 11001110
10100011 10110001 11111111 00000000 01101000 01111010 11110111 00011110 11100011 10011101
10110110 10000001 10011011 00000110 00011001 01011010 11011101 11001010 10010101 00101100
10011000 11001001 00011111 10001000 00110101 11011011 01110101 00011111 01110100 11100000
11110011 00101010 00101101 10010100 00010110 11110001 11101100 01010100 00000000 01100111
10010110 01100011 11001001 00111110 11110101 01000110 01101000 10110111 11100100 01000011
00011001 01110110 11101110 11000100 01110000 00101001 00111001 01011001 10010110 10010011
01100111 10111001 11011001 11111000 11001101 01010111 01001101 01001001 10101110 11101111
00001010 01011111 00000110 00111000 11011000 10000000 10001001 01000000 01010010 01000000
00111100 00010000 00000001 01101100 00000010 00111000 00100011 00000111 00011000 11101011
01011101 10001100 00011010 11101101 10101100 00010011 10100011 10110001 01011000 00110100
01000001 00000010 10011011 01011011 10100110 10111001 00001100 00100101 01100001 10111000
00010100 00001010 01001110 01000001 00011110 10011101 01111000 00110101 11001100 11111001
01100010 11010010 10010010 11010011 01100101 11101011 10101000 10011010 01110011 10111100
10010110 11111011 10111111 11000011 11110011 00110000 01110101 01111111 00010000 01001001
00100111 11011000 10011010 00110101 10110111 10111100 01001011 10101001 10000001 00100010
01001000 11001000 00000010 00100010 00111110 11101011 01100111 01110000 11001110 00111010
10010011 10001111 11110111 01000101 01111010 00010111 10000001 01110101 10101000 10110101
10101101 00010101 10101110 00100010 01011001 00000000 10001110 01110110 10000000 10011001
00111010 10110001 00000001 01111001 11101010 01111101 01111011 11110111 11001111 01011110
10110101 10011100 10010011 01110000 10010101 01001011 11111100 10111101 00011010 01000101
00111001 01111011 10110001 10000011 01011011 01111110 10111010 10011101 10000011 00011110

```
00101010 10101100 11001000 10001110 00110001 00100010 00000111 01011111 01110001 10011010
11110011 10101111 11010100 10000011 00010110 01111101 00000111 01000010 10011100 10110011
01001101 10100010 11011010 01001100 11000100 01100000 10010110 10110110 01000010 01001000
11101001 11101001 01011001 11011111 11110000 10001011 01111000 01111010 00111011 10011000
10101110 10100001 11010010 01100010 10000010 01111000 11100100 00010010 00100001 10001101
01110110 00000101 01100001 11010000 11100000 01100000 01010110 10001010 01110010 01010010
10111010 01100110 10011100 11010010 11011010 11111010 00011010 10010010 01110111 10101010
01101110 00001111 01101110 10110101 00111010 00010000 01010100 10010011 10110110 01111010
11110101 10101100 01011101 01011111 01001110 10110100 11010101 10101100 11101110 01110100
11111011 11100101 00101111 01101111 00101000 11101101 11010101 00011011 10110011 00001111
01110001 01010101 01111011 00111101 00000000 11111001 11100010 11110011 01001101 10011111
11000011 10010111 11110111 01011010 00001110 10101000 01110111 11011000 01011100 01110010
10010011 00101111 00000000 11110011 11110010 10111000 11101100 00001111 01001100 11111010
01100011 11010011 10010011 01011111 01010000 10001001 01011000 10101100 01101111 00100001
01101011 11111101 10100111 01110001 00100011 11111101 01110000 01011110 10100111 11101010
00000111 00111001 11101110 00111101 11000111 00111011 11001101 10110111 00110101 00101000
11101100 11111111 00000000 01001101 11111111 00000000 01000011 11010010 11000011 11001101
01000001 11110011 00111110 10011111 10101001 01010110 11001011 01010000 01011000 01100110
10010010 00101011 10101111 10011110 11001110 01011100 11111001 10001010 00000111 00000011
11011100 00001111 11110000 11111111 00000000 00001010 11010001 01001111 00100010 00011011
11001101 00101001 01011100 10101110 00011101 01000010 11100001 11001111 00000111 00101010
01000111 00110101 00110010 10111101 11100011 01101110 10101100 11101110 10101011 00011011
00110111 00100101 11011000 10100101 10101101 01111000 01001010 00000111 00100010 11101111
01000110 00100010 11010110 11110001 00001110 11101100 00101001 11011010 10100100 11111011
01111111 01110100 11111101 00101010 11001110 10001101 10101000 00110110 10101000 01011011
01001111 10111111 10110110 00110110 11111010 11100100 01100100 00001001 01001110 01110110
10001001 00010011 00100011 11100111 00000011 11010111 11010111 10110111 01000011 11011100
10000001 11011001 11001110 11011100 00111001 10110111 01101011 11111010 11111111 00000000
10000011 11110010 00111110 01111110 11011010 10011101 01010000 11010001 10101100 01010101
10110111 00010000 11010011 10110000 11101000 01011101 10110011 01001000 11110110 10110001
01000110 00110110 10100010 00000101 10101110 00000111 00100110 11011110 10101100 11011011
01101101 00001100 01011101 00001011 01010001 10110001 10110101 01000111 10110111 11110001
00000100 01100110 11101111 01001001 11001001 10010001 01010101 00110110 10011001 00000011
11100011 00011100 00011101 11000000 10000000 01000110 00110011 10000011 11001001 01010001
11011011 00111001 10111001 11111101 10101111 11100001 11001001 11100110 10110000 10110100
10111000 10110101 10111110 10110010 10110001 10110110 00001101 00100100 01010011 01000111
00100010 10110100 10001100 01011001 10110010 01110111 11100100 00000000 00110000 00000000
11000110 11010010 01110001 11101110 01001001 10101111 01010001 11000010 10100011 01111100
11010001 01101010 11011110 01111101 11010111 01001111 11101011 11001100 11010010 01010000
01110000 11110111 01100101 00011101 01101101 11010011 01011101 00111011 11101000 01111010
01011101 11001111 10001011 10110100 10011000 11010000 11001110 00100111 00010111 01011011
11001001 01101101 10111110 01110110 01110000 11001010 10100100 10101001 11000001 00111111
00100000 00111011 01110001 10000000 00111001 00101100 00110011 11011111 00111110 10000001
11100000 00101011 11100001 10101000 11101000 11110111 01110111 00100000 00010101 11001101
11010011 10101001 00000100 11110000 00001000 01010101 11001110 00000111 01100001 11101101
01011110 01011111 00101111 10111011 01110111 00011011 01011000 11101010 10010101 00101001
00101010 01010010 10101001 00100110 11010101 10011010 01010110 11110101 11111111 00000000
10000110 00111011 00110010 01101010 00110111 00111001 10101100 00011110 10111010 10011110
01010001 00001011 01010100 00001101 01001000 01100101 01011001 00001110 01110010 00001111
00110101 01001110 01001110 10100111 10111101 00111011 10000001 01010001 10111011 11111010
11010101 01001001 01000110 01110011 10010011 11111000 11010101 01011111 10101000 11001110
01010011 11000100 01011010 00011101 10100110 10111101 01100100 11110110 10110111 01000011
01100100 10000011 10011000 11100100 00000011 11100110 10001101 10111101 01111110 10011110
10100010 10111100 10111010 11011011 01000010 01010000 10110010 11011000 01101011 00010001
00011111 11101101 00111011 01100111 11011101 00010100 11000001 10011011 00100101 00001111
11011101 01110101 00111101 11111001 00000111 11110010 00000000 10001010 11101000 10001100
10101100 10111100 11010110 10100001 01110011 00001111 11000100 00111010 00110000 10110110
11111111 00000000 01001101 10110100 00111011 10100001 00111111 01111101 01000000 11111011
10000111 11010111 11101001 11111100 10101011 00101110 01100000 10001111 10100111 01000101
00111001 01111100 11001010 01110110 00001000 11011000 10011100 00010000 11101010 01001111
00011110 10111001 00111100 01111110 01000110 10101111 10011010 11111100 10110010 11110011
00111101 01111110 01101110 01111010 00111110 01101000 11101001 10101101 11101110 00100011
01111000 00010010 01101001 01011011 11001011 01000010 10111001 11011101 10011100 00000001
01010000 10011011 00111000 00110101 00111001 01100001 10010110 11010100 10111100 01110111
00110001 00110110 11100100 10111001 11111011 10111110 01011001 11110110 11110101 11001111
01110001 11010000 11100110 10100001 10110101 00001101 01010110 11100111 10011011 01101011
11101110 01110101 11011011 10001110 00010100 00011100 00010110 11000111 00100111 11010110
10100000 10010101 01000001 00111100 10000010 00101011 10011101 00110000 11110011 00111011
00011011 11011111 10000011 01101111 01110001 00011011 10001011 01111101 01010110 11011110
11010101 11000011 01100101 01110110 01011010 10110000 11100011 11010011 10010111 00111111
11010110 10111001 10100110 11111000 00101001 11100010 00000011 00111011 00111001 11010100
11101100 01011001 00110110 11100011 10010011 00100110 01001001 11111111 00000000 10111110
01101011 11010110 10001110 00100010 00110001 01010110 01101001 10010111 01010010 10100111
```

00111011 01101110 11011101 00101101 11010011 10111111 10010101 10000110 00111111 11000001
10011111 00010011 00001100 00110100 00111010 10001101 10000000 01110001 11010011 00101111
00101111 11111111 00000000 00010001 01011110 11011001 11100000 10101101 00001110 11111111
00000000 11000011 10111010 00011010 11011000 01101010 01010010 01000101 00100101 11101001
10010110 01001001 01011101 10100000 01100010 01010000 11101110 00111100 01100011 00100000
00011110 10011000 10101110 01011010 10010101 01100001 00101000 11011001 00011011 01001010
10111011 10010101 00110111 01001101 01101100 11111111 00000000 01000011 10101010 01100110
00000011 00100100 10011010 10000100 10011100 11100111 00111100 11110011 01011110 01111101
11001110 00000010 00100010 01111011 01110110 10101000 01011000 10011100 10011110 01101000
00011001 01010101 11001111 11100011 01010101 00011100 11110101 10100111 11100100 00000101
01100110 00100111 00000100 01010101 01111001 00101000 11101010 00110010 10010011 10101000
00111001 11001101 01100010 11101010 00011010 01110100 01010111 01101010 00001011 11111100
10110010 10101110 01110110 00111110 00111001 01011100 11100011 00100011 11101000 01110000
00111111 00100001 01001110 11100000 01111001 11100110 10100110 10010010 01011010 01001010
11010001 11001100 10011011 11100011 00111111 00101011 10000010 00110011 10001110 00111111
01010000 01101011 10000011 10111011 11010011 10010110 01111111 00110010 00101000 11110111
10100101 10100001 00100001 10010101 00011011 11111000 00001111 10110101 01101100 10100100
10010010 10111011 11101000 01110100 01000010 01001101 01011111 11001100 11010001 10110011
11010010 01011101 11010110 00110101 01100110 01100011 00010010 11110100 11011100 01001001
11000111 11010010 10111010 10101011 01111000 11010010 00011000 10010110 00100101 00011000
00000011 11110101 10101000 01110010 01110010 01110111 01100100 10111011 01101100 01001010
01100100 11001110 01111011 00011010 01100011 00111000 00100011 11011111 10101101 01000101
11011000 10101100 01111101 01000010 01011011 00010100 10000101 11111101 11101010 10011011
00111001 11000100 00001101 10011010 01000010 01111111 00111010 10000110 00110001 10100101
10111111 11001110 01101011 00110110 11101110 11111110 00111011 01011001 11101101 10100001
10010011 10000101 10010011 01110110 01011011 00111111 01110000 00001110 11111111 00000000
01001100 10010000 00111111 00011010 11001110 01010010 01001011 01110011 01011000 01000101
11001110 01010110 01000100 10010010 01001100 10001000 00000011 11001000 11100001 01010111
11010100 10011100 00001010 10001100 10111010 10111000 11011100 10101101 10111001 01001111
01000010 00101000 10111010 00100110 11001100 10000001 11001001 11101001 10011110 01111101
00101010 10101011 10011111 11000110 10101001 10110110 00100010 10110011 00010000 01110011
11101001 01010101 00011100 10011110 01001101 01010111 01010000 00101011 10111001 11101011
10011010 10100111 00101001 00011000 00110100 11101110 11011000 00011000 00111010 10000100
01000010 01110100 00111001 00011011 10011000 00001110 00110011 11011100 01111010 01010111
00010111 00110100 01010110 11101000 11000100 11111001 01000001 01001110 01111001 00010101
10010101 10010011 01011010 10010100 10011001 00011111 10011100 10000000 01100001 01110000
00101010 00100110 10010100 11110011 10000011 10011010 01101101 11110111 00110100 01000010
00001001 00000001 11100011 00110100 10111011 10001011 01010101 01011111 01011011 00010100
01111101 01001010 01011111 11010010 10010000 10110111 01101100 11010110 10111010 10101101
11001110 01010001 00110111 01111110 00100110 10111001 10101101 01100111 11000100 00010001
01101001 01110011 11111001 00110010 00111010 10101111 11001000 00100100 11101011 11001110
00001001 00100011 00111111 10100101 01110011 11001110 01001101 00101111 01110100 11011010
00010001 01010010 10010010 01001100 11100011 01111111 11100001 00111111 00110111 11010111
01101001 01100101 10100110 01011001 01001011 10101000 01011101 00110001 11000000 01000100
11111110 01111110 10011000 11110111 10101101 10010101 00011110 00100011 10111101 00111011
11100110 11010001 10100010 10110101 10010101 00000001 11011000 01100111 10111001 00001100
01000110 01111010 11100011 01101000 01101100 01110100 00011001 11101001 01011100 10111100
10010010 10010111 11000100 11001111 01001010 11110000 10100111 10111001 11100100 01010111
11111110 00111011 10010001 01100001 01001001 00100110 01110111 10110000 01100111 11100100
00100001 01000010 01000000 00011111 10010110 00101011 11001110 01010011 11000111 10011110
00100001 10110110 10001111 01010000 10001111 01001100 11010100 00011010 11001001 01100110
10010000 11001011 00100000 01010010 00111001 01100011 11000111 11001011 11000111 11001011
11000110 00111010 01110010 01001111 00111111 01001111 01011111 00001111 01000001 01101110
11110110 00110011 10101111 00101101 00101100 01110100 11011110 00011110 11111000 10110111
10101100 01101001 01011010 10111100 01111010 01101111 10001000 00101110 00000110 10100111
10100101 01100100 01000110 11010010 10110010 11111110 11110010 00010001 10011100 00010110
11001000 00011001 01101111 01010010 00001000 00100110 10111110 10010110 01100111 00001100
10111001 11101101 01001110 10111101 00110101 00000110 10100101 00011110 10100111 10011001
11010100 10101010 11101101 10011111 10101101 01010101 01110110 00011001 00110101 11001101
01101110 11100000 01010110 01100110 11100011 10101101 01010011 10010110 01010000 10101011
00100011 00010011 10010000 10100011 00100111 00000011 00111000 00010101 00101101 11011000
10101011 00110111 10100010 00111100 11110011 01010101 11110001 01010110 00100101 10010010
00011011 00001000 11010111 00100000 01100100 10111100 11000111 00000000 11110101 11100011
00011101 01000111 00000000 10011111 01011110 00111010 01100011 10010001 11001110 01001001
10101110 01000001 01111111 00110000 10000001 01111001 10011100 00101111 00101111 11110111
01000100 10000100 00001110 01110000 00111001 11000111 10110111 00110101 10111010 10000110
10001101 11110110 00000010 10001101 11000101 11001100 10010000 10111010 10000110 00111000
00101100 00110010 00000110 01111001 11000110 01001000 11001111 11101000 01101001 00100001
10111110 01100111 00100101 01011000 00010001 11101110 01001111 01011010 01010110 01010110
10111010 00101001 01110110 01100101 11010100 10011011 10011110 00011010 10101110 00101011
11110001 11000001 11111100 10101011 10010110 11100110 11100111 11010100 00111110 01100111
01001110 01111001 10100011 01111111 00111100 11010111 01000100 10001110 00110001 00110111
01110010 00111001 10101100 10001101 01100011 01001001 10000011 01011000 10110101 11110010

00100100 01100011 00001100 11001010 01001001 10001010 01010101 00011100 11000110 01111111
10101000 00111100 01100100 01111111 01011100 00011010 11100110 10010010 11101000 11001101
01100010 11011010 01110111 01000111 10010000 10001101 00011010 11010011 01001011 11010100
01010100 11001111 00011011 01101001 01111010 11001100 01000111 01110100 01110011 01000000
01110110 10010110 11111111 00000000 01101000 00011100 01100001 10000001 11100111 10101000
11101110 01000001 00011101 01000101 01111010 00010110 10011011 11100010 01011111 00110101
01111100 10101011 11111000 11001000 10010001 01111010 11001011 00011010 11100101 01011000
01111010 10010001 11010100 01111110 00011001 11111100 00101011 10011111 11011010 00110101
11101110 11001111 01100011 11010001 10011100 00010100 11010010 10011100 01001110 00110011
11100010 00110100 10011110 00011010 11010010 10111100 00110001 10101010 01101010 10010000
01101001 10010110 10010111 00111010 10001101 11010001 00110001 01000101 00100011 01000010
10101110 11011110 01100011 11110000 01001000 00100100 01110000 01000000 00001100 01111011
01110010 00111101 01001101 01111000 10001111 10000110 11110100 01101101 00011101 10110100
10111011 10101001 11110101 10010101 01011001 01101110 00100100 00000011 11001001 01000101
10010100 10100011 00101010 11111111 00000000 01111011 00011001 11100111 00100111 11010111
00111101 00111101 00101011 11010101 10100111 00111001 11000110 10001011 10010100 01011110
10111101 00001110 01101000 01000101 11001110 01110110 10011111 01000011 10010010 11010111
11110100 10110101 10000010 01111001 00101110 10101101 01100101 01111001 01010011 10101011
01111001 10011111 01111011 10101111 10110101 01111101 01110001 11100001 00001101 01001010
00111101 01000111 11000011 01011010 00100100 11101001 01110000 00100111 10010011 11101100
11010001 10100100 10100100 00110110 01001000 10010000 00101000 00001100 00001111 10111101
01110100 01010100 10010011 10011101 00001000 11011111 10100111 11111001 00011001 01001110
00011100 10010010 01110110 00110111 01100100 01100011 10011110 10111001 10101010 10010010
00111111 01011111 01011111 11100101 01011110 01111010 11011100 11000100 10100110 11110010
01010111 10011100 11111000 11111001 10101110 11100001 11010011 11010010 11111010 11000110
11100001 10100010 01101101 11000010 00101001 10000010 10010010 00000011 10100001 11001001
00011001 11000111 10100001 11001111 11111101 11110101 01010101 00010100 10011100 10010101
11000111 10101001 11100100 00111010 01110110 10110000 11000000 01111101 10010010 11101101
01010111 11001001 01010001 11110010 10011100 01110100 11110110 10101001 00100001 00110000
01001011 00011100 10110011 01000010 00000100 01101010 00011001 10110110 10000011 10001100
00001100 01010111 10101110 11010011 10001101 11011100 01001000 01100100 11011010 11011101
11101001 01011011 11001011 01000101 01000010 00011001 10011010 11011010 11011100 11100111
11111110 11011001 00100101 01011000 11010011 10010010 11101110 11111100 10110000 10110111
11011010 00011101 01111010 10101001 01100000 00111000 11110101 00010100 01001001 00100101
00000110 11101100 00110011 10101010 10110110 11010001 11110101 00111001 00110000 00001010
10101010 10011111 01110110 00011100 11010110 11100101 10111110 10000001 01111100 11011111
01111110 01000100 00000111 11101010 01111111 11000010 10111100 01111001 10100110 11011110
10000110 11101010 01001000 11110111 11001000 10100110 00100101 01000001 00100111 00100110
10100110 11110011 00111011 10011110 01101011 01101001 01101110 01110011 00001110 00010010
01110101 11101111 10011010 01110110 11101010 11100100 01110111 00101100 11001001 11010101
01110100 11101011 00101101 01011010 00000011 00000101 11100100 01111011 10111010 11101100
01110000 01110000 11110001 10011111 01010101 00111111 11100100 01111010 11010111 10011000
11011110 11011001 11101010 10011110 00011101 10111100 10110110 11110011 00011000 01011100
01101001 11101100 11100001 01000100 11011001 00000011 11010111 10000110 00011101 10001110
00000111 11010011 11011110 10111001 10100101 00011011 11101010 11001110 11111010 00110011
10110011 11100100 01111011 00110011 10011101 11110001 11100111 10000101 01101111 00110101
11010100 10000110 01101011 00011001 00111100 10110000 10101101 10111100 00000010 11000111
01101011 00011100 01110111 11111111 00000000 00011110 11011001 10101110 01111101 10101100
11110100 11001011 01111011 01001011 00010011 10101011 11000110 00010010 11101110 11010110
11001011 11001011 01010000 11001101 10110100 11111001 10100001 01000000 11101000 00111001
00111100 11110011 11111010 11010110 11010100 10101011 01011010 10010010 10100111 00000101
11101111 00100111 11111010 00011101 11001010 00011111 10111100 01110010 01111011 00011110
01010001 10101011 00111010 01000001 00011111 10010011 00011100 10001101 00110100 10110111
00000100 00110011 01100100 11100111 01101010 11111011 01111101 01111000 11111101 01101011
10101000 11110000 11010111 10001000 10101111 10110100 01001001 00100001 10111000 10110101
01110011 00010110 00110000 00001010 10011110 01010010 01000001 11101000 01000111 11111001
11110110 10101111 10100001 11100100 01110010 10100101 10101111 11110101 01100011 10000101
11011011 10011101 10100011 11101000 10111101 00010011 11000100 00110110 10011010 11111101
10011111 11011010 10101101 10111111 01110111 00100010 11110001 00100100 01000100 11110010
10000111 00011111 10101000 11110100 00110101 01111110 01001001 00111010 11010111 10001101
01101011 00111011 00110011 10001010 01001011 10010101 11011001 10011000 01111010 10111110
10101101 01100111 10100100 11011010 10110101 11101101 11110100 10000110 00111000 00000011
00000101 11001010 10101001 01100011 10010010 01111101 00000101 01110011 00111010 10100111
10001001 01110100 00110110 10110001 00000110 01100111 00110111 00010001 01001100 10011011
10000100 01001111 00010001 11001011 00101111 10111000 01101110 10011111 10001101 01101101
00011000 00110110 10111001 10010001 00110111 00111100 01000011 01011001 10110100 01101001
11101110 00111110 11010011 10100111 11011010 01111101 10001010 11011110 01000000 00011000
00000110 11100011 10110111 01100000 01111111 00011110 01111111 10010101 01010111 00010000
01101010 01110110 11110110 10100010 00010010 11110001 10101110 11101110 00000110 01001001
11001111 00111111 10000101 01111011 00110001 01101011 10010101 00101001 01101110 01101111
01011010 00110100 11100001 00110111 00011010 01001110 11101001 01110101 11101110 01011011
10110010 10110110 10011110 11101110 11100011 01101110 10100001 00101000 01100111 01000100
00000001 00011101 00110010 01001001 00000011 10001101 10100100 00011100 01100111 00011111

10000111 11100011 01001101 10011110 11110110 01001101 00110010 01010011 00111101 10011100
11000001 11011101 00110000 00111101 10011010 10010011 01111110 11110111 00101011 11011001
10011000 00101101 01010101 11001111 01000010 11010010 11111100 01010111 01111001 00111101
10110100 00010010 10001000 10100010 11001011 00001110 10100101 01011011 10101111 11100111
01011101 00000100 01011110 00100101 10111110 00111101 00010110 00110001 11101111 10110000
11111111 00000000 10001101 01111100 11111101 01011001 01001010 00010010 11100101 11101100
01111010 01010000 10100011 00011001 00100100 11011001 11101001 00011110 00011110 10010011
01010111 01001011 01111000 11111111 00000000 10110100 11100000 11111011 00111100 10000100
01111100 11001011 10111101 01011011 00000111 11010100 01100000 10010001 01011101 01100010
11001111 11101111 10010011 01011100 11110011 11000110 11100001 11010011 01101001 00111111
11000000 11100101 11110110 00010101 01111011 00001111 00010011 11001000 00010110 01100110
00110000 10011001 00110110 11111101 11010101 01010010 00110010 11000011 00000011 11010100
10000000 00111111 00011111 01001010 11001111 01001101 01001111 01010011 01110010 01000001
11010000 10100101 11011011 11010101 01011000 01001101 00010001 00000100 01100011 11111101
11101100 11010111 00100111 11010111 00101000 00110100 11011010 01111111 10011000 11111101
10010100 11010110 11100111 00111011 11111101 10100001 10101011 01011011 01101010 10000000
00111101 10101100 10110011 01011011 10110011 00110010 11001100 00010100 10001001 00111100
10100010 01110000 01010100 11100000 00110001 00111110 10111101 00110000 00110000 01101011
01100111 01010000 10010001 00101110 00101101 10011010 00001001 01000110 01001011 10010101
00000001 01011000 01110101 11100100 01110110 10100010 00110101 01100001 00111000 11101011
00110101 01110001 11110010 10111000 11001001 00110100 10001010 10100100 01011011 00101101
10010100 01110000 01000011 00101010 11001100 10110001 10001101 10100111 00001101 10011010
11100010 10111100 01000111 11100001 11100100 11010111 10101101 10000010 01011001 11001000
00101101 11101110 11010111 10010101 01100010 10111001 00000111 11011000 11010111 00110100
00011011 10000100 10010100 10111011 00011110 11010101 11001111 00011101 11010101 00111100
00001111 10101011 11101001 01100010 01011011 10001011 10101011 01111111 10110100 00101000
00011011 10111100 11000101 00111011 10110011 11111101 01101011 10100110 11110000 10111111
10000101 01101101 10110101 00111101 00011110 00101011 11111001 01101110 00110111 10001001
00010111 00111011 00010011 00011000 01011111 01100011 11010110 10111110 10001010 10101110
00100110 11111000 01110111 00101000 01111001 00100011 10001110 00110000 10110100 11110101
00101100 11101000 10110110 00010011 01101000 01111110 00100111 10110100 10110110 10000101
11001000 10000101 11110111 10001110 01011000 11100001 10010000 00100001 00100100 00011111
01011100 01100011 00111111 10000000 10101110 11110010 11110011 11000100 01011010 01010101
10110001 01110100 01101011 11000100 10010010 01101100 11100011 01100010 00011100 10010010
01111101 00111101 00101010 00010100 10011101 01010100 10100110 10110111 01100111 00001101
01110101 11001011 00101011 00011110 01001111 10101110 01111000 10001101 00110101 00101011
10110001 00101010 11001100 11011111 11011001 10101100 01110110 00100011 10000101 11100000
00010000 00001001 11000000 00100111 00011100 01100100 01110010 01111010 01110001 11010100
11100010 10110000 00000101 11000101 11101100 10111010 01110101 11111100 11110000 00100011
10111110 10010000 10101110 10000010 01011001 01111000 01010001 11100110 01110001 10000000
00110011 11010111 10110110 01000000 11001111 01101110 10010101 11101001 01000010 00101011
10010111 01011111 11101001 10011100 01101101 00110100 11001100 11011101 01000011 01010010
11111011 11001111 00011011 00111010 00000110 01010000 00110010 11111001 11001000 11110101
11111110 01000011 00010100 10010110 01011111 01101010 10111001 00010001 10111011 10010011
10111011 01101000 10010000 11100100 01111010 01110011 01011101 10101001 01110010 10101011
11001000 10001101 11011001 10110011 00010110 10011111 00100111 11001100 11110010 01001111
00010101 10101010 11101101 11001000 01110111 01111101 10111100 01100011 10010010 00111110
10011110 10110101 11001011 11011101 11011100 01101001 01101010 11001110 10110001 11101111
10111000 11000011 01100000 11001010 11101000 00111111 01111010 00111101 01110001 11010011
11110100 10101110 01111000 11001001 11010100 10101001 11001011 01001101 01101101 10111011
11111101 00111111 10101110 11000111 01100010 10001010 10000100 00111001 10100101 11010100
11110100 00101101 00110011 01011111 11110000 11111100 01110110 00010110 11011000 10110111
10000000 00110000 00000001 01001110 00010110 00110101 00111001 11111010 00011100 01111110
10011100 01010111 10101111 01101011 11101011 00111101 10110101 10011110 10000110 01101110
00010001 11101101 10100000 01011000 00010001 01011001 00001001 00011111 00100011 01101101
00000011 00011000 11001110 00111000 00110101 11100000 11001010 10000101 01000101 01010110
01101010 01101111 01000111 01111110 11100111 01001100 10101010 01000001 11000110 00111100
10111101 11001110 00000000 11111100 01000010 10111100 01011001 00001100 10011110 01110010
00101100 01111101 10010000 00100010 10010000 00111111 00011100 11111111 00000000 01011010
11010110 11010011 01111110 00100110 11000100 00011111 00011010 10000010 00110011 00001110
11000110 00010100 00111111 11111010 00001111 11110101 11001101 01110000 01001011 00101111
10111100 01111101 11001101 11001110 11101111 01101101 01110111 10101001 11010011 10100111
11000100 10001101 00001110 11100011 00110001 00110101 11000100 10110110 10011100 00000000
00011101 11100001 01100001 10011111 11010010 10111010 11111101 00101011 01011000 11010011
11101110 11100001 10001011 11101100 11010111 11101011 00110100 01111000 00011011 01000010
00010000 01110001 11101100 01110001 01011110 00000101 01101100 00100101 01011010 00110000
11100110 11111100 10001101 01101111 00011001 01101100 01011100 10010100 11000011 00100011
01001101 00100100 00000101 01100100 10011100 01111101 11111100 01100011 00100111 00011110
10110101 11001110 11101010 11000111 11001101 10110110 10111010 10111101 11110010 00010101
01101110 01100010 01001101 10101000 01110111 01110011 10010011 11000111 00000011 10100111
01110011 01011110 01110100 00011011 01010011 10001011 10010110 11110111 00001110 01011101
01001111 00101001 10110001 11010110 01110101 00111001 01100111 01101011 00101000 10100011
10010001 11100101 00100100 01101110 11111001 00011000 01101101 00000011 11010111 00110101

11101000 10110001 11111111 00000000 01101000 01011010 01000000 10110010 11111001 01010001
00010010 10101011 10010010 00011110 11100110 00111000 10001110 00110010 00000110 01000110
11110110 01011101 11000111 00111000 11111001 01010111 00100100 11110110 00000110 10111110
11010110 01010001 01010010 10010010 10000101 11110101 01100001 00101011 00101011 11001000
01001101 01010101 10100001 11010100 10101101 10011010 11011110 11101010 11101100 01000101
00011001 11101010 01100010 00100011 01110111 11100111 01011100 11001100 01110111 00111010
00000110 10000001 00000001 10110110 10110000 10001101 01101101 11100011 00111100 10110000
00000111 10010111 00111110 10100111 11010100 11010111 00101111 10111111 00100100 11100010
10110110 01111011 10001010 11000111 00100111 10101110 11111000 10001110 11011110 01110111
10110100 10010010 11000101 10011010 00101011 10000100 10010011 00100001 10111010 00010000
00110001 10001110 00001101 01100010 01101011 01110110 10110111 01010011 11011011 11000101
10101001 11000000 00000011 01001110 10100011 00100100 11000110 01110000 10100100 11110101
00000111 11011000 11111010 10011110 00000111 11110011 00111110 10100100 00010011 10100000
11100001 00100110 11111010 11011011 11101111 00111001 10101010 11000011 10011110 00101100
11100001 11101111 11011010 11110010 01001111 00110011 00010111 01000110 01000001 10110000
10010101 00000111 00000000 01110100 11100000 00001100 01111111 00101010 11011001 10110000
10000101 10101101 00110100 11011011 01111011 01000110 10000000 00111110 11110101 00010011
00111011 01001001 10010111 11011010 11000100 01110011 10000000 01111000 01011110 00111000
11001000 00011001 11100010 10111110 10011001 10101000 11110010 01101000 10111111 10101101
11001111 00001110 11101101 10111111 01111000 11001011 10111100 10110111 10110010 01001011
11011000 01011110 11100000 00011111 00101011 11111011 10101010 01111110 01011111 11001010
10110100 10100110 10111110 10010011 01111001 01011011 01101100 00100010 10101110 00110000
11100000 01111100 11000011 11101000 01111011 01111110 00010101 00010010 11010110 00101010
11100110 10010001 01010111 10010001 11001101 01011111 11001010 11111000 11110010 11001011
01101110 00100111 10010011 10010011 01011001 11010011 01000011 00111100 00111110 01011001
10011110 00110110 10000100 10111010 10000111 01011101 11100000 10001101 11001010 01111010
00010001 11101101 11101111 01011101 10110000 01101001 00100101 01111101 00101110 01000101
01001011 11110011 01111010 00011101 01001111 10000000 10110100 01011000 10110101 11001111
00010100 01101001 11110110 10010011 11011100 00100010 11000100 10110010 00001001 10011110
00000110 01010110 01110011 01110010 10001011 10010110 01100100 00011100 01101101 11100111
00011000 00100101 10001000 11111011 11011100 01100111 10100101 01111101 01010111 11100010
00101001 00001101 11111110 10010011 11100111 01001001 00000011 00101001 01000110 00011111
00101100 10100000 01100111 00011001 11110110 00111111 11100111 00110101 11100111 01100010
00011101 11100110 10010010 01011111 11010011 00100101 00011111 00110011 01000011 01111001
01101011 10110000 11001001 00011101 10111010 11000111 00000000 11111110 00110111 11100001
01101010 11110100 01010010 11101010 01010111 01101010 00001101 10001100 00000010 00011000
10001111 01001001 00100101 00011000 11001111 10111010 10101111 11111000 11100011 11110001
10101110 00011001 11000110 11001011 10011010 10100011 11011000 11110110 00010011 10111110
10010001 01000101 01001001 10101101 01110101 10101101 11000001 10100100 10111101 01100010
11111000 11001001 11000000 00001010 00001111 11111110 00111011 11111110 00110101 11010011
11111000 01010010 00111101 01010101 01101111 01000001 00101100 10100110 00010011 11110111
10001011 00111000 11111001 10111111 11110001 11001111 11101011 01011000 01010101 10011110
00011101 11010010 01110110 10001101 10010111 11110101 11100110 01011100 00100011 00110101
00111101 01011001 11101001 10001111 01111001 00010101 10110011 01000110 00100110 01001001
11110100 11101101 11011111 00110000 01111100 11110000 01011000 11111111 00000000 10110100
00001001 00011111 10101110 01101001 00000101 11100101 11001100 11101100 00100011 11111011
01000111 11011011 00101101 01011001 10110010 11010010 11110101 00101011 10000001 10010001
10011111 10101101 01111100 00111010 10000010 10111110 10011011 00011110 10011010 11010111
01010110 00111100 01011101 11011110 01000101 00010100 10000011 01001110 10110001 01001000
00100100 11001110 00000011 11011100 00111111 01011110 10011100 10001101 10100001 10111111
10100101 01110000 11011010 11100100 01010000 11000001 11100110 01011101 11101010 01011010
10011011 01011111 01001010 11101110 01110111 10110000 11111001 00000010 10001110 11000011
00011100 11111111 00000000 10011110 10011000 10101111 10100001 10000011 10001010 01101010
00110100 11110111 01100110 01010010 01101001 10100110 01101011 11101000 00111010 00010110
10001101 10101000 11101001 10001001 01110101 01110010 10010011 01001111 00100001 11001110
01011000 11011100 11001000 00110011 11001001 11101100 00011000 00001111 11010010 10110011
00110101 11001101 00000111 01000100 10001010 00110110 01011000 00010110 01011000 01011011
10101110 01111100 11110111 00111111 11001100 10011010 11010101 01010101 10101011 11101101
00011100 01110100 11010011 11001011 11111010 01100110 01001001 00100110 01110011 11011110
00010101 11110000 10101101 10101110 10101101 10101010 11011111 11111101 10100010 11100001
11010110 11011010 11011101 01100011 00100000 00101111 11110001 10010110 11011101 11011111
11011011 01101111 11101011 01011110 10101001 00011101 10101110 10011011 00100101 10011000
00001001 00000010 11000111 01101110 01001001 00010001 10101000 00011100 10110010 10001100
10001100 10010011 11011111 00111100 10011111 11001010 10111000 01110001 10111000 10001001
11001110 01111110 11001101 01110100 11111100 11011001 10100100 01100001 11001011 01110110
11001111 00101000 11010101 00111100 00010100 00001110 10100000 11010010 01011000 11011111
00001000 11101101 11011100 01100111 11001011 01100101 00101100 01010000 10001111 01000011
11101001 01010011 11011011 01111000 01000011 01010000 01011101 11000110 01011011 11110101
01100100 00111101 00000001 10000011 10010001 11111000 11100110 10111110 10000010 10011110
00101011 10011010 10011100 01111001 10010110 10111110 10100111 10001111 01010010 10010111
10111110 11011010 00101001 11101010 00111110 00000111 10111110 10011111 01100100 10010010
11101010 11000001 00010111 10100010 11100110 00001111 11111110 11001010 10101010 10101110
10011111 00010100 00100101 11100011 10010111 01001101 10111001 10111011 01100101 00100101

01110010 10001011 10001101 11111000 00111000 11001000 11001111 01100011 11101011 11001111
10110101 01101010 11101011 11110011 11000111 10010110 00010110 01001111 11001100 10111010
01110000 11100101 10010111 00110100 10110110 00111001 01011001 10110100 01111101 01101110
01101001 10010010 01110011 10100101 01111001 01101100 00111010 00101000 00011111 00101111
11101010 01001101 01010001 11010100 01100010 11010101 10101110 10100110 01000001 10101010
11000111 01110100 11101101 00011010 00000100 00000100 01000011 10111100 00000001 11101001
10011100 10001100 11111101 01101011 11010110 10000100 11110000 11101101 11000101 01110011
00100110 11010001 11000011 00111000 11010101 11010101 11011011 01110011 11010101 10111110
00010000 01011110 01011001 00110101 11101101 11001110 10011101 00000101 10100111 10010011
01111100 10010110 10101111 00100100 10010011 00010000 00110111 00111000 11110011 01100011
00011000 11001111 01011100 01100000 10000001 10001111 01101111 01011010 11110110 10011101
01001001 10010101 01110100 01111101 01001001 10010001 01111100 10111111 10010000 10010010
00111011 00000011 11111110 01110001 01011100 01010101 11010011 01010101 01110101 01111011
10010000 10110110 00111110 01100101 11111110 11001100 11010100 01011010 01100001 00111100
10111010 01100101 11101100 10110010 00000011 11110010 00010011 01100101 00101001 01010100
11111010 00001101 10111101 01101011 01000110 01101101 01010011 01010101 10110000 10110111
00101000 10011010 00101101 11100011 01001000 01111000 00101101 00100101 10101011 10001101
11011111 01001100 10001100 00000001 01011001 11010100 10000010 10101011 01101000 10111001
00100100 10111101 01010111 11110101 11101010 01111010 11101010 10100100 00100001 01111001
00101111 11001000 11100011 11101110 10110101 10101101 01010110 01101001 00110111 11101010
00010001 00110000 01001100 11110000 10001100 10101100 10101010 00111111 00001110 00110010
01111110 10110101 10100011 10100100 01111000 11000010 00111101 00110110 11101010 00111001
01100110 10110000 01001011 10010100 00011100 00110000 11111110 00101100 01111110 00111111
00101000 11111010 00000101 10101110 11010111 10000101 10000100 10101001 10111000 01010011
01110110 01011111 11010111 11110101 11111001 01011000 11100010 01011000 10001001 00101001
11110011 00110100 01111011 00100111 10000111 00111100 01000011 00111111 10001011 11010010
01111001 01100100 11010011 11100100 10110001 10110001 10000100 11101101 00101100 01100101
00001100 10110010 00011111 11101110 01100011 00011110 10011101 01001111 00000111 10010001
01011010 11110111 01110111 01110000 11011011 11000110 01100010 10000100 00001000 11010001
01111010 00101010 11110000 00000101 01111100 01001101 01001010 00001010 10000101 01001111
01100100 10011101 11101101 11110010 00111101 10001000 01001111 10011110 00111100 11010110
00110011 01010011 01011001 00010001 01000000 11100101 10011110 10111100 10100011 11000100
10110111 11010010 01011100 11001011 00100100 10000010 01000011 11100100 00010010 00001001
00011101 01111010 00011111 01001010 11110100 11110000 10110001 11111101 11101101 11011010
00100010 01101111 11011101 11010000 11110101 10101011 00011011 11101000 00110100 10101101
00001010 11010110 00001000 10010111 01101011 00000100 00011101 01001111 00100011 10001010
11100010 10011110 11101010 11100111 01011000 11010100 00100010 10110100 01011001 01000010
10111100 10101101 10000101 11011100 01111000 00000011 10101001 00111111 10010110 01111101
11111000 11100010 10110001 01001001 01110011 11001010 10101100 10110110 11010100 11011001
00100101 01100100 10001111 01000111 10111011 01101011 00111101 00001011 01001001 10110110
10110111 10110010 01010100 10001100 10110100 11000010 00010111 01100110 00111111 00110001
00101101 11010101 10001001 11110101 11101001 11111100 10000101 01100010 10111110 10111001
10100110 11011001 01011010 01011011 01000111 01110011 01111000 10101001 01110001 10110001
01001000 01000000 01110010 01000000 11000111 01010011 11101001 01011110 00011100 00100001
00111010 11110111 10011010 01011011 10110011 01111011 11101001 01110011 10010110 10011011
01010111 10010011 01010000 10111111 10110111 10011111 01001100 10000010 01011011 10100100
10001110 01000010 01001111 10010110 10011001 11001010 10010000 01111000 11001000 00000100
01111010 01111110 01010101 11101000 11010110 10000000 01001011 00001010 01001011 00110100
01000110 11010001 11001111 00111011 00011001 11101011 11011100 11100100 01110100 10100000
10010100 10110111 00111100 11001010 10001101 00111001 01101000 01010101 10011000 11011100
11000101 00110100 10100110 11011110 01100000 11110001 10011110 10110001 11001001 11001010
00110111 00011101 00000001 11101101 10011110 00111101 01000111 00011101 00101010 10111011
11001101 01100000 11101100 10101011 01111011 00010001 11010011 10011100 10110110 00001001
00111111 11101010 11011111 10110111 00001101 11010000 01100100 11110100 00000111 00000111
11011010 10111001 00010101 11100100 11011111 00101110 11111111 00000000 11010111 11110101
11100111 11111001 11110100 00101101 00100010 10001101 01100110 10110101 10110011 00010001
10010001 00010101 10010010 11001010 11011001 00100100 00110110 11111101 11011001 11101101
10000010 00110001 10011010 11100100 11100111 10111001 11010100 01000011 00010110 01101101
00001010 11010101 10000010 10010110 11100001 01100011 00111001 00101011 10011110 00111001
11011110 01110010 01110001 11101101 11101001 01011101 00010100 11011101 00111001 00110111
11001111 10100001 11001011 00111000 01010100 10111101 11111001 10001011 10011110 00010000
11110011 11100001 11110001 00110101 11000101 11001101 11000110 10000111 01101001 01100001
00000100 10110110 11100110 00100011 01110001 00011001 01111111 00110000 11100100 10101011
01100000 10101110 01001110 00000110 01000110 00111101 01000110 00000101 01110111 10011110
00100010 10111100 10000010 00001101 00001110 11111000 10110100 11110001 11101110 00100000
00101001 00111110 01100000 00111000 00100100 11110111 11100111 10001110 11110101 11101001
11001010 01110100 11101110 10010100 00011101 11101100 01110010 00111000 01001001 00111011
10110100 01101110 01000011 10101000 01101001 10110011 11110001 00001101 11100100 00110011
00011111 01000101 10010001 01001111 11110101 10101011 01000110 01001011 01111100 01110010
11001011 11111001 11010111 10011100 11101110 01110100 01011011 10111001 00000001 10010110
11001011 00111100 10111010 01100111 11111101 11100001 01011001 00111010 10001110 10011011
10100000 11101010 00101000 01111110 11011011 10100111 11011011 11101010 00000100 00001100
10000001 00100100 01101010 11111111 00000000 11001110 10100101 10111110 01011111 01111000

01010110 10111110 10000111 00010011 01110011 01111101 10100110 01101000 11110110 01101011
10100111 11101001 10110001 00101101 10111100 00001001 10010000 10101000 10011101 00000001
00100111 00100111 11110101 10101111 00111110 10111110 11010101 10001001 00110010 01111100
11011001 01100010 01111001 11100110 10011101 00111010 01101110 10100100 10011100 10100111
11010111 01010011 10111101 11011010 00101010 11001000 11100111 11101110 01110101 00000111
01110101 11000111 00101100 01111010 00000101 00011101 11001101 01101101 01101001 10111110
00001011 11010101 10110101 01101011 01110011 00111101 11010101 11100100 00010110 01010001
01001000 00001000 11111110 00101001 00011000 00001110 11011100 00000001 10001111 11010110
10111101 10110111 11001011 01000110 00011100 11001101 00011100 10101110 01001101 10111101
00001110 11110001 00111100 00110011 01101010 10101000 10001011 01111101 10101100 01001001
01110010 10101011 10000001 10001000 11101101 11001010 10000011 11001111 11010100 11110110
10101101 00101011 01111011 00111111 00001110 11011001 00001111 10010010 11010110 01010101
01111100 10000110 11011110 10010000 10110110 11101100 10000010 00001000 11111001 10001110
01001111 01011110 11011001 11000101 01111000 01010011 01010010 10011111 11000010 11101100
10111011 01111111 11000001 00110110 01010101 00011101 10010110 10000100 11010011 01101010
00011110 00010111 01101000 10010110 00001011 10001101 00110101 10101110 01100010 01000011
10111000 00101100 10110110 11101100 11100000 00011111 01011100 00010001 01010101 10010011
01011110 11110000 11010101 10011000 00101001 01101011 10100110 10011011 01100100 11110100
10001110 11011000 00100000 11000111 11101001 01001001 01010011 01110001 01001110 00110001
01111010 01101111 10111001 10010011 01101110 01001110 11101100 10000110 01001111 00010110
11101001 01011111 11000001 01101001 00110111 11111101 11110011 10001111 11101011 01010100
00100111 11110001 01001101 10100001 01010010 01010111 01001010 10010110 01010001 11111110
01111101 10101011 01100101 01001001 11011111 01010110 00011010 10010011 11011011 11101010
00000010 11100010 00001000 11100110 00010110 11100110 00000101 01100001 10010000 10000111
10101010 11010101 10100011 00100110 11100101 00100100 10001111 10010111 10111101 01110001
11001001 00100101 00100111 11010100 11101100 01011011 00100110 01100110 10101101 10111011
01011011 11111100 11011010 01101101 11000001 10110010 11000111 01000100 00000011 01110100
01011111 11110111 11001111 01100001 11111110 11101001 01011010 11001001 11110001 00001111
10001000 10110101 00101011 00111011 00011100 00111101 10101010 11000011 01110000 01011100
00101010 11001110 10011000 01110101 00001011 10010011 11011000 11110010 00001111 01001110
10100000 10001110 01111010 11010111 01001100 00100011 00011001 11010100 10001111 00110110
11111111 00000000 10011101 11001100 10100101 01110100 10001110 00101100 01111000 10101011
01011111 01010110 11011100 10110111 10100101 01001111 10101000 10001101 00000001 11111110
01010101 01011010 11100111 11000100 01111010 11011101 11001000 11000100 11111010 10001100
10101100 00111101 00000011 00000000 00111111 01001010 11111010 00000101 01000110 10010010
01110111 01010001 00111000 01111001 10100100 01111010 00010111 11110110 10101100 11010011
00000101 00010111 00111110 00010101 10011010 11100001 10111101 01111110 11001000 01011011
11111010 01010100 11000010 01101100 00101000 11110010 01110100 01011101 01010010 11000000
10010011 10010010 01101101 11010110 11100000 01100011 11110000 11000001 00010101 11100110
11001011 10010101 01101001 00011001 10100110 10111101 01010001 10101111 00101001 01100100
01101010 01011010 11011010 00010101 11111011 00110011 11101010 01111110 01011000 11111110
00011011 10001101 00110001 10100101 11001111 11100010 00010100 00011010 10111101 00111110
10111101 01111111 00000110 10010000 11010111 00010111 00110000 11111001 01010111 10101110
01011001 01000000 00010001 00110100 01011000 00011001 00100011 10010101 00111100 10000011
01011000 01001011 10010010 01011101 10101111 11100100 11111111 00000000 01000011 01001000
00101011 00111011 10011100 00000100 10010010 00001000 10101101 10000011 11011100 01001101
11100110 01001011 10010010 11011000 00111110 10110101 11000110 01011110 11011111 01101101
01111110 01110010 11001100 01110011 10000000 00000001 00111111 11001010 10111101 00101010
00110001 11100110 10011011 10110010 11010000 10011001 10111011 01101010 00110110 11000110
01000001 00100100 10101000 11110011 00010110 00000111 11111101 11000110 11100011 11110100
10101111 01110111 11010001 10101111 10110100 10011000 00101100 10100010 10001001 10101110
00011101 10011000 01100011 00100100 10111010 00101111 01101111 10101101 01001110 00101011
01000100 10010010 11111110 10111110 11100011 00011000 01110011 01001011 01010011 01001010
01011101 01011011 01001010 01011100 11111101 11101001 01001111 10110100 11110001 11111111
00000000 11110001 01010101 10011011 00100110 10111111 10100100 00001100 11111111 00000000
10100001 01001100 11000111 11111110 10111011 00101111 00111111 10010011 01010111 10001111
01101001 01001001 11101001 11111010 10011011 11110010 10110010 10111111 11110110 11101110
10010000 11000000 10010011 01100111 10000011 11111111 00000000 01001101 00011000 10011100
11111110 01000000 11010101 01111001 01110101 10101011 00001111 10011000 11000101 01101101
01101110 00011011 11011111 01111111 11111111 00000000 00010001 01010101 01100110 10011111
11111100 00110111 11111001 10011010 00101000 01111001 10010100 00011111 01011110 10011100
00011111 10010110 11010010 11011101 01010111 11011001 11100100 00111001 11111100 00110110
10001010 10100111 00110110 10110011 00101100 10001010 11011111 01110010 00010010 01111101
00100001 11011101 11111111 00000000 10110011 00001010 11010011 10010101 01011110 11101011
11111100 10111111 11001100 01111100 10111101 11011001 01111110 11010110 11101100 11111001
00110001 01101110 01111101 11101100 01010000 00110110 01110110 11101101 11111100 01110001
10010011 11111100 11101010 00100100 10111011 10111111 10001010 11111110 00101011 01110100
00001011 00101101 10010011 00101011 00110011 00111001 00001101 10010001 11001001 11000000
11111011 11011000 11001111 01001110 01000000 00011100 01010110 00101011 10010001 01001110
01001110 01001011 10111001 10100011 01001101 10100101 01100011 01000111 11001101 00100000
11110011 11000001 10101110 01011111 11000101 10101100 01011110 11001010 00010101 00111101
11011111 00010101 00110100 10010111 11101111 01100010 10111100 11010000 01001111 11100001
01100111 00000100 01001000 00100011 10101110 00101010 10111100 10001100 01111001 10101111

10101101 01010110 01101110 11001000 11110011 00011001 11011010 10100101 11000000 00111100
10110011 01100110 10101100 11111001 11000000 10011100 00001010 11110001 11011100 01101110
11011101 11001110 10110001 00001100 10111001 11100110 10111010 11011011 11101000 11111100
10101011 01111011 01111000 00100101 01100000 11101000 10001000 00000001 11111010 11100010
10111001 01100101 01110100 11001101 00001111 00110111 11010101 01100111 01001001 11100111
11110010 11101101 11010111 10011100 11010111 00111100 11101000 11001000 11100111 00111001
00100111 00111101 01111101 01101011 11011011 10100010 10100100 10010111 10111100 01110010
01001111 01010111 01110010 11001100 01000100 10001100 01100100 01111110 10110101 11010001
01011010 01011100 00110110 11011100 01100011 11011010 10100010 10101010 11110111 01110101
00101010 00000101 11011111 00110011 11011011 10001010 00111100 11001100 11110100 01011100
11111110 00110101 11100110 10111000 10011101 00101000 01000011 00100001 11000111 01001010
01101110 11110110 00111111 11000011 10001111 11000110 10000111 01110111 10111001 01000001
10111001 11111011 01111101 00101001 10101100 11001110 01000001 11100100 01111011 11010001
01100010 10001101 11111011 01100000 11011111 01100111 10000011 10101001 11111001 00010111
00111100 11100000 11110100 10101001 10010101 11001010 11100000 10000011 10011110 00111001
01100011 10001100 01100100 01010111 00001100 11101100 11100100 11101110 01101011 11010001
00010110 01000100 10011011 10110011 10011110 00001111 01111100 11010111 00110011 11100010
10000110 11000101 10101101 10110000 11001111 11110001 11010101 01010010 01001101 01010100
10001010 11110011 00110010 10011111 11000010 11001110 00010001 10011011 11011111 00000110
10101010 11001000 11100111 10010001 11011110 10111110 10101010 00110111 10111001 11100100
00110011 11111111 11011001 11111111 11011011 00000000 01000011 00000000 00000110 00000100
00000101 00000110 00000101 00000100 00000110 00000110 00000101 00000110 00000111 00000111
00000110 00001000 00001010 00010000 00001010 00001010 00001001 00001001 00001010 00010100
00001110 00001111 00001100 00010000 00010111 00010100 00011000 00011000 00010111 00010100
00010110 00010110 00011010 00011101 00100101 00011111 00011010 00011011 00100011 00011100
00010110 00010110 00100000 00101100 00100000 00100011 00100110 00100111 00101001 00101010
00101001 00011001 00011111 00101101 00110000 00101101 00101000 00110000 00100101 00101000
00101001 00101000 11111111 11011011 00000000 01000011 00000001 00000111 00000111 00000111
00001010 00001000 00001010 00010011 00001010 00001010 00010011 00101000 00011010 00010110
00011010 00101000 00101000 00101000 00101000 00101000 00101000 00101000 00101000 00101000
00101000 00101000 00101000 00101000 00101000 00101000 00101000 00101000 00101000 00101000
00101000 00101000 00101000 00101000 00101000 00101000 00101000 00101000 00101000 00101000
00101000 00101000 00101000 00101000 00101000 00101000 00101000 00101000 00101000 00101000
00101000 00101000 00101000 00101000 00101000 00101000 00101000 00101000 00101000 00101000
00101000 11111111 11000000 00000000 00010001 00001000 00000110 00000000 00000100 10111100
00000011 00000001 00100010 00000000 00000010 00010001 00000001 00000011 00010001 00000001
11111111 11000100 00000000 00011111 00000000 00000000 00000001 00000101 00000001 00000001
00000001 00000001 00000001 00000001 00000000 00000000 00000000 00000000 00000000 00000000
00000000 00000000 00000001 00000010 00000011 00000100 00000101 00000110 00000111 00001000
00001001 00001010 00001011 11111111 11000100 00000000 10110101 00010000 00000000 00000010
00000001 00000011 00000011 00000010 00000100 00000011 00000101 00000101 00000100 00000100
00000000 00000000 00000001 01111101 00000001 00000010 00000011 00000000 00000100 00010001
00000101 00010010 00100001 00110001 01000001 00000110 00010011 01010001 01100001 00000111
00100010 01110001 00010100 00110010 10000001 10010001 10100001 00001000 00100011 01000010
10110001 11000001 00010101 01010010 11010001 11110000 00100100 00110011 01100010 01110010
10000010 00001001 00001010 00010110 00010111 00011000 00011001 00011010 00100101 00100110
00100111 00101000 00101001 00101010 00110100 00110101 00110110 00110111 00111000 00111001
00111010 01000011 01000100 01000101 01000110 01000111 01001000 01001001 01001010 01010011
01010100 01010101 01010110 01010111 01011000 01011001 01011010 01100011 01100100 01100101
01100110 01100111 01101000 01101001 01101010 01110011 01110100 01110101 01110110 01110111
01111000 01111001 01111010 10000011 10000100 10000101 10000110 10000111 10001000 10001001
10001010 10010010 10010011 10010100 10010101 10010110 10010111 10011000 10011001 10011010
10100010 10100011 10100100 10100101 10100110 10100111 10101000 10101001 10101010 10110010
10110011 10110100 10110101 10110110 10110111 10111000 10111001 10111010 11000010 11000011
11000100 11000101 11000110 11000111 11001000 11001001 11001010 11010010 11010011 11010100
11010101 11010110 11010111 11011000 11011001 11011010 11100001 11100010 11100011 11100100
11100101 11100110 11100111 11101000 11101001 11101010 11110001 11110010 11110011 11110100
11110101 11110110 11110111 11111000 11111001 11111010 11111111 11000100 00000000 00011111
00000001 00000000 00000011 00000001 00000001 00000001 00000001 00000001 00000001 00000001
00000001 00000001 00000000 00000000 00000000 00000000 00000000 00000000 00000001 00000010
00000011 00000100 00000101 00000110 00000111 00001000 00001001 00001010 00001011 11111111
11000100 00000000 10110101 00010001 00000000 00000010 00000001 00000010 00000100 00000100
00000011 00000100 00000111 00000101 00000100 00000100 00000000 00000001 00000010 01110111
00000000 00000001 00000010 00000011 00010001 00000100 00000101 00100001 00110001 00000110
00010010 01000001 01010001 00000111 01100001 01110001 00010011 00100010 00110010 10000001
00001000 00010100 01000010 10010001 10100001 10110001 11000001 00001001 00100011 00110011
01010010 11110000 00010101 01100010 01110010 11010001 00001010 00010110 00100100 00110100
11100001 00100101 11110001 00010111 00011000 00011001 00011010 00100110 00100111 00101000
00101001 00101010 00110101 00110110 00110111 00111000 00111001 00111010 01000011 01000100
01000101 01000110 01000111 01001000 01001001 01001010 01010011 01010100 01010101 01010110
01010111 01011000 01011001 01011010 01100011 01100100 01100101 01100110 01100111 01101000
01101001 01101010 01110011 01110100 01110101 01110110 01110111 01111000 01111001 01111010
10000010 10000011 10000100 10000101 10000110 10000111 10001000 10001001 10001010 10010010

10010011 10010100 10010101 10010110 10010111 10011000 10011001 10011010 10100010 10100011
10100100 10100101 10100110 10100111 10101000 10101001 10101010 10110010 10110011 10110100
10110101 10110110 10110111 10111000 10111001 10111010 11000010 11000011 11000100 11000101
11000110 11000111 11001000 11001001 11001010 11010010 11010011 11010100 11010101 11010110
11010111 11011000 11011001 11011010 11100010 11100011 11100100 11100101 11100110 11100111
11101000 11101001 11101010 11110010 11110011 11110100 11110101 11110110 11110111 11111000
11111001 11111010 11111111 11011010 00000000 00001100 00000011 00000001 00000000 00000010
00010001 00000011 00010001 00000000 00111111 00000000 10100001 11100010 00011011 00000110
01011011 01011111 10110010 11011000 10110100 01001111 01101100 00000000 00100111 01110001
11100111 00111110 11010101 11001101 11101000 11110010 00110100 01110111 00001111 00000001
11011111 11110010 11110011 11010111 10001010 11101100 11010010 00101000 10101110 10100001
00100101 00011011 00101001 11111100 10101011 00001110 11111111 00000000 01001011 00010001
01001100 00100110 10110101 11011000 01011111 00111001 01100000 00101011 11001101 10000011
10111010 10110011 00001110 10110111 01100010 00111100 10110001 10101111 11101110 11010000
10111001 11001111 01011010 11000011 11010101 01100010 00000010 11100001 11100101 10110110
00010011 00100001 11000111 00100100 10011100 11100111 11101001 01011011 00010010 01011101
00000110 11111001 01001100 01111011 00100100 00000010 10101001 11011100 00110000 00001001
10110111 00000000 11111101 01111001 10100001 10100100 10000000 00110100 10001111 00100101
01111100 10111111 00110011 01111110 01001000 11100111 10011010 11010010 10111010 11010101
10010001 01110011 00000100 01110000 10100000 00000011 10100100 10011001 11001001 10101100
00100000 01111100 10110000 01000000 00011001 00100000 01100111 00111001 10100111 11000011
11111011 11010001 11111011 11001110 00001111 10101110 00111010 11010010 11110011 00101011
01011101 10001101 11001000 10101110 00010100 01000011 10111001 11010100 10000111 00111110
10010101 01101010 11000010 00101001 01011010 01010000 10101111 11110111 00001111 00100011
00000110 10110011 11101101 11001110 11100010 00010100 10110000 01111100 00001110 00000101
01110100 00011010 00111101 10111011 01110101 10010011 00111100 00011010 10001001 11001111
10101010 00110101 10100101 01001101 01001101 11011000 11011111 11010010 00100001 01011000
00000111 10011011 10110100 01100110 10110101 00111100 11100000 01100100 11100111 10010000
01111011 11110101 10101010 01001001 00011110 11011000 11110010 11100111 00001000 00111011
00001010 01101010 11001000 10100100 11110001 10011100 11010111 00011101 01001010 10001110
01110010 00111101 01011000 10101011 01101000 01011111 11110010 00100101 01001111 10111001
11001101 00101010 11001001 00101100 01000100 10010111 01011101 10011000 10101010 01001011
00110100 10110001 00011100 10000010 01001111 10111110 01101001 01011110 11110101 11100100
01011111 11011110 00000000 01001111 10101000 10101110 01110110 10011101 11110100 00101000
11010000 10001110 01111101 11000011 00111001 11111010 10000011 01000101 10110101 11000100
00101011 00110011 10010000 11000000 01001001 11011000 11010110 01111100 01110010 11101111
00111110 11010101 01001101 01110101 00000101 10000111 01010010 11111011 00111100 00010001
11101111 10010001 10011011 10010010 11011101 10101011 01011010 00010111 11100110 01111010
10011100 10011000 10100101 10100001 10101001 01110011 11100100 10001011 11101000 00100101
10111000 11100111 10011100 11100011 11010110 10110100 00110101 00101000 10111100 11011100
11001010 01000001 10001111 00100011 11100101 00000111 10111111 11100001 01011000 11110000
11101010 01101011 00000110 10101100 11101110 01010100 00111001 01010101 11011000 10111011
10000111 01001010 11011111 00010111 00010001 01101010 00001000 10000100 11001010 10010010
00111001 00011101 00000000 11101001 01011101 00111110 11010001 11000110 00101001 10110011
10010011 10010001 01001101 11011000 11100111 00100110 10001111 11101101 10010001 11111001
10001000 10100100 10100100 01011100 01110011 11111101 00101010 11111101 10001100 00000010
00011011 01010010 01110110 11101100 11001001 11001101 01011111 01001011 00000100 11111011
00100000 10000110 00110110 00001000 00110111 01100100 11100010 10101110 00110101 10101100
00010001 11000111 00011000 01110010 00011100 10000001 10011100 01100110 10100110 10101110
00100101 01110010 11110010 00101110 10100110 10010100 01101001 01011010 01010111 00110000
11010111 01111100 10110010 01100000 00001100 00001110 11100100 11010101 11101011 01101000
00100000 10110111 10001000 00110111 10011010 00100100 10010000 11111010 01010001 01110011
00010100 00000010 00100010 01001100 11100010 00010000 00111001 00011100 11010110 01001101
11000100 10110010 01011011 00000001 00101100 01101110 10010011 01000111 11101111 11000110
01101011 10001110 00101111 10110001 11011110 10011001 01100011 01011101 10011011 00111000
00011001 00100111 00011100 11110010 01101011 10010100 10111111 10010100 10000100 00100100
10001010 11010111 10010100 11001011 01110001 11110011 10111111 00011100 11110100 10101100
01001101 01100000 11111111 00000000 00001110 00000111 10100001 00110101 01010100 11011101
10011110 10100011 10110101 10010001 10000001 01111001 00101111 10011001 01110000 01011010
00110101 00111000 11110101 00100010 10110010 01101110 11111100 11010011 01110001 10111011
00111000 00011111 11001110 10111010 00000111 10001100 00001000 11111101 11111101 01101011
10011100 11010111 01100111 00110000 10001101 11001000 01110000 11100000 11010111 01110101
00111011 01001111 01010011 10001011 00010001 01001110 11001010 11100011 11100110 11001101
10111100 01100001 11001111 01001100 01111101 01101010 10011111 10000100 10100011 11110011
10110101 01101011 10111011 10011001 00001110 00000000 01010011 01010000 01101010 10010111
00001110 01101101 10000001 00110010 01110010 01000110 00110001 01010110 11111100 00101101
00001001 01011000 10100101 01111110 00001000 00100011 00011100 00001010 11101001 10001101
11010010 10111111 01010011 10000001 01011101 10110011 10110101 11010000 01101110 11010010
00010110 10010010 01011100 11110011 11010000 00001010 10110011 11100001 10010001 01101101
01110111 11100010 10110111 10011110 11110110 01100100 10001101 00100011 00000100 10000011
00100110 01110001 10011110 10000011 00110101 11001111 01011010 01001101 10110101 01001110
00110001 10011100 11110001 01011101 00001111 10000011 11100010 10010011 11101101 01110111
01110010 10111000 11100000 00101000 00100100 01100011 10101101 01001100 00111001 10101100

11011001 01011101 01001011 01111111 00010000 10100111 00111010 10011111 11011001 11010000
10011000 11011110 11001010 11010100 11110001 10110100 10010000 01100101 01101111 01011010
11110010 01111101 01010110 11110110 00111011 11001101 01010001 00010010 00011100 00100100
01000010 01011110 01110110 11110111 10101110 10100011 11000111 01011010 11000011 01011110
01111110 11100110 00000000 01010010 00111000 00110010 11101100 01111010 01110010 01101011
10001010 11010010 10101100 11100100 10111100 10010101 11010110 00111101 10001001 10000000
01011111 01111001 00110101 00110100 11110101 00100110 00111110 01100100 11011010 11000100
01111001 01111000 11101110 00100011 01011100 00100010 00110110 00001101 01011111 11010000
01001001 01011101 01010110 11011010 01101101 11000111 10001001 00000110 01101001 11110000
11011001 01001001 01110111 10100111 11100111 00000100 10000010 11011000 00100101 01101010
10011101 10000101 11011110 00101110 11100010 01011000 11000001 00100111 00111000 11001111
10101101 00010011 11100110 11010101 00111101 10001101 01100001 10100100 10010001 11101011
00110111 10010010 10010100 10000000 10010100 00111111 01111000 01100011 10011010 10101001
01100000 10000010 01001001 10000010 11100111 10011010 01001001 11100101 00101101 00001000
00001101 11101000 00101010 01011101 00110000 01111111 10100100 10001110 01000000 11100000
10011110 10110101 11110001 10001001 11110011 01010110 11010111 10111001 11101110 00101111
10000100 11101000 00111100 01010010 01000010 11111000 00100011 01010100 00100001 10111001
00010110 01001111 11111000 11110001 01011100 10101110 10110000 10100110 00011111 00000101
01111000 01011010 00101100 10000001 11110110 01011000 10010110 01100110 11110111 00111101
10101011 10100110 11110001 10010110 11101000 01111100 00001101 10101010 00000001 11010111
11101100 01100100 00011100 01111011 10001010 10100101 00100101 10011001 10111011 10111010
11010000 00101101 11100110 11111101 11011110 10011111 00011100 00110000 10011001 00110011
11111100 01111000 01000001 11000101 01111101 10010110 00011011 01001000 10011110 00010101
01001111 10001101 10011101 10000100 11010111 10010010 01000111 10100110 00000111 10011110
01010100 10001110 01001001 10010101 00111100 10110101 00111111 01001010 11100101 11111100
01011111 01100101 00101100 10110110 11110110 10010011 01001100 10100000 10000100 00000111
10010001 11011111 00110101 11011101 11101010 10111010 01111101 10110110 10110001 01101010
10000000 01110101 01001111 11110101 01001100 00111010 10001111 01101010 11100000 00111100
01100111 00010100 10110110 11111010 00010011 11011011 10010110 11011000 01000111 10101001
10100010 01110110 01001110 11101000 11001101 10011110 00111001 10101010 11001010 00111100
11010111 11000011 00001111 10111100 01110010 00110011 01010110 11110100 10011000 01001100
11110000 01000001 00100000 00011000 01110111 00111101 01001101 01100101 11011101 11000110
00000010 00011110 00110011 01011010 11111010 01111110 11101000 11101101 00101101 11000010
00001100 00010011 11011111 00110101 10101011 10110110 10001101 00111101 01000110 10011001
11011000 11101011 11010010 10100100 01111010 00111101 10111101 10000111 10011001 10111110
01011001 00111010 00010000 00111011 01110111 10101110 00001110 11100101 01001100 01001100
01011010 00110000 00110010 00101011 10100001 10110001 01011111 00110010 11111101 00001100
10000100 10111011 10001111 01010011 01011000 10111010 10001100 01111110 01010100 10110010
01000111 11000110 01000011 00011110 01001001 11101011 01011001 10101000 11011111 01010110
11000001 10111101 01001100 00011001 01111111 01110100 11011011 10110011 10010111 11001110
01001110 01101010 01111001 10100101 00110010 11011001 00000101 00100011 00111111 10001110
00101010 00001011 10010001 10001001 00001001 00100100 00010111 00110101 01011010 01101011
10101111 10010101 11010100 00101111 11111111 00000000 01011010 10101110 00111111 10111100
11010010 00101000 01000101 01111011 10100010 01000011 00001111 01010000 00110001 10011111
01011010 11101011 01111100 00001000 11001100 00011001 11010000 01110011 00000100 10111111
01111000 00011110 01110001 01011100 01001101 11001011 00010011 10001110 01101011 10101101
11110000 00111100 11101111 00000100 10101110 10001000 01111111 11010110 00010001 10000000
01111010 00011010 01110110 11100101 10000101 10101100 01011100 00110111 00111011 10001011
00110101 01011011 01011001 00000100 01011100 10100001 00011111 01011110 01101011 01010010
11110010 11000100 11001100 00010010 01101011 01011111 00111000 01011100 00010001 11000011
01000100 01111111 10011000 10101110 01011011 01011101 11010101 01011010 11011110 01010100
00100100 00010101 11011000 00111000 00000100 11110101 11111010 01010111 01000001 11100001
11011101 01101001 00101110 00101100 01100010 10010111 01111010 01111001 10100111 00000011
00010101 11000000 10011010 00110101 01101100 10000010 11000010 01101011 10001011 10101001
10100101 11110011 10101101 00001100 01010111 10110001 01100011 00110010 10000001 10001100
10001111 01111111 01111010 11100100 10111110 00101001 01111001 11010010 01101010 00010110
00010111 00010010 01000000 11101000 01001100 01011000 00100111 00011100 00011111 11000110
10111101 01100010 00011001 00010110 01101000 11111100 11000000 00111110 01110011 11101101
01011100 10100111 11000100 01001000 01010110 01101111 00001101 11001111 10010101 11001111
10010100 11000001 11000111 10110110 01101010 11111001 11010010 10010010 01100100 01001010
00010111 01000111 10010111 01101001 00100100 10011001 10010000 00011110 10000100 11010110
10110110 10111001 00101000 10001110 11010110 00110000 01001001 11111001 11100100 00000000
01100010 10100011 11010011 10100001 10000110 00101000 00011110 01011001 00001110 00000000
11100000 10010011 01010110 11101111 11100010 10000010 11100010 00101000 10011110 11100001
10111111 01110110 10000111 11001100 00000111 00111101 01110001 01000101 01011010 10010001
10010100 11101110 11001101 00011110 10001010 11000100 01111110 00101010 10111010 00011010
01001110 10001101 01101111 01100101 01101110 01110110 11001111 00111110 01111100 11101111
01111010 11100000 11011000 00110110 11001100 01100100 10000000 01111111 01011010 11011000
11110001 00111110 10100100 10111010 10100110 10100000 00011101 00000111 11101110 11010001
01110000 10100100 11110001 01011000 11101100 01111000 11110110 10101110 11101100 00110010
10001100 00110101 11101110 01110011 00111011 10110110 01000110 10000011 00011100 01110100
00110101 01111101 01001111 11101110 00111000 00010101 01011101 00000000 11101101 11001111
00010101 00100010 10010010 01100011 00000011 01110111 11100001 01011101 00101101 11111101

10010100 00010110 10110000 11000100 01010010 01001001 11101001 10001111 01010010 01101001
01111001 00100100 10001111 10100111 00111101 00101000 01010010 01000001 11000111 01000001
11011011 11011010 10001110 00000000 01000101 00111101 11111011 11010100 01111011 01001101
01000000 10011001 01000000 01101111 11110000 10100010 00011000 10001100 10010010 01110000
00111010 11110111 10100110 11100111 11110011 11001111 01011111 01011010 01001101 11000100
00011100 00100110 01000110 01111111 00001010 01001010 11101101 10000001 11010010 01101001
11011010 00000010 11001011 00010001 10010001 00101110 00100011 00100100 10001110 01000110
01101011 11010100 00111100 00000000 10110001 01101001 11110110 00001111 01100111 11100110
00001101 11101100 11011011 11110011 10001010 11110010 11001111 00001111 11001001 00110001
11001001 01001100 10011100 01110001 11110101 10101110 11111110 11000000 11001011 00000110
11000010 11100011 01100011 10011100 00011100 01010111 10010001 10001011 10101001 00101000
00110111 01110111 10100001 11101010 01000010 10010100 00011100 01110100 11101010 01111010
00011000 11000110 00101001 10101100 01110000 00101010 00101011 00111001 11010110 11100110
00000000 11000011 10101001 00011100 10001010 10010100 00001010 10001000 00110101 00110101
01110100 01110001 01001110 00001110 00101110 11001100 01101001 00111100 01110011 01010000
11101111 11001011 10010001 01010011 00110111 10101001 10101000 01010101 01000011 00111001
00000011 11010110 10001011 11101001 01100010 01110100 00100011 10011100 10010010 10100110
10101000 10111001 11111001 01001111 10101101 01011010 10011000 11100001 10001000 00011101
10111010 11010101 01011001 01111000 00011001 11000101 00010110 01111111 00010100 10001011
10001000 11011101 00110100 11101101 10011010 01010000 01110011 10000010 10110101 00110011
11100100 10110101 01000001 01101000 00110011 00100001 00111100 11110001 01010010 10110001
11100111 11111010 11010111 01110110 00011101 11111011 10100100 11010100 11011100 10001110
01010011 10000001 11001111 01001010 11001111 10011000 11100111 11011110 10100100 11010100
11100101 11110010 10110001 10010011 11110010 01111010 11010101 01100010 11000100 01100000
11110000 01000101 01100111 01010110 01101101 11001010 11000110 10010100 11010001 00101110
00110010 00110010 01111010 11010100 01100100 01111100 11011100 11010100 01101101 01110110
00010100 11100000 11110100 10100111 10101100 10110001 11001000 01111010 11010110 00001010
11001011 01000011 01011011 00011001 01011010 10000100 10111110 01001110 10101101 01101110
11100000 00010000 00011111 10000011 10011111 01111110 00101010 11001101 11100010 11100110
01000001 11001111 01001010 11001111 11110001 00111001 00110001 11000011 00011101 11000010
01110011 11100101 00110000 00101101 11110100 11001101 01011000 11111011 01000000 10011100
01000110 11001000 11011011 11000001 00011001 11001101 00001110 11010011 01011010 10010111
00000001 11110000 10010010 01011011 11101001 01010110 10010000 11100000 01111010 11100110
10101001 00101001 11000100 10011000 11111100 10101010 11001010 00110001 11000111 10110101
01100000 11111101 11001110 10000111 01011010 11010100 01110101 11001000 11011101 00011110
00110001 01011001 00110111 00000011 00001101 01011010 10001111 11001111 01111010 10100101
00110010 01110011 11001101 00001111 01010100 01010010 11011100 11001011 10111001 10000101
10100110 11000100 01110001 10001100 10111011 11111011 11010101 10010001 01100110 10110110
10110110 11101001 00011010 01100111 00011101 01011000 10011110 11100110 10110101 00101101
10101101 01000010 10001101 11011011 01111001 00100011 00011001 00110101 01100011 11001001
00011011 00111001 00010101 10111101 00100111 11001000 10001110 01101010 11010101 00101111
10100010 00111100 10101110 01101011 01001001 00101100 10110101 11011101 10010001 10101110
00010000 01001001 11100110 01000110 00110011 11001001 00000100 11010111 10100111 11011010
01000001 10001011 01110001 10010011 11110011 11110101 11101011 01011000 00011010 11101101
10001100 00000011 01010010 10110010 10010110 01111100 01111001 01011011 10110110 01100100
10011100 01110011 11010110 10111010 01100100 01100011 00011010 10000000 01000001 00011001
11101111 01011010 11010101 10011010 10010100 01010010 01100110 00010000 01010110 11011000
01110010 10001100 00001100 11100100 11010000 00010101 10110000 01110000 11011001 11110100
10100111 10101001 00001100 11011100 01110100 10100000 00101110 01110011 10001110 00101011
10010101 11011001 11101100 01011101 11001000 11110111 00110000 00111000 00111100 11010010
10010110 11100011 00000100 01110010 01111011 11010011 10011011 10001111 10101101 01000110
01110011 10011010 01110110 01101001 11101100 00100111 01100001 11001010 11011100 01100000
11010011 10011011 10000000 01000000 00010101 00000011 00110000 11101001 01010001 01101110
10010000 00000010 01000110 01001111 10110110 01101010 10111001 01011110 11010111 00100110
11000100 11001100 11011101 10111001 11111010 11010100 00110111 00010011 01110011 10000000
01101010 00110011 00101011 01100111 10010001 01010101 00100101 01100011 00100011 01110100
00100011 11011110 10011010 10000000 11001001 01011110 01100011 10001010 11001111 10010010
01100010 00001001 01100011 10011100 00100111 01011010 10110101 00101111 00001001 10001110
10100110 10110010 01101111 01100100 11000001 00100011 00111111 01011110 11010101 10110011
10000011 11100101 10110001 00100000 10110000 01001011 01111100 11111011 10100100 00000101
00100011 00100111 00011001 00110101 11010001 01011010 01000010 10110001 01000110 00010100
01110100 10101000 11101101 01100000 01010100 10000000 00101010 11111101 01101010 11000000
10001000 10001110 01101000 10010011 01011011 00100010 11000001 11001110 00110011 11101111
01011000 00011010 11000111 00010001 10010010 00000001 00111110 11000010 10110111 01011111
00011111 10011101 01110011 11111110 00100001 00100001 01101101 11001001 00011100 00011110
11111100 11010100 11000110 00011010 10010000 11011001 11000111 00111000 11011010 01001010
10000001 11101111 11010111 11010110 10000101 00111011 01000110 01101001 11101110 01110011
00100110 01001111 11100111 11101011 01001010 01000000 11000111 01001010 11101100 10001101
10100000 11101110 11000101 01101110 11000101 10011101 00101010 01000000 10110111 10100011
00100011 00111011 10010100 10100111 11100111 01011111 01000000 01101001 10100011 01101101
10001101 10111100 01111000 11000000 00010001 00101111 11110010 10101111 10011111 10110100
11110011 10110110 11101110 00000000 01110001 10010010 11000000 01100100 11010111 11010000
10010110 11011001 01011011 01101000 00111000 11001001 00110001 10001100 11010001 01011010

01101011	10100001	10000101	01000101	01100110	01001010	00110011	11100110	01111101	00000101
00100011	10000000	00111001	01101110	11110100	10101000	01111001	11111110	01010100	10000111
10010011	11010111	00100010	10111001	01100100	11101110	11001000	00000101	11100101	00001110
01111010	10011010	01001110	01000000	00010100	10100111	10100111	10111110	01101001	00011000
11100011	10011110	11010101	00001011	10110000	00001010	11000011	00100011	10001111	10101110
00101000	01100011	11011111	11110000	10100101	11001110	00110001	11101111	01001000	10111110
10111101	10001101	00110110	11011000	00010001	11100011	00111001	00100111	10100110	01111010
01010000	11000100	11100000	00001010	01011110	11111000	11101101	01001101	00111101	00000111
11111001	11000101	00010111	11101000	10000000	01110010	11111010	00010001	11011010	10000101
11000000	11101111	11011011	10101101	00011111	11000010	00101001	00111010	01111101	00101000
10110011	01000000	00011100	00011000	11001110	01001111	00000011	10100101	00100010	10010011
10001100	01110001	10000011	01000111	00100011	01100001	00100011	10010111	00111100	01100011
10110101	00101000	11100100	10011110	01111001	11001111	01011010	00110111	00000001	00011100
01110011	11001001	11100011	00011100	10011010	00001111	11011100	11111001	01000110	00110010
01101000	01101110	11000111	10110101	00110111	01110001	11110100	11100010	10011101	10101100
10110100	00000000	11000000	11001000	11100111	10100101	00001010	00110011	00100011	11100100
11100000	00011110	10000000	01010001	10011111	11011101	10010001	11011100	11110001	01001101
01010101	00000011	00000110	10010101	11000000	01101111	11001010	11010010	00001100	11110011
11000111	00110100	11101110	01011000	10001100	01111010	11010001	10001100	01000110	01001010
00001111	11000110	10000111	00000000	11111100	10111111	10101101	01010010	11010101	01101000
00100000	11011101	10010110	00111000	11101001	11101010	01111011	11010000	10100011	10011110
10011100	11010010	10100111	00001000	00101000	11011100	00010111	00100111	00011100	11110110
00010100	00100101	11010100	01100011	00111111	11110100	00111100	11111010	11010010	00111001
00100010	01001111	01101100	01110100	10100111	10101000	00111101	11101001	10101100	00111001
11100000	01110010	01111010	11111011	01010010	11010001	10000000	01111011	01100010	10011101
11101011	11001101	00001111	11001011	11100111	00111100	01010011	01110001	10011110	00101001
00000000	10011101	10111000	11101001	01001011	10001100	00110000	00011001	11100110	10001111
11100001	00110100	10000100	01100100	11100100	11010000	10101100	11011000	00001111	01101100
11101101	11111001	00000110	00110011	11011110	10000000	01101000	11001111	01100010	01111000
10100110	10010011	10001110	11011100	10010011	11010010	10000110	00000000	11000111	10000000
00000111	01111110	11110100	00101111	11001011	10001010	01000111	11001110	11100010	01110001
11110100	10100001	11001111	11101110	11001110	11001110	10111000	10101001	10110010	10111000
11111010	00010010	01101110	11001011	11100000	11110000	00000101	01001011	10111011	10100111
00011100	11010101	01110100	11111001	01110000	00000111	00100100	00001110	10100110	10011110
10101100	01001001	00101010	00111101	00101000	01101110	11000000	10001001	01110111	00000010
00001101	01010101	10111100	10110101	00010010	10001101	11001001	10010010	11100000	01110011
11101111	01010110	01000111	01011100	01100111	00000011	00000011	00000010	10010101	00000110
00001001	11101011	11000111	10110101	00110101	11011101	10010100	01110010	01111010	10011101
10010100	00011010	10001101	10100100	10010110	11110111	01000011	11100100	01111110	10000111
11010000	11010111	10010111	11101010	10111010	01110100	11011010	01100101	11100001	10001010
01000101	11101000	01110010	00011000	01111111	00010000	11110110	10101111	01110000	11010100
01101101	11010100	11000110	00011001	00110001	10111100	11110101	00011101	01110011	01011100
10011111	10001000	01110100	10000100	11010100	11101100	11001010	10010101	11111111	00000000
01001000	01001110	01100011	00111101	00101011	10100110	10010100	11111001	00010111	10010001
00101111	01010011	11001011	11101111	00100010	11000001	00001100	00111001	11001111	10110101
00111010	11011010	11011101	10100111	01101110	11100000	00001110	11110101	10100001	00011100
00101100	01111100	11001000	01011101	01001001	01110101	00111000	00111100	01110100	10101101
00101011	00011011	01000001	00011100	01100011	00000000	01100111	10101101	01101011	01010010
10100111	00101010	00010100	00010011	01100010	01011010	01011011	10010101	00000000	00000101
11111001	00111101	00110001	11010010	10110110	00101101	10101101	01000011	00001101	11000111
00111000	00111101	00101010	00111000	00100010	11001110	00110010	00111110	10110100	10111010
11011110	10100011	00011110	10001011	10100110	10001001	10110110	11101111	10010101	11111110
01001000	10010111	10110001	00111110	10110101	11000000	11111001	10100111	00101110	11100110
10101101	11011001	00011100	11111111	00000000	10001100	00110101	00000101	10000011	11111101
00000110	00001001	01111110	01110110	11001000	10010111	00011101	01010000	01111010	01010111
00100110	01110001	11000000	10100111	01001100	11001111	00110100	10001110	11110010	00011100
10111100	10000111	01111011	00011111	01010011	01000000	00000100	00001110	10111001	10101110
11111010	01110100	11100010	10010101	10001100	01011101	11011000	11010101	11101001	10011010
01000110	00111001	11101101	11010000	11111110	01110100	11110111	00111000	01011111	01001010
01100000	01011100	11110000	11111100	11100110	10110100	01111010	11101100	00011110	10100000
11101110	00111011	11100111	11110011	10100101	00111100	00001100	00001111	11001110	10010011
01101111	00011000	11000111	01000011	11011110	10010101	10111000	01001110	00111010	11010010
01101101	10100110	00011101	00000110	10110110	00100100	00011000	01111110	10111101	11001111
01001010	01101011	10000010	10000100	01100111	00011000	00111101	00101001	11011111	01111000
10100111	01001110	00001111	00010100	10111000	00001110	00110000	01110011	11101011	10001010
01111100	11011100	11111010	00001000	11101000	11111100	00110001	01110100	11000000	11111001
01000111	11111110	00000010	00000101	01110101	10000000	00000110	00011001	10101111	00110111
10110000	10010100	11011011	11011101	00100011	00011110	11000111	10001110	01101011	11010000
10101101	01100100	00101111	01101110	10001101	10011111	10111100	00110011	11010110	10111100
11111100	01100101	00100100	10100101	01110100	01110110	01010011	10010110	10010110	00110101
00100010	10111110	10001010	00010000	00000000	10010011	00101110	11111111	00000000	01111011
00010101	01011010	11110010	11101001	10110110	11100110	00111100	11100000	10011100	01100110
10110001	00011010	11101001	10110110	11100100	10000001	11110101	11110101	10101001	00010011

01010000 01010101 10001000 11101110 11101011 11111100 11101011 01110111 00011101 01110100
01100111 00010111 10101001 00110011 00101001 10010000 10011001 01110111 01110010 00101011
00110010 01101101 01001001 00100011 10111000 11011010 01110111 10111110 00001111 00111000
00010101 00111101 11000101 11100000 10001001 01001010 10011110 00001001 00011101 01101010
10001101 10011100 01000010 01111011 10110010 11010010 00001100 10000011 11010100 11010101
11010010 01010010 01111011 10110001 10101101 11001101 01101111 00110110 00011011 10110101
00000010 00011001 00011101 00000000 00011100 11101110 00010101 00110100 00110000 00101100
01010001 10010010 00100100 11001110 00001111 10101101 00011010 01000110 10011110 00100101
10010110 01000101 11001110 00010001 00110001 11001111 10101101 00100101 11110101 10100001
10001001 11000010 11000111 00100111 11001111 11011111 00001101 11010110 10110110 10101001
10100101 10110100 00001101 10001011 10111010 01110100 01100110 01011011 10100100 11011001
11010111 10101001 00000110 10111011 11101011 00111100 01001000 10000011 00001001 10000111
00000111 10010011 01011100 00011110 10001111 01111000 00110100 11101001 00000001 10011101
01001011 11100100 11110110 00011001 00110101 11011011 01101001 11111010 10001101 10011100
10010001 10000010 01100101 11110010 11011100 11110101 11001000 10101110 00101100 01001011
01011100 10110110 01000111 01110110 00010001 01101110 11001011 10010011 00010011 00100001
00000011 10110000 11110100 10100110 11000010 10000101 01011011 00100011 11110010 00110101
01110001 00100000 01011001 01110011 00100100 00110011 01000111 00100111 10101110 00001101
00011110 01000001 00011101 01111010 11010111 10011011 00100100 10101111 01110011 11010001
10111001 01100010 00101101 10010010 10100110 11011110 00101000 10011010 11011110 00100000
00110011 10001110 01111011 11010100 00101001 10011000 01001111 00010101 01101001 01001010
11001011 00011110 00000111 00000111 00010100 10101111 01111101 10001000 11010110 11100101
01010100 01001000 10010100 11100100 10001111 11111110 10111101 01100010 10001000 11100001
10010011 01010010 11110011 10000011 01101100 00111011 10111001 01010011 11111101 00101011
01111010 01011000 01000001 01000001 10111111 10111111 11101001 01011001 10110001 11011010
10100000 10011000 10000111 10001011 00100000 01110100 01101111 01011010 11011010 10001100
10101100 11110101 00110001 11000100 01010011 01110011 10110101 10000101 00110110 00110000
10110000 01110110 01110010 11111110 01100001 00111001 11101011 01010111 11101100 01101101
11100010 10001110 00010000 00100000 00100101 00001111 01111110 01101010 10001011 01000101
00100011 00011111 00101101 00001001 00100100 00001110 10110100 01000011 11110110 10000101
00111000 10001100 00011100 11110110 10100101 01010010 10100100 10011110 11001100 10111000
11010010 01001001 00011011 00011110 01011011 01000110 10011111 01111000 11100010 10100001
10111000 10001101 10001010 11100100 00110001 11111100 11101010 10001011 01001011 01110111
10111011 01110100 10001100 11111001 00011101 10111011 01010011 01101110 00101110 11011000
11000111 10110100 11100100 00010001 11101001 11011110 10110001 01110011 01101011 01110100
00110101 00000110 01010111 10010001 01110011 00110000 00000100 10010011 10010011 11011100
11100110 10101100 01011100 11000100 00111100 10110000 00000001 11100111 10111111 00111100
00011010 10100111 01101010 11000100 11011100 11100111 00011001 11110100 11110110 10101011
11001111 10111011 10000011 11011010 10011100 01011100 10010100 01110100 00110101 11010000
01111101 11001011 00011000 01101100 01000011 11100000 00010100 11000111 00110101 11000111
01011110 01001010 11010010 01001100 01111101 00101011 01110011 01011000 10111100 00010011
11000111 00011100 01001000 01001000 01000101 11100100 10001110 10010101 10000111 00100111
11001100 11100000 00000001 01001001 01001001 11001101 10000010 01001101 10010101 01100110
00111001 01001100 00011010 11100101 01111100 01000001 10000001 00011001 11111010 11110111
11101011 01011101 01101100 11000011 00111100 00001110 00111011 01010111 00101111 11100010
01001000 01110110 11000010 11100111 00011001 11101010 01110011 01011101 01110100 01011101
10100100 10010010 00110010 10101110 10010011 10001011 00110001 11101110 01100100 00010010
01000111 00011111 11010000 01010110 11001110 10001011 00101000 10001110 11000111 00001010
01001000 11000111 00100100 00011110 11110101 11001111 11011011 00101000 01101000 01000001
11100111 10011110 01111001 00110101 11010001 01101001 10110001 11101110 10001000 00000100
00000111 00010101 11101010 00111110 01010011 11000111 01111011 11101000 01101000 11101001
10010000 00110101 11010100 10101000 10011100 10011100 10011110 01110010 01111001 10101110
11010011 01001110 11010100 11100001 11010010 00011010 11110001 01100100 01000001 10010011
10000000 10100100 11110110 11000000 11101001 01010101 11111100 00011001 10100110 10000011
10111110 11100111 01101011 10011101 10011111 01111000 00010011 11010010 10110101 00100111
10111000 10110000 10110101 11110000 10111110 10101110 11011010 10001100 01000011 11001101
10010101 10001111 10010100 01000010 11100100 10000011 10001110 00101011 00001010 10010110
01011010 00100001 01001010 11101001 00011110 01001111 11100010 01100000 11111111 00000000
01100001 00100000 10110010 00010011 00110100 11100000 11001001 11101010 00000111 01101010
10110001 10100011 11000011 00001100 01111010 01111101 11001100 11011011 01010011 00000010
00100011 10010010 00000001 11101011 01011000 11010111 00010111 00000110 11101001 10000110
01001110 01110110 01110100 00100100 11110010 01101011 01010110 01101001 00010110 00111101
00000010 01111000 00000011 01111100 11101100 11000011 10100101 01011010 10100101 01101000
11101000 01001010 01111010 00010001 01101001 10011010 10110101 11010010 11101001 01110111
00010001 01000011 00100010 00100100 01100011 00111101 10110011 10001100 10001010 11100110
11110100 11111011 10100000 00101111 11100011 01101000 11010111 10010000 11011100 01110111
11101111 01011010 00011111 01101100 10001110 00011011 01101001 11100001 10001110 00110010
01110110 01000110 01111001 11101011 10011010 11000100 10110000 00011011 01110110 01001001
11010111 10010001 01000110 10101110 00101101 11011000 10111000 01101000 11010001 11101100
10001011 00101001 10010010 00110000 01110001 11001110 00110011 01010111 11110100 10101000
10001111 10011010 01001110 01110001 11000101 01010001 10110001 01010000 01101101 01100010
01100001 11001110 01010100 00011100 10011010 11011000 11010010 10100011 00100001 01001011
10011110 10011100 11100011 11111010 01010111 11001010 11000110 10010011 01110101 01111101

11100011 11011101 01101111 11011100 00110111 00111100 01011011 01101010 11010111 10011110
00010110 10111001 10110101 10001101 01000011 10111100 10110001 00100010 00000001 10011110
10111101 00101010 10110110 10010111 01101111 00110101 11000110 10101001 01101000 00000000
11000101 10110101 10101000 00000101 10110011 11010001 01110000 00110001 10001010 11011111
00101101 11100100 11000010 10001101 00100010 10001111 00101111 00000011 00111001 00110101
11001001 11111111 00000000 11000010 01001011 00110100 01110111 11110111 10010000 00001000
01100011 00001001 00101011 01110101 00100111 10110101 01111101 00011101 00111010 10011100
10101010 11001001 01011100 11110000 10100111 11110001 00011101 11110100 00110111 11110001
01000111 00110001 00011001 00001000 10011000 11101010 01101011 11001101 01111110 00101001
01101010 11001101 01110001 11110010 10100100 10111111 00100111 01000010 00000111 01111010
01101101 11010101 11010010 10110101 11001011 10000001 00101111 00000111 10100000 11011101
01011000 01111010 11111100 01111110 01101010 10000000 11100111 00101001 10001111 10010111
10011110 11110100 01110010 10111001 00110011 00111101 11110111 00111000 10011011 10010010
00100010 10001011 00101010 00111001 11001111 00111101 11101011 10100110 10000111 01001001
10011010 00101011 00011011 01110111 10010001 10010001 01000011 00101000 11100000 01110010
01110011 01010100 10101100 00101101 11101101 10100100 11010101 11100010 10110100 10111010
01111101 10001000 11001100 00000110 01111010 01100110 10111010 11011111 00010100 10101011
11000101 00011100 01100000 01000100 11111110 01010000 00000011 11100110 00011101 00000110
00101011 10100111 10011011 01000101 11011100 10101110 10000110 01111101 10101100 01101011
01100110 00011110 01011110 10100100 00101111 01001111 01001010 11100001 11110101 10001001
11011010 01101011 11110111 10010011 11010101 10110010 01110001 11101011 01011110 10010111
10100101 01011000 10011001 00100010 00010111 00110111 00000000 10000100 00011000 11000000
00111111 11000111 01011100 10100111 10001110 10110100 11111011 00111101 00111010 11011000
01011100 00001000 11110001 01110011 00110100 10111001 11100011 10100000 10100101 00101110
01010101 00101011 01001000 00101101 11010100 11100001 11101111 10001001 00110010 10010110
01110110 11100010 10101001 00111010 11111111 00000000 00010000 00111001 11001111 01101010
01011011 11001001 10000011 01001000 00001000 11111100 01101010 00111111 00110111 00100100
01111110 10100010 10110110 10001101 00100111 00011101 01010011 00010000 10010010 10011100
11110110 11101101 11000101 01101011 11101000 11110010 10001000 11100010 11011100 00011011
11100111 00000011 10001110 01111010 00011010 11001001 11001111 00100000 10010001 10010000
01101010 11011101 10111100 00110011 01001101 00011011 10011011 01111000 11011110 01000010
10111101 01000000 00011101 00101000 10010011 11111011 00100011 10001110 11100111 01000001
01110011 10101110 00101100 10110110 11101001 01101001 01110000 01000100 10111000 00011000
11011101 11011111 10011110 11100010 10110111 00111100 00110010 00101101 11100011 10001000
01111001 01110011 10100011 11110011 10010010 00110011 11001101 01111001 10100110 01011001
10110010 11111100 10000001 11010010 10110100 00101100 00101110 11011110 11010110 01100100
10010100 01100011 11001100 00011101 00001111 01011100 11010110 01010010 11000010 01000111
01010111 00010010 10111001 10011001 11101110 01111010 01101100 10100001 00011111 01101100
01101100 01001111 00100011 00111110 10000010 10100011 11010101 10100000 00010010 11011011
01011101 11000100 00110000 01010010 01011000 10011000 00110110 01111001 10101111 00111111
11010000 01110101 10001011 10011001 10100101 11001101 11000101 11001110 11000111 00011000
00111000 00000011 00011011 11000101 01110101 10111010 01101110 10101111 00010101 11000100
01010010 01100100 11100011 01100011 01110101 00110101 11001000 11101001 11001001 00111101
01001011 10111101 11001111 00110101 10110111 11010100 01010010 00010101 00010110 11010111
01101000 00001101 10111100 10111001 01001100 11110111 10101010 01011110 00100100 11111011
01001101 10110111 10010101 01101010 01100101 00101101 01101100 10100011 11110111 01001101
10001110 01011000 01111011 11010101 10101111 00011101 01011010 10001011 01111101 01100110
11100110 00111000 11010111 11100100 11011100 00100100 00011110 10011100 11111111 00000000
11110101 11101010 10100101 11011101 11111100 01110111 10110110 00010000 01000100 11101010
01110111 10101000 11111100 10101011 01011111 01100110 10101110 10100100 10000100 11110101
00110001 01010011 00011000 11111001 10000001 11100110 10011010 10101011 10111001 11001000
00000011 10000001 11011111 11010110 10100100 01100000 00000001 11000001 11001110 00111101
01110011 11010010 10011010 10000111 01101100 10111101 11000101 01110111 00101000 11011001
01101000 10001100 10101101 10101001 01101010 00010101 00010001 10001100 11100011 11110000
10101000 10101110 01011000 00011001 00111111 01110111 01000100 10110010 10011110 10000101
10110001 11111101 01101010 00110111 00000101 10100100 00011101 10111111 00001010 00100010
11101111 10100010 00101001 10110001 01000000 11001111 10100000 00010100 01101101 11101011
10010011 11000111 01101010 01110000 00011111 10111100 00001010 11011101 01000111 11100100
01101001 10101111 10011100 01110101 11111101 00101001 11110011 00010011 01110010 01001000
01010111 01110100 10000000 00010011 10001111 10101111 01111010 11011010 10000011 01001111
10001000 00101110 11101100 11100100 11110110 10101100 00011101 11011011 10111001 00000111
00011000 00011101 01101010 11100101 10101101 11101001 10001100 10000101 00000000 11111011
11100010 10110010 10010010 10010100 10111110 00010110 01110100 01010001 10011100 01010011
11110111 10010001 10110101 00001101 11111100 10010110 10110010 00100000 10110111 11011000
00011100 00110110 01110010 00000101 01110101 11011010 01100110 10100001 00110101 11110001
00110011 01011101 00011100 11001011 10001111 01001100 00001010 11100010 01101101 01100000
00010011 01001011 11100111 00000010 11111000 10101110 10010111 01001011 01101101 10100100
00000010 01110000 00111101 00111101 01101011 11001011 11000111 11010001 10001011 10001110
10011011 10011110 10100101 00011111 01111011 01010011 10110101 11010010 10101111 01100101
10110111 00100111 00000111 00100000 11110101 00000110 10111010 01001011 01001011 10111000
10101110 00010011 11100100 01101100 00111111 10100001 10101110 00011110 11010010 01101100
10011110 10111100 11010110 10100100 00110010 11101101 00000000 10000011 10001100 01110111
10101111 00010010 10000101 01101001 11010010 10010101 10000101 01011011 00001110 10101010

01101010 01110101 01010011 01100100 10000001 01000100 01000011 01101010 11110110 00011100
01010101 01011011 00111011 10101111 10110100 01011011 10000010 01001000 11001000 11100000
11010100 11110010 10110111 11001011 10001110 11110101 11101011 10101001 11110011 00101011
10100011 11001100 10010100 00011100 00011101 10011001 01000010 01100011 11001110 01111011
10010011 01010000 11001001 11001000 11000101 01001100 11111100 10110101 01010111 01101100
01101111 00111011 01101000 10110101 11110111 01100101 00100101 01100010 01001011 00110101
00000010 00111001 01111110 10100011 00010100 10001110 01010100 01110111 11111010 11010010
11000011 10010000 10011001 11100111 00011110 10010101 10011101 10101001 01001100 00010110
01011111 00101111 10100001 00100011 10110101 01110101 10100111 11001001 00001101 11001001
01101010 11101110 11000010 11011111 00011000 11100110 00011100 01111101 00111010 11010110
01001101 10101100 10001101 01101101 00100011 11000101 00100111 11111010 10100010 01110010
00111101 10101010 01000111 00110010 11000110 01111000 00111001 01001111 01001010 10101111
01110011 01110110 00110000 01111111 01110011 00100011 10000001 11010100 10001010 11100110
10010101 11011110 11101100 11011001 01000010 11001000 11010001 11011010 10000111 10011100
00001010 10101111 01110001 00000000 11100001 10010010 10101010 01011011 01011110 10100011
00000000 00110111 00011000 11001111 11111011 01010101 01101101 10100110 11001000 11000000
11000001 11100011 10101000 00110100 00111001 01011001 01111011 11000011 01000101 01101001
10110110 11001111 00010100 10110000 01001101 11111100 01100011 00000100 11010110 01000110
10000111 00010011 11000001 00001001 10000110 01100000 01000011 10100011 00010000 00111110
10011101 10101010 11100100 11110111 01001010 11110111 00110010 11000010 00111000 10010101
00000110 11110000 00111101 01101000 01001001 00001011 00110010 00110000 00011100 01010011
11010010 11010110 00110101 10100111 10111110 10000100 11101010 00001000 10010011 00110101
00110010 00110110 01101010 10110011 00011100 00111101 01001010 10110010 01010110 01111011
10011101 00100101 10000100 11000001 00011001 00010101 00011111 10010101 10111010 01000000
00111111 00110011 01001110 10000011 10111000 11101010 00111010 11010101 11001011 01101000
11111010 11101110 00011101 01000111 00010100 11100000 11111011 10010001 00110111 01100100
01001011 00010010 10101001 00000000 11100111 11101001 01000011 01110010 01001111 00011101
01111010 01010011 11110000 00110001 10001100 01010100 00110010 01100111 10101010 01100111
00110101 10111011 11110010 00111000 11110111 00110011 11110101 00001101 00111010 00111101
01000100 00011000 00100110 11001111 10010111 10011100 10011100 00001110 11110101 01001011
01001010 10111110 11110010 11110101 01111011 10011101 00100010 01100010 01011111 11001001
01000000 11010001 10110001 00111100 10010001 01011011 11101100 00000010 10101000 00000011
10101001 11101010 01110011 01011100 10011100 10101010 11010110 11111110 00110001 10010110
11111111 00000000 01101110 01100010 00110000 11111001 01101100 01111101 00001101 01010101
00111011 11001101 01110010 11011100 00101111 10101001 11010010 11001101 00010001 11101010
10000111 00010101 00010010 01011100 11111001 01100111 01101100 10001010 01000000 00111101
11000101 01110011 11110111 10011110 00100000 00100101 11001000 10110010 01011001 00001001
11110101 11000110 01000001 10101101 01011101 00101110 11101101 10101110 10100000 01001111
10110101 00100001 10001010 01110010 00111001 00000100 01110101 10101000 11110110 01110010
01101010 11100101 10011010 00111011 10111100 11001110 01111011 01010100 01110011 01001000
00110110 01010100 00110010 10101011 11000010 00110010 10000111 10001111 01001010 10001101
10100101 00010010 01101100 01011110 10001110 01001001 11100010 10001010 10010111 01111010
10100001 00010010 00001100 11001010 11011001 00011101 00000101 00010010 11111110 11101101
01001111 11101000 01101010 01000100 00000011 00000011 01101111 01001010 00011001 01110111
01110001 01011001 10101001 01110111 00011001 01010010 00110010 01100100 00100100 10111000
11100011 10110101 00101011 10101000 11000111 00010101 01100001 10100011 00000000 01010100
01001001 00010001 11000001 00111001 11111101 01111010 11010101 10110101 01101101 01000010
11101000 11001111 10111000 10010000 01000111 00011001 00100011 10101101 01010011 10110001
10110101 01101011 10111011 10000000 01011111 11101110 01100111 00100110 10110110 11001101
10111100 01100000 00011100 10101110 01001101 00111010 00010101 01001000 11001000 01010000
00000000 10100110 11100100 10010011 10111000 01011000 10110100 10110001 00101010 11000111
10000100 11100010 10011001 01010010 00111110 00110001 11110010 10011010 10000001 11001111
11001111 11011110 10000101 01100010 01111010 10001101 10111000 00000011 01100001 10010000
01100111 10001010 11100101 01111100 01000101 00100110 11101110 00001000 11001000 01101110
01111001 00010101 11010100 01001000 11111000 01000010 01101011 10001101 11010111 10100100
11001100 11011011 01110001 11000000 00111100 11010110 10010000 10111101 11101100 01001011
00110001 00010001 01000001 00100100 10000011 01000110 01001110 01001010 11110100 11111110
10110101 00101110 00000000 01011100 01110100 00111111 01011010 10001101 10000110 01000111
01000001 01011101 00101101 00100111 10101010 00001101 10001001 10101100 11010101 01001101
11101100 01000000 11100100 10000010 11000000 00001100 01111010 11100110 10111110 10001000
10110110 00000010 00101011 01010100 00011000 00111011 00100011 01010000 00110010 01101011
11100111 10101101 00101000 01100110 11111010 11011001 01111001 11111111 00000000 01011000
00111010 01010111 11010000 11001001 10010011 00011010 01000111 11101100 00110010 01111111
00001010 10001010 11001010 11001001 00011001 01010100 01011010 10000111 01101111 01111110
10000010 10011110 01000111 01110000 00101001 10100000 01100111 10101001 11000110 00101001
11001010 01110111 00000010 00000101 01110010 11110011 01110111 00110010 00011011 11001111
00011001 11001110 00101001 10100100 10000000 11100100 10010001 11110010 01110110 10100000
10011110 00000110 11100010 01110000 00001101 00101111 01010000 00111101 00101010 10100000
11010111 01010001 11011100 00011011 11101110 11111110 00110100 10000100 00010010 00110000
10111101 11101001 01111001 11011001 11110011 00001010 00000110 01111011 11110000 01101000
01110010 11101000 01001000 11001110 10000111 00000100 11010010 00010001 11000110 00111101
01101001 01000111 01001110 11011100 01110111 11110101 10100011 10101000 10101001 11010111
10100000 11000001 10110000 00001000 00011110 10010100 00100111 01011111 01101010 01000000

01110000 01111010 01111101 01101000 00111100 10011100 11100111 00011000 11101011 01000010
11110101 00000000 01010010 00110010 01110111 01110011 10001110 10010100 00101001 00001010
01000111 11101011 01001010 10011110 10111000 11100010 10011011 10000000 11000011 00100111
10100000 10100110 00111101 00000011 00000100 10010110 00100100 11010011 01000001 11100010
10011101 10011101 11000111 11100101 00111100 01100111 10010011 01000110 00111000 11000000
11101011 11101111 01010101 01100010 01000110 00101000 11100100 00001110 01000110 01001111
00110100 01100011 11100100 00100000 00011010 01111111 11011101 01000000 01000111 01010001
01001100 00000100 11001000 10111001 00011111 10011101 01000101 10010000 11000100 01010101
00001010 00110001 11010100 11110101 00111110 11110100 00011110 10111001 00111110 10011101
00101001 01011101 10110001 10001111 01001111 01010011 01000110 00000000 10010011 00100111
10111111 01001010 01101101 01110101 01000010 00001100 00000001 10001110 01101001 10001100
00000001 01111100 10011110 11010100 11100000 00001001 10010000 10010001 11010010 10010111
10100110 01001111 01111010 00110101 01011010 10000000 10001101 10000000 10111011 01110001
11111000 11010011 01110110 10000010 00000000 00111001 11110111 00110100 11111101 10111100
10001110 10110100 11000110 10100001 11101000 00110000 01100011 10010010 00110000 00111001
11101101 10001010 00111011 11010000 00111000 00011100 01010010 00101000 00111101 01111101
01101000 01101010 11100000 00101111 01000000 01101001 11001101 11110111 00110010 01110001
01010001 10010011 10010110 00000000 00011111 10101101 00101011 01100000 11100000 01111010
01010000 10011101 10111010 00000000 00011100 01100000 00001010 01011100 01100011 00110100
11101110 00000101 00110111 00000100 10000000 01000111 00011111 01011010 00010000 00001000
11100000 00101000 11001011 01111110 01110100 01100011 10001111 10101111 10111101 00001100
00111100 11000111 11110110 10100100 00011111 00110110 01011000 10011110 00001111 10101101
00100111 01110110 11101110 00000010 10101111 11001010 01000111 00100111 10101101 00111101
01011011 01100110 01110001 11010100 10011010 10001111 10000010 01000111 10100111 10101101
00101111 00100101 11110001 11011010 10000110 10000000 10010001 01011011 11001011 10001100
10010110 11111111 00000000 11110101 11010100 11101010 11011001 01001110 01001110 00000001
11101010 01001101 01010111 11000110 00110001 01010010 01100100 00110001 00000011 00010100
01011100 00000000 10011100 00000010 11011001 00011000 00100111 10001100 11010101 00001011
11111011 00100101 00001011 11100110 01000010 10100100 11110001 11001111 00110101 10100010
11101010 00001000 00011011 10000111 01111110 10011110 10010100 11010111 01010000 01010000
11000111 10010010 00010001 11000110 00001110 00001101 00101101 01011110 10100000 01110001
01110111 11111010 01101100 01001101 00100011 11001110 10010001 11100010 01010010 00110000
01001000 11101111 01011001 11101011 01100100 11011000 11011100 01000111 01111010 11101100
10101111 00110100 11111101 10101011 11111011 10111110 00000000 00011101 00101011 00101001
10000000 00000011 10010001 01011010 00110110 10001011 01000110 00111010 00101100 01110000
00101011 11001011 00110001 00000001 00000000 11001001 00100110 10111100 11011011 11000100
00011010 10011011 11101010 11011010 10010011 11001101 00100110 11110100 10001110 00111111
10010010 00100101 00100111 10000000 00111101 01101011 10101100 11110001 10001110 10100000
01100101 00100111 01001110 10110111 01111101 11110001 11111111 00000000 11001011 01010010
10111100 00011111 10100101 01110001 00110010 11000011 10000010 01110011 11101001 11010010
10110101 10100100 11101111 10101101 10001001 01101110 11100101 01110000 01111001 00011001
00111100 00011010 01111000 01100000 00111010 00001100 11100110 10011000 11001011 10110111
10111111 00010100 11110000 00110000 10100000 10010001 11000101 01110101 01000111 10101001
00111010 10000011 01101101 01100011 11010011 11110100 10100100 11100000 00000011 10010011
11110100 11100110 10011100 10111000 10010011 00111100 10011010 00001000 00011011 11110000
01001000 11000111 01100011 01001101 11000110 11111010 10001000 01101011 00101110 11101100
01111001 10000111 00111001 00011001 11001101 00011001 11100100 11100000 11111011 01100110
10011100 10101011 11000110 00111111 10011101 00100110 00000011 00001111 01111010 01001110
00111011 00000010 00100011 01100101 00101100 01001110 00001110 00111101 11110001 01001011
10011100 10101110 00110001 10000011 11011100 10001010 01110110 00110000 00111101 11001111
01111010 01101011 00000011 10011101 10111110 11011100 00011010 11010001 01011001 00111101
10001010 01000011 10011011 00000100 01101101 00100111 11101000 01110001 11010010 10110101
01110100 11011101 01011001 11101101 01101101 01010110 00100010 11000101 01110110 10011110
10011100 11010110 00110011 00000011 10010001 11001110 00101001 11101011 00110010 10010001
11110111 00001001 10101100 11011101 10011111 11000100 00110100 11101101 10110001 11010001
00001001 01110001 00011011 10001001 00001001 00011101 11111000 00011111 11001010 10100000
11100110 01100000 11110001 01110100 00111101 10001111 10101101 01010110 10010000 10011111
00110000 00101110 11100111 00111101 10101010 11100101 10111011 00101000 00111000 00000011
11101110 01110100 00100010 10110011 01110000 11101011 01100011 00100100 11010011 00101100
11011011 10101100 10101100 10010001 11000011 00111011 00101011 10111001 11100001 01001111
01000011 11110100 10100111 11111101 10010110 01111011 01001001 00111110 11110001 01001110
01110011 10010000 01111010 01010011 00111100 10100011 00110100 10001001 00111001 00111100
00001100 10010010 01110011 10001010 10010010 00011001 01100100 10111100 10010100 01000100
10100111 00011000 11100111 00100111 10011100 10001010 00111001 01010100 01010101 11011001
01010110 11010100 11011100 11111110 11010011 10001010 01101011 01000000 10111110 01011111
10010111 01110110 00111011 10101111 01000111 11111100 00111011 01010101 00100100 10000110
11100110 01001011 10000011 00101011 10000011 10110000 00110111 00100010 10110010 00101110
01001100 10010000 01001100 00110110 00011111 10011101 00111010 10011010 11010011 10110100
11010111 00100101 10010010 00110000 10010011 11100011 01111000 00111111 10011101 01001101
10010111 00110101 11010001 01010110 01100111 01000011 00000100 00110001 01001000 10111111
00111011 01100011 10001111 10010100 11110101 10101011 10010110 11100000 10001110 00110001
11001000 11101101 01011000 01111010 01101011 10111100 11010111 00111001 01000011 10000001
11101001 10011010 11101001 00010011 00011000 00000111 10111111 01110001 01011100 11011000

10010110 11011110 10001100 11110100 00110000 01101010 11001010 11100101 10111011 01001001
11100100 10000101 11000001 10001101 10001010 00011100 11010111 01000001 01100111 10101001
11001011 00100000 00000010 01110000 10000100 11100011 11101111 01100011 10101101 01110011
00000100 01101110 00000100 01100111 11110010 10101011 10010110 10101100 01000111 01011100
10010011 11110101 10101110 00011011 11011010 11101010 11000111 01110101 10010011 00110111
11111111 00000000 11010111 11001001 11000001 11101001 01001111 11111001 10100001 00111001
01000001 11111001 11010101 00001000 01101110 00010010 00111100 10001100 00011111 10101101
01001000 11010111 01000110 01000001 11111110 11000111 01011110 01101011 00011110 01100101
01110010 01101100 01001000 11110111 01010010 10011001 00110111 01001000 01110010 00111101
10000101 00011110 01111110 11100001 10010001 11010110 10010001 00100100 10001111 00000100
10010101 11001111 10110101 01010101 01111110 00011100 10010100 00111100 00011110 11011110
10010101 10100101 11101111 10110000 01011000 10110101 11100111 00011000 11010000 11100011
10101001 11101111 01010010 01000011 01111100 11000001 00001111 00000011 00111110 10110101
01001101 11011110 00100011 00011001 11011110 11100001 00001111 10101101 01010101 10000100
10010011 11010001 11000111 10010111 10011110 10100010 10100001 11001001 00100111 01100010
10010100 00101110 01101011 10101101 11010000 11011001 11001000 10101010 10010111 11010010
11000101 00100100 01000111 01100111 11011111 10100111 00110110 11001100 00000101 00000100
00010011 01001110 01001000 11100001 10001000 10000110 01111100 00010111 11001111 01000011
01010010 11110111 11110010 00010011 01010110 00100010 10110001 11000010 10100111 01001110
01101001 11110010 11001000 01111010 10111001 10100001 11101110 11100001 00000011 00000011
10011001 00001110 01110011 01010100 11101111 00100111 11011100 00000000 11000110 00110011
01010111 01111000 11011010 11001000 00011110 10100101 00011011 11101001 01110111 01001000
01111000 10101010 01101111 11110010 10001100 10110101 01001101 00101001 11001011 01100111
10101101 01010011 10010101 10001100 10110010 01100000 01110101 00010100 10111001 10101100
01011010 11010000 01100001 00111001 00100100 11110110 10101110 01101111 11000100 11100100
10001000 01001110 11000010 00110011 11101111 01011101 00000101 11001100 10100100 00001100
00000011 01011100 10011111 10001001 00100100 00100011 10001100 11100100 10011110 10011000
11101101 01011101 00110100 10110111 01001101 10011000 11010110 10110111 00101011 10111001
10010101 01100110 01001100 10100011 01100111 00011111 00100000 11111101 00101011 10101010
11010001 11011010 00111101 10000001 01000000 11100100 11110101 11111010 01010111 00100111
10100110 01000110 11000010 01011101 11011001 11100000 10000010 00001001 11001101 01110101
11111010 00111100 00100100 01000100 00110001 11010101 11001111 00010101 11101010 00111000
10101111 01000011 11000101 00111011 10011101 00110010 11101011 11001010 10110110 11011001
00011010 11100101 00001111 01010101 11110101 10101110 01101011 11100010 00101111 10001000
10010110 01001011 01011000 11110100 11011011 01000101 01000100 00001001 11110011 10110111
11010111 11010010 10110101 01010010 01100011 10100110 11011010 00111011 01001110 01110010
10000000 01100011 00100000 01110111 10101111 00110101 11010100 10100100 11111011 01010110
10100001 00100100 10010010 00011100 10010010 01111001 00011101 10000101 01100110 11100000
10101010 01001010 11000100 10111101 11101100 01000111 10100110 01000110 01100011 10000100
10111100 10011101 01001111 01001010 11010001 10111100 10001111 11001001 11010011 01011110
01101001 10111110 01000100 00100000 10000001 10011110 11100100 01110011 01010101 11101101
10100100 01010101 00100000 00000001 10010011 10011100 01010001 11100010 10101011 10101001
10011001 00101101 11100010 01110111 00100101 00001000 11011110 11011111 10000101 01101011
11101101 00010100 00100011 10110001 01001111 01101101 01001100 10101001 00101110 01010110
11001111 01000101 10010111 11100101 11001100 11110111 01000011 01100110 11101111 01101111
01011010 10000011 11000011 11010110 11110001 11011101 01001000 11101011 00100100 10100001
00000100 01101010 00011111 11101010 01101010 10000101 11001100 11000110 01010111 11101011
11000000 11100000 00001010 11010110 11110000 11111100 00110010 01001001 00010100 11100100
00001111 10010000 01110101 01100010 01101011 01001011 10110110 10110100 00010010 10111101
11101110 01111010 10001110 10010011 00100010 01001001 01100001 00011110 11000110 11001110
00000110 00101011 10100001 11010010 10100001 00110011 00000011 10110001 10110110 00000000
00110010 01001111 10110101 01111001 11010110 10000011 10101100 11000111 00010111 10010111
01101101 10001100 10111001 01101100 00000010 00101011 10110111 10110111 11010111 00101100
10101101 00100101 10000010 11000000 00110110 00100101 10011010 01010000 10000000 10010011
11110111 10110010 01101011 11000001 10101001 10000010 10011100 01101010 11110011 10101101
10001111 01010010 00110101 11100011 11101100 11101101 01111101 01001101 11101111 00011000
01011110 11001011 01100011 10100000 01001011 01110011 00000001 11000001 01010010 10000000
01100111 10011100 11010111 10011101 10110110 10100011 00001100 11011001 01101001 10001110
11000010 01111010 01111011 11010111 01110111 11110001 00101010 00101001 00100100 11110000
01110101 11100010 10100111 11011111 11110011 00010011 10100001 11110111 10101111 00011111
00010010 10110000 10010101 00100011 01110000 01111000 11101100 01101011 11010010 10100101
00001001 00011110 01010100 10111110 00100011 10101100 11010011 11100100 11011101 10001001
11001010 11100100 00010001 11000110 01101010 01001011 10011100 01001001 00010001 01100011
11000000 00011101 11001000 10101100 00111011 00111011 11011001 00010101 11110110 10111110
01000010 00010011 11011010 10110100 00101110 01100110 00100100 00100010 10011111 11110101
01100111 10101001 10101101 11011010 10010110 11000010 00110011 00111110 11001110 01100100
11010101 00100000 11110010 11111001 11111101 11100000 11111001 10111010 11010111 10101100
01011010 00101010 11001101 00000000 01001001 10000000 01110100 00100011 10010000 01000111
01111010 11100010 11110100 01011000 00100000 00110111 10110000 01001000 01000110 11110000
10001100 00001000 11111010 11010111 01100101 01111000 11001100 10110001 00010011 00001111
01011110 11100011 00111000 10101100 10101010 11001001 01110010 10100011 01001000 10010000
11011101 11101101 01010111 00000000 00001110 00000111 01000001 01011110 01010111 11110001
01000010 01110110 10011110 11101110 00001000 01111010 01111001 01111111 00111111 00110101

11101001 00001011 01110001 11100110 00001100 00111000 00111001 11101111 10011010 11110010
00011111 10001000 00010111 10001101 01110001 10101111 11001001 10110111 00100001 00010100
01101100 00010101 10010101 00101011 01001010 01101010 11101100 01110011 01111010 01101000
01110010 10100110 00110010 01011000 10011100 10001100 01110100 11001000 10101000 11010101
01111001 11000110 00111001 11110101 10100111 11001001 00100110 01100100 11000010 01100100
00000001 11000111 11010110 10100011 01101001 00000110 00110011 11001000 11000111 01010011
10001010 11110100 00010101 11110110 00110010 00100111 01100000 00010110 00111100 10010011
11010010 10110111 00111100 00100001 00111011 01000011 10101000 01101110 00011100 10100011
10001100 00011110 01111010 01010101 01111101 00010010 11011110 00001011 11011011 01001011
10011000 01100100 00111111 10111111 00100000 01111001 01100100 11110110 10101011 10011010
00100101 10000100 10110110 01011010 10111100 10001000 01000110 01100011 00000011 00100000
11111010 11010100 00111010 10011010 00111000 10110011 01001000 10100110 10001110 11100010
01111101 00000011 01001011 11010100 00100010 00000110 11101010 00000001 10111111 10001111
10011010 00100011 10110000 11111110 10010101 10001111 00110111 10000000 10100001 01100111
00000110 11010010 11110101 11100011 11000111 01101001 00010111 00110101 11010011 01011001
10001100 10010000 01110011 11000110 00110000 00101010 11011011 11001010 01100010 00111101
10000010 01010111 00110010 10101101 00100100 11010000 11101100 10001110 01101010 11000011
11000000 11011011 01100011 00001011 00110101 11101010 01100111 11111101 10010101 10101110
10010010 11000011 01000101 10110010 11010011 01000010 00001100 10011001 01011111 11010110
01001010 10110001 00010100 11111001 01011100 10001110 10011110 10110101 10011111 10101101
11101010 01010001 11011011 11000011 10010011 00100110 00111111 01001010 11001110 10110110
00100110 01011011 00100010 11010010 01000111 10011101 11111100 01000000 00111001 11010110
11110111 11000110 11011001 11001010 10010000 01000101 01110010 00010001 00010010 01011101
11011001 00111011 00011010 11011001 11010111 01101111 01001101 11101101 11101011 10110110
01000001 11001001 11100011 11011010 10110010 11011100 01111001 01111111 01011110 11100110
10111010 10110000 11101001 10101000 01011001 11101010 01100100 11000100 01101111 10011000
11110001 11001111 10101101 00110001 01010100 10010001 10010000 00001110 00101010 01000000
00000000 00000000 11101101 11001110 01101001 11001111 11110010 10001100 01100100 10000011
11101100 01101011 10100001 01001011 10010100 10010010 00010110 11100000 01110000 00000001
11000111 00111110 10111000 10100111 01110000 01010100 00010011 11001111 10111101 00110111
01110001 00000011 11100111 10100110 10010011 10011110 01111001 11110110 00011110 10110101
01101001 10111110 10000010 00100100 01011101 10100010 01000111 00101000 01110010 00101000
01100011 10000000 01000000 11101010 01111001 10100101 00100011 00001011 10011110 11111101
11101001 10000101 10111101 10110001 11101111 01010001 01110101 01111101 10000010 11001100
10001111 01110110 01111000 11000111 11100011 01001111 10110111 00111001 01111100 01100111
11110100 10100110 01100000 00011110 10000111 00011000 10101001 00100011 00000011 10010110
00111111 10000000 10101010 11011000 00010001 10111001 10100111 01011110 11000111 00010111
11101110 11001110 01000111 10111111 01101010 11010011 10110011 10111101 11000011 11111010
11010111 00100000 11101100 11000011 10011100 11110001 11010111 10001010 10011010 00101011
10001001 00000001 11111001 00011000 10001111 11101011 01011100 10010101 00110000 10111110
11010101 10111110 11000111 01101101 00011100 01010111 00100010 10110100 10001111 01001110
11010011 01101110 11010110 01011100 00110000 11101110 00101011 01011001 00100101 00011100
01110011 01011110 01110011 10100011 11101010 00101100 10011011 00010100 00110001 11001000
11001001 00100011 00111101 01101011 10101011 10110011 10111100 00010010 00111010 00001100
11111010 01110101 10101111 10011111 11000110 11100001 00011101 00101001 11011100 11101111
10100111 01010001 01001101 01011101 00011101 10000110 10011011 00101011 11100111 11110111
01100011 10010011 11010111 10001010 11010111 10011001 10110001 11001001 11101001 01011000
01111010 00001011 11111001 10000101 11011001 01001110 01110000 00101011 01010110 01111001
00111000 11000001 10101101 00101000 11001010 11110000 01010111 11011100 11100110 10101110
10111101 11100010 00110110 00111100 01110101 10100010 11011010 00010011 00110100 10111000
01011111 11000110 10100010 00100100 10110100 10000000 01100000 10011010 11011101 11010011
11101101 11111110 11001111 00011110 01001111 01010110 11101011 01011011 11011011 10101011
00111001 11001010 11111010 10010100 00100010 00010100 10001101 01010011 10000000 00101011
00000011 01010001 10001001 01001011 10100011 00010001 11001101 01110100 10011010 10110001
01010110 10010010 00111101 10000111 10100000 11100110 10111001 11111101 01000000 11110011
11110100 10101110 11001010 01110010 10111100 00110101 00110011 11111011 01000110 01110011
00001100 01100111 11010000 11010101 01100110 01010101 11000011 10011101 11011101 01111101
01101001 10010111 10110111 10110001 11000101 11000001 11100100 11110110 00000010 10110000
00101110 01101111 00100110 01110111 00100101 00001001 01000001 11010011 00011001 10101110
01110111 01010010 01001101 11101000 01110110 01000010 00001110 01011011 00011011 00010010
10101010 10010011 10000010 00000001 10101100 11101011 10001000 10000100 00100101 11011010
11011110 01010010 00111101 01000110 01110011 01011001 01001110 01100100 01110110 00111111
10111100 01111111 11001110 10011000 11001010 01010011 11100110 00011001 11001111 11010110
10011010 11100110 00101111 11011000 00110010 11100011 11001110 10110011 10110010 00111011
10110000 00010010 10001110 10001100 00000111 00110101 01111110 11001010 11100001 10100101
01110010 10110010 00000000 10000101 00001111 01101110 10011111 01011010 11100111 01110000
11011011 10000011 01101110 01110001 11110100 10101101 01001101 00100110 01010010 01100100
01110001 00100011 00001100 11111010 01111010 11010101 10100100 10011010 11010100 01111110
11001001 11000000 11011011 01100001 10010010 00110011 01010010 01100011 10100001 11101101
01010000 00110111 01001010 10011001 01111110 11100001 00111101 10101011 00001011 10101011
11111011 10101000 11010111 11001100 01110100 01011001 00001100 00111001 10101101 01111000
01000001 00010001 10000001 10001110 01101011 00100010 11010011 11100110 10010100 00001111
01111110 01101011 01100010 00010110 11001001 10101101 01010100 00011101 10101110 11001100

01101010 10111110 10000011 11011111 10000011 11010010 10100000 01100011 10011001 00111000
11101000 00101010 01100111 00111001 11001111 00011000 10101000 01010000 01111110 10110100
10011011 10001101 11001110 01110001 11000100 11110001 11001101 01010011 10011010 00000010
01011000 10011111 11101111 11110101 11100010 10101110 00010001 11001111 00110100 10111000
11100000 11010101 00100100 11010110 10010001 00101000 11100111 11100001 00010001 11101001
11110111 10111110 01010001 01010000 00100000 01110001 11110010 10010001 11011010 10101111
11011100 00101000 10010001 00111000 11100011 11010000 11010100 00011010 11011100 00011001
10110101 00101110 00111010 10101001 11001101 00101110 10010101 00101111 10011101 01101010
00010101 11111001 01110001 11010111 11011110 10011110 10101101 11011110 11100011 01001100
10011010 00111001 01011000 10000000 10110010 01110001 11101111 01001100 10111100 10110111
11011101 00011001 10010001 00001110 00001000 11101001 10001010 10010010 01010101 11110010
11111001 00111101 00111101 11101001 00100001 01100000 01000110 00001111 11100100 01101000
11100111 10110011 00000110 10001010 00010000 01001011 00101010 10111000 01011001 00111000
00010101 01100100 01011100 00011100 10000000 00110000 00000111 01111010 00100111 10001100
10001001 00110010 10111100 10001110 10011000 10100110 11111001 01111001 11100110 10000101
00000100 11110101 01000100 11011100 10010001 00100111 01101001 00110011 11101001 11011100
11010001 00101100 11000100 00101110 01010011 10101000 10101000 11011100 10000101 11000110
00000111 00111101 11110000 01110001 01001100 10000111 10010110 11011100 01001111 11001000
00111011 01010011 01011010 00001100 10010001 00100110 01100010 00001011 00111001 11111100
00110001 01000011 01001000 11000110 01000001 10110001 01110010 01101010 00101001 00100100
11000000 11110111 11110110 10101001 10101100 10100001 00110000 11111101 11110010 01001011
10011110 11011110 10010100 10010010 01110001 11010101 00001001 10110010 11100011 10010000
10110001 11100010 10101010 10010110 00100111 10011110 11010100 11101011 10000011 10010111
11011010 00111111 00111010 10101011 00101100 10100010 00110001 10110111 10100000 00011100
01010010 11100110 10110011 00010101 11000111 01001100 01110110 10101111 00100111 10001010
11100011 10110101 01010110 00001101 01110110 01011011 01110000 11100111 10101001 10101101
11111011 11011011 10000000 00100001 01110110 11100111 00011000 11100011 11011110 10111001
10001001 01000111 10011010 11100100 10001110 11111110 10100110 10110111 10100100 10100101
11010000 10010111 11100110 01000000 11111011 01011001 01001110 01111111 00111010 10001101
00111010 01110101 11100111 00110100 11110110 00011000 11001101 00110011 00011000 01110100
11101000 01000001 11100111 10001010 11011110 00110111 01011010 11011000 01100101 11111101
00010001 01001011 01101011 00010110 01001011 11101011 00101000 10101111 10100000 01111111
10000111 11111101 10101010 11110000 01101111 00001110 00101001 11111110 11011010 11010011
10011011 10101111 11101111 11000000 10101111 01111011 01010101 11111001 01001110 01001111
00111001 10101100 11101010 11101011 01100011 00101010 10101100 01101010 01110100 00111001
00011101 11101001 11011100 11100100 10101000 11110100 11100100 11111010 01010011 01110110
11100111 00111100 11110100 00111001 11001001 10100111 01001011 10011101 10001000 10100000
01110010 01001111 00100110 10110010 11101111 01110011 00100001 10011001 00011000 11001110
00111110 01001010 00111001 11001111 00011101 00101001 01001111 00001010 01001001 11101010
01001111 00000010 10010011 01110001 11000001 00001011 10000000 01001101 01000101 11111011
00000000 10001100 01001000 00111000 00111101 11111011 01010010 10110111 11110000 01111110
01000100 11010000 01111000 00100000 01010011 00110010 00001111 11100001 01001101 11011100
00000100 11000001 11011110 01001111 00011000 00100111 10110101 00101010 10011110 01111111
11001111 00010100 00110001 11111100 10101001 00010000 01110011 10010010 01101000 01001010
11000011 01100000 11011101 00001111 10101101 00110001 10000001 11011010 00000110 01001111
10101001 11000101 00111111 00100100 00110000 00011101 10000111 01011010 01000110 00111100
01100000 01111110 00010100 01011011 01011011 10010010 00111011 00111100 10011100 01110100
11001110 01101001 10111000 00100101 00110001 11101011 11010110 10011101 00001111 00011100
01111110 01100110 10011011 10011100 11110010 00101000 01101111 10101010 00011000 10100011
10100001 11001000 11000000 00011101 00101001 10011101 00001001 00111000 11001001 00110100
11111110 10100000 01110011 11110101 10100110 00110000 00100000 10000010 00111010 01110110
10100010 11000000 00001000 00001001 00111001 11000110 01111101 10101001 00110011 10110110
00111100 00001110 10011110 10010100 10101101 10010000 10001110 00000001 11000111 10101111
00110100 11011100 00000101 10001101 00000001 00111101 00001110 01001101 00010110 10111010
00000001 11011000 00111110 01100001 00000111 10100000 00010100 11011110 01001001 11001111
01111110 11110100 11100101 11100100 10011100 00000011 10001110 10111001 10100110 11001011
11000110 00000000 00011000 11001111 00011101 01101001 01101101 10100111 01010000 00010100
00010010 00000001 00111000 11101011 01001000 10111001 11101010 01001001 00110100 11100110
11001110 00000000 01011111 01011110 10111110 11010100 11010110 00100100 11100100 00001100
11110011 11101111 01000101 10111011 10001101 00000110 11101110 01000000 01010011 11001110
00110011 01001101 01010111 11000010 10001100 01100011 10010011 11010100 11010010 00100010
01100001 11111010 11110010 00111000 00100110 10000101 00011000 00000100 01100011 10000001
11011100 10011010 10110111 11011000 10010001 01111010 00101001 00011110 10100110 10010001
11001111 00010100 01100011 00111100 10011010 01001110 00110011 10000011 01010000 10011000
11000110 10101111 11001010 00110011 10011110 10111101 10110001 01001111 01001110 01011000
10011100 01110001 01000111 00000001 11111010 01110100 10100101 11000001 00001001 11110101
10100110 11000000 01010110 11101001 01001000 01111001 00111100 11010010 01110100 01001100
01111010 01010010 01100111 00100011 00111101 00110011 01001001 10100001 11011100 01010100
11100000 01010011 00010011 00011011 00011100 00011110 01000111 10100101 00111001 10001001
11100011 11010110 10011010 01111001 01101100 00001010 01110110 10110000 10000000 10010011
10110000 01110110 00111101 11101001 11011000 00111000 00000111 00111100 10011010 00110010
00101001 10111001 11001001 00011001 11100111 11010000 01010001 11101010 00000100 10001011
10011110 11110101 00100010 11110000 00110011 10011111 10100101 01000101 11011111 00011001

11000000 10100011 00011111 00111110 01111111 10011101 00100100 10010101 10110101 00000010
11001010 01110001 10000001 11010111 00110100 11110101 00001010 10111100 10010110 00011100
11010101 01101101 11011100 11110101 10101001 00011100 10000011 00011000 11101110 01101010
01100101 10111101 10001011 00000110 00000011 10010000 11111101 11111010 11010110 01000101
11111101 10101010 11000110 11100000 10110100 10011001 11001111 00111011 01000000 11101011
01011010 10101100 01000000 01011101 11000111 11110001 10100110 11001000 10101011 00100000
11000011 10001100 11110110 10100111 00001101 00000000 11110010 10011101 01000111 01000101
01011101 00111010 11100010 01011011 11011101 11001110 11110000 01110010 11100100 00011110
01110001 11110101 10101110 00111110 11110010 01100001 00111100 10010010 01001010 10011000
00000000 10011110 10010101 11101110 00010111 11111010 01110010 11000110 00001001 00111100
10100001 00011100 10001110 11000110 10111100 10110111 11000101 11111110 00011011 01101101
00110111 01111101 11101101 10100000 00100110 11011100 10110111 11001100 10100011 11111000
00111111 11111010 11010101 11010001 00011011 01010100 10010110 10101100 01001101 11011001
01011000 11100101 01110010 00000001 11011011 11010110 10011110 10000111 11100101 00100011
00011001 00011110 11110101 00000011 10110000 11001000 00111101 11101001 11100000 11100010
00111110 11111000 11101011 01011101 00110110 10110001 00000010 10001110 10011100 01110000
00110011 01000110 01110000 11111100 11110111 10100011 00111000 11100111 10100101 00100011
11110000 01110000 01110001 11001111 01001010 10101011 10101011 01011100 01101100 01111011
01110110 11110111 11101111 01010001 10110011 00010001 11000011 01100010 10011100 10111100
11110010 01111011 11010100 01101111 11000001 11000111 10101101 00001011 01010010 01001001
00111010 10101001 11000111 11011111 00011100 11110011 01001101 11000111 01111111 11101001
01001101 01000011 10000011 10001110 01111101 10101001 11000101 10110011 10010001 10001100
01111010 11010011 01001110 01001101 11101100 01010010 00011000 11000011 00110100 11111111
00000000 00101111 00111100 11010011 00010100 11111100 10111100 11010011 01000100 10000011
00011101 11001111 11100011 01001001 00111110 11100001 01110011 10100010 01111011 01001110
00110111 01000110 00001001 11001111 01110010 01101010 00000000 00001100 01100111 00000100
00010001 10011111 01101010 11000110 10011010 11010110 01111000 10001001 11110011 00010110
01000100 11100111 10010001 10011100 01100010 10101110 01011000 00111011 11100000 11000111
00100011 00111011 10100111 11010111 10100101 00001110 10011011 10001111 01011101 00001000
01001101 10011011 10110110 00010010 10001001 11100010 11110010 00001011 01100100 00001110
00110011 11010000 11100010 10101111 00110101 10100100 11010110 10001110 00100101 10110101
00000110 01001000 11001000 11101010 10100000 11100100 01111101 01101011 00010110 11011110
00010110 01010110 00010010 00000001 10001100 01110111 10101101 10001011 01111011 11001001
10001010 01111001 01101000 11101110 10011111 01000011 10001010 11001110 10100100 01011010
01001111 10010101 00010111 01111101 01000001 11100001 01011001 00100010 00010010 11100111
00101110 01111010 10010011 11011110 10110011 10011110 00001111 10011100 00000100 00011100
11110101 11001101 01011011 10011010 00100110 10000111 00011100 10010001 10011110 10100011
00110101 00011010 01100101 01001010 00001110 01001111 10100101 00100101 10100010 11010100
10010100 11011101 11001101 11011111 00001111 00000010 10100100 10010010 00110001 10011110
10100111 11010110 10111010 10001000 11010100 00110000 11001000 10101100 00101101 00011110
00010011 11010001 00110010 01111111 10100101 01101101 00100100 01101101 00011101 01110001
01100010 10101110 10011110 10000111 10110011 10000110 10001111 10111001 10101000 11100100
00011000 10010011 10011010 10110101 00001011 00010001 10010001 01010101 10110111 01101101
00100000 10011010 01111010 11001011 11001111 01001100 11111011 01010111 00010011 01111010
11101010 01110100 00011010 10010110 11111110 01011000 01011111 10011111 00111100 11110111
10100110 11001011 00101100 01001010 11011000 11110011 01000101 01000010 11110011 11100010
00111100 10011110 00110001 01011000 11100010 11101101 01100110 01111100 10100011 00000010
00110011 11010110 10100010 01011010 00110001 01110101 10110001 10111101 11100110 11100010
00100011 10000110 11101011 01001110 01000000 01011001 00110011 10011111 10101101 01100011
10101100 11011001 11100111 00111100 01010100 11000110 11101011 00001010 00000000 11101011
11101101 01010101 01111101 01000111 01100001 11110111 00010010 00011001 00011000 10101000
11111100 11101000 10000100 00111010 00001100 00000011 11000101 01010100 11110011 10110000
11011110 11111101 01101010 01100100 10011000 10010010 00000001 10101100 10010111 10010001
01011101 00001011 10110000 10000110 01010001 10111001 10001001 11111100 11101001 00001100
10010010 00010011 10010010 11000100 10001010 10000001 11100110 00011000 11101010 00110011
01000010 01001011 10010001 01001101 10110100 10010110 10100100 10010011 10100011 01111100
11011100 10011010 01100100 11001100 01011101 11111000 10100110 01111001 10100011 00111000
00011101 01101001 10111001 11101010 11011001 10100111 00000101 11010000 01101111 01110010
10101100 11100000 10000010 01110011 01010100 10011101 10001000 10010000 11100111 10001100
01110101 10101011 01110111 10010011 00101110 11000011 10010011 11001001 11100010 10110011
11000100 10101010 11000011 10011110 10011101 00101001 01000001 00100100 11011111 00110000
00110111 01100010 10101101 11011101 11000000 00000011 10101001 00110101 11001010 11101011
01000100 11001010 11011001 00111101 00110011 11000101 01110101 00010111 01010010 01000100
01000001 00000011 00000101 11111010 01100110 10110000 01101110 10100010 00010011 00111110
00001110 00010001 00000111 01110001 11011110 10111101 00101100 00111111 00101001 11000111
10001001 10111011 10001001 01011011 01001011 11110010 11010111 10010010 10111100 10001110
01000101 01110101 01111010 01101001 00000110 01000000 10111100 10000111 11101010 00111001
10101100 00011011 01001011 01111000 11000100 00000001 10110110 11100011 00111101 00001001
10101110 10101111 01000100 10000010 00110110 11111001 01100100 11001010 01100100 01111101
11101110 10111000 11111010 11010111 01100101 01000110 10111010 10011110 01100101 10001001
11111100 01001001 01111010 00101100 11110100 01110000 00100110 00111100 11001000 00110001
11010011 10101001 10101111 00110001 10001010 01101001 00011010 11101000 11001001 10000011
10110000 11110001 11001101 01110100 10011110 00111001 10011110 01011001 00101110 11000100

01000101 11000011 10100000 11111011 10111100 01110110 11101001 10011010 11000110 11010011
01000000 11001100 10000000 10001100 10000010 00111000 00100100 01110101 00110101 10011101
00110111 11001010 10011100 10011110 11001100 11001101 01101010 11001011 01110110 11110010
00000101 10001111 00010001 10000000 00001111 10101001 10101100 11111111 00000000 00010000
11001000 01001101 11010100 00000001 00011000 10010000 00100011 11110101 10101101 00001011
01101000 10000111 11011110 11101110 00110011 11000111 01101010 11000111 11010101 10101110
00111111 11010010 11000000 11000110 01110001 11000110 01101011 01011000 01110010 11101011
01100001 10110011 00100101 01010111 10000111 00100100 11110101 10101101 11001101 00101001
01100101 10001111 01001111 10010100 10111001 00101000 00100100 00100001 11010111 10001110
00001110 00000101 01100010 11110111 00111001 00111101 01101011 10100110 11110010 01100110
00011010 01101010 00101001 10001100 10010100 10001001 01111111 10000100 01100111 10000011
01011101 00010010 11010010 00111010 00000010 01000101 10101111 00001001 00101000 01011011
10101001 11101110 11100110 01110000 10001000 10100011 00000011 00111101 11001001 11110100
10101101 01001011 00001000 11001101 11000111 10001101 10110100 00111001 10011111 00100100
00011011 10000000 00110000 01111111 10011101 01010111 11010001 10110100 11110110 00011010
01100111 11011010 01100100 00111000 00000110 01010100 01000101 01011100 01100011 00111001
11101011 01011010 10111010 00110101 10101111 10011001 11100011 10111101 00100001 00100001
00000101 00010010 00010011 11100110 00010010 01001110 01110011 01011000 10111011 00111001
00100100 01010010 11010001 10100011 11010011 11111100 01100110 10100001 11110100 10101001
00100011 01111100 10000000 11110010 00001100 11100000 11010111 10010000 11011110 01101001
11101101 00001101 11001110 01100110 11001110 00110011 11010100 01110101 10101111 01010100
11110001 11100100 11100110 00011101 00010100 11001001 00011111 01011111 00111101 00111001
11000111 01011010 11100001 10100100 10010001 01101110 00100011 11111101 11110001 00000100
10011010 11001010 00101001 10111011 10111011 10010010 11110111 00110001 00011010 01001000
10100010 01001100 10111001 11111010 00010001 11010110 10010010 11010010 11111001 10100011
10011000 00101101 11000000 00110010 01000000 01001111 00100000 00011110 01000111 10111111
11111111 00000000 01011010 10100011 11010101 01100011 01101000 00011011 10011101 10000001
00110001 10010001 10011110 11100010 10101011 11011011 01001101 00001100 10110011 00100101
10111000 01101111 11011110 00110111 00111000 00011111 10101101 01101001 00010100 10110101
01100010 10111110 10100111 01100001 10100110 11001101 00001100 11110111 11110001 10011011
01110110 00100000 01111010 01100011 00010101 11010110 00101011 01100000 01100000 11110010
00000101 01110001 10011010 00001000 01011000 10101111 10010001 01111010 10010010 00001110
00101011 10101111 01001001 00000000 00000000 01111110 10100110 10110001 10101111 00001111
00110011 01001000 10010101 10101111 01011010 00101000 01100010 01111001 01011101 10110110
00001111 01010010 00111010 01010111 10000100 01101011 10110010 01111101 10101011 01010111
10111100 01110000 01000001 01000111 10010100 11100000 10001110 11100010 10111101 11100011
01010101 10010101 01010111 01001110 10111000 11001111 01111000 11001101 01111000 00100100
11000000 00110110 01111001 11000111 00100110 10010101 00000101 01101001 01011101 10001001
11101110 01010001 00100000 00000100 11000111 01110001 11000110 01101001 11001001 00001110
01000000 11101110 01110001 11010111 00110100 11110100 01011100 10110001 00011000 11100111
11111001 11010110 10000010 10101010 11111001 01011000 11000111 00110101 11011101 11001111
00011000 10101101 01001000 10111110 10100100 10011010 01011100 00100000 01000011 00100110
00001111 11101111 00010111 00011000 00000000 11111111 00000000 00101010 11101011 01111100
00111111 00101011 01001101 10010101 10111011 01001111 10011111 10110011 00010011 11010111
11010110 10111000 11011101 00111001 10100100 10001010 01101101 11011001 11000000 10101111
01000010 11010001 11101100 01010100 11011000 10111111 11110000 00111100 10001011 10010000
01110011 10010001 01011100 10110101 00011100 10011011 00110111 01010110 10110101 11001101
10101011 00010000 10100100 01111100 10011000 00101000 00111101 11101001 10110111 11100111
00011100 10011100 11110011 11011010 10111000 00011111 11101101 01111011 11101101 00100110
11110110 01001000 10000011 00001100 00000011 11001110 00111010 00111111 10100101 01011010
10010111 11000101 00010010 01001111 00001110 00100100 01011100 01001001 11011100 10101111
01000001 01011100 10001101 01010101 01001010 11101111 01010001 00110110 10001101 10001101
01010111 01010101 00010110 01110001 11110000 11011011 00111111 10101101 01110000 11111010
11100110 10110001 00101101 11010000 00110001 11111001 10011000 01001111 01001010 01111110
10111001 01111000 11010011 10101010 00011110 11011111 11001110 10111001 11111001 11001111
00011001 11000110 01001111 01111100 11110110 10101101 11101000 11010000 01001111 11011111
10010010 00100001 10110001 11101011 00100000 01010011 11101011 01000011 00000010 11000011
00100111 00100011 11011010 10100011 11111111 00000000 01011000 10000111 00111101 10111000
00010101 00101100 00100100 00000001 11010011 11110001 10101110 11101000 10110111 01101101
00001001 01011110 01100011 00011000 11111100 10111100 11110001 11011110 10100011 10010000
10000110 00011000 00011101 01110001 01010110 00011100 11100011 10000000 00110010 01101010
10111110 11100000 00110010 01001111 01010011 11000101 00110101 01101101 11000010 11000011
01100101 00111000 00000000 10000010 01110011 10001110 10000100 01010010 11100000 10000010
00001111 01110010 00111011 01010011 11000100 01111001 00111001 11101011 01001010 10000000
11100111 11011111 00111110 10010100 11100101 00110101 01111011 00111101 10000001 01101010
01001010 10000011 10101000 10101000 10100101 01010011 00011001 11000001 11000110 01001111
01001100 10001010 10110111 00000100 01000101 10100100 00000011 00111100 00010011 11001001
10101101 00011011 10111011 00101111 10110101 11100000 01000111 10110011 00110001 10001100
00000001 11101011 01011001 01011010 00110100 11011111 10101001 01001111 01010011 10011111
01100000 01000001 11111011 10111100 01111101 01101001 01000110 01000000 00011001 00000111
11110011 10101011 01110010 01000010 01000011 00011000 11001000 11000001 00011101 01110011
01010101 11001100 01011001 00000111 10010010 00000000 00110101 01110111 01110111 11011100
10010010 00101100 11110101 00111100 10011100 11010011 10010000 01110111 00111100 01111110

10110101 00100111 10010011 10110100 01110001 11010010 10011011 00010010 10011100 10011110
11100011 10110110 00101010 11010010 10110111 01010000 01001011 01010010 11001101 10011001
11000100 10000000 10001111 11010000 11010111 01000011 01100001 01110000 11000100 10001000
10000110 01001001 00100111 10000001 01011000 01110110 01110000 00110001 00000111 01100000
11100111 00111111 10011101 01111010 01000111 10000001 10111100 00111010 00010110 00100001
10101000 01011111 00000000 01011100 00011111 11011101 11000110 01111011 01111011 10011010
11100100 11000100 00101000 01110010 11111011 11000111 01011101 00010110 11010011 00111010
10101101 00010010 11010100 11011010 01011000 10100000 10010000 01100010 01000011 11001001
11101111 01010011 01001100 01111001 10100111 10111100 10011100 01111011 11010100 10010110
01010000 00011001 10011011 01110011 10001111 10010011 11011110 10111100 10010100 10101110
11111011 00100010 10011011 01101100 10111001 10100101 01011001 10011101 10111110 01110100
10011110 10011100 00001010 11010011 10011000 11101101 00000001 10001000 10101000 11110010
00010100 00001100 00011100 01100000 01110100 10100110 01011101 01001001 11111110 10001110
11100111 00111101 10101001 11011010 11111011 00110010 01011011 00110011 00101110 01100101
00100110 01000011 11001110 01101011 10011010 11110001 00010101 11110111 11011001 01100010
11111101 11011010 11100110 01000010 01110000 10111100 11111110 10110101 10110110 10101100
01001100 01101110 11011111 10001101 01110001 00011010 10100100 10101101 01110111 01110111
00100100 11000111 00011000 11101000 00111110 10010101 11010100 11010011 01010000 01000100
11010011 01011100 11010011 00110011 00011101 10011001 10011111 01110011 10110001 01110111
00111101 01001001 10100111 01111001 01111100 00000110 00000111 00000110 10011100 11001011
10000011 01001111 00100000 00011110 01111011 11110111 00110101 10000101 11010110 11010110
00111101 00111000 11101101 10100001 01011101 11010100 00010010 01110001 11010110 10100011
01110001 11000111 00110101 01100101 10010100 01110111 10100100 11110010 11001001 11101101
11000101 01000010 01001110 00101111 01010010 11101110 01010011 01100101 00000100 11111011
01010100 10010110 00000100 01000111 00110111 00100100 11100000 11110100 00010100 11110111
11000110 01110110 10000001 11000101 00001000 00110000 01000001 01011110 11010101 10100011
01101101 11111100 01000010 01101010 11001011 01000011 01100101 00000110 01000110 00110011
11110101 10101011 00011111 01110111 11101000 01101010 10110101 10110001 11101001 11011111
00110101 01101001 11000111 00011001 11101101 01001001 11011010 11110111 01001000 11001100
10010011 01001101 00000101 11100110 00100111 10110000 00010101 10101110 10000000 00001110
10000011 11110100 10101100 11101101 00101110 00110011 10000011 11001110 00111001 10101101
00011100 10010001 01010111 10100001 11001101 01010101 11011101 10001001 00110000 00011011
01110011 10011010 10001101 10010111 10111101 00110110 01010110 11001111 00011000 11100100
11010011 10011100 10001111 11110001 10101000 01101001 11101100 11001100 11000001 00001111
00000111 00100111 10101101 00111001 01110001 01001000 10100011 00101011 10011010 01010101
11101001 01010111 11001010 10111010 00000011 01100100 01110111 10001011 00011011 01000100
01010100 11110111 00010101 10001101 10100010 00111000 10010011 11001101 00011000 11000100
10010001 10011111 10011000 01100111 10101111 10100001 10101001 00110101 00101011 11101111
00101010 11100100 01000010 00000001 00101110 01111101 00101011 00111110 01101001 10011011
01001100 11010110 00101101 11100100 00111100 01000111 01110010 01111100 10110110 11001001
11101111 11011000 11010010 10110011 01101001 10000101 11001101 11110111 00000010 01001110
11011001 11110110 10101000 01001100 01111000 11100000 11110000 01000111 01000011 01010110
11100010 01011111 11011110 01101110 11101101 01001100 10111001 10001000 00010001 10111000
11110100 10101001 11100101 10110001 01000101 01010010 00110111 00000000 01000111 01001010
10001101 11011011 01101000 11110110 10101001 10011001 10000110 11000001 11001111 00110101
01011100 10010010 11011001 11100111 00001001 01010111 01110100 10010101 11010011 10111001
00111101 01001000 01111100 10110011 00101011 11100100 11100100 00100111 01111111 01111010
01011001 01001111 10010110 00110000 01000111 00000010 10100111 01000010 00000010 01110001
10011110 00000101 01010111 01100011 10111001 11000011 11001001 11110111 00110011 11000111
10111101 01010010 01000011 11011100 01110101 10011100 01011001 00011110 01101100 10000011
11111101 11010001 01010011 11001101 00101111 10010101 10001111 01010011 11010010 10101010
01001001 01111000 10111000 00101011 10011100 10011111 01000001 01010101 11011110 01100001
00010000 11011101 00100001 11111101 11100001 11101000 00001111 01101010 01010111 01110111
10110000 10011011 00101101 11001101 00101111 10010010 00001001 01110011 10010111 11101111
11101101 01011001 11010011 11001110 01100110 11001001 11100111 01100111 01011010 01100110
01011110 11101110 01101101 11001110 01001000 10001101 00111010 10011010 10101111 01111011
01110100 10100000 00001000 11010011 10100000 11101001 01010100 11100011 01110111 01100110
01001011 10110010 00101011 01011111 11001101 10111000 00010000 00111010 01100011 10001100
01110110 10101100 01110000 01011000 00110001 11001111 01001010 10110101 00110100 10000011
10100111 01101110 11110101 10011111 00110100 10011011 01011100 10010000 01111011 11110001
11110100 10101101 11100000 10010100 00011101 11010110 10100011 01010110 00011111 00110001
11110100 11101001 11101001 01010000 00000110 11100111 11111001 01110011 01001000 10110010
10110001 00100111 00000010 10010110 00111000 01001001 11001001 00110101 01111010 11001101
01101000 10000011 11010000 11011011 11110000 10010100 11101011 00101111 10001001 00110100
11001000 01110011 10010111 01101001 00000101 01111011 11001111 00111101 01010100 11111101
00111101 11101011 11000010 10111100 00010001 00000000 11111111 00000000 10000100 10100011
01001100 00111000 00011001 01001001 01111111 01001100 01010111 10111011 10010000 01110011
10000001 11011000 11111110 10010101 00010101 01100010 11010010 00110010 10101001 01110101
10111000 11010000 00000110 11101101 10100100 11111100 10011001 11101101 11011100 11010000
01001111 11001001 10001100 11110101 00111100 00011010 00010100 01100000 00011110 01111000
11110100 10100100 11100000 00001100 01100011 10001100 11010110 00001010 11001011 01110011
00100000 11101110 01001000 11001001 00000000 01100010 10000000 00001011 01100000 01110100
00011101 01101001 01010111 10011000 11110001 11001111 01011110 10010100 00100111 11011111

00100000 11110001 11101110 00101010 10110101 01000000 00110101 01001001 00101111 10111000
11110000 00110011 11011011 10111101 00110010 11100011 00010001 10000011 00100111 00111001
00100111 00000000 00001010 01111000 00000100 10010010 01001111 00000011 10101111 11010010
10011011 10001110 00110010 11111101 01110011 10011100 11010100 01001000 01000011 10111000
01010111 00100000 11110100 11110110 10101000 11111001 00000011 00111101 00111110 10110100
11100011 11001111 11001101 01001101 11001111 11001000 01000001 11101011 01010101 10100101
10000110 00011100 11101110 11110111 10100101 11101000 01000000 01011010 01000101 00111000
10001111 10100110 00101001 11000000 10001100 10011100 01110101 00010101 00111110 10000000
00100000 00100100 00010010 01001110 00000010 11111010 11010001 11001001 11111111 00000000
00111101 01101001 00111010 10001110 01000110 01110011 01000000 11001001 11000001 00101101
10010010 01111010 01010011 10110000 10000011 10010011 11000000 11101001 10011110 01001101
00110111 00100000 00011100 00011110 01110001 11001110 00101001 11100000 11100111 01111111
01101100 01010100 01100011 11101111 00100000 11000001 11000110 00111010 11010000 10110101
00011000 10011000 01101110 10101111 11111001 00011010 01110001 01010110 01101110 01000110
00110111 11111011 11010000 01111111 11010101 11100111 00100111 00100100 11110000 00101001
11011001 11100100 01100011 10111101 00001011 01110000 00011001 10000011 10110111 00011101
11000111 00110100 10011000 11001110 00111101 10101000 11011101 11001110 01000111 01111010
00111111 11011110 10101010 01100000 00001110 00010101 10001000 00000111 11111001 11010011
01010100 00010000 01111101 11101000 01010011 10001001 00110111 01100000 01110001 11011100
11010001 10010011 10000010 11010101 00110110 01101000 00000001 10000110 11010011 10011111
01011010 00001111 00111000 11110100 10100100 01100000 00110001 11010111 10010011 01001111
11000000 00100011 10000011 01010010 10110101 11011000 00000110 00011110 00101000 11100000
10011100 11110110 11110101 10100100 01101110 01100101 00011100 11111100 10000000 01010010
11110111 00000000 00001010 10111101 00000100 00101111 01101111 11000110 10010011 00011001
11100111 00111101 00111010 00001010 00000111 01011100 10011110 10000010 10000010 00111010
01100011 10001010 01101111 10110000 11000100 11011100 01000011 00100000 11000101 00011101
01010011 10001010 01011111 10111010 01001000 11111110 10110100 10001100 01110000 00000000
11101010 01111010 11110001 01001001 11000110 11011010 00001000 01010001 11001101 00100010
10001101 10111001 11001111 10101101 00001110 11000001 01001110 01001001 11000110 00111011
10011010 01101110 01001001 00100000 11110110 00110100 11101100 11111010 00001100 00011000
00011110 10100011 11010111 10011010 00000110 01001001 11110110 10100111 00110110 01000000
00100111 10110101 00001011 11000001 00100111 10011100 01010100 01001011 01111011 00000000
11010011 11010111 10101111 01001010 10010011 10011100 10001010 01001100 00011100 01010011
00011000 10010000 00110011 01000101 10101110 00000100 10001010 01000001 01101100 11111011
11010011 11010001 10000111 01011010 10001011 00111101 10111011 01010010 10101001 11111100
10101010 01101110 10010011 00000001 01011000 10000010 11000011 01110111 00100000 01110110
11110101 10101000 11100110 10010000 11000110 00111100 11000011 11001001 00100111 00000010
00110001 01001111 11001000 00000111 00111111 10100101 01000110 11110010 00110001 10010000
10110011 10001110 00111111 10000100 00001010 10100111 01100111 10100000 00001011 00111000
11110011 01010111 00000111 11110101 10101100 10111011 11111011 01010011 11111111 00000000
00101101 00000110 01100011 00100011 00011000 00111101 11101011 01010000 10011110 01010000
00011110 00111101 01101000 01000101 00010011 11000101 11001111 00100011 00111100 01010011
01010111 01001000 00001111 00011001 11110001 01100111 10000101 10011010 11010010 01000011
01110011 01100010 10000100 11011011 00011110 10101010 00000111 11111010 10111010 11100100
11010000 00110010 10010010 00111001 00000010 10111101 11110111 01010001 10110111 00100001
10001000 10010011 11100111 01000010 00110000 01111101 11000101 01111001 11000111 10001100
00111100 00110100 00100000 00000110 11110011 01001111 10001001 11111100 10000001 11111110
10110001 01000001 11101001 11111000 01010111 01100101 00101010 10111100 11101011 10010110
01011011 10000011 01001100 11100010 11110011 10000001 11000111 00000111 10110101 00111011
00100111 00100000 00110000 10100101 00010001 11100000 11100100 11110100 11111110 01110100
11111001 00010100 10001110 01000001 11001111 10110101 01101011 10110110 10000010 10110101
11001000 11110111 11100011 00111001 11101011 10011110 01101001 10111011 10110011 11001101
00001011 10010001 11001111 01011111 01010011 11101011 01001001 10010010 01011111 11100101
11000111 00111110 11110100 11100010 11011010 11101000 00101011 00001010 11000111 00011000
11000001 11001101 00110110 01001100 10101011 11111101 01111010 11010001 11000111 00111001
00011100 11010001 10001101 11001000 00110001 11000001 11111010 11010110 10001101 11011111
01101101 00000110 00110101 01001111 00011111 01011010 01110000 00000011 00011101 11111111
00000000 00111010 01101011 00000011 10011110 01111010 01010010 00110100 01111100 11110111
10101100 01111001 01011011 01110111 00010111 10101001 11010100 10110111 10000110 01111100
01000111 00100111 00110010 01101001 11010111 01010010 10011100 01100011 00100000 01100110
10100010 10110010 11010000 10110101 01011000 10100110 00111110 01111110 10011111 01110101
00001010 01100100 10001100 11111001 01111001 00010101 11110100 01100010 01000100 11110010
00010100 01010100 11100100 10110111 10100101 01001001 01111011 01100100 11111010 01111111
10010100 00011010 01101000 11011100 10010001 10011100 01000110 01110011 10001111 10101101
01000100 00110001 00011101 11010001 01110111 01001000 11111001 11111110 11010110 11001110
11101101 01100100 00100010 01000100 00001000 10000100 10010001 11110011 00001111 11110011
11010110 10011001 00001000 00111111 01101010 00110001 11001001 11000110 00000001 11100011
00011001 11000101 01111011 11100011 10000101 10010001 00001110 01010101 00001111 11010101
01110011 01001101 01011011 01111000 01110111 10001100 11000011 00010001 00011000 11100111
11110111 01100010 10010111 11010110 00101101 01110000 11010001 10011110 00100010 11110110
11010110 11000010 11010100 11001101 00100101 11001001 00101111 10001110 10000010 10110011
11101100 01001100 01110010 01011111 01000111 00011010 10110110 01000001 00100000 00000011
11010011 10011010 11110111 11000110 10110111 10000111 00011111 11110001 11101011 01101111

11111111 00000000 01111110 10000101 00110111 11111011 00111110 11000110 01001000 11001000
01111011 00101011 01111100 01110111 11001100 01000010 10110011 10001101 01100101 10101110
10000000 10010010 00110000 00101100 00110100 00100001 01101001 01101010 10010010 01001000
01110010 11111000 11001110 00000101 01011000 10011010 11001000 11000110 10010001 11101111
10001111 11101111 11110100 11110111 10101101 01001001 01110100 01101101 00111110 01001000
11111001 10110111 00000100 00001110 10011000 01100011 11111110 00110100 10001011 10100011
01011001 00101010 00000001 00011100 01010010 00000010 00111010 01100110 01010011 11000101
01100101 10001001 01101010 10101010 01000111 01000101 00101100 01000011 10000011 11110010
00111001 11011011 10101011 01111100 01100000 10111010 11100011 11010010 10110011 11001010
10010101 10010011 10001110 00110001 01011101 10011100 10011010 00110101 10100100 11011111
01111101 10101110 00000110 00111111 11101001 10101101 01010011 10010111 11000011 10010110
01110011 10011110 00100110 10111001 00011110 10011000 01101010 11100110 11111010 10110101
11010010 01000111 01010010 11000101 11000100 11100110 11100100 00100101 10000000 00011000
11101101 01011100 10110110 10100000 11001101 00001101 11010110 01100000 01101101 10011011
11001111 11001101 10001110 11010101 11101000 11001101 11100001 01010011 11111100 00011010
10001101 11000000 11000111 00011111 11101010 11000001 10101010 10101111 11100000 01111000
01001000 00101010 00101111 11100100 00110010 01100111 00111001 00110001 10001110 00101011
01001000 11010000 11101100 11000101 01010011 00010011 00010111 10110001 11001001 11101001
01110011 01001101 00110000 00001011 00111000 00111110 11000111 00110101 01110100 10110001
00000000 11100011 11110101 10101101 01111001 01111100 00001001 00100011 00000000 00100011
11010101 00010000 01110111 11000111 10010111 01001110 01001111 00000101 11011111 01100100
00000011 10101001 01011011 10010001 11111110 11101001 10100001 11100001 10101111 01110110
10011001 01010000 11000100 11000101 01101000 01100011 11011011 11100001 10001111 11001110
01110001 10011110 11110100 11011001 10001001 10001001 11011011 11101011 11000101 01101110
01111111 11000010 00101001 10101000 00101100 01011011 01010010 01011011 01011110 01111111
10001011 01110001 11100111 11110100 10100001 11111100 00110011 10101010 01110000 00100100
00010110 10100111 11011111 11001100 11000110 01101011 10011101 01100001 10100111 10111010
00110101 11111010 11001101 00110110 11110111 00111001 11010001 01110100 01001111 01101111
10101101 01001100 10010111 00100100 01110010 00101011 01011001 11111100 00101111 10101000
10001100 10010100 10000110 00101001 00111101 10000100 10100010 10101000 11011100 01101000
01011010 11010100 01111111 01110011 01001111 01110011 10001111 01000110 00010101 00101111
00001011 01010010 11111010 10011010 01111101 01100010 10011111 01110010 10100011 11011110
11000110 01100100 11011010 01011000 00100111 01101110 01001101 01001001 01101111 00111000
10010111 10000100 00111100 01010101 01001011 10001111 00001110 01101010 11011110 01110011
11001010 00110100 11001011 10101110 01111001 00100000 10000000 01110001 11110100 10101101
01001011 01111000 01100101 10110101 10110100 01000101 10010010 11000110 11100101 00100100
11000111 01000011 00010001 10101101 10111110 10101010 11100000 10001100 01010101 01111011
10110011 00110110 11101100 01100010 10101010 11001000 00000000 00011000 00011101 11101010
11100101 11001100 01110010 10010110 01110110 11110010 00100101 11000111 10101111 10010110
01101010 00111000 01100001 01111110 00001011 11000110 11100000 01111011 10101001 11111111
00000000 00001010 11001101 11010000 10010011 00110111 10001101 01001000 10010100 11000101
10111110 11100100 11011100 01111111 00001010 11001011 11010100 01010100 10110101 11010000
10001100 00001110 11011100 11010111 01000111 01110100 01001010 11000111 10000100 01000111
11111010 10000000 01101011 10011011 10111001 10010110 01010001 00110001 11111101 11010100
10011001 00111110 10101011 01011101 00111000 01001010 01101111 10011011 11011110 01000110
00011000 10101001 10101110 01010010 10000100 01101100 11111011 10111100 10101100 10011100
01111001 10011101 00101011 10101110 01001001 01000100 00011010 01111100 10100100 01001010
01110010 11000000 00001101 10100100 01100010 10110000 11101101 01101101 00100110 10010101
00010001 11110110 00001100 00110001 11001001 11100111 10100000 10101001 10111100 01010101
00111100 10010001 01011011 01000101 00010010 00110111 11001000 11111100 00000000 00111010
10010010 00111010 11010111 01101101 01010101 00101110 11000111 10001110 11110100 00111001
11011011 11001011 11100111 10011110 11101100 11100111 00101110 00111010 00001100 11110110
10101001 10101101 10000001 10001010 00110010 01000001 00100000 10011110 11000010 10101101
11101000 11111010 01001010 11001100 10100100 11001110 01001011 10100000 11100100 10000101
11101101 01010100 10101111 11101110 00000100 01001010 01010110 00111100 01100100 01110000
00111011 11010001 00111000 10110110 10111001 01101100 01001101 11101100 10000111 00100101
11010011 11000101 01101010 11101100 10011101 11111001 11001111 10100101 01100001 11011100
00110001 10010101 11011100 10111000 11111001 11001111 00111111 01011010 10110100 10110011
00010001 00011000 00001010 00001010 00010011 01010000 00011000 11011011 00111101 00111110
10111001 10101011 01010000 11100100 10110101 11000110 11001010 01101100 01111000 00100100
00001100 01010100 10110110 00010111 10010111 00010001 11001010 01100101 10001110 01111001
01010001 11000111 00011011 10000011 01010011 10101110 10100011 01101000 10100011 11001110
11010011 10001110 10111001 10100110 01011010 01000111 10111001 01001111 11001100 00111111
00011110 11110101 01010100 11101001 10111011 11011000 01001101 10011011 10011010 01101110
10110101 10101001 11011100 00111001 10000010 01001001 11001100 10110110 11101000 01110111
10010000 11000000 01110001 10001110 10010101 11011001 11111000 00111110 11101110 01001011
10111111 00011000 11011001 10110110 11011110 10111100 01110001 01011100 00101110 10000111
01101110 01100101 01101001 00001010 00101001 11001111 10100111 01010010 01101011 11010100
00111100 00101011 10100011 01001011 10100111 11101010 11111010 01100100 11010111 00001010
01100011 10010110 01011001 00110010 00000001 00011000 11100011 00011001 10100110 11101001
10101010 01100101 10100101 11010100 11101010 11111110 00100010 00000010 01111100 00111000
01111000 11111111 00000000 10010110 11001000 01001110 01101011 11001010 10101110 11101110
00001010 11100101 10100011 11100011 00011101 11101011 11010111 00111100 01101101 00011111

10011101 10100010 10100100 01000000 00111110 00011110 01010100 11100100 00001100 11100010
10111100 01110111 01010110 10110010 10011010 00010010 01000001 01011001 00001010 01100111
10101110 11010011 11011110 10111001 00100000 10011011 01001101 00010000 11110111 00111001
00101011 11001001 11100101 10111000 10111010 10010001 10100100 01100010 01011111 00111111
10000101 01101001 11111000 01100010 00100011 00100110 10100010 00000000 00111000 00100010
00110010 01110011 01010101 11010110 11001101 10011011 00000010 01100101 00100000 11100111
10010011 01011010 11011110 00011001 11110010 10100000 11010110 10000111 10011000 11011000
01000011 00011011 10000000 01001111 00010101 11011001 01001110 00011100 10001010 11101100
01101001 01110110 00111011 00101101 00010001 10010001 00101111 11100000 00101110 00001001
11101100 01001000 10101110 10111010 11100010 00110001 11001110 11000011 10001111 01101010
11100011 10100011 10000100 01000111 00100000 10010100 00110000 01000100 00000100 00011100
10010011 01011101 01111110 11100101 01100000 00001110 11110100 11000001 00011001 11101011
01011100 01010101 00100100 10011110 11000101 11000101 00011100 11111111 00000000 10001000
11101110 11100101 10001011 01001011 10111000 01010100 00011111 00111011 10001100 00101110
01000110 01110010 01101011 11001010 00010010 00011100 11001000 00010100 10101111 01000001
10010011 10010001 11010010 10111101 01110011 11000101 10110000 01111111 10100000 01111110
11100101 00000001 00100011 00001110 00001101 01111001 10000100 11010001 10011000 01100101
00101011 10001100 00010011 11010100 01111010 11010101 01010010 11100101 01011010 10010001
00101011 10011001 11010011 01000100 00000101 11001110 11100000 01110001 11011111 10100101
01001011 01101110 00110111 01001010 00000111 01100011 11010111 11011010 10011110 11110000
10000101 01101111 00110000 10001010 01100101 10111100 01101100 01100101 00001010 10000111
00100011 00111101 00101011 10100001 10101011 10001000 01101011 00011100 01001011 10000001
11000000 11001111 11100111 01011110 10011011 10100000 10101100 01010111 00011110 00011101
10001000 11000111 10011100 10000101 00101001 11000111 10101101 01111001 11000101 11001100
00011110 01011110 01110010 00111001 11101101 11001101 01101101 01111000 01111011 01011101
10111001 11010011 10100011 00110000 10100111 11001111 00010011 10010001 10010000 01111011
01010110 01110010 01001010 01010001 11010000 10110100 11111010 00010100 11111100 01001001
01101011 00100100 00010111 10110010 10010011 10010010 10000101 10110011 10111000 11010110
00111100 01011100 11111101 00101011 10100000 11110001 00001101 11101010 11011111 00111110
01111010 10000100 00111101 01111101 01101011 00010001 00110000 11011100 00001110 10000000
11010011 10100111 00101011 00100100 01001100 11001010 11110010 01111100 11001110 01110011
11010111 10110101 01010000 10011000 01110101 00000000 01111101 01001101 01101001 01001111
00011111 11101111 00111101 10111101 01111010 01010011 00110110 11100001 11111010 01110001
11101011 01011011 00110111 10100101 11000100 01010010 11110010 11001000 01010000 01111101
01111011 11010000 01110111 01110011 10001100 00011100 01110111 10101011 10010010 10011110
00111000 11100000 00001110 10011001 10101000 11110010 10111000 00111111 11010110 10101001
10111011 11101100 00111011 00001101 11011010 01110001 11110101 00011001 11001101 00110101
01010100 00101001 00100111 10000011 10011100 11110110 10100101 11110011 00000110 00001010
10011110 00111101 00101001 01000100 01100111 00011101 01110010 01101001 00111001 01000101
10100001 01101010 01000110 10001010 01110011 11110101 11101111 01010111 00100001 10110111
11011100 10011001 11101001 11101011 10011010 00100010 10001100 00001111 01110001 01010110
10100011 00100000 01111100 10101111 11000101 01100101 00101001 01000101 10101101 01011001
10100010 00010110 00011000 01000100 00100011 01110000 11100110 10110101 11110100 01001011
01011111 10110100 01011100 00100010 10001110 11100111 10101111 11110011 10101000 01100011
10110101 01100110 10110101 11011010 00111001 00111001 11001110 00101011 10100110 11110000
11010110 10011101 00110101 10111100 01100110 01010001 00010011 10110001 00111110 10000010
10110001 10111011 10010110 10110001 11010110 11000011 01101100 11101000 00101110 00111100
00101111 10100111 11101010 10010110 11001110 00100100 10001000 01000111 01110001 11100101
11100001 01100101 00011101 10111101 00110011 11101011 01011110 01011011 10101100 01101001
00101111 10100111 11011100 00111101 10111101 11000100 01110010 01000111 00100000 00100000
00011100 11111111 00000000 00010111 10111000 00110101 11101011 11010001 11001101 00110100
01101001 00011011 01101101 11000110 01111111 10000110 10101100 11011100 11101001 11110110
11111010 10010100 01100000 01101010 00110110 11010001 11001100 00111011 01101110 11101101
01010000 10101010 01001010 00111010 11001011 01100000 10110101 11110110 00111100 00010010
01101000 11000000 00100100 00000001 11011010 10011111 10100111 11101001 11110011 11011101
11001010 00010110 00111000 11011100 10010010 01110001 11010010 10111101 10100000 01111000
01010111 01000111 10001110 01001100 10001011 00100000 11111000 11101001 10111001 10001001
11000101 01101010 11011010 01011001 11011011 11011010 00100110 00101101 11100000 10001110
00101111 10100000 00010100 00101100 01100101 00110101 10110010 01100110 10001010 10011110
10011010 10011100 10001111 10000110 01111100 00010110 10010000 11011011 10001001 10110101
00101100 11111001 10000111 10011111 00101000 00011110 10010101 11010101 01101101 01011000
10100011 00001001 00011000 11000010 00100111 00000010 10101101 00010011 10000001 10001110
11110101 01011110 01011100 11001001 00100001 00000000 11110111 10101110 00111010 11111000
10000111 01010101 11101010 01101010 00110110 11010010 11011100 11011100 11001111 10110111
11111000 00111010 10110001 10101101 11110100 00110001 01000001 00001001 10001001 01010100
01100011 00011100 00001010 10100001 01100100 00000100 01110001 11100001 01000111 00111101
01001001 10100010 01101001 00001001 01111110 10110101 10010011 01111101 10000100 00111101
11101110 00010101 01000111 00111000 00000110 10101011 01111101 10101011 11001110 01001001
00000111 11100001 01011001 00110111 00010010 10010011 00110011 11111010 01100111 10101111
10101101 01000111 01100011 00100001 00101101 00100001 00001101 11111100 01011100 11010010
10110111 01010000 00101110 01000010 01001000 10001110 01010101 11110100 11001001 11111101
00101011 10001101 10010110 00100010 01001101 01110110 00010000 10011101 11010111 01110111
00001011 11111100 00011011 01000000 11100110 10111001 10011011 10011000 11001100 00110010

11001000 10100100 00010001 10000010 01111000 10101110 11001101 00100101 00010100 11000111
01000101 11111011 11001100 11001010 10010101 00001000 00110101 00000110 00110010 11100000
11010101 10111001 11001101 01000000 00001000 11101011 01011001 11000101 01001010 01010111
00111011 10010101 10000000 10001110 00101000 01001100 10010001 01001110 01010010 00001001
10100101 01010111 00000000 01100111 10111101 01000010 10100101 01100111 01110110 01010101
11001000 11100101 01010101 11001111 00111101 01101001 10011011 00000101 01001000 11101101
10011111 10111011 11010011 11010110 10011010 11000100 01100000 10001110 01110001 01001011
10011101 01000111 01000110 10000111 01110010 11110101 10010011 01100111 00011100 01110100
10101101 00111101 10100100 11000111 10001100 01111011 11010110 01010101 10010001 10101101
00001011 10001001 00001000 01010000 00000111 01011010 10111001 00110101 01100010 01011010
01011101 00001011 11010110 00100011 00010001 10011110 00111001 11001101 01001110 00001110
00111101 10000101 01010111 10110000 00100111 11001010 00000011 10101000 10101011 00101111
11010011 10001110 10011110 11110101 01101010 10011101 11010101 11001110 00111010 10011010
11001000 01101011 00010001 10011110 01111110 10110100 11100101 00000001 10111011 01010100
01001100 01000111 10011000 00111101 00110001 01010010 00101000 11011010 10011001 00010100
10100111 01111101 00001000 01000010 10111000 11011010 10000100 01111110 10110100 11010101
01100010 00000110 00110001 10011010 00011010 01001110 01111001 11100110 10011011 10011100
11110011 11010000 01010110 01101110 01010111 01011010 01101000 00001111 01000011 10010110
11110001 00001110 01100001 10111010 00110111 00000011 00111001 00011100 11100110 10001111
00010000 10001111 11101101 00011101 00000010 00111011 10001000 01001001 11011110 00110001
00101000 11111100 00111010 11010110 10101110 10110001 01101000 00101110 10100001 11011010
00111001 11111100 01101011 10011101 11010010 11011000 11011010 01111001 10111010 01100101
11010001 11001100 01010010 01100100 11000000 01110011 11010000 11110111 00010101 11010011
00001000 10101011 01011100 00111100 10001101 10011101 00010011 01010100 10011010 11101010
11000101 00001001 00000110 01000111 11000110 00001111 10110001 10101011 10010010 11011101
01001110 01110000 00111100 10101101 10011111 01010011 01010001 01101000 00110000 01111001
00010110 11110010 00110001 00011000 11011100 01111111 10010101 01101001 00111000 10001101
10010111 00100010 10110001 01110010 10001010 01101101 01011000 01110110 10110110 11100110
01101000 11011100 01110011 11011111 00100111 11110000 10100111 01101110 00010001 10001100
00010011 01010110 00100110 11000000 00011101 10000110 00101010 10010101 11000100 11010001
01000101 11001110 01110000 01111010 11100100 11110100 10101001 10111110 10100010 00011001
00110100 10100000 00010000 01001001 11000000 00111111 10101101 01100101 11011100 11011110
01100101 11001000 01000110 11001001 11101101 10000001 11010010 10101011 01011111 11101010
00001010 11100111 11100100 00111100 00010011 11111001 11010101 01111000 00100001 10010110
11101000 11100010 00110011 10110001 00111101 01001000 10101110 10010101 00010111 00111101
00011110 10000010 01010111 11101000 01011000 00010111 01001010 00010000 00000100 00111001
10011100 11110000 00111000 10101011 01110110 10110110 01001111 00101001 01000110 10111010
00111011 00010000 11111011 11110011 01010110 01101100 11110100 11111000 01101101 11010011
01110011 10000000 11100111 11101001 01001001 01111001 00110001 01101000 11110110 10100111
11001011 11101010 11000111 10100000 10100111 00111010 10001010 00101011 10010111 01110110
01001001 00011101 11111100 11100010 00100001 11100101 01000111 10001100 01100011 10100000
10101100 01011001 00001000 11000001 00100100 11110011 11011110 10100110 10111011 10011001
01000000 00100000 01111110 00100111 11010110 10110011 11011010 01000000 01001111 00011100
11110011 11001110 01101010 10100011 10100100 01101110 11110111 00010111 10011001 00000100
10100001 10011000 10010011 11011011 10101101 01000000 01100011 00011100 00110000 11001110
01001111 10101101 01011011 01111110 10111000 01000001 11010111 10011010 10001001 11111101
01001000 11100010 10110101 10000100 11010010 01010110 00101010 11000100 00011000 11100100
00000001 11111000 10011010 10110000 10001011 11000111 11110101 10100100 10000010 00111100
10011111 11000110 10101110 01000011 00001111 10011011 00110000 01010000 00111000 11101111
11000101 00111000 00110111 01111101 00110110 00011110 10011011 10011011 10111110 00000001
10000111 11001100 11110001 00010101 10010011 10111000 11101001 00101111 11100111 11000001
10101111 01100001 11011100 00001110 01000111 01011110 01111010 11010111 10010111 11111000
00111001 01110110 11101011 11110110 01101010 10011001 11100011 00111101 11111101 10101011
11010011 10111000 00000000 10000000 00110010 01000101 00011000 10010100 10010010 11010100
11100110 01110011 11100111 01100010 10011110 01111110 11100111 10101111 00110100 10101101
10000110 01001110 00111010 01100111 10001010 00110010 00000000 11001000 11100100 11110110
11000101 00100110 11011100 01000111 10001111 01011010 11100011 11110100 00010000 00111001
00001000 00000111 11001101 11010110 10010001 01110010 00111000 00010100 00110000 11111001
10000001 00100011 00000111 11111010 01010010 11111011 11110110 11101011 01001011 01100000
00010011 10011100 01111011 11010010 10111111 01010100 01011111 01111110 01110001 01000001
11000111 01101111 11001010 10011000 10011100 11001000 11101100 01111000 11100111 00011111
01001010 01111101 00110100 00000001 10100100 10010010 11110010 00001110 11011011 10111000
11111010 01010010 10101111 01110011 01001010 10100011 11100111 00111110 10000011 11010110
10010000 10110110 11101111 11111110 10110101 00001001 10110110 00000000 10100011 00000111
11011011 10101101 00100001 00100000 10011110 00111000 11001101 00101011 01110100 11011100
01111000 11000001 11000101 00001010 01110110 11100110 10000001 11011100 00111001 11011100
01000111 01111100 01010011 00010100 00000000 11111111 00000000 00101001 11001110 00101000
01101100 10001001 00110111 01100111 10011100 01010000 00111000 00111100 01010010 01001101
11011111 01010001 00001110 11000111 00100100 10011010 01101111 01000011 11101000 00101001
11001110 01110000 00000111 01110011 10011010 01100011 11101110 00111001 11000111 01001110
11010100 11010011 10111000 00001011 10010001 10011110 00111001 11110100 10100011 10101001
00111001 11101110 00101000 11101111 10001100 01110011 11101011 01001000 11011011 10001001
11000111 01000001 11010111 00110100 00000000 00100000 11101001 10001110 10011000 10100011

10001110 01111111 01001010 00110001 10000100 11101111 01001000 10111101 01111111 11001111
00010100 01101011 11010000 00000011 11001011 00001101 10010001 10011111 11000110 10000110
00000000 00100110 00000111 01101110 10100110 10010100 00011100 10111111 11001011 01001100
00111001 00011101 01111000 00101111 11000110 00101001 10000000 00110110 00001001 11001110
00111000 11001101 00001101 10011111 00110011 11100100 11101001 01001110 01111100 00101000
11000011 11110101 11101100 00000101 00110001 10011011 10101001 11101001 11101111 01001001
00101101 01110100 00011010 00010100 10101000 11110010 10110011 11101111 01001101 11100111
00100111 10011110 10110100 10101000 01001000 10001100 10110110 00111001 11110100 10100011
00011000 00111110 11011001 11100110 10000100 10011101 11101111 01110010 01000100 01101100
11111110 00000011 11110101 10100011 00111101 00110001 11001101 00101111 01100010 01001111
01101111 01111010 00111010 00001100 01100111 11110001 10101011 01101001 01110100 00011000
11000101 00011001 00111110 11111001 10100111 00011100 01111111 11110101 11101001 10101101
11001011 10000000 00001111 01000001 10010011 11000101 00111001 01001110 01001110 00000000
11100010 10110010 11100110 11101010 11000000 01100110 00001001 00100100 00010001 11001101
01001000 11000111 00000111 01101111 00011100 01010011 00011011 00111111 11000011 11011011
10111101 00001000 10111100 11100010 10011101 11101110 00000011 10001010 11101111 00100000
00011110 10010100 00101110 01111111 11001001 10100001 10001110 01000111 00011100 11010011
00110011 10001100 00000001 11010111 11010010 10000110 10111010 10001000 01111111 11110001
10000000 00111010 01110111 10100110 10100000 00100100 00011101 11111100 10011010 00011000
11110111 11110100 10101000 11110000 01001100 10011011 10001111 01111110 11010100 00111101
01110111 00011000 11110000 01000111 11100000 00111101 01101001 01110011 10010001 11000000
11111100 00101001 10100100 01100101 01110001 11011111 00111001 00100110 10011011 10111011
10011100 10011110 11110101 00110110 01110110 11010100 00001001 00010100 10011101 10000000
11110101 00100111 10100101 00100110 00001001 11001010 10100000 11101000 01111010 10010011
01001100 00000011 00000100 01001000 00111110 10000011 11011010 10100100 01100011 11101001
11010011 11101011 01010101 01100100 11000000 10001101 01010100 01101111 11110111 11101110
01001001 10100111 11000010 01000000 00000011 10111110 11011111 01011010 01000110 11001000
00111101 00111000 10100110 00111100 10000100 00010010 10100000 01111101 01001101 00111011
00100111 10100010 00000001 11110111 00101010 11010011 01000100 01000100 01111000 11100111
10101001 00100010 10110010 00101110 10100000 10010010 00011110 00001001 11011111 10011110
00001110 00101011 01011101 00111110 01001000 11111001 11101010 01111011 01010011 10101110
01100010 00010010 11000101 11001110 00000001 11101010 01001110 00101010 01010110 11110110
01100101 01011100 11110010 00011111 00011000 01111000 01110101 01101101 00000001 10111101
10110100 11001111 10010000 11100111 11100110 01011111 11111001 11100110 01111111 11000010
10111001 00010101 01110000 10100000 00000010 01111000 11110111 10101111 01101111 10111111
10110101 10001100 10000111 10001010 01100100 00001111 00010011 10001100 01110011 11011110
10111100 10101011 11000101 00111010 00011011 01101001 10010111 10000111 01100110 01001100
00010010 10110110 01100011 00100100 01110110 10101110 11011010 01101111 11011010 01111011
10001101 11101100 01001111 10011001 10001010 11100000 01101100 00100101 00111101 01101001
10111000 11111001 10111010 01010100 10001000 00001110 11101110 01110011 10001111 01001010
00011000 01110101 00111101 11110011 01011011 01011110 11011010 01101111 01100010 01001010
11111000 11100111 10011110 10111101 01111000 10100101 01101100 00000011 10111011 10111101
00111101 10010111 10010001 11111010 11010100 01111110 01011001 00100000 11110011 10011110
01101000 01001001 01001011 01000000 00010100 00010000 01000000 00110100 10101100 01011001
01001110 00110010 00001111 11100011 01010001 10101000 11100111 10011100 11010100 10011111
00101111 11010111 11101011 01010011 00100101 11001010 11000110 01111101 01100001 01101101
01110101 00101101 10101000 00101101 00001111 00000111 00011000 11100100 01010101 01111100
10010010 00001011 00111001 11001001 00100111 10011010 11100101 10100010 11010100 01100110
00000111 11100101 10111000 01111100 01111101 01110011 01010111 00111111 10110100 01100111
11011011 10111001 00100101 00111000 00110101 11001111 11101100 01011011 11011001 10001001
11011111 10101010 00110111 01111011 01111100 10011101 01111101 01101001 11000000 01100001
11110000 00111000 11001101 01100000 10101110 10100011 01110010 10100000 01101101 10010111
10101111 10101000 10101001 10010011 01010010 10111000 11000001 11011110 01010000 11111110
00010101 10100111 10110001 01101011 01110001 01110011 10011011 00100101 01001110 11010010
00110011 10000011 11010111 10001110 11110100 10101101 11000001 11100111 11110010 10101100
10011000 10110101 00101001 01110011 10010011 10001100 11100011 00010101 00101011 11101010
10110010 11101111 11000010 01000011 00010011 10100110 00111011 10011110 01101011 00110111
00010110 10110101 00011010 01110111 00110101 00111010 00001110 00000111 11100001 01000001
10001101 01000001 11001001 00111000 01110011 01010100 00100011 11010100 10001001 11100101
11100011 01001100 11111011 01010011 11111111 00000000 10110100 01100011 00110010 00000101
01111000 10111001 11000110 01111010 11010001 11001001 01101101 01000000 11010000 01010001
10011110 00110011 11001000 10100110 00101110 01000111 00011101 01110001 01010101 01111111
10110100 00010111 11001100 00000111 11001010 01111100 00011110 10111100 11010011 10010010
11111010 00011100 10111111 11001010 11100011 00111101 00110011 01011001 10110101 00100111
10100010 00001011 10010110 00110001 10000001 10010010 11000111 00100100 11010011 10110110
10000001 11001111 11110011 10101000 01111110 11010111 00001110 11011111 11100011 00000111
11101001 01001000 00100111 10000101 10001111 11111010 11001010 01111100 10001101 00000111
00110010 00100101 01000001 10001110 11111100 11100110 10011100 00010100 00010000 01001001
11001111 10110001 00010100 11010101 10011110 00000000 00111001 10010100 01111110 01010101
00001101 11001110 10100011 01100111 01101001 10110000 01011101 01011100 11000101 00010000
10010011 11101110 10011001 00001110 00110011 01010001 00100110 11010110 10001100 10100100
11001011 10000011 11110001 00010100 00011100 00000011 10010010 01111000 11101011 01010000
01011011 01011101 01011011 11001101 00001000 01101000 01100111 10001110 01000100 00111001

11000011 00000110 10101011 00110001 10001100 11111101 11010010 10000100 01111011 10011110
10010101 01001011 01000100 00100001 10101001 11111011 11000110 11001000 00011000 00011101
11101000 11000110 01100100 11001000 00111101 01001111 01000011 01010010 01101101 00000011
00100100 11110100 00011110 11110100 11010000 10101111 10110100 01101100 00000011 11101010
01101001 01110011 00100111 10101000 00001001 00101000 01000000 01000001 01111100 10011100
11110100 11000001 11101001 01000010 11110110 00100000 10111001 11111100 01101001 01010110
00110010 00010111 00001111 11111001 11111010 11010011 11011001 01110000 00001110 00000111
00110100 00111001 01101010 00110001 10011100 01111101 11100001 11010011 10111101 00000011
00111011 00001000 11101011 10011111 11000010 10011100 10101010 01001000 00111100 10001101
10011111 11001010 10010111 11111000 11110011 11011010 10010101 11011011 11101010 00111110
01100000 00101010 10100111 11111000 01010011 11110010 10101000 10001100 01110000 00010011
10000111 10110111 10001010 01000111 00100011 10111100 01100011 00010101 00101110 01000001
11100011 00011101 00111101 00001111 00110100 10111001 11000010 11100110 10010011 10010011
10000011 10110101 11000011 10011001 10010101 01111111 10110011 10101101 01100100 00000111
00110110 01110110 11011101 00110011 10001111 00101000 01010101 01011001 01110100 00001101
00100110 01110010 00001101 11000110 10011001 01101100 11100100 01110100 11001010 11110100
10101101 00110010 00110011 11011100 11100010 10000101 00011111 11111110 10111010 10110101
01010010 01011101 11000101 01110110 01100010 00111111 10000101 11110100 01011100 00111110
11001011 00100100 10001100 10110111 01101000 11001001 00010101 01000110 01101111 10000111
11011110 00011010 10011000 11100110 01001101 00111111 00101111 11010100 10111111 10011010
01110011 01011101 01001001 01010011 11010100 10011110 11011101 01101000 00000100 01101101
00001101 11010110 10010011 10101101 00111110 11100011 10111001 11001001 01111111 11000010
10111100 11110000 11010111 10011001 11110010 01011000 10111000 11000111 01001100 01001010
01111000 10101010 10110011 01111100 00110110 11010000 01100101 00111001 11011011 01110011
00011111 01111100 10101100 10010101 11011011 11110010 00000110 11101100 11110000 01111010
11010010 01100100 00110001 00111100 10011100 01100010 10101101 01100010 00100111 01101011
00110110 00111110 01100110 11001110 00001110 11110011 11100001 01101110 10000111 00111001
01000011 11100110 11011101 00100001 00011100 01110101 00000111 00110101 00100110 10011101
11110000 01010111 01000101 10011100 10011111 10110100 01101010 00010111 10110001 11000100
10100000 10111111 11001011 10001100 10011010 11110100 00001000 01100010 11110011 00111011
10001111 01101010 11010001 11010011 00110100 11000001 01111101 00110100 10010000 00111100
11111011 00100100 00010001 10010010 00010100 00001110 10110101 10100101 00101100 01001101
01000101 11110000 10110010 01011101 10001110 00100010 11011011 11000001 00011010 00001110
10000101 00010101 10110111 11110110 01001100 00001001 01110001 01110000 00000001 00110010
01001011 01110010 11000100 01110011 11110100 00010101 00100101 11001101 10011110 10100011
01111001 10101110 01011000 01011110 01011100 00110101 10101010 01011011 11011010 01100111
00010001 01000111 11010100 11100100 01100011 10101101 01101111 11001010 10000010 00011001
10011110 00011110 11101000 01110000 11000011 11101001 01010001 01100011 11001100 11001111
01000001 11001111 01101010 10011001 01010110 10011100 10011101 11100111 10101011 00011101
11000101 01011100 01111010 00000011 11111000 01010100 01100110 00101111 00110100 00000001
10110101 00111101 01001000 00100010 10011111 10111000 01100111 10101111 00011101 00000101
01011100 11010011 01000100 00000101 11100101 00110111 00001100 01000000 11011011 11000110
00111010 11111110 00010101 10010100 01100101 10101101 11000100 01100111 11000001 10100000
11000001 10101000 11011101 11111001 00001101 01101101 01101100 00011110 01001110 00111001
00000000 01100110 10101000 01101011 01111110 00000011 11010011 10101101 10101110 01000000
10111100 11010011 00010000 01100111 11101110 10110010 11110100 00100111 11101011 01011101
00011010 01111001 01000111 00111110 01011000 01111001 00011111 01110111 11001010 01111011
10001010 10000110 11110000 11011110 00101011 10100010 11011101 11001111 00110100 10001001
11110111 11010100 01001000 11011001 11000111 01101110 00000101 01110100 01111011 01001001
01110010 00001010 11101110 11111010 00011100 01010101 11000111 10000001 00110100 01001001
01110000 00000100 01010011 01000111 10011111 11101110 11001001 11000101 01010100 10010111
11100001 11101110 10011011 10011111 11011101 11011101 11011110 00100000 00111111 11101101
01110100 10101110 11011011 10000001 11000001 11111100 10101001 10000000 00001101 10111001
00000011 00000000 10011110 11111101 11101011 00101111 01101011 00100010 10101111 01110011
10000000 01111111 00000000 10100001 11001001 10000111 01010011 10111000 11000110 01110000
00000011 00001100 11010110 01111100 11011111 00001100 11100110 00110010 10010110 00010111
11001000 01001111 10111010 11110101 10101111 01010010 10001101 01000001 00101111 10111000
01110100 10100110 10110000 00100011 10110101 01010010 10101100 11101101 01100000 10111001
11100100 11010011 01111100 00110011 10111101 01100010 01000100 01110111 10010001 01111010
00000000 01000101 01000000 10011111 00001101 10110101 00111000 00011100 10010100 10111001
10110111 00100111 11010100 01010111 10101111 10110000 00111011 11001011 01100011 11110101
10100011 11001011 11000100 01011110 11110100 00111100 01010100 10111011 00001111 10011000
11110001 10101011 10001111 10000111 10011010 10110110 00001100 10011011 11100011 10010001
11111011 11100100 11010100 00001001 11100000 00101101 01101110 00110101 00111011 00100000
11011111 11101110 00001101 01111011 01011010 00000001 11001001 11101000 01111011 01100110
10010101 10010100 01100000 11100011 10111111 10100101 00111111 01101110 10111010 10100001
00110110 01111000 00011101 11010111 10000001 11110101 11000000 01001001 00110110 01110010
01110001 11101000 01111010 11010100 00000011 11000010 01111010 10100010 01110011 11110110
00101011 10011100 00010011 11010011 01101101 01111011 11110010 10101110 00001000 00000000
11010011 10011011 10011100 01110010 01111010 11110001 01010101 00011100 01000010 01011101
00000111 01110101 11011000 11111001 11101110 01011111 00001011 11101010 01011000 11000100
11010110 10110011 00001111 01010011 10110111 00110101 00011011 11101000 00110111 10100001
00001000 00010110 10110010 10010010 00111000 11100101 01001000 11000101 01111101 00010000

10101011 11001001 10100100 01100100 01010000 01110110 10011110 11111100 11110100 10100110
10110001 00110001 01011101 00000010 11101000 11111001 10110001 11111100 00111111 01110011
10001100 10111100 01110010 11110101 11101001 11100101 11100110 10011011 11111101 10000001
00110110 00111110 01110011 00100010 00001111 11111010 11100111 10011010 11111010 01010100
11000010 10100111 00011001 10001110 00111100 01100011 10111000 10101000 10111110 11001101
00000010 01000101 10010011 00010010 00011111 11111000 00001101 00111111 10101100 11000111
01110001 01101000 01111100 11010110 01110100 00000110 00001010 00110110 11001000 11100000
10000011 11011101 01111000 11000101 01000010 10111010 00101101 11001000 00100100 10100100
10000001 11000000 00111101 00001110 01110011 01011111 01001100 00111101 10000101 10111110
00111001 10110111 10000111 00100100 01111111 01110100 01010100 00101101 10100110 01011001
10011100 10010011 01101011 01101111 11001111 01011111 10010110 10000101 01011010 00110111
10111101 10000011 01000011 11100111 00000001 10100101 11011100 01100011 10010101 00100011
00000111 00011101 01101000 01101011 00011011 10100011 10000000 01000000 11110110 11100110
10111110 10001101 11111110 11001000 10110001 00100100 01100110 11001110 00011100 00001110
10100111 01101111 01011010 10001100 11101000 01011010 01110001 00111011 10111110 11000101
00001001 00111111 11101110 11110110 10100111 11101101 01101001 11101000 00011010 00011110
01000111 11100000 11001011 01111000 00100011 10010000 01001011 01111010 11100000 10111110
01111010 00010011 11000101 01111010 00100101 10110101 11010101 10110100 10010001 11100001
01100111 10001000 00000000 01111011 00011100 01010110 11010111 11110110 00010110 10010110
00000110 00000101 10001100 00111001 00111101 11110001 01001100 01001101 00000011 01001100
01010010 01111111 11010001 00010011 00111101 11001111 00110101 11001011 00100110 10110110
10001011 00011101 11001010 01001100 00100000 00000101 00110000 11010001 11100111 11010111
00110100 00111001 00000011 10000001 10000011 01010110 10001110 10000001 10100111 10110100
10101111 10011011 01110001 10110000 11110100 11000001 11000110 00101000 01011111 00001111
11101001 11000000 00011100 01000101 00100110 00111101 01110111 00011010 10010111 01001101
01011011 01110001 10101001 11011000 11001111 01100011 10010111 00100010 10011100 00111010
01110011 11010110 10110100 00010011 01000001 10110000 00011001 11011000 00100101 11001111
01111111 11011110 00010001 01001011 11111101 10001011 01101101 11110111 10000011 01001100
00111101 00000111 10011001 01011000 10111100 00110110 10111010 00110010 11010101 01010100
01100110 01100000 10010011 10010001 01001110 01001000 11000010 10010010 01111011 11010110
10010111 11110110 01011100 01011011 10110110 10001001 00100101 11100000 01110101 00000111
10111101 00110101 00110100 01110011 11000001 00110111 00110010 01100111 10111111 00000011
10001010 01101110 10001101 11011110 11100011 11110110 10101000 10100010 10001110 00000001
00100000 11010100 00110011 00010011 10010011 10001110 11110101 10101001 11111101 10010010
01001000 11111111 00000000 01011110 11111110 11011111 00101101 01000010 11011010 01001100
10011100 10011111 00111101 00001000 00011110 10101011 01010010 11101000 11111001 10000011
10101000 10111010 00011000 00101110 00110011 00100101 01000110 10010001 10101100 01000111
11100100 11001000 11001001 11001001 11111010 11010110 11100011 01101000 01001100 00011111
00111111 01101000 00100101 11001111 01011100 00101111 00010101 00001100 11011010 00000101
11000010 10111001 00100010 01100100 00101001 11011000 10111111 00011001 10101000 11110110
00001101 10101101 11000011 11011010 00100010 10001101 10011000 11001101 11000101 11001011
00010011 10001110 01010100 00000001 11111000 01010110 01101110 10111101 00000000 01011001
00000100 11111000 11111011 11100011 00000100 11111101 00101011 01110011 11101100 10110010
11011010 10110011 10001001 00110110 00010111 11100011 10100001 10101000 10101111 11100001
01011011 10001011 01010111 10001001 11001001 00000000 10001110 10100011 11010110 10111011
10100001 01001101 01110010 00100010 00111001 11101101 00101011 10011110 01111001 01111011
00100001 11110010 11001001 01000010 00110001 10011110 01111110 10010101 01000101 01100110
00100011 00100100 10010001 11101100 00101010 11001110 10110111 01101111 00111101 10010100
10100111 11001100 10001100 10011111 01000010 00111010 00011010 11001111 10110111 10110100
10111000 10111100 01011100 11000111 00001100 10000100 00011111 01101010 10011000 11100001
01011110 11110111 00111011 01010101 01011000 10010110 11100010 10010100 11001000 00000011
00001110 10010101 00100110 11101100 11100111 10011110 01101010 00001000 11110100 10011101
01001110 00110100 00101100 10001001 00100000 00000011 10010010 00110001 01010000 00111100
00110010 10101000 11111101 11110111 10011001 00011001 11101011 11010000 11010010 11111010
10011100 11101101 01110110 01010010 10101100 10110110 00101111 11001001 00100000 10001111
00111011 11001000 11000000 11110111 10100110 01000001 01110001 00001100 10000100 11100001
10000001 00100011 10010011 01010100 10100011 10110111 11110011 10100100 11000100 00110001
01001001 00110001 00011101 01110000 01110011 01011010 00110110 01011010 00011101 11000001
01100010 01001010 10100100 00100011 10111000 00100111 00100110 10100110 01010100 00111001
00111110 00100001 11110011 10110100 01011100 10110011 10010001 01001110 00001100 01100100
00010001 11101101 01011010 01001101 11001000 11100010 10101000 11111101 10001101 10101100
10100010 00000011 01110110 01000001 00111100 10011100 01010011 10111100 11111111 00000000
00101011 00000011 01110101 01000011 01010110 11011000 11010010 00110011 10111010 00110110
00101101 11010100 01000111 00010010 01100000 10011100 11110111 10101001 10010100 11100110
10101010 11000011 00101000 10010010 00100001 11101000 01111011 11010100 10111011 10110001
11011111 10001010 01101010 01001100 11100100 10011110 10101100 00001011 00101110 11101010
01111100 10100101 10000000 11100000 11010100 00001110 11001010 00100100 01000010 01011000
00001100 11110100 00010100 10111001 10010000 10001101 11011100 00000100 00111101 00000001
10101010 11011011 01000110 01000011 00011010 11100110 01001100 01101110 11111100 01001101
00110000 01011101 11110101 00000100 01110001 11101101 01000100 11010010 11110001 10000001
11001111 11010010 10101001 10101110 11100010 01001001 11000110 00101010 01100101 00010111
01101101 00010000 11010001 01110001 11100101 00001100 01111000 00111100 01010110 01000110
10100011 10100110 11000101 00111001 11001111 00111111 10011111 00110100 11111011 10001001

11011010 00101110 00001100 01100111 00100111 10100001 11001111 00010101 00011111 11011011
01011011 10100001 11100000 11111011 01010101 11000111 01000110 00100010 00110111 10010010
11111010 00010011 10001000 11100110 11111001 00000000 11100000 00110111 00100010 10001111
10110110 01101010 01000101 01110110 10100011 11000010 00001111 10101000 01011010 10011111
11001111 01011001 00000111 00100011 10101111 11101011 01001110 00000010 00101101 10000011
00000100 01100111 11011000 11010100 11001101 01000110 01011010 10110101 01100001 11111010
10011001 11110111 00001001 10101000 01001010 01110000 11110111 01101110 11111000 11110100
00011000 10100010 00111101 00110010 01001001 00001110 01100100 10010101 11001001 00100111
10010000 01101011 01010011 11001101 01010101 00000100 11100100 01110101 11110101 10100100
01001001 10000110 11111111 00000000 10010000 11100100 00011110 01110011 10011010 00010011
01001011 01100001 01111010 00010101 00100010 11010001 01100011 00000011 00001110 00000001
11100110 10101111 11000011 00001100 01010000 11100000 00100000 11101001 11101101 01000011
11101010 00010000 11000011 00011001 00110011 11001100 10000000 11110011 11000001 00111100
11010111 00101001 10101100 01111000 10101111 11001011 11001010 11011010 01000000 11100100
00000001 11001011 00011110 00101010 10011011 10011101 01000100 10010100 01110101 00001011
10011011 11110111 11110111 01010001 11000011 10011111 00110000 10010001 10011110 11011110
10110101 10000001 10101001 01101010 00100110 01000000 10000101 00001110 00010000 01110110
11001111 01011111 10101101 01110011 10101111 10101011 11001001 01110110 01110000 01011011
00001001 11011100 00001010 10010110 00110110 11001010 10010001 11010111 00110101 10111100
00101000 01001001 01101011 01110000 10110101 11001011 01111111 01101000 11011100 00110000
01111001 00100110 10100100 01000010 00001000 11011100 01110000 00101010 10000011 01100100
00100111 00011101 01111101 01101001 00110010 11011101 11001111 00111101 11101011 01100111
01001101 00110101 01110110 01000111 00111001 10100001 11110111 10011000 00011100 01010011
10011000 00000110 11100000 11100111 10101111 01011010 01001011 01101111 10011011 10110111
01001110 10010101 01110010 00011000 10000111 00101100 01111011 10011110 11110101 10011011
01110001 11110100 00101111 01110010 00100101 10000100 11000111 11110100 00100010 10110101
00101100 01100001 11110010 01100011 00100100 11111101 11110011 11111010 01010101 00111110
00100100 10011000 00101111 10111111 00000011 11010110 10110100 10111010 00001010 11011010
10010101 11101111 01110011 00001010 10101110 11001010 11000110 11010111 10000011 00000111
11111100 01010100 01110001 01111010 10000101 01100010 00101011 11010010 10010101 01001000
00011000 11001110 00001001 11101010 01101011 11001101 11111100 00010010 01111111 11100010
10100010 10001111 10010010 00111111 01110110 01111010 01110111 10101111 01001010 01010011
10000100 11001111 10100111 01101010 11100111 11000101 10110101 11001101 01100011 00101000
01101100 00110011 00100011 11001100 00101010 10011101 00000111 00000111 00100011 10111101
00101001 00111000 00000001 10000000 10100011 00100101 01111110 10101101 11001001 10100111
00000000 00111010 01100000 11110001 11010010 10110000 11010011 10100001 01000011 00111001
00111100 11100011 10001111 01000011 01000010 11110011 11001001 10100011 10100000 11101011
11111000 10001010 00010111 10100111 00010100 10010101 11110110 01000011 10110000 10001000
10100111 00111001 11001110 01011100 11110101 00100110 10000101 00011000 00000100 00001110
10000100 11110011 01001110 01011100 11110010 00111111 00101010 01001110 00000011 01101101
11001111 00111101 11101010 11011010 01000010 00011000 11011000 11011110 11111110 10111110
10011001 10100001 00001111 11101110 11111000 11100001 11111001 10100001 10000010 10001100
01111110 10111110 11110100 00100111 00111100 11010001 01111110 10000000 00110100 00101111
11001010 00010000 01100111 00100011 10011100 10011010 00011000 11100011 10001110 10110100
11101101 11011000 01110000 01000111 10100110 01101001 10101100 00110011 11011111 10101101
01000011 11010100 00000101 00011101 01110010 00000110 00000111 10101101 00100111 00101100
01111001 11100000 01010010 11110100 01101110 00111010 01100011 00100110 10011001 10010000
01011100 10011110 11010100 10110111 00010000 00011100 01101111 00100000 00011110 10000010
10010011 01110110 00001000 00111000 11100100 01010010 11110000 00010111 00111000 11101010
01111011 01010010 00111111 11011110 00101011 10011110 11011100 11010001 01100001 10000000
00100110 01000011 10010000 00111000 11101100 00101001 01001001 11001001 11011011 10011110
01000111 01011010 01101010 01110001 11000000 00111101 00111010 11010010 11101101 00011100
10011100 10011110 01111001 00110101 01011011 01101110 00100001 00011100 10011100 01100000
01111110 00010100 11010101 00000100 00001110 01001111 01011110 11111101 10101001 11011101
11000001 11111101 00101000 11000000 11001110 01111010 10011110 11010100 00111101 11110100
00011000 10100111 10000010 00111000 11100000 00001100 10011010 00110000 01111010 11110111
10100001 11001111 01001100 01100010 10000111 00111100 10010101 00011101 01111011 10011010
01101111 11001000 00000100 01010011 11000110 00101000 01101110 10111000 00011101 00111101
01101000 01010001 10001110 10111111 11001110 10000101 11100000 01010100 10111011 11101100
00000011 01110111 01101111 11101001 11011000 11010010 00110001 00111000 11001101 00001000
00110110 10111111 11101010 01111110 10110100 10000111 00101101 01001010 11110110 01110110
00000001 01011011 10010001 01001000 11011001 11000111 10100001 10100101 01100001 10000011
10001010 00011011 00000011 11110000 11111101 01101001 10110111 10101000 00001100 01100010
00010100 10000101 11101111 11010100 11010011 10011000 10011100 00000011 11011000 11010011
01011000 00010010 01000111 11010110 10011100 11111111 00000000 01111111 00000011 10100101
00001110 11000001 01110001 10100011 10010010 01111001 11100000 01010000 00001001 11011010
01111011 01100011 10111111 10101101 00001101 10000001 01001110 01100001 10001110 00111011
10011010 01001001 11011100 00000110 01110100 11000010 10001110 10011101 11101000 00000011
01101001 01110110 00000111 10101101 00101001 11000010 10000010 01110001 01000100 01011000
11000001 00101110 01111110 10110101 01111100 11000000 00100000 11001110 00110000 01111010
11010011 00010000 01100000 00001111 11010111 10011010 01111010 11111100 11000011 00100011
10100000 00111101 01110001 01001100 01010011 10111001 01001111 01101110 01101010 00110111
11011000 00000111 01100000 00010010 11100111 00110100 11001110 10000011 10011110 10111110

11010100 10101111 10011110 00000000 11101100 00111000 10100110 11100000 10000110 00000111
00000100 01010011 01100011 01100100 10011101 10111110 01100011 10011100 11010010 10000001
10001111 10101111 01101010 01100000 11100001 10110000 00110011 11110101 00110101 00110000
11110110 10100100 10010010 11101010 00100001 10010011 01100100 01110000 10011111 10001001
10101000 10011000 01110111 00111101 01111011 11010100 10110011 00000010 00001000 00100100
11111101 01101010 00000101 11100101 11001111 01110001 10011111 11000010 10000110 10110100
00000001 11101001 10000010 11111001 00111101 01000111 00110100 10111110 01101111 10011110
11111100 00011100 00100111 10110000 10100110 10100001 00000001 11001111 10111111 01010011
01001101 10001001 10001001 11100101 11110000 00110000 01101001 00110101 01100100 00000101
10001001 10100010 00010010 11000111 11001000 01001101 11111101 10111000 10101110 01100111
01011000 11010011 11100011 10111011 10110101 10010010 11011010 11101010 00101100 10000110
11100011 10010001 11001000 00111110 10100010 10111010 01011011 01110010 11001101 10000010
11111111 00000000 01011010 01100101 11101100 00100010 01110001 10010000 00111110 01110001
11111010 11010011 10000011 01110001 01100000 01111000 01011110 10111101 10100100 11001111
10100110 01011100 11101101 10010000 01100111 11010000 10000011 11110111 11000101 01100111
01100100 10010100 10101111 01011101 11010110 11110100 11101000 10101111 10101101 01011110
00001001 10000111 01011100 11101101 11001000 11101000 01101011 11001010 01110101 01111011
00011001 11110100 11011011 10100011 00000100 11000000 01100011 00111100 00011100 11110101
10101110 11111010 01010101 01011101 01000100 11111011 10010011 10110001 01011101 10110010
00000110 00001101 00110001 11010111 00111001 00100011 10100101 01001000 11001011 10010010
10000111 10111110 00111010 01100110 10010101 00111010 11111011 01111011 11010010 11010110
11111010 00001111 10100001 01011000 11000111 10110100 01110000 01111000 10101000 11110111
10001110 11011000 11111100 10101010 11001011 10000000 00100100 00000011 00111100 01010011
01110110 00101111 10100101 01010100 01100100 11010110 10010001 01000000 01111101 00000100
10011010 01110110 00010000 10010011 10001100 11111010 00001010 10101011 00100100 00000110
11011101 10110010 00000001 00011110 10110101 10110011 01101101 00100100 10000101 01001111
10011000 00000111 10101000 01100001 11011110 10101011 01001001 01110001 01101111 00100011
00011000 11110111 00000010 11100111 10001110 01000101 01111001 01010100 11100110 11101111
01110100 01111010 00101111 01011101 00100100 01000011 00010001 01010111 01000001 11101001
01001111 01010001 11110011 01110001 11010010 10010010 00001000 01110010 00011100 00100111
00000000 00011110 10010100 01100001 10010101 11111010 11110001 01011110 10111101 00111001
00101001 01000110 11110111 00111100 11011010 10010000 10110100 10101100 00111001 11000001
00001100 00111001 10101000 10101110 11110111 01101111 00011000 00100111 11010010 10101100
10101011 00000010 01111111 11000110 10011101 00100001 01010000 10001110 11000111 10100000
11101011 01001110 01000100 10010000 01011011 00010011 10111111 00011101 11111101 11000101
01011000 01100110 11111101 11101110 01000000 11100100 01010100 00010110 11010010 00001001
10100001 01001001 01010011 00000101 00001111 01000011 01010110 00100011 01101000 10001100
10100100 10010101 11000100 10000000 01110101 11101101 01001001 10100100 11001010 10111000
11100011 00100001 00000011 11111001 11010011 01111100 11001110 00111010 01110011 01010010
00110111 01010000 01111000 10100001 11110000 00001111 01101111 11001110 10100010 11011010
11101000 00100110 00100010 00110001 11000111 01000010 01101010 01011000 10011100 01100111
00000000 01111101 01001101 01000010 11011100 00001110 00101000 01010110 00100000 01111011
11010110 10011010 00001010 11100101 10001001 11011000 00001000 01001111 11010000 11010111
00101111 11110001 00001001 10000000 10110000 11010010 11001001 00011100 01100111 10101110
00111101 10101011 01110110 11100110 01000010 00010111 10000000 01001111 11111001 11100110
10110001 00111100 01111001 00010000 10010110 11001011 01001011 00000100 11110100 00111001
11111100 01110001 01011000 01010101 10001111 10111100 10000111 00011101 01001011 11111110
00011000 00100110 01001101 00011010 11011111 10000001 10110011 10010011 10011111 01011010
11101000 11101100 01100011 00100100 01101110 00100100 11111110 00000111 00010101 10000111
10100000 11000101 11100101 11101000 10010001 11110001 11001110 11010011 11111000 01010111
01000011 01100111 00101010 11000111 00010110 00001000 00111100 01110111 00000010 10110011
10101101 01100100 11011101 10001101 00011110 11100100 11100001 01100010 00100100 11100001
01001000 01111111 01011101 11000110 10100011 01011001 00110110 00000111 00000100 11100011
00000111 00011001 11001101 00111011 00111001 00100100 11010101 00011011 10011100 10101100
10111110 01100100 11000100 10001000 10110011 10010011 10110100 01100110 10111001 10101001
10101110 01111101 11001001 00011101 01110011 01110110 10100100 01000111 00011001 10010101
00110011 11101110 01101001 00100010 10010101 10010111 00101100 11110010 10011100 01110101
00111111 00110111 01011010 11001111 10111110 10001110 11001110 01000111 01000101 11011111
00100010 00111011 10011110 00011000 10001010 10001000 11101001 11001100 00000111 11001001
00100010 00111000 11110101 11001101 01101110 10101000 11000101 11110101 00010010 10111001
01110110 11101111 01010110 10010001 01100011 00110001 01000001 00100011 11100100 11110101
00100111 11111010 01010101 00101101 01101011 01011010 10111110 10110011 11010001 11010010
11100010 00011001 10111111 01111010 01011011 00011001 00100000 01010100 11010000 11101001
11000101 11110010 01100100 00111000 00000000 01110110 10101010 10111110 00101010 10110101
00000011 01001100 10001101 00100011 11000001 00011011 10000111 01011010 10100101 00001000
11000101 11011001 01101010 00100110 10101110 01001101 10100011 11101011 11110111 11110011
11000110 10001101 01110000 01100011 00111001 10001111 00111001 11011011 10001110 01101011
01000011 11111011 01001110 11100101 10010000 01100110 00100100 00100111 11010111 10100101
01010101 11010001 11100010 00000010 11000110 00101100 01100000 11100010 00111111 11001110
10110100 00000000 00011001 11111111 00000000 11101011 01010101 00111010 01110001 11100110
01101001 10000100 10110100 00100100 10000111 01010001 10011011 11111110 01111000 00001100
10001111 01111010 10011001 01101110 10100101 01100100 11100110 00001100 00011110 11111100
11010100 01100000 11101101 01000010 01000111 01010001 01001111 01000110 00011101 00001111

00100100 11110111 10100100 11100001 00010001 01011101 11110111 00100101 00110011 10000010
10000111 01111010 10111111 11100111 01000000 10111100 10001000 01111111 00001011 11110010
00111111 00101010 10000100 10110000 11101110 01111111 00001010 10101110 11100100 01101110
10100001 11010011 01000001 01110110 01011010 11111110 11010001 10110111 10001110 00110011
11100111 00010010 00000010 10000010 01001110 00000101 01010010 10110011 11110001 00000110
10011111 01111000 01100100 00110001 11001101 00100000 00001000 01110000 01110010 10110101
01010011 01010000 11100010 11011010 11100000 11110100 00011110 01011110 00111111 01011010
11100101 11111100 00111111 10000001 01101101 00100001 00011101 00001100 10000110 10100110
10010101 00100100 11100100 11010011 00101001 11101101 01110011 10111111 11111110 11010100
10110010 11100011 01101100 11111000 00011101 01111001 10101001 00101100 11110101 10011011
01111000 00100111 00010011 11000111 01111100 10001010 11100000 11100100 00010010 01101011
10001110 00100100 00011111 10101101 00110011 01101000 11000110 00001000 11001000 10101011
11111010 10111010 11101110 01101011 00001000 01110011 00011101 11000100 10011010 10011101
10111100 11010111 00100101 10111100 11111000 10100100 01111001 00001001 01111001 00100100
11011101 10001100 11010010 10100100 10001000 01010111 11111101 01100100 01111000 11111111
00000000 01111010 10111000 01010110 10001000 01001001 11010000 00001010 00111100 10100011
10001100 11111010 01010110 00010011 01010001 10001011 10110111 00110001 11010010 10110000
10010111 01011011 10011101 11101110 00111000 11111001 00001000 11000001 11101000 01110010
00101001 01111001 11100011 10111001 11101111 11101111 01011110 01110010 11111101 01001111
11001100 01111000 11110100 00111000 10101000 11001100 11010011 00101111 01000111 10010011
10100111 11110111 10111010 01010110 10011111 01010111 10111111 01010011 00111001 11100001
10011100 01001111 01010101 11010001 01101111 01000101 10001110 10100000 00101110 00100100
10001111 01111010 00001100 10000010 10100111 11110100 10101011 00011010 11111110 10101110
11111010 10011001 10001001 10011110 00000101 10001011 11001011 11001110 00001000 11101011
11001111 10111101 01111000 11010101 11001110 10111010 01101101 00100010 00100001 11101111
11011110 00110011 10001110 10000101 10111001 10101010 11111110 00011000 11110001 10000110
11011001 01101111 11111110 11011111 10101000 11001000 00000001 11000111 10010010 00100101
11100100 00011111 10100101 00010010 10100111 00110100 10101100 10100101 10100001 10000100
11010101 10011010 01000111 10101100 01100000 00101001 11000000 11101111 11001111 00110100
00110110 11010001 11110101 10101110 01001111 01001111 11010110 10100100 10111100 10110110
10001110 01011000 01101110 00010010 01000001 10001111 01011100 11110011 01011010 00001001
01111001 00111011 01000101 10111001 11001000 00111101 11110010 01101000 11110110 00110010
00100011 10011011 01010011 01110110 11011101 01100010 00000110 01001001 01100100 01100011
10000001 11011011 00111101 01101010 11000011 11100000 11000111 10011000 11011001 00001000
11110100 10101110 01101010 11011011 01010111 10010111 01101001 11111001 01100011 00111110
11000110 10101100 01011011 11101010 00000110 01011100 11100101 00110001 11001111 00011000
10100100 11101000 11001101 10110001 00101001 00100011 01001001 10110011 10011110 10011111
10011101 00001110 01110011 10000101 00000110 10100011 10001010 01110000 11011000 11001000
11000111 10100001 10100010 00101001 10010110 01010101 00010010 10100111 01001111 11100111
01011001 00111000 11011001 11101010 01010101 11101110 00111101 01000111 01101110 11011110
10110100 10000010 00111101 10101110 01001110 00111010 10001110 10000100 11010011 10110011
11000001 00111111 10101101 00100010 10001100 00110000 00101110 01110011 11101000 00101001
01011101 10000000 00001000 11110110 10000000 01111111 00111010 00011011 10101000 00111001
11000000 00111101 00101000 01111100 10000111 00011000 00011000 00011101 10101001 10011000
00111001 00101011 11000001 11101111 01000010 01010110 11011000 01100011 10011011 10011111
01101010 01101011 00001101 10110001 11101110 00011100 10111111 10111001 10100111 11100111
11100110 11110101 10100001 10000000 11101010 01001111 11100001 10001010 00011010 00001011
10001000 01001110 01010011 00011011 01110010 01101000 01111100 00101010 01100111 10001110
00101001 01000111 00100111 11010011 11011110 10011001 00101111 11011100 11000111 01010001
10011110 01101000 10110000 10000100 00011000 01100001 10011100 01110011 11011111 11011010
10011110 11000111 10101001 10100110 11010010 01110011 10011111 01101111 01111010 00101100
11000110 00101111 00011000 00000000 00001010 01001100 00000010 11100011 00100110 10011110
00010111 00101100 00000001 11100000 01110110 11110111 10100011 00011101 01001001 11100000
01010000 00100001 10001011 11001001 00111100 11110000 00001111 01011010 00010111 10101001
11000111 11010100 10011010 01111110 00110001 11110101 00110101 00011001 01011111 00110101
11110001 11011011 00110100 11010011 11101000 00000010 11100111 00110100 00010001 11000111
00111111 10010101 00000011 00000000 00011100 00001111 11111110 10111101 00111111 00100100
01110110 11100010 10000100 00000011 00011000 01111110 00011001 00010100 00000001 11010000
00000010 01111111 00011010 00011011 11010111 10110111 01111111 01111010 00000111 11011101
11000111 10111111 00110100 10101110 11011000 00001000 10100000 01111001 10000101 10000111
11100111 01001101 00000100 10010111 11000111 11100011 01001110 00000000 00001100 10001100
11010010 10101001 00011011 11111101 00110010 00101010 10010011 10111000 11000100 11000000
00000011 00111001 10100011 01101111 01001111 01001111 01111010 00011100 11111010 11111110
00110100 10111101 01110001 11101001 01010000 11010110 10110111 00010000 11000111 00011000
11001011 00001110 10111111 11001110 10001001 00100011 00000101 10111010 11100111 10111101
00010010 10011111 10011000 00000101 11101010 00000111 00100110 10011111 00001110 00000100
10000011 00100011 10000011 01001101 11101011 10111000 11001110 01110011 01010001 00100011
11101101 01110010 00000000 01110010 00110011 11000101 01010010 10010110 10110111 11101111
00110100 11000100 10111000 10010100 10110010 00110100 10001000 00001001 11001001 11000101
01010001 01111101 00001100 11111001 01100100 10001011 10110011 10011100 11100011 10010101
10101101 11100001 01010001 01000101 01011000 01000111 00110111 01111000 00000111 11110001
11110010 00111101 11111001 10101010 11001100 00000000 01011100 10001111 11010110 10111010
00001011 10011111 00001110 01011100 11001011 10110000 00100101 11000100 01101110 01001001

11101110 10100110 10100010 11111111 00000000 10000100 01100010 11111011 01111000 01010011
00101101 10111001 10101101 10011011 01010010 01011011 10000001 10011001 01101101 11110111
01111001 11101001 01010101 10101111 11010101 01101110 11111111 00000000 01110110 11111100
11000110 00001111 00111000 11101111 01011011 10010010 11101000 00110111 10100010 00100111
01010100 10010110 00011101 11100111 11011110 10100000 00011010 00011101 11110100 01000000
11100010 00011101 11100000 01111010 01110111 10100100 11100101 10100111 00101100 01011001
01110000 01011010 11011101 10011001 00010000 11000010 10110000 11000111 11100101 11000110
10100001 00000000 11101100 00111000 10101001 10010101 00110010 00111101 11101010 11001011
11101001 11110111 10110001 11111101 11111011 00111001 10110001 11101100 00110011 01010001
00011000 10100111 10001111 10000011 01101111 00101000 11101111 11001010 10011010 11100110
01110100 11100110 11110101 01101000 11011101 01010100 01000101 00111011 11011001 01000010
10100111 11011101 11011111 10011110 00000000 00111101 11101011 00100010 01101011 00010110
00000000 00110100 01101101 10000111 11101110 00001001 10101101 00001011 10010011 10001001
01011101 10001110 11101100 11111111 00000000 00001000 00101010 01111000 10100111 10100011
01000101 10000100 00001100 11011101 10111001 00111110 11110100 10111001 00100111 11011000
10100101 01010010 11000101 00110101 10010001 10101101 11101101 11010001 01011111 10101111
10110101 01000110 11111010 10010010 10101000 00111110 01100100 10011000 11110101 11001000
10101101 01000100 10001110 00100110 10001100 11111101 11000011 01011100 11100110 10110101
01100110 01100111 10011101 00100011 00011100 01100111 10010010 01000001 10100110 10100000
11111011 01101010 00100111 10101001 00101100 11011010 10111101 10101100 00100001 00100101
10010110 11100000 01100001 01111001 00000000 00001110 01101010 00100110 11110001 01100110
10011111 00101000 00111111 11101001 00000110 00110000 00001111 00000001 10010100 11100110
10110001 11101110 01110100 01111111 10010011 10001110 01001001 00110101 10011001 00100110
10010001 00110000 00111001 11000000 11000000 11101010 01001101 01101001 01000110 10000011
10011111 11000101 00100010 00011101 11101110 01110100 01110010 11111000 10001010 11001011
01110001 11000101 11010010 00010011 11101000 00010100 11010100 00011111 11110000 10010000
11011010 11101110 11000111 11011010 00010000 00011110 11000000 00000010 01101011 10011001
10111001 11010011 11011010 00111001 01010001 01110000 01111110 01100011 01010011 00100110
10010010 11011001 11101000 01000000 00100111 10101101 01011111 11010101 01100010 10110101
11100110 00010101 11011111 01100011 01111010 01011101 01110110 11011100 10011100 10010111
11100011 11101001 01010100 11011111 01011011 10000010 00110001 10010000 10101110 11100011
10110111 10111101 01100110 01111111 01100110 01001111 10001100 10100000 11011110 10000111
11010010 10011110 10010110 00100000 00000001 10111101 01110001 10011110 01000101 00010001
10100000 10111110 00100110 01010010 01001101 10010011 01001111 10101111 01100100 00001111
00101110 00100010 00111101 01110011 01010101 01011011 01011000 10011111 00100111 11001001
11011000 00001001 00011101 00111101 00101011 01000010 00001101 00101101 01100100 10001111
00111000 11100000 10011110 10010101 01010010 11110011 01000010 10011001 01001001 01111000
00011000 01111010 10010001 01000100 00100101 01001110 01001110 11000110 10001110 10000100
11010010 00001000 11110101 00101011 11010010 01001110 00001000 00011011 11111001 00100011
00010101 00011100 11010111 00010111 11110010 00100111 00110111 00010010 01100000 01111111
00001000 00111000 10100010 11000010 01100001 10111111 01100100 11011101 01000111 10110111
01111110 11010101 01101110 01000000 00001001 00011110 10010100 00111000 00100100 11110110
00101010 10011101 00110101 00100100 01100101 11101110 11011101 00100110 01100100 11011110
11101110 00111010 11100110 10100101 01010101 00010010 01100111 11111001 01010101 11111111
00000000 10110011 11000100 11001010 01110011 11010100 11110111 10101010 00010011 01011011
10001000 11111110 11100011 01100110 10110110 10000101 10010010 10110001 01011100 10110110
11011000 10001110 01001000 11100011 00101110 00001000 00011000 00100011 11010010 10101100
11011011 00101000 00111111 00101110 00110001 11101001 01001111 10110101 10110101 01010110
00000011 01111001 00100100 10011010 10111011 11110110 01000000 00111001 01001110 00001101
01010111 00111010 01101010 11010111 00110011 11010100 10101100 01100001 00000001 01110001
01001100 11110010 00001010 10010000 01000010 11100011 10011110 01001001 10101011 10010001
01000100 11011011 10110000 01101010 11010010 01000100 00001011 11100000 11010110 00001101
10111011 00110110 11001001 10110010 01100101 01111000 01100011 11001111 00111100 11111101
00110001 01010110 10111111 11010101 11000110 01001110 00101010 01111111 00100101 01010100
01010101 00111011 11000111 11110010 11000001 00011001 11000101 01001011 01101111 01100101
10101000 11101110 10010001 00010101 10001011 01101110 10111111 00000111 11010000 00011110
11110101 10110010 11101111 10110101 01000111 00011100 10010011 01011001 01111010 01010001
11001100 10000101 10000000 11100011 00011100 11100010 10110101 00001111 01000001 11011111
10011010 11101100 10100011 10100001 11001001 01010101 11011101 10011101 00011111 10000010
00010100 00011101 01111100 00011100 00011110 00100010 01110011 10001010 11110100 01010011
11011011 10001110 00101011 11001111 10111110 00011111 00101011 01111111 01101100 11001000
01001111 00100011 11001001 00100111 10000001 01011101 11101010 10010110 01100010 00000001
11101001 10011010 11100110 11000101 01011010 11111010 10010011 00000000 00111101 00110011
11010000 01100111 10001010 01010110 00000100 00000001 10011111 11000110 10011110 11011000
11000000 11110101 11110111 10100100 00100011 00101001 11001111 00111100 11010111 00011100
01011111 01000100 00110001 10000000 01110100 11011101 11011100 11010010 11110000 00110011
10011010 00001110 00000000 11011100 11100111 00100011 00111100 00000000 00101000 11001111
01011111 01011111 01001010 00110110 11010000 00000000 00000010 01000111 11111000 01010011
01110110 10001100 11111101 01101001 11000011 10011000 11110001 10011100 01111101 00101001
00000111 00111101 01111000 11100011 00110100 00100110 00110001 00111111 10001011 11011110
10011010 11000111 00011000 01100011 11011100 01110100 11110110 10100100 01100010 00110001
10111000 11111110 00000010 10010101 11001110 00011110 00110000 00000110 00111101 01001111
10101101 00001011 11001100 00000011 10100001 00100111 10011110 01111101 01111101 00101001

10101100 01110000 11100011 11011100 01010010 10110001 00101110 01001010 10001111 01001110
01111101 10101000 11001001 00000101 00000000 11100100 10001110 10111110 11010100 11010000
00000110 00110000 10000100 10010000 01101001 10001010 00001011 00000001 10011110 00111101
01101001 11000111 10001001 00001111 01111100 00011010 00111110 11110111 00100111 11110010
10100110 00100000 01010000 00001011 10010011 10001110 01000111 00100000 01111010 01010011
00111000 00100100 11110001 11000001 00011100 11010010 10101111 01001100 10001111 11000100
11010010 01100111 10100110 00000111 01011110 01001101 00100101 11100100 00000010 10111000
00000000 00100000 11110100 11111101 00101001 00000000 11001001 11001001 00111100 00001010
00001111 00100111 00110100 01100111 11100101 00111000 11111100 00101001 00001100 00010100
00001100 10000000 00110011 11101111 10011010 00010111 10000011 10010001 11010111 00110100
10011110 10011000 11101011 11111100 11101001 01111000 11100011 11110101 10100001 10110110
10010000 11111010 10000010 11110100 01111111 01010001 11010000 11010000 11011000 11001001
10100101 01101110 01100011 00011011 00111011 11110100 10100110 10001110 00001111 10101111
11110101 10101010 10111011 01100001 01110001 01001110 00000111 00000000 01100111 10011110
10110100 11000100 00011001 11001001 00100110 10000011 11001010 10011101 10011101 01111101
01001101 00111011 11101110 10100000 00011111 11100111 00110101 00110110 11010100 00101110
00110100 01110101 00000111 00111111 10000101 00100010 11111100 10111100 01110101 00111101
01001101 00101111 01001100 10011110 11111000 10100110 11100111 10001111 01001100 11110101
10100100 10011101 10001001 00010101 11000000 10100100 11000110 01111001 11000101 00111011
10010001 10000001 01001101 01101111 10011000 01111010 10011110 11010100 11101111 11011001
00001100 00010000 00010000 01001111 00111101 01101001 10111000 00111001 00011110 10011001
11001001 10100001 10000110 00000000 10100111 00110000 11001111 01111110 00111101 00101000
00000001 10111001 11101001 11101011 01000001 00011001 00111111 00111001 11111100 10101001
00011100 00000011 11101001 10011100 01010000 00001111 01101100 11110000 01101001 10101011
00000000 10111001 11001010 00010010 00111010 01111010 11010011 10000000 11100011 10001111
11001100 11010011 01001001 11111001 00001000 11101101 11101101 01000111 01000100 00100011
00110100 01011010 11011010 10000000 11011100 11110110 00000111 10000001 01000010 01100000
00100000 11100111 11101011 11110101 10100110 10101110 00111010 10000001 11101101 01001001
11110111 01010100 10010000 01111010 10011100 00001010 01011101 01101111 01110000 00000111
00111001 00011000 01001110 10111001 11101010 00101001 00110111 01100000 11100110 10010111
10000000 00000110 00111011 01111010 01010010 00000010 00001001 00000000 10011111 11111110
10111101 00110101 10101110 10100011 10110001 00100010 01111101 11111100 01110111 10101001
00010100 00010001 11010111 10011100 11010100 01111001 11100111 00111000 11100111 11010110
10010100 10011100 00001101 11011101 10101000 11010000 01000011 00100101 00100101 10001111
00111001 00000011 00110100 11010010 11000000 01100100 10000001 10010011 10011100 00000001
01010010 00110111 00101011 11101111 01010001 10001111 10010100 01100000 10001111 11000110
10010011 01111101 00000000 01100011 10010010 00010001 11000111 11110001 11111011 00011010
01100010 10010010 00001111 11001111 11111000 01010011 10011111 00111011 11001110 11101110
10010100 11001110 10111000 00111101 01101010 10101101 01100001 11011100 10110001 00001001
00000000 01100111 10100000 11110111 10101001 11000001 11100100 10011111 11001100 01010101
01001111 00110001 10110010 00000001 00011100 11111010 11010100 11101000 01110111 01100100
11100111 10010011 01011001 10110110 11010011 10110000 10001010 01111010 11001100 01001100
11010000 11111001 10110000 11000010 11110010 11001011 10000011 10000000 10111100 01100110
10111000 11001101 01111011 01000110 10010111 01010010 11010010 10010011 11001111 01011111
11110100 11011000 11111001 11011011 10011110 10111110 11000110 10111101 00000001 11001011
00010000 00010111 11010010 10101000 01011110 01011010 11111101 11111001 01110011 11001111
01111100 11111111 00000000 01001010 11010110 00010011 11100101 01111110 01100011 11110101
00111100 00011010 01010101 00110000 11001000 11110000 10110001 11000001 00000100 11100111
11011010 10010011 10111111 00000111 10100111 01011010 11101110 10111100 01100111 10100001
10110100 11001001 11110110 11101011 01010100 00011011 11000111 11111010 11000000 00010111
10011100 01111010 11010111 00000100 10100111 00111101 01001111 00111110 11010101 11011110
10100100 10100111 00011011 11000100 10001011 01110111 00100100 11000111 11101111 01000110
01111010 01110110 00110100 11100011 10111011 11010111 11110100 10101000 10001111 00000111
11111111 00000000 10101111 01001010 10101111 10110100 01100011 10011010 00101100 00011110
10000111 11010001 01101101 00100110 11101000 11011111 01100001 11110110 10101010 11110111
00010110 01001110 01000111 11101110 11011011 11100100 00111101 01010101 10111011 01111101
00101010 10110100 10010010 10100000 01101100 00100001 00111001 11001111 00111000 00111101
01101010 01001011 11111101 01000111 11001001 10110100 01110110 11100111 10000001 01011110
01000101 11110100 00111101 00101001 11101000 10001001 11101101 01110010 00000011 10001111
01001110 00101010 11000011 00110010 10101010 10010001 10001100 11010111 00110011 10100000
11101010 01100010 01111011 10111001 01010100 00011101 10001001 10110111 11111000 10001110
00110011 01011010 11101111 00111000 00001001 10111011 00100000 11100111 11010000 11010111
10100101 01000110 11011100 10111010 10011100 00010101 01011101 11011110 10000100 11111000
00000100 11101110 00111101 00110011 11011010 10011010 10111001 00010010 11101110 00000100
11101100 11101001 10000011 01001111 00000011 00101000 00001111 01100011 11010011 00010100
10001100 00110000 00001111 00011100 01010110 10011010 00110011 00100111 10100000 11100100
00100001 01010011 00000000 00000000 00001001 11101101 01000000 01101110 01101010 00011100
11110100 00100110 10010101 01011011 11110010 00110101 01001101 00001010 11110111 00101100
01101110 00100100 10001100 01111110 00111001 10101001 01011001 01110010 00111110 01011010
10101100 10111100 01110111 10101001 11100001 00011001 11101000 01101001 00110100 00110100
11110100 00100100 00010001 11110001 11001101 00101111 10010100 01111010 11110100 10100111
10101010 11100100 11110101 10100111 00110001 11011011 11000110 00101000 01001101 00110110
01001011 00101011 01001101 00010001 00110001 00011110 11000111 00010101 10001101 11100011

11000001 10001011 01011101 00111011 00111101 00111001 11111110 01010101 11010000 00111110
01110000 01111000 11100011 11101011 01011000 10011110 00111011 10000110 01101001 10101101
10101100 00000100 00101000 01011111 01100011 01100100 10011100 01110100 11100010 10111001
11101010 11111100 01001011 01010011 01001000 00111101 00001011 00111010 01010100 11011110
01100110 10010111 01101001 11100101 00111100 01111001 01010001 11001110 01001111 01011010
11011111 10110110 10011010 00111101 10001001 00011011 10011110 01110001 11000001 00000111
00110101 11100111 00010110 01110011 11011101 11011001 10111111 00001011 11001001 11101010
01001000 10101101 01100100 11010101 01101110 01100010 10001011 11001101 00110000 01000110
01100011 00111100 01100111 00110100 11100111 10000111 01110011 01111011 10010110 11001110
11100101 01011000 00011111 10111001 11110011 10011111 01101010 01010011 11010000 10000111
01010001 00100010 00111000 11100100 00011010 11100011 01010011 01011010 10010101 01101101
10000100 10100110 11011100 00010100 00111100 01110001 00100101 01001011 00100110 10111100
11010001 01000001 00011100 10010010 01000000 01110000 11111101 00000000 01101110 10110101
10010010 10100001 00101000 01101100 00011010 10011010 00111010 10100101 10100010 10011001
00010011 11001001 01100010 00110001 11010001 01001111 01101010 10100101 00011101 10100100
11000001 11001110 11111101 11100000 01111010 11100110 10110001 11101111 10110101 11111111
00000000 00101110 11100110 00101000 10011110 00001001 00000011 10110000 11001000 00000001
10110011 01010110 11101101 10111100 01000001 00001010 11001010 01100010 10011110 00111001
01010001 11000111 00000100 00011110 01110000 01101011 01111010 01101110 01001101 01011000
10000011 01111010 00010101 10010100 00101111 01010011 11000000 11101111 01001110 11010101
10100001 11111011 01010101 10110100 01010001 00011111 10010000 11100111 10101101 01010011
10110110 11010110 10101101 10110001 10000011 00101001 00001111 11010111 10010000 01101010
01001011 10111101 01000010 00101001 10010110 00110011 00001011 10001001 00110000 01110011
11000111 00010100 00111000 11001011 01001111 00100010 01011011 11101100 01011110 10110100
10001000 01011011 11000010 00010111 00111111 01110101 01110001 01010011 00100011 11110010
01001001 11101101 01010100 11111100 11101101 11100011 00000100 01110011 10000001 11011110
10011100 00100100 11100000 10001010 10011000 00110111 00110110 11011000 11100110 01011011
01000110 11011101 00100001 00000111 10100111 01011010 01010110 01100000 00111000 11001111
11100111 01010100 10110111 01100000 11010001 10111011 00111101 11101010 11011010 01110110
10111001 10011011 00101100 00111100 10011001 00111100 01010100 01001110 11000100 11110010
11011101 10101000 00100111 10110111 00110100 11000110 00000100 10011100 01100110 10100111
01111101 10000010 11100101 00101101 01010110 01010010 00101100 00101110 11001000 11100111
10000100 11101011 01011000 00111110 00011100 10001101 11001101 10000001 00100111 10000001
11100110 00011010 11011011 11010101 01100011 11011101 10100111 01011110 11111101 00000110
00101010 10010111 10000110 11100010 00111111 11011001 10100000 01100000 11100000 10110001
11000101 00010100 01100100 11010011 10010100 10001101 11101101 01111011 00100010 01010110
10001100 10001110 01111011 11010000 10110001 10011110 10100110 10101100 00111100 00101111
11001110 11011111 11001100 11010011 00010110 00100110 01101111 01100001 01011010 01110011
10100110 10101110 10001110 10011000 01010011 01101001 10000010 00000101 01011000 10101001
00011000 10000110 11100000 01010100 10101001 00001110 11010101 00111100 01110001 11101001
01001001 10010000 00110001 10010101 11101001 01011100 00011100 10010000 10101001 00100110
10001110 11000111 01010001 11000011 01110010 10100100 11110000 10011101 10100100 10000101
11001001 10101110 01110111 01011100 10111000 10010110 00100010 00100000 10000011 11101111
10011110 10100111 00010101 11010101 01001101 00100000 01010100 01110010 10110101 11001111
01011000 00011000 10100111 11010100 10100111 01100111 11111001 11001010 10110111 01111010
01101010 10101010 10000010 10110111 01000000 10101101 00001110 01110100 10011001 11001111
01000111 10100001 01011100 10001001 01001011 11001111 01101111 00100011 10100011 01110011
10010011 11001101 01011101 01111111 00001010 11011100 01100011 01110100 00100000 00000000
11101011 11000111 00010101 11011111 11000010 01000001 11000001 11100011 11101001 01010010
00111001 11111101 00101011 00000111 10001010 10011101 11110100 00110001 11110110 01110001
01011010 00110011 11001011 01001110 10010011 10101000 11101000 01101100 01101111 00101100
10100110 00100010 01000100 11000001 00101011 11101011 11110101 10101111 01000100 11010011
10110101 01100101 11010100 00110100 11001000 10100111 10000110 00101100 01101111 01011111
10011000 01111111 01110101 11111011 11010101 00111101 01100010 00110001 00101100 00110010
10101111 00011001 01100001 01011001 00111110 00000011 10111000 00101101 01101011 01110111
00000001 01011100 01001001 00010100 10011001 00100000 10011111 01011010 11101110 11000010
11010101 11110110 10110111 01010010 11011100 11100110 11000100 11010011 01001011 01010100
01101111 00101110 11100001 00100110 01110001 10001010 10111111 01100111 00110000 00001100
00110011 11000111 11100001 11010110 10100010 01101101 10111101 11111010 11010011 00010010
00110010 01111001 01000011 01011101 00111010 01110100 00111001 00001101 01011111 10110100
00010010 01110000 00000111 00010101 01110011 01001001 11000011 01101001 10010110 11101100
01001111 01010000 01110001 10001111 10101101 01100001 00100011 11001001 00011100 01101110
00011111 10101111 10101101 01101110 01101000 10101000 01010111 01001010 10110110 11100111
11111110 01011001 11010111 00111101 01011000 10101110 01011101 00001011 10000001 01110001
01000000 11011000 00110011 11101011 11010010 10001111 01111100 11010000 11000110 10010011
00111111 00111111 10110101 01110011 00111101 01001010 00010100 01100100 11100011 11111001
10011010 01001110 01010011 00100001 01101001 01111111 10000111 10101101 00100011 00011100
01100111 00111101 01001101 00101101 00000000 01110110 01000110 00001001 00111111 10000110
01101001 10101100 01110010 00000110 00111001 00111110 10110100 10101101 11001100 01011001
11000111 00010100 10000000 10000101 00111100 01010011 00001011 00001011 11001000 00110100
10001010 00111110 01111111 11100111 01001011 11101001 01001100 01101100 10101000 11000000
11100111 10011110 10110100 10010101 11110111 00010000 00110001 11111001 00110011 11010011
00100110 10000111 00111001 00011110 01011000 11111011 11100111 10101111 10110101 00000000

11100000 01110001 11111001 11010000 11000100 00000001 11011111 00110100 00111011 01011100
00000000 11111010 00100111 01101110 11110100 10001101 00100001 00111000 00000000 01110000
00001111 01011111 01011010 01011000 10000110 00110010 01001111 11011111 00110100 01110100
11101101 01000101 11101101 10101000 00001001 00011010 10000000 01001001 01111100 10010010
01000111 01001111 01001010 01000100 01100010 00001001 11101100 10011101 10101001 11001100
11001101 00011100 10001000 00000000 11111011 11011001 11001110 01101001 10101000 00111010
11101110 11111100 01101000 10110101 10110101 00000001 01010100 10000000 00110000 00000110
01001111 01010011 01000001 00000101 10100110 00100100 10001100 00100000 00011110 10111101
01101001 01010100 11110101 00111101 10101001 00001011 00001101 11100011 00100011 00100100
11010101 11011111 01000000 00010111 10110111 10100101 00100111 01010001 10001010 00011011
00100100 11100111 00011100 00001010 01001100 10110111 01011100 01110111 11101001 01010000
11010111 01100000 00010100 01100001 01000101 00100111 01000000 01001111 01001010 00001111
00111000 00000111 11101011 10011010 00011100 10001101 10100100 11110101 11000111 01101010
01001101 00110101 10111000 11000110 10000000 00011000 00011100 10110101 00111101 10000001
00100011 00011101 01001101 00100111 11100011 01000111 01000000 01001111 01000011 01001110
11001011 10100000 10000110 11101101 11111001 11000111 00100111 00010100 11101100 00010000
01111110 01110011 11000111 10101101 00110100 00001100 01110101 11111100 00111001 10100011
10011111 00110011 00100111 10100111 10100101 00001101 00001100 01000101 01101100 10010010
01110010 01110001 11101000 01101000 01100000 00001001 11000111 00110100 01101110 01011100
00010010 00001110 01111110 10010100 10111101 01000000 11110111 11101001 10011010 01001010
11101111 01100000 00100110 10110111 10010101 01101101 11000100 10001110 01010100 00010011
10110111 01100010 10001111 01111010 10000000 10000110 11000000 00011001 11100100 11110101
10100101 11110011 00001010 10100110 01110000 00110010 01111010 01100110 10010011 00100100
00001100 01110001 10001110 11100111 10111101 00001111 01001101 10000100 00110011 00011000
11101011 11010111 10100101 00111011 10101010 00010001 11001110 00101001 01001000 11001001
11001110 01111010 01110110 11000101 00110001 11110011 10110000 10001100 11111101 11111010
01110110 01101001 00001100 00001111 11001100 00111110 01010001 01001110 01100101 01100110
00001111 11001110 00000110 00111000 10100110 11100011 00011000 01010001 11010111 11010111
00110100 11100110 11100011 10001100 11110000 00101001 01011101 10000000 11001100 00000110
01100010 01001000 01000010 00111011 01100100 01100110 10100000 10010110 11011010 00000010
00110110 10011000 00100011 01110000 01111001 00100011 01101000 00110101 01101011 10000001
10110011 10100110 01001101 00110001 01011011 10110000 11100100 11100111 00011001 10101011
11100110 11010011 01000001 10010100 00001110 10010111 01100011 00100011 00111001 01111011
00111000 10110010 01000111 01011100 01010100 00110011 01111000 01111011 01001011 01101000
11001001 00110110 00110001 01100111 00011100 00010001 10010001 01011010 10000011 10000010
00000111 01011111 01011010 01110111 00011101 00000111 11010110 10101011 11011010 11001011
10111000 00011100 11110100 11111110 00010100 11010010 11100100 01110010 00010010 00111001
00100011 00011100 00011111 10010010 01001110 11110101 01001010 01011111 00000100 11101001
10110010 01110100 10011110 11100100 01100111 10101001 00000100 01010111 01011100 11011000
00011101 01010111 10001110 11110100 11010000 01111011 10010001 10001010 00111101 10111100
11010111 01010000 00111000 10011001 10111110 00011111 01011001 01001000 00010001 11001101
11010100 11011001 00011101 00000110 00000101 00100011 11111000 00010101 01010111 10001000
11101111 01111001 11110100 01101000 11111000 10101110 11100000 10111000 00100111 10100111
00000011 10111101 00100011 00011100 10110111 00011100 00010010 00110001 10011010 10101111
01101111 00100001 11011101 10011100 00001100 10111110 00001011 10111010 10000100 01101101
10110111 10011110 11011101 11001111 10100110 00001000 10101010 00110011 01111000 01010011
01010010 00010001 01111001 01111111 01100110 10000110 01000000 00111101 00011000 01010111
10100110 00011110 00000110 00000001 11101001 11001001 00110100 11010010 10100000 11100111
10001110 10100110 10100101 01010111 10111110 10110110 00011111 00111011 00111100 10010110
01011111 00001101 11101011 00010001 00111000 11110010 11101100 00001110 00111011 10000001
10001010 10101111 00110110 10010011 10101010 00000011 11001110 10011011 01110011 10001111
11110111 01110011 01011110 11001001 10110100 01110011 11101011 11101011 01000010 01100000
01110000 01110010 01110001 11010000 00001010 10110111 01010010 00001111 11101100 10011010
01000110 10110100 10010001 11100010 01110111 00111010 00011100 10110010 10100001 00110010
01101001 10010111 00001001 00100111 01011101 11011011 01110001 11010010 10110011 01100101
11010010 11011000 01000100 00111100 11001000 11100101 00000001 10111010 00110001 01010010
00101011 11011110 10010100 00110110 01001000 00111100 00010010 01111011 11010011 01011110
00110000 01100100 11100100 00000010 10000000 01110000 00110001 11000101 00110101 01011010
00101011 10100000 11111101 10111011 00111100 00001010 01101011 00111000 10001101 10101010
01111001 01101100 01010110 01011100 11100001 10000001 00011111 10101101 01010110 11111110
11001101 00100111 00001100 00100101 01000010 01111011 10001100 01010111 11010000 00001101
01100011 01101111 00100011 11100101 11101101 11100010 00100111 10111001 00101011 01010101
00011111 01000011 11010011 00100101 00110010 00010111 10110001 10000100 11100100 11100111
11101110 11010110 10110001 11000100 11000000 10001111 01101000 11001111 00010111 10000110
11001101 01100010 01100100 11001001 11001001 11110101 11101001 10011010 10011111 11001011
00011011 11001000 11001111 00010101 11101010 11010111 00011110 00010100 11010001 01100100
11100111 11101100 01000000 01100011 10101110 00001001 10101010 01110011 01111000 00100111
01001010 01100010 01011010 00110100 10010010 00100000 00111011 11101110 10101100 11011010
10100110 11100101 01111011 10001101 01010101 11101110 01111001 10010011 10000001 10111111
10000001 11001001 11101111 01010010 00100010 10010101 11101011 01011101 11111001 11110000
00100101 10010100 10011111 00110010 01011101 01011100 00000000 01111010 00001010 10001101
11111100 00001110 00000111 00010000 11011111 00111110 01000111 01110110 01011010 00101101
00000101 10110100 10001101 00111101 10101010 00111000 01110010 10100111 11101111 00111110

10000011 10101110 01101011 00100010 11111100 10010110 01110010 11011111 01111100 00011010
11110100 01111001 10111100 00010101 01111000 00010001 11000010 01011100 01000100 11100000
01111010 10001110 10110101 10011001 01110011 11100000 01111011 11001000 11100010 11111001
11011000 00111010 01100111 10000010 10110100 11010101 00101000 11101111 01110010 00011100
11010001 11001001 11101001 00101011 10110110 00100010 01111011 00010011 10001100 11010110
10100000 11000110 00111010 11110101 10101101 01001000 10111100 00110101 01110011 00001010
11101100 10001101 00000110 11001110 10111100 10011110 01101010 01010100 11110000 11011110
10101000 11001001 10011000 11101101 10111100 11000000 01111010 00010000 11000010 10111010
01010010 10110010 11010001 10011000 11001001 01011101 11101000 01101000 01111100 00111011
00000111 11111011 01010010 11101100 10000011 11010010 00011111 11101011 01011101 11110010
10000000 00110001 11101011 01011100 10100111 10000011 10110100 10011011 10101101 00111110
11101010 11101101 10101110 11100010 00110001 01101111 01011101 10011000 11001110 01110011
01011101 01011111 01011100 00000001 11000000 00010101 11001001 01011010 11010111 11010101
10001001 00101011 00001010 10000011 10011110 01111010 01110110 10100110 01110101 00100111
11011110 10011100 11000100 10001110 11100111 10011110 10110100 01111101 11010011 11111010
11100110 10111001 11010011 11101110 00000011 01011000 01100011 00000000 00001110 01000101
00110111 00000101 01000000 11001110 00111110 10110100 10101100 00111010 10010001 11010100
10011110 01101001 01011111 00011000 11000000 10100001 11011011 01110000 00000000 00110010
00111000 11111010 10010011 01010001 10110001 11001110 00111111 11000010 10011110 11011101
00111010 01010010 01111110 01111011 10101001 00101011 00111101 01010000 00001101 00001011
11010111 00111001 11111100 01101001 00001111 11011111 00111100 11100111 11010011 11011010
10100100 11101000 01001001 11001111 00111101 10101001 10001001 10011100 10011111 01011100
01110011 10011010 00000110 10000100 11001110 00000001 11000111 01101010 01000110 00000100
01100101 01001001 11000001 11111010 01010010 10001100 01100000 01100000 11110000 00101001
00111010 10000010 01111011 11111010 01010101 01101000 00100000 01000001 10001100 00000011
11001110 01111001 10100001 10001001 00100111 10101111 01111110 00101001 01001111 00011000
11101011 10011111 01001010 01000001 11001110 01001111 01000011 10011111 01011010 10011101
10000000 01101111 01000010 01010111 10110111 10100101 00000111 00111000 00011011 01111010
11111010 11010011 10001000 11101010 01111101 11101001 10111001 11000110 00000000 10100110
10011011 01000010 00000110 00011100 10011111 11010110 10011011 11101101 01001110 00011100
01100100 10011110 10110100 10011100 10000101 11110101 01111100 11110001 01000011 11011111
01000001 10000111 01001110 10011101 01101001 00110110 10000010 01001011 00001110 00000001
11110100 10100101 01101111 10010100 01110010 00110011 01000011 00001101 10100000 01101100
11111011 10010100 11110101 11011101 10000000 10001011 11010111 10001110 10000011 10000001
01000111 01110010 00010111 10101000 10100101 00000011 01110000 10100100 11100111 11001011
11001111 10101001 11111100 11101010 01101111 01110111 10100000 00000001 11001000 10001100
00101010 11110101 00111101 11001101 00110101 01001000 11100000 11110111 11101101 10011010
01111011 01111111 11111010 10111001 10101000 11011011 10101000 11100111 00100111 00010100
11110101 11011000 00000101 11101011 11000111 10100111 01010011 01001101 01111110 00001010
00010001 11010100 10011010 00111001 00011100 11100011 11101011 01000110 01110000 10101110
11000111 10110101 00010111 10110110 10000000 00111011 10010001 10001100 01110001 10001010
10001001 00110010 11000000 11110001 11110101 10100111 10000010 00110000 01011011 00100111
00011111 01001110 10110100 00010011 10000001 11000111 01010011 11010110 10011101 11110101
00000000 01101110 01000101 00000100 11100100 10001111 01101010 00000111 00100111 00111000
11101001 11111010 11010011 00000000 11000000 01110010 01111010 10011110 10000000 01010010
11011010 11101100 00000001 10111001 01100001 11111100 11001101 00000100 10011100 11100001
00000111 11100011 01000111 00100101 01111101 11110011 10011010 00011100 10011110 10011111
10011101 00010111 10111010 10111000 00001011 11010011 00011100 11111110 10110100 10011100
00000010 01110001 11010111 11011110 10010111 10000001 11011111 00110101 00011011 11100111
11001100 00100111 10110110 00101000 10001010 01001100 01000010 01100101 10001111 01011110
00001110 01111010 11010011 11000000 00000011 11101110 01110100 00010100 11001101 11011111
00111001 00011001 11100010 10001100 10011100 11110001 11111100 11101000 01111110 01000101
01011000 00111010 11110100 00011100 00010001 10010010 01110011 11010010 10011000 10100000
01110110 11101011 10001100 11100100 11111010 01010011 10011111 00111011 11110011 10011110
00111000 00011000 10100011 10101000 11110111 11100110 10011010 01001110 11000010 00011101
10011101 11011000 10100001 10000110 01001110 00001111 01001010 10001101 00001001 11101101
01001111 11111011 10111100 00010010 01110011 11101111 01010011 01110110 00000011 11110110
11100111 10101101 00110001 10110010 01100100 00111000 00011100 00001111 01011010 01111110
01000001 00011001 11001101 01000110 01011000 10110000 00100100 00010010 00110001 01000111
10011011 00000001 10101111 10000010 01111000 11100100 11010100 01101010 01110000 00110111
00001010 01111010 11001001 10110111 10001100 01110101 11111110 00100011 01001100 01110000
01110010 00000011 01110100 00011101 10101000 01011010 10000000 00000010 01000010 01101110
11110111 11101011 01010011 01000011 10010000 01111010 10011100 11010100 00011101 01000110
00111011 01010011 11100001 01111110 01111011 11100110 10001011 10100110 00000101 10011111
10011001 10100100 00101100 01011011 00100011 11010000 01010000 11111111 00000000 01111100
00000011 11010100 11110011 01010001 10100100 10011000 00100111 00110100 11111000 10001110
01111001 00111100 01010011 11101010 00000110 01111101 11111101 10111000 00100011 00110001
10101000 11001110 01111001 11001101 01111001 01111111 10001100 10110100 00011111 10110001
01001100 01101110 11101101 11010111 00010000 00111111 00101100 00000111 01100010 01101011
11010111 01011011 00011001 00100100 10001100 10000001 01011001 10011010 10000101 10001100
00110011 01011011 00111111 11011010 00000000 11110010 10100100 00000100 00110010 11101101
11001000 11100110 10110101 10100010 11011100 00011101 11101110 00000111 10000101 01100100
00011100 10001100 01111101 01000001 10100011 01111000 01010001 10001100 01111110 01010101

10110001 11100010 00011101 00100110 01001101 00110010 11110100 10000001 10010011 01101111
00100001 00111110 01010001 00100011 10110111 10100101 01100011 11110010 10111100 01100011
11110101 10101110 11100101 00011110 10110001 11011000 00001111 01100011 10111011 11010111
00101100 00010110 00111111 00110110 00011001 00010001 11001111 01111100 01110101 10101110
01110110 11111011 01010111 10010010 11110010 00111101 10011111 11110010 11001111 00111001
11101011 11010110 10011011 11100010 01100011 00011010 01001110 10011011 00101100 11000100
01000010 01001111 10011111 11001101 00011111 11000111 10011111 01001010 11000111 01011111
01100011 11000111 11110011 10101110 00011010 01110100 11010011 11010110 11000101 11010100
10101000 11101111 01100011 10101010 11010001 01101100 11101100 00100111 10001001 11011011
01010001 11110011 01000011 11111111 00000000 00001011 01000111 11111101 01101011 01010001
01110100 01101101 00010011 10000010 00110101 00111001 10010011 11011000 10101101 01110001
11010110 11011010 10001101 11000100 00011000 00000111 00010010 00100110 00111011 10011010
11101011 11110100 00011000 11101101 11110101 01110101 00001011 00001101 11000000 10001110
11100100 01111101 11101000 10100100 00011100 11111110 00000111 10111101 01011100 11011101
01100101 00101111 01110010 11010110 00111011 00101001 01000011 00001100 11100010 10111001
11011110 10100101 11101000 00110100 00111101 00111101 01010111 00001001 10101011 11011100
01100011 10110000 11000110 01110001 01010010 00111110 10000011 01101000 01011100 00110010
01101011 01010010 10100110 01000111 01100010 01101010 11100000 11010001 10100101 10001101
00001000 00010011 01000111 10010001 11101101 10001010 01001001 10110100 11001001 01100010
10000100 11001011 10010100 00100000 01111010 01111010 01010110 00101111 00010001 01010110
00101111 01010011 01000111 10000110 11000011 01001111 01000100 11001100 10101011 11111101
00100010 01101011 00101000 01001101 11010100 00011010 11011100 11010111 00001000 10001100
00110011 00011111 10101110 01101011 01101000 00101110 00100011 00000111 00111101 01000000
00111101 00101011 00111110 01100011 10001101 00110110 01011110 00111111 10001001 00111111
10011101 01101010 00100010 11111110 11101000 01111101 00101011 10111110 10000101 01001110
01111000 11011101 10011100 00011000 10101010 00101010 10010100 10101100 10001010 11010010
11001001 11100100 10101011 11001001 00100110 00000100 01101011 11001001 00100100 11100011
00010101 11001110 01011101 11111000 11000110 00101000 00101110 00110110 11011010 01000001
11100111 10001110 10111001 00101101 10110000 01010101 01101111 00011001 11011101 10111100
10010111 01000010 11001010 00000111 00100001 00010100 00000111 10010011 00011101 11110011
11010010 10111001 01110111 10110100 01100010 10111111 00100000 11100111 11011000 01110101
10100111 01110100 11010110 10101100 11100011 10110011 01100111 01010011 00000111 10001110
11101110 01000100 11011011 10100110 10110010 10001000 11000111 11101000 10110010 10010000
01101011 10101100 11010010 01110101 10101011 01001101 01010001 00110011 01101011 00110110
11111001 00000000 11011110 11010001 10011110 10101001 01011110 01011100 10011010 00111101
11110011 01001010 10010001 01111101 10011110 01001111 00110000 10001100 10000000 01111011
11010101 10010001 10100100 11011111 01101001 10100000 01011110 00100001 10010010 00011001
00010010 01000000 00110010 10100111 10100111 11010111 11011010 10010011 11100101 01000111
01000010 10100100 11101101 01110100 01111010 11000001 00100101 10010101 11000000 01101100
00010011 11010000 11010101 01111100 01011111 01001001 11000100 11010010 11011011 00111111
01101110 01100011 00110101 10001111 11100001 10011101 01100101 10110101 00110100 11110010
01101110 10000000 01001011 10111000 11000111 00111000 11101001 00100000 11110101 10101110
10001001 01010111 00011101 01111111 01011010 11001101 10100100 11011101 10001100 11110101
10000011 00101010 00001000 01101110 01111010 00111100 00110110 01100100 01111011 00010010
00101001 01111100 10101001 01000001 11100110 11001010 11010100 10000010 01111111 11100111
10100001 10101011 10011100 00101110 01111001 00111000 10100011 10111111 00010101 01011110
11001001 01110101 00011111 00111011 00101011 01111001 00110010 00011110 00001101 10000100
01111000 11110110 10010110 10000110 10000101 10111100 10110010 00111110 11000100 00110001
10001111 11111001 11101000 00101010 11111010 00011110 10011001 11000110 01101000 10011000
11100000 01010010 01010001 10001000 00111010 10001100 11100111 00101111 01101101 01010110
01000110 10001111 01111110 10011100 11111100 00001110 00001010 11001010 00001001 10100100
01001011 00111011 01100110 10010000 00011001 10101100 11101110 01110111 11100011 00011001
11011010 00001111 11110010 00110101 10100001 01110010 01110011 00101111 00010101 00110010
00011110 00000111 10101000 10100100 10101001 00101000 11101010 10011000 10111101 10100011
11101010 01100111 01111101 10011110 11001110 00111110 00111100 10111011 10000001 11101101
11100101 00011010 01111000 10010110 11010110 00111100 01101100 10010011 01100111 00011111
11000101 00011001 10101101 01101101 11111000 11101010 01111001 11101101 10001010 10001100
11100100 11100111 10111101 00101111 01111011 01101011 10000011 10101000 10001010 11110001
01011100 01000011 00100011 11101101 01001001 11010001 11100100 00111000 11100000 01100111
10110101 01011011 11100100 10010011 10001010 00110110 10101001 11100100 10000000 01111111
00001010 01111110 01111111 01011010 01101001 00101000 10100000 10010110 10111011 00001100
01010101 00100100 01110010 01101001 11001001 11110111 11101001 11001100 00001101 00001000
00000110 01110011 01001101 00100111 01100011 00110110 00101010 10000010 00000110 01101000
01001100 10010011 01010011 00101000 11111001 00111001 00011000 11110100 10100011 01110000
00000011 11110001 10100101 11100110 11000000 11001011 11010110 10100100 11110010 11110100
10101011 10110011 10110111 00111001 11100010 10101010 01101000 00110011 11101101 10110001
00000101 11111000 00010101 01001111 11000101 11111010 11001101 10111101 10101101 10000111
10010111 11100110 00000111 01111001 00100100 00100011 00001010 01111010 01100011 11010110
10011111 10100010 01001001 11100110 11101001 11010001 10111000 11100100 01100010 10110011
10100000 10110100 10010011 01100110 11110001 11010101 10100011 01000111 11001111 00000101
10110010 00001111 01011010 10010001 00100101 00101010 11011101 00111010 11010100 01011110
01010110 01110000 01110001 10000001 01001010 11100111 00000111 00111111 10010101 01100111
01010101 11011001 00011101 00110100 11101111 01111011 10010010 10111100 11011000 01100000

00000111 01011010 10001110 01101001 10110010 00001001 11101101 01010001 00110100 10011000
11101101 10011110 00101010 00111001 00100110 11000100 01111001 11000101 01111001 11110010
10111101 11110110 00111101 00010100 11100010 11010001 01011010 11101010 11100001 01010101
01011101 10100110 01101101 10010001 10000001 10010010 01001111 01001100 01010111 00101011
01100011 01110100 01011111 01010011 10011101 10101101 00011000 00111100 01101110 11011001
01010110 11110110 10101100 11011111 00011100 01101010 10001101 00100101 11100001 10110001
10001101 10110001 00011010 01110011 00100000 00000111 10101101 01011000 11110000 00001101
11010010 10001011 11010111 10001010 01000101 11001010 00011000 11111001 00000111 10100000
10101110 11001000 11010000 01011100 10111100 11010111 00111001 10101010 01010111 11100110
10011111 00101010 00111010 11101011 00101101 01000110 11101101 11100100 11000111 11101110
01001000 01011110 10100011 10111001 10101011 10011010 10100111 10011111 00111100 00100011
11001000 10010101 11100011 11101111 10000000 01101001 11010011 00101101 10111100 00010110
11010010 10110010 00001100 01110000 01101010 00111101 00110110 11101001 00100100 10001010
00101101 10000111 00100000 11110101 11100010 10111000 11101010 01001001 01011110 11001000
11010011 10010110 11100101 01011011 00001011 01010111 01101111 10011010 01110000 01001001
11001110 01001001 00111100 11010100 00111010 00111100 00000010 11011111 01010101 11010100
00100101 01000011 11000011 00010000 10000111 10001111 11000110 10111010 01011001 01001010
10101100 01111100 10011110 00110001 10010011 01011000 10010110 10111000 10010000 11001010
01010011 10001111 10011011 10010010 01111011 10011010 11101010 11000011 01101011 00111101
00110100 00110001 10101010 11010010 10001110 10100101 11000010 11011100 11110101 11001101
01011010 10110110 01100001 11001101 01010101 01011110 10000110 10100100 10000011 10000001
01011110 10011010 01011010 01011000 11110010 10010011 00101110 00110000 00000110 00110111
11001111 10100001 00110101 10110111 10100110 10010000 01101100 01101101 11010100 01110100
11110010 11000101 01100001 10011111 11111000 11110111 10010100 11111111 00000000 10110010
01101011 01100111 01001011 00001010 00101101 00101101 11110000 00001010 00001101 10100011
00100100 10001110 10111100 01010111 00110101 01101101 10001101 00010001 01110000 01100011
01101111 01001110 00001111 11101011 01001001 10011100 10010001 11001111 11100001 01000111
01010010 01111000 11100000 01110100 10100011 00000000 00011100 10011110 10010101 11001010
10010101 10001011 00001111 01101110 10000010 10001100 10011100 11111111 00000000 11110101
10101001 00010100 01100101 11001110 01110011 01001010 01110010 01001111 10110101 01010011
00010000 00010011 10010101 01001100 01110001 01000001 00011100 10001100 10011111 11000010
10011001 10010011 10111100 00011111 11100000 10100001 00111000 00011001 00111110 10110101
00101010 11100000 00111000 11111100 11000011 10001110 00000101 00110010 01010000 00001001
01001100 01110100 11110100 10100111 11010011 01011000 11111100 11011000 10100111 01101011
01101110 00000011 10110011 10001110 01110001 11000101 00110111 11010100 00011110 10100010
10011101 10001101 10101001 10011111 01001010 01101111 00100100 10011100 10001010 00011011
11101100 10000000 00110001 11101011 10011100 01010000 11111100 00010000 00111011 10011010
01000111 00101100 00010100 11101100 00111000 00111101 11001101 00001010 01111000 11001110
00111111 00011010 01011100 11010110 11011100 00000101 00000100 00101000 11100000 01100100
11111011 11010010 00100001 00001011 11000110 01111001 00111101 01101000 01001100 10010000
01111110 10110100 10101001 11010000 01111011 00011111 11001110 10011100 01010101 10010101
11000000 01001111 11110101 01100000 10000001 11010000 01010000 11000111 00101111 10011100
01110001 01001010 11100100 11110001 11011111 11010110 10010001 01001111 00111101 01111010
11110100 10100101 01110001 10001011 11010100 00001110 00111001 10100100 11000111 00111001
10100101 11100100 01100111 11010111 10110101 00100010 10000011 10011111 01111010 10101011
01110101 01000011 01100000 11011000 11001000 11100011 10011110 11110100 01111101 11101110
10110100 01100001 10001001 00111001 00111101 01111010 01010010 00000110 11001001 10100100
11111101 11100001 00001010 00000001 11001101 00100110 01000110 01001111 11101001 01000111
11111001 11001101 00101010 10001100 00110111 10101111 01110001 01001001 01101010 11101100
00000011 00011000 00010010 01000000 11101000 00000111 00100100 11010011 10111111 10001011
11111101 10011010 01101110 11011100 10010001 11001111 01010011 01001110 01100011 10011010
10101101 11110101 00000001 10111011 01000111 01010001 11010000 11110100 10100011 00111000
11100000 00001100 10010001 11101001 01000011 10010001 11000000 00011101 10101000 11001110
00000110 00111111 00111010 01010111 00000001 00001110 00011011 10100000 00100011 11101011
01000110 00000000 00000000 11110110 00010100 10111000 11101100 01101001 10111001 00000100
10001110 00101000 11011000 00000011 00111001 00111110 10000110 10000011 11010111 00111100
10010011 01000011 11111111 00000000 10101101 00100000 01110011 10000001 10000011 01000001
11110100 00011101 01101011 00110110 11101100 00000001 10010000 01001110 01101001 10101101
11000111 00111110 11010100 00101001 11000000 00100011 11010110 10011100 11001100 01000000
11110111 10101011 10111010 10110101 11000000 01101010 10001101 11000111 11100110 11101011
11011010 10000000 00000000 11100111 00010100 00101000 00100001 10000001 00111101 10101000
00000000 01100111 10001110 00001111 01111010 01101100 01000010 00010000 01110111 11110101
11000111 00011100 01010001 11001001 00100011 11011111 11010010 10010101 10001110 00001111
00100011 00111101 10101001 00110111 00010000 01000111 11001011 11110100 00110100 10011010
00000001 01001000 11001011 10000001 11011011 10111111 00110100 10000111 10100001 10100101
11101001 11110011 01110101 00110100 11011111 11101111 11100100 01100111 00110100 00110010
10101110 00101011 11110000 00110000 00000111 00011110 10100110 10010011 00011101 00011000
11110110 00110100 10111100 11101100 11000001 11000001 10100110 01100111 00000111 10010011
11000111 01100001 01001110 11110111 00010000 11110110 00001010 00011001 11000111 01000100
00111111 10101101 00100010 10001110 11011101 00000000 00110100 10111100 10010010 00110011
01001001 11001000 11000110 01001110 01001001 11111101 00101001 01111010 00000000 11011111
10011011 00101110 00000111 01001010 00000110 00000001 11001111 01101010 01110110 01001110
00110011 01001101 01100001 11011010 10010011 11011110 11100000 00110111 00001101 10111100

10010011	10000001	10011110	10111110	11010100	00101000	11111001	11001001	11001111	01101010
01110110	11011110	10111111	10101101	00000100	01100011	10011110	10000000	11111010	11010011
11011000	00000100	11001110	01001111	01111100	01010010	00101001	00100011	00100000	01111010
01110101	11110100	10100101	01100000	01010001	00010011	00011100	01100100	11010010	00110111
00000011	10001111	01011111	11001110	10000101	11100110	00110110	00110111	01101000	01100010
01000111	01100001	11010010	10001110	00000001	11000111	01011100	01110101	11001101	00111010
01010010	01000010	10011110	01101001	10100000	01100011	10011110	00110010	01111001	11110101
10100001	10101101	01110100	00010000	10000100	00010010	01010000	01110110	10100001	10011000
10000111	11000000	00000000	11111011	11010011	11011011	10000110	00011110	10100010	10100011
00000111	01110011	10010001	10110100	10000100	00011101	01001001	10100001	01011001	00000000
10101101	10010011	10010011	10011110	01001111	00011100	01010010	00011110	01000001	11001000
11000110	00111010	00001010	01010000	01110000	00111001	11000110	01001111	01000001	01000011
00001110	00011111	11010100	01111011	11010000	11100100	00000100	00000001	01000110	11011110
10000010	10100100	10001010	00111101	10101000	00111101	01110001	11010110	10011100	00000110
00111001	00110100	01110011	10001100	11100011	00100100	11110100	11110110	00010101	01111100
11011010	01101000	00000000	01111111	11010110	00111001	11101010	01110001	01000110	01110001
11010100	11010010	11110011	11101011	01001001	10001100	00010010	11011101	01001101	01001101
11101110	11110110	00000001	10111001	00100101	11000001	11000111	11100001	01001110	00011000
11001111	11001101	10001110	01001101	00101001	11001001	00111011	01111011	11100010	10011000
11011101	10110011	11001110	00001110	01101000	10110110	10111010	00001110	11100001	10011100
00010011	11101011	01000010	10010010	01011000	00011100	01100100	01111010	11111010	11010001
11010111	10011100	01111101	01001101	00100111	00111001	11000111	10101101	00011010	00110001
00000111	00111011	10001000	11110101	11111101	00101001	00011011	10110000	00000111	10100101
00111001	10000110	00010111	10010011	11001001	00110100	10001110	00000001	11000000	11101101
11101011	01000101	10101110	00111011	10001100	11000111	11001100	01001101	00111001	00110011
11100101	10111001	11000001	11100111	10000011	01001101	01101110	01011111	00101000	00111000
11101001	01001111	01100010	00000010	10010001	11001111	11010110	10001101	01111010	00001000
10001101	00000000	11011111	10000101	00111101	00101000	01011110	00001011	10010001	11000110
01101000	01000011	11000001	00001000	00111001	10100001	10001000	00101000	00000000	11001110
01110011	11001001	10100001	01011000	00000000	00000011	10000000	01111010	11010010	01110000
00110000	00000111	01010011	11010110	10010111	10100111	00011111	10011110	00101001	00001111
00101110	01001110	00101000	10010011	10111010	00000001	10111100	01100100	11101101	10100011
10001101	10000000	01100111	10011010	01000110	01011111	01101010	01111000	00011001	00100100
00000011	11110101	00110100	00101011	01101100	10000000	01100111	00000011	00001101	10011010
01010101	11001110	00000111	10111001	10100011	10100111	11011101	11001110	00001111	00011001
10100100	01111111	10010100	01100110	10101101	11110110	00000000	01111100	00000001	11101010
01101001	00110010	01001010	00000011	11101011	01000010	10001111	11101110	10001110	10111101
11101001	10111001	00111011	10111001	11101111	11010000	01010100	00100111	11010000	00000111
00000011	10000001	10001010	00011100	10011100	00000101	11101010	01110011	10011010	01011100
11100001	10110001	11011000	01010010	00010011	11110011	11111101	01111011	11010001	01101011
11101000	10000000	00110011	11101010	00101001	10011011	10110111	01110001	11011110	10000110
00100111	00100011	00100011	11110000	10100100	01101110	00001111	11001000	00111001	11101111
11101101	01000011	11011000	00000101	11001111	00111100	11111110	01010100	11000111	00111001
11101000	00101001	11011011	01001011	01110011	01000000	11111011	10011001	11101101	01000101
10101111	10110011	00000001	10101001	00100110	11010101	11101001	11000000	11101001	01001110
01100001	10011110	10100111	00111001	10100110	00011110	00001111	11001101	11010000	11111110
10010100	01111010	00001100	11110011	11010110	10010011	01100000	00101010	10001110	00110010
01001001	10100011	00011101	01001110	01111000	10100100	00000111	00100111	11111010	01010010
11100100	10000011	10000001	11011110	10001110	01110010	11000100	11001111	11001000	11100000
01110000	01001000	11101011	01000111	00100011	01100111	11010110	10000101	11000111	00011000
00011001	11100111	10011100	11010010	10111001	00000010	01011100	01100111	00100111	10111101
00111110	10000100	01011100	01101110	01110010	00001111	00000111	10001110	01101001	10101101
11001000	11111100	00110001	01001111	11101000	10000000	01111010	11010011	00111010	10111110
11010000	00110000	00111011	11010100	00110000	00001100	00001100	01110011	11110101	10100100
01100011	11001000	00011111	10011110	00101001	11101101	11101111	11010010	10100011	00000000
11110010	01110011	01011010	01000101	10101011	00001111	01010001	11001111	10001110	00111111
01001010	01001100	10011110	11000011	00011100	01110111	10100011	00111111	11111101	01111010
00011111	10001000	11111000	11100100	10011110	10000111	00110101	00101110	11111101	00000100
00100010	01110001	10001100	10001110	00111101	11101001	01001000	00011011	00110010	01111010
11111010	01010010	01100011	11111100	11111010	11010010	10110110	00001110	01000000	11101101
11101011	01000010	11110011	00000000	01100000	00110000	00110001	11010010	10010011	10001110
11111101	11111011	01111010	11010010	11101110	00100000	01100100	00001110	00101000	01100001
10110111	11011100	11111010	11010101	00100100	00000100	01101110	10111011	10011000	00001110
11000011	11110010	10100110	00010001	11101001	11011010	10100110	01111110	00000110	11011110
11111110	10110100	11001100	01100011	10001100	01010101	01111010	00001101	10010001	10111000
11001110	00111011	00000001	01000110	00110110	10110110	01000001	11001011	10011010	01111001
11001000	00111000	11101101	10001010	01100111	10100111	10101001	10100101	10111010	00100100
10010000	00110000	01010111	11000001	11100111	10001110	10100100	11010100	10110001	01110011
10001111	10101101	01010011	11000001	00100100	01110011	11000110	01101010	11000110	11101110
11100000	11100011	10011010	00011111	01111011	00001100	01111010	00001100	11110011	11010100
10011110	01110001	01010001	10011110	01111010	11110100	00000111	10111101	01001000	10101011
10000010	00110001	11010000	00011010	00011111	10100011	10110001	11101001	11011010	10100010
11101000	00001100	01001101	01101111	01001011	10000010	11110110	11010101	11100010	10011010

00110000 01000011 01110111 00111100 11101101 00110101 11100101 00011010 10011110 10001101
01110011 01100111 01111000 11110001 00110100 00001101 00101110 00111001 00001110 00000110
00110010 00101011 11011011 11000110 00001000 11000001 11000001 11001111 10101000 10101010
00110011 01011001 10101110 11101111 10010110 00110110 01100001 10001110 10100100 01010110
11110100 01110001 00101110 10011010 10110010 01011010 00001111 01110011 11001101 01110101
10101000 00101110 00100000 11010110 00101110 01100010 10111000 10000011 11101100 11111111
00000000 00110110 01010110 00110000 11011001 01000001 10011111 01000011 11101001 01001101
00000001 01010110 00111100 11110111 11110110 00111101 01101011 01000111 01011101 10110101
10111001 10110100 11010100 11100100 01001011 11100110 00010010 01011100 11100000 00010110
00100011 10110110 01101011 00111101 11000000 01010100 11100111 10010010 01111111 01001010
11101010 11100101 11101100 01100101 00010111 11010000 10010001 01011001 00000010 10001110
10011000 10101011 00010110 11001100 00010101 10000011 01000110 11000100 00111000 11101000
01000001 10101100 11110100 10001111 01111011 10000010 00111110 10111001 10101011 00010000
00000010 10000111 11011000 01110111 10101101 00011100 01101101 10101010 00011110 10101100
11110100 10011101 00010011 01010010 10111001 11010101 00110100 01110111 00001001 10000011
01110011 00010100 10011011 00011000 11100111 10011100 01110101 10101001 11011101 01110101
00000001 00011011 11000111 00100111 10011000 01010011 10111111 00111001 10101110 01011011
11000010 01010111 10000010 11010110 01101001 11010101 11111000 11011100 10111001 11100011
10011010 11101001 10011111 01011001 01101110 10001000 10100011 10010001 11010100 11110001
01011110 01110110 00101001 01000001 10110011 11010100 11000010 10101001 10111000 11111011
10101010 11100011 01100110 00000000 01101001 10010010 10001111 01010110 01011100 00001111
11000110 10110110 01111100 10011101 10110001 10001100 10000010 00111000 00011100 01110101
10101110 01101110 11100110 11100000 01000111 01100000 01111111 11101011 10101010 10001110
10110101 11010000 11001001 00111110 11101000 01001000 01001110 01001001 01011100 00001111
11001010 10111010 00110000 10110001 01010000 10000111 01110011 10011111 00011111 11110001
10011110 01111101 01111001 00000000 10011110 11111010 01110110 00111111 11000110 11000111
10100101 01101100 11101001 10011010 01011101 10010001 00101001 00100100 11110011 00001000
10000110 01111010 10011110 11110101 10000101 01101111 00111000 00110111 01111011 01100100
00011000 00111011 10111001 11100111 10100001 10101110 10111101 11110100 10110001 00110100
10110001 11001010 10001101 10001000 11001000 00000100 10101111 10100101 00101010 10010101
00011100 01111100 10001100 01101000 11000011 01000011 01111010 00001011 01001101 00111110
11010101 01000011 01101110 11001001 11101011 10010110 00111100 11111110 00010101 10000101
10101111 11111101 10011101 10110100 10101011 10011100 01110010 11110010 00010010 01000000
00000111 10100101 01011111 11011011 11100110 01000011 11100101 00010110 00111001 00011111
11000101 01011000 01110111 11011010 01101101 11001111 11011001 10100100 11110011 00100110
01001111 00101101 00110010 01111001 00011100 10011010 11100100 01011110 11111100 10110101
10010001 11010100 11010011 01001000 11100111 11110100 10101000 11000100 01110111 01110001
11001111 00001001 00100011 01101001 11101011 11111100 11101011 11010011 00111100 10100000
11001000 10010010 00000011 11000001 00011101 01101011 11001110 00110100 10110010 10101101
01110111 00010010 10001110 11100111 10010011 01011110 10010000 00001010 10010000 00000111
01000001 10001110 10010101 11101001 11000110 11011100 10110111 01100111 10011111 00100010
00100110 10001000 00010000 00101001 10101101 00011110 00111111 10101101 01011000 11100001
01111001 11001111 00000110 10100010 01111001 00110001 11011011 11110001 10100011 10100001
00100001 11101001 11011110 10100011 10111000 10010011 11100100 00111001 11110100 10100110
01011100 01011100 00101100 00010000 10011001 01011100 11110000 00000101 01111001 11010111
10001100 01111100 01000101 01110111 01110101 00001001 10000110 11010000 10111101 10111100
01111100 11110101 11100000 10110101 01100100 11100100 10110110 00100101 11101011 10110001
11010000 01101001 01111010 10100000 11010100 00110101 10101101 01001110 11011110 00111001
00000011 10001011 01010110 00000011 10001111 01111010 11011101 01001110 00001110 00111101
00111011 11010111 10000000 11101001 01111010 10010101 11101110 10010011 10101000 01111101
10100110 11000110 01101111 00101110 01011100 00010000 11011001 00011001 00001100 00111011
11100110 10111101 01000011 11000010 11111110 00110010 10000011 01010110 00100010 11011110
11101110 00100100 10110110 10111001 00111100 10000011 10111011 11100100 01101111 01101010
11011111 10010001 00100101 10101000 00110100 11001110 11010001 01111001 11101011 01001110
00000111 00000110 10100011 01001100 10010001 11101001 11101101 01001111 00011100 10011100
01010100 11001101 01011011 01100010 00001001 01110011 11011110 10001100 01110011 01001110
01000000 00110010 00000101 00001100 01110001 01010011 01100101 01101101 01001011 10111101
10000000 10111111 00011000 00000110 10011010 10110010 11100011 10110111 00111111 01011010
01000011 10011100 01010011 00010100 01100110 10000100 10101100 01000000 11101011 10011011
11010001 00000101 10110100 10010010 10010101 00100100 00100000 00100111 10101101 01111001
10111110 10110111 11100011 00101011 11001011 11100000 11110000 01101001 11001101 11100101
01000101 11011110 01100000 00111001 00110101 11010010 01111000 11111110 01001001 01100010
11010000 01001010 11000010 01110000 11110010 11001000 10001001 10011111 01100011 11010110
10111001 11001011 00101111 00001101 10111011 01011010 10010110 01000001 10000010 01110001
10001100 11110111 10101100 10100101 01101101 11011001 11010001 01000110 10001011 10101000
11001110 01010011 00010010 00111011 00010010 11111001 00100100 11110101 00100100 11110011
01011010 01011010 01110110 10100001 01110111 10100111 10010000 01101101 01100101 10010001
00010000 10011111 10011001 01110011 11000001 10101110 10000111 11111110 00010001 00001011
10010110 01010000 11100000 00001111 01110001 10011010 10110000 11011110 00010111 01111000
01100010 11111001 11001010 00010011 11011000 01110101 10100111 00111010 11010100 11010010
10110010 00111010 00010101 00001001 00110111 01100011 01000111 11000011 10011010 11101111
11110110 10001100 01011011 01100100 00111011 00101110 00111111 10111011 11010111 10100101
01101100 00111001 11001111 11110000 11110011 11110101 10101111 00110111 10110110 10010110

01111101 00011111 01010111 11100000 11100001 11010100 11100001 10000111 10110101 01110110
10011111 11011010 01001000 00010111 11111101 01101000 00111100 01110101 11001101 00111111
01100111 11101101 00100010 10011010 00110011 10010100 10111101 10011011 11010101 10010111
10110111 01100110 10011000 01011001 01001010 01100111 10100000 00010101 10010100 11111010
10001010 11111001 10000111 11001011 10011110 00111100 10001110 10111100 11010011 01011111
01010010 11011100 00000001 11011100 10000111 11101001 01011100 11010101 00110000 10010010
01111010 10100100 01101001 00001100 01101101 00111110 10110010 00111100 11011111 11000100
00010011 11111001 10011010 11110101 11111001 00111101 10100100 11000101 00011010 01010101
11100100 10010110 10010111 10010001 01001000 00001110 00000110 01110000 01111001 11101101
01001111 11110001 01001100 00001100 00110101 10101001 00100100 01000001 10010001 00110111
11001110 00000000 11111101 01101010 10010011 11000011 11100101 10100111 10011000 01111110
11100111 01110001 11101010 01101011 10101101 01010011 10010111 00100101 10001100 10011101
01010101 00101001 01110011 01000101 10011110 10100101 01101111 10101000 01111101 10101110
00100100 10000100 00010001 10011001 00000111 00111001 00111101 01101010 11011100 00101100
00010100 00000001 00011000 00100011 00010101 11100101 11011010 01010110 10100111 00110101
10011100 11101000 11011001 11001010 00001110 11000110 10111011 10001011 01101101 01011110
11000110 01101111 10011011 11101101 00111000 00111000 11001110 11000011 11000101 01110000
01010110 11000011 10111010 01101100 11101111 10100001 01011001 00110101 10101001 10110011
01111001 10101000 10011011 01111000 11001000 01111001 00111110 11111111 00000000 10101101
01100100 01101001 10011010 11000111 11011001 10110101 01011000 10101100 01101110 10010100
01111001 01010111 01011111 00111100 01010010 01100111 10100001 11001111 01111010 00100011
10000100 11101011 10110111 01110001 00110100 01100000 10100101 10100100 01000011 10010010
01000111 01011010 11001011 11111000 10000100 10011111 01100111 10111011 10110000 10010010
00110001 11100101 10010101 00011100 00110000 11110110 10101011 11000011 11011010 10011011
01010111 11011101 10011001 11100010 00101100 11100010 11011010 00111011 11110101 11000000
11100000 10001010 00000001 00011001 11100010 10111000 01001101 00010011 11000110 00110010
00110000 01001000 10110101 01000101 00000100 11110100 00010010 10101111 00011000 11111010
11010111 01100101 01100001 01111001 01101111 01110111 00010000 01111011 01111001 01000011
10100001 11101111 11011110 10111101 00111001 01101000 01111001 10001001 11110100 00110110
01100001 10011010 00011000 11110100 11101011 10001111 00110011 10101001 10001100 11110101
00011101 01101011 01100010 11001100 00010001 01101001 00000111 01011100 10000101 01001111
11100101 01011100 10111101 11100001 11000101 10100011 10000001 11010011 00010101 11010101
11011010 10001100 01011011 01000110 00001001 00111111 11101010 11000111 01111111 01101010
11100100 10101101 10110001 10100100 00001001 10011011 00100000 11100111 10110101 01000111
10000010 01110011 11001101 00011000 11000000 11100100 11100100 11010011 10111010 01111111
10111100 01111111 01001010 11100100 11011000 10100001 01010000 10000001 01001000 11011001
00100000 10001111 01111010 01101111 01000011 10111011 10110101 00001011 11000010 01110011
11010100 11110101 10100100 11010000 00001110 11101100 00110010 01111001 10100110 10110111
01010001 11000111 00010100 00110110 01110110 10001110 01101001 11001100 01111000 00011110
10111110 10110100 01011000 00000101 01011110 00001001 00011101 10111101 11101001 10011000
11000000 00000010 10001100 11111100 11111101 00111000 11110101 10100001 10111000 01111100
01100110 10001011 00110000 00011100 01001110 00001110 00000000 11100000 01010011 00111010
10100110 00000111 00000111 10111111 10111101 00111111 10100101 00000011 11010011 11010100
11010010 10110110 10100000 00001010 00110011 11000111 01001010 01101111 10101110 11011111
10100101 00111001 00000110 00010000 10011110 00110011 11101111 01001100 01001111 10111011
10001111 01011110 01101010 10000000 01111010 11010011 01110011 11001001 11100011 11101001
01001000 11000011 00111100 11100111 00011110 10010100 10101011 10001100 11111011 00001010
01001110 11111101 00000110 00011001 00000001 00110011 10011110 01101000 01010111 11100000
01111010 01100111 10001010 01000110 00011100 10001010 01000101 01101100 10110001 00011101
11000101 01010010 10111010 00010000 10111001 00011001 01110010 01111011 01010011 00011100
11110010 00111000 10100111 10101111 00000000 11110001 11001001 10100100 01000011 10000001
11101111 01001011 01101101 00000000 00010100 01111100 10000011 10101101 00101110 00000110
11101110 10011100 11010010 00110001 00011100 10000001 11001101 00011111 00110110 01001001
00011101 01111010 11010010 00000000 01110011 11111001 11100110 10001111 10100001 11100011
00110100 00100000 11101011 10011110 01001001 11100100 11010011 01011111 00011000 00100101
11111011 01010001 01100101 11010100 01100001 10011100 11010001 10111011 11100110 11001110
01111010 11110110 10100011 11111000 01110010 00000110 00101001 00111010 10101111 10111101
00111001 00101101 00101110 00000010 11100111 00000111 00111000 11001001 10100011 10001101
11000100 10110111 00110100 00011110 00110001 11111100 11101001 00011101 00001111 11100001
11101001 01001011 10101000 00000011 10110111 00111100 00011110 01101000 01010011 11000110
01111101 00101000 00000011 10001100 11110101 10100011 11111000 00110000 01111011 10011100
10011010 10110100 11101100 10110110 00000001 10000000 10010110 01100111 00100000 01100000
11110100 00111001 10100111 01110110 00111100 01100111 00011101 10101001 01001001 11100011
10011010 00110111 01110010 00001000 11101001 11011100 10011010 10001011 00110111 10101000
11101110 00110011 00000100 10000001 10011110 10110100 11111110 00110011 11001000 10100011
10100001 10100100 01000110 00000100 10011100 00001110 10110101 00101110 11110111 00010000
11010010 01001011 01100000 10001110 10011001 11000101 00001100 00111001 11101011 11000101
00001011 10000010 11011000 11101100 00001101 00001101 11101010 01000110 00000111 10100101
01010011 00000001 11011001 00011000 00000110 10011010 00001110 01001110 00110001 11000111
01101010 00000111 00000000 01111010 11100111 10100101 00011100 11010010 00000001 00001111
00100111 10001110 10011110 10111110 10110100 00101111 00100011 00011001 10100011 11111000
11101001 01011011 10101101 00111011 00111011 00000000 11011100 01100011 00100111 10101110
00000110 01101001 01110001 10011100 01110011 10001010 00011011 11010000 01111010 01110011

01000111 01011100 01010001 01100001 10100001 00111100 11001100 00011100 01100010 10010101
11000001 11000110 00010100 11010011 00011100 00000000 01110010 00111000 11001101 00111011
00100100 11110101 00111111 10100101 00010111 10110110 10100001 01100001 10101011 11110111
10111001 11100100 11110101 10100100 11001111 10011001 00100110 00110110 11100011 00011110
10111101 11101001 01011011 10000011 10011110 11110100 11101111 10111010 00111101 00111111
10011101 00111001 01011001 10001000 01100100 10000101 10001000 11110100 00100100 11010000
11100100 00110100 10111001 00000100 00011100 00001100 01110100 10100101 11001000 11011001
10011010 00110010 00011001 00110010 00111011 01010010 00010000 11010110 00011011 10001010
00010010 01110010 00000111 01001100 01110110 10100010 01000110 00011001 00101010 00000111
01111100 01010000 11011101 10000000 00011111 10001101 00101110 11011100 11100000 00000001
10011100 11010001 11100100 00110001 00001001 11001001 11000001 11100011 10001010 00110011
10110101 01111000 11101010 01000111 11100101 01001101 01100110 11011010 11000100 00001110
10111101 11111101 10101001 11001100 01110010 11100011 11011110 10011101 11101100 10110100
00000001 10101100 11011001 10010011 11011000 00001100 11010011 10010100 01110101 00100100
11100100 10010011 10011010 01101011 01100100 11110100 11101000 00101001 11011000 00000011
00111111 01001110 00101010 01010111 10011000 11110110 00011010 01000000 00111000 00111001
11000110 00101001 10111001 00100101 10001000 00011111 01110000 00011100 01100111 11010110
10011101 10010000 00010111 11111010 01010010 00011100 00001110 00010110 10101001 01011001
10001000 01010110 11000000 01010011 11001101 00100000 11100000 01110100 11000101 00000111
00000100 10011111 01000001 11010010 10010011 00111001 11100011 10110101 00001011 01110000
00001111 11100010 11101011 01001010 11011000 11011010 00111111 01011010 00111010 01110011
10001100 10011010 00001010 01110000 00110111 00010000 01101000 11011100 00000100 11100100
11100101 10001111 01010010 01111000 00011110 11010100 00101111 00100011 11110001 10100011
10011111 00101100 11111010 10011111 11010010 10000001 11111101 11010001 11001001 00010100
01101011 11010000 00000001 10001111 11011111 11100011 00000011 10110111 10101101 00110001
01111001 00001000 01001111 01011100 01111010 11010010 10010001 10001110 01011111 10011111
01101010 01000110 11001110 00110011 11010000 00001010 01101011 01011101 00000000 00111011
00010001 11101011 01000010 10000000 00010000 00001100 11110100 11101011 01001011 11010100
11100001 01111000 10100100 00111000 11001111 11001101 11010010 10010011 01011101 00000000
01001010 00001000 00100111 10000101 10100000 00001110 00110010 01111011 01110100 00010100
11010010 11000111 10100000 00011100 10011110 10011110 11010100 01101010 10000000 00010111
00000000 01100010 10010001 11111000 00100011 00000011 00000011 10110101 00101111 01010010
01000000 11100111 10110110 01101001 00111010 10010011 11101000 00101011 01000111 01100001
00000011 10010001 10010000 01000111 11111111 00000000 10101110 10010011 10011100 01111110
00011100 11010000 10100011 11010111 10001010 00001111 01100000 00001111 01111010 10000110
10110101 00011000 00010001 11110011 10000001 10011111 11111110 10110101 00110111 11011000
01100111 00010100 11100010 01000111 11001000 01110001 11010000 11100111 00110100 00010010
00000011 11100001 10111011 00011110 01101000 11011011 01110000 00011010 10111001 00100100
11110001 10010010 00101001 10101111 11001110 01000110 00110010 01101001 11000100 11100001
01111000 11101010 01101001 10100011 00111011 11000111 10111101 00100000 00010100 00010010
00110110 01110000 00000000 01001111 01001110 11110100 10001011 11111011 10110011 10010101
11001001 11001101 00111011 01101111 00111101 01111000 10100110 10000001 10010011 10011100
01100000 00010011 11000101 00001110 00110110 00000000 00000011 00101001 11001111 11101001
01001101 00001010 00110011 10001111 01000001 01000011 01110011 11110100 10100111 00101001
00011011 10001000 00011001 11001101 01011010 11011000 00000110 00110000 00011011 10001000
11000001 11000110 00110011 10011010 01010111 00011001 00000111 00111101 11111010 11010011
10010000 01110010 01001111 01011010 01100111 11110001 01110101 10101100 11010010 11010100
00000001 10111000 11000000 11101001 11101111 01001100 00100111 00001010 00010100 01111010
11010011 11111000 11100100 11111111 00000000 10010001 01000000 00011001 00100000 10011110
10110101 01011100 10101100 01111010 00001001 00101010 10000010 10111000 00110101 00001111
01100010 11000110 10100111 11111110 00100011 01010001 11001010 00001110 11001100 00011111
11010010 10001101 11000100 00100010 01110011 10001010 01110000 00111001 00100111 11010000
01110111 10100110 11100011 10000000 00000111 00010101 00100000 00000011 00000000 10110001
11100110 10100101 00100111 11010100 01101100 01101110 01111010 11111010 11010010 00110001
00111001 11100011 10001010 01011100 10001100 11100000 00001110 01101001 11000111 11101111
10010001 01001111 10010110 11100100 10010001 10011100 01111001 01011101 00111010 11010000
11000111 11100111 11000000 11100011 10001010 01110011 01110101 11101100 01111000 11001110
00101001 00011100 10011100 11111011 11111010 11010011 10110000 11000110 00110110 01110001
11111000 11010011 10111010 11000110 00101000 01010011 11101000 00111111 00111010 01011100
11101101 11000111 11110011 10100010 11010110 01000000 00110011 00000011 00111101 00111001
10100001 10000001 00111100 10011110 01001101 00011000 11111001 11001110 00001001 11110111
10100111 00011100 11100110 10100110 11101111 01100000 00011011 11010111 10011010 01001101
11011011 10010011 11010000 11100111 10100000 10100101 01101111 01101110 00101001 00011100
11100000 10001110 00000001 00110100 01011010 11101011 01100000 00011111 10000011 11000001
00000011 10110101 00110101 01001111 01101100 00011010 01001110 10111000 00101110 01110011
10001111 01101010 01000101 00000100 10011110 00111111 00011010 01101110 00111101 01000111
01110000 00111101 11101001 10101100 01001110 00111000 10101001 00011011 11101111 00000000
01111111 00011010 10001101 10111000 00000100 00000001 01010110 11010111 01100010 01001000
11110001 11001110 01110011 11101100 01000101 00100110 00001000 00011101 01101001 01110000
01000111 00011101 10101001 00001110 01001111 01001010 10001000 11101110 00110001 00000111
00100100 00001111 01001110 11110101 00101010 10011110 11000101 10001110 00000001 11101001
01010001 00001100 11101110 00000011 11010110 10011101 11000000 10010000 10000011 11111000
11010000 11011011 00010001 00111010 00110000 11000111 01011100 10011010 00110111 11100101

01111000 10101000 10010000 10110001 00111001 11001110 00000111 01100001 01010010 11100100
01101110 00100100 11100000 00000001 11101001 01001010 11111101 00000110 00110001 11111111
00000000 11010110 00001111 01111010 00000001 00110100 11100110 11000001 00111101 11101001
10101100 11100111 00111100 11100010 10001011 10101000 11101000 11000000 11100000 01110101
10000110 10010110 11110010 11101010 01001001 11101110 00000111 11101111 11100100 11111011
11000011 00011000 11000000 10101100 00011001 00100010 01100000 11100100 01100011 10001100
11110111 10101101 00101011 10011101 01001101 10100111 10111000 10010110 01010111 00011100
10111011 01100111 00000011 10110110 01101010 10011011 11001100 01100101 01111100 00101010
11100100 10011010 11110100 10010011 00110001 10001001 00000010 10010010 00110000 01001000
00110101 00111010 00110001 00110001 11110010 00111011 11100100 11010000 11111101 10110011
11010111 11110101 10101010 10000101 10111111 01111000 01001001 11101101 11011100 11110011
01011010 10101111 01111011 10101001 01111011 00011011 01111010 01000101 11011100 00110110
11110111 11101001 00100101 11011110 11111111 00000000 10110011 10010001 10000110 11011001
01011101 00110010 11101011 00011010 00010001 00000011 11100111 10111001 10001100 01111010
10011000 11101011 10000101 10110101 10111011 01011000 00101110 11100000 01100111 00011001
00001001 00100000 11011101 10010001 10010001 10001010 11110100 10010011 01100111 01100101
00101000 11100110 11010010 00011110 01000000 00111111 01110110 10110010 11100100 10001100
11110111 00110101 10001101 01101010 10010000 10001111 10111010 11101100 10001100 10111101
01001110 11110011 01001100 10011010 11011001 00100010 11010011 10101111 00111100 11001001
00011110 01010100 00100100 00011110 00001000 00010101 11010010 11001010 11001010 10010001
00011001 00110011 11011011 01111111 01011010 11001011 11111110 11001011 11010011 11110111
01100111 11101100 01110001 00100001 00011100 11100100 01010101 11110111 01010001 00101100
01100100 00000001 10000001 10001100 00011100 00001110 11010100 11100011 00010101 00000101
01100011 00101010 10010101 00011101 01001101 01011011 00111100 11000011 11101101 00000011
11101101 00001110 11000100 11100111 00101100 01011100 01100000 01111010 10011010 11110100
11101101 00101010 11110110 00111001 01101101 00100011 00111011 11110011 11000000 00011001
11000101 01111001 01101001 10110111 10010010 00011101 01011010 01001011 00111001 10010100
01000111 11111011 11001100 01110011 11011000 01110110 10101110 10100011 01001110 10111011
10011011 01000101 10010100 01000101 01110110 01001111 11011001 11001111 01000110 10101110
01111100 01000101 11011100 01101100 10001110 10011100 00110011 11010011 11001000 11101011
10010001 10111110 01111100 00100100 10110001 11100011 00111001 11000101 00110111 01011000
10111000 01010001 01100111 00101111 11001101 10001100 10101001 11000001 10101100 11110111
11010100 01110100 10110001 00011001 10011000 01011101 01000011 10000011 11001001 00011001
10101110 01011011 01011101 11010111 10111110 11010100 00100100 10000110 11010111 00111011
00111010 01101110 11001101 01111001 11010000 10100100 11011100 10001110 10001010 10010011
01010110 11010000 01011101 00001100 00110100 10011010 10010101 10110010 11111010 11001001
11001111 10110101 01111010 01010010 01001000 00000000 11000110 01101011 11001111 00111100
00010011 00001011 01001011 01110110 01100111 00101011 10011000 11010011 00111100 10011111
01011010 11101110 01111001 11110101 10101111 01101010 11001010 11001001 01011100 11110011
10100110 01011100 01100110 00100111 10111111 00010100 10001100 00001001 11100011 10101101
01000000 10010010 00000000 00111001 00111100 01010101 00101101 01011011 01010000 00110110
11111010 01110101 11001100 11001011 10011101 11100001 01001000 00011000 10100100 11110100
01000100 10011100 11010111 10001011 11110101 10010001 00111001 01111011 00101000 00001001
00010001 10100001 11000100 10000111 11010100 11111010 01010111 00001001 10101011 11001100
01111100 10110000 10111101 10001001 11110101 11101001 01011101 00001100 00011010 01110101
11011101 11010101 10100100 10010111 00111110 01011011 10111010 00010011 11001001 00111100
11100100 11010111 00100111 10101011 01101110 01011001 10011101 01001111 00001110 00111000
11000001 11101010 00101011 00101010 01101111 11011110 10110011 00101111 11011001 11001010
00101010 11101100 11000111 10111001 00100110 00111011 10000000 00110010 01110001 11010111
11101011 01010110 00101101 01100100 00100110 01000000 01000011 00010100 11001001 11001110
01000111 01101010 01001101 01001010 00110110 11111011 01000010 00100110 11010111 00101111
10000000 00111101 01111010 11010101 11011011 00101101 00011011 01010000 01100000 00110001
01100101 01110000 00000111 10101001 01011100 00001010 11101001 01111010 01101010 11011001
01110001 10100110 11011110 11001000 11110101 00101111 00000001 01101011 01100110 11111010
11010011 11101100 01010111 01110011 01101111 10111001 10001011 11101110 10011100 01110010
11101001 01011101 10000010 11110101 11100010 10111100 01010111 01001101 10011010 01111101
00100010 11111110 00001001 01000110 11110100 10010010 00110110 00000101 10000000 11110100
11101111 01011110 11000101 00001100 11011110 01110010 10100100 10101001 11110111 00011000
01100100 01100110 10000110 11101111 00011011 10011001 01010100 10000101 10011001 01111011
01110000 01010001 01010001 00110011 01100000 11110001 01010001 00110001 11100111 10001010
00011000 01110100 10101000 10111110 10010110 01100110 01101100 10010000 10010001 11011110
10011010 11010010 00000001 11000111 01011010 10001111 01110001 11101000 00101010 00110111
01100000 00001001 10100100 11011010 01001000 01001011 01010011 00001111 11000111 11101100
11011111 11011000 01101001 00100000 00100100 00000100 10010101 00001001 11100011 10101101
01101001 11101000 00100101 01100101 10110001 10000001 10000111 00111111 00101000 10101110
01111011 11000100 00010111 00010001 01101010 11010110 10010010 00001011 01011001 10001011
10011011 01101001 01000000 10010001 01000001 11100000 11100111 10110001 10101101 00011011
00001011 10111011 11001011 00100001 00011100 00111111 11011001 11010010 10111100 01101010
00111010 10101101 01110000 11010110 01111110 11010001 01111011 10111011 10011110 10001110
00011001 01110010 00100110 11001110 10101101 00110000 10100011 00011000 10101010 10110111
10100000 00010000 01111011 01010100 01010110 11010111 11000010 11100010 00010111 10010000
01000111 00100100 01100110 00110011 10000110 10001101 10000111 00100010 10110010 10011111
01011100 10111001 10010010 01010011 00010111 11110110 01010101 11001000 00011111 11011110

01101010 11100010 01110001 01110011 11010000 11011001 00111101 01101110 01110001 10011110
00100000 00001010 11011110 00100010 01110001 10110100 10000011 11000110 01001111 10101101
01101100 11001101 01100101 10100110 10011100 11100010 11110011 01100110 01000111 00100000
10001100 01100010 10100110 10010110 11001000 01001011 11100010 01001000 00011010 01001000
10110110 00000010 10100101 11001110 01000111 01010010 00101011 10100000 01111000 11000011
00001111 10011100 00000011 11110101 00010101 11101000 01010001 11111110 00011010 10000010
01111010 10011100 11110101 11110100 11010101 10011100 01000100 10111010 00110101 10000011
01001001 11111011 10011101 01011010 11011111 00011111 01010001 10011010 10101001 01110111
10100000 10000000 10111001 10001111 01010011 10001000 11100100 11110101 01010011 11111111
00000000 11010111 10101110 11011110 11101010 00101011 01101000 01101101 11100101 10010001
11100001 10001011 00000001 01001001 00111111 00101000 10101111 00100100 10111101 10010100
11011100 01011101 00111100 11100001 01111100 10110010 11100111 00101010 00000000 11111011
10010101 11010111 00011000 01001101 11011001 01011111 01100011 10010001 11001010 00110110
11011000 10111101 01110111 00101101 10110101 10010001 11000010 00001111 10110100 01011110
00010001 10000011 00101001 11100111 01101000 11110110 10101100 11011101 01000110 01010001
00110100 10101000 01100011 01011101 10000000 00001111 11001110 10101110 01101001 10111010
01100100 11010111 11000001 11100100 10000001 01110111 11100000 11100001 10111001 11101001
01010110 10100101 11110000 11101101 11110010 11000100 11101110 01010011 00100111 10000000
00000000 11101010 01101011 10100011 10010110 01001001 01101010 11001000 01000100 00111110
00011011 11010011 00010011 01010010 10111101 11111011 00110011 10110001 01001100 11110010
00011010 10111011 00111011 00111111 00001000 01000011 00000100 10000010 01001001 11100101
11110011 01000111 10100110 00110001 01011100 01010101 10101011 01011110 01101001 10111010
10001100 01110010 01111001 00110010 11100110 00100011 10010010 00110001 11011010 10111101
00101011 01001001 11010110 00101101 11110101 00111000 00001011 01000000 11000000 10111110
00000110 11101000 11001111 01010100 10101110 01101100 01000100 01100111 11001011 01111000
00011101 00110100 01101010 11000101 01101110 10001101 00101011 00111000 01100010 10110111
10000111 01101100 00101010 00000000 00011111 10100101 01111001 11011111 11000100 10111001
11000001 11010100 00101101 10100001 00001100 10011001 01000101 11011110 01111101 10110011
01011101 01110110 10110111 10101011 01000101 10100101 11011000 10011001 10100110 00111001
00111111 11000011 00011000 11101110 01101011 11001101 11101111 11010110 11110111 01011001
10111011 10010010 11110111 11101100 11101110 01110111 10011110 11000011 00100000 00001110
11000010 10111001 10101001 01100001 11100111 11001101 11001100 11001101 00101010 11100010
00010100 11010101 10010000 11101101 00000110 11110110 11001110 00011000 00101110 00100000
11010100 01010100 10011000 11100100 00100000 10000110 00011101 01000111 10101101 01011101
10110110 10111010 10110110 10110011 10111001 00110011 11101001 01010111 11011000 11001000
00000101 10100010 10010000 11110101 00010101 10010001 00100110 10011111 01110011 00011111
00011111 01100110 10010111 10101111 00100100 10101101 01010101 01001000 10001000 00100100
11101101 00100000 01110100 00100111 00010101 11101010 11111011 00110111 01111101 11001110
00101001 00101110 11100111 10101001 01011000 01101011 10010000 11101010 00110110 11101110
10010110 11110010 01100100 10000011 10000110 00001101 11011010 10111101 00110010 00101000
11001000 10001001 00000001 00111000 11000010 10000001 11111010 01010111 11001111 01111110
00011000 11001000 11010101 11101101 00010000 00010111 11111001 10100101 01000001 10001100
11111011 11010111 11010000 11010010 11100100 01110111 00100111 10011010 11100010 11000101
10101011 00101101 01001101 01100001 10110000 00101110 00000000 11001111 11100100 01001101
00001010 00110001 10010011 10001110 00101000 00111100 11000110 00111000 10100011 10111110
00111011 01010111 10011100 01010000 00000000 01011000 10011111 10011011 10001010 01100000
11100110 01000111 11101110 00110001 11000001 10100101 11100111 00010100 00101011 01100011
00000011 00011001 00111101 11101001 11101001 11010100 00000111 01100011 11100100 11110110
00000110 10001111 11111001 01101000 00111111 10111001 01001101 01100110 11000000 11100100
10011100 11110100 00000010 10001100 01101101 00011000 11110100 11101011 01001011 01000110
00000000 11111111 00000000 01111011 11011011 10110110 00101000 01010101 00011011 10110010
00001110 01111110 10110100 00111001 11000000 11001110 00101001 00001011 11110000 01001110
11011111 10100101 00010111 11010110 11001100 01110110 00011111 11000110 01110010 00111010
01010011 01010100 10010010 01110001 11101111 11000101 00100010 10001110 00110010 01111111
00101010 01010101 11101000 01001000 10101010 11110100 00010000 11100011 10000010 01111110
01101110 01000000 11110110 10100110 00110000 11000111 00111001 11000000 11101111 01000111
01100010 00001001 11001111 10111101 00001111 11011000 01110111 00111100 11010100 11011111
10111000 00001011 11010111 00010100 00111000 00111101 00110000 00000000 10100011 00111000
01100010 01111111 00101010 01000011 11110111 11011101 10111111 10001111 10100101 00010110
10110011 00000001 01001110 00001110 00000000 11111100 01101001 00001001 11111001 11001111
10100111 01101010 00010011 00011111 11100011 01001100 11000110 01011011 01110001 00110101
01010111 01110110 00011000 11101100 10011100 11100111 10011010 00110001 10000011 01000110
01111110 01111100 01100100 11110011 01000010 10001100 00111001 11001111 01001010 01001001
10110100 00001000 00111000 00100111 11011010 10011011 10011100 00011110 00001111 01011110
10100110 10011111 11000000 00011001 01011100 11110101 10100110 00101001 11000000 00111000
11100100 11110111 00010100 10110101 01000010 00011100 11011001 00000000 10000001 11101001
01000001 11100111 10001110 00111101 11101001 10101101 11010000 01100011 10101110 01101001
11111001 11000111 10100110 01001101 00010110 11101000 01010111 10100000 11001100 00001110
10000111 00111000 00110100 00110001 00011110 01101110 11010000 00001111 00000011 10010011
01000111 01010110 11111010 01010000 11000100 11100100 10011110 11011000 10100111 10110001
00100001 11101000 01001101 00001110 00001001 00000011 11011110 10001110 11001000 01001111
00011001 10100100 11000001 11101110 01111010 11111010 00001010 01010110 01101000 01100000
10111111 00101111 00000011 10010001 11011100 11010010 01111111 00000001 11000101 00101011

00010000 00000000 11001001 11000101 00100000 00100000 11111011 00001110 11000011 11010110
10000100 11011000 00000011 01110000 00000111 01110001 11011100 11010000 11011101 00000000
00011101 00110011 01001101 11001111 11001100 01001001 00011001 00010100 11100110 11110101
00111101 00001101 00111101 00101111 01110001 00001101 00111001 00100111 10010110 11001111
11010010 10011100 01111000 10001111 00111101 00101000 01011100 00110110 01111101 10000101
00110101 10001000 11011100 00010100 10000011 01010010 10011101 10011000 11000001 01111000
11101001 11010100 11111010 11010000 10000100 10011110 01001111 10101110 00101001 00011100
01100100 00000001 11101111 10011010 01010111 11100000 01100111 00011110 11110100 01011110
11111010 10000000 01110011 10011110 01111010 10011010 00111001 11001001 00111000 11000000
11000111 01010011 01001001 10000000 01001000 00100100 11111110 00010100 01001011 10010011
11000000 11101100 01111101 01111010 01010010 01110111 00000001 01111010 11111100 10100011
10101111 01110010 01101000 01010001 10001110 01111010 11111101 01101001 00011011 00011111
10001001 10100000 10010000 01110001 11001111 00000011 11010010 10101010 11110111 00000000
11100100 00110011 10110111 01001010 00111010 01110011 01001000 00111010 11110011 11010100
10011010 00111000 11011001 11010111 10001100 11110101 10100001 11111001 00000000 00011100
00011100 01110001 01000010 01110100 11100000 01010010 11100011 11100101 11000110 01111111
00111010 01000000 01110011 11010011 10100101 00110001 11011100 00110000 01110011 11010011
00111001 10100000 11110101 00100100 11010000 11100100 10110010 11100100 00011111 10101101
00110001 10000001 00001000 10000000 01110001 10000011 10010011 01001001 01111001 00001000
00010101 10110001 00101001 00000000 01110100 00010100 00011100 10000011 11001000 11101011
11000111 01011010 00111000 00110010 00001110 10111001 00110100 10111100 10110001 11011101
10000011 11000111 00000010 10011110 10000000 00100011 01100011 00100011 11011010 10001100
11110010 01001110 00111010 01110001 01000010 10000011 11100110 00001100 10010011 11101011
01000010 11100000 11001000 01110010 01111001 00011100 10011100 01010010 01010110 01001111
01000000 00011000 10010001 10001000 10001001 00101101 11001011 10111001 11001001 00110100
11100110 00111100 11110010 01110000 01001111 00111100 11110110 10100000 00001100 10001100
10001110 10110100 11010101 01011110 01001001 11101011 01000011 01011101 11000110 00111001
10011000 00101010 00000000 00111010 01110111 00010100 11010111 11100001 01111110 10111101
01101001 11000100 10010010 00001111 00111100 11111101 00101000 01010000 00000010 11100011
10111111 00100111 11101001 10011010 00011110 11000001 01101101 01000110 11110110 00100000
11110000 01110001 11000111 10110101 00100001 11101010 00110110 01100111 10100111 01011010
01010001 11101000 01111010 10011010 01000100 11100101 00001110 00101001 11101011 01100001
00000110 11100001 10110011 00100011 11111111 00000000 11010111 01000010 11110000 01101000
11111110 00011110 11111100 01110110 00010100 00101111 11001011 11001011 11110010 01001111
11100101 01001101 00101101 00000000 01000001 10111000 10010011 11101001 10011110 00101001
01000001 00000100 00011110 01101000 11101101 10001111 11001110 10001100 10101000 00111000
00000011 10001010 10011011 00101101 11011000 00001000 01001001 00010001 10010010 00111001
01111100 11111110 01010100 11010011 10000000 00000000 00011110 10111100 10011010 01110110
00000001 11000111 01100000 00101001 10101011 01000011 11101110 10000000 01110011 01111010
10011111 11001010 10011011 10011111 10011011 01101111 01101110 10110100 11100100 00100011
01100011 11100100 01110100 00011001 10100110 10100001 11000010 11100111 00011000 10100001
00000000 10000111 00111001 00111100 11110101 11101111 01001001 11011100 10010011 11010010
10011100 01010011 00100101 00000001 10100100 01110011 10010010 00000000 11001111 10111101
00111011 11101001 01100001 10100001 00001011 01100101 11110000 00111010 01010001 10000001
10011110 10111111 10000101 00101011 00000000 00001000 01010001 11111000 11111011 01010100
01100100 01111100 11100111 00100110 10011011 01111010 01011000 01000011 11110010 00000010
10011110 01111011 11110101 00010100 11011100 00000000 00110110 10001110 10100011 10101001
10100010 01010011 10000001 11000000 10100000 11100100 00010100 11011010 00001110 01001101
00100101 01111110 10000000 00100010 01110011 10011110 11111001 00110101 00011100 10001101
10110111 11100101 01000001 10010011 11010011 00110101 00100010 11110001 11101101 01000000
11001110 01111000 11100000 01110110 11110111 10100101 11101010 00000001 11000000 00000000
01110101 00110100 11000000 00000001 00011001 00111100 11111010 11111011 11010011 10011011
00100100 11110000 01110001 11101011 10001010 01101011 10111110 00001111 00011100 01010011
11011000 00000100 11001000 00101100 00001001 11110100 10100100 01101001 00000000 00011101
00111001 00111101 00111101 11101001 01011011 10000101 00100011 00011001 00110100 00101011
00000011 10000110 11101010 00000101 00011010 11110101 00010000 10111000 00111001 11100110
10011010 10100100 10110000 11100111 00100001 00111011 01111011 11010010 10110110 01110110
00010010 00110001 01001000 10100011 11110111 10000100 11100111 00111000 10100000 01100000
11100000 10001110 10111101 00101001 01000110 00110011 01001001 00100001 00100100 01110101
10100110 10101001 00110100 00101011 01110100 00000001 11011000 11011010 00110001 11101011
11010100 11010011 00111101 01000111 10100101 00101011 11110101 11000010 01110101 00110100
00000101 11001000 00100011 11110011 10100100 00000011 01000000 11101011 10011110 00000111
01110011 01001011 10011100 10111001 01100001 11101001 11000101 00011101 00000111 11100011
11001101 00011001 00000000 01110100 10100010 11001101 00001111 01000001 10011000 00100101
10000111 11010010 10011100 01001000 01101100 11111011 01110111 10100011 00111111 00111110
01000111 01000011 11011110 10001110 11011001 00010100 11010101 11000100 00110000 00101110
00100100 00100111 00111111 10000101 00111111 00111001 11001101 00110101 01000110 11011000
11110001 11011100 11110011 10011010 00011100 01110100 00011111 10001001 10100110 11011110
10011010 10000000 11100100 11100000 11100101 10110000 01101001 10000011 00100100 01100100
11110101 11001101 00001110 00001110 01000001 11000110 00101000 11000110 00000111 00011110
10110100 01101110 00111101 01000011 00011011 01010011 10001110 10111001 11001101 00001010
10100011 00000011 10101110 01111111 10011101 00101011 00001110 01110001 11011111 10101000
10100100 11001110 01111011 11010101 01101100 10000110 10000100 00111100 10000011 11101001

01001101 00111101 01000001 11101101 11011010 10011100 01111001 11100111 11010010 10011011
10111010 10100110 11100010 01101000 01110011 01110000 00111000 00011100 11111011 01010011
01110001 11011110 10011100 00111000 00011101 01101001 10011011 10110010 00111101 00111101
11101010 10011010 01011011 00001000 01010111 11101011 10010010 00101001 10111101 01111001
10100101 01101110 11000000 11110011 01001000 01111011 11110110 10101001 01010111 01000010
00000110 11001111 00000011 11110011 10100101 11100001 01111001 00000110 10010001 01111010
01100111 10011010 00011011 00111011 00111010 01110011 01001101 01011101 10001100 01011100
11100100 00011010 01001100 00011100 10011010 01010010 00110110 00001111 01110011 01001000
11111110 11100100 11100010 10100101 00101110 10100000 01000110 11011101 00110001 10001100
10011110 10111001 00110100 11011101 11011000 00100100 01100000 11111010 11111101 01101010
01001110 00111010 11010011 01011011 10101111 00011101 01111101 11101000 11110010 01000000
00110000 01110000 11111001 10100101 11001110 01001110 01101001 00010111 10101001 10100001
01001001 11000110 00110001 11010011 10100110 01101010 10010101 10000000 01010100 00111000
00111000 11100100 11010011 10000001 11001110 01011000 00001110 00000001 11100111 11011110
10011000 11000111 10101001 11110101 10100101 01010010 01111000 01011010 10010110 10101111
10101010 00000010 01111000 10111010 10011100 01110011 11110101 10101000 10100011 01100110
11011011 11110011 00101000 11001101 00101110 11100011 10010000 00101001 00110111 10000101
11100000 00110000 10100001 10100000 00111100 01100110 11010110 11100111 00100011 00001110
00110001 11001111 00100100 01010101 11101000 01100101 00100001 11111000 11100111 00111101
11101011 00001101 00011000 10101001 11000010 00001110 00001111 11100011 01011010 00110110
11010010 00010011 10001110 00111111 01011010 11101111 11100101 01111111 00100010 01010001
01110100 11100001 10000001 00111100 11100010 10100011 01100101 11000110 01110000 00000111
00111101 10110001 01011010 11011010 00001110 10011110 00101110 11100100 11100100 10000010
00000001 11111001 10000001 00111101 01101011 10100001 01111111 00001101 11011010 00001000
11111100 11001101 11001100 00111110 10010100 10111101 10110100 01100000 11010111 00110001
10101010 10100010 11100110 10101110 10001110 00001011 11001011 11011011 11111001 01110011
11101111 01011110 10001011 01100111 10101010 01011010 01000101 10100010 01011011 01011100
11011101 11001100 00010000 00010101 11000110 00000111 01010010 01000111 00010101 11001010
01101011 00111010 01111100 00110110 10000011 11100100 10011000 11100011 00011100 00000010
00111001 10101100 10111110 10101000 00000110 11110010 01000111 10100110 01110011 10001010
10111111 01101010 10101010 00100110 10100000 01000100 10010111 00101110 10001100 11011111
11010101 00111100 01011001 01110010 01001110 00101100 01100000 10001110 00110001 11011010
01000011 11001111 11101001 01011000 01110010 11101011 00011010 10110100 11011001 00110010
01011111 01001101 10000010 01110010 00000000 11100000 00001010 10000010 01001100 10000000
01111101 00000111 00110100 11100000 11011011 01000110 00001000 11001000 11101111 01010011
00100100 11101111 11101111 00011001 10100100 10000111 00110101 11011001 10010111 01111100
10010111 01011011 10011110 11100011 11111110 01111010 10010011 11101001 01011101 01111110
10001101 11100010 00111011 00101001 10101100 10001100 00111010 10101000 01001111 00110110
00100101 11001110 00001010 11100111 11001100 00011111 11100011 01011100 01011100 10100101
01011000 10000001 10000011 11101011 10001010 01001111 00101111 00100111 00100000 11100111
00011101 01101010 01100111 01001111 10011111 01000011 01100101 01010101 10100101 01100100
01101100 01011110 11101010 01110110 00110010 11001000 11101011 01100011 10100111 01000100
10000011 00111001 00010010 00011100 10001111 11010010 10110001 11011000 10011101 11000101
10001111 01011010 01100011 10110000 11011111 11101111 01001001 10000110 11001110 01111101
01101010 00101001 11000011 10010011 11011101 00100101 10110110 11001110 10100111 11000011
01111110 00101000 10001011 01001101 10000001 00101101 01101110 10101101 00001110 11001100
11110011 00110100 01000111 00100111 11110001 00011101 11101011 10110111 10110001 10111101
10110111 10111110 10110110 00010011 01011001 01001100 00100101 10001111 10100110 01000111
01010001 11110101 00011101 10101011 11001000 00110110 10011101 10111001 11001001 11001000
11101011 01010110 00110100 11011011 10101001 11101100 10101110 10010010 11100110 11010110
01011111 00101010 01000001 11111111 00000000 10001111 10001111 01000011 01011101 00001101
00110101 10111001 10011101 10001111 01011111 00001000 01111010 01010101 00111101 01101110
11010011 11001111 11010010 00101110 11100010 01101110 11110001 11100111 00111110 11110100
11101101 00001011 01010011 10001011 01010110 10110001 11110011 10010000 01101100 10010100
01111111 10101100 10001111 00111111 01110000 11111111 00000000 10000101 01011000 10111100
01010011 00110101 10100100 10101000 10011000 00110010 00010101 11100000 01111010 11010001
01010011 11011101 01000001 00010101 10101101 10001100 11011111 00000110 00010001 11111101
10010111 00011010 11110100 11000001 00100001 10000111 10101101 01011101 10111111 11110000
11011110 10010101 01111011 01110100 00101110 00100110 10110011 10001101 11100101 00011111
11000111 11101011 01011000 11111110 00010111 10011101 01101100 11000000 10001110 11101110
01010100 01011100 10001110 01110011 11101011 01011101 10000100 01000100 01001101 10000110
10000101 10000011 10100111 10101000 00111001 00010101 11100011 11010101 10101010 11100001
00111011 10100011 11010101 10110101 10010010 01000111 00110101 00110111 10000110 11110100
10100001 01110001 11100110 11000111 01100101 00010000 10010000 00011100 10000010 01000101
01011100 01110001 11000110 11010001 11000000 11110100 10101011 10010111 10000000 10101100
10111100 11110100 11101010 00001110 01111010 01010110 01100100 11010111 00010001 01100100
10000100 10010001 00001011 11111101 01101011 00110111 01010110 01010011 01011010 10110001
00100011 10000100 11110001 00101011 01000000 10111010 11001001 10001010 00110100 11001100
10001100 01000111 01111100 01010111 10100101 01011010 11000110 01100011 10000110 00100101
11001110 01110000 10100011 10010011 11110100 10101110 00100010 01111101 00110010 00111011
10001111 00010100 01000101 00111001 00100111 10001000 11110111 11110000 00111011 10001010
11101100 00101100 11100110 10001000 11111110 11100100 11001111 00011011 11001110 10011111
01111000 01101110 11100110 10111101 00111010 00110101 00010010 10000010 10001111 01010011

10010011 00010001 01001101 10100101 01110010 11100011 01110001 11010000 11110100 10100100
11110011 00110000 00111010 01110101 10100101 01100101 00111101 00000001 11101001 11101011
01001100 11011000 01101011 01010111 00101011 00011100 01011110 10100000 11010010 01110001
11001101 01010010 11010100 10100100 00101011 10100111 11011100 10110010 01110000 01010010
00100110 00100011 00111111 01001010 11000000 11110001 01010111 10001001 10001110 10011011
00100011 11011011 01011000 01111001 01110010 11011100 11101101 11100100 10011110 10010001
11010111 00010101 00110110 10111101 10101011 01011101 01000111 00100010 01001101 01111011
00100110 11000110 00011000 01100101 00000000 01100011 11110000 10101011 01010001 01110011
11010000 00101100 11111010 00010110 00110100 00101101 01000100 11011010 01000111 00111000
00111001 01110001 01110000 00110010 01111001 11101000 11011101 01000001 10101111 01011001
11010010 10101110 10100011 11010100 00101100 00100010 10011011 00011000 11001000 11111010
01010111 10001001 11011011 11111100 10100000 01100111 10001010 11101111 11111100 00010101
10101001 11000110 11010110 11101111 01101101 11100110 11100110 01001000 11110010 01110001
11101011 01011100 10111000 10011010 01001010 00010001 11110011 00111011 01110000 11110011
11010110 11001100 11101011 01100001 01101100 11001001 01110000 00001110 00111000 01101100
01111101 01110001 01010110 10010011 01101001 00011011 10001111 00111100 01010110 00000100
01100001 10000101 11001100 10001110 00100111 01110000 10010010 00011111 10011001 00001111
00111111 10010101 01011111 01101011 10110001 00001101 10111100 10001100 01001001 01001101
10000000 11110101 10101111 00101111 10011110 11001011 01000011 10110001 10100111 01100001
10010010 00110000 10011011 01010000 10010001 11000111 00100110 00100001 10110011 11101001
10011010 01111011 10110111 10111101 01111001 10101101 11011111 10001011 11101111 11101101
11110101 00001001 01011010 11010111 11001010 00110000 00111011 01100101 10010101 10010111
00111001 11111111 00000000 00001010 01110111 11111100 00100111 01011010 10011001 00000100
11111001 00010110 10100100 00011110 10000011 00000111 10001111 11110001 10101111 01011011
00001101 01111000 11000101 00100011 11001111 10101100 11011100 10011001 11011010 01101011
11110111 01000110 11010011 01000111 10111011 10011111 01101000 00111110 01011010 11100111
00000111 10111101 01110001 10010110 11011010 11100110 10011101 01111101 00010000 01001011
11011000 00001010 01100000 01111101 11010000 10111101 00101011 00110011 01010001 11110001
00010110 10101001 10101000 01011001 00011011 01101011 10101001 10110010 10001110 01111001
11110010 11010111 00011001 11111010 11010101 01011000 10110100 11101001 10100100 10001000
00111100 00001000 01100100 00000111 10101001 00011101 10101011 10110010 10011010 01101101
10011100 11111100 10100111 01000101 01101111 01100111 11100101 01000101 00101101 11011111
10000111 11101111 01001001 00101110 00110010 11010000 10011111 01101111 01101111 01011010
11001110 01001101 01101011 01010001 11110011 01001011 00011011 10000111 00100111 10110110
01000111 00010100 01011001 11101001 10110111 11010000 01001001 00011100 11110000 01011011
11001100 10010010 10100111 00100000 10001010 11010001 10110111 11010010 00111001 11011101
01110110 11000110 11011111 01111011 01111111 00010000 11101011 10011010 11101000 10110110
10010111 01100010 10110001 10011101 00101110 10100011 10101001 01001110 01010001 01111100
11100010 11000100 10011111 11101110 11100100 10011111 01101010 10101111 01101100 00101110
01110100 11111101 01001000 01111001 00000101 11100011 10111100 00000111 00011000 11101111
01011101 01011100 00011010 00001010 11011011 11001010 10010011 00100101 11100010 01101111
01010010 00011100 00000011 11011110 10111010 00011011 10101011 01111000 00101110 11101110
10101101 00110101 00000010 00000000 10011110 00111111 10010011 01110000 11101111 01011100
01111000 10101100 01001100 00101001 01011001 10011011 01100001 11101000 10101010 10010111
01000111 10011111 01111000 10000111 01011001 10010110 11101000 01000111 01101101 00111010
11000101 00100011 11000110 01111111 01111010 11000000 11110101 00110100 11001000 00111100
01000101 00110101 10101100 01101001 00001100 00010001 01000010 00010001 00000111 00000000
11100100 11010110 10111111 10001001 00111100 00111011 00101100 11111010 10100101 11001101
11000100 00001101 00011000 01001001 00001110 01000000 00110101 10001011 00100111 10000110
01101111 11010100 00010010 00000100 01100111 11011000 00011100 11100110 10110110 11000011
11001001 01001110 00111100 11001011 10101001 10011101 01011000 01110010 01001010 11000101
11000100 11110001 01010100 10100011 00111110 01100101 10111100 01111111 01000101 00110101
00110101 10111111 10001000 10101100 10100110 00101110 10101111 01101100 11101000 00001111
00111000 11101011 10010011 01011000 01110011 01101000 01010111 11110000 10100000 00000110
00000010 01100100 11000111 01100011 10011100 11010100 00110110 00101101 00110110 10011110
11010010 10111111 10010011 10001001 11010011 00000011 00001110 00110011 10001010 11010010
00110000 10110001 10010111 00101101 11001110 10101011 11000011 10111010 00111000 10001011
01010011 10110100 10111100 10111011 10010111 11001001 00101111 00111000 00110001 01000101
11101010 00110011 01011110 11011000 11011101 00001000 11101011 10000011 01011110 00001011
11100001 00111001 11100110 10111010 11110001 01001101 10010100 11010111 00010010 00110001
00100110 01101100 11110011 11111110 00010101 11101110 11111001 00010010 00011101 11000111
00111000 11001111 01111010 11100011 11000110 00111001 01011001 00011011 11010011 11011011
01000001 11100100 11110000 01000111 10110101 00110011 00101101 11100101 10000101 00011101
01111011 11010010 10110110 01000011 11100000 00101111 11010100 11100110 10010000 00010000
00110000 00111001 11011110 01001111 01001010 11110011 10110111 00101100 01011100 00011101
11111100 10011100 00000001 11011010 10000110 11001001 01111101 10100011 10001010 01001110
01110110 10111111 10111111 01111010 00000000 11110010 11111001 11000001 11100100 01110111
10100110 11101110 00000000 10111011 10110111 00010010 11100100 00010010 01101001 01110010
01000001 11100111 10010011 01000000 11001000 00011100 10001110 01111011 00011010 00111110
11101000 11000111 01010011 11101011 01000010 11010100 01100000 00001110 11101100 01100100
01110101 00111001 10100011 11101111 00111111 00011101 10101001 00111010 00010011 11001111
00111000 11101011 01000011 00010011 11010000 01100000 01100011 10101101 00111011 10100110
00100000 11111110 00011110 10110100 10100111 00000000 00001010 01101111 11001010 01111011

01110100 11100110 10010111 00000111 01100111 00110100 10101111 10101000 00000110 01111010
00001110 11000110 10001111 01111110 11111101 11001101 00101110 00111010 01110001 11000101
00100011 01111010 00001111 01011010 01111011 10100000 00001100 11100001 11010011 10111000
11101011 01000111 01010010 01001000 00011100 10010011 01000011 00010011 10000000 00111001
00111000 00110100 00001100 01100011 11100101 00111101 01001101 01001011 01011101 00011000
11000100 11001110 01001110 00111010 10011110 10110100 00010001 11000111 00100111 00010100
10111000 11000001 11001101 00100011 00010001 10001111 10100111 01011111 01101010 01101101
00000000 11100010 00110001 10000010 11011101 01101001 10111101 01001111 00110100 00011100
11100111 10101110 01111001 10100101 11011011 10110111 10110110 01001001 00110100 01110011
01011000 00000000 11110010 00001111 11100111 01001000 01001110 01001111 11111000 01010001
10000011 11000000 11001111 11010111 10011010 00011011 00000011 00100010 10000111 10101110
10100000 00011001 11100010 10001001 01001000 00000101 00111000 00111001 00110100 00011100
11110100 11101101 01001101 01010000 01000110 00001001 11101010 01101001 00110111 01100000
00001110 00000010 01100100 01100111 11011110 10010001 01000001 00100011 11100111 00111100
11100011 10110101 00111100 11110000 01110010 01101001 10101110 11011000 10010011 01101111
01011010 01110110 10111110 10100010 00000111 00000000 10010001 10001110 11000010 10001100
01110111 00100110 10010001 11001001 00001110 10000000 01111010 01110011 01001000 11100011
11010011 11010111 10011110 01111010 11010001 01110110 00110001 01111011 10000010 01111001
00111111 11001010 10010000 10000001 10111100 10011110 11000000 01010011 10011111 00001010
01110000 01111011 11110110 10100100 01110001 10111011 00011001 11101001 01001010 11111101
00000000 01100011 11100000 01100000 11110110 10100011 10001111 00110000 10010001 11010110
10011100 10100011 10010010 01000111 00100111 10110101 00110101 01110011 10010010 01001111
00100111 11010110 10001011 11101000 00000000 00001001 11001001 00011000 11000000 11111110
01110100 00110111 11001010 00001011 11100000 11100000 01010001 11110011 00110111 01111100
00000001 11011111 00010100 11010101 01011110 10100001 11000110 01111001 11001101 00111011
11000100 01000100 10001100 01110010 00001111 01111010 00011001 01110011 11001011 11111101
00110001 01000111 01010010 01001111 01001110 00111011 01010100 01111001 00000011 00011000
00011001 11001001 11101011 01000101 10010011 00011000 11100010 00110011 11010010 10010011
00000100 00000011 10000001 11011110 10011110 11100100 00101000 11100111 10111111 01000001
01001101 11000000 00111100 10011110 00000101 00010111 11101000 00100001 10101101 11010100
01100011 10101001 10100001 10000110 00000111 00000000 01010010 11100111 10000000 01110001
01000001 00111111 00100001 11111010 11010000 11011010 01111011 00001100 00011011 00000000
01100110 10000111 11111001 00000111 00000011 10000001 11001111 11010110 10000011 11001001
00000011 00111100 01110111 11000101 00100110 11010010 11000111 10101111 00010100 11101100
00000000 11000011 01111100 01100100 11100100 10001110 11110100 00100111 11011101 00011000
11100000 01111011 01010011 01001001 00101100 01001000 00011101 00110011 01001111 01111100
10000001 11101010 01111011 01010000 10111100 11000000 01001100 10000101 00011001 00111110
10111100 11010011 01010000 10011110 01111101 01001111 01100011 01000011 11100011 10000010
11111101 00110011 01001110 11000001 00111101 11111000 11101010 01001101 01001101 10011011
00000001 10000111 10000011 11101111 11101011 01000001 00100011 00011111 01011110 10100110
10010100 10010000 01111101 01001111 11100011 01001000 00000000 11001110 00111010 01100111
11110100 10100111 01100100 00000010 01100011 00110111 00011001 11000111 00000011 11110101
10100001 01000111 00100111 10010001 10000011 11101101 10001100 11010100 10000011 10000111
11001101 01000010 00000011 00010111 11101011 11111111 00000000 11010111 10100011 10101110
10000000 00111011 00100000 10011110 00111010 01010000 10111101 01111000 00010100 00000011
10010011 10000000 01111110 10110100 00100111 00011001 00100100 11110011 10011010 01001000
00000011 10111101 00110100 01110011 10011111 01011100 11010010 01100011 00000111 00100111
10100101 00101000 11001000 01101100 10000011 11010110 10101010 11000011 10111000 01110011
11111100 00011000 00011110 11110100 10001011 10000000 00111010 11100011 11010010 10001110
01000000 01111111 01001010 00110011 10000001 10001100 01110011 11101001 01001001 10001000
01010101 11000000 11001111 10101111 11010010 10011010 01011111 00111000 00100011 10010010
01001111 00011110 10010100 01111111 10110100 01110001 11001001 10100111 00111111 00000000
00001110 11110100 11011011 10111000 11010000 10011000 11101000 01111010 11111011 01010011
00111010 10010000 00110000 01111000 11101111 01010010 00101001 00100001 11111000 11101000
00101001 00011011 10011111 11101011 01000101 10000011 10101000 10011110 10000011 11110011
10100110 01100111 10011100 11100011 11110000 10100111 11110100 00111100 10011111 11001110
10011010 11000100 11100111 10100110 00110011 11010110 10001111 01100110 11011010 00010000
10011101 10001110 01000110 01110011 11000110 00101000 01101100 00101000 11001111 10100101
00101010 01110001 10111101 10000000 11111010 01010010 00011100 00110111 11010000 11010010
10110101 10010000 00000100 01011100 10001110 01001001 11001111 01011010 01000011 11000000
00100100 11111101 00101001 11000100 11100011 00000011 00011101 11101000 11101101 10010011
11010011 10110101 00111101 01101100 00000011 01000001 00111011 00001001 11001111 00100100
11010011 01110000 00000000 11100110 10011100 01111101 00000111 01111111 11010010 10011011
10000101 00011000 01001100 11110001 11010100 10001010 01110111 00000001 00001010 11111100
11101001 11001110 01101001 11111000 00101101 00100110 01001001 11000111 01101111 11000010
10011011 11010000 00111111 10100111 01101010 01000101 11101001 10011010 01011101 00000000
00010111 01101110 01110001 10011110 01000111 01010011 01001000 00011000 01101101 11001110
01111010 00011010 00111000 01011000 01001001 00100011 10000010 01110011 11110101 10100110
10011100 00000001 10110111 00011100 11100111 00111000 10100000 00000011 01110110 00000001
00100111 00111000 11001101 00100011 00001110 01001011 00010001 11011011 10000101 00110100
11110111 11100011 11110111 01100111 10010010 01001000 11101001 01001101 01010110 00100111
00111001 00011100 11110100 11100000 11010011 11010000 00000000 11100111 11001011 00000000
00011110 01101001 10100101 01110000 00111100 10111111 01000001 11001110 00101001 01001110

11101110 11100111 11110010 10100011 10111000 00100011 00100111 11011111 11010110 10010101
11011111 01000110 00000001 10001100 01000111 11101101 10011110 11000010 10001110 01000000
11100100 01110101 11101101 01000110 11100010 00001000 01010001 10000000 00111101 01001101
00100011 01110000 00110000 01011011 10010011 11010010 10001101 11010000 00000010 00001101
11011011 11110001 11011011 10100101 00110111 00111100 11010011 11010100 01100001 00110000
00111010 11111010 11010011 00110000 10100000 00011111 01101110 11010100 11111001 00000110
10000011 00111011 01111001 11001001 11001011 11010000 11011101 00110001 01000011 01110011
00100110 01001111 11111111 00000000 10101010 10001110 10111111 00101111 01100011 01010011
11001011 01110110 00010111 00010000 10001110 01101000 11100111 11110011 10100101 11101011
10001110 01101000 11001000 11011111 11101010 01000000 11101001 01001110 01001110 11000010
00011011 10000010 00100011 11000000 00011001 11001001 11101111 01001010 11011110 10011101
11101000 01000011 10010000 01000110 01111001 11001101 00100001 00000011 00100111 00011101
01101000 10000010 10111110 10101100 00000000 10000010 01000111 00110100 11010100 11100111
00100110 10011100 01111110 11100000 10100001 00000001 00100011 10000011 11011010 10010101
11110101 00000001 10111001 00111000 11011011 10001110 10110100 10001010 01111000 11000111
01111010 01011110 10000111 11100110 11101011 11011110 10001110 11100111 00000010 10101010
11111101 01000000 01000101 00111000 01110001 11101100 00101000 11011011 11110011 10010110
11101011 10010001 11000101 00101000 00011001 11101011 11010010 10010011 00101100 01100100
11001111 00000001 00101010 01011101 11000000 00011000 11111100 10100011 01111111 01111110
11000110 10010001 00000110 01110011 11101111 01001100 00011111 10111100 11101011 01010010
01100111 10111111 10100101 00110100 11010110 11100000 00110000 10010001 10010010 10100011
11110011 10100100 00100111 00000111 11111010 01010010 10101000 11111001 00001011 01111010
11010000 11000011 10011111 01011111 01011010 00110111 01100000 00100001 00111101 11110011
11001001 10100110 01110011 10011110 10111001 00110101 00100001 11101001 10011110 10100111
11010110 10011010 00000000 11100100 11010000 11110101 11011100 00000001 00001111 11110111
10000101 00101110 01111001 00100100 01110101 10100000 00011110 11111101 01000101 00000000
11100111 11110011 11101011 01000101 11010000 00000001 11000011 01110101 11101101 11011110
10010001 10001000 01101110 01110011 11110100 00011001 10100101 00011001 00001011 10000011
11010110 10010001 10110001 11110100 00011110 11110100 00100110 11010000 11011000 11000110
11100100 01100110 10001100 11100000 11111010 11111010 11010010 01111110 00110100 01110000
00001001 11110101 00111110 10010101 01011011 10000101 10001000 11110010 01000010 01101110
11101110 01001111 00010100 10101101 11001001 10100101 01011100 00000011 10001111 01101010
10001100 01100111 01101000 11001111 01111010 01001110 01011101 00101110 00100001 11111001
11100111 11011011 10111101 00101010 11100100 00000011 10001010 01101110 00110111 00100110
00101001 11000001 10111001 00100000 01010000 10000110 00100010 00010011 10011110 10110100
10111011 01000011 01110010 01011010 10100011 11001001 11001001 00011001 11111100 01101010
01000011 10011111 11110010 00101000 10010010 11100110 01110111 01100010 00111100 01001111
00011000 01101100 11100000 11111110 01110100 10011111 00110100 01101111 10011110 01110011
11110101 11100010 10100101 01111100 01101111 00011100 11010001 00110010 01100101 11110011
10011110 00111101 01101011 11010001 01010111 01101001 10100110 01000110 11000100 11110110
01111010 10100101 11010101 10011100 11000010 01101011 01010110 11000001 00011100 00011100
11110010 00001111 11010110 10111010 01111000 01111100 01001100 11110111 01010000 10000010
01001000 01000111 11000111 00100000 00001010 11100011 11010110 00110110 11001001 11000010
11100000 00011110 11100110 10100100 10000100 00011000 11000001 00011110 11111101 01111101
01101011 00101010 10010100 11100011 00111110 10100110 10110000 10101000 11010001 10100101
01111111 01111001 00100101 11000100 11100100 00011100 10011111 01001010 10000101 10000001
01010000 00001000 00011111 01010011 01010110 10111100 00111111 00011100 01010010 11101010
00110000 00101100 10001010 00111010 11010111 10100111 11011011 01011011 11011011 01101100
11000111 11011001 11100001 00100000 11110101 00000110 00110000 01101010 00100101 01010010
00010100 10010111 00101001 10101111 10110011 11110110 10011110 11110001 11100100 11101000
10000100 10011100 00010011 10011100 11110110 10100100 01111000 01111001 11100000 11010111
01111011 11100010 10011101 00011010 11000110 00101101 00111110 01111011 10011011 01011000
00000100 01010010 11000110 10111011 11001110 11010011 10001100 11010111 00000111 11100110
10001001 00001110 00110011 11011011 00110101 01110100 11100101 00011010 10101011 10110101
10001110 01111001 00100111 00000110 01000000 11110001 00110000 00011110 11010100 11010000
11000100 00101001 00000000 00011010 10110101 11100110 10101001 00111000 00100010 10000111
01101000 11010101 01110010 01001000 11001110 00111000 00011001 10101101 10100111 11001001
10110101 11001001 10111011 00101001 00010000 11011110 01011111 01001010 01010100 10010100
10001110 11011111 10001101 00111101 11100100 00000111 10100111 01111010 01100010 00000000
01110011 10001110 10111101 11101001 01001001 00101101 10010000 10101111 01110001 11101111
00100000 11001111 00011001 11110111 10100101 01010011 10010100 00011001 10100110 10110110
00111111 11000010 10000011 00101000 01010001 11001111 00100111 11010010 10101010 11101001
00101101 01110111 00000011 01000110 11000011 01010110 10111101 11010011 00110111 11111101
10010010 01101111 00101100 01001000 00111001 00011000 11001110 01101011 01000111 01001110
11110001 01001101 11111100 10010111 01110110 11100110 11101110 11100100 11111001 01000001
10000001 10010000 00001000 11000101 01110011 00110010 11001000 11000111 00000111 00011100
01010100 10001000 01010100 00011110 01000111 01011110 11110101 00111100 10101010 01001100
00010101 10101111 01110011 11010100 00110100 10101011 01011000 00110101 00111011 00101001
00100110 01000001 10111100 11000111 00100110 00000000 11110101 01000011 11010110 10101101
01101001 10111010 00110000 11010010 11100100 00010010 11011001 01011100 01011100 11000111
11110011 01100100 11000110 11010010 01101111 01001100 01111010 01100010 10111001 11011111
00000001 01011111 00011000 01011110 01011011 01110111 01100010 00000011 10001100 10001111
01001010 11101100 10101111 00101110 00010110 00111000 01000001 10010001 10000010 01100111

10000000 01001001 11101011 01011110 00111110 00100101 00111010 01101101 10110100 11110100
00111101 01001000 01001011 10011101 00100110 10001010 01111110 00100010 10110111 01011011
11111111 00000000 10010001 11100101 10010110 00110100 11101110 00100011 00111000 00100110
10110001 11110100 11011101 00000101 01101100 11000001 00010001 01001101 00110011 10000111
01101111 11111001 01101000 01110011 11000111 10100101 01101100 01011100 01001001 11111110
10010000 10000100 10010001 11001111 00011101 01111010 11010011 11101110 00100100 11110010
10100010 00100100 00011100 01100011 10111101 01100000 10100101 11010101 00010101 10101010
01000110 01100100 10110111 00110110 11010110 00110111 10110010 00110100 11110011 01000111
00011000 10001001 01001111 01010011 11001001 10101111 00101101 10111101 10111011 10010010
11101111 01010001 10011110 11100100 10010010 10000110 01010010 01001111 11001010 01110001
10000001 11011011 10100101 01011101 11110001 10001101 11000111 10011111 10101100 11111101
11100010 01000000 00011100 11010110 00111100 01000100 11100100 10000011 11001001 11100011
00010101 11101010 01100000 10101000 01011001 01110011 10110100 01111001 11111000 10001010
10001110 01101110 11000111 01111001 10100010 11111000 11100010 00111011 01001101 00101101
00101101 11101111 11100001 10111000 10010110 11100010 00010101 11000000 10010011 00111001
11110011 00000101 01011001 10011011 11000111 01011011 10100010 11001101 10101101 10011001
01000011 10001110 10101110 01110011 01011110 01111010 11111000 01100110 00000100 10001010
10110011 01101101 11110010 11100111 11011111 10101101 01110110 11010101 10100101 00011001
10111101 11001100 10010101 10111010 10100010 01010111 01011001 00100111 10010110 01001001
11100110 11111011 11101110 11011011 11001001 00111101 11110011 01001000 01100010 00111011
11111000 00011111 10000101 01110110 00011110 00010101 11010010 11101100 10110101 00111000
01100101 11110011 11100110 10010011 11101101 00001001 11111111 00000000 00101100 11000111
10100111 10101101 01110100 10110000 01111000 01010011 01001010 01010011 10010111 10000000
10111001 11101011 11001001 10101100 11100101 01010110 00110100 10111101 11011110 10100110
10110000 10100100 11011110 10101000 11110010 11011111 00100001 10100100 00111111 00100110
00101010 11010110 10011010 11010010 11101001 11110111 11010001 01001100 10011001 11001010
00011110 01110001 11001111 00011101 11101011 11010110 10100000 11010000 10110100 11101000
01000110 01010010 11010110 00111111 11001010 10101100 10110110 10010101 01100001 00100000
11100110 11010010 00101111 11001011 00010101 11001111 01010111 00010011 01001110 01011011
10011010 11000010 10010111 10011001 10010101 01101010 01100000 10111000 10001010 00111001
10100011 10011000 01101100 00111100 11110101 10101100 00011111 00010101 01011101 00101100
10000001 00101101 10100011 00100100 10100001 00111111 00110001 00000011 11010010 10111011
01111000 10110100 11001011 01001000 11110010 00100011 10001001 00000000 11110100 11000101
01001000 00101101 01100001 01010011 10010001 00010010 00001111 01001110 00101011 11001110
11110110 01110000 11100110 10111001 11010010 11100100 11011010 10110001 11100010 00010011
11101001 00010111 01110011 01011100 11001001 00101100 01110110 11110011 00111010 01001000
01110010 00001000 01011110 10010100 11101000 11110100 00011011 11010000 11101000 01111110
11001011 00101000 01001111 01110001 01011110 11100100 00100000 00000011 10011100 01111101
01111000 10100110 10111100 00000011 10001110 00101011 10101011 11101011 01101010 00101011
01000100 01100010 11101001 00100110 01111000 10100011 01101001 01110111 00001010 11000001
01111100 10010111 00011011 11001111 01111010 10110001 00010110 10011011 01111111 01101010
10000110 01011000 11000011 10100001 11000111 11110000 10011010 11110101 10111001 10101101
11010100 11111101 11100001 01010100 00100100 11010011 01100001 01111100 11100100 01110010
01111111 00001010 10101111 10101111 00110110 11110100 01000010 11110110 00110001 01111011
10011110 01101000 10011010 11101101 11111100 01110001 10111100 01111110 01110110 11110011
11011011 11001100 00010101 01001110 11100110 11110110 11110111 01010000 10010010 00110001
00111011 01111001 10011011 01111110 01110000 00000101 01110110 00010111 01011110 00011101
10110111 10010111 01011000 00000010 11100011 01111010 00000010 00110010 00110001 01011101
00010100 00111010 01001101 10010101 10101100 01011000 10000010 11011110 00110000 01001111
01010010 01000110 01001101 01110100 10101100 01011101 00111000 11000110 11110110 10111001
10001111 11010101 00011101 11001111 00101000 10001000 11011100 01001000 01001010 11111001
10010010 00011101 11100111 10111011 01010111 01101011 10100101 01101010 01001001 00001100
00111111 01100100 10111010 01010111 10001111 11001010 01010000 01111001 00111011 11000001
00111101 11101011 00101010 11101011 01001001 01010001 01111110 00100001 10110010 00011111
11101001 00001000 11011011 11100100 00000100 11110110 11110101 10101110 10001110 00011101
00010110 00101001 10100010 10010011 11001110 10011000 10010111 01110001 11001110 11010001
11010000 11010110 00011000 10011010 10010000 10101111 00011011 00011101 00011000 01001000
01110010 00110110 11001010 00111010 11101100 01010011 01011110 01101001 11111110 01111101
10000100 10000101 00100111 10001011 11100111 00011111 11101101 00001111 01001010 11100001
11011111 01011001 11010101 00110010 00011000 01011100 01001011 10110000 00011111 10011000
01010111 10101010 01000111 10100111 00110100 01110000 10000000 10101111 10011110 00110001
11010010 10111000 11011101 01100111 11000011 01100110 00111111 00110010 01011000 00100101
00101000 11100100 10010111 11110010 11001111 01000011 11101011 10001010 10011100 00101101
01001000 11000011 11011100 10010001 00111000 10111010 01001010 10100111 10111101 00010011
00000010 00101111 00010000 01011110 10001001 00001110 11110110 00010010 00100001 11101010
00110001 10001111 11010110 10110101 11101100 01111100 01000000 10100000 01111110 11110010
11001111 11100100 00100011 11111000 01001101 01100010 00101110 10011001 01110001 00100100
01001000 11110110 11100011 11001101 00101100 01110000 00000000 11101011 01010010 00001101
00110111 01010001 00000101 00110111 11011011 11001010 00000010 10011110 10111110 01011110
00110011 01011110 10100101 10010101 10010110 10100111 10011111 11101100 11011011 11101000
01110101 11111110 00011100 11010111 01100000 10111110 11010101 10101101 00100010 11111011
00101110 11000111 11110011 10000110 11010110 11100011 10000000 00101011 11010111 00011011
00000101 10110001 10001110 11110101 11100001 10011110 00001001 10110100 10010010 00011111

00010000 01011001 11001001 00100010 10010001 10001001 01111011 10001100 01010111 10111000
01110100 01110010 01110011 10010000 11000110 10111001 10110001 01110010 11011010 11000110
10010100 11100010 11100010 10000101 01011100 10010001 01000011 11110010 10011001 11101000
01111010 01010000 01110001 11001111 01011111 10101101 00100000 00111000 00111000 01100101
00111011 00111011 00011010 11100000 10111011 00101000 00000000 00111100 01110101 10100101
01101101 11000100 00010011 11001111 01011010 01110011 11110101 11101001 10011110 00110011
01001101 01100010 01000010 11100111 10001100 11010001 10100000 11000111 00001100 00000100
11001001 00111000 11000111 01110011 01001101 11110100 11111110 01110100 10000111 11100110
11100100 10011010 01010001 10001100 01110001 11001101 00111011 01011000 01000010 00111110
11101100 11110001 11010000 11110111 10100011 10011100 01100100 10001110 01111011 11100110
10010101 10111001 00110100 11100010 00000111 00111101 11101001 00111101 00000000 01100010
00010001 10000001 10011010 00110111 01100011 10100111 01011010 01011100 10000101 00000100
11110110 10100100 11110110 11111111 00000000 00100110 10001101 11110110 00000000 01100011
11001110 00101001 00110011 11001000 00000000 11010010 11110100 11100011 00011001 10100011
10100110 01111011 00001010 01101001 11011000 00000100 11001111 11001101 11000111 11100111
01000001 01010101 11101001 10001110 10110100 11010101 00111100 10010000 00111111 00111010
01111111 01101100 11111110 01110101 10011101 11101100 00110000 11100000 01100100 10001110
11000010 10011001 11000110 00111101 10001111 01011110 00101001 11001101 11110011 01111101
00111011 01010001 10001100 00010000 01001001 11100010 10101111 10101000 00001110 01010001
10011010 01001100 11100100 11110001 01001000 11011100 01100111 11011110 10011011 10011100
10000111 11011001 11000111 01101010 00110100 01100000 00100011 00000010 11000100 01100011
10100000 00111100 01010011 11110110 11100100 11110101 11100111 10111101 00001010 00001111
00011101 10000101 00110100 00110000 00100111 10001111 11000110 10000101 10100000 00001110
11001000 11000001 11000111 01100011 11010110 10011000 01000111 01111111 11000010 10010001
01000111 11011111 00000000 11010010 10110001 11100011 00011101 01110011 01010001 01110110
11000000 01010010 11000000 10100110 01001111 01101110 10010100 10000011 10010011 10001110
10100110 10001100 11100000 10001101 11011000 11000110 01111000 11001101 00101110 01111001
11001000 11100110 10101101 01101000 10000000 01000110 00111000 11001101 00011101 10000000
11000101 00011000 11001111 00111110 10110100 00011001 00010100 01100000 01100111 10011010
10011011 10000000 10011000 11111001 11001111 10111111 01111010 01101011 10001100 11100000
11010011 11010100 01100011 11010110 10011000 11100011 00111101 00001001 00000000 00011100
11010101 01101111 10110000 10000111 00110111 11001010 00001000 11100111 00100100 01111110
01010100 11000001 11101101 11001110 01101010 01001100 01110010 01001111 01111110 11110100
11000110 00111001 11001001 11110100 10100111 11001101 01100101 10100000 00001110 01010010
01110011 10001100 11110001 11011110 10100011 11011100 01001011 00011100 01100111 00011001
11101111 01001110 01100010 00000001 00000011 11010111 10110101 00001100 01000001 11000000
00011111 01000011 01010001 01100110 11000110 00111001 10010100 01111111 00001001 11100011
11010010 10011001 11001111 00000011 00011100 01010001 10001110 01110010 01111000 11110100
10100000 10010010 01111111 00010011 11001101 01010010 10111011 11010100 00000111 11100111
10011101 11011101 01001111 01001110 01101001 10001100 11011011 10111010 11110100 00010100
10101101 11001000 00000100 11100100 00011111 01101010 00110001 10001110 10011101 11111011
11010100 11001011 10111000 00001001 10001101 11011111 01000001 01000111 01001100 00010011
01001000 11011111 01111001 00110001 11010000 00011110 01101000 10011000 10000010 00000000
00100100 10000010 01011011 10001010 01001001 01101001 01110100 00110110 00001001 10001101
10011001 00100111 00110100 00101110 01110000 01000111 11101011 10011010 00001010 01101111
01000010 00000001 11100011 11101001 01001010 11000011 11100101 11100011 10101001 10101011
11010100 01000011 00110111 01100011 00100110 10011100 11000000 10011110 01000101 00000111
00000001 00010000 00001111 01011110 01101000 11100100 11100111 10011110 00111011 10011010
00011110 10011010 10000000 11011001 01001111 11001000 01110001 11000001 10100011 10000010
10011000 11101001 11101010 01111101 01101001 11001111 10110111 00000000 00000011 11010111
10100110 01111011 11010011 01110001 10010000 00000000 11100111 00111111 10100101 00100100
10101110 00000001 11000000 01010010 01001000 11100011 10110101 00001100 01110001 00011111
00111000 10100011 00100100 10000011 10001100 01110101 11000111 00010100 01100011 11100100
00011000 00011101 00111101 01101010 10101110 00000010 01100011 10001100 10110000 11111001
11101000 11001110 00000110 11101100 01110011 10011010 01010110 11110111 00111100 10011110
10111000 10100100 01100001 10000101 11110111 11000101 00101110 01100000 00011000 01111110
01011100 11101100 11100011 00100110 10011101 11110100 11001101 00000011 11101110 00001100
11110011 01000011 01110000 00110001 10001110 01000001 11001110 00101000 00000001 10101101
10110111 01100111 00111101 01000101 00100110 01110001 00100001 11001001 00100011 11011010
10010111 00000011 00100111 00011100 11010000 11011101 01110011 11010100 10001110 11100110
10010011 01110110 00000000 00100011 10001100 01110101 11101111 11010110 10010011 00011000
11111001 10001111 00110100 10101000 10100011 00100111 01110001 11101011 11010100 11010011
10001001 11000001 00000000 01110111 10101010 01000000 00110101 01100011 00100000 00000001
11000111 01011100 10011010 01000011 11010111 11101001 01001010 11011011 01110011 11010111
11110101 10100100 11101001 11001000 11101111 01001001 10101011 00000000 01110100 11100011
11010110 10010011 10011110 00000110 01101000 11101011 11001110 00110011 11110101 10100001
10110010 00001000 11001001 11111100 00101001 01101100 11101110 00000001 10001110 00000000
11101010 01111010 11010000 01010111 00100111 00011001 11000001 11101111 01000000 11101000
01111101 01111101 10101001 10101010 01001000 00101110 11000100 11111100 11101111 01010101
01110111 11110010 00000000 11101011 10010101 11001101 00100110 00111000 11101001 10000011
10011100 01111011 00001010 00010000 00000000 01001001 00011100 01111010 11010010 01110110
11000110 01111000 00000111 00111111 10001101 00101011 10110000 01100011 10100100 11000110
00111101 01111000 10100100 11000001 00100111 00000100 11100000 01110110 00010100 10101111

11000100 01111000 11110101 11101011 01001000 11000100 00101000 00011100 01110010 01101001
11110100 00000001 00000000 01011111 00110011 00011001 11111010 11010011 01011000 00000101
01110011 11011100 10011110 10100110 10001100 10010000 11011011 10011000 01100000 00011010
01000110 00100100 10111111 10110000 10100010 00101111 01001101 01000000 01010110 00011000
00100011 00111110 11010100 11100011 10001101 11011000 00000110 10011011 10110111 00100100
00010011 11011011 10100101 00111000 00010000 01111001 11100111 10001010 01010111 01000000
00110001 10000110 00010000 00101111 01111100 11100110 10001110 10000100 11111111 00000000
01111110 10000100 00000111 00000000 10011110 10100100 11010011 00011011 11111000 10111101
01101001 10111111 00100000 00011101 10001110 01110011 10011110 01001101 00110101 01000110
11010010 01110000 01101001 11001101 11011010 10011010 11011101 01110001 10001110 00101000
10111111 01110001 11101000 00100110 00111110 01110010 01111010 11010010 10110001 00000011
10000000 00110010 01111101 10001101 00011100 11110001 10110011 10100101 00001110 01111000
00011000 11100011 10011010 01000010 00011010 00000111 10101111 01101010 01010101 11101011
10010010 00110010 01111101 11101000 11000000 01011110 10110100 00001110 01011100 11100011
10100101 00111011 10111011 11011000 01000010 00000000 01000000 00100100 11110101 11101011
11110101 10100011 10100010 01110011 01001010 11111100 01100011 11110101 10100100 11100001
10110001 11001101 00100110 11000110 00110011 10110110 01110001 11001001 00111100 01010011
11000000 11000000 00100100 01110101 11110111 10100110 01100011 00100100 11100000 01010011
11110011 10110101 01111000 10101011 11100101 01001111 01010100 00000011 00010011 10000000
00000111 10101111 01010011 01001011 11010011 10001100 00001010 01000101 11111001 01100011
11110111 11001110 00101001 00111010 10011010 10011011 10100110 00000011 01110110 10001100
10001110 00111000 11001101 00001100 01111111 01111001 11110010 10001111 10010010 10011100
10100011 10010010 01111011 01111010 11010011 01111110 11110111 11100011 01000101 11010010
00000001 11110010 01100001 10100011 11011010 00101001 00100010 00111111 00101111 00011101
10101001 10001101 10010000 00111101 11001101 00101110 00110110 11000111 11000101 00101110
01100100 11000000 00011011 10001100 10010011 11001000 00110100 00101000 00100100 01110100
11000110 01101000 11001111 10110101 00111011 00100100 10000011 11011011 00100011 10001010
01101000 10110001 10001100 00111010 01110011 11010000 11100000 11010010 01100111 11011000
11110011 01001110 11000110 00000000 00000100 01010010 00101000 11110101 11101011 11101011
01000011 01111010 01011001 10010011 11010100 01100111 00100100 11111011 00001010 00111110
11101000 11001111 10101101 00111101 10001111 11101110 11110111 01111010 01110110 10100011
11111000 00000000 00111100 10011100 11010001 01100010 10000100 01110011 11001000 11001111
00110100 11000110 11001111 01101111 11000110 10011110 01000110 01011100 10011010 01101010
10101001 00000000 10000010 01110001 01000101 11011001 00110111 00001100 11100111 10101111
01001110 11010100 10001100 00111011 10011110 00010010 10010000 11100100 00111111 00111101
00101001 01011000 11101110 10001100 10101110 01001111 00111100 01010010 01001110 11001110
11000000 11111011 10001000 11011100 10100111 00011100 01100111 10100110 01101000 01101111
10010111 01100000 11101111 01001010 11000111 10110111 10111110 00101001 01010100 00001100
00001100 11110010 01000111 01110011 01001110 11011010 11011100 01000010 00110111 00100111
00111101 11101001 10011100 01110011 11111101 01101001 11100111 10011110 01110001 01001100
11001111 00001110 00111011 00011111 01011010 00010100 01011011 00000001 10101101 11010111
00111111 10101101 00110011 00000100 11111100 11000000 11111110 01111101 11101010 01000110
11100101 01111000 10100110 01110101 01001100 01110111 11001101 00001001 01110010 10111101
11000000 01001100 00000011 11011011 11110000 10100000 10110110 01111111 00011110 10010100
10111101 00111011 00011111 11000011 10001010 01101110 00001011 00110111 11110100 00000010
10011110 11100000 00101010 10001101 11001000 01000110 01111000 00000111 10011010 00111110
10000111 10011010 00111000 00000010 10010001 01001110 01000001 01101100 01100000 00001110
10000110 10001011 00100010 10101110 00001011 10001100 11100101 10000101 00110101 10011100
10010110 00111001 00011000 10100111 01100011 10010011 11101001 01000000 10001100 01100011
11100110 00011100 11010000 11011101 10011110 10100100 10011110 00110110 11110001 10101000
01011111 10011000 11111100 11110100 11001000 01100100 00110001 10111000 00111101 01101010
00100111 10011100 01110000 01110010 01110011 11010010 10000110 10011000 00000100 00000111
10001111 11110000 10101111 01010010 11110111 10010111 01100010 00001011 10111110 01111010
10011110 10100011 10011010 01001100 10101111 01100110 11111100 11001101 01100111 10110011
01111011 11110001 11101011 01001110 01000010 00011000 10010011 11010011 10001010 00011101
00110100 10110101 10110000 10010101 11001101 01111101 00011000 10000001 10101010 11000111
10000011 11010011 00000111 00110101 11101001 10111010 01001111 10011000 11010001 11100111
10011100 00011110 10010101 11100100 01010001 11001111 11100100 00111010 00111000 00100100
00010001 11010010 10111101 00111111 11000001 11011010 11000100 01010111 10011010 01010110
01001011 00000001 00101100 01100111 01100011 00001100 01111110 01010101 11100111 11100010
11101001 00101111 10001101 00011101 11011000 01111010 10001010 11001110 00101100 10110101
11100010 01111000 01001100 10111010 00011101 11100000 11001111 11111100 10110010 00111101
01101011 10000001 11110000 11110110 10011010 00101110 10101110 01000111 10011110 00001001
10000000 00010001 10010010 00111011 11010111 10100100 01011110 11001111 01101101 00101101
10110100 10010001 01011101 00010001 11100101 01001000 00001010 00011100 00110101 01000111
10100111 01101001 11010110 11010110 10110110 11001000 10110110 10001010 00001100 01011000
11001000 11110111 10101110 01101010 01110101 00011101 00111000 10110100 01010010 10100100
10011100 10101110 11001111 00110111 11110001 01100101 10111100 01010110 10011010 10011110
01100000 10000100 11000101 00010001 00011111 10000001 00111110 11010101 10010010 10011011
01011111 10010101 11001111 10111110 01101011 11010010 10110101 10111000 10110100 11101011
11101011 01011001 01101100 10101111 01001111 10010011 00101011 11110011 00011111 10011000
00110001 10000010 00111010 01100000 11110100 10101111 00111001 10111100 10110011 10111000
10110001 00100001 01100111 10001100 11000111 10011110 10000101 10111011 11010111 01101110

00010110 10100111 00110110 11100110 00110101 11101001 11011001 11011101 00000010 01101101
01101001 00000111 01101100 01010100 11011110 01011110 01001110 01110001 11101011 11111000
11010110 01111011 00110110 00111001 11001001 00000111 11011010 10010110 00111011 10100111
11001000 00001111 10010010 10000000 01111010 11010111 01100010 11010011 01010100 01110010
10111011 10111101 10001001 11100100 10010000 01100111 10000001 11101100 01000110 01101001
10000100 01111100 11100010 10011001 10000001 00100001 11011100 10100111 10000011 11000111
00110100 11111101 10111111 00100010 00000000 01111001 10100111 00101011 00111000 11011101
10000010 00000110 00100100 10000000 00111010 10011111 01101010 10010001 00010100 11100000
10001010 01100110 01001000 00011000 11000111 00111001 11101011 01010011 11000100 00111110
01001110 01001110 01001101 00010000 10000101 10010011 01101001 10001011 01010010 11011110
10011101 01111010 01110100 11111001 10100011 10011011 01110111 01001110 10111001 11100010
10111101 00100011 11111011 01000010 11011011 01010000 11010011 11010000 01001111 00000010
01001011 01101111 00101010 10001100 00010011 11111110 01111010 11010111 10010110 11011100
00101001 10010010 00100010 00000111 10100111 01001010 11101001 10111100 00010101 10100111
11101010 10100100 10111010 10111100 00011001 10110011 11100000 11111110 11111000 10010001
10011111 10100101 01111001 11111000 10101100 00111011 01101011 10011011 01100011 10110011
00001010 11011101 11101101 11010000 11011101 11010011 10101101 11101100 11101100 10101110
01001011 11000110 00100100 10010000 10001111 10111011 11100110 01001001 10011100 01010010
01111000 10101011 01011001 01001011 00111101 00101000 10111100 10001100 10110001 10111011
01110000 10101011 11011100 10011010 11010001 10111000 10110010 01011000 01100010 01110110
10000110 00100100 11001000 00011101 00000111 00011001 10101111 00011100 11110001 00110110
10100011 01110111 01111011 10101001 11001001 00010101 11100010 11111001 01000010 00100110
11000000 10001011 00111101 00101011 10010010 10001101 00111111 01101010 11111001 01001110
10011100 01000101 01011000 10100101 10100001 00001011 11001100 11010111 00010011 11001001
00101100 11000111 01111011 10111001 11001101 00111010 00100111 00111011 10110010 00111001
11101101 11010010 10101011 10101111 00000011 00000111 10100000 10101001 10100001 11001010
11100111 10011100 11100111 11011010 10111101 10101010 01101001 01000011 01100011 11001100
01111010 10110010 01101011 01100000 01001001 00111110 11000110 10101101 11000101 00100000
01010011 11010011 00110101 01011001 01001000 00011101 11110001 01010011 00010010 10111000
00011110 11110101 10100011 10110110 11100001 01101011 00011010 11011010 00100110 10100011
00100110 10010111 10101001 01000101 01110011 00011110 00111110 01000011 10000110 00011110
10101010 01111010 11010111 10110000 11011010 01011100 11111101 10100010 00011000 11100110
10001110 00010111 00010001 10110000 11001000 00100100 11110110 10101111 00001011 01000011
11001000 00100000 10001110 10111101 11101011 11010011 00111110 00011101 01101010 00110010
11001001 10100110 01001011 01101111 00110001 11111101 11011100 00110010 00001101 10111001
11101010 00110011 11001001 10101110 00111100 01010101 00100101 00110101 01111110 10101000
11010110 10001100 10101101 10100001 11010010 11011101 01000111 01110011 00100100 01000100
01000011 00101111 10010100 11100111 10100001 01011110 01101010 00101000 00100000 10111101
10001100 00011101 11110111 01101111 00100001 11100111 10010010 00101010 11101011 01001110
10111111 10001101 00100000 10011000 00010001 01011110 01011111 00100011 11010110 11101000
11101001 01010011 10001001 01001111 11001100 11010100 00100011 00000011 00000110 00100010
00110011 11011111 10001010 10110001 00001100 10110111 01100000 00000001 00100000 10001111
00111001 11101100 01101010 10111101 11011110 10101001 01100101 01101011 10010011 00111100
11110001 10101111 10101000 00100110 10110010 00101110 10111100 01100001 10100011 01000001
10011111 11110100 10101101 11100100 01110110 01010001 10011010 11001001 00111101 01101100
10010000 11011100 11010001 11010100 00101100 10110010 11100111 10010000 00001111 10101111
00110100 10010010 01001111 00100110 01001000 11110010 11111111 00000000 01011010 11100010
00011111 11100010 00010101 10010010 11100111 11001001 10110011 10111001 01110000 01111011
10010010 00101011 01011010 11001111 11000101 01110110 00010111 01110001 11111001 10010001
11111001 11011101 00111010 01101101 10101101 10100011 01000110 01011011 11011000 10010101
00110100 11001101 11000111 10011100 10001110 01001010 10011010 10101011 00101101 11010100
01110001 10000010 11001110 00001000 00011110 11110100 11010001 10101001 01000001 00100000
11001110 11011001 01001000 00100011 10101000 10001100 11010010 11000101 00101100 00010111
00000000 10000000 00000011 11111010 10101001 11111111 00000000 00001010 11001010 01010000
01101001 11011101 10100011 01001011 10101011 00011000 01010111 00111010 10111101 10110100
10111010 10110100 01010001 01000110 01001001 01110000 00001001 11011101 10011110 00101011
01100110 01011011 10101000 10100011 10110101 00110010 11001000 11100000 00100000 00011101
01001101 01110001 11011110 00101101 11010001 01100010 11010011 11000010 01101010 10010110
00000001 11100011 11011001 00100110 01100101 10001100 00001100 10000001 11101110 00101011
00001110 11100111 01010110 10011111 01010000 01010100 01010011 00100011 11111001 01111101
00111100 10110001 11010010 10110101 01010100 10010100 11100010 10111001 01000110 10101010
00101011 01011001 10010110 10110101 00011101 01011110 00001011 10101111 00010010 00001001
10001010 11001001 11100100 01000110 00110110 00010011 00011001 11100110 01001111 10100110
00101011 10110110 10110011 10011010 00000110 10001001 00001100 01101011 00110100 01100000
10001110 10001101 11010110 10110010 01111100 00111001 10100000 11000111 01101110 10001001
01111001 01110100 10100000 11001011 10000000 01100011 01010011 11001110 00111101 11101011
10100010 01001000 10110111 01110101 10101110 11001001 01010001 10000100 01010010 10001111
01100011 00011111 01101010 11100001 10110001 00001100 11101011 00100111 10010010 11111001
10111100 00110001 00100110 00111000 00100000 00001110 00101011 00100101 00100000 00011110
01010010 01111111 10100100 00111101 11000001 11011101 11000011 00110001 11101011 01011011
01001111 01100111 10010011 10001110 00110001 10001110 10000110 10101001 11011100 01011010
00001000 01011011 00101000 00000000 11000111 00100000 11100010 10111001 11010101 00100100
10110110 01100011 01010101 10001100 10011011 01001011 01110101 11010011 01110101 01001001

11100101 01001110 00100010 10010100 11110001 10001110 10000011 11010110 10111010 01001000
01100110 01010110 01000000 11001001 00100000 00100011 11011000 11010110 00101101 11000011
01100011 11100101 01110001 11110100 10101010 01110001 00011111 00100100 11101111 10001110
01001100 00010001 11101001 11011110 10111001 10101010 00111001 10100111 01101011 10011101
01010100 11010010 01101011 01000011 01111110 01010111 00000110 11111010 11001111 00110001
10001111 11110101 11000011 10010000 00101011 10110101 11001111 11101111 00111001 00011100
01110110 11000101 01111001 10010101 10110110 10100010 01100111 11010111 11110100 11101000
00000001 11100100 11001001 10011100 01010111 10100110 01100111 01110001 11100111 10100101
01110101 01010011 01010010 01010000 10111011 00111001 10110001 00101101 01011111 01000001
01110011 11010100 00001010 00000000 11100111 00111101 00101000 11001001 00111100 11010000
11011100 00000010 01101000 10111010 11011000 11100100 00001100 01111100 11011001 00000111
00111001 10100011 00111001 01000010 01111111 10011101 00011100 11100100 01010010 00011101
11000100 10000000 00111000 01001100 01110011 01000011 00010000 01111101 11011000 11110010
01111111 00001010 00001001 00011011 01111101 11001101 00101010 11110010 01000110 11100001
11010010 10000000 00110010 01001011 00010101 00000011 11011110 10011011 11010111 01000001
10110001 10111101 00110001 11101111 11011110 10011011 00101001 11001000 11011010 10000111
00100100 11110101 00100011 10110101 00111111 10000010 00111001 10100101 01011100 00010000
01110110 01110100 00010100 01101000 00100001 00011011 10010000 00000111 01100001 11011110
10010011 10100111 01101010 01011110 10100101 00000000 00011111 01010011 01000111 00000101
11001000 00000111 10100101 00101110 10100011 00001110 01110011 11000111 01001111 01111010
00011000 01100100 01110010 01101001 01001000 11001111 11010110 10011011 11011111 00000010
10101001 10110101 01110000 00010100 11110000 01000001 11000111 11100000 00101001 00010100
01110000 01111001 11100110 10000110 11100010 00110011 10001111 10111111 01000000 11100100
10000001 11101011 01011001 11011011 01010000 00010101 00111010 11100011 11110101 10100110
01110010 11000000 10001110 01111000 00111100 11010011 11010111 00011111 10000111 10110101
00011110 11000000 01110001 11011111 11011110 10101011 11100110 00100001 00010111 00100011
00100001 10111111 00011010 00001000 11000001 11111110 10010100 11001110 01000001 11101111
10010010 01111010 10011010 01111011 00011100 00011110 10111100 01010100 11011100 01100011
01011000 11100110 01001100 01100111 10100111 01101010 01111011 00001111 01101110 01101001
10011101 00011111 00111000 10100001 01001001 11100100 10011100 11100110 10101011 01110100
00110110 00000011 00111011 10110001 10001110 10110100 00010011 10000011 11000111 01010011
01000010 11110001 11110100 10100100 11000000 00000010 10000100 10101100 10000100 00001110
00001110 11001101 11000111 00011001 00010100 10011100 10010001 10000010 01111000 00111101
01101001 01010111 00011000 11000000 11001110 00111101 11101000 00000011 10010001 01001010
11101010 01000000 00100000 00000111 00111000 00000010 10001100 00000000 01111101 01001000
10100101 01101110 01000111 10101101 00100001 00000100 11110111 10100110 10011010 10111000
11101110 00000111 11111101 01100000 11001001 11101101 11010010 10011011 00110001 11000100
01011000 11101110 01111000 10100111 01110100 11000001 11110101 11100011 00110100 11010001
10001101 11100100 10011010 00010011 11010100 10010000 11100111 10011111 01000001 11111010
11010010 00000000 01111010 01110100 11110111 10100111 10110001 11000100 01111011 10001001
11101000 01110000 00000101 00011100 10001111 11100101 01001011 01001011 01011100 01100011
00110110 11110011 10010001 11111001 10011010 01010111 11001111 10010110 01110110 00011100
10011111 01010011 01000000 00011011 01000000 11001111 11010011 11101011 01000011 01110100
00100000 01110111 00110100 01101011 11010100 00000000 11100111 01101001 00100100 11100000
01010010 01111010 00001100 11111100 11111101 01110001 11101101 01000110 11011111 10010111
00000100 11110001 11101001 01001000 01111111 11010110 00100110 00111001 00100100 01110101
00110100 11110101 01111011 00000000 10101101 10000000 10000101 10011011 00100111 00000010
10010001 01110111 00110000 00000111 10100001 00111101 10101001 11001100 01000010 10010000
00001001 11001001 11110100 10100011 00011100 01111011 11010010 10110011 01100000 00110101
10110001 10001100 01100011 10100101 00011000 00001100 00000011 01100010 10010101 01110010
01011111 11100110 00110100 10011001 00000000 10010011 11001101 01010101 10111010 10100110
00100000 00100100 10010111 00011000 11100000 10000001 10001100 01010011 01111001 00001000
00000001 00111100 10000011 01001110 01101110 01001111 11110101 10100101 01000101 11100111
10010011 11110100 10100100 00110001 10001100 00111010 00001110 11000011 11010011 10111101
00000000 00010010 00001110 01111010 01010011 10111001 00010001 10010000 00111000 11001001
10100110 11100011 00101100 10011100 11100000 00000011 10011100 01010000 10101101 01101011
10000000 11100010 00110001 10011111 01011111 11100101 01001100 01010000 01000010 01100100
01110010 01110011 11010110 10010101 01000010 10010001 11110010 00011110 10110100 11101100
11111100 10100101 01010000 11111011 01010100 01101000 11000000 01100000 11110100 00011101
00111101 01101000 01101100 11101100 00101011 11001000 11100111 11110011 10100101 11011001
10001100 01110111 11000001 10100110 10111111 01011100 10111110 01110010 00001111 00000000
01010101 01000110 11101000 00000000 01110000 00111010 01010001 10011100 01000111 11001111
01011110 11100110 10000111 01100001 11010000 00001100 10011010 00111000 00001011 10000011
01001010 11101111 01100000 00001100 00010000 10111100 00001110 01101000 11101000 00110000
00111010 11111010 11010000 11100100 10010010 00000010 00011110 00110011 10010010 01101000
11100000 01001001 10000000 01000110 01001101 00110101 00101011 10000000 00111110 00010101
10110000 00111010 01100011 10110101 00110101 01111000 11000001 11101100 00101000 01110001
10010100 00101010 00110011 11101110 01101000 00100011 00100011 01101000 00111100 01110111
11110111 10100001 10110000 00001110 11100111 00111101 00001101 00100111 11011101 11100100
11110101 00010100 11111110 11000100 10001100 01100111 10110110 01101010 00111000 11001110
01001011 10001100 11100101 00110001 11111001 11010001 01101011 10100000 00010101 01110011
11100110 01100111 00011111 10101101 00101011 01110000 01011100 10011010 01000010 00111001
11000111 01100011 11101011 01001010 11011001 00011000 00000000 01110001 11101001 01001111

01101101 10000000 01101111 00000100 10000000 00111001 00111111 11001010 10010100 10000001
10010000 01111101 00111111 01011010 00110010 01111010 01111010 11111010 01010001 11111110
01000110 01101000 10110000 00000001 00111011 01010100 10010001 11001001 11001111 01001010
01001100 11110001 10010010 01110010 01111101 01101000 00111110 10100111 10100000 11101010
01101001 10111001 00000111 10101111 11011100 00011101 11101001 11111010 00010110 00001100
01000010 10100001 00100111 11111111 00000000 11010111 01000000 11100001 00000111 01100010
01111010 01010000 11000000 10010111 11100111 10111101 00001011 10000110 10010011 00011000
11111001 00000111 01011111 01101010 01110111 10110001 00000010 01110100 11100100 11100100
11111011 11010011 11000000 00110010 01110101 00011101 00000101 00110101 01001111 00000100
11100111 00111001 00111101 01111111 10010101 00011100 10110100 01001110 10111101 00001011
11010000 00000100 01001110 00111110 01010100 10010011 00111101 00001110 00000111 10111001
10100111 10110110 00000000 11101001 10010011 11010010 10001101 10011001 10001100 00000011
11010001 00001110 01000110 00101001 10001100 01001001 00000000 11100011 10011110 11010100
00111101 01010101 10000000 01111010 11100011 01110110 11100011 11000101 00110001 11001100
10000101 01011100 01100011 00011110 10000010 10000011 10010010 00000111 01101100 10011100
01010011 11011011 10100111 10110101 01001000 00001100 01100010 01110011 10001100 01010010
00000001 11001111 01001100 10011110 11110100 11010111 11100100 11100111 10100101 00110101
00010100 10101001 01111110 10111100 11110010 01001101 00110110 11011010 01100000 00111011
11111000 11101000 11000000 00000110 10011101 11010011 10010010 01111110 10110100 01100111
00011001 00111111 10010110 01101010 01010101 10011110 11100000 00001100 00001111 00011100
11111110 10110100 11011100 11111111 00000000 00111110 01101001 11011100 11111001 01111100
01110011 11101010 01101001 10111000 00100000 10000001 10001110 00101001 11011101 01011010
11100000 00000100 01110110 11101010 00101001 00010100 10010000 00001001 00011101 01101001
01111001 00101111 11000111 11100010 01101001 10111111 11000101 11111110 11001101 01010110
10100000 00110101 00001000 11000110 00111011 11110111 10100001 10101001 11111101 10000111
10100111 01111010 10001101 11110010 01011111 01101000 00100111 00011101 11101001 01011011
01010001 11011100 01011100 11100000 01100110 10000100 11101001 11001001 11101011 01001110
01100010 00000000 11000111 01111010 01101111 01000011 10001110 11110100 10100010 11111010
00001000 00010100 01100001 10001000 10100100 01101110 01001001 11000101 00111101 01111010
11110011 11011110 10100011 11111011 10111001 00001011 11010111 10111101 01010111 10011000
00001011 10001110 00101000 11101000 10011100 00001010 01100001 11001000 11000000 00111100
00001010 01111011 01111010 00001111 11000010 10100101 11011001 10000000 11000000 00110010
01110011 11111010 11010000 11011100 10100110 01111010 01100010 10011100 01111000 01100000
00111101 01000111 11100101 01000111 11011110 01100011 01010100 10010101 10000000 00111001
11000101 00110111 00111001 00100000 01010011 10011011 11110101 11110111 10100110 10100110
01111001 00111001 00011111 10010101 00101011 11110111 00000001 00011001 10110000 11101110
01001111 01000011 11010010 10000101 00000111 11001011 00000000 11010001 11010111 10011111
11001000 01010001 10010011 10001111 10010111 10011010 00111101 00000111 01110001 00110011
10001110 00001111 00100111 11010010 10001110 01111001 00111001 11000000 10100001 10000000
00001101 10011100 01100111 11111010 10011010 01010110 00000000 10001100 10111111 01101110
10110100 00101011 11011110 11001100 01000010 01110010 01001110 00000000 00111000 11110101
10100000 01110111 00011110 10010100 10101000 01000001 00000000 11101110 10100110 00010000
01111100 11000011 11101001 01001100 01110111 00000001 11001011 00011100 11100010 10100010
10011010 01000011 00010100 10100000 01000110 10111011 11110010 00111010 01100010 10100101
00000000 00000011 11110101 10100011 10010110 11000111 00111000 11110111 10100100 11110111
00010000 10011111 01111000 00000000 01001111 00111110 10010100 00010001 11000001 11001111
00100010 10010011 10111110 00010000 11110001 11101011 01001011 11110111 00010011 00100100
11100100 11110110 10100100 11010001 01100010 00010011 11010011 00010100 11001110 10000000
10011110 10111001 10100111 10110110 01000011 10000001 11010111 10001110 10110100 01100111
10010001 11011000 01010011 10110001 00000011 01011101 01001111 00011000 00111111 01011010
01101001 00011101 00000111 01000011 01001010 11100100 11111001 10100111 00100111 10000000
00111000 00000010 10010001 01111001 11001001 10100101 11010100 00000000 01100111 10111111
00110100 11010011 10010011 11010011 10000001 11011100 11010011 10111010 01100111 00011001
11100010 10000001 10010001 10000101 11101001 10011010 10111011 10101110 10000000 00001000
10111100 10000000 11100011 10101101 00110011 10101000 11000010 11110100 11001111 01111010
01011100 11110111 11101111 01001001 11010100 11110101 00111000 00010100 10010101 11011000
00000001 11100101 01001001 11001111 01001010 01100100 10010010 00001100 10001110 01110011
11000101 00111111 10001100 01111011 01010010 10011100 11111101 00101001 10111101 01011000
11110101 01000111 11001111 11111011 10000001 00010101 00100111 10011000 00000000 01000001
11010011 11010111 10001010 00010010 00110010 01001001 11100000 00000001 11101111 01000111
10010100 00111010 11100011 10001111 01111110 11110101 11101001 11101110 10101110 01100110
01011000 01000110 01010010 01110011 01000110 11101101 10111100 10001010 10001111 01110010
10101110 00111000 11000001 11111110 01010100 10011100 10001110 11100100 11010001 01110111
01111011 01110100 00011101 10101110 10110100 00100100 01101001 00000001 01101110 10111100
01100011 10101101 01110101 11111110 00000010 10011010 11100001 10011110 01111000 00101101
01101110 10100001 00011001 00111001 00110000 01001000 00110010 01011011 00011110 10010101
11000101 11101111 00011011 10110111 11100011 11110100 10100101 10000110 01000110 10000101
10000100 10110000 10110001 01001001 01010000 11100100 00110000 11100000 10001010 00101010
01010011 10001101 01001000 10110001 11010011 10101000 11100000 11001111 01011100 10110110
11010100 01001100 10100100 11011011 11101010 11011010 01010011 11011011 11001001 10011111
10111100 01000000 01110100 01111111 01001111 10100101 01101100 00101110 11101011 01111000
10000000 10110101 01010100 00111000 00011111 01110100 10011100 01010111 00001101 10100001
11111000 10010011 01010110 00001000 00100000 10111101 10110001 10010010 11110110 00110011

11111100 01000001 01001000 10010011 11111111 00000000 10101111 01011101 00110101 11001000
10011010 01001000 01100011 01110100 11010100 11001101 10001001 00100011 00100110 00111001
01010100 00011100 00001110 11111111 00000000 10001101 01111000 10111000 10000100 11010110
11000111 10100010 10100101 01110101 01110010 10110110 10111001 10101010 11000010 00010011
11101100 11111010 10101110 10011011 00101100 01110001 10010011 10000101 10010000 00011100
10000000 01111011 01100000 11110110 10101110 01111011 11000110 01010111 10110000 01001011
10100010 01000101 00001001 00100111 00100110 01000000 01010100 01110101 11100010 10110011
11111100 01001101 01110101 00111101 11000101 11101000 10000001 00110101 00010011 01111101
00000000 11111001 11110111 01100011 00000011 00100011 10110111 00010101 00110110 10001011
10100111 00110110 10101111 10101001 10100111 10011111 10000001 10001110 00001001 11101100
00000000 11110100 10101101 00101001 11010001 01101010 11010011 10010001 10000011 10101001
11001111 01111000 10100011 00001010 11011111 01001110 10111100 10011101 01111100 11001000
01101101 10100101 01110100 00100011 10000010 00010100 11100010 10100010 01111000 10011110
00101111 10010110 01000100 01110000 01111101 11000110 00101011 11011110 01110100 11011000
00100001 10110111 10000110 00111000 11100001 01010000 10000001 00000110 00000110 00000101
00101101 11111110 10001111 10100111 11101010 00110001 00010101 10111011 10110110 01000111
00111000 00111111 00110000 11100001 11000111 11100011 01011101 01111111 01011110 01010111
10110101 10110100 00100110 01010100 00010111 01000011 11000001 01011101 01001100 01111111
01110100 11110100 10100111 01111001 10011011 10110000 01000111 00011100 01010111 01101101
11100010 01111111 00000111 11001001 10100111 01000110 01100111 10110101 11011111 01110001
01101101 11010000 11110111 01110100 11111010 11010111 00100010 11110001 00000101 00000011
11100101 11101011 11010000 01010111 01010101 00111010 10010000 10011010 11100110 01001111
01000011 10011001 11000011 10010011 01000001 10100000 01100100 00000011 11111010 10011010
10010001 00001110 00110000 01110011 11010000 11110011 01001101 10010101 01001001 00101000
00110001 10000001 11011110 10010011 10000101 00011000 00011101 00101010 10111101 10100100
01010011 10110010 00100111 01011011 00011101 10100111 10000010 11110100 01111000 00101111
01100100 01111001 11101110 10100001 01110111 00100000 11111110 11101111 00100011 11100100
00111110 10110101 11011011 10111100 11000110 00011100 01000100 11110110 11010010 11101100
00011100 00000010 10111101 00000101 01110011 00011110 00000001 11010110 01100110 10111010
10000100 01011000 11001100 00010010 00111111 10110011 10001110 00011011 10111011 01010111
01001001 01110110 11010111 11000000 10000011 00011001 10001010 01000100 00011101 01000001
11100011 00110101 11100100 11100011 01101010 00111001 01001111 01010011 11010010 10100100
10010111 00101010 10110000 11000111 11011000 11000100 11001000 10000100 11100000 11110110
00110101 11001000 01111000 11110011 01000000 10110100 10111101 11010011 01100101 11010100
01110000 10010001 11011101 01011011 00101110 11110000 01111010 00000111 00011110 10000110
10111010 11011000 10011000 11001101 10000010 01010100 10100001 11101110 00001101 01100011
01111000 11000110 01111000 10100000 11110000 11100101 11101001 10010110 00100011 00100100
01100110 00110010 10011000 00011110 10100110 10111001 11100011 00110101 00001001 00100111
00010100 01001100 11010110 10000111 10001110 11000100 10111001 01010001 11001110 01111101
11110011 01010110 00100010 01010010 00001001 01101100 01010101 01111000 00001110 00000110
00110001 10011010 10011110 00100110 01100101 01100010 01101011 11011111 10001010 01001001
01011100 11100001 01111011 10010011 00110000 11011101 11000011 11110100 11110110 00110100
10001001 00011001 11101001 10011010 01010100 00000000 11100000 10010000 01111010 11010101
11001000 11100011 00011001 11001111 11101001 01001001 00101110 01101101 01000101 01110001
10101010 00001000 00011000 00000011 11101001 01011101 00000111 10000010 10110101 00010101
10110100 11010100 01011110 11011010 01100010 11101000 00101110 10000111 10010110 00011011
00111100 00001001 00111011 00010011 01011001 00001000 10111110 01100111 00001011 10011100
11111011 00001010 10111001 01101001 10100110 01011111 01000011 00100100 01110111 00001001
01101001 00110110 01100010 01100000 11111001 11011010 01101000 11100101 10110110 10001100
01101010 11101111 01100100 01111010 00000100 11011010 11110101 10101101 10011101 10100010
00110101 11011011 11100010 01110000 01001010 00011000 11010100 01110010 01001000 11101111
01010011 11101000 01111010 11101101 10010110 10101101 11100110 10001011 01110110 01110001
00100100 01000111 11100110 10001110 01000001 11001111 00111101 11101010 00111101 00101101
01101101 01101110 11101110 00001101 11010001 10000110 00110111 01001011 10010001 10111100
00000110 00011001 11110010 11011011 10111101 01010111 10011011 01001100 10110111 10001111
11000101 00110110 01110111 01110110 10001010 10010001 11001000 01000001 11110011 00010100
00011110 10100010 10111100 11000110 11010100 01100111 11001011 11011100 11011101 01000010
11101010 11100101 01111111 00010111 01111000 01010100 01101010 00110001 00111101 11100101
10000000 11111111 00000000 01001011 00000011 11110111 10010001 00010011 11000100 10000011
11011011 11011110 10111100 11110101 01101101 01000000 00100101 01011001 01110110 00111010
00011110 01000001 11100000 10001010 11110111 01100101 10001100 00001110 01110011 10001110
11110101 10001011 10101001 01101000 11110110 01010111 01010111 00100110 01110111 10000001
00111100 11010011 11010100 10001110 11110101 11010101 00010110 10111010 10011000 10011110
01111111 11100001 10111101 00001010 01111101 01010010 11101011 00111011 01000010 01011011
00101001 11111101 11100011 01100011 11110100 00010101 11101001 11010110 01110110 11110001
01011001 11011010 10001000 01100000 10001101 00000100 01100011 10100000 11000101 00110110
11011010 00110101 10001010 00100000 10110001 10101000 00000011 11011011 10001010 01111011
10110000 00100100 00000001 11001000 11110101 10100101 01010010 10101111 11011001 10001001
01101001 10001111 01110010 00001010 11010100 00010010 11000110 00001001 11011100 00001110
11000111 11110101 10100111 10111001 00000111 00000011 11010100 11010010 10110110 00000000
11100011 10111101 01110011 10110100 10101100 00101011 10011001 00011010 10111100 10111000
10110100 10011101 01100110 00011111 00100100 10001011 10110000 01110111 00011001 00110101
11000001 11101000 11110110 00010010 01011011 10110011 10101001 00001000 11110010 00001110

11000110 10111101 00001111 01010100 11000000 11010011 10101110 01011000 10001100 11101100
01011101 11100011 11101010 00101011 10010100 11110000 01111101 10101111 11011010 00101110
10100101 10111000 01110010 01001010 00000101 11101111 11101010 01111001 10101101 00110000
11010001 01001001 10111110 01010000 01110011 01101101 11101010 01110110 01010000 11101101
00110001 01000111 10000001 11111100 00100010 10100101 01001100 11100011 00110101 00011010
00101110 00000000 00011001 11101001 01001011 10010011 10000011 10000011 01010001 00110101
01110111 01110000 01100100 10011011 10000000 10101000 10100110 01100101 01100001 11110011
10001100 11010010 00111001 11011010 01000000 10101010 10010111 01010011 00101000 10010000
01110011 11010011 10101101 00101011 10111011 00000100 01001100 10101111 00010011 01001100
11010000 11011010 11000110 01010010 00110000 00111110 01101100 01110010 01111101 01101011
10011100 11111011 01000100 10100010 00010111 11000111 01010011 11111100 00110101 11010010
11011111 01000100 00101111 00100100 10001101 01100110 00000000 10001100 11110100 00110101
10011011 10101000 11111000 01000110 00110011 00101010 01001101 01101011 01110100 01000011
11111111 00000000 11001111 00111001 01111001 00000011 11101000 01000101 00101000 11010010
10001101 11101110 11011101 10001110 10101010 01110101 01111001 01100010 11010001 01011111
11000010 01010010 01000111 00100111 10001011 01101100 11000110 01011100 01001010 00001110
11110110 00001100 00110001 10000000 00101011 11011000 10010100 11110101 11000001 11001110
01101011 11001010 11111100 00100101 10100110 11011111 11011010 01111000 10011010 11010001
10101111 10000100 01101110 00000110 01000010 11001000 10100111 00110101 11101010 11001010
00000010 11110001 11010110 10111010 00110001 01001110 00101001 00101011 00110011 10011001
10110110 11110111 00011100 00001111 00111000 11000110 00010000 00011110 01101001 00010011
00000000 01111011 11100111 10111101 00101011 01010010 00000001 11000111 10100111 00111100
11010111 00011110 10110111 00100000 01010110 11100100 11111111 00000000 10001101 00100011
00010011 10011110 00111111 00011010 01000010 01111000 10100101 01101110 11000011 10110101
00101101 01000110 00101110 01110000 10111001 10100100 11100100 10011110 10111000 11001101
00011001 01011101 10000111 01111111 01001010 00010011 11101110 00000010 00111001 00111111
11001010 10101011 10101000 10000001 01110010 00001000 00000111 10011111 01110011 01001000
10100100 01110011 11101001 01001010 10011000 00001000 01111110 10110100 10011101 10110000
00111000 10100101 01110110 00110000 11000110 01110000 00000111 11100111 10011010 01110010
00001100 00010010 00000010 11100000 01110101 11001111 10101101 00110111 00011000 00000011
00011100 01100011 10101111 10111101 00101111 01010000 01110010 11011000 00010100 01011001
10100111 10101000 00001000 10111100 00000010 01000111 10101101 00011011 01000001 11100110
10011010 01001000 00011000 00011101 01000001 10100111 11110000 00000111 11100011 01000100
01011101 10011000 00001000 01111110 11111001 11000111 00100100 01010010 11110010 00000110
01110001 01001000 10100011 10010010 01101000 11100100 10001100 01110011 10011010 00010100
10010111 01010001 00001101 00011001 00011101 00000101 00001001 11011100 11100011 00110100
00111000 00000100 10001100 11111010 11110100 10100111 00110111 00000011 10110000 11101111
01001101 00100000 00011010 00110010 01111001 11111100 10000101 00111001 10111010 11100000
01010000 10100100 00000001 10010001 01001101 01101110 00001010 01100000 11100011 00100111
10011010 00110100 10110101 10000110 00001011 11000011 10000000 00111010 01110111 10100100
00001100 01001010 00001110 00111010 00011010 00100100 11100000 10011101 10011100 01100111
10111101 00111111 00111100 11111010 00001100 01110001 01001010 11110110 01000000 00001110
00111000 11011101 11011111 11010010 10011000 11111101 01110001 11011011 00011101 01111101
01001101 00000000 10011100 01110000 00110010 01001111 10101101 00001100 00110110 10110111
10101111 00011110 10111101 11101010 10000000 01010010 01000000 10001100 00001111 11100011
00111101 00101000 11000110 00010100 00001010 00111001 01010100 00011101 11011100 11010010
01100100 11110001 01010000 00000000 10100000 10010111 00000111 00111111 10000101 00100011
01100000 00000010 01111101 11101000 01000000 01011011 10101111 01111110 11111001 10100011
01101000 00000011 11011000 00011110 11110100 01110010 11110111 00000001 01110010 10100000
01100100 11110011 11011111 00011110 10110100 11000100 00000100 11100011 01111000 11111001
11001111 11101001 01001110 01100011 11000000 00110100 00001111 01011010 01101101 11011000
00000110 11110101 11101011 11010010 10011101 10011101 11001110 00111101 00101001 10111001
11100100 01000110 10010100 00110111 11101110 11110000 01001001 00111001 11001110 00101010
01101110 00111011 10000111 10101111 01111100 01010010 01100100 11100111 10000000 01110011
11011111 00110100 01110000 00001111 11010010 10011111 11010000 01100111 11010111 11010110
10101010 11101101 10001000 01100111 00011110 11111001 00011111 10001101 00101010 10111001
11100100 11110100 01110011 11111010 01010000 10111110 10000010 10011011 10001101 11001110
01111011 01010001 01100000 00010101 01100011 11011010 10001111 10001110 01001001 11100111
00100110 10010011 00111100 00100110 01000110 01001000 11101011 10001010 01110011 11111111
00000000 10110000 01110001 11110101 10100100 00010010 01100000 11111010 10011100 01110110
10100011 01000001 10110001 10000110 01001111 10010000 10010100 11111001 11011101 10111000
00010100 01100100 10011110 00000000 11000000 00011101 11101001 11001000 00110110 00000000
00101000 00101100 00000110 11001110 11111001 11100010 10010010 01001101 11101011 01110001
00000011 00000010 00001000 00000011 10100000 10100110 11101101 00001010 01001110 00111111
10001100 01100000 11010011 10001110 01110000 00000110 00111000 00011101 01101000 00011101
01001110 01001111 00111110 11111101 10101001 10101101 00000000 00011101 01000001 11100011
00111101 00111000 10100110 10101001 11100011 10000001 11011111 00000100 11010000 11011011
01111010 10010010 01110001 11010111 00011110 11110100 00110111 11111010 11000000 10100011
10100110 00110011 11001101 00001000 01101100 00010100 01111100 11100111 00011100 00001111
11110000 10100100 10000101 01010100 01110011 11010111 00100111 00111001 10100101 01101111
01000011 11010010 10011100 00000010 10101111 00011101 00101000 10111000 10000110 00100001
00101100 00110010 01111000 11101111 10001010 01010110 11000010 10101001 11101111 10011110
10000010 10000101 01100000 10111000 00011001 11101001 01001000 11000000 10110010 01100101

10111011 11110001 01001111 11010000 00000100 00111000 11011010 00001000 11110100 11100110
10011010 10111111 00110000 11100011 11111111 00000000 11010101 01010010 00001100 00010100
11100011 10011111 11000010 10010001 00110010 01000111 00011100 01111010 11010010 01111010
10000000 10011011 01110001 11110010 10001110 01111101 01101001 10100101 01000110 01001001
00111101 01110011 01001110 11101111 10011100 01010010 11110101 11111010 01110111 10100011
11001000 00000100 11001001 11001111 01001100 01010011 00000001 11101010 01111010 00001110
10100110 10010101 11110000 01110001 11001110 00010000 00011111 11001110 10011101 10000010
01010111 00111101 00000111 10100101 01001111 00110011 11011000 01101100 01101000 00011100
10011100 11110100 11110111 10100011 00111000 01000010 00100011 11101001 01000111 01100000
01000001 11111100 11101000 00011000 00001001 10011110 01110010 00111001 11000101 01010100
00000100 00100000 00111001 00010100 01110011 10000111 11100100 11111010 01010010 11000101
10010010 11011001 11000110 00110011 11011010 10010001 10000001 00001010 01111001 11101111
11010111 11010110 10000110 10110101 11010100 00000010 00111100 10000001 10001110 10010100
10001111 11110111 11110011 11011000 10011110 11110100 10101101 11110111 01000111 10101101
00100011 00110010 10101111 00101111 11001000 11101101 01001111 11010100 00000110 10110010
10110100 10101111 10001110 10000011 00111111 10011101 00111001 11111100 11001111 00101100
10001000 11001000 11011110 01000111 00011001 11100110 10000100 00100111 11001011 00011000
11100111 11010110 10001110 01110011 10001110 11100010 10010001 01100011 00010000 01100001
00111110 01101100 10011100 01110001 10010011 11011110 10010101 10010100 01110010 00001111
01111110 10110100 11101101 11011101 00001110 00111000 11101111 01001101 01011100 10011101
11101101 11101111 01001110 11101110 11100100 00001101 10010000 10011100 10100000 01010001
11010010 10011100 01000110 11011001 01001111 10100110 00110000 00101001 00011100 10001000
11000000 11101110 11100111 10100000 10100100 01110011 11001000 00111101 01001000 11101011
10001010 01101111 01000000 00000010 01111111 01110110 01000111 01010011 11101101 01001101
01100101 00100101 11110010 01111000 00001011 11010011 00111101 11101001 11101101 11000001
00000111 00011000 11100011 11110011 00110100 10001100 00110010 01110010 01111111 00101010
01001001 00000000 10101111 11110111 01110000 00000111 00011110 10110100 11001100 11110001
11101100 00111101 01101001 11001101 10011100 00000011 01001101 01111111 10011011 11100101
00000011 10100111 10101101 01000101 10011011 11010100 00001000 11010011 00100101 11110010
01111010 00001110 10010100 10001110 01100100 01101001 10001111 00000001 00100010 00011110
10111101 01001101 01001000 10111000 11101100 00110011 01001010 11111000 10100001 00000001
00011110 01000001 00011100 00001110 00110011 01001110 01100011 10000001 01000001 00011001
00000000 00000001 11001101 00011101 01001101 01011110 10001001 01011000 00000110 11100011
10111111 00100100 01100010 10000111 11001001 00100000 11110100 00110100 11110010 01001111
01000001 01001000 11011001 11000001 00101011 11111001 10011010 01010001 01011010 00000000
11001100 01100011 10100101 00011101 00111101 01101000 01101100 10010101 01000000 00000110
01001001 11100100 10011010 00001001 11100110 10101011 01001101 11000000 01001110 01001111
11100101 01001101 11000110 11010001 11000111 11011111 00111100 01100110 10011111 10011101
10100000 11100011 10101001 10100100 00011000 00001001 11111000 01010010 11110101 00000000
01010101 00000000 01100011 11110011 00111110 10110100 11011111 11100001 00110100 01110011
10011111 01101010 01001100 11100000 00010000 01111001 00010100 10111100 10011000 00000010
10110001 01011111 01010000 00001111 01001010 01001100 01101101 00111001 11000111 01011010
01110110 00111010 01100111 00011101 01101001 00001001 11100111 10000001 10011010 01101101
01011011 01000001 11101110 00100111 00100010 01001110 11011001 00111101 00000111 01111010
01101010 10011111 11101110 10001110 01001001 11101001 01001111 01111100 11100000 00010101
11101011 11011100 11010011 00110010 01000110 01000110 01001001 11000111 01010011 11101011
01000101 11110100 10111001 01000011 10111000 00010010 00010001 10011100 10011100 01010000
01110000 10100000 01100011 10101111 01001010 00100010 00000001 01110010 01111101 01111010
10011010 10001101 00001001 01100000 00111010 10011100 11010011 11100111 11101000 10001000
00100100 00111100 10100001 00011101 11101001 10001010 00111011 10000011 11000101 00101110
00001110 01000101 00111101 11110001 10011101 10111101 11001111 00111000 00010101 00101110
11100000 00110000 01110010 01110111 00101111 10100101 00100000 00011101 01110011 11010010
10010101 01000110 01110011 11101001 01001110 11111110 00110001 10011111 11100111 01010101
00100100 10101101 01100100 00000011 00011100 01110100 11100111 10000001 01000010 11111101
11010011 11011011 00111110 10110100 10101011 11001000 01110011 10011010 01000110 00111100
00001110 00110011 11101011 11101101 01010011 10101000 11110111 00010000 00010011 10110011
00011000 11001111 11010010 10001100 00001110 11111101 01000101 00001100 01110010 10000101
01000111 00000011 10111001 00010100 11010010 00000111 00000011 10110111 11110011 10100111
10101010 00010000 10011100 01100111 10111110 01111011 11010010 10110111 00011100 10001111
11001010 10000110 11101001 10010001 10000001 10011110 00000101 00001001 11000000 11000111
01111010 00011011 10110110 10100000 00000001 01110011 10000011 10001111 11000010 10010011
00011001 00111101 10110011 11011000 01111010 01010001 10000011 10001100 11100011 10001111
10101101 00011100 01101100 11100011 10001100 11010010 10111010 10011110 11000000 00110011
11101011 11111000 11010011 10011000 01100111 00000100 11111110 01010100 01101110 11000001
11000000 11000111 11010010 10011001 11001110 01001110 11100001 11000000 11101010 00101001
11011011 01001101 01000000 00001000 11101011 01001011 10001100 00001100 11111010 01010001
10010001 10010000 00000000 11000111 10110101 00011111 11110010 11010100 00101110 00111111
00011111 01011010 00010011 01111101 01000000 01101110 00000001 11100100 11100011 00000000
11110011 11101111 01001101 11101110 00001010 10001110 01111101 00101001 11111101 01111110
01010001 11010000 00011110 10110100 10000111 10101110 01000001 10101011 01001110 11011010
10000000 00101110 01111000 11110101 11101111 10001010 01101001 11100111 00100111 10111101
00111000 00010011 10110111 11011100 01010011 00000110 01011001 11000000 00000011 10111111
00100010 10001011 11011100 01101000 01001110 01001110 00111001 11100110 10011100 11011101

01111110 11110110 01111111 00001010 01110001 11000001 10010000 10000000 00110000 00000001
11100110 10010010 00110110 11111001 00000110 00010100 11010010 11100101 10111011 11010100
01000111 10000010 10110000 01110000 00111000 11100011 00000011 10110101 00110001 10100100
11100000 01100101 10001111 00111100 11110100 10100111 10111110 01001110 01111001 10101000
11011011 00000100 00000000 01110011 10000001 11101001 01011110 10011111 00110110 10111011
10010010 00011100 00011111 10011000 10010001 10011111 01101010 00000100 10000000 01100111
00111001 11110110 10101000 10010111 00111001 11011010 01111000 11110100 10101011 00010001
11000100 10101100 00110010 01110011 11000111 01010001 01011010 00101011 01110100 00001101
01001000 11010101 10001001 00011111 00111101 01001011 00011000 11011100 01010000 00100001
11000001 11000111 00100111 11010011 11011110 10011110 11100100 00001110 11011100 00001110
00000111 00010100 01000100 11000001 01001111 01001110 10110101 10001100 01100100 11110101
01001100 01111010 00011011 10010110 11111110 00101100 11010111 00100011 01001101 10100010
11110100 10010000 00000110 00000110 01100011 00011100 01111101 00101010 10111101 11011101
11110101 11100110 10100110 11000001 10101111 01100111 10010010 01011111 10101111 00010101
10011110 00011000 00011100 00001111 11010110 10100100 01001001 01011011 00000100 00001110
01001101 01001011 10100101 00001011 01011110 11011010 10001110 11111010 01011101 10110010
11101101 10110000 01011111 00110101 00010111 00011000 11100111 00000011 00010101 11101001
10011110 00011000 11010010 11111110 11000111 01100110 00100101 01110001 10001001 00100100
11100100 10010010 01111010 01010111 00000111 11100001 01011011 00110110 10111011 11010101
01100011 00011000 00011110 01011010 01110010 11011101 11101011 11010101 11100001 00011001
10001111 00000000 01100000 01110100 10101110 01101100 01100101 01001110 01011000 11110010
11110101 00111010 10110000 11110001 11010011 10011000 00001101 11010111 10010110 11111000
00001011 10010001 01010011 00100110 10100000 10101010 01001110 11110000 11111111 00000000
01011100 01010010 00101101 10111010 11110100 00100011 00110100 11110011 00000000 11000111
01001100 01010111 10010001 00101011 11011111 01000011 10100010 11101000 10000010 11110010
11111010 00101111 00101001 11011000 10010000 01010011 00011100 10101111 10101101 01111001
10000101 11001110 10011011 01111001 01110001 01110111 00101100 10010110 10010110 10010010
11111001 01101100 11011111 00101010 10010001 10001100 00001010 11110101 01001111 10110010
11000110 01111011 00001100 11111010 11100010 10011110 10010000 00101111 01001100 00001111
01101010 11101011 10100011 01010101 11010011 11011000 11000110 01010000 10001100 11110111
00111100 11010010 11010011 11000001 11011010 10010100 11011001 00110011 00010100 10000100
00110111 01011100 10011100 10010001 01011011 10010110 00011110 00000100 10110110 01010000
00111110 11010111 01110011 00101100 10000111 11010001 01000110 00000001 10101110 11000001
10100011 11000001 10101001 11010001 01000000 11101001 01001101 11100011 00101010 01101101
01111011 00000010 10100111 00001110 11000111 00100101 01110001 11100001 11001011 00111011
00011001 11100011 01101000 01100001 00111011 00000001 11001000 01110010 11011001 00111111
10001101 01001011 10101110 11001000 11110110 01110110 00010010 01011100 01011011 11001010
01100010 10010110 00111000 11110111 11101101 00111100 10100011 11111101 01000101 01101111
11101010 10000101 01000101 10100011 10110011 10110010 00001101 10111100 11100100 10011010
11110010 00111111 00011010 01111000 11001011 11101101 10010000 10011011 00001011 01010100
01100000 11011111 11110010 11010000 10010001 11000110 00111101 10001101 01100001 00011110
01101010 11110010 10110010 11010100 10100111 00110101 00010101 01100011 10101110 11010000
01110101 11110011 10101000 01011001 10001001 10101110 10100000 00110110 11001111 10001110
01001110 01110010 00011011 11011100 01010100 01011010 11100101 10110000 11110001 00001111
11111010 00011010 01001100 01010010 00000100 00011001 00100100 01110111 00110101 11001001
01111000 00111011 11000100 01101010 01100010 10001110 11001110 01111000 00011101 11100101
00011111 00100010 10010101 00011001 11001000 10101111 01010000 11010011 10101101 11010110
00011000 01110010 11101010 00000001 01101111 01101010 11101010 10010101 00010111 00001001
01011110 11011010 00001110 11110001 01101010 11100111 10010101 11101010 10011110 00000111
11010101 01101100 11011111 00110000 01111001 01110111 01010001 00010011 11000001 10001100
11110011 11111000 10001010 11000101 10010110 11011110 01101000 00100101 11110010 11100111
10001001 11100011 01110001 11010100 01001000 00101011 11011101 00010101 01001001 00111100
11111010 11110001 01001001 00110101 10010100 00010111 01001000 01010010 11101010 00010100
10010110 00110010 00110001 10000110 00010101 01010100 11110001 10010010 10000110 10001101
01011100 11000111 11011000 10100111 10110001 11100010 01010000 11000100 01011000 10000000
11000111 00011110 11110101 11101000 10011110 00010110 11110000 01110100 01010111 00010000
01000111 01110101 10101000 11001010 01111111 01111000 00110010 00010110 00110011 11010110
10101100 01011111 01111000 00101010 11001101 10001110 11101011 00011001 01100100 10110111
00111111 11110011 11001100 10001100 10001010 11010101 11010000 10100010 10111001 11010010
11101101 10111110 11001101 00110100 10101001 01110000 00000001 11100001 10000000 00100011
00011110 11010101 10100101 01001100 01011111 10111011 11101110 11101110 00101000 01010010
10110011 11010100 11011000 10110100 11010011 01101100 00101100 10111000 10110111 10110110
10001101 00110001 11011111 00011001 00111111 10011101 01001001 00101100 10111100 10010000
01001001 11000101 01010100 10010110 11101000 10011110 11000111 00110101 00011000 01100011
00100110 01000110 01001101 01111001 10101110 10110101 01000110 11001101 11010100 00001000
01011101 10100010 10000110 01001001 00100100 11101001 10001110 01101011 00110011 01001010
10010100 10110110 10111011 00010101 11000100 10000011 11111101 01101000 00100000 01111110
01010101 01110011 01010000 10001101 10001010 01110100 11110101 11001110 01111011 11010110
01011110 10100111 00110100 10110110 00110110 11110110 01011010 10000100 00010001 11101111
00010110 11010010 01100110 01010101 00000111 11111000 01001111 00000110 10110100 10100001
01010101 10101001 10101011 10000011 10000101 10010011 01100111 01100000 00100100 00011000
11001001 10101010 01110111 00110011 00000101 00011110 11100110 10100100 10110100 10111010
10000010 11101110 11001010 00111011 10011000 00100100 00000110 00101001 00010111 01111000

00110101 01001110 00101001 01000101 11010101 11010110 01010000 11111110 11101100 00000011
10110111 11111101 10111010 11101101 11100110 01101010 01000111 00001001 01100010 00101100
10010010 01110011 01000110 01110000 01111111 10100101 00101000 00011100 01100011 11011110
10100010 10011100 11111001 01110001 10010110 11111111 00000000 00100110 10100111 10011110
11111011 00001000 01100011 11001111 00011100 01100111 00110010 00110010 00100010 01111010
10110001 11000101 00000010 11101010 00011001 01010011 01110100 00010011 01000111 00100000
11110101 01010011 10011010 11100000 11100110 10110001 10001110 00111011 11101001 01101111
01111100 01000101 00100001 10111000 00101110 01111111 01110011 01101100 10101100 01001110
01111111 00001010 11101001 00111100 00111111 00000011 01111101 10011010 01001001 10011110
11001101 00101100 11010010 01000010 00111100 10101000 10000000 11000001 11000111 10111101
01101010 10010101 11100011 01110110 00111011 00110011 01000011 01010001 00111111 11110001
00101110 10111001 01011100 11110000 01100001 01111111 11100101 01011000 10111110 00000101
10000100 11000101 11100001 11111011 01110010 01010111 01100011 11001011 11111011 11000011
10010011 11010111 11010010 10110110 10101110 01000000 10010010 00100111 01010011 11010001
10010100 10000011 01011001 11111010 01011101 11010101 10111100 00110110 11010001 11000001
00001000 10010000 10001000 11000110 00000000 11011011 01011001 11000010 10101010 10001101
11111100 11000001 00101011 10110011 01101101 01000001 10100101 01101110 00110000 00101011
00101110 11100111 01010111 10001010 11011010 00111100 11111001 01010010 10010111 00111111
11000010 00000101 01100101 01001111 11100010 11111011 00110100 10111101 10110111 10110101
10011010 00101001 10010010 01011001 10110001 10000010 00110000 01000000 11001101 01001100
01101010 00101001 10111011 00100001 11111011 00110110 10010001 10111011 01110001 00101001
01101001 01001001 11111110 10110101 10010011 00100101 11010111 00010010 00110001 00100000
11100100 11100000 00001111 01111010 01101110 10110011 10101000 10101101 10011101 10011100
10110010 10010110 11000001 00100011 00000011 10001110 11110101 11000101 00011101 01011110
11100110 01111011 11111000 11001010 01000101 10110010 11011010 00110000 01110110 10101001
00011101 01001111 10101001 10100111 10111011 11010001 00011010 01010010 10100110 11100101
10110010 00111011 01111011 00111101 11110010 01011101 10100110 11100011 11000000 00111001
01101010 11011100 00100001 01001000 11001101 01110001 11111010 01000100 11110111 00011011
11000100 00101111 00111100 01001000 00110010 01001011 00110111 01010011 11101101 01011101
00000110 10011011 01110000 11010010 01011100 10111100 01010011 01001101 10010111 00011111
11000011 10000001 11001111 11010010 10011100 10011010 01001001 01011100 11010010 01110100
01100110 10011110 11000110 10001110 10011101 00011110 00110101 10011011 00000000 00001111
00000101 10001111 11110010 10101110 11000111 00010101 11001001 11011000 10000001 11111101
10110101 01100001 10001111 01010011 10011111 11000010 10111010 10100111 00101100 11000100
10001100 11010010 01101101 00110100 10001110 01110111 01110001 11011001 11000111 00011110
10110100 01100000 00110001 11100011 10100101 00100000 11100011 00000100 11110101 11000101
00011101 00010100 10010011 11010100 11110100 10101000 01101111 01011101 00001001 00001101
10011101 11010100 11111110 00010100 11110101 01100000 10100000 11111010 01100011 10011010
01101011 01100111 10110001 00000010 10010001 11110010 00010000 00001010 01010111 01100010
00000000 01000001 01011110 01110001 01000110 00111110 01011111 01101010 00110110 11111111
00000000 01111111 10001010 00001011 01100111 00111001 00011100 01100010 10010000 11000100
11000111 10111111 00011101 10110001 01001101 01100001 10011100 11110000 01111110 10110100
11100101 11110100 00010100 10111101 00110000 00001001 11111100 00101001 11101000 00100000
00011101 10101001 00011000 10010000 10000111 11011110 10000110 11100100 11100100 10001110
01101001 10101111 10000110 00100011 10010011 10001010 01001110 01010111 00000000 01000000
01001110 00110011 11011010 10011100 11000011 10010000 00110011 01000011 00011110 01001010
11111010 11110100 10100001 00001000 00011001 00111111 10011101 01010010 11010011 01000110
00110001 01011000 11110110 10100100 11001110 01111001 11001111 01011010 00011100 00110001
00011000 00000011 00100111 10111101 00110101 01111000 11000000 00010100 10110100 10111000
00000111 00000000 10001110 01000111 11111111 00000000 01011110 10011101 10010000 00001001
11001111 00000010 10000111 00001010 00011111 10100111 00110100 11011100 11110001 11110111
01111010 11010011 01101110 11000010 00011100 10100111 01110000 11100011 10110101 00110111
00000000 01110011 11011110 10010001 10110010 00000110 00111010 01100110 10011110 10100011
10011100 11010010 10111011 11011100 00000110 00110001 11100111 00100111 10101110 00111000
00010100 01110011 10111111 00101101 10001010 01010010 01111000 00111000 00110100 10011001
00111001 11000001 11101101 01000011 10111011 11011000 01100010 10010011 10011110 00110110
11010000 10100011 00000011 10011111 11000010 10011101 10010000 00111000 11101011 11101111
11011010 10011001 10010000 01110001 11101001 11011010 10010111 01010000 00010011 01110110
01001001 11100000 10001100 01111010 11010000 11000100 10010000 01111101 01101001 01001111
01011100 00000001 01000111 00011100 01110100 00000000 01111011 11010000 11010110 10110111
00011010 00010000 10011100 11110100 11100111 10110101 00011000 00100000 01100000 10001110
11011101 00101000 11100000 00010011 10001110 11111110 10010100 10101101 10010010 10111001
11100111 11010011 00000010 10011101 10101111 10101000 10001000 11011100 10010001 00011100
01100011 00011101 00001111 00100110 10100100 01111111 10011010 01000001 10011110 00000000
00010100 10001010 00110001 11011111 11110000 10100110 10000011 10111000 11110010 00111000
11110101 10100001 10110111 10110000 00001110 11101111 11000110 01000101 00110001 11011000
11100100 11110111 00100100 01110001 10011110 11010100 10101011 10000110 00100100 01110011
10001100 11110011 01001001 10010010 00001001 00111000 11101000 00110010 01111101 10000101
01001101 10111011 10001110 11100010 10010010 00110010 00010100 00001110 00000111 01010011
01001101 01101100 00010000 01001000 11100111 10001110 10110100 11101100 10010001 00011111
00000011 10010010 00111011 11010010 00100110 11010000 10000000 00110001 11001011 10000001
11001101 01010010 01101111 10101001 00100000 10011100 00111000 00101010 01110011 11000111
01001010 01001111 10011011 00111001 00000111 00100000 11111011 01010010 10110110 01111010

11110110 11000111 00100010 10000110 11011100 00100011 11000010 01110000 00111101 10101000
00011000 11110010 00000000 01111100 10010001 11111000 11010100 01101011 11000110 01110001
10011100 01111010 10011010 01010100 11100111 00011001 00111100 00100111 10101111 01111010
10001101 01001110 01110111 10001100 11100101 00110011 11000101 00101011 10000001 00100011
00110111 00111111 11100011 01001000 11011100 10110110 00110001 11011111 10101101 00101000
11100111 11010011 10011110 10100110 10010000 00011110 10011000 11100110 10001011 11101010
11000000 00001110 01011000 11111011 01010001 10000010 01111001 11110100 11100010 10010111
10010101 00011111 00111111 01010011 01001000 01110010 01001001 00011110 11110100 01101000
10110110 00000001 10110010 00101000 00111000 00100100 10011111 10010000 11110001 01000111
01011100 11110001 10000010 00001111 01011010 01110110 00111101 11111001 00011101 01101001
10001010 11000100 00000100 00100000 01111101 01111101 11101001 01011101 10000000 10100100
00010010 01110010 01001000 00000000 00001010 01001110 00001001 00001101 10011110 00110001
11111010 01010010 01001010 00110111 01100001 01001111 11010111 10001010 01010101 00011001
11001110 00000110 00110000 00111000 10101010 11010101 00000000 10111100 00010100 00111100
01100010 10010001 10011000 01100000 00001110 01111101 10101001 01001111 00001000 01001110
01101001 00110010 00000001 11001000 00011001 00010100 01011111 01100100 00000000 00110011
10001110 01111010 01110111 10100100 01110011 11110011 00001100 01110011 10010011 11000101
00111001 01110001 11111000 00001010 10001111 11101111 01000110 00001001 11100000 10010001
01000101 11101110 00000001 10010011 11100110 10001110 01110010 00111101 00101000 01100001
10010011 11110100 00111101 11101000 01001110 10000000 11100011 10100111 10100101 00111000
11110010 01111001 10100100 11010101 11110110 00011101 11000001 10010100 00001100 01100110
10000110 11100100 10010001 10011110 10100011 00010100 11011101 11111000 00100011 00111000
11100110 10000101 11000001 11001001 11000111 01001110 11110100 11011111 01100100 00001000
01110110 00000110 01111010 00011101 10000011 10100111 10111101 00110001 01110000 11000000
11110100 00111100 11110101 10100101 01101110 11000011 00111100 11100011 10110101 00110101
01010100 00101100 01111000 01001110 11111101 01101000 10110101 10000100 00101110 01000000
00011101 01110000 00110011 11001101 00001011 11110111 01000111 00011111 10000001 10100101
01100000 00011000 11111100 10001011 11110010 00000001 10000000 01101000 11001001 00100000
01010000 11011000 00001001 11000111 00001100 01001101 00100111 00000101 11110010 01001101
00101011 10001110 10110100 11001110 10000100 01110010 01111000 10100110 11100101 11011100
00000011 00100100 11110110 11000001 11111010 01010011 11010011 00100011 00100111 10001100
10011010 01100000 01100010 01011001 11000000 11101100 01101001 11011001 11001011 01100011
10100111 00011100 11010100 10101111 00110001 11011100 01101110 00111110 01000000 10111110
10010100 11100110 00111000 11101000 00111010 10001110 01101001 10101100 01001000 00011001
11000110 01101001 00011011 01110011 01110010 01011011 10000001 11101101 01001110 11001000
01000010 10101111 11001100 11100011 00111101 00000111 01011010 01101011 01110100 00100001
01111011 10011100 11110011 01001010 10101011 10011100 11110001 11001000 10100100 00111001
00111101 11101000 01010110 10111000 00001011 11001110 01010000 10011010 10001011 11100110
00101101 10001100 11110111 11100110 10100101 01100000 01001011 10100110 00111000 00011101
11111101 01101001 00011000 11111100 11000000 10000001 11000111 01110011 01010100 10010010
11101000 00000000 11000000 11110110 11101010 00111111 01001010 01100011 01100011 10110001
00100100 00011110 11110100 11110110 01101110 10111111 11100111 00110100 11010100 11111001
10111110 10010100 10011000 00001101 11101000 01000000 11101101 01001011 10000011 10010011
10011100 11110011 11011011 11010010 10010100 10011111 10011011 00111001 11111100 00101001
00001001 00100100 01111010 00001110 11110101 00111011 00000000 10001100 11011000 00011100
01110101 11001111 01011010 00010000 01100001 00000110 00000110 00110011 01000010 10101001
11011001 10010011 11010011 10110000 10100001 10111001 11100011 10101111 10100101 00110100
11101111 10111000 00001100 01111100 11101111 00100111 10100110 01001101 00001101 11110111
01110001 01001011 11011000 10010000 00111010 01010000 01000000 11001000 10100101 01001111
01010000 00000001 11010111 00100011 10100101 00110011 11011111 00111100 11100110 10011110
01111001 11100010 10010001 10000111 11110111 01000111 01011010 01111110 10000000 00100011
11100000 10011100 00011110 01001101 00001100 00000001 00100011 11010000 01010010 10111110
00010111 00011101 01101001 00001111 00101000 00110011 01000011 01011010 00000000 11010110
00111101 01000110 01101001 00011111 10000101 00111000 00010100 11111100 01110101 10100110
11100011 10110110 01111110 10110101 00001100 00000100 00111001 11001110 00000111 01001010
00110000 00110011 01001010 01111010 11110001 11010010 10001110 01010101 01101010 11100100
11101110 00111011 00001001 10011110 00001001 11110111 11000101 00011100 00010001 10001111
01011110 10110100 01111111 00000000 00011101 11001111 01001010 01001100 10010010 11111110
11010100 11010000 10000001 01110011 10011111 10101101 00110010 01001111 11011101 11100000
00000001 11010110 10100100 11101000 01111010 01110001 01001100 01110001 11000110 01001111
01011010 01011010 00100111 10100011 00000000 01101100 11010001 10001111 10010100 10010010
00111010 11010011 10111001 11001110 00111011 01110101 00110100 11010110 11001110 00001110
01111011 10011110 00000111 01110011 01010111 01100100 01011000 11101100 11101101 10001100
01100011 11010111 00010100 11011110 01000011 01111010 11010010 01100000 11100000 01111101
01111011 01010011 11110011 11001110 01111101 10101010 00011011 01011011 10100010 00000110
11111010 10001110 11100110 10010000 11100011 00011001 11110100 10100000 01111011 00011111
10101001 00010100 10001010 01110000 01001000 11000110 01111110 10110100 11010101 11010010
00000001 01010000 00000001 10111111 00100111 00001001 11011111 10011010 01100010 11100000
11100011 00010100 11111100 01100010 10010001 11110010 00011100 01100010 10010011 11011001
00000000 11010010 11000000 11110110 10100111 10000001 10000011 10010011 11111000 01010001
11011111 10100111 11001101 01001100 01101110 01000001 11100111 10010010 00111011 11010001
01110111 01110000 00010001 01001110 11110110 00100000 11110100 10100101 01000101 11001101
00011000 11111001 11101000 11100100 00010111 00000011 10001110 00111010 11010001 01110000

00100011 01100110 11000110 01101001 11001100 01001001 00100000 00000001 10010011 01001101
01010101 00000001 01110001 01001110 00011100 10011110 01111011 11110001 10001010 01101100
00000110 11100000 00001100 10011111 11010110 10010001 01001110 01001110 01101001 01001111
00111100 00001110 10010100 11101100 00000000 10100100 10011110 10110100 10011111 10010011
00011111 01010010 00111100 10010010 00110010 01000110 00111101 10101001 11011001 00000011
10101111 01111010 01001110 10001001 11000101 00000000 11101110 11100111 10100111 10101101
00001001 00110101 10101000 01110101 00001110 10101100 00000000 00011100 01010011 00100011
01101100 10000111 11011000 01110000 10011001 11101011 10001110 10110100 11111110 01111110
11110000 11100000 01010011 00010011 00001010 00111000 11110101 10101101 00011110 10011110
11110000 01101110 00111001 01000110 11011000 10001111 00011001 00111001 10101000 00011000
00010110 00111001 00101110 01010111 11011010 10100111 00001100 00110011 10010100 11101011
11011010 10011000 10100010 00111100 01111100 11100111 11100110 11101111 01010000 10100100
00100011 11000011 00010010 00101100 11110000 01001101 00100001 00001011 10010010 00001000
11100100 01110101 10100000 10011111 10011011 01101000 00100111 10000001 11010100 00011100
01010100 01111011 01110010 11111111 00000000 00110111 00011111 10001111 01011010 11110100
00101110 10011011 11011011 01010001 00010001 10111100 01000000 11110010 10101011 10000011
11101101 01000100 01011100 00011100 10010011 11000000 10101001 00011001 10000000 11001111
01111111 01011010 10001001 10010100 01100100 00001100 10011100 00011110 10111000 10101101
01010111 00110010 01111010 00001111 01001110 10100100 10111000 11011100 00110010 00001110
00101001 01010000 00000001 11001011 01100111 11011110 10011010 10100111 11100100 11001000
11100111 00010100 11100101 11001001 11100111 10011100 00011010 00010101 11010011 11010101
01011100 10001011 01011000 01111010 11100011 10101101 00111101 01100100 11000001 00111110
10110100 11001101 10111100 01110011 11010111 11010110 10011001 10000011 10010000 00001111
11100011 01011010 00110110 11011000 11110100 00111011 11111111 00000000 10000110 10001100
00000100 10010111 10011110 01100110 00111011 01100000 11010111 10100010 11101110 01010000
00111010 11010111 10001101 01111000 01010111 01010110 10001011 01001100 10111010 10010011
11001111 11001010 01000110 11011000 11111001 11000000 11001101 01110101 00101101 11100011
01001011 01000000 11100100 00101010 01011100 01001010 00111101 01000000 10101111 00101011
00011001 01001110 01110010 10010101 11010010 10111001 11011001 01001010 01001011 10010110
11010111 00111011 11000110 10011011 01101110 00111011 11010100 10001001 00101110 01000001
10101111 00111110 10010011 11000110 10001010 01110000 00101101 11101101 10100101 11111111
00000000 10000001 01010010 01001101 11100011 01001011 10111100 00011111 00100110 11011101
00000000 00111101 00000001 00111001 10101110 01001111 10101011 01010110 11011111 10010100
10100111 01010110 00011101 11001111 01000000 01101001 11000010 11110110 11111100 01101010
00001001 10101111 01100010 10001011 11100110 01110111 00000000 00001110 01111010 11010111
10010110 01011111 11111000 10101111 01010100 10011000 10000000 00100101 01001000 01001000
00000111 00011011 01111010 11100100 11010110 00001101 11110101 11101101 11100101 11010001
00101101 01110001 01110011 00101100 10100111 00011000 11001001 00111111 11010010 10110110
10100111 10000100 10101000 11011101 11011110 10000110 01001110 10101010 00111101 01110110
11111111 00000000 11000101 10011010 01100101 10011100 10011011 01001100 11111110 01100011
11111111 00000000 01110101 01000110 01001101 01110011 11110111 11111111 00000000 00010000
00100101 00110001 00010101 10110001 10110100 11011001 10011110 00000011 01001000 01101011
11001111 00100011 11000110 00000001 11111110 00110011 11000101 01001111 10001100 00000001
11001101 01101010 10110000 01010001 10110110 10100110 01011110 11010101 10110010 11100110
10110011 10101100 11011111 11101010 00101100 11111111 00000000 01101011 10111010 10010001
11010000 11111111 00000000 11001011 00110000 01110000 10000011 11110000 10101110 01000010
11100111 11111101 01110110 01010011 00100000 01111101 01111010 11010110 11100101 11001000
11001010 00111110 01111111 00001110 01101010 10011111 11110110 01101100 10010010 01101001
01110011 11101010 00000101 10000010 01000001 00011011 01101100 00000000 10000011 11001001
10101110 11101010 01011000 01110101 00010101 10100010 10110001 00011011 10011001 01101010
11000100 01001001 10000000 11000100 00011110 10100000 10000011 10000011 01011101 11010111
10000110 01111100 01111011 01111001 01100011 00011100 01110110 11111010 10010100 01011111
01101000 10110110 00000011 00000010 01001101 11000111 11001100 00011110 10010101 11000000
11100111 01110001 11101101 10010000 01111101 00101010 01110100 00100011 00111001 00111001
11001001 10101011 10011101 00111000 11001101 01101010 10001010 01010011 01101000 11111010
00000111 01000111 11010111 00101100 00110101 01101000 11110111 11011000 11001110 10000100
11110111 10001100 10011100 00011111 11001010 10110110 00100011 01100000 01110011 11101000
00101011 11100111 00101011 01101001 00011110 00111001 00010001 10010010 01000111 00001110
10011100 11100101 01001110 00001000 10101110 11001111 01001011 11110001 10110101 11111101
10100100 01010001 10101100 11100000 01011100 01000110 00111011 10010011 10000011 11111001
11010111 10011101 01010011 00000010 11010110 10110000 00110101 10000101 01100100 11110111
00111101 01110101 10110110 10011110 00111011 11010100 01111110 01011111 00011100 11010111
00011111 10100100 01111000 11001010 11000010 11110010 01010000 10001111 00101111 10010101
00100011 10011100 00000000 11010101 11010000 01000011 01111100 00100101 10001011 11001100
10001101 10000100 10000000 10011110 10100000 11100100 01010111 00100101 01001000 01010100
10000011 11011000 11011001 00110100 11110110 01100101 11110000 10100000 11110000 00000001
11100110 10000110 10000011 00000000 11010100 00000010 11101111 00111110 10110101 00100010
11001111 11100110 01110100 10101000 01001010 11001000 10110111 01110100 01010111 10111110
00111000 01001101 10100111 00000111 10001110 10100110 10110011 11100010 00100000 11000010
11110000 11001100 10111001 01000010 00110110 00110000 11110101 00010101 10101011 00111100
01100010 01000101 11011101 11111101 01111010 01010111 00111111 00100100 10111110 01010101
11000100 10111101 11000110 01111010 01100110 10110011 01101101 00100111 11100110 01011100
01011101 11110100 00110001 01110100 11001101 00111111 01010010 10000110 11110110 11100011

01001100 10110101 10111000 00101001 10100111 10010011 10111100 10110001 11100111 01100000
00111101 10000101 01110101 10110110 10010001 00001011 01111011 10001000 11100001 10001100
10010001 00011000 01010010 00000101 01010000 11010010 00100110 11110011 10010010 01010111
00000001 00111001 01101110 10100000 01010101 11001111 00110001 10000100 11011011 10111101
00101011 11010011 10000101 01011011 01000001 00100110 10110101 00111000 10101010 01000111
10010001 11011001 00010111 11011010 01010101 11100111 00100111 10010001 01011000 11110111
10010111 10001101 00111101 11000000 10000110 00000011 11110010 00101111 00101100 01001111
01111010 01111100 10110111 01011001 11001000 01000011 11001111 01110010 00101010 10101100
00000100 00011001 10110010 10100011 00000011 00010101 11001011 01010110 10100110 10111110
01000110 10010100 10101001 01110011 01101010 11001101 00001011 00111000 00100010 10010011
11001011 10111001 01111000 11010000 11001001 10001100 00101001 00100011 00111000 10101011
11001100 01111010 10011100 11111110 01110101 01000110 11011001 10111100 10111000 11001000
11101010 00110011 01010000 11011110 11011101 10010101 00000001 01111001 11001001 11111101
00101011 10100001 11010100 01010110 01010110 00110010 10101000 10110101 00100100 10111001
10010100 10010000 11110010 00000011 11000010 10101001 11101011 01010100 00101100 00010111
10001100 11110100 00100110 10110010 10110101 00011101 01011100 11000101 00111010 01011001
00100110 00111100 11001001 10111010 10000011 11010111 00010101 10110011 10100110 01000111
11000000 01100111 11100011 00111101 00000101 01100001 01011110 11001010 11010010 00111010
00110000 11010001 11010001 10110010 11001100 11001011 10001000 10001001 00000011 00101111
10001100 01010111 00001111 11100010 00001000 11100001 10010110 11101110 11001010 00110000
10111000 10010110 00111001 01000110 01011011 11011010 10111010 11001101 01011010 11101100
01011011 11011011 10010010 01111001 10101110 00010110 01101001 01001100 11110111 00000101
11011100 10011110 10100111 00000011 11111001 01010111 00111110 00011001 11110011 11001100
11110100 00101000 11010000 11110110 10001110 11000110 10110101 11101011 00011011 11011011
10000001 11100110 00010000 01100011 10001011 00100001 01111111 11000110 10001000 01100001
10001100 01110010 00101010 10110101 10011011 01100111 10010011 11010111 11010110 10101100
00001001 00000111 00111000 11111110 01010101 11101010 01011011 01001011 00011110 11010101
00111010 01010000 10100101 00011011 00100100 01011011 01001000 10010101 01100100 11001111
01111111 01011010 10110000 10001010 00000001 00000100 00011100 00011111 10101101 01100101
10011001 01001110 11001110 10111100 11110110 11001101 01000000 11110111 10101101 11010011
01110101 01100101 00111101 00101100 10010000 01001010 00110001 10110101 11011001 11011101
11111000 01011010 11100001 10100110 11010111 00100000 01000111 01100010 01111100 10110101
00111000 10101110 11110111 10111110 01111011 10001110 10110101 11100110 00011111 00001111
01100101 11011101 10101101 01100100 10010010 01001001 01011110 10010101 11101001 11101010
00110000 00111000 00011100 00001010 10101010 10011010 01000101 00011111 00101111 10001111
11100101 11110110 10011110 11101000 10001011 11001000 11001011 11111110 00010100 11101110
00110001 10010011 11010010 10010000 01100100 10000011 01000001 01010010 01001000 00111101
10000101 01100101 01101110 11000111 00000000 10111011 01111010 11100000 11110110 10100110
11110110 00011100 11110011 11101011 01000110 00001001 00001111 11001001 00011110 11010100
11100101 01011100 11100010 10010010 10110111 01010000 00000011 11010100 00000000 00101000
00111101 10111110 10010100 10001111 10010011 10001101 10011000 11000111 11110011 10100100
01100011 11010011 11010100 11010011 10110101 11000110 00101011 00010000 10100000 01100011
10001100 11111010 11010010 00110111 11001101 11000110 00111000 11110101 10100000 10001111
10011100 01010000 10111001 11001110 00110011 01001010 11110110 00011101 10101110 00001011
10010011 11010000 01110000 01101001 10101011 11010011 10100000 11001110 01101001 11011011
01001011 00001110 00001111 10111101 00110111 00100100 01110001 10110111 00111001 11101110
01111011 01010001 11010100 01000011 10011000 10010000 01111010 01100010 10001100 11100000
11100011 00100111 00111000 10100110 11100100 11100100 00000000 01110001 01001000 00000110
00111011 11010011 10110010 00000000 01110010 01111100 10110010 10100000 10010000 01111110
10110100 10101001 11111011 10110100 11111001 10111111 00001010 01110001 11000000 11000111
10101101 00110000 11100100 10001110 10100010 10000101 10101010 00000001 01000000 11101111
11010111 11101011 01000011 10110110 00001000 11101111 01001110 01010010 00111000 11001111
01001010 01100110 01001011 01100101 01111010 01111111 01011010 01111011 01101000 00000010
10110110 01001001 11101001 11000111 10101101 00111111 11101110 10001010 01100011 10010010
10101011 11110010 00001100 10010001 11010011 00110100 00111111 01000001 10111111 10010010
01111010 11100010 10000110 11000100 00100000 11000000 01001100 01100000 11111101 01101001
01001001 00011000 10100100 01010011 10111000 10011110 00110000 00000111 01001010 01011110
11111111 00000000 01001010 01010110 11101000 00110001 10101110 00000110 11010001 11001001
00111110 11110100 01100100 11110100 00000010 10011101 10001100 01110010 01001000 11100111
10100000 10100001 01001111 00100110 10011000 00001000 11000100 01100111 00000111 00011110
11110100 10001010 00000111 01000000 01111001 00111100 11010000 11100000 00011110 11011101
00101001 10111100 00011111 10101110 00111010 01010010 00000000 01010000 00010100 11100111
00100100 11010011 10010100 10001100 11100011 00111101 11111001 10100011 11111110 01011001
11100000 01110101 00111111 10100101 00101111 01001000 11000000 11101010 01110001 11010110
10010101 11111011 10001101 10001100 00100111 00110010 00011111 10010100 11110101 11100000
10011110 00101000 00100111 10001111 01111110 11110100 11110100 11101001 10001110 11111000
10100110 00000011 11000111 11010011 10101101 00101011 00001000 00011101 10001010 10001100
00000001 10010111 11111110 01010100 10001101 10011110 00010111 00111100 10011110 10110100
10111101 10111101 11001111 01011010 00011100 11100100 10011100 01111110 00110100 00110101
11100100 00000001 10010000 00010101 11011001 11111001 00000011 10110000 10101000 10000001
00100110 01001100 11101101 11000000 00111100 10000001 11111110 00110101 00100010 10001101
11000111 01101111 01001110 11110100 10111000 11111101 11100000 11001111 01000001 11111010
11010001 01111011 00100001 10110001 00110001 10000001 11011111 00100111 10010011 01001111

01000011 11000111 10110110 00111010 01010100 01101100 00001000 11001110 00001111 01010011
11001001 10100111 00001111 10010101 01001001 00111001 00110100 01111010 10001000 01101110
11100010 00110001 10000001 01001101 11011010 01111010 01110101 00111001 11001101 00001010
01001001 10001111 00011000 11100100 11110011 01001110 11001011 01110010 00111010 00010011
11111010 01010011 01011101 10000000 00111010 11111111 00000000 11110101 10101000 01100011
11100101 11111101 01001101 00011100 00101000 11110101 00100111 10100000 10100110 11111100
10111101 10001110 01001110 01111001 00110101 00101100 00000100 01101111 10111110 00011000
10110111 01111100 11010011 11010011 10001100 11110010 01111010 11100111 10011010 00011000
00000010 10000101 01000010 11110101 11100111 00111001 10100110 10101001 11101001 11111010
11010101 00101110 11100000 00100010 10101110 00110011 11101110 01111001 11110111 10100101
11001000 00111001 00011101 00001101 00000000 10001100 10001110 01110000 01110011 11000110
01101000 01010101 11000010 10011100 01111110 01100111 10111101 00001101 10000000 11100110
00011011 10010111 11010000 11110111 10100110 10000011 10000111 10100111 01110100 00111111
01011110 01101010 00110101 11001011 01100000 10011110 11111100 11100010 10001011 10111011
10000000 00101000 11000011 10011100 11110100 11110111 10100101 11100000 11111011 00000001
11010010 10000111 00011001 00100100 01111011 11100110 10010001 11010111 00100000 10001110
11100111 10101101 01001000 00000011 00010000 01000000 00011100 11100011 10111111 10111101
00001100 00111001 00000011 00111100 11111011 00001010 01011110 10101100 01110000 00110010
00111011 00011010 00011011 11010100 11010011 11100100 00000000 11101100 01110001 11010100
01010010 00111001 00000000 00000010 01101001 01010100 00001111 00110011 00111101 00000110
00111010 01010011 00111010 11110011 10011110 10000111 10111101 00110100 00000000 11000100
00000010 00111010 01100100 10001111 11001010 10000110 00100111 00111000 01001110 10000000
01100100 11010000 11111101 10001000 00000011 10001010 00100100 11001001 10010000 00101000
11101001 11011100 11010011 11010001 00000000 10011100 11110101 11101011 10011010 01011100
01110110 11100111 11011111 00010100 01100100 11111001 10011100 01110000 00000000 11111100
11101001 00000000 00100000 00010110 11000110 00111001 10100100 10101111 01110001 10110000
10010100 01100000 01101100 11000110 01110010 01111010 01010001 10001101 10100000 01110110
11110100 00010100 10011000 11000110 00000010 01110101 00111101 01001001 11100110 10000111
00100100 01100111 00111100 10011111 01010001 01010010 10101110 00110100 00000100 11100000
11100111 10101011 10011010 00111010 00111001 00100011 10011010 01011100 00001110 00110011
11010111 11010110 10010001 10001000 11001000 11011101 11111000 11100010 10101011 01100010
01000110 10001100 10010000 01001001 00111000 11100111 00110100 00100000 00011100 10011101
11011001 00011111 11001110 10011100 00000111 00111000 11110111 10100110 10110111 00010001
11001000 01111010 00000000 01111000 10100010 11001011 10100000 00000111 00011000 01111101
11100111 10100001 11001001 11110110 10100001 01110001 10001100 10011110 01001110 01110011
01001001 10001100 00001100 10111110 01111010 11100111 00011000 10100101 01101110 00010011
10011110 11110100 01111001 10001101 00000110 11101100 01100000 00010110 11000001 00110100
11011100 10010011 11110010 10100000 11111011 10011001 00100111 11011110 10010111 10001100
11100111 10111111 01101010 01001100 00011110 01001001 00111101 01111011 11010000 10110111
00010000 01110011 10000001 10011100 11100100 11110001 01000011 00001100 01110101 11110101
11100000 01010000 11100100 00010010 00000111 01011111 10100101 00110111 10100001 00100111
10011100 01110100 00011000 10100010 11101001 01111010 00000000 11100011 11000110 01110011
11111000 01010000 00111001 11011001 11001111 00011101 11101001 10001011 11001000 00011100
01100000 10000011 10011100 01010011 11011111 11101110 01110001 10000001 01001101 01011111
01110000 00011011 11111100 01111111 10011110 00101001 10111000 11001001 00000000 00010010
00010011 11101011 11010110 10100100 00100101 01000010 11100000 01110110 11101110 01000101
00000100 01100001 00010011 00111101 01001111 01101010 01110111 11010000 00000110 00011100
10011100 10010010 00111011 11110000 00111101 10101001 00011011 00000111 10111110 00101000
01010000 01110110 10010011 10011110 10011110 10110100 11010000 00111000 11110111 11101110
01101001 00111011 00000000 01100000 11101101 00111000 11100011 11011110 10000001 11010000
01100011 10101000 11101010 01001001 11101001 01000111 11011110 11101000 01001111 01011010
01110111 10110111 01101111 10101101 00001100 01100011 00010111 11010100 11110010 00111101
10101000 00111100 00010011 11101011 01001000 00110001 11110111 01000001 11111101 01101000
11000110 01000000 00111100 11111101 01101001 01011110 11000011 01101000 01010010 01110010
01111001 00110100 10001100 01111011 01110110 10100110 10011110 10111111 01001010 01110011
11110100 10100011 01010110 10001001 00001111 01011110 01001111 10111101 00011101 01111001
11101101 01000110 01111110 01000010 01111011 11010000 10111001 01100011 11101000 00101000
10110000 00000011 00010000 00000110 00111010 01100111 10101101 00110111 00111001 11001000
11101101 10001110 00101000 00011000 00100100 10001100 00011100 11010010 01100011 00110101
01011011 00000000 10000000 01100000 10011111 01011010 01011100 01100000 10000000 00111111
00010011 11101001 01001010 00000110 00000101 00100011 00011100 10011010 01001111 01011101
10000111 10110000 00010011 10111011 10010001 11010011 00111101 11101001 00110011 11001001
10100101 11101111 10011010 01000101 00011100 10011101 11111101 11111001 10100011 10010111
10110000 10000101 01100011 10000011 10011010 01001100 01100110 10011010 11011001 00011000
00001011 01001110 01011100 10010111 11110100 00000010 10010010 01101000 00000000 00011100
10011100 00000001 11110100 10101000 11001001 11001110 01000111 00011001 00000111 00000111
00010101 00100010 11100111 00111111 11011100 00011000 10100110 00100010 10000001 00010000
00001000 10111111 11111101 01111010 00010010 10110000 00000111 00001011 00011110 01111011
10011010 01010110 00011000 11000111 00111100 10011010 01101001 01101110 01110110 10001110
01001111 01111010 01010110 00111000 00000100 10110111 00110101 01010110 01100000 00100011
10010101 00001011 10111000 10000010 01110010 01110000 00000000 10100000 10110001 11001110
00110001 10010011 11011111 00010100 00110110 00110110 00000011 11011000 01110011 01000110
01110011 11001111 10101101 00100111 10101011 00000001 10101100 01001001 11000111 11010110

10001100 01100011 10110101 00111010 00100000 01001011 01100011 10000000 01101000 11001111
00011001 00100111 10111111 11100101 01001010 11111010 11011100 10110000 11101111 11110100
11100110 10011001 10000010 00111001 00100011 00111001 11110101 10100111 10101110 01000111
00101111 11000111 10100111 00110100 11000110 11100100 11100001 11001001 11100000 11100111
10001010 01101101 11110011 00010000 00001100 00111110 01000001 10001110 11111101 11101000
11000110 00000111 00110100 01111111 00000001 00101110 00110000 00111011 01110011 01000001
11100110 01001100 01110110 00011101 11101001 01000110 11010110 10110010 00000001 00000110
00010100 00111011 00011100 01010011 01011111 00100001 01000001 00000011 11011010 10000111
11000110 01000111 01110011 11111100 10101000 01110001 10011001 00000001 11001111 00111111
11001010 10010011 11011110 11000011 01000000 11000011 00011000 00000011 10100111 10101111
10101101 00110100 11110011 11000010 00011100 01111010 11010000 11111110 10000011 10010011
01001110 01010101 11000111 00101111 11000001 00111110 10111101 11101010 10101100 11010110
11101100 10100010 00111110 00000010 10001111 11110011 10011010 00110011 10010010 01010100
10000011 11010011 10110101 00111101 10000110 01011111 00000011 10000000 00111101 10101000
01001110 00001110 01001111 00001001 11101011 01001010 11110111 00010101 10000110 01100011
00000011 10100000 11001111 10110111 01101010 01110010 11001000 10110001 10001101 10101101
10110011 00100010 10011000 11001100 11001100 00110001 11110111 00000110 01111010 01010011
11110110 11000111 10001111 10011001 00110111 00011111 01011010 00011100 01010011 00011001
11100011 11111010 11101110 10000101 00111110 10010011 00111000 01010001 00110100 01110011
01000100 11100111 11100101 10010110 00110011 10011100 10001111 01111111 01001010 11001001
10011010 00000010 01010011 00001001 11110010 00000001 01010111 00010000 00100010 10010001
10110000 01100001 00111101 00101010 01110001 00100010 10011110 00110001 10011010 11101101
11100110 10111011 10111101 11001111 01011110 00011001 01100010 01011011 10110011 00011001
01010111 01110110 01000000 11101101 11010110 10100011 00100000 01100100 00001010 11011010
01001000 01010000 10111001 11011110 01001111 11111000 01010100 11000011 01001111 10000001
10000111 10101001 11110111 10100110 10101010 10010010 11110010 11001001 00111101 10001100
00000101 10001101 10111011 01010101 10111000 00100000 10010010 01001001 00110110 11100000
10010100 11110110 00010101 10101010 10111010 01111100 00111000 11001000 11011001 10010000
01111010 00011110 11110101 01100010 00110101 00100001 01001010 00001111 00101111 11101011
11101001 01011010 10111010 11110110 11011011 01100010 00100011 10010101 01001010 11111010
10110011 00100010 11100110 00000001 00010010 10000010 01110011 11010011 10110101 01000100
11010001 10110001 00011001 11000101 01101100 11001111 01101110 11010010 01000110 00000110
00001001 00100011 10101110 11011010 10100100 11010110 11101100 10111000 01100010 01111010
01110101 11001101 01000100 01101010 11011101 11011001 00011001 01100010 11110000 00110010
10000011 11111101 11011010 11010000 10101000 10101010 01110111 11111110 11110000 01100000
01110110 11100110 10101100 00001000 11000000 00011100 00011110 00001111 10100101 00111001
11010110 01010101 11001000 00101010 01000000 00011100 11100111 00111001 11001101 01010101
01101001 11111100 10101110 11011001 00011110 10010101 10110101 00110110 10100110 10110101
00111100 11111001 11000010 01010000 11011100 10111000 00100101 01100000 00110000 10011001
00011000 11101110 01101010 01000110 10010000 11101101 00000000 10011110 01111011 10011110
10010101 01001101 00100110 00000101 01110010 01111000 00111110 10010100 00110100 11011100
01110011 11010011 11101011 01011011 10110101 00101101 10010110 11000110 01011010 00100010
00111011 10011111 10011000 01111111 10111101 11000110 01101010 10101100 10011110 01100000
10010011 01100000 01101110 01111101 10101010 01101001 10100100 00011110 10011001 00000011
10100101 01000010 11000100 11100111 01110001 00011000 00111101 10101011 00010111 00010110
11011110 10100101 00100001 11001011 10111000 01100000 10000010 01111000 11101011 11001101
01001111 00010001 00111100 00000110 01101110 10111110 10100110 10100010 01000010 01110001
11001000 11101011 01010010 00101001 01011100 11100000 11110011 01000100 10111001 10100101
10101010 00011101 11001101 01011011 01101101 00110101 10011110 00010111 10111001 10011100
11101100 10110111 00000011 10101000 00011001 11001111 11010000 01110111 10101110 11000101
00100110 11010000 11100100 11110000 11101100 10011010 01110101 10000100 10000010 11101000
00111100 01000111 00110001 00101111 11011111 00100100 01110101 11001110 01111010 01010111
00010111 01101111 11100010 00111101 01001010 11001010 11010011 11101100 11010000 11001101
00011001 10000011 10011111 11011101 11001000 10100000 11110101 10101000 01111100 00110011
11100010 01011111 11101100 01111000 11101111 01010110 01001011 00101000 11100101 10010010
11100001 10110111 11101110 00000111 00011000 11110110 11111010 01100110 10110011 10010110
11011100 10101011 01100001 11000101 11011111 01000111 10110001 10000011 10101000 01101000
11110111 10111010 01111010 00100100 10010111 00010110 11110010 01000111 00010011 11110010
10101100 01111101 00101010 00011011 01110000 00000000 11100111 10100001 10101110 10000111
01011101 11110001 01111101 11100110 10110001 01100011 11110110 00110011 01101111 00011100
00101001 10000001 10010000 10100111 00100011 00011110 11010101 11001111 00000100 11011010
00111000 10100010 00101011 10011011 01010110 01010011 11100101 11101000 01011000 10001000
01111100 11111000 00011101 01101010 11000100 01100011 01110010 11100011 00011001 00011110
10010101 01001101 00001110 01110000 01000000 11100111 11011110 10101110 01000101 00011001
01100001 11000001 11101010 01101011 01011000 10100111 00010011 00111101 00001001 01100011
10001001 01011001 00011110 00111100 11110001 11010111 11101001 11110100 10101011 10110110
01110010 11011100 01011010 10010000 11010110 10010011 11001011 00001110 00111010 01101101
01100011 10000011 01010101 11010010 00110000 00011100 00001110 11111000 11111100 11101010
01111000 01011000 00101111 00100100 01010000 11010101 11010101 10011010 00001000 10111101
01101110 01101100 01011011 11111000 10111011 01010110 10110111 00111000 10010000 11000101
01110010 10011111 11110100 11010001 01110001 11111100 10101011 01110010 11000011 11000111
01110110 00110010 00000011 11110110 11010101 01111011 01011001 00000111 01011110 11100000
11111010 11010111 00001101 00110100 10100011 00000101 01001111 01111110 00111010 11010110

01100100 11000101 01000100 10100100 00010011 11010000 11110101 10101100 00100111 10000100
10000100 10010110 10011010 00011010 01111011 01101001 00100110 01111011 01000111 11110110
11001100 00110111 01010000 11100110 11010110 01100100 10010000 00111010 11100100 00000000
01111001 10101100 10101001 10011100 10001001 00001000 11011100 00110111 10010001 10011110
00101011 10011100 11110000 00000110 00011010 11100010 11100111 10100000 11111001 01000110
00110011 11110101 10101110 10101110 11111010 00011100 11100000 11100011 00011000 11101111
01011110 01100101 01001100 00110010 10100101 01010011 10010101 00011110 10010101 00011001
00100110 10101110 01011001 11010010 00100001 00110000 01011011 01110101 00100111 01111111
11001111 11001101 01011111 10001100 00000110 01010010 01001111 01110001 01010000 11000110
01001111 10010101 00011001 11100011 10010101 10100010 11101100 10101100 00110110 10010010
01110011 11010000 01100110 10110111 10101001 10100110 11100111 00001101 01000111 01111001
10011001 00110110 01100100 10110000 10010000 10011111 11101111 00011010 10111101 00011110
00000100 01111001 00111100 01010101 01101101 00101010 00111101 11010001 01100100 00000010
00000111 01011110 01101001 10011010 11110101 11011010 11011001 11011010 00010011 11000110
11111110 11000011 00111101 01101011 10000010 10100010 11100111 10010101 10010001 11101000
00101011 01000110 00100011 01111111 10110101 11100011 10001000 01001110 00001001 11101001
11110111 01000111 01010011 10011010 11001001 10111011 00011010 10111100 00110010 10011101
01001110 01111011 10100100 10001110 00100000 00001001 01101000 10000000 11101000 00111111
10101101 01011110 11010001 00110100 11110001 00001100 01111111 01101001 10111011 01000001
11110110 10010111 00111001 00000000 11111111 00000000 00001111 10100111 11100011 01011000
01111110 00111100 11010100 11000111 10010000 10010110 00001000 11000000 10111110 01110111
10110000 11110100 11110110 10101111 01000001 01000011 11011001 10100101 00010111 10101011
00111100 11111010 11001101 00111001 01011101 00011000 01111010 01001101 11000011 01011100
01101011 10001001 00111100 11100100 11001000 11101100 11011101 01001111 11101001 01011110
10100001 01101010 11011111 10111010 11011010 01111011 00001110 11010101 11100101 01111110
00011100 00001100 11011010 10000010 00110000 11000001 11000000 00100111 10011010 11110101
00001011 00111001 01000011 01000001 10111011 00011100 11110111 10101000 11000110 01101001
01101011 10011101 00111000 01010101 11101110 11101010 01110011 10111110 00101010 10111011
01101101 10101001 00000000 00111111 00100011 01110101 11100011 10101111 11100011 01011100
11111100 01110010 01100000 10000001 01010111 11111100 01000111 00110000 01101011 10110010
00111010 10011100 01111010 11010110 01010100 01000011 10111101 01100101 10000101 10000010
01001010 11100111 10111001 10000110 10110100 00010001 10110001 00001011 01100101 00000000
11000110 00111011 10011100 01010100 11001110 01110000 00111101 11101010 10010101 10110100
10000100 11110010 00111000 00011101 11101010 01111011 10001001 00111100 10110100 11100100
00011111 01011010 11101000 10011111 00110101 10110100 00111101 00011011 10101101 11001000
00101110 01100110 11110010 11001110 01001011 01100100 00011110 10110101 00011100 00111111
01111111 10110001 00000111 10111101 01010110 10011010 01010001 00101001 00100000 00001110
01111101 00101010 01011011 00100011 10111000 11110011 11000000 01011010 11010010 10001101
10111001 01110101 11010100 11110010 10110001 01010101 01011011 01111100 10110001 00111101
00000011 11100001 11100100 01100001 01110101 10000100 00111011 01111001 00101010 01001101
01111010 01101111 01100111 00011001 11101010 01111000 10101111 00101111 11111000 01101111
00101001 10011111 01010111 01111110 00110001 10000101 11110101 11101011 01011110 10011101
10010110 10010011 10000101 11100000 01110111 10101001 10101101 01110110 10010011 01100111
10000101 10001001 01010110 10010101 10000101 01010001 10000011 10001010 00011011 00000111
10011100 11100000 01010010 10100000 00000100 11100111 11010011 10101101 00110111 11110101
00000000 11111110 01110101 10000001 11001100 00111011 00011001 11101111 11000101 00100110
01110010 10000111 01101101 00011011 10000001 00100101 01111010 01111010 11010000 00001111
00000000 01100000 01110011 01001010 11011010 10000000 10001111 11000111 00111101 01101000
01010110 00100110 01001100 01111010 01110111 10100011 10000001 10011110 11100111 10101101
00101000 11101000 01001000 11101011 10001010 00011101 10000000 00110010 00000011 00001110
01001111 00110100 10001011 10000011 10010001 10001110 00101001 10111011 10111110 01110000
00111011 10010001 10010011 01001110 11101100 01110000 01101000 10111111 01000110 00100000
01101100 00010100 11001111 00000010 10000100 11000111 01010010 00110001 01010001 10100010
10001100 10000101 11101010 00000111 00100100 11010100 10000011 00100000 01100100 10010000
01001101 00111101 10000110 00011100 01100111 00100111 10001010 01101010 11100000 00011100
11010010 00100001 00000111 10100111 00111101 11101000 00000000 10010000 00111000 00111100
11010001 11100100 00000011 11011101 10100011 00000100 01100111 10011110 11111000 11110101
10100110 10110001 11111101 11011001 11001111 01011100 11110110 10100000 11111101 11101100
01100111 00100110 10000101 00011001 11101001 01001001 00111011 00000000 00001110 01001000
11001111 01001010 01110110 00111001 11000111 10101101 00110101 00001111 01100001 11001101
00100111 00111000 00111101 11011110 10000101 01110001 00001011 11000111 00011001 00100011
10010011 01001110 01101100 00011100 11101100 10100110 10001110 00111010 11110010 01101000
11001001 11001001 00011110 11110100 01011110 11000011 00010011 00111100 01111111 00111010
01010110 11001110 01001000 00011001 00011110 10110100 10011101 00000111 01001110 00111011
01010010 00110001 10010001 10000110 00111011 00011110 10100110 10011110 10111101 00000000
00011000 10010011 10001111 10101111 00010100 11010011 10111000 10111111 11001000 00101001
11111000 00000000 00011110 01111001 11101101 01001000 00001000 00011100 01100100 10010011
11111100 11101001 10111011 11110101 01100010 00010101 10011011 00011011 00010111 10111001
00010100 10000011 01101000 11001001 11100000 00010011 01001011 10111000 10000001 11010011
00000111 10111001 10100110 01100011 00001011 11001001 11001111 00110101 00101010 01011101
00001010 10110000 11100011 11110010 11110000 00111011 11010001 11010011 00000000 01010011
01011111 10011100 01110001 11010011 10011110 01101001 11001101 10001101 10100101 10001111
01000000 00101000 01100010 00011010 00000001 00110001 00011110 01001110 01001111 00010100

00011110 00000111 10010110 10011100 11111010 11111011 01010000 10111111 00101100 01000100
10001110 10111111 10011101 00100111 00100100 10011100 10010000 01000001 11101100 00101001
00111011 10111101 01001011 00010101 01001000 00111100 00001110 11010100 10011001 11001000
11111010 11010010 10001101 10101010 00111110 01110001 10000000 00111000 00000011 11010110
10011101 10001110 11100100 01110011 01010101 10100011 01011010 00010000 00110101 10000111
11001001 01001000 11100111 00011000 00111001 11100111 10100101 00100111 10010110 00001000
00000000 10010011 11001001 10101001 00111000 00000111 00011101 01001101 00101110 01000111
01111101 01000000 01100110 01000000 00000011 01100000 11101011 11011110 10000001 10010010
00110000 00111011 11110111 10100100 01110111 00100111 00011001 00000000 00100000 11101101
11101011 01001010 11100100 11110001 11001110 00111001 11000110 00101001 01101111 10110000
00001001 10000000 10111001 00100101 10111011 01010010 11100111 00101000 00110010 00111011
01110010 01001101 00001100 00111000 00111001 11101000 00111011 11010011 11110001 10010011
11001101 00001111 11001100 00001000 01011111 10010010 10011110 11111101 00101000 11011000
00000111 00000000 11110000 00001111 01111010 01110010 10001101 11000111 00101010 01001110
11000001 11011110 10001110 00110011 10011110 11010101 00110010 00000000 11001110 00010011
10000011 10000010 01101001 10111000 00101101 00100000 00000011 10110000 11100100 11111011
11010011 10011011 10010001 10010000 00111001 00011101 00110011 01001101 01001100 10000100
00100000 10010011 11001111 01111010 10100100 00000011 10011101 01110000 01000110 01110001
10011100 11110100 10100110 10110000 00011110 10111000 11001111 01101010 00110001 10000000
00001111 00100111 00011101 11001001 10100011 00011000 11000001 00111100 01010000 11010000
11110111 00011100 11111101 00110011 10011110 01111010 11010011 00010111 10001001 00001111
10110101 00101001 00011000 01110001 11101110 00110011 11001101 00011000 11101101 11001111
00111101 01101001 01011001 11101110 00100000 11001111 11001010 01001111 01000001 01000110
00110010 10011111 00110110 01111001 10100001 10001000 00001110 00000111 11110000 01100011
10010010 00101001 00011000 10010011 00011001 11100011 00000110 10010000 11011000 10101011
11000110 01111000 11100111 10110101 01000110 10001010 01010100 01111010 11111010 11010011
10011111 10010110 00011110 11111110 11111101 00101000 01011100 10011001 01111000 11101001
10001110 10010101 01011100 11010111 01011011 10001000 01110110 01111001 11000111 01000001
11101111 01010001 10000010 10111101 10111110 11100110 01101000 11111011 11000011 00011100
01100011 11011010 10011100 00010111 00000011 11010111 11011000 11010010 11011111 01110000
00001110 01001000 11100111 10111101 00011011 01110000 01110001 10011100 10011110 11111001
10100110 11101110 00000001 11111010 11100100 11100011 00110100 10011100 00101001 00100000
01110010 01001001 11001001 00100110 10011010 01100000 00111111 00100001 01100011 00100100
01111110 00000010 10100011 01011100 10110001 00101010 01110011 11000001 11001001 00111000
11100010 10011101 11010000 10001110 00110010 01001101 00100011 11100111 10011110 01001110
00101010 10111010 00000000 10101101 10000101 00011001 11001111 11010010 10011011 10001111
11011101 10001101 11100011 11110000 10100101 11101000 01000111 00011100 01100110 10000000
00111110 01110011 10010001 11010111 10101101 01000000 00000010 10001100 10010001 11101001
01001001 11010100 01100111 10111111 01101010 01110111 01001111 10101101 00110100 00010011
10110111 00000100 01100011 00000011 10010011 01001110 11100101 10001011 11011100 10110010
11111010 01111110 01010100 11000010 00111000 00011001 00000011 11010110 10011101 10111011
11100101 00000000 10001100 00011111 01101110 11000011 11111100 01101000 11011101 10010010
00111101 00001111 01000001 01000011 10111010 00100000 01110001 00100011 00000000 01110101
11110101 10101000 10110000 11011000 00000101 11000111 00101100 01111000 00011001 10100101
01011110 01111010 01110010 00000101 01000111 00110110 01001011 00000011 10011110 01111010
01111011 10001010 01110110 01110110 00000010 01000110 11001000 01110100 00011000 11101001
11001110 01101010 00110001 10000010 00110110 10000110 11011110 01110011 10010011 10001010
10010011 00000100 10111110 00010111 10100001 10100100 11000000 01011110 01000110 00111000
00110100 10010000 00001000 10100111 00110010 11110100 11000000 00000011 10111101 00001000
10111111 00100000 00100011 00111100 01010000 11011001 00100100 10110001 11101000 01111101
01101000 01100001 10001100 11110011 10011101 11100111 10011010 00011011 11010100 00000110
10000011 10000010 01000000 11101101 11010100 11010000 11000000 01100100 00001110 10100011
00111101 11101001 00111010 00111111 00100111 10101111 01001100 01010010 00110111 11001100
01110110 10011100 00000011 10011110 10010101 01001010 11101101 10000000 00110110 01001100
10000111 10100110 00111011 01010010 10011111 11110101 10011111 10000101 00011000 00011100
01111011 00011010 00011111 00111001 11000000 11101111 11011110 10010011 01000000 00100000
00011001 11101101 11010111 10101110 01101001 01111000 00001010 01110010 00101001 00011000
10011100 11100111 01110111 11100001 01001010 01011100 01110001 11011111 00000010 10010010
11010100 00001000 11001110 01110110 10010000 00101001 01011000 01110100 11111101 01001101
00111101 11110001 11011000 01111011 11110011 01001100 00000100 10011100 11111010 01010101
01101100 00000010 01000110 10100011 01110001 00111101 01110010 01111010 01010000 11100011
00011000 00000011 10110101 00101110 11101100 01000110 11111000 11111011 11100100 01110000
01111101 00101001 00000111 10100111 01010011 01010010 11011001 01011010 00000110 00110001
01001000 01110000 01110011 10011111 11010010 10010101 01001110 01001111 11010010 10010001
11001001 00101111 11000111 00000011 10110101 01010011 01101110 11010110 11101000 01001000
11011100 01100100 01100111 00111100 01110101 10100001 10000111 00011111 11010010 10010101
10111110 11100101 00100000 11100001 00001000 00100011 10011010 10001011 00010110 00110100
00011100 00101011 10010010 00110010 01111011 00000001 01001010 10011001 00010001 10001100
11100011 00111110 11010100 00000100 11111111 00000000 11101011 11010010 10001110 00101010
10111100 11011000 00001000 01111001 01001100 11100010 10011000 11011111 01110101 00000000
11110101 11100100 11010011 11010111 00100100 11111011 11111010 00011110 11010100 10011000
11111100 10101000 00100100 01101011 10010000 00010011 00110100 11100110 01100000 00011000
10000000 00111010 00001110 01101001 01001110 00001000 11101011 11000000 10100100 01100110

01100000 01001110 11001110 00110010 00111000 11001101 00110111 11011100 00010110 11100011
01111111 10000000 01110011 10001111 01001100 11010011 10011000 00001100 01100011 00011001
11000111 01010011 01001100 01011110 00000110 00010100 00011100 11111010 10011010 01011100
10010000 00110000 00000111 11100011 01010011 00101011 01011111 01000001 10110001 00011001
10111000 00011000 01010000 00000110 01101001 01011000 11100000 01100011 11010000 01100110
10000000 00001000 11101101 10010011 11011000 01010001 11101010 01001000 00011000 00011101
11111101 01101010 10010010 01000100 10001000 10100011 10111001 11111010 11010000 11001101
10001100 00001100 01110101 10100001 10001111 11101110 11110111 01111010 01110110 10100100
11000000 11100000 10011110 10100110 10000110 11011111 01000010 11000000 11100111 00011111
10101101 00101110 01111010 10011110 10111111 01001010 00111010 00001110 01111010 10011010
01000110 11100000 10001110 11010100 10110110 11011100 10000000 00000000 00000101 00100100
11110101 10100001 00000110 00001111 00000011 10101101 00001101 10001100 01110010 00001111
01011110 00101000 11101001 11000001 11111110 01110100 00101011 01011100 00000001 01111110
01110010 00010111 11011110 10011001 11111111 00000000 00101101 00001111 00111100 11111010
11010010 10110001 00101011 00001110 00010011 10000010 01000110 00000111 01110010 00101001
10100010 00100001 00010100 01101001 00011010 00011110 00000001 11100100 11010011 01110001
10111000 11101110 00101110 01000001 01010011 11101001 11010010 10000110 11001110 00111111
10011101 00001100 00000010 11110000 00111110 10110100 10001101 11011010 10001011 01011000
00101101 01100001 10101001 10001100 10011010 01110111 00011111 01001100 11110111 10100000
11111101 11000001 10000101 10100110 10111001 00111111 00100111 00111000 00111000 11100100
10001010 00110100 01111011 10010100 00011011 01111010 00001110 11111111 00000000 11010010
10010000 01111100 11011000 11110101 00111100 11100100 11110110 10100111 11100100 10000100
11101111 11001111 01011010 01101010 00001100 10111111 01011110 01000101 01001010 11010001
10010010 11000100 01110011 10110100 11111001 01100011 10001001 00101001 00010110 00111100
00010000 10111001 11111011 10011100 11110101 10100011 10001111 00111011 00100011 00111001
11000111 01010011 11011110 10010111 11101110 11000101 10010011 10011110 01001111 00010101
01001111 10110000 01011100 01000011 11001011 10000010 00111010 10010011 11001110 01101001
10000100 10001100 11111100 11011001 11001101 00101110 11101101 10100000 10001100 01110011
11101111 01000100 01110001 00000110 01011100 10110001 11000001 00111110 11110100 00001111
01110011 11000011 10011000 10111000 00101000 00000111 01001111 11100111 01010010 01000111
00101000 00001100 01000010 01110000 01001111 01110011 01010101 10010110 01101100 10001110
01111010 11010000 10001110 10100000 11111011 10011010 11101110 01110000 01001001 00011110
11010010 11000100 00010111 01111100 11001111 00101100 01100000 01110010 01101010 01010110
10111000 00111100 00000000 01110000 00101010 10010001 01100000 00110000 01110010 01001111
11010010 10010001 00100101 01101111 11111110 10111101 01011010 10000100 00010110 10001001
10011010 00101100 01001011 10110101 10010001 10100000 00100111 11001111 11001101 10010011
11000101 00101100 01010011 11100100 00010011 10001111 10010011 00111100 11010101 00001100
11101110 01000010 00001110 01110001 01001000 11001100 01100011 10001111 00000101 10111000
11101100 00101011 00110111 01001111 01000110 00011110 11011110 11000110 11000000 10011111
00011000 00111111 11111101 01111010 10010001 10101110 10010100 01100101 01110010 00001011
10010001 11001110 01101011 00010001 00100111 01101100 01100011 00111100 01010001 11100111
11100111 00000100 11110110 10100100 10101001 11110100 01011011 10011010 11000111 00010010
10001101 10100011 01110001 00000110 00011111 11100101 00111001 11110101 00010101 11001110
01001100 11000111 11001101 01111110 11101000 01001111 00011001 10101011 01101111 00110111
01110000 11010101 01001110 01011110 01100100 00100100 00010001 10011010 10111010 00110100
10011010 01110110 01101100 11100010 11001100 00100111 00011010 10010001 11010000 10011011
10000010 00110001 10011100 00011010 01001001 00111000 11100011 10101110 00101010 10111111
11001100 00001110 00111010 00001110 11011110 11010100 11110111 00100100 10100111 10110111
01001111 10101101 01110110 11111011 10111101 01001111 00001100 01101011 01110001 11010010
10100110 00000011 01110000 11110101 00011101 10101010 00001100 00110111 01010001 11000001
00011101 11110011 01010011 10100000 01101101 11011000 00000000 01110100 11001110 00101000
10110101 10011110 10000101 00100001 10011000 00111001 00101011 11001000 00111101 10111000
10101001 00000111 01101110 00110010 01101010 11111010 00110101 10111011 00101110 00100100
10000100 01101111 11110101 11001111 01011010 10010011 00110110 10011110 01100110 01111100
10101110 00101011 10001101 11010110 11100100 00111011 10100001 10000011 11110110 10001010
11111100 11001000 11001001 10111000 00000100 10000100 00111111 11000111 11011110 10101001
00111100 01011000 01000111 10010001 11000111 00011000 10101110 10001110 01100011 01100101
10011100 00001000 01000111 10111111 00110101 01010110 01100110 10110110 10010110 00111100
01101101 01001100 00011110 10100000 11010010 01110101 01010011 11010100 11010101 01100101
01110010 01111011 01001001 00011100 11101010 00001100 00001100 10000001 11000001 11101111
01001011 10111000 00000011 11011111 11011011 10001010 11011000 01011000 01101101 00001010
00000101 00010001 10000000 00110011 11011010 10100101 10111000 10110111 10110110 00100000
00000001 00011111 10111111 01011010 11011011 11011010 00101011 01101000 00001111 00101010
10011111 01110100 01100101 10100011 00000010 10100000 01100011 11110010 00010101 01110001
00100101 11100000 00000100 01011110 00111011 00001010 10101101 00011000 00001011 00100011
11110011 11110010 01100110 10101110 11000101 00011110 01001111 00100111 10001110 11011100
11010101 11101111 10101001 11100101 11010100 10000111 00100011 11100101 00001111 00110100
10010000 00110011 10000001 11101110 00000101 01001111 10110100 01111001 01100000 11100100
11010100 01101011 00011001 00100100 00010111 00111001 00000010 10011110 11101101 11111011
10111100 00001110 01110001 11011010 10101011 01001001 00100010 00010010 00101010 11001110
10100100 11111011 01100010 10101010 10110010 10110001 01110011 11110010 10011110 01111101
00000111 01011010 10110000 11110010 01111110 11101111 10010011 11110011 11010100 11010110
00110011 00110100 01101110 01010111 00011100 01110101 11000001 11110101 10101000 10101000

11111001 01010001 10110101 00011000 01111011 01001001 10100100 11001101 00101111 00000110
11011101 10011011 01001101 01010010 00110101 01110000 00000000 01101111 10010000 10010011
11011010 10111101 00010110 11110000 10011001 00101101 01001000 00011000 00100111 00010101
11100110 11011110 01101111 01000011 11000101 00011111 01101101 10011010 00110111 11111001
00100101 01110000 01111110 10110101 11100110 11010111 10100111 00111010 10101101 00110101
11010000 11110111 00101001 11100001 01010101 00110101 01101011 10011110 10000011 01100001
01111101 00011100 11010001 00100110 00011011 10010001 11010110 10010110 11101010 01111111
10110101 01000111 11110110 01110100 11101011 00100001 00000011 10011010 11110011 10100110
10111000 10010100 00000001 11100101 11001000 01111000 11001110 01000000 00110100 10001001
01110111 00110100 01101100 00011011 11001101 01111100 10000011 11000111 11001101 11010010
10001111 01100110 11100101 10100001 10011011 11000001 01000001 01001010 11110111 00111101
01100101 01010101 00101101 00101101 10111110 01111110 10001010 00111001 00111101 00101011
10010010 01011011 10001000 10110101 00111101 01010001 11101110 10100100 00011111 11101000
11110000 11110001 00011000 11101001 10111000 11111010 11010111 00101111 11111101 10100001
01110010 01110010 00001100 11110010 00010000 01111011 00110011 01010001 00011110 10100001
00111100 00101001 11100101 00100001 11000010 01111010 01010110 01110001 10100000 11100001
00111110 01111001 00110011 01011001 01100001 10101110 10110111 00111011 00001101 01010111
01010111 01001011 01011011 01101001 00100111 00111001 01111100 01110100 00000000 11100000
10010011 01011110 01110001 01110101 01110000 11010111 01110010 10011001 00001010 10000001
00100011 00011100 10011110 11110101 10110001 00001101 11010100 10101011 00100111 00101010
10000100 00011110 01001110 01101010 00101001 10010110 00001001 00100110 11011100 01100001
01001100 11111010 10001010 11101001 10000101 00111101 01101110 11110111 00110000 10011110
01011111 01110101 01111000 10110010 10101110 10001111 01110100 10111010 01111100 10010010
01001010 11101010 01100100 00100100 01100011 00010101 11010011 01000011 11100011 01000110
10001010 11011100 11100110 11001000 00111010 01100011 00000000 00001001 00101011 10011111
01101011 01011000 01011011 00100101 00001001 00011001 10100110 11001011 01101000 00000010
10000000 10000011 10001111 01111010 11011010 10100101 00101010 01010011 11011100 11100111
11111010 10101110 00100010 10011010 11010000 10010010 11101011 01010000 00111010 10000101
11010011 11001111 11100101 01111001 01000110 01000011 10011101 10100010 10100110 10001001
10000111 00011000 11001111 10111101 01010001 01011000 01100110 11011111 11000000 11001000
00110101 00111111 10010101 00111010 10101110 01001010 11110000 00101010 01100101 01001010
00010000 11010010 00101100 11110100 00110000 10110010 10101001 00000101 11101111 00100011
01010110 11001100 01111010 11110100 10101011 00010111 00000011 11110111 01000111 00011001
11100100 01010101 00111101 00110100 11001000 11111100 00010011 11111001 11010101 11001011
10010010 00010110 00110011 10011111 01001110 00111101 11101011 00011001 00100110 10011101
10101100 01111011 01010000 01101001 11000010 11101000 11000111 10111000 00011111 00110000
11100111 10011100 11110101 10101011 01101100 11111110 01001101 10101010 00010000 00000110
11110011 11001001 10101100 11000110 01100010 11010010 11110010 01111011 11110100 11001101
01011011 10111100 11011101 10010100 01011110 10100000 00001110 00101011 01011000 10101111
01110110 11000111 10000111 00111111 10001010 01010010 00111101 00000011 11100001 00110111
11001101 10101000 01011100 01001000 00000001 11000000 01011100 11010111 10101010 00000011
10000101 11001111 01110011 11001101 01111001 01110111 11000010 00100000 01100100 10011010
11100001 10111001 11001000 00011000 10101111 01010001 01101110 00010011 00010101 10011110
00101010 11101101 10101011 00011110 00111101 01000111 01110110 00100010 10011101 11010001
00001111 11100101 01001011 11010010 00111110 01111010 11010100 01101101 11001001 11001111
11100100 00101001 11111000 00011101 00001110 01001001 11110100 10101110 01011101 11110101
00110011 00010101 00001111 11001011 11101110 01111101 10101000 01101100 00001010 00111010
00011110 00110011 01001000 01011000 00101110 01110000 00110010 01111011 00001010 00011110
10000010 00011011 10011100 11110011 11011110 10011100 10111011 10001001 00100111 10000000
00101000 01100000 00110011 10010010 01110000 00111110 10110100 01100111 10001110 00001110
01001101 00011010 10001100 01101011 00110110 01011011 01101110 00110000 00111011 10011010
00110010 00110000 01001010 00000010 01101001 11001101 10000000 01110001 11000111 10111101
00011100 11111101 00000000 10100011 01110001 00001101 01010000 11011000 00011100 11110101
11101101 01001101 11011101 11001011 10101000 11101101 11011110 10011100 01111001 00011000
10100100 01011110 00000001 11000111 01001111 11100111 01001101 00111101 00000000 01010110
01100001 11011011 00000111 10001110 10110100 00000110 00111000 00000101 10111000 10100100
11000000 11001111 01110000 01001111 01101010 00001001 11100110 10010000 00001001 00011001
11001110 01011000 10001100 00001111 10101111 01011010 01110110 00111111 00001111 01101010
00001000 11000000 00000000 01110100 10100100 11100000 00001110 00111010 11111010 11010100
11011101 10001100 01010000 00110001 11010000 11100010 10011100 10111001 00000100 10010011
11010011 00000010 10011001 10001100 01000111 11101010 01101000 01111111 10111011 10000001
11010010 10101101 10111011 10110000 00000100 11000111 11100111 11001001 11001101 00001101
11010100 11100011 00011101 00110001 01000110 00110010 01000101 00001100 10101100 11000111
00100111 10000100 11001101 00010010 10111000 10000000 01110100 11000111 10100111 01111010
00001001 11100100 10010010 00111001 11111110 01110100 01100011 10011111 10101111 00110100
10011000 00100110 01100010 01001111 01001111 10101101 00001011 01000001 10001101 01101110
01110000 00111011 10011010 01111011 00000010 00000001 11000001 10100011 01110001 00011100
11100000 01110011 11010000 10001010 01100110 01011011 00111100 10101111 00011101 10101001
00111001 01110110 00011101 10000001 10001110 00010100 01111011 10011110 01111101 11101000
11011010 01001001 00101100 01001110 00000000 11110100 10100011 10000101 00000011 10111110
00111001 11001110 00101000 11011101 11000000 11000000 11101011 01000010 01111101 01000010
11100011 10110011 10111000 00011110 11000010 10011011 10011101 11011000 00011000 10100001
10111000 11111111 00000000 00001010 01111110 00001010 10011100 10010011 11111000 01010011

01111010 01101010 00100010 00110111 00100101 01000111 01000001 10011100 11010010 10101000
00101100 01001001 11101000 00101001 00111110 01011110 10111101 10001111 01101010 01010110
00100000 10001100 01111011 11010010 01001110 11100000 00001100 01111011 00001110 10111001
10100011 00100000 11100111 00011110 10111001 00100110 10011011 10111000 00101110 01001110
01110010 01111011 10001010 00010101 10011011 11001010 00101100 11101011 11111010 11110101
10100010 11100000 00101011 00010010 01001000 11000000 10100100 01101100 00000101 11100011
00111001 11101000 00101001 01111110 01100011 10110000 01100111 00000011 10111101 00100010
10010000 01000001 11000001 11100100 00011100 01010000 11011110 10100000 00101010 11110010
01110111 01111011 11110100 10100100 11101011 00101000 00111000 11000001 00011100 11110101
10100001 01100100 01000000 00011111 00101101 11001000 11101011 01001101 01010000 00110110
10000011 11001000 11001001 11100011 00111100 01100110 10010100 01101101 01111011 10000000
11101110 01000001 00100100 10011110 00001101 00000111 11101110 10000001 10011110 01110011
10010010 01101001 01010011 10011001 00111010 01110100 11110101 10100100 00011000 11100100
11100011 00010100 01110101 11010000 00000001 11100100 11001011 11101100 01000000 01000001
11111010 01010011 01011011 10000100 11011011 11011011 10100110 00111101 01101001 11000100
01110001 10000000 01111110 01110011 01000001 00011000 11000000 00011000 11111010 01010001
10101010 11011100 00000110 10100110 01001011 01110011 11000000 11110100 10100111 01100100
10010100 11001001 00011100 01010001 11110011 00000100 00000001 00111000 01111100 11110101
11110110 10100110 01100011 10001101 10000000 11110001 11010110 10011101 11011011 01000000
00101011 00000010 11000111 00011101 10110011 11111001 11010011 10001001 11000110 00111000
10100011 01110110 01110000 01000111 01001010 01100111 11001100 11001110 01001011 11110001
11001111 01001111 01000001 01001101 00110001 00001010 11101101 11001000 11110111 11101110
01101000 01111100 00010000 00110001 11010110 10011100 11011000 11001110 00111011 01010011
01011001 10000001 01111100 00001110 01000110 00111010 11010010 10111110 10110110 01100011
00001100 11100011 10010011 11010000 01111010 01010010 01100111 00101010 10011100 00011110
01101001 01001001 00100001 01001001 11101101 01000111 01000110 11100111 10011110 00101000
10010101 10000000 01000000 10111100 11010000 01111101 00111111 01001010 01000110 00111100
01100100 01110100 11001111 01111010 01011100 11100101 11000110 00111010 11110111 10100101
11001001 01100000 00001111 11110101 01100000 10110011 01110001 11101001 01000010 10010001
10011100 10010011 11110101 10100000 10011110 10011001 00011001 11100110 10011000 00001000
11000110 11011110 11011101 01001101 00111111 01000000 00000010 00000000 01101100 01110010
01001001 11101111 01000011 11100111 11001100 00011101 00001001 11110111 11101101 01001110
11101010 01000111 00011101 00111001 11100110 10011001 11000001 10010000 10011111 11000100
11111011 11010000 10101111 01110010 11000001 11000001 11001110 00111101 10110010 01101001
01110000 01001001 11000111 01000001 11101001 01000111 01000101 11101010 01111111 00001010
01110111 00000000 11100011 00111110 11100100 10011010 00110100 10110101 11001000 00011010
11011001 00111000 11100011 10100111 01000001 01000001 11100100 00010101 00011101 01101001
00110111 00011100 10011101 10000011 00100000 00011100 00001111 01111010 01010011 11001000
11011010 10000111 10010011 11010100 11010011 01110110 00000001 10101110 00110010 11101001
11101001 11010100 11111011 11010010 11100000 10000010 00110010 00000111 00111100 11010010
01100000 01110000 00001111 00100111 11010111 00110100 10101101 11001100 10011100 00011010
01001101 10000000 11001110 01001000 00100011 00111000 00000100 11110101 11110101 10100111
11000110 10111001 01110001 10000001 11101100 00101000 10010100 10000000 00111110 10011100
01010010 00100111 00000000 11100111 10101110 00111001 10100111 01100111 01100000 00011011
10010000 10111001 11000110 00001111 00111000 10100100 01000000 11000100 00011110 11000111
10100110 01101000 01100000 00100011 00000000 10000010 00001001 00111101 10101001 11101100
11011110 01011001 11000111 00111100 11110010 01101010 01101101 01100100 01010010 00011000
11011111 10111011 10001100 00011100 11110101 11100000 11010010 01001001 11010001 00010100
00011110 10011110 10011101 11101001 01010101 01111110 01000000 01110011 11010100 11010010
00111001 11111001 11000110 00000111 00011000 11111101 01101010 10110100 10110110 10100100
10000011 01111100 11010001 11100000 01110000 00110011 10011010 00011000 10000001 11001111
00111001 11101101 10001010 01100011 00011110 01110110 11111111 00000000 00000000 10100111
11100111 00001000 11100011 11111000 10110001 11000110 01101010 01010100 01101110 01011000
11000011 10000011 00100110 01111110 11111110 00111000 00011001 10100101 11001001 00000011
10000011 11001001 10100100 01111111 10010101 11000010 00100001 11101000 00110010 01001101
00111111 10010011 10011100 11110111 00110101 01010111 00100101 10001100 01100000 00111010
11110011 10001111 01111010 00110011 10011100 00010011 11010000 01010000 10111001 11000001
11100111 11011011 00010100 00110000 11001000 11001101 00100111 01110100 00100001 00110000
00001001 11100011 10011010 01010001 10000101 01001101 11000111 10011111 01101010 01001110
11111111 00000000 11111101 01111010 00010101 10001011 00000010 01001000 11000010 01110110
11001000 10100101 01111011 10110010 11000000 01100100 10000010 01111101 11111010 11010011
01111010 10001100 00000011 11010000 11010011 10110011 11010100 00001111 11001110 10011001
11101000 00000000 11101001 01010101 01101110 11000100 00001010 10100011 00001011 11101011
01001101 01001100 11100100 11100111 10111101 00111001 01001110 00011111 00111001 11001000
11000101 00100111 00111001 11001001 11101111 11111010 01010000 11111100 10000000 00100010
00000000 00010000 01110011 10000001 01001001 10011100 10000010 01000111 01000010 01111000
00110100 00110000 00111011 00110001 11011010 10000000 00111110 01100001 11001111 00000000
01110001 01001010 11001011 10101001 01011101 00000110 10111011 01100011 00011100 01100111
11101011 01001001 11001100 01110001 11100101 10110000 01011100 10011100 10011010 01011110
10100011 00100000 01110011 11011011 00110100 00011110 00001111 00111100 10010011 01000011
11011000 01100000 10111110 10100110 10010011 10101010 01100011 10111111 10101101 00001011
00011111 00111011 10110010 01001110 01111101 01101000 10010011 00111011 00111110 01000010
00111110 10111000 10100101 00100000 00010001 10110011 10111000 01100111 10100111 11010110

10010111 10000000 01111000 11111100 10101001 01000010 11110100 11001111 00111000 10100011
00000000 00011101 11011000 11100010 10000001 01011100 01101110 00001001 01100010 01111001
00110100 00101111 11001100 01110011 11011011 10100101 00110111 00111011 10001011 11110101
11000001 00110100 01101101 11101011 10010001 11110100 00010100 00110111 10101101 10000001
00001111 01001110 01011100 10010000 01110011 11001101 00100110 01000000 01000010 01001110
01001001 00100111 10110101 00110111 10000000 01111001 11101001 10001110 11010100 00100110
01000010 10000010 01111000 00100111 10011010 01111011 00111101 01000011 01000000 11000110
00110010 01011100 11100010 10001100 11100001 00110001 10001110 00101010 00110110 00011011
10100101 00100111 10110000 00111000 00000010 10100100 01111110 00110001 11101011 11011100
01010011 00001110 10100010 01100011 11010100 01010011 11011100 01100111 11111001 11010001
11001111 10101110 01001111 01101010 01101011 01100011 10010010 01111111 00010001 01001010
11101000 01100010 01110001 11011110 10010001 10000110 11100110 00011001 11101101 01001010
10000011 00000011 11111001 01100110 10001110 01001110 00001111 01000001 11011110 10010001
00101100 00011100 10010010 00111111 01110111 11011011 10111001 10100110 00110111 01001110
01000110 01101001 11000000 10010011 00100001 11100000 10000100 11000111 00011001 00110100
11011110 00000100 10011100 10011110 00111101 01101010 10101101 01111101 00000100 00111011
00111000 00111001 11000110 01000111 10100111 10101101 00110101 01111111 11011011 11111100
01000101 00100011 10010010 01011111 00100111 10100111 01100001 10001010 00001000 11100111
11011111 00110100 11110100 01001100 00000001 10001000 11000111 00011100 10011111 01001010
00011100 00010011 10000011 11111100 00010100 00100010 10000000 01001111 11010111 10101101
00100001 11100100 11110101 11100000 01110100 10100100 10010011 11011101 00100010 11000000
01100111 11010111 10000001 11011010 10001111 11111001 01100111 10010010 00111010 00011110
00101001 11011100 11101101 00111000 00011100 11111010 10011010 01101111 00011000 01000001
11010111 10011010 01101101 10110010 00000001 10001110 01000111 00111100 01010011 00111110
11101111 00100000 01110101 10100111 10111001 00100110 01000001 10000001 11000000 11000111
00010100 11010111 11111011 10000111 11010100 01110011 01001011 01000100 00000010 01100000
00011110 10000111 10111101 00100100 11000100 11001000 11001000 00000111 01000000 01110010
01101001 01010100 10001100 00010001 11111000 01010010 00111000 11000010 00011111 01010001
01000101 11101110 11000000 01101001 00011001 11001000 00011101 11101000 10010001 01111110
01100011 10110011 11101110 11110110 10100111 00110000 00000010 00110000 01110011 11001001
10100111 01000110 10111001 01000001 01010010 11001010 01000111 11001111 00101110 01001110
01111010 00011111 01011100 11111010 11010011 10010001 10001110 01000000 00111001 11001001
11101001 11101111 01001110 01001100 10001100 00101110 01110011 11110101 00010101 00101010
00011100 10011110 10011001 11110101 10101111 01010001 11000111 10010001 11011111 01110011
10110010 11001000 00010100 00110000 11100010 10010111 00111100 00000001 01010011 01100011
00100011 00100001 01000000 11000111 01010011 01001011 11100101 10000110 00111001 00100011
00111100 01110110 10100010 01011010 10111011 00011010 01011001 10010001 00100100 10011000
10100001 11001110 01001001 10100111 01111001 00100111 10101110 00001110 00101010 00110110
00011000 00111100 00101001 00011001 10101001 11100110 01101001 01101110 01001011 10111000
11010111 00100100 01100011 00011101 11101000 01111001 01001010 00001110 01111001 00011111
11001110 10011101 10111011 10001100 00010000 01111101 10101001 10101100 00001001 11100100
01010110 11011100 11011101 01101110 00101101 01000110 10110011 00000010 01111000 10100100
01000110 11011100 11100101 10110001 11110101 10101001 00010001 01010111 00111001 00001100
01111110 10011000 10100000 00000101 00000111 11100101 11101111 01001110 10011011 11110111
10110111 11011100 11001010 10101101 11101101 10101000 10001000 01000110 01110011 10001010
10010000 10001100 00000000 00110001 01000010 01100000 01001000 00001111 01101111 01001100
01010100 10001101 10000001 11001111 01101010 11010001 11011011 01100011 10001001 10111101
01000110 10101000 00000001 00000001 10100111 11000100 11100001 01001001 00000100 01111110
01100010 10010101 11110001 10110111 10000001 01000000 00001010 10100011 00100100 10010011
10011111 01010011 01001010 11110111 11011001 10001001 10001101 01100110 00011110 01100111
01001100 11010011 10110011 10010001 10011111 01011010 01101001 00011000 01110010 01000110
00111010 01111101 01101001 01000001 11111001 01111000 11000101 01100001 00101101 01001110
11011010 01001001 10100100 01000101 00111011 00010000 00111110 01010011 10010011 01011001
10001110 01001110 01100100 00100100 10011110 10110101 01111110 01000011 10010000 11111101
10111011 01111101 01101011 00111101 11000000 11100101 01111001 00111001 10101001 10000110
10101111 01010011 01100111 01110110 00111001 00100100 01100000 01110000 00001111 01011010
10011010 00101001 01011000 10011100 00010011 01010000 00100010 11101101 00100011 00100100
10010011 11101101 01010010 00110111 11001000 00111101 00001101 01011111 00100010 11101010
01011010 10010100 10010010 11010000 10110001 00011010 10101110 01001011 01110000 00110010
00110010 01000101 00111110 00111001 00001010 10011100 10001110 10111111 01011110 10010101
01011101 01100011 11111001 01000001 11001111 00111101 01101001 11001010 00000011 01110010
00101011 01110111 00011101 00101100 01111001 01010011 01111110 11110101 11011001 00111001
01100010 11011100 10000110 11000000 11001101 00101011 10010011 10110011 11100100 11101111
01010101 11011100 00011100 00000101 11111100 11001101 00011111 00110110 00110010 10100111
10100111 10101101 00001101 01101010 00101011 00001110 01111100 00101111 10101001 11111010
11010011 10100010 11100011 00000111 10001100 11110111 10101010 11001101 00100011 00010111
00000111 00011011 10111101 01111011 01010010 00000010 01000000 11111100 01101011 00110110
11001010 10100100 10101101 00100010 11110011 00110111 00000010 10001101 11000100 10001110
00111011 01110101 10101000 01011010 01011100 00000000 00111000 11110110 00110100 11100100
10010111 10000001 10011010 11001101 11011111 10101001 11101001 11000110 10100011 01100011
11010110 01011110 00111101 00111110 10110100 11000011 00101110 01001111 01011100 11111011
10001010 10010001 10001111 00011000 11000001 00011110 10011001 00010100 10001101 10000010
01000010 11100011 11110010 10100011 10010101 00100110 01011111 00111011 10111000 00101011

01110000 01110010 01001110 00101001 11111011 10001001 00110100 11000110 00101011 10001110
11111111 00000000 10000101 01000100 11101101 11101000 01110001 01001101 11000101 00110110
00111111 01101000 11001001 10001100 10101100 10100100 01100011 10100101 00001011 00110011
01110011 11101001 01010101 10111001 00000011 00111001 11111101 00101010 01000100 00100111
10111111 10100101 01001011 01011101 01001010 01010101 00011001 01100001 01100101 01101110
10111001 11000110 01111010 11010100 10101001 00101001 00000011 00011001 11001000 11101101
01010100 11010111 10010011 11010111 10001010 10011001 01011000 00001110 10110100 01001001
01011111 01110011 01001010 01110101 00011101 11110111 00101100 11111001 11101100 00000000
00000011 10110101 01011100 10110001 10010111 11001101 10010111 00001111 11001000 00111101
10001101 01100110 00000011 10111000 11100111 00111111 01001010 10110111 01101101 11111110
10110001 00111101 01001111 01011010 11000111 10011111 01011011 01011000 11101110 10100101
00100110 11011010 11010100 10111011 01100111 00010111 10010101 01110110 01010111 01110011
10011111 01001110 00110001 01010110 00101111 11111110 11100000 11001000 11100110 10100100
11000111 00110001 11001000 01111000 01110011 11000000 00110101 01011011 01010001 10010000
10000101 11000111 10101111 01111010 11100111 10011100 10011010 01100111 01101111 00101101
10010011 00110010 00010001 01110111 01001111 10011100 01110011 11101011 01010111 00101111
00000110 00100100 00011001 11110100 10101010 01001011 11111111 00000000 00011111 00001001
10011110 10000111 11011110 10101111 11011111 11110011 00100000 00100100 00011010 11011010
00110011 11011010 11100111 10010010 10010111 10111011 00100011 11010010 00111110 00010011
10000101 11111111 00000000 01001001 00110000 11110010 00001010 10001100 10011100 01110111
10101111 01000110 11111010 10011110 00101011 11001110 10111110 00010001 01100000 01011011
11011101 10110000 00111001 11011111 10001110 10110101 11101000 10100000 00011110 01110011
11011110 10001100 01010110 10001101 00011110 00011101 01000101 01100110 00111011 00111001
11101000 00101001 01011000 00011110 10111101 00101001 10001010 00110000 01111010 10011010
00111001 11011111 10011100 11110001 01011100 10111110 10100110 01100011 10111001 00011001
00100111 00111101 00101001 10101110 00001111 00000111 00011111 01001110 01101001 11001100
01000110 01101001 10000000 11100111 10100110 01000110 00001110 00101001 00110110 10011011
11010000 00000101 01010001 10010011 11001000 11001110 00101000 01010001 11011010 10010011
00111101 10000110 01110011 01001010 11000000 10001110 10110100 00111111 00110000 00000100
00000000 01110011 10001110 11110100 01100100 10010110 11000010 10001100 11010000 00001110
11111110 00000111 01001010 00000001 11000111 00000110 10011010 10110000 10000001 10001110
00110010 00001111 00111100 11010011 01100101 11100100 10001111 01001010 01110111 00000100
11100100 11010010 00110110 01001001 11100010 10010011 01010110 01100011 00010101 00111000
00000100 10110001 11001111 11010110 10010001 01110110 10101000 11001110 01111000 10100101
11100011 00100100 00011110 10010100 10001110 11001011 10000000 00000101 00001000 01000000
01001001 00111101 11111001 00111101 00101001 01110000 00001000 11101011 11001111 01111010
01000110 11111011 10000011 11110000 10100101 11100000 00000010 11011100 11010000 10110101
11010100 01100001 11010000 01111011 11111010 01010001 01001000 10111001 11110101 11110111
11001101 00101111 01110000 00111010 10011010 00101110 00100000 01100000 00110011 01000011
00010000 00110000 00110011 10010011 11101101 01000111 00011001 11000111 10111110 01101001
00110001 10010111 00101101 01000011 01010111 01000000 00100001 01101111 10011100 01111011
11010000 11011101 00001001 00111001 10100011 00100000 00001100 11111010 11110000 00111101
11101001 01011100 10000000 00110010 01111101 01111000 10100001 01101100 00110001 00011000
00011110 10011101 10111101 00101001 01010111 00011110 01100001 00111101 11110001 11011110
10010001 10111010 00001110 11011110 10110100 11011110 00000010 11100011 10110101 01000011
01101100 00000100 11001110 00100011 11101001 10010011 11101111 01001010 10100000 00001110
10100111 00000111 11010010 10001110 10000000 00011110 11011101 10101001 10101101 10011111
10111100 11100111 11100111 11001101 01011010 01111010 00001000 01110011 01110101 11100000
11110100 10100100 00111001 11001001 11111110 01100110 10001100 10011101 11100011 00011100
10011110 10100110 10010101 01111011 10011010 00110100 01100011 00000100 11100010 10011010
10011000 11011100 01110011 11000111 00111101 00101001 11001010 11001010 00011011 00101111
01010001 11100111 10010010 01111011 00010011 10011100 00001010 01011110 10000101 01011000
00011011 00011000 00011100 01100111 00100111 11110011 10100111 00111001 00001110 01000000
11111110 00001010 01010111 01101100 10010010 11011000 11001110 00111011 01010010 00110001
11000111 00000010 10001011 01110111 00100100 00010111 10101110 01010010 10000010 01010110
00110000 01110111 11110010 11111101 01110001 11101011 01001010 10100111 10010001 11011111
10011100 10010011 11101011 01001100 00111100 11001000 00110010 01110010 01001111 11101000
00101010 01011101 11000000 01110110 11010000 01010000 11110100 00000011 11010011 11010110
10011010 00011011 11001101 00111011 10111001 00011000 11100010 10011101 11000001 10001000
00110000 00111100 01100110 10010101 01111000 00011111 01000001 10011010 10111110 10000000
01000111 11001111 01000000 00111111 00010011 01001111 01010101 11111101 11100001 00011001
11100110 10010111 10010110 11100100 01110000 10000000 01110011 10011010 10001101 00000110
11101100 10010000 01111010 11010001 10101010 00000001 01011011 00001101 11010011 00100100
01111010 11010000 10011101 01111010 01100011 00011110 11110100 11100110 00100001 01111011
01110001 11011011 00010100 11001100 00011111 00110000 11110110 00011000 11101000 00101001
01011111 10100000 00001010 00100101 01100011 10010110 11011000 01000000 11101101 10011010
01000101 11011011 11100101 10100010 10010011 10011110 01111010 00001010 10010011 10110110
00111010 11110110 10100110 00100001 00000101 00111000 11100011 11101011 01001101 01011110
11000000 00100010 01001000 01110010 11100011 00011110 11000000 01010010 11101110 11101011
11000111 00011001 11000111 00110100 10011111 00101000 11000111 00000100 11111010 00001010
00010011 10100111 00101011 11011111 11010110 10010110 10001100 00000101 01011110 00010100
10011110 10111000 11110111 10100110 10101001 11001001 01001111 10010111 10101001 11001110
01101001 01011100 01110010 00010111 00111100 10011110 11010100 01101110 01011101 10000100

11110011 10000001 11011000 00001100 11010011 01001010 11011010 10000000 00111001 00111100
01100011 10101001 00111111 10100101 00001110 00110000 01110011 11001111 00100111 10101101
00110001 01110010 01000000 11110011 00000110 11010001 11101001 10011010 01110010 10101110
01100101 11001111 10101111 01000001 11101001 01000011 01110111 00011110 10100000 11100000
01101110 00000000 10011110 00110011 10010011 01000110 01111001 00101101 11010011 00110100
00010010 00001001 00111000 11101101 11010100 11111010 11010001 11010011 10010011 11001101
00111011 10000101 10000001 01001000 01010010 00110010 01111001 00111101 00101001 10101110
01111111 01111010 01000000 11100100 11110111 00110100 00111001 00100101 10010011 10000000
01000110 01111001 00111110 10010100 00110001 11100111 00111101 10110001 01001001 11011111
10101000 10000011 01111110 00000111 10110111 01001010 01000110 00100000 11001010 01000000
00100000 10000001 11000001 10100001 10110010 01000010 01110011 11000001 11101101 01001000
11011000 00000100 01100011 10111111 01011010 01001001 10111011 01011100 00000111 01101101
00111110 01101110 00001001 11100011 00010100 11011111 10111100 00000011 00001111 01011100
11010010 10110110 01000001 11100011 10111101 00001000 00000010 11111101 01101001 11101010
11000000 01010001 10011100 10000011 10011100 00000001 01001000 01111001 00111101 11000000
00100010 10001100 00011100 10111001 11000111 00010100 10001010 01111110 01010111 11101110
01111101 01101001 00000000 10101011 11001001 00111000 00011000 00000010 10000111 01100010
00000000 00101010 00111001 11101001 01001000 01001000 00000011 00000011 11101010 01001101
00101110 00110111 01100000 10001110 01110011 11011010 10001011 11110110 00011011 00100011
00011100 01000110 10000001 11001001 01111001 00111010 11100111 11010010 10000111 00111100
10001100 11110110 11101011 01001010 11100100 00000111 11000110 00111110 10110100 10010010
10011110 10000111 10111110 01111000 00011110 10110100 00100111 01110001 00000011 00001100
10111000 00111101 10110001 11000101 00001100 00000111 01110010 01110011 01001010 01111010
10000011 10001111 11000010 10010011 00100000 10010000 01000111 01011010 01110111 10111001
01100000 11000100 00000001 10011100 11110100 00010100 10001110 01000011 00011110 00000110
01000110 00110001 01001011 00101001 00000011 10101001 11100100 11010010 00001110 10000010
10011101 10010001 00000000 10111000 00000010 10011011 11110111 10001110 11100011 11011111
10000000 00101001 11001100 01000111 01000001 11011110 10011010 11100101 10000010 01100000
00010001 10011100 11110101 10100001 00110000 00000101 00011000 11001000 01000001 10010011
01000010 10011111 11011110 11110101 11101001 01000110 01000000 00111000 00000111 01111101
00100111 00001011 11000111 10100101 00100110 11101110 00110100 00001101 10000000 01001111
00000111 11011100 11010000 11111100 01111001 01111001 11100011 10110101 00001100 00111001
00100011 00011000 00100100 11110100 10100101 11001000 11100000 10010001 11000000 00010100
10111010 10010100 00110100 01110010 01110001 01001101 01101110 11011100 11010001 10010010
00000001 00110100 00101111 11001101 00011110 00000111 10100110 00000001 10100110 11101100
11011001 00000001 11101111 01001001 11010000 01111010 10111101 00111100 00001010 01100111
01100000 10100011 10110111 01111010 00010110 11000000 00101000 00011100 01010011 10110001
11000111 00111101 00101001 10011101 00001111 00111101 01101000 01100011 11010010 10010010
11010100 10110001 00110011 10000000 00110111 11100100 11111011 00000001 01001101 11000110
01000110 01111001 11111100 01111011 01010011 11011100 01100101 11001001 10100100 01100001
10010011 11001001 11101010 01111000 11110100 11000101 00111011 00101101 11101100 00110010
00110001 11001000 11101011 11000000 11101000 01101001 01011000 01100110 01010010 11011111
10000000 11001111 01101010 01111110 00000000 00111111 00101000 11101000 00110011 10001110
10010100 11011110 10011111 00110110 00111000 00111111 10001101 00001010 01011101 01001000
10110000 00000010 00110001 10010010 01111000 10100110 10111011 00000010 01110110 10001110
01001110 00110111 11100010 10010100 00011110 00000111 10110111 01000011 01000010 10000011
11001110 00000110 00001101 00010111 11101000 00100000 11001111 00011100 10011110 10011100
11100110 10000100 00111110 10100111 10011111 01001010 01010111 11000010 10100110 01001110
01001001 11110110 10101000 11110011 10001000 11000001 11000111 11001110 01111101 11101001
00111011 00010110 00000000 10000000 11100011 11101011 11000001 10100111 00010010 01001000
00101010 10100011 10101001 11001001 00110100 11011110 00111110 01000101 00010100 00111011
00010010 11111000 00001010 01110000 00111000 11111100 01101000 01001110 11100100 00001110
11101000 10011001 11101001 11101111 01001100 11001111 10011001 11001110 00001110 00111011
01100110 10010100 11100000 00001110 01101000 01100011 10111011 00000000 01110000 10011000
11101011 11101011 01000011 01011010 10010110 00011101 10110010 00111001 11000111 11101011
01000001 11000111 10011000 01111101 01101001 11000011 00000011 00000001 00111010 10011010
01100110 11010000 00001001 00111101 11110011 11001001 10100111 10101010 00010011 01100010
11100000 01100111 11110101 10100100 00111001 00111011 00000000 00111000 00000011 10101111
10111101 00011001 00011001 10100101 10010000 00000000 00111010 11010011 01001000 01100001
10110100 00011111 10100111 11010110 10010011 10010110 00100111 10001100 00001010 01010101
00100111 10000000 00000001 11101001 11010110 10010000 10011100 00111111 10010111 11010100
10011111 11010010 10010000 10110111 00000000 00110011 11010011 10100111 01111100 10001110
00101001 00001110 00110111 11111010 10001110 10000010 10010111 11111000 10110110 11111110
10010100 11001110 11011011 01111010 11010000 11101101 01100001 00001000 11011001 00111001
01101111 01010011 11000000 10100000 10001100 11110001 10011110 01101001 01011000 01110000
00000101 00110100 00110000 00100111 00001011 11010000 01110111 10100010 11110111 00001011
10001110 01001110 10011100 10011010 01101010 00110001 00101110 01111110 01011010 01110010
11100000 11100100 01010010 00000000 00010111 00100011 10111000 11100100 11010000 10101110
10000100 00001111 10010010 10011001 11001110 00000111 11110011 10100000 00001100 01100011
00010100 10001010 01110000 00001001 00111110 10111100 01100010 10010111 00011011 10001001
11001111 01000011 01001111 01110000 00000001 11001011 11110101 11101010 01101001 00010100
10000010 01001001 11110100 11110101 10100001 01001001 11001001 00111000 11000000 00010100
11010011 11110010 11000111 10111011 10110101 00101011 00111011 00001110 11000010 00100111

11101011 11101011 01000011 00101001 10010100 01100001 11000110 00010011 00111100 01111010
10011010 00110010 01000010 11111101 01111010 10011010 01010000 11011011 01010101 11011011
11111000 11111011 00011010 10101011 10100001 00001101 10010110 00111100 00110010 00000001
10001100 11100111 10011111 01101010 00110110 10001111 01010111 10100110 10011110 10011000
11001001 00000110 10011010 11000101 10110111 00011101 10011011 01110110 11110110 10100110
11101010 01011111 01100001 10100011 11000111 01000101 10100101 10110000 01001100 00010011
11111010 11010000 10010110 10010110 11100011 11111000 10011100 01111110 00110101 01101011
01010111 11010011 10011100 11111000 10001110 11110010 11000111 01001101 10000010 01000111
11000100 11001100 00100011 10001101 01111001 00100000 00001010 10100011 10101001 01101001
10111010 10011110 10010111 00100000 00010111 11110110 11010111 00010110 11111011 11001111
00001100 11000011 10000011 11111000 11010111 01011100 10100010 11110100 01101000 11110111
00010110 00100110 10000011 01010111 01110001 00101101 11000011 01100101 01101110 00110011
10001001 10011100 11111110 00010101 00111100 01011010 01111100 00000111 00100000 01001100
01110010 01111001 11001001 00110101 00000111 10000101 01101101 11000110 10101111 10101111
11011011 01011001 01001100 11001110 10010001 01001000 01001000 01101101 10100111 00000111
11011010 10110110 11011010 00101111 00001010 01111101 10100010 01001011 01110001 01111111
10101001 11000011 00100100 01110010 00011000 11011001 10011001 01000001 01001100 10000011
10001010 01111110 11001010 01011011 01011111 01010001 11001011 00010101 10000111 10000111
11011001 00110010 01111111 10110011 11010101 10001110 00010010 01010100 11100000 01110001
10011110 11110101 00001100 10110110 01000011 01101111 11001111 00100100 01100000 11111010
00000011 11001101 01101111 01001001 11100001 10110101 10110111 10010011 01011000 10000110
01001011 11010111 01111001 00101101 01100001 11111011 01000100 00100110 00110101 11100010
01000100 00111101 00001001 10101110 01000101 00100100 10010101 10010000 11001010 10001010
11111111 00000000 00101000 11100100 11101101 00111100 01010100 10101010 01110011 11011001
00110001 00101010 11010100 00100111 11010000 10111000 01110100 11110010 11000111 10000010
10011111 10011101 00110011 11111011 00111110 01010010 01000000 11011010 10000101 00111101
10001101 01010100 01011011 10110010 01111110 01100000 01111000 11101001 11001101 00111101
01101110 11001111 00011000 01100011 10010001 01001101 10101001 01000101 01101010 11101110
01011010 10011110 00011111 10110001 00111010 11011000 11001000 01010011 00101001 00011001
00011111 11010100 01010101 00011011 10011000 10001100 01010010 01100111 00011000 01111111
11010010 10101100 00001011 11010110 10001111 00111000 01101110 01101010 10001101 11010100
11101101 00101100 10000000 11111110 01000100 01010001 00000111 00111000 10111101 10110100
00111001 00110001 01010001 10100010 11100010 11111001 01011000 00101000 00100001 11000011
01100111 00100100 11110101 00010101 00101010 10010000 01111000 00111001 11000111 01111100
11010101 01110100 10011011 01101000 11001001 11111100 01110000 00101001 00111100 11100101
01101110 01000000 00111001 11101011 01011101 10010111 10001101 10101110 10001111 00011010
11000110 10000100 01000100 00000000 00111011 11111010 11010011 00011110 01100000 00001001
00001001 11010010 10101001 01111001 11000101 10001000 11011011 11000000 00111101 01101010
01010000 00110001 10000010 00111001 00000110 10101101 00100000 00100100 00010010 00010010
10111000 11110101 11110100 11101111 01010010 11000011 00011001 00100011 00001011 11010011
10111001 10100110 10100100 01000100 10100110 01110000 00101010 01010101 11101011 01011100
10101110 11010000 01101101 10011110 10100101 00000100 11011100 01010001 01011010 01110000
00110000 01111011 10011010 10100000 11101011 11110010 11110100 11101111 11010110 10110100
11100101 00011100 00011110 00101010 10000100 10100000 10011100 11010001 01110101 01101011
10011011 10111010 01101110 11011011 00010001 10000000 10100011 00011001 11001111 11100000
01101001 11110011 01110110 11101101 01000010 01000110 00101010 00110111 00011111 10111100
00111000 00100111 00100011 10110101 00010100 11101111 00110111 01110010 00101010 11111011
10010000 10111000 11101101 11011111 10111010 00000001 00111101 01101010 01111000 10010100
10101111 11001101 10001100 10001111 01111010 10001010 00110000 00001111 00111101 11111011
11010101 10100100 10001100 10010101 11101010 01101011 10110101 10011110 01000011 01000010
00101111 00111101 01110010 01000101 00001100 10111001 01000000 00110001 11111000 11010000
00100011 00111001 00100011 10101101 00111111 00000100 00101011 10011100 01110101 10101100
10101110 11010110 11100010 00100000 00110001 11100100 11111011 11111111 00000000 00111010
01000111 10000101 10000011 10001111 10011000 00011110 00111010 00000011 01010010 00101000
00101100 01111000 00011101 11101010 01100101 10001000 11101111 11100011 10111101 01100101
01010001 00100100 01101101 01000101 01011101 11101000 01010101 01010101 00101011 11001001
00010100 11011100 00010001 10000010 00111010 00001111 11010110 10101111 10111100 00111001
00100011 10011110 10111110 11010100 11000101 10110111 00111011 10101010 00010110 10101010
11100111 10100001 00001010 01101101 10111101 00001010 11100000 01100000 11100100 00011110
00001111 01101111 01001010 10011011 01101110 00000110 01001101 01011001 11111011 00111001
00100110 10100011 01101011 01110010 00001001 11001001 11100011 10001010 10010101 00110100
10011001 11010000 10101000 01001000 10000001 01000111 00000100 11010010 01111001 01111001
00111001 11011011 11010110 10101101 11111001 00100100 00101111 00111000 11000101 00110101
10000001 01011111 10111010 00110010 00101001 10100111 00010111 10110000 00111010 00010010
00101011 01111001 01111110 10110100 10000001 01110000 00111110 10100110 10101100 11100011
11010011 10101110 01111001 00010100 10011011 01000000 00111111 10101111 00110100 00110111
11011000 10011111 01100101 00100010 00001111 00101111 00111100 10010001 01000010 00101011
00010100 11001011 10001100 01010100 11101101 00010110 01111001 11011101 10001010 01011101
10111000 01001110 10100011 00010101 01011010 00110111 10101010 00011010 10100101 00101011
10010001 10101100 01111011 01111001 10101011 00010110 11001101 10000111 00001100 01111101
01000101 01000110 11000111 00000000 10011010 10010010 11010100 00101100 10010010 01110001
11001111 11010110 10110011 10011101 00111000 11001000 11101001 10100000 10011010 10010110
10101100 11101000 00011100 10001111 00101110 00100110 11000110 01111001 11111100 11101010

10011110 10100101 10010000 00111101 01001001 10101011 00110111 00010010 11100001 01010010
00111000 11111010 01111010 01010101 01011011 11110011 11111011 10111101 11000100 11100000
01110110 11100011 10101101 01110011 11001110 01101001 11111011 10101111 01000011 11011000
01111010 11000101 10011000 11100000 00110001 10111000 01001100 00001110 11110101 10100001
01110010 01011011 01110010 00011100 00011100 01110110 11001101 01100110 10101011 01111100
11011001 01011110 01011111 00110101 10101111 10101011 10011101 10110010 11000111 10000011
11000110 11010100 10101101 01011101 00111000 10101001 00101110 01010011 11000101 01010110
10110100 10001111 01001000 11111000 01001000 10100100 01011000 01011100 00111001 11001110
01001001 11100011 11011010 10111101 00000111 10100001 11001110 01101011 10000101 11111000
01001011 11110011 01101000 11110010 10111111 00000000 01100111 11010010 10111011 10101110
00000000 11001110 00110011 01010011 10001001 10110010 10010001 11100010 01010101 01111110
11110000 11101110 00110001 01000001 00100000 01010011 01001000 00100100 01110101 00111000
00110100 00110111 00100000 01100110 10111001 00100100 10101100 01100110 10000000 10101110
00110000 01110011 11110101 10100111 00101001 11111001 00111010 11110101 10100011 11010111
10111110 01101001 10111000 11100011 10101101 00010000 01111101 10000100 00011100 10001100
01010010 01100111 00011001 11101011 10001111 01110011 10011010 00001110 01110010 00000001
10100000 10001100 11110001 11111000 11100100 01010010 01111010 10110000 00011110 00111110
01010011 11010011 10010011 01001101 00011100 10110110 01001001 11000101 00111001 10001111
01101010 01100011 01110110 10100110 11110100 11010101 00100000 00010100 01100111 10000010
01101000 11100100 00011110 10000011 00010100 01100100 00010001 11011111 00111101 01101001
10101010 00001001 11100111 00111111 10011001 10101000 10010011 01101111 01100000 00011101
10011111 10011110 10010001 01000111 01001111 01011100 11010010 10100001 00100100 00001110
01111010 01010001 11111110 01111001 10100010 11001101 00000000 10001111 10010010 11011101
01111000 00011111 10101101 00001101 11001110 00000101 00001101 10010011 11110100 10100101
11100000 01100000 10110101 01011101 10000000 01001110 00110011 10000011 11010010 10000110
00011000 00110100 00110110 00001111 01001110 10111001 11001101 00011111 01111000 00001010
10010100 00000000 00111110 11110001 00000100 10001100 11111010 01111010 01010010 00101000
00011000 11111001 01101000 11011011 11000011 11111011 10011010 00000000 11100011 01101111
01111100 01010101 01101110 11000000 00011011 00000000 00000011 10001111 11000110 10001100
01111111 01111011 11101010 00101000 11000000 11011001 10011110 01111000 11001000 00010100
11011100 00011111 00101111 11011100 11110001 01001111 01001011 01101010 11000000 01111111
10011000 10100001 10000110 01010111 11011111 10001010 10001001 01001001 00110001 01111110
11110000 10010010 11100100 11100111 00011111 11001010 10011101 10010001 11000000 00000111
00111110 10100110 10010001 10111000 11000110 00001000 11000001 11101111 01010011 11010000
00000011 10001110 10100111 10100000 11110100 10100001 01111001 11110111 00100111 10101001
10100001 01110011 11000111 00111111 00100000 00011100 10001111 01011010 00011001 10001111
00100100 01111101 00000000 10100000 00000101 00000011 10010010 01110011 01000000 11100001
00001110 01101001 00010111 00011000 11001101 00111001 11111010 00001010 01011011 00000000
11011110 11011000 01010101 11101010 01101000 00000000 01101111 11000000 11100000 01111010
11010001 11000110 11111100 00011100 11100000 01010011 00111111 10001100 10011010 01110111
10111000 11000111 00110001 00100100 10011100 01110000 00111011 00011010 00010111 00111001
00111100 01110100 10100101 01100110 00000000 01100010 10000101 00011001 00111001 00110100
11101101 01100001 00000110 01110010 00000001 01010001 11011110 10010011 00000011 00001110
00000000 11101011 01001010 01111000 10100001 01110000 00110010 01111111 10010101 01000010
11010111 01110000 00010011 00011001 11000110 01110010 00000111 01100001 01001101 01100110
11011101 10010101 11001111 11010111 00010100 10001010 11000101 10010100 10011110 01000000
11110101 00110101 00100000 00111011 01010000 10011100 01110101 11101011 01000010 10111101
11000000 01000011 10000011 10010001 10011010 01101110 01000000 01000000 00000000 11000010
00000001 11001101 00011100 01101110 00101010 00000111 11010110 10011011 10011101 11110001
11100011 10101110 00111011 11010101 11101010 00000100 10001100 00000000 00111100 10001110
11011001 00010100 00101001 00111000 11100100 00000000 00101001 10111000 00111011 11000011
00111111 00110100 00001001 00000110 01001010 10010011 10011110 11111000 11001101 01000011
10111000 00000011 11100111 00000111 11100110 11011001 10011110 11110100 10001000 00110000
10011110 10111110 11111110 10110100 10000000 00010010 01111110 01111110 10111110 11110100
11100100 11100100 10010000 00001110 01110001 11101111 01010111 01111101 10010000 00001000
11100000 11111100 10011110 11100011 10011010 01011100 10000000 01110010 11100111 10000001
11010010 10001110 01011000 10100001 11110101 11101111 01001101 01111100 01101111 00000000
11110011 11001110 01111010 11110101 10100001 10100000 00010111 00100011 10000110 01011100
11100100 11111110 10010100 00110001 11001001 11000000 11101101 11010110 10001001 01001110
00010111 10100111 00100110 10011000 11011000 00010001 10000001 11001111 11111011 10111110
10110100 10010011 01100101 10001110 11001000 11001000 00000011 11010011 10101101 00101111
01001111 01011100 01010010 00101110 00110001 10000000 01110011 11001101 00101010 10001110
01110001 11111101 01101001 11110010 10100010 00000110 00111111 00000000 10101010 11110001
11110100 10100111 01110010 00000111 11100001 01000011 01110101 11001101 00110111 00111000
11001011 00011110 10100110 10011101 10000000 00111010 01100011 11011111 11111100 11100110
10011100 10111001 11100100 11110001 10011111 01000011 01001101 11001000 11001110 00111001
00111001 10100100 01011001 00000000 00100100 01110000 01001101 00100100 01011000 10111100
00010011 10010011 11010110 10010000 10001100 11001000 01001110 00111000 00011100 00001111
01111010 01010110 11001001 00100011 00000011 11101011 01001001 10010010 00111000 11000001
11001111 10101101 00011011 10010000 00101011 00010010 00100011 11001111 11100000 00101001
00110000 00010100 00001111 11100111 01001100 00111001 11101110 00000110 00000111 01000001
11101001 01000000 01010000 00111010 10011110 11011101 11101000 01010111 00011000 11101111
11110101 10001011 10001111 11001111 10011010 00011100 00000001 10000000 10011100 00001110

11100100 11010000 01001000 00000111 10000001 11010110 10011010 11100101 10001011 00001010
00110101 01100011 11010000 00011011 00000111 10000001 11000111 01101010 01000111 00011001
00000011 10010011 10000001 11111010 11010010 11110111 00000011 00100111 00000011 10110000
11101111 01001101 01101100 01100001 11001000 11001111 10100101 00001001 10100100 01001000
10111000 00000010 00111111 01101010 00011000 00000010 01000001 01101110 00111111 10100101
00100001 11001001 00111110 11011110 10110100 10110010 11100001 10010000 10101110 01001110
11111110 10100011 00010100 10011010 11101010 10011000 00000110 11110010 11000011 11100100
00111000 11110111 10100001 00110000 00000001 11101010 01111110 10100110 10011001 10011110
00000001 11000111 01001110 10110100 11100010 00000001 00011111 00110001 00100000 01111010
01010000 11010010 01100101 01011100 01101011 01100000 01001000 01001110 00111010 01110111
11110101 10100001 01000110 01001110 00111101 00000110 01101001 11011011 01110000 00111111
10010101 00110111 00100111 10011111 10010111 10011111 01001010 01111101 01001001 00000110
11000001 00100111 00000111 10110110 00110011 01000110 01111001 00111111 01001010 01110011
01111100 10111100 01110111 00111100 11010100 01111011 10001110 11100111 11100011 10011110
10000010 10001101 10000000 10010011 00011000 00000001 10110001 10011111 01001010 01101001
01100010 00010100 11100000 01110010 01000111 01111010 01101000 11000110 00110001 11010000
01111010 10010011 01001010 01001111 11001101 10001100 01110100 00010100 10011110 10111010
10001111 01100001 00010101 01001001 00100100 10111011 01110100 00011100 10010011 01001010
11101011 11110010 01110101 11000111 00110100 10011100 00001100 10000000 00110010 01001111
01110011 01000011 11110000 00000110 01111010 10011110 10100110 10011010 11010100 01101110
11000011 01110001 10010110 11001111 00100000 00001010 00010111 10000101 11000000 11001110
00001001 10101001 00111010 01110011 11101101 01001101 01101110 10011000 11111110 10110100
01011110 11011011 10000110 11000000 11100100 10000110 11000000 11110100 10100110 11100011
10000001 11110101 11000101 00111001 01111001 00111110 10111100 01010011 01110000 01001001
11000111 10100111 01000011 11101010 01101001 00101011 11110100 00000110 11000100 00000011
00101100 01001111 11101010 01101000 01101110 00111010 00001100 10011110 11110100 10101110
00110110 10001111 00101101 00001111 11010100 11010010 00110010 11100111 10001110 11011001
11100110 10011011 01001000 01010110 00001100 11100100 00011111 11101011 01001001 10001110
00001111 00111100 00011110 11010100 00111001 00011000 11000001 11001110 01001101 00110111
10111000 00000100 11100000 11100010 10000110 11101100 10101100 10001010 00000111 00100111
00011001 11100111 11010010 10011010 10100000 10010000 00000111 01101111 01111010 01110011
00010011 10010100 00011101 01101001 00111001 11001011 10001111 11001010 10010110 10101000
10000001 01010110 10000111 11001110 00110000 10000011 10101111 01010010 01101001 00111010
11110011 01001111 01101110 10000111 11010011 11010010 10100111 01110101 01110110 01011001
00011001 11111110 11101000 11001111 01000001 11001101 00110111 10110110 00111010 11100000
11110011 01001110 01001100 01110011 10010010 01110010 00101001 10111000 00011001 00100111
10100110 01111101 01101010 11010110 10101110 11000100 00001110 00011110 11010100 11011100
11100101 10110001 10000011 11101111 01001110 01001110 00010011 00100011 10100111 10101101
00001000 00001010 11110011 11101010 01110011 01000011 01111010 11011000 10110000 01111100
11001001 10000001 10001100 00100000 00111101 00110011 11010110 10010101 11111001 11000000
00011101 00111011 10011010 01001110 11111011 01111101 00111001 10100011 01101000 11000000
11110100 11001110 01101001 11011110 11111010 00001010 11100001 10011100 01001001 10110100
00001100 01100011 10011111 10101101 00110101 11111000 00011000 11001110 01001001 11101011
01001110 01101110 01011000 10110111 10110110 00101001 10011111 11101101 00101111 01111010
01001110 11011011 00000101 11000101 11011011 11010011 00110100 11010111 00011110 01100000
00101011 11111001 11010100 10011101 10110010 01101001 10111001 11100111 10000001 11111000
10011010 01001110 11101000 00110111 00011100 10101101 11011011 10101101 01000111 11010011
10101000 11001001 00111110 10010100 11101110 01001001 11100111 10000011 01001110 01110011
11010111 00000100 01111110 00110100 11110100 10110000 01011100 01100110 11010010 01111111
00010001 11001001 10100110 00100001 00000100 11111100 10011101 00110001 11101001 01001111
00111001 01100001 10000001 10001100 00011110 10100111 00011101 01101001 00011111 00000001
11000000 00000100 00000011 10001110 10010100 01110100 00001101 01000011 10000010 00000001
10100110 10110110 00000111 01101110 00001111 01011010 01110110 00110000 10011100 01110111
11100110 10100011 11011100 10111001 11001000 00111100 01110111 11001101 01001111 00110101
10001001 00000101 01100101 11001011 10011110 10011000 11101101 01001010 11011111 01111100
11100111 10111111 10101001 10100010 01010011 10011101 10000001 00000111 00011101 01001101
00011101 01001001 11001111 10100111 01011010 00111010 00010100 10010000 11001110 11011001
00000011 10000001 11000000 10100111 01100000 00001110 10100111 11110000 10100101 11100111
11001011 11100011 00000011 11011100 11010010 01100111 01101010 00001110 11100100 00011110
01110001 11011110 10101001 01011100 01100000 01110000 01010011 11011100 10001110 00000111
10101101 00110001 11111110 01100100 00001010 00000110 01001110 01101001 01010100 10110001
00111011 10001111 00011100 11110001 11101101 01001110 01100010 00000001 11100000 00011010
00101111 00101000 10010000 01000010 11011000 11000110 01101001 11001011 11001001 00011001
11100100 10011110 11110100 10111101 10001001 11001000 11100010 10010101 00000001 01010000
01001110 00110011 01001111 01010111 10110010 00101100 01000110 01000001 10011110 00110010
01110011 11010100 11010010 01101110 00111101 10000111 11101011 01000010 11110000 01111110
10111110 10011101 10101001 00011011 11100101 00111000 00000100 00011010 01001101 01011011
10101000 00011100 11010110 10000000 01101100 11011011 01010100 11110001 00011010 11000110
10010111 00000111 01010011 00010010 11001001 10111000 01000110 11000000 00111001 10001111
00111111 11000001 01011100 01101111 10001011 00111111 10110100 00000111 11101110 11110001
10101011 00001101 00101100 00110000 11011011 11110110 11010000 01111111 11010110 01100011
10011010 11001000 01001001 11100111 01011011 11100001 01110111 00011100 11110010 10100101
11000110 01001001 00110010 10101011 01100001 11110010 01111101 11101010 11000110 10100101

10101001 01101010 01011010 10010010 00000101 10111110 10111101 10011010 11100001 00010111
10100000 10010001 10101011 10110011 10010001 10111101 11011101 11101100 01110101 11111101
01011110 01001010 11001100 11011001 11111000 01011001 01110100 10110001 01111000 10010010
00111011 01110111 10000010 00101001 00001100 11000000 11101101 10010001 10111010 11000111
10001111 01000011 01001111 10111001 11110001 01010101 10001100 01110111 11010011 10000011
11100001 01111101 00111010 01001001 00010010 01010011 11111011 11010011 00100001 11111001
10001000 00111101 01001000 10101100 00001101 00101010 01011011 10011101 00110010 11110110
00111011 10101011 00101001 00001100 01110011 10100111 00100001 10110001 10011010 10101101
00100100 00010010 01001001 00100011 11001010 11100100 10010111 01110010 01001001 00111110
10111001 11101011 01011011 00101000 11011101 11101110 00010101 00101001 00110110 11010001
11011000 11101000 11011010 10100100 11111010 10110100 01011110 00101000 10111100 10111010
00100000 00111011 01011001 00001000 11110000 10100011 00001000 10101011 10011110 10000010
10101101 01101011 11011010 11010101 11100111 10000110 01000110 10010111 01100011 10100010
01000101 00010100 01110110 11000110 11011110 00111001 00011010 01000110 10001011 11001100
00010011 01100111 10101000 11001101 01110001 11110110 00110111 10010111 01011010 01111101
10100101 11011100 01010110 11100100 00000100 10111010 10001111 11001010 10010100 00010001
10011110 00111101 10101011 01010011 01000110 11110001 00101110 10101111 10100111 01011000
11000111 01101100 10001101 00001101 11000100 00010001 10001111 11011101 10001001 11100011
00001110 01100011 11111010 00011010 01001101 01111001 00010011 00101010 01101101 01101100
01110101 10010110 11010001 01011011 11000111 11110001 00000110 01111000 10010010 11001010
11010111 11001010 10111001 10110011 00010111 00001100 10100110 00111110 00000011 01100011
00100100 10001010 11001111 11010011 00110101 00110011 11100010 10011011 01011101 01010110
11000111 01010100 10110010 10110011 01001111 00101010 00010110 10010110 00001001 00100001
10001100 00100001 01000010 10011101 10101011 00011110 00001111 00010011 01101010 10011111
11011010 01110001 01101010 00010111 00011110 01001100 11010111 00010001 11000110 11110001
10000000 01100011 11000000 00100001 11111101 01101011 00111111 01000001 10111101 10010111
01000111 10111000 10111001 10010101 00100010 01001001 00001101 11001100 01001111 00010011
00000110 11001110 00111001 11101110 00101011 00111011 01001001 11101110 00100101 01001010
01001111 01110011 10011101 01000110 11110011 00100011 00000100 11110000 11111101 11000110
00101010 00110111 11100101 01110000 01111111 00000011 11011110 10101111 10101101 10111111
00000111 10001010 01001001 10101101 01111110 01010000 01000111 00000110 10111010 01010011
01101110 00101000 01010011 10000011 10110001 01000111 00001101 10110111 10101101 00110101
01000001 00100010 10101101 01111001 01000100 00001111 11110001 10100111 00101100 01011000
11100111 00010101 10101011 11010100 11100011 10110001 00001010 10101111 00011110 10111001
10101001 10100001 11001000 00111100 11110001 10010011 11111001 01010010 11101100 11000010
00010110 00111100 10010011 11010111 10001010 01100110 00111110 01101100 01110110 00011101
01000101 01010011 10110011 11010110 11000100 10010011 01000011 00110011 00000010 11100000
01100111 00011101 11101010 01100110 10111101 10001000 00000001 11110010 10011110 01111010
11100100 01010101 01011000 10001000 00110010 00011100 01110001 10011010 01010111 00000111
00011000 01010011 01011100 10001110 10011110 10111010 10011101 11111000 01111010 10110011
10001100 01110100 00100111 01101011 10011000 11001111 00111100 01100000 11010100 00001011
00100100 01001100 00011111 01100110 01111001 11100010 10100011 11000111 00011111 01111000
11010100 01010011 00101001 11110010 10001110 11100001 11011111 10101110 01101000 01110100
11010110 10000111 01100010 11000101 01001101 01101110 10101110 01011010 01011000 11010111
00000001 01000111 01010001 01011001 11010111 10000000 10101100 10001110 00110010 00110011
10011110 11011100 11010011 00111100 11101001 00100011 01000011 11100101 10011100 01111010
10001111 01011010 01110010 00110110 11101100 11100111 10010010 01101011 01001010 01101011
01010011 10011111 00010111 10001001 01010101 00100011 01101011 01011001 10010110 00100010
00000000 10100000 01100010 01110001 11101010 00111101 01101010 11000010 01001100 11001010
01001111 01101110 00111000 11100010 10101010 01000110 01111010 11100011 00100111 10011110
10010101 01110011 11001011 01011100 11110111 00100011 10100101 01110101 10111011 01011000
11110011 00001001 00100011 10010111 00111111 00101110 00111001 00111100 10001111 01101010
10011101 10000010 10010000 00000110 01111010 11010101 01111101 10100000 01110011 10010010
00101010 00111100 01100100 01110101 11001000 11001111 01011010 11000110 10100010 01001100
10011111 01000010 01100101 01100001 11100110 01110000 00111110 01000001 11011110 10100110
11110011 01100010 11001111 00000000 11110001 01010100 11110001 10111000 00000001 11001000
00010101 00100100 00001011 10001111 01001110 01000101 01100101 01010110 00110111 10110010
01111011 00011101 10111000 01101010 10011110 11001101 01101100 01011000 10010010 01110000
00000000 00100000 01110111 11101011 01001100 10010010 11100011 10100110 11000000 01110010
01111011 10011010 10001010 11100011 00000000 00000010 00011011 00111001 11101101 11010010
10100011 01000000 01001001 00000000 11110001 11101001 01010001 11101100 11110101 01010110
01000111 01010111 11010110 01100110 01011010 11110011 10011101 10010011 00000011 10001111
01011111 01111010 10001000 10101011 11101111 11101010 00111110 10110100 10101010 01001000
00011110 11000110 10011101 10001101 10100100 10011010 10110101 00000101 01100001 11001011
00010000 11101111 10101011 00001111 00101010 01000110 01001110 01100100 00000000 11111011
01010100 01101001 00010100 10111000 11000001 10010100 01110001 01000011 10110001 11001001
11110100 00110100 11011111 00110000 11101100 00100100 01111110 00111110 11010100 10010100
00011011 11011000 01111111 01011000 10001000 11100101 10001111 11111011 11110111 00011011
00111101 01000110 00101001 11001111 00010000 10010001 01000001 00010011 00001100 11100111
10000011 01010100 11011000 11110101 00100111 11110101 11101111 01001000 11000100 11110100
11001111 11001000 01000110 01111010 01110010 00101010 00101101 00101101 01101110 00110101
01011110 00011101 10001011 10011110 01001100 11011011 10111111 11010111 11000100 01000000
11101011 11101111 01010001 11111101 10011110 01010000 11000011 10010100 00111001 00111101

10101010 00001000 10011100 10101110 01110111 11110001 10000011 11000101 00111001 10100110
00011101 00110011 11001110 01111010 01010000 11111001 10011110 11001100 00111101 10110100
00011111 01000110 01011001 11110010 10100110 11001001 11100001 00110011 10001010 10010110
00011111 10110100 01000100 01111001 10001100 00001110 00101011 00111111 11101101 00001110
00000000 11110101 11011101 10001100 11100110 10100100 01111011 10000010 10100000 10110011
10110111 01011010 01101011 01010001 10101010 11110001 01011010 10100110 11001011 11101001
00111101 11011000 10011011 11100111 00000101 11000110 01111011 01100011 10011010 10111011
01111000 11100000 11000100 10010010 01110101 11000000 11000111 00010101 10000101 11110110
10000010 01111000 00100111 11011111 00110101 01100010 11010110 11101011 01110111 11101110
01001001 11001110 01111010 01100110 10100001 11010011 01010101 00011101 11001110 10001010
00011000 11010100 10011011 01011101 11001000 11011101 10001000 01111100 00001111 01011100
11100111 00010101 10101111 10101001 00011100 11001011 00011011 01100111 00100111 01101000
11001110 00111101 10101011 00010101 10100101 01010101 10010000 00001101 11000011 10010011
11000000 10101101 01101011 10001001 00000001 10001010 00101110 10011100 10001010 01010101
01010011 10000111 00101011 01000100 11000101 11011101 11001001 00110011 11010111 01111110
00010100 00000000 00111100 00111100 11101101 10011110 01001011 00011110 00001101 01110110
01111101 01000110 01001001 11100000 01010111 00011011 11110000 10101101 01111111 11100010
10011010 00000111 10110001 10010010 10111011 01000010 00111000 00011000 11100100 01111010
00011010 11001011 00010011 00101111 01111000 11110001 11101010 01111100 01001100 01001100
01100100 10001110 01111000 10100101 11110111 10100000 10001100 01110011 11010010 10011100
00000110 00001111 00111101 11111011 01010111 00110100 10111100 11001000 00011000 10100111
00011100 11110110 10100101 00000000 10010100 00100111 00111100 01111010 11010010 01100011
00001110 00111001 11101011 01000011 01100100 10100110 00110011 10000001 01010010 10010101
10000000 01011100 10001110 10110100 01111110 10100010 10010001 10000111 00100011 11010000
00001010 01010110 00000110 10011011 01010110 00000001 00011000 11110011 10011010 01010011
11101101 01000010 01111010 00000011 10011111 01011010 01000110 11000001 10010011 11111010
11010010 11010111 10101000 00000010 01111101 00101001 11101101 11111001 01010011 00010111
00000101 10110001 10011100 10001010 01010110 11101011 11010110 10101011 01111101 10000000
00110010 00010100 01110001 11010010 10011011 11001001 00000111 00110100 10100111 00100101
11000111 01001100 01010000 11000111 10010000 00000111 01101010 01010111 11010100 00000100
00011100 00001100 11110100 00010100 10100100 00000011 11110101 00100011 10001010 00011011
00000000 01100110 10001100 11110011 11011100 10010011 11011110 10000000 00001100 00010000
00101001 00100010 01011101 10100011 00000100 11111110 01110100 10100111 10001010 01010010
00000000 11100110 10011010 10001111 01000000 00011011 11000110 01111010 10010011 11011111
00100110 10001110 00110011 10001100 11110010 01101000 01110011 10000101 00000111 00011001
00111101 10000101 00011000 00000111 00011001 11100011 11010110 10010011 01010110 01100000
00001100 01110000 10000011 00000011 10001111 01011010 00111001 00101001 10110100 01110111
00110100 00111001 00100000 10100000 01000001 10010001 10001110 10000010 10011011 11001000
00100011 10110111 10110101 00101111 01000001 10110000 01011110 10000000 01010010 01100000
01101110 11000101 00101000 01011100 00001100 01010000 10101010 00110001 10011110 11011001
10101010 01101000 01000011 01010011 00001110 01011101 10111101 01111010 01110011 01001011
11001001 11101101 11111000 11010010 01100000 00010011 10010001 11010100 00001110 00101001
01010111 00000111 00011100 10011110 00111101 10111010 11010100 11001011 01001101 01000111
01110000 01100001 10001100 01100111 10010001 11011010 10000100 00011111 10111100 00100111
00110100 10111011 10000001 01111100 01110000 01110001 11101001 01001001 11010111 00110100
11111001 10101110 00100001 00010111 10011110 10011100 11110011 11010111 11010110 10000010
00110010 11011001 00111101 10101001 01010011 11100101 00011000 00000010 10010001 00000110
11010000 01001001 11100101 11110011 01001010 11111101 00000000 00011000 00000010 11100001
10001111 11100001 01000011 11110011 11000111 01100011 01001010 11000011 01110110 00111010
10010011 10011010 00110000 00110010 00111000 11101001 01000110 10101011 01010000 00001100
11111111 00000000 11110101 11101001 00010100 01100111 00010100 01110111 11100011 10011010
00001111 00000100 01110011 11000111 10100101 01001011 01001101 11101010 00110100 00110111
00100000 10000011 11000110 00111001 11000111 01011010 00010011 10101001 11101110 01110011
01001110 01011100 01111100 11111101 00110000 00101001 01000001 11000000 11100010 10101111
10010111 01001011 10001000 01001100 11110101 11110101 10100110 11110000 00000001 11001111
11010011 00000010 10000101 11000111 11011101 00111101 01111011 11010011 10111101 00000000
11100010 10001011 10101110 11100000 00110111 00001100 01000111 00111101 00111011 01010011
01110001 10110101 11011100 10000001 11011011 00011001 11110101 10100111 00101001 00101111
10010000 00001111 01001110 00110011 01001001 00100111 01101110 11100000 01110110 11110101
00110100 10010010 10111010 10111011 00000000 01100011 10001001 00111010 01110001 10001100
11100100 11010010 10011101 10101010 00110011 10001110 00110001 11000000 11110101 10100000
00000000 01000111 11110011 11111010 11010010 00110000 00100111 11100110 00100111 10000000
00111010 01010001 10100101 10000000 00110000 01111111 10001100 10011100 11100011 10110111
01001010 01010101 00000000 10000001 10110111 11110000 11001101 00100001 00011110 01100010
11100011 00111100 01111011 11010001 10010011 10001101 10111101 00111000 11100000 10001010
10101011 10001111 01110001 00110111 00010010 00011100 10011110 10111101 10000101 00001001
11110010 11100000 00011110 10100111 10010011 01000011 00000001 10110000 01110101 11101011
11101011 01000011 01110011 00101110 01110011 10011110 01111010 01010000 11011011 00010000
01101110 01010001 11001001 00011101 01111000 00010100 11011110 00000001 11000110 00001111
11100111 01001110 01111100 10000010 01001111 10101111 01000001 01001110 11001001 01010101
11100100 01110011 11101010 01101011 00111000 11110011 00110111 10110001 01100011 01001000
00000001 00000001 11101110 01111010 11111101 01101001 10100111 10110111 11101010 01101001
00110000 00111110 01000011 10011110 00000111 01011111 01110010 01101001 00010001 11001001

00111100 01110100 10101101 00110110 00100111 01110110 00111001 00111000 00011001 00111100
01100110 10010000 10000001 10111010 10010111 00011100 11100011 10101001 10100100 01101111
11011101 11010100 10100000 00001110 10100111 00010100 10000111 00100011 11110011 10100101
11000000 01011110 01001111 01011010 00010000 10011100 00011110 00111011 01100100 01010011
01101000 10100000 11101100 00000110 01101001 00110010 01101001 01110010 01000100 01100000
00000101 11001001 00100011 00100100 10011010 01000100 01000011 10010000 00011100 11110010
01111011 00001110 11010100 10101101 01111101 00000101 10110000 10100111 10000111 01001010
10001101 11111010 11100100 11100100 10011111 01111010 01010100 01101100 11101111 01100001
11110111 00000001 11100011 00111101 11101000 11111011 11001111 11010111 10011010 01101101
01110110 00100100 01001110 10000111 10000011 11110101 11111010 11010000 11100100 01100100
01110111 11001001 11100110 10011110 00111010 01100011 11010011 10111101 00110111 00000011
00001111 11111100 11001101 00001101 11011101 00000000 10011001 11100000 10000001 11000000
11101100 01001101 00000000 11111100 10000100 00001110 11000111 10011111 01111010 01000101
11111001 10001000 00011101 10000001 11101101 01001010 10100100 00110110 01000000 11101001
10011010 00101101 10100101 10011011 00011101 10000000 01100100 00001110 10000111 00100111
10011010 01000101 00100011 10111001 11100110 10010101 11111000 00000011 10001100 11111101
00101001 00100011 00100000 10000100 11000000 11100011 11011110 10001111 01000001 00001101
11011010 01111100 10110000 00001111 01111010 00010100 01111100 11000100 01110110 10100111
00111001 11001001 00100111 00111100 10001110 10011110 10000010 10001100 10101110 11000011
11000101 00001010 01110111 00000010 00110110 00100011 01111001 01110010 00001001 11111110
10110100 10101011 10010000 10000100 10001110 10100111 10100101 00101000 11001111 01100001
11010111 10111111 10100101 00011000 11011100 11101111 10011110 00000000 10100100 00000011
01011011 00011011 00000111 00011001 01111100 11010011 01001001 00011001 00111111 01011110
01101001 11001010 00110010 00010011 11111001 11010000 11011000 00100111 10000011 01010101
11101000 00000010 11100100 00101010 11100100 11111101 00000110 01101001 10001001 11010000
01001001 00100001 00100111 11010000 01010000 11100000 10110001 11001001 10100000 00101001
01110011 11010011 10000001 11101111 01001001 10110110 01011000 11101100 11111110 01110100
10101010 00111000 11001111 01111010 01000011 11000111 01011110 00110011 11010110 10000111
11001001 10100100 11010101 11001000 00011010 11000100 00010001 01001101 01011111 01011110
10011000 10100111 00011100 00101000 00000111 11011110 10010000 00001100 10100001 11110101
10100011 01000110 10001011 00010001 00111010 10010110 11101001 10010011 01001110 11001110
00000001 11001001 11000000 11110101 10100100 01110011 11000110 00000000 11101001 11010010
10011000 11100111 00110001 10001110 00110010 01110011 01001101 00111011 11101000 11001000
00001110 01001100 10011101 01001111 00000111 10001100 11010000 11000000 00011001 00110111
01100111 10011100 01111110 01010100 11101100 00010010 01001001 10100110 10101111 11011111
11111010 11010001 10110000 00001110 11110101 10100110 11110011 11110101 00100111 11110100
10100000 00000010 01001001 11101100 00000101 00001101 11000001 00011110 10110100 11101100
01010010 00000110 00011111 00101000 11100111 11110000 10100001 11001111 11001000 00111010
11110010 01101001 00111001 00000111 10111001 10100101 00101011 11001110 01000111 01101010
10010101 00010100 00010111 00010001 11010011 00000011 00111110 10110100 10001110 11011001
01010100 01010001 11000001 11101110 01101001 01111011 00010110 11110110 11101001 01001100
00100111 10111111 00111001 00111101 10101001 11011011 01010001 10001110 11000001 01011001
00010001 00111101 01000110 11110010 01101000 11101011 00101000 00101100 01111111 00001010
00001000 00001101 00100000 11100111 11111000 01110000 01101000 01001100 11100000 11101100
11101111 11101011 01000011 11011100 00010010 00010111 10100110 01110011 01001000 10111001
00100000 10010011 11010000 11010000 01011011 00001000 00111010 00001100 10011110 01001001
00111100 11010011 01011100 00001001 01010111 10100111 01001110 01000111 00110100 00001011
01100001 11011100 11101111 00100100 11110100 11101100 00101001 10011000 00100000 01110011
01001111 11000000 00100101 00110011 01001101 11100011 01111001 11100100 10010010 01101000
10110010 10110110 10100100 10000000 00011011 10111111 00001110 11110100 10000101 10111000
11110110 00010100 10101101 10011100 00001110 01110000 00000000 10100100 01000000 01001010
11100011 11110000 10100001 11011101 01101000 01011000 10111000 11000110 00000111 11110001
10011110 11110100 10011101 01010011 11100101 00011111 10011101 00101010 11110010 11100011
10001110 01000111 10101101 01000110 11101101 10000101 11000000 00011001 00011001 10100001
00110110 00100110 00011001 11101100 10011001 00110100 00001000 11000000 10010000 10110111
01111110 10011001 10100111 00011111 10111101 11000111 01110011 01000011 00010001 10110111
11011110 10001011 11011100 01000000 11011100 00101111 00100110 10100011 01000011 11110010
10000000 00010111 00000010 10011100 10100000 00010011 11000111 01011110 11110100 00110110
01101010 01110111 00101000 01000110 11001001 01110000 01000111 01010010 01101000 11111110
00111111 01010001 11101011 01000010 11100101 00000001 00011001 11100110 10001110 10001111
10000000 01111011 11110011 01010100 11101111 01111101 01001001 00010000 01100011 10011111
11100111 11101011 01001101 00000111 10010010 00111001 11100011 10111001 10100001 10111000
01001110 01111000 11000001 11100000 11010011 10000111 01001111 10101101 00011010 00001111
01010001 10100000 11111110 11101111 01110001 11101011 01000010 11100111 00011100 11110111
00111100 00001010 01110011 01110110 00001011 11000000 00000111 10011111 10101101 00110101
11110010 00001000 00100011 10000001 11011010 10011101 11000100 00100110 01110010 01111110
01001110 10100111 10111001 10100111 10111001 00011101 00000001 11111100 01101000 11000110
11010000 00111000 10100110 00101110 00110010 01001000 11101011 11011110 10011011 10110101
11000000 01100110 01001001 00111000 00000011 11011111 00110100 11100001 00010000 01100001
10011010 01010000 11011000 11111001 01000001 11101011 11111001 01010011 01001011 10000101
00111000 01100001 11001111 10110001 10100010 11100101 00011110 00110100 11110010 00100010
10001100 00111000 01110000 00110011 11011101 01001101 01001101 00000010 11000011 00101110
00000001 00111000 00100100 01100111 10010001 10001010 11111010 00010101 10100000 10001101

10011100 10110011 11000101 00011001 00011110 10000110 00110001 01001100 01111011 00011011
00111001 00000111 11101111 00101101 01101101 10100100 11100111 10101011 01000100 00101011
10100010 01010011 10001111 00101101 10001111 01001011 11111011 01000101 10111101 11010001
11100001 00101001 00000010 11100111 00101111 11111001 11010100 10001011 01101010 10001110
00000111 10100001 11110111 10101111 01101001 00111010 00101110 10010110 01111110 01101111
11101100 11111011 01111110 01111011 11101101 10101000 10100110 11110000 11011110 10001011
00100110 00100011 00110110 00010001 00000100 11110100 01011110 00101010 10100001 01010110
00101001 00001010 01011000 11110100 11111110 11001001 11100100 00101001 10100101 11111001
10000100 01101100 11000110 00110011 10001100 00011010 00011011 01001000 01101000 11111000
11011011 01011110 10110101 11111111 00000000 00001000 10101110 10001100 00111001 01001011
01100111 00011101 10111000 10010000 11110001 01000100 10111110 00011001 11010011 01001111
00011110 01010100 11000011 11011100 01001011 01011010 01111011 01100100 11001001 01111000
10101000 00111110 10000111 10001111 11111111 00000000 01100110 11001010 00000001 11111001
01110010 01111101 00000000 10101000 11001110 10010111 01110000 01110011 11111011 10100011
01011110 10111000 11011110 00010000 10110001 11001110 01100011 10111000 10111100 10001100
11100111 10110100 10010100 10100111 11000010 01110000 00001110 10010111 10110111 01000011
00111101 11000110 00111111 11000010 10110011 01110011 01101110 11110110 00001111 10101101
11000010 11011011 00011110 01000110 10011010 01000101 11000110 00001001 00010000 00011100
11110111 10101000 11100110 11010010 11100100 10001111 00100110 01000101 00100011 00000010
10111101 01111111 11111110 00010001 01110010 00110000 00000110 10100011 00110111 11100011
00011000 00110100 00111111 10000110 11100111 00100000 10000100 11010100 01110111 10001110
10011000 00110001 00001010 10110101 01010010 00100110 00010101 01101010 11000110 01101011
11011101 00111100 01100110 01011011 00001101 10111100 11100000 00001100 11010100 01001111
00000110 11010100 11100100 01111101 01110001 01011110 11000001 01110001 11100000 11100011
00101111 11011111 10111011 10001000 10011110 11011001 10000110 10110011 00011111 11100001
11101100 10101100 11100111 00010111 11010001 01111101 01111100 10111100 01010000 10101010
00100110 11101111 10110001 11000101 01100011 11001010 01100110 10000011 00100011 10011100
11100010 10101001 11111001 01100111 01100001 00100100 01110111 10101111 01011001 10011111
11100001 10110101 11000100 10001111 11110010 01011111 11000010 10011110 10111001 01011010
10101001 00101111 11000011 00111001 10011000 11111001 00010000 11101010 00010000 10010111
11000110 01001001 00110001 11010110 10010001 10101101 00011011 11011101 10110001 00110100
11011001 11100101 10111001 00100000 11101101 00000010 10100101 00110001 00011101 10011001
01101110 10110101 11101000 00101101 11110000 10101111 01010100 10001111 11111101 01011101
11100101 10011100 10000000 11111011 00010001 01010000 11011100 11111100 00111110 11010110
10100010 00000000 00100000 10001010 01011111 01010001 00011011 01100111 11110100 10100010
01010011 11110110 10011111 00001011 10110001 11010111 10000110 01101010 00010111 11100110
01100111 00000000 01010100 10001110 10000010 10100011 10111001 01001101 11010000 11101101
11000111 00111101 01110011 01011101 01111101 11001111 10000110 01110101 00111011 01110001
11111011 11111011 00011001 01010000 11100111 10101000 01011100 10001010 10100001 01110001
10100110 00110001 11100001 11010100 10100001 00011101 11110110 11110100 10100101 00001001
10110101 10111001 11011010 11011101 00011011 01101110 01110010 01000100 00011100 01100000
10001010 01100010 01000111 11000000 11001001 11100000 00011110 00101011 10100100 01001101
00011110 01111001 00111001 01001000 01001011 11100011 11111000 01001000 11101011 01010001
11000011 11100001 11011101 01000110 01011100 10101010 01000010 11111000 11101011 10000000
10100110 10110101 10001100 11010100 10011110 10100111 00010110 00100001 00101011 01111011
10101100 11001010 10001111 01110100 10000101 00000111 11101011 01010110 10010010 00111111
11011101 10010001 11001011 11110011 11011011 10110101 01101001 11000011 11100001 10101101
01010010 00101001 01111111 01111001 01101001 01110001 11101111 10010101 10101011 11101001
10100010 11001010 10100100 01111001 11010001 11001000 10011001 11110101 10001100 11110001
01011010 00111010 10010001 11101110 01110010 01011001 10011000 10100001 01111010 00011110
11100011 10100111 00010100 10001101 00010001 11101001 01011101 00101010 01101001 00010001
00010001 10110110 01000110 01110001 11001110 01000001 11110010 11001101 01000011 01110001
01100000 10110001 00010010 10101000 11000101 11000001 11110110 10101000 10010101 01001000
11101110 00001001 00110011 00000111 11001010 11101100 01000111 00111101 11110011 01010010
01100000 00100010 01100100 00001010 10111110 10010110 10100011 11001100 01110000 11001100
00000001 11101101 10011110 11010100 10000110 11010011 00111100 01101110 00011001 10101100
11100101 00110101 00111101 00011001 11010111 01000010 10011011 01101010 11100110 00101100
10000011 11110011 00111101 11101001 11110000 00001110 01110001 10001100 11010101 11110101
10110100 00110010 00000010 01001110 00001000 11101111 01010011 01000011 01101000 00100011
00011100 00010001 11111001 11010100 01000001 11110010 10101101 01011001 10111011 10100111
10101001 01010101 10100011 00000100 01110100 11000001 11111010 01010100 00100110 00111110
01110001 11111100 11101011 01000001 11000111 00111100 01010100 01001111 00010001 01101110
00000000 11100111 10111001 10101011 11100111 01001011 01000011 00110111 00011011 10111101
00001100 11100111 00000011 01111111 00000000 11110011 11101011 01000010 11000111 11110010
11110100 10101101 00101000 00101100 01100100 10010001 01001110 11110101 10101001 00011110
11001100 10000000 01111110 01010011 10011110 00111000 10101001 01010101 00011111 01000001
01111011 00110110 01100011 10110100 01111001 00011000 11101011 01010001 00011000 10001001
00011111 01001010 11011000 00010110 10001100 00110010 01110001 10001111 01011010 10001101
11101101 00001111 00111100 00011111 11001010 10101001 01001101 11101100 11001000 11110110
01101100 11000111 01110101 00111101 01001000 11100110 10100010 01110001 11101100 01000001
10101101 01100111 10000000 00000001 11010010 10100001 11110010 00000110 00110011 10110111
10001110 11100110 10001111 01101000 10000100 11100010 11010010 00110010 11111001 11001000
11101101 11000111 01111010 00110000 01110111 01110011 01010111 10011110 00001111 11011101

11100100 00000001 01010000 11101101 00100110 01011110 10000011 00011000 11100011 00110101
01110000 10010111 01110001 00110100 11001010 10101100 01011011 11001100 00000000 00001110
10111111 10101101 01011010 11010011 01111110 01101011 10010010 01110001 11010000 01110000
01001101 01000011 00101010 10010011 00100110 11011100 00011100 11100110 10101100 01011010
00001111 00101101 11011101 10110110 11110000 01111010 10010011 01010011 01010001 10111011
00011010 01100001 11111110 00110100 01010110 10010100 01111110 11111011 00101101 11101011
01011011 00010011 11001010 00111100 10111000 11111100 10111100 11101100 00111101 11001111
01111010 11000111 01110000 00011010 01100010 00110001 01011010 01110010 11100001 01100001
01001000 11110001 10001100 00001110 10010100 10010101 00110101 10100101 11010001 11011011
11001101 10101100 10011010 00111101 11010111 11100001 10001110 00001111 10000100 00101101
11100100 00000000 10001100 10011110 01000101 01110101 10111001 11000000 10101110 01011111
11100001 10100010 00010101 11110000 01100101 10000111 10111000 11001000 11111010 01010111
01010001 10110111 10011100 10000011 01011100 10011000 10001011 11110011 00011110 01011100
11011101 11011000 10011001 11000111 11001100 11111001 00111001 11100010 10000101 11001000
11001001 11101010 01001001 11101111 01001111 00100011 10010000 00111011 01110111 11100110
10011010 01001000 11100100 00000001 11110101 10101110 01100111 01100010 01000100 01001110
00000110 01110001 10011100 11010010 10100000 00111001 11101001 11110101 00110100 01111100
10111011 01001000 11000111 01011010 00001000 11011100 00001000 11101101 01010010 10110101
01011010 10100000 00010000 01110010 00001001 00100111 10101111 00010100 00101111 01100000
00001110 01001101 00101111 01101110 11010100 11010000 01111100 11000000 00110110 00011110
10110100 11101111 11011000 01110110 00100100 11001001 00011100 01100010 10011011 10110111
11011111 10011100 11111110 00010100 01110100 00011101 01101000 11110111 00110101 00101101
10110110 00100000 11000000 01100011 11101100 01111010 01010010 00010000 01110001 11101111
01000011 00011100 11100011 10000011 11000101 00011011 10110001 11001110 00001101 01011010
01101000 00000101 01010001 10010001 11001001 10101000 11110011 10011001 00001000 00001011
11010000 01110101 00110100 11111100 11100111 10101111 11101001 01000111 01011111 10111101
11101011 01010010 11100100 11000000 01100010 11111111 00000000 11100011 11010101 00100010
10001100 00000000 01111010 10011110 11010100 10011000 11100111 10011010 00001000 00100100
10001100 01110110 11101001 01010101 00011101 10000100 00001011 10111000 10010011 10011111
11001010 10001110 01001100 10100000 01111111 00000000 11100101 10001101 00100010 10001110
01001001 00100100 01100111 00111101 01101000 00100100 10010011 10011110 11011101 00101001
01011010 11000011 00011010 00001111 11001011 10010010 10111000 00110100 01100100 00000000
01001001 00000100 11100100 11110110 11101101 01001110 11000111 01100010 00111011 11010000
10100011 11011100 00001010 00000110 11000101 01101100 10101000 11100011 11110101 10101000
11000000 00001010 11011001 00111100 00010011 11010110 10010111 00100000 10101110 00110011
10010001 11101011 01001110 00011000 01100010 00111101 00000101 00100110 00100001 10111101
00000001 11000111 00111001 11100110 10010011 00011001 01010011 11001110 00001101 00100110
11110001 10110001 11110000 01111110 01110001 01001110 00100100 01100011 00011000 11101000
00111001 10100111 01111101 00000000 01101010 00001101 10001011 11000001 00100100 11110111
00110100 10101011 11110010 10101000 00100111 10101111 10100101 00001011 10010010 01000010
10001110 00000000 11100100 11010010 00001101 10111100 10000100 00111001 11110101 00110100
11110101 00000001 01010001 01000000 00011001 11000110 00110011 11111010 11010010 10110111
01001110 01111000 11110111 10100100 11101010 01110010 01001111 11010011 11011010 10001110
11000011 10101011 11100111 11010000 01010001 01110100 11110110 00000001 00110011 11101001
01000010 11100100 11001000 11100000 01110111 00010100 10100100 10000000 01000000 11101110
01101001 10001010 01011000 10111100 10000000 01110000 10000011 10001111 10101101 00101111
00110000 00000101 00000111 00100000 00001100 11100100 01111011 01010011 11111010 00010010
10111101 01101001 00000000 11000010 10001100 01111110 01110100 10101011 11011100 10011010
01001101 00110111 10101000 11011000 10011011 10110010 01001000 00011101 10111010 10011010
00011000 10101111 11001111 11011100 00001110 10011110 11110100 00011110 10111000 11000000
11111100 00101000 01110001 11000001 00000011 10011100 11010010 01110010 11101000 00100010
00110100 11100101 00110011 11101011 11111010 11010011 10110010 00010111 10100111 01011110
11010100 00101111 01001100 01110111 11110101 10100111 00100110 01100100 10010000 10010000
10111100 01110111 11001101 00100100 10110100 00000001 10111000 11011011 00100110 00111011
10110110 01101001 11000100 00000000 00111101 11101001 10011100 10001001 00001001 00100111
10101001 10100101 01100000 01000001 11111110 10110101 01111100 11011010 01011000 00000100
01010110 11000000 00111001 00111111 10000000 10100110 00110001 00100100 11110100 11111101
01101001 11001110 01110010 00111110 01000001 11010111 10111101 00111001 00000111 00011001
11101001 01001110 11001000 00000001 10000110 01001110 00111011 01100110 10000111 11000001
11000010 11100111 00000111 11010011 11010110 10010000 01110011 10000001 10001111 01111010
00110000 00110111 11110000 00111110 10111110 11110100 11011011 01001100 00000001 01110001
11001111 10100111 10110101 00001100 00000001 00100111 10101111 00100111 10101101 00001010
00000000 00011011 01110001 01000110 00001000 00111001 00001101 11000101 00001001 10100010
11000000 11110010 01001000 11000101 00000100 10011100 10001100 01100010 10000010 00001001
01110010 01110011 11010111 10110101 00100110 00000000 00100100 10001111 10111110 01111010
00011010 00001000 00000111 11000111 00011101 11111001 11110101 10100110 11100100 00110001
00001010 00000001 01111100 01110101 00111101 10101001 11001010 10111100 11100100 10011110
11010100 10100011 11100101 11100000 00011110 10111101 01001101 00101011 10000000 11000011
11101100 00111000 11101111 10011010 01000110 00100011 11110011 00011000 10100101 00100000
00010010 00110010 01001111 00011110 10010100 00011100 00010011 11110100 11111100 11101010
10101110 10111010 10000000 00101110 01110001 11010111 00011110 11110100 10011001 11001011
10000010 00000000 11011001 10011110 10110100 10101100 01000110 11001110 01000000 11001001
11101000 00001101 00100011 00001111 11110110 10111011 11010100 00111101 11001010 10111000

```
10011011 10110111 00111110 01110001 10010001 11101000 00101000 01110110 11100111 01101010
10000011 11001111 00000000 11111011 11111010 01010010 10010110 11100111 00000001 01111000
11110101 10100001 00011001 01010000 10011100 00011111 11010010 10011011 01011010 11011100
01100011 00011100 00010110 01101100 00000110 11000000 11101001 01001111 00100000 00001000
11001111 11001101 11110011 10011110 00000001 10100110 00100100 01100111 00100011 10000001
11111000 01010011 10110010 00110011 11001111 00111000 00110100 10010101 11110111 00010101
11000110 11100111 11100111 11000010 11110100 00011100 00011010 01000110 11101011 10001111
11000010 10011110 10100011 10001100 00100111 10101101 00110101 11001111 00011000 00011100
11110011 11010110 10011011 01001111 10111000 01101110 00100010 10101110 01010000 00011110
01111111 00111010 01011110 11000100 01100111 11011110 10001110 10111101 01001110 00111101
01101000 01011100 01101110 00100011 10100110 00101000 10111001 00100011 01000001 11000010
01110100 10100101 01101100 10001100 10101000 00011000 00101111 11010010 10000101 00011011
01000001 00111100 10011110 00111111 00110011 01000010 01101110 00111000 01100111 11100000
11111010 01010001 10101000 00001001 11011111 00100000 11100111 00011100 00011010 01101011
00011100 01111100 10100000 01100110 10011111 10010000 10111111 01010011 11010000 00001010
00000111 11110111 10001000 10100011 01000101 10101000 00001100 01101111 10111001 11001001
11001001 00111101 01101001 11001010 01111001 11101001 11001001 00010100 00010011 10110100
00001101 11111101 01011111 11110101 10100001 10001110 00111011 01010000 11010101 11110101
00000010 00111101 11001101 10000011 11101011 11110101 10100101 01010101 01101111 01001100
10011111 01111010 01011100 00011100 00001110 00111001 10100001 10001001 00001110 10000000
00010011 10001110 11111000 00110100 00110100 11101100 00110100 00111000 00001100 10011100
11100111 10001110 10110100 11000101 11100100 00011111 01000010 00110011 11000101 00101000
00000001 10000001 00001101 11000000 11110100 11101011 01001000 10101111 10111001 01111110
01011110 00001110 00110001 11110100 10100001 01101000 10001010 00001100 00000011 10000000
00001110 00000101 00001100 01000010 10010100 11100111 10010010 00110011 10001111 01011010
01100001 00100001 01011101 00010100 01110011 11101010 01001101 00001010 00111001 00111100
11100100 10010001 11010100 11110110 00010100 11010010 10110001 00000001 00101000 11001001
01001100 11110100 00011100 11111110 00110100 01110011 11011100 01010010 01110011 10000000
00001111 01011010 01010110 00100111 00011000 00011101 00101001 01001011 01001101 01000000
01110111 01010000 01001111 01101110 11010100 11011100 11110110 00010100 01100111 00111000
00011101 10110011 11001101 00110100 01110101 11000000 10100000 00000101 11001000 00111000
00011110 10111101 01101000 01101110 10111000 10100000 11110110 11000110 01101001 00000110
01011000 10010010 01000110 00010011 00111100 01100110 10010110 10011101 00000110 00000100
10010000 00110000 00111010 10000011 11001001 00110100 11011100 00010011 10000000 00111011
11110101 11110101 10100001 10110111 00111110 00000111 00011000 11101010 01111101 11101001
11000001 10000110 00000110 00111010 10011110 11110100 11010110 11000010 00011010 11001100
00100011 10001100 10001110 10100100 01111010 01110011 01001001 11110011 00010001 11001110
00000001 00111100 11100011 11010010 10010101 01000110 00000001 00001001 10001110 01001101
00100011 01100001 11001000 00100000 11110001 10001100 01111101 01101000 10010011 00101100
01010111 11111001 00011011 00011001 00111011 11000001 11000101 00011000 11100011 00001100
00111010 10010011 01001000 11111000 01011111 10011000 01100100 11100111 11110101 10100101
11000111 01000110 00111001 10100111 11100110 00100100 00100011 10000010 01111000 00011110
10010100 01100000 00001110 10100111 10010011 01000001 00111101 11000111 01110011 01001100
01111100 00011100 00010011 11010100 01110100 11111100 01101001 01101001 01111101 00110100
00100100 01111011 00010010 00010000 00110000 11100011 00111100 01010000 10000111 00000100
11100100 00011100 11110110 11100110 10010001 10000111 11101110 10010000 01110100 00011111
11100001 01000110 01001001 00111110 11010100 10111001 10111110 01100011 00011000 00000110
00010101 11111000 00011110 11010100 11110000 01110000 00111101 10110001 10001110 01101000
01110110 00111011 00110110 10100000 11000001 11001111 00100110 10011010 11000011 10100101
01010010 10110011 00000110 00000011 10000001 10010011 10000011 11101110 00101000 01000010
00110010 01001110 00111001 10100100 01100001 10010000 00000000 11101001 10011110 01001101
00101110 00111010 11101100 11101010 01111011 11010010 01010110 10111000 10000001 11001000
11101001 01001001 11001000 00100000 01110100 11110111 10100011 10101001 00011001 11101100
00111010 01111010 11010010 01111100 11001101 10001100 00011100 01111111 01001010 00011110
11110110 00101010 11100010 10101000 00000001 10110001 11001111 00111101 01001001 11101111
01001000 11000000 00001111 11000110 10010101 11001110 11011000 11111000 11101011 01000011
01110010 00000000 00111101 01111010 11100110 10011111 10010000 10000100 00111100 11110000
00001110 00001111 10101101 00001000 00010101 01111111 00011010 01011100 00011100 01100100
10011100 01100011 10111101 01000111 10001111 11011101 10000010 00111010 10011110 11100111
11010010 10010010 01001101 01101000 11000111 01110001 11100111 10100001 11101101 11101101
01001100 01011110 01011101 11011011 11011110 10010100 10000101 11001000 11001001 00111001
00110100 11100101 11001000 01000111 01011110 00000110 01001111 01011111 01101010 00010010
11101000 00110001 10111101 00111011 00010010 01001111 01001010 01000011 10000000 01111000
11101010 01111011 01010010 11101110 11111110 00101110 10111000 11100100 01010010 00100000
01010101 00000000 00100001 11100011 10111001 11110101 00110100 11110110 11011000 10000000
01010010 00010110 00100010 01001111 11101011 01000100 01100011 00111000 11001111 01111010
01100011 01100001 10111010 01110010 00110011 01001110 00100111 00000100 00000011 11011110
10010010 01100011 01001100 01101001 00100100 11001011 11101000 00000101 00100011 10011100
00001100 01110111 10100101 01101100 00011100 01111010 11110111 11110110 10100000 10000000
00111001 11001111 00110100 11011111 10011000 11101110 00111011 00011100 00000010 01111010
11110110 10100110 01101110 00111000 01110000 10000111 10010011 11111100 01010100 00101001
11001110 00000001 11111011 11100100 01100100 11010000 10000000 00000000 01110011 01000110
10011011 10110000 10111000 10001010 10111000 00111000 10100001 10000110 11110011 10011100
```

11111110 10010100 00100000 11100011 10101101 00101010 11110100 11111001 01000000 00000010
10011011 11010001 01011001 00010010 01110101 00001010 00001000 01001110 10110100 11111101
10100000 11110101 11100010 10011011 11000011 00011111 11000110 10011110 11000111 00011100
01010001 11010110 11101000 00000110 00000110 00000100 10001100 00101001 11100011 10100101
00011101 00001110 01000000 11101101 01001111 11000000 11100000 00000001 01000010 10101000
00001010 01000000 11101011 01000010 01111010 11011100 01111110 10000010 00101001 00100100
01110011 01000001 00101010 00001000 00000000 11110010 01111010 11010010 10001110 00001111
00100010 10001100 00101001 01100011 10000011 11001001 11101000 01101001 11011111 10110000
10000100 01100110 00001011 11110111 10000001 10100101 11000001 11111110 00100011 11000111
10100101 00100010 10000010 00110000 00001110 00001001 11110110 10100101 11111001 10110001
10010010 10111000 10100110 11100110 11010011 00010000 00001100 11100111 10000011 11001101
00000100 11111100 11000111 10001110 01111101 10101001 00111000 00000011 00111101 01001111
01111010 01101010 11110011 11010100 01110011 11010111 00110100 10101111 01110001 10001111
11000111 01111010 00110111 10000000 01111000 11101010 01111010 11010000 01000110 00110000
00000111 01011110 11100110 10010011 00011111 10011101 00011011 00001000 00110010 00110010
00110011 11001001 10100000 01100001 01101001 10100111 10010010 01010111 00011100 11111010
10000011 01000110 11101111 00101100 01110100 00101111 10001010 10010101 01111101 11000110
00111011 11100101 00000011 00100111 10001010 01100011 01000110 01110000 00111100 10110000
10000011 00100111 10101101 00111111 00100000 11111100 11011101 00111110 10110100 01100111
11011111 11110001 10100010 01011011 10001000 01100100 10111001 00000011 00011100 11100011
11010010 10101011 11001011 01100101 01101111 00101010 01100001 11100001 01001111 01111110
00000101 01011001 11100111 00000011 00100111 00110100 11100101 01011100 00001111 01110011
01010101 11001110 11001010 10111001 01010010 00101011 01001000 01100010 00100011 01100100
00110001 00001111 01111101 10110101 01100000 01000110 00110001 11000010 10000001 11110100
00010101 00100010 10000000 00010011 10011110 10110100 10011000 00011100 00010010 00111110
10011100 11010101 01111011 01000110 00010111 00011010 10111000 00000000 10001100 01110101
11101010 01101001 00011011 01110111 11111011 00011000 11110111 00010100 10101101 11010100
00001100 01110111 10100001 10001111 11001110 00000111 11101001 01010011 11001110 11001001
00100001 11110010 10010010 01000110 11111001 11010010 00110011 11101011 10010101 10100110
10111101 10010101 10110011 01110101 10110111 10001000 11111111 00000000 11000000 01000101
01001111 10000011 11001110 00111000 00111101 10101001 01010111 10100110 00111010 10011010
01111100 11101110 11100011 00101000 11001001 10100110 01011000 00110111 11111010 11001011
00111011 01110010 00111111 11011101 11101011 01010001 10111110 10010001 10100111 10010100
11100110 11000110 00011111 11111011 11100110 10110100 10011101 01001000 11101011 11111010
11010010 00101001 11111001 11111010 11111011 01010010 01110010 01101001 11011110 11100011
10111001 10010100 11011010 00000110 10010100 01001001 11111111 00000000 01000000 10110111
00011001 11110100 01011010 10000101 10111100 00101011 10100010 10010001 10000011 10100111
11000100 00001111 01110011 11011110 10110111 00010100 00011100 10011100 11110001 01001000
00111110 01100010 01110110 11110010 00101001 10101010 10001101 00111011 11011100 01111100
11001100 11100111 11011111 11000001 11111010 00011001 00011000 11111011 00000010 01100000
01110010 00111001 00110101 00010111 11111100 00100001 01111010 00010110 01111111 11100011
11001011 00000100 11110101 11111101 11100001 00010101 11010010 11100111 00000111 00000110
10000010 01111110 10000010 10000111 01011010 01001101 11101010 00101011 10110011 10011010
11111111 00000000 10000100 00110111 01001000 01010101 00111000 10000110 01010001 11101000
00000100 10011001 10100110 11111111 00000000 11000010 00010011 10100101 00011110 11010011
00001100 11110111 11011101 11010010 10111010 01110101 00111000 00011101 00101000 11001011
01110101 10100011 11011010 01001101 01101010 00111110 01100110 11001110 01000010 01011111
00000010 11101001 01111000 00100001 00011110 11100111 11011111 11100110 11101011 01001000
11011110 00000010 11010011 00001110 01111111 11010010 00101110 10010000 10011110 11000000
11010111 01100001 10001110 01001101 00100011 00001110 00111101 11101010 10010101 01111001
01011000 00111001 10011001 11000011 10111111 11000011 01101101 00110001 10100011 11111111
00000000 10001111 10011011 10101100 11111011 00010000 00101000 10001011 11100001 10011110
10011001 00011111 11111100 10111101 01011101 00011100 11111010 10010001 01011101 11001001
00111111 00111000 00100000 11110110 10100001 01110010 00110010 00101001 10111010 11110010
11101000 00001010 01101100 11100000 11011111 11100001 10001110 10010110 11011100 00001011
11001011 10010000 00110011 01010000 00111111 11000010 10111101 00101100 11001000 11101101
11110110 11011011 10000001 11000110 00000111 01001010 11110100 00111100 01100100 01100110
10001100 10001100 11110010 01111001 10100100 10101011 01001001 00001101 01010100 01100111
10011010 01001011 11110000 10011010 11000000 10010000 11001001 10101001 11011100 00001100
01110100 11001010 10001010 01001001 01111110 00010100 11000011 11100101 00111010 11111111
00000000 01101001 10111001 00000111 11111110 10011001 11110100 10101111 01001011 01100000
00001110 01000111 01101010 01101011 11100101 01000000 11000000 11001111 11010110 10101101
01100010 11100111 01100000 01010101 00011010 01110111 01000111 10010001 10111111 11000010
00110110 01011001 01001011 01000111 10101010 11110100 00111111 11000101 00010101 00111010
11100011 11100001 01101101 11111100 11100011 11110111 01110111 11110110 10111100 01111010
10000010 00101011 11011000 01100011 00000111 10101000 11100101 11110001 11001110 00101010
00110101 11101011 10010111 00011000 00100111 11010010 10101011 11101011 00110101 00111010
10010100 10101010 11001001 00100110 10101110 01100101 11111000 01100011 01001110 01111101
00100111 01000010 10110100 10110001 10011000 10000010 01100010 00011000 00100101 01001101
01101010 10101110 01000110 01101000 00011101 01001001 10100100 00011001 00111101 01001101
01110011 01010100 10101001 11001111 00101011 10110011 00100001 01111010 11110110 10100001
10000000 00111110 10110100 10001111 10011110 01110000 01101001 11011001 00100011 00010101
00010111 10111010 10111000 00001000 10100011 11100111 10100100 01100110 11000001 00100000

11110101 11110100 10100011 11111000 10000101 00001010 10100010 00111100 00011110 10100011
10111111 10111101 00101101 01111011 10001110 11100010 11110100 11001110 01111011 11010010
00101110 00110010 01000110 00111010 01010010 00101110 01001000 11001001 10100111 00001111
10010011 11110001 11110101 10100111 11010100 01000010 00100010 11100000 10011100 10011110
00111011 00001010 01010011 11001101 00110101 00001000 00100011 00100011 00111101 01111011
11010010 10101111 00111001 11100111 00010100 00111111 00100000 00001110 01110011 01001011
10000011 11000000 10100100 11001110 00111001 00011101 01101000 01010000 11000111 10010010
01111111 00001010 10010100 10000000 01000000 11000011 01100110 01000111 00111100 11010001
11001000 10001100 11100111 10101101 00101110 00110000 00111101 00001101 00011001 00100100
00011010 10101011 10100000 00011001 10000010 01010100 00011100 00010000 00101001 11111001
11101010 01101001 00010111 00100100 11110101 00111100 01110011 01000011 10010010 01001110
01001111 01000011 11010000 01010001 01111011 01101000 10000100 00110111 10001110 00110111
11111010 11110001 01001111 00100111 10001100 10001110 10010100 10001100 00110001 10000000
01101001 10111100 11111111 00000000 11000000 01101001 01011001 10001100 01110011 00010010
01110001 11101011 01000010 10000001 11011110 10001101 11011000 00011001 00100111 11101000
00001101 00110011 10010010 11111100 10011100 11110001 10011010 01111010 01011111 01010000
00000011 10110111 10100000 00100011 11010111 00010100 10111111 00110001 00111000 11001101
00100110 11010000 00011000 11100000 01110011 11101011 01001010 11111111 00000000 11011101
00000011 00010100 11110100 10110000 00000110 00000000 00100000 01100111 10101001 11100100
11010010 01101110 00101100 10011001 11000110 00111001 10100110 01110100 00011101 01110011
10001010 00110000 01011011 00000000 10011110 00111111 10010101 00101111 00100000 00100100
01010101 00100111 10001110 11111101 01101001 10100000 10000000 00110011 10001100 10001111
01001010 00110111 01101110 01110010 10111001 11100100 11010011 01010011 10110010 10100001
11100000 01110101 10101001 10110011 00000001 00011111 01110110 11001111 10010000 11110011
10011100 10011111 01011010 10010101 01111010 01110101 10100100 11111110 00101100 01111110
10110100 01100111 00101101 10001100 01110111 11101101 01011010 00000000 10001010 10111000
00111101 11001110 00111010 01010010 10110000 00111101 10001101 00001110 11011011 01101001
00010101 10111010 10010010 00110011 11101111 01010011 01101011 10000000 01110100 00000111
10011100 01100011 10111101 00001011 10010010 01110010 00001111 01011110 11110100 11010110
00111001 11100000 01111110 00111001 10100111 01110101 11100111 10110110 00101001 01101110
00000000 11100100 11100111 11100101 11110100 11100110 10000101 00011101 10110011 10001100
11010000 11000100 00110000 11110110 11110100 10100000 11110001 10000010 00000110 00101001
00110100 00000011 01110000 00110011 10001110 11000011 11110101 10100001 11110000 11011100
01110011 11010111 10011010 01000001 11111011 10110000 00000001 11111100 01001101 00001100
01000110 01000111 10100001 11101111 01000010 11101100 00000000 10100100 00011110 00111101
00001110 00110001 01000010 10001100 10011100 11110101 11000111 01101010 01011110 00111001
11000111 11100111 01000110 01111001 11000111 01111110 10100111 11011010 10011111 00101011
00000001 00010100 11111100 11011110 11111000 11101001 01000010 11110100 11100100 11110100
10100001 01111000 01101110 00000111 00111101 11001101 00011000 11011010 01110010 00111001
00100100 11010011 01111010 00100001 10100001 01110010 01110011 11101100 00111101 10101000
11101111 11000111 00010100 01110111 11000000 11001001 11001111 10101101 00110101 10110000
01110011 10010011 10010000 00111010 11100010 10100111 01011110 10000101 00001011 11001111
00111110 10011111 11001110 10000010 00111000 10100110 00101001 00111110 01011111 00111001
00011100 01010000 11000011 01110110 01000111 00111100 11010101 01111100 11001000 00011101
11110111 10001110 01001111 00011110 11010100 00010001 11101101 10011111 01101010 00011000
00011100 11100111 11110001 10100101 11000110 00111110 01010011 11101011 01010010 11100100
11110110 00000001 10011011 01000000 00011001 01110011 11110101 00010100 01101101 00100111
00000111 10011100 01111010 01010011 10010111 00000100 11110010 00111000 00010100 00011100
11100100 10011110 10001001 11011010 10101110 11110110 11011000 10110001 10110010 10010000
00011101 00111101 11111111 00000000 01011010 00111010 10011100 11100111 11110001 10100110
10010101 00101100 10000111 10011110 01000111 01111010 01010101 11100100 10000000 00001101
01000011 10111101 11101100 01000000 00111001 11001011 01111101 00001111 01000001 01000011
11100000 10010001 11000111 01010011 01000000 00100000 10110011 10000100 00111100 11110111
11110110 10100100 01111100 11100111 00100011 00100111 00011110 10100110 10101001 10110000
00010111 01101110 00110011 11110011 00011010 00011100 00000001 00011110 01110010 00111000
11111101 01101001 00110000 00110010 00110010 00110011 11101011 01001101 01000000 00001111
11011111 11111100 10001101 00111011 11101011 01100000 00011110 10011001 00111111 11000011
01001000 10100000 01111001 01100000 00011010 01010110 00101100 01110010 01110011 11110010
01100111 10101111 01111010 01001100 01100000 11110001 11011100 11010010 01001111 01011011
00000000 10111001 00000100 01110000 00111010 01010010 00110000 00100000 10011100 01111111
11111010 11101000 01100001 10111000 00100000 11001110 00000111 11110011 10100110 10110001
11001000 00100111 00100111 00001010 01111010 01111010 11010100 11011010 11100000 01000110
10100100 10001000 10011111 00000000 10011001 00001001 11101000 01101001 11001010 10101010
00011111 00000111 01111001 10010011 10111110 00101001 01011010 01000001 00010111 00111000
11100100 10001110 11010100 00100110 01110000 01011011 10000000 01001001 10101010 10110111
01110010 11000100 01100010 01011010 01011100 10011110 00010000 01110111 11101110 01001101
00101000 00011111 01111111 00111100 10011110 10110100 11000110 00100110 01000010 00110110
00011101 11100000 01111010 11010011 11000000 00111111 01111011 00111100 11010000 11011110
10100000 00110001 11001110 11101000 11000000 00000000 10011110 01111001 00010100 11101001
00111010 10001111 01000001 11010011 00010100 00100000 00000011 00100011 00011000 11111010
01010000 10011101 01000011 01110101 11000111 00100010 10011101 11111011 10010000 00000001
01000010 11001000 01001001 11001110 01001111 00011001 00111101 10111110 10010100 11000001
10000010 11111101 01001001 00011110 10100111 10111101 00101010 11100100 01111010 10010010

00001111 10101111 01011010 00011011 00100001 10111001 11110100 10100011 11010000 10110001
11011011 10110011 00100001 11101010 00000111 10111111 01111010 01101000 00000100 10010010
01001111 01110011 11001101 00100011 00011100 10000100 00111101 00111001 11101101 11011110
10010101 10001001 11011100 01111010 00001000 11000000 11101011 10011110 10110100 00101101
01011000 10110111 00000010 01110010 11011000 00011101 00101000 01110010 10101010 01001010
10000011 01001001 11010101 11000000 00011100 01101111 11101111 01001001 11110010 11100000
11001000 01000110 00010000 10011100 00011100 11010001 10111001 00100010 11100101 01111001
00100011 10100000 11101110 01000111 01011010 01100010 11111101 11011101 11011101 00111011
11010011 11111010 10000000 10111000 11000000 00111110 10110100 11000101 00000011 10011110
01110010 01001111 01001100 11010010 00011010 00001100 00000001 11010100 11110011 11101010
01101001 00111011 11010000 11100100 11101101 00100000 01111101 11111100 01010001 11011000
01100111 10101111 10101101 01010011 11010111 01000000 10110000 10111100 00001110 10011101
01101000 11110101 00100011 10111101 00100111 01000001 10011110 11010100 10011101 01000110
01001110 01000000 10100100 11101101 01100001 00000001 11100000 01100111 00111101 10000111
00110100 10111001 11000000 11000111 10100111 01101010 01001100 10110001 11100100 01110000
00101000 00011101 01000110 00111010 11111010 11010100 01101110 01010101 11000001 01001111
11001010 01001001 11101010 01101001 10111001 11001001 11001000 00011101 00111011 01010001
11010001 01011100 11111111 00000000 00011110 01110000 00110011 01000111 10010110 00110111
10010000 00111011 00001110 10100110 10101110 00011010 00001100 01110110 01110001 10000001
11001110 01001111 01101010 01100111 11001010 01110010 01110000 01000100 01001011 11011111
11010110 10010001 10001110 01100011 00100100 01110000 00000101 00111001 10000110 11101000
11000100 01111001 11101010 01000001 00110100 00110110 01000000 10011001 11011100 10000001
10011100 11110111 11111101 00101001 00011011 00011011 11111010 01110100 00011100 01010010
10110110 00000111 00000011 10100111 01101100 11010000 01000001 00111001 11110101 00111101
01001101 00110100 10000000 01001001 01110000 01011101 00000111 10100001 11001101 00110100
11111100 11010010 00111000 11101100 10000111 10011010 01110010 11100100 11110101 11101010
01001111 01111010 00011011 10101011 10001111 01111110 01101001 00111101 00110100 01100000
00001100 01000111 00010100 11010110 00100011 10101111 10100101 00100011 00000011 10010011
10001110 00000110 01111011 01010000 11000011 10001100 01100011 10001100 11110100 11000101
01001101 10110100 10111010 00011011 00010111 10101111 00110100 00011100 11100011 00000011
11010110 10001100 11110000 00110111 00001110 10011101 11101001 00111001 11000111 00011100
10010011 01000110 10101001 10010100 00101010 11110100 11100010 10010011 11101110 10000001
10010011 11111000 00001110 11110100 01100111 10100000 00000011 10001010 01000110 00011000
10010011 11001100 11101010 01000111 01000001 01010100 11110100 00100000 01101111 00011011
11111011 01100100 01110101 00011110 11110100 00010011 10011111 10010000 00001110 00111010
10010011 10011010 01110110 00110000 01001110 01101001 10111100 10110001 11101001 10000100
10100101 11010000 10110000 01010011 11110011 11110010 00111000 11111110 01110100 11101111
10011011 01111111 00100011 10010011 01000111 00000000 10000011 11101101 01001010 10100011
00111001 00100100 11010011 01001101 01110101 00000000 11000111 11001011 10010010 01001001
10100110 00111001 11111001 00000000 11000110 01001110 01111000 00010100 00110001 00101100
01111101 00110011 11010000 00001010 00010100 00110001 11111011 10000011 00011101 10110010
01101010 01011101 11110111 00100000 00111001 11110011 01111010 11110000 01111101 00111011
01010011 10111010 01110001 11011111 00110100 00001100 00000010 01111001 11001001 10100110
10101000 00101100 00110111 00101111 11100001 01001110 00110011 10110011 10110000 00001000
01010011 01101000 00011000 00011100 01110111 11101111 01001100 01011100 11001000 01001001
11101100 00111001 11111010 01010011 10111000 01100000 00001110 01110010 10011000 11001110
01111101 01101000 01000001 10111001 00000000 00111000 11000111 01011010 01110110 10010001
01011011 10001100 00000111 10101011 00010011 11000111 11010010 10010111 00100111 01110000
00100100 01100111 10001010 01110011 01101101 00100111 11111101 10000001 11011110 10010101
10001110 00110000 11011000 11100111 11111000 01000101 01000010 01110110 00100100 01100011
10011110 00001001 00111101 01111011 01010011 10011000 11111011 01110000 00111011 10011110
11110100 11010111 00111111 10111100 11000111 01011100 10001100 11010001 00101111 00111110
01011001 11111100 00111111 00011010 10110111 01101101 00101110 10001011 00001110 11000111
00011100 00010011 11011100 11010011 01000110 00000010 01100000 01100100 10111001 11100111
00011111 11100011 01001010 01111110 01100111 11011011 10011100 00011100 01110011 01000011
11110011 10011100 01100100 00000010 00111011 00011010 00110100 11101000 00000010 00001111
10010100 00000001 11010100 11100111 10011010 01011111 00110000 00101111 00011000 11101001
01000110 00000111 00011000 01010011 11110010 00001110 00101010 00111111 00101101 10011011
10011100 01110101 10101010 01011010 11101010 00000111 01011110 10100100 00011100 10000000
10100111 00111001 11101011 01000011 00101011 01110101 00100100 10000001 11101111 01001101
11011100 00100011 11000111 10111001 11101011 01001110 11111110 11111001 00100111 01111001
10100011 10101101 11001000 00010101 01001000 11100100 10000110 11000001 11110111 10100100
11101000 00111001 00100110 10010101 01001001 00111101 01000000 11100111 10100000 11110100
10100100 11101000 00001001 00111001 11000111 10100101 00001111 11001000 00000101 11001001
00111100 01100011 10011111 01111010 01010110 00000100 00001100 10010001 10000011 01001000
01001001 00111000 11100111 00000011 11010000 01010011 00110001 10110101 11111101 01111101
01001001 10101010 11011111 01000001 11011100 01111000 11001011 10010010 01000101 00000011
00100011 00111101 01001101 00011111 11000000 00111101 01111010 11010010 01100100 10101010
10011100 11110101 10100010 11011101 11001001 00000101 11101001 10010111 10100110 11111101
11100011 10011110 11011110 10010100 11110110 10010000 00010000 00000110 00110011 11101011
10010001 01001000 00001001 00111000 11110100 10100100 11011110 10011010 00000000 01100000
01101111 11101001 01001110 00000000 10010011 11000111 00010100 10001011 11010100 11110001
01001100 10010011 00000101 00110001 11001111 01011110 11010101 00110111 10111000 11000011

01110000 11001001 00011101 11000101 00111001 01001000 00011000 00011111 10001101 00110101
00000000 00000111 01110101 00111011 01110110 01001001 11100011 00000100 00011110 10110100
00101011 00100111 10100011 00001011 00000011 01001000 11001010 00110000 10001010 00001001
00111101 01110011 01000001 00011101 10111010 00011010 01011110 01110011 01001001 11000001
01111111 01101010 00011010 11010100 01110110 00000100 11011101 11111111 00000000 11101011
00010100 00010001 11001101 00001000 11000001 10110010 01111010 00001111 01011010 00110010
01111010 10001111 11010110 10010111 01001101 00000100 00001101 10000000 01101001 10101010
01110010 01111010 01100111 10011110 00101001 00111010 10010010 11000111 10101111 01001100
00001010 01010000 01001110 00111000 11100011 11101001 01000110 11100010 00000111 00000101
10001110 00111010 01111110 00110100 10011000 00100011 10011100 01010010 10101111 11101110
11010111 00000111 10010011 10011010 01001100 10110010 00100111 00100111 00000100 11010100
01111001 00001100 01111011 00000010 01001000 11110100 00010100 11010110 11011100 00010000
11101100 00111000 11110111 10100011 10010011 11010011 00110100 00111000 11011010 00110000
01111010 01110111 10101101 00010010 01011101 00000000 10001111 00100100 01101100 00111001
11100011 11011110 10100100 01001110 00000110 01110010 00110001 01001000 10101100 01011000
01100001 00111000 00011110 10111110 10110100 10101101 11001111 01001010 00110110 11010101
00001101 00001000 10000000 10011100 11100111 10010000 01111001 11001101 00101001 11000000
01010011 11010111 00000011 10011100 01010010 00110011 01100011 00100011 11010011 11010010
10000100 01010011 10000010 11011001 11000110 01111101 01101001 00111101 00000100 00100010
11101110 00000111 11010100 11010010 10110010 10011110 01001111 00000011 11010010 10001110
10000000 11110010 01000001 10100100 01001100 01100011 10001100 11111110 00110100 10111111
00100000 00010111 10101111 01111010 01000111 00100101 11111000 01001110 00001000 10100101
11100100 11010010 01110000 10100000 10010010 01111000 10100111 10100000 00001011 11001000
00010100 10011000 11011100 01110010 01000111 01001010 00011000 01100111 00011101 01111101
11101001 01000001 11001001 11000000 10100110 10000100 00011001 00100011 00000011 00011100
01111010 11010001 11101100 01111011 11010001 10011101 11111000 11101011 01001010 11011000
11001000 10100100 11000110 01000110 00000001 00000000 00001101 11000100 10010001 11010110
10000101 00000000 01110011 11010100 11010011 10011000 00000011 11011111 10011100 11010010
10000101 00011100 10010000 01111110 10010100 01101011 01111011 10001101 10001001 10001100
01110001 01001011 10010011 10111111 00011000 11100011 11011111 10111101 00011100 00000000
00111011 11111011 11010001 11010100 11100111 10100001 11000111 01111010 01101000 01000110
10100110 10010101 10101001 11000011 01100001 00010101 11001010 11001001 01101101 00011100
11110010 11001010 10111011 01010000 10010001 11110111 01111110 10110101 10010110 10111001
11111111 00000000 00011100 01110110 10100001 00111000 11001001 11000111 11100011 01001001
11010000 00010001 11010000 01100110 10001001 00110111 01010011 01000110 11000110 10000111
11100100 01111010 11010011 01110011 10001100 10000001 01000011 01100111 11101111 00110111
00111000 11101101 01000111 00011000 11111101 01111110 10010101 00111011 01101110 00001100
00001110 00000001 11001101 00011101 00010011 10011010 01001110 00001001 11000110 00101001
01011000 01110111 10100111 01100110 11000101 01110000 00011000 00010100 00110111 01011111
01101010 01001101 10100000 10101110 00001111 01110001 01001101 01001110 00110010 00110001
11000101 01001011 00000001 11100011 10000001 11000101 00011000 11000110 01001001 00110100
00100001 00000011 00111100 01110011 11101001 01000010 01111101 11000010 01001111 01011010
10100000 00010011 00111100 01110001 11001001 11101101 01000000 00101100 01001101 00110111
00100111 00100011 11010010 10011101 11010000 01110000 01001111 00010100 10011011 10111110
11000000 00101111 00111101 11001111 00110100 10011001 11101011 10110111 10101110 00110001
11001101 00011001 00111111 10000101 00000011 10010011 11010011 00010100 11101111 01111101
00000000 00000111 01000011 11110011 00010011 11101011 01000010 10010010 01000111 00011101
01101000 01101100 11100000 11100011 10111111 01111010 01010101 00000100 00011100 01100111
00111110 10110100 10011011 01010111 10110010 00000001 00010111 11111011 10111111 11001110
10010111 00100000 01100011 00011101 01111010 01010010 00110111 11011100 11001110 01110001
11001101 00110111 00011111 00100110 00010011 10101101 00011101 01000000 00110011 11001001
11100011 00110100 01100100 11100000 10010001 10011010 01110000 00000100 01110110 11111010
11010011 00110010 01001000 00100100 01110101 11001111 01010011 01000101 10111010 10110000
00000110 00000111 10001100 00011100 01100011 10101110 01101000 01100010 01110111 10010011
11111001 01010010 11110001 11010011 00011001 11101111 10011010 01001001 00011000 00101011
00000101 00000000 10111011 10011110 10111110 11010100 11011011 00000000 01100010 01000000
00000011 01101011 11100000 11110101 01101010 01010101 00011001 11101010 00111001 11110111
10100100 00111000 00001011 10111000 11111110 01110100 10111011 10110011 01010011 01100000
00010011 10100100 01100100 10000011 11001110 00101001 10011100 10101010 00000011 11010111
11010100 10001010 01111011 01100000 01100100 01111110 00100100 01010000 10111100 11101100
11000111 01001100 01110100 10100110 10111100 10000000 01001110 00100011 01000111 01100011
11000111 10111101 01000110 10011001 11011010 10001101 11010011 00111101 01110011 01010010
00110000 11011101 10001100 11111101 01001101 00110110 01011100 10010010 00110000 00111010
01010010 10111011 11011000 00000011 00001100 00111010 10011100 10001100 01010001 10010110
00001000 00110110 01110101 00111110 10110101 00100010 11110111 00010100 11011100 00010001
11110011 00010011 10000010 01111000 11100111 10110101 00110110 10011000 00001100 01100000
01001100 10001001 10010001 10010100 10101001 00010101 01111110 01110010 00001001 10100100
11001110 00001000 01010000 00111110 01000001 11011100 11110111 00110100 11000100 01011100
00010011 10010010 00110010 01101001 00000000 11111100 10000011 10111100 10011110 00000000
00111000 00010100 11010110 00011101 11111011 10011111 01011010 00000110 00010100 01100000
00001110 11110100 00101111 01000001 10011110 01001110 01001110 01000110 01101001 01101110
00000011 10110011 10000001 11000000 10100110 10010001 10001111 01110010 01001101 00111101
01001001 00100111 11101110 11100000 00000001 11000101 00110000 10011100 00101000 00010101

10100101 11111010 10000000 11101111 10010101 01110111 10110001 11100100 11100011 10111111
01101010 01100110 00001000 00011111 00111111 01011111 01011010 01011100 10000110 11000110
01101001 00000110 00001001 00000011 00111100 10011110 11010101 00010111 00000001 01001000
11101000 00110011 01001000 10101011 10001110 10100111 11110010 10100110 00101000 11000110
01110000 01101001 11100111 00000000 10001010 00101110 00000000 11000111 00000111 00110100
10011100 10001100 01100111 11010111 10110101 00101011 11100000 00011100 01100000 00010011
11101111 01000001 11111001 10111001 10100110 11010101 10000000 01000101 00100111 10111111
01010001 11101011 01001101 00000000 10010001 11001111 00011100 11010011 10110011 10010111
11101001 10011110 00111011 11110111 10100111 01110000 01110011 10010011 01010011 00100110
11010000 00010001 11110011 10111111 10101110 00101001 11011100 11100111 00001010 01111110
10110100 00110011 01100100 01100111 10000001 11101001 01000111 11011101 00111000 00011100
10011010 01111011 00000000 00110111 00100011 00000100 11110001 11101001 01001101 11101001
10010110 00100111 10111101 00111011 00100011 00111000 00000011 11101001 10011110 11110100
11011001 01110110 10010011 10110100 10001100 10001010 10100111 11100110 00000000 11000000
01101100 11000110 01000000 01001100 11100110 10011100 10000100 00010011 11101010 00111011
11010011 01011100 00000010 01110010 11111111 00000000 10010101 00111011 10101001 00000100
01100111 00011101 11000111 10100101 01001101 11101111 10110000 00001101 11100111 00011000
00111100 01100111 10101000 10100000 11111101 11110011 10000011 10000100 11100011 00011000
11101111 01001001 10111000 10011001 01011100 10010110 11101011 01000001 10001100 01100100
00011100 11100111 00100111 10100101 00100101 11100101 10111001 01100010 00111001 00000000
11100011 11110100 10100101 01101110 00010111 10110111 10110101 00011000 00011011 10011101
10110011 11000101 00100111 00000110 01001110 00000001 11000111 10111101 01010011 11101100
00101101 00000011 10010011 10000010 01111000 11001111 01101010 00110010 00000111 01001110
10100110 10000110 00111001 00100111 10001100 00001110 11110100 01110000 01110010 01001111
00111000 11101101 01000110 10000011 00001110 10100000 01111111 00111010 01101010 10010101
01010011 10000000 01001111 00100010 10001110 00001001 00000011 00111000 00111110 11010100
11100100 01010010 01011111 11100100 11100000 01100011 10111101 00101101 10000000 00001001
11001001 11100011 10110101 00110101 10000110 00110010 00110011 11000111 01111100 01010011
11010101 10111000 00100100 11100011 00010100 11000110 00111000 00111000 11000111 11010110
10011010 11010000 10000001 00011111 00100100 10001100 11100011 00010100 10001100 00111000
01001110 01111111 00001010 01011110 01001000 11001110 00001110 01111010 01010000 00001111
01100010 00111010 01010011 10010011 00101100 01001100 01100010 01001100 00000001 11010111
11111010 01010000 00001001 11100111 11010010 10010101 00111001 01110010 01000001 00111110
11110100 10000100 11100100 11100100 01110000 00111011 01010100 11011001 10111101 01011001
00000001 10000000 10101000 01001001 00111100 10010011 11010011 11010110 10001100 10110000
01000000 00000110 00110011 10011110 11110100 00101011 00000110 00100011 11010010 10010100
10001110 01110011 10011100 00100000 11101011 01010110 00000011 00000100 10011001 00000011
10001110 11011111 10011101 00111001 10001110 00000110 00000111 00000111 10111001 10100110
11110110 11110011 00001110 00000000 11001110 00000101 00001101 11001011 10001110 00111110
01000001 10001100 01110011 11011110 10010010 11010100 01110110 00011101 10010010 10101010
00001111 01111110 11011110 11010101 00011010 10001100 01110101 11001001 00011110 11110101
00100110 00001001 11001000 01110011 11001001 00111001 11001111 10110101 00110101 11001110
11101110 00000000 11100011 00010101 00011011 11101100 00000001 10010010 00000110 01111010
01111011 10011110 11010100 11011100 10000011 10011100 00000010 01110000 00110011 11001111
01001010 01010110 00000011 01100111 01001100 11100111 11011111 10100101 00100110 00000001
10001100 00101000 11101000 01001101 00010110 01100010 00010111 00100000 10001100 10010001
10010000 01000111 01011010 01000101 00011001 10010000 10011100 00001100 11111010 11010011
01100101 11100111 00011100 10011111 10010011 10000001 01001110 00111111 11101010 11001110
01001111 01000001 11001101 01010010 10110010 11011100 10110001 10000111 00000001 10000110
01111010 00011110 00111010 11110101 10100001 10001000 00000100 01111011 01010000 01010111
00000100 00001100 01100100 11110101 11111010 01010000 11100000 00000001 11111000 11010011
01010111 11101000 01000000 01100011 00001111 10010010 00111010 11010001 00101111 00011111
01001010 01000111 01010010 11000011 00011001 11111010 11010001 10011110 01111110 01011110
01000111 01001010 00101101 01100010 11000011 10011100 01100000 01110111 10100110 10000000
00000110 01011000 11110101 10100111 11100111 00000111 00011110 10110100 10000100 00001110
00000110 00101010 01011000 10010000 11001110 01000000 11001111 01110011 11111010 01010001
10110100 10101100 00101110 11000000 01100111 10011110 10000110 10010111 10000001 00011010
00001110 01110010 01001111 01001010 01101100 10100000 10011100 00101111 01100010 01111010
11111111 00000000 00111010 01101110 11000100 10001010 00111000 00100011 00100011 10000001
11010000 01111011 11010000 11100111 11110111 10100001 01000000 11101101 10111100 10011010
01010100 01100001 11100110 00011111 01001111 11100111 01001000 01110111 01001001 00110001
11100011 01100010 00001110 00000111 10111101 00111000 01101011 10111000 11101100 00001100
00110111 00001110 01111011 10011110 10010100 00010011 10010010 01110001 11001111 00110100
10001100 01000001 00011001 00011101 10111001 10100101 10010100 01100001 00011101 01111101
01000101 00001101 10010100 00011001 00011001 11101001 11010010 10011000 00110011 10011111
01000000 01111010 10011010 01110000 00111011 01000000 01011010 01101111 00111001 11000010
11110000 00111101 11101000 01101100 00000100 01011110 01111001 11110101 10100101 11100000
00011101 10111100 11100100 01110101 11110111 10100111 10101111 00100011 00011101 00111001
10101000 11110111 00000010 01001000 00001010 01110000 00111000 11001001 11101111 01011001
10111101 10001000 00010101 11111000 00000101 10001111 01000000 00110011 01001110 01001100
00010001 10011010 00001000 11001110 01000001 00011001 11001101 01000110 01011000 00101000
11001110 00111001 00111101 00000101 01011101 11101100 10000000 01110011 00010010 00010000
00011110 00111101 11110011 01001101 00011101 01011101 10110011 11010111 11010110 10011011

11101001 10111100 11100100 11010011 10011100 00010110 00011000 11110101 10100100 11100100
11101100 01010101 10000011 00011001 00111110 10111110 10111001 10100001 00110000 01110000
00000111 01111010 00001111 01001110 10011100 11010000 10000111 01101000 11101001 11010110
10000101 00011110 10000100 10000010 11100011 01111110 00101000 01010010 01110010 01110011
11010010 10011010 11011000 00000111 00100011 10000011 01001110 11001001 00101110 00001111
01101010 01101010 00110001 11101010 00111011 10001101 01100001 11110011 00011110 10100011
11010110 10000110 11111001 10110000 00111011 01110101 00110100 01100000 11100000 10001100
11111011 11010000 01001001 00011100 00110001 11001001 11111110 01010100 10011010 01001111
01010001 00000110 00111101 00000110 01001110 01111010 11010011 10011100 11111100 11100101
01000001 11000111 00011101 10111011 01010001 10011100 00000000 01011000 11100000 00011110
10010100 11010011 10011101 11100011 00111000 11100111 10100111 10111101 00110100 10111010
10110010 11000110 10101010 10000101 00000101 01010000 01100100 00001110 10110100 00011110
10011000 11101000 00111111 10011101 00101011 00001101 11001110 00100011 00000111 00011101
11001001 10100011 00101010 01111000 11000111 00011001 11111100 11101010 10110100 01101100
10010001 10001111 10001111 10111011 01001111 00111000 00000011 00100111 10101101 00110000
00011111 10111111 10111000 00001100 11100111 10101111 10100101 00111000 01110010 10011001
11111100 11110011 01001001 11011000 01110110 01100011 01011100 01110101 11100000 11100010
10010011 00111011 10100101 00011100 00011100 00000001 10001111 11111110 10111101 00101000
00000000 11001000 11101100 01110010 01001111 10111111 11111000 01010000 10100000 00011001
00001001 11001001 00011100 11110101 10100110 10011011 11011000 01001101 01011000 01000100
01011100 00110001 11101011 10011111 01110011 01000011 11100000 01100001 10001000 11100001
00111011 01010010 00001111 10010100 10010010 00001111 01010011 11010110 10010101 10110000
01001001 01010000 01111101 11001001 11110101 10100010 01011010 01101100 10000111 10111000
10000000 10011100 01100100 10010000 01001001 11101100 00111011 01010010 00000110 11111110
11110111 01011010 01000111 10010011 00011000 11000000 11101001 01000001 00000111 11111000
10001111 00110100 00111011 10110001 10011101 01100001 00100000 00001100 00001010 01110110
00000110 00111001 10100110 10000101 00111100 10010111 11111100 00110001 11011110 10010000
00000010 01001110 01110000 01000001 11110111 00110100 11101101 01111110 10000100 00001111
01010001 11110010 01101110 11100100 11100111 11010110 10011000 11100100 11100000 00100001
00011100 11100111 10010011 01001011 10000110 00001001 10011100 01111110 00000010 10011101
10010010 01011011 10100001 11111010 10011010 00010010 11100100 11011100 01000010 10101111
00011000 11011000 00111000 10100100 11101010 01111110 01111110 10111101 01110001 10001010
01101110 01010111 11001100 11000000 11011111 10011110 11110100 11110101 11101111 11011110
10001011 11101011 10101001 01010111 00010011 00111100 11100101 11000110 01111101 00111101
10101000 01010011 10111000 11110100 11100011 10111101 00101011 00011100 11110100 11000110
01111101 00001111 01101010 00110000 01000001 11110111 10101011 11100110 11101100 01001000
10001100 00000001 10010011 00100000 11111101 00101000 00100000 01110110 00111000 10100001
01111010 11100011 10011010 01101110 01110000 01111011 01100000 01110111 10101000 10111101
11000000 00110010 00001001 11000111 00100010 10011100 11011001 11001110 00000111 11100111
01001101 01011001 00000100 10011100 11100011 10001110 11100100 11010001 10000010 01001111
01011110 00101000 11010100 01100000 11100111 00011100 01111010 11010001 11011011 10010011
10000000 00001101 00011101 00011111 00100011 10011111 01101100 01010011 10110001 10010011
10010001 01000010 10111011 01110111 00000010 00110111 11111001 10001110 01000001 00100000
01100110 10100100 01110001 10001010 01101110 11101101 10000111 00011101 11000000 11100110
10001110 00011000 10001100 10011111 11000010 10010100 10000000 01001100 00000100 00111000
00000011 00000011 10101110 01101001 11101101 10011100 00010010 01101000 00100111 00100111
10101111 00000011 10110101 00011000 11001110 01001001 00010100 11110100 00000001 10111001
00000000 01110100 11100110 10011101 11010010 10001110 00000001 11001001 11100000 01010000
00001010 10010001 01010100 11000100 00110101 10110010 01011000 00011100 11111110 01110100
01111111 00010111 11001111 10000010 01111101 00101000 01010000 01001001 00100100 10010001
11000111 01101010 01000101 00000101 01000011 10010011 11001001 00110101 10011010 00000001
01010100 10110001 11001110 00111000 00000010 10011010 10100101 10001110 01001001 00111001
00111101 10101010 01001110 00110011 11001001 11000110 01101001 10000100 00011100 01110000
01110001 11110100 10100111 10101101 11000110 00101000 00011100 01110000 00111001 11101111
01001000 00010111 00000000 10010011 11010110 10000110 01101110 10011111 00110110 00101001
01110111 00001101 10111001 00000111 00111001 11101000 01101000 01101111 01000001 00000110
00110001 11010100 01110101 10100100 01111100 11110101 00100111 10011111 01001010 00010100
10011100 10010011 11011110 10000010 10111100 10010011 10011100 11100110 10001101 11110100
00000001 10001010 01011011 11100111 11110101 11110101 10100010 00110001 10000100 11001001
00111100 11010011 10110000 01110000 01111101 00000111 01101010 01101110 00001110 01110010
01101001 00110111 11010100 01100011 10111001 11001000 11110100 11101110 00101001 01111000
00100011 10011110 10010100 11000110 00100100 11110001 11010001 00111011 10010001 01001111
11000000 11011010 00111010 11110101 10100011 10010111 01000000 00000110 01101110 00110000
00111010 10011010 00000001 01100010 10011001 01101110 00001111 01111100 01010010 00110000
00011011 11000001 11111100 10101001 11011001 00111100 00010001 11010110 10000111 10110110
10100000 00100110 11101110 10100000 00011100 00011010 00011111 00111000 11001111 11100101
01000011 01111100 10100000 11101100 00011100 10010011 01000010 11100100 10011100 10011010
00010100 01101110 10000000 01000100 11001110 11100010 00001111 11100010 01101001 11011001
11100011 10000001 01001001 10010001 11001111 10101101 00011100 00010011 10000000 11010100
01101010 10011101 10000100 00100111 00000000 11101110 01110010 01111101 10000111 10100101
00101011 00010000 01000000 11000001 10100100 11100000 11110001 11010110 10010111 10001110
11010100 00101101 00000110 00011001 00000000 11100100 10010011 01000111 01010000 00111011
00011111 01011010 00111111 01011010 00110010 00111010 00001110 10110101 01011110 10000000

00100011 10010101 11000000 00011001 11101011 11010010 10010101 01010111 10000000 00101000
11110100 00011001 11101001 11101101 01001001 10011100 01111110 01111110 10110101 00001111
01000000 00010101 11110010 00111000 11101111 11101011 01000011 01110100 11001001 00111000
11100111 00010100 10011000 11001001 00100111 10011110 01001101 00011011 01000000 01101100
11110011 11111000 11010011 11010000 00000001 11001111 11101111 00000010 10000001 11000111
01110010 01101000 11001111 00111000 00010100 11101110 10011101 00000101 00100010 00011110
01110001 11011100 01110101 10100001 10100110 00000010 00101011 01100101 01001110 11001111
10100110 01101001 10101111 10011111 00101111 01101110 00110010 01001101 00111001 00110001
11010000 01110100 10100001 10110011 10010001 10001110 10110101 00111101 01101100 00000010
11100000 10000000 00000000 11101001 11101110 01101001 00001111 00010100 10101101 10011110
00000111 01101010 01000110 11111111 00000000 11000111 10101010 10000000 01101111 00111111
01000001 01001111 01101110 01000111 10100101 00011101 10000000 11101010 01101000 01110001
11101000 01111110 10111001 10100011 01110110 00000011 00010000 01100101 11110010 00110001
10011110 11100011 00110100 11100010 01000010 10001100 10011110 10011110 10110100 00010000
00000000 11001101 00011000 11001000 10101001 01110111 01000000 00011001 11100011 00100111
11110010 10100010 01010110 00001010 10111110 10100111 10110000 00000010 10011010 11111000
01100000 00111101 01110011 01000011 10001110 10000000 10011110 10110101 01001000 01110110
00001100 10110110 11000000 00001001 11100100 11010010 01110100 11001110 01111001 10100111
11100111 11100110 11001111 11110111 00101001 10100011 10010001 11001111 01011010 01010111
10110011 10110000 10000011 10111000 00011110 10110100 10000000 01110011 10010110 11101011
01001010 11000011 00000111 01110001 10100111 01110100 00111001 10100101 01110000 00011000
11111000 11000000 11110100 00100111 10001100 11010000 11000111 11100101 11000101 01000111
11011100 00010011 10000011 11111101 00101010 01001110 00000110 01001110 00110011 01001001
10000000 00001100 00101001 00011011 11001001 11001011 11100100 11010010 00101111 11001100
10111001 00000011 00011001 00110100 10111000 00000100 10010010 01000001 11100111 10111101
00000011 11101111 00010001 10011010 10111110 01011011 00000000 00001111 10011000 11111111
00000000 01011010 01001110 01111001 01100111 00011100 01100011 10001100 01010010 10010110
00100000 11100001 00000111 00011110 11110100 10001010 00111110 01111110 10111101 10110001
10001010 00110100 01100011 01100000 10111101 00000001 00111111 01011100 00001010 00110010
01110110 10010010 11100011 10111111 00000000 11010000 11011101 10101001 01000010 10101000
00111001 01110011 11010110 10010100 01101111 11010000 01000011 00011011 10010000 01111000
00100100 11100011 00111000 00010100 01100011 00011011 00010111 00011001 01110011 11001001
11110110 10100111 10001100 00010110 00011100 11100110 10011000 00110010 01100100 00100111
10001010 10010100 11111100 10000000 01110011 10001100 00011110 00000110 00001101 00110001
01000110 00100100 00101101 11011011 00110100 11111101 11000100 00011100 11100011 00111110
11010100 00100001 00000000 10010010 00001101 01010011 01110111 01111010 10000000 11010000
01110011 10000010 11111101 11111101 11101000 01010010 00001110 01111101 01000111 00000100
01010000 11111100 11100111 00100100 01010011 01110010 00001001 10010000 01110100 11001001
00000111 10011010 00011011 10111110 11001100 01111010 10001010 10000111 11110111 01100011
11111001 11010000 10000011 00011101 11110000 00101000 11000110 01110000 10111101 10000111
01101111 01011010 01010111 10010000 00001000 11111001 11110100 11000111 01001010 01001010
11101011 01110001 00001000 01110000 01010000 10011110 10110100 10001110 00110001 10111100
11111010 11010001 00011111 00000011 11011011 11011110 10010101 11111001 11000111 00011111
00100001 11101010 01101001 11101000 01011000 10000100 10000010 11100011 10000011 11001000
10100101 01011100 11101110 00111101 00000000 10100000 01111101 11010001 10010011 10001111
01101010 00110111 01100000 01101101 00000011 00011110 11100110 10001011 11011001 11101010
00000010 00101000 00111001 11101011 10011100 11010000 11000100 00000011 10000111 11111111
00000000 11110101 11010000 00001001 00101111 10011110 11000010 10011010 01010100 00001110
01111010 10011100 11100111 00110101 00101101 00000000 11110110 00111000 00111100 01110101
11110100 10100100 10001000 00010000 00000110 01101000 01101110 00010000 01100111 10101001
10100110 11100111 00000000 10010100 00011111 10001001 10100011 01000110 01000000 11110000
00111000 11011100 01111010 01111111 00111010 01100111 00100100 10001110 11000011 11010010
10011100 11011111 00101010 00010001 10011100 00011110 11010100 11010100 00111100 00010011
11010000 01110110 00110101 01101010 11010110 00101100 01000000 11011001 01101100 10001100
10010011 11010010 10010001 00000001 00100100 11110100 11000000 10100101 00000111 10000001
11011011 11011110 10010101 10001001 00000011 00000000 11100100 11100011 11010010 10110011
10111011 00000001 10111100 00000000 01111000 10100101 11101011 11110011 01100111 00000011
11010110 10001101 10111000 00111101 01111000 10100000 10001100 00101000 11011010 01101011
01001110 10111010 10010000 00100010 00010110 01100010 00000001 11101001 10001110 00000101
00110101 10000111 00111001 11101101 01010010 00101001 00100111 10100001 11101010 00101001
10110001 00101110 00011000 00000100 11111100 01110010 01111010 10011010 10011110 10100101
01011000 00011011 10000000 00000001 11101010 01001111 01000001 01000011 10101000 00000111
00011101 01101001 10111100 00010010 00011000 00110111 11011100 11101010 01101000 00011001
00000111 10001010 10100111 01101110 10000010 10111000 01100011 00111001 00101000 00111111
00011110 10010100 00101000 11011010 01111110 11110001 11110111 10100111 00010101 00101100
01110001 11010011 11010111 10011010 10001111 10001100 10010000 00110001 11101110 01101010
00010010 00101000 01101111 10010110 00000010 11111001 01011101 01111011 11010011 11111010
10010011 11011010 10010111 10100111 00111101 11101000 01010011 10010010 00001110 00110010
01111101 00101010 10110100 00000001 10101010 00111001 11100100 01110010 00111011 01010010
11101101 00011011 11001001 00111101 00101001 00011011 00100100 11110011 11011111 10101001
10100101 01100000 01001011 00001100 01110001 11011100 10011010 00011110 10100100 00000110
00110111 00010011 11010111 00011001 11001110 00101001 10001100 01001011 01001011 10111000
11110000 10011111 01110001 01000000 10100111 00001101 11000100 10000001 11011011 11010111

11010110 10010101 01110001 10001100 01110011 10000000 11011100 00000001 01001101 01101011
10110011 00000000 01010000 01110110 11100010 10000110 11101001 10001110 10011001 10100101
11001111 00001110 00111000 00000000 00011110 01110001 01010001 10111110 01011010 01000000
00000111 01001110 11100110 10100010 11101101 10111011 00000000 00110110 11100110 00011100
01111010 01110000 00111111 11001111 01111010 00001000 00000000 11100000 11010011 10100101
01100001 11100110 11100000 00011110 10000111 10000000 00101001 01010011 00011110 01100000
00100000 01110100 11101001 10011010 10111101 01010001 01100011 00001000 00011000 01111100
10011111 01101100 11010000 11000111 01101100 01100001 01010000 01110010 01111101 01111101
00101001 00010000 11100110 00110100 11011111 10011100 11100111 10111001 10100010 01011100
10011001 00001010 11100011 00000100 11110000 01101000 11010110 11011010 00001001 10000111
01011100 11100111 10010001 01000001 11100001 10110110 10000001 10001101 10011101 01001111
10100101 00001110 10101010 10101001 11110011 10011110 00010111 10110000 11101111 01001000
10100100 10011001 01011100 11110010 00110011 11001001 10100010 11110111 11010000 01100000
11110010 00001110 10000011 10011111 01000011 01000001 11101001 10000011 11010100 11110101
10100110 00000110 11110011 00001001 11100000 11110101 11100010 10011111 10010011 10011110
10011100 00001110 10111110 11110101 00001101 10000000 11001100 01100100 11101101 11000111
11100111 11011110 10010111 10000101 00011111 00111111 01001111 01001010 01110011 00011101
11010010 00010001 11010000 01100011 10001110 01101001 10101110 00110000 01001011 00010011
01010111 11010000 00000110 10101110 11100010 01111001 11101110 01110011 01000010 10001100
00101111 01001010 10010000 00011110 00000011 01110100 00000110 10100011 01010010 11011110
01110001 11100011 00001000 00111010 00000001 11011110 10001101 00011001 00000010 10110111
01101110 01111111 00011010 01100011 00001101 11011101 01001001 11000111 10101111 10101101
00111111 00111100 01100011 10100101 00100010 00010010 10111111 10000101 01000101 10011010
01111010 10010110 00110101 10111001 00011100 01111010 11010000 10000011 00110010 00011101
10111000 11110111 10101000 11010110 01001111 01010001 11010100 11110101 00110100 11111110
00000010 11111100 10000011 10101101 01010010 11010100 00000101 01100000 01110010 01000000
11101111 11010000 10011010 01000000 01111000 01001101 10011101 10001111 00100111 11010110
10010001 11000110 11100000 01000110 01110001 10011110 10110100 11100100 11000111 00001010
00000110 00111101 10101010 01010101 10011011 00010101 11000110 11000100 00000100 01101001
11111010 00001010 00001000 11100111 00100111 10101111 01011100 11010100 01101011 00100111
10011000 11000100 10001110 01010000 00110001 00011001 10101001 00011000 11100001 00110001
11101011 11010100 11010001 10101101 11101100 00001100 01101110 11010000 00001110 01001111
01111111 11010110 10001110 01110010 00001111 11100111 01000000 00000100 10010001 11000001
11111100 01101000 01101110 01111010 00011010 10111101 10000100 10000011 10111001 11101011
10001010 01000100 00111100 01100000 10101110 00111001 11111101 00101001 01011100 01100100
11100011 10110110 00111001 10100111 01111111 00011111 00011110 10010101 00010110 10110110
10000101 00000111 11110001 01100111 11110100 10101000 11010100 00101010 10010010 01110001
11001011 01110011 11010110 10011100 11000111 00110001 10010001 11001000 11001001 11101101
11011110 10010011 10000001 00100110 00110001 11010000 01110001 01010110 10101110 11111010
00000000 00110000 11110100 00011111 10001111 10101101 00001111 11010011 11010100 11111101
01101001 00001111 11001100 00000101 00101110 11011100 11110001 11101001 11011110 10101001
00100100 01001110 10100010 00101111 00011101 01111001 10100011 00100001 00110010 01110011
11110011 11100011 10101111 10100101 00101011 10011100 10100111 11011101 11001101 00110001
00111000 11110111 00110101 00101110 01011010 10001101 10100000 01001101 10100000 00010001
11010100 10001110 01001001 00110100 11100101 11001001 00011001 11000111 01001110 01110011
11101001 01000010 11100011 00000111 10000001 11001001 11100110 10000010 01001001 01001101
10100000 01110000 01001110 01001110 01101001 01001001 00010010 00110001 11000011 01101100
10001101 01000001 11111110 00101100 10110001 00111101 11000101 00101011 00011111 01000101
11111010 10010001 01001110 01100011 10010010 01000111 01011010 01100100 10111011 10001000
11011010 10000011 10000010 01000001 11001001 00110100 10010001 01100010 10011100 11110000
01001000 00100111 11010011 00010100 00110001 11111101 11011001 01100001 11010100 00001110
11110100 00010110 00100000 11100100 10011100 11100111 10000001 10001010 01101011 10010010
10111101 01111010 01110100 00000011 11011110 10101001 01001001 01110101 00010101 10000101
11000111 11001000 00000001 11101110 00111001 11000101 00101001 00100011 00100011 00001011
11011010 10000110 11001110 11100000 00001011 01110000 00001111 00110100 10011100 10010110
11111011 11011100 10011110 01101000 01110110 10111000 11000100 01100000 00001000 00100001
10111011 01110110 00010100 11010010 01001000 01011111 10010111 10010011 11010100 11010011
11110001 10011101 11100111 00011101 01111011 11010100 01100100 10010000 00000000 11011011
11001001 00111101 00101010 10011011 11010000 00000101 11111001 10001010 00010010 01001111
11010110 10011011 10011100 10111000 11111110 11100000 11100000 00010001 11011110 10010100
11111100 11010010 00010101 11111110 00001110 11110100 10001100 01001110 01110001 11101001
11011111 00010100 10110110 01000100 11101110 00000010 01001111 10011110 01010010 00000000
00011101 10000101 00011011 01011000 00010001 10010010 00110011 01000000 00000000 00010001
10001110 10010100 10101010 11100101 10100100 11000101 01001101 11101111 10100011 00000001
00111011 00010000 00001110 01001001 00111101 01101001 10101100 01111001 10100111 00101001
11100000 00001100 11111101 01101001 10101100 01001000 00111101 00010111 11110010 10100110
10101100 00111101 01011001 11010110 01100101 10111011 01100011 11101000 01101000 01011100
10001110 01110111 00000010 01111010 10011100 10011010 01000100 00111001 11110111 11111110
10010100 10111111 00100000 11100011 11101111 10011111 01001010 10101101 01010001 00100011
10110111 01100111 10010011 11000000 11110101 00010100 00100110 01110011 10011010 01101010
11100011 00011000 10100001 10011011 10001100 01110100 00000011 10100001 10100011 01111101
11000000 01110110 01001001 01100011 10011110 10011110 11110100 11001001 01001001 00100011
00001000 01000000 10100111 10101001 00011011 00000001 11001111 00110100 01110010 00110001

10010001 11110101 11001101 00100100 10000000 01101010 01100101 01000001 11000001 11001000
00111110 10110100 11100101 00100100 01110111 11000111 10111001 10100110 10101011 00010010
01001111 00100100 01010001 10000000 01001110 01110011 01000011 01010110 00010000 11101100
10011101 10000011 10010011 11001111 01111111 01011010 01101100 01011101 00001111 00111101
11101001 00011011 00011000 00100111 00111100 11010011 11110010 01110110 11110100 11111101
01101010 10000000 01101011 00011111 11011110 01100000 10001111 10010000 01010011 10001001
00100110 10011010 00001110 01111010 10001010 01000101 00111011 10110011 11011000 01010011
01001010 11001111 01010000 00010111 10110111 00010100 00001111 11000111 10001010 00000000
00000111 10100111 01101110 00110011 01000110 11100000 01010111 10100001 00000011 11010110
10100001 10000000 00101001 11000111 11010100 11111010 11010000 01111110 01001100 01111100
10100100 10010011 11010000 01010010 01111101 11100110 11001001 00111101 00111010 01010010
10110110 11101100 01110101 11100111 11010100 11010010 01001010 11011011 10001100 01001111
10011101 10001110 01001110 00000111 10110101 00000101 10001110 01000111 00000111 01100111
10110000 10100101 11111110 00001100 01100111 11101011 01000001 11000010 10000000 00000111
00100100 10001010 01100010 00011100 10111100 10000011 10010000 01000000 11110111 10100110
10011100 11100011 11110000 11100010 10010011 11100110 00000011 00011001 11111100 00101000
11001110 00110110 00101011 00000011 10010011 11011110 10001011 00110101 10100000 11101110
00101000 11001001 11100111 11010110 10001110 00111001 11000110 01000111 10111101 00000111
11111101 01100111 10101101 00100011 10011110 00110001 10001100 10011010 01101100 01000010
00110001 00111001 00000000 01110111 11101011 01001110 01101110 00110001 10000011 10001010
01000101 00011100 00001100 11111110 01111001 10100101 11000111 01000001 11011110 10010011
11010000 01100010 00111111 01001110 00000111 00100111 10100101 00101000 00011100 00001110
11000110 10010001 11001001 00000100 01100011 10011010 01010011 11001111 00110100 10110101
01111010 10110000 00001101 11011101 10000000 11100000 11010011 01000111 01110010 11111001
00111110 10011101 10101000 11000110 00010011 00111001 11000001 10100011 00111100 01110100
11001101 01001010 10111101 11000100 00001100 00110011 10011100 11110111 11101111 01000111
00111111 01011010 01010110 11100111 00000000 11110000 00101000 01100010 01110011 11000111
01001111 01101010 00011000 11000011 01101111 10100101 00011000 10100011 01101001 00000011
00111001 10100101 00000111 00100011 00110101 01101001 00000000 01110100 00011101 00101000
00011111 10101111 10101101 00100011 01100000 10000000 00111010 10010011 11010011 00010100
01100111 10011111 10100111 01011010 01001010 11101100 00000101 11101101 10011110 11111101
10110011 01001101 01111110 00001111 00100110 10000110 00100011 01101000 11011110 00111010
01010010 11100111 10101111 10100101 00101011 11011011 01000110 00000010 01100101 01111000
00100000 11110001 01001110 11000110 01001110 01111000 11001001 10100100 11100011 10101110
00111111 00111010 00011000 11100000 01010101 00110001 00000001 00111100 01010010 11100111
00010100 10011100 11110011 10011010 01000000 00111001 11100100 11100110 10100001 00001100
00111001 00111101 00001101 00111011 00011111 11100100 11010011 01001011 01100011 10100111
11100011 01000111 00101101 11010110 10011010 11010111 01110001 00001010 00111000 11001101
00011101 10111001 00010100 01101110 00001011 11000111 01011010 01100010 11100111 00111110
10010101 00101101 11011011 01000010 10010000 11100100 00000100 10011110 01001000 11111010
01010010 10101001 11100100 10001100 00010001 11101111 01000001 11100011 00010100 10001010
00001000 00111100 10011110 00101010 11010000 10000111 01100100 11110011 10000001 11111000
11010100 01001000 10111000 00111001 00100111 00101110 01111011 11010100 10001101 10011101
11011101 01111110 01001010 00011011 11010100 00001010 00111100 11000000 00001110 00000111
00011101 01101001 00111001 00111000 11011010 00111110 10110100 01100011 00010010 01100111
00111111 10011101 00101010 10001100 00100111 01010011 11111000 01010010 10111110 10110111
00000001 00111001 11000001 00111001 11111010 01010000 00110000 01001000 11011010 01110010
01111011 11010000 00111110 11101111 00100011 10010001 01001101 01110001 11000000 11100011
10101101 00111011 11110110 00000001 11100001 10000001 11001110 00111011 01010100 01111011
10001001 01110111 00000111 11010111 00000010 10010100 11100001 01010111 00111110 10110100
11100101 00011000 00100011 00000110 10001111 01010000 00011011 00101000 11001011 01110001
11010100 00001110 10010100 11100100 11001110 00000111 10101111 01111010 01101111 11011101
11001110 00111101 01101000 11000001 11101001 11010011 10111001 10101000 11011101 10000000
00000000 01000011 01010000 10100000 10000010 01001011 10010000 01111011 11110100 10100010
01001100 10010000 01111100 10110011 11111000 11010010 00000010 01000000 00011101 01111101
10000001 10101010 10111101 10010101 11011010 00000000 00011100 10011100 10000001 11000111
10100101 00001001 11000011 01110100 00011111 01011010 01111010 10001101 10100000 10011100
01100100 11111010 01010011 00000110 01001001 00101100 01110001 11110100 00011101 10101001
01011111 01011101 00000000 01011001 00001001 00011000 00010100 11010011 00100000 11110011
00001110 00000111 00000000 01100011 00111110 11110100 10111001 11111001 10001110 01111010
01010000 00110010 01000111 00111110 10111001 11000101 00110110 00111011 00001100 01010001
11110010 01100111 00011001 00100111 10010011 01001111 11100100 11100000 10001111 11001010
10010011 10001111 01011110 11110100 01100000 00011000 11110111 00111111 00000010 10010011
10011101 10000100 00101010 10001100 10010001 11000111 11100001 01000111 01000110 11110111
11101111 01001000 11100111 00100111 01100000 00011100 01100011 00101100 01001111 11101001
01001101 11011101 10110110 00111100 11110101 00100100 01010010 10111101 11010111 01110000
00100100 00100000 00101000 00111011 10110010 01001001 11100110 10011010 01111010 00010010
10000011 10011111 01010011 01001101 01011110 00001111 00100111 00100100 11111010 01010011
10111111 11100101 10100000 01010000 01110011 11011110 10000110 10101101 10111000 00001101
11000110 01000001 10100011 00011000 00011101 01111001 11101001 11001101 00111010 01010010
11011110 01011110 00100011 00000000 10011100 11010011 01110001 10011110 01011100 10001110
00111010 10011110 11010101 01011011 11101010 00000011 01000010 10010110 01110001 11101001
11011011 10011010 10010011 00000100 01001001 10001110 00001000 10100110 10100001 11011111

00101011 10110111 10100111 00000000 01111011 01010000 11100011 00000000 00000000 01001110
01001001 11100100 10011010 10010101 01111110 10000101 10001010 10111111 01111011 11100110
11101011 01001101 11001111 00111000 00001010 01001001 00110100 00101001 00011110 01100001
11000110 01110010 01111011 11110100 10101001 00000000 11011010 10001001 11101111 11010100
01010101 01011001 11011011 01010010 00001000 11111010 10111000 00111000 11000001 11101010
01111000 11101011 01000100 01001011 10010001 11001001 11100111 11010010 10010101 01110111
01110010 00111000 00000111 11010110 10010000 00010010 10101011 10001110 11111110 10110100
01101001 01110000 00000010 11011100 11100000 00001100 10011100 11110101 00010100 10100000
00010011 11001011 10001111 10010011 10101101 00111001 00001001 01010100 00011000 00011111
00111110 01110000 00000001 10101000 01100101 01101110 00010000 01100000 11101100 00011111
01111000 11010100 10110101 10101001 01010110 00100101 11110100 11001111 01001010 01100011
01100111 01101111 11110111 11010011 11010100 11111111 00000000 10000101 00011001 11000001
11110101 11100011 10100001 11101110 01101000 00000000 11100011 00000100 11110101 11100110
10101101 10100110 11001001 00000101 00011001 00111100 11010001 10010000 11011001 00100000
01110001 11011010 10000101 01101110 10100100 00001100 01010010 10101001 01010000 01111010
11110100 10101001 10111111 01010110 00000010 00100001 11101010 01001111 00011100 01100111
00010100 11011100 11100000 01110010 01110001 11001111 00000111 11010110 10000011 10010110
11111111 00000000 01010011 11000000 11000111 11100111 01001110 01100100 11100101 00110011
11001110 00000111 00010100 11010110 10100011 10111000 00010010 01000000 11001111 00000011
11110000 10100110 11111100 10101011 10000000 00110010 01110011 11001001 00100110 10000110
00011101 10001011 01110011 01001110 00100000 00000101 00000111 00111001 10100110 10111100
11000100 00110101 10110000 01010100 11100111 10011111 10101101 00111001 00000111 00111001
10100110 10001100 00011010 01001111 10111011 11000001 11111100 11101010 00010110 11000101
10001010 01111110 01010001 10011110 00101001 10100000 11100010 00100010 01000000 00111100
10011010 01110001 00000000 10011110 01001001 11100100 01010011 10111011 11100010 10000111
01110010 00000110 00110111 01001111 01101110 11100100 11010000 11001010 01110000 01000111
01111010 01000111 01100010 01110000 00000000 11000000 00100011 11110011 10100001 10110010
01001001 00011001 11101011 11111010 11010101 01000101 00001101 10001010 00001001 01000101
00101100 00110001 10010001 01001000 10100011 01101110 11000011 11000110 01101001 10101101
11000000 11100100 11111101 00101001 11101010 00001011 01100011 01110000 11101101 10001010
10000100 11111011 00001110 11000100 01101010 00000010 10100001 00100100 01110100 11100110
10010100 10000111 11001000 11000110 00110011 11011111 00110100 11100110 11000011 00001100
01110000 00000000 11101111 11010110 10011000 11100000 11001001 00010011 10101100 00101101
10110000 01110111 01100011 11011110 10011010 01010111 11011000 10010001 01110001 10011111
01111100 10001010 01101010 10101111 00011000 00000100 01111101 01000101 00111001 01111001
00111000 00111100 10010001 01000011 01110000 01000000 11101000 01001111 11101001 01010111
10100010 01111010 00000000 10001010 01000110 00111000 11101011 11011110 10000101 01100000
00110111 11100111 10011100 01110100 00000010 10010011 10011110 01110001 11101011 01001010
00000011 01110001 10010011 11000101 00101110 10100101 10000010 01110111 11110101 11101101
01000011 00010001 10000011 11011100 11111011 01010011 00110010 01001001 00100010 10011100
10111111 10111011 00011001 00111000 00100101 11000111 00000010 10011101 11110101 11010000
10010110 00101110 01000000 10001100 11100100 11100011 00110100 01110000 00010011 00000011
00111011 11001111 01101010 01001100 11100011 00000000 10001110 01111010 11010010 11100111
01110000 00111011 00111011 11110101 00110100 01001001 10001000 01100110 00110110 11000110
01110110 01111111 10111110 01001001 11101111 01001110 01000011 11001110 00111010 11111010
10011110 11010100 11010110 11001000 10001111 00001001 11110111 00000111 00010100 11100101
00000011 10000001 10011110 01111110 10010100 10100010 11111010 10000000 11011000 11010111
00111100 10111111 01111110 01001001 10100000 00110001 11011001 10011101 10111000 00011001
11101001 11101101 01001110 11001000 00000100 11111010 01100011 00110100 11001100 10010010
00101000 10010110 11100101 10001000 10111100 11001001 10000000 00110010 00000111 01111110
11011001 10100111 01001010 11000000 10010000 01000111 00100100 11110101 11111100 00101000
01101111 01001100 01100000 00001010 01110011 10001111 11011101 10010010 00001001 11100100
01110001 01010011 11010111 01110010 01001000 11100101 00101010 01011100 00101001 11100111
10001100 10011100 01110110 10100101 01001110 10111001 11101110 01111011 11010011 00000001
11011100 01110011 11010000 01111010 01010100 10000011 00000000 00011100 01111010 11010010
01101101 10110110 01010000 11011110 10001000 01010000 00010011 10111100 00010001 10010011
10001010 00011100 10000001 00011001 00111101 11000111 01000001 11101011 01001101 01100001
11001001 00000000 01110010 01111001 10100111 10001100 01100000 01111110 10111100 11010101
11110101 00100111 01010001 10000001 01110010 11100001 10101001 10100000 10011001 01011100
10110110 01111110 01001110 10000000 01010100 10001011 10011100 11101110 00111100 00001110
11000011 11010010 10011000 01110010 10111100 00001110 10111111 11001010 10011011 01011010
10001000 01010110 11100111 00000011 01110111 01001010 10001001 10001111 11011111 00111101
11110011 11000111 11010010 10100100 00000011 00100111 00010100 10001011 11010111 10001111
11000110 10000110 10110100 11010000 01101000 00011100 11110000 00101000 11111010 11110111
00111001 10100001 10000110 01011100 00010000 00111010 01010000 10111001 11001001 00100111
11110000 00010100 10111010 01101010 00000011 00111110 01011101 10100100 10111110 00111010
11010001 10001100 10000011 10001110 10011101 10001101 00101001 00000100 10100010 01110100
11110111 00110100 11111100 11110000 00001111 01101010 00101110 10000110 11001000 10100101
11001001 00100000 01110110 00000011 00100100 11010001 11000001 00111001 00000011 00000110
10010110 01001100 10010100 00011000 11110101 11100110 10000001 10001100 01110011 01000001
00100000 10101011 10111000 00100100 01101000 00111001 11001111 01011010 00000011 00101011
01111100 11010001 10011100 10100000 11100000 00011010 00011001 10001000 01001100 11100000
11100011 00111011 00000101 00110001 01100011 00010001 10000000 00000000 11000000 00011101

10101010 01010110 10100101 10000011 00001101 11011001 11001001 00111000 00000111 11110011
10100111 00111001 00000000 01101101 11001111 11001110 00110001 11000000 11101101 01000000
11000110 01110010 10100010 10011011 11001111 10011000 11101101 10000000 01110011 11011111
11010010 10101111 01100001 00100100 00111000 01110101 00111011 10101001 10100000 00010000
00111111 00011010 00010111 10100111 00110100 11101100 10010000 00111001 10101000 10111011
01101100 01100011 01110001 11101011 01001000 11000111 00111001 11101001 11001101 00000011
11100110 00000100 11110110 11001111 11100111 01000111 01111110 10011000 00011000 10100110
11010011 01001100 10000000 01111100 11110110 11100011 11110001 10100101 10010001 10000010
10100000 00000100 11110101 11101001 10011010 01101011 01100101 10100100 11011100 01111000
00000000 01100000 00001111 11110001 10100111 00110111 01010000 00111101 11110010 00101001
10100101 11010001 10010101 01111011 00001101 01101100 10000100 00011000 10100011 00000100
10010010 01110001 10000001 01001010 11111100 00111110 11010001 11010100 11110011 11111111
00000000 11010111 10100001 01111110 11100111 11001010 00001001 00110100 11101101 10101101
10000110 00100110 00111001 11001001 00111111 10000101 00011100 10101000 11110111 00110100
11011100 00011100 00010001 10011100 01110011 10011100 11010011 10111010 00000010 01111001
11000101 00101101 01010010 10111000 00001101 11001110 00111001 11110100 10100100 11101111
10111000 11100111 10011010 01010110 11100111 10001111 01011010 00111000 00000101 00111001
11111001 11101010 00101110 11011110 11000000 00111001 10111110 01000100 00111001 00111101
01111000 00000011 00011001 11100110 10011000 11101010 00000011 11110101 11001110 11001110
10011110 11010100 10111100 10011100 00001100 01100100 01111010 00001010 01110110 00111001
10010011 00111101 00000111 01010011 01010111 01111110 10001100 00000110 10111010 01110000
01111001 11100000 00011100 10011111 01110011 01010001 11100000 11100100 10010010 01111101
10101001 11000011 00100100 00011101 11111000 11001001 11100110 10001000 10001001 10010010
01010010 00000111 01000001 11000000 10101010 01101101 10000000 01110110 11001111 10100101
00001110 00000000 11001001 00100011 00111101 11111000 11101101 01001101 01101110 10000101
01110011 11110101 00100011 10111101 00100011 10101000 00100111 10011111 01001110 10010100
10010011 01111101 01000000 00010100 10010000 01111110 01000000 01110010 11011101 11001101
00001001 10001101 11011011 01001001 00000011 10011110 01111101 01001101 00101011 00010011
10111011 10100000 11110110 10100110 10100111 00011100 00011100 11100111 10101110 01101001
00101011 10111101 11000000 01010010 01111110 01111110 10011000 11000111 10111101 00010001
01111111 00011001 00111111 00100000 10100001 11000001 11000110 00000000 11100111 10111110
01101001 00010011 10001111 10111101 10011111 11110001 10101010 10010010 01010110 00000001
10000011 11100110 01000001 10000000 01110010 01001111 10101101 00101100 10111011 10010110
01000010 00010101 11000010 10001110 11000011 00110100 11100001 11001110 11110010 00111000
11111010 11010011 00011000 01100000 11110011 01010011 00101101 00110110 00100100 11101011
00110011 10110100 00001110 00110000 00101000 01101101 10100011 00011011 11110000 00001111
01101100 01110111 10100000 00110000 00100100 11111101 00101001 01110110 10010010 00110011
11100110 00000001 10001110 11100111 10001010 10100110 11101111 10101010 00010000 01101100
11111101 11100101 00111001 10101001 10101101 11110111 00000001 01010011 10011111 01111010
01110110 00001001 00000011 00000110 10101111 01010110 00000011 01110000 01001000 11001000
10100100 11000011 00010001 10011100 01100100 10011010 01010010 11000100 01100001 01000111
00111100 11110011 01001110 11001000 11110011 00001110 11000011 10011110 11010101 00101100
01000011 00011001 01011000 00100110 00110011 10011100 10011110 01110001 01000110 00001000
00011100 01111110 10110100 01100011 00000100 11110101 11110111 10100101 11101000 00110010
00001000 00000111 11010011 00010101 00101001 11101001 10100000 11000001 01010111 10011110
00111010 01110111 10100000 10001100 11110100 00110100 00110001 11011100 00001111 01100011
11101011 01000110 11001111 10010111 00011000 11000001 10101011 10111101 11000000 00110111
00001100 11100000 01100111 00100011 11010100 01010000 11100111 00111000 00000111 10001010
01000000 00000110 01111110 11110111 00110100 01100011 00001101 10010011 11001001 00011101
00101000 11010001 10110001 00001010 11000011 00001100 01000000 00111111 10000101 00100001
01011100 10101000 11001111 01001111 01001010 00111110 01101101 10011011 10011100 11110011
11101001 01000110 01001110 01111000 11100100 00001010 01001101 00001100 00110010 01000110
01000010 10001110 01101000 01010011 00100111 00111001 00000011 00000111 11010010 10000110
00100000 11110001 10000010 00101001 01110000 01111010 00001110 01000101 00100000 00010011
00011110 10111100 01010001 00010010 10000010 01110010 01001101 00111111 00011000 11101011
01001100 01100011 11110011 01110001 11010010 10011101 10111010 00000000 00101111 01110010
01111010 00001010 01001110 01011001 11110010 00001001 11001111 01101010 01110111 00000111
11011100 11010001 10010011 11111111 00000000 11101010 10100001 11000101 10101101 10000000
01000000 00000000 00111000 11110101 11100111 00110100 10001011 00100110 01001001 01100100
00111001 00011110 11100010 10010111 01110110 01110010 00110110 10011111 10101101 00101010
11100000 00000010 00110001 10001111 01111010 10010100 11110101 11010100 00000110 10100011
00011001 00001001 00101111 11111010 01010010 10110110 00000010 01100011 00111111 10011101
00000100 11100000 11100111 10101001 11110100 10100011 10000011 11001100 10011101 00101001
11011101 00101101 00010000 00000010 10001100 00101111 10111111 10111101 00110000 01101110
11000111 00011000 11000101 00111000 00011111 11011110 00011110 01111000 10100101 01101110
10000011 01100111 00111110 11010100 01011100 00000100 01101111 01001110 11110100 11011100
00011110 10111001 11000111 10110101 00111011 10011110 10100111 10001111 01001100 01010010
11110100 00011100 10000011 10011010 10011101 01000000 01000011 11010111 10011111 11010110
10001100 01101101 11101110 01001001 10100110 10110111 00100011 10011110 10010100 11100100
00011000 11101111 01010100 11010110 10000000 00011001 00100111 11010110 10011101 11011111
10100110 00000101 01000101 10111000 10010011 10000001 11010000 01010011 11000000 11101101
10001110 10110100 10010110 10101000 00000101 01110010 01000000 11111001 00110001 01001000
10000100 10010000 01111000 11111010 11100110 10000011 11011111 11110100 10100101 01011110

00000111 00110100 11010010 01000000 00000011 11100110 00011000 11101111 01000010 10001110
11011101 00101001 00110011 10010010 01110110 01110100 00010100 00101010 10110110 01001111
10011000 01111110 01000011 11010000 01010010 11010101 10110001 11011000 01110111 00011100
00001010 01101001 00111100 11110001 11001000 00010100 01110010 01111010 00011110 00110001
11010110 10000101 00011001 11101001 10011111 10101101 00100110 10010101 11000100 00011001
00011001 11110110 10100001 10011000 00000110 11000000 11101011 10001010 01101110 00110001
11001000 10100100 01100011 10110111 10101111 00100100 11010010 01101111 01011011 00000000
11110100 11101000 01111101 11101001 01010111 00110100 10001100 01110000 00000000 01001110
10100111 11010110 10000100 00011100 01110011 01001111 01000110 00000010 11110001 10000011
11111001 01010000 10111110 10111001 00110100 00110110 00110000 00110001 11011110 10000100
00111111 01011010 10100101 01101110 10100000 00011001 11001000 11001111 10101101 00011011
10000001 00111000 11000111 01001010 01000110 00111000 11101101 01000010 11100011 00011000
11001101 01001011 10111011 00000000 11001000 11000000 11110111 10100000 11101110 00011011
11001111 00011001 00111110 10110100 11011100 00001110 00011001 10001110 00000111 01001010
01110011 10010101 00100000 01100100 11110001 10011010 01001011 01100000 00011010 10101100
00011011 00111000 11101000 00111011 10010001 01010010 01110100 00000011 00100110 10010001
10110110 10011110 00000110 01111110 10110100 10011100 01110111 00111100 00001110 11110100
10010011 10111000 00001010 10011001 11000111 11001111 11111111 00000000 11101011 10100100
11100011 01111110 11011100 11100100 11110111 10100110 00001110 10100111 01111111 01001111
10101101 00001000 10100010 00110010 00110000 10111111 01111111 11011110 10101111 10011001
00000000 11110111 00111011 01001110 00001001 11100110 10011011 10011100 00001100 11110100
10100011 10010110 01110010 01011111 00000000 01110110 00010100 01101110 00100100 11110100
00011011 00111110 10110101 00011011 11101010 00000001 10001110 00001110 00001111 01011110
11110100 00110110 01001111 01111100 01111010 10011111 01011010 00010100 00010011 11010100
01100010 10011101 10011100 01110000 01111000 11001111 01001010 10101000 10000000 11001110
00111010 00000001 01001111 01111100 10000001 11000000 10100100 11001111 01011100 10001110
01101001 00110000 01111000 00111001 11101011 11011010 10000110 11101100 00000011 10110001
10010111 11110110 10100110 11110010 01111001 11101001 01001110 01100001 11001110 00111101
10101001 10011111 11101111 01010001 10111010 00000001 01010100 10000001 11010110 10001100
10010000 00110011 11011111 11111001 01010010 01110010 01011100 10011010 00011111 01101110
11010000 00001000 10100000 00000100 01011100 10011110 10111100 10010011 01000011 10000001
10010001 10111111 10010000 00101001 01010100 10001110 00001111 01111111 01011010 01001100
01110010 00111110 10011101 11101010 01110100 01001100 00000101 01010101 11011100 10011011
10001111 01001110 11000000 11010011 00110010 01111101 00111001 10100111 00111001 11111101
11011111 00011100 01100011 11010110 10010111 10100000 11100100 11110011 01011010 00101011
01011000 10110000 01010001 10000001 11000001 11111010 10011111 01011010 00010100 11100000
10111000 00000011 10010010 00111001 00110100 10001011 10011110 01001000 11101001 10011010
01010111 11001110 11101101 10101010 01101010 00011001 00000011 00111110 11101010 01100000
01111101 00110011 01000011 00011100 00000000 00011111 10010001 11010100 11010011 10011111
00000000 10001101 11100111 11110010 11101111 01001101 01011001 00110000 00001001 11101000
01001111 01001010 10101011 10000000 00101110 01001111 10101000 00011101 01111000 11101111
01000110 00110000 00110111 00011010 01101000 00101101 11001011 01111111 11011111 00110100
10111000 01101111 00101011 00000100 11100111 11111010 01010100 11011111 01010000 00000010
01110011 00110111 00001010 01001001 00000011 00000101 10111101 11101000 00011000 11100111
00100111 00111101 10101001 00010101 10000111 10101001 00111111 11010110 10010100 00000000
00000110 11010000 00000110 01111010 10011110 01111001 10100101 11001101 01110001 11101100
00001011 10011100 10000001 10001010 00110011 10011101 11111110 11011101 00101001 00100101
11001001 11000000 01110110 11011000 10000010 10010101 11111001 00000000 00001110 01000110
00111001 10101011 10110101 11010101 10000001 10111101 01000011 00111100 10001100 00011100
00000001 11010100 11010001 10010010 01010000 10000001 11000000 11110111 10100100 01100000
00000000 00101010 00110001 10011110 10111000 10100111 00101000 11011111 10001100 10011110
10011111 10100101 01000110 10000000 00100110 01111000 11001001 11110101 11100010 10010010
01000011 11110010 10111000 00000011 10011111 10101101 00001100 01000001 01110010 00010011
00111011 00000000 11101011 01001101 10010110 01000101 01010000 00000000 11100101 11001111
01010010 01101001 01011001 11101100 01010000 11100101 11000110 01110110 10001100 01101100
11000111 01011010 00011000 10000001 11001000 11101001 11111100 11101000 11100001 01000001
11100011 00110100 11010111 01101100 01100011 00001010 00001011 10001110 10011110 11010101
10100101 11101100 00000011 11011000 10010011 11000111 01000000 01000101 01000111 11010000
01110001 11011010 10011111 10001100 10000000 01001111 01111110 10111001 10100110 10101000
11001111 00001011 11111001 11010100 01101100 00000011 10111000 11101011 11111000 10011111
01111010 01101110 00110011 11001110 00110001 10010011 11001110 01101000 01011110 11111111
00000000 10010111 10110101 00001000 01001001 01011110 01111011 11110011 10001010 10110110
11110100 11010000 10000000 11001000 11110011 00001000 11101100 00111011 11010000 00001001
11110011 00111001 00011000 00011000 11100011 00110100 10011101 00000111 11100011 01000100
10011100 11110100 00011100 01010010 01001101 01110100 00101100 01111111 00001101 10011100
01110110 11000111 00110100 11011110 10111110 11011110 10100100 11010010 01100000 11100011
10100110 00101001 01000001 11000110 00001111 11101001 01000011 01001000 00000110 11110011
10111111 10011100 01010011 01000001 11101010 01001111 01000010 01111000 10100011 00111001
01110011 10111011 10100101 00111101 11111001 11100000 00011110 00111110 10010100 00101110
11100000 00011100 00010111 11101001 01001010 11011100 10111001 11001111 00001000 00000111
00100110 10011010 10111001 00000111 00101111 10001110 10111110 10010100 11001100 00001110
00010111 00100100 10111001 00100100 10010010 00101010 01011101 11010001 00100011 11011100
11111110 11110011 10000000 01001000 00100011 10111101 00110101 10110010 01000000 00001001

11111111 00000000 11101010 10100111 00010010 01011011 00100111 10100001 11111110 10010100
00100111 00111000 11100011 10101111 10101101 01010100 00010110 10011010 00001101 00000010
10101000 01010111 01110010 00001111 01011110 01001111 00110100 11010111 00101100 11011000
00000011 01100111 00111111 10011101 00011100 00000011 10001110 10111110 11110100 10000100
11100000 11110001 10010010 01111111 00101010 00111010 10010010 00101010 01110010 00111011
01010011 01011000 00001101 11000011 00000111 10100001 11000001 10100111 01101110 11011010
00111110 11101111 00011101 10101001 00010001 01001110 01001001 00111000 11100100 11100111
11010010 10100111 01110111 10101001 01100000 11001010 01010100 11100001 10111000 11100111
10100101 00100011 11100100 00010001 10010001 10011100 01110111 10100000 00110000 11110011
00010001 10000110 01001111 10100111 00010100 11010101 11101000 00110011 11010100 11110101
00110100 00100111 11010000 00000111 01111101 11101110 10011100 00010011 11011110 10011010
10111000 10001100 01110111 11001101 00111100 10010001 11010000 01110010 01000001 11100110
10010000 10000000 01001000 01000000 00001110 00111010 11110001 11010010 10101110 11100010
01000000 11000011 10000001 11111010 11100110 10000111 11011101 10110101 00110110 01100011
00100100 11111110 10010100 10111100 00010001 11001111 01100001 01001100 11110010 11110011
11110011 10010010 01000010 01100011 10100101 01000010 10001110 10010111 00011000 10000111
00000101 11001001 01111110 11011101 01110001 01001011 10010010 01100010 00111100 01100000
01100100 01100011 11011110 10011101 11000011 01100000 00011110 10011110 10110100 11011100
10001111 00101001 00000110 00111010 10011110 00000101 00110110 10011110 11100010 10111000
11101110 01001111 10111101 00110011 00011001 10010100 10000000 00001110 01111101 01101001
01010101 10110011 00011000 11111110 11111110 01111001 11000111 10110101 00110101 00010111
00100000 10011110 11100111 10101101 00101011 10110110 10101110 00001110 11100000 11000100
00101110 11001111 01011100 11110011 01001110 00000111 01110000 11011010 00000111 01010011
11010111 11010010 10010001 00010111 00011000 00001101 11111000 11010010 00001001 01000110
11110011 11100101 10000011 10110000 01111010 11111010 11010101 11000110 01001101 10110010
01000110 01100111 01110100 10111011 10001111 00000000 01100100 00001100 11111010 01010000
00110000 00010111 00111001 11001001 01110011 10011010 00100101 00111011 01100111 01000000
00000110 01110010 00110010 01001001 11101101 11101001 01000100 10101001 10000100 11011000
00111010 10011110 10111111 01001010 00011010 01011010 10110000 00000110 00000100 10100110
00111000 11000110 01111111 10010101 00101010 10111001 00100100 11100100 00000011 11110101
10100100 11000001 11101001 10001111 10100101 00011111 01111011 11010111 00010101 00100000
00011100 00000011 10110111 00111101 10111001 00111000 10100100 01011110 10011000 00000011
00011000 10100011 10110111 00000011 10101101 00101011 01110000 00000101 00011010 10110000
00010011 10000010 00000001 00011111 10010111 10101111 10111101 00011100 01100111 11111010
11010000 10100011 00111001 00111101 00111110 10111110 10010100 01100100 00101000 11011100
01111001 00000011 10111101 00110001 10110000 11001110 11101100 10001110 11011001 10100000
10011111 01101110 10011101 10101001 10111110 10111011 11001111 01101100 10010001 01001000
11011001 00100101 00000000 11100011 11011011 00110101 00111010 11011000 10100000 00100100
10011110 00000101 00001001 11111000 10011110 11111100 00001010 00110001 10110111 10111101
00100011 00011111 10010100 00000000 01110001 10011110 11110101 01001110 11010110 00100000
00111001 00100101 00011000 11100111 00111110 10010100 10101111 11001110 00000000 11101001
11010100 10011111 01011010 00110001 10000000 00000000 11111100 11101001 00000110 01110111
11111101 00101010 01101111 11011100 10110001 01010000 10001100 00010000 00101001 10001010
01001111 00000011 00011000 00011101 11101001 11001011 11010011 00100000 11110101 11101111
01000010 00101110 11011110 00101010 10110100 01100000 00011001 11100011 10100101 00110001
00110010 01101001 01110010 00001011 11100000 01010001 10000011 11011011 11010111 10010011
01010101 10110110 11100100 11101110 00111000 10010000 00111000 11110100 10100110 10110110
01001000 11001001 00111101 00101000 11101010 01110000 00101001 00001001 11000000 11000000
11100110 10001001 01001101 01011100 10100000 11000110 01001111 01011010 01011110 00110011
10011010 01000010 01110010 01000001 00010100 00100110 01010100 10010010 01111001 10101001
11010100 10000000 11111111 00000000 10010110 10011000 01000000 00000110 00000110 00001001
10100110 00001100 00110000 11001000 11001101 00111000 10000110 01110000 01000110 01110011
10011110 10111001 11101101 01001101 01100111 11011011 10001100 01110011 11101111 01010101
01101011 11101010 00111101 10000111 01110100 00011110 11110100 11000101 11001111 01001110
11000110 10000110 10010011 00100000 01100011 10101001 00110100 11111110 10011100 01010010
01111010 10001000 01100001 00011000 10010000 00001100 11101111 11111110 10010100 10100111
10101001 11100011 10001100 11111110 01110100 01110011 10011101 11001111 10011100 01110110
00000011 11111010 11010010 00111001 00011011 11001001 11001001 00100111 11111001 01010000
10101101 01111101 01001011 00010101 01110000 00011000 00001110 10011101 10111000 11101111
01000110 00000110 00000110 11111100 01111100 11000111 10001100 11010000 10000000 00101001
11011100 11111101 01111101 00101001 10111000 11011101 00100110 01001111 00000011 11010011
11010000 01110111 10100001 10110010 01101100 00101110 01000000 11100100 10000010 01110011
11010010 10010001 00001110 00100011 00111100 10000001 11101110 01101001 01011011 00000101
10000011 00111001 00011111 00100111 01000001 11101001 01001100 10010001 01110111 01001000
01111010 10010011 11011011 10011010 00110110 11011000 10100000 10001011 01101010 10010011
10110011 10011010 01110011 11100100 00000010 11001111 10110001 00111101 00111011 11010011
00001110 00000000 11000010 00011111 10111001 11001001 00111110 10100110 10000110 11000011
01001000 10000111 00000111 00011000 11001101 01000101 11010000 00001100 00111100 00100110
01100100 11100111 00111100 11111101 00101001 11011101 00000111 00000011 10010011 11011011
11010010 10001100 11110001 11001000 11111010 01010010 10000110 01010000 11111001 11000110
01001001 11101001 01010111 01001101 00000000 10111000 11011011 11011111 00111001 10100110
11100000 11101111 01110000 01110001 10000011 01000110 01011000 11100011 11101011 10011110
00101001 01110010 00000110 01011010 10101001 00100100 01000000 10011011 01110011 11011011

```
10000011 11011010 10001100 10010001 11000110 00110001 01000110 01001110 11010001 10000001
11001001 10100011 00010001 11111111 00000000 00011010 00110001 01101110 11111001 10101001
01001001 01000111 01000100 01010101 11001110 10101001 01110110 10010111 00111100 01010011
01110000 00110010 01011000 10011010 01010110 11111001 01000110 00110011 10001010 00010100
00011110 00000111 11101010 01101001 10100010 01000101 11100000 10000001 11000111 01101110
00000101 00110111 01110001 01100010 11100011 00011011 00110001 11010111 10011010 01110110
00110000 01111000 00011111 01010010 01101000 11011100 00000010 00011101 11100111 00100100
11010101 11011100 01101100 01000101 00011110 10111100 01100111 10011010 00010001 01001011
00011100 11110001 10001111 01010001 01000011 00001110 00111111 10100101 00100110 01001110
00110010 11000100 01100011 11010000 01010100 11011110 11101100 01000011 10111110 01100000
00110010 01000000 00000010 10010011 10000001 11010100 11010000 10111000 00000100 10010101
11100100 11110111 11000001 10100100 01101110 11100111 11010110 10101011 01001011 00000000
11010100 11011100 00110111 10011100 11100111 00111101 00111101 10101001 11111111 00000000
00110110 01111010 11100111 11011000 11010000 11011000 00111101 00001110 00110001 11011010
10010001 01111110 01100010 01110000 01101000 10111000 10000111 01100011 00100010 10001110
01110000 00111010 01111011 11010000 10111111 00100110 00111111 01011010 00000001 01110110
11001111 00000011 11101011 01010011 10110000 11000110 10111111 00000011 10001100 10010001
11101001 01001101 01000000 01111010 10011111 11100111 01010010 00011110 00000111 01011010
00010100 10000010 00111101 00101001 00000000 10000011 00100101 00001001 00100011 10101001
10100001 10001001 01010001 10011110 10000010 10000110 00001011 10011100 00011111 11111110
10110101 00011100 00010100 00000110 00111110 10011001 11101101 01001010 11001101 11101110
00000010 00000011 11011100 10011110 11010100 00110011 01101100 01001100 11100011 10101111
10110101 00101010 10000001 10001100 11010010 01110010 11000011 10001110 10011101 11001001
10100111 01111011 00001111 11001000 00010100 01110001 11010111 00011001 00110100 10111011
01110000 00000110 00111000 10100100 01000010 01111001 11001111 01001010 01011001 01111010
00001100 00010000 00111101 01101000 11101000 00100000 00100011 01110110 00001000 11101001
01000110 01001110 01110000 00000110 01101001 00000000 11001010 01111100 11111001 11100011
10100101 00101000 00011011 01001110 01000000 11100100 11111010 01010001 11101010 00000010
10111001 11011011 10010101 11101110 01111010 11100010 10011010 01000110 11100111 11001111
10100101 00001011 11010100 11111010 10011110 01101001 01011100 10010001 11111100 01000000
01010001 10100000 10000100 11101110 00000000 11101111 11011110 10001100 10001110 01110000
01111000 00011101 11101000 11100100 11110001 11101001 11011000 01010011 01011011 10000000
00111101 11101000 11011001 11101010 01010011 00000101 11100111 00011101 01111001 00111110
10110100 00000001 10000110 00111100 11100111 11111010 01010000 10100101 10110011 10000010
00111000 11101011 10011010 01001100 00010000 01110011 10011010 10010001 00010010 01100100
00011100 00001010 01100000 11001110 01001000 00010100 11100000 01001000 00000100 11111111
00000000 00100001 01001101 01011100 10000001 10010010 00111001 00111101 00101000 01101001
11101100 00000001 10000001 10011100 01110111 00111101 11101001 11000111 00100100 11110101
00111000 10100011 00011011 01000111 10101001 11110111 00111001 10100101 11001110 00001000
10100111 01110110 00000010 01100011 00011000 00000110 10001100 10010110 00111100 01111110
10100111 10100101 00001101 10010010 01001000 00011111 10011101 00011011 01000001 11000111
00011100 11010000 10110111 00011101 11000011 11101110 11100000 01100111 11110001 10100101
11101010 01110010 01001101 00000000 00001100 01010010 01110001 01000101 10101110 11000100
00011100 10110001 11000000 11100010 10010111 00100100 01110001 10011111 10101101 00001011
10010001 10011010 00010100 00001110 10110100 11101100 10010110 10000000 00100010 11100011
10111001 10100011 11111000 11111001 11101011 11101001 01001101 11101110 00110001 11010110
10011100 11011001 00111001 11100011 11110001 00110101 00101000 00000001 01111001 11100101
11111010 01010011 00010010 01000101 01100100 00000101 00110011 10000010 01101001 01110010
00001011 10001110 01101001 11001011 11110011 01100000 10100111 00000011 10111101 01010101
10011010 11010100 00000001 01110010 00111001 00111001 00100111 11101011 01000000 00000100
11010010 10110000 11101101 10011100 11110001 11001001 10101000 11000000 11001001 11110110
11101101 01010001 01111110 11000011 10111000 11110010 00001001 11001000 11001110 00101001
10111101 11000000 11000111 00011101 11001101 00111001 10000000 01100111 00011001 11100111
00010100 11010110 00100100 10011111 01000100 11101110 01001111 01111010 01111010 10000101
11000000 10011101 11010010 01110011 11110111 00010111 10100000 10100011 00000011 10001100
00001100 11110001 10010001 11101101 01001110 01100001 11000111 00010100 11000110 11001000
11000000 11101001 11111101 01101001 01001010 11110111 00010000 00110001 00100000 01111010
01110001 01001000 11000011 00111000 00100111 10000001 11101001 11010110 10011100 10011000
01010001 11101110 01111101 01111011 11010001 10011100 00001110 01001000 11111111 00000000
00011010 00101100 00000010 00101110 00111010 01110001 10011111 01001100 01010011 11010101
01001010 10011100 10010001 10001100 00011100 11110101 10100110 11100000 01110101 10100000
11100011 00011110 11010101 01000011 01000000 10101101 11110011 10010010 01110010 00000111
01101010 00000011 01100111 00011110 10111110 11110100 01111101 11100000 00111110 10110100
00101001 00100101 10000111 10100101 01001110 11001111 01000001 00000000 00111001 11101011
01000001 11100111 00100111 00110100 00101000 11001111 00111100 00001111 01111010 00110011
11110010 11110100 11111010 01010010 10111011 01101100 00000000 00010001 11000110 01111010
11010000 11100111 10100111 00110100 00101000 00111101 01011100 01010000 11011001 11011101
11101101 01001010 11011101 01011000 00001000 01110000 00111010 01010010 10001110 00001111
10111101 00011100 00010110 00011100 01110000 00111011 01010001 10010000 01101001 11011010
11000000 00110111 11010011 01111111 00100111 00010100 10100000 01100111 10010011 01000000
00000000 00001100 00001010 00011011 10001100 01100011 10000001 01001010 11001011 10101000
00000010 11110001 11001001 00011100 00001010 00010100 10011101 11011101 00101000 00111101
11000011 01010010 00001110 01001000 00111001 11000110 01001101 00110100 10101110 00000001
```

10111011 00101101 10110111 10111110 01101001 10011101 01100100 00111001 11101001 11011010
10011111 10010001 10011100 10001111 11001100 11010011 01010100 00010111 11100111 11010011
10011010 10101011 00100100 11000000 01110011 00011101 11000111 01101000 00011001 00111101
11111001 10100011 10011101 11100111 10011010 00010100 01101101 00111001 11101111 01010001
10101111 11011110 01110110 00100111 10101101 01001011 11010100 00000000 10101001 11001000
00100011 10100000 10100111 01100000 10010000 00000111 10101001 10100111 00100111 00000000
10110001 11000111 00100111 00100110 10011011 10010010 11001111 10011100 01100000 01111011
01010101 00010101 01100001 00011001 10110000 00111000 11000000 00011110 10110100 10001110
01111110 01010000 00000001 11100001 11001111 00100111 00110101 01001110 11101010 11110110
00111000 00001111 10010110 00000110 11110111 00011101 01000101 01010001 10010111 01011001
10010000 01111101 11111011 01110000 00111110 10000110 10110011 01110101 01111011 00011010
00101010 00110010 01111010 11011000 11011011 01010000 10100100 01110100 00100000 01111010
11010011 00010100 01111001 10000011 00111001 00000011 00111101 01111001 10101010 11010110
10111010 10000100 00010111 10000011 00010001 10111000 00000111 10111010 10011110 10110101
01110001 11000001 00110010 00100111 00011100 00001110 10100111 00010100 11111001 10010011
00100001 11000101 11000101 10001000 11111000 00100100 10000101 00011101 00111010 00000011
01000011 10000011 10000011 10001110 10100000 01110110 00111000 11100110 10010101 11111000
01110001 11000111 01010011 10001010 00110011 10010010 01001000 00000011 00011101 00111001
10100001 11001101 11101100 00000010 00101001 00001010 01010000 00010001 10010000 00000110
01011000 11111010 11010010 10100110 01001000 00100111 00011000 11001101 00100010 10000010
01010000 10101110 00111000 11001111 00011001 11100010 10000110 00100100 10000111 00011101
00010011 10100000 00110101 01000010 01000000 10011000 11011001 11010000 10011100 01111010
11010000 11011000 00011000 11110100 00110100 10111001 00011100 11100011 11110010 00010100
10011100 01100011 00111000 11101000 00111000 10100111 11001101 01100010 01000110 11101110
01010010 10011001 01000011 11111010 01010010 00101010 11110000 00001111 01010010 01111011
10011010 01000010 01000001 10001111 10001110 00111111 00001010 01010100 00111000 11100000
00001110 00111101 11101010 01101111 01110111 10101001 01010111 00010101 10001000 11001110
00111010 10011111 01011010 01110111 00100100 10000011 11010011 11111010 11010011 01010011
00101010 00110000 00111010 10011110 10100110 10010001 10111011 00000000 01001110 01111101
11101010 10101101 10100000 11000101 01010001 10010011 11010011 10001111 01101010 00010011
00011001 11100111 00111000 00000011 00110100 11110111 00111000 11011000 00000111 01000010
01111001 00110101 00011111 11001100 00100011 01110000 00111000 11110100 00110100 10011011
10110001 00000000 00001001 11011010 00110111 11111100 10011011 11001111 11001010 00101001
01010111 10001100 01111011 11010011 01110001 10011100 00010001 11011010 10011100 01110000
00001010 01110111 00100010 10010010 01111010 00010110 00011001 00011001 00000010 10010000
11100011 10011110 00101000 01110110 01010000 11011000 11101110 01101000 00001010 01011100
10001110 10111111 10001101 01011011 01001000 10000001 00111000 11011110 11100000 00110111
00111000 11100100 10001110 00101000 11111011 10001000 00001111 00111001 11101001 11001101
00101110 00001001 11101011 11011110 10000101 11000110 11110000 01110010 01111110 01001110
01000101 01000010 01100101 10001001 10010101 00000111 10101110 01011111 11010010 10010111
10101111 01111110 00101001 00010000 10011100 01101110 00100011 00000111 10111101 00110011
00111001 00111000 00000011 10001110 01110010 01111101 00101000 10111011 00000001 01000110
01110000 01110001 11000111 10111101 00111000 10110000 00010010 00000000 10111100 11101101
01011111 10011011 11011010 10011011 11010001 00111010 01110001 11101001 01001101 01100000
00011010 00110111 00000101 10110001 10001110 01001111 10110110 00101010 11000101 01110000
11111011 10100111 01101000 00011011 00000001 00111100 01100010 10011101 10000011 11100110
00010000 01011011 10101111 00100100 11010000 10000111 00111111 00110001 11000000 00000011
10011100 11100111 10111101 00110110 00111111 10010100 10011001 01100100 11011110 01110001
11011100 01110111 10101001 01100011 00010100 00111111 11001000 01110000 01001111 00011100
01010010 01001000 10100101 10000000 00011001 00111000 11001111 00110100 10101000 10100000
00001110 01000110 00110111 11110110 11101011 01000100 11001111 10110000 00000010 00110011
10011010 10010100 11101111 10100000 00001010 11000000 10101000 00000101 11110000 00000010
11111101 11010001 01001101 11000000 00011011 00001011 00011110 00110011 11011110 10010101
10010100 11101111 00000100 11110011 10000001 11010010 10000111 00101100 01001011 10101000
00000011 10100111 00000010 10101101 11101000 11000000 01100100 10000100 00101111 00111001
11100111 11011010 10011101 10010000 01000111 01111100 00011111 01001110 11110100 10100111
00011000 00011001 11100111 10001110 01000110 00111010 01010100 01101010 01001111 01111110
00101001 00111011 00010010 00000001 10000111 10011000 11101010 00000110 00010011 10111001
11001101 00101110 11011111 00110010 01001100 11110000 00000110 01111011 10001010 01111000
00011011 10001010 00000011 11011100 11110011 01001100 01000010 01100100 11011110 01110110
11100011 11010011 00110100 10111001 10111011 00001110 11000010 00101011 00101011 10101011
10010101 11001000 10001100 01110111 00100011 10101111 11010010 10010111 00100011 00100000
10011110 11011101 00101001 00011111 10111000 00000011 11100100 11101101 01000110 00001001
00100000 11111110 01111110 11110101 01101001 10100111 10111000 11000101 01000110 00001010
10011110 10000111 00011101 01101010 00111000 10001001 00001000 00110011 10010010 01101001
11100011 00011000 00111011 10000101 00000011 11010000 00001100 01110011 10010010 01101000
01110110 01000000 00000100 00011101 11100100 00000000 01000110 01111010 11111011 11010010
01111100 11010001 11000110 11101010 10000011 11100111 11101001 10010011 11011010 10001000
10011000 00110011 00111001 00000100 11101100 00000011 10010011 01001101 00000000 11100000
01100100 11110101 00111100 11010110 01110111 00000001 00001000 11001000 11011110 11100000
11111100 10011101 10110011 11010110 10001110 10101101 10011110 11000111 10100101 00001111
10010011 11010000 01111100 10011101 00000110 01111011 11010001 10001110 10011101 01111010
01010011 01001001 00110101 10100000 00001000 10111100 10011111 01101010 01110010 01100001

10111010 11110000 00111010 11010100 01111111 11000111 11001111 01001111 01011100 11010011
10010100 10000010 01111101 10101000 01111110 01000100 00000110 01110011 10000000 00001111
11101001 01001011 10001110 01000110 01111011 01010011 00110011 10001110 11011000 11001111
01101111 01101010 01111110 01110000 10111000 11101110 01111011 11111010 01010011 01100101
10000110 01110011 11000000 11111101 01101010 00110110 11000000 00000011 00100110 10011110
00010011 00001011 10011110 01110001 11011100 10011010 01101011 01110110 11100111 00010100
01101100 01000000 01100011 00000100 10110110 00110010 01111101 00111101 01101000 00011101
01001001 10100111 00110001 11001010 01100000 01100100 01111011 11010011 00011111 00000000
01100111 11010111 10111001 11101011 01001110 11101110 11000011 11011000 00011111 00011001
11000111 00111000 11000111 00110100 10000000 01100111 11011011 00011101 01101001 01011011
00111110 01011111 01001110 01001101 00001101 10000010 00111001 11111100 01110011 01001010
11101100 10100000 01010011 10010010 01011100 01110010 00110001 11000101 00110011 00100100
11111011 01010000 10111000 11101001 11011010 10011110 01001111 00110100 00111110 11000000
00100111 01100010 10110100 01100000 00000010 00000000 11101101 01001011 10011100 01110111
10100100 01011100 01100111 10001111 11001110 10101001 00100010 01000110 10110110 00111011
01110010 01101001 11000000 10000001 10010001 10001111 01110001 01001101 00100000 01111110
10110100 11101110 11000100 00001110 10110100 01011001 00110010 10000110 00100001 11111001
00001001 11110100 10100001 00110001 10011110 01000001 00011001 11110101 10100001 01110000
00110010 00111101 11101001 00110010 00001001 11001001 10100101 01101101 00000000 01011000
10110000 01000110 01110000 01000110 01101001 10000111 00100011 01111111 01110111 11101100
01101000 11011100 01110001 10010000 00110001 01001110 01010010 01001001 11100111 11110001
00110101 00101001 11011111 01000010 00000110 10110001 00100111 10000011 11010011 10110101
00110101 10000110 11100011 10010111 00111000 00000011 10001100 01010011 10111010 11100011
00000011 10011111 01111010 01110011 10010000 00011000 00101110 01111110 01110010 00110010
01101010 10010011 00011101 10000110 10101001 00100001 01110001 11010000 11010010 00110010
10010010 01000110 01111010 11111010 11010010 10000000 00110000 01001001 00100111 10001111
11010110 10011101 10001110 00001111 00111000 11001000 11001001 00111110 10010100 11111110
00010010 10000110 00110000 00001101 00110001 11011110 01111110 01000000 00111010 01010010
11000101 10000010 00111001 11100011 10111110 00101001 00001001 11011100 10000100 10001110
10011100 01111110 00110100 10111011 01001001 00100111 00011101 00110001 11111001 01010001
01111101 00001000 00010001 01001111 10011000 11100100 10010001 11000110 01111000 10100101
11011100 10100001 10001010 11111010 01111010 11010010 01111010 00011100 10011100 00101000
11101101 11011110 10010011 11101111 01100111 01100000 11100011 11010100 10011110 10010100
00111101 11000110 00101010 10011111 10010101 00001100 10011000 00000101 11001111 11100111
01001000 10111000 11100100 01100011 11101011 01001010 11100100 00010101 00100100 00000010
01011101 00111000 00010100 11000110 00000111 11001011 00000011 00111001 00100111 11010011
10001010 01101011 10110001 01000011 01011000 01100011 11011100 01100111 10000000 00101001
01011000 11111100 11100010 00101110 11001011 10000010 01110001 01001000 10000011 00011100
00001010 01010001 11000000 00011100 10000001 11001110 01001001 10101000 11100101 01001101
10000101 10000100 01010011 10010000 00110001 11010100 11110101 11001111 01101010 01101001
00000001 01111001 00111100 10111110 01111000 00011111 11010110 10011111 11000100 01100011
00001011 11010011 00110100 01100111 11100110 10010000 01110000 01000000 00011101 01111101
01001101 00111000 00101011 00110001 00110000 01100000 00010100 11110010 01000110 01110001
11001101 00100111 01010100 11100111 10001010 01101111 00011110 11111011 11111011 11010001
10110100 10011111 01111111 11000110 10011011 01101110 11100011 00011101 10010010 11011101
00101000 11001000 10100110 01110010 00001110 01000111 01010011 01001000 01000010 11111111
00000000 00010000 11001001 11110101 10101001 11010011 10101000 00011101 01101110 01110010
00111101 01101001 01111001 11000111 00011111 10101001 10100001 10011011 00111001 00111101
10101001 00111100 11001110 00110001 10001110 00101010 11010111 01100010 00000101 01100011
11000000 11001111 00110100 10001100 00001001 00000011 10111000 10100110 01100000 01110101
11100100 01111011 11010011 11010011 00100111 10100000 11001001 11110101 00010100 10101101
01110110 01011000 00110110 00000000 11100100 11010001 11000001 00011100 00010010 01000111
10111101 00011000 00000100 11110001 11010000 11010010 10101110 00101010 10011110 10000100
00001001 10000001 10000011 10001110 00111101 01101001 01011100 00000000 00000110 11000010
01000101 01000111 11010110 01000000 01110111 01110100 11100100 10001010 01110010 11110011
11001001 11100100 11010000 00000000 11011000 11000001 00011001 00100100 11111101 01101001
11001011 10011100 01110100 11001111 10110101 00110111 00000111 00111001 11001111 00011000
10100011 00100111 10110001 10100010 01011110 01000000 00101010 00110110 11101100 10011100
01100000 01110110 00010100 10000111 11100110 00111000 11001111 00011110 10010100 00001100
10110001 11101000 00000111 10111101 00101010 10001110 00110001 10001111 11000111 00110100
10101100 10011110 11100000 00100000 00000000 00011100 10011110 10110100 11100110 00100011
00011100 01110011 10001010 01101110 01000111 01000000 00001111 11010100 11010001 00011001
11000111 01010000 01001101 00101011 00100100 00000000 10111001 00100110 10000110 11011010
00011000 01100001 01110010 01111101 01000101 00001010 11000001 10111001 11001111 11100001
01001010 00111010 00001101 10011100 01010011 00000001 01111011 11100011 01101101 01000111
10010110 00100100 10001100 00000000 10011111 01011010 01110011 01101110 01110001 10001100
11100011 11010111 00010100 00000010 00111001 00101000 00111110 10110100 00100100 00000000
01011000 01111111 00000110 01110001 11101010 01111011 11010011 01010100 01101110 11000001
01101110 00111110 10110100 01100111 00111100 10001100 01100010 10011101 10001110 11100111
10001110 11110101 01010110 11010011 01010000 01100010 10111011 01100000 00010011 11011010
10011000 10011101 01001100 10000000 00010000 00001111 01101010 01110011 00000010 01010011
11111001 01010001 11110111 01111101 11001001 11100010 10100001 10111101 01101110 00000011
01010100 10110001 00011000 11000000 00011110 10100110 10000110 01100001 10011110 10011101

```
00111011 11010011 10000000 00000000 01110100 10100110 10011110 00000111 00001011 11000000
10100111 01110110 11110110 00000001 11101010 00001011 01111100 11011000 11111010 10011010
01100010 10110001 11011101 10010010 00111000 11110100 10100111 00101111 01001110 00101001
10111001 11101100 01101010 01011000 00001110 01000011 11011100 00000010 00110011 01000011
01100011 10100110 01111010 11010011 01011000 11100111 11100101 00000010 10010011 10110001
00111100 01110001 01001110 11100011 11011100 00110010 01110010 01110001 10011100 01010000
00000001 01011001 00110111 01100111 00111100 01110100 11001111 01001010 00010100 11100111
10100111 01011010 01011010 00101111 11011100 01000010 00000011 11111001 10011111 01011010
01010000 00111111 01011010 00111010 10010011 10001110 01001101 00111101 10111110 01010000
00000111 00111001 11111110 01010100 00001110 11100001 11010100 01100010 10010001 11010111
00111000 11100100 11100011 11010010 10000101 11100000 11010001 11010111 00010100 10101101
10101101 11101110 00100001 01010111 00011001 00111001 10100100 01100110 00000000 10010010
01111111 00101010 00111010 01110001 10001010 01100000 11001000 00000100 00010011 10010010
01111011 11010011 10111110 10000000 00101010 00111000 11011000 00001001 00011100 11111111
00000000 00101010 01110111 01111100 10011010 00111001 00111000 11101111 11101011 01001101
11100000 10011100 00100001 00111101 01101001 01111010 10000000 10001101 10010011 10000001
11011000 01110101 00110100 00000010 11001100 01000110 00111010 01010011 11011000 00001110
10011101 01111101 11101001 10100011 00100011 10100101 01001111 10100000 00000001 00101010
10111001 00100111 10100110 00111010 11010010 01111100 10111101 00111010 01100111 10101101
00101110 11010101 01101100 11100100 01100111 10011110 11110100 11100110 00111100 01111011
11010101 01011110 11100101 10001100 11000110 11100001 10000011 11010000 11110111 11001101
00111101 01110010 01000111 00000111 10001110 11100110 10011010 00000110 00111110 11110111
01000011 11001101 00001101 10001100 01100011 10110111 10110101 00111110 10100100 00000011
00001100 00001110 00001001 11001111 01101010 01000000 01110011 00100110 00110011 10010001
01001010 01001000 01010001 10011100 00010011 11001111 10101101 00000000 10001110 10111000
11000001 00110100 01111010 10000000 11011001 00001001 01100001 10000000 01001000 00011101
11101001 01110000 10111011 10000110 01001111 11100111 01000000 00111001 00100100 11110100
00011110 10110100 00110000 11011101 10000000 01110011 10001100 01010010 10110010 11011100
00000101 11101010 11000000 11100011 10001111 10101101 00111000 11110101 11100111 10010011
01001101 11001001 01010001 11110010 01111111 00101010 01001101 11000111 00111000 11000110
11111111 00000000 01011010 10011111 00100000 00010111 10110110 00111101 01111001 10100100
11000110 11101100 00000001 11000101 00101110 00110000 01001111 00011100 11010010 00111001
11000000 01111110 10111001 11110110 11101101 01010111 01100000 00010101 11111011 00101010
01111110 00111100 11010010 01110110 11000101 00010001 10011100 10001100 10010001 10001111
10101000 10100001 01111010 11101110 00011000 10100011 10101000 00001010 10100000 10010100
11110111 00100111 11110010 10100100 11101101 11010011 11110001 10100001 01000000 11000001
00000111 11010111 00111000 10100101 11001000 00000011 10011010 10011011 10000000 11100010
01110000 10111101 01000101 00011101 00111011 11010011 01001111 00100100 00001100 01110100
00111100 01010010 00110001 11100100 11010001 01111110 10100000 00011000 00111111 00111000
00011110 10111000 11001101 00001101 10001100 00001100 11110101 10100001 10110010 01000110
00010100 11100011 11011110 10001100 11110000 00110111 11110101 11101111 01010101 01111101
00000000 01011100 01110001 11001001 11111010 01010011 01010111 10110110 01101001 10101110
01001110 11001101 11000000 01100100 11010011 10111001 11100011 00111111 10011101 01001101
10000000 01010111 01100000 01011111 01101111 00100011 11010111 11011110 10010011 00011001
01111110 00101001 01011011 10000010 01110001 11010110 10010000 01111110 00011000 10101010
10110111 01100000 00011010 01000110 00111010 01110011 10001010 01110000 00011000 00000000
10000010 00001111 00110100 10111001 11101011 11001110 00110011 01001100 01101110 01110001
10001110 10000011 11110101 10101001 10110011 00101100 00011011 00011011 11110001 10011110
00101000 00011100 00101001 00000011 00011101 01110011 01001000 00111000 01000010 11011000
11100100 01110011 01001010 10011111 10101001 11101010 00000101 00100100 00000011 10011100
11100011 00000000 01110111 11101101 01001100 01110010 01010101 00011101 10010011 10101110
00110000 00111101 10101000 00111101 01001011 00111001 11001000 00010100 11001001 10011000
00001000 01000000 00111001 00011101 11001110 00111111 10101101 01001100 10110101 00010010
00111001 00110100 10011011 11001101 10111110 10010001 01001001 00100100 11100111 10010010
01101010 01111011 10010010 10111000 11101001 01001111 11110010 10100000 01011001 10100101
01101000 00000111 00001110 11011001 11001101 01000111 01110001 00010001 11011001 01011000
00111101 01001111 01011010 00011111 00001010 00110000 01101110 01100100 01101011 01011011
10100001 00110010 00110001 00000100 01110111 00010101 11011001 01101000 10011010 10011010
11101010 00011010 01100001 01100100 00111111 10111101 01000011 10000011 10001110 11110101
11000011 11101010 11110001 10010110 01000011 10001100 11100110 10101100 01111100 00111001
10011101 10001110 10101111 00111100 00011001 11101011 00011111 11101011 01011010 11010010
10001011 00111001 10101011 01000010 11111011 10011110 10001001 10000110 11100000 11100000
00001100 01110100 11100110 10001001 01001111 10010100 00010011 00011100 10010011 11010000
01111111 10001101 00011101 01000110 00001111 00100111 10110101 00000001 01010110 00110001
11010111 10011111 01011100 01010110 10010110 11101110 01110001 10001010 01000110 00001110
11011100 11100101 11001000 10100100 01101100 00000100 11111001 00111001 00111101 01101000
01011100 00000010 01001000 11101010 01111000 10100110 10000001 11111011 11001110 00000001
11101011 11001101 00001110 11101000 00000011 10001100 00011111 01011100 01110101 00010100
00100000 11100011 00011001 11100000 01111010 11010010 01110010 11100000 10000001 11111101
11101110 01111101 11101001 11100111 00000011 00000000 11100011 10011110 10010100 00101101
11101110 11001001 01100011 01110000 00001111 00000011 10000001 01000111 00011011 11111000
10100111 00110111 00000011 00011000 11000111 00110100 11011100 10010000 01000111 00011100
00001010 00110100 01101100 10100000 00011001 00100111 00011001 10100001 00111000 11001111
```

01111010 00111010 00000010 01011111 10010011 11011110 10010001 00000110 00011100 00011100
00001100 01100010 10000100 00000010 10110110 01000110 01111011 11100110 10001100 10010000
10100000 10010011 11111001 11010000 11111100 11111101 01101001 00011100 10000110 10010100
01100000 11110011 10001010 00101110 10101111 10100000 00001011 10111000 11100111 01101000
00111100 11111010 11100010 10011010 01001000 00011001 01011100 10001100 11111111 00000000
00101010 01010110 11001000 11100000 01110101 11101110 01101000 01100011 00011100 01011001
00100100 00010010 11100100 01111111 10010001 01001011 10010101 10000000 10000111 00000011
10000011 11101011 11011110 10011100 10100110 00110101 10001111 01110001 01101100 00001111
01001111 01011010 01101011 11100000 00110000 01010001 11010100 11110010 11011000 10100001
10111110 11111000 00011100 10011111 01010010 01000101 01011010 10111011 11011100 10000001
10111011 10110010 11111001 11101001 00011111 01101111 01111010 01110011 10000000 10100000
00010011 11000110 00111000 11000001 11101111 01001010 11100011 01110011 00100000 00010100
10001101 11110011 01100000 00010000 00111101 01000000 11000101 00011101 00000000 01010111
11011010 00110010 01000111 01010010 01111111 10011101 00100000 11000001 00100100 00001110
10011110 10110100 00100001 11011100 11011100 01111010 01110011 10011110 11011111 01011010
01101011 10110110 01101101 11011111 11001011 11011000 00000110 00111001 00111111 11010110
10000100 11010011 11011100 10110000 01110110 00100101 10001000 11011011 10010010 00111101
11101001 10111111 00101110 11010100 00101111 11010011 11011100 01110010 01101001 11001001
11010001 00010111 10000011 11000111 00101101 01000111 01010010 01001001 00000011 11011011
00010100 00110100 10001001 00010011 00100000 00000011 10010001 11000010 01110100 11001111
01111010 01000000 00000111 01011100 10010011 11101110 01001101 00111001 10111111 01110100
10001110 01001110 00110001 11011011 00110101 00011010 10011111 00110000 01110100 11101011
11101111 01000000 10000111 10110001 11011100 01110000 00110000 00111101 00110001 01001011
10111000 00001100 00000000 10100011 10001110 10000000 11010001 10000101 01010010 01011011
00100011 01111111 10100110 01111001 10101000 11010100 00011101 11111110 10011001 11100100
10001010 00111010 00010110 01001000 10000100 10011100 10011110 00110111 11010100 01100111
00010001 10001110 10111111 00111111 10110101 00011101 00001111 00011001 00011001 00111100
11100110 10011101 10110101 01110001 11111010 11010001 10111010 11010000 00000110 10110000
01100010 10011000 11100100 01110011 11010111 00110100 10011000 11101000 00011100 00011111
10100000 10101001 00011011 10100111 00100111 10100001 11001101 00110001 11011000 00010010
00001001 00000101 00111011 01100011 00111001 10101001 01011011 11101000 00100110 00001101
10000010 11011110 11001001 11010011 11101011 01001000 00001111 01100001 11000010 01111011
01110111 10100101 01111100 00101000 00100100 11110000 00010111 10010011 11101111 01000100
01001011 11000110 01011000 10000000 00001001 11001110 01110011 11011010 10101111 01010111
10111000 00100010 00100101 11001000 00011001 01010001 10010010 01101010 01000111 11000000
11000110 01110011 11110100 00010101 00011100 00110010 00011001 00100011 11110011 01000110
00000000 00100100 10000000 01111101 10101010 01010111 00100100 01100100 10001110 10111110
11110101 00010110 11010010 11100011 00011011 11001110 00001000 01000001 10001111 11000110
10000110 11111001 01000110 00000001 11100111 11011100 11110101 10100110 11000010 11001100
00111010 11110011 10010011 01001000 11000001 10110010 01000001 00111100 11100111 10011010
00011110 10000000 00111101 10001110 00000000 01010001 11001111 10101101 00110111 10010010
00001000 11101111 01001110 00111100 00001101 11011011 01111111 11111010 11000010 10011000
11000011 00100100 11111111 00000000 11111010 10110011 01001110 11001011 10100000 00000110
00110111 00001100 01100111 00000011 11111001 11010010 01110101 10001111 00011001 11100111
10111001 00010101 00100111 01011110 00111001 10100110 01100011 00011100 01111010 01110010
01101001 00101101 00110110 00000001 00011011 10000101 00000111 00011000 00000011 10001010
01101011 00110110 00001111 01001110 11110100 11111100 00000110 00000000 00011110 01000110
01110010 01101000 01110010 00001001 11101111 01010110 11101101 11010000 00000100 11001110
00001000 11001111 00100110 10010101 01110010 01100100 11100111 11110010 10100001 01110011
11010110 10010001 11001001 00011100 00000001 11010100 01100100 11010000 11110101 11011000
00000101 01111110 01010000 10001110 10001001 11011111 11011110 10010011 10101001 00000001
00000110 01110011 01001100 01010001 10010000 00010100 01100111 00011000 11101111 01001011
10001110 10100011 10100000 11101100 01101000 01001100 10000001 11011001 00000000 10010101
01001110 01000111 01111111 01101010 10001101 10000110 11100111 00011110 11011101 10101001
11001100 00110000 00111000 11100010 10011010 10000011 10001111 01011111 01101010 11001110
11100101 10001011 10000010 11010010 00011100 11100110 10001110 00000111 11100001 01001010
01111110 11101111 10100111 00111100 11100010 10010001 10001001 01110111 11111111 00000000
01100011 10100000 00011000 11101011 01001110 11110111 01100000 00100000 11000000 00000011
01111111 00100000 11010011 01110010 01111001 00000111 10101101 00111001 10110010 01000110
00101000 01110000 00110010 00111000 11001111 10101101 01010010 01010110 00010110 11000011
01001000 11001000 00011100 01111110 00100110 10001100 10000001 10000000 01001001 11001111
10110101 00011001 00100101 11001110 01111010 01110110 10100001 10111000 00100001 10011100
01100100 10011110 10000010 10000110 10000011 01010000 11001000 00000011 10001111 11001010
10000110 00111001 11000001 00111100 01100110 10010011 00111001 01110111 00100000 01110100
11101100 01111011 11010001 10010000 11000000 01111010 11010011 10111101 11110101 00011000
00110000 11000001 00111110 11110100 10001011 11110111 00111110 10110100 10101101 10010010
11100100 01110111 11000110 00111101 10000101 00100010 10001100 01110010 11100111 10000001
01000110 10010110 00010111 10101000 01100100 11100011 00100011 10010111 00100111 10011010
01101110 00011011 00100100 00011110 10100100 01110000 00101000 01011101 11001110 00001001
11111110 00111110 10110100 01100011 01101001 11001110 01110010 01111011 01110011 01001011
01001110 10000010 00000100 00000101 10011011 10010011 11001111 10100101 00011000 11011010
11111001 11101010 01111101 01111101 01101000 01000001 10110100 01110101 11001111 00111100
11010011 10010100 10101001 01110010 01110011 11000000 00010100 00101101 00011000 11101110

00110011 10000000 01000000 11101011 11111000 11010011 11100101 11100100 01101101 01011110
01001001 11110111 10101000 11110001 10011110 01111010 01100111 11011011 10100101 00111011
00011100 00010000 00111111 00111010 01010110 11010100 00101110 00100110 01111000 00000011
11010011 10101101 00101110 01011001 10110110 00000100 00011100 01110111 00100111 10111101
00110101 10000000 00001110 00010101 00000111 11010100 10011010 01010110 00111000 00000111
10101001 10100110 10011111 01000110 00110001 10001111 10010010 01111100 10111111 01001110
10110100 11111100 01111110 10110100 11000100 00111001 01101100 10001110 10011110 11111101
10101001 11001111 10010110 01001100 01100100 00000000 00111101 00101000 01110111 01011011
00001010 11110110 00010101 10111010 01100111 10011110 01111011 01010011 00010111 10010011
10011110 01111000 11100000 01100010 10011100 10100011 10011101 11111000 11000000 00011110
10100110 10011010 11001100 11000100 00010011 11011111 10110101 00011010 10100100 00110000
01010010 01000110 01000010 00001110 01111101 01001101 00110101 10010111 11100101 00101011
10111011 10010011 11010111 00010100 10111011 10110000 01111101 01001111 10110101 00100001
11101010 00000000 11101111 11001110 01000111 10101101 01001010 11110010 00010101 11101110
00000111 00011100 01111100 10111001 00111001 11111010 01100110 10000101 00011100 00010010
01000111 01111110 10000000 11010010 10001110 11111000 11111100 00101001 00011100 11110100
01000100 11101101 11001001 10100111 11101111 00000110 10001100 01101110 11101110 01011101
10110001 10000001 01001110 01100011 10010000 00000000 10100011 10100111 01111111 11000110
10011010 10000111 10011100 11111010 01110111 10101010 01001101 10001100 01110110 01111101
00111000 00000011 10111101 00100010 11101101 11000101 00100111 10101001 00100111 11100110
10100011 00110001 10110111 00101100 00111001 10100110 10010110 10100001 11101000 01110101
01000111 00011101 10110000 01101001 01110010 01000001 11001011 11100010 10011000 11000011
00011001 01101100 00001110 10011100 11100010 10011110 00110000 11000100 00010000 01110010
01001111 11101001 01010101 01100101 01110010 00000100 00011000 00101110 01001001 01101110
10011101 10101001 01111100 10111100 01100100 11100100 10000001 11010100 11110011 01001010
10100100 01100011 10010000 00001111 11100011 01001000 11000001 10110110 01100011 11011010
10100110 11001001 00110000 00010011 10001100 10000000 10000011 11100100 11000110 01001001
10100011 00000000 10010010 00000000 00111000 10100001 10010101 10110110 01100000 11111101
11001110 11010100 10111100 10000001 11000110 00101010 10011000 00000010 10101000 00011101
10110001 01001000 00000000 00110010 01111100 11000011 00011000 11110111 10100111 00110110
11101110 11111111 00000000 11001010 10011010 11011101 10110011 11010100 11010010 01101010
11101110 11000011 10111000 10111000 00000000 01100000 00000011 01001100 11100011 11011100
01111111 01011010 00111001 01011100 11111010 00010011 11010100 01010011 10011011 00011001
00000011 11110101 10100001 00101011 01101100 11000100 00111011 10110000 00011110 11010100
11010110 00100101 10010111 00000000 11100000 00011110 11110100 11010111 00111100 00010000
00110000 01101001 11011011 01110000 00111010 10010001 11101111 01000101 10110101 11010100
00000001 01100011 00001010 00000111 01001111 10101101 00111000 11100100 00100000 00011001
00011001 00110100 11011101 11100011 10000000 00111110 01101100 11110111 10100011 10100110
01001000 00111111 10000101 00010010 01000000 00001100 00010100 11100011 11111001 11010011
01110111 01101101 11000111 10010110 00110111 10010011 01000110 00111100 11000011 10011111
01001110 11010100 11101100 00000011 11000000 11101000 00111011 11100110 10001011 01110101
00010000 00011100 00001110 00010110 10001100 10010010 01000111 11001011 10000000 00000111
00010100 11011100 10110011 00110111 00100011 00001000 00111101 11101000 11000011 00010010
01111001 11111100 00000101 01001111 00110011 00011000 00100001 11011100 01111110 11101111
01111110 10110100 10000000 00000010 01001001 11001111 01111010 01011110 10100101 00110000
01111000 10100100 11001000 00001111 11011011 00011110 11010100 11101111 11011000 01000011
11010101 01000001 00111101 01001001 11000111 10101101 00101011 01100000 00000011 01010001
11101100 01100010 11111001 00100100 11010011 11111101 00110001 11111010 11010100 11101010
11110111 00011000 10110001 01110100 11001001 00111100 01110110 10100100 11001001 00100011
10100110 01001101 00001110 01001110 00110110 10001100 01110001 11101001 01000110 01110000
10100000 01110001 10111111 10111101 00110100 11000000 01101011 11100111 10011101 10000010
10001111 10010111 00000011 01110001 11100110 10011101 10011100 01110000 00111010 01010011
00001001 00001011 10000010 11011101 11111011 01100010 10011101 10101110 00000010 10101001
00001010 00111111 10101001 10100001 00110000 00111110 10000110 10000110 00111100 11101101
11011011 01000000 11000010 10010010 01011101 10111111 00000001 01001001 10101101 00110100
00000000 11011100 00110001 11110010 11010001 10000000 00110001 10011001 00000000 00100111
11010110 10000101 00101010 01000001 11000111 00110100 00101000 11001110 01110011 11001110
01111101 01101010 01011011 11101110 00000011 10110011 11011101 01001000 11000111 10101101
00001100 01111001 11110110 10100110 10010001 11111101 11110011 10011111 01000000 00111011
01010000 00110000 10100010 10101011 01110000 00011100 11000111 10011111 10101101 00110101
10111010 11100010 10010000 01100000 10001110 00001111 00110100 10100000 00010000 00110001
10001110 01001001 11001101 00010110 01110110 11011100 00000111 00010110 00000000 01010011
01010100 01100111 10100111 01001010 01000110 00000011 10100000 11100000 01010011 11010100
01100011 10110101 00001101 00000000 11011110 00000111 00110100 11100010 00001111 00000111
00111000 11111010 01010011 01011001 01001110 01111001 11101111 01000011 01110010 10100011
10011111 10100000 10101001 11010110 11111010 11101010 01011000 11101100 10011100 10011100
00001010 01100011 00110110 00000000 00111101 11001111 01001010 01011110 01110110 11100010
10001100 00001100 11111011 10001010 01111100 10101010 11010111 01100100 00000001 01100011
10110111 00100011 11110010 00110100 00101111 01001100 10011010 01110000 11000001 00011101
01101000 11000110 01001111 10110101 00111000 10101101 11000000 01100110 11100000 01001110
01101001 01010100 11110110 00111100 00011010 01110111 00011001 11000000 11100100 11010011
01110001 11001001 00100111 10011111 11000110 10001101 00000000 01101010 11110010 01111001
11101111 11011010 10011100 11111001 11011011 10000000 01111001 11001111 01110001 10011010

00110001 10110111 00100110 10000100 00111011 10000000 00100111 10001010 01001101 01011000
00000011 10000101 11100000 10011010 01101010 10010011 11001000 11001111 00011000 11101011
11101011 01001101 11000110 01000110 01111010 11100110 10100100 00000011 10110001 10100111
10101000 00001000 00110011 11101011 11001111 10101110 00101001 00000000 00100000 00010011
10010011 10010010 01101001 11011100 01100100 10101000 00111001 00100011 10101101 00011001
11111001 11110000 00101000 11010010 11110111 00000001 00010100 10000001 11011000 11010001
10010101 11101100 01111010 11110101 00010100 11110000 01110001 11000110 00001001 10100110
10001110 00000111 00101011 11001001 10100101 00100111 01110110 00000010 00101011 00010011
11010100 01100011 00100011 10100101 00101000 11001110 00110001 01000010 11010000 11001101
10110101 10000000 01110101 11100000 11110111 10100011 10101000 11101110 00011001 11000110
01110001 01000110 01110001 10001110 00110011 10010011 01000110 01001001 00111001 00010100
00101111 11001101 11110101 10100011 01000110 11111100 10000111 10110000 10011101 00001110
00000000 11100111 11111001 01010000 01110000 00000001 11100011 10111101 00011000 11001110
01001000 11001000 00011000 11100111 10001010 01001100 10001100 10000000 00111010 11010100
00110100 11100010 11110101 00100100 00010100 00001100 10011110 01001111 00100111 00110100
10111000 00011001 11001001 11101101 11111010 11010001 11000000 01001100 10011100 11111010
01100000 01010011 00000000 11001001 00100000 01110011 01011010 00101001 00000000 11101100
01100000 00010011 11001111 00011100 10011010 01010000 00111101 01101000 11001000 00010001
11111010 10001100 11111110 01110100 10001100 01110000 10011001 11001111 11010010 10110011
11010100 00000110 11101110 01101100 11110100 11000000 11101001 01001110 11100111 00000000
01111011 11110011 01001011 11010111 11101111 10010001 11111000 01010011 00110111 01100100
10010011 10000010 00110011 11010111 00110101 01110111 01010110 00000001 11000111 00111111
01001111 11101011 01001100 01010001 11001110 00011001 10111001 00011110 10010100 10100000
01100011 11011111 00111101 01001101 00111000 10010000 00111000 11101001 10011110 10010101
00101110 11100011 00011000 11101101 11110010 10010101 00000011 00100100 10011100 01010010
11110100 11001000 01001110 10110100 01111101 00000110 01111110 10100110 10000110 11111001
10010100 01110110 00100111 11010000 11110100 10100001 00101011 00001000 01101011 00000000
01111000 11001110 01000111 10101101 01010001 11010110 11100111 00010000 01011001 10011100
00110110 00110011 11000111 01001010 10111100 01000010 10001100 10000100 11101001 10000000
00101011 00010111 11000101 01010010 01111110 11100010 00100010 10000111 00001001 10111011
11110011 00000010 10100010 10100110 10101011 01000011 01001010 01111010 11001001 00011001
10110000 11001010 00010111 10000000 01111011 01010101 10011111 10111100 10111100 11110100
10101100 00001011 01101001 11001001 10010011 10011110 10010101 10110111 01101111 00101000
01100000 00010100 11110010 00001111 01110001 01011100 11001001 00111101 11011001 11101100
11000111 01100010 10000101 11101101 10100110 01110011 11101000 01101010 10011110 10001111
00000000 11010011 11110101 01111000 11101110 01111001 01000000 00111000 01100010 00111011
11010110 11110100 11010001 10000000 00111101 01110011 01010101 00011110 00001100 11110011
01011011 01000010 10100011 11011100 11001010 10101100 00010100 11010001 11010110 01000011
00100010 11001001 00010000 01101000 01011000 00111110 01111011 10001010 00010111 10000000
01110010 00111000 11001111 01001010 11100110 00101100 10101110 00100101 10110001 10010000
00010100 00111001 01000010 01111001 00000111 10111101 01110100 00010110 01110111 10010001
01011101 10000000 11000011 10000010 01000111 00100000 11110101 00000110 10110110 01010011
01001111 01110011 11001100 10011100 00111001 00011001 00111011 00010010 01000111 11001000
00000110 11111100 11110010 01001000 10100101 11011011 11110010 00000101 11001001 11000000
00111111 10011101 00011001 00000011 00111100 11111100 11111101 11101001 11011000 00100001
00011100 11110111 11101100 00101010 10101111 01100011 00111110 10100000 11000101 01000011
11110001 11000000 00011101 01101001 10101010 01110010 01001011 01110111 11001110 00000000
10100011 00011000 11101011 01001000 11101100 00110010 00110110 01110101 11111110 01010101
00010111 00101000 01010101 00100011 00100100 01100111 00100111 10111001 10100011 00000111
00100100 00100011 00001100 11110111 10100111 00110111 11101110 11110010 01110001 11010110
10011000 11011001 00000011 11100100 00011000 00011110 11100110 10000100 11101100 11110100
00000001 01011010 01000001 10000010 00000000 11001001 11001111 00100100 11010000 00111001
11100100 10011110 01110011 01001000 10111000 01011000 11001110 01000101 00100111 01010010
01111101 10101011 01001101 00110111 00000001 01011000 11111100 11000100 00100001 11001001
00111101 01111101 10000101 00011011 01110110 11100000 10010000 00111101 10101001 00011001
01110011 11001111 00010100 10100010 00111100 11100000 10100001 11100100 11111010 11111010
01010000 10110101 11010001 10010000 00000111 00111111 00100000 00111100 00001110 11100110
10000110 00100011 10001100 11100111 00011000 11101001 01001000 01111100 10110110 10010011
00010001 10011100 10000101 00111100 10110101 00110101 11110110 10001001 10111011 11100111
00011100 11100100 11110000 00101011 00110101 01111011 10000000 11110101 00100001 01001110
00011101 10111001 11000110 11111110 00000101 00110011 00001100 00100010 00110010 00010011
10000010 01001110 01110000 01111111 01001010 01000101 00000000 01001010 11100111 00011001
00000111 00011100 10011111 01101010 01010010 01011000 11001000 01001001 00011111 00100010
00011100 10000000 01000111 01111010 11010010 11100101 01011000 01111110 00001000 11111010
11110111 10101000 11011000 00001100 10001110 01111011 11100011 00011110 10110100 11111000
10110111 01100011 10011110 01001001 00111101 01001101 00110101 11001000 10001100 11100000
00011100 10111001 11100000 10011010 00101101 10100000 11000010 01010011 10010000 11101010
00001110 00010000 10011100 10011110 01111010 11010011 01010110 00111100 11000100 11101011
10011100 01100100 11010010 10011101 11000000 00000000 00110110 01110010 01110000 01001101
00111101 11110010 11000111 00001110 01111000 11101100 00000101 01001111 10100001 00000000
01001000 00011000 00000011 10010111 00111101 10000101 00110101 10100100 01010100 01110111
00000011 10010010 01111000 10100111 01111100 11000011 10001000 11010100 00000000 00111010
11100110 10011000 00111010 01110100 11000000 11101011 01010010 10101110 11001010 10111000

00010000 00001110 11000101 00011100 11101100 00010100 01000000 01110011 10010010 01000110
00111001 10100100 00111110 11000111 00011001 11101111 01001101 11000001 00001001 10011110
10100100 10011110 00111000 11101001 01010110 00110001 00110001 10110110 00111101 11011000
11111101 11100011 10011110 10111110 10010100 10100000 00010101 00011111 00110001 11001001
10100111 01110101 00100111 10001110 11111100 01010011 01011100 10000101 00111111 00111001
00000011 11010000 01100111 10101101 00110110 00101011 10001111 01110000 00010100 11100011
00111101 10110011 11001101 00110001 01001001 00100100 10010010 01000000 11000101 00111000
10010001 10001100 10111110 01111000 11101101 01000110 11100000 00111001 00111100 10011111
10100101 00011011 10001100 00000000 00011001 11100111 11010011 00111100 11010011 01011000
01110111 00111110 10110100 10000000 00000000 11100101 10000001 11111111 00000000 01011000
01111001 10100101 11011011 11001000 11101001 10001010 10010100 11110101 00010011 00001001
01100011 01010110 00000011 00100100 00001111 01110011 11111010 11010010 00101001 01000110
00100000 00101001 11001111 01101010 00100101 11011010 01110001 10111000 01110100 00111000
10100101 00000111 10100110 00111000 00011000 11001101 00001111 10100000 00100001 00010000
01100101 00000110 01000111 01001111 11010010 10010011 10110001 01100110 00111001 00011110
11110100 10101111 10111111 11001010 00101001 00011001 00000000 10010011 11001001 11000101
00101110 00000111 10010110 10001100 11100111 00011001 00110100 10100100 10111010 10001100
10001101 10001111 11001101 10011100 11110100 11101101 01000000 00000000 01100000 11100010
10011101 00010110 00001011 00011100 10110111 00000111 11011011 10100101 01000110 01100101
01101001 00100110 11000010 01000110 01000100 01101010 00111001 00101100 00111010 11010001
10111110 11100000 01001010 11100111 00001001 11000000 11100100 11111010 11010011 00011001
10110001 10010011 11011110 10001101 11000101 10110010 01110011 11111001 11010011 10001000
00001011 10110000 10011110 01101000 10110010 10110000 10110110 00011011 10011100 11110011
11101000 00101001 10100111 00101100 00001111 01101100 11010100 10011001 11101010 01001111
01011100 01100100 01111010 01010011 00110011 10111011 10100101 00101110 01010100 10001001
00010001 01000001 00110010 01111011 00000001 10001100 01010011 01110000 01011011 11101001
10011010 10010011 00011001 11101001 11010010 10011010 10011000 11100111 11010010 10110100
10110101 11000000 00001010 11100011 01111011 00110001 11100000 01111110 01010100 10101010
00110000 01000011 00011110 01110011 11101011 01001001 00101000 11011101 10000001 11111111
00000000 11101010 10100001 11111011 01110111 11000001 10101001 01110111 01100101 10001101
11001000 00000100 10011100 11110100 10100100 01101100 10010101 11111011 10100100 01100111
10110001 10100111 10100111 00000011 00111000 11100111 00111100 01111011 11010011 01011011
00000000 00010110 00100100 11010101 01110100 11010000 00000001 11001110 00000000 11100011
10001010 01101010 10110110 01001000 11000000 11001001 10100101 00111001 00101001 11111010
01010000 10111111 00110001 01110000 10011100 10000001 11011110 10100110 00100010 10111000
00111111 00100000 00001100 11110101 11101011 01000111 10100110 11010001 11010010 10011000
10000111 00111001 00100000 01111100 10000011 10001100 10011010 01111011 00010010 00000001
01101100 11100000 01100011 00000010 10011011 01001000 01000011 00011111 10000011 11010110
10001100 10011111 10101001 10100111 00101010 01100000 00000010 01111010 11010011 01011000
00000010 01110011 11011000 00001110 01101001 01011101 11011110 11100001 01110000 11011101
10000101 00111110 10111110 11010100 00110001 00100111 00011110 11000010 10010000 00011101
10000011 10000001 10011111 01001111 01101010 00100101 00101100 00010000 00010000 00110001
10011110 11100110 10101011 10010111 10011011 01010100 00000001 11001001 00100100 00000001
11111001 11010001 10111100 00001000 11000001 11001110 01110111 11010010 01100100 10000011
11010111 00111100 01110000 00101001 10111000 11000000 11111101 01101010 00010000 11101110
00111001 01001001 11000110 01001111 01111010 01101011 00011101 10101000 01110000 00110010
01110011 11101011 01001110 01001110 01001000 11001000 11000001 11001101 00001010 01001110
00000011 00001110 00000111 10100110 00101000 10110101 11110101 00000110 00001110 01110000
01001000 00011101 00000101 00110100 01100101 10110010 01101001 11010010 00110001 00101110
00110000 00111000 00011111 10101101 00110011 00011011 01000001 11011111 11010011 11010011
11010110 10011101 10011000 01011100 00011100 11101101 01010001 10000011 10001100 10011010
01111010 01110100 00111001 00011100 10011010 01100000 00100001 10110011 11110010 11110001
11011000 01010001 10010011 10111000 01100100 01110001 10011111 01011010 01001001 00111011
10001100 01001110 10000000 10000010 01001001 11001011 01010100 10010010 00010000 10100011
10110110 01111011 01010011 01011000 11100111 00100100 11110001 10001010 00011111 00100101
01111000 00011100 10010011 11111001 01010000 11110101 00000001 00111010 11101100 01101100
11100000 00001010 10001101 01001111 11011111 00100111 10010010 00001101 00111111 10011100
01111110 00110100 00100111 00100011 00000000 01010101 00101101 00001000 00000111 00111001
01010000 10100011 10001111 11101111 01111011 10011010 00001010 11100100 11100000 11111010
01010011 00000000 00101011 00011001 01101001 00110010 01001111 10100000 11100111 10011010
01010001 11000010 11111100 11111101 01001111 10100101 00011010 11011010 11100101 10001000
11011100 11111100 10100000 11100000 00000011 10011010 00001001 00100001 11001111 10010111
11001111 10111001 00011001 11000101 00101110 00001001 00111001 00011101 11111011 00010001
01000001 00100111 00111001 11101101 11101101 11011110 10100110 11101111 10101000 10110100
00010001 01111011 10011100 11110110 11000110 01101000 00011001 00100100 01100000 11111101
01001101 00001011 10010011 00100000 11100000 00000000 00001111 01001010 00111000 01010010
01110001 01011010 00100111 11010001 10000110 10000001 10001110 01001110 00101001 00111011
01100111 00110100 00001100 00000011 11010100 10011111 10101000 10100011 10011100 10011100
01110100 10100011 01101101 10000001 10001100 01110001 11001110 00111101 01101000 11000011
00011100 11100011 10100111 01101010 10010001 11111000 11111010 11111010 11010001 10010001
10011100 10000001 10001100 01111110 10110100 00101101 11110100 00011000 11001110 11111000
11101010 01101001 10101100 10100111 00110100 11100101 01011100 01111111 10001001 10100111
01100111 11111101 10100000 10111110 11011000 10101001 01101101 00000001 11010100 00001100

01100100 10001110 11100011 10111101 00011011 10111101 00110010 01000001 11101111 01001101
01101101 10000111 10001100 10000001 11001111 10100101 00001101 11111011 11001110 10001101
10001100 01111010 01110111 10101010 01111011 10010000 00111011 01110110 00000111 00000011
10011110 10011001 11110100 10100000 00101110 00110000 01110001 10000011 11011100 11010011
01011000 11100111 10010000 00111111 00001010 01000111 00111100 10000000 00001110 00111001
11100100 01010011 01101111 10101000 11011001 00101110 00110010 01111000 11111100 11101001
10100111 10011110 10110100 11011110 01000111 00001001 11000000 10100111 00110010 10110010
10001110 01111001 10101010 01111010 00100001 00000010 10010000 01001111 01000000 00000111
11110011 10100110 10110111 01011100 00010001 11000111 11010110 10011110 11011100 01110100
10100100 11001110 11010011 11010011 11101010 01101001 00101110 01010001 00001101 11001011
00101100 01111100 00101111 00010100 11101101 10111110 10100111 00111111 01001010 01011110
00000111 00000000 11010010 00111001 11110010 11000110 01011011 00111110 11110101 00101100
10101011 00000110 01100011 00100111 01101111 01110001 11011000 11010000 01110010 01111011
11100010 10011010 10000100 00010101 11001000 11100111 11011100 11010010 00000111 00111011
10000000 00000000 11110011 11011110 10000100 11101111 10111000 10000111 10010010 00100011
11000110 01000101 00011111 00101111 11010110 10011000 11000001 10001001 11011101 00100101
00101011 01110100 11111001 01111000 10100011 01000001 11110101 00000001 00100000 11011010
01110110 10101001 11001111 01101010 00110001 10111000 10011100 10010011 10001110 11000010
10001100 10101100 01101010 01001110 01110010 11111110 11110100 10000000 00110000 11111110
00100011 10001100 11010011 11011100 01010111 00001101 11001100 01001111 00000111 00000000
01110110 11000111 01011010 01010000 01011011 00000000 10100111 00000111 11011110 10011100
11000011 11100100 00011100 11100101 11111101 10000101 00000000 10110000 01001110 01111010
11010010 01110001 11010100 00000110 01110010 10100111 00100100 00001100 10011110 11110100
00101110 00110110 10010001 11101011 01000110 00001110 11110010 11001111 11001001 11101101
01000011 01110101 11100100 01010100 10110111 01101101 10000000 00110011 10001001 00000010
11111011 01110111 11101111 01001010 01011011 10101111 00111100 10001110 10010100 00110111
00111100 10011110 00111101 00101000 11011011 11110011 11110010 00111001 11110101 10100111
01110111 11011000 01110110 00010011 00011100 01110011 11110111 11101001 00010010 00110001
11001001 10010000 00010011 00100001 11101111 10011010 01110011 01110010 11011000 00100011
10001111 11100111 01000110 01000000 00111001 00111001 00100100 10011110 11010100 11100100
10101111 10101011 00010000 00000000 01010101 00110000 10000110 10010001 00110010 00011011
00100101 10001111 00011101 10101000 01101100 10011111 01000001 01000011 00011100 00000010
00111010 00011111 01101010 01110110 01111101 00000111 01110000 00100111 00100111 10001111
11100111 01000110 00111001 00100100 01110111 11101101 01001011 10110100 00000000 00110001
11000101 00001011 11000001 00111001 11111100 11101010 01011010 10111110 10000000 10000100
01000000 01000001 11110110 10100101 11011100 01001000 11001000 00010100 10011001 11000111
00100111 10111101 00001010 01001110 11000011 10011111 01011010 00101100 10110110 01100010
00010001 01000110 01000001 11100111 10010011 11101111 01001010 10111001 11000110 00001001
11100100 11010010 00101110 00111110 10011110 11011000 10101001 00111111 11001110 00101001
00101011 00100100 00000011 01010111 11101011 10001010 01110111 01100011 11011010 10011010
00110011 11001101 00001010 00111101 01111010 11010000 11111011 10000000 01110001 11000111
00110100 00101001 01100011 10011111 10011011 00100010 10011010 11111111 00000000 01110011
10101110 00110011 11101001 01001110 00000011 10010001 11111110 00110100 00100110 10011000
11011000 00110110 01110010 00000000 00111000 00010100 00010001 11001101 00011101 00001111
00110100 01100000 11100000 11010000 10100011 01110001 00000111 10111001 10100001 10110000
00111001 00111101 10101000 01011110 00000101 00000111 00000001 00110000 11000111 10010011
01000011 11011011 01010000 00010000 01110010 00010011 00000011 00011001 00011101 01101001
01001000 00111000 00000011 00111100 01100110 10001110 01000000 11000101 00011101 00010111
00011111 10100101 01001111 00110010 01000101 10001001 10001100 00001111 11000110 10000110
00000000 10001100 11010010 11110101 00011100 11110001 01000011 01110110 10100010 11110110
00100000 00111001 11100010 10000010 01110011 11011011 11011010 10001110 10000100 11010000
11000100 00101010 11100100 11110101 11001110 00101001 11101110 01011000 00101000 00100100
11100011 00011000 00010100 01100111 10101111 01111100 01110111 10100111 01110100 00011000
11110101 10100110 10100000 11000111 00011000 10100001 10101011 10110000 00010000 00001111
10010111 00000011 10100111 10101101 00001100 01001111 01001010 00001001 00011101 00000001
11100110 10001110 00110000 01101000 01000100 00001010 00000111 11100001 01001101 11001110
00011011 10011100 10011111 01111010 01110110 01111000 00111100 10011010 01101110 11101100
01100011 00001010 11100100 10011010 01111101 01110101 00000001 01000001 11111001 11111000
11101100 00111010 11010001 10111000 11100100 00001110 11110100 11000001 10111001 11110010
00000111 00000111 00110100 11111110 00111011 00011111 11000110 10000110 10010011 01100011
11011000 01001100 11110000 00110011 11010100 11010011 10000000 00110001 10101111 10111101
00110111 00011111 10001101 00101001 11111001 01011111 00100111 10101110 00101010 00110101
10111101 11000000 01000101 00100100 10100000 00011101 00010011 10110101 00101000 01010000
00001111 10110000 10100100 01100110 11000111 01001111 11001110 10000111 11001110 00000001
00000111 00100000 11010010 11011100 01111110 01100011 01111011 11110101 11001101 00111000
00011100 00000001 10001010 01100000 00011000 01010011 11001001 11001001 00111101 01101001
01110111 01100010 00110000 00000111 01011111 01011010 10100101 01100101 10110000 11000001
01011011 00111100 00010000 01110000 00111011 11010011 10011100 11111100 10000001 10111101
01111010 10011010 01100111 11001101 11010011 01110110 00111101 01111000 10100101 00111100
10000001 11001110 00000000 00111101 01001101 00001101 10100000 00011111 10110111 10011100
00000001 01010001 11101110 00000100 11100011 11110010 00110100 10101011 10111001 10110011
10000011 10000000 01111000 00100110 10010001 01001000 00000011 00000011 10011100 01110111
10100101 01110000 00011110 00110000 00010011 00000111 00111110 10110100 00100110 00001011

11100100 10011010 01101010 10011100 10011100 01110111 10100100 01010110 00011001 00111001
00000011 00100011 10001010 10010111 01111110 10100010 10111000 00110011 10000110 01110010
00111111 00011010 01010110 00000011 10110110 01101001 10101010 00110110 10111000 11101011
10010010 01101000 11110011 00000000 00101000 10100000 11101111 11000111 01111010 10111011
10101011 00000101 10000001 01111000 01100011 11000101 01110011 11111110 00110010 11111111
00000000 10001111 01001000 00100100 00000011 00011100 11100010 10111010 00001100 11100001
10000000 11100111 10011110 10100100 10011010 11001101 11010111 11101101 00001101 11011110
10011011 00111010 01110000 00000111 01010001 10011111 01101010 10011001 10111101 00101100
01010100 00110100 01110111 00111000 00011011 01111001 10110001 00101110 11011100 01110000
01111011 11010110 11000101 10011100 10111000 11101111 10010011 10011010 11100110 01001100
10100101 01100100 11001111 11100111 01011010 10010110 10010111 00000000 11100011 10011010
11000001 10101011 00100101 01100110 01111010 10110100 11100110 01110100 11101000 11000001
10010011 11010110 10011111 11100101 11110001 11010010 10110011 01101101 01100101 11000110
00111001 11101011 01011010 11010001 10110000 01100101 00011000 00111001 10101000 01101011
10101011 00110100 10011001 01010010 01000101 11001111 01101010 10101100 10011110 01100100
00110010 10001001 00100011 01110010 00011100 00011110 11010101 10101010 11110001 11110001
01010100 10100100 10001011 10110101 01011011 11011101 01011000 11100110 10011101 00110011
01000110 11000111 01010110 01010110 11100010 11100000 01100000 11111111 00000000 11001111
01001110 10110101 10101000 10110010 10001001 01010111 11100100 01100100 00100011 00111101
01010110 10111001 01001100 01101100 00111000 11101101 01010010 01000011 00111100 10010001
00011100 10100011 00010001 11111000 11010101 00101010 10010110 11011100 11100110 10011101
00010101 11010000 11101010 00110000 01110111 11100101 11011000 01111101 00101000 11000111
00111100 00000001 01011000 11010000 01101010 11001101 10111011 00010011 00101110 01111101
11000101 01101000 11000111 01111101 00010100 10011000 11000100 10011000 11101101 10001100
01010101 11111011 01000100 11110100 00110001 01110100 11011010 00100110 11001110 01001001
01101101 11000100 10011100 01110001 10011010 01110111 01010000 00110011 01001101 01011001
00100011 01101100 10110000 00111001 00100011 10101001 10100110 00111011 01100000 00010011
10010000 00111001 11110101 10101011 01010010 10001010 11101010 00101110 01010010 01011111
10111100 00111000 11101111 01001000 11011000 01000011 10000010 11000011 00010101 00010100
10110111 00010001 00100010 00010101 01000110 11011110 01001000 11100100 10001110 11010101
01010001 10100101 11001000 11101011 10000000 00101011 00110111 01010101 01011100 10101000
11010011 01101100 10110110 11110111 01001001 00011111 11011101 11001011 10011111 01000001
01010101 01001110 10100001 10110100 11111100 10010001 11111110 01100110 10100010 01100110
01011010 10001001 11000000 11001110 01111101 01101010 00011101 01001001 01101110 10001101
01010101 00110100 01001010 10011010 10010001 10001011 01111111 11101110 01000001 11011101
11010111 10011010 01010100 11010100 01010100 10010010 01100110 10001100 11100100 11111010
00011010 10100011 00100000 11001000 10101010 11111001 00111101 00101010 11010011 11010111
01110011 01001111 01100011 00010110 01101101 00101110 10100101 00000100 10000111 01101111
11001110 00001111 01010011 10011010 01110001 11010100 00101101 10010110 00110010 01001100
10111100 11111010 00000001 01011000 00011011 10111101 11111001 10101000 11011110 01011101
10111001 11001001 10100001 11001001 10001111 11101010 11110001 01100110 11001011 11101011
00010000 01100000 00101000 01011001 00111000 11101111 11011010 10101111 01000001 00111100
00110011 10000100 01101000 11100100 00000101 00110010 01110000 01111101 11101011 10001011
10010110 01110010 00011111 10100110 01000001 10101100 01111011 11111101 01011101 10101101
00100101 11011101 00011011 01101100 01110101 00111100 01110111 10100100 11100100 11101110
10010010 01000001 00101100 00110010 10110110 10000111 10101001 00101110 00110001 11010011
10010001 11010010 10011011 11110010 10010000 10001101 00100111 11011111 00100010 10111100
11110111 01001101 11110001 10000101 11010000 10000100 01100101 10111100 11100001 10011110
01110111 00001010 11101001 00110100 01011111 00010010 11011010 11101010 00111000 10001110
01101001 00100011 10110111 10010100 11110110 00100111 10001111 11001110 10110100 10110011
01001010 11101100 11100111 10010110 00011110 01001011 01010100 01101111 10111001 00100100
11100111 00111011 00110111 10001100 00000001 11101001 01000001 11111001 01010011 11101110
10111001 11000111 01100001 01001100 01001100 01100100 00011100 01100100 01110110 11110111
10100111 01100111 00100100 10011100 01110011 11101111 11010010 10101011 01000111 10110001
10010000 11011111 10011000 10100000 11001111 00100111 11111001 01010001 10000010 00011000
01110010 01111001 11101011 10011010 01111001 11000000 01011100 11101110 00111100 01110101
00011101 00101001 00011001 10001111 11100001 10001010 01011010 10110001 11101000 00101010
10011100 01101100 11000000 11100000 00001100 10010010 01111101 01101010 00111000 11010000
10001101 11100101 11111001 01110111 00111001 01100011 01000010 10010000 01011100 11110011
11000111 01111010 01111000 00111110 10100000 01010001 01111011 01101110 00100110 00110011
01101110 00111000 10100111 11100000 01100000 10000010 01001000 00011101 01110011 01001101
00100000 01110001 11001001 11100100 11010011 10011000 01100000 10011100 10010010 01001000
11101010 00111101 00101000 10111001 00000000 00000000 01101111 01100000 00101001 10101100
00110010 10100100 01101110 00011111 00110111 00000011 00110100 11111100 10101000 01000011
11001110 00000110 01111010 11010011 00001001 00101010 01000000 00011000 11001110 00110011
11110100 10101011 01110110 01011010 00100010 10101100 00110101 00110110 10101000 00100011
00111011 11001000 11101011 01000111 00000100 01100101 11010100 01111101 01001001 10100101
01100010 01111100 10111100 11100001 11110011 11011111 10011110 10110100 10011000 11101000
00001000 11101011 11001111 00111101 10101000 11101000 00001100 01010110 00100000 01111001
01100000 01110111 11101111 01001100 01100101 01100010 11111001 00100111 10001100 01100011
10101111 01001010 01110011 11100001 10000001 00111100 10010000 00000101 00110011 00000000
00011100 01111111 10011100 11010100 11011111 10111000 10000101 01001110 00110010 01110001
10010011 11011011 00110100 10010001 11101110 01101001 00001001 01110011 11000000 00111100

10011010 00011110 01000000 10100011 00011000 00111001 00111110 10010100 10101000 00110000
00001110 01000111 11100001 01001110 01001001 11101100 10000100 00111011 11101111 01110100
00011100 01110110 10100110 00011100 11100111 00011111 11000001 11011110 10011111 10111011
00011000 00000011 10001110 11100110 10011011 10001100 00011111 10010000 01110101 11101111
01010010 10110111 00101010 11101100 01001100 10001100 11100011 11111100 10001010 01010100
11011010 10101001 11010110 10000110 01011100 11110110 11001111 00111110 10110100 10011111
01111011 00111000 11101000 00111000 10101101 00011010 11010000 10010001 00010111 01110001
11011111 10010001 10001100 11111110 10010100 11101110 10100011 10011110 00000101 00100011
01000110 01011001 10001011 01101110 11100011 00011101 00111011 01010011 00110010 10111100
11100111 10011100 01010110 01110010 01111011 00010110 00111100 10010011 10110111 00100000
01110001 01001000 00001000 11011011 10001100 01010000 10111000 00111000 00000011 00111110
11110100 00110001 11111110 00010100 10100010 11101010 11100000 00000100 01110010 00000000
00111001 10100110 11100100 01111001 10000011 10111000 11111110 01010100 01101101 00100100
11110010 01110001 01001110 11111110 00001010 10100111 01100111 10100000 00001100 11001011
00010000 00000111 10100001 11101001 01001010 01001000 00101011 10110100 00001110 00001111
01010010 00001101 00011101 01001110 00110011 11110101 10100100 00000000 10000010 01001001
11100100 01100011 10001110 00101010 10101110 10010010 00010101 10000110 00100111 00110001
11100000 10001100 11010011 11110010 01110000 00110000 00111001 00010100 01110100 01000011
10000001 01001000 11011100 00101110 01110011 11010111 10100000 00011101 10101010 01011110
11111010 00000110 10100001 10011100 10110011 11100111 10010011 11011110 10001100 01110101
11110100 00110100 11010110 00000000 00001100 01110110 00011101 11111101 01101000 01100000
00110010 00111001 10100101 10101000 01011100 01110111 01000010 01111101 01101001 10011001
00100101 11000001 00011100 11110001 11011110 10010101 11001001 00101100 01111000 00011000
11101101 01001000 10111000 11000111 01111100 01010101 01011011 11100110 01010000 10001010
00110011 10011111 01111110 11111101 11101000 01111110 10000000 01111010 00011110 01101001
01000111 01011100 11111010 11110100 10100100 01100101 11001001 11100111 11111111 00000000
11010111 01010010 11011110 10100110 01100011 01001001 00000100 10001111 11010010 10011100
01000111 01001101 10100111 00110100 00011100 10000110 11111001 10000110 00001111 01101010
00110001 10000011 11101001 11110100 10101010 01001010 11000000 00110101 10111110 01011001
01111101 01110001 11001000 10100111 01110011 11001001 00111111 00111001 11101101 11000101
00110100 11100000 10110111 11010011 10111101 00001101 11110111 10111010 11100000 01100110
10100010 11111101 01010001 01100010 00000000 01111001 00101110 01110011 11001101 00011101
01101000 00011100 10010010 01110011 11000101 00001101 11101001 11001110 00101011 01001000
00101011 01011100 00000001 10010111 00111101 10111111 00111010 00111001 11001110 00001111
01101010 00011011 10011100 01100100 10010011 11101101 01001001 10111011 00000011 10111101
00100100 11101100 10001001 10111000 11011110 10000111 10001110 11000111 10110101 00111011
00111101 01111000 11100100 00011100 01010001 10001100 00011100 11110100 10100101 11000111
00100111 10111111 00110100 00111101 01110110 00101000 01100010 11100000 01100111 01110001
11111111 00000000 11101011 01010010 01100100 01110011 11000001 00111111 01001010 01011100
10001100 11100000 11110111 11100110 10001110 00000001 11000110 01101000 01111010 10001001
00000011 00010010 00110000 01010011 10000001 11110100 11001101 00100111 01101100 01010011
11000001 11100111 11011000 11010011 00011100 10000101 00000111 11101011 01001001 01101110
00110001 00000000 01100001 11000000 11101001 11101011 01001011 10000001 11111000 10011110
10100110 10010011 11100110 11101000 00111010 01110110 10100000 00011111 10010000 11100111
11100100 11110111 10101010 01110111 01100010 01010110 00001110 00111110 10100111 11101011
01000011 01110011 10001110 11000011 00111001 10100101 00101011 11110010 00001111 10011000
11111010 11111101 01101001 00011111 00000000 00001100 11110010 00111101 01001001 10101001
00011000 11010111 11111001 10001111 01010011 11000111 10101101 00111001 01111010 11110001
11111001 11010011 00011000 10011100 10011100 10011110 10110100 00000110 11101011 10011010
00110101 10111101 11000101 01100001 01011000 11110011 11010111 10001111 01001010 00001100
01101110 11011100 11100100 10101110 01111011 01010000 11100111 00011000 00000100 10011100
00000001 10011100 01010010 01101110 01101110 11000011 11110011 00110101 01101101 10100001
01011011 01010011 10101001 01110011 10111000 10000010 01001111 01001110 10000010 10000100
01100010 11011000 11001000 11000000 11000111 00010100 11010011 10110111 01110000 01010011
11001101 01001001 10000010 00111010 11100000 10001010 01111101 00000100 00110101 01011011
00000000 11100100 01100011 11011110 10000101 11000110 11101110 10011111 01000011 01001000
00000000 00100100 00000001 11110100 11111010 11010010 10010000 01001000 11000100 01111101
01111101 11101000 01000010 00011100 11000001 10111100 11000011 10010011 10010100 11000111
01101010 01101010 10000001 10010011 11000001 11001101 00001000 00001010 10010011 10111111
00011111 11100001 01001001 10010101 10010001 00110000 10100111 00111000 11101011 01001101
00110110 10110111 00000001 01110010 00110001 11000011 00000011 11101101 01001000 10101100
11000111 10000010 01110011 10011111 01101010 00011000 00001100 01110100 11111100 01101001
01111011 01100000 01110100 10101001 01101110 11000000 00001011 10010101 11111111 00000000
11101011 11010000 11011100 10010010 01001111 01001010 00011011 10101111 00110100 01100100
11100100 10011110 11010101 10100010 11011000 01100011 10110010 00111101 00111111 00011010
01101010 10001110 11111001 11100010 10011100 10111001 01101100 00010011 11010011 11010010
10011010 11100100 00001000 10110011 10010010 00111001 11101101 01010000 11110100 00000001
00110010 01011001 10110001 10011100 11111010 01010010 11100000 00001100 00000111 11111100
00111101 10101001 00000100 10011000 00011101 00110010 01111111 00101010 00111010 11110100
00011100 11100111 10010000 01101000 01001101 00101101 10000100 00111101 10000001 00011101
00000000 00110100 11010110 11111001 10001110 00001001 11000010 00001111 11010110 10011010
11111011 11111010 10011110 10111110 10011101 10101000 11011100 10100100 00010000 00001000
00100100 01110101 11000101 00100111 01101011 11011100 00000101 01110110 00100100 01100000

01111100 10000011 10100110 01110011 01001010 11101101 11110011 00000011 10011110 10011101
01110011 11011110 10100011 01010101 00111111 01111000 11100111 00011001 11101111 01001110
11011011 10000010 01011000 10001100 10001110 10010100 10011011 10110110 11100101 01011000
01110110 01111010 10011111 00110000 10011110 01111000 11100011 10100101 00100100 01011011
01010000 00000000 01111001 11110101 00111110 10010100 10001111 10010101 11111001 01000111
01001110 11010100 10100001 01111000 11000001 11101001 01001101 11110111 00010000 10100011
10010000 00000000 10100100 11100101 01001110 01110001 10010100 10100011 00011111 00111110
01110011 10011111 01011010 00110110 10010011 11000010 11110100 11001110 01110001 01000011
11011000 00000011 00111011 10111001 00000011 00011111 10001101 00001000 00011001 10000000
11000001 11000111 10111101 00011011 10110111 01110001 10110111 00010100 01110001 11001110
01110011 10000011 11011010 10000111 10101110 10000000 00000110 00110101 00100111 10010011
10010010 00101001 00010100 11110101 11000000 00100011 11010011 00110100 10111100 00010110
00100011 00100000 01010010 00101010 11110101 00100100 10001100 01100111 11110011 10101001
10111011 10111000 11101100 00011000 00101101 11010000 11100011 11101011 01001011 11001001
00100000 01110101 10100101 01100010 00000000 11100111 11110101 10100000 00101000 00011001
11100111 00010100 11101110 00100000 00100111 00000111 10100110 00000111 10111101 00100010
11110100 11011100 11111101 11101001 00010100 10001001 00111000 00011101 00111101 01101001
11000100 10000010 11111000 00000000 11110001 11101011 01010011 11100100 10000000 00011000
10001100 01111010 01010000 11000000 00010001 10010110 00110100 10001100 01110011 10011110
11011110 10110100 01100000 00010001 11010111 10011111 01101010 10100100 00110100 00000111
10001110 11111100 10011111 01001010 00000110 11100000 00001001 00100111 00111001 11110110
10100101 01100000 00000110 00001110 01110010 01001001 11101001 01001110 11000110 01110001
01001101 10101101 00000100 00110100 01100011 10111110 00001001 00010100 11011100 10110001
11001001 11100011 11111100 00101001 01001011 01101101 00111000 00001011 10010011 11101011
01000010 10001100 01111110 00100111 10111101 00100100 10101110 00000001 10010011 10001111
11110001 10100101 11001001 00100011 10000011 01001000 00001001 11100111 00100010 10010111
10001100 11100000 01111110 01110100 01110101 00000001 00110011 10011111 01100011 01000011
00101010 10010111 11011101 10011110 01101000 00000111 00000111 11101001 01001011 11010100
01111111 11110101 10101000 11010000 10110001 00010100 00011100 11110101 10100101 11101000
00110011 10001110 01101001 00110001 10011110 10110100 10100001 01000000 00011100 10011010
01001101 10010000 00100110 01001110 01111101 10101000 01100001 11001110 01101000 11001110
00000001 00110100 10001010 01011000 10011100 00011110 01111101 11101010 01110111 01100000
00101011 00010010 00000110 01111010 01111110 10110100 00110010 10000000 00110010 11111101
01110011 01001010 11000111 00100111 00011000 10100110 10110000 11001011 10001100 01111101
01101010 10001011 00010100 10011110 01110000 10111101 01101000 01101100 11110001 11001101
00011001 10100100 00001100 01001011 11100011 10110101 00111011 01011111 01100000 00010100
11100100 00000010 01110001 11001001 10100000 10110001 11101000 00001110 00111101 01111000
10100011 10011111 11111000 00001101 00100111 00101101 11010111 10101101 00100110 10001000
00010111 10010000 00000001 10100100 01100010 01000100 10001000 01111101 01110011 10011010
00111011 11110111 10100101 11100100 01100011 10110111 11010110 10000010 10101100 00001101
10011110 01111001 00111100 10001010 01000110 00000000 01100011 00000000 00001111 01101010
01100011 10010010 01001110 00110011 10001111 01011010 01111110 00111011 10000001 11000000
10101001 11010100 00101100 00101000 11000110 11110010 01111101 11101010 00111101 11011001
01100010 00111010 01110011 10010011 01001011 10111011 10000011 11010111 10010011 11010110
10011011 00101100 10001011 00011000 11000110 01000000 11110101 10100101 10110110 11100011
00100100 11001000 11000111 00000011 00000011 11011111 10111101 00110101 11110000 00110110
00110111 01010010 01000101 01010111 01111011 10111000 10110001 10000100 00100100 11100000
01010100 00111111 01101010 01101100 11111100 10011101 01110011 10011110 01101011 00110111
01010110 11111010 10100010 10010101 00110110 11001011 10101110 11000000 01110101 11000111
10111110 00101010 00111111 00110101 01000111 01010010 00000101 01010000 00100101 11100100
00111100 10010011 01001101 11110010 10110011 10011100 10010011 11111001 11010110 01111110
11011000 11010001 01010001 01100101 11011111 10110110 01000010 10101010 00111001 00111001
11001111 01100001 01001000 01101111 10100000 01010001 10001100 00011100 00001111 01101010
10100011 11100101 01100010 10001111 00101000 00011100 00010001 11010010 10001111 01101010
11101101 01110010 10111101 10001010 00101101 11111111 00000000 01101000 01000100 00111101
01001000 00111101 10110001 01000010 11011110 11000101 10110000 10000000 01111111 01001110
10010101 01001111 11001010 00010100 00110100 01000010 10100111 11011011 00111101 01101100
01010111 10110001 10001001 01111111 11101101 10110000 10000001 10010110 01101111 11001000
01010000 10110111 01110000 10110011 00011100 00110111 00000000 11110101 00111101 11101011
00111101 10100010 00000110 10100011 11110010 01110000 11111101 00101010 01010110 00100001
10100010 01111101 10001010 00110101 10111110 11010000 10100000 01101110 00101100 00001001
00111101 00000110 01111010 01010001 00010100 10110001 11101111 00101100 00001000 00111001
11110111 10101100 10100110 10001111 00000011 00111110 10110100 11001111 00101111 00111001
11110100 10101010 11110110 11111101 01011000 01111011 00010011 01101101 10100101 01010010
01110011 11100110 00001100 01010010 00111011 00101011 00100001 01010010 01010000 10000010
00111001 11001001 10101100 01001101 10100000 10001100 01100000 11111011 01110011 01000110
00001001 00011110 11011001 11101001 01001101 11100010 01101111 10111000 01111101 01011101
10011100 01010110 10100101 10100111 11001110 00101111 10100100 00010001 11000101 00100001
01001100 11110000 01000000 11100000 00001010 01011011 00011011 00101011 11000001 11001111
10010001 00100110 11000011 11010000 11010111 01101010 00100011 11000111 01001010 00010110
00111110 01110000 01101010 00111001 11110100 10110011 01000111 01000010 01010110 00110000
11101101 11100000 10111000 01000000 00001011 10100001 11111010 00010011 01011010 01110110
10011110 01100000 00011000 00100011 00010101 01101111 11001011 01011010 00010110 00110001

01010011 11101101 01011110 11000110 10111100 11101110 11000011 01010010 01010010 01110010
00110001 11001101 00110101 11000001 00100111 10100101 01001010 10100011 00000100 10011111
01011010 00011011 00011101 10101011 01001000 01101010 11111001 10000101 01111011 10010101
11011010 00100000 11000111 10011010 01100111 10010110 10100010 10101101 01001010 00111111
10111011 01001100 01100000 00001111 01001010 10010110 10101110 11000010 11000100 01000001
01010100 00001110 10011100 11010000 10011101 01111000 11101011 01001110 01110000 00000000
11101011 11001101 01010110 01101001 00110000 01110001 01010010 11011011 01001000 01110110
01000101 10110000 01000001 11101110 01000111 11100011 01001100 00100111 10001010 10101110
01100110 00000000 01100011 00111000 00110100 11000011 00111001 11101011 01001111 01010111
11010000 10000111 00011011 10010110 00001100 10000100 01110100 00111000 10100000 01001101
10001110 10100111 00100110 10101001 10110100 11011001 11101011 01001001 11100110 00011100
01110101 10101101 01111001 00000001 10100010 11111011 01001110 00110011 10011100 11010100
01111111 01101000 11100000 11110011 01011001 11111110 01101110 01011111 11011010 10011011
11100110 11110010 01110000 01101001 01011001 11011111 01000010 01011001 01111111 11001111
11100000 01010010 11111001 10000011 00010101 10011110 11010010 01100111 10111101 00001001
00101001 11000111 00110101 10100101 11010011 01000001 10101001 00111011 11111101 11101100
11010101 00111001 10110111 01111111 00001110 01111101 11101010 01001111 00110111 10111001
00110100 01100100 00110111 01001110 01000101 00101010 01110111 10111000 10010011 01101000
11000110 10111110 00101100 10100000 10011110 01111101 11000101 01110001 10011010 11000101
11000100 10011110 01100001 00001110 01110011 11101111 10011010 11101111 11101111 00100001
11110011 01000001 11101011 11111000 01010111 00101001 10101101 11101001 01110010 01001110
00110111 00100000 00000000 11111110 01011001 10101101 11101001 00100100 11011101 11011001
01101101 10110110 10001110 01111010 11010110 11110001 10100011 01110011 10110101 10001110
00111010 10010001 10011010 11010000 01001001 11001100 10000011 01110100 00001100 01000011
10001110 10100000 10011010 11100111 00011000 10011000 01011100 11000100 01111000 00111001
11101001 01010110 00100010 10011100 10001110 01111010 01100010 10111011 01100101 01001001
01001010 11000110 01010001 10101001 01100011 11011001 01111110 00011010 01101010 10010011
01011110 11101001 10010111 00010000 11011100 00110001 01110011 00001011 01111100 10111001
00011101 00000101 01110110 01001011 10011111 00101100 01110001 10010001 11011110 10111100
11000111 11100001 10010110 10111111 00011100 01010010 10111110 10011011 00110010 11000110
10011110 01110011 01101111 01011001 00001111 01010010 01101011 11010011 10100101 01100110
11001001 00011001 11100100 10110111 00011111 01001010 11100111 10101101 00000101 00010111
01100100 01110010 11010101 01010111 10010101 11000001 10001110 01000001 11111100 11110001
01001101 01101110 11111001 11101001 01001101 01111001 00000000 00000111 00011101 01001101
01010111 10111000 10111011 01010101 10001111 11100111 11001110 01001001 11100100 00000001
10011010 11000110 11111101 00001100 11010010 00101100 00011001 00010111 00011011 01111010
00001111 01011010 01100100 10010010 00011000 11000000 01011100 00010010 01111010 11010101
00001001 01101111 10110110 10111000 11111101 11010011 11100011 00011100 10010010 01101010
10110100 10111010 10000000 01100011 10111001 11011011 11001011 11001111 01001100 11010101
01011101 10111110 10000011 00110110 11110111 11100111 00000011 00011111 00111001 11101101
01001101 01010010 10110001 01100111 00000000 00000111 00100100 10010110 11001101 01110010
11010111 11011010 11000011 00000101 01000100 01000110 11110011 00011111 00111101 10001111
01000001 11101011 01011001 00010111 00111110 00100101 10001010 00001100 11100110 11111100
01101111 11101000 01000110 11101100 10011100 01010100 11110011 01101001 10100000 00011101
11100100 11010011 11000100 10101011 10110000 00110110 01001110 01110011 11000101 00110101
00011100 01110100 01111100 11111001 10011101 01001101 01111001 11101101 10110111 10001011
00101100 00100100 10011001 00100010 00110011 01101100 11100111 11100110 10010000 10010011
01011011 10010110 01011010 10010101 10111100 11001110 01111110 11001111 00100001 10010111
10110111 10011000 00001110 01000110 00101010 10100010 10110100 11010100 01010110 00111010
10111111 00111001 01100110 11001111 10010111 00101001 11011001 11010011 10000001 11010010
10010101 10100101 01010000 00001111 00111000 11011011 11010111 11011110 10110001 01101101
01101110 10110001 00011001 01010000 11000100 01111111 00011001 00100111 10100101 01101000
01011011 11111110 11110100 00000110 00000011 00011100 01100111 00110101 00101010 00110111
01100001 01110010 11001110 00110011 00010000 11101010 00000001 00111001 11111010 11010011
11000000 11000100 10101110 00111000 11001000 00010100 11000101 00100100 10000100 00111101
01110001 11011000 11010010 10100111 00111011 11001001 11111110 00110011 11001101 01011010
01000001 01110000 11001111 00011001 01010001 11001001 00111101 01001101 00111011 00111000
00111001 11101111 01000011 00001111 10010111 10101111 00110100 11011100 00010011 11101111
11101011 01001101 11101110 00110000 01111110 00000010 00000010 11011100 10111110 01110001
11101100 00101001 00010101 01000111 00111000 11001111 11111000 11010010 10111110 00011001
10010001 10111101 00101001 11001101 11010011 10001010 10011011 11011001 11101000 00000011
01010101 11001110 00001000 11101011 10001110 11010100 11011111 10011000 10001000 11110000
01110000 10000000 11100100 10001111 01011010 01110110 01110001 11000101 00100011 11100001
10010011 00000100 01110000 01101001 11111010 00000000 10000100 11100011 11100101 00000011
10001111 01111010 01101110 11010000 01110110 01110011 11010010 10011100 10100000 10010011
11010110 10000110 11000110 11101110 00000111 00010101 00101101 01101011 10101000 00000110
01000000 11101001 11010110 10011010 11000000 10000110 11001000 00110100 11100101 01011100
01111110 01110100 11010011 11111110 10110011 11010000 01110111 11001101 00111101 11000100
10000111 00110010 10000000 00001110 01001111 00011000 10100110 11001010 01111100 10111000
11110011 10001100 11100111 10100111 11010110 10001100 00010010 10011001 11101010 01111101
01101001 00011000 01110100 00011001 11001001 11110101 10100001 11001001 00001100 01010111
11111001 01010100 01110001 11001001 00110100 10011001 00111011 11110010 11100111 10001100
01110001 01001011 10011110 11001011 11010000 11110100 10100100 11001110 11011110 01001101

01001101 11101110 11110100 00000000 00100011 10011010 01100011 00011111 01001110 01101001
11101101 11001000 00011101 10111101 00101001 10011000 11100111 00100011 10000001 10011110
01110011 11011110 10110100 01011010 00010010 00100000 00011001 11001000 11110111 10100000
01110010 01110001 10001100 00001111 10101101 00101010 01100101 10001111 01000000 00010011
00111100 01111011 11010001 10000000 00001001 11100111 00111001 11101001 10011010 00011001
01000011 01011000 10001101 10001110 01011111 00111000 11000101 00001000 01001110 11000000
01011111 10000011 11101001 01001110 11100111 10010110 11000001 11000110 00111001 00100111
10100101 00100010 10001100 11110011 10011110 10110101 00010111 00000001 00111001 00100110
10000101 00111001 01110010 00111101 00111000 11001001 00110100 10101100 00111001 00000011
10110101 00001111 11010011 10100110 01001111 11010110 10101101 00100110 10110101 00000001
00111011 01100110 10011010 10011100 10011100 10000001 11011110 10011110 01110000 00010111
00010100 10001101 10011110 10010100 11010110 10111011 10000000 11000111 00111100 10011111
01001100 11100100 10011111 01011010 00111010 10010011 01001010 10100001 01111100 10111010
00110000 01110110 11110100 11100100 11010110 01111011 00110000 00010101 10111010 01010011
00011011 11101110 01100000 11110111 11101111 01000011 10011100 00001101 10111101 00111101
01001101 00101111 01010110 01000011 11011000 01110111 11110101 10101011 10111101 11110110
01100100 00001010 11111000 11000000 11000111 01010010 01101001 00000110 00000111 01011110
10110100 00110111 01011111 10010111 10011010 01100011 11100111 10001110 01111000 00110101
00110110 00101100 01110110 00110111 10010011 10001110 00001110 01111010 11010000 01000000
11100000 01111010 11111010 01010011 01001110 01110000 00110001 11000000 10100000 11110101
00011110 11011101 01101001 01101011 10111000 00001000 01110001 10010001 10010011 11010011
10110101 00101111 00011000 11100100 01111110 00010100 10011100 01110111 10100001 00000110
00001110 00001001 11100000 11010101 10110110 11010010 00000000 11001110 01011011 10001110
01111001 11100000 01010010 01001000 01110001 00011111 01001110 00001111 10101101 00111000
10010000 01011000 10101111 01001111 10100101 00100110 01000001 11101011 11010000 01010100
11011001 10000000 10001000 01001111 00000100 11100111 11110011 10100110 10010000 01110001
10010011 11001101 00111001 00000111 01111110 01111110 10010100 00110001 00111000 11001100
10011111 00100000 11001111 01001010 00010011 11101000 00000000 01110111 00011110 10011011
00000111 01111110 01001101 00110101 10011000 00011000 11000000 11000110 01001001 11101010
01101001 00110111 01111001 10000100 11111010 01010011 11010100 00011110 00000000 11100011
11010011 00110100 10100011 10111110 11000011 00001100 00000010 01110011 11111101 01101001
10111001 01010000 01001001 11001110 01110001 11010011 00010100 10001111 10001110 10011000
11100011 00111101 01001101 00101000 00000000 00111000 10101010 01110001 01110111 00010000
11011100 01100100 11100100 11110010 01001101 00101011 00010000 10100111 00001100 01111001
10100001 01110010 01001000 11101101 11101111 01010001 11101101 00011111 11011100 11011101
11101111 01000011 10000101 10111100 11000100 10011010 00111010 11000000 01000000 00111111
11001111 00010100 00111110 11100010 00110001 11111100 00010100 11111100 01111110 01011110
10110100 00010001 10000011 11010110 10101001 00101011 10110001 01011100 01101010 00010011
10110100 10001110 11010100 10011111 00110000 00111001 00001101 11111001 11010010 11110011
10011111 10101101 00100110 11101101 11010010 01100000 00001100 11100011 11010110 10001101
10000100 00100000 11111001 10000110 11010111 00011001 00111000 11100100 00011010 00010111
00100100 10001101 10011011 00110000 00111010 11100010 10010111 00000100 00000011 11011110
10001110 00000111 10101111 11100001 01001101 00110110 00000010 11110100 01111111 10100101
00011001 11000111 00111000 10100001 01010111 00000011 01110111 00100100 11111011 11010010
01101101 00000001 11110010 01111111 00101010 00011100 10010000 00001111 01011110 01001111
01011111 01111100 11010011 00110111 01100100 10011110 10111011 00110011 01001011 10000000
00011000 00001101 11000000 00011010 00111000 00011001 11111001 10110011 10010011 01010100
10010000 00001101 11011100 01001011 00000000 00001111 11001001 11101010 01111010 11010010
10011100 11100100 01100111 10101001 10100011 00111100 11100111 10100000 11110100 11000101
00000000 11100111 00000100 10000001 11000111 10101101 01000110 10000000 00101111 00011001
00000011 10100011 11010000 11001100 00110001 11001111 00100100 11110110 00010100 10001110
00000001 00111001 00111100 11010010 00001110 00000110 11101100 01100011 10001110 11100010
10000100 10110100 10111101 11000000 01011111 00110100 11110110 01010011 11110100 10100001
01000000 00111100 11110100 11110101 00111000 10100100 01000010 00011000 01101110 11000001
00010100 10111000 11101011 10011110 01101000 01101001 00000000 10101101 11001011 11100011
10001100 00001010 01000111 11000111 00011000 11101000 00111001 10100101 01101101 10101011
10000011 10110100 11100100 11010011 01011001 01000010 10010010 01001001 00100111 00111101
10101000 10110011 00000001 11011100 11100100 01100000 10001010 01110100 10001100 00010100
00000010 01001111 00010100 11001100 10000010 00001001 11001000 00001001 11101000 01101001
00011110 00101111 10011001 00011000 10011100 11100000 01110000 00101001 10100101 10100000
00001011 10000010 10111001 11001001 11100111 10110110 00101000 00000001 10000010 11100111
11110011 10100001 10001001 00001111 10001100 01100101 11001001 11101001 11101001 01001010
11011011 01000001 11001011 10110110 00110000 00111101 01101000 01110111 00000001 00000001
11100100 01101110 00011100 11010010 00010000 00111010 01110111 00011100 10011010 00001001
11101000 11000011 10011100 11010011 01010101 01110010 01111001 11110101 11001101 00101111
00110110 00110000 00011000 00101010 01011000 01100111 00011000 11100010 10001101 10100111
00100011 00111100 10001111 01001010 01111001 00100100 01100111 10000011 10000011 11000000
10100100 11001001 10010001 11001001 00100111 00000000 01010010 11110100 00011111 10101000
11011101 10001100 01111001 00111101 11111101 01111011 01010000 00001001 11100111 00100111
10001111 01011010 01110110 00110111 00000010 01101000 00000000 01100011 00100100 11100000
00001110 11010100 00111011 00110010 01000101 01100010 00000000 00011110 10011111 11001110
10010001 01011000 00000011 10000000 01110000 01111101 11101000 01010011 10111111 11101001
01001011 10000000 00110010 01001000 11100010 10011010 10110000 11011000 11001110 10101110

00111101 11111001 10100111 00010101 00100100 00010010 00111111 11111101 01110100 01100111
10001110 00000101 00011101 01111000 11001111 00011001 11100110 10001011 00101011 10000110
10100010 10101011 00011110 00111010 01100111 00010100 00001111 01011111 11010110 10001100
01101110 01001100 00000010 00000111 10101001 10100100 00100000 00010001 10010100 01101110
00000101 00100111 01100010 10000101 00000000 11101100 11001011 10011110 00111101 01001101
00001000 00000110 00000111 10101101 00101011 01110010 01111101 10101001 11011001 11001111
00100010 10011011 01000100 00001101 01101110 10111000 10100110 11010010 10110111 00100111
00111000 10100100 01011010 00110101 01011010 00000000 00000001 10011110 11110100 00000101
11100111 10101101 00101111 00000000 01100111 10100101 00100001 00011001 00011000 00011101
11001111 00110101 00111010 10000000 10100011 00101101 11101110 00101000 01101010 00111110
11101010 01111100 10011101 11101000 00000011 00011001 00101100 00110011 11111000 11010011
10111000 00000000 11100100 10010001 01000110 01001110 01001110 00000110 00000101 00001101
11010011 00011100 11010001 11111100 01011111 11101100 11010010 10001101 11111010 10010110
00100001 11000000 00000011 11100110 11001001 00111101 00101001 01010111 11100101 00000111
10011010 01001100 11100100 10010000 00111011 01110111 10101000 01011110 01111000 10010111
00100101 11100100 00011100 01010100 10111101 00000100 10100010 01001100 10100111 00111100
01100011 11110000 10100101 01100000 00110001 11110011 01010101 01000111 10111110 10001001
01111010 00001100 11110011 01010001 11111101 10110100 10110001 00100100 00001100 01111010
01010100 00101010 10001010 11000101 10101010 01110010 01111101 00001011 11111100 10001111
11101011 11000101 00100000 00111110 10100111 11101011 01010100 00111110 11010111 00110001
00111100 01100010 10010001 01100110 10010101 10001110 01001001 00010100 00101100 01001010
11011000 10101111 01100011 00100010 11110010 11110001 10010010 01001111 00110100 11010011
00100111 00111011 10011001 10000111 10110000 11001101 01010001 01101001 00001001 00000111
10010011 10000011 11101111 01010001 11110011 10010011 11011110 10100010 01010101 01010101
11001011 01010100 01111011 10010111 11001100 11110001 11100100 10011110 10011001 10101000
11001101 11010010 11100011 00000000 00010010 01111101 01110011 01010101 10111111 10000010
10010101 01000000 11110100 10101100 11011100 11011101 11110100 01100101 00101010 00101000
01111011 11001110 11100100 01100000 01110000 00111101 10101010 00000010 00001001 00111100
11110011 11001101 01001110 11000010 10011011 10000001 11010110 10110011 01111010 10111011
10010110 10100000 10010000 10001010 10100000 01010000 10110001 10000000 01110011 11011010
10100100 11101101 10011010 01001111 11111101 00000110 10001011 00010100 10000110 11100011
00111101 00101001 00110110 11100011 10101111 01001010 01111010 11010000 11000110 10100110
11011101 11000111 01100010 00110001 11010000 10001010 01011100 10000001 01000110 01000000
11110100 11100110 10011000 01001110 01001001 11000101 01010111 10010000 00100001 00001000
11001001 10100101 11100010 10011101 11010000 00000000 01111000 10100110 10110101 00101001
00101011 00101101 11000110 10000110 10010001 10011110 00101000 11101111 01010010 01100100
00010000 00111101 01101001 10011000 11111111 00000000 11110101 11010011 01001001 00101110
10000010 01100100 01100100 01110011 01000111 01001010 01111011 01100000 01010001 10000000
01000101 00101110 01010100 11001010 10001001 00001110 00000001 00011110 11010100 10001010
00111101 10101010 01111100 00001100 01110011 01001101 00101011 11000111 01011010 00111001
01100011 10111010 00011011 00100011 11100110 10010001 10001000 11001110 01111101 11101001
11111000 11111001 11111010 11010011 00001000 00111000 11110111 10100010 11000000 00111100
00011110 00111010 01010011 01011101 10110001 01001000 11011001 00110101 00010100 10111001
00010100 00101000 01011100 01010111 00100110 11011100 00000111 00011001 10100100 00000100
01110110 10101010 10011011 10001000 11001101 01001000 10001101 10011110 00101001 11111100
11001010 10110111 01010010 01100110 01101100 01010100 00101101 00100000 01011110 10010101
00011100 10101101 11001111 00000110 10100011 10010100 11111100 10110101 10100100 00011101
11110111 00010011 01100100 01010111 00010011 11111100 11100100 00001010 10101001 00101100
11011000 00110100 01011100 01100111 11010110 10101001 00110110 01001001 00110100 01110010
01011000 01110111 00101100 11111001 10100100 10011110 11011111 01011100 01010011 11111100
11001100 00001111 10011110 10101001 00101100 10000111 00111001 11001101 01001000 11100100
10110111 00000100 11110000 00001111 01011010 10110101 00010100 10001001 11010100 10011011
11001100 00111101 10101010 00111001 01100110 00100101 01111000 00111111 10101101 01000010
11110010 11101101 00011110 11011110 10110101 01011101 10100101 11100111 00010101 01010010
01111011 01011100 00011110 10100100 11001111 00111011 01010010 00101100 11000111 00011001
11001101 01010110 01101001 01111101 00000001 00110101 00011001 10010100 00001110 01101010
11011101 00111101 00000101 10110001 01110011 11001110 00111000 11001001 11111100 01101001
10101111 01110100 01000000 10101010 01001101 00101110 11010000 01001110 01111010 10011010
10000010 01101001 11110000 10011101 01111010 11010010 10001101 00110100 11101100 10000001
10111110 11100110 10011111 11011010 10110010 01001111 00111101 01101010 01011000 01101110
10000010 10100110 00110011 11110101 00111001 10101110 01111101 10100111 00111001 00010100
10010010 01011100 01101101 00000110 10101001 01000010 11001110 11011101 01000110 01110100
00010010 11011110 00000010 00001110 11000011 11000111 10101101 01100100 01011110 11011100
00110000 10000100 10110111 10100111 00110101 10010011 01110111 10101011 00001000 11000110
00111101 01101011 00001111 01010010 11010110 01001100 11001111 10000100 00100111 11101001
01011010 01000010 10000011 01111010 00011001 10111010 10001001 00010101 00110101 11001001
01010110 01011001 10000100 10111011 01110000 11100111 10101001 00011101 11101010 10010010
01001011 11000110 00001001 11000001 11110101 10100111 01011111 11100110 01001000 10010001
11110001 10010111 11001111 00100111 11010010 10101010 11000010 00111100 11011110 00111101
11111001 10101111 01000110 10010101 11101100 01100000 11100101 10101110 10000110 11001101
10001101 11000100 10010001 00110000 10010001 00011011 00001110 00001000 01110000 01101011
11011111 01110100 10111011 11010110 10111011 11010010 10101101 10101110 00001100 01101110
00100100 01111000 10000001 00101100 11110101 11100000 11111110 00011110 11010010 11100111

11010101 00101110 11100011 10000110 11011100 10111111 01011100 00110011 00000011 11110111
00000111 01111100 11010111 10101011 11101011 00011110 00100000 10000011 01000101 10110000
10110111 10110111 01111001 10000001 01110001 00011110 11000000 00010111 11010000 01110001
10011100 01010110 00010101 11100010 10010110 10001011 01010010 01101010 00110011 01011110
11110010 11110111 01101011 01100000 00111111 01000011 10001100 10011111 11010110 10110001
00110101 00111111 00010000 01011000 11101001 10101011 10011011 10101011 10000000 11101110
01011011 00011011 01000001 11100100 11010111 10011111 01011111 11111000 10101110 11101010
11100100 11001000 00100000 11111101 11011010 00011110 00110011 10001100 10011100 01110111
10101100 00011101 11011011 11011100 10110100 10000111 01111001 11110101 01101010 11100111
10000101 00000111 01111101 01011001 00000111 01101101 10101010 11111100 01000001 10111000
01101000 11001000 10110000 10001100 00100011 11100111 11100101 00100111 10011100 10001010
11000001 11010100 10111100 01010011 10101010 11011111 00000010 10010111 00010111 00100100
01000111 11111101 11011000 11111110 01001100 11010110 00011100 10101101 00011001 11100010
00111100 01111110 00000011 10100101 01000110 01100010 10010001 10001111 01011110 00001111
01111110 11110101 11010111 00011010 00110110 01000100 11011111 01010010 11100011 11011111
01001010 01100011 11000001 10010000 11100100 01111010 00010011 01010001 10000010 00010111
10101111 11100111 01010101 10100100 10001100 00101000 00011011 11001111 00111110 11010100
10001101 00100111 11001000 01110011 11000111 11010110 10101001 01000010 00101011 01110100
01001001 00110011 11001100 01100010 11111011 10111000 00101000 01111011 01110101 10101001
00101100 11110101 01101001 11101101 00100101 11001100 00001100 01010000 01110111 00011001
11100010 10101001 01000101 00100000 10010011 01111000 11110100 10101001 01100011 10110111
11110011 10011111 11100110 00000111 01100111 01001110 00001110 00101010 11011100 01101101
10111001 01100111 01101111 10100000 11111000 11011101 10100011 01011001 11100010 10111100
10001101 00011110 00111100 01100011 00100000 11100011 11110101 10101111 01000001 11110000
11110110 10111011 01101111 01111001 01101000 01100101 01001001 00000111 10010110 10001010
00000110 11011110 10100111 10011010 11110000 10111011 10011011 01010100 10000110 00110001
10111100 10000000 11111001 00111001 11000001 11101100 00101000 11010011 11110101 00011001
10110100 11111001 10100011 10010110 00001001 00011100 01100000 10000111 11101011 11010110
10111001 10101010 01010010 01001111 01011000 10001011 01010100 01111101 00011111 00011100
11000000 11000011 00010011 01100000 11100000 10010011 10000000 00001101 01001000 10000101
10001010 00010010 01001000 01001100 10011100 11010111 10000101 11011001 11111000 11111011
01011010 10110101 00001110 10100010 01101000 10011100 00011100 11110101 01011110 01111001
10101101 00111101 00111111 11100010 01011101 11100100 01101000 00000101 11110100 01011110
01101010 00001110 00001110 00110001 11010010 10110001 11110110 00010011 01011011 10000101
11001111 01100100 01010011 10011100 00010101 11101001 10011110 00101001 01011011 10000000
11111100 11100100 01010111 00011111 10100001 11111000 11100011 01001110 11010100 10000111
10010011 00011001 01110001 00101000 00111100 00000110 00011000 11001111 11100001 01011101
01000101 10111101 11000000 10111000 10001000 00011100 01100000 00011100 01110100 10101100
00011101 11100011 01110100 00110010 11001111 01110000 00000111 10100111 00110100 00000011
11010111 00011101 00000101 00000011 00000100 11111010 01010001 11010011 00111110 10000110
10101010 11011011 00001001 00110000 01011100 10010100 00111000 11101010 01111010 01010011
01010000 01110011 10001100 11100111 00011101 11101001 11001010 01000110 00001101 00110101
01111001 00110100 10011010 11101100 00110001 01011000 11110010 01000000 11101111 11010010
10010011 10111110 00111101 01101000 11100011 01111001 11001111 01011100 01010000 11011100
10011100 00001110 01000111 01101010 01111010 01110111 00000001 01011011 00100100 10011110
01111010 01010010 00010000 00011000 01100111 10110111 01100001 11101011 01000001 00000100
10111011 11110100 11100010 10011000 11011000 00100001 00010111 10010000 00000101 01001101
11010000 00001010 01111010 01101110 00101101 10011100 01111011 01010010 00101000 11101010
01000101 00011100 00010000 00010100 01110100 00010100 00110001 11000101 00001001 00100111
10111000 00000011 01110000 01000000 11110110 11001101 00101110 00000001 01110001 10111100
10001010 00001001 11000111 00111101 11001001 11000101 00001100 00000000 00111100 01110010
01101010 11101111 01101101 00000000 10001111 01110001 01101001 00111001 11100011 10110000
10100111 01110010 00001101 00101011 00001111 10011000 11111010 01111111 01011010 00111000
11011110 01001111 01001010 01101111 01111011 10000001 00011011 10010011 10001111 10100101
00101111 00111110 01100001 11110100 00000011 10001010 00110011 11110011 10011100 10011110
00001111 01101010 01110010 01100100 10000010 01001000 11000110 01111010 00001100 11010010
10110101 11000000 10000111 01101011 11001000 00110011 00100011 01100100 01111011 00001110
00101001 01111101 10111011 00000001 01001110 11000001 00101010 00000110 01110000 00000001
11111100 11101000 01011110 00110010 01000111 11101011 01010100 11011110 10110110 01000100
10100001 00110001 10011001 00001001 11101000 01001111 01000001 01001010 11010100 00101111
00011110 10111001 11110101 10100110 01110101 01110011 10011010 10010111 10100110 11100101
00001001 11000111 01011111 01111111 11001110 10011110 00111001 01101010 00010100 01110011
11001111 11100001 01000011 10110110 00000001 11100011 00100111 10110101 01000010 10111010
00000001 10000000 11110101 11000000 00111011 00000111 10101111 01111010 01111111 11110000
11111010 01100111 10100101 00110111 01111111 11001011 11101011 10001111 01101110 10110100
11010010 00011010 01001100 01110011 11011011 10000001 01011010 00101101 01110100 01100100
11101010 00101110 11010000 01110010 01001111 11100001 01001000 11100000 11100111 00011001
11000111 01111100 01010010 11111111 00000000 00000110 01111011 01010000 00000111 00011110
11111101 01111001 10100100 10110100 11010000 10100000 01101110 00000000 00000000 01110101
11101011 01001000 11011000 11001000 11100111 00110100 10101011 10011111 11000110 10010011
00011001 00111000 11100011 10101111 01101010 01110111 01011011 00000000 00110001 11001111
01011010 10001101 10111110 11111110 01111101 01101001 11011001 00000111 00011100 00011110
10111101 11101000 11000001 11001110 00111101 01001101 00101011 10110100 01001101 10000011

00000100 11111111 00000000 00001000 11111010 10010011 01000000 00100000 10001100 10001110
10010100 00110000 11001110 01000111 01011100 11110001 01000100 01000111 00001010 00000001
00111001 11011001 10011100 10010010 01101001 10100111 01110000 01001100 01001100 11100000
10011111 11100101 01001000 11000011 00001011 10001111 11001110 10011010 00001001 00111111
00110001 11100000 11010000 01001001 01101110 10100111 00010100 11100110 11111011 00001101
00001110 11001001 00100111 10011111 11000010 10011010 11000000 10011100 11110101 11110111
11001101 00001100 00001000 00000011 10001110 10110100 00110001 11000000 11000000 10101001
10001101 10101100 00110000 11111011 10101111 10001100 01110001 10001010 00111001 00111100
10011110 00101001 11100011 11101111 01110011 11010011 10111101 00110011 00000001 11000111
01111110 01111101 01101000 01011010 10100001 01011100 00011000 00000010 00001001 00111001
00000000 01110111 10100001 10000110 01010001 11001001 11101010 01000111 00010100 00101110
01001001 00111001 00111000 00011101 10000111 10101101 00111001 01111001 00111111 10000101
00110101 01110100 11001001 00011010 00010111 10011111 01101010 00010100 10011100 01010011
01011100 11100101 00001111 11010111 11010110 10010111 01110000 00111110 11110101 00101010
00110010 11011100 10101101 00001110 10100111 00111101 11110001 11110101 10100100 11001001
11101111 11010010 10001100 11100101 11111000 10100011 00000111 00111100 10010001 01011010
01111010 10010010 00101010 10010010 01110011 10011110 11010100 00110111 01010000 01000000
00000000 10001111 01010001 01001001 10011100 00001110 11011000 10100001 10001000 01010100
11111001 11110010 01101001 00000000 10111001 11000001 00011110 11110100 00110110 01001111
01000001 11111010 11010010 01100111 00111000 00100111 11111111 00000000 11010101 01001010
10100000 01110101 00000100 01010011 11010101 00001111 01110001 00001001 00111101 00110110
11110011 11101111 01000001 11001000 00100111 10011111 01111110 01101001 01011000 10110000
00100111 10100111 11100011 01000011 00101111 01110010 01111110 01111110 11010100 10011110
10111010 10001000 01000110 00111110 01100000 11000001 00000011 00111101 11111101 01101000
01011000 11000110 00110011 10001010 00111100 10110010 01000110 01011111 00000100 10011110
10100110 10010111 11010000 00011010 00010000 11101110 00011100 11100011 10100110 01001001
10100110 11101101 11000000 11100111 00100111 11110001 11000101 00101011 10110001 00100100
01100111 10001111 11000010 10010001 01000110 00110000 01111001 11000111 10111111 00111001
10100010 11101011 01110001 01101100 00001010 00111101 11111111 00000000 00011010 01010010
01011000 10011111 00101111 01110000 00000000 01110101 11110111 10100100 11000111 00111101
01110011 01001101 10001110 00110101 00000111 00100000 01110011 11010011 00110100 01011000
00000111 01110010 00011000 10000001 10011111 11000110 10001110 01011001 11000111 11001100
01000010 01110101 00110100 10101010 11000011 01110001 01011111 11001100 11010001 10010101
00101010 01110010 01000110 00001111 01110001 01010010 10010101 10110111 00011011 00011001
11100110 01111100 11100111 01100001 00100111 11101011 11010010 10000101 00101100 01000111
00101001 11001111 10101101 00111001 10000000 00011000 00000000 11100011 00111111 10001101
00101001 01100010 00011111 00000000 01110001 01001101 11011010 11000010 00011000 01110110
10110000 11000011 10001110 01000000 11100110 10000101 11001001 01101100 11100111 00101111
01001110 01100010 00010100 01101110 11100011 10011010 01101010 11100110 00101100 11100011
10000111 00111101 10101001 10110111 01110000 00011101 00001000 11011011 00011110 01001110
00001001 11101010 01001000 00110100 00110010 10001001 00001111 00100011 10001110 10111111
01011010 01101010 10010111 00101111 10001100 00100000 01000000 01111010 00001110 10110100
11110111 01100101 10001100 01101110 11000001 11111010 00011010 10011101 00000000 01000100
00011100 01101110 00111101 10111001 11000110 01110011 01001011 10011110 10000100 10001010
01100110 00001111 01010010 01111010 11010011 10010100 00010010 01000000 00011101 00111101
01101001 10101101 11110101 00000000 11110011 00110010 00000000 11101101 01000001 00000001
10000110 11010101 11101001 01000110 01100011 10001111 10010111 11101000 00111111 01011010
01101010 00011101 11000011 11010011 00110100 01111010 00000000 11111001 01000000 00011011
00010111 00111111 10010101 00100110 00000001 00111000 11000111 00010100 00000000 00000110
01110001 11001001 11101111 01001100 01010010 01001001 11000110 11010011 10001010 00101101
11010100 00000111 10001111 01101010 01101110 00001000 00000101 01110001 11010000 11110101
11110101 10100100 01000110 00011000 01111101 10100000 11110001 01001011 10111011 00101100
01110010 00001101 00001001 11011000 00000111 11110011 10011110 01111001 10100000 00001100
00100111 01001110 00111101 11101001 10001000 01010100 00001110 10000111 10010011 11010000
11010011 10011011 01111001 00100100 10111110 00111101 10101000 11101010 00000000 01111001
00000011 10110001 11110110 10100110 11100000 11010011 10010101 10111001 11100010 10010111
01111001 00100100 00000010 01111010 01010001 01100000 00010001 10000110 01000000 00011111
10101101 00101000 00000011 10100000 11111100 01101001 10000000 10000011 10010000 00111011
00001010 01110110 00001111 10010111 11110111 10001010 00111001 11101111 01001001 00010100
10000101 11111110 00011111 11110110 01101001 00011111 00100101 00000110 00001110 00000111
01011100 01111010 11010011 01000000 00011101 00111010 11110001 11001101 00111001 10110011
01010010 11010011 00100100 00011011 10010011 01000110 00001111 01101010 00111000 11001000
11111101 01111101 11101000 11011100 01000111 01011010 10110100 11110100 00011110 10000000
01001110 00110000 00000111 01011100 11110010 01111101 00101001 01001111 11001011 11000101
00100111 01011100 11110010 01000110 00000101 00011100 10011111 11110001 00100110 10100011
11100100 00010110 00000010 11011100 11010110 01111101 11100110 10100001 11100100 11001011
10110101 00111001 01111010 10010111 01010010 10111000 00110110 10110110 10010010 00110110
00111101 10000101 01110011 00001001 00100001 01100110 11001001 00100111 11101010 01101011
00111001 10110111 10110101 11001110 10011100 00111101 00101110 01110111 01110110 01101000
01001001 01110111 00110100 11000100 10010010 11000111 00011001 11101001 01001110 00000111
01110010 00001101 11010101 00001010 00101110 01110001 11001101 01001110 10111111 00101111
00000110 10110001 01111010 01101111 10111001 11011011 11001010 10010110 10001000 10010001
01000001 01010001 11101100 01101001 01010000 00001101 11111001 11001111 00010100 11011100

11010010 10000110 00011011 11111001 10100100 10011110 10011010 10011001 10010010 01100111
10011010 01111000 11100110 10100000 01010110 11000001 11111001 10101001 11111110 01100000
00100011 11011110 10000100 11010110 11101100 00011110 10000100 10100011 00011000 11110110
10100001 11110001 10001100 01010100 01001101 00100111 00111101 00101001 10001101 00100111
11001101 01010011 01110100 10110100 10111001 00011110 01100101 10001101 11001011 01001011
10010001 11011010 10101010 10110011 01110001 11010110 10000011 00101110 01000110 00110010
01110001 11110101 11000101 00101101 01011110 11000001 01110010 11000011 00011111 01010011
01000000 01101110 00101010 10011111 10011101 10010011 11010111 00110100 11000110 10011011
11100110 11000110 01101001 01101010 10011101 10101100 01010001 01110100 11001100 00111011
01010011 01111100 11111010 10100010 11110011 01100011 10000001 01010001 00011001 01111000
11101011 01011010 00110100 11110111 00000011 01000001 10100111 10100100 01111001 10000001
11111010 01010110 01100011 11001101 10000001 11010110 10100011 01011011 10001111 01111010
00010101 10000110 01101010 11111001 11011100 01010011 01111100 11110001 10011110 00111010
01010110 01100011 11001110 00000000 11101011 01010001 00111101 11010001 11100011 00010100
11110100 01001001 10110000 00110110 01011010 01100001 01001111 11110011 10111000 10101100
00111111 10110100 01100000 01110101 10100101 01011011 10111100 00010001 11001101 01000111
10110011 10111010 10111000 01011110 11000110 11011010 11001010 00110001 11010110 10001111
00110100 01100100 11100100 11010110 00101011 01011101 10001111 11100001 00111111 10001101
00001011 01110110 10100111 10111101 01010101 10000010 11000110 10111111 10011011 10010110
11101011 11000101 00101111 10011011 11000111 01011010 11001001 00010111 01111001 00010100
11010110 10111010 11100000 01110011 01001001 10101110 11011011 00001110 11111101 00001101
01110110 10010100 01100111 00000110 10001111 00110111 00111001 11100110 10110001 00001101
11100110 00001110 00001111 11100111 10011010 01001111 10110110 00010000 01111000 00111111
10101101 01001011 01011101 10010000 11001101 11000101 00100000 11110011 10011100 11010010
10110100 10011101 00101011 00000101 01110101 00001100 00010001 11001111 01011111 01111010
01010110 11010100 00110010 11011110 10000111 11010010 10110100 01001001 01110100 00000011
01101100 01001000 00111011 11010011 01011000 10101111 00111001 10101100 10010100 10111100
00111001 11110111 11111010 11010011 10011010 11101100 01100111 11101111 01010101 11011010
11011010 10100001 00111011 00011010 00001100 01010100 10001110 00101010 10011100 11010010
10001000 11000111 00010101 00001011 01011110 00001101 10001111 11001110 00111101 11101011
00110110 11100110 11101100 00001100 11110011 11000001 11101110 00101010 01011110 10101110
11000101 01011100 10111101 11110110 10100011 10111011 00000110 10100110 01101001 10010100
10000000 00110011 11010111 11011110 10111001 11010011 01110110 01111010 10010110 11100000
01010011 10010110 11110011 11100101 11101010 00101010 10010101 00110110 11110110 00100101
10011011 01010011 00011100 10001110 10110101 10011011 00110001 11000011 11100100 01100110
10100001 00110111 01100111 01101111 01011110 00001111 01010001 01010000 10001011 10100000
01110011 11101001 01010111 01101110 10000000 10001011 01001000 00111000 11100110 10010111
01110110 11011100 01010100 01101001 01110000 10111101 00111000 10100100 10011001 10010111
00100011 00000110 10010010 10001110 10000010 00011011 00100100 10111100 11010101 01101001
00100101 11001001 11101001 01001100 10010001 10001001 00100111 00010101 01011110 01001100
11100110 10110110 11100101 01101111 01010000 00100111 00110010 10000000 01110001 11001111
11100001 01010000 00111100 10111000 00100111 11111010 11010011 01001000 11000111 00111001
10101000 11100101 11000000 11100110 10101001 01011101 10001001 10001011 00100011 01100111
00100011 00110101 01011101 10001001 11000110 00001111 11100010 01101000 01101110 01111001
00000111 10001010 10001111 00111001 11100111 10111001 11110101 10101010 11100101 11010110
11100100 11011111 10100000 10000101 10001010 10010011 11101001 01010001 11001011 00101110
01010011 10101101 01001100 11100101 01001111 00000110 10100011 00110001 10101011 00000001
01001011 11011001 11110011 01101100 00101011 10011100 11111110 10101000 11011101 10110011
11010110 10110010 10010100 00011101 11000101 11011011 10010111 10101110 10010011 01010100
10110111 10000100 00001100 10111001 11110111 10101110 01111101 00010111 01101111 00111100
00010010 01001001 11001001 10101110 11001000 01011001 11011001 00100011 00111010 10000010
10100111 10011001 00111100 01101001 00010000 00000000 10010110 00111000 00011001 11100010
10111101 00011011 01000011 11111000 01110011 01101111 00000101 10010100 01010111 00111010
11100101 11011000 00000001 10000110 01111100 10101000 01011011 10010011 11111000 11010111
10011110 11011011 10101010 11100100 10001100 00000011 10011110 10111001 00110101 11010111
11011001 11111000 10011000 11000001 10100001 10111100 01110011 11001000 01100101 00110000
01100111 11001010 10001111 00111100 10011111 11000110 10101010 01110010 10010100 00110100
10001010 10111001 10011001 10101001 10101111 11101011 10010110 11111010 00010101 10001000
10110110 11010011 10101100 11100011 10001010 00110111 00111001 01010101 00011100 01100111
11101010 01111011 11010111 10011110 11011101 11011110 01001111 10101000 01011101 00111100
11110111 01000111 00100100 11110110 11101100 00111110 10010101 00001101 11011101 11101001
10011110 01100111 01111001 10001110 11110111 00111100 11110010 01111010 01100110 10100000
01000010 11100100 11110001 11010011 11010110 10010100 00101001 01011001 11110011 00111101
11001100 11101110 01011000 01101001 00100100 00111001 11011000 01000000 00011110 11111101
01101001 10111011 01110111 01100011 01111100 10100000 00011100 11111010 11100010 10000110
01010110 11011000 00001011 10010000 01111110 10000110 10100001 01111000 01110111 00111001
00100111 10010001 11101111 01011010 11111011 00111101 01101110 01001101 11001001 10110001
00011010 11111101 11011001 01000001 11110110 11111111 00000000 00011010 10000101 11100110
00100001 11001001 11101001 10001010 10010010 00011011 00100000 01010011 00101100 01000111
10111111 00111101 00101001 00111110 11001001 10000011 10011110 01011100 01111011 11010101
01001010 01001001 10111011 01011100 00011001 01011010 01101001 10001011 01111101 11000110
11101011 01001010 10101100 01001110 00000110 01110011 10001010 00100101 10110111 01100000
11111111 00000000 11011100 00111111 01011010 01100100 01100011 01101011 00010001 11011111

11010111 10101101 01001011 10111000 10001001 11100010 01010010 11001110 01110001 11010100
11010110 10100100 01100000 10101100 01011011 10010011 10101110 00111001 00110101 01011010
11001110 00100101 01110110 00000011 10010001 10011010 10111001 01110001 11111011 10110000
01010111 00011100 00011110 01110010 00101011 00111001 11010100 01101101 11011000 10110101
10100001 01000110 01000011 11111011 11000011 11000000 00100000 11111010 11110011 01010100
11100110 00111011 01001110 01000111 01001110 11110101 01101110 01010000 10111001 00100100
01110101 10101010 00010011 00000011 10010001 11010111 10011111 01111010 10111000 01011111
01100001 00111101 00001000 11001001 01100010 01110010 01111000 00000100 11010010 01101110
00100011 00111100 11110010 00101000 11110010 11001111 00111111 00110101 01000100 11101000
11000101 10111101 01000111 10100101 01101010 11010101 11011110 11100100 11011000 10011001
00100100 00111011 11000011 00101001 00100001 11111010 11110000 01110000 01101011 10110010
11110000 10111111 10001101 00101111 01110100 11011001 10100011 10001110 01111001 00100100
10111001 10110111 00011100 01111100 11001101 11001000 11111111 00000000 00011010 11100010
11110010 00000100 01110100 11100100 10010100 01110001 11101011 10011110 00001101 01100111
01010010 10010010 01101010 11011011 10000010 01110110 01100111 11010010 11111010 00011110
10101000 10011010 10010101 10101010 01011100 11011010 11001000 00100100 10110111 10010011
10100001 00111100 00010000 01111101 11101011 01010101 00011111 00111001 00100100 11110001
01011110 00001111 11100000 00001111 00010100 01111111 01100001 01011110 00111100 00010111
00010010 10010011 01100101 00111111 00101100 00001111 01001000 11011011 11010110 10111101
11000010 11001010 01110101 10111100 10110000 01001001 11100000 10010110 00111001 00100011
10010011 10010001 00100010 10011010 11110011 00101010 01010010 10010101 00100111 11100100
01010110 11100101 10100000 01110011 00011110 01000000 11101011 11010000 01010011 00010000
00111110 11111100 10111111 00011110 10011000 10100101 01101111 10111001 11010100 11100111
11010110 10001100 01100111 10111111 00110101 00011110 10100011 00011100 11111000 00110100
11010110 11100001 01110000 00001110 00111000 10100000 01110011 11001111 01101100 11010011
10111000 00111000 11100111 00110100 11011000 10101101 10101000 00100111 01000010 00011011
00111000 00010101 00001100 01100100 10110110 11111111 00000000 10010111 00011100 11100010
10100100 11100000 01100100 00001100 10011111 10101001 10100100 01011101 11000000 11100011
10001010 10010111 10101110 10101001 00010100 00000111 11100101 11111011 10100011 00100100
11111011 11010010 10111110 00010100 11100000 10001100 10011111 01001010 01001110 01000110
01001001 11100111 00011101 00000000 10100000 11100101 10100100 00101100 11111101 11111010
11010010 01100000 00001110 00111001 00011001 11100100 11100011 01111101 00100100 10001101
10000000 10011110 10111101 01111110 10010100 11101110 10100100 10011110 10111100 01100000
00001010 10001101 01010100 10110111 01010010 00001101 01010010 10111110 10001100 11001100
00011101 10110011 00111110 11010100 01010011 10011110 10100100 11110100 10100111 10110111
00001000 01110010 00111010 11010000 11001100 01110111 11100100 11110000 00001111 00000000
01010100 01111101 00100011 00111001 11100100 10011110 10010101 01101111 11001000 00000011
00100101 10011111 10001111 11000100 11010001 11110011 00110111 00000100 10010000 00110001
10010011 10001111 11110001 10100001 01110001 00011100 01100100 00011100 11100100 11110001
11101011 01000000 01010011 11100101 11101101 00111001 11000111 01000011 11101111 01010000
10011111 01110010 11000101 01101100 10011101 11100111 00100011 00011101 10110001 01001001
00011110 00110001 10010111 00111101 01001110 00000101 00100001 00011001 00100001 01000000
11000010 00001010 01011101 10100011 00111001 00100111 10100101 00001101 01011001 11101010
11000000 01000011 00100000 01100000 11111011 00000111 11010011 10001010 01100010 00010011
10011100 10110111 11100000 00101001 11111001 11111111 00000000 11101011 01010011 01011000
01100000 01101110 11001101 01010101 11010011 01100000 00111001 00111000 11101111 11001111
10100101 00110001 00010111 00000000 01100101 10001001 11101111 01001010 11011101 01001001
00000011 10010011 01000111 00000000 00000000 10111101 01001111 01011010 01110001 10110011
11010000 00000000 00011110 10100001 01111110 10011001 10100001 10001001 00000011 00000000
01110010 01111000 00011110 11010100 10011000 11000001 00100100 00000001 10111111 11011010
10010000 10000010 01011100 00000001 11011110 10010100 10100011 01100110 00000010 10010001
11010001 01111010 00000000 00111010 01100110 10000101 00111101 01000111 01110011 01001001
11010000 10010010 10111101 01001000 11101011 11010111 00010100 00000101 00111100 00010010
01111011 11110011 10010011 01000110 10101110 11101000 00000001 01001111 00000000 11100110
10011010 10111000 11001110 00001111 00110100 00110111 00010010 00010000 00000111 00011101
10111001 10100111 00011110 00001111 01011010 01011011 00001001 00110000 01000110 11000011
01110010 00110001 10001110 11000110 10011001 00010111 00100011 00000111 00111100 11110101
10100001 10110000 00110010 11011001 11100110 10010000 10010010 00100011 00101100 00000110
01001111 00011100 11111010 01111011 11010001 01110111 01100001 11011010 11100010 10101000
11000011 01110001 11000111 11010110 10001100 01111010 01111101 01101001 10000011 00111100
10001110 10010100 11100001 10010010 01111101 10101010 11100001 10101110 10100010 01000000
11000111 10001110 01000101 00101011 01111101 11011100 10010001 01000110 11101100 01110100
11100111 11010111 10001010 01100110 01011011 00111111 00111111 00100100 11110101 11001101
01100111 00100110 00110001 00110110 10001100 11100110 10001110 10101110 01111000 11100000
01111011 11010011 11010111 10101001 11001000 11100000 01010011 00100010 00100001 10001000
01010011 11000110 01111010 10011010 10110111 01110111 01100100 00000000 01001000 11001110
00111000 11011110 01111011 01010010 11110010 01111000 00011100 01111010 00011010 01000110
00000111 11100100 01100001 10000001 10011110 11010100 10101010 01111110 01111110 10011001
00110100 00110100 11010110 11000000 00111010 00101111 10011010 01000000 01001111 00000010
10011001 10011100 00011111 01111100 11110100 10100101 01010010 11000000 00010110 01100010
00000111 00111101 01101001 00000000 11111001 11111010 01100100 10011110 11111000 10101001
11011101 10000000 00101110 00100011 11100010 10010001 10000011 00010011 11110010 11110100
11111010 01010000 01000000 00001100 01111110 01101100 11010011 00010100 01110001 11110011

01101110 11001101 00010010 10001010 01001110 11000000 01110101 10000111 00011000 00000011
11001100 11000000 11110100 10100100 00000000 00101000 11001001 11111010 00001010 01100011
00101001 00110011 01101110 01111110 01110000 01111010 00000001 01010010 01100100 10011100
01110001 11111111 00000000 11010110 10101101 10011101 10001001 01000010 11110100 00011001
11001000 10100100 11011101 10010011 10001101 10111100 01111010 10011010 01011100 01110001
01001101 11001111 00011000 00011100 11111010 11010100 00101101 00110110 00010000 10100100
00010011 10001100 01010000 10100011 00001110 01000000 11101011 11010100 11010000 10100100
01110101 00111100 01010010 00100000 11011100 01110011 11001101 01010010 00000001 01011010
01000000 01000110 01000000 00110100 01101110 00101100 10011111 00100001 11000111 11110100
10101000 11111010 01001000 01110000 10101110 00001001 11101111 11011010 10011110 11000011
10101000 00000100 11111110 01010100 10011100 01101110 00110100 00101000 00000001 01000111
11101110 11000000 11110111 11100110 10011001 11110011 11110010 01001111 00111111 10101101
00001010 01001111 01001010 00110011 10011110 00010011 11110011 11001101 00101011 11110100
00010000 11110011 10111000 10011110 01111000 01000000 00111110 11110111 10101101 00110001
11001001 11101001 00011110 00110110 01100111 11101111 01010011 10111100 10110010 01110010
10110100 11010111 01010011 11000000 01101110 00000000 11101011 01001110 11001101 10101101
00000000 00010001 00111001 00101100 00110011 10000011 11010111 11011110 10011101 10111000
00000001 11000000 10100011 10001100 01100000 01100110 10011010 10100111 00111100 11100010
10100110 11000101 10000111 11011101 00001110 11011101 01001111 11110011 10100111 01101101
00101100 10101001 10011110 11011100 10010001 01000001 00101010 00001110 00001110 01110010
01101000 11000111 10100011 00011100 01100111 10011111 01111010 10101011 10100110 01000000
10101110 10101101 10011111 10010001 10000000 11110101 11001000 10100001 00001010 01100111
00011011 10110011 10001110 10100110 10011000 11100000 10011110 00001111 00011111 01000011
01001110 01010001 10000010 11111001 00000010 10010101 11010010 00000000 00111100 10110000
00100000 01100000 00001110 11110100 00111011 01110011 10110111 10001100 11111011 11010011
01111100 11000000 00011100 01000110 00111001 00100111 10011111 10100101 00111000 00011100
11110010 01111111 00000011 01000101 11000000 01010000 01000110 01110010 01111010 10000001
11001101 00100011 01000111 10111001 10110111 01100010 10000101 10001111 01101111 01001110
10000110 10000111 00000000 00001100 00001110 10011101 11101001 00110111 01100100 00000011
01011111 10110000 01000001 10010011 11011110 10011100 10100100 01110101 00000100 10001010
01100010 11100101 01111110 10111001 11001101 00001100 11001101 10001111 10010011 00011001
11001111 01010011 01010001 01111101 01000000 01111110 11101100 10100110 00000000 00111000
11001101 00110111 10011110 01111001 11100110 10010001 01100100 11001001 00000000 00011100
01100010 10010100 10001100 00001100 11100011 00100111 11010111 00110101 01001001 00100101
10101000 00000111 01101100 01100111 10010011 11001001 10100100 01100010 11000111 10011110
11000110 10011111 10000010 01001000 11110100 11101111 01000000 01100010 10111100 00010001
10010001 01010101 00100110 10000000 01100001 00000100 00100000 00000010 10011111 10011110
00111111 11000110 10010111 00111001 00000011 10001010 01000111 00100010 10100011 10101101
11000000 01011100 11100111 00000111 10100101 00100011 00000010 01110011 10000011 11001111
01001010 01101111 01010011 10011100 11110000 00111010 01010000 10101011 11111010 11110100
10100110 10110101 11011100 10100100 00111000 10010000 00001111 00011100 11111101 00101001
10101000 00001110 01111110 11110111 00111101 11111101 10101001 11001011 11001001 00111000
00011101 00101001 10111101 00010111 00111000 10100010 01001111 01010010 01000011 00100011
11110001 11111110 01110100 11101100 11110000 00110011 01000010 11111101 11011100 00000001
10010011 01000110 00111001 00101100 11111111 00000000 10010101 00111011 10001101 00001010
00111000 11101000 01111001 10100110 00000010 01001001 11100111 10011010 01110111 00000000
00010011 10001010 01101010 10010001 10011100 11100111 10011010 00111101 01001010 00011101
10000011 11111111 00000000 11101011 10100110 11110000 11011101 01101000 01110010 01001010
01100001 00111001 11001111 01010011 11101001 01001110 01001110 10011000 11110100 00010101
00001110 11000100 10000010 11110100 11101011 01001011 10001100 01100100 00000011 11111001
11010010 00001100 11110110 01011100 01100111 10111110 01101001 10111101 01001111 00111100
01111011 11010001 11101000 00110110 01100011 01111000 10001010 01000011 11100100 10100010
10001110 01000110 01111001 11000111 01101010 11001000 10000100 01010110 10100111 10001001
00000110 01000100 00001011 11011011 00100110 10110011 01100001 00100001 01000110 00000111
00110101 10000100 10101101 10111011 00111011 10110000 11001111 11011101 00101100 10101000
11100000 00011100 11010100 10101001 11001111 11011110 00110101 00001010 10011110 11110100
00110100 10111000 00010101 00001111 10011010 01011010 11011000 11010001 10110010 01011101
11011001 11101111 01001000 11001101 11001000 10101010 10101101 00100001 11001001 00110101
00011011 01001001 10001110 01110011 01001010 11111010 01011000 10011011 00010111 00111100
11001010 01001111 00110111 00011101 11101010 10000011 01001111 01001110 11110011 01111000
11100111 10101101 01000101 11101111 10100000 00110010 11100011 01001101 10011110 11100110
10001111 00111011 10111101 01010000 11110011 10001000 10100110 00011011 10001100 01110001
10011110 01101001 11000110 11001111 01100000 00110100 10011110 01100000 00000110 00111111
10101101 01000110 11010011 01100100 01110101 10101100 11010011 01110001 10011010 10001101
11101110 01000110 01001111 01011111 01111010 10100100 10011010 01110111 10110001 00101100
11010000 01101001 10000000 00011101 01101010 00110111 10011111 00000010 10110011 10100101
10111000 11100111 00100000 11010100 00001111 01110000 00001001 00111110 10010100 00110111
11110010 00001101 11001101 00110111 10011111 00100011 10010011 11010111 11011110 10100011
01111011 10000010 00000111 01011100 11010110 01011011 11001100 01110000 01111110 01101110
00000101 01010111 00110111 01011111 10101101 01010010 01010111 00000110 10011001 10101000
11110111 01111100 00010000 10111101 01101010 00110110 10111010 00000011 10111111 00110101
10010100 11110111 01000100 00011100 10001010 10101001 00110101 11010000 11101011 11011111
10111101 01101000 10101101 11010100 10100100 10001101 11000011 01110000 00001110 01001001

```
00111000 10101000 11010110 11101011 00000011 10101111 00010101 10000110 11010111 10111000
00100000 01100111 10011110 11110100 11001111 10110110 00011111 01011010 10010111 10100011
10110000 11001101 11000111 10111100 11101010 01001110 01111111 00111010 10001101 10101111
01001111 11111001 00110101 10000101 11110110 10100010 11000111 00010100 10001101 01110000
11011000 00100011 00111001 00111110 10111001 10101010 01001011 10101011 00011110 11100110
11101111 11011011 10110010 00111010 11110011 01001000 00101111 00000000 00100111 10011110
10010101 11001110 00011001 11001000 00100011 00100100 11100111 11011010 10010100 01001110
11011001 11111110 10110100 10111001 00100011 01101011 00110001 00011101 00100111 11110110
10001110 00000111 00000111 11110001 00110100 10000011 01010001 11001000 11101101 01011100
11100011 11001110 01111101 01101001 10100010 01010010 00001001 00111001 00111100 11010101
11110010 10101000 10111011 00100100 00010110 00111010 01000111 10111110 00011000 11111001
11001111 00110101 00000011 01011111 00000010 01111000 00111101 11101011 00001101 10100110
00111101 11001101 00110000 10110011 00110001 11000000 00111101 00111010 10011010 00011010
01011011 10100010 10010001 10111000 01101111 10110010 01001110 11010110 11100111 10111101
00100111 11110110 10001001 11011110 00000000 00111100 10010001 11010110 10110000 10010100
00110110 01001001 00111001 00000111 11101011 01000111 00101010 01001111 00111101 01111010
11010011 01110100 10111001 10010111 00110001 01001001 11011000 11101000 00111111 10110100
00011000 10001111 10111101 11010011 10001010 01010100 11010100 01111000 11101011 10011111
01001110 01101011 00001010 00101000 11100110 01101100 10000001 00011100 10001111 11101110
00010100 10011010 10010011 11101100 10110111 01100111 00100000 01000001 00110111 01101111
11100001 00110101 10101011 10100110 11101100 10010101 10001000 01010011 01000110 10110011
11101010 00100111 11010111 00001000 01111010 11010101 00101001 10110101 00000110 00001011
10111011 00111001 10101010 11001101 01100111 01111001 11000010 10111100 00110011 10011100
11111111 00000000 10110010 01101001 01100001 11010000 11110101 01001001 11010000 10011000
00101100 00101110 01011101 00111011 11111100 10111000 10100100 10101001 10110110 11110101
00001110 01100100 01000101 11110110 11100011 10111011 00100100 10011100 01111101 01101001
01010011 01010001 00111001 11000111 01000001 11101011 01011001 11010111 01001011 00100101
10111100 10110010 00100100 11001010 01010101 11010100 11100001 10000111 10100101 01000010
10110011 00101000 01001100 10101011 00001110 01111011 11111010 01010000 10101001 11011101
01101000 01010010 10110110 11100111 01000001 00010101 11101110 01000001 11100111 10101111
10101001 10100111 10101100 11111111 00000000 00111111 01011110 00101011 00001101 01100100
00100111 00011000 11111100 01111101 11101010 11100101 10101011 01110011 10010010 01111111
00001010 01101110 10011011 01111010 10001110 01001000 11011000 10001001 11001001 11111111
00000000 00111101 01101010 01010000 01011011 10101000 10101010 11110110 10101101 10111100
10001100 01010110 10010100 00100001 01110110 00011100 11110110 10101000 01010001 01010110
10110011 00110010 11011000 10000001 10001011 00011110 10111100 11010010 01101101 11111001
01111001 00011100 11010101 10001111 10010111 00011101 01101010 00110111 00101011 11010111
11110000 10101011 01001001 10100001 11011100 10101110 11110001 10001100 01100110 10100001
01110101 00000110 10011111 00100100 11011011 01111000 11101101 01010001 10110100 10100000
01111011 11100011 10101101 00011110 10000010 10111001 00011010 11000100 00000001 00100100
00000011 11001111 10101111 01101010 10001001 11100011 11101011 10001010 10110001 11100110
10101011 01110100 01101111 11000010 10000100 11011010 01001000 11101000 01101001 11101001
00010111 01110000 01001011 10111001 01001110 01101000 11001100 01110001 10000010 00000101
01100010 01011110 01101010 00001111 00010001 11000000 00000111 01100111 01110011 01011101
01100001 11110010 11010111 00000101 10110001 11001101 01100100 01101010 10101011 00000100
10010001 10111110 11110100 01000011 11011011 10100101 01011100 00100111 00011011 11011001
01011100 01110011 10000110 10011010 00011100 10101101 11001101 11101011 01001010 01110000
01011011 10010001 01010000 01111001 10011001 00011101 01110001 10011010 10110111 01110001
01101000 00010111 00111110 01011111 00100000 11110011 01010100 01011110 00100010 10111111
01111111 00111100 01010111 01010100 00101100 11011001 11001011 00100101 11011100 10010011
11001101 00101011 11001110 01111111 11111010 11110101 00001100 10110010 00011001 01111001
01110000 01110011 11110101 11101001 01001101 01110110 11101100 00111111 10011101 00010001
11111100 11001010 01001101 01101010 10011011 11100110 10111011 00110001 01101100 00010000
11101101 00111001 00100011 00111111 01011010 01111111 10011010 01110001 10000011 11010000
11010011 00011000 10001100 01100100 01110101 00111111 11001010 10010011 00111001 11001110
00111000 10100111 10100011 11010100 10011011 10010010 10011001 10001110 00110001 10001110
00111011 10011111 01001010 01111100 01101100 01011000 00011100 01100111 10101111 00100010
10100011 01000100 11001000 11001001 11001111 10110110 01101010 11100010 10011100 00100000
11100011 10100111 01011010 01001110 01101110 11010110 00011101 11000101 01010110 01010101
10001111 11100111 00000110 10101001 01011100 11011110 01111100 11000111 11001011 00011000
00011101 10001001 00110101 10100001 00100100 01000011 01100110 01011111 00100100 00011110
10000110 10101010 01011100 10101010 10001000 10001010 10000000 10000011 11110000 11111110
10110100 01000101 01000001 10111101 01000100 11111100 10001100 11111001 01100111 00101100
00001001 00100111 00111001 10100111 01000100 00110010 11111100 10011110 01111010 01100111
00110100 11011100 00010001 10010101 11101110 00111101 01101010 01001000 00010111 11110111
10001000 01000000 11001000 11110111 10101101 00011100 10011111 01100010 01001101 00001011
01101000 10011000 00010100 00101001 10011111 11001111 10101101 01101011 11011110 01100000
01011010 11111001 10111000 00011000 11110100 00100110 10011111 10100101 01000000 10100110
00100000 01111100 10111100 10111111 01101010 10000011 01010100 00100000 00011100 01100111
00000000 00001110 10010101 11000101 00101010 10010111 01110110 00110100 01011010 00100011
00110000 10100110 11100011 11011000 01111011 01111010 11010101 01011001 10000000 01010001
10010011 11011100 11110100 10101011 01001110 10111011 10010111 00011111 11010110 10110011
11100110 00000101 10111001 00110101 10111101 00111001 01011101 10010010 11110101 00100011
```

01111100 11110100 00011100 01100111 10111111 10101101 01000100 01011011 11100101 00101100
01001111 00000011 10001100 11010011 11111100 11000010 00110011 10001110 10011101 00101001
10111011 10111000 00000000 01111110 00100010 10111010 01100010 10010010 01000110 01101100
01101010 10001100 10100111 00011100 10001110 10110100 11010001 10000000 10100000 00001010
01111011 00110110 00111001 00000111 00011001 11101000 01101001 00010011 10010111 00100011
10000000 00000111 01011100 11110111 10100101 01101110 11100011 10111001 00100100 01101100
01110011 10010001 01011101 00111111 10000011 11111100 01011011 10101000 11111000 01110010
11100100 10011011 01111100 01001101 01101100 01111111 11010110 01011010 11001001 11110111
00011011 11101001 11101000 01101011 10010110 11101010 00110011 10011010 10010011 00011100
00000110 00000110 10100110 01010000 11100111 01010110 00001011 10110100 01111101 00110101
11100001 11101101 01101010 11001011 01011111 11010011 11000101 11001101 10001011 10001110
00111111 11010110 01000010 01001111 11001111 00011001 10101101 00100011 10001100 00001101
10110101 11110011 01111111 10000100 10110101 11111001 11111100 00111111 10101011 01000111
01110011 01101110 11000111 11001011 00011111 11101011 01100011 11001111 00010010 00101111
01111010 11111010 00011011 01001110 10111110 10000111 01010010 11010011 11101101 10101111
10101101 01011011 11110111 01010011 10000000 11101010 00001111 01101010 11110011 01101010
11010010 01110100 11111100 11001101 01001011 10001011 10000101 11101010 00101010 00111110
01000001 11111001 11000000 11100111 10111000 10100101 11000110 00110011 11011110 10001110
00001010 10011100 11110000 01000111 00110101 10010110 11111010 10000000 10011001 00111100
01100000 01110100 10100101 11111110 00110001 10011100 11110011 01001010 10111100 00101000
00100000 01010010 01100100 01110000 01110011 11001101 00100101 00100000 00010101 01111010
11111111 00000000 10011110 00101001 10111000 00011000 01110001 10011110 01001111 01110011
11011010 10010111 00000100 11110000 00111010 11110101 00100110 10010000 11100011 00111100
10001010 10010100 11011011 01110111 10110000 00001101 10001100 10010010 01000110 00111111
10001111 10100101 00111010 00010101 00000000 00011110 10011101 01111101 01101001 10101100
00111010 10010001 11000000 00011101 11101000 01100011 10010000 01000010 10001100 00001111
01101010 10100111 10101001 00000010 01101110 01010011 11111000 01111010 11010001 00010001
11100000 10110110 00110010 01111010 01100010 10010000 10010011 10000000 00010011 10101001
11101111 01001110 01010000 01000111 00000111 00111001 11000101 00100100 10101110 00000011
10001111 00001011 10010011 11010111 10111101 01000111 11000110 00001111 01011100 11010010
11100011 11110111 01111000 11000111 01000110 11011110 01101000 01100011 11110010 00000000
00001111 01111100 11010100 10110101 01100010 11000100 11100100 01000101 10000000 01111001
10100001 00000000 00011001 11101101 11011110 10000111 00011100 11100000 10011110 00000001
11101101 11011110 10000100 00000100 10000010 01000000 11100011 11010010 10110100 01111101
10000000 01101011 00110111 01000001 11101100 01001110 00110001 01000011 01100000 10110000
11100111 10001100 01010011 10100010 00000011 10011110 01111001 00111111 10100101 00110101
10000110 01001000 11100100 10010111 11101101 01010010 10110100 11010000 00000000 00101001
00000100 00010011 10000010 01111101 00101000 11101001 11111000 10011010 01000110 00001101
10111011 10101001 11000110 01000101 00100110 01110000 11011100 01110101 11101010 00101001
00101001 01110010 01111001 10001001 10000010 01110000 10000000 01110100 00111101 11101000
01101110 00001110 00111010 00011110 11110100 10101010 01110000 01111110 10100111 10101111
10111101 00110001 10111001 01110011 11010100 10010010 01111010 11010011 01110011 01100011
00011101 10110011 00000111 10101110 00101001 10100011 00100110 01000000 00111101 01101001
00110111 01111100 11111001 11111110 01110100 10101010 01001000 00000111 00000111 11101010
01110001 01010101 11010010 11000100 10001000 01001000 00001110 00110010 01110000 01111101
00101001 01010011 11100101 11100011 11110011 11001101 00100001 01011101 11011000 11001110
01110001 01001010 01001111 00111001 00011101 00001001 11100000 01010010 11011101 01101010
00110111 10111000 10011101 01001000 11111100 11101000 00100101 10001011 11100000 10001110
00111111 10011101 00101011 11100100 00011100 00001111 01011010 01101000 00011101 00000010
11111010 11111010 11010100 11110010 10001100 01110010 11100000 01110000 00001111 01011110
01111001 11110100 10100100 01110011 10001100 00010001 11000110 11111010 00111100 10110000
10111000 11100011 10010010 01111001 00010100 11000010 00011000 10011101 11010010 01110100
11101000 00000101 01010110 10001000 01001100 01110110 00110010 00000000 00011100 11100011
10011100 11010010 10101010 11110010 00001001 00110100 00101111 00000100 11100100 11110001
11011010 10000110 00000111 00011101 01110000 00111101 10101000 01011110 01100011 00010000
10000010 01001110 00110011 10001100 11111011 11010011 00010011 11010111 11010010 10001110
01111100 10110010 00110001 10001100 11010010 10100111 00000100 01100111 00111100 01110101
10100110 11011011 01101000 01001000 01000110 00000000 00001110 01001111 01001111 01111010
01011000 11111110 01100100 11101011 10000001 11101010 00101000 01111110 11000000 01110001
10001110 01001001 10100001 11111001 01010010 00011111 10000000 01111011 01010001 10101111
01010001 11101111 10110000 01110000 11010001 11000110 01111011 01110101 00110100 10010010
10011100 10011110 10111100 11110110 00010100 10001011 10010000 10000011 00000000 10000000
01111101 11101001 01011111 00111111 01110111 00111100 10011110 11110100 11010011 01001011
01000010 01000100 00011001 01110101 11000000 11100000 11100111 10101101 00000100 10000011
11110111 01010101 11011000 01111010 11100110 10001100 00010010 01000010 11100111 10000001
11001001 10100110 11100101 10010111 10000101 00011100 01010100 11001001 00100100 11110101
00011101 11001110 10101001 01001000 00000111 10011010 00001001 11001110 00000101 00000011
00100011 10010011 01000110 01001110 01001001 00000000 01100011 11101011 01010111 01110010
01000101 01100010 00110001 11101000 01001111 00011000 10100001 01000110 00111011 01010011
00110010 01111110 11110101 00111001 10011001 10000001 00000011 00001001 10110011 10111101
00101101 01000000 00001001 11000001 11000110 00111001 00110100 01100011 11111000 10111010
01111101 01101001 10111110 01101001 01010000 01111110 01010001 11010111 10111101 00001110
11001011 11100101 11111100 11100111 10101111 01101111 01011010 01101101 11110101 00000001

11000101 11000000 00111000 00000100 10011010 01101111 00100000 10000011 11011010 10000000
00001000 11111110 00010000 00010000 01110110 10100001 01110011 00100001 11000001 00011011
00111101 00101010 01100101 01111011 10000000 01100000 01100111 00111001 11000101 00000000
10001000 11000001 00111000 11100011 11010100 11010011 11010100 00011111 11100011 00011110
11011001 00010100 10001101 10010010 01110011 11011011 10100111 00010100 01011100 01111011
10001101 01001110 01011000 10010001 10010001 11101010 01101000 00000000 10011001 00000001
11001111 11001001 11011100 01010011 10001000 11000010 11110100 10100110 11110101 00000111
10001100 01010011 01110001 11101010 00100001 11000000 00000010 01001000 00000011 00111110
11110100 10111100 00101110 00000001 11110101 10100110 00111110 01111000 01010000 01110000
00111010 11010011 10110010 00001010 11100100 11111101 00101001 01011110 11001000 00000001
10000000 00111111 00110110 00110000 01101001 01111111 10001111 01101000 11111100 01101001
10011001 11101000 00111001 10100011 00011011 01110010 01000111 00100100 11111010 11010001
01111101 00110100 01000000 00111011 11100101 00000111 00000111 11110100 10100011 00100100
11100100 10001111 11001010 10011010 10001010 00111011 10011111 01111010 01110000 11001001
11100111 10100101 00011110 01100000 00011111 01110100 11100100 00001100 11111101 01101001
10101010 00001001 11001111 10100101 00001101 00100000 11001001 00000001 01111000 00011101
01001110 01101001 00011000 10010010 01110011 10001100 00001111 01001010 00101110 11011110
10000000 00111100 10011110 10011110 10010100 11000100 10010001 01001100 10000100 00000101
00100101 00000000 00011100 10011010 01010011 10011100 01100111 10100111 10111001 10100111
00011100 00000001 10011100 11110101 11111101 01101001 11101010 10000111 01100000 11110111
11001000 00000111 11011110 10011010 01001000 00001001 11110010 01110100 11101101 01000011
00001100 11110000 00111101 00101000 11011010 00000001 11001111 01101110 11110101 00110111
11101000 00100001 00010000 10011110 01001001 00000011 01100101 00101010 10010010 01001110
01111010 00001111 01000001 01001000 10111001 00001000 01110000 00111110 10011100 11010000
10011001 11001000 00101101 01010011 01110100 11000000 01010110 11101000 11111001 10100100
11101000 00000000 00011001 00111100 11010001 10001111 10010100 10011100 01110101 00110100
10111111 01110101 01110011 11000110 01001101 00111101 10000000 01001101 10000111 00011000
00111101 01001001 10100111 10110100 01100001 11011111 11100111 11001110 00000111 10100001
11000101 00110001 10001110 01011100 10011111 01010001 10000000 01110011 11010010 10001110
01000111 00011001 11001000 00000010 10001011 01110110 00000001 01010111 00000100 01100011
00110100 00111001 00111101 00000111 00011000 10100100 11101011 11010011 00110100 10111000
11000111 10101111 00110100 11101111 01110010 11000001 01001000 00100100 01110110 11100111
10101101 00000111 10011100 01110111 01001100 01010000 10011000 01010110 00011000 00110100
00101110 00000111 00100111 11110000 00010101 00101111 11010100 01010110 00000101 00101100
00000000 00011101 10111101 01000101 00111001 10000111 01011100 11110100 10100110 11100111
10001100 10011110 01111101 10101001 00010111 10011110 01111001 11001111 10100101 00010111
10111011 00001011 00001010 01001110 00000110 00000111 11010110 10000101 00011110 11111111
00000000 01001010 00011011 00100000 11100000 00001100 10010001 01001110 11001000 11000111
00100111 10011010 00101110 11101110 00010110 00011010 11111100 11110001 11010010 10011101
10001110 00111000 11100011 00110100 11001110 00001111 01001010 00010111 00100011 10010010
00110010 01110001 01000101 10000110 00101110 11011100 10001110 10111100 01010011 10111011
11100100 10011100 10000011 11111010 11010011 01000111 00101011 10000110 11001111 00100011
10011010 01000101 00011000 11100000 01110100 11110111 10100001 11101000 10101110 11000000
11000111 11110001 00001000 11100010 00100010 00111010 01111111 00111010 11001000 01000010
00110111 01100110 10110110 11111100 01000000 00001111 11011001 00111100 11000000 00000110
00000001 00010101 11001110 00110100 10111000 10101110 01111110 01011011 10111011 00011101
01111000 01110111 10100001 01101101 10100100 10100110 00110011 01111011 11010101 01100011
00101110 00111001 10101000 11111100 11100000 01001110 01101010 00101111 01111101 00001101
01110100 00101101 10110001 11100100 00011010 10000110 01000011 10010011 10001010 01101011
01001011 10010001 01010001 10111011 01111100 11011101 01111000 10100110 11110100 01011010
00010000 11000001 10011011 10110001 10100110 01111001 10100100 00011100 00011010 01100011
10011110 01111010 11100100 01010100 00110010 10110111 01101100 11010110 01110010 01001111
01110000 01000011 10100101 10011000 10101001 11001001 00110101 01011001 11101110 00111101
01001111 00010101 00011100 10110010 01110110 10101010 01110011 01001001 11001111 01011010
10111000 10111110 01111101 10110100 00101110 11000101 10011001 01101110 11110000 11111101
01001110 00111110 10110101 00010111 11011011 01000110 01001110 01001110 00001110 00111011
11010110 01110101 11001100 10100000 10000010 01110011 11111000 11010101 00011001 01100110
11001000 11100100 11111101 00101011 01010111 00011011 11111010 10001101 01011000 11011010
01011011 10111100 10001110 10111111 10011001 10101000 01100100 10111011 11000010 00010011
10111000 01100110 10110010 01111100 11010010 00111010 10011110 00101001 10011110 01101001
11100111 10011110 00111011 01010011 11100100 01001001 01011001 10001010 11011101 10001101
01000001 01110111 10111111 10000010 01110000 01001000 10101000 10011110 11100011 11011110
10110011 01110111 00011100 11110111 10100000 11100111 01110110 01111101 01111010 11010101
10111010 01111100 10110001 00011101 10111011 10010110 10011010 11100001 10111010 11010100
01101110 11000100 11111100 11011001 10101000 00011011 00100111 10101001 11000000 10100100
01010000 01001000 11000101 00111001 00101111 11100101 00001011 01011011 01100010 01000011
00100001 00111111 01011010 01101000 00111011 10111001 11001111 00110100 11010100 00111000
00011110 11110100 11100100 00000011 10100111 00111110 11011110 11010100 10100011 00011011
01101110 00010111 00011111 10010001 10000000 00000001 11100110 10010001 01111000 11111010
11010110 10000110 10010111 10100100 11011110 01101010 01001100 00010110 11010010 00001001
00100101 00011101 00001100 10011111 11000000 00111111 00011010 11101100 10110100 10111111
00000000 01000010 00000000 11111110 11010001 10111000 01110111 01111100 01110010 10110001
01110100 11001111 11010110 10011010 10000111 11011100 01000011 10101010 10100010 01111001

11110010 10000010 00111001 00100100 01110101 11001101 01011011 10110111 11010011 10101110
11101110 00111111 11010100 01011011 11001100 11100100 11111010 00101101 01111010 11110101
10001110 10001001 10100110 01011010 01100011 11001010 10110010 10001011 00000011 10111011
00001100 10011100 11010110 10010011 00011110 00010000 00100010 10000100 00000000 11110110
00011000 10101101 00100110 11100011 10100111 01010011 00100111 10001000 00111100 01110010
11011111 11000011 00111010 10110100 10011001 00100010 11000110 01101111 11001011 10100101
01011011 10001111 11000001 11011010 11010011 01111100 10111111 01100110 00001000 01001111
11110111 10011000 01010111 10101101 01111001 10011000 01101001 00001111 00111110 10011000
10100110 11100011 00100111 11010000 10011010 10010101 01100110 11110100 01000100 11111101
01100110 01000111 10011011 11000011 11100000 00111011 11101001 00110001 11100111 11001111
00001100 01011000 11111010 10010011 01011010 00110110 11011111 00001111 11100000 00111000
00110011 11011111 00111001 00100111 10101000 01011000 11110001 10001010 11101110 00110001
10000001 11010000 10011111 11000110 10010001 00000000 00111001 00100011 00111000 00011111
10101101 00111110 01100100 10110110 00100001 11010101 10010011 11101010 01110011 01110110
11111110 00001111 11010001 00100001 11001010 10011011 01111001 00101110 01001010 01110111
10010010 01001110 10110101 10100011 01101101 10100100 01101001 11110000 00001100 11000111
01100001 01101110 00001000 00111100 01111100 10111001 10101101 00110101 00011000 00111001
00111100 11111010 11010010 10001110 00001001 11001000 10100011 10011001 11110111 00010111
00111011 01111011 10010001 10100100 01100010 00111000 10001010 11000001 00001100 01101001
10111011 11101111 00010101 01010000 00110001 01001010 10001100 00110011 10000001 11000110
11001110 10111100 01010000 01011000 10000100 11000111 01001100 11110111 10100001 00110000
10101001 10000100 11111010 10010010 01101010 01111001 11011111 01010110 01001111 00110011
00011110 00100100 11000011 10111110 00000110 00111101 11110001 01010001 11100110 01000010
01000000 01110110 11100111 10111101 00101000 11101111 10111111 00101111 11001111 00110100
00110110 01001110 00000010 00101111 11010111 10011010 00111001 11000011 01010011 11000101
10111110 00100000 11011001 00001011 00111111 00010101 01011101 00000000 10111000 10001110
01101100 01001010 10100011 00111110 10110101 11000111 10111000 11101010 10100111 10011111
01111010 11110100 10001111 10001010 10110000 01111111 11000100 11100010 11011010 01001101
10100000 01101110 10001011 10110111 10101101 01110000 00010010 10101110 00100100 11001101
01101101 01000010 01101001 00101011 01110101 00111011 00101000 10111110 01101000 10010101
11100000 01100110 10001000 11110011 11001000 11111010 11010110 10000100 00110111 00000001
01001000 00111001 11101111 11010000 11010100 01001001 00010000 00100010 10000101 10110101
11011100 00001110 00000001 11001111 10110101 01101011 01110101 00100101 01100011 01110100
10011111 01010011 01100110 11011110 11111000 01000111 10010010 00111010 10010001 10001010
10111101 11111101 10100000 10111000 00000011 10100111 11010100 11010111 00101110 11110000
01001111 00011111 11001100 00111000 11000111 01011100 11010010 10011011 11000001 11010000
11110001 11101110 01111011 11010010 01110100 11100011 01110010 00100101 01100110 01110100
10110010 01011111 10101110 00110010 00011000 00001100 11111010 11010100 00111111 01101110
00011001 00000111 01110111 11010011 10011010 11100111 00111110 11010101 11001111 00111100
10001111 10101101 01000110 11010011 00011100 11100011 00111001 00010101 00111110 11001010
00110111 11011100 11001110 11000110 11101100 11010111 10100011 10101000 10101010 11101111
01111100 10101100 10000011 00000111 11101011 01011000 11001111 01110000 11000111 10011100
11111011 01010100 01111110 01111001 00001110 01111001 11000111 00010101 10101100 00101001
00101101 11101110 01001011 01100110 11000011 01011101 10000000 11011100 00011100 10000011
01001111 10001010 11111011 00000111 00011001 11111100 10101011 00000010 01001001 01111001
11001110 01110000 00101001 10011111 01101000 00100011 00100011 00111001 11110101 00111001
10101101 00111101 10001010 01101110 11101100 10011110 01101101 01001110 10001110 11100111
01010010 11000000 11011011 10011100 01111011 11100110 10110010 00101111 11101111 10110111
00101001 11011000 01001001 11001000 11101111 01011001 11110010 11001100 11010010 00101001
11111001 10110011 01010101 10011100 11100111 10111110 00111101 01001101 00011110 11000110
00101110 01000001 00101010 10011010 00010110 11100001 10111011 00111001 00111011 00111010
01111111 00111010 10000110 11100110 01100010 11001100 00000110 01111010 11010100 00101100
11011011 01111110 11101000 11001101 00011011 00001000 00011001 01111100 01100100 11110100
00100100 01010101 10111000 10101011 11011100 11000101 11001000 01110111 10010111 10000100
11001111 00011001 11111010 01010011 11110010 00111110 11101000 11111101 00101010 00111100
10010011 11110111 00111010 11010000 10111111 00101000 00100111 01101110 01001111 10101101
01011101 11101100 10110101 00110001 00010101 00100011 00100100 11110001 10001010 10110000
10000000 01101100 00100111 10010011 10001010 01101110 11010000 01000000 00000111 10101001
11100110 10100100 01000110 00001101 10000101 00011001 11001000 11101111 01001001 00101110
10100011 01001101 00010011 00100100 00111110 01100000 00001100 00000110 00001110 01111011
10011010 01110000 00000011 00000111 11100110 00100111 11011110 10100011 00100100 10000001
10001100 11100000 01111111 00111010 01101110 11011100 10001100 10011110 10111110 10110101
00101101 10100110 11101100 10001010 00100100 10011001 10010001 01000000 11111001 10110010
11111110 11100111 00110101 01001010 11100010 01101100 10000011 10001110 10100011 10100101
01001001 00101000 00000011 11101011 11101001 01010101 00011001 10011000 11110101 00011101
01101010 10101001 11000110 01001011 01110110 01001101 11110100 00100001 01111001 00001011
01001001 11001000 00111001 00011101 00001001 00010101 01110010 11010001 01001110 01000111
00100011 11010110 10101001 11000011 00011110 11100011 10000111 00000111 10101111 01110011
01011010 11010110 00110001 11000100 11010111 00000000 01001001 11011111 10100001 00110101
10100100 10100101 10100000 10010110 11100110 11111110 10010101 00101010 11000011 01101010
01111000 11001000 11111110 01110101 10010111 10101010 01001000 00011010 01010010 11000111
00000100 11100111 00100100 00000011 01011010 01111000 01011000 00101101 01110001 10000000
00001001 00111101 01000101 01100010 01011100 11001000 00100100 10010000 10010110 00000011

10011111 11010110 10111000 01010101 11111001 11011101 11010001 01101111 01101101 01001000
11011101 10110011 00010111 00000111 10011111 10100101 01010010 10111000 00111011 01110000
00110000 01110011 11101001 11101001 01010111 00110110 10010000 00001110 00001111 11100011
10011010 10100001 00110011 00010111 10010000 10010011 11010011 10111101 01110101 01010011
01010110 01100100 11110100 00101011 00111111 11100011 11010110 10100011 01110001 11110011
01100100 00011111 11111110 10110101 01001010 11000100 00110011 00010001 10011100 01110001
11010010 10100000 11100111 00111100 11100010 10111010 00011010 00100000 00011011 10010011
11101111 01001110 00100111 00000111 11101001 01001101 11100110 00110011 10001100 00001110
01111010 10010011 11001000 10100111 10110110 00100101 00100011 00111000 00000100 01110111
00010100 10110100 01001000 00110111 00010101 01100100 00011101 01001101 01001100 10001101
10001110 00110001 10001100 11010101 01111111 00101000 01110010 00110001 11000101 00101000
11100000 11100000 01100100 11100000 01010100 11110010 11011011 01010000 00101100 10101001
00000000 00001111 01011100 11010111 10100101 11111100 00100100 11010111 11011010 00011011
11001001 00110100 10111011 10001001 00001001 10110111 10010000 00010111 10001011 00111111
11000000 11111110 11011110 11010101 11100110 01101000 01111000 00011001 00111000 11001101
01011101 10110010 10010110 01011011 01001011 10000100 10011010 00000110 00100010 01000100
00111001 00000100 00011110 10010101 10000101 01000101 10100101 10011001 01101000 11111010
01111001 00100101 00010010 00000000 01000000 00111111 10001101 00011001 01100011 10010000
01111111 00111010 11000100 11110000 11000110 10101100 00110101 00001101 00100010 11011110
11100100 10110111 10011000 11101110 00000000 01100010 00111101 01000111 01011100 11111011
11010110 11001001 01100001 10110100 10011111 01011110 10000011 00110101 11100110 11011001
11110101 00101000 01110001 11001011 00100010 00000100 11101000 00111001 11000111 10101101
00011101 00110111 11111010 11111010 01010000 01011011 10010010 10101000 00111010 00001110
10110100 11010010 00001001 00111101 01001110 00110001 01010001 10101101 11101100 01001111
01010001 11011100 10011101 10000111 10110111 10100111 10101101 00001011 11000111 01011110
01101001 01111001 00100100 01110001 11010010 10010000 10110000 01010100 00101101 10001100
10011111 01001010 00110101 11101000 01011110 10010110 00011011 10011111 00110011 10001100
01110001 11011100 01010001 10010000 01001111 10110000 11110101 10100100 01000010 01001001
11100101 01000110 01110001 11011010 10001101 11011111 00110000 00011000 11101011 11111010
01010101 01011101 10011001 10001011 10011100 00001100 10000001 10001100 01110100 10100111
00101001 11101010 01010011 00100100 10011010 01101111 01010011 11001111 01001010 01001110
11000100 10001110 11111110 10010100 11101101 01110010 11000000 00010110 01000010 01000111
00111111 01011100 11010010 00101111 00000111 00000000 11010000 10111111 00101000 00100000
00001111 10100111 10111101 00101111 01011110 11011100 10011010 00000110 00110001 00000001
00001001 10011101 10100111 01111110 01111101 01101001 11001100 00000010 10100001 01100010
01111001 11110100 10100000 10010000 01001110 11011100 11110011 11110101 10100001 10000111
11001100 00000110 00111001 10100110 10011110 11100010 00000001 11000000 00001010 10011000
00000111 10111001 00110100 11010101 11001111 01100011 01001000 11000001 01011001 11001111
01010010 00000001 11000111 00111101 11101010 01001100 10000001 00100000 00011000 11100000
01010100 11011101 10001001 00010001 10110000 00011011 00010000 01100111 00011100 11111110
01100110 10001101 11000000 01100100 11100100 00001100 01110001 10010011 01000111 01110001
10011010 00000110 00000110 01000000 00011101 00000111 01001010 00110111 11011100 01100000
10111000 00100100 00011100 11100100 01111111 00111010 01001110 01110010 01111001 11100100
10011110 01101001 01011000 11101101 00001000 00111001 01110010 01111011 01010010 00010011
10001100 00001101 10111111 01010011 10011010 01010110 01010111 00000010 00111111 11110110
01000111 00111100 11111110 01110100 11100110 01101110 01001110 00110001 11101101 01001101
11000011 00000100 00000000 00001110 01110011 11101001 01001110 11000110 00000000 00011000
00011100 11010101 10100110 00000000 11000111 10001100 01010010 00111111 00011000 00100100
11100000 01010010 11110100 00100100 00001110 10111110 10100110 10010001 01001001 11011010
11101101 10001110 10111101 00101001 00110101 11010101 00001011 11010100 01010010 01000110
00110011 10011110 10111100 01110001 11001101 00100010 01110001 11001101 00100010 10001100
00100000 00100100 01110001 10001110 10000011 10111101 00101010 11100100 00100111 00100111
00000111 00111100 01010011 00011000 10001111 10010101 00000111 00000100 10010111 01110011
11000110 01111010 01010010 10110110 01110000 10011101 11110000 01110011 01001010 10111001
11000001 11100111 00111111 01001010 10001101 11001011 10010111 11011010 00100100 11000000
01000001 11010000 01110111 11111010 11010001 11010110 11101100 10000000 01111100 10000011
10011100 11100101 11011100 00010011 11010010 10000101 00000111 01101111 11001111 11101001
10011110 00101001 11000011 00000010 01001101 10111101 11000101 00011000 01010111 10001100
11100100 10000001 11001111 01110011 01010010 10110101 01011010 10010110 00000000 10001110
00110000 10111100 01111011 11010100 01101101 10111001 10010111 01101010 01110101 11001111
10101111 01101010 00100010 11111001 11010111 00111000 11100011 00111101 01101000 11001111
00100100 11111111 00000000 00101010 01111100 11011101 00000110 00001010 01100011 01000011
10000000 01110011 10000011 11001001 10100101 01000001 11100110 01111100 11111001 11111001
00110011 01001100 01001101 10101010 01001000 11011011 11001111 10100110 00101001 11101111
11110011 01100010 00100001 11001001 00111101 01110001 11000000 00000010 10101011 10101101
11001000 11010100 00110111 00000010 00001001 11110111 11100000 11010010 00110111 00111000
11101011 11101111 01001101 11001000 01011100 10101111 01110010 01111000 00000000 11010011
11000000 00100111 00100100 10001100 11100011 11011110 10010011 01011101 01101110 00110101
11100110 00110011 01110110 01001111 11001010 00111010 01110111 11101011 01001110 01100010
11000000 11100000 01000101 10111011 11011111 00100010 10001111 00110000 10101000 11000111
00000000 11100011 10101000 11101111 01000010 10111010 00101000 00000001 10011011 00100111
11101011 01001110 01001001 10110110 00100100 01110100 11011111 11000110 01001111 11100101
01001000 11011100 10001110 10111100 11010010 10110011 00001110 01110001 10010000 00000111

01110010 00111010 11010010 01100111 00100011 10000010 00001111 10111001 10100110 11011010
10110110 10100010 00011110 10111001 00001011 10000001 01001100 01010110 00111001 11000101
00011100 10011110 00000111 11100111 01001010 00000110 00010111 00101111 10001100 10011010
01101010 11001100 01101100 01001100 10110000 00111111 00111111 01111111 01001010 01010111
11011010 11000011 00110010 01100011 10001111 11010010 10010001 01001110 00110010 01111010
10011111 01001111 01011010 00011000 01100000 11110001 10000000 00001111 01010001 11101011
01001101 00000011 00010100 00010110 01100000 00001000 01101100 00001010 00010000 10011001
00001011 10010001 11010000 01110001 11001101 00100001 00101100 00001001 11011110 01110000
00111011 00001010 01010110 00000011 11001011 00001011 11001001 00011101 10101010 01011010
01111011 10110000 10111000 10001000 00111100 10100000 01010100 01100100 11110011 11010110
10010000 00110001 00100111 00100101 00110001 10001110 11111001 10100111 01100101 01010111
10001100 10001100 11110111 10100011 01110011 00110000 10101010 01110110 00100100 01110011
00101001 11011101 10011110 01000000 00000011 10111001 11101011 01001101 00100100 10010010
00000111 01101110 11111100 01010011 10110000 01011000 10001100 00011111 10010000 01110110
00010100 11010110 11100100 00010000 00000110 00111110 10110100 10010101 10000110 00111001
10000000 00000011 00011101 00101001 10111111 01111001 00111010 11110001 11110100 10100001
10001000 00000111 10101110 00111101 10101001 00010010 01001100 10110001 11011110 10111000
11111100 00101010 01101101 01110000 00011110 10011101 01001010 10010011 01001101 01101100
00000000 00111011 11100111 10011010 01001101 11000011 00100111 10100000 00011101 11001101
00001010 00000111 01010100 11111100 00101000 01101101 10100100 00000010 10010011 11000111
01110001 11101111 01001111 01110011 10000100 11110111 10100110 01100011 10011110 01111111
00001010 01110001 11100000 10000011 11101011 01001111 01110100 00110110 11000110 10010010
10111100 10000001 11001001 11101111 10001010 00111001 11101011 11011010 10010000 00011110
01011111 10001110 01001111 10101101 00011001 00111100 01101101 00011111 10000001 10101001
10111000 10000101 11011010 00100100 11000110 11111110 10000011 10111101 00100111 01111110
00111001 00111110 10110100 00101110 01011011 00011001 00111100 01010000 01001000 01011110
10011100 11010101 00100101 11010100 01000010 10000000 11000000 01100100 10011100 11110111
00110100 10000000 10001100 00011110 10111111 10001101 00101000 00100001 10001000 00011110
10110100 10001110 01110001 00100110 00000000 10100100 11101100 11110100 00011000 10111100
10011111 11000010 10011100 10110100 11000111 11000111 00000100 11010010 10110001 00000110
00111100 11100111 10101001 10100101 01101011 00111011 10100001 11011100 01001001 01000110
01110001 10011110 10000111 11110011 10100100 01100010 01111100 11001100 00100111 10100111
01010011 11011010 10010100 10000011 11000001 00110100 10101100 11000011 10000101 11101100
01111001 00100110 10001111 00110110 00100001 00010111 11010100 11111101 00101000 11011011
10110000 10010010 00001001 10100011 01111000 00000000 00011110 10100111 11011010 10001110
10100111 10101111 11101011 01010001 10100010 11010010 11000101 10001010 00001111 00111101
00101001 11011111 10101101 00110001 10111000 11000111 10111101 00011001 11001101 00010110
10111000 00001001 11000110 00001110 00110001 11010111 10101101 00101110 00001110 00000110
11101010 01000110 11011011 00011111 00111111 11100100 11010010 11100111 00100100 10010011
10011111 10100001 10100011 10101000 10101110 00011100 00000001 11000000 10100101 11000001
11101100 01110000 01101000 01100000 00110001 10010010 01101001 00110001 11000111 00011001
11000111 01101010 00101110 01010000 00101111 01001110 01001111 00010100 01100011 00000111
11011111 11010110 10010001 11001000 01011110 10110100 10111101 10000001 11101111 11010111
00010100 10011010 01011011 11101110 00100000 11000111 00111001 11101011 01000010 10000110
11101011 10001110 10100111 10111101 00101111 01101100 11100010 10011010 11100111 10000000
11011001 11001110 00111010 00001010 00011010 01000000 00111011 00100111 00011110 11011001
10100110 11100100 10110111 00000111 10001110 01101000 11001001 00111100 11110110 11001111
01101010 00011010 01000010 01111001 11100011 00011101 00111010 01010000 11101100 00100100
01010111 10111111 10000000 01001111 01101011 00100100 01111110 10100011 00010101 11000001
11001111 00100011 01000101 00100001 01000011 11110111 11110011 11010010 10111101 00001001
10110010 01100011 00011111 11010010 10111000 10011111 00011011 01101001 11110010 01011011
10111000 10111101 10000001 01111110 01000011 10010001 00100000 00010101 10001100 10110100
11010110 11100110 11110100 10100100 10010011 00110011 01010110 01111110 11011001 00010100
00100100 10111101 01111001 10101100 00101000 01101110 11110111 00111110 00111010 11010101
11111000 10100101 11001110 00111111 01011010 10100101 01000101 00111101 01001110 10111011
00011010 01011110 01101111 00011101 01111001 10101000 11011110 01100001 11101111 11001111
01101010 10101011 00011001 11000001 01110011 11010111 00110100 01011100 00010011 10001100
11010110 01001001 00111101 01010001 00111110 10100100 10001101 00111110 00000110 01000101
00110001 10101110 00110111 00001100 01100010 10101001 01001011 00100001 00000100 11110000
01110001 11110101 10101010 11101111 01110101 10001110 10011101 00000000 10101010 01101001
00110101 10100011 00011110 10000101 10101001 01100100 11000001 00100111 00110101 01011010
01100110 00000111 10101001 10101010 01101111 01110110 00001111 11011100 10101000 10011010
01110010 11011111 11010110 10101001 01000001 01011011 01000000 11010100 01011001 01001000
00011001 11000111 01111110 10110101 01001101 11011011 00111000 00111001 11100110 10011110
11101100 00011000 11100000 10011110 01101010 00010110 00000000 00001010 11011010 10011111
00101000 00101011 10000011 00110110 01001111 11010110 10000110 00111000 11001111 00010100
11010110 11101001 11101100 00001101 00101011 01110011 11001111 11101001 01010101 00100100
11101111 10100000 00000010 10110001 00111001 10100000 10110110 00111001 10101000 11011001
11111101 01000101 00110011 11001100 11000000 00100100 01111110 01110101 00111100 10111100
11001100 01101100 10011001 10100100 11111001 01101001 10011110 01101001 11101000 00001101
01000001 11100111 00000001 11010100 11111110 10110101 11010001 01111000 00110111 11000011
01110011 11111000 10000010 11100011 01110001 11111101 11011101 10010100 01100111 11110111
10010010 01100111 00011111 10000000 10101101 11111101 10000100 10010101 10011001 00101110

01101001 00010101 00110100 10101101 00111010 11101011 01010011 10111001 01001000 01101100
10100010 00110010 10111001 11110100 11101000 00111110 10110101 11101000 11111010 00011111
10000010 00101101 10101101 00001000 10010111 01010100 10010000 01011100 11001000 00111111
11100101 10010010 11111101 11000001 11111000 11110111 10101110 10010111 01001001 11010011
11101101 00110100 11001011 00100100 10110110 10110010 10000111 11001010 10001100 01110101
00111101 11001001 11110111 10101011 10001011 11000000 00000010 10100110 10100100 11010010
01110110 10001001 11001101 00111010 10101101 11101100 00100100 01100001 01100001 10001000
01000111 00011010 10101100 01110001 10000001 11110111 01010100 01100000 00001010 01010101
00111000 00011101 00111001 10100001 10001001 11101001 11010100 00001111 01011010 01011101
10111100 11100111 10100101 01100011 01100111 11011100 11001000 01001100 11110111 00100111
10100111 01011010 00000000 11101111 11010100 11110101 11111010 01010000 11111000 11001111
00100010 10001100 11100100 11010010 01010110 01100010 11011100 00110001 10111000 11110011
11010010 10010001 10110001 11111001 01111011 11010011 10000001 00011011 01111101 00111001
11000101 00100011 01100001 10111000 11001111 00011101 01001101 00011010 00111101 10000101
01100000 01111110 10100000 01110111 11101110 00110011 01001000 11100000 01111001 01111011
01000011 01100010 10010100 00110000 01101111 10011011 00000111 10000011 10000001 10011110
11110100 00101001 11001001 01110011 10001100 11010011 01011010 10110001 10001000 01000000
11000010 01110101 11000000 11101010 01101001 01111010 11100111 00011101 00110011 11010100
11010010 00001100 10010010 01111000 11100011 00010100 01111101 11010001 10011110 01110001
11101101 01001011 01011011 10001100 01010100 11000001 00111001 00011000 11110100 10100100
01011101 10100000 01100001 00000111 01001110 10100110 10000101 00100011 10011110 11000011
10110111 01111010 01010100 01010011 11010000 00000001 11010010 10011101 10101110 00100001
00000001 11011011 00100000 11000111 01010010 00111011 10001010 00010000 00011100 11110011
10010000 00000101 00010010 01001011 10110100 10001100 11110100 00011101 11101001 10001100
01000001 00011001 00000111 10101111 01101010 01010110 01001001 10001100 11100011 00111110
00100100 01101001 11111110 01101110 10010010 10010111 10010000 10000001 11111011 10000110
11111101 11100001 00100111 10110011 11010111 10010100 11001011 00011110 00100101 00100010
10111101 11010111 11000101 00110110 10101101 01110101 10100000 01011111 11000001 00011000
00100101 11001100 01100101 11000010 10000001 11010100 10001110 01101011 11000100 10110110
10000111 00000001 10001000 11000110 11101111 11001110 10110101 10100111 10111101 11101110
01110101 01100001 10111011 00001011 01100011 01101010 11010011 00111111 10110111 10101101
01110100 00110110 11010000 00100100 01110001 11100001 11000110 01000101 01010001 11010011
10110000 10111000 00010101 10100001 10111100 10011110 01111010 01111010 11010100 01010110
10011101 10011110 10001000 11101111 10110000 11001011 10011000 00100010 10010101 01111001
00000011 00010101 11001111 01101010 00011010 01110000 11001000 00100011 10010100 11101111
01011011 11001111 00101010 11101111 11101011 11111001 11010101 01011001 01100110 01010001
11010111 10000001 01000010 10111010 11010100 10001001 01000000 11100100 00101110 00101101
10011010 00110111 11100000 11110110 10101010 10011001 10010101 01001111 01011110 00101011
10100000 10111111 01010101 11011111 10010000 01110000 00111101 11101011 00101010 01010101
00000001 11001111 11111001 11001101 01111010 00110100 10110101 01001001 11011000 11100010
10101000 10101100 01010000 00000101 11000011 11110010 11011101 01101000 01101001 00100100
00111001 11001110 00111010 11110001 01010011 01001001 00011000 11110011 00110111 01111110
01111000 10100110 01111001 01100101 01110011 10001111 01011010 11011110 00111100 10001111
01010011 00001101 01001000 00011101 10011000 11101100 11100011 10100111 01011010 01101011
01001010 01000011 10001111 01000010 00110001 01010110 00111100 10110000 01000111 00111101
11101001 10011110 01011111 01011100 01110110 10100111 11101110 11110100 00100111 11011110
00101010 00111100 10101101 10010000 00010000 01110111 10100111 10010010 11000101 00001000
00000111 10101111 01110011 01001111 01100101 00011011 10110011 11111010 01010001 10001110
01110011 11000000 00011110 10000110 10100010 11001010 11100010 01110111 10110000 01000110
10100100 00011111 01111111 01011100 11010011 10110011 10011100 10001100 00011110 00111010
10001010 01101011 11001001 11010100 10001110 10011101 11110001 01001100 01010110 00111110
01100001 00100000 10010001 10011010 10100110 10111010 01110100 00010101 11001001 00011010
01000011 11010011 10100000 11110110 00010100 10011110 01101001 00011101 00000101 01000110
11000101 10000011 11100001 00001110 01001111 01111010 01101110 01001000 00100111 00100111
10001010 01001101 00101011 00001001 11101010 00111111 01110110 11100100 00000011 00111100
11010100 10001000 01011001 10001110 11010000 11000100 01111110 00110101 00000111 01000011
11001111 00010101 00100010 11001000 00110011 11000001 11101011 11011100 11110100 10100011
10010101 00010000 01011010 10001010 00100001 10010011 10010011 10011010 10110001 00100100
10110001 00101100 01111101 01110010 01000101 01010111 01001000 10001100 10111000 00000111
10100001 11110111 10101001 00110110 10000101 11111001 01001111 01101111 01101010 10001110
01011101 01111100 11001011 10111001 01010110 01011001 11001111 10011001 10000000 10101110
01110011 11101000 00111010 01010011 01111100 11001111 00110011 00100000 00001100 01100000
11110111 10101011 00010010 11001100 00000000 11001100 01100011 10011111 01011100 01010101
00111001 10100100 01100101 10010011 00011101 01111101 11110001 01011010 01000110 00101011
10101000 10011001 00100101 10110111 00001100 01001001 11101100 00101011 01000110 11000000
00001001 01011011 10001101 11111011 11011000 11110100 10101100 11100000 01110000 10001111
10000001 11110111 11101011 01000111 01001101 01100101 00110010 01100000 10011101 10011001
11101110 01101001 01110010 11101000 11101110 00111000 10011011 11110111 11111110 01011010
11011000 00000101 10011000 11111100 11100111 10100000 11110101 10101110 01100010 01001100
00000111 00100001 01111010 01111111 00101010 11101001 11100110 10001111 11101101 00010110
01111000 10001111 00000111 11101011 01011100 11100100 10101010 10100100 10011110 00001110
01111010 01110101 10101110 01111010 01010001 01011101 11001010 10101001 10101001 01010010
01100111 00011000 11001101 01010110 00110010 00000101 10001111 00100000 11100100 00011111

01011010 10110110 11101011 10000001 11000000 11001111 10111001 10101010 01110010 11000110
11111000 00100000 01000111 10010100 00111101 01001000 00011101 00101011 10101110 10011101
10010001 10011001 00001111 00100111 00111100 10011010 01101110 01010100 01110100 00000111
00111101 11101010 01000110 00001010 10100011 10010011 11001111 01001100 01010100 00111001
00011000 11001000 00011100 10011110 00101011 01001011 01110111 00010000 11100010 00110000
10011110 11000110 10011010 10100000 00000000 01001111 01001111 11000110 10010001 10110010
00000110 00110011 01000000 00111100 01110011 11010110 10000111 10100000 01111010 00001111
10001100 11110101 01101111 01010011 11001000 10100111 00000001 11001110 00000110 01111111
00011010 01101111 00000101 00110011 01001011 10111000 11110011 10010000 01001101 01000101
10011011 00001011 10001111 01011101 11000000 11111010 11111101 01111000 10101011 00010110
11101101 11001001 00100100 11010100 01101010 00010100 10001110 10011000 10100010 00110010
01000001 11100011 10010001 01000100 10010010 10110000 00011110 10010001 11110000 10111011
01010100 00110110 10110111 01110011 11011001 10010111 11111001 00100100 11111101 11100000
01010011 11010000 11111010 10001010 11110101 11010100 10010000 00011111 10111001 10001101
10011101 10001111 10101101 01111100 11101001 11100001 10101011 11010001 01100111 10101101
01011001 11001100 11100011 10000001 00100111 11001101 11110100 00111100 01010111 10111111
01011010 11001100 11011011 00111100 10101110 00001001 00000011 00100000 11111111 00000000
10110010 01111010 01010111 10011001 10001001 10100111 01101001 01011101 00011010 01011100
11010010 11100011 00011100 01110111 00110100 11101100 01100001 01110011 11010011 11101011
01010001 11100111 01101100 01011001 00000011 00101110 00111000 00000000 01111011 11010010
11110110 11000100 10011100 10000001 11111100 11101011 10010111 01011011 11011000 01100011
11010111 00011000 00000111 10000010 01110011 01001101 01101110 01000111 00000011 10011010
01000100 00100000 10000000 01111011 01010011 11110111 00001100 10001010 10101110 10000010
11101000 00110000 00000011 10011111 01010011 01001111 00111101 11111001 11101001 01001101
11011101 11001001 11100011 11110000 10100011 00111111 00100111 00111101 00101001 01011001
00100001 10000111 11001011 10110100 11100100 11100000 11110100 10100110 10001100 00000010
01000001 11100111 10001110 10010100 10101110 01110011 10001110 00110000 00000111 01001111
01110011 01001000 11000100 10010110 00011100 11100000 01110111 11110111 10100110 11101110
10110101 00000001 10111011 10001001 11101101 10000001 11011000 01010000 11011001 00100000
01101101 00111001 00111101 11110001 01000011 00000011 11100110 00010011 11101011 11111010
01010011 10010101 10000111 00100011 00011101 01111111 01011010 00111010 11101000 00000011
01010100 00110000 00000001 10011000 00010000 00111101 00101001 00001001 01100011 00100001
00100111 10001100 10001111 11001010 10010111 10111110 01011111 10010111 00111111 10100101
00001100 01111111 01011110 10000010 10000111 00011011 10111101 01000101 01110000 01111100
10101000 00000001 00001000 11100111 10111001 10100110 10000011 10010010 01001000 11101110
00110001 01001011 10111100 11111001 10000100 00000001 10010001 10001100 01010010 10111001
11100000 00010011 11010011 10011110 00111101 01101010 11110100 01011010 00000010 00010001
10110010 11011000 01100111 00111000 00000111 11101110 10000001 01001000 11001100 00000011
00010011 11011100 10000001 11011010 10010100 10110001 00000011 10010010 00110010 00111101
10111010 00001010 01100100 01011100 10110110 11101100 01110011 01001010 01010111 10110110
10000011 00010010 00111111 10010100 10000011 10010011 11001111 11101011 01001010 00010100
10001110 11111100 00001110 01111110 10110100 01111101 00000111 11010010 10011101 11000000
00011100 00011110 10111110 11110101 00011111 00110000 00011000 11011011 10001111 00111011
10111011 11111111 00000000 10011100 01010011 11011001 01001111 00011100 01100100 11110110
11001101 00110101 01110000 00110110 00001110 01110011 11001101 00001100 00000000 01011100
00010011 10010010 01001110 01101011 01000111 00100001 01101110 00011111 00101001 01110010
01001001 11001001 00011101 11000101 00100011 00110010 11110100 11100111 00110100 00100110
11010001 11001111 01000001 11010111 00000000 01010010 00010010 01011101 11000111 00000000
00100111 01011111 10101101 01000110 10100001 01100001 01110011 11111011 11000000 00111111
10111011 01001000 10111101 01111110 01101111 11000011 11101001 01000111 10011001 10010010
01000110 00111001 11101101 01001110 10010001 01111000 00000111 00111000 11011000 01111001
11110111 10101101 00100011 10111110 10100010 11010000 01101110 11100000 01010011 11100100
11100011 10110001 00111000 10100110 00000001 11001000 00100011 10001111 01011010 01011100
11101110 11000001 00111001 00011000 11101101 01001110 11110100 11110101 11001111 00110100
01001011 10111000 10000001 10110110 11111001 10111111 00100001 01111111 01110010 00111011
10011010 01101110 00000111 01110000 00000110 00111101 01001101 00100110 01000000 01100111
11000110 01001111 01101111 11000110 10010011 00000001 01010111 01101001 11000110 01001111
01011010 01011010 00111101 01001011 00000000 01010100 10101010 00001100 10011100 11100111
10010000 00111101 00101001 10111001 00001101 10000000 00010100 00100010 00011110 11110100
11110010 00111111 01110010 01000000 00111011 00000000 11101010 01111011 11010010 00011110
01000010 01100000 11100111 00011101 01101000 11010101 10101101 00000100 11011000 11010110
00100000 00001110 10000111 00101100 01110010 01000000 10101001 00110110 10000000 01111001
11100011 00111101 01110011 01001101 01100001 11110011 10001101 10011101 00000000 11001111
00110100 10111001 00100000 00000110 00111100 11100100 01110001 01000100 10110110 11010000
01000011 00111000 11001001 00000011 00000000 01111011 00001010 01110011 10010010 01001000
00011101 00111101 00010100 01010011 01110110 10001000 11111000 00100111 10010110 00110100
00110110 01001100 10000000 10000000 01001000 00111100 01010001 11101110 11110100 01000011
01100010 00110010 11100000 11100011 10101110 01001101 00101011 00110010 10101011 00010001
10010001 11111001 01010000 01000001 11001111 01101100 01010011 10000111 01001110 10010101
01101010 11101101 00010010 01110100 10111101 01000111 01010001 01001100 00110001 11100111
10101111 00000110 10011101 11110010 10000010 01110001 11001001 11110111 10100001 00011001
01011001 01111110 01101110 11110101 00001110 11011101 10001010 01000010 10100111 00000111
00011100 11010010 10010000 00001001 11100110 10010011 10111111 01110011 10011010 00110001

10000001 01010100 11011010 00100100 01011100 10001110 01000110 01000001 00110100 10001011
10010011 10010101 10100100 00000000 01100011 00000000 01110100 00111101 11000101 01001001
10010101 00011110 11000100 11010011 11011000 00001000 11000010 10000101 00011001 11001000
00100011 11101011 01000000 00011001 11101111 10000000 01111011 01111010 01010001 10000000
00001110 01000000 11000111 11010110 10010111 10010010 01111101 00101010 01111100 10001011
00000010 10100001 01111000 00001011 11010100 11110101 00110100 01110101 00011100 11100100
01110011 11010010 10011001 10000110 11011111 11110010 00011111 10010011 00111101 00101001
11011011 10110000 01111011 11111101 01101000 11110101 00100000 01110011 01100011 00011001
00100111 00000010 10000101 10010011 00100011 00111000 11000000 00111110 11110100 10000111
00100100 11111011 01010010 00001100 10011110 01011010 10010100 10000000 00011010 00111100
11110010 00111010 11010011 10110000 00001011 11100000 10011110 01101001 00110010 01111101
00111000 10100100 11000110 00001110 11101100 01110010 01101001 11011011 10100010 00000001
01111110 01010111 11001111 00011101 00111101 01101001 01000000 00111000 00000111 11110010
10100100 11000110 01001110 00101001 01010100 00110001 11101110 01110001 11101101 01001111
11001100 00000011 00000101 10000001 00110100 00101000 00011001 00010100 11011110 01110001
11000011 01110100 11101101 01001011 10110100 00001110 01011100 11110101 11110100 10100101
01101110 11100000 00001110 01001001 01111110 10011000 11000101 00101011 01110100 00010100
10001101 10011110 10000011 11110101 10100001 11111001 00100011 00111101 01101000 10110111
01100000 00000101 00111100 00011110 10010100 01110000 10100111 11011100 11111010 01010010
01110001 10001111 11111110 10111101 00101111 00100000 01100100 00000001 11110101 10100111
01100010 11000101 11101011 10011110 11010100 10001010 01000111 00100100 10010010 01111001
10100001 01001110 01111000 00100010 10011000 10111000 11100111 00011001 11100011 11010110
10110010 01101011 01010000 00011111 10011110 11111101 00110011 01001000 01110001 11000001
11000101 00110101 10001001 00111101 01111000 11001001 10100000 10000010 01001010 01100000
11110111 10100011 11010000 00000111 00000001 10011001 00001011 01110111 11111110 01010100
00100001 00111100 11110001 01000001 11111011 11111110 11011101 11101000 11100011 00100000
00000011 11110101 11110111 10100010 11101110 11011010 10010000 00110111 10000000 00111010
01110010 01101001 11011101 00111010 11110011 01000110 00111010 01110001 10001111 10101001
10100001 01001010 11101111 00101011 11010100 11010001 01111011 00101101 01001011 00010100
00010001 10001110 01000110 00111101 00110011 01010001 11100111 10001110 00111010 01010011
11001000 00100010 10011001 11001001 00100101 01111111 00111010 10110100 11011011 11010101
00000000 11111110 10011000 00100111 10100000 10100001 01110010 01110010 01101001 10101010
01110000 00110001 10000001 10001010 01110010 10010110 11110100 11111100 00101010 01101101
10101000 00000001 11000000 00011001 00111101 01101001 10111101 01000000 10100011 00000100
11001000 01001001 00000010 10001100 11100100 11111010 00001010 01001001 10001100 01111000
00001010 00000110 00111011 10011010 01010010 00000111 01111111 11010011 10110101 00110111
00111110 10100011 00110100 00110001 11111101 11011001 00000000 01010100 10101111 00110001
00010010 01100000 00011100 01100110 10100011 01100110 11011100 01000010 10000101 00100101
00110011 11010111 10100101 00110100 10000000 01110010 00001111 00100011 00011100 11010001
10010001 00010000 11101110 01111001 11001101 01010101 10010101 11000100 10000111 00011111
10010100 01100011 11110010 10100001 01001111 10101000 10100011 10110110 01011111 00011111
01011010 00010111 10011100 01111010 01010010 10111000 11000011 01110110 01110010 01110000
01000000 11101101 11000101 01010111 10111011 10110111 10001110 11101110 00010011 00011100
10000011 10000010 00101010 11001110 01110001 10011111 11100101 11010110 10001100 01110001
10011110 10100011 10111001 10100001 10101011 10000101 11001111 00100111 11110001 00001110
10001101 00100110 10010101 01111100 11101100 10001010 00000101 10111100 10000111 00111001
00000111 10100001 10101010 11010110 11111100 10001110 01101011 11010100 01110101 01001011
00101000 10101111 01100000 01111000 10100100 10001100 00111000 00111110 10111101 10101011
11001101 11110101 01011011 00101001 10110100 11001011 10110011 00010011 10101001 11011001
11111100 00101101 11011000 10001010 11001010 01010111 01000111 01011101 00101010 10110111
11010001 10001111 10001100 01111100 10011001 00110101 00100000 00000001 10000101 01010011
10000110 01101110 11011101 11111011 11010101 10001101 11011001 11000101 01000010 01110111
11101000 01101101 01101011 10001010 11110110 11100010 01000101 00111101 10101011 00111010
11100111 01001000 01100110 00011001 01000110 00000101 11001101 01101010 11000101 00100000
11001001 00010101 00100110 11101110 11010100 00101011 00101111 10000100 01010110 00111001
00101011 10111011 00011011 10111000 00110111 10010001 00010110 11110001 11011111 00000110
10110011 01001100 10001111 10111111 11101110 10011111 11000100 01010111 01111100 01001000
00100000 00001110 10100000 11110111 10101000 01100110 10110100 10000010 01100101 11000100
10001010 00001111 11100011 01011010 11010011 10101000 11010111 11000100 10000111 01110111
01100011 10000011 01111011 10110000 00001110 00001000 10101000 11111110 11011000 10011011
11110001 11001111 10101110 01110001 01011101 01011101 11011110 10000001 01101110 11111100
11000110 00000000 00011000 11110100 11001101 01100110 01001101 11100001 11000110 00000100
11101100 11000000 00011101 10111110 10110101 11010110 10100101 01001001 11111010 10010011
11101111 01011000 11000101 00110111 10001010 00111010 01110100 00111101 01101001 10101111
01111010 10111000 00100001 00110011 10001111 10100101 01101001 01001101 10100101 11001001
00011110 00010101 11100010 11100100 11110100 00011000 11101011 01010100 01011110 11010000
00101000 00100011 11001011 11000110 00111010 11010101 01011010 00111011 01110100 00100111
01010111 10110001 01001101 10101110 11001111 00111000 11001111 11100001 01010101 10011010
11100010 01010011 11000001 00000011 00011001 11101001 11011010 10101111 10111101 10111110
00001111 00110101 00001011 01000000 00110011 01011010 11010011 11100101 11011001 00100010
01011010 01101100 10100111 10111010 01000110 00000111 00110101 11010011 11111000 01011111
11000100 00010111 10011010 00101011 00100001 10110111 00111011 11100011 11101111 00010011
01110100 00110101 10001000 11110001 10000010 00011111 00011101 01110000 00110001 01001110

00000000 10100000 00000111 00110101 10100011 01101001 01110100 00100010 11000111 11010000
00111010 00001110 10111101 01101001 10101100 11011011 00000111 10000100 11100010 01000101
11111011 11001010 01111101 01101011 01011111 10101111 01101110 00101011 11100111 10011101
00101011 01010010 10011110 11000110 11100001 00100110 10110111 10010101 11010000 10000010
00111010 01010111 10101111 01111000 01010111 11000101 10010110 11111010 10110100 00100010
00101001 11011000 01000111 00111000 11101010 01001111 00011001 10101110 00111010 10010100
10011011 01010111 01000110 01110010 10000101 10110110 00111010 10011101 11000000 11111101
00000101 00100000 10010000 00011110 00011100 10011101 11110100 01110001 11010100 00011110
10110100 10101011 10000010 00111111 10011001 00110101 11001101 00101110 11100110 01101011
01010001 00001001 00011001 00111011 00001111 00010100 10101000 10111100 01100111 10111101
00100010 11100001 10000110 01001001 00111101 01111000 10100001 01000111 11101111 00011111
11100110 00111100 11110111 10100110 11101100 00000010 10111111 00001001 11001111 01011100
11010000 11011111 00101001 11011010 00110001 10001110 11111100 01010010 01110000 01111011
00010000 00000111 01001110 01101000 01101100 11111001 01111100 00001100 00010011 01010011
10111110 11000000 00101001 00000011 11101000 00111101 00101001 00110111 00011100 01001001
10001110 00000111 01111100 10001010 00110001 11000010 00001100 11110001 10001110 11110100
11011101 10100011 01111000 11001111 01001100 01010011 11010100 01011011 10001111 11111011
10100000 01100011 10011010 01100011 00111001 00100111 10011110 11000011 10001100 01010011
10111000 11001111 10111101 00011101 10000111 00011100 00011010 01101101 10001110 11000011
01000110 00000001 00111100 11110000 01101001 11001010 01111011 01111010 11010011 01011000
00000011 11000101 00111001 01111010 11100100 11110100 00000011 10100111 10101101 00100101
10111110 10000011 00011011 11000001 11001000 11101000 10011101 00000000 00110100 01100100
11101111 11011010 10101010 00110011 10001111 11000010 10000101 11000110 01110011 10001110
01101001 00010111 10100001 11001111 01110011 01010110 11101100 00000010 11111100 10111000
11000001 00111001 11101100 01000000 10101111 00010111 11110001 01001110 10001101 00101110
10010001 10101101 01001011 00001001 00101110 11110001 00111001 11011111 00011100 10000100
01100011 00100000 11110011 10001010 11110110 01111100 11110001 11000110 01001101 01100011
11111000 10011111 01000110 10001111 01011001 10110000 00110001 10011111 10010010 11100100
01110011 00001100 10011000 11100000 01111101 01101001 00101101 01011110 10101100 10101010
01010101 00111001 00100101 01110011 11001010 11100000 11011010 10111101 01000111 00110101
00100100 10110011 01100000 01100011 00110101 01011010 11111000 01001101 01100101 00111001
10000110 01111000 11001100 01110010 10100001 11000001 00000110 10101000 11001101 01110000
01111001 10100110 11100000 11101111 10100011 10111001 11101100 00101001 10101001 00101011
10100010 11000100 11010111 00000011 00011111 01001010 11001111 10111001 10111000 00100111
10011100 11100110 10101011 11001101 00101011 00010101 11001001 01101010 10001001 10110010
01010011 00000010 10110111 01010001 11010011 01010100 01000100 11100111 10100000 10010111
00010011 01101110 11100000 11100100 11111101 00101010 00010111 11100000 11111010 11010000
01100011 01101100 11100000 00000011 11110101 00010101 00100010 01011010 10111001 00111000
00001010 01011101 11001111 01100001 01011011 11000001 01110101 00111001 00100111 10101001
01011100 10010010 01000111 01001010 00110110 00001111 01011010 11011111 10110010 11110000
10101110 10101101 01111100 11100001 01100000 10110010 10111000 00001000 01001111 11111010
11000110 01011100 00000000 00101011 10100011 10000111 11100001 10110110 10100011 11100101
10111000 10010010 01111011 01110100 00111101 10000110 01110011 10011111 01001010 10111110
01101000 01000010 11101010 11100110 00001101 11101010 01111001 11100001 10001100 01110100
11101011 01010001 10110010 11101101 00100100 01100011 00111001 11101111 01011101 10001110
10100101 11100000 10001101 01101011 01001110 10110101 11110011 11011110 11011001 00100101
11000001 11100100 01000010 11011011 11001000 11111100 00101011 10010110 10011110 00100010
10111001 11011110 10100100 00111000 00111000 00100000 11110110 10100101 00001010 10001010
11011011 10000011 01001001 10010100 00001000 00000101 10111101 11111010 01010100 01010011
00011100 10110001 00011110 10011101 01101010 11001100 10000011 10001101 11011101 11111110
10010101 01000101 11000110 11011100 10001110 10111111 01001010 11010010 00001110 11100110
01110011 01100011 01011011 00000111 10011100 11110011 10001111 11001110 10010000 11110001
10010000 00001110 01001001 10100100 01110000 01110011 10010011 11001111 11010010 10011010
10111001 11100011 01111000 10101101 10111010 01011000 11001111 01110001 11001111 11111011
10110010 00010100 01110011 10011110 10111110 11110100 10111001 11011101 10000000 00000000
11001000 11101101 11101011 01001100 00111100 11110001 11000110 00111010 01010100 11110000
11000011 10010111 00000100 00000111 11000001 10100010 11011010 00001011 11010000 01001000
11000011 00110000 00011110 01100111 01001111 01011111 01001010 10011010 00100010 00010111
00111001 01010000 01110001 11101011 01010011 00110100 00101101 00011000 00100101 11001000
11111100 00001101 00110001 10001100 00110001 11110010 01001001 00100011 11011000 11010010
10010100 11010111 01000001 10110100 01011011 10001001 10000100 10001110 00011000 10110111
10010110 00111101 00101001 11011110 01011000 00000011 10000000 00011111 11101001 01011001
11101111 01110011 01101110 10100011 10100100 10011111 01010000 01110011 01010011 10100101
11000010 00110010 10000011 00010100 10101110 01110001 11011001 10101011 00111001 01010011
01101001 11101000 11000110 00010111 00011001 11011010 01000000 10101010 00010010 00011100
10010010 01001111 10101101 01101000 00111100 10100001 10110000 00001110 00110011 11101100
00101010 10010100 11011000 00101111 10001110 10111101 11111000 11100010 10011100 00111111
10010101 10001001 10110000 00001101 11111011 10111110 10011001 10101011 10010110 00110010
11110100 11001000 11001000 11001111 01101110 10110101 01001001 00111001 00000100 11110100
10101101 00001011 00101000 10110010 01000110 00001110 00001110 01111011 10001100 11010011
10101000 11011111 01000001 00101101 01001110 10000010 11011010 01100101 10001010 11010100
10011101 10100100 11110001 11001000 10101100 00001011 10111101 10100110 01100010 11001000
00110000 01001001 11111100 11101011 01011110 01000010 00100010 10000011 00001111 11110111

00110001 11001110 01101011 00010010 01100110 11110011 00011011 10001110 01000111 01101010
11100111 10100101 11110001 11011101 10100010 11011110 11000011 11100100 01100101 00100011
00011000 11111100 10101011 00110110 01111001 00011000 00111001 00000000 11110001 10011100
10001100 00011010 10111001 00110010 10110010 10000000 11000111 10101001 10101010 00101110
00011000 11100111 10001100 00011010 11101011 01001010 11001100 11001001 10010000 10110011
01111100 11100000 10111111 01011100 11110101 11000101 00110100 11100011 00000100 01110111
11101111 01001110 01110010 01000001 00000011 00111100 01111011 11010100 01011011 01001000
11101001 10001010 11010001 01101100 00010111 00010111 00111100 01100000 10101111 11010000
10011111 01011010 00111011 00010000 01111011 10011100 11010010 01101110 11101101 10001100
10011010 00110001 11001110 00111011 11110101 10100011 01010000 01110110 11101010 00111111
00111100 01110100 00111000 00110100 10101010 01111001 00100100 01110001 11101011 01010001
11100100 00011110 01111101 11101001 11111000 11100111 00111101 10101000 10111000 00100110
01001011 00010011 00000001 10001110 01111110 10100100 11010100 10001010 11011100 00011100
01100011 11110010 10101010 11000000 11100001 10110001 10001100 01010100 11001000 01000110
01110001 11101001 11000101 01100111 00101111 00110010 10010001 01101001 00111001 00011001
00011100 00011110 00101011 11011111 00111100 00110001 01111000 00101111 01111100 00111101
01100001 01110001 10111111 11100111 11110010 11110110 00110001 11101011 10001010 11110000
00011000 00111011 10011100 11100111 10011110 00000101 01111011 01000111 11000010 10101001
11000100 11111110 00010101 00110000 10111001 11001011 11000011 00101001 01000010 00111110
10110101 11001001 10001001 01001001 11000110 11100101 10100011 10110110 00011111 00110010
10100000 00100011 00110010 01110101 00100110 10100101 01100010 00001000 11001000 11101001
11110100 11101001 01010101 10010111 11001100 00000000 00011100 00000010 01010100 01110010
00111101 01000101 01001101 10111000 00110000 01001101 10011101 01011100 01100111 00011110
11010101 11000000 11101111 11010000 00000111 11000110 00110001 11110011 00011111 11000010
10011111 11001111 11001110 11001111 11010100 10011110 00111110 10010100 11010000 00110001
11001001 11100110 10010011 10010010 01110001 11011110 10000000 00010011 10101001 00000111
00111101 01101001 01001111 00101101 01000110 01000111 00100001 00000001 11100111 11010110
10010100 00010000 10101000 01011011 10110000 11101111 01001010 01001001 11110101 00010101
11000100 01101110 00000000 00011101 11001001 10100100 11000001 11011111 11001111 01001111
01000001 01001010 10000111 10010000 11000100 01110010 11111100 11100011 11010010 10011000
11111001 11100011 10011110 10110101 01010110 00011000 11101100 00010010 01110001 01001011
10001100 00001100 00001111 01011110 00101000 01010110 11100111 10101111 01101110 10110100
11000101 11110101 00111001 00111000 11110111 10100100 10111100 11000101 11100110 00010010
11110001 10000000 10000011 10011111 01110011 01000010 11110000 01111011 00010010 01111011
00011010 00100101 00011001 01111110 01001111 00010100 11100010 00000011 01111011 00001111
01011010 01011011 11101010 10000011 01000001 10100000 11100100 11100000 00001110 01111010
01010000 11000000 00000100 00011100 10001110 00001110 00101000 11000000 11111110 00010011
11000111 10101000 11101111 01001000 01011000 00001111 10010101 00010000 11100000 01110010
01001111 01001110 01101010 10110101 11101010 00110001 00011001 10011001 10000011 11101100
00111111 10001001 00010100 01111101 11010001 10010010 01110000 10011111 10101001 00110100
01001000 01000001 00011001 01010010 00000000 11000111 00011111 01011010 01101011 00001111
00110010 00110000 01001111 00111000 00111101 01101001 10100101 10100001 00000000 11111000
01010000 00000110 00111001 00111100 11100010 10001110 10000000 01100001 01000110 01101001
11101110 01001001 01010100 00000011 00000011 10011100 10010010 01101001 10001111 11010111
00000111 10101111 10110001 10101001 10110010 11011101 00010101 01110001 10111000 00011111
11000111 10010011 10001111 01101010 01011110 10000100 11110100 00100111 11010000 11110001
10000001 01000001 11001111 11111111 00000000 01011010 10001100 01111100 10100100 10100010
11100111 00000110 10010110 10101101 11101010 00110001 01110000 01000110 00111010 01010100
01101110 01111000 00001010 00111010 01100111 00110100 11100101 11100111 10010011 10011101
11100111 10111101 00101100 10011011 01100011 11111011 11100111 11110000 00010100 01011010
11111110 10100010 10111000 11000101 00111101 01000000 11100100 10110001 11111100 10101001
11011111 00110100 10110010 00000101 00111000 00001000 01001101 00000000 01100000 01100111
11010111 10100101 00001100 01010110 00101000 11110011 10000010 01100100 00011100 11110001
01010101 10101101 10110101 00011001 00011011 00010011 11010000 00011110 00000111 11101011
01001010 11100111 11110000 11100011 10101101 00101000 00111100 10001100 10101000 11011111
11011111 11011010 10011010 00011000 01101111 01111100 01110011 10000011 10001010 01010000
01010111 11011101 10001011 01100110 00111001 00010101 01111100 10110001 10110000 01111011
11100110 10011010 11100000 00001111 10011010 10010100 10000010 00010100 00101001 01101110
10111100 11010010 01100101 01000010 01111101 00111011 11111010 11010101 10111011 10100111
01100001 10000011 11110011 10000101 11000001 11101011 10011100 01010010 10111110 01011000
00000001 11011000 01110101 00011000 11101011 01000011 10010011 11111100 00011101 01001000
11111001 10001000 11101101 01001001 11000000 00000001 01000001 11001001 11111110 01010101
01001001 11011001 01101010 01000000 10100100 00001100 01101101 00011101 00000111 01011100
01010010 01100000 11111001 10000011 00011101 00110001 01000011 01001000 10100000 10001100
00001110 10111100 01100010 10011010 10100111 00000111 00100011 10101000 11101001 01010011
01110100 11011110 10000101 10000011 11100101 10100101 00001011 00011000 11100000 01110101
00100110 10011101 11001001 11111011 10111111 01110011 10110111 01101100 11010011 00000000
01010000 00111001 00011001 00100111 10100000 10100101 00111000 11000001 01100010 01111001
11001101 00110111 10100011 00100000 01110010 11110111 00100000 00000011 11000111 01011110
10110100 11010101 10001101 10011000 01100101 10111010 11010010 00010011 10110110 00111100
01000110 00110011 11101111 01001101 00000001 10011011 10010110 00100011 00111110 11011001
00010100 01011111 10011011 01010010 11010010 00111010 01110100 00111101 00001000 00000100
01100110 10011111 10001100 01111111 00001110 00000111 10110101 00101110 11101110 01111101

10111101 10101001 10101101 00100110 11101111 10011001 00110011 10001010 01111101 00000100
11000101 01010101 11011010 10011001 11011101 11001001 11101101 01001000 10100011 00111111
00110001 00110100 01100001 10000000 11110101 11110111 10100110 11100011 00111100 01110100
00011110 10010101 01011010 01110100 00100100 01110001 00111000 00000100 11100011 11110000
00010100 11010101 00111100 10010011 10110100 11100111 00011101 10101001 11001111 11000111
00011110 10110100 00110110 00011001 00110000 10010100 01011111 01011011 11011100 01100011
01100010 11011101 11011100 01111110 01110100 11110000 01001001 11100101 01111010 11111011
11010001 11001000 11111010 10011010 01100011 11101110 00100011 00011001 00011111 01010011
01001000 10100001 11011100 10000011 11010010 10000110 00011000 00111110 11110100 10100000
01110011 10001100 11110100 11101011 01001001 10001110 11100111 00010100 00101011 00100010
00000101 11100111 00000111 00100110 10010100 10110111 00011000 10100100 01101100 00010011
11111100 11101001 00111000 01010011 11000000 11001101 01001010 01001101 10110001 11101000
00101001 11001000 00011110 11000110 10001100 01110000 00110010 01111001 11111010 11010000
00001110 11100011 11001110 01101001 10011001 11011101 11001000 11101100 01101001 11101010
10000100 00111101 00011011 10101111 00000100 00011111 01011010 01100110 00001000 11000000
00100100 10010011 11110101 10100111 00000010 01001111 11011111 11101111 01001010 00110110
11100000 10011100 11100000 11010100 10110111 01110000 00010011 00111100 10000001 10001110
01001101 01001001 10000000 01001110 00111111 10101101 00110000 01100100 11100100 11100111
00011110 11110100 11000110 00111100 01111010 11100110 10010001 01100100 10011011 11001111
11110000 00001100 10000001 01010001 10010001 10011110 01110011 10010011 11101111 11011010
10001101 10111000 00011000 11100111 00010100 11100000 00110001 11110101 10101011 11011000
10010000 11011001 11000000 00101101 10001100 11010000 11011001 01101110 00111011 01010000
11000111 00011110 10011000 11110110 10100111 01100011 00000011 10011100 01111101 01101010
01110101 00011011 00011011 11000001 11001000 11100111 00010100 11010111 00011000 01001110
10000011 00100011 11010110 10011101 00101111 00000011 10000001 11111000 11010011 00110110
10011110 00000111 00100111 11011100 11010011 10111110 10100100 10001111 01011110 01000001
01100011 11011110 10011010 00011011 01111011 00001100 00001100 01100000 11110101 10100000
10000000 10111101 01001111 01111110 01101000 11100111 00011100 01110011 01010010 11011111
01100001 10110000 01010000 01110010 01111000 11100011 11010110 10000100 00011001 10010100
10001100 01110100 00011001 00111110 11110100 11101110 01000010 00010001 10011110 10111110
11110100 11011110 10011000 11000111 01011110 11100110 10011110 11101000 10100001 11001100
11011000 00100001 01000000 11001111 10101101 00011100 11110111 11000000 11110101 00110100
11001110 01111001 11000001 00000000 10011010 01111011 00000010 01000000 00100111 10100111
10100101 01000111 01011011 10001001 00001101 01100110 11111001 10000110 00001110 00000000
00011101 11101001 11001011 10010000 00001110 00101001 10011000 11101011 10001110 10110100
11110111 00111001 01001101 10101010 01001101 00001110 01001100 01100011 01110001 10010011
11110111 10110001 11101111 01001110 11001111 00011011 01000111 01110001 11001001 10100110
11110100 10001100 01110111 11001111 00010100 01100000 00001110 10000111 00111110 10111000
10100101 11001100 00000011 01010110 00100000 00100100 11001001 11101011 11101011 01010010
00000000 01001001 11000001 11101001 01001101 11100100 10011100 01110110 10100000 10101110
00010111 10001110 01110011 11101111 01000011 01011010 00000000 01110000 00011111 11010011
00111100 01100000 11010011 10011001 10000010 11100100 01100011 00100110 10000011 10000000
10000111 10111110 00111011 10011010 01101001 00111001 11000111 01010011 11011110 10100010
11110111 11010101 00001100 00010000 10110000 00011001 11101110 01101001 11011001 11001000
00011100 01110101 10100110 10101011 01110000 01001001 11101001 01001001 00011001 00101101
10000010 01000110 11000000 01111011 01010101 01101000 00100001 11101100 00000001 00100011
00100111 11101010 00101000 01101110 10111101 00001000 00010100 11010000 01011000 10011111
01101111 01111010 00010100 11100111 10000111 00111001 10100101 01100001 01011100 00000001
00000100 11100110 10011110 10101011 10011100 00110110 00101001 10001010 01000011 01100100
01100000 01110001 11101111 01001000 00111001 10010011 00011100 10000001 11101010 01111010
01010011 01001000 10100000 00110010 00010000 10001110 11011011 00111000 00011101 01101011
00111011 01011100 11010010 11000110 10100101 01101010 11100001 11110001 11010011 11100101
00011000 11101000 01101011 01000110 01010011 11011000 10000010 01110010 01111111 00111010
00011000 00010011 10010011 10001110 00101001 00111010 01101000 10010100 01111001 00010101
11111101 10101100 11011010 01110101 11011011 11000011 00110100 01101110 00110001 11010000
11110110 00110100 11000101 10010100 11100011 10010011 01011110 10011001 10101111 01101001
01110000 11101010 01110110 11000101 01001111 00000111 10110001 11101000 00000101 01111001
10000101 11110101 10010100 11011010 01101101 11001001 10001010 01111111 10111001 11111100
00101100 01111011 11010110 01101101 01110010 11101100 01110110 11010010 10101011 11001101
10100011 00100110 01011001 00001111 01010010 01101010 01011111 00111000 10010011 10010000
01111000 10101010 01001010 11100011 10000001 10011100 10001010 10010001 00011011 10011111
11000010 10100101 01000101 01000101 01011100 11101000 10110001 01110111 11001110 00100000
00001101 10111100 10001010 01010101 10011011 11100101 00000011 10111001 10101010 01001010
11011000 00111000 10100111 10101001 11100111 10101111 00011101 10101000 11010010 11101000
00011001 01110011 11001100 11001001 11001110 01111000 10100110 10110100 11000011 00111100
11010100 01001010 11000100 00001110 10011000 00010100 10001011 11110011 00011111 01111010
10100110 10010111 11011001 01100100 10010010 00110110 00100100 00011100 11110011 10001010
10101011 00100101 10101010 01001010 01110000 01010111 11110100 10101011 01101001 00010111
00011111 01011110 01101010 01000101 10001000 10000000 00110011 10011010 01001010 11010110
10111010 01100010 00111001 11101011 10001101 00101111 00100100 01100000 10011111 01111110
00101011 00101110 01101011 00101001 01000001 11100001 01001111 01011110 00111000 10101110
11100101 00100001 11100011 11111001 11010100 01110111 00010110 11101010 11000011 00000100
01100100 01010110 11010000 10101000 11101110 00100111 10111001 11000000 00111100 00000101

01001001 11100011 00111110 11110101 00010001 10001100 01100000 11110001 10001010 11101101
00101110 11110100 10000101 01100000 01001000 00101110 00001001 11101101 11010110 10110010
10101111 00110100 10001001 01110011 10000100 00100011 11010110 10110101 11111010 11001010
00010111 00100001 10000001 10001100 01110000 00111101 00000101 01001111 01101001 00110100
10010000 01001000 00011010 00110110 00101000 01000011 01100111 00100010 10100101 10011010
11001110 01010101 00100011 10001110 00111010 01010101 01110110 01010110 01010011 11010010
10110110 11100111 01110010 01010111 11101000 01001011 01011101 00001111 01010011 11110000
10010111 10001100 00000100 10101000 10010110 10011010 10001001 11111101 11100111 01000001
00100111 10101101 01110111 01001011 11111011 11000100 11101101 10110000 11110010 00111001
10101111 10011101 10010011 01110010 11100100 01100100 10001110 11111100 01010111 01110001
11100001 00011111 00010110 10110101 10011111 10010111 01101111 10101000 10011111 00110010
00000010 01110001 11100110 00011110 11010101 10010101 01001010 01001110 01011011 00011000
11001110 10010111 01100011 11010100 11010101 01111110 01011010 00011000 10001101 11000001
01000111 01001100 01100111 00110101 00000100 00110011 11000101 00111100 00100001 10101101
11100101 00010010 01000110 01000000 00100000 10001010 10010101 11111010 00001110 01111001
11110101 10101110 01110111 00010111 00011101 00001100 00011000 01110100 11001111 11010010
10011101 11001000 11100000 11111010 11010011 01010111 11100101 00000101 01001111 11100011
01001001 10111011 11001100 01110010 00000110 01000110 00111010 11010001 11001101 01111110
10000011 00011110 00110001 10010011 11001101 00001100 01110000 01011100 10001110 10010100
11011111 10010101 01110111 11100000 01100000 11111010 00001010 01000110 00100011 00111000
11111100 01101001 00110110 00000010 11100000 11110000 11001111 11000000 11110100 10100011
00111101 10011000 11100100 10011111 01001010 00010101 10110111 00001100 10111110 01111101
10101001 00010000 01110010 01111011 01010101 00110111 11010100 00000111 11110000 00001000
11100111 10011110 11000010 10011011 11100110 01110011 11010011 11101011 01001000 00110000
01011111 00100011 10111111 01111010 01011110 00000001 11000101 00101111 01000110 00101011
10001001 10111001 10010101 11000001 00101010 00001001 01110011 11010000 00011010 01001100
00010010 01110001 11101011 11010100 11100111 10100101 00101000 00100011 10000001 11011100
11010010 10011111 10010101 00001110 00000111 00111110 11110100 01011101 10110010 10000100
01101001 00001110 00011101 01010011 10111111 01111010 01001110 10011011 00111010 11100000
00001110 11110100 10111001 11000000 00111110 10100100 01110111 10100001 11001000 00000000
00001110 11110101 01001010 11111101 01000100 01100001 01111000 10101111 11000011 10010110
11011010 11001101 10110001 01100010 00111100 10111011 11011100 01111110 11101110 01000001
11101011 11101111 11101101 01011110 01100111 10101000 01111000 00111111 01011010 10110100
00101111 10011011 01000011 00101010 00001110 01110111 11000110 01110010 00001101 01111011
01000100 10011000 00100100 01101100 00011011 11001111 10110101 00110110 01100000 00010101
00010001 01111010 10010011 11010111 00100011 10001010 01111100 11110110 01111011 00010111
00011010 10010010 10100111 10110001 11100001 00101001 11100001 10011101 01011110 01100000
00011101 00110100 11101011 10011101 10000100 11110101 00100011 00000010 10111010 10101101
00100111 11100001 10111101 11010111 10011011 00010001 11010101 01101110 00100010 01000001
10000000 11101101 00011100 01000111 00100111 11101001 10011010 11110100 11001101 10111001
11011000 00000111 01100011 10011100 01110110 10100111 00101011 01100111 00111001 00011110
11011101 01101011 01100111 01011110 11011010 00100010 10011101 01101001 00110011 10010101
10001011 11000000 10111010 00011100 00110010 00000010 01101101 10100101 10010100 11110001
11110111 10100100 11100010 10110110 00101101 01110100 10111101 00110110 11001111 00111111
01100101 10110000 10110110 10001001 11001111 10100010 11111111 00000000 10001101 01011111
00000011 00000111 10010110 11000111 10110111 01101010 01000000 00001011 01111110 11110001
10111111 00000001 11101000 00101011 00100111 01010010 01010111 11010000 11001011 10011101
10111110 10100000 10100000 11101100 00000101 11011000 10010011 10011010 01101110 00001001
01101100 00011110 10011101 11101001 11101100 01000001 11100000 01100100 10011010 10001101
11001000 11110011 01001001 11001001 11111010 00001110 10010100 10011011 01001100 01000010
00010001 11100101 00101001 01100100 11011110 00001101 01110010 10011110 00100100 11110000
11001101 10010110 10101111 00011100 10010010 00111000 00110001 01011101 10111110 00001000
10010101 01111000 11001110 00111101 01101011 10100111 10010101 10110010 11100000 00011100
11110101 11100000 00011010 11000011 11110001 00101110 10101000 10011010 01010110 10010111
01110001 01111010 11111100 11111001 00100011 11100101 00011101 10011101 11101001 10101001
00111101 10010000 11001111 00001101 11110001 00100101 10011100 10011010 01101101 11101100
11110110 01010011 01100000 10111100 01100111 10011100 00011010 11000011 11100000 10001110
01001001 00001111 11101001 01010110 11110101 00101011 10101001 10101111 01101111 00100101
10111010 10010100 10000011 00100100 10000111 01111001 11001101 01010000 00111000 10010001
11111010 11110101 11101011 01011110 10101101 00011010 01110010 11100101 00100101 10110000
11001011 00110010 10011100 00001100 11100011 11010000 11110101 10100000 10110110 00001000
00000000 01110010 01111010 00000010 01101000 01111110 00000110 00010011 10101111 01100001
01010010 01011001 01000111 11100111 01001000 00001011 10001110 01000111 01110011 01011010
11101000 10110101 00010101 11111010 00010110 10101100 11101100 11111100 11110010 01001011
11100000 01000110 10011101 01001101 01011101 01110010 10010110 11110001 10010011 10011101
10000011 10100000 11110111 10100110 00001001 01001100 01010001 11101101 00000000 00000100
10101100 10111011 10011001 00001000 01110010 11001111 11001111 10100101 01100111 01111001
01010100 11110100 00011011 01001001 00100010 01001011 10011011 10111110 10011000 00011001
00011110 10110101 01001010 00101101 11000100 10011110 11000000 10011110 10010100 11110100
10001000 11001010 01000111 11010111 11010011 00110101 10101011 01100011 01100010 00011000
11110010 10011001 11001001 11100000 01110011 10011010 11010001 10111000 11000001 00000010
01010111 00101001 01000101 01101010 11010010 10010001 11000111 00000011 10010011 01010011
00100101 10010100 10100100 00000011 00011000 01110011 10010011 11110101 10101111 01000110

11110000 11111111 00000000 10000101 10010001 01100011 10001110 01001011 10000100 11001001
00111100 11100011 00111110 10110101 10111100 11011010 01000101 10111100 01100011 11001011
11110010 01010001 00100011 00011101 00000000 00010101 11000001 01010011 00011100 10010011
10110010 00110101 01011000 01110011 11000110 01100100 10001101 10100011 00111001 00100011
00011111 01011010 01100011 10000011 10011111 01010010 01000111 00111000 10101111 01011011
10111110 11110000 11101101 10001101 11000001 00000101 10100001 00000000 11100011 00011111
01010000 00101011 10010111 11010101 01111100 00101001 11100100 01000110 11110010 01000100
01001011 10001100 00011100 01110001 11010010 10110100 10100111 10001010 10001011 11010101
11101110 00001110 10001011 01001000 11100010 11000001 00001011 11000000 00111100 01010110
10010101 10011100 11111101 00110001 10011110 00111000 11001110 01101010 10111101 11010110
10011101 00101101 10110001 00111001 01011110 00111101 01101001 10110001 10110011 01000110
11100000 11110011 10000011 01011011 10111010 10011100 11101011 01000011 00100100 10101100
01101101 01011100 10110110 11101000 10001110 11111100 11110100 11100111 00010101 10000101
00101100 10011011 01110010 00010110 10101111 11111101 10100000 10000011 11001001 00111000
00111101 11101010 10000101 11010110 01001100 10011000 00000011 10101111 01111010 01010100
11010010 00011011 00000100 10111010 00101101 11111110 10110000 11100111 00011101 10001101
00100100 10010010 00001001 00000111 11001001 11000000 10101010 01101110 00001100 01100100
11110010 01110011 11101101 01000111 10011001 10000011 10001100 00011111 01111100 11010110
10001010 00011010 11011100 10000111 10101000 10110011 01100001 01111000 00011000 00111110
10110101 00000011 01100101 10001111 11001010 00000110 00001101 01011010 11110010 10011011
00100100 10100010 01100111 11011010 10100001 01101000 11011001 10010011 11010000 11110111
11100110 10101010 11101001 10110010 01101100 01000110 11100000 01111010 11100000 10001110
11111110 10110100 10000000 11100100 11110010 00111001 00010100 10101110 10000110 00110010
00110011 11000001 11110100 11001111 01001010 01110000 11100111 10010100 00011100 11111111
00000000 00111010 10111101 10110100 00010000 11000101 00000000 10011110 01001111 11010111
00010100 11111101 11001010 00000111 11100011 01001100 10010011 11100101 00000111 10001010
01001110 01110000 01111101 01101000 00011001 00110010 10110010 10010000 00001111 11110011
10100001 01011011 10010010 01110011 11001000 11110101 10100110 11000100 00110000 00111110
01111100 01111011 01010100 10011000 00001100 00110011 11011110 10100001 10100000 01000101
10011000 11000110 00010011 00111110 10110101 11101001 10111111 00001000 10101110 11001100
01010111 00110111 00101001 11100110 00011100 01001000 00000110 01010111 10110111 00011101
11111110 10110101 11100101 10110000 00011100 00011100 00111111 01010000 01111011 11010111
01101011 11110000 11110110 11101100 11000001 10101101 00100000 11000000 00111011 11000110
00111001 00110101 11001011 10001000 11010010 00001101 00011010 00100011 11011100 00100101
00011011 01111100 10100011 10000010 01011100 10011111 10011000 10001111 01001010 00010100
11111001 01010010 00010010 10011101 00011010 10100000 10110110 01100011 00101100 01000011
10011100 11100000 01100000 11110011 11011110 10100100 11001110 01001000 11100011 00111000
00111101 00000111 01111010 11100000 11011101 01011100 01100100 11110001 01100111 00011000
11001001 00100110 10010111 10101001 00111001 11111100 10101010 00110101 00000100 00111001
00011001 11100100 11110101 10100111 10100111 00100101 11000001 11111100 11101001 01011100
00000000 10011100 00001100 10001110 01101001 10001001 10010101 10110111 11011010 11111101
01111010 10011010 01110110 00000001 01000010 11001100 01111000 00010100 11010110 00000100
11001000 01011000 11110100 00111101 00000101 00100100 00101011 10000110 01111010 00011111
01011010 01000010 11011011 10110010 01111011 01111010 11010000 11011100 01100011 10011100
01100111 11010010 10000010 00000001 00100001 01111101 00000110 01110001 10001010 00111010
01011100 01100010 11110110 00011111 11001110 10011100 00000111 00000111 01110111 11010110
10011000 11011111 00110001 11000000 00111101 11110010 01101001 01111000 00101101 10011101
11011101 11111111 00000000 00111010 00110100 00010010 00000111 11100100 11100000 00000001
10011110 11111001 11110100 10100001 10110110 11101100 00011001 11101000 00111011 01010010
00101000 00000011 00111101 11001001 00111101 01101001 01011011 00000000 00001100 10000010
01111101 10000111 01111010 01111011 00000111 01010001 00111001 00100011 10001110 10100100
11100000 10011111 01001010 00011001 00111010 00101001 00111101 01111011 01100110 10010101
11000001 01011100 00001100 01110001 11110101 10100011 01100000 00010010 00111001 00100111
10110111 00100100 11010010 10111000 11000100 11001000 00001000 01000000 00011001 11000111
01001010 01000110 00000111 10010000 01011111 10011111 01001010 01101110 01110010 10000000
11000111 11010011 11010110 10010010 01000001 10111010 01000001 11101011 10001010 10100100
10111010 10000000 10100000 11110100 00011001 11101001 11010111 11011110 10011010 11100111
00000111 11111010 11111010 11010100 10000001 01110000 10111001 00000100 01100100 11110000
00110011 01001100 10010010 01000101 11100100 00000110 00000100 00001110 10100111 11010100
11010100 00110111 11010000 00000100 11001110 01111110 01100010 01110010 01001001 11100011
10011110 10010100 00110001 01011100 00000101 11100111 10010011 11000111 00010100 11010011
00100000 00100001 00001000 00000111 00000011 11011011 10101001 10100111 10111111 11001011
10000001 11010101 11011000 11110100 11110100 10100111 00001111 00110000 00010101 01110010
01001110 00110110 10011110 10010101 00011010 00010011 10010010 01010011 00011001 00111101
11101001 11101110 00111001 11011010 10000111 01100000 11000110 01011000 10011110 11110100
10010000 10000101 00110010 01100001 00000111 11001000 00111011 11010001 10101110 11101000
00000110 11111101 11100011 10000000 01001110 00111111 10111101 01000110 00011011 10010001
10011100 00000011 11010100 10001110 10100110 10010001 01001111 11001000 00111101 00101001
01010000 00001101 11100000 01100011 10101111 11101011 01001101 10000010 00010001 00011011
00101011 11010011 00111001 11110101 10100101 10001100 00000000 01110001 10011110 00111011
01110110 10100111 00111110 01111001 01011101 11011011 00110001 11010111 00111101 10101001
10000011 00100110 01000010 00110011 10000001 10000001 11001001 10100111 11001101 10100110
10000100 10110001 10001011 10010110 00000001 01001111 01010000 01101001 11101111 11000110

11000001 11011010 10010100 01110010 11011100 01111101 11001010 01101011 11101110 01100111
11001110 00110000 01110001 11110010 10001111 01011010 00011011 11101110 00010110 00000010
01110000 00111110 01001111 10111110 01001111 01011110 11000010 10000111 00100100 10010011
11110011 01111100 10000000 01100011 00111110 10100110 10000110 00000000 01110001 11011011
00111101 01101001 10101110 11011000 10001110 01000000 10011001 11100011 10111101 00100101
01110110 00010110 10110000 01111001 01101100 00000010 00110001 11100011 00111101 00111001
10100001 10110010 01000000 01101110 01110000 00111010 01010010 00110001 11001110 00001010
00110011 10001111 01000110 00110100 10000100 01110011 10001100 11100111 10011100 10000010
01101001 00100110 10101110 00110100 00111000 10011110 00001110 11000001 10010111 11000110
00000111 00010100 11011110 10000011 00000111 10101001 11101101 01001110 00100100 10101001
00011000 11100010 10011010 00110001 00011000 11001001 00110101 10100011 01001000 01100001
10110100 10001110 10100110 10011011 10010001 11101110 01111111 00011010 01111100 10111110
11111111 00000000 01010001 01001010 10110010 01110000 00110111 00001110 01101010 00011100
10010100 01011101 10001001 00111010 01000110 00011100 01100000 00110001 10100001 10111000
00100000 01110011 11000101 00110101 11000000 11001111 01001110 01001101 00001011 11010000
10000010 00111000 00011101 01101011 01010101 01111110 10100010 00011101 11001011 01100111
10011100 00100000 11101101 11101011 01001110 11011101 10110111 00001011 11100101 10010010
01111011 00011010 01100000 00111001 11101000 01111000 11111010 01010010 10101001 11100000
10011100 11111101 00101010 01111010 11111011 10100000 00111001 10000110 01000111 00111100
11010011 01110011 10001111 11110000 10100100 01000001 11001000 00111000 00111111 10000111
01101010 10010011 10000110 00111001 11101001 10001010 01110110 10111001 01010111 00011000
10100101 10111010 00010011 11111000 01100010 10000110 11101001 11010010 10001100 11101110
01111110 00111000 11001111 11101011 01001110 01010000 00001111 00111001 11100111 11010010
10100111 10010101 11110101 00100100 01101110 00001001 11000110 01111010 00011110 10110100
00111111 01100001 11000110 00111010 11110011 11011110 10010011 00000111 10011100 01100100
10011010 01010110 00011000 11101011 11000111 10101101 00111101 00111010 00000000 10011001
11111001 00001001 00000000 10011111 01100001 01001011 10011110 00110010 10100011 10000011
01000011 00010001 11000101 00001100 01111001 00100011 00100011 10001111 11010010 10101111
11001101 00000000 11101100 10011100 01100010 10000001 11000111 11010011 11101001 01001101
11110011 00110011 11010000 00011100 00011110 11110100 11100110 00111100 11111011 01010100
10110110 11010000 00000011 00011110 10000011 10111001 00110100 11011100 00011110 10000011
10100111 11110011 10100000 01110100 11111010 11010011 10110011 11011111 00000100 10011010
10011011 00110110 11000000 01101011 00010101 01100011 11000111 01001111 01100011 01001000
00111001 11100100 00001110 11110100 10100011 11100100 11001110 01111011 11010011 01011010
00110000 01011100 00010000 00111010 01010010 01001001 00000001 00100001 11001110 00110110
11110100 10100011 00100011 10100000 00111100 11100010 10011011 10010000 00000110 00000000
00100110 10010001 00000000 00011001 00101111 10000010 01000111 01111010 00110111 00000001
01111010 00111000 11100000 01100011 00010100 01100100 11111010 11111110 00011000 10100011
00111001 11001111 00011101 01101000 00000011 00000111 00011101 00111101 11101001 10111111
00100000 00011101 10010011 10111100 00001110 10110100 11011100 01100101 10110111 01100111
10100111 01101010 01110001 00000111 00011001 00011111 10011101 00110101 11110010 00000110
00110001 10010011 01010011 11010110 11001000 00000000 10010101 00101111 10010011 01000111
01011110 01000101 00100110 00110000 00111110 01101110 10100111 10111101 00101001 00111011
01111000 11100011 10011010 01010010 01000011 10111000 00111001 01010011 11000000 10100011
10001110 00000110 00001110 01111101 01101001 00110010 00111001 00100111 10100101 00100111
00000101 11110111 00011110 10011111 01011010 10100101 10101001 01000011 10110000 11011110
01100111 01101101 10010100 10011111 01111011 00011100 00010000 00000111 01011100 10011010
01011100 10000010 01110001 10010011 10001111 01001010 00110001 11101101 11111001 11010011
01101000 10010000 11101011 11010000 11110100 11101111 01001101 01101100 01001000 10011000
00011101 01101001 01110000 01110001 11000000 10100011 00011100 10001110 01000110 01110001
11010010 10110000 00011101 11000001 01000001 11001010 00011111 11000011 10001010 00100100
00000100 00000010 10101000 01110001 11101010 01111101 01101001 00011000 10001100 10001000
11110111 01111100 11111101 01110001 01000010 11100000 10010000 00111001 10101101 01101101
11011000 10100001 11001011 11010011 00000111 10100111 01111010 00011101 01111110 01000001
10010011 11000000 11101101 01001101 11001110 01011100 11100001 10001110 00000111 10101101
00111001 10001010 11100011 00100100 10010011 11110100 10101001 01101011 01010001 00001101
01100011 11000000 00000000 00010011 11001111 00000000 11010011 10011011 00100100 10010001
10011010 01001100 11110001 10111000 10011111 11001110 10001110 10001001 11001111 00011110
10010100 11100100 11010111 01000001 01011000 01010001 10000101 00011001 11101110 00000111
01001010 01001100 01110000 00000011 11110101 00100111 10110101 00110011 11001100 00000111
10101111 01010011 11101011 01001110 11100111 01111000 00000011 10100000 00111100 11010100
11101100 00110001 01011100 00001100 11100001 00001001 00000000 11110101 11100110 10000110
00111000 00100000 01110101 11100011 10010011 01001011 11011111 10001111 11010110 10010000
11110010 01001110 00111110 10011001 10101010 11010001 10001001 10000110 11000011 10000000
01111111 11001001 10100101 11001000 00000011 00100111 10000010 01101000 01010000 00000110
01001110 01111111 00111010 01101010 00011101 11000111 00100100 00010001 01010010 11011100
10110110 01100011 00011100 10100111 00111101 11001110 00000101 00011001 11001001 11000111
01000001 11011110 10010001 10000000 00100100 11100011 10100111 11010110 10010011 00000000
01110010 01001111 00111101 10101001 10100101 10101000 00000011 00101000 01110100 11000001
00111101 01111011 01010110 01000110 10111011 10100011 01000001 10101000 11000010 11110001
10010100 11000011 11100011 10000011 01011010 11111101 01001111 10100101 00110101 01011000
10011110 10110101 00111100 10010111 00011101 11101101 10101001 11100011 01111010 10101101
10001100 11011010 01101101 11010001 10000110 01000101 01110001 11101000 01111011 00011010

10001010 00010110 00101101 10000001 10011100 00011010 11110101 10001101 01110111 01001000
10000111 01010011 10110110 11110010 10100100 01011100 00111110 01110010 00011011 10111101
01111001 10000110 10100101 10100110 01001101 10100110 11011100 10011000 11100110 00011100
01111010 11111010 11010110 00010010 01010110 11010000 11101011 10100101 01011010 11111010
00110001 00110010 11011000 11111001 10111011 01010011 11010100 00110001 10101010 10110001
00110110 01110010 01001110 00110011 11101011 01010110 11100001 00100111 10000000 01101011
01001001 11011001 01000110 11100111 01000001 00101010 01110000 00110000 01001110 01111110
10110101 01100001 00000101 01000100 10100001 01011011 11101011 11101011 01010110 01010001
01001010 11111011 11010110 01101010 01001101 11101010 00101110 10011010 10000010 01000100
01111010 11111110 10010101 00110000 00011110 10111001 11111100 11101000 01001111 01011111
11001110 10101100 00100110 00001010 11110001 11011010 10011011 10110010 01011010 00010011
01110001 10001010 10111000 00111000 10100101 01101110 00000110 00110001 10011010 01111011
01100011 10101101 01001000 10101011 10011010 01010010 10110101 10101100 10000010 11100100
01001101 00011111 00011001 11000110 01111101 01101001 10111110 01000010 10110001 11110101
11111100 00101010 11011110 11011110 00000000 00010101 00100000 10001011 10001110 10010101
10011011 10001101 10110100 01100100 11111010 00011001 01010010 01101001 11110001 01001000
00001110 01100011 00010101 10011111 01110011 10100001 01000100 11011100 10100111 00011110
10000011 11011110 10111010 01010110 10001111 10001110 10011100 11010011 00011110 00110001
10001111 01111010 10111111 01101000 11010010 10110100 01110110 00001101 01001110 00001110
11101111 01000110 10011010 00110001 11110010 01111100 11100110 10110011 11001100 00101101
00011111 10110110 01000111 01110001 01011110 10001000 11110000 01100111 10110000 10101010
01010111 00110110 01110001 11001011 10010000 01000000 11001101 01101001 01001111 00010011
00100101 10111000 10111010 10011001 00011110 00011000 11110001 00011101 11001110 10010111
00100110 11000110 01101101 11110110 11011101 11100011 00111100 11010111 10101000 01101001
01011010 10011101 10111110 10100101 01101011 11100111 01011011 11001001 10111111 00100011
10010001 11011100 01111010 11110001 01011110 01011011 01110111 10100100 10000101 00011001
10000100 01100010 10100001 11010011 11101110 11101110 01110100 10001011 10011111 00111010
00010010 11100000 11100111 10010001 10011110 00001101 01101010 11101010 10101010 10000100
01001110 10011010 01100111 10110011 11100011 11010010 10000111 11001001 01011101 10100011
10000000 11011100 10010011 01011100 11110111 10000111 10111100 01010001 01101101 10101011
00001000 11100001 01111100 11000101 01110001 10110111 11100110 11011101 11000000 00100111
11011010 10111010 00001100 10001100 11111011 01010100 11001010 00101101 00011100 11001110
00110110 01111010 10001110 11000110 01000110 01011011 11010111 00010100 10001100 11000001
01011101 11111101 00101001 01111010 10001110 10111111 10101101 00100011 00001101 11000111
00111100 01110100 10100100 11011110 10010110 10110000 10000100 01000110 11101111 11101111
11000000 10100101 11000011 00010011 10010010 01111000 11101111 11000101 00101010 10010000
00000001 11110100 10100100 00000100 10010100 11100111 10111111 10100101 00110110 10101100
10110101 00000100 00100110 00111001 00111011 01111000 00011110 11110100 00110010 01110000
00111101 01101001 10100111 11101111 00011110 11000010 10011110 01001110 01011000 00001010
10101000 01101101 10101000 01110101 00001100 01100000 01111010 01110011 11001110 01101001
10001000 01110000 01110001 10001110 11011100 01010011 10001001 11001011 11100000 11110100
11000101 00101110 01000010 10001110 00001111 00100100 11100010 10100111 01110110 00000000
10100011 00111000 11001001 00111100 01110010 01110001 01001100 00000100 00111011 00010010
01010111 10111101 00111100 00001110 10000000 01110001 11001110 01001101 00011011 10001111
00100111 00111000 00011111 01001010 10100101 01101011 10000000 10011001 11000100 10000011
01100000 11100111 00010100 00111110 11101101 11111101 00000101 00001000 11000000 00100111
00011001 11111010 10011010 01101110 11010010 01011111 10111111 00100111 10101101 00101001
10101011 11101100 00101111 00110001 11011001 11011011 11011100 11100110 10000000 00001110
11101100 11100011 01111110 01001111 00011110 11010100 11010101 01101110 01110000 10000011
11100100 11110101 00111100 10011010 00100100 00111001 00111000 11101001 11011111 00111110
10010101 00110010 01111010 01011000 01100010 00111001 00000110 01000000 00111110 11111111
00000000 00111110 10011000 10100011 00011001 01110000 00111101 00101000 01100000 00111100
10110111 00100100 11111110 01010100 11001000 10001111 00111011 10011001 10111110 01110011
11010110 10101101 01011101 10100001 00001111 10010111 11100101 11111001 01000111 01011111
11100111 01010001 01001110 11011011 01100010 00101101 10000000 00000000 00011101 00111101
01101001 01000000 11100101 11011001 11111010 10011111 11010010 10011000 11100011 00111011
00000111 00111000 11110111 00110101 00101101 11110100 01100000 10010001 00001001 11001000
00000001 10111011 10011110 11100110 10111100 01110011 11100010 10100110 10110110 11010111
10010111 01100011 01001110 10110111 10011011 00110110 11110001 00011100 10110110 00111010
00010110 00010101 11101001 11111110 00101011 11010101 00011011 01001101 11010010 10100101
10010110 00110010 10001010 01111010 00000110 00111101 10101011 11100111 10101011 11111011
10011111 10110100 01001000 11110011 01110010 01011110 01000011 11010111 00111100 10011111
01111010 11011111 00001011 01001111 10011010 01110111 01111101 00000110 01010100 10010100
10011100 01110101 10101000 11010111 01110000 00011001 10100101 01101100 01100111 00001010
01101010 00111011 10011001 01001100 01111100 01100011 10011010 11110101 11010010 10110110
10000100 00110001 10001110 01111100 11001001 00001000 00000000 00010001 11011010 10110100
00101101 00010100 01000101 00010111 11001101 11111001 01010101 00101011 00101000 11000100
10010010 01100000 11110010 00001111 00110101 01111110 01100010 00000000 11000010 10001110
00111101 10101010 01100110 11101101 11101110 10001101 00101101 01101110 01000111 00111100
11011000 00011001 00111001 11101011 11000101 01010001 01011100 11001000 11111100 11110111
00110100 11101001 01001011 01001001 11110100 11110100 10101011 00010000 11000111 11000000
00101011 11010110 10101011 01000100 10110100 00001101 01011001 01101010 11001010 00001100
10010001 11000111 00011110 10110101 11011110 01111000 01010111 01001100 01010011 10001001

11001000 11001111 10100110 01111011 01010111 00101011 10100100 11000011 10111010 01000100
00000111 00011100 11110100 10101111 01010000 11010010 11100011 00010001 11011011 10100110
00000111 11010110 10111000 00110001 01010101 01101100 10001110 11001010 01010100 11110100
10111001 10100001 00010000 00001010 10100000 00001010 10010001 11111111 00000000 01111000
00111001 00110100 11010100 00111100 00001100 11010011 11000110 00110001 11101111 01011110
01001101 11101111 10101001 11010011 10110001 00010111 10010111 10110111 10110101 01000001
00110100 01111110 01100110 01111111 11001110 01101010 11011011 00110110 00010010 10101011
10111011 01110001 10010000 00101010 01010101 01001111 01111011 01010110 01000011 00110000
11101111 01110100 11101000 11100110 01000011 00011011 10100000 00100011 10101110 00101011
10001111 11010101 00110100 01010110 10001010 01000011 10110000 00000010 00110011 10011110
00000111 01101010 11101111 00100100 10010000 10110001 10101010 10010111 00010001 00000010
00001101 01110101 01010011 11000100 01001110 11010110 01000110 01101110 10011101 11001111
00111100 00110110 01110010 00101110 00001001 01010010 00000101 00110110 11100110 11001100
10011100 11101100 00011001 00000111 00011101 10110011 10001010 11101100 10100110 10110100
00001100 01110000 10100010 10100010 01111011 00100101 00000011 00111000 11111111 00000000
11101011 01010111 01011010 11000100 00100101 11010100 11001101 11010001 01100111 00000111
01110011 01100100 11000000 11100000 10100110 00001101 01010010 10011010 00101100 00010011
11000001 00000111 10101110 01101011 10110100 10111011 10110011 00001100 11100111 11100101
11101001 11010011 11011110 10110001 00101110 00101100 11111000 00100101 10000111 00110101
11010011 01001111 00010011 11001111 10100001 10010011 10100111 01101101 00001100 00111000
11011010 01000101 00011000 00100011 00111111 01000011 10001010 10001111 01110001 11001110
00001001 11000111 10110101 01011101 10111001 10110101 11110010 11011011 10101111 00110101
01011010 01101000 11111001 11100110 10111010 01010101 10110111 00110010 01101000 01100001
11001001 11001110 01111001 11001101 00110001 01110111 00000111 11000000 11100100 11111011
11010011 10000000 11000110 00000110 00111000 10100111 11100000 00000001 10111011 00111111
10001101 00010111 11010110 11100100 00010000 11110010 01000110 00011000 11110111 11100110
10011010 11000111 01101111 01001100 11110101 11110100 10100101 01100011 01001010 11001100
00111010 11100011 10011010 11010010 00101100 10011101 10000100 11011100 00001010 01111011
10001010 10010001 00001011 01110101 11011011 11000001 11101111 10011010 10101110 10100000
10101001 11001110 01110001 10011111 11010110 10100100 10001001 10000110 01000111 00110100
01001001 01011100 01101000 10110011 11010100 11101110 00111101 11111101 00101011 10100100
11110000 10011011 00110100 01010111 11111011 10010001 01111001 11011011 11011111 10101111
11100001 01011100 11010100 00100100 00010000 01111011 10000011 11101111 01011101 00000111
10000111 10100100 11001101 11101100 01000000 00101110 00000001 11111001 00001110 01111111
10100101 01110011 01010101 10110101 10011101 11001101 00010001 11101111 00111010 01111100
11101000 00100011 10110111 11000000 11111001 00100100 10001111 00111000 00011100 11110011
01010111 10010010 01010011 11110011 10110000 01011101 10001001 11101010 01111010 11010111
00111011 10100001 01001101 00011100 11010110 00000000 11000011 11111111 00000000 00101100
11011011 10000000 00000110 00000000 11000101 01110100 00001011 10110001 10100010 01001100
10010111 11100100 11100100 10000001 11010100 11010111 10010101 11010111 01000001 10111011
10001110 00000111 00101000 00000000 11100011 00100111 10010011 01001010 10000011 10010010
11000100 11110000 01101001 01011111 00000001 01111110 11101111 01011010 00010100 11111001
01101000 01111011 00011110 11000000 01110101 10100001 10101011 10100001 01101010 00001001
11010010 01000110 01111110 10011001 11100111 10011010 01000010 01011001 10001000 11101100
10000000 01110100 00010100 11001100 01101101 00111011 01001001 11100000 01110110 10101001
00010101 10001011 00111110 11101100 01100000 01111011 11110111 10100011 10010110 11011010
00001101 10000010 11111110 11101011 10101111 11100011 01001001 10010110 01101100 01110000
00000001 00111101 11101001 01110011 10000011 11110011 01110101 10100100 01110110 11011010
00001011 00011110 10000011 10000000 00111011 10010011 01000010 01101000 01011010 10001001
10001100 01000110 00010000 00011110 01111011 10011010 01110110 11010000 01001000 00000011
00011000 00010100 00101000 00100010 01001110 01001010 01111011 10000001 11011010 10010011
00100000 00000010 11000111 10010000 00111010 01111011 11010000 10000110 00101110 01000111
01111111 01001110 01001101 00000011 10001000 10000001 11100111 00100111 11010111 10110101
00100111 11001011 00011110 01010000 11110010 01111010 11100011 00011101 01101001 00010000
11111100 11000100 11110001 11001111 10100101 00001101 10100001 10001101 11001001 00100100
11100011 10100000 11101110 01101000 10010100 00110011 00010100 01010001 11010000 11110010
11000100 10011010 01111011 00010000 01001001 00011111 10011101 00100001 00111000 01100001
10000001 11010111 10110110 01101010 11100010 10101100 10001001 10110011 01100001 10000000
00011111 00010100 11001101 10111111 10111101 00111110 11011101 01111001 10100111 10100000
00001011 00100110 01110010 01001111 01111110 10111001 10100110 00100000 11000001 01110110
11101000 00001011 01110101 00111100 11010100 01101101 10110000 00100110 00111101 11000110
00011111 00011001 11100011 11010010 10100011 11000111 01000110 00111100 01100111 11110100
10100111 00011100 00101110 01001010 00101001 00110010 00111111 00000000 11010010 00101000
00101100 01110000 01111001 01110000 01110011 11010110 10101101 01101001 10110000 11000100
00101010 00000110 00001111 01000000 00001111 01010011 01000110 00110111 00101111 11011100
11000110 01111001 11001101 00111001 11010111 00111100 00010001 11000000 10100100 01001100
00011000 11110111 01101110 11001110 01111010 11100110 10010101 11010010 11010100 01001001
00000010 10000001 10111011 00111000 11100100 11110001 11001101 00100000 11001111 10011001
10110111 10000000 00111101 00101000 00000100 10011001 01001000 11101101 11010111 10001110
01111111 01011010 01101011 11100011 00010010 01001010 00110000 00000001 00011110 10111101
01101001 01011110 11001100 01100010 00101000 01010010 01011100 10110001 11000010 00001110
11110100 11111101 11000100 10100111 00001011 11011011 10000001 11011100 00011010 10001100
01100000 10101111 00111101 00111011 11010011 10110011 10010000 01010111 00111000 11101111

01001010 11110111 01000000 01000111 11100100 10000000 10111000 01001110 00001111 00000100
10011111 01010011 11101111 01001110 11000011 00110001 01000000 00001000 11000110 01111001
11110111 10100101 01101100 00001110 00000001 11100111 10101001 10100100 01011110 01010111
00100011 00111100 01110011 11001101 01011101 10111010 10000000 01100111 01110011 11100001
01001111 00011001 11101011 01000011 11111100 11001100 01011000 00011110 10111100 01100110
10000000 10100011 00000101 10110011 11011010 10001000 01110111 00010100 11001011 11110000
01001001 11110100 10101100 11011011 10111011 10110000 00001101 11000000 00100011 11001011
00111111 11000010 00111111 00101010 01000111 00111000 01001100 00000011 10011100 11110110
11001111 01011010 01011111 00101111 01101001 11110011 01001001 00100111 00111100 01100000
01010011 01110000 00001101 11001011 10110011 10001111 01100000 00000111 00011100 01111011
11010101 11101100 01001001 00100110 01100011 01011000 11000001 10010000 11100011 11010001
00111101 01101010 00111100 11100001 10010000 10011110 10100110 10011101 00100011 00110011
01100011 01111110 00111110 10010101 00011011 01100111 01110110 00000111 01001010 01101101
01011000 10100001 11101100 01000001 01110010 11000011 10011100 00001110 00111000 10100110
00111110 00001001 00000000 01110011 11011110 10100100 11011000 01110011 10010001 10000001
10000001 01010001 10100110 00001000 11100100 11100000 01110111 00110100 10110111 11010001
10010000 00000100 11110111 00111110 10111101 01110001 01001110 01011100 10010001 10010011
01001100 01101100 11100011 11101111 01100111 10011110 10110100 10001100 01110110 10011100
01010000 11010101 10111010 11011100 10110011 10101001 01111111 10010111 10010111 11100011
10011010 00110011 11001000 11011010 01110010 00111101 01101001 00011000 10010101 00111000
11001110 01000111 10100001 10100000 01110111 11101011 10001111 01010000 01101011 01001011
10101101 10001000 00010100 10110000 00000000 00000001 11001101 00001101 10010000 11011001
11000111 00011101 10110001 01000010 10010101 00000111 00000000 00010011 11000111 00100110
10010000 10010010 10101001 11110010 00001100 11010100 11011011 10100000 00001110 01000011
10011110 10100100 11010001 10010010 00000110 01000111 00000111 10100111 00100011 00110100
00001100 11101100 11111001 11000111 01011010 00011001 10110001 10000001 11111010 11010001
01110100 01011000 00101001 00101010 00110000 01001111 00110100 00000001 11001111 00000111
00010101 00011010 00001100 11100101 10111010 00001111 01001010 01111010 11100100 00011110
00111010 01111011 11010011 11110100 00100000 01011101 11011000 11110111 00010100 01100100
01100011 10100110 00000111 10111101 00001010 00000000 11101010 00110000 01111101 10101010
00111101 11000001 10001011 10000011 10011110 00101010 01101110 00000100 10000100 01110100
11000111 00110100 00100000 00000100 10011100 11110010 01101001 10101011 10001110 01000000
11100011 11110101 10100111 00000001 10000001 11101111 11011110 10000101 11011100 00000110
10101001 01100011 11010111 11100100 00011110 10010100 10111001 00111001 11110101 10100000
10011100 01111110 01111100 11010010 10000010 01001111 01011110 00000101 00110101 11101010
00000000 11000000 01100011 00100111 00111111 10010101 00111001 01111111 11110001 11101010
01101001 00100011 10100000 00111111 10001001 10100110 10110001 00000111 11110001 10100010
11110110 00000001 11011101 10101000 01011100 00110111 01111010 00001000 11000000 10100110
11111101 11100001 11010011 11111111 00000000 10101111 01000011 10010011 11101000 00000011
10011101 10111001 11100011 10110101 00110111 00111111 10101101 00011001 00011011 00111110
01001100 11110001 01001010 11000111 10011100 00001111 11001110 10011111 00111000 00000010
01111101 11010001 11010100 00011010 01011110 01000001 11001001 00111001 10100001 10001111
00011001 11001001 11111110 10010100 10011100 00000001 11000001 11001001 00110100 10011111
01110000 00000101 11101011 10010011 11111010 01010011 11111000 10010011 10100001 11101001
11101011 01001101 00000000 10010001 11010110 10010011 00000000 01110100 00011111 10001110
00111010 11010100 01011101 01011110 11000000 00101010 11101101 11000001 00011011 10011111
10000011 11010111 00010100 01110111 00111101 00110011 11101111 01000110 11100101 00000011
00000111 10000011 11110100 10100100 01101110 10100111 11010010 10010011 01011010 10000000
01110001 10000001 10011100 01111011 11010000 10000000 01100111 11010000 01111011 11010000
00000110 01001110 00000001 00011100 01110101 00010100 00110000 00111001 11000110 00000110
00101000 11010101 10010100 10000001 11110000 00010111 01101000 11001000 00100111 10101011
10000011 01001000 11100000 11111100 10001010 00011001 11001000 00011101 01110011 11001110
01101001 01111000 11011101 10010011 10011110 00000111 01011010 01000000 11011001 01000011
10000011 11000000 00110100 11011010 11010110 11100011 00010101 10001110 00110011 11011110
10010111 10100110 01001110 00111001 11110111 11101101 01000110 00000110 00110110 10010110
11111001 11001111 00110100 10010010 11111100 11001000 01010111 00011101 01101010 01100011
00011011 01101110 00110000 00000011 00100111 00100011 10100001 11100000 10011010 01000000
01001111 00111001 00000011 00111101 10101000 11000110 01111001 11001111 00000011 10110000
10100101 01001110 11000100 11110000 01111101 11101001 00110100 11111010 00001000 01000101
11000111 00111011 00110011 11000001 11101011 01000110 11011110 01000111 10111111 01101010
00010011 10011110 10100111 10101111 01111010 01110001 00000000 00111111 01011110 01101001
11110010 10001100 01001001 00001001 11011001 11101101 11010011 10000001 01001010 10111000
11000110 00101001 00011111 00111100 00000001 11010010 10010111 01101111 01001010 00111001
10101110 00100000 11101010 01111101 01101000 11100100 00000001 10000001 11010011 10111101
00100000 11101010 01111101 01101001 10001100 11001100 01111000 00000111 10110101 00100101
10101110 11100000 11010111 01100001 11011000 00011001 11101011 11110101 10100001 10011011
10100000 01001111 11111111 00000000 01010101 00110111 00011100 00011110 01111000 00100111
10110111 01111010 01111111 11010000 01110101 11101010 01101000 01011010 00001001 10001001
11001011 00001110 11111000 10100111 01100000 01100111 00000011 10011010 01101011 01100001
01010111 10001010 00010101 01001000 11101001 11000001 00010101 01010001 11010111 01010001
10001101 11001000 00101110 01110110 00000010 01111101 10101001 11100000 10011101 10110100
10001000 00001110 00001111 01011100 11111010 10011010 00010100 11100000 01100100 10110101
00001101 10001001 00001110 00011000 11001000 00011101 11001101 00000011 00011100 10001100

11110100 11101101 01001000 10000100 01100111 00111000 11101111 01001000 10001101 11110010
11100100 00000010 01110011 11010111 00110100 10101110 00110001 01001010 11100111 10010011
10011111 01101010 10100001 10101100 01101001 10010000 01101010 01010110 10100110 00111001
10010100 01101111 11111110 00010110 11101110 00101010 11110100 01100100 10010000 01001000
11100011 10011100 00001100 11010011 00110011 10010111 00001010 00001001 00111110 11100110
10001011 01110110 00011101 11001111 00100100 11010110 10110100 10011001 10110100 11001011
10100010 10101110 00001111 10010110 01111010 00110110 00111010 11010101 00111000 10100100
00111101 00111101 00111101 11101011 11010111 11110101 01001101 00111110 00001011 11101011
01010111 10001110 01100101 00011110 11000111 11010010 10111100 11001011 01011101 11010001
10100110 11010010 11101110 01001011 00110110 01011110 00110010 01111000 01111100 01010110
00110011 01010110 11011100 11101100 10100101 01011110 11111010 00110001 10010110 11101100
00110011 11011111 00110101 01100101 00011111 00111000 11001111 11100011 01011001 01110001
11001011 10000010 01111001 11111100 00101010 11110100 01110010 11010110 00111100 11110110
11010001 00100011 10100001 11101010 01011110 01000011 10011110 10011111 10101101 01011000
01000011 11011010 10101001 10100001 11001101 01001110 10011001 00111101 00001111 00111110
10110101 10100101 11011111 01010011 00111011 00010110 11111000 10101001 01010000 01110001
01010101 11000001 11001001 11100100 11110001 11101101 01010011 10100011 01110001 01001001
11011101 10100001 01011000 10011001 00110001 10001010 10010001 01110001 11101011 01010000
10101011 00001100 01010010 10101011 00001111 01011010 10001001 10100110 11101100 00110100
10001001 11001110 00110001 01010000 10111000 11100111 00110100 01101111 11110111 10100111
11101110 00000110 10100010 11010111 00010001 00010111 10111110 00101010 10111011 10101111
01010011 11011100 11010101 10000111 00111000 00111001 01011010 10000100 11111100 11010101
01101011 01011101 11000110 10101100 01010011 10011010 00110000 01000110 00111010 01010101
00101001 11101101 01000011 00001100 00111000 11001101 01101010 10111000 00000110 10101011
11001010 00110011 11000111 10100101 00011110 11010110 11001000 00101100 01110011 11110010
11011001 10011000 10110000 01100011 00100111 10000011 11000001 11001111 00100010 10110111
10110100 01001111 00010101 11001111 01100101 00011000 10001011 01010010 01011001 00100101
10001000 01110100 10010011 10111000 10101010 11110010 00101110 01111110 10010101 01011110
01101011 01111100 10000010 00001110 00001000 00110101 01101010 10101011 10111001 00110010
10000101 11010110 10100111 10100101 01011000 11011110 11011010 01011111 01000111 10111010
11010010 01010100 10010011 00111000 00100100 00000011 11101011 11001101 01011011 11100000
00001010 11110010 00001000 10000101 11000101 10011101 11000010 01001101 01101001 00101011
11000110 11100000 11110011 10000011 11010100 01111011 11010111 01001101 10100100 11111000
11000110 01001000 01010100 01000011 10101000 11000001 10111111 01101000 11000000 10010001
01111111 10101101 01110100 00101101 01010001 11001011 00111010 01101101 00111101 00001110
11100001 11110011 11110111 01010011 00010100 10111011 10001000 00100100 00001111 11010100
11010101 00111101 00111011 01010000 10110110 10111110 10001111 01110101 10101101 11000100
01110010 10010011 11010111 00000111 10011111 11001010 10101110 00110000 11110101 00111000
00000011 11010110 10100010 01001001 10010001 10101010 00001100 00001111 10101110 01101000
01010010 01111010 00001010 01000101 00111000 01100011 11011100 10001110 11011001 10100101
01011001 00111110 01111110 10011101 10111010 11010011 01101111 01011101 01000100 00101110
01000010 11111101 01111101 00000101 01000111 10011111 10011100 11100000 01010000 10000000
01110011 11001111 00111001 10100111 00000011 11001001 01010001 01001000 01111010 10001010
11000111 10001100 11110111 11111110 01110100 10001110 01111010 00000001 11010011 10111001
11000101 00001100 00001000 01110001 11000111 01101010 01010101 01011111 10011100 01100100
11010011 10110111 01000010 01101110 00110000 10011100 10001110 11100000 01100110 10011101
11001110 01001101 00001010 01010100 10000001 10111111 10000000 00111010 10011010 01101111
10011000 00011000 10010010 10000111 11100100 10101010 01011101 10000110 00100010 00011100
00000000 10100000 11110100 10100101 11000000 00010010 00010110 01110011 11010111 10110000
10100001 10111010 10000000 00000111 00111110 11010100 11011111 10111100 01000110 00010111
10001110 11100110 10100101 00100001 10000011 01110001 00011000 11110101 00100111 10011010
01101011 00000010 00011111 11110111 01100000 01100010 10011110 11101100 00001110 00000110
00111011 11010010 00101000 11011101 11111101 01110001 01001101 10001000 10000111 10011001
01100100 01110010 11100111 10000001 10001110 00000111 01001010 01101101 11001011 00110110
00111110 01001110 10100000 11010011 10001001 11110010 10100100 00000001 01111000 01001110
11100011 11010010 10110011 01110101 01011011 10000001 00010100 01000111 00101101 10001100
00000011 10011110 01111010 00001111 01011010 01001110 11001000 00001111 00110011 11111000
10101001 10101010 00010011 01110101 00011101 10011100 01110010 10101110 01010011 00100101
10000110 01110011 11010110 10111100 11001101 11011000 00001100 10011100 11110010 00101011
01010111 11000100 00010111 10000111 01010000 11010100 11100111 10111000 01100011 11000100
10001101 10000001 11101001 10001110 11010101 10001111 00101000 11111001 10110110 11110110
10101111 01010011 00001111 01001001 01000110 00100100 11011100 01001000 01111001 10010000
00011111 01111110 10110101 00001101 11000110 00001100 11000111 10101111 00000111 00000011
00110101 00100100 10100100 10001000 11011111 00000111 00000111 00010101 00010100 00001011
11110111 00001110 00110010 01111010 00010011 01011101 10001000 01010010 00101111 11011001
11000110 00100011 10110110 00101101 11001000 00100111 10011010 10000110 01100110 11101100
00111001 10101011 01010010 10011100 00100110 00000111 01010001 01010100 11010001 01000011
00110110 00111011 10010011 01011000 11000101 01011101 10110110 01010110 11011011 00001110
10000101 01110111 10011110 01111010 01110101 00111110 11010101 01101110 00001000 10010100
10010000 00000110 01111101 11001101 00001001 00011110 11010001 10001110 10010101 01110010
11010010 00101101 11011100 11100000 11100011 00111100 01010100 11001110 01111101 00001011
10000010 11010100 11011100 11110000 11111101 10111000 01101001 00010000 11111010 00011110
10000110 10111011 10011011 01100110 11011011 00011000 11100111 10010001 01011100 10111110

10000101 01101011 10001101 10001101 10001100 10001100 11110110 10101110 10101001 00000111
00011100 01010111 10010011 10001000 10101011 00100110 11101100 11001110 11111000 00101011
00010110 10100010 10010000 10011100 01100110 10100100 00110011 01110100 11111110 11101101
01010011 00101100 01010011 11101011 01001101 01101001 00111001 11100000 11100011 11101011
01011100 11110000 11010100 10100010 11000100 11010010 10010001 10010001 01010101 01011110
01010011 10001110 01001111 00010101 00011100 10110010 01100111 10111101 01010110 01111001
01000001 11101111 01001101 01010011 10001011 01101101 10010011 01101101 01001001 11110111
00000000 01001000 11001111 01011111 01011010 10000010 01001001 01000111 01000000 01111111
00011010 10000010 01101001 01111011 00000110 11101001 11010110 10101011 10011001 01110010
01111010 11010101 11111011 00110100 10011110 10000000 01011000 01111001 00000111 01000001
11011110 10100010 00100011 10000011 11001101 01000101 11100110 00011100 11111011 01111101
01101000 01011001 00000011 01100111 10011110 10010101 01001101 11011101 10000000 11001001
01010101 01111001 00000111 10011010 11001110 10011110 11011101 01001000 00100011 11110010
10101011 11010010 00110000 11001111 10100101 01000010 11101100 00000000 11000110 00101010
11100011 10100101 11011111 01100010 01011010 10111001 11001110 01011110 01011001 10010000
01001011 01101101 11001110 00111010 10010011 01011001 00010011 01011011 10010000 01000110
00000111 00000110 10111010 10001011 10110010 00011011 10001010 11001101 10011010 00100001
11011111 11010110 10111011 00101001 01010101 10111010 00111001 11101010 01010011 00111001
11111001 01100011 00101011 11000101 01000110 10000111 00000011 00000111 10001111 10101101
01101010 11001101 01101111 10010111 00100011 10001110 00111001 11001101 01100111 11001101
00000001 00011001 00000000 11010111 01110100 00011010 01111011 10011000 10111000 01101010
01010111 01110101 11001000 00000011 00011100 10001010 10001000 00001111 10010000 11100110
10100110 01010000 00001001 00000000 11100111 00000011 10111111 10101101 00110100 10000000
01111001 00011101 00111110 10110101 01100110 01001100 10001101 10000111 00001000 10100111
11101011 11111111 00000000 11101010 10100011 00011011 01110011 01000001 00100100 00111110
00110010 00110001 11101110 00101001 11001100 00000110 11011110 01001111 11100011 01010101
10101001 00100011 11010000 10010010 01000010 10001100 01010110 11100110 10000110 01011101
10110101 00001000 00010110 00110011 10001001 00110011 10010000 01110001 11000101 01100000
01000010 01110000 01000111 10100101 01101110 01111000 01111001 10111111 11100010 01110001
01100110 00110000 01111001 10010011 10100111 11110101 10101100 00101010 10101101 00011001
01110000 01100111 10110011 01111000 01010101 11100101 00010011 01001111 00001010 01101100
00101000 01000000 10010000 11100111 10110000 10101110 10011011 01001110 00100001 10001100
10100000 10001111 10010010 00110011 10001111 10101111 01111010 11100100 01111100 00111111
10111010 00001001 01100000 01110010 11011001 00001110 11000110 00100011 11110100 11101101
01011101 01100101 10011111 11001011 00110100 10001011 10001110 00001000 11001101 01111001
00111100 10001001 01101100 01011001 01100101 00000001 00111111 10001111 10101001 10100101
00100011 00111100 01100011 10011110 11100100 11010010 01110110 00000111 11010100 11110011
01000011 01101110 00000001 11100100 01111100 00000000 00111010 00000000 00111010 11010011
01010011 10110110 10000000 00101011 10000000 00100010 00100111 10100001 00000111 10101111
10111101 00100011 10110110 01111100 10110101 11100100 10111011 01110101 11001111 01100001
01001000 10100011 01110000 11011100 01111001 01110011 11011010 10000111 00101100 00100101
10001101 01110001 10000010 01101010 01011011 11101110 00100010 01001111 10111010 00001110
01111010 01110110 01010001 01001010 01001010 11111110 10011001 10100110 00111110 01001001
00111000 00111101 10111010 00000011 01000110 00111100 10110001 00011001 01110110 11111001
11011111 10001100 01010010 01001010 11000000 11000011 11100101 00000011 10101110 00111011
11010011 01110010 00010100 11100100 11110101 01110000 00111110 01011010 01011100 00110001
00100011 11111001 01111010 11010011 00110110 10110001 00101110 11000000 11100000 10011110
11100100 01010001 01110110 11011000 00000011 10010001 11110101 01111111 11100100 00101001
11001101 11111011 10110001 10000000 01110110 11100111 10101001 10100001 00110110 10001111
01101100 01110110 10100110 10000010 01110000 01001001 11100000 00010001 10011100 01100011
10100101 00111011 11011101 11101010 00110000 00100100 00001001 01001001 11011011 10010011
11011011 00111101 00111111 00011010 01111010 10000010 00111110 01100011 11111001 11010011
00100010 01000010 11001010 01100100 00100011 00011001 00111101 01001101 00100001 10010000
01101111 00000000 00001100 10001111 10101101 00100111 11100110 00100001 00011101 10001010
10001100 01100011 10010010 01101001 01010010 00111101 11011100 01110110 00010100 10100011
00000101 11001110 01110001 11111110 00010100 10011110 01100110 01010000 10101010 01100100
01111101 00001111 00110100 00111101 01101100 10110110 00011000 10101100 11000010 00111000
11110111 01100000 10111001 00011100 00000000 00101010 00110100 00011000 11000001 00111001
11001110 00111001 00111110 10110100 11100101 11011010 00010011 00011100 10010000 00111000
00011101 11110011 01001101 01100011 11010100 10010010 01101010 10110101 11101000 00000000
11000111 01101000 11101000 00110010 01001000 11000000 10100000 10000010 00000001 00011000
11000010 01111010 00001010 01001100 10110110 01000001 00000110 10010001 01001110 11010011
11001001 00011000 11001111 11001100 01111101 01101001 00111011 00110001 00010010 00011100
00001111 10010111 00111101 01111011 00001010 10001101 11110001 00011100 01101000 00110001
11011111 10011010 00111001 10010010 01010000 11011100 01111110 00111101 10000101 00101110
00110111 01001000 10011001 11100100 01100111 10110101 00110101 11011100 00000011 00011001
00011000 00111111 01010010 00110011 01000111 00011000 11001011 00010001 10011110 10000110
10000101 01100010 01110111 10011101 10111111 01111100 11110101 11110110 10100100 01010000
10100011 11101111 11111110 10011100 11010010 10110101 10010000 00000011 01100100 00010000
00111010 11100100 01110010 00001101 00110111 00000100 00001110 01000001 00011001 00111001
11111010 11010011 10011100 01111100 11101001 00011000 01101111 10010000 01111110 10100110
10010110 01011100 11101110 11001110 01001001 11000111 11011101 00011100 11010101 01011101
10110101 10110000 00000100 10000100 00101110 00110011 11111000 00001010 01100011 00000110

```
00001010 01000110 11100001 10001111 01001010 01110011 00101110 01100100 00000000 10001100
10011110 10100100 01010011 01011101 01001111 10011001 11010100 01111110 01110100 10101110
11100011 10110001 00101000 01000010 01111010 00000011 11000000 00000111 00100011 00010100
10011000 00100000 11100000 01110101 00111100 10011111 01101010 00111011 11100100 11100111
00011110 11110100 00000011 11001001 11000001 11111001 00110001 11010111 11010110 10101001
01101100 00110110 00101110 11100011 10111011 00011000 11100011 00011110 10011111 11010110
10010001 11011001 01010010 01001111 10010011 10011100 01110010 01000111 10100101 00111011
10001111 01011100 11100000 11110101 10101000 10000011 00001101 11111011 01000011 00001100
00011110 01001001 00000111 10101101 00110110 11111010 00001100 01111110 11101100 10100011
11111100 10111001 00100111 10100101 00110110 00111110 01000111 00111101 10111011 10011010
00111001 00001010 01110111 01111110 01100110 10000100 00000100 00100000 00111001 11000000
11001111 11100111 01000110 10111011 00001011 10101000 10001011 00100010 11001010 11000111
11001011 00000111 00000011 10111111 01100011 11110100 10100101 00111001 11101111 11111100
11101001 00110110 10000000 01000110 11101010 01000110 01100001 10011110 01000101 01001100
10010010 01011101 01000110 01110101 00001010 00110000 01110010 01111010 00011010 01101010
11100101 01110011 10000010 01011111 00100111 10111101 00100111 00011001 11101111 01001010
10100100 00001110 01111001 11111010 11010110 10011011 00100010 00000111 01110000 01110000
00011111 10001100 11110011 10011100 11010010 10010001 10001110 10111101 00111101 10001111
01011010 01000110 00011001 00111111 11100011 01001101 01010010 00110011 10110111 00010100
11010011 01000000 00111001 10111101 10110011 01001011 10110000 01100111 11010110 10010000
11100100 10011110 00001111 11100001 01001101 01011111 10111111 10010001 10011010 10000110
10101100 00111011 10001110 11011001 11001001 11001001 11111100 00101001 01010100 01111011
11010010 01100100 00001111 01001010 00010111 10111001 00111101 10101001 00101111 00110001
00000011 00011100 00001110 01101000 11001110 00000111 00011101 01111101 01101000 01100110
01011110 10011111 11000111 11101001 01000011 01100100 10001010 01001010 00000011 10111000
00101001 00100111 11111010 11111011 11010001 10011110 00001110 00110011 11010110 10001100
11110000 00111001 11000101 00101010 01110111 11100111 10011010 01101000 01101100 00111001
11001000 11111101 01101000 11100111 10111001 11111100 00101000 01100110 00011100 00000011
10011100 11010010 01100111 00000110 10011111 00101010 00100100 01011101 11011001 00000011
11111010 11010001 10001100 00000010 01111010 11111010 00011010 01000110 00111000 11000001
11100011 00011110 10110100 01111101 11110000 01001000 00010100 01000001 11101110 00111101
00000011 00111000 00111001 11101101 01001010 01011010 10010001 01001001 11101001 10000000
00000101 00110101 10101010 11011001 01000011 10001111 01011100 11110111 10100101 00011001
11000001 00011000 11100111 11010110 10011001 11001001 00111001 00100111 10100101 00111000
11100000 10010001 11101011 11111001 01010110 01001110 11101111 01100010 00000111 01110100
11100011 00111001 11110101 10100100 11001000 00111111 01011010 00001111 00011000 10100001
10110000 01001111 10110111 10101101 01010111 01001011 10000000 11000111 00000010 01000001
10000011 11110101 11001101 00000111 10100000 11100100 11100011 11011010 10011101 10011100
11100000 01110100 00010100 11010101 01100000 00110010 00110000 01001000 00011110 10010100
00110101 10101000 00001111 11001111 10011000 01101001 00111010 00011100 00010011 11000111
11110011 10100011 01110001 01100000 00110110 00101110 00001110 01111010 11010001 10110100
10000101 11001000 11100010 10100110 11111101 01000000 01101111 01000001 10111000 11110001
10011110 10010100 11101110 00001111 00111100 11100111 10100110 01101000 11011011 10111011
11101111 00110000 10100101 01101111 01001110 10011111 10001101 00011101 01001010 10111000
01110101 01000111 00111000 11101111 11010000 10011010 00111000 01010000 00111011 11010010
01100111 00100100 10010011 01001011 10011110 01110010 00000111 00111101 01000110 01101001
10110001 10001000 11011001 11110101 11001111 11010110 10000000 01011011 11011011 00011101
11101001 10111011 10001111 00100100 00000001 11111000 11010000 00001001 10010000 00111011
00000001 11010100 01010100 01011011 01000000 00011100 10101101 11110010 11100111 11110101
10100011 10011100 10011100 11110010 01101001 10101000 00001000 11100011 00011100 00001111
01011010 01110010 11110101 00101100 01001111 11010010 10010011 01101010 11000011 00010100
00010011 10000011 01001100 01010010 01110001 11010011 11011110 10001111 10010111 10010001
11111010 01010000 10111101 01001111 00111101 00111010 11010010 01110111 00000001 11101011
10011100 00001100 11111110 00110100 01100011 10100110 00110011 10011010 01000110 00100000
00010001 10000011 11001001 11101101 01000011 10110001 00011100 01100111 10011010 00011010
01100010 01000001 11010011 00000011 00011001 00111101 11001101 00001010 00110001 10000000
00111010 11010010 11100111 10100000 11111101 01101001 00010111 10100111 00011100 11110011
01001101 10110100 10000110 00101111 00111110 10011100 11010010 01100000 10000001 11101001
10011010 00000000 11101111 10011110 01110011 01001101 11001001 11000110 00001001 10100001
11101000 00000010 00010000 11011111 00100110 00011000 10011111 01101111 01001010 01111110
01111110 01110011 11010111 00111101 00101000 00001100 00000000 11001011 00000011 10011111
01101010 01010101 11100100 01100011 10100001 00111100 10011010 10010001 00110001 00011100
10010010 00110000 10011101 00000000 10100011 01110010 10101010 01101110 01110000 01111101
10101000 01100001 10010010 00010111 10100000 10100101 01010011 10000000 00000110 00111011
11100111 00000111 10011010 10100110 11111010 10001001 10100001 00010111 10011100 00011100
11110110 11100111 00110100 11010101 11111001 10001001 11100111 00001000 00111000 11100011
10111101 00111001 10110010 11000111 00111001 11001101 00110001 10110011 10111111 00000000
01110001 10001010 01010010 10110010 11011000 01100011 11000000 00111111 10000101 00101110
11100000 01111110 10000010 10011000 10100100 01111001 10000000 01100111 10100111 01011010
01110010 11110010 01001001 00100000 10000001 10011010 10101011 11011100 01100000 11011001
00100111 00000010 10101010 01101010 01010110 00110000 11011110 01000010 01100011 10111000
00011001 00001100 00110001 10001111 01001010 10110010 10101101 10010111 11000111 01001100
11010001 11000110 00110001 10011100 11111101 01101001 01011001 01001011 01000110 00000111
```

10010101 01101011 10111010 00110100 10111010 01001101 11000110 00110000 01011110 11011101
11111110 11101011 01111111 10001101 01100111 11000011 00100001 00011100 00110111 00111110
11110101 11101011 10010111 10010110 10010000 11011110 11000000 11110001 01001101 11001010
01100011 10011010 11110011 10001111 00010000 11101000 01110010 11101001 10010011 10010111
10001100 01101111 10110110 11101100 01111101 00101011 10011110 10100110 11100111 01011101
00011010 10111101 00011001 00001100 00110010 01110000 01110111 01111110 01110101 01101010
00110110 11111100 10111010 11010110 01010100 01010010 01110100 11100111 10001010 10111001
00010100 10101010 00000111 11011110 11000111 10110101 01100011 11001011 01100111 01100011
10100000 11010001 00001101 10001111 10100101 01001000 10010010 01100111 00011001 10101010
00101011 00100000 00111000 11100110 10100101 01001001 00000111 10101101 01101110 10011101
11110100 00100010 11000101 11010101 01111111 01111100 11010011 11110111 01110010 00111011
01010101 01000100 10010011 00111101 00101010 01001111 00110011 00000011 00110101 10011100
10010110 10110110 00011001 01101000 10011110 00001111 10101101 00001010 11011101 11111010
01010101 01110100 10010111 00100100 01010011 10110111 11111111 00000000 00111010 10010100
10010100 10010101 10000100 10010001 00111011 10110111 10101101 01000110 11000110 10011000
10101100 01110011 01000110 01110011 11001101 01010011 01111101 10000000 01110011 00011100
01010100 00001100 10100000 10011010 10010001 10111010 01111011 01010011 00011111 10100110
01101001 01111011 00110100 10011101 11000100 01000100 11000011 10000011 10011111 11000010
10100011 00101010 00001000 00111100 01100100 11100010 10100101 01100010 00110011 11101111
01010001 11111111 00000000 00001111 00011111 10001101 00100100 10010010 01110111 00011101
11001000 01001100 01111001 00011000 00100010 10100011 01111011 01010101 00100000 11110110
00110101 01100101 01101001 01110001 11011000 11010101 00101001 10111101 11000011 01100011
00101101 00101101 11100110 10000000 11111001 10010000 10110001 01000111 11101001 10010101
00111000 00110101 10111001 01100101 11100010 10001011 11111011 01011100 00001011 10100000
00101110 00010011 10111110 11101110 00001101 01000111 10110100 01100010 10000111 10110111
01010010 10000011 00100000 00011111 10101101 01010100 01100110 11101101 11101111 01101010
01000011 10000101 11110111 00111010 00111011 00101111 00010010 11011000 11011101 00000011
10010110 00110001 01001010 01000111 01000110 11101001 10011111 10101101 01101110 01000110
11010001 11001010 10000001 10100011 01110100 10010011 10001110 10100011 10011100 11010111
10011011 10111101 10010010 01100011 10001100 11100011 11010010 10011001 00000011 01011110
01011001 00110000 00110110 10110011 01001000 10000111 11110100 10101101 00010101 01001000
11110101 00110001 01110100 01111011 00011110 10011000 01001000 00000100 01111010 11111010
01010000 10111100 10010011 11101001 01011100 01010101 10011111 10001011 00101110 11100000
00000100 01011111 01000000 00100110 01000011 11010001 10000000 11000001 10101110 10001111
01001110 11010111 01101100 01101111 10110000 00100011 10011000 01000101 00101110 00110011
11100101 11001000 01110000 01111111 00001010 10101011 11101001 10100001 10010011 10000011
01001100 11010010 01101100 10010011 10011110 10100111 11111010 01010000 11111001 00001100
00001000 00111100 00001110 00111000 11101111 01001101 11011100 01111110 01001100 01110010
01011010 10011100 00000111 01110011 11011010 10001011 01110101 00100100 00010000 11111100
10000111 00000011 00000110 10010010 00101100 10010000 01110111 10011010 01011100 11110001
10000001 11111100 11101000 11000001 01011111 01011100 11111010 11010010 11010101 01101010
00000001 10000000 00010000 01100011 11101111 10011010 00110111 00001100 00001110 01111001
11111110 01110100 11011110 01000001 11111001 11111001 00111110 10000010 10000101 00100100
01101100 00111000 11000101 00110110 11110101 00011011 10111000 10101010 10011000 00111100
10001010 01000110 01101110 10001010 00111011 11010011 01011111 11100101 11001000 11001111
11010110 10100010 10010101 10011000 00100110 01000111 00100101 10001111 00100111 11011010
10001011 01011111 01100010 01000010 01100010 00000000 11001110 00111110 10100110 10111000
00011111 10001000 01111010 11001010 11011010 11011001 01001001 00001010 01110001 00100100
10100000 10101000 11101011 10011100 11110111 00111001 10101110 11000110 11110110 01011101
10110001 10001111 01011110 10100000 01111010 11010111 10001011 01111000 11110111 01010001
11111011 01010110 10100111 00100010 00010110 00111110 01010100 01000111 00000011 00000111
10001100 11110111 11111101 01101010 10101000 11000101 01001110 01110110 00101000 11100100
00100110 01110000 11011111 00110110 00110000 01111111 10010101 01010111 01010001 10011110
10100111 10011010 10010010 01000001 10111011 10101111 11111111 00000000 10101110 10011000
10100100 00101000 00111100 11100011 11011110 10111101 10111000 11000111 10010101 00010011
10111001 00000100 10000100 10010011 10001100 00010011 10011110 11110101 01101010 11000110
00101101 10100000 00010111 11000111 00011100 11010101 01010000 00001011 00111000 11111010
11110111 00110101 01111110 00111111 10100111 01001010 01101110 11110110 00100101 00101101
01001000 10100111 01100011 10111100 11101100 11101001 11001111 00110101 00101101 10011010
11110010 00111000 11111001 00000111 00110101 01011001 11010111 01110011 00010001 10111000
10000010 01101011 01010110 11011101 01000010 11000010 00001000 00000000 00010010 00101010
00100101 10100010 00110100 01001011 01011011 10001000 00000001 11001111 01001110 10111101
11111101 01101011 01100110 11000010 00001101 11000101 00010111 00011101 01001111 01001010
11001111 10110110 01001101 11011000 11100111 11011010 10111011 00011111 00001111 11011001
10011100 01111001 10001110 00111010 01110000 00111001 10101110 01101010 10010011 01001001
11011100 11101010 10100111 00000011 01001111 01001011 10000000 01000110 10000011 01110000
11100100 00001010 11010111 10001110 00111110 00111010 01010011 01100001 10001000 01000110
00111000 11101011 01010110 00010000 10101001 00011101 01101011 11001001 10101001 00010111
00100110 01110100 01101100 01010101 10011110 00110000 01001000 11000111 11110011 10101010
01110011 01110001 11011010 10110100 01100110 11000000 11100100 01110011 11110100 10101010
01010111 00011100 11110110 10101000 01001001 00100110 00001010 11100110 01101100 10010010
10010001 11101111 11111000 11100010 10101011 10111011 01100011 00100100 00010011 11001101
01011000 10011010 00111110 10110101 01010101 11000110 00101011 01001000 01011110 11111010

10100000 11011101 10010101 11100101 01100011 10011010 00110011 11000000 00111001 11100100
01010011 01011111 10101110 01001101 00110111 00100011 00011100 01010111 01000011 11100101
10111111 10011001 00101110 11100100 10001010 01110011 10011100 11010100 01101101 00101110
11011110 00110011 01010000 00110100 10011000 00101110 00110010 01000101 01000100 11110010
01100000 11110100 00100110 10010010 10001011 10111101 11011000 10110100 00101100 01001001
00110111 00100011 10011010 10001101 11100101 11001010 01110010 01111000 10101010 10101101
00100101 01000100 11100101 10011000 11110100 11111101 01101010 11100011 01001001 00110110
00101011 10000100 10100111 00101101 11101101 01010101 11100101 00011001 11100000 01110101
11001101 01001011 11011100 10010110 11111100 01101001 10111001 00011011 11001111 00011111
10001101 01101001 10101011 00100001 10111110 10100101 01010010 00111001 00100011 00111100
11010101 01110111 10001011 11110111 01101110 00001110 00111001 11100110 10101111 00010000
10111001 11111111 00000000 00111100 11010100 01101110 00110001 11001110 00111111 01011010
11011010 00101101 10111101 01000100 11010010 10110001 10001001 00101101 10100110 01011111
10101110 00111101 00101010 10100100 10110001 11001000 10100111 10001010 11011111 01110100
11100011 00100100 01100111 10111110 00101011 00111110 01100000 00110011 10010111 11101111
11011010 10111010 10100011 00110011 10011001 11010011 01010110 00110010 11001000 00000100
11101101 00111101 11111010 11010010 11110100 00111011 01001111 00110100 00111001 01100000
11100111 10001110 11111100 11100111 10110101 00010001 10010000 01011011 00000111 10100001
11101011 11001101 01101010 01100011 10110001 00100110 11010011 11000110 00001111 00011000
10101101 00111101 00000001 10110011 10101011 01000000 00110011 11110111 01001110 01001000
10101010 00010001 01100000 10010010 00111011 01110110 00110101 10100101 10100001 11000000
10110001 11101010 00000001 11100100 00100111 01100110 00001111 00100000 01010100 01001101
11101110 11000111 00000101 01110011 11010111 01110100 11011000 10001001 10110100 00100100
01100111 10000011 10010001 11111100 11101011 10101000 10110110 01101111 11110100 10001000
11100101 01110001 11010010 00111100 00000001 11101011 01011100 11011110 10000100 01011001
10110100 11111001 01100110 01000010 00001100 01000010 00111100 00001100 01110111 11000101
01101110 01011001 10011100 00111100 01000001 11011100 11100011 10101111 00111110 11111101
10101011 11001000 01110010 11100110 10010101 11111010 10011010 00111110 11000110 11001110
01110001 11001001 10100100 01100010 01001000 11011010 00111011 11010000 10000101 10011010
01010100 11000000 00000110 00110001 11000110 01001111 01010011 01001000 10101101 10010110
11001001 11101001 11101100 00110001 01000011 01000100 10000011 10011100 01001100 00010101
00111000 00011011 01111001 11110111 00110100 11010111 00000001 01100100 11011111 10011100
11001001 10001111 11001010 10011110 10111000 00001101 10111111 01101111 00011000 11101111
01010001 00111011 00110001 10010000 11001000 01000000 00011001 00011000 11000111 01100001
01000101 10101100 10101100 11000000 01110100 01100100 11110001 11001000 00000101 11111001
11000111 01011010 01110011 00101000 00110010 00000110 01110001 11001000 10100010 00110101
11000011 10001001 01110011 11011011 10101111 01000001 10001010 00000001 11001100 01100000
10000011 10011100 11110111 10101001 11010001 10000000 10101000 11001100 00111110 01101101
10101111 11101101 10011110 11110100 00100100 01100111 01110000 00100100 11111011 00000001
11011000 01010010 11101110 01010000 01000010 10100110 01011110 01001110 11000011 11010010
10100011 01110011 10010001 11001111 00111001 11101000 00000101 00001110 01001011 01100001
01011000 00001000 11001100 10000111 00011101 11111000 11100110 10000110 11001100 10010011
01100011 00011000 10001111 10100110 01001111 01111010 00111000 10001001 01001111 10101111
10100101 00111101 01001111 01000101 11001111 10111110 01110011 01000010 10110011 01100011
00011000 01001000 11100000 01100100 10000001 11011010 10000111 00111000 11000110 00111000
11101100 01111011 10010011 01001000 10011000 10010010 01001100 10000010 01000000 00011101
11001111 01111010 01100110 01000100 10010010 00010010 00110011 11000001 11000000 00111001
11101011 01000011 01001101 00001001 00110001 11101001 11000111 00011000 11111001 11001000
11001001 00010100 01110110 11011011 10011100 00011111 01010000 00101000 00100111 01101111
00011000 11001011 11111010 11010010 00111011 00010000 00001110 01110011 10001111 01101010
10100100 10110100 11010101 10000101 11000101 01101110 10000111 01101001 00100011 00011101
11101001 10001111 10000000 00001000 01000001 01001110 11011010 10100000 00010001 11010100
10011111 01111110 10010100 11010101 00011011 01001001 00100011 10101101 00010110 10111110
11000000 10000111 00101000 11000000 01111101 11100000 00010011 10001100 10000001 10011010
10001101 01111000 01110001 10111100 01100011 11100101 00100110 10011011 10001100 10011101
10101001 10010000 00110001 11110011 00011111 01011010 00100110 01101111 00110100 00010010
00000001 00000000 01111110 00111001 10100110 10101110 10001001 00000100 11011100 11011001
11000000 00100011 00111101 01110011 01001110 00111011 10110010 00010101 00011011 00000000
00001110 10010100 10111101 01111110 01010010 01000000 11000000 11001001 11000001 11101010
00101000 10001000 10000010 01000001 11000110 00000101 01000111 00110111 01010010 11000001
01111110 01010001 10001001 10111110 01000001 10011110 00111101 11101001 00000110 00001001
00000000 11111110 00010100 00010000 00000110 01000111 11001110 01111001 11001110 01001001
10100101 11100000 01100000 01110111 01110011 11001101 00111111 01110100 00000100 01100000
01001001 00011110 01001110 11001110 01000111 01010011 01000011 10010010 01100100 10010011
10011110 00010100 10000000 00000111 11110101 10100101 00000011 01101001 00101100 01001111
11010000 01010100 01111000 11111001 00010001 01000000 11000110 01111010 11110011 11010110
10101011 01000111 10111001 00000100 10001010 01110001 10010010 00111011 11010100 00001010
11000100 10000111 11110101 11001111 01101010 10010001 11000010 10010010 00000000 01011110
00000111 01011110 01101001 00011011 00011001 00100000 00001100 01111011 10001010 00111001
01010101 11101110 01011000 00110111 00000111 10011110 10000011 10101110 01101000 01011111
10111000 01110111 10011110 11110100 10001110 01001110 00000001 00111100 11111101 01101001
10101110 01001011 00111010 00011001 00001000 11110100 00000000 01010010 10111010 10111000
10111010 00000011 00011110 00000000 11001110 00000110 01111011 01010000 10111011 01100010

11100000 00000010 11100100 11110100 00000011 10001010 01101100 10100000 00011110 00010000
11100100 10001110 00110011 01001110 01101110 00001111 00000011 10011111 01011010 00010010
01010111 00010101 10000110 10010011 10111000 10010010 01001110 00111001 11111011 10100111
10110101 00101111 00000100 11100000 11110010 01000111 01001100 11110110 10100100 11111001
01010101 01011111 00000111 10000010 01111011 11110111 10100110 10110110 00111011 10001100
11010101 00101111 01010001 11011100 01110110 11101110 01110000 00000111 11110101 11001101
00100100 10010010 00100010 11001000 11001011 10111000 01100100 00011010 01000110 11001110
01111000 00011000 00010100 11110101 10001101 01010100 01100011 00011100 11010010 10111101
11001001 00111010 01001110 00110110 11111011 11010000 01001110 00001111 01000111 11100010
10010011 00111100 11100110 10010111 10010010 01110010 01111101 00111010 01010101 01011000
00000101 00111000 00100011 11111001 01010011 10010100 01100010 10011001 11000010 10011100
11110101 00111110 10011001 10100000 00010000 01001111 01011111 11000010 10000101 10100000
00001111 00001100 10100111 11101110 01110101 10100011 00011100 11100100 10011010 01100011
00001100 11000111 10001100 11101100 11111010 01010010 10001111 10010100 01111010 10011111
01011111 01011010 01111011 10001110 11100011 10110111 00000010 00001111 00010100 11000000
01110011 11110100 11110100 10100011 00100100 10001111 01000011 01000010 00010001 11010111
10111111 10100101 01001101 10111011 00001000 00111010 10011100 10001110 00001101 00111101
01001111 00011101 11001111 10110001 10100110 10111001 11111100 00101001 11011111 11000100
00101010 10101110 10010000 11111010 10000011 11100100 01110001 10011010 01101000 11001001
11001000 10100111 00000001 11110010 11100001 10001111 01011010 01101000 01110010 00111011
01010100 01101001 01110001 00001110 01101110 00000111 10111000 10100110 10101000 11100011
00110100 01100100 10010011 11010010 10011101 10000010 01110000 00001000 11000000 11101101
01010100 11100101 01111101 10000110 11000110 11110000 01011100 00010011 11010110 10011100
00000110 11101100 00010001 11011010 10011000 01111111 10010111 01111010 01010001 11001101
01001110 11001100 01000000 11011100 10011100 00011100 01101100 10100001 10000000 11000000
11000001 11100110 10000101 00111101 01001001 00111001 10100001 01111000 01110011 11111010
11010101 01011000 00000111 00110101 00110101 01001111 10110101 00000001 10000001 00011001
11110111 10100001 10001111 00100011 11110100 10100101 01100000 00001100 10010010 11111110
10000000 01010000 10100111 00100100 10101001 11101001 11101010 00101001 00110010 00000001
11110101 00111110 10000111 10111101 00011110 10100001 00111011 11010010 01000000 00101011
01110101 00000000 01010011 10111010 00000001 01000010 11110101 11100111 10101001 10100001
10110010 00001101 00010110 01101100 10100100 00000000 10011101 11101111 10010011 11000111
01001100 01111010 01010011 01110010 11011011 11000110 00001111 00000111 10110001 00010100
01111100 10101100 11000100 10110001 11000000 00110100 00000000 01111001 11110100 10101001
11011101 10001100 00011011 00111000 11000111 11110011 10100111 00010110 11001111 01001110
01101001 10111100 10001100 01110011 11000001 10100000 00001101 11000100 11100010 10011011
11011110 11100100 00000010 01110100 11111110 01010100 11101100 00011111 11100010 11100010
10010111 00011000 11101111 11001101 00000101 01110011 11000111 11100011 01000101 10101111
10101001 01100011 00111110 01010001 11011011 00110100 00010011 10110101 00111000 00011100
00011110 00110000 01101001 11000011 10000000 00001001 11101010 01111011 01010010 11110001
10011100 10010101 11111010 01010000 11011010 00000001 00000000 00111100 01111111 00111010
01101011 00010011 10011100 01100010 10011101 10010011 10110011 10011111 01011110 10010100
11010110 00000100 01111101 00101010 01011011 11101100 00000001 10001110 00001000 00000011
10010001 11011110 10011100 00010100 11100000 01100100 11110101 10100001 01000000 00011101
00001111 11010110 10001110 00001000 11100011 00111001 10101001 10111101 11110101 00000000
11000111 01001111 11100111 01000011 00000001 10001100 11100011 00111111 10001101 00110101
10011000 00000011 10000000 01111010 01110101 10100011 00000111 00011111 00111001 00000001
11111101 00000101 01010110 10011101 01000110 00111000 01100100 11110111 00000000 11010011
01000110 01111011 00011100 11111011 11010011 10011000 01100011 10011110 10011110 10110100
01100011 01100110 00000111 01101010 01001101 01011011 01100000 00000011 11000111 01010011
10011111 01100001 01001101 11100111 11111000 10111101 01111000 10100000 01100100 01110101
10100001 11111001 00011000 11000001 00100110 10001011 11110111 00010010 01000000 11100100
00010111 11000000 11001110 00101001 11000111 11100101 01110001 11101011 01001101 01100000
01000001 11000000 10100100 01010101 00111011 11111111 00000000 10101101 00100101 10101110
11000000 00111101 01111010 10010011 10011100 01111010 11010011 00011011 01101011 01111101
11010101 11100000 01110101 00111110 10110100 10111000 11100111 11101001 01001110 01101100
10000001 10011100 10001100 01110101 11000000 10100110 11111011 00110000 00011010 00111001
00000011 01110000 11000111 11100011 01000111 00000100 00010011 11001111 10110101 00011101
10000011 01110001 11111001 01010000 11000111 00001011 10000001 11110111 11101001 00110100
00110001 11001011 10001100 11110101 11001001 11110100 11000111 01001010 00001001 00101101
00100111 00011111 01110000 01110001 01001101 01010011 11110010 01100000 00010011 11111000
11010000 10111000 01010000 01110000 00111111 11111010 11110100 11010010 01001001 01011000
00000001 10000001 11000111 00000011 00011000 11111101 01101000 01100001 11000111 11001101
11010110 10001100 10011100 00000010 00111010 11111111 00000000 00101010 00011001 11001111
11100111 11010110 10010101 11101110 00000010 01110101 00111111 01011010 10000010 11110010
00001000 10100110 10001101 11100010 10011101 01000001 10001100 11110000 01000101 01011000
11000110 00110000 00101001 00011100 00000110 00111000 11100000 10010010 01111111 00101010
00101100 10100110 11000100 10011001 11100110 11011110 00100001 11010000 01100101 10110001
10010101 11100110 10000001 01011101 11101101 10110011 10010001 11011111 00000010 10110001
00100011 10010000 00101001 00100010 10111101 01110110 11101110 00100101 10011110 00011001
00100010 11000000 00101000 01111000 00111100 01010111 00000101 11100010 01111111 00001110
00110101 10010001 00110011 11011001 00000010 11110000 00011110 01011000 01100011 10100111
10101101 01100001 01010010 10010101 10011101 11010001 11010111 01000110 10110111 01001001

00011000 11001001 00101000 11101011 10010010 01111101 01101010 11000010 01001001 10001110
11110101 10010110 10000111 01101001 00100110 10100101 01011001 11110000 01000000 10101000
11010001 00011101 01000110 10111100 01001111 11010010 10100100 11011101 10011110 11110101
10011010 00100110 11100010 10100110 10001110 01010010 01111011 11110011 01001101 00110110
00100111 01110010 11101010 10111111 10111110 00101010 01110101 10010011 00011100 00010011
01010100 01100011 10010010 10100111 11110011 00111010 11100000 01010101 01011011 10101001
00001101 10010110 01010110 01000000 01001101 00011110 01100000 00000100 11110001 10011010
10101110 10001101 11000110 01111011 10011010 01111000 00100000 11111101 00111010 11010100
01110010 00110110 10110111 00000010 01000110 10010011 11010010 10010011 00111100 11010011
01111000 11000110 01110011 11010110 10000110 11100000 01110101 11100010 10010111 10110011
01111011 01011100 00000100 01111110 00001111 01001010 01000110 00011000 11110101 10101001
00111000 11000111 00110101 00011011 00110110 00110001 11101010 01101010 11100101 00010100
10110100 00010000 10101011 11000111 11010010 10000101 11001000 00111111 11001010 10010111
11011110 10011100 10111000 00100011 10111101 00010111 01001011 01010000 01001100 00100011
01010010 11000111 10011010 10110001 11100101 11110001 11110100 10100110 11000101 11000000
10101001 11000111 00011000 11000101 00101001 01001101 00000011 01101100 10001101 01100011
11001000 11001101 00011110 01011111 11110111 01111011 11010100 10101011 00011000 11001111
00011101 00001101 01001001 11100101 11010100 10111010 10000000 01100111 11001101 00000000
01100100 00000000 10001110 00101010 10011100 11110110 00101010 11011110 11011000 11100100
01100011 10000011 01011011 01011110 01011101 01000110 11110001 11110011 01000111 00111011
01110110 01100010 10110111 01110011 00111110 11001011 01010011 11010100 01110100 11011001
00000011 01000111 00101001 01111000 11111111 00000000 10111011 00100111 00100000 11110110
10101101 11101101 00111111 11000101 00110110 11010111 01001000 00100010 10111101 10001100
11000011 00100000 11101010 01111111 10000000 11010110 01001011 11000100 00001111 11011110
00011001 00010101 01010010 01101011 01010000 01111001 00011100 01100110 10101101 01010110
01101101 11011001 10100010 00100101 01001001 00110011 11010000 00101101 11100100 10001001
10100010 11011101 00011011 10000111 01001110 10111001 00011100 11010010 11111001 10000100
10110000 00111110 10011101 01101011 11001110 11101101 10101110 11101110 11110100 11011001
00001001 10110111 10010000 11101100 11111110 00100101 11101100 01101011 10100110 11010010
10111100 01000001 00001101 11100011 00000101 10111000 11000100 00110010 11110000 00000000
11001111 00000110 10110110 10001011 01001111 01000100 11001110 01111001 01010011 01101000
11011110 11000000 01011100 10010001 11110101 10101000 11111100 11100010 01010011 10111101
00100100 10110010 11100100 00010101 00011001 11100111 10101101 01000100 11001101 10001000
10011111 10101001 00111110 10110100 10011011 11101100 01000001 00110010 00000110 01100001
10011001 00001111 01101110 00110011 01010001 11001101 00101010 11000100 01010001 01001110
01000010 01010101 01100110 10011101 11000111 01110010 11111100 01110100 00000110 10101001
11001101 00111100 10001100 01110010 10101010 01110011 10001111 11001010 10101101 00100111
01111011 00001111 10100001 10001111 11100010 10111101 01010001 10100010 10110101 10011101
10010000 10000100 10010011 01101111 00011101 11110110 00001111 11110001 10101111 00010000
11010101 01100110 00110011 01001010 01110010 01111001 11001110 01001001 10101111 01010011
11110001 10101101 11000000 01011000 11011110 00010100 01011100 00010001 11110011 11001000
11011110 10100010 10111100 10011010 11110001 10110111 11001010 01011000 11100000 00010111
00100100 11100000 01010111 01010110 00010010 00001010 11101101 10000111 01000010 10111110
01110111 00111111 01110001 10001111 01011010 01101100 11000000 00010101 00000000 01110001
01001110 11111001 10011011 00000000 11111010 01111010 11110100 10100110 10110010 11111100
11100000 11100100 00001010 11110100 10110110 00100010 11100001 00011000 00001110 01110011
11011111 11011110 10101101 11101101 00100010 00111100 10101111 01001010 10001110 00010011
10001110 11011001 00111110 11100110 10100100 01110010 01011011 10000010 01001001 11000111
11100001 01011001 10110010 11010101 11010001 01011110 00110100 11011110 01110001 10001100
00010010 01101011 01110001 00100011 00111000 01000000 00101011 00111010 11001001 01000001
10010100 01100111 00111110 10110101 10110100 10000011 00100100 01111110 10010101 10010101
01001110 10000110 10110100 11010001 01110011 01001001 10110101 11011101 01110010 00111000
11110111 10101110 11000010 11011000 00011000 00010000 00000000 10111100 00000001 01011100
11011110 10010010 11011110 01001011 10010010 01000110 01000111 10101101 01110100 01010001
01011101 10101110 00001001 11001111 11010110 10111100 11111010 10010010 10111011 00111010
10100001 00011011 00010100 11101110 11110101 11100110 10000011 11111110 01011001 00010111
01000011 11011100 01010011 00100001 11110001 00100010 10110111 11110000 10010001 10001111
01011010 00101111 00100100 10110110 10010111 11111101 01100000 01000010 00001000 11001110
01101011 10011111 10111111 10110100 10001000 01001001 10111110 11011101 10110001 10011110
01000111 00110101 01010000 11100101 01101101 01000101 10001010 01101001 11011100 11101101
00100000 11010100 10010010 01110100 11011100 00011000 00010000 01111010 01100011 10110101
00111101 11100111 01010010 00111101 11101011 11001111 00100001 10111011 10111001 10110011
01110000 00110111 00010011 00011110 01111010 01111111 11110101 11101011 01100010 11010111
01011001 00010010 11110101 01010010 00111101 01110010 01110011 01010011 00111100 00110111
10011000 00101001 00011011 10010111 00010010 00001100 11110101 11100010 10101011 00111110
11010011 11001111 01111010 10101111 11110110 10101111 00110011 00000111 00011001 10100001
11100101 00000100 00010101 11110100 10101100 11100001 00010110 10110110 00110100 10010011
01010110 00011010 11100100 01110100 10101000 10011100 10000001 10011111 01011010 01010111
10010000 01110000 11011110 10011101 00101010 10111011 11001001 10111011 00111111 11001110
10110101 10001101 10111010 10101101 01001000 10111000 10010010 10110111 00100011 00100010
10100010 10010000 11100100 11010100 10001100 01110010 00110011 10001010 01101011 01101101
11000111 00111101 01101011 01110101 11100110 00011110 01100101 01111100 00000001 11001010
11110000 00001101 00110101 01000111 00100100 11100011 00110101 00110011 10101000 00111101

00101001 10111110 01011001 11101011 11010010 10101011 11011001 10101110 10100000 11001000
01110011 11001001 00011101 00101001 00011000 01100111 10001100 11010100 10001110 00111011
11100011 00100110 10100011 11001111 00011100 01010100 10101101 01011110 10000100 11011000
01100011 01110101 11100110 10011010 11100111 00111101 00000111 00010101 00101110 00111011
11110101 11110110 10101000 10011111 00100000 01110000 00111111 01011010 10111011 11011111
01110010 01011001 00001011 11100000 10100111 11001101 11010011 11010010 10101001 11011100
01000100 00110000 01110001 11010000 11010101 11110111 00100000 10001100 01110100 11001101
01000101 00101010 01100101 01110000 01111101 00111101 00111010 01010110 10001001 11101101
01100011 00101001 00100100 01110011 11110111 00001011 10000011 11010110 10100000 00000100
10000011 11001111 11010110 10101110 01101010 00100100 00001001 00110110 11100011 10101111
01110001 01010101 11100001 01010001 10111000 00010111 11101101 11011010 10111011 01100011
01101011 00011100 11010011 01011010 10001010 10000111 00011001 00000111 10101110 01101010
11111101 10010100 10111110 01011011 10000010 01001001 11100111 11010110 10101001 01011100
00010101 00110010 11110100 11100111 11101011 11010110 10100100 01000101 01100000 00110010
01000111 00010100 10011100 00101111 11010100 01010111 01101001 10011101 11101110 10000101
10101100 01001011 01101001 00011111 10010111 00011011 00001111 00101000 11110010 01100011
00111101 00001101 01111010 00100110 10000111 10101001 01011011 01011111 01000100 00011001
00001110 00100111 01010010 00001111 10010100 01111010 11010111 10000101 11011001 01011101
10011000 11011111 10011110 11011100 01110101 10101110 10011110 11000010 11101100 10010001
00011100 10010001 10010010 10010010 00001111 01000011 01011110 01100101 01001100 00110011
10000011 10111100 01011001 10101101 11101110 01111011 01101011 00010010 00011101 11001001
01110111 11000111 01100001 11011010 10000010 11001100 01000010 00011001 10111000 00001001
11010000 00101111 01110011 11101111 01011100 01000110 10000111 11100010 10100011 00011011
10000101 11010101 01000111 10011011 10000001 10000001 00101000 11101101 11110101 00011101
11101011 10110110 10000110 01101000 11100100 10001000 01001010 10001110 00011101 00001000
11001000 01101100 11110101 11001101 01100001 00101011 11011111 01010000 01101010 11000100
10101111 10000101 00000011 10011100 00011110 10000111 00011100 11010100 00011011 10011011
00101110 00110011 11000001 00111111 01110100 10011010 10011001 10011000 00101000 00000111
10101110 01000111 00000000 01110110 10101000 11110000 10101101 10110000 11111100 11111100
01110110 00110100 11011101 10111010 00011001 10110010 01001001 10000000 10010111 11100101
01111100 11101100 11000111 11011101 00010100 00000110 00100100 11001000 00010000 01110001
10000001 01001010 10100011 10010010 01111101 10110011 01001000 11001100 01110010 01001000
00011100 11010100 00100100 11101101 01110000 11011100 00111100 11000101 10001100 11110100
11100101 11111101 00101000 00011000 01010010 01000111 01011100 01010011 01001001 00100101
00000001 11101011 11110100 00011101 01101001 11011111 00110110 01001001 00101100 00110001
11111001 01010011 01000011 00011011 10010011 11111011 11000010 01110010 00110000 01111010
11010011 01110010 00000010 00000000 01000111 11100001 01001110 01001110 01000000 01101100
10010010 00000001 11011111 10010011 11011110 10001100 10000110 10001000 00011110 00001110
01001111 01011100 11010101 00100110 01001011 00001101 11000011 00100100 00001110 00010000
01110100 10100011 00000000 00011101 11011000 00111001 11001111 01101010 01000001 11000111
00111011 01110011 11011010 10010101 10000011 00011000 11000000 11001110 00010011 00111111
10011101 00100111 01100110 01010000 10001011 11100110 10011100 10000000 01000110 11111100
11110111 11101101 01001000 00111110 01010100 00111000 00100111 00001001 11000110 01001000
11101010 01101000 01011110 10111001 00110100 11001111 01010001 10011110 10011110 11111101
00101001 00110111 11011100 10010001 01011111 00000100 10100001 00000111 11101011 01000011
10110110 00000111 00001101 11001110 01111001 10100111 00010000 00110110 00100010 11110001
10011100 01100110 10011010 00000000 11100100 11110010 01000111 01101110 00101010 10010000
11011110 10100010 00010010 11111011 00110000 10000001 00110000 01111010 11100110 10000110
00001010 00100011 11100100 11100111 00011101 11111101 01101001 01011001 10111101 00001110
01110011 01000010 11110011 10010110 00111101 00111010 11010000 01001000 10011001 00000011
10100000 00111011 11001111 01111100 11010010 00000110 11011010 11100100 00010011 11000001
00111101 10101000 11011100 10110001 11101100 00100011 10010010 01111001 11100010 10011000
11111001 00101110 00111011 00001110 11011110 11110100 11100011 01101110 10100011 10111001
00100111 11001010 11001110 01001000 11001000 10001111 11010100 10011010 10001111 10000101
11111001 01000011 11100110 01000011 11111010 00001010 10010000 11111001 01101010 00000110
01111001 11011001 11011000 00011110 00111001 10101000 11111010 00100000 01100011 10000000
11100100 10011010 01001101 00100110 11000100 00100111 00111110 01100111 01001100 10011100
01010010 10000000 01111000 00100111 10010010 01111101 01101001 01110001 10010000 11111011
01111011 10001100 01010011 10110011 11111011 11010000 10101110 00110000 01001111 11100001
10000001 01010000 11010111 01100010 11001000 11000100 01100110 00111001 01001110 00111001
00111101 01000110 01001101 00111011 00011001 11000000 11011101 10011110 11100111 00011101
11101001 10100111 00001101 10010010 00101000 11001110 00001010 00001111 01111100 11010101
10101011 01110100 00000001 01011100 00011110 01001101 01000110 01110110 11111001 01111100
01110011 10011010 01000100 11100000 00111110 11110011 10010010 01101000 01110000 11000110
01010000 00110011 10001100 00001110 10000010 10000100 11011101 11001001 11011000 01011110
11100011 10101000 00100100 01110100 00011101 10101000 01110011 10111101 11111010 10011100
00001110 10000010 10011111 10110111 10011100 10001010 01100010 01100011 01111001 01100000
00110010 11100011 10100101 00001001 10111101 10001010 00010011 00011011 10111110 10000010
10010101 11001000 01011100 00001100 11110110 10100100 00011001 01101100 01100011 10110111
01111010 00011101 01001000 00111111 00111111 01111110 11111110 10010100 00100100 11011101
11000100 11111100 11000011 00111100 01100111 10111001 11101000 01101010 01000101 01011100
00001110 10110101 00011011 00010000 10111111 01110100 11100100 11010010 00000001 11000101
01010100 10010010 11100101 01010110 00011001 11010001 00110001 11000111 01000001 11000101

00111101 01011001 01110001 10001110 11110101 00011010 10010101 00011100 11001000 01111010
11010010 10000001 10110100 01101110 11101011 10011110 01101010 10110100 11101000 01001010
00011111 10111011 00100111 00010100 10111000 11100000 00011111 01001010 10001101 01001110
11101110 01000111 01001111 01011010 00001001 11111001 11110010 00111111 00101010 10000100
10011000 01011100 01011110 11100100 11110101 11110110 10100111 11101110 01101100 11110000
00000001 00011110 10011001 10100110 01101110 00011000 11000111 01111010 00110010 00000000
10100001 10110110 10011110 10100000 10010001 00100111 10011001 10011100 11111011 01010010
01100101 10000111 01010011 11101111 11000101 00110000 10010010 01110001 10000001 11111000
11010000 11001100 00010111 10000001 10011111 10101101 00010111 10111000 11110100 00011110
10100111 00111001 00100111 10011010 01010000 01000000 00011100 01010010 00101111 10101001
10100011 01110000 11101100 00001111 11100101 01010101 01110110 10001001 00010100 10110111
11100111 01000110 01001110 01101001 10111001 10100111 01110010 01110001 11001110 00000101
01000111 01010000 00000101 01100011 10111011 00011011 01111011 01110101 11001101 00111001
00000111 00000111 10010010 00111101 10101001 10011001 00111001 11000101 00101110 00110011
11001001 00111000 11000101 00111011 00000000 10001010 00111011 01100111 11110001 10100101
01110010 00000010 11110110 11001111 11010010 10010011 00111001 00111110 11010100 01110000
00111011 01100111 00111101 11101000 01101110 11100000 00000000 10000101 11100011 01100111
01011110 11110100 10100000 10010011 11000001 11101001 11101011 01001000 11000111 11100100
11001110 00110011 01001010 00110011 10001110 01000101 00011010 00000000 01110001 10001110
00101001 00001111 01000000 01011011 11110000 11110111 10100100 00101101 10010001 11010011
11100111 11110101 10100011 01101111 00100000 10010011 10010010 00000111 00111000 10100101
10111011 00101100 01010101 00100001 01111111 11000110 10010111 10100110 00111010 11110011
01001101 11101111 10011110 11010100 01101110 01100101 11100100 01110011 01001011 01000110
01000000 11100110 00111000 00011001 00111101 01001101 00001010 01000001 01010010 00001111
01111010 01000001 11001100 10011111 00111001 00000100 11110101 11110100 10100001 01110001
11001001 00110101 01010001 10111110 11001100 01111110 10000010 10101010 11100100 00001100
01110011 01000110 01001110 11000001 10001100 11110011 01001000 10000100 11101101 11100100
11100000 10011111 01001010 00000001 00000100 11100111 00111100 00001110 10110100 01001011
11001000 01000010 10001101 11011001 00000100 11110100 11110111 10100111 00110001 00000100
10011101 10000011 10101111 01000011 10011010 01100011 10010011 10001100 11110011 10000011
01000011 00001100 00010000 00000001 11000101 01001011 11010001 00010101 10111000 10101000
01001111 10101111 01001010 01110011 10010110 00100000 10000100 11110100 10100110 01110100
00000000 11110110 11101111 01001001 10011100 01110111 11100100 11010010 11101001 01100001
10010010 00000010 00110010 00111010 11111110 00110100 11011110 10011111 00110111 01001010
01001101 11011001 10010000 00001100 11110110 10100001 10001000 01100001 10011010 10011011
01110101 01100000 00001011 10111011 00111001 11111110 01110100 00110011 01100100 11100011
10111101 00101110 01001001 11101111 10001111 10100101 00011000 00111000 11100011 10101110
00101001 11101000 00000000 10011111 00110110 01111000 11000000 11110101 10100011 00111111
10111011 00111101 01001110 00111000 10100100 01100011 10000100 11100100 01010001 10000110
00000011 00000000 11100011 10111101 00010110 11101000 00000000 10111101 00001110 01010111
00111001 10100101 11011011 10111000 01101110 00111100 01111010 01010000 10100000 10001110
01000111 00111100 11110111 10100100 01100011 10001100 10010111 01101110 00110001 11001111
00010100 10101101 01110001 01011100 01011100 10011110 01100100 00100111 00101000 00111010
00001100 01110011 01000010 00010110 00111000 01111001 00110000 00111101 10110011 11010010
10001110 11011001 11111100 10101001 00011100 10001110 00110000 01111110 10100110 10100010
11010111 01110111 00011000 11110011 10000011 11001111 01101010 01101111 01101111 01011010
01000111 01101110 00110000 00001110 00000001 10100001 01000001 00100000 10011111 01111010
00000110 00101001 11100100 11110101 10100100 01010010 00100011 11001111 00100111 10011010
00010000 01110101 11011001 10010010 00001111 01110011 01000111 01000010 01000101 01010111
10100000 10101100 00101110 00001001 11000110 01001110 00111111 10101101 00000111 10101110
01111011 01110100 10100100 00111000 00100000 01100111 10101101 00011001 11000010 01111111
01011010 01110110 00010011 00000111 11100101 10010000 01110100 00000011 10100101 00001111
10001101 11000011 00110100 10100000 10011100 10000011 10001110 10011101 00101000 00100111
00110010 00000101 00100011 10011110 10100100 11010010 11110101 00101000 00011011 01101010
11110101 00111100 10011110 10010100 01110100 10010001 00110011 11111000 01010010 00101000
11110100 11000111 10111101 00011011 10001110 01110001 11011110 10001101 10001001 10111000
11110110 11001110 01110010 01001110 01001110 00111010 01010001 11001110 11011110 01000110
01001101 00110001 10111110 01011100 11010000 01111001 11100111 11110011 10100110 11100010
10000111 01110001 01011000 10000011 00100011 11100000 00011100 01111010 11010011 01010100
00001100 00001100 01110100 11101111 01000110 00110000 01001110 01001110 00000111 11110011
10100101 11000011 00110000 11100011 10001010 00011010 01001000 00000011 00011000 01101100
00001110 00111101 00101001 00100101 01000000 11001010 01000000 11100111 00100011 00011100
11110100 00010100 01100000 00110011 11111110 00110100 10100101 01001110 01001000 11101000
00101001 00111000 11011100 01100111 00010001 11100010 01011111 00001101 00000001 10111110
01111011 00010000 00000000 11100101 11001100 01100000 01110101 10101110 00110111 00000110
00101001 00001010 10010001 10000011 11101000 01101011 11011010 01110000 01001001 11101100
01000000 11110110 10101110 01010011 11000100 11011110 00011100 01011011 10110011 11100111
11011010 01000101 10001011 10001110 01110111 01100000 11110000 01101011 00000111 00001011
01101100 01110100 01010010 10101100 11010110 10001100 11100000 10010010 01001100 00011010
10010101 01100101 11001101 01000011 01110111 00000100 11010110 10101110 01010010 01100101
00101000 01000111 01100011 01001100 01010110 11000000 11110101 00010101 00101001 00100101
10101011 00111010 11010011 10111010 10111001 10100111 00011100 10011001 00011110 11111001
10101001 10010010 01001100 10111110 00101011 00110101 00100100 11000011 11100111 10011100

01111010 11010101 10000001 00101111 00111001 10100010 00010010 10110110 11100000 01101000
10101100 10011000 00011100 11010010 11101110 00000011 10111101 01010001 01001001 10110010
01101010 01001100 10001110 11100110 10110100 10011011 11100100 11011011 01010001 01011000
10110101 11100110 11100111 10000001 11010010 10100100 11001111 00100011 10011010 10101011
00011011 01100011 10100101 01001000 10101101 11000110 01101001 01101000 10110100 11101110
00010110 00100110 00100111 00011100 01100111 00000111 10110101 00111001 01001110 00101010
00000100 11100100 11100111 00111001 10101001 01000001 11001111 10110110 00101010 01011011
01001101 01011101 10001000 01110110 01111001 11001101 01001011 00010110 00110001 10111011
11110100 10101000 00001111 01011100 10001110 01101001 11101000 01111000 11001110 01111001
10101100 10110100 01101100 00101100 01011011 01010010 00001001 10100111 01100100 00011110
10010101 00001000 00100100 00001111 10010111 11110101 10100111 01101111 11100011 11011110
10010100 01010110 10111010 10001000 10110101 00011001 00111110 10110101 00101010 00011100
10011110 10110101 01010001 00011011 00000010 10101100 01000110 11000010 10010011 01001001
10111101 00000000 10011101 10000111 00011100 10001010 10001001 11100011 11001101 01001011
11000011 01110001 11111101 01101001 00110000 00110001 11000101 00011110 11110010 01111010
00000001 01010110 01011000 11111011 01110100 10101000 01100101 01011110 01000111 10101110
00101010 11110011 00001100 01010101 01110111 01011110 10110101 00001111 11100010 10111010
00000011 00110110 01011000 10110011 10011010 10100111 00110100 00100000 11111101 01111101
01101011 01100010 01000101 00011011 00111010 01110011 01010100 11011110 00111010 11010001
00100111 00000111 01110100 11000101 10111001 01110111 01000100 11010111 00011110 00100110
01001011 01101011 11100010 01001100 01011001 00000000 01001000 01111011 01010111 01000111
01110101 01110101 00011000 00100001 01010100 10001111 00101101 10110000 01000001 11111110
10110101 11000000 01001100 10111001 00000100 00001100 11100010 10100011 01001101 01000110
01011000 10100010 00110000 00111111 11001110 00111111 10000101 10011000 11110100 10101110
10111000 01101011 10111011 00110000 10101011 01001111 10101001 11011110 01001101 00111110
00000011 11000110 10011101 01001001 11101011 01011001 10011010 10110110 10100101 01101111
01100101 00010000 11110011 10001000 00110010 01111111 00001100 00101010 01111110 01110011
01011100 11111010 10101101 11000110 01010000 11001101 01111000 11110001 11100111 10111010
10011110 10110100 11110111 10011010 11000110 11001101 00111100 11000100 11011001 00100100
10111101 11100101 01101110 01001001 00111111 10001101 01101001 10100010 01011010 10110011
00000011 10010000 11110001 10001100 10110011 10100000 01110011 01110100 00111100 10111011
10001001 10111110 01111101 10111110 11000111 10100000 10101110 00001110 11100110 01001100
11110111 11000110 00101011 10100111 11110001 10110110 10100010 10110111 01110111 01110001
10010000 01011000 10010000 00111001 11001101 01110010 00001111 10010011 00100011 10010001
11001110 00111001 11001110 01101011 11010001 11000010 01010011 10111100 01101110 10001001
01101101 10001111 11011100 01111001 00110100 00101000 11001011 10000011 10001100 10001111
11100101 01000110 01001001 01000001 10000001 11110101 10100111 11000010 00011000 11100111
10100110 01101011 10101011 11010100 10010010 01101000 01000110 00001011 10110001 11000110
00110011 11000101 00111111 10011100 10011110 00000101 00110011 00000100 00010000 00011000
11100111 11101001 01000010 01100100 10011100 00010011 11000000 10101100 11101111 01100011
01010100 01011110 10110001 00011111 10111100 00000111 01101111 11100111 01011011 00110000
10000010 11000011 10100101 01100111 11101001 11110000 10010000 10000011 10111011 11100111
10001110 01101011 10100100 11010011 10101101 00001011 00101111 00100011 10010010 01101011
10010111 00010001 00100101 11110110 01011001 11010101 01000101 00001100 01001000 01011010
00111000 01110111 00101000 11101011 11011110 10110011 10101111 11101110 11100101 01010011
11110010 00110001 01000001 11101011 10011010 11101011 01100101 10110100 11000010 11101101
00100000 11110001 01011000 11111010 10110110 10011010 10100110 11000110 01001001 01000000
00100101 11000000 11001111 00011101 11101011 10001110 10010100 11101101 00101111 01111000
11010010 01110111 10110101 11001110 01010110 01011011 11001011 10111001 00011011 00010001
10011001 01100100 01111110 11011000 00011100 01110011 11101111 01011001 11110011 01101010
01110111 10101010 01110110 00111001 11000001 01010011 11000000 11101011 10001010 11101010
01111100 00111110 01100001 11011110 11100001 10000010 01000110 01111011 00001110 10011011
10101011 10010110 11010110 10101101 00011010 00001011 11101001 00010101 11000110 00110010
11000100 10101001 11001101 01111010 11010000 11110110 01101101 11011001 00100011 10000110
01110010 10010010 11010110 11100100 10110000 11101011 11000111 00100001 01100110 10000111
00111100 11110101 00000111 10100101 01011101 10110110 10111110 10000010 01101110 10000111
00001110 01111101 01101011 10011110 01001000 10011000 10110000 00011011 01001110 01111101
00110001 01011010 00001001 01101001 10110010 00010000 01110110 11100011 00010100 11101011
01010001 10000110 11101000 01010100 11101011 01001110 11111010 10011101 00101100 00001110
11000011 10010000 01111010 11010101 10001111 00110000 10000100 00000111 00111001 11001101
01110011 11010110 01110111 01101100 00011011 11001011 00101100 01001000 10101101 01111000
11100101 11011100 00111111 10100000 11101101 01011100 10010010 10000111 00101110 11111010
10011101 11010000 10011111 00111001 01100100 01001000 01011000 01110001 01001100 01010110
00100011 10000011 01001000 11011110 11011111 10011101 01000110 11000100 01111010 11010110
01010110 01011101 01001010 00100111 11110011 01111011 01010011 01110010 10100000 11100111
10110101 01000010 01011011 00000011 10101111 00110100 00010011 10111000 01110010 00110000
01111011 10001100 11010100 11000101 00100100 11101100 00000010 10110100 11000000 00001110
00111010 01010011 00011010 01100000 01001110 00110111 01010100 01101111 10001111 01001110
01101010 10101100 11000000 11111111 00000000 00001011 01111011 01110011 01011011 11000011
01010101 10100001 00110011 10011011 00100110 10010110 11101000 00001110 00110011 11111000
11010100 00101111 01111010 10000000 01110101 00010101 01001101 11100000 01100110 11100111
00100010 10011000 11011010 01110001 01100000 00110000 01111110 10111001 11101111 01011010
01000010 00001001 01101110 01100101 11001111 00101110 10000101 11110100 10111011 01010110

00011100 00110000 10101001 10000011 00001001 00000110 00110011 11001101 01010001 11111110
11001110 01101100 01100000 00110001 11110110 10101001 10101101 11101101 11100101 10000110
01000000 11011011 11110010 00111010 00001010 01110010 01010000 11011100 00010111 00110111
01010010 01110110 10001100 10011100 01100111 10011010 01001001 01000110 01000001 00111001
00100010 10100110 11000110 01001110 00111111 00011010 10000110 11101101 10000010 11000110
01001000 11110100 10101100 10011010 11010111 01000010 10011111 10011001 11001111 11011100
11110011 01110010 01000110 01111000 11110110 10101000 11011100 00000000 01001001 11011101
11001101 00110101 11110010 11010010 00010011 11111100 11101010 00111001 01001001 00000111
10100111 00111110 10110101 11101000 01000001 01101001 01100100 01110001 10110111 10101101
11000100 10001100 10010110 01110011 10111100 11111101 00001110 00101010 11111110 01110001
00010001 00000010 10101000 11000011 10001100 11100111 11110010 10101011 01110110 11100011
00110010 01100000 11110110 11100100 11010010 10010101 11011011 00110011 01011010 00010110
00101101 01100011 11110010 10100010 11100100 10010010 11100111 10011100 00011010 11010111
11010011 01110010 00111001 00111001 11111010 00011010 10100001 00001010 10000110 01111110
01111111 11111101 01010101 10100111 00011001 00001011 10110000 00001110 10010101 11000111
01010110 01010111 01110110 00110111 10001001 10101001 00001100 10111000 11101001 11011110
10110101 10110100 10001101 01010010 11100011 01001110 01111101 11010110 11100100 01110010
00111001 10001100 11110100 00110101 11001110 10100100 10111100 11111100 11011111 10011001
10101011 01001001 00110111 11010110 10111001 01100101 00001110 10110111 00110101 10110101
11001111 01010111 11010001 10110101 10101011 00111101 01000101 00100011 01010001 00100000
10001110 11100111 00011000 00110000 10110001 11111110 01000111 10111101 01101010 11110000
01010000 00000010 00110000 01001101 01111000 11101100 01110011 00010101 01110000 11101000
01110000 11100000 11110000 01111101 00101011 10110010 11010000 01111100 01001100 11000101
11100011 10000011 01010101 00100000 10000001 11010010 01110011 11010111 11110001 11111111
00000000 00011010 11001001 10111011 00110011 00011001 01010011 01111101 00001110 11001000
01100001 10001111 01011100 11010011 01001000 01010010 00000001 00100111 10010011 11010100
01010010 00100100 10010001 11111001 01011011 11000011 00100001 01000111 11100100 00011100
11110101 10100100 01001111 10010111 11100110 00111000 01110011 11111001 01010010 11011111
01110010 01001001 00011000 11100100 00000101 00001101 10001100 10001110 00101001 10001011
10000110 11101010 01111000 10100101 00111011 01001100 10011001 11110110 11001000 00111000
10100011 11001100 10001111 00100000 00000001 10110000 00001110 01001110 11101010 01111010
00101110 10100100 10110000 01111100 00001000 11111010 00010000 10000000 11110100 11110101
10100110 10010010 00011010 01000000 11000100 01110010 00000111 01001110 11000010 10000110
00001011 11001100 10110010 01001000 01001110 00111001 11110110 10100101 00100100 10010101
00000001 00001110 00000110 01110000 01111000 10101010 11010010 11111010 00001100 00111100
11010110 01101100 00000000 01010001 00010011 11101001 11010110 10011000 11111001 11000010
00110011 11100111 01100110 00111111 01011010 01110000 11000000 01000010 00000111 00000100
01111010 11010011 00011100 01110011 00010011 00010011 11010000 11110000 00111101 01101000
10111101 10111101 01000101 01100001 01100100 11000010 11000100 00110010 01111001 11100011
10001100 11010001 10010000 00100010 00101101 10110100 10100000 11011101 11011011 10101001
10100100 10011011 11001011 00000100 00010010 11011000 00100000 11110110 00011100 10011010
01000110 11100101 11010000 00011100 11100000 00011110 00110010 01111010 11111101 01101010
01010010 01101101 10000101 11001001 00000110 01011000 10000010 11011000 11000000 00011001
00100111 11010110 10011001 00100000 11011101 10111111 10101111 10010110 01111011 00011010
00100101 00000101 10010111 00100001 10111011 11110101 11000101 00001100 11001010 01110010
00111001 00100010 10101110 11011101 10000110 00100110 01111101 00000111 00000010 10001100
00000110 01000010 11000111 00111100 11010010 10111011 00001100 01110001 10011100 01111010
11100011 00010100 10010010 10010011 11100101 11110000 01001000 11001111 00011000 11000101
01000010 11010011 01110010 00000011 10000000 01000000 11001001 00100111 00111001 00110100
11010111 11001011 01001010 00001111 01000100 11000001 00000011 11011110 10000010 00001000
01111111 00101100 00001111 10101001 00110100 11101001 01001110 00110010 01001110 01111110
11101110 00000101 01011100 01111100 10000000 00110110 01110011 10110100 11110001 10001110
01111001 11110101 10100110 10110000 00000100 01100000 10011110 10011110 10110100 00101001
00101101 00100001 11100011 00000000 00001110 11110100 10000000 11100111 01111111 10101111
01111010 01111011 00101011 00001110 11000011 11110011 10000010 00000110 11100000 00110001
11001111 00100010 10100011 01000011 10000110 11001111 00111011 11001111 01110010 01101001
10101111 11101010 00111111 00010011 01001111 11111110 00100001 10010001 11111000 11010010
01010110 00011011 00010000 00001111 10010011 11101110 10011101 10011110 10110100 01100111
00100011 01110011 11110100 10100110 10101100 10101100 11010001 10111000 10001111 01111110
11001100 11110101 11101000 00101000 01100010 00001100 01011001 11000111 01001010 10000111
01100100 01001000 10011001 00011011 01000001 11110100 11101101 01001011 10110101 01000011
10111100 10000100 11100111 00110100 00101000 11101000 01000000 00100011 00111110 10110100
10001110 00000111 10110000 00000000 11110000 00101001 11011010 00111101 11001011 00001001
10110000 01100011 11011010 01001110 00111110 10000011 10110101 00101110 00110001 00011000
01011110 01000110 01101001 00011000 00010010 00110111 00011010 01000101 11111001 10111001
11011101 11000101 01011011 10110011 01000100 00000110 00110000 10111011 01000001 11110111
11101011 01001101 00000101 10011011 11100110 11011100 00110011 11011110 10000101 00100111
10010011 10001111 11001110 10011100 10111111 00101111 10100110 01111101 01101001 01011101
10100010 11000110 00010110 11000001 11100011 11110001 10100111 11101110 00100110 10011000
00110001 10011100 11010001 11000111 10110101 01010010 01001011 10101000 00011011 10101000
11011001 01010000 01000111 01000011 01010010 01101110 00000000 11110100 00100100 11111111
00000000 00101010 10100101 10100110 11001001 10111010 11011001 00001110 11100010 01110001
11011000 11010101 11000101 00100001 10111010 01100100 01111010 11010101 00110100 01000000

11110110 01100001 10001110 00001110 00111101 01001101 00110101 01011011 11010111 00111001
10100000 11001000 00000011 10010101 11000111 00011000 11101011 01001110 01011111 10010111
10111110 01101010 01011111 10010000 10110101 10111000 10111001 11101111 01001011 11000110
00111001 00000100 11100110 10011011 11001110 00110010 00000111 11100001 01000110 01001110
00111110 01001110 00001111 01110001 01001011 01001011 11101010 00110010 01001110 00001000
11110100 11111010 11010001 10001110 00111010 01111110 01110100 11000101 11101001 11001111
01101010 01010101 01101100 01110101 11100011 00110101 01111011 10000000 11101110 01111011
00001010 01011100 00000000 10111001 11000110 01111111 00011010 01001100 11100011 11100110
00011100 10001111 01101010 01101011 00010001 10001100 10010011 10001111 10101001 10101001
01101011 01010000 00011101 11000001 00111111 11100001 01001011 10110100 11110101 00010100
11001100 00001101 11100000 00000011 11010111 10011010 00011001 10000010 10011110 10100100
11111010 10010001 11001101 00100100 11000000 01110010 11100111 10110000 10100101 11001000
11000110 00110001 11011110 10010011 01110110 01111001 00011111 10101101 00101111 00111101
01110011 11110101 10100010 11101001 11101100 00000000 11100100 00101111 10101000 00110100
10100101 10000110 00111010 11100000 11010100 01000011 00011001 11100100 01110101 00111101
00101001 11101101 10010000 01000001 11001111 11100001 01001001 00000000 10101011 10010001
11011011 00110100 10100000 11100111 10000011 11000101 01000111 10011110 00001000 11101111
01001110 00100100 00000010 00000110 11101100 00010011 11101011 01001111 11001001 00001101
10000110 00110011 01000010 11111100 10100111 10100000 11001001 10100000 01100100 10111111
01010001 10001110 11111001 00110100 00001001 00000001 00000100 11100111 10001010 01001110
11001011 01100010 10000101 01010011 10111000 11100001 11110000 00111101 01001101 00011100
10010011 10001010 01001111 01100011 11001110 01101001 01111010 01100100 10001010 00101111
01100010 00000011 00000000 11110011 10001111 11010010 10010001 01001001 00111101 01000101
00001000 00111110 01001111 10011111 10101101 00101011 01110101 11100000 11010010 00000000
11001111 01001100 00001110 01111101 11101000 01010001 10010110 00011100 11100000 01110111
10100100 01011110 00110011 10011110 01110011 11011110 10011010 10000100 10010110 01110000
01111010 00010001 01000010 01011101 00001011 00011111 10001100 11110010 00111001 10100011
00100000 00000011 11000111 00111101 11101000 11100001 01001000 00000000 11010000 00110000
01001001 00100111 11110001 10100111 10100011 00100100 00111001 00100011 10010011 11111000
01100010 10010111 01101110 01001000 00010100 10011001 11000000 11001000 11111100 11001101
00110000 01100101 10000001 11001001 00110100 10011011 11101100 10000111 01100001 11101100
00110000 10011001 01001111 01011010 01000101 00000000 11100111 00100111 10110111 00010100
10111000 00011000 11111011 11011101 11101001 00110010 00110001 10000000 00110010 01110011
01010011 01101011 10101011 10001100 01011101 10111100 01110010 01111000 00010100 00011100
00101000 11100010 01000001 10010010 01111010 01100110 10010011 10010000 01110001 10011110
11111100 11010011 01110000 10111011 10111101 01001110 01111010 11010011 10110110 10100000
01001001 11001001 00000100 00010001 11110101 00110100 11010000 01011000 00111001 11111001
10111000 00111101 10111010 11010000 11101101 10011111 10010001 01001000 00011001 11110100
00110100 00100010 11100011 10100111 11010010 10100101 11000101 10111101 01000000 00001011
01100111 11101110 00011110 10011110 10110100 10100111 00000111 10001110 10111110 10110100
11000101 00111100 11100011 10110111 01001010 10010011 11100101 11011111 11010111 11101001
10011010 01110110 10110100 01101110 00000010 00110110 00110111 11101101 11001111 00111101
11101001 00111011 11110000 00000001 10100000 10010010 01111101 00000110 01111010 10011010
01011100 10000000 00000000 11111101 01111101 01101001 01011101 01110100 00011000 10001011
10110100 01111101 11110010 01111000 11101100 00101001 01110001 11110010 11111011 01010000
00111101 10101001 01111110 11101001 11001111 01011010 01010110 00010101 10000110 11101110
11101000 00111001 11000110 00111010 11010000 00000000 00011111 01110000 11110011 11101111
01000010 10010011 10010010 01110001 10000001 11011000 01111010 01010010 10001101 11000111
00111001 01101100 10001100 01100011 10011010 01101111 01100001 10100000 01110011 11100101
10001100 11110101 11001101 00100110 01110010 11010010 01110000 01110000 01111010 01010010
11110111 11001011 00000001 10011010 01000101 11001000 01110000 11000011 11101001 01001010
11100000 00001011 10010010 01000001 00011100 01110011 01001011 10001111 11010100 11010010
01000110 01001000 01001110 01000111 00111110 10010100 10100111 00011001 11001001 11101011
01000101 10111010 10001000 00001110 00110001 10000001 11001101 00100010 10011111 01111110
01101001 11001010 00000110 01101001 00110001 10011100 11100011 10111001 10100001 11011010
11110111 01000011 00001110 10111100 01010010 11110101 01111110 00010100 01100000 01111010
00011110 10110100 10011100 10000011 11110011 11110101 11110100 10100000 10010010 01000110
00000001 11000111 00011100 11010100 10100110 11000100 11000100 11111011 11000111 10011110
00101001 11000010 01000101 11110010 11111100 11001111 11101110 01110110 10100100 11000110
01110000 01101001 00011111 01101000 00011000 00111111 01010011 01010111 10110010 10110000
11000101 00000111 10101001 00100000 10100111 10110101 00001100 01000001 00111001 11100111
10011010 00010100 00010110 11001001 00100100 11111011 00001100 11010000 00011011 00001100
00001000 00011001 11111010 11010010 01010011 01101011 01000001 01011100 00110011 11011100
11110100 10100100 01001100 10011111 10011011 10011110 01101001 10100000 11110101 11101110
01111101 01101001 11000000 01100001 01111010 11100011 00100011 11010110 10001011 01110101
01000011 00110001 00110101 11101101 00001010 00001101 01001110 00010111 11001010 11100010
01111111 11100001 00100011 10001010 11110011 10111101 01010011 01001101 10011111 01001101
10111000 00110001 11001110 10100100 01111010 00011100 01110000 01101011 11010111 01000111
01100000 11011101 10111010 11111011 11010101 01011101 01000110 11000110 00001101 01000010
00011111 00100110 11100001 01110010 10000111 10111111 10100101 01100101 00100100 10001011
10100111 01010101 11000100 11110001 11111100 10010001 11101101 01001010 10110010 00011100
11100111 00111101 00111101 00111011 01010110 11100110 10111111 11100001 11011001 11110100
11111001 00011101 11100001 00011110 01101101 10111111 11110111 10000111 01101111 10101101

01110011 11111110 10111000 00100111 10011110 01101010 00110100 10010001 11011101 01001110
01001010 01101000 10110110 10010010 11100111 10110110 00110011 11011111 00110101 00110010
11001001 11001101 01100111 11101110 11000110 01110110 10011100 00010001 01010010 00100100
10011001 11000111 10101111 11010110 10100111 01011011 01011000 11010010 11000110 10010000
10010011 10100110 00001101 01001011 11100110 10010010 00111101 10101011 00111001 00100100
11001001 10101011 00101001 00100000 00011100 00011010 01101110 01010110 11111000 10010001
00101101 01101010 01011011 01010110 11100011 10011110 00101010 01100101 00100000 10001110
00001101 01010011 11110011 00111110 01110000 00110001 11001111 10101101 01001110 01011000
00000001 10001100 01110101 10100011 10011010 11000000 11010101 11001001 11010011 10110111
00111101 01111111 01011010 01110111 01000011 11110101 10101000 01010000 11100000 01100011
10111101 01001000 10000100 10000011 11001001 10100111 11001101 11111100 11000100 10110101
01101101 10001011 00001010 01111101 01111101 00101001 01010000 11110001 11010110 10101011
11101110 10100101 00001100 00000001 10100001 00100111 00101110 10000000 01011011 00001101
11010010 10100101 10001001 10001110 01101010 10010111 10011011 11101001 01010011 11000111
00100000 00100011 10011110 00101011 00111001 01000111 10100101 11000010 11110110 01100110
10100100 00111000 11000000 00111101 11111110 10110101 00101010 10000000 01101010 10100100
00001101 11101111 01010110 10010111 10010001 01000100 10010111 01000100 11000001 10100001
10101100 10111100 11110011 01010001 10111000 00000011 11101001 01010110 00001110 00110001
01010000 10110000 00000011 00110101 10010011 10110010 11011100 00001010 01110010 10000010
01101010 00000111 01011110 00001000 10101011 10010010 00101110 01000001 11000101 01010110
01111100 10011100 10001110 01111010 01010101 11111011 00110100 11110111 01100010 01110111
00110011 00100110 01011110 01110011 01011001 01110111 10010001 00001110 10000011 11110101
10101101 10011001 10010011 11010010 10110011 11101110 10100011 11001000 11100000 11110010
01101011 01101000 11011101 01101000 10000101 10100001 10001011 01111011 10101000 01011100
11000011 01101010 01100001 00010010 00000000 00111010 00000011 10001110 01000111 11010010
10111001 01111101 01000011 01010011 11100100 01100001 10110010 01110001 11010100 10011010
11101001 10101111 10010011 10000010 00110010 00111111 00101010 11100010 01110101 10101011
00111001 00100011 00000110 01101000 10111011 01110101 00000010 10111101 00101100 00110010
01010101 00011111 10111100 01110011 01010110 10001111 01010100 01100111 11011100 11001100
00100100 01100000 01001110 01110010 00000110 00101010 10111010 10101110 01011000 11100011
11101110 01010011 00010101 10001011 01110101 11100011 11101011 01010011 11000100 00111110
10011110 11110101 11101010 01000110 00111100 10111010 00011100 10110111 10111000 11100100
10010001 01110000 01101010 11000010 00000000 00000111 01101111 10100101 01010110 10001001
01000000 10010100 01110111 11110101 00011001 10101011 01110010 01100000 10001100 00001010
10001001 10110100 10110100 00011010 11010100 01101110 01111010 00010001 10000000 01111111
10011101 00110101 11100100 00101011 10010010 00000000 00001100 01101000 11011011 11110111
01111110 10111001 00110101 00001100 11101101 10011001 00000110 01111010 01110110 00010101
00101001 00110110 01101001 01110011 10101011 11110000 11110000 11110011 10100001 10001101
10001000 11100101 10101011 10111011 11010011 10101101 11000100 01101010 00000110 00111000
11110101 00110101 11000110 01111000 00010111 00010010 00001100 00111000 11100101 00011011
00010101 11101000 00101001 11000000 11101001 11111000 01010111 10010011 10001011 10111010
10011111 00101001 11011111 01000001 11011110 00100100 01101111 00011110 01111101 01110001
01010100 11101111 00100001 00010010 01000100 01010100 11110001 10011010 11010000 01100011
10111011 11101010 00101010 10010100 11000111 10101110 01101011 00011110 01101110 10100110
11001101 00011100 01010101 11110101 10011011 01000011 01110000 00100110 10001100 10001100
10001110 10111100 01010101 00011011 10011001 00000100 11101011 10001001 11100011 00000100
10001110 10000100 11010111 01010001 10101001 01000001 10011100 10110000 00111111 10000101
01110011 01010111 00000000 10000111 00111011 10000111 00011101 11101011 11010000 11000011
11010100 11110111 01101110 11001110 01111010 10010100 10101110 01010000 01010001 00000100
00110010 01111001 10001001 00010111 11001110 00101001 00101110 01100111 01101001 01001111
11001000 00110110 00000011 11011011 10101101 00111101 11010100 11100111 00111101 01000001
11110101 10100110 00000000 00110011 11001000 11000101 01110100 10101001 11101010 01110011
01111011 00110010 00001000 01100010 00100110 01011100 01100011 11101011 01011010 10010000
10000010 10110010 00001111 11100111 01010001 11011011 11000000 11001100 11100011 01100000
11111010 11010110 11000101 10011110 10011011 00100100 10001011 10011100 11100100 11100111
10001010 10011010 10110010 01100110 10110100 11010001 00001111 00100111 10100000 11101001
01010000 10010010 00110011 11001111 01011110 11100010 10111010 01000110 11010011 00000100
01110000 11100111 00011111 00111111 10110101 01100001 01011111 11000111 11100101 01001010
01000000 10101110 00000101 01010001 00110111 01101101 11001101 01011011 10110001 01010010
01001001 10010101 01000110 00111010 01100111 00011101 01101010 10011101 11000101 11001110
11000000 01001011 00011100 01010011 11100101 00111001 11100000 10011110 00101010 10000101
11100001 00100111 00000100 01010111 01100101 00101010 01101010 01001110 11101101 00011001
11001010 10100011 10111001 00010100 11110111 10010011 00110110 01110001 10010001 10001111
01001010 11001110 01111011 11001001 10001011 11100111 00100111 10001110 00000001 10101101
00011011 00011110 01011100 10000011 11010111 10100001 11001111 01101010 10100101 01111011
01101001 00100010 01001000 01110010 10011110 11111001 11101100 01101011 10101110 00010100
11100010 10110110 01000111 00101101 01011001 11001001 10010001 10100101 11100100 11011110
01100111 00100100 11100111 00010101 10100101 00001101 11110011 01101110 01000010 11100111
00011110 11010101 10011111 01100111 01101111 00100100 10101110 01010110 00101100 10010011
10011100 10001110 00101011 01001010 11100110 00000101 10001110 00011101 10101110 01111001
11000110 01111111 00011010 00100110 10010011 11010000 10001010 01110011 10010010 01000110
10001101 10111101 11011000 01100000 01000011 11110101 11000111 00010101 01100001 01100100
11011101 11110111 01001101 01110011 11110110 01100110 01001100 11100001 11000110 00000000

10101101 10111000 01000111 11101110 11000011 00011100 01111101 01101011 10011010 10100100
01011010 11010001 00011101 01010100 11101010 00110110 10001001 10011001 10110010 00111000
10101010 01111010 10001001 00011111 01100110 10010011 00111101 11000101 01011011 01011100
00110111 01111010 10100101 10101000 00001101 11001000 00010100 00011110 11111100 11010100
01000111 11011111 01101010 11011101 00001101 00100111 10110001 10001000 01011000 00101100
01100100 10110010 10001100 10011010 10100111 10001110 01110001 10011010 10011110 11101101
10000110 11110010 10110001 11110110 11101011 11101101 01010000 10000000 00000001 11110101
11001111 10101101 01111010 00010001 01001110 11000111 00001100 11111011 00010010 01000011
10011000 11010100 10011110 10110101 10100001 01101100 00001001 00000001 10111111 01011010
10100101 00010000 11011101 10000001 11111010 01010110 10100101 10111100 01111000 10001111
00000010 10110010 10101011 10100010 00001010 01101000 10110011 00001100 01111000 00111101
01110011 01010110 00010101 10000000 00100011 10110000 11110101 10101010 11110001 11111100
10100111 10001010 10110001 10110111 10010010 01111010 10100101 01110001 10111101 01110101
01100111 01000010 10111001 00111010 10110000 00110101 00101010 00110111 00000000 00011110
11111001 11100110 10101011 10100001 11001110 01000101 00111101 00001001 11100000 01110110
11110111 10101001 01010000 10001001 10100111 10010001 01101101 00011011 10001100 01010101
10100100 10011100 10000010 00000001 00111001 00000111 10110001 10101100 11010101 11100011
10001110 11011001 11001101 01001010 10001100 01110011 11110010 11010110 00010101 00101001
00101011 11101000 00110100 01110101 10111010 00100110 10111011 00110110 10011101 11110010
11110001 00101101 10111110 01110010 01100011 00111100 10010001 11110100 10101110 11111110
11000010 11101110 00001011 11101011 01010001 00110101 10101100 10100001 11010011 00111001
00111000 00111100 10001111 01101010 11110001 10100000 11000100 01111111 11111010 11101011
01100011 01001000 11010100 10100101 10110001 10111010 00010010 11011011 10110110 00011111
10111010 00011110 01000001 10101110 01111011 00110100 01100111 00101010 01110111 11010100
11110101 01100001 00100000 11000010 00010100 01011110 01001001 10100100 01010000 00010000
10011100 11110010 11100011 10111110 01101011 00111111 01000011 11010101 10101101 10101111
10100010 11001010 01100010 00111001 01100011 00011001 10010000 00110001 11100100 01111101
00000111 01111010 10111010 01111111 01111000 11100011 01100011 00011100 01110111 11001000
10101011 01001111 01001011 00011100 11001101 00110001 11111100 10011110 00111011 11111011
11010010 01101101 00010010 01100000 00011100 11100011 00111001 00100100 00011010 01101111
10011000 00100011 00100000 00000101 11011100 11100111 00111001 11100111 10110000 10100111
00100000 00100111 00011001 00011000 11111010 01010011 01101001 11011110 11100101 01101000
00110100 00110000 10010110 01000010 00010010 00100010 10010001 00000001 11010100 10011110
01001001 10100100 01100010 01100100 00111000 10001111 11111000 01011011 10111101 00101010
00110001 11111011 11000011 10000001 01001000 10000100 11111101 11011100 10011100 01100110
10000101 01100001 00000100 10100011 10010000 01111011 11110100 10100101 01110010 10110001
11110010 11111001 11000000 11110110 11101011 01001000 11100000 01101111 11100111 11110010
00010100 01111111 00011110 01000111 00100111 00011101 11101010 11010011 11101000 10000000
00110011 11110011 11111100 10100011 10001111 01111010 01000001 00100110 01000001 01110010
01110000 00000001 11011000 00000000 10100110 10010010 01111100 11001101 10101001 10001100
10010001 01001110 01111101 11011011 00110001 10010100 11000110 01111010 11100110 10000100
10101100 00100110 00110111 00100000 00011100 11110101 10100100 11001000 00000111 01110111
00100100 11100111 11110010 10100101 11111011 10101010 01001111 01010010 01001101 00011111
11000110 00010111 11110011 00000010 10010011 01111010 10001100 01101110 11100110 00111000
00101110 00110000 01001000 11100000 01010010 10010011 10011100 01110011 11001101 01001000
10000000 11001001 10010000 10011001 00100111 00011100 10011111 01001010 10001010 00010010
00100100 00011001 11011100 00110000 00111011 10001110 11110100 11000101 10110000 11100100
11100100 11111100 11000011 00010001 10000011 11010110 10100011 10001111 00000000 00111111
01010011 10111101 10110010 01001001 11101101 01010010 01111100 10111100 00011100 11100001
00000000 11001001 11001101 01000100 11001100 01011011 11101110 10011110 10111110 11010100
01001010 11101111 01110010 01000101 01111100 11100111 00001000 00001110 00110010 00111001
11111110 01110100 11100110 11101000 01001001 11100010 10001110 01000001 00111000 00111101
00101001 10001110 11001100 00000000 11100111 00010101 00010111 01111011 00010101 01110001
00001110 00110000 00111001 11101010 01110000 00000000 10100001 10001110 01001001 00011110
11110100 00001111 10011000 11111111 00000000 01011010 01011101 11011111 00110001 00000011
11110001 11000101 00010110 10111110 11100011 00010101 01111111 00010010 01000111 01001010
10001111 10101100 01000100 11110001 11101110 00101001 11101010 01111001 01110110 11000111
01101110 00000110 01101001 10100000 01100100 01110011 01000011 10110011 11011000 10010100
00100011 11100101 10011100 01110011 11110010 00001110 11000011 10111101 00111001 00001110
11011000 11001001 00100011 11101001 01001100 11100100 11110111 11101011 01001111 11001111
11001111 11000001 11100100 01111011 11010011 10001101 10101110 01010000 11000101 11111001
10000111 10110001 10100110 00101001 11111110 00010101 00111001 11000001 11100100 11010100
10000100 01101101 00011001 00011100 01010100 01111000 11100000 11000110 00111110 01000001
10011100 11100100 01110111 10101001 10110110 10110111 01100000 00111111 00111101 00111011
01110011 11010010 10001111 11111011 11100110 10010001 01000001 00000011 00000011 00111111
10001001 11001101 00101110 00000010 11110001 11100101 11101110 11110111 10101101 00111100
10001001 11010111 10100001 00100110 10010001 00111110 00001110 01110010 01001000 00100011
10100101 01101100 11000101 11001000 00000111 00111101 10101011 10011010 11010011 11100100
11000111 10010100 01111001 00011001 11000110 01110001 01011101 00100010 00010010 01111001
11111101 00101011 10100110 01101010 11000011 01110110 00011110 01001001 01011110 10000011
00110100 11100000 00110010 10100001 10111010 11010011 01110110 11100000 10000011 11011110
10011010 10101010 00000011 01100111 10100111 10101111 00110101 10000111 10011011 00100100
10010000 00000010 01011111 11100100 11001110 00111101 11101001 11001100 10111000 00111001

00111101 01101001 10011011 10000111 10100111 00000111 10111101 00101000 11000111 01101110
10100011 10110101 00100100 11101111 10111000 00001110 01110001 10111011 00000101 11110011
10001111 01001111 01011010 01010010 01110011 11001101 00100110 00110011 11010011 10101111
01111010 01101110 01000111 01001111 11001110 10001011 10101011 01011000 00000111 10101001
11001000 11111001 01111010 01010001 11001001 11101101 11110100 10100100 01010010 00110011
10000001 01001101 11011100 00000111 11001100 01111010 01111011 01010011 10010010 00010001
00100110 11010011 10110000 00010010 11010100 00100000 00111101 01001111 11100101 01001101
00000101 10001111 11110000 11100000 01111010 00011010 01110011 11101110 11000111 00011101
01110001 01001001 01101000 00110000 11001001 00100111 10100111 00010100 00110000 00100011
10111101 00110111 00101101 10110100 00000101 00111100 11010010 10111110 01001110 00110010
01111101 11101001 11101000 00000010 10101110 00111111 11000010 10000110 00111101 01111011
11110110 10100100 01101110 10011100 01010010 11110001 10110011 10010011 11111000 11010010
11010000 00000001 01110010 00110000 00000000 11000001 11001111 00110100 11100111 11011010
01010111 00111101 00111101 01111000 10100110 10010001 11000110 01000110 01111101 11101001
00011000 00010110 01110001 10000001 11111001 11010000 10010101 10110110 00000001 01010111
01101111 00100011 00010100 00111111 00000000 00000100 11110101 11000110 01101001 00111101
01000001 11100010 10010101 01001010 10011100 01110011 11001101 00100101 10111000 00000110
01110001 10011100 01110101 11110111 10100001 00000011 00011100 01010011 10000001 00011101
01001001 11001001 00110100 00101100 10000000 10011100 00101111 01001111 01011100 01010010
10110110 10100000 00001100 00110110 10100001 00100111 10011111 11000110 10000101 11100100
01110100 11111010 01010011 01001000 00100100 10010010 11011111 10011101 00100010 10110010
10010001 10010001 10010011 10011110 10000010 10010010 01111010 11101010 00111011 00001111
11011101 11011010 10010100 00000001 11111001 01111010 11010010 00100001 00011110 10010100
01101110 01011100 11111100 11000111 10100101 01010110 10001000 01000011 10010111 10001110
01111010 00011010 01001111 11010100 11111010 01010011 00010100 10001100 10001100 00010010
01111001 11100100 11100010 10011100 11010010 01100101 11001110 00000111 11010110 10000111
01100000 00001100 00010110 00111100 11110001 11101101 01001011 10000011 11110100 10100100
00011110 10100100 11010011 00011001 10001001 00100011 11001011 00011001 11100111 10011100
11010000 11010000 11101110 00101000 11000011 01100111 10100110 01111011 11010011 10110010
01000001 00000000 00010001 11111001 01010011 01001111 00000111 10001110 00111101 10101001
10111110 10100100 11010100 11101100 00010111 00011100 10100111 00000011 10010011 11001111
10101101 00111111 00100000 01110001 01001100 11100100 11110010 01101000 11000111 00100100
10001110 01001001 11101011 01001011 01110010 10001000 11101101 11101100 10100001 10001000
10011001 10000000 00011110 01101111 01110011 11101011 01010011 01101110 11000000 11101011
11110101 10100101 11011010 01011000 11101101 00101100 00000000 00110100 10001110 00111001
11011010 00111101 00110011 10011111 01011010 10100110 10010000 10011000 00101111 00011001
00001000 00111001 00110100 01110001 10010011 11000111 11100111 01001101 00111111 10001000
10100111 01100111 11010011 11110001 11001101 01001111 00101101 10001001 00000010 01110000
10000111 11011110 10010101 01001001 11000111 00011100 01100111 10111101 00011000 00001010
00110000 01110011 01001000 00001000 00100100 00000001 10011010 00101110 10001010 01000001
10011100 10010010 01110001 10000001 10011110 00101000 01100010 01111001 10100101 11101011
10010010 01101001 00110001 01001001 01101111 10100000 11000101 11001111 00000100 10010011
10010011 11011000 01111010 11010011 00110111 00000110 00011001 00000000 11100111 11011110
10000101 00000100 10111000 11001001 11101001 11011010 10011100 11000111 11100111 11000000
11101000 00101010 01011100 10000001 10110001 10111101 01001110 01001101 00111011 00100101
01111011 01110001 01000001 11000110 01110011 11011000 01110100 10100101 01101110 00000111
10111101 00011010 00110001 10001100 01011101 10101000 00000111 11110001 10111001 00111100
10011010 01110010 11110101 11001101 00001011 11000111 01011010 01010110 00000111 11111100
00101001 11011100 00000100 01100010 01110000 00110000 00111010 11111011 11010010 10001100
10000100 00000000 11010000 11111011 01000001 00001010 00111001 11000111 11101001 01000110
01110010 01111010 01110000 00101000 11010001 00001001 00001100 00011001 11100111 00011101
01101001 11011100 10011110 00110011 10010001 11011110 10011010 01011000 11100100 00000001
11110111 00111010 01100111 00110100 11101110 10000011 10000001 11111111 00000000 11010111
10101000 01111110 10100010 01101000 01010101 00011101 10000001 11000000 11110101 00110100
11001100 01111010 01010011 11010100 10000000 10011001 00111100 00001111 01111010 01001110
01111101 01111001 10101010 10111110 10011010 10010100 00001111 00100111 10010110 01010000
00000000 00001011 10010011 11010100 10001110 00110001 01001100 01100110 00111101 11001110
01001111 10110101 00101001 00011001 01100000 01001001 11100000 01110110 10100000 00000001
11111010 11010010 01111010 11101010 11000100 10000100 11001110 00111001 11000110 01001000
11100110 10000110 00100100 10000000 01111011 11110100 10100001 01001110 00000001 00111100
11110011 01001011 10000010 01010100 01100100 11100011 00110101 01010110 01110110 10110000
11000100 01100000 01111010 11010000 11111100 01100011 11010110 10010111 11111101 11101111
01011110 10010100 10011001 00111001 11000110 00111000 11110101 10101001 10111101 10011000
10110101 00100011 10010110 00100100 01100101 00101010 11100011 00100000 11110101 00010101
11001000 01111000 10000011 11000010 11010001 10110011 00111100 11110110 00000000 10000111
00111111 11110010 11001111 10110001 00110101 11011001 11110011 10011010 01010110 11001111
01011100 01010010 01110001 11100110 01000101 00101001 10111000 01101100 01111000 10111101
11011100 00001111 00001011 00010101 10010010 00110010 10010010 00000011 10000010 00001101
01000010 10111100 10001100 11110100 10101111 01011000 11010110 10110100 00011011 01001101
01001010 00110011 11100111 00101110 00011100 10000011 10001001 00111101 11101011 11001111
00110101 10101101 00010110 11101011 01001001 11001000 10011000 01101110 10001000 00011110
00100100 00011101 11101011 00101101 10110100 01100111 01101101 00111010 11001001 10101011
00110011 00101101 00011000 10011110 10110101 01100101 01100100 11000110 00101010 10101010

00011100 10010001 01010010 01110100 11101001 01001010 11101111 10100001 10110111 10011001
10100010 10001111 10010001 10010001 01010010 10100100 10011001 11001110 01110011 10011010
11001111 00001100 00001111 00000100 01010100 11001001 00100111 00011000 10101001 10010010
10111011 10111011 01100000 01011100 01011001 00111001 10101001 01010010 01010000 01000111
00000110 10101001 01101110 11001000 11000000 10101001 00010101 10000000 00011100 00011010
01001001 11011011 01110000 10110001 01100100 00111111 11001100 01101001 01111100 11001111
10011111 11011010 10101001 10101100 11000100 01110101 11111100 11101000 11011101 11000101
01101001 01101101 00101110 10000101 01101011 00110010 11011111 10011010 00110011 01010110
00100001 10010000 01110000 00000111 00111001 00111101 11111011 01010110 01110010 11100000
11110111 11100110 10100100 10001010 01000010 10101100 01110000 00101010 00011010 11010011
01010000 00111010 00001000 00001111 00000011 11111001 11010101 11000100 01101010 11001001
10110111 10010011 11100101 00011110 10111110 11010101 10100001 00001011 01110100 11001101
01000111 10100000 01011110 11100101 11001100 11101110 00011000 10100110 10111000 11100011
10001010 01110000 11101000 00110001 01000111 01101110 01000101 00111111 01100111 01101101
11001001 01101100 10101101 00101111 00000010 10101010 00111111 00100111 10001111 11001110
10101110 00111000 11001101 01010111 01110000 00111011 01010000 10011110 10110110 01100010
01101100 10100011 00101110 01110010 01101010 10000100 11100000 01010110 10100100 11000011
10010011 01011001 11010111 00100011 11101001 01010111 11001101 11001010 11110100 00001011
00011000 00110111 11101011 10010101 00100000 00001110 01111111 10010101 01110011 11011010
10010100 01011110 01100000 01110001 11000111 00100011 00010101 11010100 01011101 10100000
11100100 01111110 10110101 10000101 01111001 00010000 11100000 11100111 11101010 00101011
10101111 00001110 11010011 01110111 00110011 10011010 11101110 01110001 00010111 11110110
01111011 00100101 00100101 00111110 11100001 11100111 00011110 10010101 01011101 00100010
01111001 00000001 11000111 01001110 11111100 11010110 11111101 11101010 10010110 11001110
00000111 00111101 00101011 00010010 11100001 01011010 00011001 01001000 01001100 10000000
01000111 01011100 11110101 10101111 01100110 10010101 01000100 11110100 01001100 11100001
10011100 01101100 11001000 11100011 11100010 01000000 00011111 00111001 01011010 10110110
11001101 11000001 11011011 11011110 10101000 10010101 01100001 10010110 00000011 10101111
01000011 11101001 01010110 10100001 01101100 11000111 10010111 01011100 00011110 00110001
10001111 11010110 10101010 01110001 10111110 10100010 01000011 10100101 00101100 00111010
00010001 01010000 11001101 10000000 01111001 11100000 00001110 01101010 01010111 00100111
00111000 11001000 00011001 11101111 10001010 10101110 11111001 01101110 01111111 00110011
01000010 10110000 10001110 11010011 11100001 11110000 11000100 10000111 10011111 11100010
11100100 00010001 11101101 01011110 10000110 11000111 00000010 10111100 11111111 00000000
11100001 11100001 00011111 11101001 00100011 10001100 11100100 00011110 01111010 11010111
01111100 11000111 11100101 00011110 11110101 11100010 11100011 01110101 10101011 10100001
11101001 11100001 11111110 00000100 00110111 01110101 01000011 00100110 00001000 11001111
10100101 00111011 10000000 01101001 10101110 00110011 11001000 00111100 01010110 00010000
01110111 11010101 10011101 00110111 00110010 11101111 11000111 00000100 10100000 00100011
00100110 10110000 10101111 00100000 00101100 11011100 10001111 11001010 10111010 10001001
10100011 11011101 11000101 01000100 11010110 01101010 11011000 00100010 10110110 11110110
10001010 00001000 10001011 00011100 01111011 11011010 00011110 01000000 00011100 11010100
10010110 01111010 01011100 11010111 00010010 00100000 00001010 01000000 11001110 00101011
10101101 10000110 11001110 00101100 11100100 10101000 00111111 01010001 01011010 00010110
10110000 10101010 10000010 10101000 10100000 00001111 01100001 01011101 00001010 10100011
01110001 10111001 10010100 10100001 10101110 10000101 00111101 00110011 01000100 10001010
00000101 11000100 10000011 00100100 10001110 01001000 00111101 00101011 01010010 00111011
00011000 10100011 11000000 00000011 00011000 11101101 01010111 00100001 01011100 00001100
01100010 10100101 11000110 00001111 00111101 10101011 10011010 01010101 01011011 01110110
00011100 00100000 01100111 01011111 11000010 10101011 00001001 11000000 11100111 00011100
01010111 00000001 10101010 11000111 10001001 10001110 00001001 11000111 10101001 10101111
01000010 11010101 01100100 11000100 00111000 11111110 10110101 11100111 10011010 10010001
11001100 11001110 01110011 11011111 11110011 10100111 01001010 01001101 01101000 00010011
01000110 01010100 11000011 01110110 01001101 01010001 10011001 00001111 01011110 01101011
01001101 11100011 11001000 11100011 10001010 10000000 11000111 10000000 00110010 00111011
11111110 01110101 11011101 01001101 11011011 01010011 00001001 11000111 10101001 01001001
10100011 11100111 00110100 10011110 01111100 10010001 00101001 00101110 10100010 01000001
11101000 01001101 01011010 01111000 10001110 01001001 10100110 11111001 01000011 10100110
00111001 10101110 10000111 01010001 11011011 01010011 00111111 01100111 01111101 01000110
10100101 11101100 10101011 00011110 00100011 10000101 01000110 01000111 01000001 01010100
10111100 10101001 10101110 10100100 11110011 00100110 00111100 00010011 11001000 10101101
00000100 10000100 00000011 10011110 10011100 11110011 10011010 10011101 00100011 00000000
10000011 01001001 01010100 10001100 01111010 00001011 11011001 01011111 10101001 00000101
10111100 00100001 01010111 00011000 11111010 10011010 10111010 10010001 11100000 00001100
01110100 00110100 00101010 10000000 00111010 00001100 11111011 01010100 10011001 00100000
01110100 10101100 10100110 11001101 11100001 01001110 11000010 00110001 11011011 11000101
01100110 01101010 01110010 01111110 11101110 01000110 11001111 11001111 10001110 11010101
01110010 11110010 01100101 10000110 00101101 11010010 00010000 00111101 00110011 01011100
11110110 10100001 01110110 01100101 11000010 00100000 11100011 10111001 11110101 10101101
01101001 11010011 11010111 01100001 01010110 10101000 10010010 10110011 00101010 00111010
10011111 00110000 11110001 11010111 10010011 01001110 01111100 01101100 00011101 10110011
11010011 00110100 01111110 01110100 11100101 00011111 01110011 10001100 11010111 01011111
10011001 11000010 11101110 01011000 10000000 00000000 10101001 10001110 00111000 11101011

01010111 10100010 01101100 00010000 00001001 11001101 01010100 10001000 01111100 10111110
11011001 11101001 01010110 01010011 10001101 10011111 11001010 10110000 10011101 11111010
00011010 00101101 00001011 01100101 10111010 01100110 10100100 01011001 00000000 11101011
10011010 10000010 00111100 00011110 01010111 10100111 10111101 01001100 10000100 00010011
11010011 10001010 11000001 10101011 10111011 00011010 10101101 01001001 10010011 11010100
01010100 10001000 11000011 00011000 11001101 01000111 10010001 11100101 11111010 10011010
10010011 10000000 01110011 11011011 10110101 00101011 00101011 01011000 11010000 10010001
10001111 00100011 00111111 11001010 10011110 00111101 01000001 11000101 00110001 01011011
10011111 10010111 10011100 11010011 11110011 11001101 01100110 11010011 01111011 10001110
11101000 01010000 01011011 10100001 11111100 11101010 01111101 11000101 01000000 00100000
11100011 11011110 10100010 00000101 01000000 11001001 11101111 01001110 01011100 01100011
11110001 10101100 01011110 11100001 01100011 01010010 11000010 11110110 01011000 10100101
10001110 01101000 01011011 00010010 01000110 01111000 01101010 11110100 01101111 00001111
01101011 00110001 01101010 10010001 01100010 01000010 00100011 10111011 11000000 11001100
01111001 11101011 11110100 10101111 00101000 10001000 11111001 01111100 11110011 01010111
01101100 11101110 10100100 10001101 11000011 11000011 00100001 01001001 00010000 11100101
01011000 00011110 01000001 10101100 11101010 01000011 10101111 01110011 00111001 01000001
00110100 01111011 00000011 00011100 00011111 10010011 10001110 01111001 10100100 11100100
10001100 00011110 10011001 11100100 00000011 01011000 01111110 00011110 11110001 00000010
11101010 01010001 10001000 10100111 00101001 00011101 11100000 00011100 11100100 11110000
11111111 00000000 01001010 11011011 01010000 01001110 01010101 01001000 11100011 10010011
01010001 01100011 10011011 01100110 00101100 10100100 11100111 00011100 10100010 01110110
00010100 00101000 11011011 10000010 01111111 00001010 01000010 01000001 11000110 00000001
00100111 11010100 11010010 10111100 10000101 10001000 00100100 01100011 00010100 11011110
10100011 00010000 00001100 00010010 01111010 10010011 11011100 11010000 01000111 10100001
11000001 10100101 11011101 10010111 00000000 01110001 01001100 01100010 01001000 00000101
11111101 01111011 01010010 01101010 11101100 00000011 00011100 10011111 01010001 01001000
11011100 01100000 00000010 00000110 01111001 10100101 11000000 00111100 01111110 10010100
00110000 01011100 11100111 00000111 00111110 10010101 10100010 01001111 10100000 10101101
11010100 00110011 11111011 10111110 01111001 11110100 11001101 00100110 01110000 11000011
01100000 00000011 11011111 10111101 00011111 01001100 01110100 10100001 10000001 01011100
00011110 10100100 11110111 11001101 00011010 01110110 00001101 10011000 10001110 01000001
10001001 11100011 00000001 11000000 01100011 11110011 00011100 11010010 10100110 00100011
00011011 01000000 11100011 00011101 00000000 10100011 10011110 00111101 01111011 11010010
00110111 00000111 11011100 10011010 11001101 10100111 01101101 11000001 10001101 01110001
11111011 10110010 00001111 00000011 00111100 11010011 10000000 00000001 11000001 00000011
11110011 00110100 11000111 00111011 10100100 11110110 11001101 00011001 11000001 11100100
01010101 10101001 00110001 01011000 01000110 00000100 01110001 10010111 11100100 11110110
00111101 01101001 01001110 11100010 11111000 11100000 00001100 01110011 01000010 01111101
11111111 00000000 11100111 01000011 11110001 11010011 10101111 10101000 10101010 11100110
10111110 11000000 11000100 01011100 00000010 00111111 01010011 01001101 00111000 11000110
01111010 01101111 00111100 10001010 01000110 00100011 00111101 01001110 00000101 00001000
00001001 11100100 11100100 00011111 01101010 10010110 11101100 00100001 01110000 01001111
00011101 10111011 11010000 11100100 10000011 10000100 00011100 11010011 10011011 01101000
00100000 01101110 11100000 01110010 01111001 11101011 01001100 11011100 01110011 10111000
00011110 00001101 01001010 01001101 00000000 00100110 01010101 01110010 01111001 01111111
01111010 00000000 11111110 00100001 11000101 00011000 11101010 11000111 10011010 00110001
10001100 01110011 11010110 10101110 11010110 01001010 11101000 10110000 00100011 00111100
11110111 00111110 10110100 00000011 10000011 11010111 00111100 01110000 01001101 00100011
00011100 10011110 01111010 01111011 01010011 01110011 10011001 00110001 10011100 00001010
01011101 01001000 00011100 10100100 10101010 11110101 11100111 11011010 10011000 11000001
10110011 11001001 10100101 11001110 01000111 00111101 11101001 10110011 00101110 01100100
00111111 00111110 01110001 11000101 00111111 11000100 10100100 01010011 11010010 10011011
00110001 11000000 01001000 11100111 00011101 11101011 10101010 00000100 10110010 01110000
11011000 00111101 10001000 10101110 01101111 01001100 10000011 11111101 01011010 10111111
01101110 10011100 11010111 01000110 10000100 00001100 00000011 11111001 01110100 10101110
10011010 10010010 11100110 01010110 00000110 00111111 10111000 00100111 11101111 11110110
10100111 01110011 11010000 10001010 01000101 00111101 11110001 01001001 11100110 10101110
01110000 11101101 11110011 11110110 00010101 10000110 10010110 11010101 00010000 00111011
00000011 00111000 11000110 00110001 01001110 11100111 01111111 00000010 10011010 11011001
01100011 11011110 10011100 10111101 00111011 10011010 01011101 01000110 00101011 00011100
00000011 11111110 00110100 10101100 00110011 11001111 01000011 01001101 11000001 00000111
10010001 01001010 10100100 10001110 10110100 11010010 11010100 00000101 01010000 00011011
10001100 01010000 00110001 10000001 10000001 01000010 10110111 00111100 01010001 10111000
10001110 00001110 00110000 01101001 00100110 00100001 11011011 10000000 00111111 01011010
01010101 00000100 10000011 01001100 01101110 01111000 00011100 00011110 11100110 10000000
01001000 11001000 00111111 10100101 00100110 00110001 11111100 10101111 00011011 01101000
00100000 10011110 11110100 00100011 01100011 10100011 01100111 11011000 11010010 00000110
11001001 00111011 10000110 00001101 00110101 10100011 00000001 01000111 00011101 10001001
00010100 01100011 00111000 00111101 00101001 10001101 00100001 11000110 01111011 01010011
11110000 01111101 00110010 01001111 01011010 10110111 10101010 00000000 01101110 10011000
10001100 11110011 11011110 10011111 11001000 00011000 11000111 00111110 11110101 00011011
10110011 00010010 10011000 00100011 00000011 10101111 10111101 00111001 10001011 10011110

11111100 00001110 11010101 00001011 01010000 00011010 00100100 11011101 00100001 00011101
10000101 00111001 10001110 01011100 11110000 01000000 11101110 01101001 10101010 01000001
11111010 11010001 11001110 11101100 11100111 11110000 10101001 11011011 01010000 00001110
10100111 00000011 10100111 10101101 00111011 10010000 00111000 10100110 11100111 10010011
11101010 01111001 10100110 11110011 11011000 11100011 11101011 11011110 10101001 00100000
00011111 11010111 10111110 01101001 00001001 00000100 01110000 00111010 01111010 01010001
10111000 00000001 11000000 10100101 01010011 11000111 10110000 11101001 10001010 10011110
10100000 00101111 11001101 11101101 11111000 11010000 11011000 00101011 10000000 01000010
00001111 01010011 01001000 11000100 00100111 10111001 00110100 11001110 01001111 00000111
00011111 11100001 01000000 11010001 00100011 00101011 00101011 01100000 00011110 10010100
01110011 10011110 01000110 00111111 10101101 00110111 11101110 10101111 01011110 10111110
10111100 11010011 10010111 00100011 10000011 11010011 11010110 10100101 01110111 00101000
01000011 11010011 10011110 00000101 00100010 11111100 10001111 11000110 01101001 01001000
11111100 01111001 11101111 01001000 10100100 11100111 00100110 10101001 11101000 11010000
10010000 10101110 01111000 11001111 00100100 10011110 10011001 10100011 01101010 11100011
00100111 00011001 11110110 10100011 10011110 11010100 01110101 00111100 11010000 11100100
11101110 10110100 00011000 00110001 11000111 01000011 11001101 00111100 00000010 00000000
00011101 00001001 00011101 01101000 01010011 11010100 10011100 01111110 00110100 00110011
01101101 10001100 11100100 11110011 11101101 01000011 10110010 11010100 01001100 00111000
01010001 10001110 11100010 10011010 11000111 00111000 00011101 00111011 10011010 01001110
00110000 00001000 11111100 11101001 01010100 11110010 00000001 11111100 11101010 00110100
10111101 11000010 11100000 01000000 00000000 01110101 10100011 11101111 00010011 11001111
00000000 11010011 10110111 10010110 01100011 11110010 11100000 01010011 01111001 11100110
10101101 00110010 01000111 11100100 01111011 11010010 00010010 00110111 01100000 01110101
00011100 10011010 00111000 11101010 01000101 00001101 10000110 11000110 11001110 10111101
11101010 00011110 10101011 01110010 11000001 10000110 01111110 01100011 11011000 11110001
01001010 00111001 00011001 10100100 11110100 00011000 11100010 10010100 11100000 10001110
00001111 11010110 10011110 11011010 00000000 10000111 11101110 11111111 00000000 00101010
01101000 00100011 01110001 00110100 01110000 01001110 00000001 11000000 11110101 10100111
01100011 00011110 10011100 01111110 10110101 00101110 11111101 10000000 00001111 00100111
00110100 01110001 10011100 01010010 10000011 10000001 11101001 10011010 01100011 10010000
00111000 00000011 00100110 10000110 10000001 00001110 01010001 10010011 11001111 00011110
11110100 00101111 00011101 01101001 10111001 00111000 10100001 01111010 01110011 01010011
10101010 11011000 00011000 00101001 00011001 10100111 01100110 10011010 00111010 01110101
11000101 00011000 00111000 11000000 11100110 10000100 10011011 00011000 01110001 11011100
01110001 11101101 01001110 11000111 00011011 10111010 01111011 01010001 10000011 11100101
01100001 00001111 00100111 10101001 10100110 00010000 01111001 11001011 00010011 01001010
11011101 11000100 00111101 11001000 11000000 11001111 00111110 11010100 11010101 00111100
10011100 10001110 10110100 00110011 01100111 00101010 00000111 11100010 01101000 00000101
01001001 11100111 10100101 01010101 11010101 11000000 00110011 11011010 10000100 11001111
01111010 01001111 00110000 00110111 00101001 11010011 00111101 11101000 00100111 00111000
11111101 01101001 10111101 01000001 00110001 01111000 00001000 00110011 11111001 01010000
11101101 11001111 00111101 00101001 00011000 10011100 11110100 10100011 00011100 01110101
11101011 11101011 01001111 10011010 11011010 00001100 00011011 10110000 11001110 01000101
00101110 01000000 11001001 11101011 11101100 01111011 11010010 01100100 10000100 10100100
11001111 00111100 11111010 11111010 11010100 11011101 01110100 00011000 11010110 01101110
00010011 00000011 00100101 11111011 00001010 01110000 11111001 01001001 11000001 00111000
11101110 00001101 00011101 11110010 01111000 11110111 10100110 00000001 10010010 01000010
00010011 11010110 10011100 10010001 00010111 00000111 11001001 01100000 11000100 10010011
10001110 10000010 10011001 01110001 00001010 11001111 00011001 10001110 01101000 11110111
10100111 01111100 10001010 10011001 10111000 00110101 00011011 10110011 01100100 01010100
11110010 11110100 00011010 01100111 00001111 11100010 00011111 00001011 00011000 10000001
10111000 10110000 00011011 11010000 01110010 01100011 11111111 00000000 00001010 11100101
11111001 00000111 00000111 10001111 01011010 11110110 00010110 00011001 11100100 10010011
11111101 00101011 10010111 11110001 00111111 10000111 00000101 11010000 00110111 00110110
00000011 00010011 10001110 01001100 01111101 10011110 10110010 10110101 10001110 10001010
01010101 01101101 10100011 00111000 01110000 00000000 10100101 00100111 00011100 11010010
00010000 01100011 10010000 10100011 10000010 10001110 10111101 01000001 11101101 01000001
11000110 00101000 01001001 01110100 01000111 01101010 10011010 01101000 01111000 01101010
01011100 10011111 11100001 11111100 11101010 10110011 10111110 11001111 01101010 01101011
01001000 01000111 01010011 11110100 10100101 01101011 11001010 11100011 00101101 10000110
11101101 11111001 11010011 00111100 11010010 10111100 00000001 01010000 10011001 00110010
00111000 00111000 10100110 00110011 00011110 10100100 11110010 00101001 11110010 11011111
01100001 10010111 00010110 01011110 01000111 00111111 01011010 10010110 00111001 10110111
00011100 00001010 10100010 10010010 00001110 10010101 01101010 11011001 10000000 00111000
00010101 10101110 10001011 01001011 00010010 11101101 11010100 11010110 10110110 10011011
01101000 11011011 10001010 11010110 10110110 01100010 01110110 00000001 11000110 01111101
01111001 10101110 01110111 01110001 00111111 01110000 11110001 01011011 00011010 01100100
11011011 10001000 00011101 11000101 01100000 11010101 10011000 10001101 11000100 11001101
00111011 10000010 00111000 10101000 11010000 10011110 00101010 01000110 11001110 01110000
00001110 00101011 00111001 11011011 01110000 00011010 01000000 00111001 00011111 11001110
10101010 11001000 10100111 00100100 11010101 10100111 11110101 00110101 00000011 10010011
11001111 00111000 00010100 10010011 11101110 01001011 01000110 01111101 11000001 11001111

```
00100010 10101000 01001110 00110011 11011011 11111111 00000000 10101111 01011010 00010010
01110100 11000001 10101010 01110010 10101111 10111001 00111111 10100101 01011111 00110011
10110110 11100000 01100011 01011101 10000000 01000110 00110001 11000111 10101110 00101011
00010010 11110110 00100001 11001001 11110100 10101110 10001110 01111000 01001011 01111101
00101011 00101010 01111000 01111111 00011111 01001010 11011110 00010011 11010010 11001000
10010111 10101010 00111001 00111011 10000100 00100011 00100011 11110101 10101100 11011011
10111000 01110010 10000000 00000001 10000011 11010111 00111110 10110101 11010010 01011100
11011010 01100001 11001111 01011110 01111011 00011010 10100011 00101101 10101001 11000111
00001010 01110001 01011110 10000101 00101001 01011000 11100110 10010100 00011001 11001010
01001101 00001001 11110011 10000001 11000001 00100011 11011010 10100101 10000111 00100000
10010011 11010100 00001010 11011010 10111100 10110001 00100010 00101101 11001000 00111010
01110111 10101100 10011001 10100001 01101000 10111110 01010000 00111001 11110111 10101110
11111000 01010100 01010011 01010110 10111001 11001110 11100001 01100010 00110111 11000001
10010000 11100011 11010011 10110101 00110111 00000001 10000111 00011001 00011110 11010101
00011111 00111111 01111000 11110001 11001110 00101010 11000100 01110001 11100000 01110000
00111111 11111010 11110101 01001101 10100100 00001011 01010011 10101010 11111000 01111001
10010101 10111011 10111011 01001101 10111100 10110100 01100000 10000010 01111101 10101011
11010000 00000111 00100011 10101111 00110101 11100111 00111110 00001000 10010100 11000001
10101101 00100010 11100100 00000001 00101000 00101001 11001000 11101010 01101011 11010001
01111010 00001100 11110111 10101111 00011011 00011110 10111101 11111110 01100100 01111010
01011000 01111111 10000100 01100011 00001111 01111010 00011000 11110001 11001001 10100100
01110010 01001000 11000000 00011000 11110111 10101000 10011000 11110110 00110101 11001001
00001001 00101011 11110011 01110100 00111010 01101100 00000001 10000000 11001001 11101011
10011111 01011010 01010101 10010000 01010101 01111001 01011000 10001100 11100111 10010011
11011010 10100000 11110011 01001111 10101101 01101100 10101110 11011000 10011010 00110100
00111100 11100100 00000100 01100011 00000111 00110101 01100010 11011110 01010101 11001101
01110011 11001111 01110100 01000111 00000100 10001010 10110001 10100011 11001001 00101101
11010101 11100000 01010100 11001110 00000111 00100110 10100110 01101001 11101110 10010000
10110100 01000111 01011011 00001110 00001000 11110110 11101101 01001111 01100011 10001111
10100101 00101101 10100100 01100101 01000110 11010010 00111001 10100010 11100111 11100101
00010101 10001100 01110111 10111001 00100111 00111111 10101101 01001011 10001000 11011100
10011110 10010101 11000100 11011110 10110001 00101101 11000111 11111111 00000000 10101110
10111010 11101101 01101101 10111000 00100000 01110011 10011110 10010101 11000111 11011100
00000001 10001100 00001110 10100111 10111101 01110111 01010010 10110100 10011101 11101100
00101010 10011010 00100010 10111111 01011010 01110110 00111010 11100100 01110011 01000000
00011001 11101011 01010010 00001100 01100111 11110100 10101110 10011000 00111101 01101100
01100010 10010101 11001010 11100101 01001001 00111000 10101000 11110000 01111010 11100010
10101110 11100000 00011110 10011101 01101001 10011110 01011110 11100001 11010010 10110100
01111110 01101100 00101100 01010110 00000000 00110001 11111111 00000000 00011010 10010101
01000000 10101001 10001010 00000001 10011111 01011100 01010001 10110100 00000001 11000101
01100111 11001111 00010111 01110111 01110010 10111001 00111010 10001101 01000000 00111010
11110111 10100111 00110011 00001101 10011001 10100011 10001110 00000000 11111100 01101011
00111111 01010110 10111011 01011011 01101011 01100011 10110101 10110001 00100001 11100001
01000110 00101001 11010010 10001011 01101100 01110011 11110111 01010101 11011001 10010011
10101101 01011110 01111001 11010011 01111001 01000000 11100101 00100011 11101110 00111010
00010011 01011001 11011101 00000111 11011101 00111001 10101000 11000011 01100101 10111001
11001110 01001111 10101101 01001000 00111110 11110111 00111100 11010111 10100100 10101101
00010011 11001011 10010100 10111001 11011101 11000111 10001111 01010011 11101011 11011110
10100101 10000100 01100100 11010100 01100100 01100111 10101001 10101001 00100001 00100100
00001110 10011100 10011110 11110100 10011011 10111000 01110101 00100111 01000011 10001111
11111111 00000000 01011101 01011001 10001011 00000100 10011101 11100111 10001100 01110000
00001101 01010100 00000011 11101010 01101010 11000010 11100000 10001100 11110111 11110100
10101100 10001101 00001011 01100000 11110100 00011100 01110100 00010101 00100010 11110101
11101001 01010101 11100010 11000110 00110011 11101011 01010011 10100011 00011100 01010110
00010010 01101110 11100110 10010000 01100100 10101010 01001110 01000110 01101010 01011100
11111101 11000101 11110111 11111110 01110101 01011010 00101001 00110001 00100110 00101010
01110001 11001001 11001001 10101001 01111010 00111011 00110010 10101110 01011000 11111011
10100111 10001111 11000110 10100100 01101100 00010001 11001111 10101101 01000010 00001001
11001111 01011010 01111000 11100111 00011101 01111010 11010100 00110111 10101110 10011011
00010111 10100001 00101000 11101001 11110100 10100111 10000001 11000111 00011101 00111101
01001101 01000110 00001000 11100111 00011101 00101001 11101010 11000011 00011101 00001110
01101001 00101111 00110001 10110000 11001001 11110100 10101001 00010000 11111010 00001110
01101010 00110101 00100111 00111110 10111111 10001101 00001100 11011000 00111111 11010110
10100110 01001001 10000001 01111010 11011110 01100010 00001000 01101101 11000110 00110111
00000111 10000010 00001111 00110101 11101000 00011110 00011011 11110001 00011000 10111101
00011111 01100111 10111111 01100100 10001110 11100111 00011000 01011001 00110001 11000100
10111111 11111101 01111010 11110011 00100000 11000100 00011100 11100110 10101100 01000101
00111111 00011001 00111001 00001110 00001110 01000111 00111101 00101011 00001001 01010010
10110011 10111011 00110011 10011100 00010011 00111101 10010101 00011011 10001110 00010111
00000000 00001110 10100110 10000001 11000000 00000001 11001001 00111100 11111010 11010111
00011111 11100001 11101111 00010011 00010011 11100101 11011011 11101010 00101100 01011100
00000001 10000101 10010100 10011110 10011111 01011010 11101011 11010011 11111101 01011000
00101001 11001010 00010001 11000001 00011101 11101010 01011101 11001100 00111001 00011010
```

```
11011100 01011100 10000000 11100111 00000011 10010011 11101001 01000111 00111110 01011011
10010011 10001100 11110100 00010100 00111110 01001100 01000100 00010010 00111000 11100111
00100010 10010001 01001000 00111001 11001000 11111100 11101001 01000101 01011111 01110001
00001001 10111011 00001011 10000001 11000001 00111101 11101001 01111000 00000011 00000000
11110011 11011110 10000110 00100011 01101001 11001001 11000000 10100110 00101111 00101011
10011100 01100000 01010011 10111111 01100000 00000110 00011101 10111011 00011110 10110100
11110101 00111001 11011000 00111010 01100010 10001110 01111110 01001110 00111000 00100110
10001111 00110000 00101010 01001000 11000011 10001111 01000011 11010110 10100111 01011011
10000000 10011001 01101110 01000000 00100111 11011110 10001100 10010000 00110000 00001111
00111000 11101010 01101001 10001010 11011111 00101010 00010011 11001111 10111111 10101101
00111101 10000001 00000111 10101110 00111101 11001101 01010111 10100000 10110110 01100100
01100110 01000000 01001000 01010001 11111000 11010001 11111100 01011111 11101101 01010011
10110001 10010011 10010001 11000000 11101110 01101001 00010111 10011100 10010000 00110001
01010110 10011011 11101010 00110001 00111001 00111100 00100110 01001001 00110100 10111101
00000110 01011111 10000011 11101001 01000110 01000001 00000000 11100111 00011110 11110100
10001101 00011000 01011111 10010100 10011100 11100011 10100111 10111001 10100101 00100101
01110001 01011111 10110000 11001100 01100101 11111010 11010011 11011011 10010011 11000001
11111100 01101001 10000000 10010000 01111101 11001101 00101011 00001111 01011100 00011111
01110001 01010010 10001001 00010011 00010001 10101100 01011001 00100011 10100001 11000111
11010100 11010001 11010001 00001110 01111000 00000010 10010011 10000000 10100100 10010011
11011111 00011000 10100101 01111100 01111001 01111000 11011111 10000011 01010111 11010010
11000011 01010111 00010000 10011100 00001111 01110011 11000110 00110011 01001011 11000001
00011011 10001001 11000110 00101001 00001000 00011111 01111011 11110010 10100110 10110111
11001101 10001100 11110101 10100001 11011001 00001111 11010100 00111000 00101000 01011011
10110101 00100110 01000001 00011100 01110100 10100100 11001010 11100100 10001110 10100011
00110100 11100110 11111111 00000000 11000111 01101001 00110110 10111011 00001100 01000010
00001001 01011110 00101001 10111011 10111111 11001110 00101001 11001101 01000110 11111101
10111100 01100110 10011101 10011111 01000000 00100100 11010010 11100010 01101101 10111110
01101001 11000111 00111101 00001110 00101011 01011111 10101011 00000010 01000111 00011110
10110101 00001010 00001100 00000000 10100000 11110100 00011101 00101001 11101000 00110010
01110010 01101011 01011001 01101010 11101111 01110010 01101110 01001011 10011110 01110011
11111100 10101000 11011011 10010011 10010010 00101001 00010011 11101001 01010010 01100100
10001111 01101010 01010110 11101110 00100001 00000000 11111001 11111001 01101010 10010011
00111000 00011100 11010100 00101100 01001000 00100011 00011101 00101001 11101010 01111000
11100110 10100111 01000000 00011111 11110101 00110100 10101010 01111001 11001101 01000111
11000111 01011110 10100110 10011111 11010011 10100110 00000101 00101011 10001000 01011110
00111011 01010001 11010101 10111110 01110011 11110100 00000110 10011001 10001100 11110010
01111111 01001010 01111111 01010010 00111001 10100010 11101100 01100010 11110000 01001110
00111010 01010001 10000110 11001111 10101000 10100100 01010010 00111010 10011010 01011100
11101101 00111110 11111110 10010100 11011010 01011011 10110000 00010000 01110011 10011010
01111111 00011101 00101001 10111011 10001001 11100011 11001010 00100011 11011110 10010011
01110000 10001111 10101111 01011110 11000010 10000111 11100100 00111011 00001111 11101101
10010000 00000110 00101000 01000110 00101010 00110010 01000110 01011110 10011001 11100111
10101010 10011110 10001110 01011100 11111111 00000000 01110110 10010101 01001111 00011101
11111111 00000000 00011110 10110100 10101100 11000100 00001011 11110111 10110000 01000000
00011000 11101101 01001111 11110011 00001001 00111100 00000000 01111110 10110100 10011000
00011001 00111001 11101111 11011110 10011010 11100001 10100011 01000000 01111101 01101001
00100110 10010010 01100000 00011101 00000110 01001111 01010011 11010110 10011101 11010111
11011010 10011010 10000011 00000011 00100100 00011100 11010000 11000111 00100111 00111000
11100010 10000101 10110110 10100000 00111111 00111110 11111001 11111010 11010100 01100001
11001011 01100111 01111010 11101100 10100111 10101110 01111010 10011110 10011101 11101001
10011001 11100000 10000011 11010011 10110101 00101001 00101101 01000000 01111010 01100000
01111111 00010000 11100110 10010111 00001101 10111100 01111010 01110100 11100111 10100101
00110000 00010101 11000111 00101011 10010011 11110100 10100100 11101010 01110111 00010110
11100111 10110010 11100111 10100101 00111101 01111110 00010001 10100010 01001110 00110011
11000000 00111100 01010010 01100001 01001111 00101110 01110001 11001101 00110111 01110110
01001000 01010011 11000000 00111101 11101001 11001101 10001111 11100000 00111101 01000110
00101010 01111010 10001000 01011100 10001100 01101110 01010010 00001110 00111101 10101001
00001000 11001010 10010011 10010000 00001001 10100000 01111100 10110100 00001111 10011010
10101011 10010101 00001110 11100000 10100000 10001100 11100100 11010010 11101110 00000100
10011100 11010001 11010100 10001110 00000111 10111001 10100001 11111001 11100011 11010100
11010110 01101110 11010111 11010000 01000010 10101000 11000111 00100011 10001100 11110110
11001101 00100110 00001110 00000111 00110100 10011001 00100000 11111010 11100010 10010100
10011101 11011110 11010100 01101010 11001011 00010001 10000110 01000111 01010001 01001110
11000110 01001101 00110111 10010101 11000111 00011111 10001110 01101001 01110010 00001101
00110001 01101110 00101110 01000001 00110100 11100101 11101011 11001000 00010100 11011111
00110000 01100100 01010010 01101110 11110010 11000011 10011110 10100010 10010101 11010101
10110100 00011000 10111101 01100100 00111100 11100101 00111011 01010011 10011000 10011110
10000111 10001111 01111010 01101110 00111000 11000110 01101000 01010011 10110111 00000000
11110111 11111101 00101000 01100000 00111011 01101110 01000000 00011001 11101011 01001100
01011100 00000011 11000001 10100101 11000110 00011011 10010011 10011100 11010001 10001111
10011100 00001110 10010100 10110101 10110110 10000011 00001110 00001000 11000110 01111001
11110100 10100001 10000001 11100100 11110001 01001001 11111110 11101000 11100100 11110101
```

10100111 11100111 01101111 01001110 01101000 10010101 10010000 10000110 10101000 00000100
01100111 00011111 10000101 00001010 01001111 01010011 01000010 11100100 11111011 01010000
10100000 11100100 11110111 10100011 01110000 00011100 00000111 10101101 00110101 10000110
01110011 01000111 01000011 11111101 00101001 00011000 10010010 01110001 01000011 01011101
10000000 01010010 01001111 01000001 01000000 00011000 11101001 11001101 00100011 01110000
00111110 11110001 11001001 00111101 00110001 01001010 11011100 00010010 00110001 01001010
11111010 10001100 00111010 10111110 00000111 00100010 10011100 11000111 11101001 11001101
01000111 11010000 01110111 11111100 00111011 11010010 11100011 10100000 00010100 00100100
11000100 00101011 00011100 10000000 00110011 01000010 10000000 01111000 00100100 11111101
01101001 00111101 01000101 00011101 00001000 11110100 10100001 00111011 00001100 01010001
10010111 00000111 00011001 11100011 11010110 10000011 10110100 10000011 10010000 01111000
11110100 10100110 10110110 01001000 11111010 11010001 11010000 00010001 11101101 01000100
10011000 00000111 00011101 00111001 10100111 00001100 01100011 11111100 01101001 10100011
11101110 11110100 11111010 11010010 11100111 00100110 10010000 00000111 00011001 10100011
11011011 10110000 10100110 01110110 11000111 01111111 01011010 01110010 10110001 01101111
10010100 00001111 10101101 00101110 01100001 00110001 01000001 11001000 11100111 10000001
01001001 11000111 01000001 01000010 00010010 10100100 11101100 11000110 01111101 11101001
10101011 10010011 10011100 11110000 01111101 01101000 01101011 01010000 01000011 11010111
10100111 11001101 11010111 11010010 10010001 01111001 00000111 01100000 11100011 11011110
10011010 01111010 00000001 01000011 00011101 11101011 10000011 11111000 00001010 10100100
11110100 10110000 11000001 10001000 11000110 11101100 11100111 00110100 10011001 00011101
00001001 11111001 11001000 11001110 00110001 01000011 01110011 11000111 01100001 01000111
10111001 00011100 11010100 11011011 10101000 00001111 00011001 11011010 01001101 00110011
00001010 01111000 01100001 10011100 01010000 11001100 00010101 01011100 11110111 11110100
10100110 00011100 01100000 10001100 10001110 01001101 01001110 11001111 01110001 01101010
01100011 01101011 11011110 00011101 10000111 01010101 01010011 00100010 10010100 10001010
11101111 00011111 11101011 00110001 11010111 11101011 01011110 01111001 10101010 11011000
11011101 01101001 10110011 01111001 01010111 01110001 00010100 01110011 11001000 00111101
10001000 10101111 01011110 10010011 00000001 11110000 00111010 10011110 10100010 10101011
11011101 11011001 11000001 01111011 00010011 10100101 11011100 01001001 00101000 00111110
10100011 10100111 11010010 10001110 01000011 01101000 01010101 01110000 00111100 01110011
11001100 11001001 11001001 00011111 10001101 00101011 00010000 01000111 01011010 11101010
10110101 10111111 00000111 11001111 01101111 00010001 10011110 11000011 00110011 01000110
00111010 11000111 11011100 01010111 00100001 00100000 01101000 11100100 00101010 11100000
10000010 10000111 00000100 00010001 11001000 10101001 00111010 11100001 01010110 00101100
10010000 10110000 00000011 00100011 10100111 10111101 01000100 11010010 11110010 00111101
00101001 10001110 01110010 00111111 01011010 10001100 11001001 10011100 00001010 10111101
11001101 10001011 00101000 11011100 11100110 10101101 11011011 10110110 01011111 00011111
10101101 01100111 10100011 01111100 11111000 00110101 10100001 01101011 00100000 11011100
00000010 10011110 10110100 11100110 10111001 10110100 01000100 11011100 11010011 10110110
01011100 11110001 10001100 11010110 10100101 10010100 01100110 00101001 01000110 00111011
11111011 11010110 01101101 10010111 11001011 11011011 00011111 10001101 01101011 01110001
10001000 11011000 00001110 01101011 10010110 01001101 10100101 01101011 10000011 11010100
11011000 01000110 11001010 11111010 01010100 10011100 01110001 11101011 10001110 01101010
10101100 00110010 01110001 10011100 01010101 10000010 01111000 10100111 00101101 10000100
00100011 01111110 01110101 00000100 10110101 01100001 01111010 11010100 01101111 10011100
11110100 10101100 11101101 01110111 10100011 00000010 10101100 10000000 00110111 01101110
00101010 10100011 11000111 10011111 11101011 01010111 11011100 01110101 11110101 10101000
00011000 00001100 01100111 00110100 11101100 10011110 10000100 01011000 11001011 10011001
01110010 01101010 10011100 10010000 01110101 11001110 00111101 10101011 01110001 11100011
00011000 11100100 01010101 01111001 00100010 11110100 00011100 11010110 10110100 11111101
11010001 00011100 11110101 11001101 10101000 00111101 10111011 01110111 10101100 11110111
10110100 00000000 11100010 10111010 01101011 10001000 01111001 11001001 00010101 01001101
10100000 00001100 11011011 10101011 01100101 01011110 01001101 11101000 00101011 00011000
01011111 01100100 00000101 01001010 10111000 11001000 10101100 10101011 11111101 00101100
00011100 10010100 00010101 11011000 01111001 00111001 00111000 11000101 01000011 00111101
10101000 11101011 10110100 01010000 10101011 10111010 01101110 11000100 00111010 01110111
00111100 11010110 11110110 11001100 01000010 01000001 00100011 00000100 11110101 10101011
00110000 01011010 10000011 00011000 00100000 01100111 11010000 11010111 01010111 10101010
11101001 01100001 11010111 00111011 01110000 00111011 00011010 11000100 01001011 01110011
00001110 01010100 00001100 00011111 01111111 01001010 11101111 10100111 10001001 11100111
01000110 01011110 11001010 11000101 01001011 00010000 01101101 00101111 01100000 10010100
11100111 11110111 01101101 10011010 11110100 11110101 00100001 10010100 00110000 00100000
10000011 11101001 01011110 01110100 11000000 00111000 00000011 10010000 01101011 10110010
11010000 01101110 00001100 11011010 01111010 00000011 11001011 11000111 11110010 00010011
01011001 01100010 10111101 11100101 01111001 00011101 00111000 01111101 00110100 01100110
10000001 11100110 10100010 10010100 00001100 01110011 11010110 10100100 11011101 10010011
01010001 01001000 01000000 11001111 01110011 01011100 00110111 01000111 01001110 10100101
01011011 10000011 10000100 11110111 10101100 11101011 10001001 01110000 00101011 01000010
01010000 00011011 11110001 10101010 10010011 11011011 11111110 11110000 01110001 11011111
10101110 00101011 01101010 01110110 10110111 01110010 00011111 01100011 00100100 11101110
10010001 10111110 01001100 11110101 10101110 10111011 11000010 01110000 00000101 10001010
01001001 01001000 11100111 10100110 01101011 00111110 11011110 11010001 01010000 00010011

10001110 10111101 01101011 01001010 11001110 01111111 10110010 00101110 00000010 10010010
00001111 01011100 01010101 11010100 10010010 01110001 10111000 10110111 01100111 01001011
00001000 00000100 11110101 10101010 11111010 10010011 01100001 01110000 10000111 10001010
11001110 10110000 11010101 00100010 10010100 10010000 00011011 00100100 01110000 01101010
01001011 10011011 10100101 01111100 11110110 00000011 10101111 01111010 11100110 01101001
01101100 10001011 11101010 01100010 01101010 10000000 10010100 00100111 00011100 11010111
00100111 01111000 00001010 11001010 00111000 11100011 00110101 11010110 11101010 00110011
10100001 10001100 11110010 00110001 11101011 01011100 10110101 11111001 00001101 00100111
00011101 00001111 00110101 11010001 01001001 01001001 01001010 11000100 01010100 01010111
00110011 10100100 01100011 10011110 00111110 10010101 00101100 01001100 01000100 01100011
10111101 00100011 10101110 00000110 01111111 01011010 00100010 11100001 01101011 10110110
00001101 00100011 00011000 01101000 11110101 00100110 00000000 11100111 10000011 10011010
00110001 10000011 10011101 11011100 01111011 01010000 10100011 00000111 11011110 10011110
01110000 00001111 01001010 01110010 10010010 11101010 01101011 01101110 11000010 00010101
11101110 00001110 01101000 00111100 11110001 10011010 01101100 10000111 00000011 00000010
10100011 11001001 01011010 11000110 11010110 11010101 00000000 10001110 11111000 11101011
10000000 01111101 11101011 10010011 11010101 00101110 01001101 11010101 11010011 10010001
11000010 00000011 10000001 01011011 00111010 11001101 11001001 10000010 00000011 10000011
11110011 00011111 11101011 01011100 11011111 01011100 00011100 11111101 01111110 10110101
11011111 10000110 10100111 01101111 01111001 10011100 00111000 10011010 10111101 00000111
00101111 00000111 10011110 00101001 11000000 11100000 10011110 11010100 11010110 01100001
10000001 01001011 11010100 00011110 00111111 00011010 11101010 10111101 11001110 01000001
11101010 01000111 11010011 00110101 00101010 10010110 11101111 11010010 10100000 11100011
10001111 01101111 01011110 01101001 00110111 00001100 00001100 10011100 00011111 01001010
10011011 00001100 10111010 10000101 01110000 00001001 00111100 10011010 10010010 00100011
10001110 01001001 11000000 00110101 01001100 01001010 00111000 11101010 01110001 11011010
10100100 11110011 10000000 01101100 01100000 01100011 10111000 10101100 11100100 10001011
10111110 10000101 11110101 01111100 01110101 11110100 11101101 01010010 00000111 00100101
00110000 00111011 11010101 00001000 11100110 00000011 11101111 00010000 01000101 01001100
00100101 00011000 00011000 00111100 11010010 11100101 11101100 01011010 01100101 11010101
11101011 10001110 00000111 11010100 11010100 10101010 01110000 01110001 01010100 11111100
11000000 01000000 11110101 11101110 01101010 01000100 10010111 00111110 11000111 11010110
10110011 01101001 11101100 11001101 00010011 00101111 10100001 10100111 11100110 10101001
10100100 10000000 11110111 11001111 10111101 01001100 10010010 11100111 00111000 10101100
10111101 10011011 01001100 10100100 11101110 01011011 10001000 10000001 11111000 11010011
11010111 10000010 01101010 10101110 11101110 10000011 10001010 10010000 00110111 11100001
01011001 11011001 10100110 01101011 11010000 10011101 10001110 00000111 10110101 00101110
01111000 11101011 11010110 10100010 11011100 00001000 11000110 00101001 01010100 11100111
10101001 10100100 10011011 00010000 11111100 10000000 00001000 00011101 01111110 10110100
10000001 10001000 00111001 11101110 00111010 10001010 01101111 10110000 11101011 01001000
01111010 11100000 11010011 01101101 00110101 01110110 00100111 11011000 10111110 10010111
00011100 10001110 01111111 00011010 11101001 00110100 00111111 00010000 01001101 01100111
10001000 11100100 01101111 00110110 00001100 00001100 10001110 10000111 11110000 00110101
11000111 11111001 10000000 00001111 01111111 01101010 10110000 10010010 01110010 00101011
10011010 10100010 01010110 00001110 01011110 11100111 10110000 11011010 01011110 01000101
01110111 01101111 00011100 10010110 10101101 10010100 00111100 10011111 01101111 10101101
01011000 00111111 10010111 11110101 10101111 00110000 11010001 11110101 01001001 11101100
10100101 00001111 01101110 11011000 11111110 11110010 11110110 00111111 01010001 01011110
10000001 10100100 11101010 00010000 11101010 00110110 11111110 01101100 00111000 11011110
00000111 11001100 10111101 11010110 10100001 00101011 01101000 11001110 01101001 01000010
11011010 10010111 10001110 00001110 01110011 11111001 01010000 01001011 00110001 00100000
01100000 01100011 11110100 10100110 01100011 11110011 10100111 10110110 00011011 10001100
11100011 11111010 11010101 10111101 01010101 10001001 00000101 00100100 10010001 10011110
10000011 10110101 00110100 11000111 10010100 00111100 11110101 00110100 11100011 10111000
11110000 00110001 11101111 11000101 00110101 01000001 00100111 11010100 10011110 01101010
01010011 11010111 01010000 00000111 00011011 01001000 00000111 00011000 00011101 10110011
01001000 10100111 01110010 10000010 01111111 00101010 01010010 00000001 10010011 00100011
00111011 11110011 10010110 00100110 10010010 01100010 01011010 01001110 00111000 00011001
11101011 01010100 11011011 01111011 00100001 01111010 10001000 01111001 00000100 00011111
11001010 10010101 00011011 00100000 11100100 01110001 10001110 10010100 11000111 01111111
10010101 11111101 11111000 11001101 00111101 01110010 11010010 00011110 10000011 11010010
10010111 01011101 00001001 00011001 11001110 11000011 10011100 00000001 11011000 01010000
01111011 01110001 11001111 01111010 01111011 00010010 10101000 01110001 11001111 00110100
10011001 11001011 11111011 10011110 10011110 11010100 11101111 10100001 01100011 00001110
01110111 11110000 01101001 01011011 10100111 01001111 10101101 00110111 00100110 01001001
00110111 00000110 00111011 00111010 01100011 00010100 00110001 01110010 00001000 10001100
00001100 10010011 10010010 01111101 10101001 01101000 10110110 00000000 00111011 01110011
10000010 00101001 10100100 00101110 11110010 01001001 00011001 00111101 10000101 00011001
00000110 01001110 00001111 00110100 00110110 00010100 11110011 11101001 01001110 11101101
00101101 10001001 11101010 00100010 11110010 01001001 00100110 10000011 11010011 10011100
01100010 10000101 11100100 01100111 00111101 11111010 11010011 11111001 11101011 11000110
00001101 00101011 10100111 10101011 01100101 00001100 11011011 10110100 00001110 10011100
11111111 00000000 00101010 00011000 11100100 01100000 00001010 01010111 00111000 00111000

0000011 0010100 1111011 0011010 1001110 1010111 0111001 1101011 1011110 0011111
0101111 1010110 0000010 0101111 0100011 1011110 0010011 0011110 0000010 0011010
1001001 0000011 1111001 1010100 0101011 1001000 1101001 0001111 1000110 0010001
0000110 0110010 0110110 0111010 1110001 0011110 0111100 1010011 0010100 1101101
1110011 1010111 0011110 0010101 0010010 0011100 1110100 1101011 1101111 1001111
1001111 1001001 1010111 0100110 0110110 0110111 1010000 0100100 1000010 1110011
1010010 0011101 0111000 0000011 1010111 0110101 0001111 1000101 1001001 1101010
1111011 1100110 0100100 1011100 0000000 1001000 1101001 1000111 1000100 0000100
0001101 1101010 1110001 0011110 1010100 1110010 0000011 1100111 0010011 1101000
0000101 0110101 1100100 1010110 1001001 1100100 1010011 0010100 1110111 1001111
1100001 1010011 1010110 1000000 0101010 0001100 1110011 0001010 0010100 0011110
1110000 1110010 0111101 1101001 1000110 1110010 1001111 1101001 1000010 1111101
1110001 1000110 1000000 0011011 0110001 1010111 0100101 0111111 0010011 1010000
1100011 1011110 0010001 1111000 0011111 0111001 1001101 0011011 0111111 0111011
1000000 0101010 1001110 1011010 0000000 0101010 1101101 0000111 0011100 1111011
0011010 0000001 0111000 0000011 0111111 0101101 0011001 1000010 1100100 0011010
0110010 0001010 1110100 1101011 1010010 0110011 1101100 0001001 0010101 0000110
0000010 0000000 1111110 0110100 1000101 0100000 0010010 0001001 1001011 1111010
0001010 1100001 0000100 0100110 0000111 1100101 1001001 0011000 0101010 0110010
0110000 0000000 1110110 0111101 1101001 1011101 0110110 0100010 1011100 0101000
0100111 0000111 1100111 0100110 0010011 1011111 0111100 0001010 1101110 0110011
1001000 1100011 1010110 0010011 1001110 0000100 0111000 1000100 0010011 1100111
1110100 0101101 1110100 0101001 0110001 1111001 1100111 0000011 1111110 1111011
1100110 0010101 0000111 0111001 0010100 1100100 1100111 1011010 0010011 1110111
0111100 1010100 0101101 1000100 0101111 0000101 0110010 1001001 0010100 0111001
1000111 1101010 1101011 0011111 1111110 1001101 0001010 1011000 0110101 0101001
0110101 0101000 0001110 0111001 1000111 1011100 0010011 1000111 0000001 0111000
0100110 0010010 0010111 0010001 1000001 1101111 1001010 0100100 1111011 1010011
0010000 0101011 0100001 1101000 1000111 1001010 0000101 0100010 1101110 0111110
0011001 0100100 1101100 1110100 1000111 1100011 1001110 1000011 0000100 0100111
0111000 0111101 1111001 0100111 0111010 0011000 0011000 0000100 0010000 1100110
0010101 0000110 1011100 0000101 0011000 1001110 0100100 1010010 0110001 0100100
1100000 0001100 1100011 0111101 0111101 1001111 1001000 0000101 1100101 1110000
0001010 1101001 1100110 0001110 1111100 1010010 1100011 0000100 0010010 1111001
0110101 1110111 1101110 1011000 1110001 0010000 0111010 0001010 1101011 1100011
0100011 1011111 0011010 1110110 1101100 1110101 1000111 0010100 1110001 0001100
0001100 1101111 0111110 0110101 0110010 1111101 0001000 0000000 1111001 1110101
0111110 0100111 0111101 0011100 0001111 1100010 1111001 1001111 1101010 0011100
0010000 1000001 1001110 1110011 1001101 1011101 0110100 1100100 0101110 1011111
0111101 0001010 1111011 0000000 1111100 0010010 0110010 0111111 0100011 1001001
0010000 0111000 1110101 0111101 0101001 1010011 0101100 0110010 1111000 0110100
0001110 1011000 0011100 1101101 1000110 0111000 1001101 0111101 1001011 0010111
1110000 1000101 0011000 1001111 1011010 0000001 1011010 0111010 1110011 1101111
1001000 1110010 1110001 0110111 0111000 0111101 1101010 1010101 0101110 0101011
0001010 1000100 1101110 0011110 0111110 1100110 0010011 0101111 0111101 0000101
1001110 1111101 0000101 0101010 0001101 0100011 0110101 0101011 1011001 0001100
1010100 1101011 1010110 0010000 1110001 1000010 1110010 0001001 0000011 0010100
0011000 1111100 0101000 0110011 1011100 1001100 1010111 0111100 1100111 0100000
1111110 1110100 0111001 1000110 0111011 1010010 1110000 1000000 0001111 0011110
0111001 0100111 1100011 0100011 1110110 0111101 0101001 0001100 1101111 1111011
1010100 0101000 1000111 0100000 1110100 1110111 0100100 1100010 1111011 1110100
0100100 1100001 1001000 0111001 0100111 0010100 0011011 1100010 0110000 1101100
0110000 0010000 0110001 0000011 0000111 0100101 0100110 1001001 0100001 1000111
0111011 0111111 0011101 0101110 1000111 1001111 0001100 0001111 1001100 1010010
1001101 1011110 1000011 0000101 1111100 0001101 0001100 1011000 1000000 1100100
1100011 0101101 0100011 0010001 1101011 1110101 0110100 1100000 0001110 0010100
0111110 1100000 0010100 0100000 1100000 1010011 1010100 0010000 1110000 0111011
1010010 0110110 1000111 0011111 0101101 0110100 1111011 0000000 0101011 1110000
1110010 0110001 1000011 0011100 1010001 0000001 0000011 1001000 0111000 0111100
1100110 0011011 1010111 0011000 0100111 0000001 1101000 1101001 0001010 1110001
1010111 1110001 0100011 1110001 1100110 1110100 0111110 0010100 0001111 0001100
1100011 0111101 1001110 1111010 0100001 0001111 1101101 0011100 1110001 1000001
1100001 0110011 0111000 1101101 1001101 1101110 0110000 0111101 1101000 1011110
0000101 1001000 1000011 0011100 1110100 1000101 0111011 0100000 0011110 0111101
1111011 1010011 1011000 0010000 0100100 0011110 0111101 0111101 1101001 0110010
0111000 0011000 1100100 1010010 1111010 0000000 0011001 0111000 1000010 0111100
0010010 1111001 0100001 0011011 1100111 1000001 1010100 1010010 0010010 0110010
0110001 1011000 1110011 1001000 0111101 0111000 1100110 0101010 1101000 0000101
1101100 1100111 0111000 1100110 0001100 1100101 0111000 0000100 1100010 0000110
1111110 0101111 1011010 1001110 1000110 1001110 1111000 1110111 0110100 1110011
0100000 0010111 0100011 0100111 1110011 1010110 0000001 0100001 1010000 1001001
0000000 1100011 0111001 0100100 0011001 1111010 0011010 0111000 0111000 1001001
1101000 1110010 0101010 1011011 1000000 0110101 1001111 0000111 1111111 1011100

11100100 01010001 11011111 10001010 00000011 00000110 11001001 11100111 11110001 10100001
01001000 11101010 01111000 11110111 10100111 11100110 00000011 10010101 01001000 11100111
10101001 11001110 01101001 01011011 00011000 11001111 01000011 01001100 01101001 10000001
01100000 00000111 11101000 00101000 01011110 10111001 10100011 01101101 01011000 00001111
11001011 01110100 00000100 10000010 01111010 10010001 01011000 11111010 11001110 10001011
01100111 10101100 00010011 11110110 10001000 01000010 00010000 00111111 11010110 10101111
00001110 01001101 01101001 10110001 11001110 01000111 00000100 00011110 11110100 01101101
00101110 10000001 01001101 00110110 10010101 10110101 00000100 11011001 11100110 00011010
11110111 10000101 10101110 01101100 00111110 01111011 01110110 00110111 00110000 01100000
10010011 10110100 01111100 11001010 00000111 10101000 10101110 01100001 10000000 11000101
01111011 10110110 11011100 11001000 01111000 11000010 01100011 00011000 00011101 11101011
10000010 11110001 10111111 10000111 11111100 10010010 11110111 11110110 10001000 10111110
01010001 00111001 10010110 00100001 11000110 11001100 11110111 00010101 10011010 01110110
11110100 00111010 00101001 11010110 01111011 00110011 10001001 01000011 10010001 11011100
11010101 11001011 01100101 11000011 00000011 10011100 01100111 10100001 11001101 01010100
00001010 01010100 11100100 00011100 11010101 11101011 00111100 10010011 10010000 00101010
10111101 10100101 10010001 11010111 10111001 10101101 00000001 00100001 01000000 11101111
01011010 10010000 00111001 00110001 11100000 11010110 00111010 10110110 00001110 00111010
01010101 11111011 01101001 00110111 01000111 10110111 11010011 11010110 10111001 11111001
10101110 00011010 10011011 01110110 11010010 00001101 10000011 00000111 00111100 11010101
11001110 10100011 11111001 11010110 01001101 10101001 11111001 00110011 01011010 00010001
10011100 10001010 10001001 01010101 11010000 10101011 00010110 00111010 00100111 01011010
01101011 01010010 10101001 11001111 00010100 11110000 00101011 00110101 01110100 11101110
01001011 01010111 00100001 11000110 01000001 10101000 10011010 00110001 10011010 10111001
10110111 00111101 00111111 00111010 01100011 10101111 10110111 01001010 10101000 10100111
10110011 00100100 10101100 11010001 10000010 00001110 01111111 00001010 10000001 11100011
11101110 01111011 11010110 10000010 10101000 11000001 11110101 10101000 01100101 01011010
01001110 01001101 10001000 11001001 10011001 01001110 00011000 00011110 10011110 10110101
01011101 11100010 11000111 01101110 10110101 10101001 00101100 01011111 00100101 01000010
00100010 11000111 01111100 11010011 11010101 00110101 01100000 01001100 11001111 01011000
10101001 01011110 00011111 01001110 11010101 01100101 10100001 00011011 11001011 01010011
10110001 11001110 01111101 00111101 10101010 10101111 01100111 10101111 01010001 10110010
10001100 10110000 00000110 00011100 10000000 01101011 00001110 11111111 00000000 01001101
11100111 01110100 01101010 00000001 00011101 01110000 00101011 10101010 11011010 00000010
11111101 01101010 00011001 10100001 00001100 10011000 10101011 01011100 11010000 01111010
00110001 00011100 00101101 11001101 10001110 11100011 10111111 00000111 00111110 10110101
01100111 01000100 00110010 01011011 11011100 10010000 11111100 00100011 11110000 11000010
10110111 11011110 11010100 00001100 11010101 00011001 00101100 10110110 10011111 00110010
00111110 10111101 11000101 01101101 01001010 10110111 00110110 10001100 00010010 11010111
01000010 11110110 11101101 10101111 11001000 11111100 10101010 00011001 10110010 11000111
10100110 00000111 11010110 10010010 00100110 00101101 00011000 11001001 11100111 11010111
00011101 01101001 10001110 01110001 11001110 01101011 00110110 10101101 11010000 11101000
10111001 00110010 10100110 00010111 00100110 10011000 11001100 00001001 00011001 11111010
11010101 01101001 01101110 10111110 10110101 10011001 01110001 10101000 00101000 00100011
00100100 10001111 11000110 10110100 10000100 01100101 11110110 01001000 01111010 10011011
11110001 10110110 11100111 11000111 01010001 01010111 00100010 10000101 10001000 10101100
10011101 00101010 11111010 11011011 11001001 01001001 00011110 01000100 00000000 11110101
11100111 10100101 01101110 01011011 11101010 01010110 10100100 01100111 11001100 00000011
11010000 11010101 01001010 00110011 11101010 00100011 10010111 10111111 10001110 01011101
00111110 11111111 00000000 11001110 10001011 10000100 01101111 11110010 01101000 10010011
01010000 01101001 00100010 00111011 00011000 10010000 01101011 01111111 01010101 10001110
00011011 10101011 01100111 00101001 00101100 01100100 00010001 11010011 00110101 11100111
11110111 01011110 01111101 10111100 10100100 00000110 11101000 01111101 00101011 01011000
01000001 11001011 01010000 01001101 11000011 01110011 01001110 01001001 11001001 10001100
10000010 01111000 11101011 01011001 10110010 11001101 10000011 11101010 01001101 01000010
01100111 10010010 01000001 11001001 11111010 11010011 00110011 10010011 10000011 11111001
11010111 01001100 00101001 00111011 11101010 00101001 11010100 10111110 11000100 10100110
01010000 01011111 00000011 10100111 01011100 01010011 10110011 10010011 11101101 11101101
01001100 01000101 00000100 11110100 10101001 00010100 01100011 10110101 01011011 10100111
10101011 10110001 10010001 00101000 00000001 10001111 00111111 10011101 00111001 10000110
11011110 00001111 11100000 01101001 10001001 10111000 10001110 10011101 11101001 11111100
10011110 00001101 01000100 01101101 01110011 01010001 10011100 01100000 11101110 11111011
11010101 01011010 11100110 01000001 00011010 10010011 11111100 10101010 01101001 10001110
11010001 01011000 01011010 10101101 11101000 11000111 10010010 10000100 11100111 00111111
00110111 11010010 10101010 10011101 00111110 01111001 00011001 01010100 10011101 10010101
11001100 11111101 01000010 01100001 01110001 01110001 10010101 11111011 10111101 00111001
11101111 01010101 10111000 00000111 10011111 11001110 10100100 11011010 00110001 10011110
11010101 00011110 01110000 00001000 10101111 01010101 01000110 11001000 11110011 01100111
00101011 11101010 00101000 11000111 00111100 01110001 01001100 11000110 00001110 01111101
00101001 11111101 10000001 11111101 00101000 01010000 01001110 00000000 00111000 11100110
10000010 01000110 00001100 10110110 00101010 01000001 00011000 01100011 11010011 11110001
10101001 00010010 00111110 10111001 11111100 01101010 01100101 00011011 01111111 00011010
10011001 01001010 11000101 00100100 01000011 11100100 10010001 11001110 01101010 01100100

10000000 00000001 10010010 00101010 01010101 01010001 10001100 10011110 10010101 00100111
01011111 11101001 01011001 01001010 11100101 01011011 10111001 00010010 01000000 10111110
10011001 00000010 10011100 10010110 10100000 11110001 10001100 01111010 00011100 11010101
10000100 11101011 11001110 00111101 11101001 11100000 01100101 01001000 11000101 01100111
11001110 11001101 00010010 01000101 01110011 01101001 11000000 00000000 11111110 01110100
10111110 01001100 10101010 00111110 01000000 00001111 11110101 10101011 11011101 01010111
11010010 10100100 01000101 11101111 10010001 11001101 00101111 01101000 01101000 10101001
10011001 01100010 01010010 00011011 00001111 10010000 01111101 11001101 01011001 10001110
01000000 00000001 11000001 11100111 11101011 01010110 01011010 00000101 01100101 11111001
11000110 01000001 00110101 00001100 10110110 00111000 11001001 10000100 10011110 01111011
01100111 10001010 01110001 10101000 10011010 10110000 01110010 01110110 00100101 01001001
00111011 11100111 00111110 11110101 01100001 00100100 00000100 00011100 00011010 11001011
01011101 11001000 00001001 01111100 10001100 01010101 10001000 11100100 00000101 00000110
00001110 00110011 11010000 01010000 11010101 10010000 11010011 00101110 10101001 11100011
10011010 01111100 01101100 01111101 00111010 11110111 10101010 11001000 11011111 00110000
11001000 10101001 01110111 00000000 11100111 00011110 10010101 10000011 01010111 11010100
10110100 11101110 01001111 10010011 10011100 10011110 10110100 11010110 01101100 01110010
01111010 01010100 01111011 10000001 00000011 11010011 10111101 00111011 10001100 01110101
10101001 11100101 01000001 10111000 10101010 11011011 01001110 01111010 11100110 10101100
01000110 11000010 10101011 10000010 00110001 01010010 00001100 01100100 01111010 11010000
11100001 01110101 01100110 11000000 10110111 00010100 10111011 01001001 11100111 00000110
10110101 01110100 01101101 01001010 01011101 00111110 11101101 00100111 10001101 10001110
01111010 00110000 11101100 01000111 10111101 01100010 00100110 00110011 01001111 01011001
00110000 11111110 11000010 10110010 10101001 00001011 00001110 11001001 10100011 11011000
01101100 01101110 10100010 10111011 10110101 10001110 11100010 00010110 11011110 10001101
11111010 00011010 10110000 00001110 01000001 11110101 10101111 00111011 11110000 10101110
10110010 01110100 11111011 10100001 00011100 11001100 11101111 01100111 00110111 00001100
00110011 11110111 01001111 10101000 10101111 01000010 10000101 10000100 10011100 10001110
11111100 10001111 01110001 01011001 01011010 11001110 11000111 00100100 11100001 01100110
00111001 01111001 01001111 01110011 11001111 11010010 10001110 01110000 00110000 01111001
11000111 01011010 01101010 00011110 00001110 01111000 10100101 00011001 11001110 01110011
10001110 01111010 11010100 11000110 01000010 00001111 10010110 00100001 11110011 01111110
01110100 11001111 11110110 10110011 11000001 11110101 10100111 01110101 11001000 11100111
01100001 00111100 11100100 11010001 11110010 11000110 00111010 01110000 00111011 00011110
11110101 01001110 01101111 01100110 00000011 01010111 00100100 11111100 11111100 00001010
01001001 00110000 01000110 00110001 10010000 01111111 01011010 01111001 11111011 10011000
00011001 11101001 11001111 10111101 01000111 00010001 00100111 10000010 00101010 01011010
01011011 00000000 11101101 10111011 01000110 00000111 11100010 00101010 00111110 01111001
10100111 10010111 00011001 11000111 01010000 00111010 11111011 11010000 11000000 11100000
01100100 11110111 11100000 01010110 10111100 10111010 01011000 00000011 10110110 00010001
01110010 11100110 10010010 01010000 00000111 11001010 00111010 01110111 00100011 10111101
00111001 10000111 00011001 11001000 00011110 11111001 10101000 11100011 10001101 01010100
10000000 00001001 11011000 00111101 01001101 01001011 01000100 11011100 00111010 11110100
00010100 00111010 10010000 01110110 10011100 01100111 11010010 10010011 01111011 01001001
00100000 00100000 01101100 01000000 01110001 11001001 11101011 01001100 01111100 11111001
10011001 11001001 11111100 11101010 00101111 01100001 00001111 11111110 00011111 11110110
01101001 00110001 10010010 00000111 01100001 11001001 10100101 11000110 01001110 00111011
01010011 11011011 00000011 10011110 11010100 11011110 10111010 10000000 11001100 00011101
11100111 10110111 11010110 10001111 10011000 11100100 00001110 01110011 01001000 10101110
01001001 00100000 00000011 01001010 11100100 11100000 00000001 11111010 00001110 01001101
01010011 10110011 11010101 00001110 11100000 11011100 00001100 01010011 01010111 10000001
11110101 11100110 10011010 00111110 01010001 11101010 01101001 11111001 11111111 00000000
00111000 10101001 01101110 01010111 00001011 10011010 01011110 01100010 10001110 01111001
11000000 11100010 10100100 11001111 01010010 00000111 00111101 10111101 11101010 00010101
01101101 10100011 01101111 10010100 11100011 00111101 01001101 00011110 01110001 00000011
10010011 10011010 11101000 01101011 01001011 00100010 01001011 01001011 11010011 11100111
00111000 00100110 10001100 00001110 00110001 11011110 10101010 10110100 11110001 00110110
00000110 01000110 01000111 00110100 11010001 00111000 11011111 10000001 10010000 10011111
01011010 00010110 10011011 00000001 01111011 00000001 01000111 11010010 10000110 00011110
01100111 00100011 00100011 10001110 00101010 00110100 10010011 01110010 11110001 01001110
11100100 01110101 00100111 00011111 10011101 00100100 10000110 00111000 01100100 00000010
00001011 11111110 00110101 00100010 00000011 10001100 10001110 01000111 10101110 01101010
00111100 00010011 10011100 01010000 10010010 11001001 00101001 11000001 10001100 00100000
00011110 10011101 11101001 00110100 00000100 10101011 10111011 00000011 00111111 10001101
00100011 00011100 01110110 10100011 01110111 11111111 00000000 10101010 10001101 11000101
01111010 00000000 01001111 11110010 10100001 10110001 00001011 10001100 11110100 10100100
11101000 00111101 01001101 00101001 01101110 11100001 01111001 00110100 00101000 00000110
01001100 10010011 11001111 11110010 10101001 10010010 11010000 01100010 11110100 11101010
01110011 11111000 11010010 00010000 10100111 10011100 11111110 00010100 01100011 00101110
01001110 00101001 01110110 11110010 00111011 01010010 01010000 10110000 11011000 11010111
00000001 10100011 11110010 11111001 00011001 11101110 00101001 01100010 10000110 00111000
11110011 10110100 01110011 11101011 01001111 00011000 11100100 10101111 01011010 00111010
10001100 11010101 11011110 11011101 01001001 00011011 11011011 11010100 00010011 11111001

01010011 10111001 00011101 00111111 00111010 00000111 11011110 00100101 10111011 11010000
11000111 00010010 00001100 00001100 00001010 10000111 10101000 11000001 10000000 00111100
11010010 10000011 10010101 00000100 01010000 01111000 00011101 00101001 00010100 10010000
01110011 11011011 11010010 10100001 01011100 00000001 10000001 00111000 11001000 00011100
01010011 10011000 10110000 11001111 00001001 10001010 01101111 00111000 00111110 11110100
11010111 10001001 01000001 00011001 11100111 00000110 10101010 11001100 00000111 00101110
01001000 11101001 10000011 01001101 01110000 11011000 11000010 00110110 00001111 01111010
01111011 00000010 00001111 11010110 10010001 00111110 01010000 00000000 11100100 10011010
01101111 11011110 11010000 00011000 10111101 00001000 10100001 10001000 00011110 11011110
10110100 00110111 00000111 10101111 00010100 01100011 00111100 10011110 10010100 01001011
01000100 00100000 11011100 00111010 00000011 11011010 10000110 11000111 01010011 11010110
10000101 00001010 10100100 01111010 10011110 11010100 10101110 11000010 00111010 10010110
10010101 10000110 00000100 01110100 00110100 11101101 11000000 00100110 00110001 11001001
10100110 10000010 00011000 10010011 10001110 01101001 00011011 01101111 01011100 01111110
01110100 01101000 10010110 10000000 00101110 11100000 00001000 01100111 11100111 11011000
01010000 10100111 00100000 10010000 00101001 00100101 11100011 00011000 00011001 11100111
10100000 10100101 01100011 10110111 10100000 00011111 01011010 00110101 00011000 00110001
11001111 00000000 01111110 00110100 00000110 11000000 11000110 01111001 00000011 10111001
10100100 01000010 01110010 01001110 01001111 11010110 10010111 10000110 11001111 00111000
00011001 11101011 01000010 01101110 11010110 01000010 00011100 10001101 10010001 10010011
01000110 11101110 00001000 00000000 01111011 01100110 10010111 00000111 00011111 00100000
11111100 11101001 00111000 00000111 11010110 10100110 11101101 00001110 11100010 11100100
10110000 00000100 10011100 01111011 01010010 00110110 01000001 11110111 10100101 11000001
11101011 01001100 01010000 11011000 00111101 00110001 11101011 01000110 11111010 10000000
11100101 11101010 01000001 11111100 11101001 01010100 11101111 00100000 01100000 11111110
00110100 00111000 00000100 11111011 01010001 11000110 11110000 00111101 00111001 10101010
10110101 10000110 11000000 11100000 10001110 10111000 11000101 00011001 11101010 00001110
01110010 00101001 01011000 11100111 00100111 00000000 11111101 00111010 01010000 01111001
11001111 00011111 01010011 01010001 10100000 11000100 11001110 11100011 10001110 01000111
10110101 00111111 10001100 11110001 01001100 11100011 00011100 10001100 10011010 01010110
11100000 11110000 01111010 11010101 10101101 10101110 00000010 00010001 10011111 11001110
10001100 10000111 01111100 00001111 11000100 11010001 10011110 00111001 10100001 10001000
01010101 11001000 01011100 10011010 10010111 10101110 11100000 00011100 01100111 01101000
00010100 01110100 00110100 00000110 01010000 10101110 11001111 10011110 10010100 01000100
01001001 10001100 00011110 11100100 01100110 10010101 10010000 10011000 01111010 10011111
11010110 10001100 01111110 01111110 10110100 01110100 00010100 10011001 11111100 01101001
01011010 11111010 10110000 11010001 00000111 00100011 10100101 00110111 10100010 01100111
10111101 00111001 10001000 00011100 10010011 10011111 01001010 01101011 00001110 11011001
10100100 00010111 00001100 00000011 11001111 01101010 01001110 00111010 11100011 10111111
00011100 11010010 11110100 00010101 00011110 01110011 11011111 11111111 00000000 10101101
01010101 10110000 11000111 00101001 11101111 01000011 11100000 00010001 10110100 11110101
10100110 01110100 00011101 11001101 00001100 00000001 11100100 11100100 00001111 01111010
01001101 00101011 11011101 00000000 10100100 10001100 11100100 10010011 10010011 11111010
01010001 11011100 11110011 10010011 11110101 10100100 01101100 00001110 01111011 01010010
01101110 11100111 11101011 01001000 01001000 01110110 01001110 01111010 01110011 01000010
10010010 10100000 10011111 11100101 01001101 11111110 00010011 01000110 11100011 10001110
01101001 01110101 00011011 00011101 10111000 00011110 10110100 10001100 11000000 10001111
10111011 11010110 10010001 01111110 11111000 00111110 10111101 10101000 01010010 01001001
01110010 11111100 01110011 01010101 01101011 11101000 00100100 00111011 01110110 01000001
11000101 00000000 10011111 10011111 00000011 00011100 01110101 11001101 00110101 10001000
00011110 10110100 10111001 00000010 00111100 10000001 01001001 00010100 00101010 00000010
01111000 11000111 00011000 11100100 11111010 11010011 10011011 00011011 01111000 11100000
11010011 00011101 10001111 10010110 01000000 00011001 11001111 00010100 00110011 01100001
10001000 11101101 10001100 00001010 01110111 10111011 00010000 00010010 01000100 01011000
00000111 11110100 10100111 10110110 00110110 01110011 11001000 11110100 11110101 10100110
01100000 01100011 00100111 11110010 11001101 00100010 11110011 00100000 11100000 11111110
01110101 00001011 11001100 01100011 10011010 01001100 00001100 10010001 10110011 11011000
11010000 11011011 10001100 01100111 00011011 00001001 11000110 01101001 00010100 10101111
11001110 01001001 11101001 11011100 11010010 00101011 00010110 10001100 11110001 10000000
01111011 01010101 11011001 11011000 00000101 00111011 10000001 00000000 11110101 00010101
01011110 11100010 00010101 10011110 11011010 01010001 00100100 01100000 10100100 10000000
10000011 11101010 01000101 01001011 00101001 01100101 00011100 00011100 10010011 11001110
01101001 00111001 00101000 00111000 00111110 11100000 01010110 01101111 01000100 00000111
10010001 11101011 00011010 01101100 10010110 00111010 10001100 11110110 11011111 11110011
11001100 11110001 11000110 00111000 00111101 00101001 01101101 00100010 01101000 11010111
00111111 10001101 01110101 01111110 00110000 10110001 00110010 01011111 01011011 11011100
10110000 00101000 00011100 01101100 11000110 00110001 11010011 11011110 10110010 11100110
10000100 00000101 00011000 00011000 11110111 10101100 01100101 01010101 00101011 01000101
10011101 11110100 10100100 11011100 01110101 00110011 00011111 00100111 10111101 01001111
01100111 00101111 01010010 01001111 00100010 10100000 01110001 10001100 11110110 10100111
01011011 11100100 10000011 01010010 11001101 00101110 01101110 11011001 11001011 11001110
00101011 01010010 00110110 00000011 10111111 01011010 11100110 11101100 10100101 11000011
01110011 10010000 01110011 01011011 01110110 11001100 00111000 11110100 10101000 10101010

11011011 10110011 11101000 00110100 01101010 01000100 01110001 11010110 10100101 01010001
10011010 10101001 01101110 01110111 00011010 10111100 10000000 01110100 10100101 11001010
10010010 00100000 01010101 00011101 10111011 01010011 11011000 00001010 01110010 00000001
11011010 10011110 11000011 10001111 11100101 01000101 10110100 01110110 00010001 01011111
00011100 11010100 00010010 10101111 00000111 10001010 10110100 11101011 10001010 10000101
10000110 01000101 01010100 01101101 01100001 10100010 10101001 01011110 00101010 10111011
01000110 00110010 01110000 00111111 00011010 10111100 01000111 00010101 00010001 01011110
00110011 01010011 10101111 01000000 01011010 00010100 00011001 01110001 01001001 11100101
11110001 10011010 10110011 00100010 10010011 11010100 01100010 10100001 00111111 00101001
11111110 01110101 00111111 00001000 00101101 01001000 01110000 01110111 10011010 01001101
10100111 10111000 10101001 00011000 01110011 11111100 11101000 01100000 01111011 00011010
10100100 10010111 11011010 11010100 10101011 00010100 11100100 01010011 10011110 10010101
00010011 11000011 10111000 01110001 01010111 10011100 00001010 10001100 10101101 01010011
10110100 00111010 10000001 10001101 00110100 01001101 00010001 11100000 01110001 01010101
11100100 00000111 10011111 11010011 00111101 10101011 01100110 11100010 00000000 11100010
10110011 01100110 01010010 10101111 10110101 10000101 01101101 11101101 00010101 10101100
11000110 10011011 00110001 00101110 00111010 11100001 10111111 10011101 01100101 01011101
11000100 01001001 11000101 01101111 01011101 01000001 11011101 01000101 01010001 10011010
00101100 01110011 10000011 01011010 11010010 10011101 10111010 00001101 10100110 11010001
10001110 10011010 01010110 11111100 10110000 11001000 11100111 11010110 10100001 10011010
11011110 01111000 11100100 11111101 11011100 10001110 00000000 11101110 01001110 01101011
01110000 01001000 00100011 01011100 11010100 00110111 00000111 01110000 00100100 00001100
10001110 11110101 11010111 01001110 10111100 10101111 01100111 10110000 00101000 10100011
00110110 11011010 11111110 01011000 00011000 00101011 11111110 01110101 10100001 11111101
10100011 00001100 10001011 10000111 01010000 01001000 00111101 01001111 01111010 11001110
10111011 01010001 10011110 10011111 10000101 01010011 11110010 11111110 01100001 10011110
10010101 10110011 10001100 00101010 01101010 00100110 11011010 11010011 01110010 11011100
11110010 11000101 10011100 10100000 00000000 01111010 01010100 00101111 01110101 00001111
01011110 01000001 11101111 10011010 10001001 10010111 10110001 11001101 00110001 10010111
10000011 11110010 11111111 00000000 10001101 01101011 11001011 00000100 01100100 11011011
11101100 01011000 11111011 01010100 01100011 00000100 10011100 01100100 11010100 11101001
00101000 10010111 10010100 11100100 01010101 01001000 01100000 01100111 11000111 10011000
00111000 11110101 11001101 01011011 10001010 00110000 10101110 01001111 10101101 00101010
10001110 00001001 01111011 10101111 01010001 00101011 11011111 01010010 11001010 00011100
01110100 10100001 11011011 00011000 00111001 11100110 10011010 01100100 00001010 00001001
00010101 10011011 01111101 01111100 10101010 10000100 01000111 10010010 11111000 11110101
10101100 10010100 01011101 01000010 10100111 00110100 10010101 11000100 11010100 10101110
11000100 01000011 00001000 01000110 11110011 01011100 11111011 01100101 10001001 00100111
00111001 11110101 00111101 11101010 01000111 11011100 01011011 00100100 01110011 11011100
11010011 00111101 01000001 11001000 11101111 10001010 11110100 00101001 01000010 00110100
11010110 10000111 00000101 01001010 10001110 01101100 10101110 11111001 11110100 11000111
00111100 11010011 11110000 01111010 10011111 11001010 10010101 00000000 00000100 11110011
10011100 11010100 10001101 00010001 11001111 10100111 01111010 11010010 01010010 01000110
00000011 01110000 00001010 00000011 11010010 10011100 10111000 00001101 01010010 00100010
11100111 10110101 01001000 11101010 00110001 11110010 10001111 11000100 11010100 10111001
01110110 00110100 01001000 01101000 00000000 10001100 10100111 01111010 10010001 01000110
01001000 00000010 10000100 01010000 00111010 01110111 00010100 11101100 01100011 11101011
11110101 10101000 10111110 10100101 00110000 01100010 01000000 11100011 00010100 11100100
11100000 10001110 11111110 10111001 10100101 11011011 10010001 10011100 11110011 10001110
10110100 10101000 10111000 11000111 00100100 11111011 11010100 11001010 01011101 10001010
11010000 10011001 00000110 01111001 10101001 01000000 11000011 10001110 00101001 10001000
10111100 00000011 11011010 10100100 01011110 10100011 10011111 11010010 10100001 11001011
01001011 10001101 00010010 00000001 11001111 10100101 01001000 00111011 01010011 01010100
01100111 10000011 10011010 10011001 00100011 00011001 11100000 01110100 10101000 01111011
01110011 00011010 00101111 00100000 01010000 01001111 00010100 11110110 00000111 11101011
11101101 01000100 01001011 10000010 01110011 01010011 11111001 01100000 01110101 11101011
01011001 10101101 01001101 00010101 11001010 10101111 00000000 01101110 00001000 11001000
00110101 10011111 00110101 10100001 10000010 01000010 01000110 01001010 00001110 01001110
01111011 01010110 11011110 11011110 01111101 10110001 01001000 11110000 10001001 00111010
10001100 10011010 01010001 10101001 11001011 10100011 00010100 10010011 01100110 00100010
01001001 11010011 10011100 10000011 01010011 11000100 11000011 10101101 00111010 11111010
11001100 11000100 00110111 00100010 10010010 00001111 00111000 00010101 01010110 00110110
00000100 01100011 00000011 10011010 11011101 01011001 10101011 10011001 11101101 10111001
01110101 01001111 00111001 11001101 00101010 11110010 11111111 00000000 01001110 11110101
01011101 01001110 01001000 11101111 01001110 01100110 00100000 00001100 01111110 00110101
00011100 10011010 11011100 01101001 10010110 01010011 10101001 11101100 01101010 01000100
00011100 11111111 00000000 01011010 10101001 10011100 10000000 00000111 01011010 10010001
00001001 00000111 11100110 00111001 00110100 10100100 10010011 11011100 10100010 11110010
00110110 00111001 00000110 10010100 10011100 00110000 00000011 11110001 10101010 11001000
11011100 11010100 10111001 11000111 01010011 11010100 11110111 10101100 00110101 10110011
00011010 10110001 01100110 00010110 11000001 11101011 11010011 10110101 01110110 01111110
00010110 11010111 00011010 00000001 11100100 01011101 00110110 11111000 00001111 11011101
00100100 11111101 11011111 11111110 10110101 01110000 11101000 01000010 10010010 01000101

```
01011011 10110110 10010000 11100011 10010011 11000001 10101100 10100110 10100100 11010101
11000001 10100100 11010101 10001111 01011110 11111011 11001010 10001100 10000111 00100000
11110010 00110001 11011110 10011100 01000111 00011101 01101011 10000101 11010000 00110101
11101001 00101100 10011100 00100100 11101100 01011110 00000011 11101011 11001001 01001010
11101101 00100001 10010001 01100110 10001001 00100100 10001101 11000011 11000110 11011101
00001000 11101111 01011001 11010011 01101011 10101110 11100111 00101100 10100000 11100000
01001001 10110100 10010001 10001111 11010011 11010110 10000000 00001011 00011100 01100000
10010010 01101001 00011010 01010110 11101000 10011111 10001001 00100010 10010111 11001100
00101010 00001111 10010110 01110000 11100111 10000000 01001111 01101010 10101001 00110101
10110011 00010000 10001111 10111011 00000000 11110110 00000111 10010010 01101001 01111001
00011000 00100111 11101011 01000010 11100001 01010000 00000010 10111001 11000000 11100011
00100111 10101101 00100011 00010011 10000011 10111111 10011111 01111010 10010100 11111011
00000001 00011010 11110100 11100011 10111111 00100100 11010011 11000010 11100100 11110101
00111101 00111001 10100000 00001100 01110001 10001010 01101011 01001001 11010101 01010000
00010000 01001111 01010011 10011010 10100101 00010111 01111101 00001000 00011101 00101100
01100100 10001100 10010001 11000111 01010001 10011010 01100110 01010100 11100101 01000011
01100100 11110111 10100011 00000000 00011100 00010010 01001110 00111101 01001110 01101001
01110010 01001100 01100000 10010010 10011000 11001111 00111000 11100010 10001110 01011011
00111101 10000000 01101001 01100010 11000101 00010111 10000000 00000111 11101011 01000011
01100011 10001111 11100111 01001010 10000000 01101111 00111100 11111110 00110100 10101010
00000001 01010111 00100011 10011110 01111011 11010100 11101001 10110000 11101100 11000100
01011100 01010011 00011111 01101010 11001000 01111001 00100111 11101011 01001111 01010001
10000110 10010000 00011110 10111000 10100110 00101110 00111010 11100010 10101111 10010011
10101010 00010000 11100000 11011110 10000011 11110001 10100110 11001010 01110010 01111101
11111011 11110001 11000101 00001010 01110000 01111110 10110100 10001111 10010010 01111010
11110001 11101001 01001001 10111011 00010110 00011011 01001000 00011001 11100011 10101111
00110100 10101100 11011100 11110100 00010100 00010010 00000100 01100000 00000000 01110010
01111011 01010011 10010011 00011011 01000101 01011101 11010010 01011010 00010011 01100001
10011110 01110111 00000001 10000001 01111111 01011010 10001111 11001110 01100110 00111111
00101001 11111111 00000000 11101011 11010101 01000100 10011011 11010000 11100111 10110001
00100010 10100110 11001110 01000111 01001110 10111111 10000101 01101110 10010001 00100100
11011110 01100001 11011000 01111011 01111010 10011010 10011001 00011000 01100000 00010000
11011001 00011111 01011010 10101000 10100100 11101101 00100100 10001100 00011010 01111000
01101110 00111001 00011101 00101010 00101100 00000110 10010100 00010011 11100101 11000010
10100110 00000000 00011101 01001001 11101111 01010111 00010110 01000011 00100110 01111011
01111010 01010110 00011010 10011110 00110000 01000101 01011110 10110111 10011100 10000010
00010111 00111001 11110110 00110100 10010111 01101011 10000001 10101000 10000111 10110000
00011001 10100000 11001001 10000011 10110111 10010000 01001111 10100101 01000110 10001100
00011001 01110010 01000000 11111010 01010011 10010100 00000000 00001111 10111101 00101111
01010001 10010010 00000110 11100100 01111100 10111111 10001101 00001010 00000111 00111001
10100110 10011100 10110000 11000110 00111010 01111110 10110100 00110111 11001101 11000111
01111010 00010111 10010000 11011001 00100010 10011100 01100100 01100111 10000011 11010000
11010000 11101011 10111010 00111111 10010000 11100111 00100111 10101111 10110101 00110011
11100110 00000111 10011010 01011100 10011100 01110001 01000111 10101011 00100100 10010011
00111000 00000011 00000100 00111001 10100100 00100011 00111101 01001000 11001111 10110001
10100110 01100011 11001011 00011100 01110000 01001101 00111011 00011101 01111011 11010011
10010010 01110111 11010000 00000101 01111100 00011110 11100111 11011110 10001100 00010001
11011111 10001111 01001010 00111001 11101001 10001110 00101001 01010111 11011011 10111101
01100101 01100001 10001110 01101110 00110001 11101111 01001011 10000011 10001100 01010011
00001111 00010100 10001100 00000001 11000001 11001101 00000000 00111101 10111101 11001101
00101010 10001100 10010000 01110011 11001101 00110001 10011011 01101000 11001011 10011010
01101001 00100110 01000101 00100000 11110001 10011111 01111010 01101101 00001101 00010010
01100011 00001101 11000001 00111001 10100110 10110000 11101111 01001000 10000111 11001011
11000010 10100000 11100000 01010010 10110001 11001011 01111010 01010001 01111110 11100100
10001000 10100101 11000001 00000011 00111100 00011110 10111001 10100111 11110001 10011111
01111010 01101000 01000010 01111011 11010000 10010001 11100000 00011100 00011110 00000101
00111111 01000010 10011000 11100101 00000011 10001010 00011100 01101111 00100011 10011110
00000101 00110101 10111110 11100101 00000100 00010000 01000001 11101101 11101001 01010011
00100110 10011110 10100010 00011101 11010100 01110100 11101101 11010111 00110100 10101010
01000011 01110001 11001111 11100101 01001001 11110100 11101111 11011110 10010101 00111000
01000010 00111111 01011010 10010110 10101111 10110000 00000111 01000011 11000001 10100001
01001000 11011011 11101111 10011111 11001110 10000101 00011000 00011101 00101000 11000000
00100111 00000111 10000001 01001110 11001011 10100000 00001000 11011111 10111011 11101000
00001001 11110111 10101001 00011100 10010010 00000000 11101000 01001101 00110011 10100001
10100100 11001110 11010001 10010010 01111111 01001010 01110110 11101110 01010101 11001001
00001001 11100111 10111001 00111101 10000101 00110001 01110000 01000000 00000101 01111101
11101000 01001100 11101111 11111001 11001101 00111111 00111111 00100110 01000111 00111001
00111000 10100100 10111100 10001001 00001100 11110001 11101111 11101011 10011010 00001001
01011101 10101001 11010100 10111001 11110100 10100011 00011100 11110010 00111010 11110101
00010100 11000110 01011111 10011011 11010010 10100101 01111001 10000000 11110010 00110011
11010011 10001010 01101001 01010000 01110000 00110011 11111000 01010011 10010100 01100100
11100011 00010100 11010110 01010101 11001111 00100111 10011010 00110111 00101100 10010001
10001111 10111111 11100001 01001101 00100100 11101110 00000000 00001100 01100111 10101001
```

10100110 11110001 10001100 11101101 11001111 11100011 01001110 00011100 10111110 01110011
11010000 01111110 01010100 11010011 01100100 11011000 01011101 11011001 11001111 00100111
00011110 10010100 10111001 00011101 00001111 11100111 01010001 10001100 00010010 01000111
01010011 11011111 11011010 10011110 11000100 10001110 01111010 11010011 01010001 01011101
01001010 00010100 01110011 01001101 11011101 10000000 01111011 11111011 11010001 11001001
01000001 10000011 11001111 10101101 00101001 11000010 10000001 11000111 01010011 10001100
11100010 10100101 10101111 10010000 00000110 01111110 01001010 00011011 10100001 11000111
01011010 01000011 00100010 11101110 00100011 00010100 00101011 01111010 01010010 01101001
10000000 11101110 01001111 01011110 10110100 10011110 10000110 10001110 01000000 00011001
00000000 11100110 10010101 00111010 10010110 00111100 11010001 01100110 00000010 00110000
00000110 00110010 01001111 01001111 10100101 00110000 00010001 11100101 00001100 01110111
10100111 00110011 00110001 11000000 11101101 01000011 00001110 00001101 00001101 11110110
00000001 10101101 10001111 11000010 10001100 10001111 10100111 11100001 01001000 01000110
00000110 00111011 11010010 00010011 10001110 10111101 00101001 10101011 00000000 00011110
10111000 00110101 00011100 10001100 00000001 00011011 01001111 00100110 10100011 10010010
01100001 00010110 01001001 00111111 10011001 10101100 10011001 10110101 01000000 10110010
00010000 00111001 00100111 10100001 00110100 11101100 00000110 11010011 01001000 00110011
01000110 01111001 11100011 11110010 10101110 01110010 11101011 01010110 11000100 10001000
00001110 00000010 01101101 11111001 10001110 01111010 10011010 10000010 11011011 01011001
00000000 11001011 11010011 10100111 01000010 01101001 01000011 01011101 00000000 11101001
10011011 11100110 11000110 00111101 01101001 11000000 10010010 01111101 10101011 00010110
00111101 01011010 00011001 00001111 00101100 00111111 00111010 11010010 01001011 10001000
11100100 11101000 01111010 00001110 10011000 10100100 11010101 11000101 10101001 01100011
10010010 01000001 00101100 01110110 00001110 11010100 11100010 01110000 00111000 01010000
01101010 00110101 01111110 10000010 10010101 10001110 01000111 01011100 11010011 01001101
11011000 01100011 11011001 10010111 10010101 00011101 01000111 01011010 01101000 00111000
01001101 10101010 01101000 00111101 00110000 00111010 01100011 10011010 01110111 00000000
11111101 00111010 11010011 10010100 01101100 11000000 01101010 00001100 11110001 10011100
11111010 10011010 01110001 11100000 11100111 10110101 00110001 01011000 10001101 11111001
01010010 01000001 00111111 10010101 00011000 00111000 11100100 11100110 10100001 11101000
00111101 00001001 00110010 01000000 00011011 00000111 00010100 00000011 10001100 01101110
00010100 11000010 00011000 11100011 11100110 00000001 00000001 11001110 00110001 11010110
10000010 01111110 01100000 01000001 11000000 11110101 11001101 00101011 00110000 00010001
11011011 00110010 00100010 11110111 00100100 11110110 10100111 10101001 01010000 00110001
10011110 01111101 00101001 10100100 10000001 00100001 11001000 11001110 00111001 11101011
01001101 01000011 11100110 01111100 11001110 00111001 11110100 00010100 10111010 10000000
11100100 00001010 11000101 11000110 00001111 01011110 01110011 01001001 11100110 01100100
10111001 11101010 00110011 11000000 10100111 10010010 00001010 01111010 10000001 11010110
10011000 10011000 11000111 10100111 11010011 10110101 00110110 11010010 11011000 01000010
11111101 11101100 10011110 01000000 10100100 11110011 00110011 00011000 11000111 00011001
11100100 11010011 11010111 10011111 10111111 11010010 10011010 10000111 01110100 01111001
11011011 10000001 11010000 00001010 10011001 01101010 00001001 00011001 11011110 00100100
00000010 01111101 00111000 11100000 10111111 11101110 11001000 01111100 01110110 10101110
01001100 11100000 11110001 11001101 01110111 00010011 01000100 00100101 10000110 01010101
01110010 00001010 00010001 10000000 00101011 10001110 01011000 01111001 11000111 01111111
01011010 11001010 10100100 00010010 01110111 00111010 10110000 11101111 01110100 11001100
10111011 10001011 01111010 10000110 00011000 00001110 01000110 00110010 00111101 01101011
01111010 00111011 01111111 00110011 00100001 10111111 00001010 01100011 01011001 11101101
10010011 00111101 10001111 01011010 10001110 01101011 11101010 01110101 00110011 00011101
11010111 11001011 00100010 10110100 01101100 01100100 11001111 00000000 11010100 01010111
10110001 00010000 00111000 11101101 01010101 11101101 10100100 00101011 00100000 11100110
10100101 11101010 10101100 01001010 01110110 11010000 11101001 01101101 01111010 01100110
10110100 00100010 10101100 11111011 00010011 10010001 11010100 00011111 01101010 11010010
10001000 00011010 11001110 11011100 10101110 11001100 10101011 10010011 00100000 11001101
01001001 10000011 11101011 01001000 10111100 00000001 11101111 01010010 11100011 10010001
01001101 00100110 11001000 10111001 00001001 00011001 00110101 00011001 01010000 00001101
01011010 01110000 00000000 00111000 11111101 00101010 10110001 00011111 00111001 11111010
01010011 01101010 11011010 10010101 01110010 00100111 01010011 10001010 10000000 11110011
11000101 01011000 01110001 11101111 01010001 00111000 00011000 11001000 10101001 10111110
10010111 00011101 10001000 00011000 01010101 01111001 00000000 11011110 00101010 11011110
01111000 10101000 00011100 01110011 10001100 00001010 01111010 11011011 01110000 10110001
01011000 11100011 00110100 00011111 01101010 10011011 01101000 10100001 01000110 00111110
10010100 10010101 10101111 01111011 10001101 00010001 01101100 11110110 10101010 11110010
10000010 00001111 01001010 10111001 10001110 01101000 01101000 11000101 00111110 10110111
00011010 00110011 11111001 11101011 10001110 00001101 01000001 01110011 00000000 10010000
01100111 10111101 01101001 10011000 10111000 11101001 01010001 00111100 01011100 01010000
10010011 11010001 00100110 00110011 10011111 10111001 10000000 10101111 00000110 10101000
01001101 00010000 00000111 10000001 11011010 10111010 00011011 10011000 10001111 00111001
11100111 11010110 10110010 11101110 11100001 11011011 11001110 00110011 11111000 11010111
01000111 11000100 11101100 01001101 11110101 00110001 11100100 10000001 10011011 10011110
11011110 11110101 10011110 11101010 01100011 11001000 11101101 01011010 11110010 00010010
00110010 00101010 10000100 11001010 00001000 11001001 11001111 00110101 11010011 00000101
10100110 10100101 11011011 10101001 10011011 00100011 10010000 00110011 10001110 00111101

01101010 00010101 01010101 00111100 11100010 10101101 01001011 00010111 00100100 00010001
11001111 10111101 01000001 10000010 00111001 00011100 11010111 01010101 00100110 10110110
01100100 01101010 00100111 10010111 00011001 00000011 10001110 11110100 01111001 01100011
10011100 00001010 01110110 00110011 10000011 01001110 11100000 01010101 10110111 00010100
11110100 00010110 11100100 01101001 11000000 00011100 01100011 11110101 10100111 00110001
00000100 01010011 01100101 10010001 00010110 00101111 10011100 11100011 10011010 11001001
10111010 10111001 01101001 01001000 01011000 11110011 10001111 01000001 01010101 00001000
11110011 00110111 01100100 01100101 00111001 10101000 10010010 01011110 01011110 10010011
10111101 01100001 11101001 11011100 10011010 11001110 11100100 11100110 10011111 10000010
00000110 01111111 00001010 00010000 01110011 11010111 11101011 01011101 00010001 01010110
11010000 11100100 01110011 01101111 01110010 00111110 01111000 11001111 10101111 01101010
01101001 01000101 11001110 01001000 11101011 11001101 01001100 01000000 00011001 11100011
11110101 10100111 00101100 01111001 00000000 10001110 00001101 01010110 10111011 00011001
11011010 11100101 01110001 00011000 11011100 00001001 01011110 00111010 10000001 01001110
11110010 11000110 01110011 10001010 10010111 01101001 00100011 00011101 00001111 11010110
10001100 00010000 01000110 01001111 01111010 01101001 10110110 10001010 01001010 11100000
00010101 01110000 00110110 00001110 01101000 11000111 00011001 00111110 10111100 11010100
10001000 10100100 00010011 11101101 11101001 01001011 10110100 11101100 00111110 11110100
00101001 01101010 00111011 00010000 10100010 10010011 00100110 00000111 11101010 01101010
01000101 00011001 01111100 00010001 11001000 10100111 00100100 01111011 01001111 10111001
10101001 00010110 00111100 11100000 10111111 01111100 11111110 00010100 10100100 11100011
10111000 00010001 00110010 10000000 11100000 10001110 00111001 11111100 11101010 01000100
11000110 11111110 01110010 01000101 01000110 00000110 01001001 11001000 11001000 11001101
01011000 11011010 01111111 10000100 01110000 01111010 11010100 10111101 01000110 10010000
10100000 01100100 01010011 11010000 01110100 11110111 10100100 01000000 01011011 00100011
10100001 11000110 01000001 10101001 01010001 01110000 10011100 11110111 11101111 01011001
10111011 00010100 10001001 00010000 00001110 11000100 10010001 01010010 00100000 00100000
01110101 11001110 00111010 11010100 01110001 10001110 10011011 01101010 01110101 10100101
00110100 10011100 01001101 00010110 10000100 10000000 01110100 00100100 01010011 10110001
10001110 01110001 10011010 01000101 00111100 00001100 01110011 11001101 00111100 01110101
11001111 10101101 01100100 10100110 10010010 10110011 01000101 10001110 01001110 01001101
00011101 00001111 11011101 11101001 01001110 01100010 00001111 00011000 10100101 01011111
11111110 10110001 10101100 01011011 11101010 10010000 01011100 01000110 01011100 10111000
11001001 11101010 00101011 00100011 01010001 10110010 00110001 01111110 11110110 00100101
11111001 00001001 11100111 11011010 10110111 00010111 00000111 10001010 01100100 10010001
11100100 01110011 10000010 00101000 10000100 11011111 00110101 11001001 01101011 10011100
11100101 11010010 01000000 00111010 11100110 10100100 01011001 01110010 11111001 00111101
00001111 11101011 01010011 11101010 10010110 01000110 00000011 10111110 00110010 01111100
10110010 01111001 11110110 10101010 00000010 01001110 01000000 01000001 11011011 10111101
01110111 11010011 01110111 10001101 11010001 10010011 11010011 01000010 11011010 00011100
11001001 11000101 01011011 10001011 00000101 10111001 10101010 00001000 01111110 01110011
11000111 01011010 11010001 10000110 00110000 00010101 00001011 00000111 10101100 11100110
10101110 00110100 11101110 00111111 00011100 01110100 11101011 01001011 10011100 00000001
10011010 00111001 11001000 11100011 10101111 01001010 00000110 00001111 00001100 00101011
00101011 11110100 01100110 10001011 11001000 01110010 10011100 11110011 11011010 10101100
00100001 00011100 01110011 01010000 00101000 11111111 00000000 00011010 10010001 00111010
11110001 11010000 11010100 01101111 10100000 00010111 11100001 10010011 00011101 11101011
10100001 11110000 10100110 10101110 01101101 11101110 10010010 11010110 01100110 00111110
01000100 11101101 10000101 00000111 10100010 00110001 10101110 01010001 01101001 11001110
01001000 00000000 10001110 10100000 11100100 01111101 01101011 00111001 00001110 01101010
11100111 10110001 00011110 00110010 00111101 00111010 11010000 01110110 10010011 11010011
11110101 10101100 10111111 00001111 01101010 00101011 10101010 01101001 11000010 11100000
11110001 00101000 11100010 01001111 01100011 01011010 01000100 11100111 00011110 10000010
10100001 00110101 11010100 11100010 01111110 11101011 10110000 00011101 11000100 11100111
10110101 00110001 11111001 00001000 10111011 01111011 11100111 10101101 00101111 11101000
00111101 01001001 10100111 01111010 11001001 10011110 00000111 01100001 01001011 01100000
10111000 01100100 11110101 10100110 11110100 01101110 10111001 00111000 10100100 11101010
11100000 10000001 11000001 10100111 11100000 00101111 00100011 00011001 11001111 01111110
11110101 01011010 10110010 01000110 01101101 00100100 11100100 00011010 00101110 00000000
00001001 10000111 11001110 01000001 11101101 01000000 00111001 00011111 10111100 11100000
01100111 10001101 10111100 11010000 11100100 10010001 11000111 00011000 11101110 01111011
11010011 11101000 01010101 10000101 01000100 00000100 11100000 00000011 10001111 01111010
10001101 11001001 00100011 00001000 00110000 00000101 00001011 10010000 00000000 00100111
00111110 10100110 10000110 01100001 11001010 10001110 10011110 11010101 10011010 11011101
10001000 01110110 00010000 01101111 11111001 10001001 00100111 10010010 01111011 10011100
01010100 01111011 10000111 10010101 10111011 00111001 11001111 11101011 01001110 00011100
00001110 00111010 01111101 00101000 00111100 00000100 11000000 11001110 00111101 10101010
11100011 10100110 10000010 00001101 11000000 00000001 10001110 10100110 10011010 11000111
11100101 00011001 11101001 01001101 01011111 10111101 10010111 00011100 11010011 10011011
10000001 10011111 01011010 00010100 10101111 10100011 00000000 01100000 01001111 00001111
11000000 00111101 10101001 01110000 10111110 10110100 11001101 11000000 00001110 01111001
11110111 00110100 11100110 00000111 00111111 01111000 11010011 10111010 11011001 00000001
10010011 00010001 00001100 00001111 01101010 10011111 01110110 00010111 00011011 01110111

10001100 11100100 10001100 11100011 00010101 10001001 01101101 01111101 10001000 10000110
01001111 11001110 01101010 01100001 01111100 01111010 10110001 11100100 00011110 10100011
10011010 11101001 01010100 10011000 11011001 10110100 10000100 10110110 01110011 11111100
11101001 11111011 10110000 11100000 01111110 01110101 01010010 00101001 10010110 01001111
11000010 10101100 00000110 11100011 00100100 01100110 10000110 01001001 01100011 01110010
11100011 01110000 00110100 11100100 11000110 00110111 00001100 11100111 00110101 01011101
00011000 00010011 10010001 11011110 10100100 11001011 01110011 10000011 11010110 10110001
01111101 11000000 11010010 10110110 10010111 00000100 01110001 11110101 00111110 10110101
01111001 00100100 11011100 00110010 00000001 00011001 10101100 00110100 10010010 01000000
01010000 10000010 01010011 00011101 10101011 01000010 11011110 01111100 11100111 11010110
10011100 00101111 00110001 10010111 01111001 11000000 11011100 00001111 11010110 10011111
10010010 00111000 11001110 00101010 00010100 10010000 00010001 10000000 01101001 11011011
11111101 01111001 10101000 10011110 10001100 01000100 10111100 00011100 10010110 00100110
10010101 00001000 00111101 01001101 01000100 10111111 01110111 00100111 10000001 01001111
11000110 01110010 01000001 00011000 11101011 01001001 00100110 10000110 00111001 10011000
00010001 10000101 00000111 11110001 10100011 00111101 10000001 11000110 01101010 00100000
01001011 01100100 10000000 01110001 01010010 00000000 01001001 10100110 10101110 10000000
01111010 10011110 11000100 11100010 10001100 01111100 11111000 00010101 00011110 01110011
11000101 00101000 11001000 11101111 11010010 10101010 11010111 11011100 01000011 11011100
11100011 11101001 01001010 10111100 01111110 00110100 10000011 00011000 10100000 00011110
01110001 10011110 00101010 01111001 01111010 10000000 11101100 10101111 01000011 11001110
00111010 01010011 01001111 11001101 11110111 10111111 01001010 00000011 00000011 10011110
01000111 11100111 01000110 11100001 11011000 01010101 00101011 00000000 10101010 01110001
11000111 00111110 11000110 10010101 01001000 11001111 01111010 01101010 10011100 10011110
01001101 00111011 00100011 00011000 11000111 00110101 00011010 10111101 01000110 00000011
10101001 00111001 10100001 11111010 00000000 10111101 00101001 00111000 01010000 01101001
01010000 01110111 11000000 00010100 01101011 10110000 00000110 01110010 00101000 11001010
11110011 10000001 11001111 10101101 00100110 01110001 11010111 10001010 00111000 00000110
10010011 01001001 10000000 11111111 00000000 11000110 10000000 00101001 10000000 11100111
10001100 11111110 01110100 10111110 10100001 01001111 11100101 01001001 11011001 10000000
11101100 11100110 10000110 00000110 10011011 10110100 00001110 01101000 11001011 01010011
01011110 01100000 00111011 10001100 11110010 01110000 01111101 00101001 01110110 10000000
11111001 11000111 11100010 01001101 00110011 10100111 00101000 01111001 11110101 10100111
01101110 11011101 10000011 11011110 10001101 01101100 00000000 11011101 01110001 11011100
00011110 01101001 11011000 00111001 00011011 01101001 00110000 00001111 11010010 10011110
10000000 10011110 10011101 00101001 01101001 10110000 00001010 11101011 11000001 11000011
01111101 01101001 00010011 00000001 01110010 01111001 11110100 10100110 11110010 01100100
01111100 00011111 10010011 11010010 10010001 00001110 01110011 11101001 11011010 10100101
00111011 11101110 00111011 00010010 01100100 00010111 11000111 11100110 01001101 00110001
10110000 11101001 10010011 11010111 10110000 10100111 00010011 10001110 10100010 10011010
11011001 00000100 01100110 10101110 11000011 01100001 10000010 01000000 11000110 00111000
11101011 01000000 11101011 11101000 01101001 00001001 11000010 01100011 11010100 11110101
10100101 11001111 01110000 01111001 11101111 01010000 10011010 11101010 00110001 11001101
11000001 00111000 00011111 10001101 00001100 01001001 00011000 00111101 01111101 10101001
10101011 11011111 11111011 11010100 00010011 10000011 11010011 10011110 11110100 10101110
01000000 11110101 00100011 00000011 00110100 10011011 10110010 00111000 11101111 01001100
00100100 10010011 11001101 00011111 11101110 11010000 11010011 00101100 01111010 10000000
00111010 10011110 10110100 10111110 11011101 01111101 11101001 10011101 00011111 00010100
01100100 11110010 00000000 10101101 00100001 10101000 10101110 00001101 11001110 01111001
10100111 10100001 00000100 11100110 10100011 01010000 01001111 01101010 10010111 11011000
01010100 00111101 00001001 00010001 10111010 00010011 01001100 00111110 10111111 10011101
01001000 11000011 00111100 01100111 10001111 01001010 01001101 10011001 11100011 10110101
00110000 00100010 01110111 11000000 11001001 10101100 11001011 11101011 10000111 10001110
00110111 00100011 10100001 00011100 01100010 10110101 11011110 00010101 11000111 00100011
00110101 01010110 01001000 11111101 10000110 01111101 11101011 00001010 10010010 01011101
00001011 01010001 01100111 00110010 10010011 01011101 01011100 01101111 01010000 00001001
00000011 10001111 10100101 00011111 11011001 00110010 10110000 00100101 11011111 00011110
10011101 11111111 00000000 00111010 11011101 01110101 11011010 01000001 11101111 01010001
01111001 10011000 00010101 10011111 00110011 00110100 01010000 00110001 00001110 10001111
10111000 10000010 11110010 11100100 01110111 10101010 10010111 01111010 00110011 01000111
00011001 01101011 01110110 00101110 11100011 11111000 01001111 00011001 11111100 01101011
01111100 11001000 00110001 10011100 11110001 01010001 00111011 00000011 11010000 01100000
01010100 10111010 11001101 00001111 11011001 10100011 10001100 10010111 11101101 00110110
10010010 10010001 00110010 11101100 11000111 01011110 01110010 00001101 01011011 10110010
11010101 11011001 01011000 10000010 11000111 10101111 01111110 01110001 01011011 10110111
01110110 10010001 11011101 01000110 01010110 01100001 10010000 01111011 10001010 11100100
00110101 10001011 01000011 10100111 11011100 00000010 10000000 10011000 11001000 11100111
10001010 11010110 00010101 01111011 11101110 00100110 10001110 11101111 01001010 11010100
01111100 11110101 11011010 01111110 11111111 00000000 10111101 01101010 00000110 00001010
01110011 10000000 00000101 01111001 11010110 10010101 01111100 01000100 10001000 11000011
10101110 00111011 11010111 01101101 10100110 11011100 10001001 10010001 00110010 01110111
10011100 01010111 01001101 11101110 01100110 11001101 00101100 10000011 10000010 01001111
01111110 10010100 10111111 00101111 00100101 11001110 01110001 11001111 11010010 10100000

01110110 11001011 01100000 00001110 10011101 01001101 01001000 11100000 10011111 10010100
00011110 01111011 11010100 10110110 10000101 01110010 01001100 10010110 00011100 01110000
00101010 00110111 11101110 01000111 00000100 11010010 01101110 00111101 00000000 00111111
01011010 00001001 00011001 00011001 11001111 11010110 10110011 01111011 01011100 01100100
10111000 00011111 00100000 01111111 01001110 10011001 10100100 01011101 10101011 11010100
11100011 11010011 00111101 00101001 10011001 11000110 01011011 11010110 10011100 00110010
01010100 10010111 10101010 01011011 01101000 00110001 11011011 01000001 11001001 11101011
10011110 10110100 10011001 00000000 10000000 00000110 00000111 10101101 00100010 10010010
01111110 01011110 10011000 11101110 00111011 11010011 01001001 00100000 00001110 00111001
10100001 10110100 10000000 01110100 10101101 11110010 11101101 00000000 10011100 11110111
00010100 10100000 01101101 00111001 00101100 01110001 10001110 11110100 11000110 00100101
01000001 11110010 11111010 11111110 01110100 11100000 11011000 10001100 10010111 11100100
10001010 01001011 01100000 00010101 10100100 00011000 00100000 00101001 00100111 10110101
00100010 10001111 11011101 01111100 11100100 11111110 00010100 11010010 11000111 00011101
01110000 01101001 11011101 00000000 00000111 11101010 01101001 10101011 00111101 01011000
00001101 01001101 10111000 11001110 00111010 00001110 00101011 10011010 10111000 10000101
10100010 10111100 10010101 01110001 10000001 10111011 10001110 01111101 01101011 10100101
00011100 10001110 10000011 00011111 01001010 11000011 11010101 00010111 01101101 11101110
01001000 00111100 10001100 11010111 00111101 01101011 00111101 01001101 10101000 10111111
01111000 01001000 01100010 11000000 10100111 10111100 01111111 00101111 01001110 01101010
00111000 11011011 01101000 10100111 00110100 10111011 10000110 00101011 00100101 11101110
11101100 01110110 11101110 01100101 01011110 00101110 01001011 10000011 01011001 01110010
01000110 01000100 10011001 11110100 10101101 11001011 10111000 11001011 11110110 11101111
11001101 01010100 01111000 10110011 01011001 00101011 11110011 01011000 01010110 00101110
01101001 10000111 00101000 00111111 00001100 11010110 11011100 00100000 11100011 11010011
11010010 10110001 10110100 11010101 11000001 11000111 01001010 11011100 01000101 11000000
10101101 01011101 11010110 10101001 00001110 11000100 11001001 11010100 01110001 01010010
01110100 11111111 00000000 00011010 01101000 00000000 00001010 01110110 00111110 01011100
11010000 10001001 00011010 11100111 10000010 01000101 01000000 11000011 11111111 00000000
11010111 01010010 10111001 00100011 10000001 01010000 10111110 01110011 01000011 10110001
01001001 00001101 11100010 10100010 01110001 01001111 01101110 00001111 00010100 11000010
01110000 00111101 11101011 00010111 00101110 01011101 11001011 00011000 01000111 00010101
00011110 11010001 10011100 10110101 01001100 11100111 00000010 10100001 01100001 10010001
01000111 01011101 01001001 00100011 11000000 11001101 00100110 11010010 01001101 01001001
11010000 11010011 11111000 00010101 01000010 00100000 11011011 11001110 00101001 01110001
11101101 01010010 01100011 10101001 11111101 01101001 10101110 00001110 00000001 10100111
01111110 01010111 01100001 11011100 01100110 00111011 01010100 01101110 00110011 11001110
00101010 01001110 01111011 11110101 10100000 11100100 11110100 10101010 10000011 10111101
11000100 01010011 01111000 11000111 01000011 01011001 11110111 10010110 11111001 10001101
11000000 11100011 11011110 10110110 00011100 01100100 11110011 11010110 10101011 01001011
00010110 11101100 10001010 00010100 10011101 11101100 10000010 11100111 00100001 00110100
01100100 01100110 10110010 11101110 01100111 10001110 00111001 00001010 11001001 10010001
10001110 11100100 01010111 01000011 01111101 01101110 11000001 11001001 00000011 10001111
01011010 11100111 01110101 01101011 00110110 00100011 01111000 00011100 10001110 10111110
11110101 11010101 01001110 01101001 10111011 00110010 10011011 00101011 10110100 10010001
00110001 01110011 11100110 00000010 01000111 10111101 00110111 11001011 00000111 00000111
00110101 10010011 00110010 00011101 11000100 11110100 00100110 10100001 00111011 10000110
01110010 01111000 11110100 10101110 11111000 01010001 01001111 01100110 01100110 11101011
01011011 10100001 10101111 00100001 01010101 11000001 01110110 00000000 01111010 11010101
00101011 10101011 11000000 10111100 01000101 11110011 01100111 10111110 01101010 10000001
11100000 10000001 11010111 00111101 10101000 11000111 00100101 01010111 10100101 01101111
00001010 00011010 11101110 01100101 00111010 10110111 00011001 00110100 10001101 00101001
11100100 10011111 01101010 01101110 11010110 11111011 11000000 11100010 10100100 11011001
10011110 00000000 10100001 01000111 00011100 11010110 10101011 01000101 01100011 00000111
10101001 01011111 10010000 00101001 11001010 00110001 11001111 00011001 10101001 10010101
01111001 11100111 10111101 00011110 01011110 11101110 00111011 11110111 10100011 01110010
01110110 00100011 00000011 00111101 11101001 11011000 11100000 10000001 11101011 01001110
11110010 11111110 10110100 11101110 00000000 11000111 01111010 01000011 10110110 10100100
01100001 01001001 11111010 11010011 10011100 01110000 00111101 10101010 01101100 00101000
00000011 00111100 11100110 10001101 10111100 11100110 10101001 10101011 10101011 10100010
10101100 10001000 11000010 10001110 10101010 01001111 10111101 00111111 00011100 00011110
11000011 11010100 01010100 10001010 10100000 10001111 10101111 01101010 01010111 01010010
00111110 11101000 10101100 11111101 01000001 00101011 01101110 01000010 00000001 00001110
00110011 11010011 00011101 01101010 01001100 00010000 00110011 11101111 01000110 11010000
00000111 01001110 01111101 01111101 01101001 01010111 10011110 10111101 00101001 11101010
00011110 01000101 01100100 11101010 11111101 11111001 10101001 10010011 10000001 10001110
01111111 00011010 10001100 10010000 10110111 00000100 00000001 11000001 10101001 10100011
00111100 11010101 10110111 01101101 10000001 00100100 10001001 01010011 10101000 00000011
00111111 10011101 01001010 10001011 11001001 00000111 10001010 10001110 11011111 00100110
01001111 01000001 01010010 00001100 10011010 11100101 01100101 00101101 11000111 10101000
11000000 11001000 11101101 11010000 11010011 11010000 10011100 00011110 10100110 10010101
00000111 11001010 00000111 01101010 00010011 10001110 00001101 00101001 00111110 10101000
11010011 10100001 00100100 01011000 00000010 10011111 10010011 10001100 10110111 11100111

01001100 11001001 00000000 11100111 11110101 10100111 10100111 01001110 01101000 01010110
10110101 11011000 01011011 10110000 10110001 00010011 10111000 01010100 11101000 01000111
00100110 10011000 00010111 00000000 01100011 00111100 10011111 01001010 10010000 01000111
11011011 10111101 01100011 00111101 10110111 00101011 10010000 01010100 10100111 00001100
00010010 01111101 00000101 00101010 10001100 00001111 11101011 01001010 11010001 10010010
01000110 00001110 01101011 00011101 01011000 01011011 01000010 00110111 10001100 01001000
10111000 00100011 00111110 11000110 10111001 11011011 11011101 00110101 10101101 01001111
10011000 00110010 11001000 01111010 10010001 11000110 00101011 10101001 11110010 11001110
11101010 01011001 01100000 01011001 00100010 00100000 10001110 00001101 01101011 01001010
10101100 10101001 10111011 00011001 11001010 10011010 01101000 11100100 01101101 10100011
00011011 11000010 10101110 01110001 10011111 10101101 01101010 10001110 00000110 00111010
01010000 11110110 00111111 01100111 10010000 10010001 11010000 10011010 01111100 10100000
01100000 01100000 11111101 01110001 01011101 00101110 10101101 11100101 01111110 10000100
10101000 11110111 00100000 00100100 11110110 11100100 01110111 10100111 10101010 11110001
11001111 00110100 11010000 00000001 00110100 11110101 01011110 01001101 00100110 11101111
11101000 01011010 11011100 01111010 00011110 01111101 10111101 01101001 01110110 11110011
11000101 00100000 11001110 01111110 01100001 01010010 10100000 00111001 11001000 11101001
11111100 11101011 00111001 00101011 11101100 00011101 01000101 01010101 11101111 01001000
11011100 00001010 01111110 11011100 11110010 00101001 10100111 10010000 01000111 01000010
01111101 01101011 00100100 10101110 11101100 11000101 01110011 01011111 11000011 01110111
11001101 01100101 10101001 01000001 00100110 01110010 10001100 01111100 10111001 00000111
01101110 01111011 11010111 10100100 10011100 11110011 11001111 01011010 11110001 10111000
01001110 11011110 11111101 11101011 11010110 11101100 00100110 00010111 01010110 00110110
11010010 10100001 11001110 11111000 11000111 00110100 11101010 01110011 01000001 11110011
00110011 00001010 10101000 10110011 10010011 10011100 01100000 01111110 01011001 10100100
11011010 01110110 10111000 01010011 11010100 01010000 11001101 10000100 11000111 01010010
01101001 00011011 00100111 10011100 10010001 11111000 11010010 10111111 00111001 10010011
00010111 00011100 10000001 10011100 11100000 01110011 01001000 11111111 00000000 01110100
00000100 00000100 01100110 10001100 00010000 10100000 00100111 00010100 10101100 00110110
00011100 01110001 11101110 01101000 01010001 01001000 01100000 10011111 00101101 00100011
11100011 00011111 00111111 10101101 00011001 11111001 11110010 01001111 01101110 00101010
00011100 10001101 11100100 11101110 00111000 11001111 01001110 10110100 10010100 10010101
11110110 00000010 01000111 11000000 11000111 01101010 01001110 01001011 10100110 01001000
11000111 10110101 00011100 10011100 11101111 00111101 01111010 00001010 01000100 00000100
10111000 11111010 11010100 11011011 01001101 01001000 00011100 11000100 10001100 01100011
11010111 10010011 01010001 11100111 00100111 01101111 01100001 01010010 00000110 11100000
11100011 10010011 10011100 01111011 01010010 00010011 10000010 01000010 01110011 11000111
00100010 10101010 11011010 00000000 10001110 01011000 00010100 00011000 11001000 11110101
10100001 10111010 11101110 00100011 00111110 10000011 10110101 00101011 00110011 00011100
01100011 10000100 00011101 01001111 01110011 01001100 11110011 00010100 00101110 11100000
00100100 00111001 00111000 11100100 01010011 01101101 01101000 00111011 00000001 01010010
01001000 11100111 11110000 11110100 10100111 10000000 00110001 11110011 00011110 01101010
00111100 11111001 01101110 00011001 01000111 11010100 00011010 01111010 10000000 01000111
01110001 01011010 00101101 10110100 00010001 11100110 10110110 11010111 01011011 00010011
10011111 11001111 00110101 01101011 01110011 00101111 11011100 00111001 11001101 01100011
11000110 11001000 11000011 11100100 11100100 01010110 10000101 10111001 00001100 01110110
11100111 11100111 01001100 01101101 11101101 11110101 10101110 10110111 11001101 00000111
01110111 10110000 11011101 10011001 10111001 10100111 01011110 10000001 11000100 10011100
10001010 11011110 01000010 10101100 10000011 00000111 00011110 10000011 10111101 01110001
11010001 00010001 11100110 10000000 10100011 10111111 00100100 11010111 01010001 01100110
11001011 00100100 00100001 10000001 11111100 01111101 11101011 00101001 00110100 11110100
00000110 01011100 01010010 00000000 00111110 10111110 10100010 10010101 10011011 01101001
00011011 01111001 10100110 10000000 00001110 00110000 00001111 10111101 00111000 00101010
10101001 00111011 00111111 00011100 11010110 01001110 00111101 10001001 00011111 10111100
11101110 10101011 00110001 11001000 10101010 00111001 01101100 01111011 11010101 01111110
10100000 10000001 11010110 10011110 10011111 00101000 00011101 11000000 00111101 11101000
10110011 10000000 00011010 10110110 10110010 01000100 11000011 01110010 00110001 01110001
11101011 11010010 10101101 01110110 00111011 00010110 10110011 00101101 11100101 11001111
11100111 11001101 01011101 01010111 11001000 11000111 00110100 11010011 01000000 01001000
10100000 10000001 11101010 01111101 00101001 11111111 00000000 00110010 11100000 10011110
10000111 10110101 00110001 01001011 00000011 11001111 00100100 01010010 00101101 11000011
01111001 10100111 00110001 00000000 00111101 01000001 10101001 01110111 10111000 00010010
00101001 11100000 10011110 01000111 00111110 10110100 10111011 10000110 00111010 11111110
01010100 10011001 00000100 00000010 00111001 11001111 01101010 00011001 01110111 00111001
00000011 10001010 10001110 01100111 01111011 10001110 11100100 10001011 10001010 01000011
10111011 00011001 11101000 10011110 11110101 00011010 10000000 00111000 01110011 01001010
00110010 11011101 01110011 10001111 01111010 00010011 11010000 00000101 11001001 11001110
01000111 01001010 01000110 11000111 01000001 11001000 00111101 01101001 01111001 11111110
00101111 11010010 10011100 00010111 00011111 11111101 01101010 01111010 00001000 01011101
10000100 00000001 11000110 00101000 01110101 11111001 00001000 00000100 10000010 01111011
11010001 11011100 10011100 01010010 00101001 00011101 01001000 11101011 01001001 10100101
01101101 01000000 01110110 11010110 00000011 10011110 10111000 10100001 01110000 01111011
01110110 11101011 01001101 01001101 11011001 00100100 10110110 01000111 01100000 01111011

01010000 11001101 10010010 00000101 00111011 01101000 00110010 01000101 11001000 11100111
10101101 00011110 01100001 00011101 10101001 10001010 01110110 10011111 01011111 01101010
00010100 11100111 10101000 11000101 00101110 10011011 10001000 01111110 11100011 11000001
00001010 00001011 11111011 11010011 10001001 11100111 10100111 00100110 10100011 11001110
00110010 01110001 01000000 00100011 11011111 10011110 11110100 01111100 10000000 01111011
01101101 00011001 11100111 10010001 11010110 10000101 11101001 10001110 10000110 10011001
11000111 11100000 01111011 11010010 00111001 01101100 01100010 10000111 11100100 00110001
11111100 01101110 11001110 00111010 01110001 10011010 01101011 01001000 00000000 00100101
11001000 00000000 01111010 11010100 01110010 10111000 10001100 00001100 00010011 11101111
01010101 11011110 01001111 00110011 00111110 10010100 11101101 01110010 10010001 10100001
10010001 10001010 00110011 10001110 10000011 10011010 10001010 11011101 10000100 10010001
10100001 11101000 01110001 10001010 10010101 01111000 01110001 11101001 01010010 11101110
10110100 01100011 00011100 11000101 10000000 11111010 11010010 10101111 01010011 01001000
01001011 00001110 10011000 11100111 10111101 00101010 11111101 11001110 01111111 10011101
01001101 11001000 00010100 00011110 00101001 11001000 01001000 00000011 00111111 10011101
00001000 00000000 11100110 10011010 10000100 01111010 00010000 00101010 01010100 10011000
00001110 11001110 11100111 00000011 00111100 11010010 10110110 11011100 11010000 10100000
01110101 00011000 10100011 10010000 11011100 11110001 01001110 11111101 00000000 01000110
11111010 01010011 00111000 10001100 00010010 01110010 01111011 11010010 11100100 10000001
10010001 11001001 00100111 10100101 01000111 00101100 10101011 00011010 01100101 11001000
11001001 11101011 01000010 01101001 00100000 00100100 01010110 11101110 00111010 00011110
11010100 11010000 01110000 00110001 01011001 10110010 11011111 00010000 01001001 00000000
00001110 01101010 00010111 11010100 00001110 11110010 01111000 11011110 01101000 01011010
11101000 00000110 10101010 11110000 01110010 11100111 10001100 11110001 01001111 01101111
10101110 00101010 10000101 10110101 11110100 01110010 11100000 00110111 00000110 10101110
10100111 11001101 11001001 00011111 10101101 01010011 10110110 11000101 10001110 11101010
11111001 00100111 10000001 01000010 10010010 01000001 00100011 10000001 11111100 11101001
10100100 11100011 10011010 01001101 11000100 01010110 01101010 10100010 00010101 10011001
00111000 11101001 10000000 01111111 00111010 10010001 01000111 01101110 11011110 10110101
01000001 10100101 00100110 10010001 10100111 01111110 01111101 00101010 01011101 01000001
11110010 10011010 00000100 10000101 00011000 11001000 11111010 01010100 10000011 00000001
01101011 00100111 11001110 01101110 10110100 10000110 01100110 11011011 11001001 11111101
01101010 01100101 01010111 10100001 01101010 00000101 11001011 10001001 11010101 01111010
10011110 00111110 10110101 10011001 01110001 10101000 01000111 00011011 11110001 11001110
01111101 01101001 00011110 01001100 10001100 00010011 10011100 11110100 11001101 01000000
11101011 00010001 00100011 11100101 01000011 11101011 10010001 01011000 00100110 01011101
10001010 11110111 00011010 10001000 11100111 01100001 00000110 10110011 10101110 00110101
00100001 10011110 00011010 10110100 00100110 10110100 10110111 10010101 11001110 11111000
10000111 00111101 01110001 11000101 01010010 10011011 01000110 10000101 10110011 11100101
10111011 10100001 11101101 10011110 01101010 01011011 11101100 01010010 00101000 01001011
10101001 01111010 00011110 00101010 01011000 01110101 00000000 11000111 00000101 10110001
10011111 01011010 10100111 01111101 10100011 01001111 00001111 11001101 00011011 00001001
00000101 01100111 10000101 10010011 01111110 11010010 00001010 00111010 10011110 11110100
00100100 10110110 10111110 10100000 01110110 01110000 10110110 11100101 00010101 01010011
01010011 10110110 01011011 10001011 01010111 01000111 00000000 11111011 11010001 01100001
00111011 00110100 10010001 00000111 01011110 10100010 10101100 01101010 10010010 00101100
00110110 11000101 11111101 00101010 10101010 11000111 10010101 01101000 01000111 01000011
10000110 01000101 11110010 01101110 00001010 10000011 11001000 00111101 01101011 10100101
11010010 01101110 11000000 11100100 10011100 00001100 11010111 00100111 00100100 10111001
10111000 00100111 10101101 01101000 01011001 01001000 11010001 10001100 10010011 10001110
01101011 10100110 10001111 00110101 10110100 00110011 00111101 00001110 00010110 00111110
01011110 01001000 11100011 10101110 00101001 01110011 10111001 10011111 00111001 11001001
00111111 10011101 01010001 11010010 00100111 00110010 11011011 01101110 11101011 11001111
01010011 01010111 01000011 00010000 00001001 11000000 11001001 11101001 01011011 00111011
00101101 01000100 01001010 10101100 01001011 01100011 10111101 00111100 10011101 11001100
01110110 00011100 11100011 10101110 00101010 00101100 11100010 00111110 00000000 11001001
11101110 01001101 00101000 01010101 00101110 01110110 00010111 11100010 10100010 01010000
01011101 11000101 11010000 10010001 01011000 01101101 00100100 11100110 10010111 01110001
00111100 10111111 11100000 00101001 10111011 10000111 10010110 01110011 10000011 11101101
01001011 00001111 00100000 00010111 00011101 00000101 00101011 11011100 01100000 11000000
10010100 11001111 10101111 00110100 10011110 01100001 00100100 11100000 01111100 10000010
10010111 00011100 01100101 10001111 11010010 10010101 00110001 10110111 10100111 00000110
10001101 01111010 10000000 10011001 11000000 11101011 10011110 11111001 10100001 01111001
00011000 10100110 01111101 11100010 01110001 11110111 00111111 10010101 00001111 11110010
11001010 01110000 00111010 00001010 00011011 01101111 01100010 10010000 11100001 00011001
00100111 00100011 11010111 10101101 00101001 00100101 01100100 11111001 11000111 00010100
10011011 10001110 00000000 11001001 00011110 10111000 11101111 01000010 10000000 00000110
01110011 10011100 01111110 10110101 00010110 01100010 00010101 00001111 00100000 00011010
11001011 11010110 10000000 00110010 00100100 10011001 00100111 10011100 00010011 11011000
01010110 10011011 00010000 00000111 00100100 01110011 11010010 10101000 01101010 11100001
01001101 10111100 01100000 00000110 00100100 00011110 11011101 00000101 00101010 10001001
01110010 11101000 01010101 00111101 00100100 01100111 10100011 00001101 10111100 00001110
01111101 01101001 01000111 11110011 10100100 10001111 00011001 11000101 01001001 10001111

10011011 10001010 11100101 01001001 01001001 01011100 11110100 11001000 11111100 10101101
11000111 01110111 01111111 10101101 00100111 10010011 11000110 00001000 10101011 01001000
10111001 10100111 10110010 11111011 01010010 11100101 01101001 00010010 11011001 00000101
10010100 01100000 01001011 11010011 10011010 11010111 01001110 10011111 11001110 10101011
01011001 11000111 11010101 10111011 11110110 10101011 10101000 10111100 01010011 01011010
10101011 00110010 01101111 01100000 01010101 11000101 00111101 10001000 00100010 10010111
00011100 00000011 11101001 01001000 11011000 11101011 01001010 11101111 01100001 01011100
10000101 11111000 00011001 00000010 10100001 01111111 10101101 01011000 01110010 00001000
00010101 01010101 11111000 11100111 00011100 01010100 11110011 01110101 00101101 00010001
10110111 01001100 01010100 01101100 01001101 00111100 10110111 01011100 01010011 00101011
00110111 10101110 10100101 11101000 00100110 01111011 11010010 00110001 10100011 00000000
01111101 00101001 10011101 11101001 10100111 01111101 11001001 00010100 00001100 01100100
10001010 01110110 00110010 00101001 10000100 11111010 01010000 10110010 01100010 10110100
10001100 10011010 01100001 01100001 11101011 10001010 01010110 00011000 01001100 01010010
01110000 01111010 11111110 10010100 11100001 11001000 11001101 00011101 01000000 10001111
00000000 11010010 01101101 00011000 11110100 10101001 00110001 10011110 01101001 10001110
00110010 01101001 01101000 11110110 00010101 10001000 10011100 00000011 10010010 00101010
00100010 10111101 01110001 01010110 00110000 00110001 01010001 10011110 00111001 10100011
01000100 11000100 11010001 10011001 01110111 01101110 00100100 10001100 10001100 01100000
11010111 00111111 01111001 00000001 00001110 01110011 11101001 01011101 01100011 10000000
01111010 01010101 00001011 10111011 01000001 00110000 00111000 11100010 10110111 10000101
10110111 01000010 01111010 00011110 01101111 10101001 11011001 00110010 01001001 10011100
01100000 00011110 01000101 01100111 10110010 00001110 11110101 11011100 01011110 01011000
10010111 10001110 01000100 10010000 00011100 00010001 11001111 00110101 11001101 11011110
01011001 00011000 10100100 11000001 00011100 01110110 10101110 11111010 00011000 10001101
01001001 01101000 11000110 01100101 00000011 10110110 01001111 10110101 00100111 10010110
00001011 00011110 11000111 11010110 10101100 10011000 10001010 10111111 00100000 11100111
11011010 10011000 01100011 00100001 11110011 10001111 10101101 01110111 00111010 10001001
11101100 01100100 11010001 01010111 11001011 00000011 11100110 11001110 01111001 11101101
01001110 01000001 10010011 11001000 11000110 01001110 01101010 01111111 00101100 00010000
00001110 00111000 11101100 01101000 00010001 10010000 01110011 11011010 10000101 01010011
10010111 10101001 00101110 00101100 10101110 11001010 01001111 01001110 10011001 11101011
01000110 00000110 01001110 11001010 10011101 10010100 01100011 00001000 01000110 01001101
00001010 10111000 00000111 10110001 11101111 11011110 10001110 01110110 11110101 00001110
01000010 00111100 00001100 01100010 10011001 10110111 10011111 10101101 01001111 10000000
00000111 00111111 10011101 00001111 00011110 01000111 00011100 01010011 01001101 11101110
11000110 10010111 10010000 11000000 10000000 00000001 10010001 01001111 01010001 10001110
00111010 11010010 10110010 10110110 00111001 00110100 10101010 00110010 01110011 01000011
10111010 11010100 01111010 01011100 01000110 01010010 01000110 01110001 01001010 10100001
10111011 01110001 01001111 01011100 10010111 11000001 10101001 00010101 01110000 00111110
01101010 01010111 01101101 10000101 10101110 01010111 11110010 11110011 11010111 10101101
00110001 10000000 00000010 10100111 11001001 00000100 11010100 01001111 11010111 01110111
01011010 00010100 01110100 11010100 01000101 01001001 01000110 00001000 00100111 11010111
11010110 10100100 10000100 11100100 11100110 10011001 01110110 10100100 00101110 01111101
00000110 01101001 10110110 10000111 01110010 10000011 01011010 00100111 11101110 11101100
01100110 10011110 10100101 11010100 11100000 10001111 11010110 10101101 11000100 01000111
11110000 10001010 10101110 10000100 01110011 10011010 10011001 01000111 00000000 10001110
10010101 11001110 11011011 01100110 11001001 01110110 00011110 11000100 01110110 00011000
00011001 10100111 10001110 00000001 00000111 10011110 01111000 10100110 10000101 01101100
11110100 11100011 11011110 10110101 11110100 11101101 00100010 01111001 11001111 01100001
11110101 00010101 10011101 01001010 10011100 10100101 11011000 10100001 00010100 01000110
01001110 00000110 01001011 11010110 10011101 10011110 10010010 11101100 01000110 11111110
00001111 10100110 00101011 10100001 10110001 11010010 00100010 10000100 11100100 10000000
01110011 11010100 11010110 10010010 11000010 00010100 01110000 00000110 01101011 11001101
10101001 10001000 10010011 11111000 01001011 01001000 11000100 10001011 01001000 00000011
00000100 11110000 01111101 01001101 01001111 11111101 10010111 00010001 00011111 01011110
10110101 10101100 11001010 00110000 00000001 00011001 10100100 01100001 11011110 10110011
10010101 01000111 10110011 11011100 01110110 00110010 00011111 01001100 10001011 00011000
11000111 01001010 10001011 11111011 00111110 00100101 01101100 10001000 11000111 00010101
10110110 11000011 00100010 10100000 01100101 11001101 01100101 11101101 00011010 11011000
01110110 01000110 01010111 11011000 11010100 01100111 10001110 10111100 10011010 10000110
01001011 01110000 00000110 00110001 01011010 11110010 10101111 00111100 01010100 00001111
00010110 00000001 00110101 11010001 01001110 01101101 10101011 10100001 11011000 11000110
10111001 10110101 11100100 11100100 01110010 01101011 00010010 11101110 11011111 11001010
01111100 11100000 11100011 00011000 10101110 10110001 11010100 00011110 10100010 10101000
11011101 11011010 10001001 01100010 00100000 10001010 11101000 10001101 01010111 11010100
11001110 01101010 11000111 00110001 11111001 01010011 11010100 10010010 01111010 11010100
10010011 01000010 01100010 00111011 01111010 00011110 11000110 10011001 10000011 10001110
01000000 00100111 10111110 01101011 10100001 01101101 10100001 10011010 01000010 10000001
10001110 10111101 01101001 11110001 00110001 00000011 00011000 00011111 10011101 00100010
01100011 01101110 01111010 01110011 11101011 01000111 00000011 11100110 11110101 00111100
11010010 01001000 00110111 00100101 11001001 00000011 11101011 01010001 10110001 11100111
00111101 10111101 11101000 11000001 00100100 11110011 11010111 10011010 00001111 00011100

01010101 01011011 10110010 00010000 11000010 01000000 01111100 11110110 10101111 01000111
11110000 01111100 11100110 01111101 00000110 11011111 10000000 00111100 10110010 01010000
10000001 01011110 01101100 11011001 11000110 00001101 01110110 11011111 00001111 10100101
00100010 11010010 11111110 00111110 10111111 00110010 10011010 01110101 00010101 11110111
00110010 10101011 10110001 11010111 01100100 01100011 00111101 11101000 01101110 01001101
00110111 00011001 00000011 11010011 10111101 00011001 11111001 10111000 11111100 01110011
01011000 00111011 11011111 01000011 10010000 01000000 11011001 01101010 01111011 00011110
01111000 10100110 11100011 00011001 11110101 10100011 10100111 00100110 10011011 01011010
01101000 11001011 01000011 01011011 10101111 01010001 01001010 10011100 00000011 10000001
10010011 11101111 01000000 00011011 10011111 11010000 01110111 00110100 11000101 01101100
10111110 00101011 00100111 10100000 01101110 00111001 11000001 01100110 00000101 11001111
01001110 00000101 00101111 11001010 10111001 11111001 10111011 01111101 00101000 11011101
11001000 01011100 01110101 00111001 11100010 10010001 01110001 00100010 01100111 00011101
01101010 11010100 01101111 10101000 10011000 00100001 00111011 00111110 01001100 01101100
11101101 11001111 11110011 10100011 10100000 11011010 00110000 01001001 11101111 10011010
00010111 10000001 11000000 11100011 00111101 10101010 00110000 00110111 10000011 10011100
10001100 01110001 01010101 01101011 00101101 00000100 00111011 00010010 00010101 00111011
01000111 01001110 01111010 01010010 01001010 10111011 10011000 00000011 11111100 00011100
11100000 00011010 01010111 11000001 00011000 01110001 11111011 10110001 11011000 01010011
01100010 11001111 00101110 01000111 01011110 11111000 10101001 11110010 00000001 11001100
01111010 01100000 11110100 00111100 11100110 10001101 11111111 00000000 11101100 00111101
01000110 11101100 11000100 00000000 01001111 01111100 10011110 00111010 11010011 10110110
10110011 01110011 10111000 11010011 01101101 11000111 01000110 01011001 11100011 11110110
11001101 11100101 11110101 01101111 01111111 01011010 10111101 00011100 11111001 00100000
10000011 10001111 01000011 11101001 01011000 10101011 00011001 10110111 10010101 11100100
00000101 11001000 11101111 11001111 01001010 10110101 00001100 11111000 00000001 10110001
11010111 10110101 01111010 01101101 00110111 10101001 00110111 10110001 11010001 01011001
10110110 11100011 11101111 11010111 00111110 10110101 11010010 11101001 11001100 00001100
01000000 10001100 11110001 11000110 00101011 10001111 10000010 01100101 00000111 00100000
11100000 10001010 11011011 11010010 00110101 00000010 00010100 11000111 00110011 01100111
00100111 00100010 10110011 10010100 01111011 10001110 01000111 01001000 10010010 01100100
11100000 11110100 11110110 10101001 01001011 00100010 10100000 01010010 00011111 11101010
00111011 11010101 01101000 10000110 00000111 01011110 01001111 10111101 01001000 10100000
10010100 11001001 11100110 10110001 10010101 10010011 11011000 10011011 00010110 00010011
10110111 00111111 10101101 00011011 10001000 01111100 01100111 10100101 00110000 00000110
11100011 00011100 11010010 10101100 10000101 00001000 11001001 11111100 00001101 00111001
01001101 01011000 01000100 11001000 11000111 11110101 11111100 11101011 01001010 11011010
01010011 10000000 00101011 00101110 00110110 11001110 01111000 10101011 01110110 11001100
10101010 01000000 11100100 00011010 10011110 01100100 10110100 00011101 10001101 01010111
00100100 11110001 11101011 11011110 10011100 10111100 00100111 01001100 10011010 10101111
00010100 10000000 11110100 11100100 11010100 11000000 11100001 11110001 10011010 00011011
01000001 10110000 11110101 00100100 10010011 10000011 10000011 11110100 10100011 10011100
11100000 10011010 10001101 01010101 10001110 01000001 00111001 00011101 01110011 01010010
00100111 00100100 11111011 01010100 10111101 10000100 00101011 00010000 00001000 11001101
00111001 11001110 01101001 10011000 00100011 10011110 10100011 10110110 01101000 11001001
11001101 01001010 01111010 01011001 10000000 11111100 10010000 01111001 11100110 10011010
01110011 11111100 01000111 00000110 10000011 10001111 01011100 11010010 00000011 10000011
11001111 11100111 01000011 01111010 11101100 00000100 10000011 10000001 10111001 10001110
00101001 00011001 10111001 11111110 10110100 00011100 00110000 11111001 10000110 01101001
10111101 00110001 10011111 11001010 10011011 01110111 00011011 00011101 11001110 00111000
00110100 11100000 00110000 00001111 01111010 01101110 01111010 00001100 00011100 00011010
00001110 01000000 11000110 01110001 11101101 01010000 11010011 11011100 00000111 01110001
11000001 11101111 01001000 11001101 10000011 10001110 11010100 11000101 10010011 10011100
01100011 00000000 01110000 00101001 11001100 10111001 11100100 11010001 11001100 10011000
11110110 00010101 01001001 00111100 10001110 01101001 01111010 10001100 00011110 10010100
11010101 00100100 01100111 11110100 10100001 01001001 01110000 01110010 00110001 11001101
00001110 01001101 10000000 11101111 11100011 11101011 11000111 01101100 01010010 01111001
10011101 11001110 00111110 10000100 11010001 11000100 01100011 10100111 00011110 11110100
00110110 00001110 00001001 00011000 00111001 11001110 00101000 10111111 01001011 10000000
11001011 10001100 10110100 00101111 11110010 11110011 10001110 00101011 00110110 01101011
10111000 11100010 00100001 01100100 00111000 11001000 11001110 01101011 01010001 10000001
10010000 11110010 01111000 11110110 10101110 01010011 01010011 10010000 11000101 01110010
01100010 01110000 00011100 10101001 11111100 01110000 01101000 01000110 10010100 11101100
11011101 10011001 11010000 11101001 10110011 01111001 11110001 00111001 00000100 01100011
00111100 01100010 10101111 00101000 00100000 01110010 01110000 00101011 00011111 01001011
10011010 00110001 00100000 11110010 11001000 00010001 10010001 10110010 10110110 00001001
11100000 01111110 10110101 01110011 11010000 01010101 00010101 10011000 10111001 00100111
00011001 11100000 01010011 11010000 01100110 10011010 10101100 10100000 01110001 11001110
01101001 11101010 01110011 11101101 01011001 00101001 11000101 10010001 01100110 00101111
01000001 01001110 01000010 00110000 01110010 01001111 00111101 10000101 00110101 01110001
11011100 01010011 01100110 10111011 10000110 00011000 11000011 01001110 11000010 00110100
11101000 00111110 10110100 10011010 01010111 10111000 00010010 11100011 11011111 00011100
11010010 00111100 10000001 01011100 10010111 00111111 10011101 01110011 10010111 11011110

00101000 10000110 00100011 10001000 00010011 11001100 00100011 10111001 11100010 10110001
11101110 10111100 01001100 11010011 10011100 10111110 01100011 00000111 10010011 10001010
10100101 00010111 01101101 10001010 00111010 10111011 10111011 11100001 00011111 00001001
10000011 10011111 01001110 01101011 00101110 01101011 10000011 00100001 11001001 00111100
01010110 00000000 11010110 00100000 00001001 11001100 10100000 00011100 01100111 11101011
01010000 01111111 01101100 01011011 11001101 00100001 11110010 11100100 00100000 01110100
00000000 11010100 10111010 01110010 01111010 10100100 00100100 11001101 10001011 10011001
01001111 01001100 11111111 00000000 11110101 11101010 10001011 01001010 01110010 01111001
00111111 10011101 00110101 10100111 00000110 00110000 11011101 01110011 11011100 01010101
00100111 10111010 11000001 11101011 11110100 10100111 11001011 10101000 00100011 01000101
00101110 10001000 01110000 00000001 11101000 00111001 00000110 10111010 00101000 10101111
10010110 00101000 10000011 00010010 00110110 01100011 10001110 01101011 10000101 10001010
11110100 00101100 10000111 01111111 11100001 01000101 11100101 11010000 01100101 00111000
01100010 00111110 10000110 10101111 10010101 00110100 01010001 11101000 01001001 01110111
10010001 11001011 00001110 01111001 00011100 11010010 10011011 10100001 11010011 00100011
00111101 00101011 11001010 11111110 11011101 01111011 01101110 01110110 11000011 00111011
10010100 11101101 10010011 11111110 01111000 10100111 10011111 00010011 01011110 11000111
00100100 01111110 01100111 01001111 01010001 11011110 10110001 11110110 00110111 11011000
01110111 01001000 11110101 00001111 00111000 00011010 01100001 10011000 01111010 11100011
10011110 00001101 01110001 01110110 01111110 00101000 10001010 01000111 10001101 01100110
11000100 01000101 10000111 01011110 11010101 10101000 10011010 10000010 10110000 11001010
00010000 01010011 11101011 11010110 10110010 10010101 00101001 01000101 11110111 00101101
00110011 01111111 11001110 00011100 11010011 00001100 10100011 11111000 01101011 00010001
01101111 10110001 00011001 00111011 10000111 00010101 00010011 11101010 11110001 00101000
01000010 01011101 00001010 01110111 00100100 11100010 10110011 01110001 01101100 10101101
00001101 11000010 11000000 10011010 10001001 11011011 00000100 10001100 11010111 00111000
00111100 01000001 01100110 11001111 10110101 00100111 01010010 11111001 11101101 01010110
00000110 10100010 10101101 10001100 00110000 00111001 11110100 10101000 11100101 11100101
11010110 11000011 10001001 10101110 00100101 11101111 10011010 00111100 11100001 10010001
11001111 01011010 11000001 10010111 01010000 00000000 01100001 10111010 10010001 10011110
10110100 01000001 01111001 11100110 01110011 10010011 11110100 11001101 00010110 01001111
01010100 00001100 11011100 01111001 00110010 00111101 01101010 00100111 10000010 00111001
00111010 10001100 11010101 01100100 10011111 01110101 01001010 10010011 01100100 11101101
11101011 10011010 10010101 01001110 11101110 11110111 00011101 10001011 00010110 00101011
10000011 10000011 11001000 00010101 10011001 11100010 10101011 10100101 11111011 00110111
10010010 00000110 01001001 11100111 00111011 10110001 01011010 01110010 11011101 01000011
01100111 00000110 11101001 00001000 11001110 00111011 11010111 00010001 10101100 11011110
10011011 10101001 01001110 01001000 11100000 11110110 00110101 01110001 10100110 11100110
01100101 00111011 00011001 11100100 10010101 00100100 11110001 10011010 10011110 00010001
00101001 10010000 00110001 00100100 00000011 11010011 00000111 10100101 01010000 10010110
01110000 00001111 00000111 00100100 01110101 10100111 01000011 01110100 11001100 11011100
00011010 11110101 00101001 11000001 01000110 00111010 00110011 00110100 11001111 01000010
11110000 11011011 00010011 01101100 01010100 00010011 11000001 10101101 11100100 00000111
10101111 11100101 01011100 10001111 10000111 00101111 10000100 00010110 10100101 01001110
00110010 11001101 01011011 11101001 01111000 00111000 11001001 11111010 00011010 10001010
10011010 10000011 00110100 00011011 10110111 00100000 00011110 10110100 10100110 01000101
01011000 11111110 01100110 11000111 11100001 01010000 11000100 00010110 01000110 00101100
00010111 00101111 11011100 11010011 10011000 10101000 10010000 10101110 00110111 10111111
01110001 11101001 01011001 10111101 01111010 10001010 11100100 10000111 00100000 00000000
10011100 11111011 10011010 10010011 01101110 01000111 11011110 11000000 00011100 11010100
01011110 01100111 11001001 11111111 00000000 11010110 10100011 00001010 01011000 11110001
11001111 01111010 01001010 00001101 01101010 10000110 11000111 11100101 01000001 00001100
01110111 11100000 00011110 00111101 11101000 10010100 11001000 01000000 00001000 01110000
10010100 01100100 00010010 00000000 11111100 00110001 01001011 10000011 00011111 00000111
11100111 01111010 00011101 10010011 00011000 00100100 01111111 00101110 00000001 00100000
01110100 10100001 11111110 01010100 00001010 00111111 00011010 01010011 10010101 00100000
10001110 01001110 00111001 00010100 11010101 00100011 00011110 11010101 00001010 11101101
11101000 00101101 10000111 00010000 01001111 01001100 11110011 11001111 01011010 01110110
01111000 00101011 10001100 01010011 00010111 00111011 01010111 11111001 01010010 01100111
00001010 00000000 00000111 10011010 10101110 01010100 11110101 00001011 11011100 00011011
11111101 01100000 00000000 00010010 00000111 01101010 10000010 11111101 11000111 11011001
10100101 00000000 01100011 00010101 01100100 00011111 00101111 00100100 01110101 10101000
01101110 11010111 00110110 11110010 10101000 00011100 10010101 00111101 01101010 00100111
00001011 00100010 10100000 11110101 00110001 11010000 11100010 10101100 10100111 01001110
01000101 01010110 10001100 11100100 00000001 11101101 01010110 01010000 01110100 00010101
11001011 10110110 10000111 10100101 00011111 00110010 01001000 10001110 00101001 11100100
00010011 11010011 10101001 10100110 11110001 10011100 01010101 10101011 01111000 10001110
01110010 01101001 01011101 00101101 00000011 11001100 10011010 00111000 11110001 00011000
00000011 10110101 01001100 10000011 00000011 11011110 10000101 00011001 10100101 01101110
10011110 10010101 00111110 10000110 01110111 00001100 10001111 11000110 10011000 01111001
10100000 11110010 00110001 01001001 11111010 11010101 10100100 10011011 10110000 00001100
01111110 10011110 11110101 01011101 11000001 00111101 01111010 00011010 10110100 11001011
11000111 00011100 01010100 01101111 11001111 00010100 11100101 00001110 10001000 10100100

01010011 01110001 10000011 11101101 01000110 01110001 01010011 00110010 10001010 10000101
11010111 10011010 11000101 11000101 11011110 11100101 10101110 11000100 01101110 01111001
10100001 01010100 01010000 11000100 01100111 00000100 01100110 10000000 11010100 00110101
01100111 01100000 00000101 11000111 01001100 01110011 01001100 00101010 00000111 11010110
10010111 00110100 11100110 00111001 11100010 10001111 01110101 11101001 00010001 00100001
10101000 00001101 00111000 10010011 10011100 00001110 10010100 11011100 11100010 10000100
01100001 11000101 00110110 10011101 11110100 00011101 11101110 01001001 11010010 10011010
11011101 00101001 01110010 00101001 00111000 00000011 10011010 01101010 10011011 10110110
10000010 10111001 00011111 11100111 10011111 01011010 01100011 10011100 10001101 10111000
11101011 01010010 00111111 00111101 00101001 10001100 00110000 00111010 11010011 01010000
10111000 00100111 11011100 10000111 11001011 11000111 10111101 00110000 10000001 10001010
10011111 00000011 00000011 10011110 10110100 11011110 00110111 00011100 11010101 01101010
10010101 10001001 11011101 10010100 01100111 10110011 01011001 01000110 00111001 11001101
01100001 11011110 11101001 11001100 01110010 00011101 01110010 00111101 01101011 10101010
11011010 00001111 01111110 00101001 10110010 01000010 10101100 00001000 11000110 01101000
11010100 00101111 01110011 11001101 01101111 00110100 11010110 01010011 10111001 00010111
00111000 11101011 10001010 11001011 10011010 00100010 10100111 11101001 11010111 00110101
11101001 11110011 11101001 10110001 00110111 01101100 01111101 00101010 10000101 11001110
10001011 00011011 10010010 00001110 00001000 11110101 00100010 10111010 10101001 01100010
10010010 11010001 10001001 10100100 11001111 00111101 01010101 11001000 00001011 10000001
11110100 11110101 10100110 00111010 11101111 00000100 01010111 01011111 00111110 10000010
10010001 00001100 00010000 01110110 01111010 10001110 11010101 01000101 11110100 10010100
11011001 11011100 01111011 11010110 11101011 00010100 10011011 00100101 11000110 11011010
10011100 11101111 10010011 10001111 11001010 10011011 10110111 10100001 11111110 01010101
10101101 00110110 10011110 11101011 11001000 11100111 10111101 01010011 01111011 01010110
00000111 00101100 00001111 00111100 11111010 01010110 11110001 10101000 10011110 11000001
01101011 00010101 01000000 11011100 01110010 01101001 00000010 11100100 01110000 01111000
11110100 10101011 00101101 00010000 00000000 01110001 11010110 10010011 11001010 10100001
01001011 01010010 01101100 01000101 10110111 00001011 11010110 10001110 10111101 01111000
10101001 00111010 10100110 00101001 10100001 01110000 01111010 01110001 01011011 11110011
01001010 11010111 01100010 11011101 10001101 11101000 01110001 01010010 10110110 01000111
11111000 01010000 00100011 11100011 00111000 10100000 11110011 11010000 11100100 01110111
10101000 01001010 01010010 00011111 10101001 00010100 10011111 01111011 10001110 10010101
01011101 10001110 01011100 11110011 01010110 01011100 11110001 11000110 00101010 10011100
11000100 10000011 01011010 01110010 11011001 11011001 10010010 11110110 00100011 10111000
00100100 10100110 00101010 00101011 00000010 00000001 00101010 01000110 01111101 11110011
01010010 00111001 00011011 00111001 11101001 11010110 10100001 10110101 11000111 10011000
01111000 11111010 00011100 11010110 11001011 11001000 11001011 01100111 10101001 10101000
10000011 00100011 11100100 00011101 01111101 01001101 01011010 10000110 00100010 01001000
11000111 01011111 01001100 11010100 00010110 11100000 01100011 10100111 00110101 11010100
11111000 01111111 01001101 00001111 11111011 11101001 10010011 10001010 11100011 10101011
00100101 00001101 11010001 10111100 01111100 10000111 11101000 11111010 00110001 01100110
01001001 01100111 00011001 10001100 01110011 10001100 11110101 10101110 10100010 00111000
10010110 00110001 10000100 01011100 00000001 01001111 10001110 00111100 00001110 10011000
10101001 00110001 10001010 11110011 00101010 01010100 01110010 01110111 01101111 01000011
01000001 10001010 00001110 01111101 10101000 11110010 11110010 01111001 00110101 00111110
00111000 11110111 10100011 00011001 10101110 01001001 00110110 11011101 11010001 01100100
01100001 01111000 11110111 11110101 10100011 00000000 11010101 10000101 01011111 10010110
10011000 11001000 00001111 01001111 11010110 10010101 11011101 11101110 00110111 01110010
10110110 00111001 00111001 00011100 01010011 00011101 01111001 00100100 00001111 10100101
01011011 00100011 10100110 01101010 00010111 11101101 10001100 11100110 10011011 10000010
01011010 11011100 01000101 01011111 00101111 10000010 11010101 00011100 10000011 00100011
10000001 01010110 10011111 10010011 11010010 10100011 01110101 00000001 01111110 10010101
10100010 10101000 11011010 10110010 00101001 00011001 11110010 10101111 01110010 00110000
01001101 01010111 10010001 01110000 00110000 00111011 11110101 10101101 00001001 00000111
11001001 11010110 10101011 10111010 10011110 11110101 10100101 00101000 10111011 11011100
10010110 01100001 11011111 11000000 00100101 11011110 00110001 10000011 11011011 10001010
11000101 01111000 11001010 10111001 00000111 10110111 11100011 01011101 01010100 11001011
11110010 00010011 10001110 01111101 00101011 00010110 11110010 00010000 01001110 01000000
11100110 10111011 01101001 11010101 01001111 01010110 01100101 00101000 11110101 00110011
11111101 10000000 11100000 11010001 10000000 00000101 01001000 11111001 11011011 10001100
01100011 00010100 11000101 01100010 00110001 11111010 11010110 10111010 01011100 10000100
00111101 01111010 01010011 00011100 01100000 11110001 11111100 11101001 01110011 11011111
10110101 00110101 10111001 00011110 11110100 11010100 00101100 00001101 00010001 11100111
01110111 01111010 11101101 01111110 00011111 00101110 00101101 10101111 11001110 00001000
00000110 01000100 11111110 01010101 11000100 00101111 00010010 01010111 10100001 11111000
00010000 00101000 11010001 01001011 01100011 00001111 00100100 10100111 10101001 11101011
01001001 11011011 10010011 01010011 00011010 10011011 00011101 00011110 11101100 01110000
00001111 11100011 01001100 01111110 00000001 00111000 00111100 00011110 11011101 01001101
00011100 10000010 00111101 11101001 01111000 00001110 00000111 01011110 11100111 00010101
00011011 00101011 10011100 11000001 10010110 11111011 11000100 01100011 00111101 01000101
00100110 11100010 00010111 00010100 01001010 11000111 00100000 00011110 10111001 11101101
01001100 00011100 00011100 10010011 11111010 01010100 10110100 01011000 11110101 11101010

01110011 11001110 00111011 01010010 01110010 11001110 01011001 11000111 00100011 11010010
10011011 10001100 00110011 10011100 11100011 00000011 00100100 11010010 00111011 01100001
01000010 10001110 01110011 11011110 10010110 11111010 00111101 10001000 00010101 00110010
11000100 00011110 01000110 01101001 11101000 00111110 01110000 01110111 01100011 11011111
10110101 00100010 00010001 10110011 00111001 11000101 00001010 11011001 11001110 11010001
11000000 11101111 01001111 01100001 00001100 11000001 00000000 00000000 01111110 10000111
11010100 01010001 10010011 10001100 00001110 10011110 10110100 10011001 00111000 11001111
01011010 00110010 01100100 00011000 11101001 10001110 11100010 10101101 00100100 00000011
01111111 10000101 11000000 00111100 10011110 10111001 10100110 11101110 01100011 00011110
11010100 00100100 00001110 11011001 10101001 00010000 00000101 00111111 00111001 00000000
01110101 00111111 01001010 10000110 00101001 10000100 10101100 01011011 01101110 00100011
11101101 11000101 01001101 10100011 01111011 00110001 10001110 01010000 01111000 00100100
11100100 11100011 11010010 10010000 00010110 11101111 11001101 00110110 01011001 00000010
10000000 01001011 01101100 00010101 01000110 01101101 01001110 00101000 11011011 00000110
01010101 11101001 10011110 10110101 00010011 10100111 01110111 01110001 11011101 00011110
01011011 00011100 10000010 01010101 11101010 00011111 00111100 11110011 01000111 10010111
10110100 10001111 00110011 00011111 00110111 10100101 01111010 00101101 10011111 11000011
11001011 00001000 01000000 11110011 00101111 10101110 10100100 11000111 01011100 00000000
00110011 01011011 10010110 10011110 00010011 11010001 11100000 01111101 11011111 01100010
01001001 01011100 00001110 10110010 11110011 01011101 00110011 11001100 10101001 10011011
00101100 00111100 10011110 11100111 10010011 11000111 10011110 00000100 01100100 10111000
11101111 10000001 11010110 10110110 10101100 11101101 01101110 11100111 11011001 11100100
01011010 01001011 10011110 10111100 11000111 01011110 10100101 00010101 10010101 10011100
00100100 00011000 00101101 11100010 10001111 11101000 10110101 01101101 01010000 01100111
00111001 11111111 00000000 11101011 01010111 00000101 01001100 11010110 11101010 11010110
10110001 10100010 11000011 00110101 11010100 11100101 10110100 01011101 00110010 11110110
00111011 01110000 10110111 01100001 00010011 11111001 11010110 11010100 00111010 01111010
10101111 01110010 01111000 10101011 11100000 01110101 11110101 10100011 10000000 00111001
11101101 11010110 10111000 10101010 01100011 10100111 00100111 01110011 01010101 01000101
00100010 10110010 11011010 00100110 00111010 01110100 11101110 01101001 01111110 11001001
00010011 00001110 01000101 01011000 11100000 10100110 01110010 01111111 00101010 01010101
11100100 01110011 01011100 11110101 00110001 00110101 01110110 10111001 01111110 11001001
01110101 00101011 10100101 10011100 01011011 01111000 00000100 01110110 00110100 11100001
01100111 00011111 00100111 10011111 11001110 10100110 01011110 00001111 01111010 01110111
01011110 00111010 01010100 11000010 10111100 11011110 11101101 10000111 10110011 10000111
01100001 10001010 00110110 01110000 10111100 01010100 10001110 11100100 10100111 01011110
01000111 01111010 01001110 00000110 01110010 01111001 10100011 00111101 01000101 01101011
11110101 11011010 10101001 11011001 10110000 01110100 01100000 11000011 01110001 11011001
10110100 01111110 01110100 01100100 00101011 10001100 10110111 11010110 10011001 11001111
10111000 00111110 11010100 10101110 11011100 00001110 00101011 01000101 10011000 11001101
00101101 01001100 11011110 00010110 00100100 10000100 11100010 01001110 00011000 10010000
01111101 01111011 01010011 10010000 10010010 00011111 01111001 11100010 10100011 01011100
10010011 10001010 01110111 01001110 00101010 10010110 01100000 11011110 11100100 00111100
00101000 11100101 00000000 00011010 01010011 10010110 00111000 11000111 00010100 10001011
11000000 10100111 00100001 00000011 10101101 01100111 00101100 01110101 01000100 11101100
00110101 01000010 00100001 11111010 11010011 10111010 00001110 01101001 10101100 01101001
10101110 11100100 10011110 10010100 10011110 00101010 01101101 11101010 01010111 10110010
10001000 10101000 01110000 00001001 11001101 00100010 01111010 10110111 01011010 00000000
10100110 11001001 11000101 01000100 10101011 01001111 01101011 11011100 10100101 01001101
00001111 11001111 11100101 01001000 01001110 11101110 10100100 10011010 01101100 01100111
01110101 01001111 11010011 11101001 01011000 11010100 10101001 00111110 11100110 10011100
10001000 10001101 01001001 11001110 00111001 11101011 11001101 00111111 10010000 01110001
10011110 00111011 11010001 10010001 01000110 01001110 11110001 10011110 10010100 10111110
10110011 01010110 00001011 01110010 01111101 10010010 01111011 10000111 00000111 00111101
11101001 11001010 00000011 01110011 11011011 11011110 10011010 10100111 11010000 01111101
01101000 11011101 01010110 10110001 01010011 01111101 01110101 00100111 11011000 01000100
01110000 11000000 00100111 11110101 10101100 10111101 01000111 01001010 10001110 11101110
11101000 01001100 00001001 10001101 11110110 11100001 10111000 11001110 11101111 01001010
11010100 11000001 00100011 00111000 10100111 00110010 11100100 01111011 11100110 10110110
01011000 10111001 10101101 11001001 01110100 01010010 00101001 11011011 11011001 11000101
00000100 01100001 01000000 11111100 11101010 11101110 00000110 00111001 11100110 10100011
01110101 00111000 11110110 10100110 01101110 00100000 01110111 10101001 10010101 01101001
01010100 01001101 10111001 00000101 10010101 11001001 11110001 11001110 01000000 11000101
00101010 10000011 10011100 10010001 10001010 10001010 00111001 00001110 00110001 10011100
11010101 10000000 11011001 11000111 10111101 01110011 10111001 01001001 00010100 10000011
00011100 01110101 00111001 10101010 10010111 01111010 01111100 00010111 01000000 00001001
10010111 00110101 01101111 10101001 11101011 10001010 00110010 01110001 01000100 01110001
00010011 01001111 01000001 00111010 01101001 10011100 11110101 11001111 10000101 11101101
00100100 01111100 11000011 00101100 10101001 11101101 10011010 11001001 10111011 11110000
01111100 10101100 00001111 10010011 01110100 10000011 11111101 11100001 11010110 10111011
01101100 01100110 10011011 11011011 10011010 11101010 10100111 10001111 10101010 10110110
01100100 10111010 01001000 11110011 11011111 11111000 01000101 00101111 01100010 10010000
11101111 01011000 10100100 00011101 10000010 10011010 10000110 11111110 11010010 11100010

11010110 00110000 10100110 11001001 10000110 11011110 11111011 01110011 01011110 10010001
10001110 00110011 01001101 00101011 10010001 10000010 01111000 11101111 01011010 10101100
11000110 01001011 01000110 01000011 10100000 10001111 00110000 10000010 01111100 11000011
11100101 11110010 00001000 11100011 00000110 10101001 11001101 00101111 11001111 11000001
10101111 01010000 10111001 11010011 10101101 00101110 00000110 01100101 10000101 00001001
11101000 00001111 01001100 01010101 01100011 11100001 11111101 00110001 10111010 11011001
11000111 11111000 11010110 11011111 11011010 00010000 10010110 10111101 01001001 11110110
00001100 11110010 10001011 10111001 01001000 00111001 00111101 01101010 10000011 11011110
10110010 10001101 10111011 10001110 00001101 01111011 00110111 11110110 00000110 10010100
00001110 01000101 10001100 00111000 11101001 11010010 10100100 00011010 00010110 10010101
00011111 11011100 10110001 10110111 00000111 11010111 00010101 01111111 11011010 01010001
10000110 10110110 00100111 11011001 00110011 11001000 01101101 01100110 00010011 10011100
00000000 01011100 11100011 11010000 11010101 11111000 10110100 10001011 10101011 10001110
00100011 10110011 10011010 01010011 11101001 10110110 10111101 01101110 00101011 01001000
00100001 00011000 10000110 00001000 11100011 00000011 10110000 00010101 00101010 10101001
00111100 00011010 10001001 01100110 01010111 11010101 00100010 11111101 10010001 11100101
10010001 01111000 00100111 01010110 10111000 11011001 10001000 10100010 10000000 01100111
10011111 00110001 10101011 01101110 11000011 11000001 00110111 01110000 11001000 00111100
11001011 11110100 01000000 00111111 10111010 00110011 01011101 11011010 10001101 10111100
00001110 01110011 01001010 10101011 10000001 11110011 01010110 00010101 00110011 00001010
10001100 01101010 10010010 00111001 00000101 11110000 01001100 00011001 00111110 01110101
11110101 11001011 10000011 11011001 01110000 00000001 10100111 00111111 10000001 01110100
10101001 00010011 00010011 01001001 01110010 11011111 01010111 10101110 10110101 10000101
00011000 11100111 11010100 01010111 00110011 11000110 01010100 10111101 11101110 01011111
10110011 01000111 00100100 10011110 00000101 11010001 11010011 10000100 01001001 10000000
11110101 11110011 00101010 11001000 11110000 10011110 10011011 00011000 00000001 00001101
11000000 00011111 11101111 01010111 01001000 00111101 00101001 00111000 11110100 11100010
10010011 11000100 11010100 10010110 11101100 01101010 10011010 00111000 11101101 01000011
11000010 00001100 11000111 00110110 10010111 01011000 00000011 10100010 11001000 00101011
00001010 11110010 11001110 11110111 01001011 01011111 11011111 01011011 10011111 00101111
00111111 11101011 00000111 00100010 10111101 00110001 11110000 01000111 10100001 11110101
10101010 10110011 11000110 10101100 10000101 01011111 00000100 01111010 00011110 01101011
01101010 01011000 10001011 01111001 10010001 00101000 00011110 01101001 00011110 10101111
00011100 01100011 00000111 00111110 10111100 01110111 10101011 00110110 10111010 11001100
01001010 01111100 11001101 11011100 10000001 11101001 01011011 00011010 10010111 10000101
10110100 11001011 10111011 10011100 10100011 01001001 01101100 01001110 01001011 00001000
10111011 10011111 10100101 01010011 01111111 00000001 00000010 00110011 01101011 10101000
10111110 00001000 11101001 00100010 11010111 01111111 10110101 10100010 11010010 01111011
00011001 00110101 00100100 01100000 11101010 10011010 10011001 10111100 10010100 10010000
11011000 11100011 10100111 01001100 01010110 00100100 11010111 01000000 00010000 00011111
10010011 01011101 01110100 11111110 00000011 11010100 10000000 00111110 01010100 11110000
01001010 01111010 11110010 01001000 11001101 01010101 10011111 11000000 10011010 11000000
00001000 01010010 00011000 01100100 00111110 10100010 01001110 10010101 10110101 00111010
11110100 01110111 01001111 01100010 01111001 01011011 00111001 01100100 10000011 11001100
01100010 01000110 01000000 00110101 00110100 00101010 10110001 00001111 01111010 11101000
10111111 11100001 00010110 11010101 01100001 10001011 00100010 11001010 01000010 01111101
10111001 11100110 10110011 10110101 00111101 00101011 01010000 10001011 00100000 11011000
01001110 10011100 00001100 10010000 10110101 01111111 01011001 10000100 10110100 01001100
00010100 00000100 10110110 10010100 11111001 00011011 11111001 00100111 01110001 11101001
01011011 01010110 00011010 10001001 00100000 01101111 11100011 00011100 00010001 10011111
11001010 10110000 00111111 01111001 00010100 00010001 11100100 00111010 01100111 10101000
00100011 00010101 00100100 00101101 11101001 10010011 11101101 01001110 01010011 01001101
01101000 00100110 10001110 11100110 11001110 11111011 01101100 01100000 10100011 01100111
00111100 10001111 01101010 11010010 10110110 10111000 01101001 10010000 00000111 00100011
00101111 11001001 00110101 11000101 11101001 11010111 00000110 00110111 11000001 11101001
11011100 01010110 11110100 00010011 10011001 00000000 11110010 11111000 11110101 00111001
10101001 11010101 00000101 10001110 10000001 11000110 00010001 00111111 01000001 01001110
01001111 10010111 11110001 00111101 11101011 00110010 11011110 11101001 11001011 00100000
01110110 00100101 00000111 00000000 01010110 10000010 00011100 11100000 11110110 00011101
11101000 11100111 10010011 01100010 10110001 00101010 10011101 10111000 11000111 11100111
11011011 00110100 11101000 11011000 00001100 10010010 01111010 00001110 10111000 11101011
01010000 00101001 00111001 11101111 11001001 11110100 10100111 10111001 00101011 11000000
10100010 11110111 00011000 11101100 01101110 00011011 11001000 00111000 11101101 10011110
10110100 01111100 11000000 00000010 10011100 10011100 11110011 01000111 00111100 01100000
11100110 10011010 11001100 01001111 11001011 10011110 00111101 10111011 11010100 00101101
01011101 10110110 00000001 11001100 01011000 00100001 11001001 00111001 00111101 11101001
11010001 00101011 00110011 01111010 01100000 01111010 11010100 00100100 00000000 00110000
00001101 00111001 00100100 00100010 00111101 10100011 10111111 01010011 01010110 11101111
11010000 10010100 01001000 11001100 01110111 10011110 11100011 00110101 00011110 01110111
00100011 10000010 01101001 10101101 11001001 01000000 11100111 10000001 11001110 00000111
01110011 01001110 00100100 00000001 11010011 10011010 10000110 11001011 10001001 10001111
00001111 01010011 11011100 10001010 10110010 10000000 10000010 01001101 01010110 00011001
11110011 00001000 00011001 00011001 00110101 01110110 00100101 11001110 00111101 01101011

10000110 10100010 01010111 00111011 11100000 11110100 00100100 10000110 00111101 11000111
00100110 10110100 00111001 00001000 00000101 01000101 00011010 01100001 00000000 10101001
01011011 10100111 10111101 01101000 10101111 00011101 11000001 11011001 11101100 00111111
00111100 01111011 11010011 01110111 01110001 11101011 01010000 10110100 10000011 10111101
00110111 11001100 00011001 11000110 01101000 01110011 11010100 00101100 01001111 11010000
11100110 10010101 01111101 01110001 11111001 11010101 01100110 10010111 10011100 01010010
10100100 10100100 11110001 11010011 11110000 10100100 00000100 11111100 01110011 11010110
10010001 10000010 11100011 10100101 01000111 11100110 00011100 11110001 11010010 10001101
11111111 00000000 10010101 00111111 00110001 00110001 10001111 11111110 11001101 01000100
01000111 00010101 00110110 01000111 00111100 01010100 01101100 01111011 00001010 01101110
11010110 10111000 11110101 00101011 10111000 11000000 11100110 10100010 01111100 00000011
11111000 01110001 11101111 01010011 11001011 11010011 00010101 00000011 11110100 11000101
01100011 10100101 10110101 00101010 11100100 01111011 11111000 11110111 10100011 01111111
10111101 00100011 01110110 10100110 00111001 11001111 10110101 00001110 00001110 11000010
00100100 00000111 10101101 00101010 11110101 10101000 01110111 01101101 00110100 10101011
00100001 10100100 10010000 00110010 11000000 01100000 00000110 01101000 01110110 00000100
01010100 00011001 00111101 01101000 01011110 00001111 00110101 10101010 01101101 01110101
00010000 11111101 11011000 11000101 00001111 11010011 10101101 01000111 10011111 01111010
00010111 10000011 10011110 10110100 10010011 01010111 10111011 00011111 10100000 10101010
01110011 11010111 10110101 00000000 01100101 11101001 10101100 01011011 11010000 01010100
10010001 01100100 11010011 11110111 10010011 10111101 11000111 01111101 00000111 01101101
11001111 11011100 11101101 11010110 10011101 10001100 10000001 01001110 01000001 10001010
01110110 00000101 01001100 10100110 11000111 01100010 10111011 00101110 01000110 01001101
01000110 01010100 10011110 00101010 11100011 10101111 00010100 11000110 00011110 11010100
10011100 01010010 01110111 01000000 01010010 01111000 00010101 11111000 00110101 01010110
01001011 01010100 00101100 01111110 01010001 01011010 10011011 01101010 00100111 00011100
11010001 11001101 01100000 10110101 11001100 01111001 00101100 01010100 10000011 11000111
00010101 01000010 01011101 00110001 01001011 01100111 00000000 11100011 11010100 01010111
01001100 01100010 11011101 11000111 10101101 01000010 11110000 01110011 11000000 10101011
01110011 01100001 01110011 10010010 10010011 01001011 11101010 01001010 11110001 01011001
11110011 11101001 10011001 00100111 01100111 00000110 10111011 11000110 10000011 00100011
10011010 11001111 10111001 10110001 11001011 00010110 01000001 11010111 10101111 00010101
10100101 00101010 10110010 01011011 10010001 01100011 10000111 11111011 00010100 10100011
00001010 01100011 00100100 11111010 10001010 01100011 01011011 10010000 00111001 01011010
11101010 00100110 10110101 00101010 11000111 01110101 01010111 10010110 00100000 01111000
11011011 01011101 01110000 11000100 11001101 00111011 00001001 10101110 11000111 00110100
11110001 11100000 01110010 00111000 11110101 10101000 11011001 01110000 00111110 11101111
01011010 11011011 10111100 10110101 11111001 01111110 01000001 01011001 11110011 01000110
01000110 00110010 00001110 01001101 01101111 00001010 11010110 01110110 01111010 10001010
11001100 11001101 10010110 00110000 00001101 01010010 10011011 11101111 01100000 10001110
00111011 01010110 10101011 11000110 01010100 00011110 00111000 10101010 00110111 00101011
10011110 00101011 01101110 01101110 01111101 01001000 01111010 00011001 10110011 00011110
00001110 01111010 11010100 00110110 10110010 01100010 01010011 11001111 00110100 11101011
10110000 01000000 11101000 00110001 11101011 11101011 01010101 01100010 00100101 01100100
00000111 10101111 00110101 11010010 10010110 10000111 00111011 01110110 01100111 01010001
10100111 01000111 10111001 11000110 01001101 01111010 00100110 10011010 10100010 00101011
01011000 10100011 01011111 11101110 11010111 00000001 10100000 10000001 11100111 10000010
01111000 11100010 10111011 11111011 00110011 10011000 11010011 10011010 11110001 11110001
10110011 01110111 01010001 10111001 11010101 00001101 01010101 11001101 00010100 00000111
10001110 01111000 10101001 01110001 10010011 01010101 10010101 10110000 00111101 01101010
11000100 01100111 11010011 10101101 01110000 10110101 10100110 11000110 11001000 10010100
00101110 01111011 01010011 10110110 11110001 01001110 01000011 10010001 01001110 11011011
01010001 01110111 01101101 01000000 01101110 00111000 11001101 00001100 00101010 01001100
01100000 01111111 00111010 01101111 00111001 11100011 10001010 01001010 01010110 01000000
01000110 11101011 11000101 01000110 01010111 10011010 10110000 11110101 00000100 10111100
10010001 01010010 11010101 11111010 10010100 10101100 01000000 11100011 00110101 00011110
11011100 11110101 11100100 01010101 10100110 10001111 01101111 11100011 01001100 00100000
10001110 00001001 11111101 00101000 10001110 10000000 11011001 01001110 01010101 10101000
00100101 01011110 00111001 11101111 01010111 00011100 01100011 00100000 11110101 10101000
01100101 01010010 00001000 11110100 10101101 10101111 11011001 10000110 10110110 00110011
00100110 01010010 01110011 11000101 01100110 01011101 11000111 10000001 10011111 11010110
10110111 00101110 00100011 11101111 10011111 10100101 01010001 10111001 01010000 00000110
00001000 11101011 01011010 11000010 10100101 10011101 10011011 00110011 01110111 01100111
00110111 01110010 10111000 01101111 01000000 01111101 11101010 00001110 11111000 11101111
11101001 01011010 00010111 01110001 10011100 10111110 00111011 01010101 00000111 11001111
11100011 01011101 11111100 11010111 01111110 11101001 10000101 10110101 00010001 01110111
01101110 11100100 01010010 00010001 11110111 11000010 10011010 01010000 01001111 11100111
11101001 01001100 01110011 10001110 01010111 10011010 10111000 10110110 00110001 10101101
11000001 11101001 11010110 10111101 00001011 11000000 11001101 00011111 11110110 00010010
00001100 01110010 00100100 00111001 11001101 01111001 11011001 11000001 01101110 10111111
01010000 01101011 11010000 10111100 00001101 10000011 10100001 01101101 00000011 00100011
11001101 00100111 00100010 10011100 11011101 10010111 10011001 10010101 01011101 10001101
11100110 00100101 10111001 00011100 11100100 11010011 10011000 00011100 00001000 11110000

01110001 11101011 11101011 01001101 10010010 01000110 01100111 11000010 01110000 10000011
10100111 10110101 00111101 10011000 01101110 00111001 00100100 01110001 11010111 00110101
10001100 10111100 11001110 01101101 11000100 11100001 10011111 10001110 11011101 01101001
10110010 10010000 00110010 01001001 11101000 01101000 11101001 00010000 11000111 01111110
11011110 10010100 10011000 11001000 01000011 10001111 10111111 01010010 10010011 10110101
11010000 10000001 11000000 01100000 01000001 11001111 00111101 01101000 00011110 10100111
10100101 00001101 10000000 01111101 01101010 00001001 11100101 01011000 10100011 00100101
11011011 10100111 00100111 00010100 00101101 01110110 00000010 01100000 11011111 00110001
00100111 10000100 11101100 00101001 01011100 11100100 00010001 11010000 00010001 11001101
01010011 00010111 11010110 11111110 01011011 10011101 11000000 10010101 11101011 01010000
01001001 10101011 01011011 10110100 01100111 00010010 01100011 00011100 10010011 01010111
01101001 01110101 00000010 11110010 11001001 11000111 11001011 11010011 10110101 00110001
11100101 01011101 10100111 11100111 00101001 11101110 00101011 00011011 11101101 11001011
00110001 00100110 00110010 01110001 10011110 11010101 00001101 11000100 10110010 11001101
00011001 01011000 00100100 11011000 01011100 11110010 01001000 11001111 11111111 00000000
10101010 10101001 00111011 11101110 00000110 10100100 11010111 10110000 10100100 01100010
01001001 00011011 00100000 01110101 11100111 10011010 10100110 11011010 10111100 00110010
01100111 11001000 00111101 00000001 11100000 11010110 00110101 11100100 01000001 01000110
11000111 01101111 10011101 10110001 11001111 10101101 01100111 00111100 01110010 01000010
01001011 01000010 01110000 00001000 11101000 00101001 01010011 10100010 11011110 10001100
01101100 11011000 10111100 11010101 11100100 10011000 10111110 01000000 00001000 01000111
01110011 01011001 11010010 00000010 11101100 00001100 10000001 11000011 01100010 10110011
10100010 10011111 11001100 10010100 01111001 10000111 00000011 00111001 00111001 11101111
01011101 01000100 00110011 00000101 10001100 00000110 01010001 10011010 10101001 01000001
11000111 01000000 11010000 11110100 00000001 10000010 01110011 01001110 11000101 01010101
01011001 01110110 11110101 00111111 10000101 00111011 11001101 00111001 11001101 01111100
11000111 00111100 10001111 01100001 11000101 00010011 01110000 00111111 11111101 01110100
11100101 11001001 11100011 00111101 01101010 10111010 10110000 00100111 10010011 01010010
00101011 01100011 10100001 10101101 01011011 10010110 11001101 00000011 10000001 00101110
00111111 00111010 00011011 10010010 00111000 11100010 10100011 11110011 00111001 11001110
01110011 01001011 11100110 01111010 01010100 01001010 00101110 11100010 10110101 11001001
00111010 10000010 00101000 01100000 00001110 00111001 10101000 11001011 01111011 10001010
01001100 10010010 00111000 10100011 10011001 11101101 01100001 01011000 10011111 00111000
00111000 00110100 11001001 01000111 00011100 00011100 11010100 01101001 10010011 11111111
00000000 11010111 10101001 00111010 01110001 01001010 11100000 11100010 00100100 00111101
01110001 01010010 11101101 11100110 10100010 11101000 01111110 01001110 00101001 01010001
10110001 11001011 01100111 11111100 01101001 00110111 10100110 11000011 00100100 00000011
00000000 01010010 11101101 00011000 11001000 00111001 11001101 00011001 11011101 11011111
10001010 00110001 10000110 11100011 11110001 10101000 01001111 10111000 11110111 00011011
11001111 01011010 01011100 10010000 01110010 01111111 00111010 01010110 11110101 00110100
11010110 00011101 01000101 01000100 10011010 01111010 10010100 00111011 01110000 11000111
00011111 10011110 01101001 11011100 00000001 01010000 11111101 11011110 10010100 11100101
00100111 10111101 00111110 01100111 01111101 10001001 11100101 00100101 01101100 01110101
10100110 01100110 10100011 00111101 11111001 11101111 01001110 01011100 11010101 00111010
10110111 01111010 00001010 11000100 10101010 01110010 01000000 11100011 11101011 01010001
11001010 00111011 01010000 00001101 00111101 01111010 01110101 10100101 11001100 11000001
10100001 10001000 00001010 10110110 00000111 01001110 11110101 00101011 00010001 11101110
00101010 00110000 00111010 11010100 10011110 11111101 10101001 10110110 10111001 01110101
00010000 11101100 10001010 00100101 11100011 10100111 01000011 01001101 00111000 11001101
00111111 11111000 00110000 01101000 10111111 01110001 01101101 10101000 11000101 11001000
00011000 10100100 01011110 10100111 10111101 01001000 10111100 01110001 11001111 10110111
00110100 10001100 00101011 00111101 11110111 01000011 01111110 01000010 10101011 01100000
01111010 01010010 11101110 00110101 00011011 01111010 00011010 01000101 11001101 01001101
01001001 00110101 10101010 00001011 00101110 10100101 10000000 01000001 00010100 01101101
00000111 10110111 00010101 00010110 11101101 10100111 11010110 10100100 00010010 00000011
11001110 01101001 11000010 10101110 10110110 00100101 11000110 11111010 10010001 10110100
01100000 01111101 11001110 10110101 00100010 01111011 10001111 11000110 10010111 00100011
00110100 10100000 10000011 11101101 01011010 01111011 01000111 00110010 01101100 11010000
11100110 11101011 01001101 11001110 01001110 00111001 00010101 00100110 11010000 01111001
01011010 00110001 10001110 01001101 01001110 10111101 00000000 01101010 10010001 10001100
01010000 01110000 00111000 01011010 00011001 00000000 11100110 10100001 10011001 10011001
01111001 00010101 01110000 01011100 10111011 10010001 01110010 01101100 01110010 01001101
00110011 00011100 01010110 01111100 11010111 11000001 01101010 00111000 01110101 00111110
10111001 00011101 00111101 11111010 11010101 01001010 00001001 10101011 11011100 10111011
10011010 10111011 01110000 00101001 10101101 10011110 11010100 11011000 00100110 01011001
01000111 00000111 10011110 11111110 11010101 00110110 00110010 01101011 10011110 11001110
00111011 10000001 00011010 01100000 10011100 01010010 11101101 11101110 01101001 01111100
10110001 10001010 01110111 01001111 01110011 01011010 00100110 10010110 11100000 11000110
00101111 00000111 00111000 10101001 00010111 00010100 00010001 10010010 01001111 01101010
01100011 10101111 11110111 01101011 01001011 11000110 01001010 11010110 00100000 10011000
00101110 01000110 01101000 00111000 11000000 11100011 11110001 10101000 00000100 10000100
00001110 01101010 01011100 11100100 01111011 11010100 00111000 01001001 01101110 11001010
11010001 10000011 00011110 01000101 00100110 01111101 00110001 01001011 10001110 00110011

10011010 00000000 10100101 00011000 11011001 01101000 00110110 00100111 01101010 01001100
01100111 10011110 11010100 10100111 00000100 11100010 10001110 10111100 01100110 10101010
10011010 00010011 00100011 11000111 10110101 01010110 10111100 00111011 01000111 01001110
00101010 11110011 10001110 00110010 00101010 10011101 11101100 01000101 11000111 00010101
10101010 11010001 11110111 00100001 10011100 11101101 11100101 11010110 00011000 10000011
11000000 00100111 00011001 10100111 01011001 11101010 00101101 00001110 00111001 11011110
01000111 10101001 11101011 01011001 11011010 10100110 11100001 00100111 11001110 00110000
11100010 10101011 01000011 00100001 00100011 10001110 11111101 10101010 11011111 00110101
10101100 01010010 01010111 00111011 10001000 01101111 00010010 01011000 11110010 00001110
00110011 11010100 01010100 10101011 00110000 00100011 10101101 01110001 11110110 11010011
00011000 10011111 00100011 10000011 01011011 00110110 10010111 01000010 01010001 11110010
10010001 10011100 11010111 00111100 11100010 11100000 11001010 10110001 10110110 00100100
00000100 11111011 01010010 11100100 01111010 11110101 10101100 11110101 10010111 00010100
11110101 10011011 11011110 10110011 01110010 01101000 10010111 00000010 01110111 10000010
00101001 00111000 10010010 00101000 11011100 01111010 00010101 00000110 10101001 11001101
10100011 01101001 11010011 10000011 11100110 01011001 11000101 11001111 10100000 11000101
01011001 00010010 10000001 10000001 10011110 10110100 01111001 10011001 11101111 01001101
01010101 10101001 11110110 01000101 11001001 01111101 11001100 11110100 11110000 11011110
10010110 10100100 01111111 10100011 10010011 11101011 11110011 00011010 10011110 00101101
00011010 11001110 00100000 11111110 01011100 00100000 00001111 10101101 01011100 11011101
11000000 00111001 10100101 11110011 00111110 01011111 01001010 11011110 00111000 10101010
10011101 01000100 11101001 10010101 00010111 01001110 10110111 00000011 00000001 01110001
11111000 11010100 10000010 00001000 10000000 11000111 00100100 01111011 11010101 10000001
10001100 11010010 00111000 00011101 01110001 01010100 10110001 01010010 10111111 01100001
01001010 00001000 10001001 10100010 00011011 11110111 01100100 11100111 11110100 10100110
11111001 00111100 11100011 00111111 10100101 00001100 00001010 10111110 01010100 11111110
00110100 10000110 01001001 00000111 11111000 10011010 11011011 11101011 00110010 01111010
01011100 10001111 01100110 10010000 10111110 01000001 01101110 00001011 01110001 11110100
10100100 00010001 00110000 11001111 00100010 10100010 01111011 10110010 00001001 10101010
10101111 01111100 01010100 10010010 01001110 01101010 10100011 10001001 10010100 10010000
10111101 10011010 00101111 10110100 01011101 01110011 11010010 10100010 00100000 11100011
10100101 01010000 01111101 01010000 00000011 10000111 00011111 01011110 01101010 10111100
10011010 10010001 11001001 00000000 11110100 00010101 10110010 11000101 01001110 00111101
00000011 11011001 00100110 01101001 11100100 11101110 11100111 10001110 00111010 11010100
00101111 01110101 11100101 10011100 01101110 11101101 11010111 00010101 10001101 00101110
10100001 00100001 11001111 00110101 10011111 00110101 11010001 00111111 11000101 11011111
10111101 00111010 10011000 10011001 01001111 01000100 10000001 01010010 01010111 00110111
00010000 11100101 11110111 01111010 10011010 11010111 10110110 10000111 00001010 00001110
00111001 10101010 00011010 01110100 00111011 10010001 00110011 11001110 00000000 11001111
10111101 01101010 10110001 00010001 10101110 01110011 01001001 00100011 10101011 01100100
00100100 10000100 00101000 11101011 01010101 00100100 10111011 00001010 00110001 10011010
10101111 01111011 01110111 10011110 00000111 01001010 11001101 01100010 01011101 11111001
10101010 11010011 10101000 11010010 00101111 01001011 01111101 11010100 00001110 01111101
00001101 01000011 11110110 11010011 11111100 01011100 01111011 11100110 10101010 00110010
10001110 11011001 00110101 00010100 10000111 00000011 00111001 11100010 10110001 10001101
10110101 01010110 11010000 11010010 11000110 10101100 00010111 01011001 00111100 10011010
10110110 10010011 10000110 11111010 11010111 00110110 10110011 10010000 11011100 01010110
10010101 10100100 10011100 00000011 10011110 10110101 10101010 10111010 01010110 01000100
10110100 01101011 10101100 10011101 10110011 01001010 11001111 11101001 01010100 11010001
10111001 11101011 01010011 00101011 01100010 10011010 11010101 11011101 10100010 00001001
10011001 10110001 01001101 11001110 01001111 11111111 00000000 01011010 10100011 11001110
01110011 01001100 11110011 00111001 11100010 10010010 01101001 01101110 00000011 11011111
10011110 11110101 00001001 01011010 01110011 00110110 00111110 10011110 10110101 00001001
10010011 11011110 10011011 01010001 01100000 00100001 00100000 11110101 10101000 10011011
10100111 01011110 00101000 01110011 10011010 01100110 11101100 01010000 10101111 10110111
01000000 01100011 00110111 11100111 10011110 11010100 11100101 00100010 10100011 00111000
11001111 01011110 00101001 10101001 10011110 01110011 11010010 10100010 10100100 00111001
01011101 11000000 10110001 10111000 00010001 11001111 00010100 11111100 11100111 10001010
10000001 00001000 11000001 11001101 01001100 10000100 11111010 01111101 01001101 01011010
11101100 00110001 01110110 10001111 11111110 10111101 00101010 10010000 01000110 00110001
11001101 00001011 10000011 11000110 01101000 00111000 11000101 01010010 01111101 01011000
10000100 00011100 10011100 01010101 10000100 00000010 10100000 01001100 00010111 00111100
11110011 01010011 10100001 10101001 01001101 01101100 11000110 11001001 00010100 01110001
10011010 00011000 01110010 00001101 00101010 01110011 11010010 10011111 10011101 11011101
00000101 01100011 10100110 10110111 01000000 00110000 00001010 01010110 11101001 01001010
10100011 11010111 11010110 10011100 00010111 00111101 10101010 10010100 10010101 10101100
10001010 10110001 00010111 10010111 11101111 01001100 01101000 11000001 00100100 11010101
10101101 10111100 11010011 11110110 10001010 01101001 00100110 11110101 00100101 10111011
00010100 10010110 00101010 01110111 10010100 00101010 11010111 10010111 10010001 10011010
01001111 00101111 11110000 10101011 10110111 00101110 11000010 00101001 10011000 10111001
11000101 00110001 10100011 10101011 10001110 10111100 01010100 00101110 10100100 01010011
11101000 00100011 00110110 01111000 00010111 11010000 00011100 11010101 00111001 01101101
00010000 11110110 10101101 01110111 00000000 01110110 10101010 11110010 00101110 01111111

```
00000011 01010010 10101111 00010001 11101010 01100011 11001011 01100111 00011001 00111001
00100011 10111101 01100111 11011101 01011000 10001100 11100100 00001110 10110101 10111111
00110110 00110001 11001000 11100110 10101001 11011100 00101110 01000001 00000010 10101110
00010010 10001111 01011101 11000010 11100111 00110001 01110011 01101100 00000000 11000110
00101011 00100010 11110010 11011100 11100000 11100011 00011110 11000000 11010111 01010101
00111100 01100000 11111010 01010110 00111101 11011100 01000111 00100100 10000000 01001111
10100101 01110110 01010011 10101001 00101011 11011001 00001010 11010111 00111000 11001101
01000110 00100011 10010010 00110000 00111000 10101100 01110111 11001010 10111110 00111101
11111111 00000000 00101010 11101011 01101111 11100000 11001000 01111110 00111110 01110011
11001101 01110010 11110111 01101010 11010001 11001000 01110000 00001000 00000111 10010011
10010001 01011110 10110110 00011110 01110111 11010001 10011100 10110101 11100000 11010110
11000110 11110110 10000011 01110000 10100101 10000110 01001001 10101111 01000010 11010011
01101110 00110111 01000100 10000111 00111101 10111001 11001101 01111000 11110101 10001101
11011001 10000010 01001100 11100111 00001000 01101011 10111101 11010001 00110101 00010000
11010001 01101101 01110110 11100011 10110101 01110010 11100011 10101000 01001001 11101011
00010100 01011101 00011001 11101001 01100011 10111000 10001110 01011101 11000011 11101011
01010111 00100001 00111110 11010101 11001111 11011011 01001111 10111011 10111101 01101011
01011010 11001011 11000110 00111111 01011010 11110010 01100110 10101100 10101110 11110111
00111011 00101100 01101010 10100001 11100000 01010100 10000000 10001111 11001110 10101010
01000010 11011011 10000111 01011110 01001101 01001111 00010001 11001101 01110011 11011001
10110101 10100000 01011011 01010010 01010110 11101001 11000101 00100110 01101000 01011110
10010100 01100110 10110010 01010111 00100110 11100001 10001110 00111001 00010100 11000111
11100111 10101101 01001000 01000111 10111110 01101001 10101111 11101001 11010110 10100110
01010011 01001001 11011000 01111011 10010000 10110111 01001100 01010100 01101111 10000010
00110011 01010010 00111000 00100100 00010001 11111010 11010011 01011101 01110001 10000001
01010110 10001010 00100000 01110011 10010010 01001111 10101101 01000100 11100100 01110100
11000110 01001101 01011000 01100000 00001001 11101000 01110011 01010101 01100110 11100000
11110100 00111001 10101010 10001100 10000100 01000011 00101000 10101010 01110111 00101010
00001000 11110100 11110110 10101011 11001101 10010110 01011111 01001010 10101101 00101100
01111001 11001000 11101111 11011010 10110101 10001011 01010111 00000011 00011010 11101010
00100001 10110000 10001111 01011010 11000111 10010110 00100000 10100100 10011100 11010111
01001001 01110011 00001001 00100011 10001010 11001000 10111100 10000000 01010111 01011101
00101001 01001001 01101110 01100101 00100101 01110011 00100011 00100000 00000010 01101001
00011000 01111111 01111011 00011111 10001101 00111101 11000001 11001111 01001110 10000110
10100001 01111111 11100111 11010011 10011110 10010101 11010110 10111011 10100011 00100111
10100110 11000010 00110111 00111111 11010010 10111101 00000011 11000000 10100000 00001101
00000000 01100111 00100011 01110100 10000100 11110001 11101100 01101011 11001111 10110001
11101010 01111001 10101111 01001001 11110000 10001010 11111001 00111110 00011100 10110110
11011111 11001001 00111001 01111111 11010110 10001010 10010101 01110100 11010100 11001110
10100110 10101011 01000011 01010111 10010110 00111001 11011011 10001110 11011100 10011010
01111011 11001000 10111100 11100111 10101000 11100000 00101111 10101101 01010100 01110110
01111001 00000001 00000000 00011110 01111111 10001011 10100110 00101010 00111111 11110101
00100000 01101110 00111011 11111101 01001001 11101011 01011001 10110111 10100001 11001101
01100010 11111110 01110010 10111001 01110011 10010011 11101001 01010101 11100110 10111010
10001010 00110111 00000101 10111010 11111011 01010110 01010100 11011010 10011111 10010111
00100011 10100110 00110011 11000111 00000111 10100110 01101011 00010110 11111011 01010000
10010000 00010111 01100010 01110001 10011110 10011100 11110101 10100001 00101110 11000101
00011101 00100101 11100110 10100100 10110000 11000111 10011000 11001000 00101111 11011000
00011010 11000110 10111101 11010110 00000100 11011001 00000101 01000010 00011110 11100100
01110011 01011100 11011100 11010111 01110011 00010011 10111000 10110001 00100100 11111010
11110100 10101000 11010011 00110010 11001000 01001010 01110101 11111010 11100110 10110100
11110110 01010110 00010110 10000101 10111001 01110101 00111001 10100011 01111100 00000001
10010100 00111101 01001111 01001010 10001101 10101111 01001100 10000011 10101110 00001000
11111101 01101010 10001100 10000010 01000001 00110110 00011101 10000001 11001000 11001000
00011110 11010100 11010101 01100000 00000001 11101100 01101011 01010111 01001110 11001110
11000100 10011011 00110110 11011010 10001110 00000111 00111000 11000000 11101011 01010110
11100001 11010100 01010000 11000110 11111001 00111001 11101111 11010110 10111001 01011111
00111011 01101000 01110011 00011110 01011100 10010011 11000110 01101001 11101011 00101001
01011100 10000010 11011000 00000111 10010000 00001001 10101000 11110110 00101010 11011110
11101000 00011101 00111100 01100110 00011011 11000011 10110100 10111001 00000100 11110000
00000111 10100001 11110101 10101011 00010111 11110110 11110001 11000100 01111111 01111001
10001101 11100001 01110000 01110001 01011100 10000111 11011011 00011111 11001100 00011100
11111011 11100100 00011111 01001010 11010100 10010011 01010100 00110011 11110001 00110001
00000011 10001110 10111001 11100110 10011111 00100100 10110110 00000100 11001000 10011010
00011001 00100010 10010010 00111001 01000000 11100100 00011010 11101000 00100001 01010110
10010110 00110000 11111011 10111010 11111111 00000000 10110101 01011100 11100010 11001010
11011000 01000110 01110000 01100100 00000011 10101000 11110101 10101110 10010010 00110111
11111101 11010100 01111011 01100011 00101000 00110110 10001111 10010111 11010010 10100001
10110111 00011111 10001000 00001110 11010001 10011011 01110110 00110001 11011010 10011111
00010010 10010110 11101011 01010010 00001000 01000111 10011000 00110001 11010010 10100101
00101010 01000111 01001110 10000111 10111101 01111100 11011011 01010010 10111110 10100111
10111011 01110100 01000110 10100011 00011101 00101001 00011011 00111011 10111101 11001101
01001001 10110101 10111011 01010000 00000001 11011111 10011010 01001110 01010001 01101110
```

11100000 00110100 00001111 01011010 01110110 00110111 11100100 01111010 01110101 10101001
01110110 11110001 11101001 01010001 11001001 11111011 10110101 00100111 00111111 01011010
10000110 11111001 01110110 00010001 00000011 10110110 00000111 01011110 01101001 11110001
10110001 00100010 10100011 11000001 01100011 01010010 00101001 11110110 11101111 01001001
10100110 10011110 10100000 01001000 10000100 10010001 11101101 01001011 11100110 01100011
10101101 00100010 11110000 01001110 01101001 10001100 01110111 00000011 10001010 11011010
11101001 10110001 00001111 00010010 11100111 10100101 01001000 00110011 10001100 11010100
01010001 10001100 00000001 11000101 01001010 11000011 00011100 11100010 10110011 11011111
01100010 01101100 10000111 10100001 11111101 00101001 01111100 11011100 10011111 01001111
01111010 10001101 10001000 00000011 00111101 11101001 00111010 11110100 11111110 01110100
10011011 01111011 00000101 10001001 10001100 10000000 10001100 01010010 01111001 10000000
11010100 01001100 10111000 11110110 10100110 00101111 00101101 10001100 11110001 11101011
01001101 01000001 00110001 00100111 01100010 11001111 00000111 10010001 01001110 11001000
00111101 11101001 10011000 11111001 00111101 10111011 11010010 01110110 10101001 01110100
10010011 01111010 10000011 01100100 10111111 00101111 01111110 10110100 10001010 00000000
11101111 01010001 11101110 11111100 11000101 00000011 11010111 00111100 11010000 11101000
01000101 01101100 10000010 11100100 11001010 10100000 11010011 11110000 00000000 11100100
00000011 01010100 10111100 11001110 01110001 10011110 00101000 11111011 01000111 11101111
00000000 10100111 11101100 11011011 10111110 10100000 01011100 11101011 10011010 01110010
00011100 11010011 01010000 11100101 00110001 11111000 11010010 10101001 00011001 10101100
10011100 00101100 11110101 01100010 00010101 00000111 00111001 00110100 11101111 10010100
10011111 10010100 11110100 10100110 10001110 01000001 00111101 10101000 01011100 00010001
01010001 01110110 10110110 00000111 10101000 11110100 11000111 01111110 01101001 11111101
01101001 10101000 00110000 00111001 11101111 01010010 00100000 00000010 10000101 01111110
10100011 00100011 01110101 00000110 10011100 10101011 11010000 01111111 01011010 10010011
00011001 11101011 01001011 11010111 11101110 11110100 11111010 01010000 11101111 01111011
10010011 01110010 10011001 01011100 11100111 10101111 11100111 01001100 11001110 00111000
11000110 00101010 11111001 10001111 00111101 01101010 00100111 10001110 10010100 10100010
10010110 10100011 10111001 00001010 00011110 00111101 01101001 11100000 10000010 00111010
01110011 10011010 01010101 01011100 00101111 10111101 00100010 11110101 11110110 10101001
10111000 00010010 00101001 00110100 10111011 10001110 11111110 10110100 11011100 11110001
11010111 10001010 01101010 10011100 11110001 01010111 00000101 11001101 10111110 10000100
10110100 01001100 01011011 10001110 00101010 00111001 00110000 01010100 11100100 11110011
01001101 01100010 00000110 01111101 01101010 00101001 10011011 00100011 00100010 10110111
01011010 01101110 01001011 01000110 00110110 10101011 00000011 01000111 00100000 10010001
00111001 01001010 11001111 11011101 11110011 00000000 00000101 01101110 01001010 01110111
00001100 00010001 10011100 11110101 10101010 00001111 01100111 11100101 01001010 00001000
11111011 10000110 10011010 10111101 11101100 00010110 01001011 01110010 01111101 00111000
00111001 00111111 00101000 00111101 01111101 01101011 10100001 10001111 11101110 11110011
01010100 10110100 11111000 10110110 10100000 00111000 10101011 11001001 11110111 00111110
01101110 10110101 10011100 10110101 10010110 10100000 11000000 01110001 11001101 00011101
00111001 10100000 01110001 11000001 11101001 01001011 11011111 11111001 01010001 00011011
01000101 11101100 00001111 01010001 00010110 10001100 00001100 11010011 11000000 10100011
10100000 10100010 11111110 01100010 00100000 01110001 10001100 11111011 01010010 00101110
01000000 10101001 00011000 01100110 10001100 01010110 11010111 10001011 00100111 01010001
00000011 10000011 11011010 10100100 00000011 10100111 00110101 00011000 01011110 00110011
01010010 00101111 11111110 00111011 01010001 00101011 00100001 10000110 00000110 01101001
10111000 11001110 01101001 11011011 10111110 01111110 00101001 10001110 11011011 01111111
00011010 10010110 11010010 11010100 01101010 11100010 11100111 00000110 10100011 10010000
00000011 11010100 01010011 10010100 11100110 10010111 10101001 10101001 01010011 01101000
01110110 00111001 10001111 00010000 11101001 11011110 01101100 01000110 01101000 11111000
00101011 11001001 11000111 10100101 01110011 10110110 11011111 11101011 00111000 10101111
01000010 10011010 00110000 11101011 10110100 10001010 11100101 11110101 00101101 00110100
11011010 11001111 11100111 00100000 11111101 11011001 11101010 00101011 01101010 01110101
01010011 11010010 11100001 01101011 00010101 01100010 10001100 10110110 01000111 01110011
11011110 10110100 01100001 10110011 10010010 00010010 00001111 00100100 00001110 01101010
00001000 00100011 00100010 01000000 01111111 01001010 11011011 10001001 10000001 00000011
10001100 01111011 01010011 01101101 10101101 11001000 01110111 01111011 00010001 01000111
11111011 11000101 00100000 11110000 01000111 01011010 01011101 10100100 01110010 10100011
10001110 11110101 00100111 00011111 10011111 10100101 01001111 00011001 01010011 11000001
11100000 11010110 00010101 00010010 01101111 01000010 11010011 00101001 11101111 00100000
11110100 11111100 01101010 01000000 01110000 00000001 11001101 01011010 11111011 00110000
00000100 00011110 11111111 00000000 01011010 01101001 10110111 11100011 11100100 10101100
00110101 01111101 00001101 00110100 00101011 11111001 10000100 00011110 10010100 01111001
10000100 10001110 00101010 01011111 10110011 00011101 10111101 00101010 00111111 00101001
10010111 10110111 00010101 00101010 01101101 10010010 11010000 10101000 11000100 01010100
11101011 00100110 01000111 00111101 10101010 10111111 00100011 10101101 00011001 00100111
10100000 10101101 01111101 10100010 01101111 01000100 00100110 10001011 00101110 00111000
00011110 10011110 10010101 00010100 10000000 10001100 10010011 01010010 10100011 00010010
00001101 00110110 01010001 10010101 00111110 10110101 01010111 01111101 01001001 10110001
10011011 01110100 11011100 00011010 11000111 10111001 01101100 00011100 10000011 10001010
10111101 10101000 01001010 11001010 01001000 11111100 00110011 01011001 00101110 11111011
10111111 00001010 11011010 00111110 10000100 11011010 11100101 01101001 01100101 00100100

10010001 01010001 11111001 10000111 00011101 01001110 01101001 11101101 00011000 11001001
00110101 00011001 00111000 11001000 11000110 00111101 11101011 01111000 11111001 00010110
00110010 01011001 01001010 11100111 10011110 10111110 11110101 00000010 11100110 01001001
01010001 01111001 00111011 10011000 00001100 01111010 11010010 01001100 10111001 11100111
00010101 10100011 11100001 10111000 00000100 11111010 10001100 01111011 11110010 00110110
00011101 11111101 00111000 10101101 11100000 10000001 00100011 10110100 10110101 10001101
01100010 10001000 01111100 10111000 10101010 00111010 10000101 11011001 01100010 01010100
01110100 10101011 00110111 01010010 11111001 01010000 11111010 11010111 00111111 00110100
11011111 10111100 00101101 10011110 00101011 01101011 10101110 10100101 01000010 00110111
00010101 11100100 11000000 10100110 10001001 01000011 00001100 11111010 01010101 00011011
10011001 00111110 01111100 11100111 00111100 11010100 01011110 01100011 00001100 10011101
11010101 01110110 11100110 01110110 10001001 10110101 10001101 01001100 10110001 00000110
10100010 01100001 10011100 01100110 10100011 10110110 10011000 01101101 10100111 01001100
11011111 10001111 11100011 01001111 11011001 10101000 10111101 01001001 11100110 00101011
01001001 11111110 10110011 00111001 11100010 10101100 01011001 11011101 00000101 00111000
01111110 10011001 10101010 01101110 01101010 00100101 10010011 11100111 11001000 10100011
10010001 00111101 01010011 00010110 11111010 00011101 00110100 00110010 10000110 11000001
01011110 01101010 01101111 00110000 00011010 11001000 10110100 01100011 10110000 00010000
11010101 01101111 11001100 11011010 01110011 01001001 01101000 01100101 11010110 11000101
11010101 10010000 01100011 00011001 11000101 00110001 10011111 10110000 10101010 11011110
01100110 01101000 11110011 00111111 01001010 00011010 01001001 10001101 11101000 01001000
11110010 10010011 11110100 11101111 01001100 01101001 00000101 01000100 11110010 00001010
10001011 11001101 10101000 10010101 11010110 11000010 00101100 00011001 00111011 01010100
00101100 11000011 11111100 10011010 10001001 10011111 11111111 00000000 11010101 01010001
10110011 01100100 11010001 00000110 11011010 10110011 11101000 00000100 11111001 11001101
01001000 10101101 10001110 00101010 10101000 01111100 01110010 01111011 11010100 11001000
11011001 11100010 10000111 00010111 01111011 10001110 11000100 11001001 10011111 10101101
01001100 10000111 00000010 10100011 01010010 01000110 00000000 10101001 00000111 10111101
00010110 11010110 11101000 00000111 00101111 00111100 10001010 01000110 00010100 11111110
00110001 10001010 01100011 01110100 10100001 10111101 01000101 10110000 10101001 11010011
11100101 11101011 01010011 00100111 01001111 01111010 10101110 10000100 11110000 01110001
01010110 00100011 00111000 00111100 01110100 10101010 11010001 00100010 10001001 10010011
10010101 11001101 00111001 01110011 11010010 10011010 00001000 00000110 10011110 10111101
01111001 10101100 01100101 10100011 11010100 10100001 11100000 00001100 01010100 10001010
00000110 00110011 01010001 10000011 01010010 00101001 00011000 11101101 11111000 11010000
10101111 01110010 01000101 00011110 10110100 01110101 00110100 10011001 11001111 00011001
10100011 00100100 00011110 00001101 01101011 10100010 11010101 00010010 11011101 11110110
00100100 01010010 00101001 10101101 11001001 10100011 00100100 10011010 00111010 00011110
01101000 01001111 10100000 00010001 10110111 01011110 10010101 00010011 10001010 10110000
01111111 10011101 01000100 11111101 11101001 10110100 10000110 01010101 01110001 01010101
11011100 00000010 01101010 11010011 10101110 01101010 00000111 10001111 10001100 11100111
10100101 01001100 10011111 01110001 00010100 00100100 01011100 01110101 10101010 01010011
11110001 10011110 10111000 11101011 01011010 00110111 00000100 00000001 10011111 01101010
11001010 10111011 10011011 00001000 11110100 10010010 01011011 10001101 00100010 10000100
10111011 01000110 01000001 10101100 11101011 10010000 00111001 00011001 10101001 11101110
01100100 00011000 11000010 10011010 11001101 10011010 01010010 01111110 11110001 11111100
01101011 10110010 00101001 00110101 11001100 10110111 00101110 11000110 01101101 11111000
11100100 11100011 10100001 11110111 10101110 01100011 01010100 10001111 00100100 10110010
00011110 00001001 11101010 01101011 10101000 10010100 10000110 00100100 10011010 11000010
11010100 11010100 00001000 11011111 00100111 11010111 00000010 10111011 11101000 00111011
00110100 01110011 11010110 01011010 00011100 11101011 10011100 00011100 01111110 01110101
01111111 01001101 10111101 10011110 00000110 00111011 00001001 00101001 11011100 01100110
10101011 11011000 01011010 00110101 11011100 10000101 01010000 00010010 01000111 00100100
11100011 10100101 01110101 01110110 00011010 00011010 10101100 01000011 10001100 11111101
01101011 11010000 10101101 01010010 00010001 01011010 10011100 01010100 11010100 10011011
11010000 10111101 10100101 11101011 00101010 11100000 00000110 01110001 11100110 01111010
01100111 00010101 11010101 01011001 01011110 00000110 00000000 01100111 10101111 10111101
01110010 00000111 11000011 01000010 01010000 00011110 00000011 11100101 00111111 10101001
10101001 00101101 10111110 11011101 10100100 10110000 11110011 00000100 10010011 01011011
10100001 11000110 01000111 01101010 11110001 10101010 01000010 10001101 01011111 10000101
11101010 01111010 00110001 10010100 10010110 11100111 10100011 11011011 01001100 01111000
11101111 01010110 10000100 10011100 01100100 01110001 01011100 11011110 10010101 01111010
10110011 00101000 10010101 00011011 01111010 00011111 01111110 01101011 01101001 00100101
00000101 01101011 11001011 10011100 00100101 00000011 01010110 01101001 00101011 01100100
00001100 01010100 10011100 10000001 01010100 10100010 10011000 01100000 00011100 01110011
01001010 11010011 00010110 00011100 01010100 00111000 10111001 00010000 01011100 11001000
11000111 00011111 10011001 10100100 01100010 10101010 00110011 10011010 10100000 11110010
11001000 01000000 00000000 11010010 01100101 10110001 11001001 10101100 10011010 11011010
11101000 10100110 01011001 10010010 01000000 00111011 11010100 01001111 00100001 00000110
10100000 11011011 10000011 10111000 10011110 00101001 11011100 00011010 11010110 11001011
10100110 10000100 01101010 01001011 10111100 01010100 01010010 01111100 11011110 11110100
00110011 01101101 00111101 00101001 10111111 01111000 00011110 01110000 01101000 11110110
01010111 01111010 10010101 01110001 10110101 00001100 10001010 00110001 01010010 00111111

```
01011100 01110110 00000010 10100011 01100011 10010011 10000011 01011010 00110100 10101110
11010011 01000001 01110010 10111100 10101011 11001110 00101011 00111110 11101010 00011101
11011001 10101101 00100111 10001100 10000011 11101101 01010000 11001100 00111110 01011111
10101101 01101011 00001011 00101101 11000100 11110101 01000111 00100101 01111001 00001111
10010111 00100001 00011000 11100100 11110101 11110111 10101010 01001110 10100111 10110101
01110100 00011010 10001100 00011001 00100111 00011110 10011001 11001111 10100101 01100000
10111111 00001110 11100011 10111000 11101111 01011101 11110100 10100100 10011010 00110001
01101000 10000000 10010010 00000001 00111000 10101111 01010011 11010010 10100011 01011000
10110100 11001011 01100101 01000010 10000100 00101100 01000000 01110000 01101011 11001011
10010000 10010010 11000011 10111110 01001101 01110101 10011010 01010110 10100010 11010000
11000110 00110111 10010010 00000111 01000011 11000111 01011010 11100111 11000101 10101011
11000111 01000000 10001101 11110111 00111010 11000110 11001011 00101001 00000000 11110011
11101101 01011001 01111010 10000000 10011001 00010111 00101000 10100101 11000111 01110011
01010110 11100001 10111010 01010110 00011001 01000011 11000111 10110101 01001010 10001100
01001110 01001111 01101010 11110011 10100011 01011010 01010100 11110111 01100001 00101010
01101010 01000111 00110001 00110000 01100111 00000011 10110110 01101010 10111100 11010110
11100010 01000010 00001111 00111011 11000111 00100011 10011010 11101000 11101110 10101101
00100010 10010101 11001011 11110100 01111010 11100111 11110101 00101011 01011011 10101011
01101001 00001011 01111111 10101100 10001011 10101110 11100001 11111010 01010111 10100011
01000011 00011001 00011001 11011001 01101100 01110010 01001110 10010011 01000110 01100100
11010000 01110000 01000001 00000000 11100100 11111010 11010100 01110000 11000010 11010001
11001000 10000110 00010001 11001000 11110111 10100111 00111101 11000001 01110111 11000111
01011100 01010100 01110000 11001100 01110010 01111001 11000101 01110110 10111000 11101011
01100110 11001001 01000011 10100101 10110111 00110010 01101111 01100010 01000000 00111111
01011010 11001111 01110101 10011011 11001010 00111000 01010001 11010011 10101101 01101001
01001011 00110111 01100011 10000011 11101111 01010101 00100101 01100010 00111000 01010011
11010111 10011010 00110110 11010101 00010010 01010011 01000101 11110010 10001000 00001110
01111001 11101101 10010011 01010000 00110011 01111110 11110101 00011010 01000001 10011010
10011010 01001111 11011110 00111110 01000111 01101110 11100100 11010100 00101010 00000100
10001110 00000000 10010011 00111100 11110100 10101110 10001000 00101101 00101110 01001011
00010001 10011011 00001101 10001100 01110001 11010111 00110100 10000001 10001000 00100111
10011110 01111011 00010011 01010110 01101110 00100000 00001010 10011011 10001011 00011100
11110110 00010101 01001001 11100100 00000001 10001111 01101100 00001010 10110101 01100110
10110100 00000011 01010010 11010010 01110011 11000010 11111110 10110101 11010101 11101001
11000000 01111101 10010001 00111100 11001011 10100010 10101101 11101001 10001010 11100001
00101101 00100110 00101011 00100000 11100011 11011111 00111101 01101011 10100000 10000110
01110111 01101000 11000001 00000110 10110000 10011100 00101111 10101011 00011010 01100111
10101101 01111001 01010010 10001110 01110000 01110001 01000010 01101111 11000111 01000011
10001110 11010101 01110001 10100101 11111100 00111110 10110101 00011100 10010010 01010111
11001000 10101011 11010100 10110101 11010001 11101101 10101011 10010101 11010011 01110110
01111001 00011100 01010011 10010000 10010001 11010100 00011111 11000010 10010111 11001110
01010100 01001100 10010011 11001101 01010100 10111001 10111110 00010001 10000111 11111101
00101011 01011010 01110000 01001101 01011101 00001101 10110010 11011111 10011011 10010011
11010010 10011000 01110000 11000000 10000110 10101100 10011111 11101101 00111100 10000011
10110000 11100000 10001111 11010110 10011000 11111010 10001001 11001000 00100101 10111000
10101011 11110110 01101101 11101011 01100001 10100011 01100001 00010000 00001100 11110011
01010010 01101101 00000000 01110001 01011000 00011111 11011010 01001101 11010000 00010100
00111100 11110101 10100111 01111101 10111001 10111011 10011110 01111101 01101000 11100100
01111101 01000011 01010111 10110001 10111010 11000011 10001111 10011011 10101101 00001010
10100100 01110010 01110001 11111001 11010110 00100111 11011011 10001010 10011100 10010110
11100111 11111011 10110100 11100100 10111110 11110111 11001111 10111101 01001100 11100000
10010101 10011010 01100100 11011001 10011011 10001000 00000001 00011001 11001110 00101010
01000110 00011110 10011100 10001010 11000101 10001010 11110100 11111010 11111110 01110101
00110010 11011110 01100011 10010010 11000111 00010101 01011110 11001111 01001101 00011001
01011010 10011010 01001100 10111001 00111100 01110100 10100001 01000000 11100000 00001111
11001110 10101001 00100101 11111010 10000001 11110011 10011111 10100101 01011000 10000110
11101110 00100110 00100000 01101110 11100100 10011110 00111011 01010110 00101010 10011011
01110010 11010000 10010111 01110100 01001001 00101010 11110011 10001010 00010001 01110001
01010010 10010011 11001110 01111111 00111010 01101011 01001000 00000111 01010001 01010110
11111101 11010111 10101001 00111011 10000001 11001110 00110001 01001101 01100000 00110000
00001110 01110001 01001000 11101100 00101010 00100110 10010111 10110101 01100010 11110100
11010101 10000000 11101101 11100011 10100110 01101001 10101110 11011000 11101000 01101010
00010010 01000000 00100111 10011010 10001110 01000010 11000000 11111011 01010011 11100110
10110110 10001101 00001110 11011101 10001001 00011001 10110001 11011111 10011010 01110101
10100000 00110010 00111001 11001101 01000000 00111110 01101010 10110111 01101110 01110001
11000000 10100001 10101110 11000001 01101101 00001011 10100000 01010010 11111101 11100001
11101111 01010001 00101100 10011001 00011100 11111110 10110100 11110011 10000001 11010011
10101101 01100111 10111110 10101100 00000111 00011111 01111010 01001111 00110000 11111110
00000010 10100011 11001111 00110100 11110110 11101001 11110010 11100010 10000101 00101011
00000101 10001001 01010110 01101110 10000000 11010100 10101011 00101010 10011100 01111010
11010101 00111110 11010100 11101100 11100011 00000011 10111001 11101111 01000011 01101010
01001111 11011110 00000111 00011110 11000101 11011111 00110000 00011110 11010100 11110001
00101111 01100011 01010101 00010000 11100110 10010000 00011100 00010010 01101010 00100111
```

11001010 10011110 10000100 11110010 00110010 11100111 10011001 11001110 00101001 11011100
00011110 10110101 01011001 00100100 00111110 10010100 10111110 01101001 00100011 10001110
11010101 01101101 01111011 10100001 01100010 01100111 01000011 10011110 01111010 01010100
01101111 10001100 01100011 00011100 11010001 11100111 00001100 01010100 01101100 11011001
10100010 00010000 11010010 11001100 01010110 00010100 11111011 11010010 00110001 11000000
10100110 00010110 00001010 00110010 01101010 00000111 10011100 00000001 01010110 10010101
10110100 01000011 10111011 00011110 11110010 11100011 11101011 01010101 11100101 10011000
00110110 00101010 10110101 11001100 11000000 01111101 11010011 11001001 10101000 00000100
10000111 00100000 11100100 00010010 00111010 00000011 01001110 01001110 11111010 10010010
01011000 11011101 10110101 11000101 00111101 10100100 11001001 10101100 11111111 00000000
00111000 10010010 01000001 11111110 01110101 00101000 10010001 10001001 11000111 10110101
00101110 01100101 11010100 10111110 01010011 01101110 11011010 01100000 10100011 11001011
00100110 10101110 10001001 00000110 11001010 11100111 11100010 01101100 11100000 11110011
10011111 01011010 10110110 10010111 00001100 00000000 00001100 01110011 01010011 00110110
10011110 10110001 00110010 01110001 00110101 00011110 01000101 00011101 11111111 00000000
00111010 00011010 01010001 10001110 00111111 00111010 10100001 11100110 11100111 00000111
10101001 10100011 11001100 00100000 11100100 11110100 11110100 10101100 00010101 01001101
01110101 00101010 11000101 11110101 10010111 00100011 11111100 00101000 01101001 01001001
11111010 01010101 00001111 00110011 10001110 11110100 10100100 10011100 01110101 10100101
00101001 00111011 00010101 11001010 01011011 11110011 10111111 01110111 11001000 11111100
01101001 10011110 01110001 00011100 11111111 00000000 00101010 10101110 01011011 10001100
01110110 10100011 00100011 00111001 00010100 11101101 10110011 10111000 10101100 01011010
00110010 00010011 10000011 10011110 00101001 10111110 01100111 00111110 11010101 00001010
10001100 01110000 00111111 00101010 01110111 11111100 10110100 00011110 10110101 01001110
11101101 00000101 10001001 10001011 01010010 10101111 01001110 01101001 10011000 11110101
11101001 01001000 11000111 10110110 00110001 01001011 10011111 10111000 01101100 01001010
00111101 00101000 11111110 00100001 01001000 10111101 00110011 11011110 10001100 10001110
10111001 10100010 00100010 00011110 11011111 01110111 10011010 10101011 00111100 01000010
01010101 11011010 01000110 01111000 10101011 01011001 00111110 10011101 11101001 10000100
01100100 00010001 10001010 01101110 01001110 11110111 01000010 10110001 10000111 11100100
01111001 00101100 00110011 11010000 10011010 10111010 00010111 01101111 01111010 10011010
01111000 10110010 00111011 10000011 01010101 11100011 00111100 11100000 11110110 11101111
01011101 00010100 10100101 11001111 00011101 00001001 01101000 01110001 00000011 00011001
11000110 00101001 10111001 11110100 11101001 10011010 10010111 00010100 11000110 11000000
10100101 00101000 10000000 11101111 00110100 10001100 01111010 01100111 11010110 10100101
01000011 10111001 01110011 10011110 00000001 10101010 11001100 10111101 11000111 01011010
01100011 00011001 00010111 10010001 01010010 11010010 11011100 01000101 11110100 01100110
00000111 00000100 11100100 01111011 11010011 10100010 01100101 10010001 10111001 00111000
11110110 10101010 01001011 00111001 00101000 00000001 00111100 11010010 00100011 00010010
01110011 11011110 10010011 10100100 10011000 10010011 01100110 10001100 10110000 10101001
01000010 01101010 10110001 01011100 00001100 11010100 11010110 10110010 10001001 00000000
00011111 11001100 11010011 11100110 01010000 01000110 00000101 01110011 11011011 10010001
10010111 01110010 10110111 00011111 11110000 00101010 01110000 00111001 11100011 10111101
00110101 11010100 11100111 10101101 00110111 01110001 00001100 00111000 11101001 11010110
10101110 11101110 01011011 00100000 00110011 10110101 00101000 01000001 00000100 00010001
11000001 10101100 00111111 00101000 00000011 11000000 11001000 10101110 10110001 11010100
01001010 00001000 00100011 11110011 10101010 11101111 01100101 00010000 01100010 01110001
11111000 00001010 11011001 01001110 11011010 00000101 10001110 01011101 00100010 00111100
11100100 01010100 01110111 00110000 11110001 11000101 01110100 11101111 01100011 00011011
01110111 11111010 01111011 01010100 01101101 10100110 01000010 01000001 11001001 00100100
00011010 10111111 01101000 10010011 10110000 10011001 11000110 10111010 10011100 01100000
10001110 01111011 01010111 01000001 11100001 01011000 11111100 10111000 10100101 01100000
01001110 01011100 11110101 10101011 01010010 01101000 10010110 11001110 00110001 10111010
01001111 11000000 11010100 11010000 01011011 11000111 01101000 10000110 00111000 11001111
00010101 11010111 01000010 10100010 01101100 01110001 01100100 01011010 10110100 11000111
00000000 00000011 11000111 01111010 11000111 10010000 10001100 01010101 11111101 01011000
10011101 10000000 10000011 10000001 11010000 11010110 00100001 10010000 10011001 00110001
11011000 01010110 10101110 10100100 01101111 10110001 10110100 00010001 00011101 11100110
01110001 10010001 01011001 10001101 00111100 10100101 11010001 01001111 01001110 11110101
10110001 00101110 00001000 11101011 11000101 01010110 11110010 11010111 10101110 00111001
10101110 10011010 01001110 11001011 01000010 10000010 11011001 10001110 00111110 01100011
01010110 00111100 11011110 00111001 00111100 01010101 01111101 11000001 01000001 10101000
00100110 10010111 10010001 10001111 11000110 10110100 01110110 01111111 00010001 00110110
00100110 10011010 01010001 10001100 11100111 00011100 11110100 10100110 01000010 11000001
10011011 00010101 01001110 01010010 11001101 11010100 11010100 10110110 10111011 01000001
11001001 00100100 00010000 00101001 01011010 00011101 00000011 01100011 01110010 11011110
01001101 10101001 11101011 01010110 10111100 11000001 10001110 10110101 10011011 00001011
00011010 10011111 11001101 11101000 00110001 11000101 00100110 10010011 00110010 01100101
10010101 10010100 01110011 11000101 00100111 10011100 00110001 10011010 10100110 11110010
00010000 00110001 01010001 10110100 10011100 01100000 01010100 01001010 10011110 10011010
11101000 00001001 00010111 00011110 01110001 01010001 10110100 10111100 01110001 11010110
10101001 11111001 10100000 01100000 01110111 10100001 01011011 10110111 00111111 10011101
01010111 11110000 11010110 11011010 10001010 11001001 10010110 11010110 01001100 10011110

10111100 11010011 10110011 01010100 11011010 01001100 01110111 00110100 11111111 00000000
00110111 00100011 00011100 11100111 11010110 10100011 10011001 00111011 11011100 10111011
00010110 01010111 00100111 00100100 11010100 11110001 00001100 10000000 01000111 00010101
01011010 00110011 10011100 00011010 10110011 00001111 10110111 01001010 00010010 11101100
10000101 01111110 10001100 10110011 00010101 01001100 11000011 00100100 00000101 11111110
01110101 00011100 00111111 11000101 01010010 01111010 01100011 10101101 00100111 11100100
00100001 11000000 01110011 11001001 11100010 10011010 11000111 11100111 10100101 11011101
10001010 10001101 10110001 10111100 10010011 01010000 11100100 11011110 11000000 00111101
00001110 00011111 11101011 01010011 00101000 00000011 11101011 01010101 10010001 11111001
11000000 11100010 10101100 00100111 01000001 11101011 01000101 11101111 10111000 11110100
00100111 01001111 11110110 10101001 11011011 10110001 01010000 10110001 10100011 00111001
11101111 01011000 11011010 11101111 01010010 10001011 00100001 10111011 11010011 11000011
00001110 01111000 10101010 11100001 10101001 01110111 01110001 11010110 10101010 01001100
10010110 01011000 01000011 01010010 00101111 10101111 11110101 10101010 11000001 10111010
01010100 11001001 00100110 01111000 00110101 01101010 10100101 11110101 00010101 10000111
11111011 10001010 00001110 01000111 01011010 01100110 11101010 01001100 11100100 11010011
10111011 01101111 01100010 01000001 10001111 01111010 01100111 11011110 11111001 01101000
01100011 10001100 11010011 01110111 01100011 10011010 10110101 01101101 11000010 11100011
01011111 10001100 10001010 10001001 10000000 00111001 00011001 11100010 10100101 11100011
11110011 10101010 11110011 01001000 00000000 11110100 00010100 11111101 10011011 11111000
10000000 11001101 10111111 10010011 01101110 01010101 01101011 00001110 01110110 00100111
00100011 10111111 01101010 11010001 10111100 10010011 01110001 01110110 00111110 10111101
10101011 00100010 11100001 10111000 11101011 01010000 11011111 01000100 01101101 00010010
10011011 10100111 00100100 00011110 10110101 10011011 01110010 00111000 00111101 10101010
11101101 11000100 11011101 01110011 01011001 10010111 00110010 10011110 01101011 10110010
10010100 01101101 11010100 10110110 01010011 11001001 00000100 01100110 10110001 11110101
10100010 00001001 00001010 10011100 10010010 01111000 11000101 01101010 01001100 11011101
01001101 01000001 10100101 01011001 11001011 10101001 01101010 01101000 11000010 00100111
01110100 01000011 11001001 00000011 10001010 11101101 10100100 11010100 01110101 01111101
00001110 01101010 10011010 11101000 01101010 11111000 01100111 01000101 00110001 01011010
01100111 00000000 11100100 11110010 01111011 11010111 01010001 01101101 01101001 00011100
01100011 10001110 10111101 11101010 11101101 10011101 10011001 01011000 10010000 00000001
10000001 10001010 10111000 10110110 01000011 00100001 10001000 00100100 11111010 01010111
10011001 01011011 00010010 11100110 11011011 01101100 10101010 01110100 11010100 00010101
10001100 10110100 10000011 00111001 11000000 11001110 01101010 01000001 10100111 00111011
00001110 10000000 00000011 11011110 10110110 11010110 00010101 00011111 11000010 00000000
11000110 00111000 10100111 00100100 01011000 00000010 10111000 10100101 01010111 01011101
00010001 10100001 10001011 01100101 10100010 11000001 00001100 10000110 01100100 11011110
01110010 01110000 01111001 11000000 11111100 10101011 01010101 01100000 00001010 00110000
00010111 00000000 01111110 00110101 01100001 01100011 11001001 00011101 10000101 01001000
10100000 01110100 00110100 00111001 10111001 00111111 01111000 01000101 01100000 10100111
00011000 11000110 00101000 11011010 01010100 11100000 00001110 01001101 01001101 11101010
01110001 10011010 01101011 00011100 11010100 01101010 10111010 10000111 01010010 00010110
00011100 11111011 01100110 10001100 01100100 11010100 10001011 11000000 10100011 00011100
11111010 01010101 01110011 11001010 00111011 00100000 00100010 01101111 01000010 00101001
01011011 00000011 00000000 01010011 11110110 10001100 11100111 10011110 10011110 10110100
01101101 11011100 01111110 10110101 01001001 10110110 10001001 00100011 00101010 01001111
01101010 01000110 01010010 00111010 11010101 10000001 11101001 01001100 01111000 11110001
01001110 11101000 10100010 00100110 01011111 01011010 10001101 11100010 00000011 10100101
01001010 11111100 00001111 01111010 01100111 01010011 11010110 10001111 01101001 10101101
11001001 00101011 10110000 11101100 01101010 10111100 11001010 01000111 00101101 11111000
01010101 11110110 01010000 01000110 01111111 10011101 01010011 10011001 01001000 11100100
01110100 10101010 10001100 10011101 11110100 00010101 10001100 10111011 10110001 10111000
01100000 11010111 00111011 01111111 00010000 01001001 01110111 00001110 11110101 11010001
11001111 00011001 00111001 11001101 01100010 11101010 01010001 10000010 10011001 11111101
00101011 10111110 00001010 11101101 01011000 10011001 10011001 00010000 10110110 11011001
11010000 10011110 01000000 00111100 11111011 11010110 11100010 01001010 10110010 10001100
10100110 01000111 10110001 10101110 01111101 01000111 00111101 01111001 00010101 00111010
01001010 01010100 10000011 10010010 00001000 11111101 01101011 01101010 10010100 11101111
10111001 10011100 01001110 10010110 11010110 11100001 10101101 11000110 00010100 10011100
00011010 11010101 10110110 10111110 00010010 01110111 11000001 11101110 00101011 10010011
10110110 10111100 00111100 10000111 00111011 11110011 11010111 00110101 01111010 00011001
01111001 11011100 10011111 10011101 01110000 01010101 10100101 01111110 10000110 10000111
01010000 10110011 00101011 00000100 11000011 01110101 10101001 10001000 11001010 01110011
11111111 00000000 11101011 10101110 01100110 00111011 10100010 10100111 00011001 11110111
10101011 11010110 11110111 11000101 10110000 00110011 10011100 01010111 00101100 10101000
10111000 11101100 10000110 10000110 01011111 01101000 00110001 01001111 00101001 10010110
11010011 00010001 00111111 01110000 01111010 00011010 11000000 10111001 10110011 10011110
11010110 01000010 10110011 01000111 10000010 00001111 11100111 11110100 10101110 11100010
11010010 01110101 10010001 01111000 11101010 00111011 11111010 11010100 01110111 01110110
11110001 01011110 10100011 10101100 11001011 10010001 10001100 00000011 11011100 01010111
01000101 00111100 01001100 10100000 11111101 11110100 01100101 01010010 10010010 01111011
00011110 01111110 11100111 01110111 01010000 01001101 01010101 10011000 10010001 00100110

```
01001110 01000000 00011110 10010101 10101111 10101110 11101001 00010011 11011000 00010001
00100100 01100001 11100100 10000000 11100111 00100111 00011111 01110111 11101011 01011000
01101110 01001001 01001110 00111010 01110111 10101111 01010110 10001100 10100011 00111000
11011101 01110101 00111000 11100101 00000111 00010111 10101000 10111011 10010100 10001110
11101110 01001111 01101010 01101101 10111000 00100001 10001011 01000110 00110010 11100011
11010111 10110101 01000011 00011000 00000010 01000010 11001110 00001110 00111011 01110011
01010011 00101100 11011001 00111011 10000110 01001110 00000101 01110100 11011010 11001101
00100100 01100110 11110101 00100100 10111000 10010100 10010101 11001001 00111100 11111101
01101011 00110110 01111110 00111001 00111100 10010001 11010110 10101101 10111000 00010011
00000010 01001110 01110011 11010111 00010101 01011110 01011100 10010000 00000001 11100110
10101110 00101010 00110111 10110000 00010010 01011001 00011111 11011110 11111101 11010001
10011111 01011010 11010011 00110111 01000100 00011100 00101111 01001010 11001000 10001000
00011000 10011011 00111101 01111001 11101001 11101011 01011010 00001010 11010110 10001100
00110010 11100100 10101011 01110111 00010101 00110101 00101001 01110011 01101110 00110100
11101100 01111011 01101111 11011010 11010101 10001001 00000111 10001010 10001010 01001011
10101000 11000001 00100011 01110110 00111101 11110011 01011100 10000011 11101010 01110010
11100011 10000110 11101101 11001101 01000100 11111010 10001011 00011110 10100100 10100000
00111110 11110101 11110011 01010000 11000011 11011101 00011110 11010111 00111010 00111010
00011011 10011101 01001001 01000110 01001001 11000110 11001110 11010101 10001111 01111001
10101001 00011001 00111110 11100111 00010101 10010111 00101100 11000101 10000001 11001001
11001110 01101010 00010110 01111111 10010000 10011100 01110000 00101011 10100010 10011101
00100101 01101011 00100001 00111001 10101011 10010110 01011010 11111101 10000011 10011111
01011111 01101010 00111110 11011110 01110001 10110111 10101111 00111101 01001101 01100111
11111001 10011001 00100100 11100010 10100010 11000001 00101111 11010100 10001111 01011010
11010111 11011001 11110101 01100100 11110011 10011010 00100110 11101001 10000110 00010111
10100001 11101011 01001001 11111101 10100111 00101010 10011100 01110001 10011111 01101010
10100011 00101001 00100100 00000011 11011111 11010110 10001000 01100010 01101001 00011011
00100100 01100010 10011011 10001101 11110101 01100000 10100101 01100011 01011110 00011101
01000100 10010010 01001011 11010101 11111000 01101110 00000001 00111101 01101011 00001101
00100011 11111100 01101010 01100101 00000001 01000000 00100100 11111101 01101011 10011101
11010010 01001111 01010001 10101010 10100110 11011001 10111000 00111001 00011011 01001111
10101000 10101001 00111100 11100010 00001000 11100110 10110010 00010010 01010000 10111110
11110100 10001101 00111011 00010000 01000000 00100011 00100111 11010110 10010100 00100011
01100110 11001010 01010101 00001101 01001001 00101110 10110001 11011110 10100011 11111011
01101001 00100111 10000110 00110101 10001110 11110011 00110001 11110110 00110101 00011100
10110011 00110110 11101100 00110001 00111001 10101101 00100001 01001010 00101010 11111100
11001000 10000111 00111101 01001101 11110100 11010110 10100111 10000001 11001000 01001001
00110000 00111101 00111011 01010101 11101011 01111111 00010001 11111001 10011100 01001100
10000000 00010011 11011101 01101011 10001111 11110011 00001011 01111111 11111010 11101001
10100010 01010011 10011110 10111000 00010100 00101010 01010000 00010011 01101100 11110100
01001000 00101111 10100011 10011100 01100110 00110111 00000110 10100110 00101101 11111001
01010111 10011101 11000001 01110100 11110001 01100111 01100011 01100000 11111011 00011100
01010110 10110101 10010110 10111001 00110100 01100011 00010011 00010011 00100110 01111101
01001111 01001010 11000110 01111000 01000101 00010100 11111001 01001011 01010011 11101110
01110101 00111001 11100111 01110110 01101001 00010100 10110001 11100011 10101111 10111101
01010101 10110001 11010100 01101100 01101110 01000110 00111100 11001101 10001111 11101000
01101011 01100001 00101101 01010100 10000000 11001000 11011111 10001101 01110001 11001110
10010111 00100110 10101101 00001111 10011100 10101010 10000111 11011011 10100101 01001101
00011000 01100110 10010000 01111010 01010100 10000010 00010000 00111110 11101001 10100111
11101101 11011010 01111010 01010110 01011110 11010011 10111000 11001001 01000000 11000000
10100111 00101000 11000001 00100110 10100000 01011001 00011011 10100101 00111101 00011000
10010010 01111001 10101001 01111110 11111110 11000010 10110001 00100111 01010001 11010011
00100011 10111101 01001001 11010011 10011100 01111101 00101010 00001111 00110111 00000110
10001111 00110111 00111001 00011101 11111101 01101001 11111011 00110010 10001001 11010011
10001100 11110110 10100000 00010010 00111001 11000110 01110011 01001100 00010010 01110001
11001101 00101010 10010001 11101011 01010011 01100110 10110111 00011011 00100100 11011100
01000001 00011000 11100010 10000010 10100000 00011110 01001001 00000011 10111101 00100111
00011001 00011100 11010011 11110000 00001010 11100100 11010100 10111010 01111111 01101001
10000011 01100010 10000011 10110111 11010111 00110100 10000100 00010010 01110011 11000101
00101000 00000011 00011101 01111011 11010010 00111001 11000000 11100111 10101111 10101101
00110100 11101101 10101001 10011101 10000101 00011111 10101111 10101101 01000101 01110001
00101000 10001000 00001100 01100111 00111110 10110100 11010111 01101111 10101101 00100110
01000001 11100000 10001110 00111101 11101010 10101110 11101101 10101000 01011000 10100001
00101101 11011100 10000100 11110100 11111100 00101010 00010011 00101011 00011100 11110001
10011110 00110011 01011010 00110010 01000001 00010001 01111110 00010100 10000001 11110101
10101000 11011110 11010101 01001000 00111000 11100010 10011011 10010011 01111010 00100001
11011000 11001000 00110010 00110111 01010011 11000001 10100111 10101001 00100101 01110011
11011110 10101110 01001001 01100100 11011011 01111010 10000010 01111101 01001111 01111010
10000001 10101101 01100101 01010011 10000010 00111111 01011010 10000111 00010110 11110110
00011001 00001100 00101010 01001100 10000010 10100110 01100011 10001001 00111010 01010101
10000100 10110110 00100000 10000110 11000101 01011010 00010110 10011011 10000110 11101100
01111110 00010100 10101110 11010110 10000100 11011100 10000110 00100000 00000000 11110111
10100111 01100010 10100101 00110000 10011100 11110110 00000100 01010100 01100101 01001000
```

00100011 00111101 00101001 10110110 11010111 10100000 10110111 00100100 10000110 01000010
10101111 11001000 00000100 01110111 10101011 10001010 10101011 00101000 11011100 00111010
00011010 10100100 10000011 00100010 10100100 10001110 01010011 00010011 00001100 01110100
00111101 10101010 01010101 00110101 00101101 11001000 10111110 10100100 11001111 00010110
01110000 00010000 01010000 00010000 10001010 10110101 00010001 01010110 11000011 00100001
11101011 01001010 11010001 11100000 11100111 10110101 01100100 11010111 10010001 01100101
01000011 00011110 01111001 00010100 01101101 00111011 00111001 10101011 01001100 10011110
10010100 11011100 01100110 10101011 01000100 00110010 00100000 10111111 11001110 10100100
11100011 01110111 10111101 00101110 00111111 00101010 00110001 11001111 00100110 10110011
01010110 11010101 00001000 00010100 10110111 01011100 11010000 11000100 01111101 01101000
11101100 00001101 00110100 10001100 10011110 00101001 11110110 01110111 00000001 11011011
10110001 01000010 01100000 00000011 11101111 01001101 01011100 00011110 10100111 11110101
10100101 01100011 11101011 01010101 01110101 01100000 01111011 10001010 10100100 10001100
11110011 01001111 01000110 11001000 11110100 10101000 11110011 10011110 10010100 11110101
11101001 01001010 10011011 00000110 00101011 11110010 00101010 10011101 11000100 01100011
10101000 11101011 01010110 11010101 10111011 01100010 10000000 00000001 11101011 11001101
01010011 11101000 11010011 00100000 11001111 01000110 00100000 11100000 10011110 01101000
01100010 01110111 11010011 10101110 10100010 11011000 01110011 01010001 10000011 10011110
10111101 01101011 01110101 10110110 10000100 11011000 01111011 01001000 00111111 00011010
01100110 11110001 11011110 10011100 11110001 11100111 11110010 11111100 10101010 00000010
00001000 11100000 11110011 10010011 11101001 01000011 01110111 11010101 10001110 11000100
11100011 11001011 10010011 10000011 01001101 01101100 00101001 11000010 00011010 10001011
10010001 11010011 11110011 10100100 01100010 01101010 10100011 11010100 00101100 01011010
10110111 00111110 01011011 01100111 00111100 01100011 10100101 01101001 00100001 00001100
10111001 10101100 00110000 11001101 11000110 00101010 11000100 01001100 11000000 11110001
10011100 10001010 11100111 11100101 01010111 00000110 01101000 10111100 01111101 11010110
10101010 00111010 11100000 11100111 11011110 10100100 01001001 10100101 11001110 00001000
11111100 11101001 11101111 10000110 11101000 00111111 00000011 01010011 11001010 11000001
00110100 01000100 00001110 00111001 10100011 00000111 00111110 11000111 10111110 01101000
01111001 00100011 00000111 00000100 11110011 11011011 00011110 11010101 00000011 11011101
10000000 01000000 00011101 10111010 11010000 11101001 01011101 11011101 10110001 11011110
11100100 10000100 01110101 10100110 01100000 10010010 01000110 00110000 00101010 10110100
10010111 10100011 00011000 11001000 00111001 11110100 10100110 00101101 11010001 01101110
11111100 11111010 11010101 00100101 01100000 10110011 00101101 10110000 11101110 00001101
01010010 10111000 00111000 10010100 10001100 11010100 11001000 01011000 10101110 00111111
10011101 01100111 11011100 01001010 01110111 10010011 10001010 11011111 00001101 00010101
00010110 00011010 10010100 11110101 01000110 11011101 00011110 00111011 01010110 00001100
10110010 01101101 01111110 10110101 10111011 01110011 11001010 01100100 10011010 11100111
11101111 00000001 00110010 10010011 11011111 10111000 10101110 11011000 01101010 11101110
11001101 10100000 00111111 11001110 11001111 00011001 11100110 10100000 01111001 11110000
01111001 00111100 11010101 01001001 10100101 01100000 01111101 11101010 10101001 10011111
01110110 01111001 11101001 11010110 10111010 11100001 00010110 11110110 00101110 11000110
10001100 10010011 11100111 10100111 01001100 01110101 10101010 11001101 00111000 01010011
11000101 01010001 01111001 10001001 00011100 00010011 11111001 11010011 01111100 11000010
11011101 01111010 11010111 01000010 10000101 11011001 00011011 00110010 11100010 11001010
01011000 11100000 00011010 10110011 01101110 01110000 01000110 01111110 10110101 01000010
00101110 01000111 10111101 01011100 10001010 01000000 00000000 10100111 11001000 10010010
11011100 10010111 10101001 10100100 10010010 10000011 10000011 10011010 10010001 10100110
11001111 01000011 11001101 01010000 01001001 01001000 01111111 01101010 01111111 10011011
10001111 11000110 10110001 10110101 10001000 01100101 10010011 00100001 11000111 00110101
00011001 01100010 00000111 10100110 01101010 10111011 11001011 10010011 11010111 10100101
01000110 11010010 00000001 11010100 11010101 00101101 00011000 01011011 01011101 01001011
10011011 10000001 00000011 11010110 10000110 01100011 10011110 00001101 01010011 11110011
10110111 01100011 01101110 01000111 00111110 10110100 11110000 11000100 10010011 11001101
00101011 11011001 01101010 01010101 10101100 01011010 01010110 00100100 01100000 11010100
11101001 11001000 11000111 10111101 01010100 01000010 00110011 11101110 01101010 11010100
01111100 01010110 01010010 10100110 11101101 01110000 10111001 01110010 00011110 00111010
00001110 00101010 11010100 01111111 11101100 11010101 01101000 10111010 01100111 00111100
01010101 10001000 10011000 00000001 11000001 10100001 11011111 01101011 00000001 01100101
00011000 01111110 00110100 11101111 00110011 10010000 00111010 11010101 01000110 10010000
11110011 10000011 01001010 10010010 00011110 01000111 11101011 01010000 10011011 00100001
11101000 01011010 11011111 10111010 10010101 10001000 11001101 01000100 10001100 00010111
11111111 00000000 11010111 01001100 11011100 01001111 01111110 11111100 01010101 01011110
11001100 01100101 10001100 00001100 10001010 10010101 00001110 00000111 01011010 10101011
11100110 01110100 11100111 10011010 10010001 00011100 01100011 00000111 10101101 00111010
10001101 00000001 01100111 00100000 10001111 01111010 01001101 11000011 00011101 11101010
00011101 11011011 01111111 00011110 01101000 01100010 01011000 00001110 01110001 01011100
11110010 10111111 01000000 00100110 01011001 00101001 11001010 11011110 10010101 01011111
01110111 00011000 11111101 01101001 11001010 11011100 00001110 01101010 10011010 01001100
00001011 00101000 11000011 00011100 10011110 01101010 01001101 11011100 00001100 01010101
01000101 10010011 00110101 00110010 00110111 10101001 11100010 10010110 11111010 00110001
00010011 00000011 11000111 00100110 10000000 11011100 11010100 00100100 11100011 10101001
10100110 00010110 00111000 11100011 10011010 10110100 10101100 10110100 00010101 11001001

11011001 10111001 11101011 01001100 01100110 00011101 10001111 00010101 00000111 10011011
11010111 00000110 10100001 10010010 01011110 00111000 11000111 11010100 01010101 11110010
10111011 00110001 00010110 00100100 10010011 10011100 11110011 01010100 00101111 00100110
00100000 01111010 00001010 00011110 01100011 10000010 00001101 01010011 10011101 01100101
10011011 00000000 01010011 01001001 00110101 10111001 01101001 00010100 00101110 10100100
11011100 01111010 11010110 01101100 11001100 01001110 01111111 01001010 11011100 01001101
00110001 10100100 01111111 11011110 01001001 10000001 11101101 01010110 10100010 11010011
00100000 10001001 11010000 11111001 01000011 00100011 10111001 11100110 10110011 01010101
01100011 01111101 01001101 10101110 10010001 11000111 11111101 10010110 01111001 10001111
11101110 11100011 01110111 00111111 10100101 01011000 01001111 00001011 11011100 11001110
00000001 10011110 01100100 10001011 00111110 10011100 10011010 11101100 11010110 00011111
01101110 11110101 00111111 10010100 00000000 11111110 01010100 11111110 10110101 00101110
11010110 00100001 10111011 10011100 11101101 10101111 10000110 00110100 11111000 00111001
01110000 11110011 00111111 10101100 10011101 00101011 01011010 00011011 01011000 11100011
00111000 10001101 01010001 00000110 00111010 00101000 11000000 10101011 11011110 01010110
01101010 01000001 00011010 10001110 01101011 00101010 10110101 00100111 00101011 00001000
10101100 00100011 11110110 10100111 10101100 01100100 10000001 11000111 01001010 10010101
01010100 01100010 10010111 11101000 01101010 00011011 10111110 10101011 01110010 01011011
00100011 01010101 11100011 10100101 00111001 10000110 00001000 10100101 01100011 11010010
10010011 00111100 11110011 01001001 01101011 11010000 00010011 00011011 10001100 11010010
01100100 00001100 11110101 10100001 11001110 00001111 01011010 10001101 11011000 10000011
11101101 11110101 10101101 00011100 00011110 10000000 00001100 11000011 00110100 11001100
01110011 11000000 10100001 10001000 00100011 10010011 10001010 00011110 01001110 10000000
01010100 01011010 01001001 11011101 00001110 11100000 11011001 00000010 10001101 11010101
00011110 11100010 01110010 00111010 01010010 01100111 10011010 10111101 01101111 01110001
01101000 01001011 11000001 11101001 01000110 01110001 01010001 11100110 10011100 10101111
11101011 01010101 10100011 01011100 11001000 01010111 00011101 11001111 01011010 00110010
01001111 01101010 01101011 01001000 01001101 00110001 10011011 00011101 00111010 11010011
01001010 11001000 00101110 00001111 11110111 11101010 00111111 11100010 11101011 01001111
11001000 00100000 01100111 10101101 00110111 11011110 10100010 11000101 01011100 01001001
01101010 10110100 11000111 10001010 10010101 11011011 00100000 10000000 01111001 11110101
10101010 01010011 01001001 11001110 00110011 10011010 11010010 00010100 11011011 01111100
11001000 10010110 11010011 00101010 01011110 00110111 00000100 01100011 10000011 01011000
01110111 10011001 11101101 11000101 01101010 11001100 11000111 10011010 11001001 10111101
01100000 01001001 01010001 11010111 10111110 01101011 10101010 10010011 01110111 00001011
01011100 11001000 00010001 10010110 10011000 11100000 01110011 11101111 01010010 01111101
10011110 01011100 11100111 00011100 01010000 01011000 01000111 00100010 00110111 01110001
01010010 11000011 01110110 10111101 00001000 11110101 11100110 10111011 01100110 11101100
01100101 11010100 10000101 00000001 00000011 00000111 10110001 11100110 10101100 00101011
01100000 00000010 00110010 00110001 11101111 01010010 11111001 11010000 11001010 00111001
11100001 11111101 00110011 01000111 10010000 11000100 01100100 00010000 01111101 00110000
01101011 00000110 11001010 10110011 00100101 10000110 01100000 11011111 01111111 00011001
11110101 10101011 00000001 10001000 11100101 00011011 00011111 01001010 10100010 01100010
01110100 00100011 01110000 00100011 00111101 11101010 01010100 01100010 10111101 10101011
00011001 11101010 00110100 01011101 01011011 11010110 10001001 10111000 00111101 01111010
11110011 01011010 11111010 01101110 10101100 10110001 11100000 01001100 00110010 00111101
01101011 10011110 11111001 01100101 11000111 00111000 00111111 11001110 10011011 10111111
11001011 11100000 00011110 01001111 10101101 01100101 00111010 01101010 01000101 11101110
01110111 01000111 11001011 10011111 00111100 10000111 10001100 11110101 11110111 10101110
00110011 11000100 11111110 00011111 10010110 00101001 00011110 11101010 11000000 00010011
00011001 11100101 10100010 00011101 10111101 11000101 01011000 10110010 10111111 10011010
11011111 00011011 00011000 10010000 00001111 00100000 10011010 11101001 00101100 11101111
01100010 10111100 10001111 10000011 10000111 11000111 00100011 00111100 11010110 01110100
01111001 11110000 11101111 10011001 00111101 00001100 10101010 01010011 11100111 01000111
10010011 00100001 00101101 11001011 00110001 11101011 11010010 10011100 11001110 00000001
11100100 11110001 01011101 01100111 10001001 01110100 00011100 10111100 10010111 01010110
01110001 11100101 11000000 11111001 10100011 00000111 10101111 10111000 10101110 00111001
01001110 01100101 11000100 10000000 11111010 01100011 11010010 10111101 11001010 00010101
11010101 01101000 11011101 00011100 00110011 10100110 11100000 01011001 01100110 01011101
11111111 00000000 00100001 11001111 00011001 10101010 11010011 00101110 11100011 11001000
00111100 11111010 01110110 10101001 01011111 10101001 00000100 10011110 00111010 00011100
11110101 10100111 01101101 11000000 11111001 11001111 01011110 11011101 11101011 01001110
01100111 11001101 01100011 00110010 10101111 11110001 00010001 11001110 00111101 00001001
10101001 00100011 10010000 10000101 11100100 10000001 11101101 01010000 11001011 00100000
00101100 01010111 00011101 11111010 11010100 00100001 10001110 01001110 11011110 10011001
11110101 10101101 00100010 11101111 10100010 11010000 01000111 01111110 01000001 00111101
11111111 00000000 00101010 10001100 10000110 11101110 01111010 01010001 11100111 01000001
11010111 01110000 00000111 00111110 10010100 11110101 10111000 10000111 00000100 00010011
11001111 01111010 11110000 10011010 10010100 01001111 01001110 11101100 01100111 00111101
00001000 11100011 11010010 10010001 11000001 00100100 01110101 00011100 01100010 10100100
01011011 10101000 10001000 11001110 00000111 00000111 00000011 00110100 00011011 10100001
10001111 10010101 01010000 11100011 11011010 10011010 11100110 01001011 01000100 00011100
11100101 01110101 01010011 10011100 00001111 11000110 10011010 10110001 10110011 00110001

```
00111101 00000111 11110011 10101001 11010110 01111111 10011001 10110000 10100011 00011110
10010100 01111101 10100011 01101111 00111000 11100011 11010110 10101110 11110110 11101000
00100001 00000000 11100011 10100111 00111101 01111001 10100101 01011001 00001000 11101001
10000001 01001100 01101011 11000001 11000110 01000000 11001101 00011111 01101011 10001110
01000001 10110100 10001100 00011111 01011110 10011001 10100110 10100011 00100111 01110100
11000111 01110110 00011110 01100011 00110001 11000010 01100111 10000001 11010010 10011010
00110111 11100011 10111111 11100011 01001110 01011011 10000100 00111101 00110011 01010011
10001001 10100011 00000111 00111001 11100011 00010101 01001010 00010011 11101100 00101011
10001100 10000100 00011100 01100100 11100111 10011111 01011010 01111110 00001000 01110001
11001110 01101001 01001100 10001010 01000111 11001000 01101000 01010110 01010001 10001110
01110011 11000101 01100111 00101000 01011011 01010000 01100011 11010101 10111110 01100010
00110001 10010011 11101110 00101000 11011010 00001000 11000001 10101000 11011010 01010101
11001001 11100111 11110001 10101000 00111110 11010001 10010010 01111001 11000110 00101010
00010010 01110011 10111101 10000111 01110010 11010011 11000010 00001000 00100011 10001110
00101010 10111011 11000010 11000000 00011111 01101110 01101001 10011111 01101010 00011110
01100001 00100111 10001111 01001010 01010001 01111011 11010011 01100001 11000001 11001101
01101010 10101001 10111000 10101011 11011000 10101110 01110010 00110110 00000011 01110110
11101010 01111010 00011100 11110010 00111010 11010010 01001011 00111110 11100111 11111011
10100000 11100111 11010110 10010111 11001101 01000101 11100101 11001000 00011001 11101011
10000011 01010011 01100110 11110101 10110000 01011100 10010101 00100100 00100011 11111000
10111001 00011101 11000101 01101001 01011000 01101011 00110111 01110110 10111100 10100100
10100100 10000001 11011001 10001110 01110011 01011001 00000010 01000100 00111100 10010011
10000000 01111010 11010100 10011001 01010111 10001100 10000010 11000011 11111100 00101011
00111001 01010010 01010110 11110111 10010110 10000011 01001101 00011101 11100110 10010111
11100010 00111011 01101011 10000000 00010110 11100001 01111100 10100111 11101001 11010110
10110110 01111100 11100100 10010111 11111101 01011011 00001001 00000111 10101000 10101111
00101010 01000111 00100011 00011011 01011011 10100111 01001010 11011001 11010011 01110101
00011001 10100011 01100000 01000011 11100011 00011101 10101011 10011110 10101110 00011010
00110110 10111010 11010000 10100100 11110101 00111011 11000000 00001111 01101010 00011100
01100000 01010110 00111101 10011110 10110000 01100100 00000011 11001110 11000001 11110111
00010101 10101000 10010011 00101100 11001011 10010100 00111001 00010101 11100111 00111010
01001101 00011010 10100110 00001100 00001101 00110100 00010010 00001111 01011010 01110111
01010011 11010110 10100011 10010011 10101110 00000101 00101110 01100111 01110001 11011101
00010011 10100100 10000011 00011110 11110100 11111100 00010001 10000011 10011111 11000110
10101011 11000101 11010111 10101111 11101001 01010110 00110011 11000111 01001010 01110011
11010101 11011100 01100001 10111000 10010011 01001101 01111001 10001100 01100111 10010011
11000101 00100011 10011100 01110101 10101010 00010111 00110011 01100111 00100011 10111101
00001101 10110111 00011011 10110001 00010111 00011010 11110101 10111000 11100111 00111110
11010100 11100110 10111100 11100100 01101111 11101001 11011110 10110010 11100010 10010000
10010110 00010100 01001101 00100001 00011100 00010001 11011110 10100101 00100111 01101101
01000010 11000110 11000000 10011100 00011100 11110011 11000101 00111011 01110000 00101001
11000101 01100110 11011011 11101110 00101000 00001001 11100000 01111111 00111010 10111000
00010000 10000011 10011100 11010001 01010011 10100101 10010000 11111101 01001011 00001100
11000111 10001111 11100111 01010001 11100100 10010000 01110011 11011010 10100000 00010011
10010000 11011000 11101101 01010110 01010011 00000100 01100111 00110101 01010110 01101111
10101000 01011100 01000101 11100111 10101101 01000111 00101011 01101101 00011101 01101010
01111101 10111111 10100101 01000001 00101000 11001000 00100011 10110101 00110100 11010010
11011000 01001101 00000101 10100101 11100010 10010110 00001000 01001000 00111001 11101000
00111101 11101011 01000101 01001110 00000111 01001010 11100100 11101111 10100011 01101000
00100110 11110011 01010011 00100001 00001001 11101011 10011110 10000110 10110111 00110100
11011011 11010011 01110101 00010010 01110010 00110111 10001110 10110100 10100100 10010011
01010111 00110011 10110001 01110011 10111111 11010110 10101011 11001101 00101111 00100111
00100011 10001111 01011010 10011101 01001110 00000111 11010110 10010001 10010100 01001001
11010110 10100001 00100111 11010100 00011100 01001000 00010011 11100111 00011100 01111010
11010010 01001010 00001110 11110011 11010111 00111111 01011010 10110101 00011100 01100001
01111110 10010101 00110111 10010110 10100111 11101110 10011010 10011011 00110010 01001010
00110001 11001101 00100100 01001111 10010010 01110000 00111110 10010101 10101001 00010011
01111001 10001000 00001000 10101000 10000100 00101010 01000111 11001101 10000010 00101010
01010100 01011100 00000011 10001010 01010101 00101111 00101101 11000111 01110010 01101101
10111100 01100100 10011100 10011010 01101001 10001100 01100111 10001110 10111101 11101001
00110111 00011111 01101010 01011111 00110011 10001110 00110001 01011000 11110010 10110110
00010111 00010011 00000011 00111000 11110101 10100100 01101000 11110001 01001010 10101100
00001001 11100111 10101101 00111111 00100011 10100101 01011111 00100101 11010000 10001000
00111001 11001101 00001100 00000101 01001111 10001100 10011010 00001000 00011101 11101011
00101110 01011101 00101100 00001101 10010101 01111100 10110001 11010111 10111111 01011010
01000110 11111010 01110011 01010110 11110110 11100111 10011010 10000111 01101110 01001101
01011010 10001110 11010110 00101000 10000111 10010101 00011001 00110100 01110101 00000000
11110101 10100111 00010101 00100011 10011010 01000101 01100000 00001110 00000101 00011111
01101011 01110001 10001111 01101110 10011000 11101001 10011010 00101001 10001100 11011100
11110011 01001000 10101101 10011010 01101101 00000000 10101110 10011001 00011000 00100000
01010101 01001001 10100011 01100000 01111000 00010101 01101101 10001001 11101001 01000001
00011011 10111001 11110100 10101101 01110101 11010011 10010100 11001101 10010101 00100011
11111001 10010011 11011110 10010001 10000001 00011111 01001010 01111100 10110001 11100001
```

10000011 00100111 00000111 00110101 01010110 11100110 01100011 11100101 11110001 01010100
11101111 10111000 00010011 00100100 10101011 10011100 00111000 11100010 10011100 11000110
00010010 01111010 01111110 10110101 10010110 00100110 00101101 11010110 10100110 01100110
00100101 01111010 11110011 01010000 10100101 00101011 01011000 00110100 00110100 00011110
01010100 01011110 01000000 00011001 11111010 01010010 11111101 10100100 01101100 00100100
00000000 00101011 00110001 11001001 00000000 00010000 01111000 10100110 11111001 10000111
01110110 00111011 11010010 11011011 01110000 10110010 00110100 00011010 11100000 10001100
01100011 00011110 10100110 10100000 01111011 10111100 10010011 11001101 01010011 10010101
10001110 01111010 11111110 00010101 01011001 10100100 00111100 10011100 11100110 10100110
11001101 00110001 11011000 10110011 00101101 11000111 01100000 01101010 10111100 10110011
10010110 00100111 00110101 00000010 10010010 01111001 10101001 10100010 10001111 01110001
00011110 11110101 01101101 01101010 00000011 00100001 11011100 11100100 11111110 01110101
10101001 01101101 00000110 01111001 00100010 10010010 11010110 00001100 01100000 00011110
10110101 10101011 00001010 10000000 00111010 01111110 00110101 00101010 01101010 11110110
00011101 11011001 01011111 11001010 00000010 00100011 10000011 11001111 10101101 01100010
01011101 01100000 11000110 01110010 00111001 11001101 01101111 01011100 10110001 00110001
00111110 00101011 10011111 10010101 10000110 00001000 11100100 10001100 01010110 11111000
01101011 01011110 11101101 10001000 10100001 00101100 10011111 00100101 01100110 01011100
00010001 10000010 01000101 01001111 01110000 11001101 00011001 00100000 10010011 11111101
01101010 10011100 11010010 00011100 01100111 10110111 01011010 11110100 01100000 10101111
10101001 10110010 00110011 11101110 01010100 10110001 11111110 10010101 10011100 11000000
11100100 11111100 10111000 11110101 10101101 01010111 10010000 11110011 11101001 01010101
10011100 00000010 00111010 00001010 11101000 10000011 10110110 11000101 01011011 01010010
10000011 00101001 11111100 01101001 11110001 01000111 10000011 11001101 01001001 10000010
00101001 01110011 10000001 11111101 00101011 01000001 00000010 10010000 10100110 10100111
01000110 00111001 11001101 01010101 11011100 00111001 11000101 00111000 00010011 10000000
01011000 11110011 01010100 10010100 10011110 11000000 11010001 01110111 11001100 11100011
00011000 11001101 01000110 11110010 11110001 10000001 11010110 10101011 01101110 01101110
10011001 00110100 00101000 11001001 11001110 01101000 01110000 10010010 00110011 01101011
01010010 01011111 00110111 00111001 11100110 10001101 11011111 00100110 00111010 11010100
00001101 11001011 11110100 11111010 11010001 10111011 10001110 11110100 00101000 11011101
01011101 10000101 10001011 00010001 00011110 01110011 10011010 10110100 10000111 10010000
01111011 01010101 00001000 10001000 00100111 00011101 00101010 11100100 00111001 11110101
00011000 00011101 11101010 00101101 10101101 11000001 10010111 00010000 00001110 00111001
10101011 01110000 01100011 11010011 10011010 10100111 00001000 00111011 11111001 10101011
10001011 11110010 00001010 11001010 10100111 01110001 01011000 10110100 10100111 00100011
00000000 11010011 10011010 01000000 10111100 01100110 10101011 10001100 10011110 10010100
11100001 00011011 00110001 11100110 10010110 11111011 00001111 01010001 11101101 00101101
01001110 00001110 11010101 00011000 00111001 11001101 01000000 10010001 11100111 10101000
11000101 01001110 10101010 01110000 00101001 01110010 00101011 00110000 11010000 01110000
00111111 11000101 11010110 10011111 10111011 10111111 10101101 01000110 00010100 11101111
11001000 10101001 00001000 11100010 10100101 00111011 01011010 11100010 00011000 11001101
10001010 01110111 10011010 00001001 11111101 00101010 00110111 01010010 11011001 11000111
01011111 11001010 10101000 01101010 00010111 11110000 01011001 01000100 00011010 11100010
01010000 10111100 11100000 00001100 01100111 00100110 10001101 01100110 11101110 10000110
11101100 10110111 00110101 11111100 11110101 11101111 10011010 01110111 10011011 10011111
01101010 11100101 11010111 01011101 10110110 10010100 11100111 11001101 00000000 01110110
00000011 10010110 00110100 11011001 10110101 11100101 10010001 01011101 00101101 11111100
11010100 01110000 00111110 11110001 00011101 11101011 10100011 11101010 01110011 01111110
11110101 10011001 10001011 10101101 00010100 01110101 00001101 00101111 01011010 00010110
01010010 01010100 01010111 00111001 10100110 11101010 00110011 01001010 00001010 11011101
00110111 11101111 00001001 11100011 10001110 10110101 10110011 00001010 11001101 00100010
11110000 00110000 00111011 11100110 10110010 10011101 00111111 01100111 10101011 00110101
01011010 10100010 11110100 01010010 10001010 10010000 01001101 11011011 11110101 10101010
11101001 00001011 01110100 11101101 11101011 01010011 01111101 10011100 11111010 11010110
01010111 10111000 01011000 01111011 01001011 10010010 01111001 10101000 11011110 01000010
11000000 10000001 10011111 10101101 00111100 01000011 10000001 01010010 01111001 01000011
00011000 00000011 11101011 01010111 00101001 11011011 01100001 01110010 00010100 11111110
01100010 01111001 11001111 00110101 00100010 11000111 10011100 01100100 11110001 11101001
01010111 00010110 00010000 00101001 01011001 01000001 00110101 10010101 01010111 00101011
01101110 00111101 00001010 10010001 11000000 00001111 00100100 01110001 01010010 00001000
11000111 11110000 10001010 10110110 00100011 11000111 00100011 10100101 00100110 00000111
01111010 00111010 01011001 00000010 00100000 01011000 11111011 10001110 00111101 10001101
00111111 00011001 00011001 10101001 01000000 00011000 10100011 10110110 01111010 01010110
01110110 01111011 00100000 01101100 01100110 11010001 10001111 01111010 00110000 01111101
00111000 10100111 01100011 10001110 01111010 10001111 01111010 00110111 01110001 10011010
10110101 00001110 10100010 10111000 11100110 11101001 11101111 01001101 01100010 01110001
01001101 11110011 00111101 01101001 10111011 11110000 01111010 11110001 01001101 01011101
00111011 10100100 01001000 10111101 10101001 10001100 01110001 01000100 10110010 01110101
00100011 10101101 01000101 10111010 10000101 00011011 11101110 00000011 11001011 00011100
01111011 11010011 01011001 11111101 00101010 00110111 10010100 01110101 10100110 10100100
10111000 11100111 10101101 01011100 10010010 11101000 00000100 10111001 11001111 01011010
10001001 11011000 01100110 10100011 11110011 01001001 00000111 11010010 10011000 11101101

01010100 10100010 11011110 10100000 10000111 10110100 10000011 00011111 10001101 00110011
00111001 11100100 00011110 00101010 00110110 10010000 01100011 00111111 10101101 01000100
11001101 11000111 01011110 00111011 01010100 11111011 00100111 01111011 10111101 11000110
01011000 11011101 11011010 10001111 00110011 00011100 01010100 00001010 01000111 10101110
01001101 00110010 01010111 00100111 10000001 01011010 00101000 11101100 00100110 10001011
00011110 01100110 00001000 11110111 10100111 01111001 11011000 11001110 01000101 01010001
01011001 01101001 11111011 11110111 01110011 01010101 00101010 01101010 11010110 01000000
10001011 01100110 01000000 00111001 01011110 11110100 11010110 01101100 10011010 10100110
11110010 01110011 10011111 01001010 01001111 00111000 11111010 11110001 01000010 10000110
10111110 11110110 11000000 11001011 10011001 11100000 01111010 11010000 01100110 11000101
01010100 11110011 01111111 10111011 11111010 11010010 00111100 10011001 11111100 01101010
11011100 00010011 01000000 10101110 01001011 00101011 01010101 00101001 01011000 11110011
01001111 10010010 01011100 00001110 10110101 01010010 01101001 01111000 11101011 01001101
01101001 10100010 00101110 11000100 01110111 00001101 11101011 11000000 10101100 01101011
11111110 00001001 11100111 00111110 10010101 01110110 01010110 00111001 00100100 10010010
00111101 10101011 00101110 11101110 01001100 10111110 00111111 01011010 11011110 10010101
00101101 01110101 00001001 01101000 01100111 11011101 00010010 00010011 00100100 11010100
01110001 00011110 00111001 11001111 11100111 01001111 10111100 11100110 00111100 01100011
10111111 01111010 01100100 01011000 01000001 10000011 11011110 10111010 10011100 01011101
10111011 10011100 11101111 01110010 11100100 00101010 10111000 00000111 00111101 10110011
10010011 01010110 01100011 10010001 01000000 00111100 10011111 01101110 01101010 10110000
11101001 11010111 00010100 10110001 10101000 00100100 10001010 11001010 11001101 11110100
00101110 11000101 11111000 10011000 01100111 10010010 01111001 11110101 00110101 01100010
00101101 10101101 10011100 10001100 11100010 10101001 11000110 10101100 00111010 11110100
11101111 11000101 01001110 10101101 10000001 10000001 10001100 01010111 00100101 01000100
10111010 00010100 10010001 00110010 11000001 00010110 01000110 00001111 01111010 10010001
10101101 11010000 11110000 01001001 10101010 11101001 00100110 00111001 11101111 01010110
00100011 00111011 10010011 10011100 11010110 01001101 01001001 00000101 10000110 10001011
00110001 11111100 00101101 11011111 10001010 10001101 11111100 11101000 00100101 11001010
10010011 11000111 00111001 00010101 00110011 01000110 01000111 00101000 01001001 10100100
11011100 01001111 00001110 00101000 01010111 11110101 00100100 10110111 01101001 10101010
10000111 01101100 01001110 01111001 00011101 11101011 00111111 01011111 11010001 11010010
11110111 11111101 00101010 11001100 10100010 01001111 11011100 00001111 11100010 10101000
11100110 10000011 11001011 00100100 10100000 11101010 01110011 11010110 10001000 01101110
00001000 11101110 01000000 11111010 11010101 11010011 01001110 00010010 11100110 10100110
01001011 01011110 11010001 01011000 11100101 11100001 00111111 10111101 00100010 01000000
01110010 10111100 00011100 11010100 10001011 10001100 11001000 01001111 01010010 00111001
00100111 10011010 11011001 11010101 01101101 11100001 01100010 10010111 00000010 00010000
01001110 00111110 01100011 10001110 10110101 10001001 00110110 00001011 01100001 00000110
00001001 10101111 01011010 00010101 01111001 10010101 11001110 00011001 11000001 11000001
11101010 01010011 10010110 01010000 01110011 11100101 10110111 11001000 00111000 11101001
01010100 11011000 10110011 00110001 00101010 11011011 01000111 10100101 01011011 10011100
00101010 11101100 10001001 00010100 10000000 00000111 00111001 11101010 01101010 10101100
10100001 00010101 11001000 00100011 11110101 10101110 10100100 10101111 10101001 10010001
11010010 10101011 10011100 01100111 00111001 00110100 10100011 00111011 11000101 01010111
01000010 01001110 01000111 10101111 01101010 10010101 10001110 00000000 11101011 11011000
01010111 00010101 11011110 11101100 11110100 01101110 01011000 01001001 00001111 00101011
10011111 10010010 10101100 00100100 11000001 01000110 00001001 11111010 11010101 00101100
00011100 01110000 00001111 00111110 10110100 10101001 00011001 01100001 11111100 01100110
10011101 10100010 10111101 00000111 10101001 01110001 00100101 11001001 00100111 00110100
11110111 00111001 01001110 10110101 01010001 00100001 10010101 01000110 11100000 10100111
00011101 10101001 11100010 00101001 10011000 01110100 00100011 10111111 00111100 01010110
00101110 00101001 10111011 00100000 01001100 10010001 10110110 10000010 00001110 01111000
11000101 00110001 11010111 10000000 11000010 10100100 01001000 00011001 10100011 11101010
00001001 11110100 11001101 01001101 00010100 00100011 01101111 11001110 11000000 11111011
11010011 01110111 10111101 10000101 01101011 10010101 00010000 11110011 01001010 11010010
00010000 00111010 11010100 11101111 00001010 00010011 11111110 10110011 00011001 10100100
01101000 01100001 00100000 01100100 10011111 11000000 11010101 00101001 01011101 01011011
10101000 11110101 00100000 01101001 11000000 00111000 00011001 11100010 10010001 01101110
00001110 00110011 11111010 01010101 10000001 00010101 10111111 10011000 11111001 11011100
00110010 00111000 11000001 10100000 01000111 00000000 00111011 10110110 10001100 11111101
01101011 00111011 01111001 00001011 01111101 11001000 00011010 11100011 00001011 10010000
00111110 10100010 10100010 01101001 11001011 00001100 10001110 00001110 01101010 11100011
10011011 01110011 10010000 00010111 00000111 00111100 11110011 10011010 01010100 00110000
10000001 10000100 00001000 00000111 10111101 00110101 01100101 10110010 00011011 01011110
01100110 01111110 11100111 00101001 10010010 00001111 00011110 10110101 00101101 10111011
00011110 11100011 00000110 10101101 10100100 11101010 10100000 11101100 01010100 11100100
01110101 11000111 01101010 01100011 01011110 01000111 11001110 11000000 00110010 00111101
10101001 10111010 10001101 01101001 01100001 01011011 01011101 01001000 01011101 10001000
01111100 01110011 11111001 01010010 00110100 01110010 00110010 00111011 01100000 10010001
11010000 10011110 10110101 00111000 10111010 11000001 00000111 00100000 01100100 11110100
10100111 10011011 11100010 00001110 11010000 01101010 00011011 10011010 01111011 01101000
00111111 10011001 00000010 10010111 11110100 11001111 11100001 10001010 10011101 00110111

01100011 10100001 11111010 01010100 01111111 01101100 00100111 10101110 00101000 11111011
01100001 11110101 11001111 10111001 10101011 01101001 11011010 11101100 01101001 11111001
10010010 10001000 11100110 00100111 00101000 10001110 00000101 01011011 10001000 00111010
10101000 00101111 10011110 01111011 01010110 01110111 11011011 10001000 00000000 11110000
00111101 01000000 11101111 01010001 10011011 11010011 11101010 01001000 11110111 11101101
01011000 01111011 00111001 01001001 10001010 11111010 10011011 10001001 00101100 10110001
10010010 01000011 00011111 11000100 11110100 10101011 00010000 01101010 00010111 10010001
11110001 00011101 11000011 10000100 00011101 10000101 01110011 00111111 01101100 00111001
11101011 11001110 00111010 01100111 10101101 01000100 10110111 10110010 00011001 00110111
01110100 00100000 11110010 00110011 11010110 10011111 11010101 11111001 01010110 10000011
01110101 00010010 11011000 11101110 11100001 11010111 11101111 00010100 10000000 01100101
00001110 00111101 00001111 01111010 11010001 10110110 11110001 00000010 10110001 00111110
01111010 11100011 00011110 10000111 00111001 10101111 00110100 11111011 01101001 00011000
00100100 10010011 11011010 10011011 11110110 11000110 00001011 10110101 00001001 00010101
10010100 11110000 00101010 01111010 11011000 00010101 01000011 11011000 01100011 11010101
10101100 01110001 11110011 11001111 00011100 01111000 00011001 00111011 10001101 01001110
11011010 10110101 10000000 01001100 11111101 10100110 00101111 11001110 10111100 01100000
01011110 01100000 00010010 01000110 01011111 10111101 00111111 11101101 10001100 01000111
11011110 11100011 00111001 11100010 10110010 01111001 01101010 10110110 10101100 10100101
01011001 10100011 11010110 10100110 11010101 01101101 01001000 00000001 00101110 00100011
00111110 10011100 11010110 01101101 11001110 10100111 01101011 11100110 01111100 10110111
00010001 11100100 11111011 11010111 10011100 00110110 10100000 01110001 11010111 00111110
11010101 00010000 10111010 11111001 00110011 11010100 11010100 00101100 10110001 01110111
00011111 10110110 10111011 00111101 00110001 00110101 00101011 01000010 10011111 00110100
11110001 10001100 01110101 11100110 10100101 01011011 10111011 01011001 01011100 01100110
11101110 00100000 00001111 10101011 01010111 10010110 01111101 10110001 10001001 11000110
11101110 10111110 11110100 11110100 10111011 01100001 10011100 10110001 00111110 10011110
11010101 10100010 11001011 00100010 11011101 11101110 00011110 11011111 10110001 11101100
01110110 11110111 01010110 01100000 00001100 01011100 11000100 01000111 10110011 01010101
10101111 00111110 00011001 00111110 11100100 10101001 11111001 10001010 11110001 01111000
10101111 00001001 00000101 10001011 01100100 11110110 11000111 01101010 10110101 00010101
11101001 11011001 11000011 10111110 01111110 10111100 01010100 01001111 00000000 11111010
00001101 01010110 01101100 11110101 10100111 10001101 01001110 00001110 11100001 10010011
11010011 00001101 01010110 10100010 00001010 10101001 11001001 11110111 10101111 00100001
10000111 01010010 10010010 00100100 00001101 10111000 11100111 10111000 00010101 10100001
01101101 10101001 11001100 10101111 11000100 10001111 10110011 10101001 11100110 10110010
01011000 00001110 01011111 00110010 11111101 10100001 11101001 10010010 01001100 00111011
00011110 11010101 00011010 10110000 01110001 10011010 11100011 01101101 10110101 10101001
10110110 01100101 11011011 10001100 01010110 10001101 10011110 10110101 11100110 00100010
00000010 10111000 01110001 11011100 11110100 00110101 10000011 11000011 10110101 01110010
10010011 00110111 01100110 10001000 01001010 10011000 00100011 00100010 10101001 11011011
10100011 01000001 00110110 11101000 11111010 11100111 00011000 00110100 11101000 00110101
00000101 01100001 10010010 01000110 00111111 10010101 01011001 00001101 00010100 10111100
10100001 10101100 01111101 10010011 11011101 00000011 01100110 10000010 01001100 10101101
10001100 11010100 10001001 00101010 00011110 11111100 10001010 11001011 00111011 10010111
10111110 01101010 01000100 00111111 00100111 00110101 10010100 10100000 10000110 10110101
00110100 01111100 11010001 10001110 10110100 10001101 00101110 01000111 00011001 10101010
10001010 01000000 00010100 11100010 11011000 11101111 01001101 11011001 01101110 01001111
00101001 01100100 01001100 01111000 00000111 11110011 10101001 11111100 11001111 01111110
00001101 01100110 11101110 10100111 00110100 10000100 01111101 01101011 00110110 10011011
11101000 00111110 01000011 01000101 01100100 11101111 11011011 11010110 10000010 11011011
10111000 00000111 11101011 01011001 10001101 00101001 11101110 01101001 11001001 00101001
11111111 00000000 11101011 11010100 00101000 00101011 00001011 10010100 11010010 10001011
10101111 00110101 00100111 00111111 11000101 11000101 01100111 00001001 11001000 00011001
00010101 00101010 01011101 00010001 11010111 10011010 00011010 10111110 10001000 01010110
01100101 11101100 11111011 11010011 01011001 10110011 01010101 10010110 11100011 00100011
11011110 10000001 00101000 00111000 11000001 11100010 10100111 10010001 10101011 10001010
11000101 10111000 11100100 00111101 00101001 11001010 11011101 01000111 10101111 01011010
10101100 10001100 00111111 10111101 11010110 10011110 10101101 11001111 00010100 10101100
11010101 10001010 00100101 01110000 00110011 11101111 11101101 01010101 11111110 01011100
10011110 00101010 01001100 10011100 01110001 01001100 11000111 00011100 10001111 10100101
00001111 01010111 01100100 00000011 01011000 00000110 01011100 01010011 01110011 10110110
10010001 11000111 00111100 01010010 01110101 11101010 01101001 00111101 01010101 11010011
00011101 10000111 01101111 11100100 11100100 11110101 10100100 01010010 01110011 11000111
01001110 11110100 11000101 11101010 01001001 10100100 11001001 11101101 01011010 01011010
11001010 11100010 10110000 11110011 11001101 01000001 01110011 00010000 00101001 11000000
00011001 10100111 11111001 10000011 00011001 11101000 00101001 11001010 10111001 10001111
00110100 11010011 11010111 01000001 00110100 01100011 01001011 00010001 10001101 11001111
00010100 10001111 00100001 11001000 00010101 10100101 00101100 00111011 10110011 11010010
10101001 11001011 00001111 11100111 11101011 01001101 00111101 00000101 01100001 00100011
11111001 10111010 11010011 11011110 00110000 01000110 01000111 01011010 10001100 00010010
00001000 10101001 10110011 10010100 10100001 11101111 10101000 10101101 11011000 10100011
00101000 00000000 11010100 00101100 10100111 00001111 11001111 01011110 00000101 01101001

01111001 01100000 10001110 01111011 11010100 00010010 11000101 10001110 01111010 11010100
00100111 01101101 01000000 10000010 00011000 01111000 01000000 11100111 11111010 01010101
11001000 01100001 00101011 10001100 00001010 00010010 00100000 01110001 01010110 11010000
00010001 01001101 11010100 11010111 01010010 10001001 00101101 11100011 11000001 00000000
11111110 01110101 01110001 11111000 11100011 10101110 00101010 00101000 01100011 11001001
11100111 11111001 11010100 10101110 00000000 00111111 01011010 11100110 10011110 10111010
10110010 01011011 00101011 01011100 11110001 00011011 10001100 11100000 01100011 10101101
01110011 10001111 10001100 11100100 10011110 01111010 01010111 01000111 01111000 00000001
10001101 11000110 01111011 01010111 00101011 00100011 01110010 00000110 00111001 00110101
11011111 10000111 01101010 11001110 11100101 00100011 00111111 01010010 01010011 10011101
11001000 00101011 00100110 01101001 00001000 11101111 01011101 00001100 11101011 10111001
01111001 10101110 01110010 11110010 00010110 10000110 01000011 10010011 11000001 11100110
10111011 01101001 01101001 10100001 10100010 11110011 00101011 10010110 11001111 01111010
10000101 10001001 11001111 00111111 10011101 00011011 10000110 01001111 00110100 11010010
01110011 11001000 10101110 11011000 11101100 01010011 00001001 01111001 11101000 01110000
01101010 00110101 11001000 11100100 11111110 01110100 11101110 11110100 11011111 10111101
11110100 10101011 10000101 11000101 10110110 11100001 11101011 11000111 00011101 01101001
00110011 11000110 11101100 00011100 11111010 01010000 11011001 00100000 11110011 01001100
11011101 10000001 11001001 10101101 10010011 01001101 10001101 10001111 11001001 00000111
00111001 10100100 11011101 10010000 00001000 11001101 01000010 11001101 10000011 11010111
10101101 00011011 10111000 00111100 11110101 10100011 10010110 01001011 01010010 01001001
11110011 10010011 01001000 11000111 00011100 11110110 00110101 01011100 10111110 01111011
11010000 11010011 00001110 00000110 01101001 01000010 00110111 01001101 10110010 00111100
11001011 00110001 10110110 00111110 10100110 10101111 11000010 01000000 00111101 00101011
00110010 11010000 00110100 11001101 11111011 10110101 00100100 11110100 10101101 11111011
00001101 00110101 10000001 11011101 00110001 11000111 01111110 00001110 01101010 00101010
11001010 11001011 01010000 11010000 01011000 10110010 01001111 10111101 01011101 10001010
00010011 11110111 10111101 01101010 11000100 00010000 01000111 00011001 11100111 11110000
10101011 01011000 01011100 01100000 00000001 10001100 01010111 00011111 00101010 10111110
10100010 11110100 00100011 10001010 00101110 00000101 01001010 10110110 11100100 11110100
10101001 01100011 01110101 00000011 10110101 01001000 10110011 01100111 11111111 00000000
10101101 01001110 11010111 11010110 01000010 01101100 10001001 01100000 11011011 11010110
10010111 11001011 10101001 00110010 01100100 00011001 00011100 11010100 11110001 01000010
11000100 10011100 11110111 11111101 00101010 01111101 10101000 10110101 00101011 01111001
00111100 10001010 10010111 11001010 00000010 10101100 10001000 00011001 01001110 00111001
00100000 11111010 11010000 01100010 11110101 10101001 01001101 10111011 11011100 10101110
01011011 10010101 01001100 01000001 10010111 10001010 11100010 00111100 01110101 01101001
00110100 11101100 00100101 01010110 10001110 00111011 01001011 01101100 00000010 01001001
11101010 11000111 11010010 10111011 11111101 10011101 00111000 00111100 01010110 01001110
10111101 10100100 01001011 10101100 01101001 01110111 10110001 01000001 00011001 00001111
10110111 00101010 00000000 11101110 00101011 01011100 00100111 11110001 01101110 01100001
10001000 01010110 10001001 11100101 11110110 01100101 01110110 00010000 10010010 11100000
10011110 11100011 10010000 01101010 11111110 10001011 00010001 10111010 11010101 00100011
10001001 11110010 11101001 11001110 01110001 11101001 01011010 10011010 00100111 11000011
11101111 00010101 01101010 00010000 10000110 10000011 01000101 10111000 00000000 11110100
00101101 11000110 01111101 11101011 11010000 01111100 00010111 11110000 10010011 01011100
10110101 10111111 10010110 01101101 01001010 00010100 01000111 00010001 00011100 00000001
11010001 01110011 11011110 10111101 11101001 01100010 01100001 00011101 00111001 10001110
00000100 10111010 10011110 01111011 10101000 10000110 11010011 11101111 10100011 01000010
11011001 00011001 00000100 00011100 01110110 10101110 11010110 11000011 00110010 11011011
01000110 11011110 11011100 11010111 00010101 10101100 10010110 10111011 11110001 00011100
01110000 10001100 01100000 01001000 01010000 00000001 11001111 01000011 01011110 10000011
01100111 00001001 10001110 00010100 01011010 11110010 10110001 00001111 10011011 01110011
11010010 10100100 11111101 11010000 11000111 01100011 01010010 10101110 00000000 10100011
11001011 11100111 10011010 01110111 10010111 10001110 10110101 11100110 11001110 11110111
11010000 11010110 11101000 00010110 00111100 11010001 10001100 01010011 10000110 01000001
11100010 10000110 11000110 00111110 01101010 00111001 01011111 11000100 00010111 11010100
01000010 01001111 01100001 11111000 11010010 11100011 00110101 00011110 11101110 11010100
01101111 11000001 11101011 01000011 10001110 10011010 10001001 10110010 01001100 11111010
11110101 10100100 00111110 11110101 00000011 11001011 11001111 00000110 10001111 00110110
10110100 11100101 10110110 10000010 11011100 10010011 01110000 00011001 00010100 11010110
01100010 01111101 10001101 01000010 11010010 01010010 00000010 00001111 00111101 11101010
00110101 01001100 10010110 01011000 11011100 00111101 11101001 10001110 11000100 11110100
10101000 01111100 11001100 00001111 01010011 11110101 10100110 00101100 10000111 10111000
11000001 10101101 10010011 10111011 10110010 00000010 01010111 00111000 10101000 11111100
11000001 10011111 11100111 01001101 01101001 00111001 11000101 01000110 01011010 10011011
01000010 00100101 01101001 00110011 01010001 10010110 11001000 10101000 10100110 10010011
00011100 11111010 11010100 01111110 01101111 01100000 01101001 01101111 01111011 10000101
10111011 00010010 00110011 01110101 11001101 01000110 01100100 00011011 10111101 00101001
10001111 00100111 00011110 11110101 00010110 01111001 11101011 01010110 11100010 11010010
00011001 00110001 10010000 00000001 11110101 10101000 11011010 01001101 11100011 00000110
10100001 10010101 10000000 11100100 00011010 10000111 11001101 00111101 00101000 01010010
01101111 01100010 10101100 01011010 11110011 00111111 11111010 11010101 00011011 10110001

00100011 10011111 01011010 10101110 01100101 00001010 01111001 00110100 11000011 00110001
00100011 00110101 01101001 00111011 01101010 00001100 10110011 11100110 10010000 00000000
10100110 11001001 00101000 11000001 11100110 10101010 01001011 00110000 00000011 00010101
00010010 11001011 11000110 01001101 00110101 00011011 10111011 00001001 10010110 10111100
11001100 11110100 00110100 11111111 00000000 00110011 00011101 00111010 01010110 01110011
11001110 01010111 10001100 11110101 10100110 10110101 11000110 01000000 10101001 11100101
11100100 01110110 00001011 00110111 10101011 00101111 10110100 10100011 00111101 01101001
00111100 11100101 00011101 11001110 01001101 01100101 11001001 00110001 11011111 10111001
11001101 00110001 10101110 11110010 01101011 01111110 01010111 10100011 10111000 11101100
10001101 00111111 10110100 00001100 11100100 00011010 01101011 01011100 00000010 01001111
10101101 01100100 10111101 11000110 00110010 01001001 10101000 01011010 11100000 00110001
00011100 11110010 01111010 01010110 11011110 11001111 10011100 10101011 00011011 01001111
00111110 01111010 01010101 01111001 01100111 00011101 11000101 01100110 00001001 11001010
11110111 11100010 10011001 11100111 00010010 01111001 00110101 00010000 10000011 10001011
00101101 01000100 10110101 00100100 11011001 00100100 01010110 01111101 11000001 00011110
10111100 01010011 10100110 10010111 11100100 11100000 01110011 01010101 11110011 11100110
01010110 10110001 10001011 01110010 10111011 00100101 10010101 11101110 01011011 00111000
01011111 01011010 10001101 00000011 01101111 00000011 11110101 10100111 11011100 10011111
11011110 10001100 00001110 00110001 10001100 11010010 11000100 00111111 01011111 01011010
11011010 11010110 11011000 11100100 10011110 11100101 10001000 10111101 00001001 10101011
01010000 00101110 00001110 11101100 10001111 10101101 01010101 11100000 01111101 00101010
01100100 01010000 01010000 11110101 00100110 10110000 10101001 01110111 10111011 00110101
10000010 11010000 11010001 01000010 00011011 00011000 00110101 01100101 00100001 10001101
10000110 00000111 00000111 11111001 11010110 01110100 00111001 00011110 11010101 10101011
01101011 10010110 11101101 10010011 01011100 10010101 01011101 10001101 00011010 00100001
01111011 00110110 00000011 10001110 01111001 10100001 00010101 10010111 10000011 10011110
00101011 01001000 00001110 01111001 00010100 11111100 00000110 01101111 10011100 00001110
01101011 10011011 11011011 01110111 00100111 10010101 10010100 10010000 11101101 11100111
00011100 01111101 01101001 01011110 00011101 11000011 00111000 11100110 10101100 10110100
01101011 10001100 00000001 10001010 01110110 11011110 11011101 10101010 01111001 11101111
10110000 01110010 11011100 11001011 10111001 00000100 00011100 01100011 10100101 01010000
01100101 00011001 11100000 01110000 01001110 01110001 01011011 11110010 01000100 10110010
11110000 01111011 01111010 01010110 00111100 11010001 10011000 00100101 00111011 11000001
11011001 11011100 11010111 01010101 00101001 11011101 00010010 11010011 01011010 10001100
01110110 11111101 11010001 00011100 11110011 11010110 10101000 00111010 11011011 10010100
00101010 01000000 00000111 11010111 00010101 01111101 11111010 01100100 01110111 10101100
01001011 10111001 00000100 01010111 00111000 00100000 10011110 01101011 10101010 10000101
11011011 10110011 00111001 10110001 00001011 01001011 10100001 00101110 10101100 11001000
10000110 01000011 00000100 10101001 11110010 01110011 10010011 10011100 11010111 00111011
00100011 00000110 01110010 01110010 00111001 11110111 10101110 10100110 00010110 01011111
00101111 00111100 00010000 11111100 00011100 11111010 01010110 01011101 11010110 10010010
00100100 10011101 10011010 00001001 01111100 10110100 00111101 00010111 11010010 10111101
00101010 01001101 01101101 10111001 11000110 01110100 01001011 00011100 00001010 10000000
01100001 10001111 10101001 00100110 10010001 10001100 00001010 01010011 01100010 10100001
00100111 10111101 01100110 00111101 11000001 00111101 00001111 00011101 11110001 01010001
11111001 11111000 01111100 01100111 00010101 11000010 10101000 10110100 11101111 01110011
11010000 11100111 01011011 10011011 01011110 01110100 01101011 11110111 01000000 00000111
11011010 10011010 11110111 10000000 00001110 01001110 01110001 11010011 11011110 10110001
11100110 10011101 10111101 01001001 10101000 10111100 11100010 01111000 00100111 00100100
11010011 01110100 00111011 10000111 10110100 00110101 11011010 11101100 11110101 11001111
00000111 10011100 01010011 00011010 11110011 10101000 01110011 11011111 10000011 01011001
10001101 00101001 11000000 00011101 10101001 11001010 00110111 00000001 11101001 01010100
10101001 01000001 01101111 10110000 01110011 00011010 00111111 01101011 00100100 11110101
11001111 00011100 11010010 00001011 10000000 00001001 00100011 10111000 11111100 10101010
10011000 01011110 10111000 11110100 11101011 01001100 11011100 01110000 00000000 11101101
11011111 11010110 10101010 11010001 01111010 00010000 11011111 01110010 11111111 00000000
11011010 00111010 00010011 11010011 00111110 10110100 11011111 10110100 01111100 11111100
00001110 00101010 10010100 10010010 01100111 10000000 01111000 10100100 01010110 00001100
01111111 00001010 01101001 01011001 01101010 00011100 11110111 00101110 10110101 11000010
10110001 11000111 01101111 01011111 01111010 10001101 10100111 01010010 10111000 11001001
11001111 10100101 01010011 01110110 00100100 10011100 00011110 10011110 10010100 10100001
10111110 11111110 01111101 01111011 11010101 00101010 01111010 00000111 10110100 00101101
10100100 10011100 11100011 00110100 00110100 11011001 01101100 01100110 10101001 01001001
00110001 01010001 10001111 01011110 10010101 00011000 01101100 10011100 01110111 11110101
11110101 10101010 01110100 10101110 11101110 11000001 11001111 01001101 00001011 11000110
01110000 01110010 00000000 11000000 11110101 10101000 11010010 01001111 01011111 11001110
10100001 00000011 10011110 01111010 00001010 01011100 01110011 11000000 10100101 01101011
11101000 00100100 11011110 11100100 11100110 01001100 01100000 11100111 10001111 01011010
01110111 10011010 01110001 11010111 00011001 10101010 11101000 10100111 00011101 01110001
10011110 10100010 10100110 11011011 10110100 01100000 11010100 10110101 10100110 10100000
10000011 00000111 10101110 01101000 11110011 01110001 11010111 10101110 01101010 00110111
01101100 11100101 01001111 00100000 11010100 01101010 01110110 10100001 00000111 10000011
11101011 01000101 10111001 10110101 01100100 11101010 00111001 11100100 11100111 00111001

11101111 01001000 11110111 00000100 11100100 01110110 11110101 10101000 10110000 11001100
11011011 01001000 00000011 10111000 11110111 10101001 01001100 00111111 00101010 00001100
00001111 10100101 01101000 10100010 10011110 10000011 10111011 00100010 11110011 00011000
10000011 11001001 11100111 11010100 11010000 00110010 01111110 10110101 01101001 00101101
00000011 00000010 01010100 11100111 00011101 10101010 01000100 10110110 00000111 00000101
11000110 00101010 00101110 11101111 01100001 11011000 10101000 11111001 00011000 11000000
00110100 11011111 00110000 10000110 00010101 10100001 11110110 01111100 11100011 10001100
11111101 01101001 00000101 10111000 11011010 01000001 00000000 00011111 10100101 00100111
01010011 01011101 01011000 01011001 10010100 01111001 11001111 10110001 11111101 01101001
11001010 01110110 10011010 10110101 11110110 01010010 10100011 00100111 10100101 01000101
11100100 00011101 11111100 10101111 00010100 10111101 11010110 11110100 01100011 10110011
00101011 10111100 10100100 00011100 00000001 11111010 11010010 00101001 01100000 01111010
01110101 10101011 00011111 01100110 00111001 11110110 10101001 00111110 11001000 11011100
01111011 11110110 10101011 01110011 01001011 01000001 01011001 11110100 00101011 10000011
10110100 01110100 11101011 01001010 10000111 00000000 11111111 00000000 00111111 01011010
10011111 11101100 10100100 11100011 11010000 00011010 00011110 00001111 01001111 11001011
00010100 11011011 01001001 10001001 00101001 00100010 00110000 01001010 10001110 00111000
00011110 10010101 00100100 00110011 00010001 11000000 00011111 10001101 00101010 10101011
00001111 10010101 11000111 11010010 10100100 01001000 01000000 00011101 11110011 11110101
10101001 11010001 00010100 10010011 00000001 00110111 00011001 11101011 10011010 10110001
00010100 11101100 10101011 11010111 11101011 01010101 10011010 00101111 00101111 10100101
00110111 01110000 11101111 10011111 11001111 00010101 00010010 01010110 01100110 10001001
10011010 01000010 11100000 10000000 00110000 11011111 10011101 01011001 10110110 11010100
10110110 10110110 01111001 00100000 01110101 00010101 10000110 11100100 10101001 11100011
11110011 00110101 00101010 00010010 00000000 01100000 00101011 00101111 01100110 10110101
11010000 01111100 11101110 11100111 01010001 01101101 10101001 00011001 00111000 11111011
10011110 11011001 10101101 01101011 01101101 01000111 11001010 00111011 10011100 10011100
00011110 10011100 11010111 00010110 00100100 00111001 00011000 00111000 00011101 10000101
01001101 11110110 10000000 00110001 11110011 00011111 11001110 10111001 11100111 01000010
00101111 01010100 01101010 10101010 01110100 00111011 11111011 01001101 01010000 11110100
00100100 01101100 11101101 01010111 11101101 10110101 00101000 01100101 01100000 00001111
00000110 10111000 00011000 00101111 00001010 10100111 00100111 11110011 10101011 00011111
11011010 00011100 11100101 00001001 11001111 01100011 01011100 10010011 11000011 11011101
00010111 10100011 00111101 00011010 00011001 01100011 10010001 00110010 00001110 01101010
01101111 11100001 11101011 01011100 00111101 10100110 10100110 11000000 00010110 01000010
01110011 11011000 00010011 01011010 11110110 10011010 10110011 01111001 01111001 11100000
10011100 01111010 11010111 00010101 01001100 00111011 10001011 11010100 10110011 01110111
00000100 01110100 10100001 01000001 11101111 01010101 10101101 10110101 00110101 00100000
00011001 00000000 11100111 11011110 10101100 10100101 11100100 00100111 10101001 10101100
10011100 00111001 00111110 00100110 01001111 00110000 00110000 00100101 11111001 11101001
01001110 11100100 11100111 10001010 10010001 00100110 10000000 11100111 00101101 11111001
11010011 10110111 01000100 00111010 00011110 00101011 10011101 11110011 01111100 01001100
00111101 10100010 11011000 01101010 11110100 11000110 00101001 01111111 10000111 10100101
00000101 10010100 00010001 10000011 11001101 01001001 10001110 11100010 10000100 11101110
11110101 00001011 11011111 01100010 00100101 00000111 11010010 10011100 10100000 10011110
00110001 10000001 01010011 00100100 01111001 00111110 11110101 00101000 01011101 10100110
10110100 11011101 10001100 10001001 00100011 00111011 01110011 11001111 00010100 10101110
01001000 11000110 00001111 01111010 01111011 01001000 01000010 01110101 11101001 11010111
10110101 01010001 10011110 11101001 01010100 01110101 11101011 01001010 11001001 11101101
10110001 00110110 10111001 01110001 01101110 00011011 10100001 11101011 01010011 10100100
10100001 10111110 10110101 11001100 00111110 10100001 10111010 01000010 01000011 01100000
10000011 10001100 01010011 10100011 10111110 01100010 01110001 10111011 11110011 10101010
11100100 01001011 01010001 01011001 10011101 01000001 10001100 00011110 01101010 00110000
00101011 00100110 00101011 11100110 00000000 01110011 01010111 11100000 10111101 01010011
11000011 10001111 11000110 10110010 01110100 01011011 11011000 01100011 11001010 10010000
01110010 01111010 01010010 11100011 00111101 00111000 10101001 01011100 10000010 00111000
11100111 11010010 10000000 10100000 01110110 11111100 01110011 01011001 00111111 01110011
01110000 00101011 00010001 10001110 11011100 00011010 01111110 11101100 11110001 01001110
01110001 10010001 11111010 11010100 01001100 00001101 00001001 10111101 11000111 01100001
01110001 10111000 11110001 11000101 01000101 01110001 00001110 01001001 11101100 01101001
11101010 01110110 11100011 11111001 11010010 10111100 10011001 11001111 10101101 01101000
11011101 10001001 10110001 01001101 11100011 01010000 00110001 11111101 00101010 00110110
00000100 00011111 01101010 10111000 11100000 00110100 01100011 10001110 01101010 10111100
10111111 01110000 00000010 00111011 11110001 01001101 01011101 10101011 10000110 11000100
01111100 10011010 01000110 11001111 01101110 01000111 10101101 00111000 10010000 00101001
10100100 11111010 01010010 10011010 10110011 11010001 10000001 00100100 01111100 00011101
10111000 11101111 11010110 10101100 11000111 11110011 00011111 01010001 01010100 11000000
00111000 00111100 10011010 01111100 01010011 10011000 10111001 11101011 11101101 01010011
01101101 00000100 11010001 10101000 10101011 10001110 11110100 10100111 10011010 10101101
00011101 11000010 11001010 00111110 01001110 10111110 10011001 11101001 01001110 01100011
11101001 10010011 11111000 11010111 00111010 10000110 10110111 01100011 00001001 10000001
00101010 01111000 00011101 00111101 00101011 10010001 01110011 10000111 11001000 10101110
10111001 11001110 01010111 10011110 00101011 10001110 10010111 00100110 01001111 11000100

11010111 01111110 00011001 00101011 11011000 00010000 00110001 00100111 10011010 10101111
01110101 00010010 11001000 00110000 01111010 11010011 11011000 11100100 10010001 10011111
11000110 10100011 00100100 11111010 11110100 11101111 01011101 10110000 11010001 11101010
01101000 10001110 01100111 01010010 10110001 01101000 10100100 00100110 00000010 01111010
11110100 11000101 01100011 10110100 11010010 11000100 01110010 11100000 10001100 11100110
10111011 01111001 00100011 00010010 00011100 00010001 01011001 00010111 10110110 00000001
10001110 00111100 10111101 11111101 11000001 10101110 11101010 01110101 10111001 01110100
10010010 00000110 10001110 01110101 10110101 00000010 00000110 00001010 10111001 11100111
10101101 01000111 00011110 10100100 00001000 01111110 00001000 11111100 00101010 11110100
11111010 01110011 00101100 10011000 00000011 11011111 10011111 01001010 10100111 00110101
10011001 01010011 10010011 00011001 11000111 10101101 01110110 11010011 10011100 00011001
10001011 01110010 11011000 10001100 11101010 00111001 00011001 11000001 10101000 10011010
11111001 10100100 00011111 00100010 00111000 00011101 11001101 01001011 11110110 01110001
11001110 01000111 00111101 10101001 00000100 01100000 00100111 01000001 01010110 10010101
00111011 10001001 11001110 01011011 00010001 01111101 10101010 01001001 00011100 01110000
01110000 00101001 11011011 10100101 01100111 11100010 10100111 01011101 10101010 00111001
00000010 10011110 10100111 00011101 00000001 01100010 11111110 10010100 10011101 01000101
11011000 01001110 01001111 10111001 00001010 11000111 00101011 00111000 01100111 01100011
10010011 01010110 11101101 11101101 11110010 11100011 10101001 11100110 10100101 10110110
10110101 10011010 01011110 00010010 00011001 00011111 00111110 10000010 10111010 00101101
00111010 11001010 01101000 10000111 11111010 10001100 00111111 11111011 01010101 11001111
01010010 10110101 10000110 10000110 01101001 10110110 01000101 01000000 00111110 01010001
11001111 10101001 00011101 01101011 01011110 00101000 11100110 00111101 00000110 00111110
10100111 00010100 10110001 01000001 00111110 00000110 11110010 00000111 10101000 00010101
01101111 11101100 10000101 10001000 00101111 00100011 11111110 00000111 00010101 11100111
01010101 10101001 11001101 00101011 10011010 01101010 01010101 00010110 11110010 10010010
01111111 01111000 00000101 01011000 10001110 11010100 11101100 11111111 00000000 01011010
01110011 11101011 10001010 10011101 00101101 11000010 10011110 11100100 10011111 01010011
10011010 10110111 00010101 10111011 00110110 00001110 00111000 10101000 10001100 10000010
11010110 00101011 10001011 01000001 10110000 01111100 11000100 10011110 11100110 10100110
01001011 00110000 00111010 01100111 10011110 11100110 10101111 01000101 00010000 01011100
01100000 01110011 01010010 10100000 01100000 01111010 01110001 01000011 10010011 10010110
10010010 01100000 10100000 01000111 01101111 01101010 10101010 10111111 00100000 11100011
11011110 10100101 01011000 11101010 01110000 00110000 10110100 10000000 01110011 01011010
11010011 10100100 11010110 10110111 00000100 10000110 11101101 01010101 01001100 01110101
11100110 10100011 01110101 00000110 10011101 00101001 00001010 00001110 01001110 01110011
01010101 01011010 01101100 01110011 10011110 00101000 10110101 10011110 10100101 00010010
00001000 11000001 00100000 11010111 10100110 11111100 00110010 10110001 11010011 01100011
10110011 10111001 10111101 10111110 10011110 00100011 00100011 01110001 10110010 01001100
01111100 10101011 01011110 01011001 11110110 11000000 10111101 11000110 00111101 00101010
11010101 10001101 11110100 01001101 00110010 00101100 11010010 10011000 11100010 00100111
11100110 00100011 11010010 10111010 01110000 11101110 00110000 01111110 11110010 10111001
10001101 01111000 00111001 10101011 00100001 11011111 00010010 11111110 00101101 01101011
11011110 00011100 11110001 10110100 11111010 01000110 10000110 01101101 01111111 10110010
01100010 00001000 11010001 01111001 01001000 00110010 01000001 00011100 11110011 11110101
10101110 11101001 11111110 00100010 11011011 11111111 00000000 11000010 10111101 01001001
11101101 11011010 01001011 10011011 11110111 10110100 01110001 00101011 01001010 00111001
00001111 10001111 11110001 00110101 11100101 10111010 10011101 10001110 10011011 10101011
11111000 11011000 01001101 10100101 01011110 11011010 10100101 10110100 00110000 01101100
10111000 10011110 01111001 00000000 00000000 11110110 11000110 01111010 11010101 01001101
01100011 11000101 01110110 01010110 11111010 00010100 11111010 01000101 10111100 00101001
00100100 10010010 00000010 00100100 10111001 10001101 10111000 00100011 10110000 00010101
11011110 11011101 10100011 11001010 10100010 01111001 11111100 10111010 01101110 01110011
00111110 00001011 10110101 00110111 01011010 10000100 10010111 00110111 00000011 10010101
11100110 10111011 11110100 00100000 01010111 00010011 11100000 11111001 01000100 01010110
11000100 01100011 10101111 00011001 10101110 10010011 11101101 01111110 11100111 00110101
11000111 01011010 00101101 01001010 11001101 10011110 10000101 00110100 10101100 01101001
00110100 10000011 00111110 11110100 10001110 11011101 00101011 00110000 01011100 01110111
11111110 01110100 11100111 10111000 11110111 11001111 10100101 01110010 10111000 00101101
11001011 00101110 11111001 10111110 10010100 10011110 01100000 11101001 10011010 11001111
01101001 11110001 11111100 01011000 00100111 11011010 10001111 00110011 00100011 10000011
10001010 10000110 10101111 10100010 00011101 10001011 01001110 11011100 10011110 01101001
10101000 11000111 10101101 01010100 11110011 01001111 01001110 11111001 11101001 01001011
11100111 01100011 10011100 11010110 10010000 10100111 10101101 10101100 01000001 00111011
10011100 11010001 10010011 10000001 01010001 01101111 11100010 10011001 11100110 01100111
00011100 11110001 11011010 10100001 10101001 01110011 10000001 00111000 01101110 01001000
00011111 10001101 00101110 11101010 10101101 11100110 11100001 10110011 01000011 11001011
10000011 10011100 11100010 10101001 00101101 11011000 10101100 01001010 11001100 00000111
11010110 10011000 01011011 00000100 00010001 11101011 01010001 11111001 10100000 10000010
01101001 10100110 01000000 01111001 10100010 00010000 01001111 01010000 01101011 01010010
01011101 11011000 11111100 01101010 00000010 11011100 11010100 01001101 00101110 01001001
00111111 11010110 10100010 01111001 01110000 00111101 11101010 10011010 11100111 01011110
11101110 10000011 01001000 10110000 11000111 00111000 11001001 10101000 01011000 10001101

11111100 00011010 10000101 10100100 11001000 11101011 01010000 10011001 01111010 11110011
01001101 00100111 01101101 01010000 10001011 01001110 11011000 11100010 10100001 11110011
00111001 00100110 10101010 11111001 11011001 11101111 11110100 10100110 00110100 11000011
10111001 11100010 10101001 00101110 10010110 00011101 11001001 11001100 10111101 01110111
01010100 01101101 00100111 00011110 10000010 10101010 00111100 10100011 00100100 10010011
11000101 01000110 11110111 01011000 00011000 11000110 01000111 11010110 10011010 10100111
10101110 10100011 01000101 10010110 10010111 00111101 01111011 01010100 01010010 11001101
10000010 00111001 11101011 01010100 11111100 11100011 10001111 01111010 10001001 11100101
11111001 10111001 11100100 11111101 01101011 01011010 01110100 11011100 01110111 00010011
01010110 00101110 00011001 11110010 01111110 01101110 11010101 00001001 10011000 11100111
10001110 10010101 01010101 10100110 00100000 11110001 01001101 00110010 00010000 00101001
00111000 10101011 10010101 11010011 01000010 11000111 10011000 01001001 00111100 11010100
01101101 00100110 00001001 11111010 01110001 01010001 01111001 10011101 01111101 01101001
10011001 00111001 11100111 10100101 01011010 01011010 11101010 01001000 11110110 10010100
10010001 01010001 00011001 00001110 01001111 00110100 11101111 01011100 00001010 10001100
11100000 01111101 11011110 10111110 11110101 10110010 10010010 11101000 01010010 11010111
01110001 11001011 00100111 11001000 01111000 00100111 11011010 10011001 11110011 00001100
01111100 10111000 00000110 10001100 10000011 11001000 10100101 11001000 11101111 01001111
10011101 11011010 11100011 01000011 01110111 01001001 11101101 11110101 00110100 00111011
10110110 00111110 01011110 11011110 10010100 10101101 10010011 10010000 00101010 00111100
00010001 11110111 11111111 00000000 00101010 01111100 11111010 00010110 00101111 00100100
01100111 11010110 10010001 10011011 11001011 01010010 01111011 11110101 10100100 01100110
00100000 00010001 01010100 01100110 10010001 10011011 10001100 11110001 01000100 01010011
01111010 00010001 01010010 01101010 00101000 10010001 01011011 01110000 00100100 11110101
00111101 11101010 01000100 00000100 00011110 10111100 11010101 01101000 10000011 00010101
11001011 01110110 10101011 00101000 01000000 00011001 00111101 11111011 11010110 10001101
11011001 10011100 11101011 10111001 00111000 11100011 10101111 01011111 01001010 10110000
10011001 10101010 01001000 01001110 01111110 01011010 10110001 00010010 10011100 11100111
00111100 00011110 11110101 10001011 01010111 01000101 01111010 00011010 00010001 00010001
10001100 10011010 10111001 01101101 01110011 10110100 11101110 10101100 10010000 11011101
00000001 00111100 01010100 11001001 00101111 00000111 00100011 10011110 10011100 01010111
00111101 01001010 01001001 11110100 00101101 01101110 01110100 10010000 11001000 00011001
00000001 11110101 10101001 00111000 00111101 00111101 00111101 00101011 00100011 01001101
10011001 10001100 10011011 01011000 01110001 01011010 10011011 10000000 00000011 11011110
10111000 01100111 00001110 01010110 01011001 00100110 00000110 11001110 01110001 01001100
00100111 10011010 01101011 11001011 11000110 00000000 00100100 11010100 10110110 11100100
10010011 11110111 01111001 11110111 00010101 00010010 01001101 00101011 10001101 00101011
10010001 11100000 10010111 11100101 01111010 11111011 01010100 01110011 11011001 00110100
11101010 01000110 11000010 11111001 11101101 10001010 11010011 01000010 01001111 00011000
11111101 01101010 01010100 00100000 00011110 01001101 01001111 10110100 11111011 11000011
11011001 11101001 01100110 01110010 11011111 11011001 00110111 11010000 10011100 01111001
01000101 10010011 10110001 10101110 01111011 01011011 10110110 10011010 00001011 10001100
01001010 10100110 00111111 01010000 01000101 01111010 00111011 11011101 01000100 00000001
11100111 00111111 01001010 10101110 01100100 10001110 01000000 01000100 10001010 10000101
00001000 11100100 00110000 11001110 01101011 10101110 10001110 00100110 01001001 10100111
00100011 00011010 10010100 10101110 10011010 00111100 11101110 11010000 10101100 01000000
10011001 00001110 01110011 11000111 00010101 01100100 00101010 10110111 00111000 10101011
00111010 11011110 10010000 00100001 10010001 11011110 11000100 00011100 01110101 11011010
01001101 01100111 01000111 01110011 00010110 11000001 10111110 01001101 10001101 11011101
01110001 11010010 10111101 01101010 01010010 10001101 01000101 01111000 10011100 00110010
10100110 11100011 10111001 01001011 10011110 11011111 01011010 00001001 11011101 10000110
11000111 11010110 10011011 11000000 00111111 00111110 01110010 01111011 01010010 10000011
11011011 10110101 01101110 10100001 01110101 01110100 01010011 11010100 01011100 10011110
10111101 01000111 10111101 00100001 00000001 10111000 00000011 11110010 10100100 11100000
10010010 00001000 00111001 11001111 10101101 01001100 10100011 00111101 10111000 10101000
01111010 01101100 01010010 00001000 01010111 00101001 11001110 00001101 01001110 10011000
01010001 11000000 11100011 10100111 00010100 00100100 01000011 00011100 01010000 01000000
00011101 11001111 01001100 01010110 01111010 00110100 01010110 11000011 00100100 10010000
10101001 00100011 00011001 10101000 10000001 11100000 10011100 00011100 11010011 11010101
01001001 00100100 01100111 00111100 01010100 11011110 01010001 11000000 11001101 01101001
01100100 10110100 00010110 10101100 10101100 10100000 10011110 01000000 00111101 01111101
00101001 01011001 01110001 11010010 10101101 10000101 11000010 00011110 01110110 00001110
11100110 10011000 10010001 10010011 10010011 10001100 00000010 01101000 11010010 11010111
01100001 01100010 10011010 10000011 01001110 01011000 11110010 01111110 01111101 11111001
00011100 10000001 10011010 10111010 00100000 00100100 10011110 10000010 10010001 10100000
11100111 10100101 01000010 10011101 11110110 00001110 01000010 10011011 01000111 10111100
11101110 11101110 01000111 01100001 01001010 00100010 11011011 10110000 00000001 11110011
11110111 00010101 10100001 00001100 01000000 01100111 10001110 01001111 10101101 00111111
11001000 11000011 11100111 00011101 10101000 11110110 10010111 11011101 10001111 10010101
10010100 00000010 10000011 11000000 11101011 11101101 01010010 00100100 01000111 00000111
00100000 01100000 01111010 01010101 11110100 10110111 00100000 11101110 11000110 00101010
01000001 01101110 01001000 11000000 11101011 11101111 01010001 11001110 10111010 10110010
11111001 00011101 11110101 00110011 01010001 01111011 11100011 10011111 01111010 00011110

00110010 01001110 00001101 01101011 01111001 00000011 01111000 00111101 01101001 01111100
10000101 00101110 01001001 01011110 00111011 01010010 01110101 10010011 11011101 10001111
10010000 11001010 11110010 01111001 11111111 00000000 00010001 01001011 11110110 01110010
01000000 00011101 10111010 11110100 10101101 01011111 10110010 10101111 01011100 11010011
11111110 11001110 00000111 00100011 10101101 01001111 10110110 11010010 11010111 00011101
10010001 10011001 00010101 10101111 01010001 10000001 11111110 00010101 00100000 10000000
00001111 01111010 11010011 01011000 11010111 10010010 00111111 00011110 00101001 00110000
00110111 11110100 11000101 01100010 11101010 10110101 10101101 11000010 11001000 10101000
11010000 00001100 00001100 01111110 00110100 00100100 00000101 10001001 00111000 11100000
01110111 10101011 10100011 01101110 00110001 11101001 01000110 11100000 01111000 11101000
00110011 01010011 11101101 10100101 00111101 11000010 11011101 10001010 11111110 01000111
00010100 01111001 00001010 01110010 01111011 10001010 10110110 10100111 10011111 01101010
01011100 10101001 00000111 00011101 01001110 00110011 01000100 01011100 10111011 00000011
01000101 00110100 10000111 01110000 11000001 11000101 00111101 01100001 10001101 01000110
01011101 00110010 01101010 11011001 10010001 01110011 11001010 11111110 01000010 10011010
11010010 10101110 01111101 01000101 01001100 01100101 10101101 10011000 11101110 01000011
00011101 10110100 01111001 11001010 10101110 00111101 10001101 00001111 01101110 00001111
00100010 10100110 00110010 10101110 00111010 11010100 01101111 00111000 00000111 00000000
11100100 11110111 00010100 11101101 10101101 10101111 01110001 11101000 00110101 10101101
10010111 00000011 10011110 00111101 00101001 10001101 01100110 10111001 00011110 10011101
01110011 01001010 11010010 10110001 10100000 11001010 11000010 00110011 01010100 11010011
11010010 11001100 10010100 00000110 11001101 00000000 11110111 11110101 10101000 11011110
11001111 10001100 10100111 01011010 10011011 11001101 11011100 00000000 11001110 00110011
01001101 01011001 10001111 00111100 01100110 10100110 11101110 11111010 11101000 00000101
00110111 10110100 01110101 00111001 00000000 10010011 01010000 11001101 01101010 01000111
01100011 01011010 01000110 01110000 10100011 11010110 10011011 11100111 00000110 11000101
01101000 11100111 00110101 01100010 01101100 10011001 10010110 11010000 11100011 00001100
01110010 01111001 11100110 10010111 00011000 11000110 01111011 11010110 10011011 11111001
01100100 01111100 11000011 00110101 00001111 10010110 10000100 11100111 00010101 01101010
10100001 01010110 01001000 10100101 00101111 00000000 00010011 11000001 10100110 01100111
00011000 00100100 11010101 11111001 01100001 01011111 11100000 00111111 10011101 01000100
11110110 10100011 10110111 01011111 11100111 01001101 01010100 01001011 01000001 00010000
10100100 11100100 10001100 01110100 11111010 10011010 10011110 00101001 01001000 00011100
10011110 00101010 00000101 10110101 00101010 01001110 01110010 01101000 11110010 10001000
11101100 01111110 10110100 11011100 10100011 10110010 00101001 01001101 10100010 11111000
10111011 11001111 00000001 10001000 00011101 01000001 00000110 10101110 11011010 11011110
00010101 00011000 11100111 11111100 01101011 00001110 00100000 00000000 00111011 00000101
01011010 10000110 01100000 00000111 10111000 00111100 10001010 11001110 01110100 11100010
11100011 10101010 00101101 01001100 11101001 10101101 11101111 00001110 01000110 01001000
11111010 11100110 10110100 10101101 11101111 00111100 11001111 10111010 01101011 10010100
10000110 01001100 11100011 00110101 10101101 01101110 11111100 01100111 00111001 10101111
00111010 10111101 00101110 01011101 01001101 10110100 01100110 11101010 01011101 10011110
10000100 11010101 10101011 01101001 11001111 11110111 10111000 10101100 00101000 11100100
00100111 00010101 01100110 00111001 00110110 10011110 10111101 01101011 10010001 11010010
11010010 11100100 11011000 11011111 01001001 10111000 00000011 00111111 10011101 01011001
10000010 11101011 00000111 00100100 10010001 11011000 11010110 00010010 01011101 01110001
11000111 01010001 01010010 10001001 11001011 01111011 01010110 00011010 11101100 11001001
10110101 10001110 10101010 00101001 00010100 11100000 10001110 11111101 11000101 01001000
11110010 00000001 11011110 10111001 11011011 00111101 01000010 01001000 11111010 00011110
10000110 10101101 10111101 11101111 10011000 10100100 10100111 01011010 01011010 00100110
01010101 11101110 00111110 11111110 11110000 01000110 10111111 00101001 11101011 11000101
01100010 01011111 11011110 00010010 01000000 00000111 10001111 01011010 10001010 11111110
01010110 00101110 01000110 01101010 10001011 01111100 11000100 01101111 11111100 00101011
01001000 00100101 01101101 10000110 10010101 11001001 11010001 10001110 11111100 10001110
01101010 11101100 00100011 00100100 00001110 10100100 11110111 10101100 10110100 01101101
10110010 00000001 10000010 01000111 10101111 10100101 01101011 11011010 10101000 01100011
10001100 11100010 10001001 11000111 10100011 00101100 10111000 10000011 10001111 01111010
10010001 01011011 10001110 11100000 11111010 11010011 00011000 10000000 01000111 10111101
01000111 00101100 10011011 00110000 00000000 11101011 01011001 11110010 11001010 11010111
00010011 00101111 01000011 01110100 11010001 00001110 10111101 00111101 01101011 01000010
00011101 01000001 01100100 00001000 00001000 11000111 10101001 11001101 01100000 01101110
00111001 11101001 01001111 00010010 11111100 11011101 00110001 01000100 01100011 11001111
10100100 10001001 10110001 11010010 00100001 11011100 01111010 11100100 01010010 10110000
00011111 11000010 00101011 00001010 00101011 10100110 01011100 01100000 11100010 10101101
01000111 01111001 10111001 01001111 00100111 10001111 01011010 01001110 10011111 00101110
11000000 01011110 00110001 01100111 11101001 01001100 01111000 11001111 10100101 00100010
01011101 00001100 00000011 10011110 11010100 11101111 00111101 01111001 11100100 11010110
01101110 10011111 00101101 11011000 11001000 11110110 00011110 10110101 00011011 11000100
01011001 01001001 11101111 11011010 10101101 00101001 01000110 11100100 01111110 00110100
11001001 00110001 10001010 01101001 00110111 10101000 10011001 10011100 11100011 01101011
11100000 11010011 01010100 11100011 10101111 11100111 01010011 01011101 11110100 11100100
01100000 11100011 10110001 10101010 10110001 11001001 10111011 10001110 10000110 10001001
01101010 00101011 00010110 00010111 10011110 00111111 01001010 01101011 00001110 10100010

10011000 10110010 00011000 11001111 00111101 11101010 01011100 01110010 01000000 11110100
11001101 01100011 00101000 00110100 11101110 10000001 10100010 00100111 11001010 10001101
11001001 11000110 00111001 11100010 10101101 11011011 01011101 11101110 00011000 00100011
00000110 10100000 01110101 11001100 01111000 00011101 11101010 10110110 00001100 01111101
00001111 00110101 01001010 11001011 01110010 00101101 01110011 01011011 01110110 00000001
11001001 11101010 01111010 11010111 00101011 01110001 11000101 11001100 10000011 11111101
10100011 01011010 11010001 11011101 00010101 00011000 10010011 10100111 10101101 01100100
11011110 00110111 11111010 01100100 11100100 01100000 10000010 11011101 10101011 01111010
01011010 00111011 10100110 01010010 01001110 11100100 01101100 10100011 01111001 00110101
00001011 10100001 00000110 10100111 00111100 01110001 01001001 10001100 11110101 11100110
10111010 11111010 00011010 10100101 01100010 10100110 00110000 01101000 00101010 01011000
11110001 10001100 01010101 10000010 10111100 00011100 01110100 10101000 10110001 10001110
00101011 01111110 10010110 01000000 11001000 00100110 10110111 01010110 00011000 11000111
00000110 10101011 01001001 10100111 10101100 10000100 10001100 11100011 11011111 00010101
01111011 00110101 00100010 11100100 10011111 01011100 01010010 01110101 00110101 11011100
01011100 10000110 00111011 11101001 00001010 01000001 00011001 11111010 01100000 01010100
10010001 11101000 00110000 00010000 00001011 11100111 00111000 10101101 01101100 10001100
11100010 10100110 01001001 00110010 00111010 01010011 10001101 01010100 11011101 10010011
00100011 10010100 11001010 01001101 00010110 11011011 00100000 10010101 11100100 00001111
10101101 01011100 01001011 00011000 01010111 10011000 11100010 01000000 01110011 11001111
00011101 01101010 11011010 11110010 01111000 00010101 00100010 01000110 01110010 00110001
11111001 01010100 11001010 01001110 00111101 01101110 00111110 01000001 10010000 11011011
10000101 11100011 00011100 01010100 11100010 00101100 01100111 10010001 11110100 10101001
01010010 00100110 11101000 01000110 00001101 01001110 10010000 10001110 11110100 10011010
01010010 01111010 00010101 11010100 10101010 10110001 11110111 11000101 01001110 10010001
11100110 10101100 00101100 01000011 00100000 00000001 11000101 01001010 00010100 00101000
11001111 11101011 01001101 01000001 00101101 01000101 10100001 00011100 01010001 01100100
01111100 11000011 10001010 10011011 00011000 11101001 11010100 11010000 10110100 11101000
10110001 10111111 11110001 11110101 10100101 11101100 11010010 01010111 00000001 11001001
00011110 00111010 11010011 10111010 01110011 01001110 11100011 00010101 01010010 01111001
11010110 00111100 11110101 10101011 10000101 00111110 10101100 01100101 10110110 10010101
01010100 01010101 00011011 10011101 01000001 01100010 00011111 00110111 01010001 01011001
10110111 11011010 10000001 00000011 10000010 00111000 10101110 01110110 11111010 11111101
11011001 01001000 11011100 01001001 10101110 10010101 00000101 01101101 00000100 01101101
11011110 01101011 01001010 00111000 11001111 11100010 00101011 00101101 10110101 01110010
01111010 00110001 11000111 01101110 01111010 11010110 00010100 10110011 00110011 00010011
11011110 10100011 01001001 00001110 01000101 01101001 11101100 11010010 11110111 10011010
00011110 10001000 11011100 00010111 11000101 10011011 00000100 11110001 01010010 00110101
11100111 11101110 10011100 00000010 01110000 01000110 00101011 00010101 00100110 00000011
10101101 01001101 11100111 00000010 00111101 10101000 10010100 00111110 11010010 01000100
11110011 00011001 01110011 01000110 10101011 00110110 00110011 11001001 11100100 01110001
01010000 00000101 10010110 01000111 00110001 11000001 00001001 01111100 11110010 01001001
11100010 10101110 01011110 11001110 11101010 10100101 10110000 11001100 00010111 10011101
10101011 01010100 11010011 01010000 10110111 10111001 01011111 00101110 00101000 10100100
00000100 11111010 10001110 00101011 01100101 00110110 11010110 11010111 00111000 11100110
10100010 10001011 01111110 00011110 10111010 01101000 00100101 01111000 10011111 11100100
00100001 10110001 11001001 11101001 01011101 00110010 11001110 00001000 11101011 01011100
00111100 01001100 11010000 01011110 10011101 11111100 00011110 10111000 11110101 10101101
11001000 00101110 11000001 00011001 00111101 00111011 10011100 11110100 10100101 01010110
00010111 01001010 01001000 11011110 10011011 10111010 00110111 10111110 11010001 11010011
10011111 10101101 00111011 11101101 00011001 11100110 10110001 01011110 11101100 01111010
11111110 00111110 10110100 10111111 01101100 11100100 00001110 10011100 01100111 10101101
01100001 10110010 01100101 11111010 10011011 00011110 01110000 01100011 11101111 01001111
11110011 01111000 11000110 01001101 01100010 10110101 11011000 11000000 11100111 10011110
11110100 01111101 10111011 00000011 10011110 10010100 10100011 01001101 11011000 00011001
10110101 11100111 10001100 01100111 10101111 10111101 00000110 01100001 11010111 10111101
01100001 10110101 11100000 11000110 01111101 11101001 01111110 11011000 00001110 01110011
11010011 00010101 00101110 00010010 01000010 01100110 11011010 01011100 00000011 11011111
11110101 10100001 11101110 11000110 01110001 11111001 11010110 00011111 11011010 10110000
01110010 00001111 00000011 10001010 01100111 11011010 11001001 00111101 01111010 11010011
01010000 10111010 11010000 01100110 11011011 11011100 00001110 00001110 01111010 11010011
00111100 11111101 11000011 00100011 10111111 11101001 01011000 10001011 01110110 01000110
01110011 11001111 00111001 11000101 00110110 01011011 11011110 00111011 11100100 11110110
10101011 10001100 00011100 01001001 01000110 11010011 01001110 00000001 11111001 01001111
11010110 10100011 01111011 10100001 10001110 10110101 10001111 11110110 10111110 00110011
11001101 00110100 11011101 00010011 01010011 11001000 11010010 11010000 10101101 11001101
01100101 10111000 00000000 10010010 00110010 00000101 00100100 10110011 10101011 10010001
10000011 11001000 10101100 10100110 10111001 00100110 10100000 01101001 10110000 01110011
10011100 11010110 10010010 10001101 10010101 10011010 00100100 11010101 01111001 10000000
11100001 10101010 00100110 10011111 10001010 10100000 11010010 00110011 01100011 00100111
11101011 01001101 00101100 01111001 00000000 11110101 10100100 11101001 10100110 10000000
10110100 11010011 10000000 00001110 00101010 00101111 10110100 00010000 01111001 00111001
00000110 10101010 01100100 01100111 00111101 11101000 11101010 00001101 01101011 01111011

10000001 00110111 10011010 01001001 11000001 00110100 11000110 10010000 01110011 10111011
11110100 10101000 10110111 00010000 01001110 01110001 01001010 10111101 00101000 01001010
11100000 10000101 11001001 00000011 10101111 01011010 01101110 00001110 11111110 10111100
01010100 01110010 11001010 00110011 10000001 01001101 01101001 00000001 11101010 01101000
01001011 01011101 01001010 10110111 01010010 01000101 00000011 01110110 01111101 01111101
11101000 00111000 11000111 00011101 00111101 11101010 00100110 10010000 00000001 11101010
00101001 00001100 11001011 10011110 10111101 00111010 11010000 11101001 11101011 10100001
00111010 00010011 00000011 11011100 11010011 01011000 10010010 01111101 10111011 11010101
01010111 10111100 10001010 00110000 01001011 10010001 11111001 11010100 00111111 01101110
10001000 00011110 00001001 11111010 11010110 10010001 10100101 00100110 00011100 11101001
00010111 10000011 01110010 01110011 11010010 10010001 11011001 01001111 00000000 01110011
01011001 01100111 01010001 11111001 11001000 00010001 10011100 01111010 10011010 00001101
11011011 00110001 11100011 10111111 01010011 01011010 10101010 00101101 01101100 00101111
01101010 10001101 00010001 10001100 10011110 01101001 00011010 01010000 10100011 11101111
01110101 10101100 10110110 10010101 10001001 11001110 11101100 01010000 00001011 00011110
11111100 10011111 01111010 00100101 01001000 10010111 01010110 11000101 11000110 10111000
11101011 10000010 01101010 00100111 10111000 00100100 01100100 00001100 11010101 01110110
00100100 00000111 00011110 11111101 11101000 01011111 11110101 01111100 01110000 01111011
11110011 01011010 01000010 10011010 00110011 01110101 01011011 00011100 11001110 11001100
00000110 01001001 10100110 10010110 11000111 01011010 01010101 00111100 10010001 10000001
10010000 00111110 10110101 00010011 00110110 01010111 00000011 10011010 11010011 10010101
00101101 10011001 00010010 10011101 11001001 00010110 01011100 01110100 11100111 00100111
10111101 00111001 01011001 10011000 01110000 01001111 00010100 01000001 00001110 11011110
01011100 01100110 10101101 10001111 10010100 01110000 00111000 10101000 10101000 11101100
00001010 11101100 00010010 00110110 00011000 00100100 10000001 10011111 01011110 11110101
00100010 00001101 10100111 00001110 11100110 10011000 00000011 00110001 00011100 01110101
10101001 11100011 10110111 00001100 01110111 01001000 01111101 10101011 00101001 01110111
00110101 10000111 01100110 00111100 00110010 11100111 10011110 01101010 11001100 01011000
11101010 00000111 00110100 01000111 00001100 01001000 01000110 00000111 00111110 10110101
01100001 01011011 00000011 00000000 01111110 01110101 10001101 01001010 10110001 01101011
01000011 01101011 00010011 11011001 00010110 11011111 11000010 11110010 01111101 01101011
01010110 00110101 10010100 10101111 00111000 11001110 01101011 00100010 11011110 01100010
10110010 10000011 11101001 11010010 10110110 00100001 01100011 10000000 11000100 00011110
01111101 00101011 11001111 10101100 11100100 11011110 10000011 10111011 00011111 11100100
01001001 11001111 11001100 00000101 01001001 00010100 01010010 10000001 11000011 11100000
11111101 00110010 00101001 00110110 11001010 11011000 00100001 01011111 11101011 01001110
11110010 11101110 00000000 11100110 00110111 11111010 00001010 11001101 10100100 11110100
00001011 10111110 10000010 10111100 00110111 00000100 00001101 10010010 10101111 10111110
01111000 10101010 00110111 00010001 01011101 11100111 01110110 01111100 11001110 11011000
00000110 10101111 11101101 10011101 10000000 00011011 01011111 10011110 11011000 10100110
00001000 10100111 11011110 01000001 11001000 10101001 10100111 01101110 10100011 01001111
01010011 00110100 01111101 10100100 00000001 10111010 00011001 01000111 11010100 01010100
10001011 00111110 00110001 11100110 00000011 10011111 01111010 11010010 11001011 00101110
00111110 01100111 11001111 10101110 01101010 01110000 11000010 01000001 11001000 11001001
00111100 00011100 10001010 01001110 01101001 11101100 10001010 01111010 10111101 00001100
00001001 10001010 11001010 10100101 01110011 11011111 10100101 01100001 01011101 11101001
01010001 01001011 00111011 00111011 00100000 01100010 01111011 10001010 11101001 10110101
01011011 00011100 00010011 00111101 10111000 11111010 11000110 00111111 10100101 01100011
11111001 10100101 10111001 00100000 11010111 01011101 00101001 01001011 01111000 00010001
00101000 10100111 10100011 00111001 01101111 00101111 00111101 10111001 11110101 11001101
01001011 00010100 01100000 00011100 11111010 11010101 10101101 10111111 00111000 00000000
01100000 01110111 00110101 00101111 10010011 10010001 10010000 01000110 00111011 01010111
10101101 00101001 10111011 01011000 11100011 01010001 11010100 10100110 10110001 11100111
10001100 01010100 11101001 00011110 00000000 00111101 11111110 10010101 01100101 00100001
11000011 10000011 11101001 11001111 11010010 10100101 01100101 01011100 01110001 11010111
11010100 01010110 01011011 10100010 11010010 10110011 11010000 10100111 10001110 01110001
11011110 10010011 00011001 01101110 01111001 11000101 01011011 01101000 11010100 11110011
11011110 10011011 11100100 00000010 01111110 01001110 00111101 01101001 10101011 11000101
01011100 01101101 00110010 00010100 10001101 01110001 10010100 00010101 00100011 00001100
01100011 10110101 01001000 01100011 00000011 10000000 00111000 00110101 00100000 10001111
00100111 00000000 01010100 01001110 10101010 11011010 11100001 11001010 01010111 11011011
11010111 11010010 10011100 10000011 10100110 11010001 01010110 10010010 00011100 10011101
11011000 11100111 00011100 01010100 10101011 00010110 11011100 11110100 11101001 11010110
10100101 01010101 01010110 10110010 01100011 10110001 01011011 11001011 10100111 00001000
10111001 11001111 10100101 01011010 11110010 11001110 00000001 00000011 10110111 01111010
00011000 01110100 11001111 01011010 11001001 00111011 01101010 11011000 01101101 10110001
00000000 10001001 01001001 11001000 10101001 00110001 10001110 11010100 11110110 00101010
00000111 00000010 10010111 00000011 00011111 10101001 11110110 10100010 01001101 10100111
10100001 01010111 10111110 11100010 00101110 01001111 00011000 11100000 11010010 10101000
11101100 00101010 00110010 11000111 01111110 01000111 00011110 11010100 10111011 10000111
01011100 11010100 11001001 11011111 01000110 11000110 11000111 00101010 00001111 01010001
10001111 10101101 00111000 11100000 01110100 11101001 01010000 10110011 01110011 11000111
00010100 01101110 11000110 01101010 00111001 00011110 11000011 10111001 00101001 11000000

11101110 00110011 11111100 11101001 00110111 00010011 10011100 11010100 00100011 00000111
10011100 11100111 00011110 10110100 11111000 10001111 00000111 11011010 10101110 11001001
00111101 10001001 01100011 11011001 10001000 10001111 11100101 11001001 11101101 01000001
00011000 00111000 11101011 11101011 01010001 10110100 10011101 10000111 01111010 00000001
11001000 11000111 01111010 01110010 10111111 01010000 01000010 11100100 11110101 00011101
01101000 01010011 10010011 10010011 11111000 11110011 01001100 01000101 01100110 11100100
00001100 00011010 10010011 01101111 00011101 00101000 10001010 10001010 11101010 00000000
00000001 00100011 10101101 00100011 00010110 00001110 01110000 00110010 01001101 01001010
00100001 01100010 00111101 00000101 00111011 11001010 01011000 11011000 01100101 10101010
00101111 10101110 11100100 10110111 10101001 01011101 01001001 00111001 00001110 01111001
00110100 10101100 00001110 11111100 01110111 11110101 10101001 11011010 01001000 10000011
11110001 11000111 10111101 01000010 11010111 11010001 00001110 00000001 11100111 11101001
01001110 11110111 10010000 11000100 00010001 10110110 00001111 00010100 10000010 00010011
11010111 10111101 01000001 00100110 10100110 10001010 01110000 01111010 01010101 01001001
01110101 01000000 00111000 01000110 00100100 00011010 11010001 01010011 10011011 01111010
10010010 11011010 00110101 00011110 00110110 00000000 01100010 10000111 10001000 00010100
11000011 01100011 11011111 10011010 11000011 10010011 01010110 11000000 00001100 01011000
11100011 10001110 00101010 10110011 11101010 11101100 11001100 01011000 00010010 00001111
10111101 01101011 11110101 01011010 10001101 01101010 11001001 11110110 10010001 00111010
01010101 10000101 01111010 00000010 00110011 11110101 10100011 00010001 00101111 11011111
00100000 00011111 01001100 11010111 00101010 11111010 10010011 10001100 10011101 11100111
10010011 01000010 01101010 00100100 10110001 11111011 11111000 11110100 00111101 11001101
00001111 00001011 00100111 11010100 10011111 01101010 10001110 10100111 01101100 01111100
10110001 10010011 11110101 10101000 11000010 10101001 00111100 00010001 11000111 10101101
01110011 01011111 11011010 00001101 10111011 00100100 11110010 01001101 01001001 11111101
10100010 11001101 11000110 01111011 11100100 11010101 10111100 00101011 10110110 11111010
10001111 11011010 10100011 10100010 00010001 10000011 10011111 10011011 11100111 10101000
11001010 00111001 11100000 01100000 11010110 00001000 11010100 00001111 10011001 10011110
01111000 11110111 10100111 00001101 01001101 10011000 00011110 01001000 11000111 01101010
00111110 10101100 11011011 11011100 01111110 11010001 00011011 00001101 00011100 11000011
10101111 00011001 10100100 11011100 01111001 00001011 10011100 10001010 11001100 01001101
01000000 11110111 00100100 11010100 11001001 10101001 00110100 10011101 00111011 00011111
11001110 10001111 01100010 11010110 11100011 11110110 10001011 10100001 01111001 00100100
00100111 00000111 11010111 11010110 10011100 01011000 00011111 10111110 00111111 00101010
10101010 10110111 11000011 01101000 01100010 00000111 10111000 10101001 00011110 11101110
00011100 00000010 01000110 01000111 10110101 01100001 00101010 01001100 10011011 10010011
10001111 00101111 00011100 10001111 11001010 10010001 00100001 00011001 11001000 00111001
00100111 10100101 01000110 10010010 11000010 11000000 11100001 10111000 11101101 01010010
00100000 00011101 01100011 01101110 10011101 01101000 11100101 10110001 10110010 01111010
00010111 01100000 11000010 00000000 00001110 00101011 01001110 11011100 01100111 00000000
01100000 00001100 11010110 00011010 00010110 11100001 10010111 00100111 11111001 01010100
11001001 01110000 11010001 00001100 00000110 01110001 11001101 01100001 00111010 01001110
01111010 00100010 11100001 01010001 00100011 10100100 01001000 10011011 00111000 11111101
01101010 01111111 00101000 10011110 00111011 01100111 10011110 01101011 00011110 11011111
01011000 01111000 11011100 00010110 01010100 01111110 11011000 00110101 10101111 01101001
10101011 11011011 11001100 01001010 10111000 00100000 11111101 00101011 10000110 10100101
00011001 11000010 01010110 10110101 11001101 01010100 10010011 00101100 00001000 10001000
11000110 00000111 11101011 01000010 11100111 10010000 01101010 11010100 01000001 00100100
11111011 10000100 01100110 10100100 11110010 00110001 11001010 01100000 11100111 11010010
10110000 01110110 10111111 01100001 00010100 01010110 00111100 00000011 11001001 00011100
11110011 11001101 00101010 01011100 00111000 00000011 10011010 10010101 11100010 00111001
00111001 11101011 01010000 10111100 01011000 11101101 11111010 01010100 00111001 10101011
10001000 10010110 01000110 10001110 01010001 11110011 11110111 11110100 10101010 11101111
01101010 01000001 00100101 00001000 01111100 11010100 01101110 00001000 11111001 10000111
01101010 01100010 11001100 11001011 11001110 01101010 11010010 10111111 01010010 11010010
00100100 01000100 00101010 01110001 11001101 01101001 01011001 11111100 10100000 10010010
01101010 10011010 01011101 00000110 00011100 10001010 10110001 00010011 00100001 01011110
10111000 10101000 11110111 10101111 10100000 00110010 11010011 01001010 00000001 11100100
11111110 01010101 01011101 10100111 00001100 11011001 11111110 01110100 11011001 00010101
10000000 00100100 01010101 00110110 00100100 11111111 00000000 10000101 01000010 01001101
11101001 01110001 10100111 01110010 11101010 01001101 11000001 11001111 10101111 01011010
01001111 00111000 10011100 11101100 00111101 00111101 11101010 10011111 00100011 10101001
11100100 11111011 11010100 01110010 10110110 00001111 01011010 11010101 01010011 11101001
01110001 10110100 01101000 01111101 10100000 01100011 00011111 10010101 00111000 01011101
11100000 01111010 00011111 10101101 01100110 10110001 11011010 00011101 11111001 11000000
11101001 01001100 01101001 10111101 00111110 10111001 10100001 01000010 11001111 10111000
00110100 01101110 11011011 11011111 00010101 00100000 01110110 10101011 11001001 01111010
10100111 10101101 01110010 11101001 00110001 11101011 10011010 10110000 10010111 01011110
01011110 00110011 11001111 11010010 10100110 01010000 10111011 00100101 10100011 10101000
01001011 10111000 11001111 00000000 10001100 01110111 10101001 01000101 11000010 10011111
10111100 01000110 00101011 10010100 01001011 10100011 11010111 00111100 11010011 11010110
11110101 10111010 00010011 11110101 10101001 10010101 00110111 11001010 11011001 00010110
00111010 00001011 10011001 10100011 01100000 01000010 01110101 11111010 11010110 01110001

10010000 00101100 10111011 10010111 11110001 10101010 00001011 01110100 01001011 01110101
11111100 01101010 01010000 11000111 00000111 11111010 11010100 00101010 01101101 01101010
00111011 00011010 01000100 11100111 11100110 11001110 01101010 01011000 01100100 00001010
11011111 00111001 11111001 00001101 01100100 01000011 00111011 01100100 11000110 01000110
01000101 01011110 00010010 00000010 10011000 00010100 10011010 10110000 10011010 00110101
00011011 10011110 11011100 01010101 01001011 10000001 10011010 01001011 01011001 11001111
11111010 10110111 11101001 11011010 10010110 11100111 00000000 01110101 11100110 10100010
10100010 01001001 00001001 00100010 10011100 10111100 00001100 01010110 01100100 11011111
11101011 01001111 01101010 11010000 11011100 01001101 01100110 01001101 11111110 10111000
11111101 01101011 01001010 01010100 11011101 10101110 01010010 01010111 01100100 10111110
10011111 11010110 10100100 00011101 00111101 00101010 00011010 01111100 01001011 10011100
11100111 00111111 10011101 01110100 10101000 10110110 11110110 10110001 10100111 10101000
10000111 00100100 11111111 00000000 00101010 01100110 00111101 10111001 10101001 11110110
11111110 10010101 00001011 00000010 01001001 10101101 00101111 10101101 10000100 01000100
11000011 01110001 11100100 01010010 10101111 00000010 10001110 11111000 10100111 00100010
10110001 11000000 11101011 01001110 01011011 11011001 00000101 10000011 00011001 00100011
00011101 01101010 11100100 00110110 11101100 01111010 11110110 11101111 11101011 01001011
01101011 01101011 10000011 10010110 00011100 11111010 01100110 10101111 10100010 11100010
10101110 00010000 11100110 01010111 10010000 01011000 10001110 00101011 01110101 10101001
01010010 00111100 01110010 00000101 00111101 00110011 01001110 01010101 11000001 11100100
11111110 00010101 01001110 00101010 11110111 00100001 10111011 00001000 10111100 10011010
10010101 01000110 01101001 00000000 00000100 11010011 11010110 10011010 10001010 01011011
00000101 11000011 10100101 00101000 00011001 11101011 01000110 00101001 00011110 01010000
10100011 00011100 01010011 11100100 01001011 01100001 00001110 11000000 00000010 10100011
11110011 00111100 10111010 10000110 01011011 10000000 00000110 01101010 10000100 11110111
01000000 10101110 01101001 10101000 01011101 01011000 10100010 11111100 10010111 01101011
10001100 01110111 10101100 01111011 11111011 11001110 00110001 10011010 10101001 01111001
01110010 01000110 01110000 11011000 00010101 10010001 01110011 01111001 10111011 10001100
11100011 11101011 01001110 00010111 11101010 01001101 10001001 00101111 10101110 10001011
01110000 00001111 00110101 10010101 00110100 11011001 11111110 00101111 11010010 10010010
11100110 01100010 01110000 00110011 10001111 01001111 01111010 11001111 10011010 01011110
01111010 11111101 01101011 10110110 10001100 01101101 10111000 11011010 11010000 10110000
11001101 11001001 11000110 01001111 10100101 00101010 01001101 10001110 00111011 11110111
10101010 01010001 11001000 01001111 01000011 01010010 00100100 10000111 10100000 00000101
11011111 11010010 10101110 01101110 01011011 00010011 10110001 01100001 10100110 10100101
11110011 10111000 11100010 10101011 11111101 10011010 11101001 10110001 10001011 01101001
01111001 11111111 00000000 01100110 10100101 00010110 00110111 11100111 00100111 11101100
10010010 11100000 01010100 10111001 00100110 11110101 01100000 01001001 00000100 10000001
10001011 10000010 11000110 10100111 10000010 00101100 01011011 01100010 00010010 00001010
00101111 00100000 00011110 11110101 00011101 10100101 10011110 10100011 00010100 11000001
11100001 10110111 10010001 00001111 10111101 01010111 11010110 11101111 01011110 00001111
00101101 00100000 11000111 10011010 11000111 00000100 01100111 10100111 11010110 10100001
10110101 00101001 01111011 10000110 00110101 00110100 11010100 11001111 10111001 10111010
01101011 10101101 10010011 10001011 01010111 10001110 00110101 11100000 11001000 01111010
00010011 11101111 01010110 11010110 01000000 00010000 01101101 00110101 01000110 11110011
01010010 00110001 01011000 00111101 10101101 11000010 10001101 11101100 10111100 00010101
10101000 01110100 01001111 10110100 01011110 11001100 10010110 11110001 11100111 00000000
11110010 11001100 00110010 00010111 11101011 01011101 01011110 11001111 01001011 10011001
11010011 10010110 10100110 10010111 10011101 10010001 11101001 01001110 01101001 01001001
01010000 00110011 01010110 10011011 01000011 10111000 11001111 11001111 00111100 01011000
11110101 00011001 11100110 10101010 11101010 01010110 00000110 11001010 11011001 11100101
01111001 10000001 01111100 11100001 01000000 11101111 01011001 01000110 01010001 01101010
11000111 01000000 01111001 10100100 01111010 11010000 11010010 11100111 00011001 00111000
11101111 01011100 11111011 11011110 00110100 01111100 00100001 00111100 01111010 11010100
01011110 01110101 11010100 10011101 00011111 11110001 00110101 11010001 11101100 01010101
10110100 00110010 01110101 10010111 01000011 10100101 00110011 01110000 00001110 01001101
00101001 10111000 01011110 11101100 00111111 00111010 11100110 11010010 00011011 10011001
11000010 00100110 01100101 01110010 01111011 10001100 10011010 10111001 01101101 10100010
11011110 11001100 00001001 00010000 11001011 11101101 11000001 00011001 10101000 01110100
11100000 10110111 01100001 11101101 01011011 11101000 01101100 01111101 10101000 01110011
10010111 00011100 01111011 11010010 01111101 10110010 00100001 11001110 11110001 11111001
11010101 00110101 11110000 11001110 10100101 00100100 01111001 10010010 00000111 11111100
01101010 11000100 01011110 00010100 11010100 01001011 00011100 10100000 11000000 11100111
00100100 11010110 01101101 11010001 01001111 01001001 00001111 11011010 01001011 10110000
11101111 10110111 01000001 10010000 01001100 10100001 00110011 01001101 01111101 01000110
00000000 01110011 11100110 00000010 00111101 01000101 01001010 10111110 00010000 10111101
00111111 00110110 00000001 01001100 01111010 11010001 11111111 00000000 00001000 10011101
11101010 10000000 00000100 00100000 11100111 10011110 10110100 01110011 11010001 10111101
11011011 00011010 01110010 11101010 01000000 01110101 00011011 01111100 11100000 11001000
00000000 11110101 10101000 11010111 01010100 10000011 01111001 11111101 11101000 00100010
10100110 10010011 11000010 10110111 11001010 00110011 11100101 00001110 10111101 10001101
00110101 10111100 00101101 01111001 00011010 10010110 00110000 11110011 11010100 01100000
11010011 01011111 01010111 01111010 01011100 10010110 11100100 01000110 10111010 10111101

10111000 00011100 11001011 11001111 01111100 00001010 01000110 11010100 11101101 11110011
11000100 10011001 11110111 11000101 01001001 11111111 00000000 00001000 11010101 11101010
10001100 10111100 00101111 11101101 11101011 01001001 11111111 00000000 00001000 11101101
11000111 01111000 00011000 01100100 11110111 11101101 01001110 11110100 00101101 10100011
00001011 11001000 10000111 11111011 01011010 11011111 10100111 10011010 01111110 10111000
00111000 10101000 11011011 01010100 10001011 00011011 10010000 10010011 11111000 01010100
10101111 10100000 01011100 00000001 11110011 11011011 10111111 00111110 10010101 00010011
01101000 11010111 00000011 00000000 11000000 11111011 00000000 11101011 10001010 10101110
01101010 00001111 01100001 00111001 01001000 10001001 11110101 10010100 00011101 00010100
11110101 11100111 00100011 10100101 00101001 11010101 00010100 11110000 00000011 11100111
10101111 00111101 11101001 11001101 10100100 11001101 10011111 11110101 00101111 10011100
01110000 01110001 01001100 11111110 11001111 01100010 00110001 10110100 10001100 01111010
10001010 10100101 11101100 10010010 10110000 10101111 00110001 00100100 11010100 10111000
00011011 00010001 11001111 11010110 10011000 11011010 10010011 01110100 11011011 11001101
01001000 01101101 00111111 10000111 00011100 01010010 00111101 10100001 01010000 00001110
00110011 01001101 00111010 01001011 01100100 00110111 11001101 11011100 10101110 01110101
00001001 10001011 11110001 00011000 10101000 11011110 11101110 01110011 11001000 01101100
01100111 10101111 00010101 01100000 11000000 00111101 00101001 10001101 00001000 01011100
11010101 11101001 10111010 01000100 10110101 00101110 10101100 10101101 00101100 11010010
11001001 11001110 11110011 10001010 10001111 00001100 01001001 00111001 00100111 11010111
10011010 10110010 11010000 10000000 00001110 01110011 11101101 11101111 01001010 10110000
01110110 01101100 11100111 11011010 10101001 01001001 00100010 01101100 11001010 11011000
11000110 00110111 11111110 00010100 11110001 11101001 11101011 11010110 10100110 11110010
11110001 11110010 10011110 10011101 10101001 11011110 01011111 01011100 10001111 11001010
10101001 10110100 00001010 00100100 00100000 00011100 11110010 00110000 00000101 00111001
01111010 10001111 01000011 11010010 10100101 00000011 00101011 10001110 11100011 10111101
00101110 00111000 00011110 10111110 10010101 00111100 11001101 10001010 11010110 00100011
01111110 10000000 01100011 10110101 00000111 10001100 10011010 10010001 01000001 00100111
10011110 10100110 10011010 11111001 00000011 11110001 10101001 01101010 11001100 10101011
00001101 11001110 01000110 01110011 11001111 11110011 10100110 10110011 00001100 11010011
01011100 00011110 00001110 00101001 10101110 01000000 11101000 00001110 01101010 10101100
11001001 01111110 01000001 01110001 00101110 11010001 10011100 11100000 11111010 01111010
11010100 10010110 00100001 01001110 00110010 01111011 01110111 10101010 00010111 01101100
01011001 10000010 11110110 11110101 10101011 01110110 11011111 01110000 01100011 10101001
10101011 01101011 01001011 00010010 10110101 01100110 10100010 10010010 10111101 01001101
00111001 01000110 11100001 10010010 01111010 11010100 00110000 10000010 01010011 00000111
00111100 01010101 10000101 00000100 01110101 00011101 01101011 10011010 01101010 11111011
00011011 10101011 00010011 00100111 11001010 10111000 11101011 01010011 10100000 11001111
00100000 01100111 10001010 10001010 00110000 01111010 11010101 10011000 10110000 00000110
01010100 01100000 11010110 00001111 11011101 01110111 01100110 10101001 00100110 01001110
10110001 10001100 00000001 11011111 10111101 01011100 10110100 10110100 11110011 00011000
01100111 10100101 01000011 01101101 00001001 10010101 10111000 11101011 11011110 10111010
00001011 00011011 01001101 10111101 00000001 11001001 10101110 00001010 11010101 01101100
10110100 00110100 01001001 10100010 00111011 01101011 00111000 11010100 10000000 00010100
01100111 00111101 01101011 01101110 11011010 11010101 00100011 00111011 10110001 11001111
10101001 10100101 10110110 10000011 01100110 00101010 11110000 01011110 00111001 00011100
01010111 00000100 10100100 10110111 01101100 00110111 00100000 11011011 10010001 11010011
11101001 01001010 00100011 11110110 10101001 11110001 11011011 00010100 00000000 01000000
10101100 11111001 10101111 11010100 00101100 01000101 00101100 00000100 10100001 00100000
11010111 00111111 01111011 00110101 11000101 10110100 10000111 01111010 10010000 00111111
00110001 01011101 00101110 01000000 11100000 11100111 00110101 00000100 10000000 00010001
10000011 11010111 10111110 01101011 01111000 01010101 01010000 01011110 01100010 10110001
11001000 10110110 10100011 11111011 11001100 00110001 11111001 00001001 10101011 10110110
11010111 10010001 00110000 11001000 11101010 01111011 01010101 10111011 11001101 00101110
11010110 01110110 11100110 00111101 10101111 11101010 10100111 00010101 01000001 11110100
00110111 10001000 10000110 10110101 10011111 00111100 01110010 10110010 01111111 10001101
01011010 10101001 01001010 10100010 10110110 11001100 01111011 00011010 00011100 10110111
10100111 11010110 10110011 00101110 00110100 11110101 01101001 01001001 11000000 10101001
00010001 10100111 10110110 11111111 00000000 01011000 10111111 01010010 00111001 10101001
10010110 01000101 10010000 01101111 11000111 01011010 01001001 01001010 00111111 00001000
01011100 11100010 00100010 01000000 00001111 10100110 01101010 11000010 01000110 10100100
11110101 00111101 00111011 10001010 01111000 10001100 01100100 00000000 00111000 11101111
10011010 01110110 11010011 10011010 11110101 11010100 11011011 00110001 10110010 11101000
00110101 10000001 01010011 10011111 11000011 00000111 10111101 00011101 01001000 11101000
00111101 11101010 01010100 01010101 00111100 10010011 11111111 00000000 11010110 10100110
01001000 10111001 11100000 01010100 00111001 10111011 11011001 00000111 10011001 00010011
00000001 11100110 01110100 11100010 10011110 10100000 10001100 10001100 11100000 00011010
00010100 00001100 01100110 10100100 00011100 10000000 00101000 11100110 01110111 11010000
01101000 01100001 10001111 11111011 10111101 10111010 11111011 11010100 10101010 10111000
00011001 00000000 11010010 00110100 10011011 01000000 00011101 10111011 11010011 11111100
11100001 10000001 11000101 00111101 10010000 10011110 10100010 10000001 11000111 00100100
11100110 10001101 11011000 11100100 10011111 11000110 10100011 01111001 01000111 00111100
11110011 11011010 10100010 11110011 00110011 11101101 01010000 10100001 10101101 11000111

10100001 01100001 10100110 00100100 10001100 01110100 00010101 00011011 00110111 00111101
01111010 11110110 11000101 01000011 11100110 00000010 10111000 00000110 10010011 11001100
00000000 01111011 11010000 10101001 11011101 11101000 00101011 10100010 01011100 11110001
11011111 00010100 01101110 11110100 01101111 10101101 01000101 11100110 11100100 01100110
10010100 00010001 10000000 11000000 01110011 01011010 00101010 01111101 00011001 00101101
10100001 11001110 11011100 11100000 01010001 10111011 11100100 11100110 10011000 10111000
01110011 11110101 00111101 01101000 01100001 11110011 10010001 11011010 10010010 10000110
10111010 00000010 00010100 00010000 11000111 00100000 11010011 10010100 10000010 00001000
10101000 11110110 10001110 11000110 10011100 10011100 01100100 01010110 10001010 00001110
11111011 10000101 11000111 10100001 00001101 11110101 10100100 11100111 00111000 00011000
00110100 11100100 01011110 11110101 00100000 10001100 00001110 01101011 00101001 01101001
10100011 00010101 11101110 01000110 00100011 01100010 11000000 10000001 11000101 01001110
10010001 00010000 00111001 11101000 01111010 11010011 00110011 10110100 01110101 11100111
11010010 10100011 01111011 10101101 10100011 10010011 10001010 10000100 10011100 10010111
10111010 01010011 11010000 10110101 10010101 01011110 00110001 11001101 00110010 01011011
10001000 11100011 00100011 00111101 11101011 00011010 11100011 01010000 11000001 00111100
11100011 11010010 10110011 01101110 01101111 10011001 10011100 01110010 01111000 11100011
00000010 10110101 01011000 01110111 00100010 01100101 01010001 00100011 10100010 10011011
01010000 00000000 00010101 11011101 11010011 10101101 01100101 11011100 11101010 10001100
00110010 01110111 01100010 10110000 01100110 10111011 01100011 11010100 10011100 00000001
11111110 01110011 01010101 10011110 01011100 10001110 00011000 10010000 01111011 10011010
11101100 10100101 10000101 01010001 11010100 11100111 01110101 10001101 10001001 00110101
00010110 00100000 10011100 10010010 10011101 10111110 10110101 01010010 01011011 11010110
01101110 10100100 00001100 01110101 10101010 01101010 11011001 11001111 00111100 01110111
00100110 10011010 01001000 00100100 00000001 10010010 01111011 11010111 01000010 10100011
00010100 11001001 11100111 01101100 10110000 11110111 01001100 01000001 00011101 10001101
01000011 11100110 11001000 01001000 00111101 00111111 00011010 01000000 10111100 10000000
01111111 11111101 01010100 10100000 00010011 11010111 11101010 00000110 01111010 11010101
10100010 00110101 00000111 00110010 01100000 01111010 10011110 01111001 00110100 10001011
10010010 10011100 11110111 00111101 01101010 11000010 11000101 00100011 01100001 01000010
10011100 11110111 11100010 10100100 10001111 01001110 10111000 10010000 00011111 11011101
00111011 10001110 11101101 01001001 11001101 00101101 00000010 11001100 10101100 11100100
10000100 00000011 00011110 11011101 01101001 10101010 00000001 00111001 11101110 00111010
01110011 01011010 01101001 10100100 11001111 11100101 01111100 11100001 00010011 10111110
00001001 10100111 10100110 10010010 11100111 10000010 11000011 01111101 00101001 01010101
10001011 00011010 10001100 10011111 01000011 00110000 11110010 00110010 01110011 11001101
00100000 11100000 11110001 10010001 11110101 10101101 10100001 10100011 00000101 11001110
01100110 00001110 01111010 11100011 00011100 01010011 10000110 10010110 10100100 10001100
10110111 00000111 10110000 10101100 11100101 01010010 00101000 10111111 01100111 00100011
00010111 01110001 11001110 01000000 10101001 00010100 10000010 00001111 00111100 11111011
11010110 11000111 11110110 01011010 11111111 00000000 01111011 00011001 00011101 10000101
00111001 00110100 10011000 10001001 00111000 10010011 10100111 10111101 01001011 10101011
00010000 11100100 10010001 10001011 10011101 10100011 10101001 10100111 00101100 10001100
10111111 11111110 10101010 11011001 00011010 01000010 01111111 00011001 11001111 00110100
11110101 11010010 01010100 11100000 00001110 01001001 11110111 10100110 11101010 11000110
11010111 00011111 10110011 01100110 00111000 10010101 10000100 10000011 10011110 00111011
01010100 11001001 00100001 00000100 11111011 11010101 11110001 10100110 00001101 10111100
10010010 01000000 00111101 01101001 10011111 11011001 11101101 10111111 10000011 10000001
11011010 10110011 11110110 10010001 01101010 11100001 11001010 11001000 01010110 01101111
10011011 00000000 11010100 10101001 00111001 00011000 11001111 01010001 11010010 10011110
11010110 01000101 01000001 00101000 10111101 10111001 10100110 10101101 10101001 00011000
11000110 01110011 11011110 10010010 10010010 10010111 01010011 01000101 01110100 01001111
00001101 11101011 10001100 00101110 01111000 00111101 10000101 01011001 10001010 11101100
10011000 11110110 10111000 11011110 00110011 11011110 10101010 11111001 00111000 01100000
01010011 10110101 00010001 10101011 01100100 11111100 10111100 01111010 11010010 10010010
10001010 11010011 01110110 00110100 11011101 11001101 00010001 00101010 00110111 01000010
01000110 01101010 11000101 10111000 10010000 00010000 01010001 10110010 00111010 11100110
10110011 10100011 10000100 10101110 00110010 00111010 10011010 11010101 10110011 01010010
00010111 00000000 00011111 01111010 11100101 10101000 10100010 10010001 10110100 00110101
01100110 11000101 10000101 11010011 00101001 11111001 11110111 11101111 11110101 00110101
10111111 00000101 11101010 10011110 00001111 11100101 01011100 11011100 00110010 11100100
10000000 11100010 10110100 01100001 01100101 00111100 10000011 11001001 10101111 00110010
10101100 01010011 01100110 11101001 00011011 10101001 00110100 01001100 00111010 00000000
01101001 11101111 00001100 01110010 01000111 11110010 10011110 10100110 10110010 11010111
00100000 01100111 10111111 10110101 01011000 01001011 10001101 10100000 00001100 01111101
01101011 10010111 11011001 11011001 01101110 00111011 00100110 01001011 00100101 10010011
01100011 00000011 10010000 00101010 00010111 11010011 01011011 11111000 01000111 00000100
11010101 10100101 10111011 00100011 10111111 11010010 10100111 01001001 11110010 01000110
01111010 11010100 10111011 11011011 01000010 00110101 01000110 01011001 11010011 10100101
10001101 11000111 01000011 11110100 00010101 00100100 00110110 00110010 01101111 00011000
11001110 00111010 11100100 11010110 11000010 01001010 00110000 00000111 10101101 00101111
10011011 10000001 11011010 10100110 11101110 11110111 00001011 11011100 10101101 00001101
10101001 11001110 00001111 01100001 01010001 11011101 01101001 11100011 00111011 11010000

01100000 11100010 10101110 01001011 01110101 10110100 00001110 10010101 01011010 01011011
11000010 01000110 00001111 01101110 11110100 11010010 11101000 10000101 01110110 01100101
11001011 00000001 00000100 10001111 11101001 01010001 11111001 00011001 01111100 11110110
10101011 00001101 00111000 00110010 00011101 11111101 11101010 11000100 00100000 00110000
00101100 10100011 10100111 00010100 01101010 10110110 00110101 01010010 01101101 00011001
10010111 00110001 00010110 00011011 00000000 00111000 10101010 11101101 00000011 01101101
11100001 01111110 10010101 10110110 10110000 11111100 11111110 11100110 10001001 10100010
00000011 10011100 01110011 01001001 01010101 01110111 00001011 10011000 00111110 01010001
00001011 11010000 11010000 11111001 00000111 10111101 01101010 00111100 00111001 00000110
10101011 10111101 10111001 00101010 01001000 00011101 00101010 11111001 11110101 10110000
01011100 10100101 10011111 10010111 10011111 11001110 10010101 00110010 01111111 00111010
01111011 11000100 01010111 10101111 11100011 01001001 10110100 10000011 10011010 10111011
11011000 10101011 10010010 10101001 00000000 10011100 11110100 10101011 00101011 00100000
00100011 11011110 10101001 01110001 11111000 11010010 10010110 11000000 11001101 00100111
11101111 00001001 10100010 11011011 10011101 10100111 01110010 01110011 11001101 01011100
10110110 10011001 01011000 01100111 11110000 10101100 11001100 11100101 01000111 10101111
10100101 01000110 10110010 10110100 01010010 01111011 00011100 01110111 10100011 10010010
00111010 10100001 00110100 01110100 00011101 00111001 00011101 01101010 00110111 10011111
11001101 11100000 11110000 11100000 01010101 01101000 01101110 00010110 01000001 11010111
11110101 10100110 01011100 00110111 01000110 01000011 11000101 01100010 11101001 10111011
11011000 10001011 00010011 11100111 00100000 11100010 10101000 01001001 11000100 10000111
00111101 10001101 01101000 01011000 10110010 11001010 01000000 00111101 00110011 01011001
11110011 00000000 11010111 00010010 10001101 11000111 10000110 00100011 00100110 10001010
01101010 11000011 01000011 10111001 00000011 10001110 10110101 00110000 00100111 00011100
01010100 01101001 10001111 01011010 01111000 01100010 00001111 00010101 10110101 11110101
10111010 00101100 01111011 00110110 00000111 00110101 00011011 10011100 11100011 00000011
10101101 00111001 01000001 00101111 11010011 00111001 11110101 10101011 11010110 11010110
11100000 01111100 11000111 10010010 01111101 01101011 01101000 11010011 11010010 11110001
00000010 10101101 10111101 10001001 10010000 00000110 01111110 00000001 11101101 01010110
11010110 00011000 11100001 11000000 01000101 00000011 00010101 01100001 11001110 11011100
00001010 10001000 10101001 00100111 00111111 10101101 01011010 10001101 10011101 10001010
10110000 01100111 10011110 00101010 01100000 00110010 00110011 11111010 01010100 00101010
01000010 10001111 01111010 01010100 10010011 11010111 10100101 01101100 10100100 10111110
00010100 00101101 11001011 01101001 11001000 11001101 00110111 11111000 10000101 01000010
10101101 11001111 00010101 00101111 01001110 11111001 00110101 00111011 01101100 00101011
01110111 00100111 00011000 00110100 01100100 00001010 10101110 11010010 11100011 11011000
11010100 01101111 00110000 00011101 00111010 11010101 00101001 00110111 10100011 01100100
10010011 00111100 10111101 10111010 01010101 00111001 10100110 11000111 10111101 01000110
11110011 01110101 11001001 11101011 01010100 10101110 00101110 10000110 11011110 00001000
00100111 11101011 01010110 11010101 10001000 10111000 11111011 10001001 11111001 00111100
11010110 01100101 11001101 11000111 01010001 10011100 11111011 01100110 10100010 10111100
10111011 01010001 11010001 10111011 01111010 11010110 01000100 11010011 11110011 11000111
01111110 11110101 01001010 00001111 01110110 01010010 01000100 11110010 01001110 01110111
10010011 10011110 00101010 10011100 11010010 10001110 01110010 00001001 10101000 01100101
10010100 00011110 01110011 10001010 10101011 00110100 11011110 10100111 00110101 01101010
00001111 01001011 10011010 01011000 01011011 10011001 10000110 11111100 11110011 10000001
01011001 10010111 00010111 00000011 00111000 11100111 10101101 01000111 01111011 01110110
00010100 00000000 00110000 01001110 01101011 00110001 01101110 00011010 01011001 01110000
00000001 00100111 11010000 01110010 01101011 10110110 10011101 00101110 10101101 00011100
11110101 01101010 10100101 10100001 11010111 01101000 10011111 01100110 11011110 01011010
01111111 11011110 00111110 01111000 00011101 00110001 01011101 00100100 01110011 11000010
10101010 00110110 01000110 10000011 11101000 00101011 10000011 10110011 11010011 10110101
00111001 00111100 10111101 10010110 11110010 01000110 00100100 00111111 01111001 10111000
10101101 11111011 01101101 00100010 11111011 00001000 01100111 10111011 11000000 11001111
11011101 01010001 11011010 10111001 01110001 00110100 11100010 11011101 11111001 10001001
01010101 00111100 10001110 10010001 10101111 00010010 00101000 11110010 01011001 00000000
00011110 10100110 10110011 00101110 11111100 01000001 00010100 01011001 00001001 11001001
11101110 01000111 01001010 10101110 11011010 00110100 01011011 00000110 11110011 00100100
10000111 00011101 11011010 10100111 10000111 01001110 10110111 10000100 00001100 10100000
00111000 11101011 10011010 11000001 00101000 01011110 11101111 01010000 11110110 10001100
11001000 10111001 11010111 11101110 01100110 10010001 11010010 00110010 01000000 11001111
00011000 10101100 11110110 10110100 10011010 11101010 01010111 01111111 00100010 01010111
01110110 00111001 00100100 10001110 10110101 11011011 11000011 00001100 00111000 00000001
00010101 00000111 11010000 01100010 10101100 01100000 00000001 10010011 11010011 11010110
10101111 11101011 00101010 00011111 00000100 01000001 10100110 11110111 00111000 01000100
11010010 00101110 11001100 10011001 00010110 01000000 00011111 01011100 10001010 10011101
01101101 10101111 11100000 00100111 01101010 10010100 11001111 01110000 01000101 01110110
00111000 10001111 10111000 10101010 01110111 01101010 10100011 10001110 11100110 10101001
11100010 01100110 11110101 00000101 01001101 10011100 11000011 01101010 01110111 10010110
10100111 01101100 10001000 01110110 01111010 10010001 10011111 11010110 10101010 11101010
01111010 10011111 11011011 10100001 01000101 01010000 00110010 00011011 10011010 11011100
10111011 10000100 00010000 01110011 11010010 10110010 11101101 01101100 01100001 01011101
01010110 00100110 11101001 11001101 01101011 00001010 10110000 01101110 11101101 00000101

01001110 01101011 01011000 10101011 10100110 11111000 01110110 01111011 10110110 00001101
00100000 00010001 00100110 00111010 10011110 10100111 11110000 10101110 10100010 11001011
11000011 00110110 10010001 00010000 01011101 01001100 10100111 11111101 10101110 10000111
11110000 10101101 01001011 01010000 00000010 00000001 01011010 01110000 10101110 00000110
01111000 10101110 01001010 10111000 10111001 11001001 11011010 11110110 00000101 01001101
00100010 00101011 01101011 00011000 01100010 10001100 00000100 01000100 00000011 11011000
01100010 10101110 00100101 10111000 00000000 00001111 01001010 10010010 00100101 00000111
10001010 10110010 10001010 00111000 11110110 10101110 01000111 01010110 11101110 11010010
00101001 10100010 00000100 10000111 00101010 00110010 00101010 01001111 00100100 00000000
01001000 00010101 00111000 11000110 01110001 01001111 11000110 01111000 10100100 10011101
11110111 00011110 11100101 01011111 00101101 01001000 11001101 00011110 01011000 00110101
00111110 11010000 00111010 01110111 10100001 01010111 10011100 01010010 10111110 10011100
11000100 10110010 10010011 11000010 00110011 01001110 11110010 10000001 00011100 11110101
10101011 01001101 00011111 01011010 01100110 00110001 01000010 01011101 01000100 01010111
01101000 01000000 10100110 00110100 01001011 10111111 00111000 11101011 01010110 10110001
10010100 10100110 01100011 10100001 10101011 10010011 01010111 11010000 01100101 01100110
10110111 01010011 10010001 11010010 10100000 01101011 01010101 11100011 10001110 01111101
01001101 01011111 01111110 01111000 11101101 01010000 10111000 11100110 10011010 10011101
11000110 10101100 01010001 10010110 00000001 10000000 00000000 11101111 01010001 10110100
00001011 10011100 00010101 00011111 10010101 01101000 00111000 11110101 10101000 11011000
00001100 11010110 10101001 10110111 10101010 00010001 10010111 00100101 10001100 00111101
00110110 00100101 01010000 10011011 01001011 10000001 10010100 11100101 00110000 01111101
01101011 01111101 11110001 11010100 10001100 01010101 01111001 01110000 01000111 00011001
11001101 00010100 11100111 01101011 11011001 10010110 10001110 01011110 11100111 01000101
01010010 11011011 10010001 10001110 00111101 00110001 01011001 01110011 01101001 01101100
10000111 00111000 00000110 10111011 00100111 00011001 00011110 10010101 01011001 11100011
00000111 10101000 10101101 01100001 10001001 10010010 01010111 10111000 10011010 01000111
00010101 00110100 00000110 00101100 10000010 00001000 00100010 10100001 01010001 10000001
11110011 11010111 01011111 00111101 10111010 11001000 00110000 01010100 00011100 11010110
01110101 11001110 10011000 10111000 00100101 00001001 00011100 11110100 10101110 10011000
01100010 11010011 01111010 10010000 11100001 10101001 11001111 10110100 01100111 10101110
00101001 01010000 00101001 01000001 11000111 00100010 10101111 11001111 01101010 01100011
00111000 00100010 10101011 11111001 01111011 01001001 11000101 01110100 00101010 10011011
10001010 11010110 00101011 10001000 11000000 11001111 11001011 01000111 01111110 01000111
01001111 01011010 10011011 10010010 11110100 11011001 01110000 01111011 01110111 11100110
10101110 00101110 11001100 00011010 01000100 00001010 00111011 10001010 10001001 11001000
11111100 00101010 11000011 01110101 00100110 10100000 10010111 00001011 11110111 00000111
11010110 10101110 11111010 11011000 11001110 01000101 01100111 11001110 01001001 10101000
11011100 11100011 10111111 11101011 01010010 01001000 01001000 00000010 10101010 11001000
01111000 11001111 11111001 11001101 01101110 10111110 00010011 00001011 10001101 00000000
10110100 10100000 00000001 10011111 11000110 10110101 01101101 00100001 00000101 00000000
00100011 10011010 10100101 10100111 11011011 00000110 10010111 01111011 00001110 01111111
10010101 01101110 11011011 11000001 11101000 00110001 11111101 01101011 10011110 10111101
01000101 00010101 01100100 11001011 10100101 00000110 11110101 00000100 00011101 10110001
01010010 10101010 10011111 01001100 11111010 01010101 10001000 01100000 01100110 01101101
10101000 00001001 00111110 11010101 10100111 01101101 10100100 01011100 01001100 00000110
00100010 00100000 00011110 11100111 10110101 01110000 10111010 11101001 01101110 01110110
10100100 10111010 10011001 11001001 00011111 00000000 00001110 10111101 01111110 10010101
10100011 01101001 01100111 00101100 11000100 00000100 01010010 11100100 10011111 01001010
11011011 11010011 11111100 00111100 10101010 01110011 01110000 11011110 01100000 11101011
10001100 01100010 10110111 10101101 00101101 01100011 10000110 00110000 10101000 10100000
01111101 00000101 01110001 01010100 11000100 10100100 11110100 00011101 10001100 10111011
00001101 00101000 01000101 11010100 00000100 00100111 10101001 00011101 01101011 01011101
00100000 11110010 11001110 01000110 00000101 01011000 11110010 11110001 11001111 00010100
00101010 01101110 00011111 10001101 01110001 01010100 10011101 11101111 11001100 01011011
00010010 00000101 00111100 11100110 10100101 11110010 11111010 11111010 01010010 11100000
10101000 10101000 11100110 10011111 01100110 00000000 11101011 11010110 10111001 10111001
10010101 11000101 10100000 10001110 11000010 00110001 11010111 10011110 11010101 01011011
11001111 00100000 10011010 10101011 01110001 01110100 01001001 00111011 01111001 10100110
11011011 01111110 11110111 11100110 11101000 00110011 10001110 01101011 01001011 01011111
01010000 00101110 00100011 00010010 00111110 10111101 11101001 01011000 11100111 10000011
01001100 00000011 00011101 00101001 11111011 01001011 00010010 00110001 01010010 10110100
11010110 01000000 01010111 10011000 11100100 11100000 01010100 10001000 10000100 10001100
10001010 10010101 01101101 11110000 11100000 11110111 10101011 01011110 01011000 10001100
01110100 10100100 11011011 01011111 00001110 10000000 01010011 01101000 10001001 01001110
00000111 00110101 01000101 10101100 11000110 01111110 11100101 01101010 01001101 00100000
10001100 11100011 10111001 11110111 10101010 11101101 00100001 11001111 01001010 11010010
00101110 01101111 01011000 10110010 01101100 01111001 11110010 10001110 00110001 11111101
01101000 01100010 00110001 10001010 10101101 00100100 11011001 00100011 01100001 11111010
11010000 10110010 01101110 00111000 11001111 00010101 11110100 01001010 10011011 10000010
11100110 00110001 01101100 10011000 10010010 00010011 00001001 10001100 00011010 01101010
01001010 00011101 11011100 00011110 00000111 01101010 10000101 10100100 00000011 10001100
11110000 00111010 11010011 01011110 01010101 11110010 11111010 01100000 01100111 00010101

01001110 11010010 01110111 01100100 01011101 10100010 11000010 00010101 11000110 01001111
00111111 10001101 00110111 11001110 00000011 00111100 11100011 10011110 11010101 01001111
11001100 00000011 10000000 01111010 11010010 00110011 00011101 11100000 00011111 11001110
10010111 10110011 10111011 11011000 01110111 00101100 11001011 00100000 00100100 01100111
11110011 10100100 01010110 00111001 11100111 10100000 10101010 11101100 11011101 10111010
11110011 11001101 00000101 10110011 11000110 01001101 00111110 01001011 00111011 00110001
01011110 11000100 11111110 01100110 01001001 11111111 00000000 00011010 00111100 11000000
00111010 11100111 11110000 10101010 11101001 10000011 11011111 00000011 11011110 10001101
11011100 11100000 11010011 11100101 01011100 10111010 00100000 01001110 11000100 10000110
01001100 00011111 01000001 11101011 01000111 10011001 11001110 00000110 01001000 11110101
11001110 00101010 00111110 00011011 10100001 00111000 11110111 10100001 01001000 10001100
01100000 00001110 01111101 01101010 11101100 10010010 11010100 01011101 01001001 00010101
10001110 11000000 01000111 00000111 00110100 10100100 10010011 11000110 01101001 10001000
10100111 01111001 00100111 10100111 10101101 01001110 10001010 00110111 11110011 01010011
10100101 10101100 11000110 11011000 00000000 01000000 11111010 11110011 01010010 10000101
00000100 01110011 10010000 01111110 10110100 00011100 00000011 10010011 11010010 10011101
00010001 11001001 11110110 00111110 10110101 00101101 11000111 10100010 00101110 11011010
01101000 00000010 00100001 11011000 11100110 10010111 10000000 00111101 11101001 00001001
00011000 11001000 00111101 00001101 01000001 00111100 11100001 01000110 01110011 01011001
01101011 11010000 10010110 11001011 00101101 00101110 00111001 11111101 00101010 00010110
10111100 00011101 11001101 01100111 11001101 01110110 01000000 11001010 10011100 11111110
00110101 10010011 00110101 11100011 01100100 01111100 11000011 10011010 11011010 10011101
00001110 01100011 00100111 01010001 00011010 10010111 00011010 10001001 00000100 00011110
01001001 11111010 11110100 10101100 11011011 10001011 11000010 11100111 10101001 00011100
11110110 00110101 10011111 01110001 01110000 11000101 10111000 00100100 11010100 00001111
11111011 11011101 10011000 00100100 00010001 11010111 10001010 11101101 10001110 00011101
00100111 10100001 10010100 11101010 11011100 10110011 00100101 11011001 11011000 11100011
10010011 11011010 10101011 11111001 10100100 10101111 00111101 01111011 11010010 00100000
01100110 00011000 01001100 10011111 10100101 01011011 10110110 11010010 11101110 00101110
00010000 00010000 00110000 10011110 10100110 10110100 01101110 00110000 11011100 11001010
11101101 11101100 01010100 01010001 10111000 01100100 10011010 00110001 10010011 11011110
10111010 00001000 01110100 01001000 11000001 01000110 10010110 01001110 01110001 11011000
11010110 10000100 00110110 10010110 11010110 11111000 00010000 11000110 00000001 11101110
11011101 01001001 10101100 10111110 10110011 00000100 11001010 01010100 10100100 01110011
01110110 11011010 01111101 11000100 11000100 00101100 01110001 00010011 10011110 11111101
10101010 11101101 10110110 10001011 00101000 10010011 00110010 10010000 00001110 01111110
10111100 01010110 11100011 10110010 11000111 11010000 11010101 01111001 00100111 00101101
10001111 10011000 00010011 01011000 10111100 01000100 11011011 11010000 11011101 01010010
01011011 10110010 10110010 01101001 00110110 11110001 10010001 10111110 01000110 01110011
01010110 00011010 00011011 01011000 11001110 01010010 00100101 11011110 00001111 11110001
01110011 01010101 10100110 10111000 00100011 10010001 11010100 11110001 01010100 01011110
01110110 11000001 11111111 00000000 00111001 10101011 10110101 11110111 00010111 10111010
10111010 00011010 11101111 01111001 11100101 10100111 00000011 00000111 11010100 00001010
10101000 11010111 11000111 00100000 10001100 11111010 11111011 01010110 01110110 11100010
01011100 10010001 11000000 00110100 11001111 00100101 10011000 00111111 01011100 01010101
01111011 00101000 11011110 11101100 10010111 00110110 01011110 00110111 10001101 00100001
11000001 01101110 10111100 11110100 10100110 00110101 11110011 01000111 00100000 11100111
11111111 00000000 10101101 01010101 00111100 10010111 00001000 11111001 01011110 10011101
11101001 10111111 01100111 01110000 10000000 10110000 00111001 11000110 01110001 11101011
01010110 10011010 10110001 00010111 01110111 00101110 10101101 11101011 01101110 11111001
11111001 00011101 10101001 01111110 11011010 01111011 10000011 11000101 01010001 10010010
00110011 11000000 01110000 01000001 11110100 10100110 00100001 01100100 00111101 00110001
01010011 01100100 11010101 10000111 11001100 11001101 01001111 10110110 10110110 11010000
01001011 00011111 01111010 01111000 11010100 01110001 10010010 00001110 01110001 11000001
11110111 10101100 10000101 01010011 10011111 11101001 11011110 10011000 00000001 00011100
01110011 10010001 10011110 11011101 01101001 01111011 00011000 00000111 00110011 00110110
10000101 11111001 11001110 01001001 00110100 11100101 11010100 10001110 01110001 10111011
00000100 11110110 11001101 01100010 10010010 01111000 11110101 00011110 11110100 00110001
11001001 11101110 01001111 11110010 10101010 10001101 00101000 11011100 01111110 11010010
11000110 11110010 01101010 00100101 01111010 10010011 11001111 01101111 01001010 01111111
11110110 10001000 00100111 00011011 10111000 00011100 11100110 10111001 11100010 11000100
10011110 01101001 11000110 01000110 11101000 00001110 01001111 10111001 10101001 01110100
10010011 11010000 00111101 10101011 11101010 01110100 11010000 11011111 00101111 00111001
11000000 00010101 00101010 11011110 00100011 11110000 11111000 00011111 01001010 11100100
10010110 01110010 01000001 00111001 11101010 01111011 11110111 10101001 01000101 11000011
01100100 11110100 11001000 11101011 01010000 11110000 10101010 01001111 01100010 11111101
10110001 11010111 11000111 00101100 00000111 10001110 00010011 00100010 10100100 01000001
00001011 00010001 10000011 01011100 10011010 01011101 10110001 11000001 00100100 00001100
01010101 10000100 10111100 10010000 10110000 00100000 11100011 11101001 01011001 01010100
11000010 11011011 01100010 11010101 01010100 11111010 00011101 10000100 00110000 01000100
01001010 01101110 00100011 10011010 11010110 10110110 10110010 01011110 01110010 01000101
01110001 01010001 01101010 00010010 00010010 00111110 01101100 00000001 01011010 10110110
00111010 10100100 10111001 11111001 11011000 10001100 01111011 01110101 10101110 01001010

10110100 00100101 01101110 11100111 01000101 00111001 00101110 10000111 01010101 00010110
10011111 10111011 00000100 00001010 10110101 00011101 10010001 01010001 10010000 00111111
01011100 11010110 01010101 10011110 10101101 10010001 11110011 01110000 00110001 11101011
01011011 00010000 01101010 01010001 10101001 11100100 11110011 01011110 01110101 01001010
01110011 01001110 11000110 11111101 00001011 00110000 11000010 01100011 01010000 00000000
11101111 01010011 00101100 01000001 10001001 11100010 10011010 10010111 11001000 11000100
00001100 10001110 01111010 11010101 10101000 10100111 10000101 10111011 11111110 10010101
11001100 11011011 10000110 10011011 10010000 11001010 10100110 11011111 00000111 00100000
10011111 11000110 10100100 11011010 01010111 10011111 11001110 10101110 00100100 01100000
10010010 01000001 10100111 00111100 01000000 10001110 00110001 01010001 00101110 01101101
11011001 10011111 00110011 00110011 00011010 01110110 01010011 11101101 01010010 11111001
11100111 00001001 11101110 01101001 11110011 01011001 01101110 00111001 01000011 11001111
10100101 01010110 10011110 00100110 01010000 00000001 11001111 00010100 01011101 11011011
01010001 10100110 10011001 01100100 10110010 10110000 10100110 01111001 01000001 10111000
11101101 01010100 01010110 01000011 11011000 11110111 11100111 00110101 01100010 00011001
11111001 11100100 11110011 01010011 11101100 11101111 01100010 10101100 00001111 01100100
01001110 01110001 10011010 01101100 01110001 01001101 00000000 00111100 00010010 10011101
11101010 11011010 01011100 00001110 10001111 10001010 10011111 11001100 01010110 11001000
00011100 11010101 00100100 11101111 01100001 01011110 11000100 00010000 10110000 00111001
00000111 10101110 00101010 01000101 11100111 10001111 01101010 00011110 00100101 01010001
11000001 11000000 10100001 01110010 00111111 11000110 10110011 01110100 10011101 11000111
01110001 10000101 01111010 00001100 00001110 10011100 11010100 01001101 00011000 11110011
00001000 11101101 01010110 01001000 00100111 10101101 01000100 11101010 01001010 11100110
10100101 10110101 01111011 10100001 10010100 11100100 10000101 01001011 11100010 10100010
10010010 11011111 00011101 10101010 11000100 10000001 10010101 11000001 11101100 01101001
10001111 00100110 01000111 00110101 01010111 10110110 10100011 01000110 01110011 11000100
01000001 11001000 10100110 01100011 10011110 10011101 00101011 01000011 11001011 00000100
11110011 11010010 10101010 01001100 10111000 00111111 00100110 01111110 10110101 10111100
00011011 00101101 00010000 10001001 00111110 01111110 01101010 00111011 10001100 11101100
10100001 10000110 00001001 00111101 10111010 11010010 11100100 00110000 11001001 10101101
00011010 01110111 10111000 11001000 00101101 11100110 11011011 11011111 11101011 10011010
10111110 10110011 10000011 00011111 00000110 10110011 10101110 00000111 11001100 00001101
00001000 01111000 11101011 01001101 11000001 00111101 01000100 11001101 01101000 00101110
00111100 10011101 10000101 10111000 00000100 11010011 01110010 00100100 10011101 11001111
11110111 10001001 00110101 10011010 11010011 00011100 01100000 11110100 11111110 01010101
01110010 11001111 10011100 00011110 11010100 10111101 10011010 01001010 11101000 01001000
10111100 00110000 00111010 11010011 10010011 10011110 10011101 00111101 11000101 00111000
00101110 01111011 01010101 10101011 01111000 00000000 00011001 01111110 10110100 01000010
00101110 01011010 00100001 10110110 10000010 11010110 00011110 00110111 00011010 10111110
10000000 01100000 01100000 01010011 00110010 00010100 00001010 00011010 01001110 11000011
10001010 11101000 01110000 01101101 11101000 00010111 00010001 11110000 10100111 00111101
01001101 01000100 11000111 00100111 10001010 01110111 00011001 11001001 10101000 11000001
00011001 11101011 01000100 01100000 10011011 11010100 10111011 00001000 00110111 00000011
11001111 01010010 01111011 11010100 10001010 10011001 11100000 11010100 01001111 00110000
00011001 10101010 11101101 01110101 11000001 11100110 10101111 10101110 10000001 01100010
11110011 00110000 01001110 11111000 10101000 10011110 11100000 01110110 11101011 10011010
11001110 10011110 11110100 00101111 01010011 01011001 10110011 11011111 00101000 01111111
10111101 11001111 11010110 10110100 01010100 11011110 11100100 10110100 11001101 10100111
10111000 11001001 00100100 00011110 01101010 10101101 11000101 11101000 00000111 00011100
00011010 11000110 10010011 01010000 11101100 00001000 10101100 11111001 01101110 10001011
00011110 00001111 10111001 11110111 10101101 00100011 00000101 01111011 00110001 01110010
00011011 00010111 00110111 11100000 11111111 00000000 00010101 01100101 11001101 01110111
10011100 10000000 11011111 10001101 01010000 10010110 01110001 11011101 10110001 11001101
01010011 10111000 11010100 01100000 10001000 01111111 10101101 00011001 00010101 11010001
00011010 01001110 11111011 00001110 11001001 00101101 01001011 11010011 01001001 10011110
00001001 11111100 01101010 10101011 11001100 10101010 00111010 11100010 10110011 01011111
01010001 01111001 10001001 01011011 01010101 01110111 00100111 11010010 10110101 00110100
11011111 00001011 01101010 01110111 11100000 01001011 01110110 11000110 11010110 00111110
11011001 11101010 01111111 00001010 00100100 10111001 01101110 11100110 11101100 01100101
00101010 11001011 01100100 01100111 01011101 01011111 10100010 11110111 00100100 11111010
00000001 10011010 00101101 10110100 11001101 01011111 01010011 11100110 00011011 01100111
10000110 00100011 10001111 11011110 01001011 11000110 01000101 01110111 11011010 01101111
10000110 11110100 11111101 00110001 01000011 00100100 00111110 01100100 10111101 11100101
10010100 11100100 11010110 10101010 10100001 11000111 00000011 11111010 01010110 00010010
11000110 01000010 00011111 00000010 00110011 01110010 01101111 01110011 10000101 10110010
11110000 01001100 00001011 10001001 00101111 00101110 00100100 10011000 11100111 10100000
00011000 01010011 01011101 00001101 10011110 10010001 01101011 01100111 11111111 00000000
00011110 11110110 11010001 11000101 11101110 10100011 10101101 01101010 11101101 00011110
10011100 11010010 01100000 11110010 00110010 01101011 10010010 01110101 11101010 01010111
01111010 10111101 00000100 10101001 11000101 01101100 01010100 01101000 01000110 00001111
01110001 01010001 10110010 10001100 01111011 10001110 01101010 11011011 00000000 00001110
00000111 01001110 11010101 00010011 10011100 00001110 00000101 01000111 00101101 10111010
10011010 00010101 00011111 11010100 01110111 11101001 01010101 11011111 10001111 11111110

10111101 01011000 01111001 00010100 00011110 01111011 11110100 10101010 11001110 11011011
10001111 00111101 00111101 00101000 10000011 10110001 00010110 00011101 00001100 10011011
01001110 00110011 11001101 01011000 01101001 10110011 10010000 10000011 10000011 11010110
10110010 10100101 01101101 10100111 00111001 10101001 11101101 10100110 01100110 10001100
10010011 10000000 00101011 01010111 01001010 11111011 00110010 10010101 10001011 10110011
00011101 10110000 11100111 00110101 01000010 01011001 00000011 11110001 10011100 10011111
01011010 01111100 10110010 10000110 11101111 10111110 10101001 01001001 00100001 00000111
00100011 11110010 10100111 01001110 00001000 01110111 00011101 00101111 11001101 10010001
01011001 11010011 00000000 10110010 10100011 01111010 00011100 11010101 11111111 00000000
00110000 00011001 01110011 11011100 11110101 10101010 11110111 00110001 01111001 10010010
01100111 11010011 10101101 01101100 10100011 01101101 00001000 01111010 10011011 10111010
01110011 01101110 10001100 01101101 11101111 01011011 00010000 11100000 10001111 01111110
11110101 11001101 11101001 00110011 11110001 10110100 10011100 10010001 01011011 11110110
11110010 01100100 11110001 11010010 10111001 10100111 01000110 11001110 11101100 10110100
11001101 00001000 01111010 11110001 01010110 10010000 01100001 00111101 11101010 10110100
01111000 00000000 01111011 11110011 01010011 10100011 01110011 10001111 11001110 10111001
11010110 10101100 10010110 01001100 10011101 01111000 00110100 11111100 01111011 11111100
11010101 00010000 11000110 01101010 11000010 10001100 11110101 11000101 00111011 00101011
10111011 00001011 01010001 10001110 00101001 10011101 01110010 01001001 10101001 00011000
01010100 01011000 11100010 10010010 10111010 01110110 10110000 00001000 11000111 11010011
10000011 11101011 01001101 01100001 01001110 00000011 00011101 01101000 11001111 00100111
10001010 10110100 10101101 10100011 00000010 00010111 11001111 01101010 01110111 00011100
00011100 01100011 11011010 10010101 10001101 00100111 00111100 01100010 10011100 10110100
11011100 00000110 10111110 00111111 11000010 10100010 10010100 00011110 00001101 01001011
00100000 11001111 11010100 01010100 01100111 10001110 00101001 01011101 00001101 00010001
11110101 00011100 11010100 01001110 00110000 01000111 00111001 10101011 00001110 01111101
00101010 10111011 00000011 10001010 10111000 10111011 00111101 00011000 00110010 00100110
00000111 00111111 11100011 01010000 10111111 11111011 01010100 11110110 00111100 10010001
01010001 10111111 11011100 00100110 10101010 00010000 01101001 11011101 00010100 10110101
00101011 00111111 11011111 10101000 01011111 00011011 11111001 10101001 10111001 11101011
10011110 01101010 00000111 11101011 10011010 10101110 10000000 11011111 01000010 00001001
00000110 00111001 00000011 10001010 10000100 00101001 11000110 00001001 11001110 01101010
11001100 10100100 10001100 11110001 01010101 10011000 10001101 11111000 10100010 00001010
00101011 01000110 00111011 10010000 01001101 00010110 11101100 01100100 01010101 01101001
10101101 01010010 01001100 10010100 00000001 00111111 00001010 10111100 01110010 01001001
00011000 10101000 01011000 01111011 11010110 11010000 10011101 11110100 00010101 10001100
01110111 10110100 01100101 00101110 01111011 01111010 11010101 01010110 01011110 01111010
11100011 11101011 01011011 11101110 10111100 01110011 11011110 10110011 10101110 01100000
11100100 10010001 01011011 10101010 10001010 11000100 00110100 01100100 00111010 11100000
11100100 11010101 01111001 00111011 11110110 10101011 11110011 10101110 11010011 11101011
10011010 10100011 00101010 00001110 01101011 10110010 10011011 11010010 11101100 11001001
10010100 10100100 11001001 00011101 01111110 10010101 01011111 11111101 01101111 00011110
11111000 10101011 00010011 11110000 10100000 10000001 11010111 10001100 01010100 11111010
00100101 10010011 11011110 11011111 10101100 00110000 10001100 11110001 10011100 11111010
01010111 01001011 10011111 00101100 01001100 01011100 01101110 11001101 01001101 00011011
01001111 10010110 11100010 01010100 10001010 00000101 11001001 11101110 01110001 11000000
10101110 11100110 11000011 11000011 11110000 01000111 00010110 01100111 00011110 01100011
11010101 11001101 00010011 01001011 10001010 11001110 00010000 10101000 00110010 01111011
10011111 01011010 11011000 01010000 00000000 11100111 10001010 11111001 11101010 11111000
10110111 00111001 01011001 00011101 10110000 10100111 11001000 01010011 10000110 11000110
00001000 00000000 00110001 01000011 00011010 10011111 01100001 01010110 11010110 00101101
11111000 11100011 10001010 10010100 00000001 11010000 10011110 01001101 01001010 10001011
10001110 10010101 11000001 01010101 11011001 11011111 10100001 10100001 00010000 10001111
00011100 01010100 10110001 11000110 01110011 01001111 00001011 11111010 11010100 10100000
01100100 01010111 00101011 10011010 01101110 11100000 00110100 10000001 10001010 01010100
00011000 00011001 00110100 01110111 11110100 10100110 01001101 00100000 00000011 10101101
01010101 11101111 01110111 01100010 01101110 00110110 11100010 01110000 10000010 10110001
00101111 00101110 00001011 00110111 00000111 10011111 01001010 01011101 01000010 01111111
00110000 11101101 00000111 11111111 00000000 10101101 01011001 11000000 10110011 00111111
11100011 11001101 01101001 00011010 01101011 01110010 11001011 00110001 10000110 01101110
00111101 01101011 01001010 11010010 00011100 00100000 11110101 00111101 01101001 10010110
01110000 00011111 00101100 00011100 11110010 01101011 01000110 00010000 00110000 01000101
01000100 10101010 01110100 00011011 00100011 01001000 01001110 11110001 10011110 10011110
11010101 01101011 11001011 11000111 00110100 00000001 10110100 00000011 10000001 10001010
00011101 11001001 00110101 00001010 01110111 01011011 10001000 01101111 01000010 00111111
10101001 10100100 10010100 10010000 11100011 10111101 00101110 00110001 11001110 00110011
01010001 00111001 11001111 00111000 10100101 10100111 01000001 00010100 11101110 00110010
11010010 01100111 10011010 01011101 10110101 00111111 11001011 10111011 10100101 00110110
01000101 00111011 10111000 11001101 01010010 11010100 10010111 01110011 11001000 10000011
00110110 00110010 01111000 00111110 11110100 11100001 00110000 00000011 11100111 11111100
00111110 10110101 01010001 01011000 10010001 11101101 01001000 11110010 00000010 00001000
00100110 10111110 11000001 11111001 00011100 10011100 11001000 10110011 11100110 01101110
11001001 00100000 10000000 01111010 01100110 10011000 11110010 10110001 00011100 10001110

00110011 11011010 10101010 11111001 11100011 00100111 10101110 00111101 10101001 10111110
01100001 11000111 01001010 00011101 00110101 01111101 00001000 01101100 10110100 11000111
00011101 00001000 11001111 01101100 11010010 10001001 10001110 00111110 01111100 01101111
00011101 00001101 01010011 01111001 00001011 01110011 11011011 11010010 10010111 11001100
00111110 01011111 00000000 11100111 10001010 10101011 01101001 10100000 01011111 01000010
11010111 10011000 00110111 00000001 11010011 00111101 01101001 10001010 11000111 00100100
01110101 11110111 00110101 01011101 10100100 11111001 00110010 00111001 11110110 10100111
10100110 01111101 00001000 00110100 10111001 01010010 00010101 11011001 01101001 10001000
00011000 11100111 10001010 01110011 10010000 01010011 10011100 10011010 10000011 10001100
00010000 01001111 11010110 10100100 01010101 11000000 00000011 01110110 00110000 00111011
10001010 11001011 11100001 11010010 11100101 00000100 01111111 01111011 10011110 01110011
11101001 01010010 10101010 10011111 01011110 00000111 01101010 01001000 10010111 00111100
10100111 01000011 01010110 01010000 00101110 00000111 00011001 10101010 01001101 00100100
00111101 11000100 01100101 11110011 00110001 10001110 00001101 01001111 00010010 11101101
11000110 01001101 00110100 01100000 01110100 10100100 01111001 01000010 10001110 10111100
11110101 00111110 11010101 10001101 11111001 10001011 01010110 01000100 10101100 11011001
01111101 10111011 01111111 00011010 10000110 11100010 01011111 00101110 01000000 10101000
11011000 00000011 00111001 00100110 10101010 11001011 01110000 10101010 10100011 00000111
11110001 11110101 10101100 11101011 10011011 10111110 00001001 00101101 10011100 01110110
11001101 01101111 00001010 01101001 11101010 01001011 10101010 01011111 10010110 01110000
10100111 10101111 00111110 10110101 10011001 01111001 01110101 11111011 11000001 10000011
11111111 00000000 11010110 10101100 11111001 10101111 00110000 00110001 00011111 00100000
11110010 01101010 10100111 10011000 01100100 01110000 01111011 10000011 10011010 11101000
10000110 00011101 00100111 01110011 00001001 01010101 11101000 01011000 01111011 11001100
01100100 00001110 01111111 10101101 01010111 11011100 11110010 00011111 10011111 00111000
00111101 00101010 11010101 10111101 10010100 11010011 11001001 11000010 11100111 10001100
10011010 11011010 10110000 11010000 01000000 00001000 11010111 01001100 11011100 11110011
10110101 01111111 11000110 10101110 10100101 01011000 01010011 11011100 11001101 01000010
01010010 00110000 01100001 10110100 10011110 01110010 00000100 00110001 01001000 11111100
11100011 00111101 10101011 01110010 11001011 01000000 01101100 00000110 10011110 01100010
10011110 10011011 01111010 11111110 00110101 10111101 00001100 00010001 01000100 00000100
01110001 10101111 00000010 10100110 11000001 11000101 01110001 11010100 11000110 11001010
11011110 11101001 11010001 00001100 00111010 11101010 01010001 10000010 11000110 11010010
11011101 00000000 10000110 00111111 11000100 11110101 10101001 10011001 10010100 01111100
10111101 00101001 11001101 11110011 11111100 10100010 10100011 11110010 10011000 01100100
11110101 10101110 01110111 00110111 00110101 11101111 00011011 00101000 11011011 01100010
00110111 00101100 00111010 00011111 11001100 01010101 01110111 00100111 00100111 00110101
01101101 11111000 11100111 00000111 11101011 01000000 10000101 01001100 01100101 10001001
00111001 11001111 01111010 10101010 01111010 00110001 00110100 01010010 01110011 10111011
10001010 01100000 10000100 10001100 10110110 00110000 01101010 11101010 01011010 11001001
10010011 11110010 10011110 01101010 11010000 11010011 11110010 10100011 10011111 11000010
10011011 10101001 00010100 10101110 11000011 10010101 10011000 10001011 01101111 10111000
11110000 00001110 01111011 01010101 10000101 11010011 10000100 10000000 01100111 10110111
01101010 11011000 10000110 11000000 00001101 11100111 11010011 00010101 00100110 11010101
00011100 10000011 11000101 01100101 00101010 11010111 01010111 01001100 01101010 00000110
01110100 00111010 01110100 00101011 11111100 00111100 11010101 10000100 10000010 00111000
11110000 01011111 00011100 01111011 01010100 10010010 00110110 11010011 10001110 00101010
10111001 10010011 00111000 11001001 11111010 11111011 11010100 10101110 01111010 10001110
11010111 00101011 01000100 01001010 00000100 01100001 10001001 00001010 00001111 11010100
01010001 00101110 11010110 01011110 10011100 01111101 00101010 10100011 11001011 10001110
11100110 10001111 00111000 01111111 01111000 11100011 11010000 00011010 11010001 11000110
01001011 01000010 01110100 00011111 10000101 11111001 11110010 10001000 01111000 11000111
01001010 00010010 00111000 01111000 11001100 01101001 10011100 11100111 10100101 01000111
11100111 00000011 11001000 00110100 00101100 10011001 11101101 01001111 01010101 11010100
01010110 01000011 11111100 10011000 01010100 10111001 00010001 00100110 01001111 10110101
01000001 11100100 11011011 00010011 11111110 10100000 01100011 00011110 10010100 11110110
10010100 00101101 01000110 01001001 00100111 10001110 11111110 10010101 01110001 11011011
01110001 01101000 00101111 11011001 11101101 00001110 01001001 10000110 00111111 11001010
10100011 01111011 01101011 01010110 01011110 00100001 01010101 00011101 01110010 00111011
11010011 11011000 11101110 11100011 00011100 11010000 10010001 10011111 01011010 01101110
01010110 11010100 00101100 10111011 00001100 01001011 01001011 01010011 11001001 10001000
00010001 11101011 11101001 01001110 11111110 11001100 10110001 00011001 00101001 00010110
00001001 11110100 00110100 11110101 10001000 10000110 11100000 01111110 00010101 00110010
00101001 00101111 10000000 00111011 01110010 01101010 00010101 01000110 10011110 11100001
01100101 01111101 01010001 01000100 01101001 00110110 01011001 00000011 00000111 10001111
01111110 10110100 00110110 10000111 01101010 01111001 01000110 10010000 00011100 11100111
10101110 01101011 01001101 00101101 11110010 00110011 10010001 10011111 01001010 10010010
00101000 10000000 11100001 11001111 11101001 01010101 11110101 10000110 11110110 01100011
11110110 01010001 00110001 10011011 11000011 11110000 11100011 11110111 01110010 11001000
01001001 00011111 11000101 01001110 11111111 00000000 10000100 01110010 01110010 00111111
01110111 00110100 01011001 11000111 00111001 00111101 01101011 01110001 01100011 11001111
00010101 01100010 00001000 11000000 01111100 11110110 10101100 11100101 10001010 10101000
10011110 10001111 01000000 11110110 01010001 01000111 00110110 10111010 00010101 11111100

01100101 11110110 01000001 11100110 01111111 10111010 01101010 01011111 10110001 11011111
01000010 11000100 01001001 01101101 00101000 00000011 10010011 11000101 01110110 01110000
10011110 01000111 10100101 01101010 01000010 01001010 10101111 00011101 11000101 01110011
11111101 01110010 01101111 11100010 10110001 10110100 00101001 00100101 10110001 11000000
11000011 00110011 11000111 11000100 10000001 11000111 11010100 01010101 11001000 00101111
00001000 11100011 11110101 10101110 11100101 11101101 11101101 11101110 00010111 01100100
10110000 01000100 11000000 11110101 11001010 11010101 01101001 11111100 00111011 10100111
01001100 10111100 01000110 11110001 00011111 01010100 01101111 11101001 01011000 10111100
01010100 01100111 11110001 00100011 01011011 10110101 10100001 10000111 00001101 11110000
11101010 01011011 00011000 11101101 01010111 00100001 10111110 00111100 00010000 01110000
00111110 10110101 00100100 10011110 00010011 01011001 00110010 01101101 11101110 10011001
01001000 11101001 11100110 00101111 11110011 10101010 01010011 11101000 00111010 10011101
10100111 01000101 01011001 11010000 01110011 10011000 11001111 11110100 10101100 10010100
10101001 11001101 01111011 10101100 10011011 10101110 10100110 10101100 01111010 10001011
00010000 01001000 01101100 11100000 11110100 10101101 00001000 01110101 01001100 00000010
01001000 00000111 11011011 00110101 11000101 01001011 00111101 11000101 10101000 11000101
11000100 01010010 01000111 11011111 10010001 10000001 01010010 11000011 10101000 10101011
01100000 10010011 10001010 10011001 11010000 10010011 01000001 01100100 11110110 00111011
10011000 01110101 00100101 00111101 01101010 11000011 01011101 01000101 00100010 01111100
11111101 11000111 01001010 11100010 00100011 10111101 00000111 10010000 11011101 00101010
11010010 01011110 10010001 11001001 00100100 11100011 10011100 10000011 01011100 11111110
11000001 10100001 00111010 01101001 10011101 00100100 10110110 10101010 01000110 11101000
11011000 00001111 01100011 01010101 00001100 00110010 01000100 11100111 00100011 11110001
10101100 11111000 11110101 00010110 00111101 11111001 00010101 01110001 01110101 00110000
01000110 01100100 11100111 00000111 10100101 00101111 01100110 11011000 01011001 10100001
01011001 10001000 00011100 11110111 11101011 01001110 01001001 11110001 10011100 00010011
10001111 01101010 00111100 11111000 00100100 11000000 00111100 01100110 10011101 11100100
10000110 00011111 10111011 01101110 00001101 00100111 01110101 10101011 00001011 10010110
11100011 10111010 00000100 01100000 10011010 10110000 10001100 00011000 00011100 00011100
01010110 00111011 00000010 10111101 01101001 01000100 11000110 00110001 11000001 11111100
11101000 11100110 01001101 10001110 11010111 00110110 10000001 11011010 00110011 10011100
10001010 01101011 00000001 10000010 01110011 01011001 11101001 01110110 01110010 00110011
11001000 10101011 00001001 00111010 10110000 11100011 10100101 01100110 11010010 11101000
01000110 10100011 10100110 10001100 00011100 01101100 10101010 11101101 00010001 00010101
01110101 01001000 11011001 10010101 00110100 11001001 01100010 11100111 00111001 11100110
10100001 10100111 01111101 00001011 01001110 11100101 00100101 10001000 11100110 10010001
10100000 11001011 00011110 01111001 10101011 10000010 00100010 00010011 00100100 11010011
00001110 00000111 01111010 10101001 01101000 00111011 10011001 01110010 11000001 10001100
10011100 01010101 01000011 00011001 00001101 11010110 10110110 11011001 10010100 10001110
01111010 11010101 00101001 10010111 11100110 00100110 10101101 01001101 10100010 10101110
01100110 01001100 10100000 00000011 11000101 01010110 10001111 11111001 01010110 10000100
11010001 10011010 11001111 10011000 00110010 11100100 11110110 00011111 10101101 01101111
00000111 01110010 10001000 01101110 01001001 01010100 00111100 11111011 11010110 10100110
10001111 11001101 10110100 01100111 00111001 11001000 10101100 10101001 01100100 11001010
11110100 11111100 01101011 01110111 01000001 10000011 11001100 10000010 00101101 10011101
00000010 11110011 10011010 11101000 01001110 11001011 01100001 01011011 01010011 01000001
00000111 00010101 01100010 00111001 00001001 00010100 00111000 10001100 00010000 10111001
11101001 01010001 11011100 01001110 10010001 11000111 10110100 00010000 00101010 01100001
01001101 01110100 00011101 10000010 11100010 01111100 01110111 11000101 01000010 10010111
01111100 11010110 01111101 11001101 11001010 10011110 11111100 10011110 10010101 10010011
00110110 10100010 10100000 10010101 00001101 10001010 11101010 10000010 01001001 11011010
11000110 10110110 11010000 11101001 00100100 11010100 00000110 00111000 10101010 01101101
01111101 11100101 11110011 10011110 00110011 11011110 10111001 10101001 10110101 00011101
10111001 00111001 00111000 10101010 01010010 01101010 10001111 00101100 10011011 00101101
11010110 01001001 11011000 10001111 10111011 00011000 11001101 01101101 11001000 11011110
11101000 11001101 10111000 10101101 11011001 11010110 01001011 01111100 00111110 11110110
11101110 00111101 11001101 01010000 10010011 01010001 00011011 11001000 00000100 11100011
10110101 01100110 01000001 10100010 11101011 01110111 10011001 01101001 10000100 00110110
10101010 01111000 00001011 00101011 00010010 11011100 01111011 00001010 11010101 10110111
11110000 10011000 11000000 00110111 01110111 11110010 00111000 11000111 00100010 00110101
11101111 11110101 10101000 10011010 10100101 00010101 10101110 11100000 10101010 11000111
10100001 10011011 01110011 10101000 10010000 01111110 01110110 10101100 11101001 10110101
00111000 11010111 00111110 01100011 10001100 11110110 11100110 10111011 00011000 11111100
00101101 10100100 10100100 01100011 11110111 00110010 01001010 01111011 10011001 00011100
11010101 11101000 00110100 00001101 00100110 00101110 01100011 10110001 10110111 00000100
01110010 00001001 00011001 00110101 00110001 11000100 01000010 00001010 11001010 11100100
11001110 10101011 11101000 01111001 10110011 01101010 11001010 11001101 10001000 10010110
01001001 00001111 10110000 10100101 10000110 00111101 01010110 11100100 11111111 00000000
10100011 01011010 01001000 01110111 11110111 00101011 10001010 11110101 00111000 11101101
01100010 01010001 11111011 10111000 00100010 00011110 11000001 01000101 00000101 01111010
00011111 01001111 01011010 10010111 10001100 10001010 11010110 00110001 00110010 01101110
01001111 01110110 01111001 11000101 10110111 10000100 11110101 01111011 11000010 01111110
11010000 11100010 00010001 11101110 01101011 01101110 11000011 11000000 10110110 11010001

01001010 00011010 11101010 01100111 10011000 10001110 10100000 01110100 00110101 11010111
10101110 01000000 11100000 01010010 11111100 11011000 11100010 10010100 10110001 10010101
01100100 10110111 10110001 00011010 00110111 10101001 01011010 11001011 01001101 10110011
10110001 10001100 10101100 00010000 10100010 00011111 01011100 01110011 11111001 11010100
11101101 00100110 00001000 11000111 00110100 11101110 01001001 00110100 00100000 00011101
00110011 11001101 01110010 10110111 11101101 00110101 10111000 11001000 11011110 00111100
10001100 11110101 10100111 10101100 01111100 01010100 10100011 00001011 11011011 11110101
10100100 11011100 00001001 11000111 11100101 01010010 11010101 11110101 01000101 00010001
00111100 01100000 01110011 01010001 10011100 11110001 10010001 11111000 11010100 10010011
01101110 11001111 00011101 11101000 11011011 11000111 01011010 01001010 00111010 11011100
00110111 00101010 11001101 00011110 00111111 00011110 11010101 01001101 11010100 00101110
01000110 01001110 00111110 10110101 01111110 01111110 00101010 10000100 11000111 10101001
00100010 10101101 11010011 01101001 11011001 10110010 01010101 11001100 11111001 11111001
11001010 10011010 10100101 00110111 00000000 11010101 11001011 10010011 10000001 11000000
11111101 01101011 00101110 11100110 01000011 11000000 11101111 11101011 01011101 00110100
11111001 01101111 01110100 00001100 10001010 11100110 01001111 11011101 01100100 01110110
11110111 10100110 11000000 11001101 01101110 01001110 11111110 01000011 01010100 01110111
00101011 10110101 01011100 00000011 11010100 01110101 10101001 10100001 01100101 10011010
11011001 00010100 11110101 00111101 11101011 10100101 01110101 00100001 11101111 01100001
11010000 01001000 00111110 11010000 01100011 01110010 01111010 01100110 10010010 11100011
00100010 01000001 11011100 10011110 11110101 10011111 01110011 00110001 10110101 10111101
10001101 10001110 01110110 01100100 10100110 01001101 01101000 11001010 00001111 10010111
10111011 10110001 11000001 10101011 01110000 10111111 10111100 11000110 10100111 10101101
10001000 11111111 00000000 11110100 00101010 01110011 00110001 11110101 10101000 11110111
10011110 11110101 00001111 10011001 11001111 11110011 10100001 11000110 11111011 00001101
01011000 10111001 01101000 01001000 10111101 01000010 10000111 10100110 00000101 01110100
11010110 10001101 11111100 11101011 10010101 10110111 01011100 11001110 10000100 01100110
10111010 01101011 01000000 01000000 00000110 10111001 01110001 00010110 01101101 01011000
00001101 01101000 11011011 11100100 11100010 10101100 01000010 01000000 11111010 01010101
01011000 01110011 11000111 00110101 01100101 00110001 10010001 10111010 10111000 10010110
10000011 01000101 10010100 00111111 00110111 00010101 00111010 10110111 10100101 01010110
11000001 11000111 00010101 00100010 10110110 01101001 11011001 10101101 01101100 01010101
11001001 10011001 10110010 01110001 01010001 10010001 11001101 00100110 11101100 00011010
01001001 01100100 11110101 11101011 01010100 10011101 11101110 01001011 00010110 10100011
11000111 10111101 00111111 01110000 10101000 11011101 10110000 01110000 00101001 11011010
11100010 01100010 10110000 10100100 11001000 10100110 10110110 00001101 01000101 10010010
01110011 01000100 10010011 01001111 01010000 11011100 10010110 10011010 01001010 10010000
01111101 01101010 00110101 01100011 11010000 11010011 01011011 10100111 00110100 01010011
01101010 11010111 10110000 01101100 00100110 11101100 00001010 10001101 11001110 01110011
10001010 00001011 01110001 01010001 00111001 00100100 01100010 10101010 01011100 10110110
10110000 11010110 10100100 00110010 10011111 10011111 11111010 11010100 01010010 10011111
10010110 10011110 11100111 00000111 00111001 11111010 01010100 01101110 11111101 11101001
01000101 11110101 01000000 01000110 11111100 10100001 11110101 10101000 00011000 01100100
01010100 10001110 01110001 01010000 00011001 00111010 11100010 10101101 10111000 10111111
01010010 11101100 01000110 11100111 00001001 10000011 10011100 01010100 00101011 11001001
10101001 00100101 00100101 10000001 11001001 10101000 00011100 11101101 11101001 01010101
01101101 00110100 01000001 01110001 10001110 01001110 01111010 10011010 01000111 00111101
10000111 01111010 01000110 01101110 00001101 01000111 11101111 10011010 11010010 00111011
00101011 01101110 00011011 10001011 10111111 00000011 00000111 10011010 10101111 00110111
10100101 01001000 11001100 00011011 00111000 11101011 01010101 11100100 11100101 00001111
01011010 10101011 00100001 00110101 11011000 10100111 00111000 00000111 00100011 11110101
10101100 11001011 10010000 00000100 10000111 11101001 01011010 11010010 10001100 00001010
11001111 10111001 00011011 11010111 10001010 11101011 10100101 00111011 10101011 00010000
11010001 10010001 00110000 00111000 11001111 01101010 11101101 00111110 00011100 11011010
00000011 01101101 01110001 01110011 10110111 11100111 00101101 10110000 00011111 01101010
11100010 11101110 11111010 11100011 00111110 11111000 10101111 01000110 11111000 01110011
10001111 11101100 00010100 00111101 11111100 11000011 10011010 10101100 01110101 01001110
01001010 00010111 01000110 01010001 01001011 10011100 11101101 01100000 10001000 01101101
11001010 11110100 00010101 00101011 00101111 00011101 00101001 01100001 00011011 01010011
00000010 10000110 11101011 01011111 00100110 11101010 10110110 01110101 01011100 01110100
01010001 00000001 11001111 01011111 01111010 01110110 11011110 11000010 10000110 11001110
01000101 00111100 01100000 11110011 11011110 10100111 10011111 10100000 11000101 01001111
10111011 11001101 00110111 00111100 11110001 01001010 11000110 10010011 10100110 00001111
01011010 11010001 10111101 00110100 00100111 01100000 01110011 10110100 01010101 00001011
11001001 10110000 10000100 01100111 10101000 11101011 01010110 00100111 10011000 01000111
10010001 11111110 01000101 01100001 11101010 00010011 11100010 00110011 11001110 00111111
10101101 00010100 11110111 00011110 11100101 00111011 10011011 10000011 11110011 00001111
11010110 10011111 10100101 00100001 10010110 01010010 01110011 11001000 10101100 11100101
00101100 11010010 01100000 00001100 11100100 11110100 10101110 10010111 01000110 10110111
00001001 00001000 11100011 00000100 10011110 10111000 10101110 10011001 11111011 10010001
10110010 00101100 11010001 10000110 00110000 00100011 11001000 11101011 01010011 11110100
10100001 00001110 00000111 00000010 10000010 01111001 11101001 01011100 00011110 11010001
10000011 00011010 11000111 10001110 01000101 00000011 11010010 10011010 11000100 00101111

00100110 10100011 01101001 01110111 01100111 00000110 10000100 11010010 00010001 00100001
00100111 10111001 10101000 11001001 00111000 11000000 11101001 11101011 01001100 01111001
00001110 00101001 00111100 11011110 00000101 01101001 11001010 11011111 01000000 00010100
10001101 10111111 11100111 00010100 11000110 11001110 01111011 11111110 01110100 10001100
01110010 01111001 10100110 01101111 11110101 10101010 01001011 10010111 01110010 01011011
00111100 01010110 00101001 00001000 10001111 00010101 00011011 01001011 10011110 00000001
11100000 10011010 10000111 11001100 00011011 00110000 10100110 10100011 01010010 00001000
00111001 11111100 01101011 11101110 00100011 10101010 11011000 11110011 01011011 00101101
01101110 00000101 11001000 11101101 01010001 10110011 11100011 00000011 00100110 10100000
01010011 11011100 01010100 10101000 10000100 10111110 01110001 11110100 10101000 01001000
01001101 10110111 10110001 00110110 01001110 11000000 01000110 00001111 00111100 11100110
10000100 11001001 01110010 10100100 01100111 10011110 00001000 00111101 00101000 01000000
01110111 11101101 11000110 01101010 01101000 10100011 00100000 00010001 10110111 10011111
11100101 01001001 01011010 11011010 10110000 10110101 11011000 10001001 00011001 01101101
11100011 11110101 11110100 10101011 00110000 01000110 11010001 11100011 00100011 01111111
10101101 00111010 00011000 10110110 10001110 01111000 11110111 00110101 01110110 00101000
01110001 11010110 10100001 11001011 01001110 01100100 11001101 00010100 00001010 11111110
01011001 00111001 11000111 11111000 11010100 10011110 01000001 00100000 01100111 00011100
01110010 01101010 01110010 10100101 01111001 11101101 01001110 01001110 00110001 10010011
01011100 10010010 01101110 01101110 11101000 11010101 00101011 00001101 10000110 00100000
10111101 10111000 11101101 01001110 11000111 01011010 01001001 10101110 00100001 10001111
00100000 00110000 11100011 10101101 01100110 01011101 11011110 11100001 10110000 01001111
11100101 01000010 10100110 11011011 00011011 10110101 10001011 01110111 00110011 10000101
00100100 00001100 11111101 01001001 10101100 11111011 10111011 11000010 00000111 11001010
00111001 00100011 00111101 01101011 00111110 11101110 11111000 10000010 01011011 00111001
11100100 11010110 01111011 01001100 11101100 11011001 11011101 11001111 01011010 11101101
10100111 10000110 10001110 11100111 00111100 10101010 00010111 00101110 01101111 00111011
01100101 11111010 11110011 11001101 01010000 01101001 00011010 01000001 10010011 10011100
01110110 10101001 00000100 01000101 10111010 10011110 01111011 11100110 10110101 10110100
11011101 00110000 11001110 00010000 10010000 01000010 00001110 00110011 11010010 10110111
01111100 10110100 10010110 10100110 01011110 11110100 11110110 00110011 00100001 10110011
10010010 01001110 01000000 11100000 10011110 11110101 10111111 10100110 11101000 01111100
11101110 10111000 00000100 10000010 00000111 00011110 10010101 10101101 01101001 10100110
11000101 01101110 10111000 01010000 01001111 10111001 00110101 01111010 00111000 10110000
10110101 11000001 10001000 11000110 01011111 01001000 00110011 10100010 10011101 00000101
11010100 10000110 00001000 01100011 10001000 00001101 10001011 10000001 11010011 10001010
10010011 00011100 11100111 00110101 00100111 01001110 00110001 01000011 00000000 01111011
01010111 00010100 11101010 01101011 11011100 11011111 10010111 01000001 10100111 10010010
01110000 01110001 11101111 01001101 01010101 00111101 00111010 11111011 11010101 10000101
10001000 00110000 11100011 11110011 00010100 11100001 00011000 00100111 00011101 00101010
01111001 10111010 10001101 00101111 00110010 10111000 10000111 00101111 01001110 01101000
11111000 11110110 10101011 11010000 11000010 10111000 00011001 11101011 11111110 00010100
11000010 00000110 00110000 01000111 01011010 10010111 00110111 01111011 00110010 10110110
00101001 00001000 01010110 01000011 11000111 11110010 10101011 01010000 11011010 10101000
10001100 00010011 11001111 10101000 00100010 10100100 01000000 10001010 00000110 00111001
10100100 00110010 01110011 10000010 01111000 00011101 00101010 01111101 10100011 01111010
00010100 10000001 01010110 00100001 10011111 01011010 10001011 01110110 00001110 00111010
11010100 00100101 10110011 00100001 11000001 11101111 10011010 01111010 10101001 00101010
01011000 10010011 10001010 00011010 01001000 01010111 00011110 11110010 00000000 10000100
01100111 11101011 10001010 10100111 00101100 10111000 00010100 11101001 00001111 01100100
11001101 01010111 11011010 01001111 11110000 10011100 01111010 00001010 11010110 00101001
00101110 10000100 10001101 10010101 10001011 00001100 10000011 11010100 11110101 00110101
00000011 10110110 01001110 00110001 10001100 01110101 11100110 10101110 00101100 00000111
10001110 00101000 11111011 00101110 01001001 00000100 00000010 00101011 01101000 11001101
00101101 10010000 10011010 01100101 00111110 00001000 00100111 10010001 11101001 10010011
01010101 11001000 00100011 00000011 00011000 11001101 01101001 10011000 01000000 01001110
00001000 00100111 11010010 10011000 00100001 01011100 00011100 11010101 10111010 10010001
01001111 01000010 00101100 11001010 01100000 00010011 10000000 10000010 10100100 01011000
10001000 01011111 01011010 10110010 10101010 10000011 10100000 11100110 10010000 00101001
01010110 11100100 01010001 00111010 10111100 11011010 10000101 10001010 11001111 00010000
01100101 11001111 10100101 00101111 10010010 01000110 00000000 11111100 01001101 01011100
01011000 10111111 10001011 11110010 10101001 00010010 00111101 10111100 11010100 11111011
01100110 10010101 10000010 11000101 01111000 11101101 11111001 11001110 01111000 11111101
01101010 01010101 10001101 01000000 00100110 10011110 11010010 00000000 00000000 10101010
10001111 00110010 10011100 10001010 10010111 00010110 11100010 00011101 01001011 00000000
00001110 11111000 00111100 01010011 01001110 00100011 00100111 10011110 00101010 10101001
10011011 00011100 10001110 10010100 10000101 10110011 11001000 11101000 01111101 11101001
11000110 10011011 11011001 10001001 10110100 01011011 00010010 11100000 00111000 11101010
00001101 00001010 11100100 10011100 11110110 10101010 10101010 10100100 11100000 10011110
00111101 00101010 11100100 01110001 01100101 00110010 00111000 11111110 10110101 01001110
00101010 00111010 10110100 01101000 10011101 11001011 01010000 11111100 11010001 11100111
11110000 00110101 01100101 00111010 01100011 10100111 10110111 10101101 01010111 10000101
01001000 00000100 00000001 10001010 10110001 00011100 01100100 10001111 01011100 01111110

10010101 11001011 01011001 10101101 11010001 01011010 00010110 11100011 01101100 01110101
10101101 00011000 01110010 01000000 00010101 10011111 01101101 00001001 11100000 10011110
10111101 01101011 01000110 00111000 11011011 10001100 01010111 00101100 11011010 10111101
10011001 10100010 11010000 10111101 00001111 01001110 00001111 00110101 01100101 01011011
10001100 11111110 10010101 01011010 00111000 10001110 00101010 11000010 00101001 11000111
00110101 11001010 11101100 10110100 01100101 01011000 10011001 00011011 11111001 01110100
10101001 00010110 01000011 10001100 01110010 00001111 10101110 01101010 00110100 01011100
00001110 01101010 01001111 00101111 01110110 00001111 01001010 11001101 11001010 00101111
01100010 00011000 11100111 01010101 01101000 11001010 10111000 00001110 10001111 11010100
00110111 00111001 10101100 01101011 11011111 00001101 11101001 10110111 01111001 01100001
00001001 10000101 11111111 00000000 10111101 00010001 11000111 11101001 01011011 01111011
01110000 00110011 11010110 10011101 10001100 01010011 10001101 01101001 01000101 11101001
10100001 10011011 01000111 00000011 01111011 11100001 01001011 10111000 00011001 11011110
11010010 01100001 00101100 01111100 01111100 10100111 10101101 01100011 10111100 10010111
00010110 10101110 01010110 11100010 00111001 00100011 00111101 00110010 11001011 10001010
11110101 01101100 01100100 01100110 10101010 01011100 11000010 10010011 11100101 01100110
01010100 10010000 01111010 00110000 11001101 01110100 11000111 00011010 11110110 10011110
10101000 00010100 10011010 01100111 10011101 01000011 01111000 00001001 11100100 11110001
11010111 10101101 01011010 01001001 11110011 10000011 10010001 01011011 01011010 10000111
10000110 00101101 10011100 10010111 10110101 01100011 00000100 10011110 10011101 01000101
01110011 10010111 10011010 01110101 11011101 10001100 10100000 11001000 10100101 10100011
11101101 00100010 11110100 10101110 10000101 00101010 01010101 00011111 10111010 01101001
11101101 01101110 11110101 00110100 11100011 10011101 10110001 10001100 11111110 00110101
01100110 00011011 11010110 01010100 11101011 01011000 01010000 11001110 01110010 00111001
00011110 11111100 01010101 10011000 11001111 00011100 10011010 11001110 01110100 10010001
01001010 11001100 11101000 00100000 11010100 10110011 11010100 01100111 11101011 01010110
00011001 10100001 10011001 11000000 00000111 01100111 11010100 11010111 00111000 00011011
00011101 00101010 01110101 10011100 11111111 00000000 00001101 01100001 00101010 01011101
10000101 01100011 01100101 11010001 10010111 10100111 11100111 01001101 00010010 00110000
01110010 00111011 11111101 01101010 10001100 00010111 11100110 00100011 11010111 10110101
01011010 01011001 11100010 10011011 11100110 01111110 00001101 01001010 10001011 01011010
00110100 00001110 11101000 10110011 00010100 11100101 01111010 10110110 01101010 11001010
01011110 10000000 00111001 10101100 10110111 10001111 11111000 10010000 11110001 01010001
01001010 11000100 00001100 11010101 11111011 10110111 10110000 10101100 10001110 10000100
01011101 01000100 01111000 01110011 10110011 11101011 01001101 01101000 11000001 00000100
10100011 00000010 00000001 11101101 01011100 11011111 11011010 00001000 11001110 00001110
01001111 11010110 10100110 10000111 01010001 00110001 11110001 10010111 11111010 01100110
10110011 01110100 01101111 10110110 10000001 01100110 01101011 11001010 10110101 00000011
00001110 01111110 01101110 10010100 01000111 10101000 11000101 00100001 11011011 00100111
00000111 00010101 00100111 10011001 00010100 10100011 00001000 01110001 11001101 01000100
10100000 11101101 01110010 10110101 00101011 01001010 00000111 11010110 10101001 01011101
01000100 00100110 00000101 01111011 01111011 01010110 10000011 11000010 11100010 01000011
10000001 01001011 00010101 10100001 00101101 11110011 11110100 11101111 01010101 00011101
00110110 00001011 10011100 10011011 10001001 01100100 10010011 11101100 11101000 10100100
11001001 11011000 00000001 01011101 10011100 00000100 01011011 11011001 00100100 00100001
01110000 01010100 01100000 11100000 01110101 00110101 00110100 00010000 11000101 00000010
11100010 00011000 11000010 00010011 11010100 11110111 11111100 11101001 00011000 01010111
01110011 10101000 10111001 01111100 11000100 10011010 10111001 01001001 11100101 10010101
10111001 00001010 01110001 11101011 01010000 01001001 00000100 11010010 10001100 00010001
10001100 11111011 11010110 10001011 10010001 10111011 00011000 10100100 01100011 11110011
11010110 01111110 11010001 10101101 01010000 01111011 01010110 11110110 00110000 11011111
01000110 10011110 01010000 01000001 10011001 00000111 10111001 11100110 10011000 11011110
00011000 01011111 11100011 10111001 10010011 11011111 11001011 00011000 10101101 11110101
00111110 11110100 01110010 01000000 00111001 11100010 10011010 10101101 00110101 10100010
11010000 00011101 01001001 00111101 00001100 01011000 10111100 00110111 10100111 10100010
10000001 00100010 11001001 01110000 11011111 11110100 11010001 10101011 01001010 00001011
01111000 10101101 10100010 00001001 01101111 00010010 01000110 10000011 10110010 10001010
10110001 10010001 10011111 01110001 01001111 11100000 00001110 01101010 00111001 11101010
00110111 01101001 10110010 01001000 11110010 01110110 11110001 11011110 10011011 10010011
10001010 10011001 01010100 11111101 01101001 10100101 01111001 11001101 01011101 11011010
00000010 00100110 00101101 11010010 10010111 11001100 00101010 00000000 11001001 11001101
01001001 10000001 01001000 01010111 01110001 00100011 11010010 10100101 11010100 01010001
01100000 11000100 11110011 10110000 01001001 00001101 10001010 01011111 00111100 11100011
10100101 00100111 10010110 00111111 11000010 10000001 00011001 11111010 11010100 11011101
00111101 01101100 01001010 01000010 10100100 10100100 11110101 11101001 01001111 01001001
01000111 01000011 11010010 10011001 10110111 00000111 00110100 10011011 01001000 11100011
10101101 00100110 11011011 10010101 10001010 11010001 00010110 00111100 11010001 10001100
01010011 01010110 01010000 00111000 11101111 11011011 00110101 01011001 11000101 00110001
10110010 01010011 10000011 11111000 11010110 10010001 10010011 11010101 00110100 01001001
01101101 10100110 11100111 10011010 10001111 11001110 11011011 10011110 01101010 10100001
01100010 00111011 11010101 01110111 10010000 10000011 11111100 11101001 10100101 10101010
11100101 00101011 01000011 01000000 01011100 10010110 00100111 11101011 01010010 00101100
10100000 00001111 11100111 01011001 01000010 01011100 01110010 00111111 10011101 01001001

00010100 10111100 11100111 00100100 11010001 01010001 00110101 10100001 01000101 11001001
01011010 10110011 10101111 00100100 11101011 10000000 01111010 11010101 10000111 10011011
01110111 00011101 11000101 01010001 01110010 01111001 11011110 00101000 11011001 01011010
01000100 10010100 10101110 11110111 00000000 01110000 01101011 00111000 10000010 01111001
11011101 11001101 01011110 10111010 11100101 00001001 00111111 01111100 11111011 11010110
01110011 00011110 01111010 11110100 11101011 01011101 11110100 11100010 10010110 11101000
00011000 10010010 00101110 01010111 00100100 11111110 00110101 00011101 10101001 11000100
00101001 10000011 11001111 00110100 00011001 01110001 00011111 00100010 10110011 01100001
10011000 10011001 01100101 01010000 11011001 11111110 10010101 10111100 00101001 01011001
10110110 01100001 00110111 01100010 01001101 01100001 00111100 11101000 11000011 01000110
11000100 10010101 00111101 00111101 01101011 01001110 11011001 10011010 01101011 00101000
11011011 00000111 11010011 10010011 11101001 01011000 11101000 01000010 10000111 01010010
11001110 01011100 11010101 11001101 00100110 11100011 11110111 01010010 01000101 10011110
01000001 11100011 00110101 01110101 00100010 10111001 01101101 10111001 00110000 10010101
11100101 10101000 11111001 11001001 01010110 11111001 00001111 11010110 10011001 10010000
01001000 00111110 10111101 01101001 00101110 00001111 01100011 11011100 11010100 01111001
11001011 11110001 01011001 11000110 11110110 10110001 10100011 00110100 10101101 10001110
11011011 10011000 11010111 10110001 11101011 01011101 01010101 10100000 00000110 00110001
01011100 10000101 10010111 11111010 11101000 11110111 01110100 11001110 01001110 01001101
01110101 11110110 10000011 00110001 00000011 10011110 00011011 10011010 11100110 10101111
01001110 11011101 00001010 10001001 01111010 00101100 11110111 11101000 00101010 01111000
10001111 00100100 10011010 10101111 00001110 01000101 01011000 01001110 10111001 10101110
00110111 10111001 01110110 00101110 01000010 01111001 10101001 00111000 00100110 10101011
10100111 00100000 01010100 10001101 10011100 11100111 00110100 01000110 00111100 11011011
10000011 00010110 01010011 11001110 00110001 01001101 00000011 01110111 00000111 10110101
00111001 11001111 00011101 00101001 10111111 11111010 00010101 00100111 00000100 11101111
01100011 00111101 01000001 10000000 11001111 00010100 11000111 00100110 10100100 01010101
11011010 10111101 01110010 01001101 01000100 11111001 00010100 11100000 11010010 01010110
00011101 11111011 10001100 00100111 11110000 10100100 01100001 10001110 10011101 11101001
10110010 01111010 01010010 00111011 00001110 00000101 00100111 00010111 00100111 01111011
10001100 01100011 10010010 00001111 00110100 10011110 01100001 00100110 10001001 01111001
00111000 10101000 11011011 10100101 00110100 10010110 11010111 00101010 11100001 00111001
00011100 00010100 10101010 11101110 01001001 11100110 10100101 01111111 01110011 11000101
01010110 01110010 01000111 01111100 11010011 10010100 01010011 01111010 10000000 11000111
10010000 00010001 11001101 01000100 11000100 10001110 01001111 00010100 10110010 10110111
00111100 01010100 00101100 01001001 11111010 11010101 11000110 00011010 10000011 01101000
01010010 11000011 00100011 11011111 10111101 01010111 10010001 10110000 01111001 10100111
10111011 00011100 11100011 00011001 11111100 01101010 10111011 01100000 00111111 00111100
11100111 11010110 10000101 00000110 10011110 10100011 00000111 00100010 10100000 01110010
10111101 01000001 11100010 10011110 11111001 00000100 10001100 11110000 01101010 00010110
00111100 00010011 10001100 11111011 01010110 10101001 00110111 10101010 01000000 00011011
10010111 00000100 11110110 10101000 01110111 01111100 10011001 11000111 00110100 10101100
11000011 11010010 10011000 10111100 00000010 00011000 11110001 11011010 10101110 00111110
11110110 10001100 01000011 10011011 10001100 10010000 00111001 10101000 00011111 10100000
00011110 10110100 11111100 11100100 11110001 11010000 01010100 01101111 10000110 11100100
11010011 01001001 10000010 01100101 01111001 01110000 00001110 00101010 10011101 11000110
00110001 11010010 10101110 01001000 01000000 11101101 10011100 01010101 01111001 10000000
11101011 10001110 01111010 11010110 11010100 11000110 11001100 01101011 10101110 01011011
01110000 00000100 01100011 10001110 01101011 10110101 11111000 01101110 11000100 01101001
10010010 10000110 11001110 11000001 00111111 00011110 11111110 10110101 11000110 11101010
00011111 01110011 00111110 10000110 10111101 00001111 11000001 00110110 10000110 00111101
00101110 11001110 00010111 01010000 00011100 11100101 11100100 00000000 11111010 10011110
00101011 01001100 01011100 10010011 10100010 11101111 11010100 11000101 00101111 01111100
11101101 11000111 00110001 11110100 11100110 10100011 01001110 00001111 00100111 10010001
01010010 11110100 00010101 00011011 10000001 10011010 11111001 01011111 01110110 11100111
01000110 11000100 10101000 01110011 11001101 00111111 10011010 10001110 00101100 01100000
11010010 10110001 00111111 01011010 01010001 11010111 01000010 10000111 01110001 01001011
11100110 01110011 11010011 10001010 01000010 00001110 00111011 11010100 00110010 11001000
01100011 10100001 00101011 01011101 10010000 11110111 00101001 01101010 10010010 00101010
10111000 00000100 11110101 11110111 10101110 01111110 11111110 01011100 10000001 10000011
11000000 00100110 10101110 01101011 00110010 11100110 01001000 11111110 01101100 10011110
01110011 01011001 00010011 01001000 00001000 11100110 10111011 01101000 11000011 01001101
01000110 10110111 00100110 10110000 01001111 00110110 11100000 00001100 01110001 01011101
01100101 10110010 11100010 00110100 00011101 00111110 10010101 11001101 11101000 01101011
10111010 11100011 00100011 10010011 11001101 01110101 00010000 10101110 11010100 11000111
10100101 01100111 10001000 10111010 01111011 10010100 11010010 00100101 11001110 11010011
11010110 10100010 11011101 11110011 10011010 01110011 00001100 10010000 01110001 01010001
01001010 01111001 00000000 01110101 11101111 01011100 10001001 00110110 10111100 10001001
11101010 00101100 10011001 01100001 10011100 11010100 00101001 11001110 01111001 11101001
01001110 10010001 01001001 00000100 01110011 10001111 10101101 01000110 00111110 01010000
01101001 10101000 10100111 10110000 10101110 00111111 00111101 11101010 00100110 11000110
11110011 11001101 00110011 01110111 00011100 10001010 10001101 11011011 00000111 00111110
10110101 10110110 11101010 11000000 10111011 10010011 10110011 00001101 10011001 00111101

00101001 10011011 10000111 01100010 01101001 00111100 11001100 10001110 10010101 01011101
10100101 00011001 11101111 01010010 10010101 11110111 00000110 01111000 10100011 00110110
00110000 00111011 11010010 00111001 11001111 00111001 11111010 01010100 01111011 01011000
10110001 11110101 11001111 11100111 01010111 01101101 10100000 01100001 10000000 01000001
00100000 10001100 10001010 11111011 10011111 10000000 11110010 11010010 01101100 10001001
00100011 00101100 00010011 10001110 10111101 01111001 10101011 10010001 11000110 10100100
11100000 01100111 11011111 00110101 01100001 00101101 11000000 11111011 10011001 11100111
11110010 10101011 11010000 11000000 00110000 00000111 00111001 11111110 10010101 11001111
00111010 11010110 11010000 11010010 00010100 11011101 11001010 01110001 11000010 00010100
01110001 01010110 11100011 10001011 10011110 10000111 10001010 10110010 00100001 01101000
11000110 11100000 00110001 10001110 11111110 10110101 00100000 00000011 10000011 01011100
11011110 11010010 11011011 10011011 01111011 00110100 01000101 00010100 00100000 00100111
00100011 10010011 11011110 10010111 00111000 00011101 01001000 00111101 10101001 00100100
10010011 00011100 11100111 11110000 10101100 11111011 10001011 11111100 00010111 01010001
11000111 10100001 11000111 01001010 01110110 01010011 11011000 00011011 01001000 11010000
10011010 01010101 00001001 10000011 11001111 10100001 10101100 11111011 10001011 11100000
10110001 11100000 11110101 11101110 01000101 01100111 11011100 11011110 10000000 00001110
11111111 00000000 11001111 00110101 10011111 00110101 11010011 00110001 11011010 00111011
01110111 10101110 10011010 00110100 01110100 11010100 11000110 01110101 01110100 00101110
01011100 01011110 01110000 00011011 10101000 11000111 01111010 10100001 00110101 11010011
00110111 00011000 11111100 01101010 00010111 01110110 10010000 01111100 11100111 10001110
10011101 00111010 01010100 10001001 00010001 11011101 10000010 00001111 10100101 01110100
01110010 00101000 11101010 01100000 11100100 11011110 11000100 00101010 10111011 10110010
01001001 00100111 00100110 10101100 01011011 01000001 11100110 10111001 11101010 01001111
01011110 00000101 01101001 01011000 11101001 10001101 00100110 00110111 10000010 00000111
01111010 11101000 00100001 10110010 01011000 10000010 01100000 01100000 11100010 10110001
10101011 10001010 10001100 00110100 00101110 10011101 00010110 11110111 00110011 00110100
11001101 00100100 01111001 10001000 11010011 00010000 01111111 11011001 00100010 10110111
11101101 11100000 01000101 11100100 01111110 01000010 10000100 01010000 00111010 11110100
11111110 01010101 00101010 00001101 10100111 11100101 00011111 10001001 10101111 00111010
10101101 01101001 01010101 11010010 01001110 11000111 01011100 00101001 10101000 00001010
01000000 11000110 00111011 01010011 11000111 11001011 10001100 01110010 00101001 01100011
10001111 00100011 01110011 11100011 00100111 11010110 10011110 11110001 00101110 01110011
10001100 01111011 00001010 11100110 01110110 01011010 11001000 11010111 01011101 11000100
01011001 00010100 10111110 00101001 10011111 00101001 00111001 11110111 10100100 01100101
00000000 01100011 10101001 10101000 01010101 10001110 01110000 01111111 01001010 01101110
11101111 01110110 00100010 11011111 10011000 00000111 01111110 10110100 10011001 11111001
11111000 11111100 01101010 00010101 00000101 11001110 00111010 01111011 01111010 01010101
10100000 00000010 10001110 10010101 00001010 01001010 00111010 00010101 01100001 10111001
10010101 10011111 10000001 11000101 00100001 11011101 11000000 11000110 00101010 11001100
00101000 01001000 00001100 10100011 00010101 00100111 10010110 00011001 10111001 00011101
00111001 10100110 11100110 11011011 10111011 00101010 11010110 00101011 01000100 10100000
00101110 01110001 01010001 00111001 11000110 01110001 01010110 01101110 11011000 00101110
00010100 01110100 10101010 01111001 11001011 10011110 01101000 11101010 00000010 11000001
00010110 01000111 10011000 11000010 10100110 01111100 00010100 11100011 10100101 01001001
00000100 01000111 01100110 00001001 11000000 00010100 11011001 00100011 00000000 11110101
11001101 01001100 10011110 10111010 10001001 10100010 00000101 10001011 00100000 01101110
11110101 10101001 10011010 00110001 11011111 10000001 01001001 11010111 00100000 01110011
11101000 00101001 10011011 10001000 11000010 10011110 10010100 01000101 00111001 00110111
10101000 01101100 00110010 01100110 01010000 11000000 00000001 11011010 10100010 00001101
10110111 10110000 11100110 10100100 01110001 11100110 01110100 11100100 10001110 10010100
10011110 01010111 00011000 11101111 11101011 01011010 00111111 01110011 01000010 00101110
11001000 00011000 01101110 11111110 10100110 10011001 10110100 11101100 11100111 10100101
01011000 11011011 11100101 10011111 10011111 00111000 10100001 01010100 01101110 00111100
11100000 01110101 00010101 01010000 10010111 01000001 00010000 10100100 01011011 10001000
11000111 01011010 10010100 00101111 00011100 10001100 10011111 01011010 01000011 00101010
00101110 00001000 00100000 11110001 11010110 10101010 10111101 11100100 01111011 00111110
11110110 00111101 01101011 01000100 11011011 11011100 01010111 01001011 01010010 11011110
11100101 01010000 01000111 00010101 01011010 01011001 10000000 10101010 10001111 01110111
00011001 00111100 10010000 00000111 10111001 10101010 11101101 00110000 00111111 00110110
11101110 00111101 00101011 01011000 11010001 10110110 10100100 11110011 11011011 01100010
11000100 11010010 00110110 01111000 00111001 11111010 01010011 00000010 10010010 00000110
00111001 10101000 11000100 11101010 00111000 11111010 01010011 10011010 11110001 00010000
01110110 11001101 01010100 10010100 10101111 11011100 01010111 01000101 10011000 11101101
11110011 11010100 11111110 01110101 01100101 01101101 01111011 11110000 00110011 11011010
10110011 11010110 11110011 00101011 10011100 11111110 10010101 01100010 00101011 10000111
01100011 11000001 11100000 11111010 11010010 10010011 10011110 11110111 00101001 00110101
11010000 10111001 11100100 11101111 11001001 11000000 00000000 01100000 01110001 01010110
10100010 10001110 00110000 01000110 01001000 00111110 11010101 01000100 01001010 11011100
00001101 11011111 01011100 11010100 10001011 00100110 00111011 11111110 00110101 11001100
11100010 11100110 11101110 11011001 01101001 00011010 01110000 10000001 10011110 00001000
00111110 11100010 10101100 10001101 10101011 11001001 11111100 01001101 01100001 00011011
11010001 00010100 01111000 00000111 10000001 01010101 01011011 01010011 00101101 10111001

11110111 10111001 11001111 01001010 10010111 01001001 10111101 00010000 11101110 10001110
10101100 01011100 01000101 00011000 00001101 10111000 01111110 01110101 01101000 11011101
10001100 00000000 00001000 11001101 01110001 00110000 11011100 01001000 11001111 10011110
01111111 00011010 11010000 10001010 01010111 00111000 11001001 10101000 10101001 01000101
11011011 01010011 01000100 11101110 01110101 11010001 11011101 10001110 00110000 01000111
00011110 11110101 01100001 01101111 00010111 00011100 01110010 01101011 10010111 10001110
01010110 11000111 01011110 01101010 11010010 01001101 10110100 00000000 00110011 10001100
01010111 00010011 10100110 11101100 11001011 11011100 11101001 11010010 11101001 01000000
00000000 10011110 01101001 11101011 01111000 10111001 11000001 10101110 01100011 11101101
00001101 10011100 00000010 01101010 01110100 01100110 11110101 11100010 10110000 10010101
00100100 00101011 01011000 11101001 01000101 11100010 01110100 00000100 01111110 00100110
10010101 01101110 00100010 00101010 00001110 01110000 00110011 11111001 01010111 00111010
10011001 00111000 00100110 10101100 00101001 10010111 10000000 00110011 01010000 11101001
10101011 00010001 01100011 01111001 01100100 10001001 10000111 11011110 11110111 11101011
01001111 01010001 00011001 11100100 01110100 11001101 01100010 01000111 00010100 11100111
00011100 00010000 00111101 01001111 01101010 10110100 11001011 00101100 01100011 01101110
01110011 11101111 01010001 00100100 10111010 00011001 11011000 10111100 11110001 00001110
01101010 10111100 10010000 10001101 10000111 00101010 00001000 11000111 10100101 00001001
00101100 10000011 00011011 11000101 00000110 01101110 11010101 10100100 00010100 01011110
11100010 11011000 11000010 10111101 11010000 11101101 00100110 00100101 11100011 00011110
01001100 10000100 11100111 00100011 10100001 10101100 01111001 11110100 10111011 10111000
00111000 00000000 01001000 10011111 11011110 01011010 11101100 11100101 00000000 11111010
01111011 01010101 01001001 10100010 00100111 10010001 11000001 11110110 00110101 10101010
11000100 10110100 00111000 01101110 01110001 11101000 01110011 11010111 00111001 11110100
00110100 01100011 00010101 10111011 01111001 00001010 01001000 00000111 10011000 10011111
00111111 01100011 11011110 10110010 11100110 10110011 01100000 01110011 00011001 11001000
10101110 10011111 01101000 10100100 01101100 10011001 01011111 11110001 11100110 10000101
10010100 10000011 10000000 01001101 00110111 00011000 11101101 11001101 00110101 01011000
11110111 10101011 01001000 10101011 10010111 00100010 10111011 00100011 00011110 11000111
00110101 01110110 00101011 10111000 11100110 11000000 01111110 11111101 11101011 00010111
01110000 11100111 00010100 11111101 11011000 00000000 00101111 00100110 10100110 01010100
10101111 10100000 11101100 10011001 10101011 00101101 10111001 00101000 01011010 00110010
00001101 01010011 01101101 11000000 01110010 00111001 10101000 10100010 10111001 01100101
11000000 11001111 11100010 01101011 01110110 11001010 11010000 11011110 01000100 00011110
01100101 00110001 10100001 11100011 00100100 01110011 01010010 11101111 00000001 01101100
01100010 00100000 10010110 01000111 11011011 00011010 11100101 11110011 11000000 00010101
10111101 01100101 10100101 11001010 10111000 01101001 11011011 10011110 11100010 10110101
00101101 10101101 01100000 10110111 01001101 10101000 10101000 00000111 10101001 00011100
11010100 10011011 10000110 01000110 00111010 00011010 01001110 11110010 11010000 11001111
10011011 10110000 11010101 01010101 10001100 00000001 10001110 10010100 00010001 11001101
00011011 10110010 01101001 10101110 01110011 11001111 10100101 01000110 10001001 10011001
11101110 00101011 00011110 11010101 00000011 11110101 11100010 10011110 11001100 01000000
00111110 10110101 00011110 01001111 00111110 11011101 01111111 00011010 00111001 10110100
01000101 01011000 00011011 10010001 01001100 11100011 11111000 10111111 01011010 00110111
00001100 00011110 01101001 00011000 11101110 11001001 01011110 00110001 01010111 11101100
11010010 01010111 01101100 01011010 10000111 00000000 11010010 11101110 11111100 10101010
00111110 00001000 11100011 00111001 00010100 01110000 01001110 00110001 11111001 01010000
10010111 01100001 11111010 10010010 00101001 00011000 11100011 10101111 10101001 10101001
00000001 11001000 11111110 10110101 00010011 00010000 00011011 00011000 11001101 01001000
10000111 11111001 11110100 10101100 11101101 00101000 00111101 01110101 00011101 11001001
11010101 10000110 00101001 10101100 00000111 01010011 01010001 01101110 11100111 11110001
10101001 01111010 10001100 11010101 01001110 01000000 10010000 01100011 00100010 10001100
00010011 11010000 01010011 11000110 00110001 01001011 10111011 10101101 01100010 11111011
00110000 01100100 01101011 00011111 11100101 01000110 11011110 01000001 00000010 10100100
01011010 01000010 00111001 11000001 00111101 01101010 11010100 10010010 01010110 01000010
11110100 00100011 11000110 00101001 00001011 01110011 01001110 00111100 01110001 01010001
00010001 10000011 11010110 10011011 10110010 00011110 11000100 01101111 11010111 10011010
10001110 01001110 00111000 00011111 10001101 01001110 11000011 00001110 01110011 01010001
10111001 00000111 00100100 01010110 10011110 11001101 10101101 10011001 00100101 01010110
00111000 11101101 01010101 11011111 00010010 01100100 10010011 11011010 10100111 10010110
10100000 01100011 10000001 10010000 00111010 11010101 01000101 00110111 10101101 11001010
01000100 00101110 01001000 00000000 11110100 00000010 10000101 10010000 01010011 01011000
11100111 10001100 11110001 11011011 10001010 10000101 11011000 00101001 11100110 10110100
10001011 01110110 00100100 10010111 11001100 00111001 11001110 01111000 10100111 10111011
00010010 10111001 10101010 00110010 01001011 10000000 00001111 10101110 01101000 01011001
11111000 11000111 11110101 10101010 01110100 11100100 11010101 11011000 10101111 01100010
00101011 10110010 01010100 10011110 01101010 10000011 10011100 10010011 11011011 10001010
10110101 01110010 11011001 10010111 00100000 10001100 01100011 10011010 10100110 11000111
10010010 01011011 10101101 01110100 01000011 10011001 01110101 00011101 11001000 11101110
00110011 11100101 11111100 10100111 10010011 11011110 10110010 10101101 10110111 01001001
01111010 01000001 01100001 11010000 10011100 11010101 11101001 11011011 00001000 01000110
01001110 00101011 00111010 11011011 00000010 11111011 00111001 11000000 00101010 01110011
01011101 10010100 10010011 11011110 11100110 00010101 00001011 00011010 10010100 10000010

00111011 01101001 00001000 00011000 01110011 10001100 10010001 01011001 01110110 10110111
10110010 11000011 01110000 01001111 01110111 11110111 11101101 01010110 10110101 00100010
11001100 00010011 01101001 11100100 11100111 00110101 10010110 10000001 01001111 01000110
00011110 10100110 10111010 10100000 10110100 11010100 11000010 01010010 01110111 00110111
11100011 10011100 01001011 11001001 01101110 10110100 11110001 11001011 01110000 01110011
01011001 10010110 10110010 00000001 00100110 00111011 01100011 00110101 01111110 00000110
11100111 00111001 11111010 01010110 00110101 00101100 01101011 00000111 01110011 01010110
11000001 01110111 00111010 00101000 11100100 11100110 10111010 11011000 01000110 00000000
00011101 10000101 01110010 11011010 00111100 01111111 10111110 00011000 11111100 11111101
00101011 10101011 01001110 01111110 10010101 11100101 01100010 11100100 11110100 01000111
01010100 00010010 01100101 11000100 00111001 11101000 01110011 01010110 10100011 11100111
11011110 10101001 11000000 00111001 11110110 10101011 11110001 10000010 00110000 01001001
11100010 10111001 11011011 01001101 01101010 01010101 10110101 00100111 01000101 11111100
00101001 11001110 00000001 00110100 11101000 10001000 00011111 01111011 10111101 00111000
11100000 01110010 00101011 00100101 00111011 01101100 00100010 00100110 00111011 01000110
01111001 10100011 00111001 00011001 11101111 01001111 00111100 11010100 00111000 00001101
01000011 01101101 00010010 00111000 11001000 00000000 10101000 00100100 01101100 11111101
00101010 01010111 00010101 00001001 00000100 00011110 01101001 01001010 11111010 00100100
00101011 00101101 11000110 01110011 01010001 11110100 00111110 11010101 00100001 00111000
00111000 00111101 00101010 00101001 00011011 11010011 10100111 01111010 11011001 01001011
10010101 00000000 00110111 11010010 10100000 01110011 10011110 11110101 00100110 11101100
00001100 10011010 10000010 01000110 11100111 10100101 00110101 01110110 00110100 11000110
10111001 11000101 01000010 11011000 00000000 11100111 10101101 00001110 11000011 00111000
11100110 10100011 10010100 11110000 01111001 10101011 10001100 01010101 11101111 11011000
10101101 00001000 11011101 10011011 00000010 10100001 01110110 11111110 11101101 00111001
10011000 11101100 11100110 10101011 10111011 01110010 01000110 00101000 10001100 10110111
11110011 00000001 00100100 01101111 01000011 01010001 00110001 10100010 01000010 00110110
01110100 10100110 01100111 10101110 01101010 10010010 01110111 00010011 01000010 00111011
01110011 10011010 10000101 11011011 00111101 00000101 00100011 10011110 10110101 00011001
10010000 00101010 11100100 11010110 11111010 11011110 11100001 10111000 10011100 10011110
10100010 10000110 01101110 11000111 10100101 00110011 11001100 11100011 00100000 11110101
11101011 01001001 10111011 00100111 11101011 01001001 00100110 10011001 01000001 10011110
01111101 00101001 10001100 01001000 01111111 01111010 00111010 01110100 00010100 00110001
00100000 01100100 11111110 01110101 10101011 01111010 01101000 00110110 01000110 11100100
01110100 11000111 01011010 10101111 00100000 11100000 11100100 01010101 10000010 01111101
00101010 00001001 10001111 01000101 00000000 10010010 11000111 00000011 00011101 01001101
01010100 00110111 10111000 00110011 00010111 01010000 00100100 10010000 10111001 00000000
01010111 10101011 01111000 01010101 01000011 01000010 00100101 11101001 11110010 10000001
10001010 11000111 11010001 00111100 00100101 00001001 11111101 11110110 10101101 00011000
01110010 01000111 00010001 00010011 11000000 10101110 10011110 00000100 10001010 11001100
01000111 00001101 10111010 00001000 11100011 00011100 00000000 00101011 10001011 00011011
10001010 10000100 11100001 11001001 00001110 10000110 01110100 11010011 11100110 10111001
10110000 00001110 01000110 00001111 00010100 10001110 10100000 11010100 00010001 10110000
11001111 01001111 11001110 10101100 00110110 01001000 10101111 00011110 00001101 01011111
01010011 01100010 00111110 10000110 10100101 11001111 00011101 01111010 11010100 01001010
00111111 01111001 01010010 10110001 00000001 00110011 10001010 01001101 11011101 11101000
00000000 11000111 11100100 10101100 11111011 11111001 01001010 10001110 10111000 10101011
00001111 00101110 00000110 01101011 00101011 01010010 10011100 00001000 11000001 01110011
11001111 01101010 00101001 11000110 11101110 11000000 01100101 11101010 00110010 11100110
01001100 10010001 11101101 01011001 11110010 00011101 11000011 00011111 10001101 00111110
11100110 01000001 00100001 00101100 00001001 00100011 11010010 10011001 00011110 00001001
00011001 11100011 00111101 01101011 11010001 10000100 01111001 01100010 00111011 00011101
00000111 10000110 11100000 00010001 01000111 10010010 01110010 01001111 01111010 11011101
11001000 00000110 10110011 01110100 10110101 00011110 01010000 00011100 01100011 00011110
10110101 01101011 11001100 00011001 11000101 01110000 11010101 01001101 11001001 11011100
01001100 10010010 01011001 00001001 00111110 10010101 00011000 11000001 11101011 01001101
01111001 00000111 11010110 10100011 11110011 00110011 10010001 01011001 11000101 00111011
10001000 10011010 01011001 01001111 01000100 11100000 01100010 10101011 10010011 11101011
11010100 01010011 10110011 11000001 11001111 01011010 10101001 00100001 11001001 11101111
10001010 11010111 11011001 11001011 01110000 00100100 00110010 00001110 01111011 01010100
01101110 00110010 11100011 00100111 11101001 10001010 01001100 00000011 11010110 10011101
11100101 11111100 11100011 10011110 00101010 10101100 11011110 10000000 00111110 01000001
11000000 00100011 10010011 01010000 01111001 01100001 10111001 10100111 11001011 10111001
01011100 00101000 00111100 00011010 01111010 10101110 11010001 10000110 11101011 01010101
00110111 01101101 00010001 00100111 10010001 11011001 01101001 11011001 00011000 01110000
00000100 10011001 11001111 00010101 10110010 10010110 10000000 00100000 11100000 00000001
11101001 01010011 10100100 01011110 01011111 00100000 00011010 01110011 00110110 00010111
10010001 11000101 01111101 00001011 10101100 11100110 11011101 11011001 11001100 10101001
01011000 10001101 00100010 01010011 10001110 00111010 01010011 10110000 10101010 01001011
00011010 10001101 11101110 10000000 11000111 01000001 10011010 10101001 00110101 11110111
01000010 00110001 11001111 10110101 01001111 10110011 10111011 10110001 01110111 01001000
10110011 00110100 11000000 00001100 00000011 11000111 01011010 11001111 10111001 10111100
11110010 11110000 00000011 00001100 01100110 10101001 11011100 01011101 00110100 10000101

11110001 11000000 11001111 00011001 10101010 00110011 01001010 01111010 11110101 11100110
10110111 10000101 00000110 11110111 00110001 10011101 01010010 11010101 11000101 11101011
00010101 00100011 01110001 00000000 01110111 10101100 11111001 00101110 11000000 00111101
11001001 10101000 11100100 11001001 11110101 11000111 01111010 01101011 10000010 01000000
00011101 10001101 01110110 01000010 10011010 10000110 10010110 00110000 01110010 01101100
01100100 10001100 11010010 00110111 00100111 00100011 00011001 11000101 00100000 10001100
10010000 00111000 11101111 10010011 11110100 10101011 00011011 00110000 01001000 11000110
01101010 01011011 01111000 00011010 01011001 01000100 01101001 11011111 00000000 11010101
00111001 10100100 01000101 10011011 01100011 00100001 10000001 10100100 00100111 10001110
10100111 11010011 00110101 10111101 10100111 11101001 01011000 00000001 11100110 00101110
00001110 00101011 01000110 11001110 11000100 01011010 10010010 01110011 11110011 10011110
10110101 01100101 11100101 00001010 00001000 00100011 10011010 11100011 10101011 10001000
10010100 11010101 10010001 11010011 00001010 01001001 01101010 11000001 00100010 01010101
00011000 01010000 00000000 11111010 01010011 10011000 11010101 01111001 00100110 11000000
11100010 10011000 10110010 10010110 00000011 11010000 11010111 00000011 11010100 11011011
11010000 10111110 00001010 11100111 00000111 00000011 10001100 11111101 01101001 01111100
11010000 01111011 11100111 11010011 00110101 01001100 10110110 00000000 00000111 10101000
11111101 01101001 11111100 00010011 10011110 10011101 11101010 10010101 00011001 00110010
11010011 11101110 01011100 11110011 00101000 00110010 10011100 01100100 00000011 10000011
01010101 11010000 11101110 00011011 01110001 01001110 11001001 01011100 10101000 10101100
01101010 01000001 01011100 01111010 10010110 00010100 11111110 11101100 01111010 10011010
10001010 00110000 01001100 10011001 11101101 11101111 01000000 10010011 11100100 11100110
10101100 11011011 01111100 11011100 01100000 01111010 11010100 11001001 00110100 01010101
10001001 10010001 01000001 11100111 00011100 11111010 11010010 10000101 11101000 00011100
01110101 11101011 01010010 00000001 10110100 00001110 00101010 01010000 10111000 11111001
10101011 00011110 01100110 11000110 11000001 01010111 01100010 00000000 01111111 01010001
01001110 11001110 00010111 00111001 10100110 01011100 11001000 11001101 10000001 01010001
01001101 10010101 10000100 11100111 10011110 00101000 01110001 01010010 01101000 01111011
10010100 11101110 01001111 10011010 11100111 11010011 00111100 01010100 11010110 11010110
11100011 10000010 01111001 10101000 10100001 01011101 11001110 01110001 11010111 00011101
00001111 01111010 10110001 11100110 00000101 10001111 00011101 11101011 01011101 01011110
10001000 01011010 00100010 01000110 11111001 01010011 00000010 10100010 01110000 00001011
11110000 01101010 00110110 10011000 10001100 11100011 10101101 00001001 00100111 11001110
00001110 00110010 01101011 00110100 10110100 00000100 11010000 11101110 00010111 10011100
01110011 01001111 11011000 00001000 11001110 00001111 10111101 00100111 01010011 11111110
00110100 11101001 01100101 11000010 01100100 00001100 01110001 01000011 01011010 11101000
00100100 00100011 00101010 00000001 11000000 11000101 01000101 00100100 10010001 11000101
11011111 10100101 01010011 10111011 11010100 01010110 00011000 11001000 00111101 01111101
10001101 01100010 11011110 11101010 00111001 00111100 00010010 01111000 11110101 10101110
10001000 01100001 11011100 11011110 10100110 01101110 01101001 00011011 01110010 11011101
01000010 00010011 01110001 00100011 00111110 10010101 10011101 01110001 10101000 00101000
00111001 00000111 00100010 10110000 11100100 10111011 00110010 01100100 01100111 00000011
11011110 10100001 00110011 00011101 10100100 01110011 10011010 11101011 10100111 10000101
10110011 00110010 01110101 01011001 10100001 00101110 10100000 01000011 10111111 00111111
01010001 01010100 11100101 10111011 00111001 11100000 11110111 10101010 01101100 11000100
10111111 01010001 10011010 00110000 00011011 10000000 00101011 10100101 01010011 01001000
11001001 11001110 11111010 00010110 11000100 11011100 01100110 10010000 11001110 01000111
00100011 10101001 00111100 10001010 10000010 00010000 11000100 11100000 01111101 01111010
11010101 11001000 01101100 10011010 01010011 11000001 11100111 10101101 01011111 10111010
10110111 01100100 11011101 10111101 10001000 11001011 00110110 01111110 01010011 10000001
01001111 10000110 00101001 00100111 01111100 00100000 11001000 10101101 00101000 01110100
11101111 10010011 11100110 11101011 11010110 10110101 00100001 10110111 01011000 11100011
00011101 00101011 10011110 01111000 10001000 11000001 01011001 00101011 10011010 00101010
01101101 10011001 11010000 11101001 11011001 11000111 00111101 00101011 01000001 00100010
10001010 00100001 10001100 01100000 11010010 10111100 11001011 00001000 11100111 10100101
01100101 11011100 11011101 00010111 11100111 00100100 01110011 11011110 10111001 11010011
10010101 01001101 00001101 10010101 10100000 01011100 10111010 10111011 00010001 10000001
10001100 01110011 11011110 10101001 01011100 01011110 01100100 00000010 00110011 11010010
10101001 01001011 00100011 00011110 01111010 11111010 11010100 01111001 11011100 10011100
01100100 11111010 11010110 11101010 10010010 01011010 10010000 11100110 11011001 01100001
11101110 01001100 10000011 10011111 01011110 10000010 10100101 10000110 00001111 00110111
11101001 01001100 10000110 11010110 01001001 00000010 01110000 01111101 10110000 01101011
01100010 11011010 00001111 00101110 00111100 11100111 10011010 00100110 10010100 00010110
10000101 01010011 01010111 11010100 01110101 10011100 00001010 00010100 00001110 10111110
11110101 10100001 00001100 01100000 00000011 10011110 11011101 11101001 10110000 11011011
10010110 00000000 00101010 11111011 11010110 10011101 10110101 10010011 00011100 00000111
00011000 00010101 11100110 01010110 10101001 11010101 10110011 10100110 00001000 10101111
00010100 01100101 11111001 11000111 00011111 11001110 10101110 11000111 01101111 00101100
10000111 10100111 11010110 10110100 11101101 01101100 01000000 00000011 00111101 10111011
01010110 10101100 00110000 01000011 00010010 00000011 10001110 11111101 01001101 01110001
00111010 10101110 11110111 00110100 00110000 11101101 00110100 11010111 10010000 00011100
00001100 01100100 11110000 01101011 01011110 00011101 00101101 01000110 11001100 11110100
00010101 01101111 11001111 01010000 01000000 00011100 00001010 01101011 01011101 01111100

11011100 00011010 11000010 01110011 01001101 11011111 10100000 10000111 01000011 01100011
00010100 01011011 11110000 10111001 11001001 00011101 01101010 11001010 01011011 11000011
00011000 11100001 00000101 01010110 11111011 01010110 01111000 00011001 11110110 10101001
00010110 01010010 01111001 10101100 10011101 10101101 01110010 00110101 00101100 10010101
00011100 10010000 00111010 11010100 01101110 10101000 01111001 00100011 10011010 01000010
11011000 11001000 10100110 00111100 11101010 00001110 00110011 11101111 10010001 01010010
10010101 11011101 11101100 01100110 00000110 00001111 00110011 10011110 11111110 11110101
00010011 11011010 01100011 10011100 11010100 01110010 01101010 11110000 11000100 00111010
10011110 01111101 01111010 11010101 01001001 00110101 11001000 11000111 00100001 01111111
00111010 00010100 00011011 11101000 00111011 00010110 00100101 10001001 10111010 10000000
01111101 01101010 10111011 01101110 11001111 01001010 01100111 11110110 11010100 01000111
01100110 01010111 00000000 11010011 11000101 11101100 01010010 00000001 11001110 00110010
01111011 11010110 10101110 10010011 00100111 01010100 11001000 11011110 00110101 01101110
00001000 00011001 10101010 00110111 01010110 10000101 01110010 11010001 11111110 01010101
10100010 11100001 01011010 01001100 10100001 10101000 01100101 11011100 10011101 10001001
10101101 00100011 00000111 00010110 01011010 11010100 11000000 01100010 10101110 01001110
11110001 11110011 01100111 10101101 01000001 00110100 01000100 00010000 01111011 01010110
11000101 11010101 10110000 10111000 00000100 10000001 10110010 01010000 00111101 00111000
00110101 10010010 11000110 01001000 00100101 11110010 10100100 01011110 00111010 00011010
11101011 10100011 01101001 01011101 00010100 10101100 01010111 11110010 10000110 00110000
00000101 00001001 00000011 11001001 00100000 10001110 00010101 01110111 10010000 11110110
00011101 11101011 01001110 11001110 11001101 10101110 00001001 11110010 01110001 10000001
11011100 11010110 11111101 10100101 10101010 01011011 10001100 00100111 00100100 11110111
00110100 01110011 11011001 11011000 01001101 11011001 11101000 01010000 11010010 11110100
10000101 10000001 00110111 11011100 01100000 11001010 01111011 01100011 00100000 01010110
10111110 11101100 01110001 01001101 00100111 00011000 11100011 00110100 11011100 11110011
01011001 11110011 00101101 11011011 00100101 10110110 00111001 10001111 10101110 00101001
10111001 11000101 00101111 00011101 00001001 11100110 10100010 11000110 11011100 11010101
00111101 01000010 11000011 10001110 01110011 10001100 11111101 01101001 10100100 11100000
11110101 10100110 00110001 11110101 10100110 00110001 11001000 11000000 10101100 00011011
01101101 11101100 00100001 11111001 11001000 10101000 11001110 00011010 10010111 10101000
00011001 10100110 10110101 01101101 00001000 11011010 11110110 00000100 00011100 00000010
01000101 01000110 11011110 10000010 10011010 11011100 10011010 01101110 11100010 00001111
11100011 01000101 10011100 10010000 00001011 11001000 01001110 10110100 10101010 01001010
11110010 00101001 10101100 01110000 01111011 11010011 01110111 00011101 10011101 01111001
00110101 01010000 10010111 01000110 01010111 10101001 00110111 10011001 11111101 11010001
01010010 01100100 01100011 00111001 11001001 10101010 11111001 11100011 00110100 11100100
00100111 10110101 00111101 11011101 11111010 00000001 00111110 11101100 10000001 01010010
10000011 10000001 11001001 11100010 10101011 00101011 00011010 01111000 01100011 10010001
01000100 11101001 11110011 01101100 00001011 01000010 11000111 10111000 10100111 00101001
11011100 10111101 00101010 00110101 00111000 00111100 10010011 10001010 01110000 00111101
01110001 01010011 00010101 01101101 11110111 00000110 01001001 10111000 11100111 00010100
01100100 00011110 00101010 00110000 01110010 01101001 11011001 00111101 11101010 01010010
10111110 11100011 00011100 01001000 00011001 10100110 00110110 00111010 11010000 01110011
10001010 10001001 11011011 00011100 01110101 10100001 11000111 01011101 10001000 00001001
01110010 00101010 10111100 10100111 00011101 00101010 01000111 01101111 01101010 10101111
00110001 11111001 00110001 10001010 11010001 00110111 11010000 00101101 10101101 11001000
01100101 00111001 00010101 01001110 01010011 11001111 00000111 10000001 01010110 00011100
10000101 11111001 01001101 01010011 10011000 01100111 00111000 10100111 00011000 10110111
10101011 00011110 11100100 01100101 10110110 11110111 10101000 01100110 10010011 11101001
01000011 10111001 11101010 00111000 10101010 10010010 10110001 00111001 11110100 10101110
10001010 00101001 00000101 11001000 10100110 10010100 10101001 10100010 00011011 10000000
01011010 10101001 11011100 01001010 00000110 01001101 01010111 10001001 10000000 10010000
00110001 00111111 10001101 01110110 00101000 01110011 00011000 10110011 01010010 01110110
01010000 00000110 00111011 11010101 00110111 01100011 10011111 10011010 10000000 11011001
00011001 11100011 00011111 01011010 10000001 11001111 11001110 01011011 00110101 01010000
10100111 11011000 01010111 00100010 10111001 10010000 00000001 01010100 00000000 00000010
11110010 00110010 00011000 11100000 10001010 10011110 01010000 00011011 00011001 00111101
00111010 00001010 10100110 01100100 00011111 01101010 00000111 00011101 00001101 01110101
01000101 01011011 10100001 10010100 10000111 01011110 00110110 01100100 11111001 10000111
00110001 10011010 10100110 11100110 00100011 11000001 01011100 00011100 11110101 00010101
01111001 00001110 11101011 10011001 00010101 10111001 00100100 01100100 10011111 01011010
10000010 11110010 00000000 10101100 01001001 00011100 11100111 00110101 10101101 00111101
00110100 01100100 11001001 01110101 00010010 00010011 10000011 11010000 11111101 01101011
01000110 11010100 11110011 10010001 01011001 01110001 10110110 00110000 01110001 11010111
10111101 01101101 11101001 10110001 11111001 10000011 00111000 11001001 11001101 01100011
01011101 01011011 01100010 10100000 10110101 11010000 11101001 01110100 01001000 10110011
11110011 00011111 11100010 11101011 11101101 01011011 11101000 00001000 11100000 01110100
10101100 11011101 00110110 00100000 10010001 00100110 00110001 01011010 01110001 01110101
11110111 10101111 00001010 10101011 01001101 11011110 01001000 11101011 01001010 11000101
11001000 00110001 10001100 01110111 10101011 11110001 00001110 10011001 00110101 01010010
11011101 01111000 11110111 10101011 10110001 00000000 01010000 01100111 10001010 11000011
10010110 11011010 00100010 11011011 00100110 01011100 00011111 10101101 00101001 00000100

00001110 01101001 00010000 00000000 01101000 01100011 11001001 00010100 01011001 10001001
10001100 11100111 00100111 00000100 01100010 10011001 10011110 10111111 11001110 10011100
11000011 00000111 00110101 00011011 10011110 00111000 10101001 11011001 01011101 10000101
10000110 10110011 01110001 11001101 01000100 11101100 00110000 00111111 10011101 00111101
11001101 01000000 11101111 11000001 10100001 11001001 10110010 01010000 10101100 01110000
00111001 10101010 11110010 11001000 00001000 11110100 10100111 00111001 11001000 11001001
00111111 01011010 10101010 11100111 10010001 01011010 11010011 10001011 00101011 01000111
10111000 11110111 10010011 00000010 10100010 01110011 11011110 10001001 01011000 00001010
10101010 11010010 10010011 10011010 11011001 00101011 10110010 01000111 10010110 11100111
00000110 10100010 01100110 00011110 11111001 10101000 01100100 01100010 01111001 00100111
10101101 01000110 11101101 11101000 01110011 01001101 11011010 00001011 10010101 00000010
00011110 11110010 00000001 11110111 11111000 11110110 10101010 11101111 10011101 11011001
00011100 11010011 00011100 11111001 10011001 00111001 11111100 01110011 01001101 11110011
01111001 11101001 01010111 00011000 11101001 01110100 10000111 01101110 10100010 11001100
01111000 00010101 01011101 11100101 00100001 11110010 11000011 10001010 01010110 10010011
00111001 11001001 10101000 11010101 10110111 00011110 01111111 01011010 10110101 10111101
11011000 11101100 00100011 10110111 10101111 01010011 01001100 11011101 11001110 00101001
00011101 10111111 00111111 11100111 01001100 00100111 00011000 00011101 11111101 11101010
10010101 11110110 01000011 01000010 00110011 01101110 00111000 11001111 10110101 00101111
10111101 00110111 00000011 00111101 01101001 10111001 00011001 10101011 01101011 10101000
11010000 11101100 01110001 11000001 10100110 10101110 01110011 11110100 10100111 01100100
01100011 11011110 10011011 00100011 00000101 11100100 10011100 00000001 11001001 10100101
01101101 01101100 00111101 11000111 00010010 00001111 00011000 00100100 10011110 00000000
11110101 00110101 11010110 01111000 01101111 01000001 00110110 10110010 01000111 01110101
01111100 01110001 00101001 00011001 01010101 11110100 11001111 10101101 00101111 10000011
11110100 00100010 10110001 10001101 01000010 11101101 00001000 01100110 11100110 00101000
11011000 01110100 00011110 10110101 11010011 11100011 11110111 10000000 11110101 00110101
11100110 11100011 00110001 00111100 10010111 10100111 00000010 01111001 10101110 11000110
11011101 01000110 00100011 10001100 00010000 00111001 11001111 10101101 01100100 10010110
00111110 01101110 00111001 10101110 10010100 11000110 10110010 11000011 10000010 00110010
01001000 10101100 01011001 10101101 01011010 00110111 11000110 00111000 11001111 00000110
10111100 11011010 01110011 11100101 01010110 01100101 00101101 11000111 01000111 00100110
00110001 10011111 11001110 10101111 10110111 11011101 11100000 01010110 01100010 10000010
10101101 10001111 01010011 01011010 01100011 11101110 01111011 11110111 10101010 01010010
10001010 01111010 00010100 11000110 01000100 00001001 01110011 10011010 01010111 01101101
10000000 10000001 11111100 11110011 01010001 10111011 00010000 11111110 10010101 00011011
10111001 00100110 10001000 10100111 10101011 01000000 00110101 11001001 11011000 01001001
11101001 01011000 10011010 10101100 10011001 00011101 10001000 11000111 10100101 01101010
01011100 10110001 00000011 00000111 10111111 00110101 10001101 01111101 10000110 11000001
10101101 10101000 11010011 01111011 10110001 01011000 11001011 11000110 00111000 00000110
10100101 10110100 01011101 11010010 00000110 11110111 11100010 10100011 01101110 10011100
01010101 11011101 00111110 00110010 01001000 00100011 00010101 11010111 00111001 01011010
00100101 01101100 10001101 11111011 00000000 01000100 01111110 10000010 10100111 10011001
10000110 11011101 11001110 01111010 01111010 01010100 00010001 00111110 00100011 00011100
11100110 10011001 00110100 10000101 10100011 00100000 00000000 01001101 01110001 01011001
11001001 11101010 01100111 10111000 00010110 00000100 10010000 00101001 00010000 01100011
11110001 00110100 11000100 11111011 10111100 11110000 01101001 11000011 10000011 11010110
10011010 11101101 01100000 10110110 10100010 10110001 00111011 01001101 01000100 01011011
10011110 10011000 10100101 01110010 01001011 11110001 11000111 11010110 10010011 00011011
10111101 11110011 11011110 10101001 01111011 10111101 01000010 11100000 11000111 11100110
11100111 10001110 00000111 11100111 01001011 10010000 01011111 10010011 11101111 01010001
10111000 11001111 01011110 00101000 11000111 11001001 10010001 01000110 10011101 00000110
00101011 10110110 01011000 01100000 01010100 10001011 00100110 01000101 01010110 11001001
10101001 00010111 11100110 00011001 10100001 01000111 01001011 10100010 01011001 11000101
01001101 00101000 11011011 10010000 01000111 11010110 10110011 11101110 00101111 10000001
11000010 10100001 00000111 11010100 11111010 01010101 01010111 10010101 11100100 00111111
00110111 00000000 11110110 10100110 10010100 11100011 10011110 11011111 10000101 01111101
00100101 00111000 00100101 01111110 01100011 10011101 10110010 00111001 01100110 01110110
10010000 11100111 11101110 01110101 00010101 00000100 10001100 01000001 11101010 00110000
01111010 00001010 01111011 10010001 10011100 00001110 10011110 10010101 00011011 01110000
11111001 11110100 11110101 11100110 10111010 01100001 01101110 10000110 01001111 01110010
10111100 10000000 10010110 11000111 00111111 10011101 01000110 11101000 01110011 10011110
10011110 10000110 10101100 00111010 11100111 10110110 00101001 10100001 01000000 00011100
01100011 00111110 11100110 10110100 01101011 10010101 01101000 11001100 11100110 10101110
01010111 01011000 11001011 01111101 11010010 00101001 11101010 00000000 00011100 11100000
01010101 10000000 10000011 11010011 11110000 10101001 11101100 01101100 01011110 11101110
01001100 00000001 10000100 00000111 10010011 10001100 11100010 10001001 01010100 10110010
00010010 10000011 01100100 00010110 11010110 11110010 11001110 11111011 01000000 11001110
01111011 01010111 01001001 01100111 01101000 10110110 10010110 11001000 10111011 01000110
11111110 11101100 01000101 01001011 00011100 00010001 01011001 11000100 01110110 01111100
11111110 11111000 11000101 01010111 10011110 11101111 00100011 00011001 00011100 01111110
00110101 11100111 11010100 10101101 00101001 10111011 01000111 01000100 01110100 01000010
10011010 10000110 10101100 10110001 00101100 10111000 11100000 01010101 00111001 01100110

11001110 01111001 00111100 01110010 01101010 10111100 10110011 10010010 01000111 00111000
00111101 11101010 00100011 00100110 01001001 01100010 01111111 00101010 01110000 10100101
00101101 11011001 01001101 10010010 00011001 11001011 00010011 10011110 00000111 01010000
01111011 11010100 10110000 11001010 01110110 00001101 11010101 01011101 01000000 00000000
10010010 00111000 10101001 10011101 10000000 00000000 00010010 00110011 11101101 01011010
01011001 00100001 00100100 11101110 01001101 00100011 10010010 01110000 00001110 01000111
01111010 10010001 01100100 00000010 00111110 01111110 10011000 10101010 11101011 11010011
00100110 10011110 10000011 01110111 00000010 10100101 11111011 11011011 00110011 01001011
10010111 00101101 01001001 01101110 00000001 11111100 01001101 01011000 11001001 01011110
00111010 11100010 10100011 10110111 10001111 01101110 00110001 01010010 01111001 01010010
00110001 11000111 11110101 10101100 00101010 11001001 01001011 01011110 11000101 00001111
10000101 01010101 10001110 11100011 11010111 11111001 01010110 10101101 10101100 00000000
00001100 10110000 11100100 11110100 10101000 10101100 10101101 00000001 01001111 10011011
00111001 11001111 11100001 01011010 00111110 01011000 10001110 00110011 10111000 11010111
00001101 01101001 11101011 10100001 01011100 10011101 01001000 11001000 00000011 10001100
01010010 01100011 00011110 10111110 11100010 10011000 11010011 10101010 11100011 00111111
01001010 10001110 11100010 11110010 00111000 10001011 00000111 11001110 11111110 10100011
00010101 10011100 00100001 00110110 11110100 01000101 00110001 01011101 10111110 01101110
01111011 01110100 11100010 10101011 11011100 01001100 00111010 00000011 10001100 01010101
00111001 10101110 10110011 00011110 01000111 01111010 10101100 11010011 11111001 10000100
10010010 01111111 01011010 11011111 11011001 10111001 01111011 11001100 10011101 10001101
00000100 10010000 00101111 01101111 01111110 10110101 00010001 10010001 10100100 00111110
10111110 11110101 01000101 11100110 00100111 00001011 10011100 11100110 10101101 00100110
00000010 11110101 11101001 10001010 11010101 01000111 10101011 00100000 01110111 00100100
01111111 01011010 10011101 00111000 01011110 10011111 11010010 10101010 00111100 11001010
10000111 00100111 10001010 10100011 01111011 10101000 11100011 00100101 00001111 11101011
01001110 00010100 11011100 10100101 10110000 00110110 10010001 10100101 01110011 01111000
10110001 00100111 11001100 11011000 11110111 10101100 01011011 11001101 01010001 11011000
10011100 00011100 01100011 10110101 01100100 11001111 01110100 01100100 11101010 11011100
10011110 01001101 01010110 01101001 10111101 11101011 10110010 00011000 01011000 10100111
10110001 10001100 11101010 10110111 10110001 01100110 01011011 11000110 10010000 10010010
11100111 00100110 10101011 00111100 11011101 00001110 00111000 00111110 10110101 00000110
01000110 01001001 00011101 01000101 00000100 11100100 01010111 01011010 10000100 01010001
10000011 10011001 00110011 11001000 00100100 00011000 11000000 11001111 10101101 00110111
00111000 11100000 11111110 01010100 01000101 00000011 10111001 00011011 00010100 11100100
11110100 11000101 01101010 01011011 01101001 10000100 10101000 11110011 10111010 01010010
10010100 11010010 11011100 01010110 01101101 10011001 10101001 00001001 01100000 00000110
00111010 11110101 10101011 11010110 10111010 01110100 10000100 00011100 11110001 10011100
01100000 11010110 10111101 10110100 00110000 01000001 11001000 01011110 01111011 00011010
10010010 01001001 11010001 00010111 01110001 00111100 11100111 11110001 10101110 01101001
11010111 10010101 10111101 11010011 01011000 01010011 01011101 01001000 10101101 10101100
01010110 00101100 00001100 01110011 11011110 10101110 00100000 01010100 00100100 11100000
01111110 01010101 01001110 01011011 11000101 00011000 11100111 11101011 01010101 00001101
11110110 01000110 00110001 11001001 00111110 10110101 10010010 10100111 00111010 10001111
01010010 11101110 10010110 10001000 11010101 00110011 10101100 01000111 10011100 01111101
00001001 10101010 10110111 00111010 10000000 11001111 11001000 01110010 01111101 10101011
00100010 01101011 10100010 11001101 11110011 10011100 10011110 10000010 10100010 11011100
01001100 10011000 00100000 10001010 11011001 01010000 01001000 10010111 01010000 10110101
00111101 11011011 00111001 11000001 00111100 01110110 10101000 01011101 11001001 01111110
10011100 11010011 00010010 00011001 00100100 00111001 00000000 10011100 10011010 11011000
10110100 11010010 01001100 10111101 01110010 10010101 01101101 11000010 10011110 10101100
00010010 01110011 00110011 10100011 10000101 10011011 00000011 00011100 11010110 10101101
10010110 10011010 11011000 00000000 00101110 01111101 01101011 01100010 11001111 01001110
10000110 00101110 10110101 01111110 00101111 00100110 00011110 11110101 11000101 01010011
00010010 10101111 01101000 10011011 11000010 10010101 10010101 11011001 01001110 11010011
01001101 01101100 10011100 00000000 00111111 10100101 01101000 11000001 01100100 10100000
10001100 01110010 00111101 11101001 01010110 11101110 00100101 00011000 00000100 01100011
11010110 10101001 11001001 10101011 11000110 10000111 00101000 01110010 00111011 11111011
01010111 00100101 01000111 01010110 01111010 00110011 01011000 01011000 11011011 10000110
00111000 10100010 11000001 00100100 01111101 00101010 11011000 10011110 00011000 10000000
11000000 00000100 11110111 11100010 10111001 01010011 10101001 01111001 11110010 10000011
00011001 00111000 11101000 01101010 01111000 01100101 10010001 10110010 01110010 01110001
01011001 10111010 01001101 00101011 10110010 11010011 10111110 11000111 01000010 11011010
10000010 10000111 11011010 00001110 00110011 01010001 10111101 11100100 10001111 10010000
00001111 01010011 01011001 01110110 11101010 01011011 00100111 00111111 10001101 01011011
10000101 01111101 00000101 01110011 11010100 10001111 00100110 11100011 10111001 01110110
00100110 01100110 00000111 00110101 00100100 01100100 10010011 11010111 11110001 10100100
10000110 00100110 00101000 00110110 10001100 01100111 10101101 01011100 10001010 00001101
10111001 11111010 01010111 00111011 01010111 11010101 00010000 11011101 10000101 10001101
01110110 10111110 01011011 10100101 01011000 11110011 01000010 11110011 01010001 11100111
00000011 00011001 10101010 11010010 11101110 01100110 00011000 11101001 11010000 11010010
10110011 01101010 11000010 01101100 00101110 10110101 00000001 00011110 01110000 01111110
01110011 01011000 11010111 00110111 01110011 10110111 11011100 00100100 00001010 11010101

01001101 00110100 11001010 01110010 01111010 11010101 11011011 01101011 00011000 01100001
11111011 11101011 10011010 10101000 11001010 00010001 01110110 01100100 11101100 01110010
00101111 00011100 11100100 01101110 11011011 00100111 11010110 10101011 11001000 11101110
10111101 01110010 00001111 10111101 01110111 01010111 00110011 01000101 00011111 11001010
10000011 10001111 01111010 11001110 10011110 01001000 00100101 11001111 10011000 10001010
11000011 11011100 01010101 01000111 00010001 11100100 01010010 01100111 00011010 11110111
00100100 00111111 10100101 00000010 11111011 10110000 00111101 11101011 10100010 10111001
10110001 11010011 10100101 01000011 10111110 00000011 10010011 10001110 01010100 11100000
11010110 01101101 11000111 10000110 11000100 10000011 00110110 10101101 00100010 00010010
01111010 00110000 11001110 01101011 10110010 00110101 00100000 11111110 00101101 00000111
01110100 11000110 01011011 01101010 01000100 01100000 11101110 00111100 01111011 11010110
10001100 00011010 10100110 01000110 00100100 11110100 11111010 11010110 00010001 11010001
00110101 00111000 01011011 00000010 00011100 10000001 11001110 01000011 00001010 10011010
00111011 00011011 11011000 11011000 10110100 10010110 11000101 01000111 11111011 11000000
11010011 10010101 00111000 00111101 01010011 00011110 10001100 11101000 00010010 01110101
10010011 00011000 00100000 11100111 10011100 11010011 10011011 01001101 01011011 10000010
00011010 01001100 11111011 01100010 10011001 10100010 01101001 11001101 11100101 11111001
11010011 10010010 00010000 11110100 01010010 00111001 10101101 10001110 00000110 01000101
01100000 10010111 00101011 00100001 11101000 00110010 00101000 11010110 00110101 00010001
10000101 00000000 00000001 10001100 11010011 11011011 00100000 01111010 10011111 01011010
01000111 11001111 00000000 11110101 10101000 11001001 00100111 00011100 00011111 01111010
00100011 00100111 10110010 00000111 10101000 11101100 11110110 10100110 10110000 11100111
10100101 00011011 01001001 00110100 00111000 11110111 00010100 01011010 00111011 10110010
01001000 11011011 10110101 00110101 10001110 00111000 00110100 11110011 11101011 11011111
10111101 01000111 11010111 10011010 01110111 10110110 10101001 10010100 10000100 01100011
10010001 11101101 11101011 01001100 11100011 11010110 10010101 10110010 01001110 00111010
01010011 01110001 10000011 11101011 01000010 01011100 11000001 11100110 00001010 00111111
00101111 01111010 10001101 10001101 00111000 10011100 10001110 00101010 00110111 00111001
11000110 00000111 11010110 10101101 10111011 11101000 00001000 01101011 01100111 10101000
11111101 01101001 10001100 11111110 10010100 10101111 11010011 00111001 11001101 01000110
11001110 00111010 11010001 00010110 10000001 10101011 00000110 01001111 00000011 10111111
01111010 00001110 01111110 10010101 00011011 00110000 11101101 01001110 11011101 10010001
01001101 00100100 00110001 11001011 10010011 11000110 01101001 11101010 11011100 01110101
10101000 00110010 01000101 00111101 01001111 00000011 10001100 11010010 11010111 10100011
00100001 00010110 00010110 01001111 10010111 11111010 11010011 11010110 01001111 01011010
10101111 10111011 10100101 01001001 10011111 01001110 10010100 01011001 01101100 11011001
01001000 10110010 10101100 00110001 11000101 00101111 00000111 00000111 00111101 01101010
10111010 10110110 00001111 11010110 10100111 01001010 01010010 10000010 10110101 10011000
11000101 01010010 01111010 01110100 11100110 10011101 10010011 10011100 00011010 01100111
00111000 00100100 11010010 01101110 11001001 11101011 11001111 10111101 01000101 00110101
00010100 11101101 01110001 01011000 10010011 01110001 00011111 11111101 01111010 10001110
01011100 11110010 11011111 10100101 00110101 10011100 00110111 01011111 11010110 10100011
01111001 00111011 00000011 10010011 11101111 01011010 00100101 01100110 11010011 01100100
10111011 10001110 01111001 00000110 00000110 01111000 10101000 00100100 00111001 00111100
01111110 00010100 10111011 10111001 00100000 10001010 10001010 01010010 00000000 11001000
10101010 10000100 01010011 01001110 11101100 00001000 00100110 11000111 01011111 11001110
10101001 11001000 11011100 01100111 11010010 10101101 11001010 11111111 00000000 10101111
01011010 10100101 00101001 11001001 00100010 10101110 00110000 10001011 11011101 10000101
11001010 11110011 10110000 11000111 00010101 10011111 00101100 10000100 00000111 00000000
11111101 01001101 01011010 10011011 00000010 10101000 11011100 10000010 00010111 00111001
11100011 11010010 10110111 10100101 00010100 10011110 11100100 11011110 11101000 10100011
00110110 00111001 11000101 01010101 01000010 01110111 01100011 01110000 00001001 10011110
10110101 01100110 11100000 11100000 11111011 11010101 01000111 00100100 11110001 01011110
10000100 00010011 10110001 10001100 10010110 10000101 11100101 01100000 01100011 11101011
01010101 11100111 10010000 11101100 11100000 11111110 00010100 11001000 10001011 00101010
01100001 11101010 00111011 10010110 11000110 00110011 11010011 10100101 01011100 00101001
10101110 10100010 10111011 10110001 00010111 00111000 11011101 11101001 11011111 11010110
10101000 11001000 01001001 10011011 00111111 10001101 01011000 10010010 01000011 10001110
10111100 10001110 10010101 01011111 10010110 00111100 01110100 11110101 10101110 10001000
01000100 10000110 11110100 00100110 10110111 10010100 10000011 00100011 10000011 10001001
01111010 01010100 00110011 01001010 11110010 11001101 10001001 00001110 01110001 11010100
11010100 01110010 10011111 00101001 00110000 00110001 10010010 01111010 11010100 11010110
10110000 10010110 00111100 10110110 01110011 11101001 01010101 00111101 00110101 01100100
01101010 11110100 00010101 00110010 01111000 01000001 01011101 00111110 10000011 01101110
11001010 00110010 11100100 01110101 11101001 10001010 10100111 01100101 01101000 01110010
00111000 11100011 11010000 11110111 10101110 10010010 11000010 00110101 01011100 00001100
01010111 10011101 01011110 10101010 01001010 11000111 01001101 00101010 01111101 11001101
01011011 01111000 11001110 00110010 00001111 00000010 10101111 11000000 10100100 10000000
01111101 01101010 10011100 00100011 11110010 11101110 00101011 01001010 00000000 01110000
00001111 11101001 01011110 01011100 10010101 11110111 00111010 00111101 00001011 01010110
11101011 10110111 11111010 11010101 11010100 00011001 00010101 01011110 00100101 00100100
01100110 10101101 11000100 00111110 01011010 11001111 01001000 10101101 00000001 10111110
11100010 11100010 10011000 01110010 00111001 01011010 10010001 10000110 01000111 00010101

00011011 10011100 00001110 10110101 10011010 01010010 00010011 01101000 01101111 00111000
11101011 01010000 01001011 10010001 11010010 10100100 01110110 11000110 01101010 10111011
01001001 10010011 11101100 00101010 11010100 00010111 01010001 11101010 00100011 00011100
11110001 01010000 01001010 01111101 10101001 01011110 01001110 01001001 00010101 00001100
10110010 11110110 00011111 10011101 01011010 10001111 01001011 11011000 00010000 11000111
01101010 10101111 00101001 11100011 11110001 11101011 01000100 10101101 10011110 11111100
11010101 01101001 00011000 11100011 10001010 10111110 01000100 10000010 11001100 10010010
01000110 11101011 01010101 00100100 01101110 11110100 11001001 01100101 00111000 11111111
00000000 11101011 11010100 01001100 11011100 01110101 10101011 11100100 01010111 10111010
00000001 00111100 11011110 01001000 00111111 10000101 01000110 11110010 10010101 11101110
01101010 00011001 01011100 01110000 01101010 00110010 11000100 01110111 11100111 11011100
11010101 00101010 01110111 11011100 01011110 10000001 10111000 10011001 00111011 00001010
01001111 00110000 00010011 11001101 01000100 11100100 10010110 11000111 01000000 01111011
11010010 11100000 00001110 01001101 01101011 00011011 10101101 00010000 10011011 00010101
10011011 10101110 11010011 01001101 01111110 10111100 11110101 10100000 10010001 10111111
10001010 10001101 11001111 10110111 11010111 11011110 10110100 10001110 10111010 00010101
01110001 01111111 11011110 10100100 01110110 00000010 10000101 01101111 10010011 10100111
11100111 01001100 01101110 01111010 01010100 11111011 00110110 00110100 00001100 01000001
01001110 11111001 00110100 00101111 00000011 11010110 10010000 10011110 00101001 10111110
01100111 00100011 11010010 10101010 11101110 11111010 10000010 00011110 11011101 01000101
01101101 11111000 01100111 01001000 00111010 10001101 11011010 01001011 00101000 00011111
01100110 10001101 10110010 11011001 11101110 01000111 01001010 11001111 11010010 10101100
10100100 11010101 01101111 01010010 11011110 00000001 10000001 11010101 10011000 11110100
00000010 10111101 00110110 11001010 11001110 00011101 00111110 11010101 00100001 10000001
01110000 10000010 10111000 11110001 10111000 10101111 01100110 10101100 10110111 00010011
11101100 01011001 01001110 10000001 01111111 01001010 01101011 11000110 01110011 10011010
10000001 00011111 01110100 10011111 01111011 00011100 11010101 11010101 00111111 00100101
01111000 11010010 01110111 01011011 11101110 00000001 00001001 00001000 01000111 11101011
01001110 10111001 10000101 01011001 00001001 00000011 10101111 01111010 01100110 01000001
11101100 01101010 01000100 10010011 01101111 00001110 00110011 01011100 11101101 01111001
10010100 10001100 11011001 10100000 11101111 10001110 10010100 11111000 10111111 11010101
01110101 10101011 01110011 00000101 00101000 01001101 01010010 11001001 00011110 10011111
01001010 10111010 01110111 01111010 11011000 01101101 11011100 01101011 11110000 00001110
00111111 01011010 10000110 01010011 10000101 10100101 10111000 10011010 00110101 01100000
00001001 11111001 11001111 01101010 10000001 10011011 00111111 11000101 01011101 00010000
01010110 00000010 10111101 11001011 00010010 00000111 11101011 01011001 01110011 10101110
01011011 00111001 10101101 00001011 10010011 11001111 10111101 01100110 11011100 00010110
00100111 00010101 10111100 00110111 11010001 10001001 00110010 10100011 10000000 00001110
00111011 01111111 00111010 11010000 10110000 01011111 10010011 11011110 10110011 00100110
00011000 11100011 00100111 11101011 01011010 00011010 01111011 01111100 10000000 01100100
11110100 11101111 01011010 11010100 01011110 11101001 01000110 10011010 00011111 10010111
10001010 01111010 00101110 00010100 00010011 11010100 11010100 00111000 00111001 00011110
10100111 11010010 10100111 11000111 00111001 00100111 10101101 01110010 10100101 11011000
10011111 01000001 10001110 00000001 11100000 01100100 01110011 01001110 10001000 01100000
11100010 10100110 11011011 10000001 11001111 00110100 11011001 00001010 11100011 00000110
10011011 01110111 01100001 01110001 10001111 10001110 11111100 11010010 00000000 00110110
10001111 10101111 11010010 10100100 01101100 00000001 11000000 11111100 01101010 00010010
00001001 11101101 10010011 01000101 10010101 11000110 01000111 00110011 01100100 11100010
10010001 10000001 01010001 11011110 10100100 11110010 11001110 01000000 00111101 11101000
10010100 01100000 01111101 00101010 11010100 00101111 10101010 01100100 01011100 10101110
10101011 10010011 11110011 01010010 11100011 11011011 11110101 10100111 10110010 10011100
00010011 10001111 11010110 10010101 01000000 11000101 00110101 00010100 11110110 01100011
10111101 10001111 00110001 01110010 00111101 00110001 10001010 10000111 01111110 11100000
01001001 11101101 11010000 10011110 11110101 00100011 10011100 00111110 01110001 10011100
10011110 11111110 10010101 00010011 10101110 01000110 00110001 11000000 10101111 10100111
10001010 01011011 10011001 00111011 10010000 00110110 11010000 00001001 00111101 11111010
01110011 01001101 01100000 01111000 11110111 11110111 10101001 00011101 00000001 10010011
00100011 10010100 11000111 01001111 01111010 00110110 11100100 01111110 01111100 01010110
10010001 10110010 11101010 01100100 11001000 00110110 10010000 00110010 00001001 11110110
10100101 01001000 11001001 11100100 10001110 00001111 10100101 01011010 01001000 01000001
01100000 11011000 00111100 11111011 11010101 11101011 00111011 00111101 10100000 00110100
10000001 00110001 11101001 10011100 11100110 10100010 01110101 00101100 10101110 11000101
01101011 10110010 00011101 00111011 01001111 01101001 00011011 01110001 11101000 00001111
11100111 01011011 00101101 00100111 11011001 00100001 01110100 01000010 00000000 11001110
01001111 11010110 10100010 01101001 10000100 01101000 10010001 10001010 10101001 01110010
11000101 10001111 10101101 01100010 11011111 10110100 11011100 11010010 11011100 10100010
01001101 01110001 10111111 00100000 11100111 00011111 01011010 10101010 00110010 01000001
00111000 11000000 00111101 01101001 11001011 11000011 10001111 01000011 01010010 00000000
01001110 01000000 10100111 00011000 10101000 11101111 10110000 10101101 01110010 10101001
00101010 01000110 01110001 11010010 10000100 11101001 10010001 11010110 10100110 11110010
10110011 11010100 01100000 10011010 00111100 10111101 10101001 10001100 01110000 00000111
00110101 01101011 01010111 10111000 00110100 11000110 00000011 10000000 00000110 00111001
10101001 01010100 01100100 10001111 10101101 00110111 11001011 11110011 00001110 01110000

01000101 00111000 00001100 11111011 01100010 10100110 01110001 10110110 11000101 01011010
11000100 11011100 00010001 11101011 01010010 11011011 10101001 11011101 10000000 00111111
00011010 10001001 00010100 10111110 00000000 00011111 10010101 01101010 11011000 01000001
10000101 11100111 11110000 10101100 10100111 00111000 11000100 10100100 10011011 00000100
01011001 00000111 00011011 01001001 11100111 10110101 01101010 11011011 01011011 10000101
10001111 00111101 01111110 10110100 11010100 01010101 10001111 10011110 11111110 10110101
00011100 11110111 01100101 01010011 01101110 01101011 10010110 10101100 10111001 11011101
10100010 10001101 10110110 01000101 11100100 10011001 01010111 10101110 00111000 11101111
01010101 11101110 11101110 11000111 11001110 00000001 10101100 10011001 11101111 00001001
01011110 00111111 00011010 10100110 01100110 00101100 00111010 10011010 11001101 01010001
01110110 11010100 10010110 11111011 00010111 00100110 10111100 00000011 11101010 01101010
10000100 11010111 01001100 11000100 11010100 01001110 01111001 11100111 10011111 01111010
10000101 10011011 00011101 00111111 00111010 11101100 10100111 01001001 01101110 10001100
11111001 11000111 11111001 11001101 10001100 11110100 00010100 01111001 10111011 10000001
11000101 01000000 11100100 10010001 10001110 01000110 01101010 01111000 01100010 11000110
00111101 00111101 00101011 01001101 00100000 01001001 00111101 10110110 11101101 10000001
10111101 00101010 01101001 01101110 00111100 10110001 11000111 01110001 01010101 11100110
10011011 11001001 01011110 00001110 00010011 11111001 01010110 00101101 11100110 10100100
00110000 01111100 10110010 00001101 01010100 00101001 11111011 01000111 10101001 00101110
01101010 00000101 11011011 10101011 11010101 11011011 10011100 11110000 01111111 01011010
11001010 10010110 11101100 10110001 00100000 00010011 01010100 01011110 01110110 10010001
10110010 01001111 00011101 01101001 00011001 10110010 01111001 00000011 00011110 10110101
11011101 00011100 00111100 01100001 10110001 11001011 01010010 10101011 01100100 10000101
10111001 11011011 10111000 10011100 01111010 11110110 10100000 10010010 01001000 11000001
11000000 11110101 10101000 10100011 00011000 01111100 10000001 11000111 01111100 11010100
10001010 01001111 01101110 11111100 11010101 00110011 00010110 11011001 00100001 00000100
00001101 10111001 11001000 11101111 01010111 00101100 01100000 00001101 11001100 10011101
00001111 11110011 10101010 10001011 00100001 00011100 11100111 11111110 00000111 01001010
11010111 00001101 11011000 11110001 10001111 01011010 01001110 00001101 10101101 00000110
10100110 10001101 11110100 10011010 00011000 11100011 11011010 10000011 11100111 00011101
11111101 00101010 00111001 00110101 00010000 10101010 01111001 11000110 00111010 10011010
11100111 11011110 01101100 10000000 00001001 00111000 00111110 10000110 10010011 01111110
01001001 00000011 00111101 00111010 00011110 01101011 00100111 10000111 11101110 11001011
11110110 11000110 11000011 11011111 00010001 11010000 11110011 11101010 01101010 10100011
01011100 01100100 11110010 11011100 11100111 00110101 01000000 10010011 11010001 11111001
11001111 01111010 01111010 00000110 11000000 00110101 10100010 10100110 10001001 01110101
00011011 00101111 10110100 11100101 10001111 00100111 11110101 10100110 00110011 00010010
11100000 01010101 01100110 00011011 10001110 00111001 10101001 10010001 00110000 00000001
00011101 01111101 11101000 01101000 00111001 11001001 10010110 00100110 01110011 11001111
01001100 11110101 11110100 00010101 01110010 00101000 00000110 01110111 00010010 01101010
10100100 01101100 01000111 01011110 10111110 10010101 01100001 10100111 01100000 00111110
01010000 00001000 11001111 00100000 10011010 11001001 11010011 10010011 11011000 10110101
01010001 01110101 00110101 01100000 00111011 01000111 00011101 00111111 00101100 01010101
10111111 10110110 10001000 11111000 00000111 00000111 10110101 01110011 01101111 01111010
11000000 00011110 01110000 01111110 10010101 01010001 11101110 11011011 00100100 10010110
11101010 01101010 00011110 00010011 10011001 01111011 11000110 10001011 00010001 01100011
10101000 10010011 01010011 01100101 00011001 00101101 10010010 00001111 01111110 10110101
01000110 01111101 01001100 10000111 00101100 11101111 11001001 11101001 11001101 01110011
11101101 00110011 00010010 01000110 11101111 01111100 01111010 11010100 00101111 00101111
10011000 10100011 10111101 00101000 01100001 00100010 10110101 00100101 11100010 00011011
00110110 10011110 11111000 11100000 10001101 11000111 10101111 10101101 01000110 00101110
10100101 00111101 00110011 11010111 10011100 01010110 01011100 01111110 01100001 00100000
11111010 11010101 11011011 01000101 00101010 00110011 10011100 00000011 11011111 11101011
01011011 10111010 01110001 01001000 10001111 01101010 11101110 01101101 11011000 11011101
10011000 11111010 10000010 00110001 11101010 00111011 01010110 11110101 10000100 10011110
01111110 00001000 11001111 01001110 11010101 11001100 11011011 10110000 00011000 00001110
00111001 11110101 11001101 01101010 11011010 11011101 11111001 00111000 00110000 11001000
00110111 11111110 10010101 11100111 11010101 10100011 11001111 00010110 11010001 11010111
01001010 10110111 01110011 10110100 10110000 10110110 11011101 00011110 00001110 01111001
11110101 10101101 01111000 01101101 00010101 00110000 00110011 11110101 00110101 11001010
11101001 11011010 11111010 11000101 11110010 11001111 10011100 01110110 00100010 10111010
01101011 01001011 11010101 10011010 00101100 10000110 00000111 00111110 11110101 11100011
11100010 10101000 01001101 01101011 01100011 10101110 11111100 11111011 00010111 10011001
01010101 01111010 00011110 01101001 00110111 01110011 10000000 00001111 00111101 11101010
10110111 10011100 10111011 11001010 10010110 11100110 10011001 00101101 11101100 01010001
00100001 00101111 00100000 11100011 10111101 01110001 01000010 00010101 00100100 11110100
01000000 01011111 11110010 11110010 00000110 01101001 11011111 10111010 10001001 01010000
00110110 00110011 11010100 11010111 00110101 01111101 11100010 00101000 10100001 10001101
11011000 00011100 10000001 11101000 01101011 00101010 01101101 01111010 01001011 11101001
00111111 11010001 01110011 10011111 10101101 01101111 00001100 00101101 01000111 01111101
00110100 00100010 11101000 11101101 10101110 00110101 00101000 00100000 11000111 11001101
11001111 01110000 00101011 00110110 01111101 01011001 10100101 01111101 10110000 00000010
11000100 11110110 00000010 10110000 11100001 01001000 01100011 00111110 01110101 11110100

11111011 11111101 01010101 01001111 11110101 10101011 10010001 11101010 11110110 11101001
10000101 10110010 01000001 00011000 11001111 01011111 10101101 00110111 10000100 11100100
11010100 10101011 00011010 00001011 01101111 01110101 00110001 00110010 01001010 11100010
00100100 00111110 10100111 11111010 01010100 11000010 00011011 01111000 11111000 01110010
01100100 00111101 11110011 01011001 01001011 10101000 01001001 00110111 11001011 10111011
00100110 10101110 11000011 00011110 11100011 11010111 10011110 11111001 10101100 10011100
01101100 11001001 10110001 00110111 11011010 00100011 10001100 01100110 00011000 10110000
01000111 11101011 01010000 11001001 01110001 00110001 01000010 00111001 11101011 01010111
10100000 10110100 01011111 11100011 11000101 01011100 00010000 11000101 10001110 00111010
00010001 01000011 10010100 00101101 11100110 00110011 00001111 01101100 11100011 00111001
00000111 00100111 11010100 01010100 11010110 10010110 11100111 01110110 11101001 00110010
01000111 10100101 01101001 01001101 10110100 10011100 00000001 11010011 10100001 10100110
11110001 10001100 01110100 10100111 00000101 01111101 01000001 11001000 00111001 11101001
10011100 11010010 00110001 00100111 11101001 11010110 10010100 10000011 11010100 11110001
01001000 01001000 11101011 01011101 01001111 01100010 00000100 01110110 00011100 01111111
00111010 01100010 10110001 11000001 11001111 01001010 00011011 00011001 11001001 00110100
01100111 10001110 00101010 00101111 01111101 10011000 11111101 00000100 01100011 11110010
11110101 10100110 00000011 11101011 11011110 10010011 01110111 00110100 11010110 00010100
00110100 11010010 00010000 00110110 01001001 00111100 11110001 01001101 00111000 11100111
00000110 10010101 10001111 00011100 01010100 01100100 11100000 11010100 11000100 10111111
00100000 11001001 00011101 00101001 10001101 11010111 00010100 11110110 11101111 10011010
10001101 10011000 01111101 11011100 11110011 11101011 01011010 01000101 11011011 01000111
10110000 00001100 00100011 10110110 01110001 11011110 10010001 11111000 11101110 01101000
01101100 10011010 01001001 01011011 00011100 00010001 01001101 00101000 11101010 11000011
01010100 00110011 00011100 00011111 01001010 10001010 01011111 10010110 10011100 01001110
00111000 11001111 00010101 00010100 11001101 11110010 01110101 10100001 01010011 01010111
00010101 11000100 01010011 10011110 01110001 01001101 01101110 01111101 10101001 10100010
01001110 00111101 11101000 11101101 11001001 10101101 00100101 00011011 01011011 10011000
00110100 00100100 01011110 01110011 11001111 01111110 10010100 11101101 11011110 10010101
00001111 10011000 00001001 11100011 10001010 10010011 00111110 10000110 10100010 01001010
00101000 01010111 01000100 10001010 01110001 01010010 00000110 11110100 11101001 01010000
00101001 11101100 01101010 01000100 11100110 10011011 11110111 10010101 10010011 00010011
00100111 10001100 11111010 10011010 10010101 01001110 00001111 00011100 11010101 01001101
11011000 00111000 11000111 01011010 10011000 00011110 01111110 01010011 11000101 00100111
00011111 10011001 01001000 10011011 00111001 11101010 01111011 11010010 00110011 01110110
00100011 10011111 01011010 01100110 01110001 01001000 11101111 11011110 10010111 00100111
01010000 11101010 00000100 10000000 00101010 00000110 11101011 10011010 01111111 00100111
00110101 00010011 00011010 01111011 11101010 00110110 00111011 00111100 10001111 11101011
01010000 11001000 11011000 00010100 11100110 00111101 11000101 01000011 00101111 00111001
11100110 10100110 00001001 01011111 01000010 00011001 00011011 10010001 10001110 00111011
01010101 00111001 10001110 00011011 11100101 10101001 10011110 01001101 10100100 00001010
10101111 01110000 11011001 00111110 11010101 10110101 10010101 11000101 10100001 01010110
11100010 01000000 01111000 11101111 01010100 01011101 11110001 11111111 00000000 11010111
10101011 01001110 01000110 11110011 11000111 00111110 10110101 01010010 01101111 10111111
11000110 01111101 11001001 10101110 10101000 10100101 01100001 00111111 00100010 10010100
10111001 01100000 01111010 01100111 10101101 01010101 01100011 11000001 00010101 01101001
11000001 00000100 11110010 00000110 01111101 10101010 10101011 10001100 00001111 10101101
01110110 11000001 10100011 00000110 01000110 11101100 11010101 00011100 11001101 10011110
11110100 11100110 01101100 01110101 11001000 10101000 01011100 11100100 00011110 11111001
10101110 10001000 11011010 11110111 00100001 10010001 01001001 11110101 10101000 10010101
10110110 10101001 00111100 10000000 01001111 10101111 01111010 00100100 11001110 01111111
10100110 01101010 00010000 01110010 01110000 10111001 11110110 10101110 10000100 11101101
10101001 10011011 01111010 10010011 01100001 10100101 10010010 00111100 11111101 11001100
01110011 10001111 01011010 11010101 10110101 10001100 10010110 00000111 00010101 01001010
11011010 00000110 00100011 00100000 01100100 11110101 10101101 10101101 00110110 00101101
10101011 10111001 11111001 00100100 11110001 11101101 01011100 10011000 10001010 10100110
10010100 11010011 01101100 11010100 10110110 10001000 00101000 00000111 00011001 00111110
10110101 10110001 01101101 00010111 11001010 00110000 01111011 01010110 01111100 00100111
10011100 11110111 10101101 00111000 00001111 00011000 11000000 11101001 01011110 01010101
01010110 10011010 00111011 10010010 01000101 11011000 00000110 00110000 00111001 11111100
01101011 01011010 11010000 00010010 00110010 01111111 00101010 11001100 10110111 00000100
11100011 01110101 01101010 01011011 11110100 11100000 11100111 11010110 10111001 01100111
10110000 01101000 10110110 00101110 00100111 00000011 00011101 10101010 01010000 11011011
01000000 11101111 01010000 10101001 11111001 01110001 01001110 11001111 10111101 01000101
10110100 00100100 10011011 00100011 00111111 11001110 10101010 01011101 11100100 10011101
10101011 10010001 01001111 01111001 00001000 11100010 10100001 01100010 00001001 11000101
00111011 01101011 01110000 01001100 01101111 10011011 10010100 00011000 11100100 01010100
00001110 11000111 00111001 11001111 00010100 10101100 01000100 01100000 10101000 11101000
00101010 00010111 10010000 00010000 01000111 01111111 01011010 11010110 00010010 01001101
01011101 10010100 11111011 10001101 01111001 00001000 00001101 10001010 10101111 00101100
10100000 11111011 01100010 10011100 11100100 11010101 01111001 01001111 00111001 10100010
01011010 01101010 01010101 10001000 11011110 01000001 11001101 01000000 11000110 10000111
10010000 01110011 11001110 00111110 10110101 01010010 01001001 01001010 01111101 00111010

11010110 10110110 01101000 01001100 01111101 11000001 11000111 01111010 10101001 00101100
10001100 00001000 11110100 10100111 00110100 10011011 10000111 01011010 10101111 00101100
10011100 11100000 01110101 10101011 01001001 01011000 00110110 00010001 11001011 00010011
10010000 01000110 00101010 00011101 11000100 10110110 01001101 00001110 11011100 11100011
11010111 10101101 01000110 10111000 00011101 11001101 00110100 10101100 01100110 01001000
01011011 11010111 10100101 00110000 10011100 11110011 11001101 00100011 01110010 01111101
10101001 00110011 10011110 10010101 10100100 01010101 11010101 10001011 10110110 10000011
10110010 00110011 01001000 01111101 01101000 00101011 11111001 11010010 00110000 00111000
11000101 00011011 01101100 11000000 01101011 00110111 00000111 00100110 10000100 00000111
00110100 11111101 10011011 01110000 01110010 00101001 10111101 10111111 11000010 10000110
11110100 10110000 11010010 01100011 01001001 00000111 10001010 01100111 00100100 10000000
00000001 00100100 10011100 01111101 01101001 11101110 00111001 11111001 01111010 11010111
01010111 11100000 10001101 00011000 11001111 00101111 11011011 01101110 10010111 00110001
01000100 01111111 01110110 00001111 01110011 11101011 01010011 00111010 10001010 10011100
01011011 01111011 00001100 11101001 00111100 00110001 10100101 10001101 00110011 01001100
01000000 01000000 11111011 01000100 10011111 00111100 10000111 11101011 11011010 10110101
00100110 10010011 00001001 01001110 10010011 00000000 01111010 01100111 11010010 10101011
11001011 11010011 10101101 01111100 11110101 01001010 10010010 10010100 11101110 11111010
10010010 01000100 10011111 10111100 10011000 01110000 00101011 01000000 01100000 10101101
01010000 10000111 10000011 10010001 01010110 10100001 10010000 10010111 11000001 11111110
01010101 00001110 11111101 01000111 01100010 01010110 11101001 10000001 01001100 01010110
11000111 00000110 10100111 01010001 11001110 01001101 00100100 10001011 10011110 01001111
00100010 10110001 11010101 01101110 01011010 11010000 10000010 01100110 00011011 00111110
10110101 10011101 01110111 00111000 10110111 10001000 10010011 11001001 11000111 00000110
10110100 00100110 11000100 01101000 01000001 11101001 01011100 11000110 10110111 00101001
00100011 00000000 11100100 01010111 01001101 00001011 10110110 00001101 10011001 01110011
11011110 00110001 10011000 11100001 10001110 01111110 10110101 01110110 11010010 01110110
00110001 10001110 01111001 10101100 00010110 11100101 10001111 00110101 10100011 01100001
00110000 00011000 00011001 11110110 10101110 11111001 11010011 01010110 00101001 00101101
00001101 00011001 10001001 11011000 01001101 01100111 10010110 00100100 11010110 10010100
10100011 00110000 10011100 01111110 00110101 10011000 11111001 00011001 10101100 11101001
01011000 10010100 10101100 11001010 11010011 00110001 11011111 10001110 01111000 10101011
10010110 00100111 10110111 10100101 01010001 10010100 11100000 11100111 10111101 01011000
10110010 01111100 00111111 00100111 10101101 01101101 00110101 10100001 01001101 10011011
01100001 10110110 10101000 00011001 10101001 11011011 00100001 01111010 01010101 01000101
00111100 00000011 11011010 10100111 11110011 00110111 00000011 11010110 10111000 11011111
10100001 10011011 01100100 10111110 01101110 01010011 00000011 11010011 10101101 00100010
00001100 11110011 11001111 11100010 00101000 10001000 00001110 00000000 11101011 11011110
10100110 01000000 00000111 11010110 10001011 00101011 00001001 10000110 00000001 01001010
00010000 11101101 10100001 11010100 11100011 10001010 01101001 00011000 00011100 11110011
10011010 00010011 01001110 11110110 00001011 01011100 01101100 11000111 10111001 11101011
01001101 01000000 00100100 00011110 11110100 01001010 00000001 11101011 01001011 00011000
11100011 00000111 10100101 01011011 01011100 10001010 11110111 00000100 01000101 00110001
00101011 10001100 01110111 10101000 00110010 01111011 00001010 10011110 01110011 11000001
11011011 11011100 11010101 01110000 00000111 01100001 01010100 10100000 11100011 11010010
11100001 01110011 11001101 01110110 10011100 10001111 01001010 10001111 00000100 10011101
10110101 00111110 11010011 10000000 00111111 01011010 01111010 11000011 10010011 10011111
01000011 01011111 01001001 00010110 11101111 01100100 01100010 11101111 01100010 00010000
10100001 01111011 01110011 01001110 01001000 10000011 00111111 00011101 00111011 11010100
10111011 01110010 11111001 11011011 01001010 10011000 11001110 01101001 00111001 01011011
01000110 00110101 00000110 11110111 00001000 11100011 00000000 11010100 11101111 00101000
00100011 00000000 11111110 01010100 11000110 01100001 10001100 01100010 10100011 11011100
10100010 01000001 11000111 00011000 11111101 01101010 01011010 01110111 10111011 00101011
01000100 00111001 10110011 10010011 11101011 01000011 01110011 11001001 10100110 10011001
00000001 00100100 10001010 01101001 01101100 10001110 11011110 11010101 00101110 11100010
11011000 00111000 11011111 10000110 11111100 11101001 11001011 10000011 10011100 01110001
01010001 11100111 00000000 00011110 00101000 11011101 11001110 01111001 11000001 10101010
01101101 10110001 00010010 00001110 00111010 01110101 10100111 11111101 01111001 11001101
00110011 01110110 00001001 00000011 00111001 00000010 10011110 10101100 01001001 10100001
10110100 01010101 10000100 00101010 01000010 11100100 01111110 00110100 00001110 01110001
11101010 00111101 01101001 11001100 11111001 00111101 11101001 11001000 00111110 01111111
10111101 11001111 10110101 01001011 01101101 01101000 00101011 01101010 01001101 01101100
10100000 00000001 11000101 01011100 00010010 10000101 00000011 10011010 10100010 10010010
00011000 11000001 11000111 10101111 01001010 10001101 10100100 11000110 01001001 00111000
11111100 01101011 00111001 01000001 01001111 01010010 11101110 10010001 01110010 01111011
10111100 10011110 10100100 01100011 10111101 01000001 00110101 11010110 11101100 01110000
01000111 11101011 01010100 00100101 10111100 10001100 01110000 00111010 11010101 01110011
01110001 11100110 01110111 11111010 11010101 11010011 10100111 00101011 01101000 01100110
11100110 10001101 00001111 00110011 10000011 10000011 10011110 00111101 00111010 01010100
01100101 10000110 00000001 10101010 00100010 01011100 11110100 00110100 10101010 01001001
11100001 11111111 00000000 00011010 11011001 01000001 01101011 01110001 00111001 11011111
01100010 01000110 10010000 11100111 10001010 01001100 10010001 11111110 00110100 00101000
00000100 11100110 10011100 11000101 01100010 01011100 10111001 00011000 11110100 00110100

10101110 10101111 01100010 01110101 00011100 10111111 00110000 11100100 01110100 10100110
01011110 01011110 10100100 00101010 01110010 00001001 00011000 11001111 00010101 10011101
01110111 10101001 11101101 11111001 01100000 00000000 11100100 11100011 01110001 10101100
11001001 10100101 00101100 11000101 10001001 00100000 10011010 11011010 00010100 01101111
10111010 00110000 10101001 01010101 00101101 10001001 11101110 11101111 11100101 10111001
11001111 00111000 01001111 01000001 01010101 11011011 00000001 01110001 11010100 10011010
01101011 01100011 00000011 10110111 01111010 01110111 00001101 11001001 11101001 01011101
10010000 11010001 01011001 00100011 10011010 01010010 01101100 01101011 01111010 00001100
01010000 10100000 10001100 00010000 00111110 10111001 11101001 01000011 00101110 00111010
00001111 10010011 10101110 01110011 01000011 00001100 10001110 00111000 11001101 00010111
01100100 11111001 10001110 11000110 00111011 11010001 10011100 10000001 10011110 11011111
10101101 00000101 01110000 00000001 11001001 00100011 11011000 11100011 00010100 01110100
00011100 01111010 11110111 10100101 01111110 11000000 00111001 01011111 00100000 01100000
11100011 11011000 00001010 01101110 01000111 00011101 00001111 01101110 00000101 00000111
10011110 01000111 01000001 01001101 11001110 01100100 11100011 10001010 10101101 10010000
00001110 11001001 11111110 00000001 10001111 10101001 10100101 00000000 00110001 01110010
00111010 11100011 10010001 01000000 00001100 11001101 11010111 10100001 11100100 11010100
10101000 00000010 10000011 10001110 00110001 11011100 10011110 10110100 10011010 01100000
00000000 00000010 10000000 10111111 01101110 00110000 01101010 01000101 11000010 11100011
00000000 11111101 00001001 10100110 10001110 00111000 11111101 01001101 00101001 11100001
11000001 00111100 11111011 11010110 01011010 10111101 01000100 01001000 10001011 11001110
01000111 11100111 01010010 00110000 11000111 01010011 11000111 10101000 10101010 11100100
10000000 00001001 01001111 01001110 01101001 00011010 01000001 11100101 01100011 00110101
10100101 10101110 00000100 11011110 01110000 11000000 00111000 11000111 11010111 10111101
01000101 00101100 11000111 00111101 10001110 01111011 01100110 10100000 01100110 11110101
11100000 01010010 00010001 10111011 11110001 10100010 00111010 00100000 10111000 11110111
01100110 00100111 10010010 00001111 10101101 01000110 11110010 01100001 01001001 00111001
10100001 01001001 11100000 01110110 11101001 01001010 10110001 00110100 10000111 00011101
01000001 00110100 11111001 10101110 11110101 00000001 10001001 11101010 00111010 11010101
10101011 01101011 01110011 00100011 10000010 11011000 00000011 00111001 11000000 10101001
10101101 11100000 00001000 01110111 00011111 11010111 10110101 01001001 11100110 10001000
10010011 00100000 10001100 01111111 00111010 00011011 11010010 11100001 10100000 11100001
00010000 10001100 11100111 11010100 11100010 10100101 00001100 00111000 11100011 10000001
01010101 10011110 11101001 01110001 11000111 01111111 01001010 10000111 11001111 00100001
10110001 10010011 10001010 01001110 00110111 01000011 00101111 11001001 00111000 01011110
10000111 00111111 11010010 10011000 11010111 01111000 00000111 01100001 11110111 11001101
01010001 11011100 01001001 00111001 00011101 01111011 01010100 00110010 11001000 01010100
11100111 10001010 10000111 01001001 00111101 11001010 10111101 10001101 10000101 10111110
00100000 10010010 01011010 10110100 11101100 00110101 11111001 01101101 00001001 00001001
00100110 01000111 10100011 01110100 10101110 01010011 11001110 11001000 11000110 00111110
10100110 10010001 01110111 01001000 11011001 00111000 11000111 01101010 10001010 10010100
00100011 00100101 10101001 01010000 10101110 11100000 01110110 11110010 01111000 10110100
00001000 10001001 00101100 01001011 10011110 10100000 01110010 01101011 00101110 11100011
01011110 10111011 10111001 00100111 11001011 11001100 01101001 10011110 01001001 00111101
10101011 00001101 00100001 11000001 00101101 00100111 00000011 10110000 10100111 00110001
11100011 00000011 00110101 10011111 11010101 11101001 01000110 11010110 01000110 10010010
11000100 11001101 10011010 01001011 00101010 00010011 10011001 10001001 10010000 11111010
10010011 01010010 10100110 10100000 01110000 01000010 00011100 00000001 11010011 00010101
10010001 11100110 01110100 00011000 11111010 10011010 00010110 01011110 01110000 00111001
10101011 01110100 11010000 10010101 01100110 10110101 00110101 11111100 11110110 01101100
10110001 01101100 11100110 10100101 10000110 11101010 01011000 11001000 00101001 00100101
01100010 11111001 10100100 00010000 01000001 11100010 10100100 00110011 00011101 10100100
00001100 01110001 11001110 01110011 01001010 01010100 01101110 10110100 00001111 01101110
11001110 10011010 11010011 01010110 10010110 00100111 00011001 11000110 00000111 01111010
11010010 10000111 11000100 11010011 01000100 00001000 01110001 10011110 10011000 10101110
00010101 11101110 11011000 01100000 01110110 11000111 11100101 01000111 11011010 10011000
10101111 11001000 01110010 11100100 11010111 00110100 10110000 01110001 10011011 11010101
00011010 11111101 01100101 11011000 11110100 00101000 11111100 01011010 11111100 10010011
11110010 00010011 11000001 11110111 10101110 10001011 01000010 10111100 10111000 11010100
01100011 11011110 11100000 11000111 00010000 00111101 00111111 10111111 01011100 00010111
10000011 01110100 01100110 11010110 00101110 10000011 01001000 10100100 01011001 11000110
01110010 11000111 00011101 01001111 01110001 01011110 10101011 00001100 01001011 00001010
10100010 11000110 10100000 00100010 10001100 00000000 00101011 11001110 11000101 01010011
10100111 01000111 11011101 10001110 11100110 11110100 11100111 00101001 11101010 11001001
00010111 10000000 00000001 11000101 00011100 01100111 00100110 10010011 00011001 00011100
11111110 10110100 00110000 00111001 11100010 10111000 10011110 10011011 00011011 01101100
00101011 10010010 00111011 11111101 00110011 01010001 10110011 00001110 10000010 10011100
11011001 00100000 11010011 00011100 00000000 00111000 11101111 01010010 11010101 10000010
11100011 00011101 10110001 01001101 01010110 11101110 11010100 10111000 11100110 10011001
00100111 00000011 00110101 00110000 01101110 11110110 01100001 01110000 01111100 00010001
10011010 01001101 11011000 00000000 11110111 10100100 01110011 11000110 00101010 00111111
10101001 11100010 10101101 10110100 11011110 10000100 10001011 10011100 10011110 00101001
00011000 10001110 01000111 11101011 01001101 00000111 00011001 11101111 01010001 10000010

01110000 01001001 11110101 10101011 01101101 00100111 01100010 10000111 11101110 11101100
01101001 10001111 11010011 00110101 00011110 11100010 01011111 10011110 11110100 00110011
01110110 10100010 11010110 11110100 00001011 10000111 00100000 01100110 10100011 01110110
11011101 01001000 11110010 01111100 10100111 11111001 01010011 00111001 00111101 01111010
11010101 00100101 01111101 11000000 01001100 11100000 11010100 01101110 11011101 01111111
00101110 01101001 01001000 00011111 10001101 01000110 11100100 00011110 10010100 11011010
10110010 10110000 01011100 01000010 01110000 01111000 00111100 11010011 00011011 10010011
10001100 11110001 01001101 01111100 10011100 11111111 00000000 10001101 00110100 00010011
11010100 01010101 01000111 01011111 10001000 01010110 00100110 00000111 00000110 10011101
00011100 10000000 00011100 00010011 01010001 00000011 10001110 10110100 10101010 01000111
10110000 10100010 01001111 01011011 00010011 11101000 01001110 10100111 10011111 10011011
11111001 11010100 10001000 01110001 10001010 10000001 01111010 11010100 11001010 01111101
00000101 01000011 10001101 10100101 01110100 01011101 11000111 00010010 01000111 01011110
11111101 00001101 01001000 10000100 11110101 00111111 10101101 01000011 10111011 11010110
10010100 10011100 11111101 00101001 00100100 11011000 00010011 11101110 11100011 00100010
10000011 11001010 11010100 01101010 11011100 01110000 01101001 01011001 10111000 11110100
00011001 11110101 10100110 10010111 00100010 10110010 00100100 01000111 10010011 00000011
10001110 10110101 00000011 10110001 11011101 11101101 01010010 01001010 01110010 00001110
11011010 10101110 11101100 00110110 11100100 11110001 11101011 01010101 01001110 01010111
11010001 10110000 00000011 00100111 00100111 11010011 11010010 10100011 01110110 00100011
10000001 01010001 11001011 00100001 11000110 01111010 01010011 00110111 00001100 01110101
00111001 00110101 10100101 00111010 01111101 10000001 10010001 11001101 00100110 01001111
00011101 00000111 01101010 10000101 11100100 11001111 00100000 11110011 01001100 01101001
00011000 11001000 01110011 01010001 00010110 11101011 01011010 10100100 10100010 00101011
10110001 10010011 00110110 01001111 01011010 10101100 11100101 01001001 00100011 00100011
00111110 11010101 00100100 10100111 00011110 11110101 00000110 01000000 11101100 00110001
11111001 01010110 11010001 01010001 10110001 00101100 10101111 00100000 11101111 10010001
11001101 01010110 10011001 10111001 11100000 11010101 11000111 01011100 11100111 11011110
10101000 11011100 10001111 10011100 01010110 11110100 11010010 01111011 10010001 00110100
01000010 11000000 00110000 00100100 10011100 00000001 11010110 10100011 00111100 11110011
10001010 10010011 01101110 01000111 00011101 01110011 11011110 10001100 11111100 10100101
01000110 01111010 11110101 10101101 11100010 10011111 01000011 00010110 01010011 01110100
00111100 11100010 10011011 00010100 01000100 00011100 11100011 10011111 01011010 10110101
10110111 10001100 01110101 00110100 11011101 11011011 01000000 00001101 10011100 01111010
01010110 10101101 11011111 10101001 00010110 11010111 01010010 11011101 10011000 00010001
00101110 01110011 11001111 01111100 11010101 10110100 10111011 01011111 00110000 00101010
01110000 00111010 10000011 11101111 01011000 01110111 00010111 00000111 10100111 11101001
01010010 11011001 00110001 10010101 11111010 00011100 01111010 11100110 10100111 11011001
00100110 10101110 11000111 11001111 01101101 10001110 10110010 11011010 01101110 10000100
11110011 11010011 00110101 10110001 01101000 01000011 00010001 11001110 00111101 00101011
10011100 11010011 01011000 10001100 01101110 00111001 10101110 10001110 11000001 01110010
11100000 11110011 11001101 01111001 10111000 10011011 10100110 10101100 01110110 11010011
10010001 10101111 00001010 11100100 01110001 01010111 10100001 11111001 01000001 11100111
10010011 01010100 11100001 01011110 10000111 00110101 01101100 00101111 00011100 10011110
01101011 11001110 10110111 10010110 10100110 10000101 10010100 01101110 00000000 00100111
10001010 01111001 10010011 00000111 10001110 01000101 01010110 01100110 00111011 11110001
11011000 01010001 10111011 11011111 00010100 00100100 10001001 01100011 10100111 10010000
10010101 00111011 00000111 00110101 00010111 10011000 01000000 10100001 11100100 11100111
11011010 10100000 10010001 10000001 00110101 10100101 10100010 11011110 10000101 00001110
01111001 00000000 11001110 11101110 10110101 01010101 11100100 11101011 01001001 00100100
10011100 11110011 11111100 10101010 00100010 01001110 01110010 01101011 01010101 01101000
00101011 00100101 10101011 00010101 10011110 11100011 01100100 10010000 10000000 01111001
10101000 01100101 01111100 00001110 01001000 10100110 11001110 11011001 00111100 01010101
01100111 00100111 00011000 00000111 10001010 00100100 10111010 00001100 00001110 00011011
00111100 11100100 10001010 10101111 00110011 01101110 11000000 00111100 01010010 10110100
10000001 01011111 00001100 00001101 01000010 11001100 01110011 10011110 10111001 10100101
00000101 00100100 11000100 11000110 10111001 00011001 11000000 00111100 11010101 01110111
00100011 01111111 01001010 01110100 10101100 01111111 11001111 01111010 10000001 10001011
01110101 00111111 11111110 10101010 11101010 10001110 10011010 10101101 11000100 10011111
01110000 01100011 11001110 00111010 10011010 01001100 10010001 11000111 01111010 00111010
01111010 01111011 11010010 10101001 11111101 11100001 00011110 10010101 00111011 10001101
11101010 00100011 00101110 00000111 00000111 11100110 11101101 01001100 01001110 10111111
00111111 01110001 11010110 10100100 11000110 01001001 00001100 01101000 11001000 00011100
00011110 01110011 11011011 00110101 01010001 10010111 01000100 00000010 01100111 00000111
11010010 10010101 11111001 11100011 00011100 11100110 10000001 11001110 00111000 11100000
01110111 10100101 01010010 01110011 10011110 11010100 10011011 11010100 01111011 01101010
00110101 10000001 00100111 10101101 00101110 00001000 11101001 11010110 10011110 11100111
00000111 10010001 01001111 10110110 10001010 01001011 10101001 10010010 00111000 00100011
11011111 00100011 00011110 00000101 00001101 11011001 01101010 00111101 00110111 00101101
01101000 11011010 01101011 01101010 01110111 11001001 00011110 11010011 11100101 00001111
10111110 11000000 01100111 00010101 11101010 00010000 10101010 11000011 00010010 01000110
10000011 00001000 10000011 00000000 00001110 00110001 01010100 01110100 00011101 00101001
00110100 10111011 00010001 00010000 00111001 10010101 11111110 01111001 00001111 10111101

01011101 01110110 11000110 01000001 11111100 11101011 11000101 11000101 11001111 11011011
00110101 01100111 10100010 00010011 01100011 00100101 00111100 11100110 10101000 01001101
00101110 11101001 00110001 11010011 00000110 10011111 01110001 00100001 00100110 10101011
11000010 10001101 00100100 11111001 11101101 11011100 11010111 00101111 00101100 01101110
00000101 10011000 10000001 01110010 00000111 11101011 01010111 10100001 11111101 11011000
11000001 11100111 11011110 10000101 01010101 01011000 11111110 10110101 00100010 10010000
00000110 01001111 10101101 01000010 11010001 11101110 01010001 00100110 01001110 00110011
01001110 01100011 01010001 10100001 00100111 00100100 11110100 10100011 00111001 10101000
01101101 11110101 00010110 11100101 01101011 11000011 10000101 11000101 01110010 10011010
11001001 11000110 00111010 11100110 10111010 10001011 11110010 01110000 01111101 00110001
10011010 11100101 01110101 10000011 10010010 01000110 01111001 10101110 10011100 00110110
11100000 11001100 00110111 11100001 10111101 01001111 10111101 00101100 00110010 11101101
01100011 01001000 11100011 00000110 10100000 00100101 10000111 00000011 10111101 01111010
10101001 01011100 11011111 01110011 10100011 10110011 00001100 11010001 01110001 11010000
11110011 01010001 01011100 00101001 01010000 01110001 10000001 01001111 11010011 00100111
01010110 10000100 10000001 11011011 10100101 00110110 11111111 00000000 11100101 00000001
01011011 10111111 00111001 10101110 01000101 00010111 11001110 01100110 11101100 01100110
10110001 00001100 01110011 11011111 10111101 00111110 11011001 11000000 10010011 00000100
00010011 11101111 11011010 10011000 11101010 00000001 00000111 00111100 11100011 10110101
00110110 00011110 00100100 11001111 01111010 11101010 01110110 10110101 10101100 00101110
10111010 00011011 11001010 11000000 10100000 11101100 00101010 01110100 00000100 10010000
01000111 01001010 10100111 01100110 10011110 01100000 11101001 01011010 10110110 11101010
00000001 00011110 10110101 11000011 01010001 11011011 01000100 00000011 11100010 10001111
10111110 00111000 11101011 01001010 10000000 11100111 10100110 01000101 01001000 10111101
00111000 10100100 00001101 11011100 01010100 01011001 00101101 00011001 00110111 00000110
11001110 00111110 01011010 10001111 00111100 11100000 11010100 10101110 11011000 11101001
11111000 11010100 01001101 10011100 10010010 01001110 01101001 01011001 00100100 00000100
01010010 00001110 10110100 11001111 00110011 11100100 11111100 00101001 01100110 00111011
01010011 00011001 00011001 11101111 01010101 01011110 01000000 00000111 00011101 00101001
11000001 01110111 00010000 11100010 01001001 00110100 10001100 11100011 00111100 11010100
00000010 01001110 10111001 00110100 11010110 01100010 01001111 11111111 00000000 01011110
10111010 01100011 01100100 10110111 00000011 10000111 01110010 10111000 00000100 00011100
11111011 01010011 01001100 10000000 00100001 00100111 10001010 11100110 10100110 11010100
01100111 01101110 10000111 01100010 01100111 00111000 01010001 01010101 10100101 10010010
01101001 10001001 00110011 10111011 10111001 11111010 11010111 11010011 11000011 00001110
11110111 01101100 11100010 01111000 10010101 01111101 00010001 11010011 00111101 11110101
10111100 01100000 10000111 10010101 01000001 00011101 10110011 11001101 01010110 10011111
01010101 10000011 11111000 00001001 11011111 11101001 10001110 10110101 11001111 10001000
11110010 01001111 00111000 11100111 10111101 00001011 00011110 00111101 11001001 00110101
01101011 00001101 00011101 11011011 00100001 11100010 10100100 01101100 10111110 10100000
01100100 01101100 01110000 00000111 01111010 00100011 10111110 01101110 01000001 11100111
00111110 10010101 10010010 10010001 10010010 00110111 00001111 11100000 10100011 11100111
01100011 11000110 01000111 00111100 10011010 11010101 11010010 10001101 10001100 11011101
01101001 01110101 00110111 00100010 10111011 00011000 11000001 11100110 10100100 01011001
10010111 00111100 10001100 11111010 01010110 00000000 10010010 01001110 00000110 00111010
01010011 11111100 11011001 01110011 10011010 11001010 01110100 01100010 11001011 01011000
10000011 01111000 11001011 11110010 00010011 11000001 00100000 11110100 10100001 00100110
00000001 11111110 01111111 11111110 10110110 01101011 00001000 11011100 01001101 10010001
10010001 11110101 00010100 10100010 11101110 01110001 00011001 00000000 11110111 11100111
11011110 10100101 01010010 01101011 01100110 01011010 10101110 01110100 01111110 01110000
00011101 00001001 11100111 10110101 00000110 01011100 00001111 10011100 01010111 00110110
11110111 00010011 11110100 11001101 00110010 01100110 10011101 10001010 01111100 11100100
00000001 01001101 11010000 01110111 10110101 11000001 11100010 01010111 01100011 10100111
00110111 00010001 10101011 00001100 10110000 00000011 00011001 11101011 01010001 00111110
10101001 00000100 01101111 10010001 11111011 11001111 10100001 11000110 01101011 10011001
01100000 01110011 11001110 01110001 11101011 01000000 01011001 00110001 11000001 10101010
11111010 10111010 10111111 10111100 11101110 01000111 11010110 01011111 01000100 01101111
01001101 10101011 01101110 00011011 10100011 00000100 01110110 11001001 11101011 01010101
00100100 10111000 10010110 01000101 00101100 01100101 11001000 00111101 01111001 10101100
11000101 11011110 00010011 00011100 11111110 01010100 10001001 00100110 11011100 11100101
01111010 10011111 01001010 10100101 01001101 00101101 10001001 01110101 01011011 11011100
11010101 01001110 01111000 01000011 10001111 01001010 10010001 00000111 00011000 00000111
00010101 10010101 11100111 10010000 00000110 00110111 11110000 00111010 01010010 10110101
11010011 00110111 01000010 01111110 10011110 10110101 00111100 10010010 00000101 01010001
01110101 00110110 10010000 10101110 00110010 01110000 00110001 01001011 11100111 00000100
00011001 01101100 01110011 11011010 10110000 11111110 11010111 00101110 01001000 00111000
00000111 10101101 01000110 11110011 10111011 00101000 00011001 11100011 10100111 01001110
10110101 00011110 11000001 11011100 00111101 10110001 10110001 01110011 10101000 00001000
10111000 00001011 10010011 11101001 11101001 01011001 01010011 01011101 11001011 01110000
00111111 01111000 11011001 00000011 10100000 11000111 01001010 10101010 11001011 11001111
11111000 11010000 11000000 10001110 10010101 11010001 00001010 01110001 10000001 10010011
10101000 11100100 00111101 10011000 11100111 11011011 10110001 10100111 11110101 00000100
10010110 11001001 00010101 00011111 00100001 01101001 11011001 11100111 10011110 00111110

10010101 01101111 01010010 00110101 00000101 11100100 10000001 10000011 11101011 01001111
01101101 11000000 01110010 00101001 00110011 10010101 00111001 00011101 01101001 10101100
11000100 10101000 00011110 10010100 10101100 00100100 01001100 11011000 00001000 00111011
00000011 11010110 10001100 11100000 00000010 00111111 11111101 01110101 00011110 11100000
01111000 10100011 11001100 11001110 00000111 01101010 01010110 01011101 00000110 01001001
11101001 11001111 00000111 10111110 00101001 10011011 10111101 10110011 11011110 10011001
10011100 11111111 00000000 00010001 10100111 01000111 11001110 01001111 01110001 01001100
00001001 01010100 11111100 10011001 11001110 01111000 11101111 01001100 11100111 00111111
01011010 00000110 00110010 00111101 00111101 00101001 11111111 00000000 00101000 11000000
11001111 00000010 10100101 10111011 10001110 11000011 11100011 00111000 11001000 11100111
01111111 01110010 01000111 01011010 10010011 00111100 01111111 01011010 10000111 11001101
11000001 11110101 10100100 00101110 01110000 01000011 00011111 10100101 00110111 01100001
00010011 11100111 00001111 10011100 11100110 10011011 00101011 00010101 00011100 00001111
11000110 10100001 11110011 00110010 01110001 11101001 11101001 01001110 00010010 00001100
11100011 11010111 10101001 10100011 10010001 01101110 00000000 00011011 00100100 11110110
00111111 01011110 10110100 01110001 10000001 10000011 10010011 10011110 01000101 00100010
00000000 11001101 10011111 01000011 11101011 01000011 11100111 01111001 11000111 01010011
11010110 10011101 11000001 00100001 00111001 01100011 11010111 10101101 00011000 00100000
01100011 00111000 00000110 10000000 00111000 00000111 00111111 10100101 00101001 00100011
00011000 00000111 00000110 10010101 10000011 01100001 11101000 00111010 00010011 01010110
01011110 01000101 00001011 10001110 11011110 10011101 00101010 10011010 10111001 11100011
10110000 11110101 10100110 00110001 11100100 10011100 01110001 10011110 01101000 01110001
11010111 01010000 00101101 00111101 11010110 11100000 00000111 01001110 01111011 01110110
10101010 10101111 00100001 00100100 10010011 11000001 00010100 11011101 11000100 10010010
01000101 00001111 10111000 01100011 00100000 11111101 01001101 00110101 11011100 01110110
00001111 00110000 10001111 10011011 00111000 11000001 11101001 11101011 01001110 01101001
00000111 00000111 01110001 00111001 00110100 11010000 00111010 01101110 11111100 10101001
01110110 10010000 01110000 11011101 00101001 10101101 10000101 01100001 00011110 01000110
11011100 01111110 01100010 00110011 11011011 11010000 01010000 01110010 01111010 10110110
01110011 11101011 01001110 11011011 10001110 01111010 10010011 01010010 01100000 11100011
00000100 00000010 00101001 01011101 10000001 00010110 00111000 10101011 00010001 00011101
10001001 11001000 11001001 10101000 10110001 11000110 00000001 11111100 00101001 10100111
10010001 11000001 11100100 01110111 10101001 01000000 01011000 01100011 11000000 00100100
11111110 00110100 10001100 11000111 10110101 01000110 11001100 10100111 00011000 11001110
00000111 10101101 00110001 11011011 00100111 00011001 11101011 01001001 00101110 11100011
00100100 01010110 00101100 11111000 00111000 00011110 10010100 11101101 11011011 01111000
11110101 10101000 01110010 01000111 01111110 01111000 10100111 01100000 10010110 00111100
01100010 10101010 11011010 00000000 10101100 11001100 00111111 10001000 00011111 01101010
10001111 00100111 00100111 11010111 11011010 10100100 10000110 00100110 10010110 01000011
10010001 11000000 11101111 10001110 10110101 01110110 11011010 11010001 01010101 11001011
10111001 11101001 11011011 00010101 00111100 11001001 01101000 00000101 01011000 10010001
10011000 11100000 00010011 10011100 01110101 10101110 10000011 11000011 01011110 00011011
10011011 01010100 10111110 01001000 10001011 01100001 00010111 10011001 01001110 00111001
00000011 11101011 01001101 11010010 10101100 11100100 10011110 11100101 00100000 10110101
10001011 01111011 11001000 11011101 00000101 01111010 11000110 10000101 10100100 10100110
10011001 01101010 00100010 10001111 11101111 10111111 00110010 00010001 11011100 11010111
00011110 00101011 00010011 11101100 11010110 10011011 10110011 01111010 01010100 10111001
10011110 10100101 10111101 00110110 11001010 00011011 00011011 01100100 10000110 00000100
00001011 00011010 10001110 00000111 10101101 01011011 01010001 11001111 00110100 00101000
00110100 11101110 00111111 00011100 01010111 11001111 01001001 11001010 01101110 11111101
01001110 11111101 10010101 10001000 11001111 01111111 10101110 01101001 00000001 11110101
10100111 10111001 11001001 10100110 00110000 11100011 11011000 11010100 10111101 11001011
01000010 00111001 11100011 10101101 01000110 01000111 00010100 01110111 10100110 00110011
01100011 11011110 10101101 00100100 00000000 01001110 00000111 10111101 00110001 10110000
01101001 00011001 11111101 11110011 01010001 10010010 00110111 01010011 01101101 10101101
11000101 01100001 01110011 10001100 10001100 11110011 01010101 11100101 00111000 01001111
11000111 10111101 01001000 11000100 01110011 10011110 10010101 00011011 10110000 00110100
01001010 00101001 11001000 01000011 01000001 00111000 11100010 10011010 11000111 00000010
10010001 01001111 01011100 00011010 01000111 00111000 11100011 10110101 00010110 01001001
01011001 10010100 00011000 00111101 01110011 11010011 10110101 00110011 11111111 00000000
01000010 10100001 10001111 01100001 01010001 10010010 01111010 11100111 10011010 00101101
11001010 01001110 11111011 00000011 11110000 01111000 10100100 00000100 10001110 01111011
01010011 01011100 10010010 01110011 10011110 01101001 00001011 01110001 11010111 11101011
01010101 10110110 10110001 01110110 00000001 00011000 11111100 11111101 01111010 11010100
00110010 10011111 11010110 10000110 01101110 01111110 01011100 11111110 01110100 01100111
11011010 10101011 10010101 01011111 11011110 01100011 10111001 00010111 01010010 01111001
11111100 00101001 00111010 00011010 01110001 00111101 11111011 00011010 10001101 10001001
11011101 11101101 01010100 10011101 11110100 01001000 01000100 11011000 00001101 11110100
00110100 01110100 00111110 10110100 11000101 01100001 11010100 11010011 11011000 11100110
10100110 01111110 01111011 10000110 10101100 10010001 00011011 00100111 00100011 10111101
01001000 10101100 01000000 11111110 01110101 01011101 00001110 00000001 01100001 11010110
10100100 11011101 10000101 11001001 00110100 10100100 10010011 00010001 00100011 00011100
11110000 01001111 11010010 10000000 01111001 11100010 10100001 11011101 11000111 11110101

10100000 00011100 11110100 00110100 01001110 00111101 00010000 11110101 00100111 01101001
00111000 10100001 00011011 00111101 11101010 10110011 00110111 00011100 10011110 01101000
01001001 00110000 01110011 11011010 10101111 10010110 11111010 10001010 11100100 10101110
11011100 11100010 10100010 10010101 11000001 11100011 10100101 00110110 01001001 00110111
00111001 00100011 10001010 10000101 11100100 00011011 00011100 10011110 00001101 00111011
10111011 11101010 00011110 01100000 11101101 11000111 10101000 10101010 11101111 00100000
00011101 00101001 10101101 00100111 11001001 11010010 10100001 00110010 00011101 11011100
01100011 00011000 10101101 00010100 01101100 10000100 00101100 10100111 10011100 11010100
00011001 11100000 11111010 11010001 00100011 00011111 01011111 10101101 01000101 10010010
01111101 00111110 10110101 10110100 01100011 00010100 11000110 11110100 00010001 11001111
00111000 00110101 00011111 11010111 10011010 01010001 11001011 11111010 11010011 00011011
00111011 10111101 10101001 10101000 11101011 01100100 01001110 10000010 01001011 11010100
10010000 00111000 10101010 00010111 01100111 00110010 01100011 10100000 00011110 11010101
01111001 10001111 00111100 00011110 10110101 01000010 01100010 11000110 01100111 00111000
00011000 00011001 11101111 01011101 00010100 11010101 10110100 10111001 00010101 00110110
00011001 10011110 11011000 10100110 11110100 11101011 01001110 01101100 01111001 01111001
11101000 01110010 00101001 11000101 01110010 01000001 11101001 11000101 01101010 11110100
00110010 01110001 00011011 10001100 11100011 01100000 11110111 00110101 01000110 11100101
10110000 01001000 00111100 11111010 01010110 10000011 10101001 00101001 11010100 11100111
11101011 01011001 11110111 11111100 10010001 11110100 11101101 01011010 11000001 10101011
10010011 00110111 10100001 01000101 11110010 11111101 01011011 10010011 11101011 01011010
01111010 01010010 11111001 10011100 10111001 00011101 01111000 11001111 01101010 11001010
11011011 10000010 01011011 10001100 00001111 01010011 01011011 10111010 01010111 11001100
10100000 01100000 01100111 11111001 11010110 10010101 01011010 01010001 10111010 00110001
10000010 11010100 11011000 10110000 10001000 00001001 01000110 11011100 01111010 11110011
01011101 00101101 10011001 00111011 00111011 10001100 11010110 00011101 10000111 00010010
00001010 11101000 00101101 01101011 11000010 11000100 11011101 11101010 01111010 01010100
11001101 00111011 01111110 10011100 11010101 10000101 01100011 10011010 10101001 00011111
11001011 11001101 01001101 11100110 11111011 01010111 00001010 10001010 01101111 01110011
01000110 11101110 01001101 10111000 11100111 10000011 11000111 10101101 00011011 10110110
10001110 10110101 01011100 00110000 00000111 10111101 00100000 00111001 00111101 01001111
11010111 00110101 10101111 10111010 00001101 00010010 00110011 10000010 01001111 11110101
10101000 10100101 01101010 01101011 10110111 00110101 00010011 10110000 00000011 11011110
10101011 01000110 11110100 00010000 00111001 11000111 11010110 10100010 10011001 10111000
00100000 00011110 01101000 00101100 00110110 10001110 01111001 11001101 01010100 10010110
01000010 00001110 01111011 01010110 10010100 11010010 10000110 10001111 10101000 11000001
11011000 01110111 11110100 11110101 10101010 11110011 00110001 00111000 00100011 00010100
00111001 11001110 01111000 10101000 10011100 11100100 01110101 11111010 11010011 01011101
10000001 01101000 01000110 11110010 01110010 01000011 11110100 10101000 01001011 00001100
11110100 10100111 10111000 11100111 10001111 11001110 10100000 01110110 00000000 11111111
00000000 11110101 11101011 01101000 01101001 00100001 01011101 00001101 01110011 11010100
11110110 10101000 00011101 10001110 01111110 10111101 11101001 11101100 01110010 01111011
11010011 00001110 00000111 00011110 10110101 10101011 01001010 11111010 10001110 11000011
00110011 11001111 00110101 00100110 01000110 00110011 10001010 01001100 00001101 10111000
11101101 01000110 11011110 00000111 00111101 00101001 00110100 10101101 01110001 01011010
11000011 11010101 10111001 11001101 00001101 11001001 11110100 10100110 11110000 00000111
00000110 10010001 01001001 00011100 11100110 10100001 01110111 00011000 11110110 00111110
10000110 10000111 10010011 00000011 00111110 11110101 00001110 01110010 01001001 11111110
10111101 01101010 00101001 11100101 11111001 01111110 01011110 10011101 11001101 01010111
00101101 11011000 01011110 11001000 10110000 10001100 11010010 01001000 00010101 00000001
01100111 01100011 10000000 00000111 01111010 11110100 01011111 00001010 11101000 01000011
01001100 10001111 11001110 10011111 00001101 01110011 00100111 00100111 11111101 10011111
10100101 01100101 01111000 00110111 01000011 01011000 01101101 10100001 10111011 10111000
01011100 11001101 00100000 11001010 10010011 11111100 00100010 10111010 10111001 10101110
10010010 11011110 00110011 10011010 11110011 01110001 10011000 10001110 01100111 11101100
10100001 10110000 00100111 10100001 01110010 01000110 11000000 10101010 00101110 01001110
01111010 11010101 01010100 10111110 11011111 00100000 01010000 01110011 11101111 01010110
10111001 00110101 11100110 11010100 10010011 01001111 10010101 01101100 00001110 11101000
10000110 01101110 01111000 00011111 10001101 00110010 00011100 10101011 00011110 00111001
00110101 00100011 10001111 10011111 11111100 00101001 10011110 11011111 10101101 01001111
11000011 10100000 00010110 11010110 01010000 11000111 00000111 00111100 01010100 10011110
01101111 11100011 11101111 01010100 11000001 11000001 11100111 11110011 10101001 00110010
01000111 00100011 00011100 11110101 10100111 00000100 10101111 10101001 01110110 00101100
10110011 00011100 01010011 11000001 11001000 11100111 11110011 10101010 11000001 10001001
11101001 11000111 11010110 10100100 01000010 01000001 11000111 00111110 11111001 10101000
10101001 10101110 10101000 00010001 00001101 11101100 10111000 01000111 00000000 01110001
11011110 10111001 00011101 01001101 10001110 01001011 01100111 10001010 11101010 00101111
01001110 00110011 10011100 01100000 11110101 10101110 01000110 11111110 01000010 01100101
01110001 11000111 11010011 10101101 01110110 01100001 10010000 11010110 11100101 01011111
10010111 00011111 11010110 10101010 01001100 01000110 11100011 11010100 01010100 11101100
01111010 10101111 00010101 01010101 11110011 10011010 11110100 01100000 10101100 00110100
11011001 10101111 10100000 00110001 11001100 10000001 11111011 01110010 00101010 11100101
11101000 11001001 11001101 01100011 11101000 00110010 10010110 10111111 11011000 00111101

00111001 10101101 10011011 10010001 10010110 11000000 10101100 00101010 11011110 00110011
10111000 10001100 11101001 10011011 01101001 00100111 00011100 11110110 10101010 11000001
10111001 11000000 11101011 11101010 01101010 11010101 11110111 11101110 11000001 00111001
11101010 01101010 10001100 01000000 10011001 00111010 01110001 11101101 01011010 01000001
01011101 01011100 00111010 10011101 00110110 10010000 00110111 01000101 10000010 00111110
10111100 01010110 10100010 10001100 00010001 10000011 01010100 10110100 10100000 00000101
10110110 00111011 01010101 11010100 11100000 01010111 00001101 01000100 10011100 11011010
01000100 10110111 01110001 11011101 00001101 00110000 10011110 10110100 00111100 10000001
01010100 10011100 11110011 01010100 11100100 10111101 01010000 11111000 11111001 00111111
00010011 01010011 00101010 01101001 11101001 00010100 00110010 11011100 10101100 00010100
01100110 10100000 10010110 01011110 11100100 10001100 01111011 01010110 00111101 11001110
10100110 00110000 01000010 00011110 00111011 11110011 01011000 10010111 01011010 10011011
00110111 00011011 10111010 10011100 11010111 01001100 00110000 11010010 01110110 10111001
00101101 11110101 00111010 00101001 11110101 00011000 10110011 10110000 00011100 11100111
10101111 10110101 01010001 01101011 11000101 00111111 01110000 11110011 11101001 01011100
11011111 10011100 11001101 00100001 11011100 01001101 01001100 10101110 01011100 11100100
01110000 00111101 10101011 10101011 11101010 10110001 01011010 11011100 00010011 00110111
00011010 11101011 00000000 01111010 11010011 00001101 11100001 01010011 10001111 11101001
01011000 11100110 01010010 01000000 11111001 10001110 01000101 00110011 01111001 01101110
01111001 11111100 11101010 10100011 01000110 00111101 01000011 01010110 01110011 00110001
01101001 11100101 01111000 01001100 10010010 01001101 01001000 00110100 11110010 10111001
00111011 01001001 00111101 00111001 11101010 00101011 11011011 00111111 11100001 00011100
11010011 01001010 00001111 11110100 01011000 11110011 11101101 01001101 01101111 00001110
11101001 10111000 00011000 10110011 01000001 10001111 01111010 11110100 01011110 00111010
01001011 10100001 11100110 00111010 01000111 10001000 10100101 10001001 01111001 01001111
10101101 00111011 11101100 01000100 00000001 10010011 11001111 01010011 11110101 10101111
01101110 01001111 00001110 11101001 11100000 11111111 00000000 11000111 10010100 01011001
10100011 11111110 00010001 10111101 00111000 00011110 00101100 11100010 00011001 11101010
01101010 01111110 10111010 11010010 11011000 00111101 10011110 10100111 10001010 11111101
10000100 11101111 00100101 11010100 11100100 11010010 00001011 00100010 00111010 11111100
10000000 10010011 11010110 10111101 10111100 11101000 01110110 00000101 00000000 00010110
11001000 00110001 11000000 10100101 01011101 00010110 11001000 00101110 00001101 10110100
01011000 11110111 00010100 01000011 00011010 11010110 10101100 01101110 00001001 10011110
00011110 10110110 01100101 01011111 01101001 11101011 11010110 10011100 00101100 10111000
11001001 00000111 00000111 10100001 11110101 10101111 01101101 00111010 00101101 10010100
10001101 10010011 01100111 00011001 00011110 11100010 10100100 11111110 11000111 10110001
00000111 10001011 00111000 00000111 11010000 01010010 01111000 11010111 01010011 01100000
11110110 01110110 00111100 01000000 01011000 10011111 11100000 00000000 10001100 01111010
01010010 10100110 10011010 00011001 10111011 01110000 00111011 01010111 10110111 00100110
10001111 01100100 10100111 11100100 10110100 10001111 10011111 01010001 01001011 11111101
10010001 01101100 00110111 10000011 01101111 00010111 00111111 11101100 11111111 00000000
01011010 10010101 10001110 01101011 01000100 00011100 10001000 11110000 11100110 11010011
10110000 01111001 00100111 10001111 01111010 00011111 01001110 00100011 10011110 11111101
10101011 11011100 01000110 10010011 01101001 11011110 11011010 00010011 10011111 01010101
00010100 00100110 10010011 01100110 00001110 01111110 11001101 00001110 01111101 01110110
11110100 10101010 11111010 11110111 01100000 11110110 01101000 11110000 11101111 11101100
11100110 11011000 00000001 01010011 10001111 01001010 01010101 11010011 10011100 00100110
01001010 10010010 10011101 10001111 11110010 10101111 01110000 00111010 01101101 10110010
10011110 00101101 11100011 11001111 11110111 10110110 11110011 01001111 01011101 00110110
11011001 01110001 10001000 01010011 11101011 10001010 10010101 10001111 10010011 00001111
01100110 10001111 00001011 01101101 00111101 11001001 00000111 01101001 11110100 11111010
01010100 00101101 10100111 00110001 10010000 00000101 10001100 10010111 00111110 10111100
01010111 10111110 01111111 01100110 11011011 10000000 01000000 10000110 00111110 01111010
10001101 10111100 01010001 11111101 10011111 00000111 11111100 11110000 10001011 11110000
01011010 01001111 00011101 00101110 11000010 11110110 01101000 11110000 00011111 11101100
11100111 11000000 01101100 01100000 11110111 00110100 11000111 10110011 00100000 10010000
01000110 00111101 10101011 11011111 01011111 01001100 10110100 00111000 00001111 01101101
00001001 11000111 00100011 11100101 00010101 00010100 11011010 00101101 10010100 10111100
10011011 01001000 10110111 11111010 11101101 10100011 11111011 01000010 01010111 01111010
00000111 10110010 01011011 00011110 00000110 00101100 00110011 10111111 01110111 00100000
11110100 11100110 10000001 01100101 10001100 01100000 01110000 00111011 11100110 10111101
11000001 11111100 00110101 10100111 01001000 00001000 00010110 10110001 10000011 10001100
00010010 00111011 11010101 01100111 11110000 01101110 10010111 10011100 10001000 01001000
11001000 11100100 01100111 10001010 11010010 00011000 11110110 11011110 10101000 10000111
01001000 11110001 01000111 10110011 00100001 11001111 00000111 11101011 01001000 11110110
01000101 01111000 01111100 11110001 11010110 10111101 10100001 10111100 00010111 10100111
10000000 00000010 00101011 10100000 00011101 10110011 01010000 00111111 10000010 00101100
00000001 00100101 00011010 01100001 11110101 00111001 10101010 11111110 11010000 10001000
01111011 00110011 11000111 00111110 11001001 10001111 01011100 11010011 10111110 11000111
10000111 11101100 01000110 11011010 11110101 11100111 11110000 00110101 10010001 01100010
11100110 01101001 01110111 10011110 00111000 11000101 01000010 01111100 00001001 01101011
10001110 00100101 10010111 10011111 10100111 00010101 10100100 01110001 11001001 10001011
11011001 10011110 01001110 11010110 01100111 00000100 10010001 01001100 00110110 01000111

```
10011110 01111001 11101101 01011110 10110110 01111100 00000111 01101110 01000001 11111101
11111100 10111000 11101101 01010001 10111111 10000000 11100010 11100100 10100101 11001100
10000011 10011110 11100011 10101101 00001111 00011110 10101110 00101110 01000011 11001001
00001101 10010100 10000100 00011100 01110000 01110011 11011111 10111101 00101000 10110011
10010011 11110011 11111101 00111101 01101011 11010101 10111111 11100001 00000011 01010101
10001111 11111110 00111110 00110010 01111101 11000101 01000010 01111100 00001100 11111110
01011011 10010001 01110000 10000111 11010011 01110010 11110100 10100110 11110001 11110000
01011011 11101110 00011110 11001101 10011110 01011100 00101101 11011100 10000000 11000011
10010001 10011110 01110001 01000111 10010011 00100001 11111010 00011111 01000011 01011110
10011000 01111100 00000111 00111000 00000110 00100100 10011010 00101100 01111010 11010100
01101111 11100000 01001011 10101100 01100101 00100101 10001011 10100111 01111110 00111111
00101010 10110101 10001110 10100100 11111010 10000011 10100110 01111001 10100000 10001001
10000100 10011111 11001111 00110100 10001101 00010001 11000001 00111111 10100101 01111010
00111001 11110000 00100101 11100011 00001100 01100101 00110111 10111111 01111100 11110000
00101010 00111111 11111000 01000001 01101111 11110000 11100011 00010000 10011100 01110000
00110010 11011101 01001101 01010111 11010111 01101001 11011000 01011110 11001101 10100011
11001110 01000100 01100111 00111000 11101111 11011110 10000011 00011110 00111000 00111101
01001101 01111010 00000111 11111100 00100000 10010111 11011011 10110111 00110111 10010111
10010011 10001100 11110011 11101001 01010101 10101110 00111100 00010101 10101000 11000100
11011001 01011000 00000001 11101111 11000001 10101001 01011000 11011010 01001101 11011010
11100100 10111000 00110011 10001010 11000110 00001111 00011101 00101001 10111101 00001111
00010101 11010011 01011100 11111000 01011011 01010010 10000001 11001110 11111011 01010111
00100011 11010110 10101000 11001101 10100101 01011100 01000101 10010000 01100000 01100100
11101111 10000010 00111010 11010110 11010001 10101111 01001101 11110101 00000110 10101100
01100100 10100011 00000010 11011000 00000011 00110100 01111001 10000100 00000011 11110100
11100010 10101111 00011011 00110111 01010111 11011100 00010100 10000011 11101101 01001000
11110110 01000111 00111001 01001100 11100011 00111100 11100110 10101101 01010100 10001011
01111010 00000101 10011001 01000011 01110001 00100011 00000000 01010001 10011111 11011101
00000011 10011100 11110111 00010101 01101101 10101101 00111001 11100000 01111101 00000101
00100111 11011001 01100100 11101010 00000111 10110111 00000110 10101101 01001101 00111101
11000100 01010111 01100110 11111010 10011100 01111110 01010100 11010010 00111001 11000000
00111100 01100010 10100100 11111011 00111011 11100000 10000000 00110010 00101001 00010010
00010110 00100111 10010000 01000000 11101001 11001101 00110000 11010100 01100010 11100111
00111001 00000111 00011000 11111101 01101001 11011001 11001111 00100111 00100111 10011110
10010100 11010110 10001001 10000001 11001000 00000111 00010100 01100101 10001001 00111100
00011110 10011101 00101000 10111010 01100011 00100110 01101100 00101111 00111101 00001001
11101101 01000000 01101111 11011101 11100111 00011111 00111111 01111010 10001111 00101100
01110000 00110001 01001101 00001101 11010010 10100101 10000001 00100110 01111110 01011100
11100011 00100011 10111111 10110101 00111011 10011100 00001100 01111110 00110101 00011011
10110110 11100011 10001110 00111111 00001010 01101110 11101100 00111110 00001000 10100110
00001100 10011001 11110011 11011111 10110101 00110100 10011100 11111101 00101001 00001001
00011000 11001110 00101001 01011100 10001100 01101101 00011101 11101010 01111010 10001010
11100011 10111010 10001110 10000111 00011110 11010100 11010101 00000001 10011100 00011110
10111111 01001010 01110010 00000011 11010011 00111000 00000111 10111101 01011000 01000101
01001000 11111010 00010001 11101110 01101000 01101100 01111010 10001100 10000110 00010010
01001001 11101101 11001101 01011100 10001110 00100101 00100000 00000111 00000000 10010001
11001110 01101010 00100111 10011100 01101111 00000110 00111100 00111010 00001111 01001010
10000100 11001100 01011000 01111100 10000000 01100010 10100110 11001111 10101000 00010111
00100100 10011100 01000110 00000110 00111001 00111110 10000000 11010100 00100010 01111001
00011010 01010001 00011000 00011001 00101101 11010011 11010100 11010101 01111111 00101101
10001100 10000100 00111001 11000000 11101011 10001010 11110100 00001111 00000000 01111000
01111100 00110100 10100011 01010011 10111011 10000111 00101000 10111100 01000010 00001111
01111111 01111010 11001010 10101100 10100011 01001010 00101110 01001100 10111000 01000001
11001101 11011001 00011011 11011110 00001011 11010000 01001110 10011011 01101100 00101110
00101110 00110011 11110110 10111001 00000000 00100000 00011111 11100001 00011111 11100011
01011101 01100010 01110001 11001101 00110100 00101110 01001111 00111101 01101010 01010101
00011000 10101111 10011101 10101011 01011010 01110101 00011101 11011001 11101001 11000010
10011010 10000010 10110000 01100111 00000011 11010110 10011000 11111100 10011110 00101010
01001100 00010011 11001101 01000110 11011001 11101111 11000101 01100101 10101101 11001011
01101000 00001000 00100000 11010011 01110010 01101001 01011100 11100100 11111111 00000000
01011010 10001101 11111011 11010000 11011101 10000010 11000000 11000111 10010011 01010001
00111111 01010011 11000110 00101000 11001001 10101000 11001001 11100011 10011010 10001000
11101111 01100001 10010001 10110000 11101111 01010000 11001011 10010000 01101010 01000111
00100111 11110000 10101000 01011100 10011100 00011111 11110001 10101101 01111001 01111001
10000100 00110101 10001111 11001001 01010001 01100100 01101111 11100000 11111110 01110100
00110011 01100101 00000111 11010010 10100010 11011101 11010011 00110100 11011010 10111011
01010110 00001101 00001001 01110010 00111000 00111101 11111111 00000000 10011101 00110000
10110111 00111000 00110101 00010011 01001000 00110111 01100011 10110101 00110011 00111101
11111101 11101010 10111100 10000000 10110000 11001101 10110111 11110001 10101000 01100100
00111000 01101111 11101001 01000110 11101100 10001110 10010101 00001011 10010011 11000110
11010001 11010111 10111101 00101110 01101001 01111100 00100100 10111111 00100010 01100110
01101110 00110011 01010001 11100111 00111001 10100110 01100100 10011010 01000011 00100001
11101100 00101010 11011110 10001010 11000000 00110001 11011000 11100111 00000011 10001100
```

10011010 00001001 11101011 11001000 00010100 00111001 11011100 00000111 10101000 00110101
00010011 10110111 00111001 11101101 11010110 10001011 01011001 10100000 00010101 11011000
01110110 11101001 01001100 11001000 01011110 00001111 01110011 11010110 10010011 10111110
01101000 11001000 11101111 11011110 10101001 01101111 11101110 10010010 00111101 10011011
10110101 00111001 00000110 01111001 00100111 00000010 10100010 11111111 00000000 01111010
10010101 01011011 00100010 10100001 11011101 10110010 10010011 10110001 01100001 10110001
10110100 11100000 11010000 10100111 00001011 10010011 11001101 01000010 10000100 10000010
01111001 10100111 00110001 00100100 01110111 10100010 11101111 10111001 00110110 00011111
10111011 00100010 10010011 01110001 11011110 01000000 00010101 00011110 01000001 11111010
01010011 01110111 01100011 10011111 01001010 11010010 11010110 11010110 01000001 10101001
00100100 10110010 01111010 01110010 01101001 10101100 01111110 01011110 00101010 00001100
10110011 01110011 10011110 11110100 11000111 10010100 00000010 00001000 00100111 11011110
10011110 10011101 10101110 00101101 10001011 00011011 10111111 00111010 10000110 01000110
11100000 10011010 10000111 11001101 11001000 11001001 10101000 11011110 01001100 10001110
10111100 00011010 00010100 00011011 01100101 00001110 01111100 01111110 10010101 01010111
01110001 11011110 01001111 01101010 01110011 00110001 00111111 01011111 01011010 10000101
11011010 10111010 01111001 00111011 10010010 10101100 00111001 10011011 10101110 01001110
00101001 10101110 01001110 00111010 11100010 10011011 10011100 10011111 01001010 00001000
00100101 10101001 11101000 00001100 00010011 10000000 01111011 11111010 11010011 00011011
00100100 00010010 00001111 00011111 11001010 10010101 10110000 01011011 00010100 00111111
00000110 10110100 10110011 10110101 11010000 01011010 11100011 01011000 11100011 11011011
10001010 10100000 00000110 01100100 00100011 10111001 10101011 00110111 00111100 00001111
10101101 01010111 10000100 00001100 10010011 10011110 01101010 11101001 11011011 01110100
01100110 11000111 10101001 00100000 00000001 10001100 01111010 11110011 10011100 11010010
00111010 10010011 11001110 00000110 00001111 10111101 01001011 11000111 11111100 00001010
10010001 10000000 11011011 11111000 11010110 10101101 01011111 01010110 01001101 10101100
01000000 01000000 00001011 11000111 01011010 11001100 10111111 00111101 00111001 11100011
10111101 01101011 00110010 11110111 00111101 00000111 01011010 11001100 10111100 10001111
00100001 11111101 00111101 11101011 01001000 00111011 10110100 01001100 10001100 11111111
00000000 10111100 00111000 11101111 11011010 10110110 01110100 11001100 10101110 11000000
00111001 11111111 00000000 00011010 11000110 00011110 10000111 10101101 01101100 11101001
10111001 01011000 11100011 00100000 01110101 11101110 01001101 01101011 01010111 01100011
00101010 01101011 01010011 10101100 10110000 10001111 01110111 11001101 10001110 10111110
10111101 10101011 01101010 00110011 10110111 00011101 00110001 11011110 10110001 11110100
11110001 10111001 01000001 00000000 10001111 01011010 11011000 00011101 00000111 00011001
11001111 10100101 01111000 01011000 10001001 00110110 11110100 01011010 00011110 10000100
00010101 10001011 00101000 11011000 11101111 01010010 10101011 00000011 10000010 01111010
11010101 01100101 00111000 11101001 10001100 01010100 10000001 10000001 00011000 11000101
01110010 11101001 00100111 01110010 10001001 00011001 10000110 00101000 00011101 00001111
11100111 01010000 00111001 11000111 10111101 00110101 10100101 00100000 01110101 11100010
10101101 00101011 00111101 01000110 01001010 11101100 00000010 01111011 11010100 00001111
00100110 01000110 01001000 00010101 00011100 10110010 01100100 11111011 01010100 01101110
11000011 10001100 10011010 11010110 00101011 01111011 10001001 00001001 00100100 10100000
11110000 00111010 11010100 00010010 01001011 10011111 01001100 11010011 10100100 00000011
10001100 11110101 11101011 01010000 00011100 00000010 01011010 10110100 10110101 11110100
01011011 10001111 01100001 00011100 11101110 00000011 11010110 10100011 01100110 11000000
10100110 01001000 11011100 11100000 01111110 01110101 00011011 10110111 11001010 01001001
10100101 01100111 11010100 10000101 10101011 00010101 11011000 11100000 11100011 11110011
10101010 11101101 00100000 11001001 11011110 00111010 01010100 10011001 00111000 11001101
01010110 10011011 10011001 00000111 10100101 01101101 00000101 01111101 11000111 01101110
10100010 10100001 00011000 11101011 01001110 01111100 01101100 11001111 01111010 01100100
01011000 01010011 10010011 11001101 00111101 11000000 11101010 00111010 11010110 10001110
00111010 11101110 01010010 01000100 01111011 10110000 00001110 11011010 00110000 01110001
10011100 11110001 01001011 10000001 10111111 10010001 01001001 00101011 00000000 00000000
11000101 00001110 00101101 00101101 01000001 00111011 00001101 01110001 10001110 10000100
01010011 01010110 01000010 00000001 00011101 01110011 01001100 01100010 01111101 00101010
00101001 10100110 00101001 11000000 01011110 10111101 11001101 00010001 01001101 11101000
01001011 01110110 01000011 10100101 10010100 10000001 11011011 00110100 10011010 01110100
01100110 11101111 01010001 10110110 10110111 01000000 01001001 10010110 01010000 00001000
00000011 10011010 10100111 00101100 11000011 10011100 10110000 00010101 10110101 11100000
00000100 00010111 00011110 00100110 10000101 10001001 11111111 00000000 01010100 10101101
00100110 00101011 01011001 00100111 00011000 00110011 00010110 11111010 00011110 10100110
11101100 00101101 01100000 00111000 11101100 00111011 10011010 11100110 11100111 10111001
10010010 01111001 10001001 01100010 01001000 00110101 10100011 10101100 11011100 00011110
00010001 00001000 11110111 10101100 10001011 01100010 01001100 11000000 00011110 00111011
01010111 11001110 01000001 00111101 01100100 01110101 01000001 00011011 10011010 01100100
00111100 10100011 11100011 00111001 00010101 10101100 10101011 10110101 01111010 01010101
01111011 00011000 10110110 11000110 00001000 00011111 10000111 10101101 01011010 01100010
01110010 01110011 11111010 11010111 00010100 11101110 11100101 01110001 01001000 10101111
00101000 11011010 01110010 01111010 10011010 10000111 00101011 10011110 00101000 10011110
01011110 01110000 01101010 10010101 11000101 11000000 10001111 10101011 01010110 10001110
11110010 11010000 10010100 01011100 00100100 01100100 01100110 10000001 00101111 01101100
11010110 01010111 11011010 11001011 01100000 00001110 10011111 01011010 10010101 00011011

```
00100011 00100100 11110111 10101010 01110100 10011100 01110111 00110100 01000110 11001100
00100111 01111110 00101010 11000110 00111000 11001101 01100101 01011001 11001110 01011001
11110000 01001110 00000000 10101101 01011100 11111110 11101111 10011010 10010111 01111011
01011000 00011010 00110010 11110101 00101001 00110110 11000010 11100011 10011010 11100011
10101110 01011111 00010010 10111001 11110111 10101110 10010011 01011010 10010111 00001000
01000010 00011110 10111101 01101011 10010010 10111001 01100010 01100100 01111100 00011100
10001100 11010111 01100110 00010010 10011010 01000010 01001110 11101100 01101110 01111010
10011110 11110101 01011010 11101010 01110101 10001101 00000001 11100110 10011110 11010010
01111001 01111001 00100100 11100010 10110000 00101111 00101111 00001100 11110011 00011101
10011100 01000111 10011110 00101011 11010101 10100101 01001011 10011000 01110101 00101010
01110010 00100011 10101110 11110000 10001100 01100101 10010010 11100010 11100100 11100000
00011100 11101100 00011001 10101101 01011011 10001001 01110000 01001101 01010000 11010000
11001000 10110100 11010000 11100011 00000111 00000100 10010000 01011001 10101011 00111110
11101010 11101100 11001001 00100011 11100000 11110100 11101000 00101011 10011010 10100100
00111101 10100101 01010110 11000010 00011011 01101010 01011100 01111001 00111100 11010111
01110000 11111101 00101001 00100001 00001011 10111111 00111110 10010101 01000001 00101110
00110001 11101111 10011010 10011110 00011001 11000000 01100001 10111111 11010111 10010011
01001101 11010011 01101011 01100001 10011101 01110101 10101110 00010110 11011001 00001001
11101110 00111001 11100110 10100011 10111100 10111100 10001101 00010011 10101001 10101100
10111001 10110101 01101000 10000100 00100011 11001011 10101100 00101011 10111101 01000000
10011110 01011101 10111011 11110010 01001111 01001010 11100101 10100111 10000111 10010100
11100101 01110110 01000011 00110111 01101110 10110101 00101100 00001110 00001000 00100100
11010110 00101101 11001101 11101000 00000100 10110001 00100100 00011111 01011100 11010110
00100101 11101110 10101010 00010011 00001011 00011001 11011110 01110011 11010111 00110101
10010101 00110100 11010010 11001010 11100101 10011100 11100100 10011010 11110100 11101000
11100000 10101100 11101110 11001100 10011101 01100100 10110110 11010100 11011000 10011010
11111000 10110011 10011101 10011110 10110101 00000111 10011011 11001000 11001111 00100111
10111101 01100111 00100100 10011101 00110010 01111001 11110111 10101011 00000001 10010111
10111001 11000111 10111101 01110110 11110010 00101110 10100100 11110011 11011100 10111011
10111100 00011100 11110101 10101001 01000100 10000111 11001011 11100100 11010101 00010001
00100111 00011110 10111110 11100011 10111101 00001101 01110000 10111110 01011111 01011111
11000111 00110101 10011111 00100111 10010000 11111001 11010001 10100100 10010010 11100111
10101101 01001110 10101110 00110001 01011001 00011111 01101010 01011101 10100000 11100111
00000110 10100011 01101011 11100010 11000111 00111011 01011011 11110010 10101001 01110100
01100100 00111111 01101100 10001111 10100000 10110110 11111010 11010010 10010101 10100111
11110100 00111001 10100001 01111101 01111101 11101011 10001010 01110110 00111001 10110110
00011010 10001011 10000100 00011101 11001111 01111010 00001010 10000010 01110000 00101001
11100011 10001110 01010111 10100111 01111010 01010101 11111011 11011001 10101100 11010011
01110110 10110011 00000010 00111101 10100000 11010000 11001010 00101010 01000000 00110011
10011110 11011001 10100111 00101010 10001100 01010011 01001001 11011010 11000000 01000010
01000111 01010011 11010011 11010010 10000101 01011110 11111111 00000000 10100101 00111100
00000010 01000111 00111000 10100101 00000011 00000010 10001000 01000101 01110101 00101000
10001100 00000010 00000001 11001111 01111110 10011110 11010100 00000101 11001111 00010101
00100110 00000111 01111111 11001110 10000110 00000100 00001111 10101111 00110101 00001101
01011001 11011001 00010010 01000111 10001100 01110101 11101011 01000000 11000001 10100111
10101000 11001000 11001001 11101011 01000110 00110001 11010011 10011111 01011010 01111010
00100110 00010111 00011000 11000000 01100011 11010110 10010001 01100011 00011110 01011110
01111101 11111001 11110110 10101001 01000010 10010000 00110011 01000011 01000111 11111000
01100110 10011010 10001010 01111010 11011000 01110111 00011010 10111101 01110010 01111001
10100101 00001000 00000111 00000111 10111101 00101001 00011000 11000101 00011100 11100011
00111111 10011101 00010111 10110000 10001000 11011001 01000111 01111010 00110110 01110011
01010010 00101000 11101111 01000111 01111110 01111010 01010101 00111011 01101110 00101101
01000100 01101000 10000001 00011100 00001111 11000110 10100011 01100101 11001111 11010010
10100111 00100011 00100000 01111011 01010000 00010110 10100101 11001001 00100001 10100010
10111011 01000111 10010011 01000111 10010110 00111011 11010100 11000011 10001100 11010001
10001100 10011010 10101111 11000100 01001001 01101010 01010110 01101000 11111001 11100000
01110001 01000110 11001111 01101010 10110011 10001100 00001110 10011100 11010001 11000111
01011010 01001011 01111011 10000101 11001010 11111110 01011000 11101001 01001000 11110001
10000001 11101111 01010110 00111011 11110000 00101001 00000000 11110101 10100001 00110101
01111101 00000001 00010101 11111100 10110001 11010110 10011011 11100101 10010011 11010011
11110011 10101011 01101100 10100000 11100011 10001010 01001110 00110011 11000101 00001101
10000101 10001010 11111011 01000000 11100000 10001110 00101010 00111111 00101100 00010010
00111010 01110001 11101011 01010111 00111000 11101011 10001010 01100110 11010001 10011111
01001100 11010011 11010111 10101000 10101101 01110010 00001111 00101100 01100010 10010001
10100010 00011101 11000101 01001110 11010001 11110011 10001111 11001110 10000110 10001111
00011101 11101001 01001010 01010110 01010111 00001011 00010101 01011010 00000101 00111101
10110011 01001110 01101000 01010111 00000000 11111110 01111100 01010101 10001111 00101100
10001111 10101101 00001011 00011001 00111100 00011010 11001011 10011101 10101110 10000000
11010001 01000101 11100001 01010010 11000000 11100000 01110100 11000101 00100001 10110011
01001001 00000001 00000101 01100011 11110100 00111001 00011101 01101010 11111111 00000000
10010111 11001110 00110001 01001100 00110001 11101101 11110101 11100110 10110100 01001001
11101110 10000101 01100011 00100010 01011101 00010110 11001010 01000011 11111011 11001011
01111000 11011111 10001110 01110001 11000101 01010010 10011111 11000010 10011010 01011100
```

10100000 10010111 10110110 11001110 01111101 11101011 10100101 00001011 11000101 00110101
10000110 01001110 00001101 00101101 01100011 10110011 00000110 10001110 01001110 01001111
00000100 11101001 00101110 10111000 11110010 10011100 00110111 11111011 11010101 01001001
10111100 00000101 01100010 01110111 10011111 00110010 01101100 10011100 11110101 00100011
10001010 11101110 10110001 11101101 10011010 01100011 00101110 00000111 01001010 11010111
11011010 11001110 11011010 00110010 01111001 00001111 00111011 10010011 11100001 11111100
00011100 01111001 01110011 10111000 11001111 01011100 01010101 01011001 01111100 00000011
00100110 01001110 00100110 00011110 11011001 11101011 10011010 11110100 11000110 00011100
11100000 11010000 11010001 10001100 11010011 01011000 10001010 10111101 11000011 10010001
00011110 01001001 00110111 10000001 11101111 01010100 01100000 00110100 01001111 11101010
01111011 11010110 01110100 11011110 00010010 11010100 01100010 11001001 01111011 01000111
11101011 10001100 10001110 01101011 11011010 10110000 00110010 00001110 00101001 00001100
00101010 01010111 10010001 10011110 11111100 10011010 11010111 11101011 01010101 00110111
10111000 10111101 10011010 00111100 00001010 11100111 01000101 10111001 10000000 01111100
11110110 11010010 10100000 00100011 10011100 10101111 01001010 11001111 01111101 00111000
10000011 10011100 11110101 00110101 11110100 01001111 10010000 10001111 11110111 11000000
00100011 10100111 00100010 10101000 01001101 10100011 11011001 01001010 11100100 10111101
10111100 01111100 11111011 01010110 10111111 11011010 00010010 01001011 01100010 01111101
10010010 01100111 11001111 11101101 01100100 11001010 01110010 11100111 00111001 11101110
00111101 01101010 00101111 00101101 10000011 11110011 11001111 00111101 01101011 11011100
11101110 11111100 00100001 10100110 01001000 00001001 00010000 10010100 11001111 10100001
10101100 00111011 11001111 00000001 11000011 10110000 10011011 01111001 10011000 00010010
01110011 10000110 00010101 10111100 00110011 00001000 11001011 10100001 00101110 10010011
11101000 01111001 00101011 00110001 00010001 11110100 11100000 11010011 10010000 11100011
10010011 11010010 10111011 10001011 11011111 00000011 11011111 01000111 10111100 00001101
10110010 01110001 10010001 10110111 10101001 10101110 01111010 11111111 00000000 01000000
10111011 10110011 00101110 00100101 10000110 01001100 10000011 11001110 00010111 00110101
11010011 01001111 00010101 01001110 01111010 00100110 00100110 10011010 00110010 01000110
11101110 01010011 10100101 01001010 11100011 00001000 00111001 11100011 00011000 00010100
01111001 01010011 01000100 01111111 01111000 10100100 00000001 11111100 01000100 01010011
01100100 11001001 11100011 00110101 10111110 11111011 01101100 01000000 11011101 11111101
01111101 01000101 00111000 00110001 11000110 01010000 01100010 10011010 00010111 00100111
00000111 10101001 10101101 00001101 00101111 01001011 10011010 11111110 11100101 00101101
11100000 11101010 11100111 00011001 11101100 00111110 10110100 01101001 00011101 01011000
11010010 01101100 11010111 11110000 10011110 10001000 11011010 11000110 10100000 10011110
01100111 10011001 11110110 01101000 11111001 10010001 11000001 11101011 11101101 01011110
11001001 01101001 00000100 01110001 01000110 10001011 00011100 01111110 01011010 00101000
11000010 10000001 11011000 01010110 01100111 10000110 11110100 01101000 01110100 10001101
00110010 00111011 01101000 11111011 01110010 11000111 11010100 11010110 11100010 01100000
00001110 00111010 01010111 11001110 01100011 00110001 00111110 11011010 01110110 01011011
00011110 10001101 00011010 01111100 10001000 01001101 10111100 10000011 01000001 00000100
00011010 00001001 11000000 11100111 10011100 01010010 01110011 10011110 00001111 00010101
11000111 01100110 01110100 01110101 00010111 01110001 11101110 01101010 00110111 00111001
00111000 10100101 11111110 00010011 01010001 00111001 00011000 11111001 10101010 00011101
01001011 00101011 01011111 01010001 11011100 01010110 00111110 10110101 00011100 10101101
01001111 01101111 01000011 01010000 01001011 01001110 01001111 01001101 00000101 11010100
00011000 11100110 10100011 01100011 10010011 11111100 11101000 01100011 11101011 01010001
01001011 00100000 00010100 11011100 00011011 11010100 00000110 00111001 11000110 01111001
10101010 11110010 10110111 01011111 11010110 10011111 00110100 10011001 11000001 00011100
01111010 11010101 01110110 10010011 10101111 00010101 01101001 00111011 11101000 00000010
10111001 11100010 10101011 01001010 11011100 11100110 10100100 01110011 10010011 01010000
01001000 01111001 11101011 11000000 11101011 01010110 10011100 10000101 01100001 11111001
11001111 01001110 01001111 01101010 01100110 01110010 01001000 11101111 01001001 10011101
10110100 10011110 01100110 11100011 10010001 11010010 10101011 01001001 11111001 00000101
11000101 00011001 00111000 00011011 10111001 11111010 01010010 10010110 11111100 10000111
10111101 01000111 10111011 00000111 00010100 10001100 01110011 01001001 00101110 10010010
00100101 00111110 10100010 10100110 01001001 11001110 01000111 00110100 00111111 00011100
00011110 10110100 10000001 10010111 01101110 01000000 00111111 01001100 11010100 01001101
00100111 11001011 11001110 01101010 11010111 10010000 00111011 10001010 11101111 11000111
00110101 00010001 01100000 10100011 00111100 11010010 10010011 10010011 11001111 01111010
10001100 11111111 00000000 11111010 10101001 11000110 00110111 01110111 01000010 00000010
01000110 00110001 11101010 01110011 01000010 10011100 11010100 01001110 01110000 01111001
10100101 00000100 10101111 11010000 11110111 10101011 01001001 10110100 11000010 11000100
10111001 00100000 11010011 11000001 00011100 11100010 10100010 01000011 10010011 11101101
11101011 01001011 10010001 10010010 00000101 01000101 11110100 10110011 00011010 10110000
11110010 11011000 00111101 11101001 10111011 10001110 00101010 00110110 00111111 00110110
00111011 01010000 11001101 10001010 00011110 11111010 00000110 10000100 10011011 10111000
11100011 10101111 10100101 00110101 11011011 11110010 10101000 11011011 00000011 10010010
01001101 01000110 01011011 10110001 11111100 11101010 10010101 11111101 01000001 10110001
01001100 10100100 00000010 10111111 10001101 01000110 01111001 01001100 11100111 10011100
11110100 00110100 11000110 10010011 01101001 11100111 00011111 01011010 10000111 10101001
00111110 10111110 10110101 10111100 01100000 10010011 10111010 00100101 01111001 10001110
01101001 00111101 00001101 00111001 11011011 10101111 01110001 01010101 11110011 11001000

00011001 11101010 00101001 01011000 11100011 10100001 10101101 00011100 00011101 11101110
10000010 11100000 11110010 00011110 11010100 10000101 10001000 11000110 11110001 10011111
01001010 01100011 00110111 01010011 10011110 00101001 00110111 01110100 00100100 11100100
01111011 11010101 00101000 10110101 10100001 00111110 10100011 10001001 00000011 11111100
00101001 11000011 10011111 01011010 01100110 11010000 01000110 01111010 10010011 11011110
10001110 10001001 11010111 10111101 00100100 10010010 01100011 01110111 01000010 11111111
00000000 11101000 01010100 11011101 11011001 00011000 11001111 00110100 00110011 01100011
00111111 10101101 01000001 01110001 00100010 11000110 10011001 00000111 11100111 11101101
10010001 01010110 10100010 11101111 01100110 00111110 10000100 01010111 00010010 00011001
00001000 11101011 11000101 00101010 00000010 00001110 01000111 01001010 10001010 00101111
10011000 00010010 01110011 10011010 10011000 00011100 00001010 10110111 10110001 10011010
10111110 11100011 11010100 00001100 01110100 11101001 01000000 11001111 00111111 01001111
01011010 00010000 11110010 01001110 00110000 00101000 01000010 00110111 11110100 10101001
01011101 10011001 01000010 10111000 11001100 01011000 11000101 01100111 11011110 00001100
11000110 01000101 01101001 00010011 11111001 01010101 01001011 10010000 01000000 11101001
11110010 01111010 11010011 10000011 01011100 11000100 11001101 00011000 00011111 11110010
11010011 00011001 11111100 11111011 11010110 11011110 10011000 10111000 01010000 00111010
11100011 11110100 10101100 01111001 10110000 10110011 01100011 00000000 00011010 11011001
11010010 00000110 01010000 10000001 11111001 01100111 00111100 01010111 01101101 01001001
11111011 10100111 00111101 00111101 11001110 10101111 01001011 01101101 11010001 00001110
10111100 01110101 10101101 01011000 11011000 00010001 11001111 00010101 10000101 01100101
00100111 10010110 01010011 10011110 00101011 01011101 00100100 00001100 00111010 11111110
00110101 11100000 01010111 11111000 10001110 11111000 00100010 11001110 01111000 11110101
00011111 01011010 01011101 11011101 00001000 11100011 11011110 10101011 10101011 00000000
00110001 10011010 01110011 00010011 10011111 01101010 11001010 11001101 00010101 01110010
01100110 01100010 01010010 10100001 01111110 11111001 11101111 01001101 00101100 01000111
11010010 10011010 11010010 01111100 10011011 10110001 01001110 11101101 11101100 00111011
00001110 01100011 10000001 11101101 01010000 11001010 11000000 10000000 01101010 00010111
01101100 10011110 10111100 00011010 01101110 11101111 11000100 01111010 11010101 10100100
10110110 01000000 10010101 11000101 00101101 10010011 10010011 01010001 10010010 01001110
00001000 11101001 01001100 11110011 00110010 01111111 10101101 00100011 10110011 00010001
11001001 10101101 01010010 01110110 10110011 01000001 01110001 10000100 00011110 10111101
00111111 00011010 10001101 11000111 01100011 11001000 10100111 10110000 00111100 10011110
10010100 10011001 11100011 00100110 10101101 00101110 01001101 11010000 01101110 00110001
10110011 11000000 11110101 11101001 01001100 00010001 10101110 01001110 01111010 11010100
10001101 11010011 10001110 11110100 11011110 00101010 10010011 01101101 11011100 01101111
01000010 00111100 00001100 01100010 10011010 00001000 00011100 00011110 11010100 10001111
00100000 01011100 10001111 11010110 10101011 01001011 00111000 00000000 11100110 10101001
00100110 11110110 00100101 11001100 10011001 11100100 11000001 00100110 10100010 00110011
00101111 01110011 11001101 01000000 10011110 01111100 11000100 00001000 10010001 11110110
00011110 11100111 10100101 01011100 10000111 01001100 01110111 01100000 01011111 11110111
10000111 11010000 01010101 11001001 11000110 00111010 11001000 11001110 11110111 00110011
10011110 11101100 10010011 10000000 00001111 00010100 11011111 00101010 01111001 10011011
00010001 10100011 00011100 11111011 01010111 01011111 01100101 11100001 11110010 11011111
11000000 01010011 10001100 11110100 10101101 11111011 01111101 00011110 00101011 01100101
11001110 00111001 11110111 10101110 01011010 10011000 11111010 01010100 11111110 00010000
11100100 01101111 01110110 01111001 11010010 01101000 01010011 10110000 00101101 00110001
00111111 01000000 00101011 10101011 11111000 01111111 10100101 10011011 00111011 10101011
11001011 10001101 10011000 01000010 10111110 01011000 00100110 10110110 10010110 11001000
11011100 01001000 10001011 11110111 01010100 01110001 10111010 10110100 01000100 01010001
01011010 01011010 01101100 10001111 10100000 10101110 01101010 11111000 11111001 11010101
10001011 10000010 11101010 01011100 00101001 00100100 01100001 01101010 10110011 00010011
01110011 00100001 11001111 00011101 10101000 11010010 10000001 10011010 11101101 00010100
11110010 00110001 10011010 11001110 10111110 10011111 00110011 00011110 01111011 11110101
10101101 10001111 00001010 10101000 10010001 11100101 10010100 11110100 01010001 10001111
11000100 11010110 00010010 10001111 00100101 00100011 10100011 01000011 10101001 10000100
11101101 01010000 00111101 00000101 01010111 10111000 10111000 00000001 01001110 01111001
00011001 11101111 11011010 10100100 10010010 01000101 00010001 11110101 11000000 11110100
10101100 00001101 01010110 11101100 10001001 00001010 10001110 00110011 11001101 01110000
01000010 10011111 10110100 01100100 00110101 10101000 01011100 11011110 00000110 00100111
01100001 11111100 11101011 00111010 11100110 01110010 11100110 10011011 00001100 01110010
01011101 11001010 00010110 00000101 00100111 11010100 11110110 00010101 10111001 01100111
10100011 10101000 01100000 11010011 10010010 11000111 11101001 11000101 01110101 10111110
01001010 01011011 10001110 11001001 00011001 10110110 10010110 10101100 11000000 00010000
00001111 00110101 01110001 11100000 01100000 00110110 10001100 11100010 10110110 11010010
11011110 00100101 00000011 00000011 00011000 10101000 11011111 01101000 00111000 11110100
10101100 00100101 01010001 10110110 00010111 11010100 10101111 10100110 11000000 11000001
11110010 01010111 10100101 01101011 01001100 01000010 01000110 01111011 01111011 01010100
00110110 10001010 00000001 11001111 10101001 11100011 11011010 10011011 10101000 11001010
00100011 10001000 11100111 10001110 00111001 10101100 11101100 11100110 11101100 00101011
10011100 11001110 10110111 00110000 11001001 01011110 11000111 11010110 10111001 10001001
10001001 00001110 01001001 10101011 00111010 10011101 11011001 10010110 01101001 00111101
00001001 10101100 01011101 01000010 11110011 11001001 10001000 10010010 01111001 00111100

00001010 11110110 01110000 11110100 01011010 01001001 00100010 01010011 10110110 10101100
10101111 10101001 01011110 01110010 01100010 01000010 00111101 11001101 01100111 01011010
10100111 10011011 01110010 10100000 11110100 11001110 01001110 00001111 01101010 10001100
01000101 01110001 01110001 00100000 11110010 11100001 10010110 01010111 00111101 00000000
00000111 10111101 01101110 11101001 01111110 00011111 11010101 00100100 11100100 01011001
01001110 00110010 00000111 00101100 10111000 10101111 01011011 11110111 01110100 10100011
10101011 00111001 01011101 01001111 01101000 11101110 10001101 00101011 10001011 11001100
11011011 00100100 01100011 00000001 00111011 01100010 10110010 10100110 10111010 00000001
10001111 00111111 01011010 11011100 00011110 00010110 11010101 00100110 10001000 00000010
00100010 10001000 11111111 00000000 11010011 01000110 10100100 10001111 11000000 10010111
00101100 01000001 10011110 11111010 00000101 11100111 10010001 00011000 00100110 10111000
11100011 00111010 00010001 11010101 10110011 01010111 01010101 11110100 00110000 11111110
11010110 10100011 10011101 11010100 10111111 01101100 01001111 11101111 00001111 10101001
00110101 11010100 11000101 11100000 01001011 00101110 00111100 11111011 11011011 10100011
10001110 10111000 00000000 01010101 11011011 01011111 00001000 11101000 11010000 00011100
10011000 10100101 10011100 11100011 10101011 10111001 11111110 01010100 00111010 11010100
01011110 11010111 00100011 11011010 01001000 11100000 11101110 01110101 00010000 10101011
10010010 01111111 01011010 11000111 10111010 10111100 10010010 11100000 10010001 10011111
10010000 10011110 00000101 01111011 00000100 00111110 00011100 11010001 00010001 10110111
01111111 01100110 11000100 01001000 11101000 01011111 00100110 10101110 11000111 01100011
01101101 00010110 00000100 00110110 00110000 11000111 10000011 11000110 00100010 00010100
11100001 10001011 10100101 00011101 10010110 10100100 11001011 10011010 01111011 10011110
00011101 00011100 00010011 01001000 00110010 10110001 11001010 01001111 10100110 11010011
01011010 00110000 11101000 01011010 10110100 11000011 00010001 11101001 11110111 00111001
00111110 10101011 10001100 11010111 10110101 01101101 10010000 10011100 11111001 01000001
00000111 10110010 11010011 10011110 00101001 01011011 10010110 00011000 11110111 10100010
01011001 10001011 01111111 00001010 01000100 01111011 00110100 10111010 10011110 01001011
00000111 10000100 01110101 10110111 00100000 00011011 01000110 01000000 01000111 01010110
00111000 00010101 01101010 00111111 00000010 11101010 01100101 00001001 01110011 00001100
01100011 11010011 01110111 00110101 11101010 00000010 00101001 00110001 11001111 01011111
01111010 01101011 01000000 11000111 00011001 01100000 01000000 11101001 01011001 11111101
01110110 01101111 01100000 11100100 01000111 10011110 01000011 11100000 01011011 11010000
00110010 11110111 01010000 00100111 00011101 00110010 01001101 01011001 10001011 11000001
00101010 00100101 11001100 11110111 01001001 10110111 00011101 00010101 01001111 01011111
11000110 10111011 10011111 00100111 00011101 11111010 11010010 11111101 10011101 01011000
00011100 10110111 11101001 01010011 00101100 01000101 01011001 01110101 00101011 10010010
00100111 00100010 10011110 00001100 10110010 10001100 11110011 01110001 00100110 00001111
01100000 10100000 01010100 11011111 11110000 10001001 01101001 10111111 11011110 10011011
11110011 00010101 11010101 00001000 01100011 00000011 00111001 00100111 11101011 01001010
10110000 11000101 10001111 10111001 10111011 11011111 00110101 10010100 10101010 01010100
01101110 11111100 11000000 10001101 11000101 11000001 00011001 10100011 10100111 00010100
11111100 00000010 00111000 10100101 00000011 00100010 10110101 10110110 10000100 01011100
01000101 10100110 10101110 01000001 11100110 10011110 11011110 11011101 00101000 01011110
10011100 01010100 01101111 10100101 10000000 00111011 01110011 01001010 10000011 10001110
01110011 01000111 01101100 01101101 11000111 11100011 01001110 00000010 10000101 00100100
10110110 00001011 00010001 10110111 00000111 00100000 01110011 01001010 11000011 00111000
11001000 11100100 11010010 10111000 00100011 11101001 01001111 01100001 10010001 10011010
01001101 11101010 01010001 00010001 00011110 10010100 10101111 11001010 00001100 11010011
11110000 00110111 00000011 11101101 01000111 01010010 01101011 00111101 01010110 10001000
00000110 01100011 10111101 00100011 00011111 01101010 01110010 10000011 11111110 00110100
00010000 00110001 01010110 10010110 10011010 10000000 10011000 11001110 00101001 01110001
11111101 11100001 11111000 11010011 10110001 10001100 01111010 01111010 11010010 10110101
01010100 11100010 10010101 10101100 01001001 00011110 00000101 00001011 11110100 10101001
00111000 11000111 10111101 00100110 00111001 00010100 01011111 01001101 01000000 01100111
01101010 00111010 10001110 10011100 11010011 11001000 11100110 10011010 11011000 00011000
10101001 10010101 11110111 10111001 01000011 01000000 11101000 00000101 00111001 01001000
00010100 10111100 01111010 11111110 10010100 10001100 00111001 11000111 01111010 01101001
10111011 10010010 00100110 11010010 01111001 00100111 10001100 11010000 11000000 00000001
01001010 00110010 00111111 00001111 01011010 01110010 11100011 00011000 11101111 01001111
01101101 10000000 01100000 11101010 01111101 00101001 00001000 11100111 10011010 01110011
00011100 01110110 10100011 00011101 01001101 01100111 01100000 01001000 01000000 10111000
11001101 00110000 11100000 11110010 10110101 00110011 01110100 11101001 01000111 00000100
00010010 00000110 00111110 10010101 01001001 11011111 10101000 01110101 00100001 01010001
10001110 10111101 11101000 01100001 11101001 11000101 01001001 10000011 10011100 11010010
01100011 00111111 01011010 01111010 10001010 11000100 01111000 11100011 00110100 10111000
11101111 01001111 11100000 10001111 11101011 01001001 11101101 01001101 11101101 01100001
11011000 01100011 10001100 11110011 11001101 00001101 00011001 10100111 11110100 00110100
01100000 11110101 10100100 10011010 00000110 10001000 11111001 11111111 00000000 11101011
01010000 00001101 01001011 11001101 00110011 00100011 10011100 01010000 11010010 10001000
10000110 11100100 01100110 10000101 11100100 11110010 00111000 10100101 11000111 00100000
10001110 11010100 01100011 10110000 10100100 11011111 01100001 10001000 01000001 11000111
00000010 10011001 11100101 10010001 11001101 01001111 11111110 11110101 00000000 01100100
00010001 10011110 01101010 10111001 00010011 11011100 01000100 00011101 00001111 01001010

01011110 00111111 11100000 00110101 00100110 00110010 00111000 10100011 11001011 00000010
10010011 10100110 10010110 11000011 01001000 10000111 01101111 00111001 11100010 10001100
00001100 11100100 11010100 10111011 01111101 00101001 00010100 01100111 10011100 01010010
01001101 00101001 01011001 00000001 00011001 00000000 11110110 11101111 01001101 11000000
10101001 10011000 01100011 10100111 01111010 01100001 10001111 11110010 00110100 11011010
01110111 10110101 11000000 10001011 01101010 10011111 01101010 00001100 01000000 10001110
00001111 00110101 00101001 00011100 01010010 01101101 11000110 00110001 10011010 10001101
01111010 10001010 11011010 10010000 10011000 01001001 11000000 00010100 11010011 00001001
00011101 10110010 00101010 01101100 00011100 11010011 10000000 01101110 11110100 00110111
10100000 11001010 00111110 01001001 11100111 01110010 10011010 10101101 00110101 10101010
10011100 11100100 00000010 00001111 01011100 11010110 10111011 01100100 00100001 11000101
00110111 00111001 00000011 00100010 10101010 00111010 00010011 01100011 10010110 10111101
11010000 01101100 00101110 01010111 11110111 11110110 11010001 10011111 01110001 11000101
01110010 11011010 10010111 10000000 01101101 01100100 11000111 11011000 11100111 00110001
10010011 11011001 11000101 01111010 01101011 11000100 10101101 11010101 01101010 00100111
10110100 10001100 11110011 11010000 11010110 11110001 10101011 00111000 00111101 00011001
00101110 10011010 01100111 10001011 01011110 11111000 00110111 01010101 10110011 11001001
01000001 00011100 11001001 10001110 10101010 01111001 11111100 10101011 10110011 11110000
00110110 10000000 11011010 01110100 00000110 11100110 11101001 01110001 00111100 10100011
10000101 11111110 11101000 10101110 10110010 01111000 01010001 01001111 11111001 11001101
00111001 01000110 00010111 10100101 00101010 10011000 11001010 10010011 01011100 10101100
11010010 10010101 00010100 10011101 11000111 00101000 11110100 10100111 10100110 01110001
01001000 10001011 10000001 11011110 10011101 11000110 01110001 10001010 11110011 01101100
10010010 01110110 00111011 00000110 10110000 10100000 10000001 11011111 00110100 00110111
01011100 11010010 10110001 11000111 01011110 11010100 10010100 11011011 10110010 01101000
00001000 11011011 10000010 00001111 01101010 10001100 10001110 01111001 10100111 10111000
00100111 10111111 00010101 00000001 00100100 00111111 00110101 10100100 00010100 01010101
11111001 10110110 00010101 11000100 01110011 11111100 11101010 00001001 01111010 11100111
00111100 01111010 01010100 10001110 01110011 11110101 10101000 10011100 11010011 01110100
11010010 00001011 10010001 10010010 00110001 01010000 10010110 11001111 00001110 01111110
10011110 11010100 00110011 00001100 11010100 01110010 01100011 00110100 10010111 00110100
10010101 10000110 10111100 11001000 11011100 11100100 11100011 10101000 10101000 01011100
11100011 10000101 11101111 01001110 01110011 10001110 01110011 11001101 01010111 01110010
00001000 00111110 10100111 11011111 10100101 01011100 00010011 11011001 10000000 11100011
11000001 00111100 11110001 11111100 10101010 00010111 11000110 00110000 00000110 01101000
11011111 10010000 01110011 11101001 10000010 01101010 00110010 11010101 01001001 10110010
01000111 01111011 00011110 10000010 10011000 00001110 00001111 00011100 10001010 01000110
00101100 00110000 01001000 11000001 11110111 10100110 11101110 11100111 11011110 10110101
01101001 00101101 00111010 00010010 11011001 00100011 00011110 11110100 11010111 01101111
11001010 10000000 01101001 10001110 11000000 01110101 10100001 01000110 01010110 10110010
00011010 01110111 00011110 00001001 00000000 00011111 11001110 10011000 01111001 00111101
01111111 00111010 01000011 00100001 11101001 01010000 10111011 00000000 11100000 11100010
10000101 00001110 11100000 11011000 00110001 11111100 11101001 10100111 10101000 11001110
01111101 11111101 10101001 10111011 10001111 11110001 10011110 01111101 10101001 10111011
10000100 10000000 11100111 10011010 11010110 00110110 11101011 10110001 00101100 01010110
01100000 11001111 10010010 01101001 00110011 01001100 01010000 00000001 00000011 11010010
10011111 11000111 01010001 01001101 10000010 01101000 01010110 01101100 00001100 01010010
10101011 11111110 11101101 00001001 11100000 11100011 10011010 10001001 10011000 01100010
10010011 01111111 00011100 10011010 00111101 00010000 00010010 00100011 00011101 11100111
10001110 00001111 01111010 00110111 00010001 10011010 10001111 01110110 00000111 00000110
10011011 10111011 10000010 01101001 11001101 01111001 00010101 10101001 00100011 00110001
01100001 10000010 00101010 00100010 00111101 11111111 00000000 00101010 01100010 00110001
00011100 10101111 01111010 01001100 11110011 11010111 11110011 00110101 01110110 01110110
11010000 11001101 11101010 00100011 00010010 01111110 10011110 11110100 11001110 11111000
00000111 10001010 00110011 11001001 00011001 10100100 01110011 10001110 11100011 00111110
10010101 10101100 00101001 10110100 00001000 01101011 10010001 10011100 00110110 01110011
01001000 11010010 01111110 01110100 11000111 11011101 10011100 01111010 11110111 10100111
00011110 10000000 01110111 10100111 10100101 11101110 11011000 01111010 00001101 01001100
00110111 01011010 01110110 00111001 11100100 00001010 00110001 10000011 10001100 01110011
11101101 01000001 01101100 01110101 11101001 01010010 11100011 01100000 11110101 00010101
00011011 10011110 00111010 01010010 00110001 11001111 01011110 10000111 11011110 10011011
10010000 01111010 01010100 01101110 01000110 11101110 00111010 10010001 11010010 10011010
10001101 10011001 01111101 00000111 10010110 01010000 10100100 10111001 11000000 11110101
10101010 00010010 10110111 10011000 11011110 11011110 10110100 10010111 10010010 10010111
01110000 10001011 11010011 10111001 11001101 00100100 01000000 10101000 11100110 10111010
00111001 00011001 10010111 00111101 11001001 00010011 10001110 10000100 11010100 10101010
00111101 10111111 11111010 11110101 00000110 00001110 01110010 01000110 00000101 01001000
11101100 01111000 00000100 11010010 10010010 01001111 01100000 01001101 10010011 11101110
10100101 00001010 01001000 11001110 00111111 01011010 10000100 00110001 00111001 11100000
11100110 10101100 01000100 01110001 11000111 11100110 01101010 00011100 01011010 11101000
01010010 01111101 00000011 00011001 11000111 00011001 11110110 10101000 00100111 11001110
11010011 11111010 10001010 10110000 00001110 01010000 11100000 11110011 01010101 11101110
00011011 10101000 01010001 01001010 11111010 10100010 10100101 10110001 10000111 01110010

00000111 10011001 10000111 11101111 01011010 10011010 01000001 00000011 00100000 01110100
11101001 11001101 01100101 01011110 10000000 01100101 00011101 01110011 01010111 10110100
11101100 10000111 00000101 01011011 10100111 10101111 01111010 11101100 10011010 01010010
10001001 11001001 00000111 10101001 11010010 01000110 11011000 11000101 01101001 11011011
01001010 00001010 11100000 11110000 01111010 11110011 01011000 11010110 10101101 10010001
11001101 01011010 10000110 01011110 01111001 10101111 00100110 10100101 00110111 10111001
11011011 00000110 10011001 10101101 10011110 01110011 01000011 11001011 10001110 00111001
11110110 00010101 01010101 01100100 11001000 11001000 11111100 11001101 00111011 11001100
11001111 01111010 11001001 11000101 01011011 01010010 11111100 10001011 00000110 01000001
11010011 10111001 10101000 01011110 01010010 00011000 10001010 10001101 10100100 00111100
11111010 01010100 01100010 01001110 01111001 11101110 00101001 00111000 00101110 10000101
01011100 01110110 01111001 00111001 11101111 01001101 01110110 11101011 10001010 01000101
11100111 00011110 10110100 10011001 11000001 00110101 10100010 01001010 11010111 01100001
01101101 01000011 00100111 11101010 00101001 10001011 11001001 00111100 11010010 11100111
00110100 11010110 01100000 10111100 11110101 10100010 11010111 11011000 00111100 11011000
10100011 00111001 00100010 10010011 00011100 10010010 01001111 11111111 00000000 01011110
10100001 01111011 10000101 01011000 11110011 10011111 11000110 10101011 10100100 10110011
01001110 00111100 10111011 01111000 01100100 10010001 11111010 01100101 01000110 01101011
01001000 11000101 11001001 01101010 11000100 11011010 01000101 10100110 00100001 01000001
00100100 11111110 00110101 01010010 01111001 11000010 11100011 10011110 01001101 01011111
10000111 01000001 11010100 01101110 00011011 11110111 11001011 11100100 10001111 01000111
00110101 10110111 01100001 11100001 00110100 01000001 10011001 10001000 00100100 11110101
11001101 01001011 11000100 01010010 10100010 01100111 11001101 00101001 11101100 01110001
10100010 00001011 10001011 10110011 10000100 11100000 01100111 00111100 11010110 10011101
10011110 10001101 10001100 00110100 10011111 00111111 10111001 10101110 11001010 11010111
01000101 10000101 01110011 10110000 00000000 10000011 10101101 01001111 00110100 00010001
11111001 10100010 00010100 00011000 00011001 11101011 01011100 11110101 00110011 00011011
11111011 10110001 01010110 00101101 01010011 00111001 11111011 00111101 00110101 10011000
10001101 10001011 11101101 10011010 11101001 00110100 11101101 00100001 01100001 10001100
00110100 10100000 01101111 11111110 01010101 10100011 00001100 00001001 01101001 00010110
00000000 00011100 11110111 10100111 00100100 10000101 10110011 11001111 01001110 01001001
10101111 00101110 10101101 01111001 11010100 10111010 01000001 01100010 01001000 01100000
01000101 00011001 11101101 01010101 01101110 10010101 01000110 00001001 00100111 00000011
10110111 10101101 01001110 10110011 10001101 10111100 00011100 11010110 01011101 11101100
10100101 10001001 01010001 11101011 01011000 01010011 10100111 01110111 01110110 01010111
01010010 01011000 11011000 11001000 01110110 11000110 00001101 00111011 01010101 00111111
01100111 10110100 01110110 11110101 00011100 11110011 01010111 00110100 11001000 00010100
01000110 00011000 11110101 11110101 11110101 10101100 01111111 00011000 01001111 11100100
11000000 11011100 11110000 01111011 01100110 10110100 10100111 00011111 11011110 00100100
10001010 10111001 11000100 01001100 11100101 10100111 01100000 10011100 11100100 11111110
01110101 11101000 00011010 00110101 10111111 11011000 11101100 10010001 00011111 11111101
01100110 00000001 00100111 00110101 11000111 11111000 01001010 11001011 11101101 01111010
10000111 10011101 00110001 11111101 11011100 01111100 11100011 10101110 01001101 01110110
11110111 01110010 11111001 01001001 01011101 10111000 10111001 01011101 10101010 01010001
01111010 10010100 11100100 01010100 11010100 11101110 11010110 00100100 11001010 01100000
11110010 01110011 01011100 11010011 11001000 01100111 10010111 01101000 11101011 10011100
00001010 10110001 10101001 01011100 01111001 10001100 01000111 10101111 01100001 01010010
01101000 01110110 01010111 00001101 01110100 00100110 11110010 01100100 11110010 11010100
01100100 00010010 00111000 00111111 10011101 00010100 11101001 10101010 01110001 01101101
10001001 00110100 01110100 10011010 01011100 00110001 01011001 01011010 00011100 11100000
00011110 00110010 01111101 01101010 00010111 11010101 00100001 01010010 01000010 01001000
10000111 00011110 10010101 00010101 11111110 10011101 01110111 01111001 00010000 01001111
00111000 01000000 10011001 11001111 00000111 10011111 11000110 10100010 10110011 11110000
11000101 10010100 00011000 01101001 01100101 10011010 11100110 01001111 01010010 01110000
00110011 11110100 00010101 10011010 10100111 00001001 11111011 11010010 11011100 11001101
11010101 01010111 00101100 01111101 10111000 00111110 00001000 01111100 11100110 10101100
01000110 01011010 01000001 11110010 10101111 00011001 11101011 01010110 00100000 10110101
10110111 10000100 11100110 00111011 01110100 11001111 01110011 10110111 00110101 01100001
00100011 01111100 11111101 11011100 01100110 10110011 01111000 01111011 11101011 00010110
01000111 10110101 01000011 00100000 10001111 01101000 11001001 00110101 01001111 01010011
10110100 11111011 01101000 00001010 01100110 01111000 11010011 10111110 00000111 00100110
10110100 11000100 00001100 00000111 00111100 01100110 10011011 11110110 01110001 11011111
10011010 11011010 00110100 11010100 01010101 11010001 00101110 10100101 11001110 01110010
11011111 11000011 10110110 00001001 00101110 01100111 11110011 01100110 11110110 00100111
10001111 11010010 10101110 01000011 10100011 11101001 11110000 11001011 10011000 11101100
01100001 00001111 10011100 10000010 01010111 00111111 11001110 10110110 10010110 00000101
01010011 10011100 01010100 10011110 01011000 11100011 00000010 10110110 10001011 01110111
11010101 10011001 10110110 11011001 10011111 10000110 00011111 11101010 11100011 11011001
11101011 10000101 11000101 00011011 01100110 01100010 01000110 00111111 00111010 11010001
01011000 11111001 10100110 10111100 01100100 10111110 01111011 01010001 00010101 01100101
10100000 00110010 10001001 10110101 01101110 11101100 00101000 11111011 00101010 11100000
00001101 11000110 10101111 10101010 01100100 11110111 10100001 10100010 00000000 01100011
11111010 11010010 01110111 10110110 11011010 10001001 00110010 10100010 01011011 11000101

10110111 10011100 10011110 01111111 01001010 01000001 00001100 01100011 00111000 01011100
11010101 11011101 10100011 00011101 00101001 11000010 00110101 00011001 11001111 01111010
01010001 10111010 01010110 00001011 10010100 01110001 10000001 11010011 00110100 01100000
11110001 11000110 00110011 01010111 10110000 00001111 11100001 01000110 11010101 11100011
00010100 10100010 10100100 10110101 00001011 10010100 01001000 01111110 00101001 11000100
00011101 10111100 01010101 11001100 00001110 10010100 11000101 01010001 10011010 01110110
01110001 01111010 10000011 01100101 00101111 00101001 10001000 11001111 10101101 00110111
11001011 01100011 11111000 01010110 10000011 01100011 00011000 10100110 10011100 00011111
11000010 10001011 11110100 01001100 00001010 00111110 01010001 11001110 00111001 11101001
01001001 11100100 10010011 11010000 11010101 11000101 01010001 10011010 01001101 10111100
01010101 11011110 11111101 01001001 10111101 11001010 10001101 00010111 10100001 10100100
01011000 11110010 00111010 10011010 10110100 01100011 00011000 11000111 01010001 01010010
00101010 10001100 01110100 10100101 00011010 01110001 01001011 01010010 10101111 01110011
01000011 00111110 11011111 00101101 00100000 00000111 00111001 00000111 10001010 00110011
11011111 10100110 01001101 01001001 11000111 00011000 11111100 10101011 01101011 00101110
10011011 00010010 11000110 01100011 00100011 00011110 11110100 11101110 10011111 10001101
00101011 01111101 00101001 00111011 10010011 01000110 10001011 01000100 00100000 11100011
00110100 10111000 00100111 10100101 00100000 01101100 11100111 10001111 10101111 10101101
00000001 10110000 00101000 10001011 11100100 01100011 11010000 01010110 00011101 10001101
00001100 00111001 00011110 10010100 10101101 11000000 11111010 11010010 00000011 10010001
11000001 00111001 11101100 00101001 01001001 10111001 00001000 00110000 00110111 11010001
10011110 10111000 10100011 11111000 11000110 01101000 01100000 01111111 00011010 10100110
00000001 10001101 11000011 00011100 10000011 01000110 00111011 01100010 10010101 00110011
11001111 00010100 10101101 11010010 10001001 01101001 10100010 00000100 00100110 01111010
10000001 01010001 10101111 00000111 00010100 11111110 11111100 01010010 01110001 10001010
01001101 10110110 11000111 01100001 01010111 10011110 11011100 11010010 11110100 11111010
01010000 10101010 01000101 00100011 01100100 01100000 11110101 10101001 11100110 01101011
01010110 00100110 10000101 00100011 00000011 00110100 01111111 00000110 01110001 01001110
01011010 01101111 00000010 10101001 01110111 00011101 11000100 11101010 00111010 01110001
01000111 01000011 10000001 11001111 11100001 01001011 10001111 01111100 00001111 01101010
01110110 00110001 11011111 11110001 10100111 01100001 01011110 11100011 00111000 11110100
10100001 01101001 01010111 10101101 00110100 11110011 11101101 11101111 01000110 11011010
10010100 00011000 00111001 11000000 00011101 01111011 01010010 10101000 00000000 11010000
10100000 11110001 01001001 11011110 10100101 11111001 10000000 10100111 11010010 10001100
01100000 11010011 11000000 10100110 10001110 00001110 01101001 11101110 10101110 01001000
10011101 11111001 10100100 11000111 01010010 10111111 10001101 00011100 00010010 01111010
11100110 10000000 00001000 11100011 00111001 10100110 11101100 11011000 00001101 01100001
11101111 01000000 11101011 11001111 00011110 10010100 11101111 11100011 10100101 00100011
00011110 11111001 10100100 11011011 01101011 01010000 00011001 10001110 10111000 10100111
00101110 00001110 01101000 01010001 10000000 01110011 01001010 10100000 01010100 11011101
00100110 00111011 00000111 01111100 01100011 00111110 10110100 11001101 10100011 00011100
01111110 01010101 00100011 01110010 01000110 00101001 00001000 11001001 10100111 01100001
00001100 00000000 01100011 10100101 00011000 00010100 11111100 01100100 01010010 00000000
00001001 00111001 10101010 10111110 10011010 10000101 10000110 11100011 11010110 10011011
10001010 10011011 10000010 00111010 01010011 01110001 11001111 01001010 00010011 01101000
00010010 00011000 10101011 11011110 10001100 01100100 01010011 11111111 00000000 10000111
11111101 10011010 01010101 11101001 11101101 01010011 00100110 11011001 01000100 01101100
00001110 00110001 01001000 00000111 00110101 00100011 01100100 01010010 10000000 00111101
00110001 01001001 00111101 00000101 01110010 00100110 01011111 01101010 01101110 11011110
11100111 10100101 01001101 10110100 00011010 01100001 11100110 10010110 10011011 10110010
10001000 10000010 10011110 11011111 10001101 00101110 00011011 11111100 01101010 01010100
00011000 11111010 01010000 11000111 00100111 10001010 00101101 01101101 10000100 01000100
01010111 00000010 10010011 00011001 11100000 01010100 10101111 11010010 10011000 11011000
00011000 10100011 01110000 00100011 11000111 00010100 10000111 00011000 10101001 01011001
01001111 10100111 00010100 10011000 11111100 11101010 10011010 01010110 00010101 10001000
11011011 10001110 11010101 01011010 11100010 01000000 10100010 10101101 01001011 10000000
00001001 00111100 01100010 10110010 11100110 10010011 11001101 10010111 00111101 10111011
00001010 10001001 11001111 01001011 10010101 00000101 01110001 00011000 01100101 10110011
11011100 11010011 11010000 01110001 10010010 00110011 11001101 00110011 00000100 11110100
00111000 00110101 00111010 11100001 01010010 10110010 11110110 10001110 11101110 11000110
11101001 00001101 11001111 00011001 11111100 10101001 00110000 01000001 00000111 10111111
01111010 01011100 11100011 11101011 01001101 00110010 01100100 11111011 01010110 01001101
01110011 10101111 01111000 10101011 10001010 01001000 11001111 11001101 11011111 10111110
01101010 00110111 11101010 01111010 11010000 11101100 00000111 00110100 11000111 01101110
01111110 01011111 01001010 01110110 11010010 11010111 00001011 10001000 01100100 00111110
10011111 10001101 01000110 11101101 10010100 11100111 00011001 10100100 00101101 10000011
11110101 10101000 00100110 01100011 10000011 10000011 01000010 01011100 11001011 01110000
00010001 11011011 11011110 10100001 10010101 10111000 00110100 00010011 10011111 10010100
11010101 01111001 10001001 11101000 00101011 10100111 10010101 11001101 01011101 01110100
00100010 11000010 00010110 00000000 01010100 01001111 00100110 00000001 00100111 11110001
10100110 11001010 11011001 00000111 00011100 10010001 01010000 10111011 00011101 10011000
11101010 01101011 00100100 11101101 10100000 11000101 01110110 00111000 00100110 10101011
10111011 01100000 10011100 11110100 10100101 11110011 00111011 00001010 10001110 01010011

```
10010011 11110010 11010110 11001001 00111011 00000011 01100011 01000001 11100100 11110011
01001101 01111010 01001100 10001100 01100000 01111110 10110100 11000101 00111100 10011111
01001010 10111001 01000101 01011001 01011000 01010111 10111000 11100011 00101110 01111110
10110100 11011110 10100111 10101101 00100110 01110010 01110001 10001010 00001110 00001000
00111110 11100111 10011010 10100100 11101111 10111010 00010101 11000101 01110011 10001111
10101001 00010101 00011011 00011111 01111100 11111101 01101001 00011111 00011001 11001000
00110100 11001101 11011001 11101001 11010111 10110101 00111000 10101011 11101100 00000100
10011011 11111000 10101000 10011100 10000000 10100100 10001100 01110011 11010110 10001100
10001100 01111011 11111010 10011010 10001101 10011000 11100110 10101111 10010101 11011111
01110000 01111010 10001000 11110010 01100111 10100101 00110100 10011100 11111101 11001111
11000110 10011010 01001000 00000111 00100111 11010111 10100101 00110001 11001000 11001110
00111011 01010110 10001101 00111011 01110010 10001001 00110001 11100000 10000011 01001110
11011101 11010011 00000011 11110001 10101010 11111001 11100111 00111100 11100110 10011110
01100100 11001000 11001111 00111000 10100001 11010011 01100011 11011100 10010000 10011100
10010011 01001000 01001111 00010101 00011011 01110010 00101001 01010111 10000001 10010000
01001101 01101011 11001011 01101101 01000100 11001001 00110111 00000010 10000100 00000001
11001101 00110011 00100000 01111111 11111010 11101001 10111001 00011011 00001001 00111101
01101001 10011001 11101000 01111011 00011010 10101001 01000110 00110110 11010011 01010000
00010111 01111111 00111110 11010101 00011011 10010011 10010011 10010000 00001000 11101101
01001110 10010101 10000111 01000001 01010001 10010011 10010001 11000111 00011100 11010100
11011001 10100101 01100110 01001101 11000101 01010011 10000001 11010010 10011000 01111110
01100110 11001001 11101011 01001010 11011111 01111110 10011001 10010000 01111001 00111001
11111100 01101010 10101101 11101110 10000011 00011100 01111011 00011110 01101001 11000011
10011110 00101001 10111000 11100011 10010011 11010110 10010001 10110010 00011111 00011000
11101001 01001010 00110110 10111000 01110100 00011110 11011110 10100100 11010100 01101111
00100000 11000101 00111001 11001111 11001011 11000110 00101010 10110100 10001100 00101010
10010010 11100111 01100001 01110100 01001000 11010010 11101101 01011110 01111011 11010101
00001011 10111011 10001110 10001010 10011101 01111011 10011010 10001110 11100110 11101100
00000010 01000000 11111100 00111000 11101001 01010101 01010101 10110010 01110010 01000000
11001001 11101111 01011101 00110100 11101001 11101011 10101001 10010100 10101010 01110100
00101100 00100111 00111001 11000111 00110101 00101110 01001000 01010000 10111110 10011101
11101010 00001000 11001001 11001101 00111100 00110001 00000011 10001111 11100101 01001101
10110110 11010101 10000101 00011011 00010110 00010100 10010011 11110101 10101001 00011100
00000000 00000110 00111001 11001000 11001001 10101010 11111001 11000001 11001111 01000001
01001010 00001001 11101101 11010110 10110001 01110000 00101001 00010110 10010001 10111011
00001110 00001001 10101001 00010111 00001100 01101010 10111111 11010111 10101111 10100101
00101010 10110111 00111000 00110100 10011101 10011010 00101001 01001000 10110001 10111000
00000000 01110001 10001110 01101010 00001001 10100100 11000111 11110101 10100001 11011011
10011010 10101011 01110111 00101111 00000000 01100111 00100000 11110101 10100111 00001010
01010111 01100000 11100111 10100110 10100110 01101100 11110010 00000110 10010100 10001100
11100100 10001010 10110001 01101101 00100000 01010001 10011100 11010101 00011001 10000111
11101111 10001110 00110001 10001010 10110011 00001001 00000111 10001010 11101101 01101010
11101011 01000011 10011001 00111101 01101110 01101111 11011010 11001101 10010100 11110100
10101011 01001001 00101111 10101110 01111101 00101011 00001110 11001110 01011100 01110111
00111111 10001101 01101001 11000100 11100000 00011100 01111011 01100111 10101101 01111001
11110101 01010010 10111110 11000111 01010101 00110111 10101001 10100110 10010010 11100100
11101101 00111001 11000101 01011000 11001000 00101001 11000101 01100111 11000101 00110000
01001110 10111101 00111110 10110101 00101100 01110111 00000000 11111110 01110101 11001011
00101010 01101110 11100110 11101000 10111001 11001000 00111101 01110011 01001100 01100010
01110011 11000101 00100111 10011000 10111000 10100100 11011100 10100111 11101111 00010001
10010001 11101111 01010000 11101111 00011101 00001101 00110100 00011100 11000111 00011000
11101011 10011111 01101010 01101001 00111000 00111001 11001111 11101011 01010011 11011011
11011001 01011110 01011100 00011111 11011100 01011011 01001010 11011101 11001001 11000111
00011000 10101011 00101001 11100001 10011101 01001010 11100001 10001000 11011101 00000100
01001011 11101010 11000111 10011010 10010111 00111000 00101101 11011000 10011011 11101100
01100101 00111100 11011011 01111011 01110001 01010110 00101100 00110100 11011011 11011011
11110010 01001100 01110001 10010101 10001111 11111110 01111010 01001001 11000000 10101110
10000110 11000011 11000011 10110110 00111010 01101010 11111001 10010111 10010010 01111101
10100110 01110001 10000010 00000001 00011100 00000011 11110100 11101111 01010010 01011101
01011110 10110011 01001000 00010110 00100000 00010001 00001111 01100001 01011001 01001111
00010100 10010011 10110101 00100100 00100100 11011111 01010010 10111101 10001111 10000111
11101101 00101101 10011000 00111101 11001011 00011001 11011100 00011111 10111010 01000111
11001011 10011010 11011100 10110011 01000100 00001110 11100110 00110101 00001000 00000000
11101100 00110001 01010100 00010001 01011000 10101000 00011101 11101011 01010110 00000101
00010001 11000010 00000110 00111110 10100100 11010111 10011111 01010010 10110100 10011011
10111100 10011000 01011011 10110000 11111111 00000000 00101111 01110100 10000011 10000000
00000111 10101101 00110010 01110111 11100100 00100010 00001111 11000110 10011101 00111100
10100010 00011000 11111101 01111000 10101100 11110100 10011000 10010010 01011101 11001111
00110101 00010011 01011100 11010110 01100001 01110010 11110001 10010101 01100010 10001000
01100100 11110011 01001100 10110000 11011010 01100100 00110011 01001001 11011111 11010100
11110100 10101100 11010111 00110111 00010011 00110111 00010000 11001000 01000111 11010010
10101110 11000011 01100111 01110001 00110001 00010001 10111100 01000101 00100011 11111010
11010001 11001001 11011100 00111001 10001011 01101011 00100001 10111010 00100011 10011101
```

10110001 10001110 11110101 10011111 10101010 01011111 00001000 11000011 11000101 00010011
00000011 01011010 01110011 11011010 01001111 00101010 10010100 10000111 00010001 10100000
11100011 00111101 01101010 10010000 11110000 11100111 10011000 11000000 11001101 00111011
01100111 10111111 00010100 01010010 10100111 01111001 01110011 00111101 10000101 11001111
00010001 11011010 01111000 00100010 11011111 01110111 01010010 01111011 11100110 10100010
10010011 10001001 10000110 01000111 00110101 10111001 00001101 10001100 01110001 01000010
00010111 10010011 11011011 00111001 11000101 00101111 11110110 01111100 00111100 01100101
00110011 11110101 10101011 01110100 10100101 01111101 00001001 01110101 10010001 00000101
10011011 00010011 00011111 10100000 00011100 11010111 00011001 11100010 11001001 01100110
10111011 10111110 01011011 01101011 01100100 00110010 11110001 10011101 10101010 00110011
01011110 10000100 00100001 01010101 01011101 10100000 00001100 01111010 01010000 10110000
01000110 00001001 01100000 10100000 00111000 11101110 00000110 00101011 01011010 00110100
01100101 01001001 11110011 10110101 10101000 10011101 01101110 11001000 11100110 10111100
00111101 10100011 11001101 01100111 10100111 10100010 10111010 11101100 10010101 10111110
01110110 00001101 11010111 00110101 10100010 11011010 01011100 01110011 01001000 01001101
11000001 01111001 00000111 01100000 00001110 00101011 01011111 11001011 11100111 00110100
10111000 00010101 01011100 10111100 11010010 01101101 11101110 01001011 10101000 11011001
10011111 00001101 10001100 00110110 11101100 00001100 00110000 01000110 10111100 01111010
01110011 01010011 11111001 00001101 10000001 11001111 11010000 01010101 10011100 00001110
10100110 10001100 00001110 11011101 00101010 10111001 01010010 11011000 10001110 01111110
11100100 00001001 00000000 00000111 11100111 11100111 00110100 11110101 10001101 01000111
01101010 01111110 00111001 11101011 11001101 00111011 10101101 01101001 00100111 01110101
11101111 00100001 01011101 10001101 00001010 00111010 10001110 10110100 11100101 00000011
10111101 00011000 11100010 10010011 00111111 00100111 10111101 00010110 11111001 00010011
11101000 00001100 00110011 01000010 11010010 11101110 11001000 10100100 01101100 01010001
00101011 00010101 10101000 00110111 00000111 11011010 10010011 00100111 10001100 01110100
10100011 11111000 01111010 11010011 01010100 11100010 10010010 01001011 10100000 10011000
11100000 01101000 11000111 00010100 11011100 10001111 11000110 10010011 01110000 00000111
10101101 01001010 01000101 00001111 00000111 00000110 10000110 11000111 01111010 01100111
10011000 00110011 10011010 01100011 00110000 11001111 01011010 10100100 11110101 10111010
00100001 10101110 11100100 11001100 11000000 01100011 10011010 00111000 00111101 00101010
00011111 00110000 00001110 10100010 10000110 10010011 00010100 11101110 10100100 11000001
00010010 01100111 00000010 10100011 11001001 11001101 00100111 10011001 10010001 10011100
01010011 00010101 10110000 01001001 10100100 11011010 01101110 11000101 01011000 10011011
01110001 11000101 00110111 10010001 11010110 10100011 01101001 00001111 01111010 00011001
10001101 01000011 10110011 00000100 10001001 00110000 01111011 10011010 01001100 11111111
00000000 11110101 11110011 01001100 11001111 00111101 00101001 00110010 01110010 01000001
10100010 11010001 01001000 00000111 11101110 00011110 11110100 11011100 11110000 01101001
10111000 11101111 10010011 01000111 00100100 01110100 11111101 01101010 11101111 01101101
01010001 00101101 00001110 00100111 10001010 00110111 10110111 01111010 00111001 00100011
10001110 00111101 01101001 10000100 01111011 01010010 01110001 11100110 01110111 10111001
01011011 00011010 11111001 00011000 11101001 11001101 00100111 01000001 11110101 10100110
00100111 01011100 00010011 01001111 01100001 10011110 11110101 10110010 01010111 11010101
10001000 01010101 01101110 01000000 10100111 01100111 11110011 10100110 00110110 00111111
11000110 10001100 00011110 10010100 11011011 10111110 10101000 01001011 01010001 01011011
10101110 01101001 11011111 11001011 10111101 00110011 10010001 11011010 10010101 00001111
01111111 11010010 10100101 11101011 10101000 11000111 00110110 01111010 01100011 10011010
00010111 10001110 01111011 11010011 10001001 00011101 01101010 00110000 01110011 10011010
01111010 01000111 01110110 00000100 10000000 11110101 10100011 00111000 00111100 11111110
00110101 00010110 11101100 00010000 01101010 01000110 01101100 00000000 01001111 11100101
01000111 00111010 01101111 01010001 00110001 11100100 00010001 11001010 11110100 11101010
00101001 10111001 11100100 10011111 01011111 11010010 10011010 11001100 01001101 00001110
00110000 00111101 00101001 01101011 10111010 01000001 01100001 01110001 01001011 11010100
11111111 00000000 01011010 10001101 10011000 10011100 11100011 10001010 01110000 00111001
11100110 10001110 01101011 10001100 01110011 00010001 11000101 00001100 01001110 00101001
00010000 10001110 01001001 10100001 00001000 11000001 11001101 00111101 00000000 01010101
00100111 00010100 11101110 00101001 10000100 11100011 11110001 10100001 01111010 11010010
01001110 11011011 10001101 10001111 10100000 10011111 01111100 11010011 01110111 01111111
01111000 11111110 01010100 11011100 10000000 00101010 10110101 10110000 10000111 01100111
11111001 11010000 01111001 10100100 01011110 10111001 11001111 11100001 01000110 01111010
11100010 10100111 10011001 00001010 11000000 10111100 01111101 00111101 01101001 01010100
00001100 11100111 00110101 00010110 11100001 10001110 00111101 00101001 11111011 10111000
11000001 11111100 11101000 01011010 11101110 01010001 00100000 00111100 01010011 00011000
01110101 00010100 10011001 10100011 00100011 10111101 00101101 01010011 00100111 01000001
01111111 11011110 10100111 10101110 00110001 11001111 01011010 10000111 10100000 10100001
01001111 00000100 11010011 01110110 10001011 11010000 00101100 00111111 10010000 01110000
01111001 11001101 00101010 00000011 10011111 01111100 11010011 01110111 11100011 10011110
11110100 00000110 11101111 01001101 11011101 10100001 10010010 00110111 01001010 01100000
00111000 00111001 10100100 11001110 01111000 00000111 10101111 01011010 01101111 01000111
11000111 01011010 11001101 11011101 01101110 00010110 00011111 10011100 01010000 11000111
11011011 00011111 10001101 00110000 10011110 11000000 11010001 01011010 01011110 11100010
11100101 00011110 11011100 10001110 00101000 11100100 01110011 01001100 11011101 10000100
11000000 00111100 11010011 10001001 00101011 11000001 11000101 00011011 01101110 00110001

11001011 10011010 01000110 01101100 01010010 01101111 11110111 10100110 11101110 00011000
00011000 11100010 10010011 10011101 11110110 00000001 11011111 11001000 10001110 01101000
11100011 00011000 00010100 10111101 10000111 11101011 01001100 11001000 11100110 10010101
11100101 10111000 01101000 00111011 00100111 00111100 01010010 11100111 10001010 01100111
00000000 01110101 10100111 01110001 01010000 11011101 10111101 01000110 00101010 10001100
01110010 10100111 11110011 10100100 11011010 00110011 11111101 01101000 00100111 00100011
00010100 00101001 11111100 11101010 11101101 10100101 10011000 10000011 00000000 10001100
00011010 01101110 00000111 01010000 00111001 10100111 00010011 11000101 00011011 10111010
01101110 11111100 11101001 01101101 10110000 10101100 00110101 10111000 00011110 10011100
11110100 10100011 00011001 11101001 01000001 00111100 11100111 10110101 00110101 10001001
11111010 01010100 11001001 11110010 10110010 10101100 00101001 11101001 10001110 01111001
10100011 00000011 10000011 01000110 11111111 00000000 01111010 10101111 01110101 00111000
10001001 00111010 11110010 01000101 00111101 00110111 00001101 11001010 11010111 11110011
00010010 11111011 00010011 10100111 01110011 01010101 00010000 01110011 11001101 00001010
01001001 01111100 10011110 10100110 10100100 00000011 00100011 10001010 11000101 11101010
10011101 11001101 11100001 00001011 00100001 01010000 01100000 11010100 10011100 00000001
01010001 10010011 11110010 01111011 11010011 01001011 00010010 01101001 00111101 01110101
00101000 01010111 11101001 01010000 01100100 11111010 11100000 10011110 11010100 11110111
01101100 00001010 10101100 11101101 10000011 11000101 01100110 11100011 01111101 10000110
11011000 11100111 01101110 10100010 10011010 11010010 01110001 11110010 00001010 10001101
11011000 10001010 10000111 01110111 00011100 11110011 01011011 01111011 00111110 01011101
11010000 10001001 00100101 00100111 10100001 00110101 01011010 01010110 11100111 00010100
10101111 00100001 00100011 10001110 01101010 10111100 10101101 11111001 11010110 10010000
10000101 10011110 10001000 01011011 10000011 10110111 00100011 11010010 10100001 10010010
01001100 00111110 01110011 01001101 10010110 01010000 00010011 00100111 10001010 10101100
01100101 00000100 00010000 00111001 10101101 01011101 01010101 01101101 00001001 10111000
10110010 10110001 11000111 01011111 11001010 10100011 00100100 10000001 10010010 01110001
10011010 01001100 01100000 01110011 01001100 01100011 01001010 11010001 11011100 00011110
10000010 00010011 11001101 01000110 11000100 11110111 11100011 00110100 00111001 11000110
01111000 11100110 10011000 11001100 01110001 10010001 11010111 11011010 10110100 01110111
10010010 11010000 01011101 01000110 11111010 11110011 01001100 11011100 01000101 00011001
11001101 00000000 11100011 10110101 00100111 11101000 00011101 01000101 11011101 11010000
11110001 11010010 10011010 11010010 01100011 00100111 10110001 10100110 10111111 00100111
10000011 01010001 10110111 01101111 11010110 10101010 11000000 00111101 11001111 11101110
11111010 11110100 10100110 00000010 00110110 11111100 10111101 01101001 00011010 01000001
10011010 01100011 01001001 10001110 11011100 00011010 11010110 11001001 00010011 01110110
00111101 11011011 11100101 11100011 10010011 11011111 00110101 00010011 00110001 00100011
11111001 11010011 01011110 01001110 01101001 10111011 10111011 10011110 00101010 11100011
01001101 11011001 00001101 11011000 01101100 10111001 11100000 01010100 01111011 10110000
01101001 11101110 01000001 11101000 01101010 00110110 00000000 11110011 11111110 01000101
01010101 10111001 01110110 00100001 00010010 01100101 01110001 01000001 01100010 01000111
11110101 10101000 11011000 11100100 01110110 00000010 10010000 10011110 10011101 01111001
11110100 11101111 01010100 11110110 00011111 00111001 00110010 00001110 00001111 00110100
11011101 11011001 11100010 10011010 10001100 01000000 11100100 11100111 11110000 10100110
11100111 11100111 10100101 10100111 01010010 10010110 10100011 10110011 10001110 00001111
00100010 10011010 10100100 11100011 00011001 11101111 01001010 01111101 00101001 10000100
10011110 10111001 11100110 10101110 11101101 11101011 11011000 10010100 00001101 11000001
11000111 11100011 10011010 01110010 11100000 11110100 11101001 11101011 01001101 10010111
10010001 10011100 01111101 01001101 00001010 00111110 01000000 00000101 00001010 11101101
00000101 10101110 00000100 11100000 11111011 11110100 11001101 00110111 10000000 01110000
01000001 11000101 00111011 00111100 11100011 10111101 00100011 01110010 00001111 00011100
11111010 11010000 11110100 01001001 00000010 01110111 00010100 00000010 01110010 00101001
00110011 10110111 00110100 01110010 00000000 11001111 00000100 11010101 01111011 10011001
00111100 10111110 10111001 00110100 10101100 11011001 00101101 10001001 00110100 11011011
01110010 00101011 00101110 11100010 11100011 01110110 01000000 01100010 00111001 11110100
10101000 11101110 01101110 10001011 01001000 01110110 01110001 01010101 01000111 00111001
11001111 11110011 10101110 11101010 01010100 00010010 01010111 01100110 01010010 10101000
01001110 10111000 11001111 11010111 10101101 00111111 10100000 11000000 11100000 11010100
01111110 11101011 10011100 11010000 10100000 10000011 10010010 01111010 11110101 10100110
11011001 10011001 00101010 00011100 00011100 01010011 11010011 00111000 00110101 00011000
01000110 00100111 00101000 00111110 10000100 10001010 10011001 00100000 10010101 10111001
01001000 11011100 11111011 10001010 10001101 00011111 01010001 10001110 01010011 10011100
00000011 10011100 10001110 11110100 11101101 11000111 00111101 00111000 11000101 01001111
00001110 10011001 01110111 00110111 11001010 00010011 10010001 11001101 01101011 11011010
01111000 01011011 01010000 10011000 10100000 10010000 00101000 01000111 11111110 00101111
01001010 11000110 01010101 10100001 00011101 11011001 01101010 11100110 00111010 00010010
00111001 10100101 11110011 00110001 11001000 00000100 11010111 01011001 01101001 11100000
11001001 10011100 00100110 01100111 00100000 11110111 11100011 10110101 01101001 11000011
11110000 11111101 01001111 11011111 10111001 01100010 00111011 10010000 01101011 10011001
11100010 01101001 00100110 00111101 01001111 00111100 00101100 01011000 11100011 00011111
10000101 01000100 11110110 11010011 01001000 01110011 00011000 00011000 00110101 11101010
10110110 10111110 00000110 11010011 11100000 11100100 11111001 10010010 00111110 01111010
10110001 11101101 01011010 10110000 11111000 01100011 01001100 10001000 11101110 00010110

11100011 00100011 11010000 11110000 01111111 00001010 10011001 01100011 10100011 00000111
11101110 10100001 11011010 11111010 00011110 00111101 01100011 10100000 01101110 01110000
11010111 00010010 00111000 11001111 00100000 00001110 01000101 01101000 11000111 10100000
11011011 10001110 10000101 11110010 01001111 00000111 00110101 11101011 01110001 11101000
01110110 00101010 00001000 01001011 01110101 00011001 11110100 10101011 00110001 11101001
11010110 11110001 00010001 10001000 10100011 11100011 11010101 01101011 10011110 01011000
11111010 10110011 01111010 00001110 00110100 11100010 10001111 00110100 11010011 10111100
00101101 01101010 11000111 00110010 10000111 11110110 11100110 10110110 10101101 10111100
00111101 01100000 10000111 00100010 00000010 11111001 11001110 00110010 01001101 01110110
11100010 11001110 00010101 11101001 00011000 00000011 11011000 01010100 10001001 00000100
01100011 00100111 00011000 11111100 00101011 10011010 10100101 01011010 11010011 01111011
10011010 00101001 00100101 11010000 11100100 01100001 11010001 01101101 00000001 00000100
01011001 10101001 00011101 00111110 11101101 01101010 01011010 11101001 10110110 11001010
00001111 11111010 00110100 01011110 10011001 11011011 01011011 01101000 10101010 00001101
00111111 00000000 00001111 01101010 11001010 01110100 00100111 00111101 11100100 00011110
11010011 01010011 00101100 11011001 01000001 10110011 01100010 01011011 10100110 00111101
10010110 10100011 01111101 00101110 11011100 11001000 00001111 11011001 10100011 00101110
00111001 00000100 10000001 01011011 00000111 01101111 01011010 01101111 00011111 01011010
10011010 01110100 00101100 11011101 11011000 00111010 10001101 10010100 01011010 11010001
10000111 11011100 11000000 11111110 10010100 11010011 01100100 11100100 00000001 10111000
00011111 11000010 10110100 11110010 00101001 00001001 00000011 10101111 01001010 10111111
10101010 11000001 11101010 10000011 10011110 01000110 01000100 11011010 00110010 11001101
11001100 10001110 11111001 11110110 11101101 01000100 01111010 00000101 10111000 01101100
10010010 11000111 11011000 11010110 11000000 00100000 10011110 01111010 01010001 10010000
00111001 11101101 01001101 11010010 01011010 01101010 00101111 01101000 11001010 00010001
01101001 10010000 11100100 10011100 00011111 01100001 01010011 01111101 10010001 01111000
11001111 11101011 01010110 00110111 00001100 11100110 10011101 11000110 00111000 11101011
01001101 01010001 10001011 11011000 00011100 11011001 01011011 11101100 01010001 00010011
11001000 00011001 11111010 01010011 11111110 11001010 10111001 11100011 11110100 10101001
01110010 00111011 11110110 11101111 01001010 10111000 00011000 11011100 01101000 10011101
00001000 10100110 10101100 10000101 11001100 01000110 00100001 00000000 01101101 00011101
00111101 00101001 11000010 00110000 00000111 00100011 10011010 01110110 01111011 11010001
11001001 10101010 01010100 11010010 11011000 00000110 11100000 00000011 10001010 00110001
11110011 01110011 01001010 01010100 00000011 10011010 01000010 10111001 11100011 00110100
11101101 01101101 00000000 00110111 00101110 00111010 11010000 01110000 00111011 11010011
00011010 00100000 01111000 11101001 10000011 11011010 10010101 10010011 10111110 01101010
01111101 01010000 10011000 11100110 11101011 10011100 11010001 00011011 01100100 01100111
10110101 00110001 10100010 00111001 00011100 11010010 10101100 00011000 00111101 01101010
10101110 11101111 01110001 10001111 01100110 00010100 00101100 10001011 10001010 01100011
01000000 01110011 11010110 10011100 10010110 11100011 00111001 00100111 10011010 00110101
10111110 10000000 00000010 01010000 00000111 01011110 11110100 11011111 00110101 01110010
01000111 01001111 01111010 01110011 01000011 11001001 00011101 10101001 10001111 00000111
01111010 01111110 10100010 01111011 10001001 11100110 10101110 11101100 01100111 10011010
01110111 10011100 00010100 11100011 00010100 10011110 01001111 11111101 11110101 01001010
11010000 10001100 01110011 01010011 01110000 00011100 00100110 00000111 10110111 00010100
01111001 10000011 11010111 10111101 00110001 01100010 00111001 10100100 11110010 01001001
11001110 01001000 00010101 01001101 11101001 01100110 00101011 00001110 11011101 10000011
01001001 11000001 00111100 00011010 10001101 01100010 00100111 10101001 10100101 11011010
11000011 00111100 11110011 01010011 11001011 10101110 11100011 00011111 11010100 01010001
10001100 01110111 10101000 11010100 00010001 11110101 00110100 11000111 01010110 11001000
00111111 10011101 00100110 11010010 11010000 01110110 00100110 11011010 00001001 11100100
11010000 11001011 11011111 00111100 11010100 00111000 00100100 11110101 11111100 00101001
11011101 00111010 10011010 01001101 10101001 00111101 00000011 11010100 10010001 01010100
01111110 00110100 01111001 01011110 10110100 11001100 11110101 11110101 10100001 00100100
11100011 00000100 11010101 11111001 00100001 00001111 01010100 11101111 10011010 01101011
01000111 10000110 00011100 11110001 01010001 11111001 10011100 11100110 10010001 10100111
00000110 10010111 00100000 00010010 10011000 10110011 11000011 01110100 11111010 11010010
00101100 01011000 10101000 10111100 11100001 10011010 00111100 11100001 10000010 00110011
01001101 00101000 10101101 11000101 10101001 00101110 11011110 01110011 10011010 00011000
01111011 01010100 01000010 01100001 10001100 01111110 10110100 01111001 11011001 00011001
11101101 01010010 10010010 01101111 01000010 10101110 01001010 10100000 00011110 10111101
00111101 00101001 00011011 10001111 10100101 01000110 00100101 00000100 00010010 00101001
10100110 01110001 10001110 00110000 01101011 01010100 11010101 11000010 11011101 10001001
10110000 00001000 11110111 10100011 00011100 01110011 01010000 01111001 11011000 00011101
01000101 00110000 11001110 00001111 01111010 11001110 10100010 01010111 11011000 00111010
00010110 11001001 11101101 10001010 10001000 10001110 01111010 01010100 01101101 00111111
00011100 11010011 00111110 11010011 11101110 10010101 01011100 10001110 01011011 00110000
00110110 11110110 11100000 11100111 11110010 10100011 00011100 01100000 10001010 01100110
01001101 01001000 10100111 10100110 11100000 01101010 11001001 10111000 11001100 01111100
11011001 11100111 11101000 00101001 11001100 01110110 00011110 00101001 01001111 11001010
00110010 00111010 01010000 11011001 10100111 10110000 11000110 00101110 01001111 00011001
10101001 00010111 10100110 00001101 00100111 01111100 01100010 10000110 00011000 10101000
10110011 01101100 00000111 10010001 10000001 01001100 00000100 01100100 11110011 01001011

11001001 11101101 01001101 11011011 11001110 01001111 01111010 10010110 10110101 11010000
01111011 00001110 11000010 10011010 01000001 10000110 00011110 10011111 10001101 00100001
11001110 01001000 00010100 00101000 00100001 00101001 11110010 00001000 10010001 01110000
00000110 00000101 00001011 11101010 01001110 01101001 10111011 01001000 00010100 10101011
11110111 11101001 00101011 10100111 01100000 11010000 01101110 01000110 01001110 00111111
01001010 01010010 01000000 11101000 00111000 10100100 11011011 10110100 11110001 01001111
01101110 00000101 01101000 10010011 11101010 00000001 11000000 11101101 10011010 00010100
01110001 11101001 01000110 01111001 10100101 10100011 01000010 01000110 01110111 00100011
11111010 11010001 11010000 01110101 10100111 00110000 00011001 11001110 00101001 10111001
00000100 01100110 10010101 10101100 00000011 10010000 00000010 00000001 11001101 00110101
10111010 01100000 01110001 11011111 00110100 11100100 01100101 00100011 00000010 10010100
10000011 11010111 10110101 01010011 01010110 01011010 00010100 00110010 10010011 00000111
11110000 11101111 01001010 10100011 10001111 11100101 01000110 01001000 00110101 10011011
10000110 10011010 00110000 00011010 11000011 10000010 00101001 01010111 00111101 01101000
11000110 01000111 00011100 00011111 01111010 00011011 10001100 00001100 01010010 11010110
00111011 10000000 01110101 10100100 11001000 10100101 00000111 10011100 01110111 00010100
10111000 00011001 00100111 00010101 01110111 11101110 00000100 01101111 11001000 11001101
00111100 01110010 00001111 01101010 00110011 10010001 10001010 00111010 01110001 10001010
10100101 00010111 11010100 00110100 00010011 00110100 10101011 11000000 11111010 11010010
01110011 11000111 00000011 00110100 11101100 00010110 00111100 11010010 01110110 11101000
11000000 01101110 01111010 11010011 01011000 11100000 11100110 10011110 01110000 01001111
00010100 10001111 10000001 11010010 10010011 11010001 00000000 11011101 11011000 00110100
00110001 11000000 10100111 10110110 11010001 00011000 11111110 01110100 11000010 00110111
00100101 00100110 11000000 01110010 10010001 10011100 11110111 00110100 01001000 01111110
01111100 11010011 00000000 11111100 01101001 01110011 01001001 11101101 10110000 11000011
10101000 10100011 00100100 01110100 10100011 00011100 00001010 00001000 00111001 10100010
11001111 10101000 10000011 11001100 00100000 01110011 01000110 11101010 01101011 00000010
00111011 11110011 01000001 00000111 01100000 10100001 00101011 10111101 11000110 00101110
01111011 01100111 10001010 01010000 11000111 10110111 01001010 01101000 00110100 11001100
11100011 10110101 01001101 10101101 00101011 10000001 00101110 11100011 10011010 00010101
10110000 01101010 00111100 11100100 01100110 10000011 11001000 11001111 01001010 10101011
10000010 00100100 00101100 01110011 11000101 00001100 11000010 10100010 10100100 11011101
11001111 00010101 00110010 01101101 01101100 10000110 01001011 11100110 00001110 00001000
11100111 00110100 10001110 11010101 00011011 00001100 00100111 00010100 11001101 11001101
10110111 10000000 01111111 00011010 10010111 01111011 01011100 00001001 01011001 10000010
10100001 00111001 11101000 00101011 00100110 11100010 01010011 00111100 10111001 11101101
11101011 01010110 00101110 01100101 00101111 10000101 11101001 11101011 01010000 11000100
10111000 11100000 01010010 10111100 10010110 11000110 10010001 01011101 01000001 00010111
11010010 10011101 01001010 01111011 11110001 10000011 01001100 11100110 10001011 00111110
10100110 10110111 00000110 00111001 11111001 10110011 10000001 01010001 10111011 01100011
10001100 11110011 01001001 00101001 11000000 00110101 01011001 10100100 00000011 10101111
01010011 01001001 11000110 11011101 01000101 10111001 00100001 00111100 11110011 01010000
10111011 01100000 10011100 01110100 10101000 11011101 10110011 11000000 10101010 11101111
00100111 00000111 10011110 10010101 01010001 10100111 01100101 01110000 00100100 11110011
00110000 01111010 11010100 01100110 01011111 10010000 11110011 11001101 01010111 01111001
00110111 01010011 01011010 01001110 00101011 01001011 00110110 10010010 01000001 00100110
10101110 01001000 11001101 11101001 11010110 10100001 01100011 10011110 11110101 00010011
11001101 11000001 11111110 01110101 00010011 11001011 11000110 00110001 10001010 01101110
00111010 00011001 10110111 11011000 01101100 10000100 11110100 00110101 00010011 00010001
10000001 10001110 10111101 11101001 01100101 10010011 00100011 00011101 00111101 11101010
10111011 00011100 10011110 00111000 10100001 00100101 01111101 01000110 01001000 11010010
01110001 01001000 10101100 01111011 11010100 01011001 11001111 11111111 00000000 10101010
10001101 11011101 11101010 11110100 00100110 11000011 10011010 01000000 01001110 00001000
11101011 01001101 10010100 01100000 11100111 10111101 01000111 10111011 00100110 10011010
01011111 11100111 11100100 11110001 01010110 10010000 11011000 11100110 11111011 10000111
10011010 10000101 10110010 10111101 00000110 01101001 11101100 11011100 01100000 01010100
01000100 10000000 01111010 11100110 10110100 01010000 10001011 00010000 11101110 10100000
10001110 11111111 00000000 01011010 01101001 00111100 11010000 10101100 00110001 11010111
10011010 01100011 00110001 11110101 11100110 10101001 00100100 10001001 10111111 01110000
11011100 00001111 00001101 01000011 11111010 01100110 10010000 10010001 11011100 00001110
01101010 00010111 01101110 11011100 11111110 01110101 10100111 00110101 11011101 10010010
00000001 10101100 00111011 01111110 10110100 11001100 10010010 00000000 00100011 00101000
00001111 01011010 00011010 01001110 01001111 01100000 00101001 10000001 10111001 11001111
01101010 11010101 00111101 00110100 00010011 11011100 00110011 10000011 10001100 11010010
01100100 01100011 00011101 11001101 00001100 11000000 10011100 01110001 01000110 01000000
11001000 11110101 10100100 10010011 11011001 10000101 11000100 11110110 11110101 11101111
01001110 01111100 00001110 10000100 11010011 01111010 11110100 11101001 01000010 10111000
00111000 00111101 00101000 10110010 01101100 01100100 10001000 01111000 11110100 10100110
11100111 10010011 11101011 01000110 01111110 01011110 00101001 00011001 10000111 00100100
01110101 10100100 11100011 11010000 00101110 11011000 01100111 11010111 00011110 11111100
11010001 10011100 00001110 10000000 11010010 00101111 01111100 11010010 10011110 01111101
01101001 10100110 11010000 00000011 01001001 10001110 00110001 01001100 01011110 00001110
01111101 01111011 11010010 01111111 00011111 00111101 00101001 01110010 00111001 00011000

10101010 01010001 01101101 01101110 00100110 00111000 01110111 00100000 11100110 10011010
00001110 01111010 11100100 00010011 11101111 01001000 10111101 10000101 00100011 10011110
11010100 11010010 10111100 01000010 11101010 11100010 11001100 11011011 01000001 00001110
01110000 01000000 11001111 01011010 11000010 10111100 10010110 01001001 10001110 00110010
01110110 00001111 01111110 10110101 01100110 11101110 01010010 11011001 01010000 01111111
00011100 11010100 01000001 01000001 00011100 10001110 00111011 11010110 11010100 11101001
10101000 01101010 01100011 01010010 01110111 11010000 10101111 00011101 10100111 01011100
11111110 00000010 10101100 01011011 01011001 10001100 11100100 10001100 11010101 10101000
01100000 11000000 11101111 11110101 00110101 01111010 00011011 01110110 00111000 00101000
00111000 11110111 11100010 10001001 01010101 11010100 11001101 01000001 01110101 00101000
10100101 10100010 10010000 00001001 00000111 10011110 10110101 01110010 11011110 11010100
01100100 01100000 01110000 00111010 01100000 01010101 11111000 01101101 01000000 11000001
11001011 11110101 10101110 10000111 01001011 11010011 00101101 11100100 00000110 01001001
10000001 00111001 00011110 10110101 11001111 01010110 10110100 01101101 10100001 10101010
10000001 11001111 00100101 10010001 00111000 11000100 01001110 11100100 11111011 01010110
11011110 10011101 10100011 01001010 11000100 01100110 00110111 00011001 11101010 00000000
11001101 01110100 01010000 11000111 00010100 01110001 10000101 11011010 00000000 00010101
10101111 01101010 01010110 00111000 10000110 00000110 00101011 10000101 11010101 01110101
00110100 10110001 01011101 01001100 10101011 00001101 00011110 01001000 11100011 00000000
01000010 01000111 10111101 01101010 01000001 01100011 10110100 01100000 10001111 10101000
10101011 00100110 01101100 00001111 11110011 11000101 00011110 01101111 00000011 00000111
11101011 01011000 11110010 11011111 01000110 00001101 10110010 01001000 01100010 11011010
00001000 00000011 00010101 00100110 00001000 00110101 01001101 10101110 00001001 00111100
00011100 11010011 11011010 01111110 01111010 11010010 10010111 00110010 00000110 10001011
10000100 00010011 11011110 10001110 00110000 01111101 10101010 10000001 10111000 00100011
11101011 01001000 00100110 00100111 10111101 00101110 01000110 11011101 11101110 00010111
10110001 10100001 10010000 00000000 11100111 00011001 10100001 10001000 00111001 11001001
10101100 11001111 00110101 10111101 01111000 11101101 11001101 00110001 10101110 00001000
01100010 00110010 01000000 11101111 11101111 01001101 11011110 11010110 00010101 10001101
01101110 00110000 00000000 01101111 11010110 10000101 00101010 00111010 10011010 11001000
11111011 01010011 00100111 00011001 11100010 10010101 10100111 00111000 11000111 01011010
01110110 01111100 10110111 01000101 01011000 11010100 00110010 00101110 01111001 00110100
11101111 00110101 00000001 11000111 00100110 10110001 00111110 11010100 11000100 11110101
00011000 10100100 01111011 10010011 11100110 01111011 00011111 01111010 00111001 10101110
10101110 11000111 01100011 01100101 01011101 01111001 11001000 00011001 11111010 11010010
11111001 11001010 01000101 01100010 11111101 10100100 10010001 11001101 00110100 11011100
00011110 00110001 10010001 11101011 01010011 11001010 11110110 00100101 10011011 01001101
01110000 10110100 00101100 11100000 11100011 11010010 10110001 00111100 11100010 01110010
00000000 00111111 10011101 00000110 01010110 11000110 01000001 00111001 10100010 11010110
11010001 10000010 00110110 11010110 11101000 00010000 01110001 11010100 01010011 10111100
11110101 11100011 00000111 10101101 01110011 11101001 00111100 10011001 00000001 01111010
10010001 01001110 00110010 10110000 00111111 01111000 11100110 10001010 01110001 01010111
00011001 10110101 11110110 10100000 01110010 01111011 01010000 01101110 10010111 00100011
00000110 10110000 01111100 11110110 01011110 00001001 11001101 00001101 00110110 11001110
01111010 01010110 10011100 10011100 11011011 00001100 11011101 01111011 10110001 10010000
00000111 01010011 01001001 11110110 11000101 11101110 01101011 10011111 00110011 10010000
01110010 00001111 00111101 00001101 00101001 10011111 00000011 00011111 10100101 00111001
01010011 11010110 11001001 10010010 10001101 11010001 01111000 00000110 01110010 01110011
01001110 11111011 01101110 00110010 00110010 00111001 10101110 01110011 11001111 01100001
11011111 00110101 00011011 11001110 11011011 11110011 11001111 11111000 11010100 11110010
01110111 00101000 11101001 00011010 11111000 01100111 10010011 11000101 00011111 01101110
01011100 01100100 10011010 11100110 10100101 10011100 10000000 00001111 00100011 00110100
11001111 00111100 11101111 11101010 01111010 01010011 10110100 01111010 00001000 11101001
11010111 01010000 01010010 11000100 00100001 00000111 10001010 01010001 01111100 00010111
00111001 01101110 00111011 11010111 00101100 00101110 00000000 01110011 10000011 11000001
11101101 01001011 11110110 10111111 10010100 10011100 11111101 01101000 10001010 11010111
01000001 10111101 10001110 10100101 10101111 10010111 11111011 11000000 11111010 11010000
10110111 11000011 10101110 01111000 11001111 01111010 11100101 01011010 11101111 00000011
00100000 11010100 00101111 01110110 11111011 10000001 00000111 10001010 00100111 01001111
01011101 00000000 11101100 00011010 11111000 01100111 10101110 01101001 11011111 01101110
00011100 01110010 01110001 01011100 01101011 01011110 11001000 00110011 11001110 01110011
01001000 11011010 10001011 00000011 10001100 10011100 00010001 01010111 00011010 01001110
11011011 10000011 00111011 00011111 11101101 00000001 10011111 01110010 01101000 11111011
01101000 11011100 00000001 01101111 11111110 10111101 01110001 11001101 01111100 11011111
11000001 11000001 11110101 11001101 00110011 11111011 01000000 10011110 10100111 11100111
11110100 00110101 01011110 11001101 00110111 10101000 10001110 11001111 11111011 01000000
01100111 10010011 10001100 01010001 11111101 10100001 00011000 00011000 11011100 00111101
10101011 10001111 00110111 11001100 01110001 10010110 11100100 11010100 01101111 01111100
11011001 11000000 00111100 01111010 11010110 01110010 10100101 01100101 01110000 01000111
01100110 11011010 10010100 01101010 00111110 11110110 01101001 10000111 01010011 10001100
01110101 01101010 11100011 10011010 11101101 10110010 00001110 01111111 00111010 01101000
10111011 11011100 11011001 00101101 01000111 00101011 01000011 00111011 00111111 11101101
00010100 11001111 00000111 00110100 11000101 11010100 11010100 11110010 01001111 00000011

11111001 11010111 00100010 01101111 01110001 11000101 00110011 11101101 10100100 10010000
00001111 11101001 01010111 11001001 01110001 01101100 01110110 00001011 10101000 10101011
01110111 11000110 01111111 01001010 01010101 11010100 00010000 10010000 00110011 11001001
10101110 00110101 10101111 01001001 10010011 10000011 11010011 10110101 00110101 10101111
01001110 00111010 10010011 01010001 00101010 01011101 11001010 00111011 00111001 01101111
10000110 01000000 11100000 01100110 10010001 10101111 10111010 00000001 11001001 10101110
00100111 11101101 10110010 00110001 11001111 00111000 00010100 01111101 10110110 01010110
11100111 00100100 01100100 11110110 10101001 01110000 01001101 10001010 11000111 01100111
11111101 10100000 00001001 00100011 00111100 11100110 10100010 01101011 11010000 00011111
00011001 11001101 01110010 01101001 01111100 11001101 10010010 01001111 00111101 00101001
10111111 01101100 01100000 10111111 00101001 00111111 10000001 10101101 00100011 00000100
10011101 10000000 11101011 00011010 11110100 01100100 10001100 11100011 11011110 10011010
11010111 10000011 00011100 01110101 00010101 11001010 11111101 10111001 10111001 11001111
00111100 01110101 11001101 00110111 11101101 10100111 00100111 10011010 01001010 00101010
11100000 11001110 10100101 00101111 10010111 00011101 01110011 10011110 01101001 00011111
01010000 01011101 10000111 00000111 00000111 11101011 11010010 10111001 01010101 10111100
01100001 10010011 10011111 11000110 10010001 01100111 00100100 01110010 01111000 11110101
10100110 10100001 11001110 11110100 01000011 01011011 00011101 01000001 11010100 01010100
10000000 00000100 10000000 01100111 11011110 10100011 00111010 10000110 00110010 10111011
10000001 11001101 01110011 10011110 01111111 01010110 11110101 10101000 11111100 11100010
01110010 01110011 11101101 11001101 01010111 10110001 10110011 10110011 00010110 11000111
01001101 11111101 10100011 10000001 10011100 10001100 10011010 01100011 01101010 01000011
11001100 00111111 00110110 00000000 11101011 01011100 11011001 10111000 11001000 11000000
11100010 10100011 01101011 10000011 10010001 10000001 11000101 00100101 01001001 01110100
00011001 11010011 10110110 10100111 10000101 00101101 11001001 00000110 10100001 11111110
11010010 11001000 00000100 00010011 11000111 00111100 11010111 00111110 01100110 11001001
11100011 11111001 11010010 01111001 11001100 01001111 00011101 00110011 11101011 01011010
00101000 01101001 01110111 10101000 01011000 11101000 01100101 11010100 10000000 00000000
11100111 11100100 00010100 00001101 01001000 10011111 10111010 01001110 00111011 01010111
00110110 11010010 10011100 10011111 01000010 01101001 00011010 01010100 11001111 00100101
11111111 00000000 00111010 10000101 00000111 11010100 00101110 01111010 11111011 01001100
10111111 11000011 11111000 11010000 10010111 00000011 10110111 00111110 11110101 11001000
10100110 10110010 10100100 11100000 00011100 00000010 00111001 00100110 10100100 01011101
01100101 00110000 01011101 11011100 00001000 11000110 00111001 10101001 01010000 01011011
00001001 10100011 10101100 01011001 01110011 11011110 10011111 11100110 10000010 01110001
11111010 11010111 00100110 11011010 11000010 10110011 00000000 00011111 11100100 11101101
01010010 10100110 10110000 10001100 01111000 10010100 01100100 11111011 11110101 10100001
11010011 10010011 11011000 10000011 10100111 11011100 00110011 11010111 10101101 00111100
11001000 00000000 10101110 01100101 00110101 10000101 00000000 00000010 01110001 11001111
10101101 01001110 10111010 10011000 01101100 00010000 11000000 10001110 11110101 00011100
10010010 11011101 10010100 01101111 10110100 10000111 00010100 00101011 01100111 10101101
01100011 10001101 01001010 00110000 00000111 00100000 10001100 01110011 10000011 01001110
10001010 11111000 00010010 01111010 01101100 11001111 01100011 01000011 10100110 11101111
01110000 11010000 11011000 00011100 10011111 01111010 01000010 01110010 00110000 00111010
00001110 11110101 10011101 11110110 11110001 10010010 00000001 00011001 11101101 01010010
01000011 00111000 11000110 00001001 11110101 11100010 10110100 11100100 11010011 01010001
01011000 10111011 10111011 10100110 00111011 01010001 10111000 11100111 11111010 11010101
01100100 10011101 01011000 00001100 01110111 10100111 00110100 11000011 00000000 01100111
00010100 10010100 01011110 11010111 00011110 10000100 10011001 00111110 11100110 10011111
10111011 11110011 10101000 00010110 01000001 11010100 00011100 11111011 11010000 11001100
00110111 01100111 00110101 00011100 10101110 00111011 11101010 01001001 00110001 01100001
10001111 01111010 00110111 01110110 11111110 10110101 00011110 11100001 10001111 10011010
10011000 01100100 11100111 10001110 01101001 00110100 11100100 01010001 01100101 10011011
00010100 10011011 10000000 00111100 00011110 01101010 10111001 10010100 11111110 00010100
11001111 00110000 01110101 11001101 00100111 00011011 00100001 01011111 01010010 11010010
10010000 00001110 01101001 01011010 01001110 01111000 11101001 01010100 11110111 10011010
01001101 11000101 10101001 10101101 00010000 00110110 01011100 00101101 11000111 00010100
00001001 00000001 00111000 11001101 01010011 11111001 10110000 01111001 11100010 10011010
10000100 11110100 00000110 10000101 00011011 00100000 10111001 01111011 01110000 00011100
01110111 10100011 11001100 00000111 10001100 11010101 00010111 01101100 11110011 10011010
01001100 10011100 01110101 11000101 00010010 01110110 00001101 11001011 11101011 00100000
00111100 10011110 11000110 10000110 10010111 00111110 11010101 10011110 10110010 10011100
11111101 00101001 10011011 10111010 11110011 01001011 10010110 11101010 11101000 01000110
10011010 11001000 00101001 10111110 01101010 11110110 11101011 01011001 11011110 01110001
00100111 10101111 01111010 00011001 10001000 00111001 00000110 10101001 00101101 00011101
10000000 11010001 01000010 10111110 10111111 10101101 00011110 01100000 11001110 00000101
01100111 00011001 11001111 00111110 11010100 10001101 01110101 11011100 01110011 11101101
01010011 10110110 10101100 01111010 00011010 01001010 11001011 10010010 01111111 01011010
01000010 11000011 00111100 01110100 11110101 10101100 11100100 10111000 11000000 11100100
11110101 10100110 11111101 10100111 10011111 01101010 01101110 00110111 11011000 00010001
10101100 01001000 11011001 11101011 01001101 01011111 11100001 11110100 10101100 10110111
10111011 11000111 01111010 00001110 10100010 10100001 11000010 11100000 10000011 11101011
10001010 00101100 10011110 10001100 01111110 10000110 10100010 10010000 00001110 00101001

11011100 00000001 11111010 11100010 10110010 11100011 10111011 01011101 11111111 00000000
00111011 01110001 11011110 10011100 11010111 11001011 11010111 00100111 00010100 10010010
11110011 00000011 01000011 10110110 01101000 11011100 00001110 01101010 10001010 11011110
11000110 01110010 00010111 00100100 01100011 00111111 01011010 00000101 11010000 11100011
11010010 10011011 01001101 10000001 01110100 10011100 10010001 10011010 01111111 00100111
00000001 01111010 11010110 01111111 11011010 00111111 01111001 11101101 01001010 01101110
10111101 00101010 00100001 01111011 10110000 11010000 10111000 01000110 00111010 10011010
01001100 01100000 11100100 11110011 01010101 00011110 11100011 00111100 11100110 10010001
01101110 00111011 00011110 01101010 01011110 10101100 01111011 10010111 00111000 11100111
00110100 00010001 10010001 11110101 10101010 01101101 01110000 01111110 01001100 11110001
11001101 01001000 11010111 01000000 00001010 10100110 10101110 10101100 00100010 01100100
01011100 00001111 01111010 01000101 00011100 11110100 10101010 11101001 01110100 00011001
10000000 11101001 11101110 01101010 01011111 10110100 00001111 01011100 11111011 10001010
11001010 11110110 11010000 01110111 00011110 11100011 01101000 11001101 01000001 00100100
10000011 00011000 11101110 01111101 00101001 11001101 00110001 01100001 11101000 00101010
00011100 00001100 11100100 01010110 10101110 01001011 10101001 10100100 01100001 11010100
01101000 01011110 00110010 01000110 01001111 01111010 01010111 11101000 00001000 11100010
10100100 11000000 11000111 00010100 11000110 00111100 11100010 10110010 01010010 01111100
11000110 10101001 00010000 10111111 01001111 01111111 10101101 01000000 11110011 00000101
00111000 11101100 01101010 01011001 10001000 00000110 10101001 01001111 00100000 00100111
10100101 00001110 00101101 11110101 11010100 00000110 01001101 00101001 00010101 01010110
01011001 01111110 01111100 11010001 01110000 11011000 00111000 00000111 11101010 01101010
10000100 10010010 00010000 11000011 11010110 10101110 10011100 10101110 10110101 00001011
00010110 01111100 11011100 01110111 11001101 01010110 10010110 01101100 00011111 01111111
01101010 10001101 10100101 11101101 11000101 00110011 00111100 11111101 01101011 01100101
01101011 11101011 10110001 00100100 10011001 00111000 11100000 11010010 00010010 01111010
11100111 10011010 10001111 01110001 01010011 11010110 10011000 11001101 10111011 01111111
01011100 11010001 00011001 00110111 10100101 11000000 00011100 11010100 01101101 11011111
00000110 10100011 00110010 01110000 00110001 10011100 11111011 11110001 01010001 11001101
00101000 11110101 11000101 01011100 01110100 01011010 10001010 11101100 00011101 10110001
10011111 01001010 10000111 01111111 00100111 10011010 01010110 01100000 01100011 11100011
11110101 10101000 10000011 00011110 10100111 00000111 00111101 11101000 11100101 10111110
10110110 00100101 10110110 00111001 00011011 00111101 11111001 10100111 00101011 00010000
00111010 01010100 01101001 11010100 01110011 11001101 00111000 11100011 00111100 00011010
10111111 01100111 11001100 10000011 01100001 11111110 10100101 10110000 00001101 01000001
10010000 01001111 01011010 01111110 11101100 00100001 11001111 01111010 10000011 10000001
01010101 00001110 11101100 10010001 11001100 11011000 11101111 10010000 00101010 00000111
00100100 00011111 01100011 01001010 11101101 10001110 10010101 00001110 11100010 01011111
11010110 10110101 01001101 00111101 10000011 01110001 11001010 01110000 00110110 11010011
11000100 10000001 10000111 01011110 01101010 00110110 11000111 01000000 01111111 00011010
01001100 10001100 01110100 11000110 00101010 10110110 00001011 00001110 01100010 01001000
00111101 10110001 01010001 01101110 11100011 10010001 11010111 10001010 01111010 10110111
00011101 01101010 00010111 01101110 11011000 00011000 10100101 01111011 11101010 00000010
00011111 10010111 11100110 00111111 10100001 11101001 01000010 10101110 01001111 11001101
01001001 10011101 11000011 11010010 10011011 10111011 10110111 00111111 10000001 10101011
11011011 01110010 01011011 11101010 00100011 10001101 10100100 10001100 11010010 10000010
01001000 11011011 10011100 00001010 00110000 01011001 10111001 00111111 01001010 01001101
11000000 00010011 11010111 00011101 00101010 11111001 10010110 11101100 00101110 10000001
00001001 00111100 00000011 01001001 10001101 10100100 10001100 01110001 01010010 01100011
00011101 00001111 11100011 10001010 10001100 11111010 01100111 00110101 00111010 10110111
10100000 00001010 10011101 01110000 00001111 00000110 10000001 11001011 11100001 11001001
11110110 00110100 10100011 00011100 10011100 01100010 10100011 01101110 01001111 00011100
10001010 01110010 00011101 11010000 11100110 11101011 11000111 01010001 11011110 10010111
00100111 10101101 00110001 01001111 00100000 01111010 01010011 11010100 11100111 00111001
10101010 10010010 00011110 10000011 00110111 01100111 10000111 00000111 00111111 01001010
01110011 01100111 00100000 00001111 11010010 10000111 11100000 01100010 10100011 11000000
00111110 11000110 10001000 10110111 01101110 01010100 01001011 00100101 00111100 01110100
00011000 11111010 11010101 00111011 10111001 11011000 01000111 11110010 01111101 11111111
00000000 11100101 01010010 01001011 00101111 10010110 00000000 11111100 11101010 10100110
11011101 11010010 01101110 00111101 01111101 01111101 01101011 01011000 00110101 01111011
10011001 11001010 01111101 00001000 10100011 10001000 10011110 01001000 00100111 00111111
10101101 01011111 10000110 00000101 01010001 10000001 10001100 10010011 01001101 10000101
01010100 01100111 00111111 10000101 01001110 10011100 10011110 00111010 11110111 10100010
10100011 10111010 00100001 00010010 01000011 00010111 01010001 11000110 01111101 11001101
01011100 10000101 01111011 00011010 10000010 00010000 00110111 11110100 11000110 00111010
11111011 11010101 10111000 10100011 00011011 10110111 00110110 01110001 11010110 10111001
11101101 10100101 11011001 10100010 00101101 10100001 01011110 11100011 10011010 11011110
10110001 01101111 11011101 00100001 11001001 11000101 01100001 00100010 11110010 00001010
00101110 01111101 10101011 01111110 11011101 01110110 11000100 10000000 11111010 01100011
00010101 11001101 01010001 10101000 00110010 11001011 01001000 11000100 11100010 10110100
11100001 00100100 11000111 10011100 11111110 00110101 10010101 11101001 10001010 11010001
10110111 01101111 11011101 11100000 01111110 01111001 10101110 01111111 01101000 10011100
10111011 00010011 01100010 11011010 00011110 01000110 01111001 11000101 00110110 00111110

01110011 10010011 11000101 01000101 11001110 01000110 01001111 00000011 10101101 01001001
10011110 00111110 10110100 10011010 11010100 01100000 00110011 10111111 10011111 11000010
10000000 00110010 01001111 00111101 00101001 00010000 01110010 00001000 00111100 11100110
10010111 00000111 10101111 01001010 10000111 01110100 10000000 00100101 00000011 11111111
00000000 10101111 01000110 00110110 10001111 10101101 00100110 11011111 10011111 00100100
11110110 11110101 10100101 01110011 11011010 10100101 11000101 10101101 01011000 10110100
10111000 11000010 11011111 11100111 11010110 10100011 11001110 01011000 10001110 11000110
10100110 00101000 00001110 00110011 01001010 10100001 01000000 11001111 01111010 10111011
10101110 10100101 00101011 00010000 01100111 00100011 00011000 11001101 01000110 10100100
11110011 01010111 00110010 10100111 10010010 00101001 10111111 00101110 00101000 10111100
10111010 00000001 01010111 01101110 01101001 00110110 01110001 11001000 11100110 10101101
11100000 00010011 10011100 11110011 10001110 10010100 11000110 01011110 01001001 11101111
11101001 01010010 11010011 01001111 11011110 00001011 10010101 10110010 01111010 00011010
01101010 11001011 10000011 10000010 00101010 11010110 00000111 01110001 01001101 11110010
10010101 10111010 10001010 10101000 10110110 11011110 10000010 00101011 11111001 10101100
10100111 00001010 00111000 00110100 10001101 00100011 01100111 11111001 11010101 10111101
10101010 01111011 01010011 00111100 10110000 00000111 00110101 01110101 01011000 01101000
01010000 01111001 01001111 01010000 00001110 01101001 10111110 01101011 10010001 10011010
11010001 00101011 00011111 01010011 11111000 01010011 00011101 01100011 00000111 10000001
11010111 00011001 10101000 10111011 01010110 10001010 01011010 00001100 11001110 01110011
00101001 11100111 00010100 10111001 10010000 11000111 11001000 11001101 01101000 01111100
10100011 10000000 10100000 00000001 01000111 00011011 01110001 01000101 11011010 01101101
00100000 00110010 11001000 01110000 10000100 11100000 11010010 01111110 11110000 10001111
10100101 01101000 00111010 10101001 11000000 10100100 11110010 01000110 00110010 00000101
00110110 11100110 11110111 00001011 00100011 00111100 11101110 11101011 01001100 00110010
00110111 00000000 11110011 01011010 01101011 00000000 11000111 01001010 00111110 11001110
10111000 11000110 00111000 11001110 01101000 01110010 10111101 10011010 00100101 00100011
00110000 10110001 00100011 00110101 00011011 10010011 10011100 01110011 10010011 01011010
10000110 11001100 10010100 00111111 10100101 01000110 11010110 01000111 10011110 01111001
11110101 10101010 11010111 01110010 10010010 00110010 11110001 11001001 00111111 10101101
00101110 11010010 11000011 00000011 10100101 01101001 01111101 10001111 00100111 00011000
11101011 01000000 10110001 11000000 11101011 10011010 01001010 10110101 11011101 10010000
10001100 10001111 00101000 11100111 10011110 10010100 10001100 10101101 11000000 01000011
11001111 10111111 01001010 11011000 00111010 01110111 11101110 11000000 01110010 01111010
11100100 11100000 11010011 01010111 01001111 01001101 10111111 00101000 00111000 11110100
00100110 10010101 11110101 11010101 10001101 00110011 00100111 00111001 11001000 00100000
11010011 00011011 11101001 10011111 10101001 10101101 10000110 10110011 00000000 11110100
11001111 10111101 00110001 10101100 10110000 01110001 10000011 01001010 11101110 11100000
11001100 10010110 00111001 00111100 00001101 10011001 10101000 11011010 01000011 11000000
11101111 11011100 11010110 11100111 11110110 01110111 11001010 10011001 00111000 01110000
00111001 11001111 10101101 00110011 11101100 00101010 00000111 10101111 11110101 10101101
01100011 01010101 00100100 11010000 11001100 00110001 00100011 00000010 01110111 11010011
00011110 01000011 10111000 01100011 10100101 01101111 00011011 00010100 11000111 11011101
00010100 11001111 11101100 11011000 01000011 11100100 10000011 10001111 01000000 01111010
11010000 11101010 00101101 10010000 10001100 01000110 01110010 01001001 11100111 00110100
10011110 01100001 00111000 00111000 11000111 10101101 01101101 10001011 00011000 01010101
01001110 11010101 11111100 11001101 00110001 10101100 11100010 00101001 10000000 10100000
01100110 10000111 00100111 10111101 10000110 11110101 00110001 11011001 10011000 10000001
11001001 11000000 11101000 01101001 00011000 10110110 00111110 01010011 11000101 01101010
10110101 10011000 11100111 10010000 00000001 11101101 01001000 11010110 01110001 11110101
00011101 11101010 10010100 11011011 01100001 10100010 00110010 00111101 00001111 00110100
11110101 01100010 00011011 11101011 11011010 10110100 10011110 11010000 00010000 00111000
11101001 01001000 01101101 01010101 01001000 11100011 10010001 11001101 01011100 10100101
01110101 10100011 00010001 10011001 11100110 01110011 11000101 00100111 10011011 11001111
00011000 11111111 00000000 00001010 10111011 11110110 01010101 00000011 00011000 00110100
01111101 10001100 11100000 01110001 11111111 00000000 11010111 10101100 11011100 11010010
11011100 00001010 01011011 10111110 01010001 11011011 11011110 10011000 11010010 00011111
11111110 10111101 01101000 01111101 10010100 11100100 01110001 01010001 10110101 10011110
11100011 11010011 10100111 10110101 01010011 10101011 00010101 10110000 01110101 00101001
01100111 11100101 11001101 00110101 00001001 00111110 10100010 10101111 00101101 10111110
00111010 00001010 00010110 00001100 01110010 01101011 00111111 01101000 00111011 10010101
00011001 10011011 10100001 00011000 00000111 11010010 10011100 10101110 01110001 11111100
10000111 10101101 01011010 11110010 01010111 00100011 00111001 00010100 11100110 10000101
01000000 00100111 00011101 01101011 01011000 01001110 11011011 10000001 01001100 00000010
01000001 00111001 11100011 11011110 10011000 10100100 11100111 00111101 10101010 11011111
10010110 00111000 00011000 11100010 10001100 00000001 11011010 10000111 01010101 00110111
10100000 00010101 00110000 01011111 10011100 01010010 10110000 11000000 00111110 11110101
00111011 00001100 11001001 11000111 10100101 00011110 01011110 00110000 00111001 11101001
01011010 01111011 01001011 10100000 00100000 00011001 00100011 10011100 01100100 11110111
10100111 11100001 01010100 00011110 01101010 01110100 10000011 01110010 10000001 11101111
10010010 01101001 11001101 00001010 11101100 11001000 11101001 01010001 10100101 10110101
01100001 01111110 11100101 00101100 00010001 10011100 11110100 10100110 10000000 10101101
11001110 01101010 11101110 11011100 01100100 11110100 10100111 01111001 01110001 10011110

01111001 10100101 11001100 10010110 11111010 10010111 01110100 00100011 11000011 00111000
00000101 01010011 01111110 00111101 10000101 00110001 10100000 10011011 01100010 00000110
11001110 00001101 01110100 01101101 00001110 01000001 11011000 00001110 01001111 01111010
01000101 10110111 00111000 11101001 10001100 01111011 11010100 10110110 11101111 01100011
00000011 10011100 11110010 10100110 01010100 00100011 11100111 00000111 11101011 11010110
10100010 01110001 00111100 01001011 11111100 01111001 00011100 11110001 01011101 00010001
10000000 10010110 00100101 11000101 00100010 01011011 11101110 00100101 01001010 10010011
10001111 01010001 01011010 01111011 01001110 01001011 00001001 01011100 11100111 10010010
01111001 11000001 00000111 00100111 11011111 10001010 10010001 10101111 00100101 11110010
11110000 01001001 11000111 01010001 11001101 01101100 10111110 10011100 00011010 00100011
10000101 11100100 11110111 11110100 10101010 11001111 10100100 10101000 00111000 00000111
10010011 11010110 10010011 10011010 01100011 10111001 01001101 00110101 00101001 10000000
11001000 01110010 00000111 10100001 10100111 00100110 10101001 00111000 00000101 10000011
01100111 00111110 10010100 10010011 01101001 10101101 10001100 00100000 00111100 11111110
01110101 01010011 11101100 01110011 00101001 11000110 00001000 00011001 11100000 11010010
01010010 10001100 10110100 00011101 11001101 00100100 11010110 01101110 00000000 00100011
01110000 11100100 01100000 01111011 01010101 10000100 11010110 10100110 11001111 11011111
00111001 00111101 01001000 00111101 10101011 00000001 11100001 10010100 01001010 01010100
11110001 11101011 11000110 00101001 10001011 10111011 10111000 00100011 10110111 00110101
10110010 01101001 10101011 00001101 01011000 11101010 11100010 11010111 10100111 00000100
00110010 00010000 01110001 11000110 01001101 01001011 00010111 10001000 11100111 00000111
11110111 10011101 00111011 10010001 01011100 10001000 00101100 10111100 00010011 11111000
00010110 11000101 00101010 11001010 11011000 11001001 00111000 11111110 10010100 10011101
00100110 10011101 10011010 00011101 11101100 01110110 11101001 11100010 01000010 10100111
11111101 01011001 00100000 11110000 00000111 11110011 10101011 00010000 11101011 11100010
01000111 00000000 00101001 00111000 11101110 00101011 10000011 01001011 10100110 11101000
11100111 10011111 01010000 01101010 01011000 01101110 11111100 10111001 00001011 01100111
11110000 11110101 10100001 11010010 11101110 10001000 10111001 11101000 00101001 10101100
10101001 00111100 10010000 00111110 10011100 11010101 10111000 11110101 00101000 11001110
00001111 01000001 11011111 00100110 10111100 11101010 00101011 11010010 00001001 11100111
10101110 01111010 10011100 01010101 11000100 11010100 00110110 10000100 11001001 00000111
11011111 00111100 00001010 10000101 01001101 11011111 01100010 10001111 01000001 00010011
10000010 00111010 10001010 01010110 01100000 01001000 11000001 11100100 01110110 10101110
00011101 01110101 00010011 10011101 11000001 10111001 11101000 00110000 01101010 11000010
01101010 00100100 01000111 10000010 11011100 11110111 10101100 01100111 00000110 11011110
10000100 11011000 11101011 10010101 10110111 01100111 10011010 01110000 00000100 00000011
11001101 01110011 10110001 01101010 10001010 10100001 00110000 11011101 01111011 01100110
10101101 00100110 10101100 10111000 00001000 11111101 01111011 11100010 10010111 10110011
01101101 00000111 01010011 01011111 11100111 00011001 11001001 11101011 01001000 11001100
11011001 11111110 01110101 01000001 00110101 00011000 11110111 00011100 10110110 00001110
00101010 01000011 01110000 10110010 00000011 10000010 01001111 11101001 01011001 10111010
01001101 01101010 10001010 00101110 00101011 00000001 11010100 11010000 11100101 01001110
01111001 10101010 11001001 00100100 01000101 00000111 00100100 10011010 10010011 00001011
10001100 10101001 11100100 11010011 11100101 10111111 01000010 01001001 00110000 10100111
11010111 00011111 01011010 01010010 10101011 11000000 11110100 10101000 10000000 00100011
11101001 01000111 11001101 10001100 10001110 10000010 10100011 01011110 10000000 01001000
00100011 00000111 00111100 01010010 11111001 01011001 00011110 11011110 10010101 00011000
10010001 10000111 00010100 10101000 11000111 10111001 10101010 10010110 11100001 01100001
10101111 00010001 00011100 01110100 00010100 11000111 10001111 10000001 10110111 10110101
01011001 00101100 01110110 01100000 10011100 11010010 00100000 00011011 00110010 01101001
11011001 00111101 00101110 00001100 10100110 11010001 10110110 11000010 01101001 00011000
00010000 00110010 01111000 10101101 00000000 00111000 11100111 10011010 01100011 11000110
00011011 10101000 00011000 10101000 10010011 01110111 11010000 00001010 01111100 01100011
00100100 01110100 10100110 00111111 00111100 11100011 10111101 01011110 00101010 00001111
00001100 00111010 01010011 00111100 10111100 11001001 11010000 10000001 01001111 10100101
11011001 01000101 00111110 10000011 10100101 00100110 01111000 11001001 00000111 10101111
10100101 01011100 01101000 10110010 01110011 01001010 11010001 01100100 10001111 01101010
01101010 11001001 00000001 01000000 00010001 11001001 11000001 00010100 11010111 10010101
11000001 00000000 01111101 11001010 10111010 11110001 00000001 11001110 01000101 00110011
11001000 00001111 10000011 01011001 10101001 00111110 10000011 01100101 01010111 10010110
01001110 00110001 01000010 11001001 00100110 01111010 11110001 11111100 11101010 11100011
11000010 00110000 00001101 00110001 11100000 00111000 00010101 01001101 10110101 10111000
01101000 11001000 00001100 11000111 00011001 00100111 11110000 10100110 11111001 10111101
00001011 00010011 11001101 01001101 11110110 01110001 10011110 01101001 00111110 11001110
00001000 11000000 11001001 00000010 10001110 01100101 01100000 00010011 11001101 11001111
11111111 00000000 01011110 10000101 10010000 10011001 00110011 10011110 00001101 00101111
11011001 11001110 01111000 11001111 11010010 10010011 11001001 00111000 11001111 10100101
00100110 11010101 10000001 00000000 00100101 10011111 10000011 11001111 01101010 10110101
00001100 01100100 00001100 10111001 11001111 11010010 10100010 10110110 10001011 01101000
11100111 10101110 01110011 10011010 10110011 11011010 10100010 11101010 01001000 11011010
00110000 11101110 00111011 11101001 11010010 10011100 10111101 00110011 01001101 01000011
10011110 01001101 01001000 10100000 00011111 11111111 00000000 01011101 01001100 10010101
10010001 10110101 11101100 00111001 00110000 01000101 00110110 01000101 11000000 10101001

00111110 11101000 10100110 01011100 01100100 11000111 11011010 10010010 01101010 00101010
11100010 01111010 10010100 10101110 00000110 00111011 11010110 01101101 11000011 11100100
11010101 10001011 11011001 01110000 01001111 11001101 11001111 01011010 11000111 01111001
00001110 00001110 00001101 01101010 10101101 00101101 10001001 00011011 01110010 11000100
00011111 10010100 11110111 11110101 10101010 01110010 01001100 00110011 10001110 11111001
11000101 01000111 01110001 00110110 01001111 01011111 11010110 10101001 10110011 00000011
10011111 01110011 10011110 10110101 10101010 10100101 00010111 11101010 01001101 11101100
01011101 01100110 00000111 00111100 11110100 10100101 01010011 10011111 10011011 00111110
11110101 01001101 00100100 11100000 11010100 11001010 01000000 00011001 11001110 01101010
11100101 00001110 11100010 11011100 10010101 10001000 00100111 01110111 00111111 10001111
01101010 01100001 01100010 01000001 11110100 10100110 10110011 01100110 10011010 11000111
10001100 01010100 01011111 01010001 00110110 00110110 01001100 01100111 10100101 01010011
10011001 10110111 01100100 01110110 10101011 00010010 10011110 00110011 10011111 11000010
10101010 10011100 01110010 01110000 00111101 11111101 11101011 01101000 10111110 01101101
10000101 01110001 10111011 11001000 00011000 11001001 00100011 11101011 01001011 11011000
00000010 00110001 01010001 00111110 00110011 10011110 11010100 11101110 01000001 00000111
00110101 01010001 11011011 01000001 00001111 01000010 00001001 11001111 01101010 10010001
01001111 11100001 11101100 01101001 10011011 01000110 01001011 00001010 00000110 01111101
00001111 11010110 10100110 00010110 10111110 10100000 11000100 01100010 01010111 00100000
00001111 10101101 01000000 01001001 00111001 10101001 11001001 00100011 10010001 11111001
10011010 10101110 11100101 10110001 10000001 10001111 10101101 01101001 11101100 11110101
00010101 11000110 00111001 11000000 11000000 11101011 01010001 00110001 00100000 11100011
10111101 01001001 10001111 01011110 10110101 00010001 11000110 01111001 10101011 10000011
11101000 00000011 10010000 11100100 00010000 01000101 00100011 00000001 10110100 10010011
11011010 10010011 10100101 00110111 00111000 00100011 10011110 00101011 01001011 00111011
01101000 00000010 00001110 01111010 11111110 00011000 00110100 10001101 11000111 00000100
00011100 11111011 01010001 11111100 00010100 11010111 00111000 00111100 11010011 11010001
00000111 10101000 10011011 10110010 00110001 01001001 11010100 01110001 11011010 10000101
11000001 11100111 11010100 11010011 01110011 11000001 01010001 11010010 10011111 00101110
10000010 11101010 00111111 00100000 00011100 10001110 10111000 10100100 01010001 10011110
01101001 10111101 00001110 01111011 01010011 11010100 10011100 01100100 01100011 00011001
11110101 10100100 10000000 00110010 01101001 00110000 00001000 11100111 00100111 10011010
00011000 11111100 11111001 11101101 01001101 11001001 11101100 00111010 10011110 10111001
10100110 11101100 10000100 00111001 10111000 00011000 00011100 10001010 01100011 01100000
00011110 10111100 11110100 11001000 00010100 01110011 10111000 10000011 10001111 11000000
11110101 10100100 11000000 01100001 10001100 10011111 01111100 01010110 10010000 11011011
01100001 00111101 11000011 01110000 11101001 10011110 01101000 00101100 01000001 11100110
10000000 00010101 10000111 01111110 00111101 01001101 00001101 11010011 11100110 00011100
11010100 11011111 10100000 11011010 00011100 01011000 01100011 10011110 00001101 01000010
01100100 11111001 10001000 11000001 10100101 11011111 11000110 00001111 00010101 01011110
01101001 01001011 00011100 00001100 11010011 10100111 01110110 11110101 00100101 10001001
00100100 10000110 01000110 11100111 10100111 10110101 00111001 00001000 11001111 01000011
01010000 10001110 10011100 01111101 11111111 00000000 01011010 10011010 00010001 10010000
00001000 11001000 11110101 11001111 00110101 10101110 10100110 00111011 11101110 01001000
10100000 11110001 10000010 01111010 11110011 10011010 10110110 10101011 10000001 10011010
10001101 00100011 11101000 01001111 01001010 10010100 00001100 10011100 11100011 00011110
10000110 10110010 11100111 11010110 11101100 10110100 01011010 10000100 01101110 01001111
01111010 10110001 00010111 00011000 01010001 11010010 10100000 10000111 00000011 00010101
00111010 10011111 01111100 00001010 11001010 01110011 01110111 11011000 10110101 01101110
10000101 11101000 00000111 11001110 10000011 00011100 10010011 11101011 01011011 01101000
10100100 10000001 11001110 00101011 00001010 11011010 01001111 10011100 01110111 10101101
10000100 10010100 01110110 11101001 01011100 01010011 01101110 01001111 01011101 10001011
00101101 00100111 01011100 01110100 11100010 10101111 11011010 10001111 10010011 00111101
10101011 00101011 11001110 11100110 10101110 11011010 01001011 10110100 01100011 00011101
01101011 00110100 10010110 10101101 00001000 11010001 01100011 11011110 10000000 01000001
01101111 01000001 11101001 01010001 00101110 01000001 00111100 11100010 10010101 00000110
00111000 00110101 00101111 01010000 00100111 11001110 00001001 11000101 00011100 10010001
11001110 00111000 11110111 10100110 00101110 00111010 01010011 10110010 00110011 11010011
00110101 01011101 00000000 01110010 10010000 00000110 01110001 11001101 00100111 01011110
11010100 10000101 10000000 11001000 11000101 00101010 10010001 01000011 11010101 00000000
10001101 10001110 00001000 11100111 10011110 00101001 10100100 10011100 00010000 01000000
10100111 10001100 01100111 00111000 10100000 00001100 10011010 11001010 00101111 01111011
10000110 11000100 01000011 01111001 00011111 11010010 10011010 10100001 11001001 11101000
01111111 00001010 10110111 10010000 00010011 00110100 11000000 11011000 11111110 10110101
01110010 01101101 01101000 11000000 10000111 00010010 01100000 00011110 00111001 11110111
10100011 11100110 11101100 00110001 01010110 00001011 00000110 11101101 01001101 11000110
01000001 11101001 11101111 01010000 10010010 01001110 11100000 01000010 10100101 10110000
01001001 00011101 00111111 01011010 00010101 10110001 10000000 01111111 11111101 01110101
00110011 00000101 11011011 11101101 01010001 10101110 11010110 00100000 10000001 10011100
01010011 11100111 11100101 10111000 00110010 00110111 01100010 00111001 11000111 00010100
01100100 10110000 00111101 10101010 11000011 01100000 11100111 10001110 01101010 00100111
11000001 00011100 00011100 01100111 11011010 10011010 10111011 01010110 10111000 00001001
11000111 00000100 11110100 10100110 10100000 00011011 00110011 01001111 01100001 11010000

01110110 10100001 11000110 00001110 00000111 01001010 10000111 00100111 10110101 11000011
01100010 00100101 00000000 10011110 10110100 11100110 10001011 11011111 10001010 00011101
01001000 00100011 11010010 10000101 01011100 00001100 00001110 11110101 01110000 01010111
10001101 11101111 10101000 00110000 01111000 10100011 11100000 10011110 10110100 11101111
10010000 00011110 10011100 10011010 00011000 01111010 11010011 01011001 01000001 11101000
01101001 11110010 11011101 11101110 00000011 10000110 11010101 00110100 11010111 00100011
10010011 10001010 01101100 01111001 00101110 01000001 00111101 00001101 01001000 11011100
10010011 11000111 00010101 01010001 01101001 10101101 00000011 01110010 00110101 00111101
00111001 10100101 11001001 00110100 00101000 00011001 00100100 01010010 00010001 10001110
01010111 10111111 10101101 00010001 01101001 01000110 11000011 11011000 01100110 11100110
00000000 01111111 00110001 01000110 00011001 10111000 11001111 11101011 11010110 10011110
10101010 01110001 01001010 11010001 11100001 00101000 01001101 11110101 00010110 10000011
00010110 01001110 11000100 11111110 01010100 11010111 01100010 01001000 11111001 10001111
11010011 00011101 01101001 01110001 10000001 01001010 01010110 10010111 11001100 01100100
01011001 11111001 11111000 11101101 01001011 10011100 11100011 11001100 00111111 01000001
01001111 01100000 10100000 11100100 01010011 00000010 11100100 11100111 10001111 11000110
10001001 00100001 01011100 01000111 00111100 01110010 01111001 11101101 01001100 11011011
10000001 11101111 11111001 01010100 10001100 10100011 00110100 11101100 00000000 00111010
10001100 11010000 11011010 01000011 00100000 00100000 11110001 10110100 01010001 11100101
11100100 00011100 11010100 10101110 01000010 11110011 01010001 11101110 00100100 00010000
01111010 11111010 10011110 00101000 10010101 11100011 10101100 10000101 10111001 00011011
01000100 10100100 00001110 01111111 01011010 01111111 10010001 10110111 00001101 11010111
11011010 10010011 01110000 00011000 11111110 01110100 11000111 10011000 10011110 00001111
00010100 01001010 11010010 01010111 01100101 00100110 00111111 11001010 01011110 01001111
01011010 01100011 11000010 10100100 00010001 01001001 10111000 10001000 11111001 00111000
00011111 01011010 01100001 10010101 01111000 11001001 11000110 01111010 01010000 10101100
11010000 10110100 00000110 10001000 00000101 11000110 01111110 10010100 00101100 01000000
10001010 00011101 10110011 11011111 10001010 01100000 10010000 00000000 01111001 11110110
10100001 11011111 01001110 11000011 11010011 10100000 00100100 01000011 10110111 11100111
01001110 11011011 10011110 10110100 11011111 00110011 00000111 11010010 10100011 11111011
01000000 11000001 11100100 01100111 10101101 00110100 10100010 11000000 01111011 01000100
00110011 10011010 01000101 10001101 01110011 01010001 11111001 11001100 01111111 00011010
01101110 11100110 00101111 10000001 11010010 10011010 11100101 11011000 01011010 10001111
11110010 11010101 10011111 00100011 11101001 01010001 10111100 01101011 10010001 11101010
00101001 11111001 11000000 11100111 11110100 10100110 10010110 11000001 00000100 00001100
11010001 00101011 01011011 01010001 00000111 10010110 10101101 00011111 00101011 11010110
10010011 11001000 00011101 10000111 11100001 01001111 00101100 01001001 11101011 10000001
01010001 10101011 00110000 11101011 01000010 01101010 11010110 01000011 11010100 01101111
11011001 11010100 10000010 00110001 11101111 11001001 10100100 11110010 00010000 00101110
00010000 01111110 00000110 10011110 00100100 11100111 10000001 10001010 00011111 01110111
01100001 01011001 10110101 01110110 00001010 11111101 01001000 01010110 00100000 00001001
11110111 10101000 10111100 10101100 00110101 01011000 01000101 01101100 00011100 10000011
10011010 01011111 00101001 10000111 00111000 10101011 10001010 01101011 01010100 00111011
10110100 01010011 01010101 00111101 00001000 10100111 00011000 11110111 00000011 11011011
00010101 01110011 11001001 01100010 00110000 01111011 11110101 00110100 10100010 11011000
11100000 00001110 11110100 00111010 10001101 01101100 00101101 11011110 10100110 01110011
01000010 11011011 00111101 11101000 00010001 00111110 00101011 01001001 01101101 11001001
00111000 00100011 00000011 00011101 01101000 11111011 00111111 10110001 11111100 10101001
10101001 11110101 01001100 00110100 00110110 10010110 11011100 11100011 00100000 11100011
11111010 11010011 10000100 01111100 11100011 00011111 01011010 00001100 11001101 10000011
10010001 01000001 10010000 10010001 11010111 10011111 10101101 01101011 01110111 01110010
01000011 11001000 11011100 11011100 00001111 10010011 11011110 10011100 01101101 00110000
10111100 00010001 11010111 10110101 00001101 00110000 11000111 00000110 10010101 01100101
01100110 00011000 11110101 10101000 10010101 00111101 01111001 10101110 00100100 00100111
11011001 01011011 11101110 10011110 00000101 00110011 11101100 10000011 00000100 10010011
11001111 11010010 10100111 01101001 01001001 00011001 00111001 00100110 10010101 00100110
00001110 01001000 11101110 00101010 10100101 00011101 00110110 00010101 10001010 01011111
01100011 01100000 11000111 01111000 00010100 11011111 10110010 00001110 11100010 10110100
10011000 10001100 01111011 01010010 10101010 10011100 11111100 10100110 10000101 10100110
11000011 01100110 00111100 10110110 10001011 10110011 00000101 01110010 00110011 11011110
10101010 00110110 10011001 00010100 10011001 01101100 01100011 01111111 01100000 00101011
10100100 01111000 10000000 11000001 01101110 01101001 10101011 00000010 11101110 00100111
10100000 00110101 00010001 10110101 11110100 00010101 10111010 10011100 10011011 11101000
10101000 00000001 00010001 10001111 10011101 11111010 10010011 01010101 00100110 11010010
00100110 00000000 10000001 11001011 11100111 00000011 10001110 10110101 11011010 11111101
10011100 00010011 10000010 01110000 00111101 10101001 10101111 01101001 11001001 11100111
00111000 10101011 01110011 01111100 11011011 10000010 00111000 00111001 10110100 11011001
01010111 10000111 10001000 10001100 11110111 10101010 00110011 01011011 00110010 10011110
10001110 01110110 11110011 11010011 00010101 11101000 11000110 11011100 00010000 01111110
01010000 01111101 01110011 01010101 00100101 11010011 11100010 10010001 00001010 10111010
10000001 10010011 10011100 11100010 10110100 01011000 10001001 01000111 01010110 10000001
10011100 00011001 10001101 10000001 11001001 11101010 01111010 01010010 11100000 10001110
00110011 11000111 10110101 01110110 00001101 10100011 01000101 00100110 01001000 00011000

01110010 00110000 00111001 10101010 01101101 10100000 00111000 11001000 01000110 00011100
01110101 00100110 10110100 01111000 10001101 00101110 11000001 00011100 11010000 10010010
01000001 10001100 00010010 00111110 10010100 11110011 00111100 10101011 11001001 00111111
10000101 01101100 01011100 01101000 11110011 01000110 00011111 01101110 00001110 00111010
01100010 10110011 11100111 11010011 11011110 00111100 11111001 10000000 11111101 01111101
00101010 01100011 01010010 00110010 11011000 00110101 00100000 10001010 11110101 11000110
00000110 01000111 11110010 10101011 00100011 01010100 10010000 11110011 11001010 00011110
00110010 01000001 11101011 01010101 01000100 00000011 10111000 00100000 11100111 00010100
11000110 10001011 11110111 10011000 11111101 01110011 01011010 10101001 00101101 01000110
10011001 10101001 00001110 10101001 11001111 00101101 10001100 11111010 11010101 10011111
11101101 10010101 01010100 11100101 11000111 11100011 01011000 00111011 00110001 11101001
10000011 11011111 00010100 11000110 00011101 01000001 11100100 01110110 10101000 01001001
01101110 10001010 01101100 11101011 00100001 11010110 00001000 10001100 01111110 11110011
00000100 10011110 01110000 01111010 11010101 11011000 01110101 10010010 01001001 11001001
11001111 00011000 00000111 11011110 10111000 01101110 01110011 11000110 01110001 11101011
10011010 01010101 10010001 10000111 00010001 10010010 00111101 11101010 10010101 00011000
10110111 01100110 11001000 10111101 10001111 01000011 01001101 01010001 01100100 00000011
00101101 10001100 01111011 01010101 10110001 10101001 10101001 01000000 10100000 11110001
10011100 01100111 11010110 10111100 11010110 00111011 10111001 11100011 00011000 00001100
11100111 11101010 01101010 01101000 11110101 00011001 01100001 11101111 11111111 00000000
11010110 10100101 00111000 01000101 00111011 00100100 01010001 11101001 01010001 01011110
11000010 11011100 01101110 11101111 01010011 10100101 11000010 01100101 11000110 01110011
10001111 11010110 10111100 11100010 00001101 01001101 10010100 10010001 10111000 11100011
10101111 00111101 11110011 01010110 10100010 11010111 10001110 01000110 01011011 11100111
01001100 11100000 01111011 01010110 01110010 11000011 11101000 10101110 00101101 11001110
11111001 01100100 00011000 00111001 00100011 11011010 10011101 00011110 00010111 01111001
11011100 01001110 01101011 10001011 10000111 01011101 00110010 00100010 01111100 11001000
01110000 00111001 00111001 11101011 01010111 01010011 01011101 11000010 11111010 10001100
01110100 11001101 01000011 10100101 11001011 01110100 11000010 11000111 01011010 10101100
00000100 01111000 11101111 11101011 01001000 11001101 10010010 00101011 10011011 10001111
01011000 00010010 00001100 00111011 11100011 11111010 11010101 10110100 11010110 00100010
00100011 00111001 00000111 11110101 10101100 10111101 10010100 10011000 11001101 10010010
00111111 01111000 00110010 01111000 00100010 10010111 00111101 10000101 01100110 10100110
10100011 00010001 11100100 11001000 00000111 11100011 11010110 10100101 01001011 11100101
11001111 00111100 00011010 10010111 00001011 01101110 00101011 00010111 11010111 10010001
11001111 00010100 10101010 10111000 00100111 10111000 00111101 00101010 10110111 11011010
11100010 11011000 00001110 11100000 01110011 11101001 01010010 00101100 11110001 11110100
11001101 00011010 10110101 01100001 10100101 01110001 11001110 00000001 00000100 01100011
00010100 10000000 01100011 10001100 01010011 11010001 10100011 00111100 11111110 01111001
10100010 00110111 00001100 01001111 00100010 10111001 11010100 00101101 10101011 11011100
00111101 00000110 00110010 01111010 11110001 01000011 00001110 01000101 01011000 01011100
01010011 00011010 00110001 11101011 01010111 00010100 11011011 11010100 00001000 01011010
00110001 10011010 01101110 00111001 00011000 00011000 11110111 00010101 01100011 01101000
00111101 01101001 11001110 00000110 11011111 11110011 11001101 00001110 11011101 01000100
10001010 01100100 00110001 11001110 11000001 11111001 11010000 00111010 01100000 01110111
10101011 00101111 10000101 10001100 10011010 10100110 11001101 10010011 11110010 11010011
01110110 01011011 11101010 01011100 00010011 01101100 01111000 11000000 10100101 01100011
11000111 10110101 00110001 01111010 01100010 10011101 11000111 00000011 00110100 01000001
01000110 11110111 01100111 01010101 11001001 00110010 10111011 00101000 01010110 11100111
10001010 10001111 10001110 10010100 00111000 11011011 11010010 10101010 01010001 11101100
01010111 01010010 01001111 00110011 00111101 11101001 10110011 01001010 00001100 01100100
01100110 10101011 00111001 00000000 01111101 01101010 10111100 10110010 11100100 01110010
01111111 00111010 10001011 00100111 10101011 00100001 11101011 10110001 01010011 01010000
10010100 01100000 10000000 00110010 01000111 01011010 11100111 01101110 01101110 01110000
01111000 11001001 11001111 00011000 10101101 00101101 01001010 01000011 10001110 00001111
01111110 10110101 11001111 01011100 00110111 11001110 01001111 00000000 10001111 01111010
11010110 00010100 11010011 11011000 00000101 10111000 10010100 00010011 11000101 01000011
11100110 01100100 00001111 01011010 10000101 11011000 10010001 11001111 01011010 10001111
01110001 11000110 00111011 10011110 11110101 11011011 00001010 01010001 11100101 11011100
11001001 10110010 11110010 00010011 11101011 11010110 10101100 01000011 00101001 00111111
00101000 00011100 11111101 01101010 10000100 00100100 10001110 00111010 11100010 10101101
10100110 00110011 11000000 11100111 10110110 01101011 00110100 10100100 10000001 00010010
11101110 11100110 10000111 01101100 10010011 10000001 11111010 11010010 00110000 11111100
11101010 00110111 00000100 01110010 00111010 11010110 01010010 01001110 11111010 10001111
01100110 01000110 11101100 11011001 11000110 01111010 01110001 11001101 01000010 11100100
01100011 00011001 10101001 10011111 10011111 10111111 11010100 11110101 10100110 00100010
11100111 10010101 00011100 11110111 10101101 01100011 00011011 00101111 00110001 00110110
01010111 11101011 11010100 10010001 01010010 01000100 00000110 00001001 11100110 10011111
00101000 11111001 00000000 01000001 11010100 11110011 01010010 01000011 00011001 11000110
00111011 01010000 11100100 10000101 01101011 10001101 00011100 00010001 11001111 00011111
11001110 10011100 11100100 10000001 01010010 00110000 00000000 01111111 01011010 10001101
11001111 10101101 01100111 01110101 01111011 11101110 00011110 01000100 00110010 11100111
00011111 01011010 10101100 11100100 11110110 00000100 01010101 10001001 01001110 00000000

10101010	11101110	01001001	00100000	00001110	00111011	11100111	00110101	10101100	00011110
10011010	10010010	11101110	00100001	00100111	00111000	11001111	00110101	00011011	10101110
01111110	10110100	11101110	00001111	01011111	11000110	10010001	10110000	00000110	01001101
01101010	10101110	10110110	00011101	10000100	01110011	11110010	01100010	10100011	00100111
11100101	00000101	10101000	11001001	01011110	11011001	11001101	00110101	10110011	11101110
00001101	01101110	10011101	10010110	10100010	11110100	00010001	10001001	11100010	10010001
10001001	11101010	01111001	10100110	10110011	00010010	01111000	00000111	00010100	10001010
00110000	00111110	10110101	00101010	11111011	10010010	11000111	10010010	00110001	10001111
01011111	01111010	01101110	01000001	00011110	11110100	11011110	10100111	00111111	10100101
00101010	11110010	01111001	11111100	01101010	10010011	01101101	10110110	00001111	01100000
11100000	10001010	00000111	10111101	00101011	11100000	00100111	10111111	10101101	00110101
01110010	00000110	00110001	11101111	10001010	01101010	11010010	01001001	00001000	00110111
01100000	11100100	10001010	01100011	10010001	01001010	01111001	11100111	11110011	10100100
01100011	10000001	10011010	01010111	11010110	11001101	10001001	10110000	00100100	01110110
10100101	01001110	00000110	01111111	00111100	11010011	01010111	10100110	01111010	11111011
11010010	10101111	00100111	00111111	11010110	10001110	10110110	10111110	10000001	10101000
10101111	11101011	10001100	01010010	00110100	10011111	10011101	00110010	01000011	10010001
11010111	11101011	01010101	10100110	10010000	10000111	00100000	01110011	10011010	10100100
10011101	11000100	11110100	11011100	01011011	10001001	10110010	01110000	10011101	11111010
01010100	00100001	10001100	10000000	01110110	00100011	11011110	10011100	00100010	11001011
01100100	11010101	10100101	10001100	01000110	00000001	11000111	00000111	10111101	01101001
10100100	00110111	00100101	11101010	00110010	00111000	10000110	11111100	10011010	10111000
10001011	10011100	01100011	11110010	11000101	00110000	01000111	11000110	00111010	00001110
10110101	00100010	01100011	00011100	01110110	11110101	10101100	10101110	11110110	01111101
01000001	00100100	10001001	10110110	10000101	00011110	10100100	01010010	10101000	00000000
00001111	01111110	11110100	11000101	00100000	10100110	01111111	00111100	11010011	10010000
11100111	00111001	11111100	10101011	00110100	10010010	01100011	01011110	01000101	10001000
10001111	01010001	10000010	01111101	11101001	11000101	10111001	11000111	01101111	01111010
10001010	00101110	11000111	00111000	00011111	11001110	10100111	01001100	00011101	11111011
01001110	00001001	00111101	10101010	01011011	01110111	01110110	00101001	01101000	01011010
10110110	10010011	00001110	00001000	00011101	01111000	10101101	01000001	11010011	00100000
01010110	00111100	00100011	01101001	00011110	10011101	11101011	01100010	11010011	11100101
01010001	11001111	01011110	10110101	11001001	00111000	10100110	10011011	00011101	11011001
01100001	00000111	00000000	01110111	00110101	01101110	11011011	01110000	01110001	10011110
10100010	10101011	00101001	01011101	10111100	00001110	10000011	11010010	10101100	01011011
11001101	10000000	00011000	11110110	10101110	01101000	11000001	00111101	11011000	11101110
01101001	00100110	01110011	10011110	01001101	01001101	10111111	10011111	01111100	01010101
01010100	10011011	01111100	01001000	00111101	11111001	10100111	10111001	00100100	10000011
11011000	01110100	10100110	10111001	01101110	00001000	10011111	00111001	00110101	00100000
11110101	00111101	11101010	10111010	10011101	11011100	11100010	10011100	11001101	11000000
10100010	01111010	01101100	00000100	11011001	01011110	10100111	10100101	00110100	11101101
00111001	11000101	00110101	01110010	00000111	10110101	00110001	01000001	11001001	10100101
11001100	11101100	00000100	10101010	01111000	11101011	01001110	01000011	10111000	10011010
10000000	00011101	10111111	01010010	01111010	01010010	10101100	10111111	11111110	10111010
01110001	01101101	10101101	01000001	11101000	00111101	10110011	10011100	01010001	10111000
11100011	10100101	01000100	11110011	01100111	10001110	10000111	11101011	01010001	11111001
11011110	10010101	00101110	10011011	00011001	01110011	11001100	00001010	00110011	11011011
11011110	10011010	01111001	11101011	11011110	10101011	01111001	10111011	11000111	00111101
00101000	11110011	01011000	10000000	11011001	11101111	11010010	10110101	10001100	01111011
00110000	01101000	10110001	11000010	11110001	10011111	11001110	10010101	01011000	00101001
11111110	10110101	01011011	11001100	01101100	10010010	01000110	01101001	10011011	10001110
11100001	11001111	11100001	01010001	00101101	00000100	10010101	11001011	10011110	01101110
01110001	11001111	00111101	01001101	00110101	11001111	00111110	11010101	01011100	01001000
01110111	10011010	00111100	11001100	00101111	01000001	11110101	10101010	10110101	11010101
11010000	01011011	10101001	00101110	11100011	10011111	01101010	01010110	01101110	00111111
10101000	10101000	01110111	00110000	00110100	01101110	00100100	00001100	11110100	10101001
11110110	01110111	01110110	10111000	00111101	01001001	10111000	01101110	00011011	11101011
10011010	01110000	01100101	00011101	11111111	00000000	00011010	10101010	11000011	11010000
11010010	01101101	11100011	10101101	01010011	01011100	10011011	10001110	11000101	10110111
10010100	01111010	11100111	00110100	11010111	10010001	01111000	00000000	01010101	01111101
10100011	01100111	10111101	00001011	00011110	01000001	11100100	11010001	00100110	01001001
00100011	01001100	00010100	11100100	00001110	01001101	00111011	11001100	11100011	10100111
01011110	10110101	00000011	01000100	01110000	00110011	11010011	00110100	10111110	01011011
00010010	00000000	00111000	00010100	00101011	01101110	11001010	10111000	11100011	00111000
01010010	01111011	11100110	10000110	10011101	01111010	01111011	01010100	00101111	00010011
01110111	11111110	01010100	10011110	01001001	00111100	11110101	00011110	11010100	01101000
10011110	10100010	00100101	01011011	10010101	00101111	10001110	01111000	10100110	10110101
11010111	01011100	11110101	10101000	11011110	11010101	10001111	01000010	01111110	10010100
10100010	11010110	01000010	10011001	00100010	10010101	01000110	10011000	11110100	00000011
01110110	00111100	11001100	01111110	01010100	10001111	01111000	10100000	10000001	11011011
10111110	01101001	11001001	10100111	10110000	00011001	11000110	01001111	01110011	10011010
01110000	11010011	11001110	11101110	01010111	11011111	00110101	00101001	11011101	11101010
00001101	11011000	10001110	01011001	11111001	11001110	00111110	10011000	00111101	01101000

01011001 11000000 00011110 10110101 01100011 11111011 00111111 00101000 01110010 00110000
01001111 01000011 11101001 01000100 01111010 01101001 11011111 10010011 10010010 00111011
10011010 10010111 00110111 11001100 00000101 01000110 10011000 11111010 11010100 01101101
00110011 00010001 11111010 11100110 10110100 11011110 11000101 01111001 11001000 11001111
10110101 00000010 11000111 10010000 01110110 11110001 11010110 10110101 01101110 00111011
10000010 00110010 01011110 01101001 00001111 00010100 00110100 10001101 11011111 10101101
01101100 00101110 10011100 00011011 00001101 10110111 10111101 00011111 11011001 11011100
11100011 00011000 00010101 00001110 10101000 00011000 01101100 01011011 00111000 11100111
11110011 10100001 11110111 01100100 00000011 11010000 11010110 11100011 11101001 11111110
11011000 00111101 10111011 11010010 00110110 10011100 01001100 01100011 10001110 01110011
11011110 10101010 01010101 00010011 01010110 01000001 01110011 00010001 11010000 10110110
00110001 01001111 11100011 00011101 00110010 00101011 01100101 10101100 11000000 00000000
00100000 00011001 10100100 00010110 01100111 01111000 11001001 11101001 11011010 10100110
00111010 01111011 11000001 01110011 00011100 01000100 11001100 10111011 10110000 01111000
10100101 00110000 11110001 11010111 00111001 11100110 10110110 11011010 11011100 01100111
10111111 11010110 10011000 10110110 10111000 00111000 00101010 00110010 00111011 11010100
00111001 11110101 01100000 01100010 10110101 10101110 11101110 10111001 11100110 10001111
10110010 10101010 00011110 00111001 00111111 01001010 11011101 01011011 01001110 00111010
01110011 10011110 01101001 11101101 01101010 10111101 00110001 11011010 10000101 10110000
11001100 00010100 10000011 10001110 10011001 00111101 10101010 01000100 10110101 00111000
11110100 11110111 11000101 01101101 01111001 00000011 10000101 11000111 00010100 10101011
00000010 11000110 00001110 01111001 11001101 00101011 00110101 11010000 01010111 00110000
11000101 10111001 11001110 00110000 01101001 11111111 00000000 01100101 11111010 11010110
11001000 10001110 00110000 01111001 11001101 00100011 11000110 00111111 10000100 01010101
00100111 10101101 11011000 00011000 11111111 00000000 01100010 00100011 10011110 11011001
10100111 00110101 10010001 11000000 10101101 01101110 10000000 01100111 10101101 00110001
11110010 01011100 11100000 01111101 01101001 11101000 10110101 01001110 11000001 01110010
10000000 11010011 10111000 00111100 01111110 10110100 11110101 11010011 11010100 10001100
10011110 00000001 11101100 00101010 11011010 10101100 10011000 11001001 00000100 01010010
10100000 01101101 11110100 11101111 01110100 00110010 10111000 10110010 10001100 00011110
10100011 00111000 11101111 11011110 10000101 10110101 10001110 00110111 11100100 11110000
01101010 01111001 00000001 00000011 00110100 11000000 00001001 01000010 01110001 11001111
10100101 00010110 01011011 01011100 01000100 01101101 00010010 01110010 00101001 11100010
00100101 11000111 01000000 01111000 10100101 11110010 11001001 00100000 11111010 01111010
11010010 10101000 01111100 10011101 10000010 10001110 01010101 01110001 11011100 10001101
00100010 01010001 11010100 01110011 01001111 01010101 01011100 01110001 01000001 10001001
11110000 00001001 00111001 00111001 11100100 11010010 01111001 01010010 01110111 01101111
11010010 10010111 00101100 00010110 10000100 11101110 01010101 11011111 10000001 10010010
01101000 01100110 11100100 00010111 11101000 01000101 01000111 11100110 11000110 11011101
11000101 01001000 00110110 00001110 10000111 00100000 00011100 01010111 01010101 01000101
01100110 00100010 01000000 01010111 01101000 00111101 00110011 11010010 10011100 10010010
11000100 00110111 11100101 10001111 01001110 00000111 10101101 01000111 10000000 11000100
10001100 11111101 00101001 10011110 01010000 01100001 11010111 00010100 10010010 01001011
01001000 10010010 01011001 01101001 00010101 10010011 11100100 00100100 00010011 11101010
01101001 00001111 01000010 01000000 11111001 11111010 11010100 00011011 01110000 01111000
11100110 10011101 11001000 11001000 01000010 01001111 00010100 00111011 11110011 01101010
00010111 00101100 00010110 00000100 00001100 10011010 10010010 00111001 01110110 11100011
00111100 11111010 11010101 00111100 10010000 11111001 11100011 00011000 11101100 01111111
10100101 00101111 10011011 11110010 01110001 11111010 11010010 10110010 10111101 10111010
10010111 10101011 01000101 10111101 11000100 00011110 01001001 00100000 10011010 10010011
10010010 01111010 11111110 01110101 01000011 11001101 01100000 11111100 11111110 10110100
11110001 00111001 01011100 00000001 01010010 11101100 10110111 01100100 10100011 01000111
00111011 01001000 10100001 00001001 01101100 10010010 00110000 00101010 10011010 11011101
11100001 11111101 10111011 11010100 10001011 01110101 00011110 11000011 11001000 11100011
11010100 11010101 00110101 01110000 10110001 01100111 00111000 11111001 01101001 00110110
11100111 00011001 00011100 01111011 11010100 01100010 11100010 00100110 00000000 10000010
00001001 11110100 00010101 00100111 10011010 10101100 10100010 10110011 10011101 11011011
10110001 01011101 00000101 11110010 10000110 01111110 01000001 11111010 11010000 11010001
00101000 00000100 01111110 10110100 10001011 00101000 11100111 00011000 11000101 00101111
10011001 10011110 10100011 10101101 00111000 11000111 01100100 11001001 01101000 01101111
10010111 11010111 00111000 11001001 00011000 00111110 11110101 00001001 10110011 00001100
01111000 00000011 10011111 01011010 10110110 11010010 00001110 10101100 00111010 01010010
01111001 10100000 11001001 10011110 10011100 01100010 10101010 01010110 11101000 10000110
01100100 11001101 10100011 01000001 00101001 10010000 10111100 01000011 10010000 00000000
10101010 00110010 01111000 01101110 00010011 11001110 11100011 10000001 11011011 00010101
11010010 11111001 10000011 00111110 11110101 00100010 00110000 00111110 11011101 11101010
00101111 11111100 10100010 10110001 11000011 11001011 11100001 11111001 01010100 11100000
01110100 00111101 11101011 00110010 01011101 00100010 11101010 00110110 00101010 00100001
01100011 10001110 10100100 00001010 11110100 01110010 01010111 10101110 01000111 11100101
01001100 11011001 00011001 00100111 10001110 11111101 01001101 00111001 01010100 10011010
10110010 01001000 01100111 10011001 10111101 10011100 10101010 01111001 10001001 11000111
00011100 11110001 01010001 01111001 00100100 01100100 11101101 11111010 10001010 11110101
00010110 10000110 00100110 00000011 01111010 10000010 00000111 10101101 01010101 01111101

00111110 11010110 01000000 01010101 11100000 10001100 10001111 01011100 01010110 11011110
11010110 01001011 01000100 00100101 01110100 01111001 10100011 11000100 01001000 11100011
11101011 10011010 01100000 10001100 10010001 10001110 10111001 10101111 01000100 10010111
01000011 10110110 10010101 01001000 11110010 10010000 00011110 11000110 10110011 10101110
00111100 00111010 00000000 00111110 01001011 00000000 01111101 11111011 11010101 11111011
01101101 00110110 00010001 11000101 11101100 01100000 10111111 01001100 10000001 01010001
10110100 01011001 00000000 00011100 10011110 11111001 10101110 10100110 01001111 00001110
11001110 10111100 10100000 00010010 00001111 01001100 11100010 10101000 11001101 10100100
11001111 00011001 00100000 11000100 01000110 00101000 11111010 11001100 01011011 00101000
11000101 11011000 01000000 00100011 00111100 11110111 10100110 10100100 10010010 01000100
01111000 00100110 10101111 01001101 01100111 00101100 01000000 01100101 00011111 00000111
10111111 01101010 10001001 11100001 11101001 11101011 11101011 01011010 11000110 10100010
01111010 10001110 11011101 10000110 00101110 10100001 00101000 11101010 01111000 11000101
01001001 00011110 10100100 11001011 00100000 11110100 11000101 01000101 11100100 01100011
10010011 11000111 10100111 10100101 01000111 00101100 00000000 00110001 01101100 01010110
10110001 10110110 11101100 00101110 01101000 10001101 01011111 10110110 00001110 00110001
10000011 11011010 10101101 11011010 11101011 00111110 01011110 00110000 01001111 00100011
00000011 00110101 11001111 10111100 01111001 00100000 10000001 11110101 11001101 00100011
01000000 11000011 10001110 11010101 00001110 00010000 10111011 00100101 00110011 10101101
10000111 01011010 11011100 00000001 11110011 10110001 10001100 10000000 00001000 11000110
00101010 11011010 01101011 00110010 10010011 10001101 11001000 01111101 00101011 10000111
11101001 11000110 01001110 00101000 01001001 01100100 10000111 10100001 10101000 01110100
10111010 10100110 01010101 11101101 10111001 11101000 11010001 01101011 00000100 00100000
11001111 00011001 00010101 01101110 00011101 01010000 00010010 10000111 00111101 10111010
00001010 11110011 00100100 10111011 10011000 00011101 11000101 10011111 10000011 10011110
10110101 01110001 00110101 01111001 01001001 00011000 00000001 00000010 00011110 11011101
11101010 00111110 10101101 10100101 10011000 11011011 01011101 00001111 01001101 10000111
01010001 00010010 10100110 00000101 01011000 10001010 11100011 01110001 00111011 10001000
11100010 10111100 11001110 00011101 01101011 00000100 01111100 11000101 00001000 00111001
00111000 10101011 10001001 10101101 00101000 01000001 10000111 11100100 11110111 11001101
00100111 10000111 01101011 01000010 01011001 11101000 01101011 01110100 00111101 01101010
01001111 00111100 01100100 00010010 01111010 11110100 10101110 00001110 11011111 01011000
11100011 10001001 00000001 11001001 11100100 10010011 01011010 00110001 01101011 00001011
11110010 00001101 11000000 01010110 00001111 00001100 11111001 10000111 01100011 10101000
10111011 10011111 11110111 01111000 01000011 11010110 10101011 10100001 00100000 01110100
10101100 11111011 00111011 10100001 01110000 01001000 11110100 11101111 01011010 00001000
11011000 11100011 10111101 01100111 00111000 01011001 11101000 11001101 10100000 10000111
11100111 10111101 00110111 10000110 11101001 01000011 11100100 10011010 00010000 01100011
10101001 10101100 10011010 01011011 00011010 11011100 01110110 01110000 01101010 00010111
10011011 00111001 00011000 00111100 01110110 10100111 01001001 11101011 10011010 10101111
00101111 01010000 01111001 11111100 00101011 01001101 01101101 01100000 10111101 11000101
10010110 01000000 01010010 10110011 11101110 00100101 11000101 01001111 00100100 10000100
01110100 10101100 11001011 10111001 01000110 01111010 10001010 01101001 01011011 01000100
10000101 11010000 11001111 10111111 10011011 11100111 00100000 10011010 11000100 10111001
01101100 11111101 11000011 10011110 01111000 11100010 10101110 01011110 01001000 00000011
10011100 01110111 11110111 11101001 01011001 10101111 00100000 11001001 11111110 01110101
11010101 01000101 00101001 01101110 01100101 00100110 10000001 11001110 11101100 00011110
11111101 11101000 01010011 10011110 00000001 11000101 00110011 00011001 11101010 01111001
10100101 01010101 11011000 00111101 10110011 01011101 01001010 00001011 11100010 00110011
11110100 00101100 01000011 11000011 11110011 11111001 11010101 10111000 11011000 11100111
10001111 11001110 10101010 01000010 11000000 10110110 01110001 01010111 00010000 01110000
01101011 00001010 10010011 01011101 00001101 00010000 11101110 11011101 01111001 11101111
11101101 01001101 01100010 01010100 01110011 11001001 10100111 11110010 00000111 01001110
00111011 11010100 01100111 00111001 11100011 00111101 01111010 10011010 11000110 01010110
01111011 10000011 11011100 01000010 01110111 00010001 11011111 10011110 10110100 00100000
11011010 01110000 00110011 01010010 00101010 01100100 01110001 10000010 01101001 01000010
11110101 00101111 11111001 01010001 10101011 01000100 01110101 00011001 10001110 01111001
00010101 00100010 00001110 00000111 00111100 01010000 10100011 00100100 10001100 01111101
00000101 00111111 10010000 10111101 00111001 10101100 10100110 11001010 01001101 00010001
11001010 01111101 01101010 10111011 00010001 11010010 10100100 01110011 10000000 01111101
01111101 11101010 10110001 11100111 10011010 11010110 10010010 01001100 10010111 01100001
10010011 01110000 01111001 11001110 00101010 10111111 10011000 01000001 11101101 01010010
10110110 01000000 11000001 00111001 11111010 10011010 10000101 10111111 11010110 11100010
10111010 00100010 10011010 01110111 00100110 11111101 01011000 11011110 10100101 11110011
11010000 01110101 00110100 10011001 11001000 10100011 00101100 00110010 00000000 11101011
01001000 11100111 10010001 10001111 11000110 10110101 10001011 11101010 10000111 01110001
10101111 00100111 01100101 11100010 10100011 00010010 10011110 10000100 01010011 11111001
00110100 10001101 11001111 01101010 10110100 11011101 11000101 01110001 10001010 00001000
00011100 11110011 10011111 01000001 01001000 11000111 01110011 10001110 01111010 01010010
10001100 10101011 01110011 11010010 10011000 11011101 01110010 10111101 00001111 01011110
00101000 01011010 11101000 00000011 11001111 11001011 10011110 10011111 10011111 01001010
00110011 11001110 01111010 11111011 11010010 01110100 11111010 11111010 01010011 00111110
01101100 01100100 11111010 11010010 01110111 01000000 11011101 11000101 00100111 00000111

10001110 10010100 10001101 11101010 01001111 11010010 10000110 00111001 00110100 10011001
00111001 11000101 01010011 11101110 11001001 10111101 10000011 11001100 11100011 00111101
00101000 01011100 10110001 00000000 01110011 01001100 01110011 11000111 10101101 00110001
00011011 01101110 01111000 00110100 01111011 00111110 10100010 01101111 10111001 00110011
00110110 01000110 01000111 00011111 01001010 01100110 01110001 10011110 01111011 01010010
01111110 00000011 10001110 11010101 00011001 00111111 00111111 11001110 01111010 10011110
01101001 10101101 01110100 00100101 10001101 10010101 10110111 01110000 00110011 01000000
10001000 10010110 00000100 10011010 01000000 00000000 01110010 00110010 00110001 11011000
11010100 10101100 01110110 10001110 11110101 10100011 10001011 01011010 00100010 01110111
11010100 01111110 00000110 11011111 01111110 11010100 11111101 11011100 01110101 11111010
11010100 01100000 01100100 00010011 11011110 10011100 10111100 11110001 10001010 01010110
11101110 00011010 00010010 00100100 10011000 01000010 01110001 10011010 01111000 11001001
00011001 11101000 01111011 01010100 01011111 01010011 01010011 00000000 00110000 10000011
00111101 01111001 10101000 01110111 11101010 00110001 11011001 11001111 11010110 10011100
10000000 00000001 10000010 01111110 10110101 00011010 10001100 00010000 01101010 01111000
10010101 01001110 01110110 11110001 11101010 00101010 01011101 10010010 10111010 00101001
00010010 00100000 00000011 10001110 11000110 10100111 01001110 00111010 00001010 10001110
00100100 11001001 11101001 11110100 10101011 00001011 00011110 01111011 01100010 10110001
10010011 11101011 01110010 11000101 01000000 01110010 01111001 10101101 01111011 01000011
10011000 11010000 11110101 00011000 11111101 01101010 10000100 00110001 01100100 11100011
11110101 10101101 10011101 00111010 00001100 10100110 01110001 11001111 10110001 10101110
01011010 10010010 01101111 01100010 10010101 11000111 00000101 01100000 00110000 00010110
10100101 10001110 00100010 01001111 00111101 10101010 11011000 10000111 00011111 01000011
11011110 10100100 01001000 01110001 00100000 11000111 01001100 01110011 01011000 11001010
01001001 01101110 01000111 01010001 11010110 11010001 01101110 01011110 01101010 11000000
10001100 10001110 11111110 11010101 00111101 10110100 01000000 00100000 11100011 10001010
10011100 10000000 01000111 01001010 00101110 10010110 10100011 11110100 00101010 11111001
01001010 00111101 01101000 11110010 11000000 00011100 01010101 10110110 10001100 10111010
00001100 00101110 01101001 00010110 00011100 00011110 10011100 01010100 01001010 11100011
01100101 01000111 01010011 11000000 01101110 10011101 01101001 01110110 10010011 10010010
00111111 00101010 10110110 11010000 10010011 11011011 10001111 01011010 01111111 10010101
11000111 00010101 00111100 11110110 11010001 00000001 01000011 11001011 11001011 10011111
01111010 00010010 11010100 00000010 01001110 00111110 10110101 01110000 01000010 01001011
01110011 10011110 10010101 00100111 10010010 00001110 00111010 11010100 10100110 11011101
11011000 00011001 11011111 01100100 11001110 01001000 11001110 01101001 10111111 01100101
00011000 00011011 10000111 00100110 10110101 00111100 10111100 00000010 01101001 00110000
00011010 10110100 01111010 11000110 11101000 01001101 10011001 11111111 00000000 01100010
00000100 11110101 00111110 11110100 10111111 01100010 11000110 00111001 00111000 00011101
10101011 01001001 00100011 11100110 10010111 00000011 00100100 01100010 10110011 10110011
01101101 00111011 10001110 11100110 01110111 11011001 01000001 00011100 00001110 10111110
11110100 11010101 10110101 01011101 11000101 10101011 01001011 11001011 00011000 11000110
01101000 01011000 10010101 01011110 10101110 01101001 01101000 10101110 00010111 00101000
00100101 10111000 00111001 11001111 11100111 01001000 01101101 11110001 10001100 10001110
00001101 01101000 10001000 11110001 10011100 01010010 00110100 01111100 11111011 11010101
01011101 10101101 00001001 11101011 10100001 01000111 11101100 11000000 11110101 10100111
01111101 10010101 00101010 11001111 01000011 11010110 10010001 10000111 10100000 11111010
11010100 10110101 10100000 11101110 11001010 11101011 01101000 00001111 11111000 01010000
01101100 10010100 11100100 01110100 11110111 10101011 00000000 10010000 11111000 11001111
00110100 11100110 00010100 10101101 11001100 11110101 00011001 01011111 11101100 00110001
10000010 00001000 00111100 11010000 10110110 01111011 10011111 00011001 10101011 01001010
01111011 01010001 10011111 10011000 00010001 11010010 10101010 11001101 10101011 10010011
01110010 10100001 10110010 00100000 11100000 10010001 11110101 00010100 11110100 10110101
01011110 11100010 10100110 01110010 01110011 10001010 01001100 11100000 11100010 10010011
11010111 01001011 10000101 11000110 00101101 10101010 11100111 00111000 11100110 10000001
00001000 11001101 01001110 00001110 11010011 10011010 10001101 11011011 00111111 10001101
00001001 00110101 11010100 00010011 00010101 00100001 01010100 00111011 10000111 11100111
01001111 11110010 11010100 10100111 00100000 00010001 11101111 01010001 11111001 10011001
01001111 10010111 10001100 01010010 00111011 00010000 10011000 11000001 10100100 10101101
10101011 01000101 01101010 01001011 10110110 00110000 01111010 01111111 11110101 11101001
10000011 01101000 01111100 11100011 10101101 01000100 00011000 10110000 11000000 00000111
10001010 01001101 11001101 10011100 10000101 10100110 10011010 11100101 11010000 01000101
10000110 00100011 10010001 11011010 10011001 10111001 01111101 00101010 00110101 10001110
01000010 01001101 00101111 10010110 11000111 10101000 11000101 01001111 10110011 01011111
00110001 11111001 00110001 11011011 10000111 00100000 01100010 10000111 10010000 10000001
11110111 01110010 01111101 00101000 01101000 01110000 00111101 00101001 01010001 01001011
00001110 01000110 00001101 01011010 10010101 10010101 10000100 01000110 10010010 10011100
11100011 00000011 11110011 10100101 11001011 00011110 01011000 01100011 10011010 01110000
01011111 00101100 11100111 10011111 10101101 00111000 10110110 01001000 11110100 00010100
10101111 01110111 11101111 00010010 10001000 11000110 01110011 01001110 11100101 10010110
10000110 11100000 11111101 01101000 11001001 11001110 00000111 01101110 10110101 10011110
10101111 01010100 01011000 11010010 00110000 00000111 00011100 11010010 01100000 00000010
01001000 11101111 01001010 01110010 01011010 10011010 11000000 11010110 10011100 10101001
10110001 00010010 00101001 00000011 00000011 00010100 11010110 11000110 00110010 00101001

00111011 10010011 01001000 10111001 00111111 01001010 10011010 10010000 11010011 01000001
10001110 00100111 00111100 11010000 01111101 11101010 00100110 10010011 00010010 01111111
10001101 00001111 00101001 00111101 00101011 01001101 00110111 10111000 01101010 01001001
11110111 10001101 00001100 00111001 00000011 10110101 01000000 01100110 00100011 10110101
00001011 00100100 10001100 01000110 00000101 00100100 10010010 01100000 11001001 10001010
10011100 00001100 00001010 01100000 10001111 11011100 10011010 01100011 00011001 00110001
10001110 10010100 11011100 00110111 10101001 10100001 10100101 01110000 00100101 01001100
00011100 11100111 10100101 00001101 11010111 00000011 10101111 01111010 10001111 11001010
01100010 00001110 00101000 01010101 10010000 10000000 01001101 00100111 00001101 01101110
00011010 00001111 11001000 00000111 10101111 00010100 11011100 10101000 11100110 10010011
11001010 00100110 10001111 00101000 01100011 11111001 01010101 01101101 10111000 11000101
10010111 00011000 11101011 01000000 00000011 10100000 11110100 10100100 11110010 10001001
00000011 10010001 10001010 00111100 10111100 01110001 10011010 01001101 00101011 01011101
10001000 01011100 10101000 11100010 10001110 00000001 10100110 11101101 01010000 01000001
11001101 00101000 11000110 01110000 11100011 11110101 11101011 01010101 01100101 00100001
10001001 00101011 01100000 10000010 00111010 01010001 11100110 11111011 01010001 00100001
10001011 00011101 01000110 00101010 00011111 00110110 00100101 11100001 10001111 00111111
01001010 01010010 01111100 10101100 01010110 00111000 10110101 10111100 00100011 01100110
01011011 11011000 01010101 10110001 01111110 00111010 00000011 11001101 01100100 00000000
10111101 00001001 11101001 11101111 11010010 10001100 10000101 11100100 00011100 10001110
11111000 10101111 01000001 11010011 10110010 01100011 10110011 01100110 11110000 11010100
00011101 10000001 00100111 00011101 00110000 00110001 01010010 01000101 10101000 10000110
00000100 10011110 00001000 11101101 10011010 11000011 01000111 11101111 10011010 00010000
11100000 10010010 11101101 10000000 01001111 00110101 10010101 00111000 10111000 10111011
10100110 00101011 01110100 00111010 00000001 01111010 00110111 11100100 10110110 00101010
01010110 10111110 10001100 00001111 10010011 11101111 10011110 10100100 10011010 11000000
01001001 01111010 01111010 00011111 01101110 01101001 11100011 11101110 10010110 01110110
11100111 11011010 10010100 11100010 11011010 10111000 00110100 01101110 10100101 11011010
00000011 11010011 11100111 11000111 01111010 00111110 11010111 00011110 00000111 01001100
11111010 00000011 11010110 10110001 10100011 00111000 11100000 10011100 11010000 01001001
00100100 01110110 11110100 00100010 10110000 11110110 01111010 11011100 01000110 11011111
10011111 10010001 11001111 01111110 11011001 10100110 11111001 11011001 00100011 00000000
01100110 10110010 10110000 01110011 11000001 00100100 11110111 00111001 10101001 01010110
01010010 10100011 00100011 10110111 00010101 10110010 11100100 01111011 01101110 00101011
01011000 10111101 11100110 11110000 01000111 01110011 01001101 00110010 00011100 11110000
00110011 01010101 10110111 00011100 00100000 11001111 00111101 11101001 01010100 10011100
10011100 11110100 00110100 10100100 10011010 10110010 00011011 00101100 00101100 10111110
01011000 11011100 00001110 01001111 01001010 10011010 00101011 10000111 00001010 00001001
00100011 00011110 10011001 10101010 01111000 11110100 11000110 01111011 11010011 00100110
00011001 11101010 00111111 00011010 01001001 11001001 01101110 10000101 10111110 10100110
10100010 01011110 00110000 00111001 11001000 11000111 10100101 01001011 00011101 11111000
01101110 10011101 01000000 11100111 00100111 00010101 10000111 10010001 10110011 00100011
10000001 11101101 11011110 10100011 01010110 00111100 10000011 11111111 00000000 11101011
10100110 11010110 10101010 11101100 10100101 10101001 11010010 01111101 10101111 10000010
00000001 11111101 01101010 01000001 00110010 11110000 01110011 10010010 01101011 10011011
01001011 10000110 01010001 11000111 01011110 11111001 10101001 00010010 11110001 10000110
00001110 01111010 11110111 10100001 01000110 11111010 00010011 01100011 10100100 01101001
00110011 11010011 11110011 10100010 01010010 00011011 00000000 10011100 01100111 10110111
10101101 01100001 00100101 11101011 00010100 00100100 10110111 01011110 11010100 11110110
10111111 00111101 10001001 11100000 01010101 10111110 01011000 00110110 01010010 01001101
10011011 11001001 00011110 00000111 00100111 00111100 11010011 10011000 00001100 00000010
01111010 00001010 11000100 01011101 01000010 01010010 00110111 00010110 11100011 11110010
10100111 10100110 10100100 01111010 01111111 01011010 11000001 00110111 01111101 11000101
01100011 01100001 01001110 01101001 01111000 11000101 01100101 11000011 10101000 10000010
01000110 01110001 11001111 01101010 01111000 11010100 00000011 00010000 00001111 11100011
01010100 10101001 00101011 11101010 00110101 01110110 01101000 01100000 11111001 01111000
00000111 00110100 10101010 10100111 10111101 01100111 10011101 01000000 00110001 11111001
00110010 00111001 11101110 00101010 01111001 00101111 00000010 10100111 00111000 11001001
11101000 00101001 01110101 11010000 10000110 10001011 00111011 01000000 00111111 11010110
10010011 11001010 00000100 11110100 00010101 01011100 11011101 11100011 00000011 00100011
11101011 01000111 11011010 11110010 01001000 11101101 10011110 10110101 10010011 10100110
11011110 11100101 10100000 10011010 11001110 00100110 00000100 01111001 01100000 10000011
11001001 11001101 01010111 01111101 00100010 11011100 10100110 00001100 01001000 00000001
11101001 10000001 11010010 10101100 01111101 10100000 01100111 00100110 10011010 01101110
10110001 11101011 10000011 01010011 11001000 11111010 00110000 10111001 10011011 00110110
10000001 00010001 00111100 01110100 00111101 01101010 10001101 11000111 10000111 00011011
10010010 10001100 00001000 11101001 11010010 10111010 00000110 10111000 00100000 00001100
10011110 01111101 00101001 11101001 00111010 11110111 00111100 01111011 11010111 01000010
10111010 01011011 10001000 11100010 10100100 11010000 00101110 10100011 11011111 11010000
11110011 11000111 00011101 01101010 10111011 11101001 00010111 00101010 00111000 10001100
10010010 01001110 00110001 11101011 01011101 11010011 11001111 00011111 01100011 01001101
01111001 10000110 01000111 01001111 01101111 11111111 00000000 01011101 00101001 01001110
10100010 11010101 00001001 00011110 01111001 00110101 10011100 10010001 10011111 10011101

00111001 11100111 00110101 01011111 11001000 00100000 00011110 00111001 00011101 01101011
11010010 11100110 00110000 00110000 11011011 10110101 00110001 11101111 01010101 00011111
01001111 10110110 10010111 10101100 01000000 10111001 10101011 10001101 01111001 00110101
01111001 00001111 01010011 11001111 00011010 00010010 01000110 01111001 11000001 10101000
10111100 10011110 01011100 10001110 00110010 01101011 10111100 01101101 00010110 11011100
00000010 10101001 00011001 00111111 11110000 00101010 10100101 01110111 11100001 11110100
01010000 00001100 01101100 01110111 10011110 11000111 10100101 01010100 00110001 01111010
10010100 11001110 00110100 11000100 00000111 01101110 00001000 11101011 01001101 01100000
11000011 00011000 11100000 01010111 01001011 01110011 10100000 11001100 00110001 11100101
10010001 11010010 10101001 00110110 10010101 01110000 10111111 00101100 10010001 10111110
01110001 11011010 10110101 01011000 10101000 11110100 01100010 11011100 11000111 11111101
11100000 01001100 00000011 10011110 01110010 00001101 00101000 10011010 01100000 11000001
10110111 00111111 10110000 00100110 10101111 10110101 10101011 00000001 10000010 10100100
01010100 00111110 01001000 00000111 10101001 10101101 01111101 10110100 01011010 00000101
10100001 11011001 01111000 00011101 10100110 10010010 11001110 01010110 01110011 10010010
01100100 11101011 01011101 01000111 00000000 10001100 01110101 11000111 01011010 11000000
11110000 10100010 10001000 01110100 10001000 11001000 11111110 00110010 01101011 01101111
01110111 10101000 10101110 01001010 11010101 00111001 10011101 10101101 10110001 10110100
01001001 10111010 11010010 00110001 11000101 01000101 10011100 01110010 00101001 10001110
01110011 11011111 11110000 10101110 01011101 11110111 01000110 10000100 10000110 01000000
00000001 11001101 01010100 10011010 01010000 00111000 11001111 11100011 01001001 00110100
10100101 01000111 11100011 11011110 10110011 11100111 10011011 10011100 00011110 10000111
10100111 00111101 00101010 11100011 10110001 00001101 10001111 10111001 10010111 00011001
00111001 11100111 11011100 11010110 01011101 11001100 10100011 10010010 00111001 00011110
11110100 11001011 10001011 10100010 01110010 10111101 10111101 01001111 00110101 10011111
00111100 11111100 10010001 10011111 11010110 10110111 10000101 00101001 00101101 01010010
00010101 11101101 10111001 01011110 01101001 00111010 10001100 11100111 00111110 10111110
10110101 01001011 11010011 01111101 01011001 00111101 01111010 01100011 11010110 10100010
01001100 10000110 00111000 00011101 11111011 11010111 01000011 10111100 01110110 00110011
10111101 11000110 11100111 10001100 11111110 01010101 00100100 01000011 10101110 01000110
01110011 11101011 01000010 10000010 11000111 10011100 00011111 10100101 01001101 00011000
11100110 10110100 01110110 01101010 11001100 00010000 00100010 11111100 11111100 01010101
11010100 00000100 10000000 01111010 00011010 10001001 00000001 01011110 00010100 01010101
10010000 00110001 00011111 00111100 11010111 00110100 11011100 01101111 01100110 01010101
11101110 00100110 00110010 01001000 00111101 00001111 01111010 01110111 10010101 10010011
11000001 10100111 00000000 00001000 11101001 11110101 00111001 10101001 00001110 00000000
00000111 00011000 10101100 00100101 00101101 00101100 11011001 01001101 11011000 10101110
10101010 01000001 11101001 10001010 01110110 00001001 01111100 11010011 11001000 11100010
10000100 11100010 10100001 11001110 01011011 00100000 01100011 00110000 01010111 10010011
11111100 11101001 10101110 01001000 00010101 00100100 10000111 00111110 11110101 01010110
01101001 00110000 00111011 11010101 00100100 11100100 10110101 01100100 00110010 00111001
10011000 01010101 01010010 01001110 01001101 01001011 00100001 00111100 00011110 11011101
11001101 01000100 01001000 11111100 00001101 01101111 01001101 00100001 00110010 00010111
11100100 01100100 01110101 10100110 10111110 00000000 11100111 10111101 00101100 10010010
00101001 00000111 01101000 11100010 10100000 10010001 10110010 00101011 10100010 10010100
01010011 10111101 11001001 00011101 10011110 01000111 10100110 00101010 00010011 10001101
11100000 00000010 01000110 00001111 10101101 00100001 01110010 00001110 00111001 10100101
11110101 11110111 10101101 00010111 00101000 11110101 10110000 01100101 10011011 00111000
11001111 11010010 10010001 11011011 10100110 01001001 11110110 10100001 10011000 11100011
00011001 11100110 10100011 00011110 10111111 11001110 10101011 11011101 11011001 00001001
01111001 10001111 01100011 10010001 11011111 11011110 10011010 10111101 01111101 01110001
11010110 10000111 00101010 01000110 00111101 01111101 00101000 11101101 11000001 10100100
11101101 11010001 10000011 00001100 11100111 10001110 10000110 10011010 11000100 11110010
01110011 11001001 10100110 11100111 00000111 00110100 11010111 01101100 10011110 01111111
00101010 10100101 01111011 11011110 11100100 11011100 01011100 11110001 10001100 00011111
10101101 00110011 01110001 11011001 11110010 01110100 11110101 10100011 00111000 01111100
11110110 10100110 10111011 00101000 01000011 10001110 10011110 10100010 10101001 00100010
01101110 00101110 11100010 00000110 00000111 00011111 01011010 01100100 10010010 01100000
00010110 00111100 10011010 10001010 01101001 10010101 01111010 00001100 10010011 11111100
10101010 00101101 11011100 11110011 11010000 11110111 10101011 10110011 01000110 01110111
01001000 10010101 11100100 11100100 00010101 11001110 01000111 01000011 01001010 00011000
10010011 11101010 01001101 01000010 10011100 10000001 10011111 11000110 10011100 10000011
00001100 01001010 10001110 01001111 10100101 01010101 10010010 01100100 11011100 10011001
01001110 00111000 11000111 01111111 01001010 01110010 10110111 00011000 00111101 01111011
11010011 01010000 01100111 11111100 01101010 01000100 00011001 11001111 00111001 00110101
00111010 11110100 00011110 11000010 11110110 11101110 00001101 01001111 00011110 00110110
01100111 10111111 10110101 00110101 00000001 11000000 00000111 11010111 10001010 10010001
01000000 00000100 01100000 00001111 10100111 10101101 01100111 00111011 11011111 01000001
10101101 11000011 10000011 11010111 00111001 11111100 11101010 01001101 10100011 11101011
11101001 01001110 00000000 00001100 00010101 11100100 10011110 10000010 10100101 01000101
11000111 11111111 00000000 01011110 10100011 01010100 11000110 00100010 00010010 00001111
01001110 10110101 00101010 10001110 01111010 01110101 11110100 10100100 01000100 11101101
10001010 10111001 00011010 11110001 11001000 11001001 00111101 00101010 00011100 10010010

01010110 01101100 11010110 11000001 00001000 00011100 00010111 00011111 01001010 10110001
00011010 11100000 11110100 11100011 11101011 01000100 00101010 01000000 00010101 01100010
00001000 10001011 00010000 00000000 11101111 11010010 10110010 10011101 01101000 11101100
10010000 00100101 11011100 10011010 11010010 00001101 11000111 00011000 11100110 10110111
10101101 01100011 00100010 00110100 11001000 10101000 01101100 01101101 01111100 10100100
11110101 00100100 11010110 10000100 01100011 00000011 10010001 01011100 00010010 01001001
00111101 11001010 11010101 00000110 11011100 10001010 10010010 00011000 10000011 01001000
00000111 11101011 01000100 01100011 00100100 01111010 01111011 11010110 10000100 00010001
01100011 10011100 01100010 10011011 10110100 11110101 00010000 11110100 10001111 01100000
11000110 00111000 11111010 11010100 10111000 00011110 10011101 01101001 11101001 10001100
01110100 11100110 10011111 10001110 11111000 10100010 11101001 11011101 00000000 11000000
00110000 01110001 10001010 00001000 11000111 11010010 10100101 00000011 11010111 00010100
11101111 10010100 00001100 01110101 00011101 10110011 01010000 10010010 10110110 10000000
01000000 10000011 10010010 00110001 11000101 00101010 10000011 10011111 01101010 01111000
11000000 01001111 01110011 01000110 11100101 11001110 00101000 01101010 11011011 10000000
10011011 01110001 10011010 01100000 00011001 00010101 00101001 00100011 00011101 01101001
00110111 00101000 10100010 11010111 01111010 00000000 11001100 00000011 11000001 10100100
01100001 10011110 11010100 10101100 11010001 10000011 11001000 11001110 01101000 11110011
00010100 00001100 00001010 00011110 11100010 01000000 11011111 00100000 10100100 11000110
01111001 00000010 10010111 11001100 01011110 01110011 10001010 01001111 00111000 01100011
00011000 11101011 11010010 10011101 10010000 11000100 11011011 11000000 10100111 01111001
01000100 10011010 00111100 11100000 00000111 01001010 01000111 10011111 00100011 10100101
01000011 11011100 01001000 01000110 01010110 00111101 00101001 11011011 01001101 00110101
01100110 00111000 11101011 01001100 11110011 10001110 01111001 10101011 01001110 11111011
00110001 10010010 00011000 10111001 11100100 01010011 00011001 01110000 01101001 00100101
10010100 11100011 00110100 11001111 00110000 11111110 00110100 10101100 00101011 10010010
00101010 11110011 10010011 11010111 11010110 10011100 11100011 10111101 01000010 01100110
00000011 00000011 00011100 11010010 01111001 11101101 11010011 01101001 00000011 00111101
01001101 01001111 00101101 10001010 00100111 01010101 11001001 10100011 01101000 11100111
10001010 10101011 11100111 00110000 01111110 10010100 11111111 00000000 00110001 11110111
00010000 01001111 01011010 00010011 11101110 11001001 01100100 10111100 00110001 11101001
01001001 11100101 00000011 11001001 11101011 01001100 11011100 01000111 00111001 11100010
10010011 01110110 00000111 01011110 00101001 10110100 11011111 10100001 01010111 00100101
00001010 00001111 01111010 01110111 10010010 10100100 01110011 01010000 00101100 10000000
01111011 11010010 10110100 10111101 11111011 01010110 01101010 00010010 01111010 10000110
10000100 10001011 00010100 01100000 01110011 11010111 11010111 11010110 10011111 10000101
00011101 01101010 10111010 11001011 10000001 10010011 01001011 11100111 10001111 01101010
00010101 00111011 00110100 10000001 10110010 01100110 01010000 00101001 01010011 01101000
11001101 01010100 01101011 10100000 01110000 00110011 11010110 10010011 11101101 01000000
01100110 10110101 11100100 01011101 01000000 10110110 00001111 01011100 01010011 00110111
00011111 01001010 10101100 11010111 01101010 00001111 01111010 00111110 11010110 00111011
11111101 01000110 00111011 11010100 10100100 11010110 10100000 01011001 01111101 11011011
11000110 01000111 11101011 01001001 10010011 01010101 01100100 10111101 01000000 00111010
10001100 11110100 00000010 10100001 10010111 01010001 11100100 00011110 00110000 00111010
10001010 00101110 11110110 00001011 01011100 10111010 11000111 00111001 00000111 10100101
00001010 01000000 11111100 01101011 00111101 11110101 00000001 10110000 10011111 01101110
10010100 10001001 01111011 10010001 10001110 10100100 11111011 01010001 10101101 11111011
10000101 10001101 00010100 00000111 00111000 11001111 00010100 00110111 00011100 11110110
10101010 00001011 01110111 10000011 11001001 10100111 00110101 11010010 11110010 01001011
01010110 11011110 11001101 10000101 10001011 01011001 00000111 00000101 00110011 11101111
10011010 01101011 10010011 01010101 00010110 11101001 01110001 11000001 00011111 10011101
00100111 11011010 10010100 11100100 10010110 11101001 11101111 01010011 11101100 11011110
11000000 10001011 01001011 11000001 11111111 00000000 11101011 11010011 11010100 11100011
00111110 10011001 10101100 11110011 10101000 11000101 00011000 00111000 11100111 10011111
01011110 10110101 00011011 01101010 01100000 11110100 11000000 00011110 10011110 10110100
01110010 01011011 01010001 11011001 10011010 00001110 00111111 01111001 10011100 01010010
10110010 10000000 00000111 10101101 01100110 10111110 10100100 00111010 01100111 11110101
10101000 11011111 01010000 00011101 00001111 00011100 01110010 01110011 01000011 10100000
11011011 10111101 11000011 01100011 01010101 00110110 10010000 01111101 00110011 01001010
11001100 00110111 01110001 10001100 01010110 00101000 10111101 01010000 01001110 01011011
00000011 11010110 10100000 11111110 11010001 11100000 10110010 01110101 00111110 11110100
11011101 00101001 01000101 01101010 11000010 11010111 01100110 11111011 01001000 00111001
00111001 10100110 11111001 10011001 11001111 00110101 11001111 10101110 10100000 11011101
00011101 10110011 01000111 11011011 01001100 10000111 10101000 00011111 10001101 00001110
10011100 01010010 10111010 00001110 01000110 01110100 00001011 00111110 11011110 00111011
01010100 01111111 01101011 00000101 00101011 00001000 11011111 01110010 00110010 01111101
11111010 11010100 01101011 01111101 10011100 10010000 01101000 10100111 01001111 11101110
00011111 00100011 10111001 10111010 11010111 01011000 00000111 10101111 00111110 10010101
00011011 01011100 01110100 11100111 10001010 11000101 01101011 11100010 01110010 00111010
01111011 10001010 01101011 11011111 00000000 10011100 00011100 01100011 10001110 01101001
11001010 00101101 00101011 00110000 01110000 10110011 00110111 00001100 11100000 01110001
11010100 00011010 01110000 10011100 00101010 11100100 10011111 11001110 10111001 11010101
11010100 00011011 10011101 10010101 00010011 11011101 11001001 10001110 10111001 00011001

10100001 11010011 01101111 01010110 01010111 00101110 10000111 01000000 11110111 00011100
11110010 01111011 11010011 00011110 11101100 01100100 10110110 01111111 00000010 01101011
00000100 11011100 00010010 11111001 11011100 01110001 11101001 10011010 01101001 10111000
11001010 01110000 01111001 11111010 11010000 11101001 11011001 10010010 11101001 10011011
10001011 01110000 10111011 01001111 01011100 11111011 00001010 01101111 10011110 01111101
11101011 00010011 11101101 01011000 01001100 10010011 10000001 01001100 01101011 11000001
10011111 10011001 11111001 10100111 00011000 00101110 10101001 10110000 01110001 01101011
01100011 10011110 11110011 01001110 00000111 10101111 10101101 00100001 10011000 10101001
11100011 10111101 00101011 01000110 00010100 11100000 10010011 11001111 01111010 01010110
10001011 11010111 00000000 00011010 11110100 10010100 11011110 10101001 10001011 01010000
01001011 10000111 00000111 10010110 00100100 01111011 11010100 11001011 00111011 00110110
00111001 11101001 11010011 00100110 10100001 01101000 10001000 10100100 11011010 00110111
01100111 10110111 10111101 01000101 10010100 01011101 11010000 01011101 10010110 01010010
11110111 01101000 00111101 00001111 10111101 00111000 01011110 10001110 11101010 11111101
01101010 10001011 00100111 01010001 11011000 11010000 10101000 11001100 00111000 00111000
00011110 10111101 01101010 10011100 01010100 11110101 10110000 01110011 01110100 00110100
11000101 11110000 00001001 11101111 01010010 00100101 11011010 11110011 11001000 00011001
11101111 01011001 00001111 00011001 00111101 00111000 10101000 11011111 00100000 11100011
00111101 11101001 01001110 10010010 11101110 00110101 00101101 00110101 00111010 00100001
01110010 10101110 00000000 00001100 00111010 01010100 10000010 01100011 10001100 00010011
11101001 10001010 11100110 00010111 01110000 11101000 01000000 00100000 10011110 01101001
11111110 01110100 10110001 10011000 11110110 00010010 00111101 11101011 00101111 01100000
10111001 01110100 11101000 01010010 01101011 01110011 10100100 11110011 01001111 00000100
10010000 01111110 10110101 00101010 01001110 01001010 11111011 11010111 00101110 00101110
01100101 00000000 10000000 11000111 11101011 01010010 00100101 11110101 11000010 10001110
01001110 01001110 00111010 00010001 01001101 11010000 11100110 01010111 00100110 11110001
00111010 01111111 00111000 01100111 00000000 11111110 00110100 10101111 00110110 01111000
00011111 01110010 10111001 10110100 11010100 10100101 00000000 00011100 00000011 11101011
11101111 01010010 00011101 01011000 10000001 11000010 11110010 01111101 11111010 01010100
00111010 00100010 11010000 11101000 11010000 11100001 00111001 11100111 00111101 00101000
11101010 01000001 00011000 00111000 10101100 01000100 11010101 11010101 10010111 10010000
01111110 10000111 10001100 01010100 10001011 10101010 01000101 10001100 01100111 00011110
10111100 11100010 10100011 11101010 11001101 01001011 01000001 11011010 11111010 10011010
10110010 10000110 01101110 10000110 10100011 11101000 00111001 11101100 01101010 10010100
01011010 10100100 00000101 01111001 10010100 00101110 00111011 10011110 00110011 01001111
01011011 10111000 11100100 00111100 01001000 10000111 11010011 00000110 10011100 11100011
00101000 00111011 01011000 00111001 00001011 00001110 01011011 10101110 01111000 11101111
01001101 01011001 10001000 00011100 01110000 01001111 01011010 01001000 10100101 01010010
00110011 11000001 11110111 11001101 00100011 10110000 00111001 11000101 00101010 10111100
11001101 01101010 10000011 10010001 10100110 01011001 01001001 11111110 01010100 00000100
11100010 10001111 00110010 00110110 11001111 11001101 10001111 10101101 01010011 01110000
01001000 11101000 01111110 10110100 10100010 00111100 00100110 01110011 11001111 10100101
01100010 10101100 11110111 00011111 00100001 01101101 01011000 10000011 11110010 00110000
11111100 01101000 11110011 00001000 00111101 01110011 10010001 11001101 01010010 01010001
00100111 01011100 11010011 10010000 10110000 00011001 00111111 10000101 01101001 01110100
10110110 01100101 00100100 01011110 01001001 11100100 00010010 01101110 00000111 10100111
01101010 00111100 11100110 00110010 01100111 10111101 01000001 11100110 01111010 11010010
01111001 10100011 00011110 11011101 11101010 01010101 01000110 10110111 01000100 11110010
00010110 10010010 11100011 10010000 00011100 11110101 11101001 10010011 01010011 11000011
01110110 01110001 10110111 00111100 00000011 11010010 10110011 00001001 11011101 11001000
00011111 10011101 00110101 10001001 11101101 10011111 01111010 10100111 01010101 01011100
01001110 00000110 11000100 01110111 01000001 10000110 01110011 11111001 11010100 10011111
01101011 01010001 11010100 11110001 11011010 10110000 11110111 00010101 01011110 00001111
01011010 00110010 01010101 11000000 11001111 11101011 01010010 10111001 01001010 11100100
10111001 10111011 11100111 00000110 00111100 01010010 11111001 10100000 11110000 00111010
10001110 11111001 10101100 01010101 10011110 01000001 11110100 10101001 00100010 10011001
10001000 11000001 00100111 00110100 11110100 01101011 01000010 01111001 00011010 11011100
11010100 10010110 01001110 01110000 00001111 11010110 10000101 10010000 10000001 11010111
00110101 10010010 11010011 00010000 01111010 11100100 11111101 01101001 11111110 01111111
00000000 01100100 11100011 10111101 00011100 10101001 00000111 00100011 01100110 10000111
10011000 11000100 01110101 10100101 11110011 01100100 00001011 10010100 01101110 01000101
01100111 11111001 11111000 11001001 00000111 11011010 10100011 11110011 11001111 00011100
10011110 00101010 01010101 10100011 10110000 10111001 01001101 00000001 01111001 00111010
10000010 01000011 01110101 00111101 01101000 10001010 11100001 10000111 01010011 11010010
10101000 11111001 11011000 11001001 00000111 10001110 10010100 10111110 01110110 01001000
00111101 11000000 10100111 11101100 10010101 11010011 01000011 10110011 10110001 10100010
10110111 01100100 10001110 01000111 00110100 11111111 00000000 00111010 00111101 11111100
10101110 01000001 10101100 01111111 10110101 01100000 11100011 10111000 10100011 11101101
00101100 00110010 01110010 01001101 00101001 00111000 10101110 10000001 11001000 11001101
00111001 00100011 10110110 00101111 11001100 01100011 00111000 11111010 01010101 01001001
01110100 11111011 01101110 00110110 00001100 01111010 11100100 11010101 00110001 01110000
11011001 00111100 00011111 10101001 10101011 00010110 00101100 01100110 10111001 00010001
11100100 11110010 01110011 01001101 00100100 11110110 00001011 00011101 00001101 10001100

01000010 11011110 00010100 10001101 00111001 00000000 01010101 10101101 11011100 01111010
00001010 10000011 00111011 01000000 11000000 11000111 00010100 10000001 10001011 10001110
01110011 10001111 01111010 11001001 00100111 01110011 01010101 10110001 01100001 11100101
00000000 01010100 00010010 11001000 01110011 11001101 00100011 00011100 10100101 01000000
11010010 01110001 11001001 10101010 11100101 11010111 01011101 00001010 00100010 10011010
01001100 10111111 11001110 01101010 10000101 11001100 10000111 00100100 11110111 11111010
11010100 11110111 00010010 00000010 11100111 11011011 11010110 10110011 01100110 10010011
10010011 10001010 10111000 00110100 10101110 10011001 00001111 11001000 10101101 00111011
00000011 11011111 00011000 11110101 10101010 01001111 11001111 01111100 11111101 01111011
01010101 10001001 10001110 01110011 10010001 11000101 01010100 10010111 00011101 01111011
11100111 10100101 01101100 10100101 01110101 10110001 00110111 10111000 01100100 10011111
10101101 00011101 00111000 00110100 10001100 00110011 11000110 01101001 11001001 10001111
11000100 01010110 10110001 01110001 10110101 10001001 00011110 10101011 11111000 00001110
11011100 11010100 11110001 00101000 00011000 00100111 10111101 00110010 00010001 10011110
11010101 01100001 00100011 11000010 11111010 00001010 11000010 10101101 01001011 11101000
10001011 10110000 10101001 10010000 01110001 10001111 11000110 10100110 11000011 00011110
00101001 01110000 00111011 10001111 11001100 11010011 11110000 01101011 00111110 01100110
11011101 10000110 00101111 00000000 01101101 11000111 00011001 10100011 00011100 01010001
11111100 00111101 01101001 10000110 01000001 11111111 00000000 11101011 10101100 11100110
10100101 11001100 00100001 11101000 01000001 00000100 00110110 00111000 11101111 01010001
10110110 00111111 00000001 01001000 11001100 00110001 11110010 11110000 01101010 10100000
00101100 01100110 01110010 11100111 10001111 01001010 00010101 11011110 10001100 00110110
00101100 01001010 11100000 00101001 00011100 01100111 00110101 01010010 01000011 11001110
01110001 10011010 01110110 11100000 00110111 10000011 11111001 11010101 01010111 01101110
01001111 00110101 10101100 01101001 11011001 10010011 10100000 11010111 10010000 00011100
11100111 10000001 01010000 10111001 11100011 00010100 11100111 00111001 11001110 11110001
01010000 11001010 11011101 00001111 10101101 01110100 10101011 11011111 01000010 01101111
11011100 01000010 01000110 01111001 10101000 10111000 11001001 11110101 10100101 00101100
00001111 00011000 10100100 01011010 11011001 00101011 10001010 11110110 00011001 11010000
11100111 10101001 10100111 10001100 01110011 01001100 00111001 11001111 01000001 11000101
00100011 00000011 11010100 01100111 11011110 10101010 00101101 01011011 01010001 10110001
10101110 01110011 11000111 10101101 00110101 01111010 11100111 00100011 11011100 01010010
11110100 00111000 11110101 10100100 01101110 01110001 10000010 01101000 11100110 01101011
01000010 00110111 00000011 11010111 00000011 10101101 01000110 01011100 11111101 11011010
01110100 10000111 00000011 10010010 01110011 01010001 00000110 00111101 01110001 10010100
10100010 00101001 01110101 00100101 10110001 11101101 10001110 01111001 11001110 00101010
00110110 00100000 00010001 11011111 11010010 10011001 00100001 11011100 11011101 01111010
11111110 10010101 00011110 01011011 00100111 00011000 11001111 01101010 11010011 11011001
11011000 01001101 10001111 01111001 00110000 01001110 01101010 00011001 01011000 10110111
00000011 10100101 00000010 00110010 00011101 11000001 00111001 11110101 10100111 11100000
00010011 10011110 00000101 01011110 10001000 11001101 11011101 10010000 00110100 01100100
11110101 11001110 00000101 00111111 01100000 00011111 01001100 01110011 10011010 10011111
01101000 01101100 10000010 00111001 00000111 11010110 10011101 10110111 10011111 01010000
01101001 00100110 00011110 01000011 01010010 00100000 01000111 00011101 11101001 11001000
10011000 11100011 11011010 10011111 10001100 00010000 00110000 00111111 00001010 01111111
11110001 11010100 11110011 00100100 00010111 11101110 00001000 00000110 00110000 11010100
11100101 01011100 00000000 00000111 00110100 01100000 00011110 10111101 01101010 01000101
00100000 00001111 11110001 00110100 10011101 01000100 10110100 10110000 11010000 10001000
00110000 00001000 11000111 01111010 10010111 11001011 11000100 10100000 00011110 10011101
10101001 00110111 01100000 10001110 00000110 00111101 11111011 11010010 10101001 00111100
10010011 10000011 01010001 01111011 01101000 11001011 10110001 00111010 10101010 11100011
11011110 10011110 10101011 10011100 01101101 11101001 01010101 11010110 01000011 10010011
11101101 11111010 11010100 10101011 00100001 11011001 10010011 11011110 10010111 00101101
11110110 01000011 11011000 10110011 00011110 00000001 10101011 00010001 00110000 01110001
10000010 00110001 11001101 01010011 01001001 01000001 01111101 10111001 11111010 01010011
10010010 01101100 00001010 11000001 10100111 00110111 01100010 10010011 00110101 01100001
00000001 10001000 11100110 10110110 01101100 00100011 01000101 00011001 00100000 01110011
11010100 11010111 00110011 00001101 11010000 01010011 01010111 10010011 01010000 00000011
00000101 00110011 10010001 11010100 01010100 01001010 10011110 10001100 00111010 10011101
00111010 01001000 00010100 01010100 10101001 00110000 00111101 11111001 00111100 11010111
00110100 11011010 10100001 00000001 00001000 11100111 00111110 11111101 00101001 11111111
00000000 11011010 10011000 11101010 01110010 01110001 11010100 11010110 00101010 10001010
11011010 11000101 00110011 10101010 10110110 10010000 01100100 01110001 11000101 01011111
01001001 11000001 11110110 10101110 00110010 00011101 01100001 10100011 01111100 01100011
00100011 11010111 00110101 01101101 00110101 10100101 11011011 11110111 01110011 10001111
01111010 00010100 00010101 11010000 10001110 10100101 10101110 00110000 01110001 11101111
01000011 01011101 00110110 11010010 00110011 11010111 10111101 01110010 10101101 10101110
01100101 11110000 00010111 00000011 00011110 10110100 11100100 11010110 10000001 00000000
01100011 11101011 11001111 01011010 01111100 10010110 01110111 00011101 10001110 10100000
11011100 00011101 11111111 00000000 00110001 11001000 00011111 10000101 00011111 01101010
11001000 00000111 10100110 01101011 10011010 01101101 01100100 00000101 11000000 01010011
11111001 11010000 10111010 11000010 10101000 00011100 01110011 10001110 11110101 00011100
10001011 10101110 11100100 11011011 10110001 11010000 10001011 10000010 01011101 11111110

01101100 01111010 01010011 10001100 11111101 00001110 01110011 11101010 01101011 10011101
11111110 11010111 10001111 01100110 01011000 01110011 11101100 01101010 00110011 10101010
00001100 11100000 00001100 10000000 00110011 01010101 00101010 01010010 00011101 10101100
01110100 10001101 00111110 01001111 11011110 10100100 01101001 11001000 00011000 00100111
00111110 11110101 11001111 00100110 10101000 10000100 11100101 11110010 00110010 00101000
00111010 10110010 11001001 11011011 00000011 00111110 10110101 00101010 10011110 10000101
00110100 01110100 00111110 01101000 00111111 00110110 01111001 11101111 01001011 11100111
10101001 00100000 01100100 01110001 11010110 10111001 10110011 10101001 10001100 10001101
10000000 11100011 10111001 00110100 11010001 10101001 10000010 11111100 00011110 10011101
11101000 01110000 01101110 01001001 00100000 10110011 00111010 01100110 10011101 01110001
11001001 10100011 11001101 00011100 00011101 11011100 01111101 01101011 10011010 10011011
01010100 01010010 01000001 11011101 10001111 10100101 00100001 11010100 10010100 10000100
00000011 00111100 10011010 01001110 10010010 01101111 01010000 01001001 10011101 01000111
10011101 10010001 11000111 00111100 11110101 10100110 10101100 11101011 11010100 10110000
11111111 00000000 00011010 11100101 10011011 01010100 11011011 10010000 01001110 00000000
10100110 00110110 10100110 01001010 11100111 01110000 11000111 10101110 01101010 11011101
00110101 10111011 00010101 10101100 11001110 10101111 11101101 01010001 11110101 00000111
11101011 01001100 11111011 01010100 01111011 10111001 01100001 11001111 01001010 11100101
01001110 10100101 10011111 11011101 10100011 00001110 01000110 01111001 00110101 00011011
01101010 00100111 00111000 01110111 00011001 00011101 11101001 00101000 01011011 01011110
10100011 11100100 01100111 01011010 11010111 00000011 01100111 01011110 00001101 01000110
11010111 00011001 01100000 00110111 01010111 00100110 11011010 10100000 01100111 01000001
11100110 10100000 00011110 10111001 10101000 11111111 00000000 10110100 11010100 10010000
01000100 11000011 00011101 10000110 01101001 11011001 10110111 10110000 01110010 01110111
00111011 00010100 10111011 00011110 01011110 01001101 00001111 01111000 10100000 10100111
00100011 00111110 10010101 11000110 01111111 01101011 11000100 10111100 00011001 11010100
01100011 11011111 10101101 00110111 11111011 01100110 00000010 00110111 01111001 11001011
11010011 10101101 00001010 10010011 01101100 10101111 01100110 01110110 10001101 01110111
11000111 11001010 01111001 11110100 10100001 11101111 00000111 00011100 11110010 01000111
01111010 11100010 01011111 01011101 10001011 10000010 00100101 11100011 10110001 00000111
10100101 00110000 11101011 10010001 00000101 01001101 10001110 11101110 11111001 00011001
11100010 10011111 10110000 11100101 00010011 10000111 01100011 10110100 11111011 01110010
11100011 00111011 10111001 00000111 10101101 00110001 10101111 10000011 00001110 10111000
00011110 11110101 11000101 10111110 10110110 10100001 10000000 00011011 11110001 10011110
01001000 00011101 01101010 00100100 11010101 11111100 11000110 01110011 11100101 01001010
01000111 11010010 10001111 01100010 10010010 11010001 00001011 10010100 11101101 01010111
01010000 11001110 00110000 01111110 01001110 10111001 11001101 00100100 10011010 10011000
00010001 10011110 10100100 10001010 11100011 00010011 01010011 10011000 10010111 00000010
11011010 01100010 00000000 11111110 11101101 00101111 11011011 00101111 00011111 10010001
01100001 01110011 11000000 11101110 10110100 11100101 01001111 11011101 11110111 01110111
00011111 00100010 00111010 11110110 11010100 00000110 11001111 11110101 10011001 00111111
01011010 10001001 10110101 00010011 11011001 10101011 10010110 11011111 10101000 10110110
00110110 01011000 11001010 00001110 01101001 11000001 00110101 00110001 00011000 00111111
01100100 10010011 11110001 00110100 10010101 10110100 10111011 01001000 10101011 00101101
10001110 10001111 11111011 01000011 00000111 00011011 10110000 01101001 10001111 10101001
01111100 11111100 11111100 11111110 10010101 11001111 00100101 10111110 10101100 11000011
11111110 00111101 00110000 01111101 01110011 10001010 01010011 01100111 10101100 10010000
01110110 11011011 11000100 00000110 01110001 11001001 10100100 10010010 10111111 11000100
10000111 11001000 01101101 10111110 10100000 11000101 11000011 01101110 11111100 00111101
01101010 00010111 10111100 00100111 00000011 01110001 11000001 11110100 00110101 10011000
01110100 11101101 01101011 00100000 00111000 10000100 01111101 00001101 01001100 01110100
01011101 01100111 00011001 11110011 10100001 01001100 01110010 00001101 00100111 00101000
01101011 01111001 00100000 11100100 11101100 01011001 00010111 00001110 01011111 10010111
11001000 00011101 00110011 01010010 01111001 11111001 01011111 10011100 11100100 01111101
01101010 10000001 11010000 01110101 01011100 00001100 01001110 10011001 00011110 10110100
10101001 11100001 11111101 01001001 10011001 11110111 11011101 00101000 00011001 11001001
11000000 11111110 01010101 00101010 01010100 10111010 11001100 01101010 00101101 10011010
01011111 01101100 01011100 01110101 11101001 11101111 01001000 10111010 10001010 10000001
10011100 10000001 10010011 10000001 11001101 01010100 00111110 00011001 10111001 00101000
01111111 11010010 11100100 11101010 00111000 00001011 01001110 01111111 00001010 01001101
10000000 10000110 11101000 10111000 00000111 10101110 00111011 11010011 01110101 10101001
01011011 11100010 00010111 00101111 10010001 00101011 01101010 01111000 00100100 11101110
00000011 11101011 01010001 11001011 10101001 01110011 11010100 01110100 11110101 10100110
01111111 11000010 00100110 00110111 10011101 11110111 00110010 10010011 11101100 00101001
11001001 11100001 00010101 00111100 00111101 11000100 11000111 11011110 10010111 10110111
10100101 10111010 10010111 11100000 01010111 00101011 00100011 00111010 10010110 01000110
11011101 11000000 10011111 01101010 01101001 10111110 11000000 00111111 10111101 11000110
01111010 11110011 01010110 00111111 11100001 00010000 10000100 01100100 11001001 00101100
11000100 10011110 10011000 10010011 00010100 11100001 11100001 00011011 00100101 00111001
01110001 00100011 11111011 10110011 00011010 10100111 01010110 10010101 10101111 01110111
11110111 00001011 10010001 11110110 00101001 10111110 10100011 00010000 11100100 00111010
01110001 11000111 01011110 10010101 00011111 11110110 10100101 10111111 00100100 11001100
00000001 11101101 01011010 10101101 11100001 01011011 00100111 00011100 01000100 00111001

11111111 00000000 01101000 11010100 10001011 11100001 10011101 00111100 00010001 11111110
10001110 00001110 00111101 01001001 10100100 10110001 00110100 00111001 01110110 01100011
11100101 01100110 00011011 11101010 10010000 10001110 01111100 11010001 11101010 00001110
00101001 00001110 10110001 00000001 11111111 00000000 10010110 11000011 00111101 10000001
11101111 01011101 00001111 11110110 00000101 10000010 10101110 00111110 11001111 00011110
01001001 11001101 01001000 00110100 01011011 00110000 00110000 00101101 11100010 00000000
01111011 01010100 11111101 01101010 10010010 11101000 11000011 11011001 10110011 10010100
10010011 01010110 10001101 01010111 10010111 11100100 01110101 00010100 10101011 10101011
10100000 00000100 10101110 11100010 00111101 01101011 10101110 01001101 00100010 11001110
00110001 11000100 00010001 11100000 11110101 11001000 10100101 00111010 01101101 10110000
11100000 01000100 10000000 01111101 00101001 11111101 01100110 10011101 10110100 01000011
01010000 01111101 01001110 00110001 10110101 10010100 00100011 00011111 00111011 10001111
10100110 00111001 10101000 11001110 10101001 00101110 11010011 10001000 01011000 11100000
01110101 11000111 10100101 01110111 01000010 11001010 00000000 00111000 10001101 00000111
11100000 00101001 01000100 00010001 00000001 10011101 10100011 11101011 01000011 11000101
01000110 00111011 01000100 01011100 10001111 10100011 00111000 01010110 11010100 00101110
00100101 01011111 11011101 11011010 11001100 01000111 01011100 10010001 01001111 01101011
10011011 11011100 01111100 10010110 11001101 11110100 11000101 01110111 01101101 00010010
10011110 01011111 10101111 10101101 00110111 11001011 10001000 00111110 00000110 01111110
10110101 10010010 11000110 01101011 10100100 00001010 01010100 11011111 01110011 10000110
01000111 11010100 00000001 00111000 10110011 10010100 10000011 11101010 00111000 10100100
11110010 10110101 01011001 00010111 10011011 01100111 01000010 01001111 00000000 11110100
00110101 11011101 01111001 01110001 01100111 10100111 00100111 11011110 10001101 10101010
01111000 00100011 00100000 11010110 10101111 00010111 00100101 10101011 10001010 00001111
01100111 11010110 11100111 00001110 10110110 10111010 11010001 00100011 01100100 00011000
00111110 10011001 00010100 00011101 00111111 01011100 01100011 10011100 00000100 11001001
11101000 00001000 11000000 10101110 11100101 10010110 00101110 10111100 01100111 11101011
01000010 00011000 10111010 00001100 00001010 10011001 01100011 00100111 10110011 01001000
01111110 11001101 00110011 10000110 11111110 11001001 11010110 11100100 00111100 11001010
10100000 00011111 01110001 01000011 01101000 00111010 10010100 10001100 00001100 11010111
00110001 10001110 01111011 01010111 01110000 01011010 00100000 01001111 00100011 00011111
01011010 01101011 01001101 00000000 00011000 00001110 10011000 00011110 10100110 10100101
01100011 00101010 01101101 01101011 01111100 10000101 11101100 10010001 11000110 01111111
11000010 00110111 01111000 01011011 00100110 11100101 01110001 11011111 10011100 11010010
11111111 00000000 11000010 00101011 00110011 01110010 11010111 10000111 00111111 11101110
11010111 01100000 10110111 01110000 01000111 11010110 01000001 10011111 10101101 00110100
01011110 11000000 11000011 00111011 11010000 11111110 00110101 01001111 00010101 10001001
10001000 01111011 00110100 01111001 11111011 10010011 11001110 00111010 01111010 10011010
01000111 00100011 11010110 10101110 00110110 10001101 10101000 11110110 10110111 00111100
01111010 10010001 01001100 01011101 00011011 01010000 11000001 00101111 00000001 11110101
11000110 01111010 01010111 10100000 11100111 00011011 01011110 11100111 00101010 10010111
10010001 01010111 01110111 11100111 01001101 01011001 00111001 00100011 11111001 11010110
10001010 01101000 00111010 10000001 11100111 11001011 11001111 01101111 10111101 01001101
00111010 00001101 11111000 11000000 11011000 10111110 11011001 01101110 10010100 00101010
11010100 11111011 10001010 11101111 10110001 01000011 11001110 11000000 11101001 11011110
10010011 11001110 11000000 11100111 10111111 00110101 10100011 11111111 00000000 00001000
11111110 10100001 11010111 01100100 01111100 11111111 00000000 10110100 00001110 01101001
00111111 11100001 00011111 11010100 00001111 00100010 00101100 10011100 11110100 00110101
01001110 10101101 00111101 11101110 00001010 11111101 10001010 00000110 01011111 11011101
10011111 11010010 10010001 10100100 11000111 11010110 10110100 00111111 11100001 00011111
10111111 00000011 00111011 00000001 00111001 11101001 10011010 00001111 10000111 01110101
00000000 01111000 01011000 11001011 11110101 11000000 00111001 11111010 11010011 01010101
10101000 10100101 01111011 10001001 11110011 00011001 01111110 01100000 11000111 00111101
01101001 01110111 01100000 01100111 10101111 11010100 11010110 10010001 11110000 11100110
10100001 10000111 11111001 00010111 11111110 11111010 10100011 11111110 00010001 10111011
11110010 10011000 11011010 00000000 11101011 10011101 11011000 11100110 10100101 01010111
10100100 11011110 10101100 00110101 01100110 01101000 01100101 01101111 11000110 10011010
01001000 01101100 01101110 00111000 11101011 01011010 01101001 11100001 10011101 01000000
10110001 11111001 01010111 01101001 11100111 10010110 10100111 10101111 10000110 01110101
00001101 10001001 11000100 01111110 10100111 10011110 10010101 10100010 10101111 01001101
10100111 01100110 00011110 11110111 01100011 00011101 10000000 00100011 10001110 10110100
00101000 00011101 11111011 01110110 10101101 01100111 11110000 10111110 10100100 11000001
11001000 00110001 00100110 01110011 11111100 01010100 11100101 11110000 11000110 10100001
10000010 11000101 10100010 00000000 01110001 11110111 10101010 01111101 10101100 00011010
10110010 01101000 00101100 11111011 00011000 11001100 10111101 01001111 01001010 00110001
11110010 10000101 00111000 11100111 10111101 01101101 01111111 11000010 00110101 10101000
00010001 11110011 10011000 10000001 11110100 11001110 01110011 01001010 00111100 00110011
10101000 00011101 11100111 01101100 01011100 11110011 10001101 11010101 00101010 10101100
01101111 01101011 10000101 10011011 00110000 01111000 11001000 00000000 11100100 00001010
10001011 01110001 11110011 00001010 10000011 11001001 11101101 01011101 00011111 11111100
00100010 11110111 11001000 01000000 00011110 01011000 00101101 11010111 00100111 10001010
01010110 11110000 10111101 11110000 11000000 11000100 01000100 10011111 01000011 11111101
01101001 11111101 01101010 10011101 11101101 01110100 00011100 10110010 00111001 11110110

10010001 11000110 00110000 01001000 00100000 11110001 10000011 01010010 00001011 11001001
11100011 11111011 10010010 10010001 10011110 11010101 10111100 11111110 00010100 10111100
11001110 01011001 11100011 11000000 11101111 10011010 01101111 11111100 00100010 00110111
01101101 10001111 10011110 00011110 01001111 00000111 00110101 00101111 00010101 01001010
01001111 01110000 11100101 10011001 10001111 11111101 10100101 01110000 00110000 01111100
11011110 10011100 11010010 10100110 10101111 01110000 10100011 00111001 00011001 11100011
10011110 10110101 10101000 00111100 00011101 01111101 11000000 11110011 01100001 11000000
11101010 01001011 01110100 10100111 11111111 00000000 11000010 00011011 01110110 00111010
11001101 00001001 11001001 11101010 00001001 10100101 00101100 01000110 00011101 11101010
11011010 00101111 10010010 10100001 10011110 10011010 11010100 10111001 00011001 01010100
11001111 10101111 10101111 11100001 01000111 11110110 11001011 00010011 10001111 00101101
00110001 10011110 11010101 10100001 11111111 00000000 00001000 01101101 11010111 00011111
10111110 10001111 00011110 10100010 10010100 11111000 00110110 11100000 11110011 11100111
11000111 11010011 10110110 01110011 01010101 11101101 10110000 11101111 01010000 11111101
11100010 00110011 11000110 10111000 00000001 00100001 11100010 00100111 11011011 00111101
01101001 11011111 11011011 11001000 00100011 11100101 01011111 10000001 11001001 00110101
01110111 11111110 00010000 10101011 10000011 10000000 11010011 11000111 10011111 01011110
01110011 01001110 11111111 00000000 10000100 00101010 01111100 11100101 11100110 10001100
01111010 01100000 00011010 11000101 11010101 11000010 11110101 01100011 10110101 01000010
10000111 11110110 11100010 00000100 00100100 00010111 11101101 10011110 00101001 01010111
01011010 10001100 10010011 10000010 01000111 00011101 11101010 11110111 11111100 00100001
00110011 11101100 01110110 00010011 10000000 01111000 11001110 01101001 10101111 11100000
01111001 11001010 10101001 01001001 10000000 00100100 01110011 11001111 11110100 10100111
11101101 10110000 10101101 01101010 11000110 10011101 01001110 11000101 01000110 11010101
11100001 00000001 00110111 10110111 11011110 11101001 01000001 11010101 11100010 11011110
00111001 00011001 00000011 00010101 01111000 01111000 00011110 01011101 10100000 10011011
10000100 11000111 01100001 01001010 10011110 00001000 01100001 10000010 01101110 10110011
11110010 11110100 11011011 01001101 01010101 11000010 10101101 01101110 00110101 00101010
10011101 10001100 11100001 10101011 11000110 00011100 00011101 11111100 01111011 10011110
00101000 01101101 01001100 11100100 10010100 10010011 00101111 10011100 01010110 10011011
01111000 00100000 10000000 00111111 11010010 01000110 01000111 10110110 01000101 00101011
11111000 00100011 10011110 00101110 10000111 10111000 00100010 10100011 11011011 11100001
10011110 10110111 00010101 10101010 10111101 11010001 10010000 01110101 01000110 00111101
11110000 01111101 01001101 00110011 11111011 01011101 10110011 11000001 11101000 01111010
10011010 11011101 01001111 00000110 00101001 01011110 01100110 00111100 01110111 11110101
10100000 01111000 00011100 00010101 11111001 11100111 00111001 00100111 10011110 00101001
11111011 01111100 00111011 01100000 11010101 01000100 01100010 00001101 01100010 01001100
00010010 00001000 11100011 10101101 00110101 00110101 11000110 01100000 00110111 01100000
10000011 11101001 01011011 11101101 11100000 10001000 10111100 11001110 00100111 00101011
11000111 00011100 01110001 01001010 10011110 00001011 10001100 00000111 11111101 11110001
11110110 11000000 11001101 00011111 01011000 11000011 11110100 00000110 10101010 00110011
10011111 00111010 11100011 00001100 01111110 11101100 00000011 11110101 10100001 00110101
11100010 01011100 10010011 00011000 11001111 10110111 01001010 11101000 01000111 10000010
10100000 00100100 01111110 11110010 01000110 11000111 00110100 11101111 11111000 01000011
10101101 10110110 00000011 11100110 11001010 00001111 10100111 11111000 11010000 11110001
01011000 01111110 10100001 11001011 01010100 11100111 10111111 10110111 00000110 01111111
11010101 10011110 00111010 11100110 10010011 11111011 01110001 01110010 00110010 00001010
01110011 11010110 10111010 00111111 11111000 01000011 00101101 11001111 01010111 10011011
00000011 10100110 00111011 11010100 10101001 11100000 11001011 01000000 00111110 01110110
10010000 10000011 11010010 10010111 11010110 10110000 11001101 01011010 11000101 01011010
10100001 11001100 00001101 01111010 00110110 11001000 00001010 01000111 10101001 00100010
10111010 10001111 00000110 00110111 11011011 01111100 11001011 10011100 00011111 00101100
01111110 11101100 01100100 01100011 00110100 00111111 10000011 11101100 00001001 11001001
01000111 11100111 10100101 01101110 01101001 01010110 10010000 11011000 11011010 00001011
01111011 01110101 11011001 00011000 00111001 11111100 01101011 00111001 01010111 10100010
11110100 10000010 11010100 01101001 01001101 01101110 01011010 10010000 01110001 10000001
01010001 10110000 10101001 11011001 01001010 11110101 00111100 11010010 01101101 11001101
01100100 10011011 01001011 01100011 01000010 00000110 11101001 01010101 00100101 11101001
10000001 11010110 10101111 00110010 11110000 01101010 10011101 11000111 01001110 10011101
00101001 01110011 11001010 11010110 01100000 11011001 10011011 00110011 11110101 11101111
01010100 10101110 00100100 00011001 11000000 11101010 01111010 11010101 10111001 10000001
11001110 01110011 11111010 01010101 00000111 00011000 01100010 11011000 11000001 00111101
01111001 10101010 10100111 00010100 10011110 10111011 10010001 00100101 01100010 10111011
10000010 01111000 00111101 11111010 11010101 01110111 00000100 01100111 00011001 10101011
00110011 00000001 01010001 10110111 11011100 11000110 00110001 01011101 01101010 00111010
00110011 00111011 10010001 00101010 10010010 01000011 01110111 10100111 10100000 11111001
11101001 01000000 11000011 11100100 01110100 11101001 01010010 11101101 00000101 01101001
10110110 10110110 01000000 10010000 11100100 11001110 01111101 10111011 01010101 10000100
00100100 11100011 00111101 00000101 01000010 10011001 00011111 11111110 10101010 01111010
10011110 11111110 10011101 01000101 01110011 11001011 01110110 11001011 01000101 10000101
00111100 10010101 10100111 10001111 10111001 11010111 10001010 10000101 10110000 00000000
00111001 11111100 10101001 00001100 10000000 00001010 10000101 11101111 00000001 00101110
01110000 00110001 11101111 01010001 10110001 00011101 00001101 01000110 11000100 10001110

10100111 10101101 01000110 01100100 00000000 11100011 11111000 11110001 01010100 10111001
10110111 01001000 00001001 00011001 10110001 11000101 01010101 01111001 00001111 11100001
01000011 01001000 01111010 00110101 01000001 00101011 00011100 11110000 01111111 00001010
11010011 10010001 10101101 01100101 10111001 00000010 10111100 10000111 01100110 00111101
10101010 00100110 00111000 00000011 00010100 11001001 00100100 11000110 00111101 00001101
01000100 00110010 01111010 11110100 00010101 10110100 00100010 10100100 11110101 00010011
01111101 10000001 10011000 10010011 11101101 01001100 00111100 00011100 01100011 00111001
11100110 10000111 00111000 11100011 10111111 10111101 00110111 11001100 11000000 10101110
10010101 00000101 00010101 10111000 10011011 01111011 00001101 01111100 10001100 01110011
11000111 01101111 01101010 00110111 01110111 11000000 00111111 10001101 00100110 01110001
10000010 00111010 01010011 00010111 00000100 00011100 11111101 01101011 00110100 00010110
11010000 01111110 11100000 01110010 01111010 01111011 01010100 01111011 10000110 00001000
11000001 11110110 11110110 10100001 10110000 00000110 01001111 00100010 10010011 01110110
00000001 11101100 00101010 10010010 01001101 00010011 01110100 00001010 01111011 00111110
01111110 10110100 01100000 00001100 11010011 00011100 11100111 00100000 00011100 01111011
11010100 01010011 01001001 10110111 10000010 11011111 10010101 01011011 10111101 10101100
00101001 00110000 01111001 01000010 11110010 01111101 00111001 10101010 00110011 11011110
11101101 00011000 00000000 00010001 11101011 01010001 11011100 01001001 00110011 00111001
11000111 01000011 11011010 10100001 01101000 10110010 00111001 11111100 10000101 01101111
01001110 10010010 10110001 10010100 10100100 11000111 01111101 10101101 10001011 10011110
00110011 11111000 11010000 00101110 11011011 01110111 11011101 00000111 11110101 10100100
11111011 00101000 01011111 11110111 11101001 01100010 10110111 11001001 11000110 01111011
11100011 11101001 01010110 11111001 01001100 10110101 00011100 00101111 00100101 00000111
11100100 00000011 10101101 00111011 11101101 10100000 00111110 01110110 00000011 11101101
01000001 10110111 11001000 00100011 00111110 11011101 00101000 01001011 01001100 10100110
01110001 11011111 00011001 10101001 10111100 01010110 11000001 10101101 11000100 01011011
11010110 11000000 11111001 01111001 11101111 11101111 01010010 00100101 11110001 11001001
00000101 01111111 01011010 01001111 10110010 10001100 11100011 10110101 00111001 01101101
11000111 11001111 11110010 11110111 11110101 10100101 01111000 11011110 11101100 10101011
00110001 00010111 01010000 01101100 11100011 01101000 00000011 11110011 10100111 10101110
10100011 10010110 00111001 01001110 00111101 01110011 01001010 10110110 10100000 00010011
10010001 11000101 00111111 11101100 10001010 01101010 01011011 10000001 01111100 10001100
01100000 10111111 00100101 01111110 01010100 11001110 01111011 11100110 10011110 11011010
10001111 00011011 01111100 10100011 11010110 10100100 01001011 01011000 11000001 00111001
00011101 01101010 01010100 10110100 10001000 10011111 01101010 10010100 11100001 01110000
01010000 01100101 01110011 10101000 10010001 11000000 01000010 00001110 00101001 11100010
11111000 10011110 01110110 10011111 01111110 11010101 01100011 11101100 01010001 10000001
10001110 11000011 11010110 10100101 01001011 00110100 11001111 01001110 00111101 00001001
11100010 10001111 01101001 00000110 11101101 01100001 10101000 11001000 10100101 11111101
10100010 11001010 00000110 01100011 11001111 10100001 10100001 00110101 00010110 11000001
11111001 01001001 11111110 10010101 10101000 10110110 01110000 10000000 01110010 10100011
10011110 11010100 00100101 10011010 00000001 11110011 10000001 10000001 11010000 00010001
01001011 11011010 11110110 01000101 00101000 01001010 11111011 10011001 01100011 01010001
00111001 11011101 11100101 00110110 00000111 01010011 10011010 01110001 10111111 10011011
00111001 01010100 11001101 01101100 01000111 01101101 00000000 11001111 11001010 00111101
11101010 01110100 10110111 10110111 00100111 00000100 00001111 10100101 01100100 11101011
01000001 01101011 01101101 01001010 11110110 01101100 11000011 11111011 01110100 10011000
11001011 01000110 00000000 00010100 11111000 10101111 10101110 00001001 11111001 00000110
01010011 11010011 00010101 10111100 10110000 01000010 00011000 00011101 10100011 11110010
10101101 01111011 00011000 11101101 11010101 01001001 11011010 00000001 00111100 10010010
01111011 11010110 01001111 00010001 11101110 11101001 00010010 11010101 00100110 11110111
01100111 00100001 00011101 11010101 11011011 00101001 00100010 00011110 10000011 10101101
00111101 01100111 10111111 11000110 01011110 00001110 01111110 10000110 10111011 10011000
11011010 11011110 00110100 00011100 00100000 11101111 10011100 01010011 11010010 11100010
00011101 11100100 01101111 00000111 10011110 10110101 11001111 11110101 10100110 11010101
10111001 01001010 11110110 01011010 01101010 11001110 00101001 00100101 11010100 00001001
11001000 10110100 01100111 11111100 00001101 01011000 10001101 01110101 01111001 01111111
11010101 11011001 10110110 00111011 10000010 10111101 01101011 10110000 11111011 01100101
10111001 01101100 01111100 10011100 01110011 11010011 00010101 01111010 00011101 01000110
00000100 00011100 00110111 11100011 01010011 11110101 10101001 01011110 11001010 00101000
10110101 01001111 10111011 00111000 01010100 10110011 11010110 11110011 11110011 11011010
00110000 00000100 11110101 11000101 01001010 10111010 01101110 10111010 01010100 10000100
10110111 00101000 00110011 11000111 00100011 00110101 11011110 00001101 01001110 11011000
11100011 00110010 10001100 11100010 10010001 11110101 01001011 00110010 00000111 11001101
11001111 11010011 00010101 10011111 11010110 01101010 11101011 01100100 10000011 11011001
10101110 11100111 00010000 10111010 01100111 10001000 10110111 10001100 01000000 00000110
01111000 00111011 10001000 00111001 10100111 11111111 00000000 01100010 11101011 01101100
01010011 00101000 00000000 00011110 10101101 11010110 10111011 00100001 10101011 11011001
11100111 11101111 01110100 11110110 10100110 10011101 01101010 11001111 00111100 00010111
00111111 10000101 01000100 10101011 11100010 00101111 11110000 10100000 01010000 01000111
00100010 01110100 01001101 01101011 00000111 11100110 10001100 00010000 01111010 00000011
01001110 01001101 00000011 01010111 10010001 10000000 11110011 00100001 01001100 01110101
00100101 10101011 10101100 00111010 11001101 10101110 01111001 11011111 10001100 11110101

00000010 10011000 00110101 10101011 01000000 01110011 10000111 11000111 01111110 00101001
11111011 01111100 01000011 11101101 11110111 00001101 01000101 00011100 11011001 11110000
11001110 10101100 11000000 00000100 10111000 10000100 01110011 10011110 01001001 00100110
10011110 00111100 00110011 10101010 10101000 11000111 11011011 00100010 11011110 01111001
00111100 10011010 11101000 00010111 01011110 10110110 11111111 00000000 10011110 01110010
01010011 01000110 10111111 00000001 11101010 10000100 01110101 11000001 00111101 11101001
01111011 01011100 01001101 11111111 00000000 11100000 00000101 10100010 01100001 00101111
10000101 10101111 01001000 11111001 10101111 10000111 10111000 11100110 10011111 11111111
00000000 00001000 10000101 11001001 11101011 01111110 00000111 01111110 00101011 01100101
01111100 01000101 01101110 00000001 11111101 11010001 11111111 00000000 00011010 01001111
11101101 11111000 00110010 01001001 10001111 10101111 11100111 01010110 11100101 10001000
01111010 10110110 00111101 00001100 10110100 11110000 10000100 10011001 00100100 11011111
00111110 01001111 01011100 00001010 10010001 10111100 00011110 10111100 11100110 11111010
11100000 00011110 11010101 01110100 11111000 10000010 00110001 11001000 10000100 10011111
11000110 10011000 11011010 11111010 11110010 01000100 01011000 11111010 10011110 10110101
00010111 11000100 11110101 01111111 10010000 10101111 00010100 01010101 00011110 00001111
10000100 10100111 11101111 00101110 10100111 01111111 01011110 01101010 01000100 11110000
01110101 10101110 01000110 01100110 10011000 10100111 11010110 10100101 01101101 01111100
10011100 11111110 11101000 01100011 00111110 10110101 00011011 01101011 11010010 00011100
11100001 00010000 10011111 10101101 00011100 10011000 10000110 11110101 10010000 01101001
11011000 01111001 11110000 10010101 10001000 00111111 01111010 01100011 11000110 00111010
11010011 10010011 11000010 10110110 00001010 10111100 10101100 10000111 11101010 11010101
01011101 11110101 11100111 00100111 11101110 10001100 11111011 01110110 10101000 11011011
01011100 10011111 10011100 00000100 11000110 00111001 11001101 00100111 00001010 10101001
11111100 01001100 01101001 10010111 11111111 00000000 11100001 00011001 11010011 01110000
00110111 11000001 10010010 00111111 11011010 00110100 11111111 00000000 11111000 01000111
10110100 11100000 00110010 01101101 11000110 01110011 11101011 01011001 10101101 10101101
01011100 00011111 10111000 01010000 00011100 01110010 00101001 10111111 11011011 01110111
00000000 11100111 00111000 00011110 10010100 01001110 10001101 01101110 10010010 00011101
11010001 10110011 11111101 10001101 10100111 10000000 01000111 11011001 10010100 10100111
10111000 11100010 10010100 01101001 10010110 01000000 01100000 01000001 00011110 00110011
11101001 11010010 10110000 01011111 01010111 10111000 01101100 01100110 01000011 11101010
00000110 00101001 10101101 10101011 01011100 00011111 11111001 01101100 01110010 01111101
10101010 01100011 10000111 10101001 11010101 10001110 11101000 11101000 11001110 10011101
01100100 00000110 01111110 11001111 00011111 11100010 00101010 01001000 11101101 01101101
11000001 00111000 10000010 00100001 11000111 11110111 01000101 01110010 11111111 00000000
11011010 01010111 00100100 11100100 01001100 11011001 11001111 01011010 01000111 11010100
00101110 00111001 00000010 01100111 00000100 11110101 00110100 10011101 00010110 11111010
10000111 00110001 11010110 10100100 00110000 00101000 11000000 10001001 00111001 00011110
10010100 10101111 00010100 00101100 00110000 01000000 11000000 11100111 00011000 10101110
00110100 11011111 01011100 01100011 00001111 00110011 10011100 01110111 11001101 00101111
11011011 01100111 00101011 10110100 11001100 11100010 10010111 10110000 01101001 01101000
00011100 11000111 01100010 01010110 00101100 11100000 10010001 11111000 10001010 01001111
11011101 01100111 00111001 00000010 10111000 11100101 10111100 10011000 10011111 11110101
10001110 00111101 11110011 01001100 11110011 11100110 11001111 11111010 11010010 01111011
11110011 01000010 11000010 00100101 10101000 01110011 01011000 11101101 00000100 10110000
00011110 01110111 10001100 01111011 11010010 01111001 11010000 00000011 10001111 00110001
00101011 10001001 11111011 01000100 10100101 11111110 11110001 00100011 00111100 00011010
00011010 01000110 00111101 11111001 10101010 11111010 10100100 00011011 11010000 00111001
10111010 10011101 10111111 11011010 00100001 11000001 00100110 01000100 00100000 01111011
11010100 01001011 01111001 01101110 11011001 11000011 00100001 00011001 10101110 00101111
11001100 00100111 10011100 11010100 10011011 10011000 10010000 11011001 11101101 01000111
10110000 10001100 00110100 00100111 10011010 11100111 01100001 11110110 11011011 01010101
11100111 11001101 10001111 11110011 10100110 00111110 10100001 01101100 01110001 10001001
10010000 00001010 11100100 11110011 11000110 00111010 00011100 01100110 10100011 01000010
01110001 10000010 01001001 00011001 10100100 10101000 01000111 10100000 01110011 01011100
11101011 11011011 01010010 10110100 11011111 10001101 11100011 00110100 11000011 10101011
01011010 00000010 01000000 10010110 10111001 00110101 00111111 00110110 00110011 11000111
10101101 00100010 10011110 11111001 11111100 01101011 01001111 01100001 00000100 10110110
00001110 01100110 01110101 10000111 01011001 10110111 01010000 01001000 00100111 00011111
01001010 01011001 00110101 10101011 01000001 00011110 01000011 10010011 11110100 00010101
11001001 00010110 11110111 11100011 10110101 00101010 11100101 01111001 00000011 00111110
10111100 11010011 01110100 11100001 01100001 11011100 11101001 11111111 00000000 10110110
01100000 11000001 00101011 10111111 00000111 10111110 00101001 10111111 11011011 10010000
00010011 11110111 01011111 10100110 01110001 01011100 11010001 00001100 00010111 10101111
01111100 10011010 00111001 11101010 00101001 00101010 00110001 10001110 11001000 00111001
10111011 10011101 00011011 01101011 10010001 00001110 10001010 11111100 11111010 11110110
10100110 00110110 10111010 00110010 00010100 01000110 01001111 00111100 10010011 01011100
11111110 01110000 01111001 10100011 00100100 10110000 11110111 10100001 01010010 10001011
01100011 10111001 10111011 11111101 10110101 10000110 11001111 10010111 11001111 11010110
10010001 10110101 10100110 00111100 10101010 10001110 10110101 10000111 11001001 11110111
00111001 10100100 00100111 00000000 11010000 10101001 11000101 00111101 10000101 11001110
01101110 01111111 01101111 00110110 01000110 11101000 10010011 10001110 10100100 01010100

```
00001111 10101110 01001110 00010000 01100000 00100101 01100101 01101101 00111000 11001111
01110011 01001101 01100000 11011000 00011001 00010101 10101011 01101001 10101101 10000111
01110011 01011001 11110101 10011001 11000100 01011011 10111000 11100100 00001110 00110001
01001100 01101101 01011010 11100000 11100011 11100110 00011000 11111010 01010110 01100011
01110010 00111010 01111110 00010100 11010110 00111100 10000000 01111000 00011101 01101001
00101010 01110110 01111010 01101110 01000111 00111011 01000110 10010011 11101010 11010111
00111101 00001001 00011110 10111101 00101010 00110111 11010101 00101110 01001110 01111110
01111100 01111110 00010101 01001111 00100000 11110011 01000011 11110101 11001111 10101101
01011111 00101011 01010010 10111010 11011100 01101001 10010110 10011111 01010001 10111001
01101110 00111100 11000111 11000111 11010110 10011010 11111010 10001100 11100101 00001000
00001100 01111001 11101011 01010101 10110110 10011101 10000100 01100111 11110001 10100101
01010000 01000000 11000011 00011110 10010101 01011100 10010111 01101010 11100011 01001111
10100001 00111111 11011011 00100110 10010100 11100000 11001010 11111001 11101001 10011100
11010011 00011010 11101010 01010101 11100000 11001010 11111111 00000000 10011101 01000110
00001110 00001110 01111101 01111101 10101001 00110110 11100100 01110011 11110101 10100110
11100101 11001011 11010000 00110111 00011110 10110010 00011100 11111101 11110111 00100111
11010111 00100110 10011010 10110011 01001001 10111111 00000001 10011100 11111110 00100110
10011100 00010111 00100010 10011000 10111111 01111011 10101110 00000101 00101011 00101110
10000100 11110101 00011110 11010010 00110001 00011100 11100111 00111111 01011010 01100011
00011100 00011100 11110111 11110101 00110100 10111001 00000101 11001000 00000110 10011010
11000100 00010001 10010001 01010001 11001011 10101110 10000101 01011010 11000010 11100100
11100000 11100100 10011110 01101001 00111110 01101110 11111111 00000000 11001110 10011011
11000001 00011100 11010100 10001010 01111110 01010001 01001001 11011101 10010010 11001110
11001111 11001000 11100111 10100111 10111111 01011010 01111111 10010011 10111000 11110001
01011011 10011111 11011010 00011110 00010111 01010001 10001111 10110111 01100111 00011110
10001010 01001001 00110100 01000011 10101010 11111000 01100011 11001011 11011100 11110111
01110011 00010001 10010011 11000001 10000111 00011000 10101110 01101111 01100111 00110101
11110001 00101011 11011100 00111101 10100101 11111010 00011000 01100010 00000010 00001001
00111000 11100010 10001111 10110011 00010011 11001111 10100111 11101011 01011011 10101001
10101101 01111000 01100100 11100000 01000011 00101100 10011111 00101111 01011100 00101101
00111100 01111000 10001011 11000010 11111101 01010001 10100110 11001110 00111001 00100101
01110001 01001101 11010001 10101011 11010001 01101000 00011110 11010001 11110110 00110000
00000101 10111011 01101110 00011100 01010010 10101100 00001100 01000110 00010000 00010000
01101011 01101010 00111111 00010010 01111000 01101000 00011111 10111101 01110000 01000111
10100010 00101101 00110001 01111100 01001101 11100001 11111110 01000100 00110001 01011100
10001100 00001110 01001001 00110100 01000111 00001111 00100100 10111101 11100100 00101111
01101000 11001100 10111111 10110001 10110110 01111010 00011100 01110101 11001101 00101010
01011010 00110000 11100111 01101111 01011111 11010110 10110100 10010111 11000100 01111010
00011001 11100110 01001000 01101110 00111000 11110100 00110100 11011011 10011111 00010101
01101000 01000001 11010001 01100001 10000010 11100101 00000110 01111001 00100100 11010100
00111100 00110011 01111011 10001111 10011010 11000110 01111111 11011000 11001111 01110101
00111001 00011110 11010100 11101111 10110001 11001000 01111001 11000110 00000111 01111100
11010101 10101111 11111000 01001010 11110100 10000110 01111100 00001011 01111001 10010000
01110100 00011001 00100011 10011100 01010000 10011110 00101100 11010010 10010100 10111010
10111101 10110011 10010011 11001001 11000000 00111001 11001101 00111001 11100001 10100101
01111011 10100101 10100000 01110011 00110110 01010110 11111011 00101011 01100011 01101000
01011110 01110011 01001111 00010110 10010010 00011110 11011100 11010100 10010000 11111000
10111111 01001100 00100111 10001011 00101001 00110000 01110011 11010111 10110101 00001111
11100010 11101101 00111011 00100100 11000111 01100111 00101111 01001110 10100101 10110001
01000111 10110010 10011100 01101100 11010000 01110011 00110001 10011111 01100001 10010000
11000110 00001110 11010001 11101011 10001010 01011111 11101100 11100110 00100000 01100100
01110011 10011110 10010100 11010101 11110001 01100101 10010110 00110010 11010110 11010010
00000001 10001111 11101111 01010010 11111111 00000000 11000010 01100001 01100111 11000110
00101100 11011111 00000011 10011010 01011110 11001010 01011011 11011100 00111001 10011000
10101011 01100010 11111001 00100000 10101000 00111111 01011010 01110111 11011000 10011011
01111110 00001000 00000011 11110001 11001101 01000001 11111111 00000000 00001001 10000101
10111000 11100011 11101100 10111100 01110101 00010100 10001111 11100011 00101000 11110010
00111100 10111011 00100000 01001110 00111011 10011100 01010011 10010101 00011001 10110101
11001100 00101110 01100111 01110010 11010010 11011000 10110001 01101100 01100011 11110001
10100111 00110101 10001011 01110100 00000000 01010101 00010111 11110001 01111010 10001111
11111001 01110011 11000000 11001111 01100110 10100111 01111111 11000010 01100000 01110110
01110001 01101100 00111000 11101111 10011010 10010111 10000111 10101001 10111110 10000011
01101100 10110101 11110110 00010111 00000011 10100000 10100111 00101110 10011110 11000101
11111011 01110100 11101100 00101011 00111101 01111100 01100100 11000000 01100100 01011000
10100001 00111110 11100111 00010100 00111111 10001100 10100101 01101111 11111001 01110111
10001100 01111101 01111001 10100101 11110101 01011001 10101101 01011011 00001110 01100011
01000100 01101001 11001110 00111001 00111101 11111010 01010011 11000110 10011100 11001100
01001111 00000010 10110001 11011111 11000110 00010011 01101100 00100011 11101100 11110001
01111110 01011101 01101001 10111111 11110000 10010111 11001110 00001000 11000101 10111100
01100011 00111101 01001110 01111010 01010110 01101011 00001111 01111101 11011000 11010100
10101110 01101100 01111101 10000100 11100000 01111100 10111001 11001111 01101100 11010011
10111111 10110011 10011000 01100011 01110111 00011101 10101011 00010001 00111100 01011101
01110000 00111001 11110010 10100011 11001111 10101001 00010100 10111111 11110000 10010110
```

01011100 10000000 01000000 10001110 00111110 01001111 01111010 11011101 01100001 10100100
10011101 10101110 00111011 10011011 01000111 01001111 00100000 11100111 00000011 11011000
10011010 01011111 10110001 01110001 11010010 10110000 00011011 11000101 10010111 00100101
00111111 11010101 11000110 00001001 11101011 11101101 01001101 01101111 00010100 11011101
11100011 10000000 10011001 11001111 01010011 01000111 11010101 11101100 11110111 00001011
10011101 00001010 11101001 11100111 00011100 00001110 01101000 11111110 11001111 00111101
11111010 11111011 01010111 00110101 11111111 00000000 00001001 01100101 11111000 11101000
01100011 00011111 10000101 00110100 11111000 10101010 11111111 00000000 10101000 00100011
11110001 00010100 11111110 10101100 10110110 01101100 10011110 01100011 10101010 11111011
00001111 01101100 01010000 10110110 00111100 00000000 00001101 01110010 00101101 11100010
01101011 11110110 11000110 01100101 11011001 11110100 00010100 11100110 11110001 00110110
10100100 00000111 00110010 10001100 01111011 00000000 00101010 01111110 10101100 10010110
10001001 10000010 10011001 11010110 00110110 10011100 00111001 00011001 00000011 11110000
10100011 11101100 00011000 00100011 10011110 00101011 10010000 01101111 00010010 11101010
00100100 00010000 00100101 11011001 11101111 10000001 01010001 11111111 00000000 11000010
01000111 10101001 11100100 10010101 10111000 11111101 00101001 01001011 00001010 10100010
10111101 11011001 00000111 00111011 10111001 11011000 11111111 00000000 01100111 11100101
01110001 11000101 00111001 01101100 01001110 00001110 00110000 01111110 10110101 11000101
10011111 00010000 01101010 00000100 01100100 01001111 11001111 01111110 00111010 11010011
00010011 01011101 10111110 11111110 00111011 10000111 11100011 10110101 00001111 00001001
01111011 00110110 11000001 11001110 11000111 01101011 11110110 00111100 01110010 01111111
01011010 01110111 11011000 11000110 01001011 01111010 11110110 10101110 00010101 11110101
11011011 11101110 01110110 11011100 00111000 10100110 10111110 10110001 01111100 01001110
11101111 10110100 10111110 01110001 10000000 00101010 10111110 10101010 10110110 10111110
11000001 11001110 01110111 10000010 11001000 00101111 00111100 00000001 11101111 01000011
11011000 11100011 11101111 00000001 10001010 11100000 00000110 10110001 01111010 00110001
11111011 11100111 11110111 11100110 10011000 11111010 10100101 11011011 00111110 01011110
01111001 01001001 00100000 01110111 11101001 01011010 01111101 01011010 00001111 01001011
10001111 10011001 10011110 10000001 11110110 00101111 10010011 10001100 01010001 11110110
01010101 11101100 01000111 00010101 11100111 01100011 01010000 10111001 00100111 00111110
01111100 10111111 10001011 01010011 11111111 00000000 10110100 00101110 01110011 10001111
10110100 00111000 00011110 10011001 10101000 11111010 10110010 11101110 00101110 01100011
10111011 10111011 10001001 01100010 10001011 10011100 01100111 10110000 10101100 11110100
00111111 00111110 01111101 01101011 00011111 01001000 10011010 01011001 00000011 10011001
00011000 10111000 11001111 11001011 10010011 10011010 11010101 10001100 10000010 01110010
11100111 11110100 10100110 10101000 10111000 10101101 11110101 00000110 11011001 00111001
11000001 11111100 00101010 00111100 10011100 01100011 10100101 00101010 00011111 10011111
00111001 11001000 11110101 10100100 01110010 00111001 00111001 11001001 10101101 00011011
10111010 11010000 01100100 00101111 11000101 01010101 10011011 11101110 11010101 10000110
00111001 00011100 11111110 01110101 01010110 01110010 00110001 01001101 11011010 01011011
00100001 00011001 11010111 00111000 11001101 01010010 10011111 00111000 11000001 11111100
01000101 01011110 10011111 10100110 01000101 01010010 10010100 00011110 10100111 10011111
01001100 11010101 11010010 10110110 11101000 01001101 00010101 10100101 11001001 00011100
11010011 01111000 11100000 00011110 01101010 01100110 00011110 01100010 01111010 01010011
00000010 11110011 10110100 00001010 11010011 01001000 10111011 00010001 01100010 00101101
10111000 00111000 11101010 00101010 01000000 00001111 01101010 01010110 01011111 01111010
00110110 10010101 11100011 00111100 10001010 01001101 11011010 01011010 00000010 01100011
11000001 11100000 00001100 10011111 11001110 10010100 11111100 10111100 01100011 11011100
11110011 11011010 10010011 10001100 01110100 11100110 10011000 11000111 00100011 10111110
01101010 00011010 10111110 10101000 00101110 01001000 00100100 00000111 00001011 11101011
11011000 01010011 00011001 10110000 01111101 01000110 01101010 00110101 00111011 01011000
10001100 01110011 11101011 01010001 00110011 00010101 01111100 01110101 10101010 01110111
11011000 10110111 11011100 10010100 11001001 10010010 01111101 00111011 01010100 01001100
01111001 11001111 01001010 01000101 00100111 10100000 10100110 01101110 11001110 01111010
11100110 10101110 11010110 01000010 10111000 10010010 00110110 00001110 00001111 10100101
01000000 11000111 00000011 11011100 11010011 11011101 10110011 11010110 10100001 01100110
11000001 00010101 10100010 01001001 11101110 01000011 00010001 11011100 01100011 01101001
00011001 11110101 11001101 00110000 01110100 11100011 00011000 10100100 11001111 00111101
00101001 00000001 11100000 11110001 11000101 01101000 11100011 01101101 00101110 00100100
00001101 11111110 10110000 10110111 00100110 10100011 11001111 00011000 01101110 10010100
11100110 01100010 11000111 00100011 10001110 00111001 10100001 10001110 11111110 00001111
00110101 01110000 01110001 01011011 10000010 01100000 01000110 00000101 01000111 10110111
10011110 00111010 01110101 10100111 00110001 00111011 11001000 11101101 11111100 11101001
10001110 01110001 11000000 11111100 01101000 01111010 11101100 00100001 00010100 10001110
01110011 11011111 10101101 01000110 11000111 10011100 00011110 01111101 00111101 11101010
01001110 00110011 11111000 01111010 11010100 00001110 01111000 11101011 11010010 10101101
01101001 10100011 00100100 01001001 00100100 00100011 00011100 01100011 11010010 10101011
11001000 00110111 00110110 11101100 11010100 10001110 01001011 01110011 10001110 10011100
11010010 10100000 11000000 11000111 11101011 01011010 00100111 01111101 01011001 00101111
01110010 00101101 10111000 00111100 11110111 10100101 01101000 01000110 00110011 11010000
11111010 11010100 10001100 10100000 11110001 10011110 01101001 11100001 01000110 00110000
01001110 00111101 00111101 11101001 01000110 01011010 11101000 01100110 11010111 01110010
10111010 10101110 01110001 11101010 00111010 11010011 10011010 00010010 00011111 00011101

10001101 01001100 10111000 11001001 00100111 11110010 11000101 00101001 00000011 10110001
11111100 00101001 10110111 01101101 01000001 01111001 10010001 10100010 11110010 01101001
01010001 01001000 01000011 10001110 11111110 11110101 00100110 11011100 10001100 11010011
01010100 10001100 10000000 01000001 00010101 00101111 10111001 10100110 10001000 00010001
01111011 00010001 11010011 10100101 01001000 10100011 01101001 11101001 01000011 00011110
01110011 11010100 01111101 01101001 11011101 10111110 10110100 11011110 10101100 00101100
00100000 00000111 00111111 11001110 10010110 00110101 00000011 00111101 01001110 00101000
11000110 01000110 00000111 01111010 01110010 11100011 00000000 01010100 01001001 00110110
11000111 01110000 01010011 11000001 00011000 00011100 01110011 01001010 10100100 11110001
11000111 01011010 01001100 11100100 01100100 11110001 11111101 01101001 01110010 00001111
00111001 11100011 11010110 10001001 01010011 01011101 00000000 01011111 00110011 10110111
10100111 01111010 01110000 00101100 01000111 10111101 00110111 10000001 10000001 11011110
10100100 01000101 00011111 01010011 01001001 11000010 11011011 10001110 11100011 10010000
10110110 11010010 00001001 11100100 11010010 10010010 11011100 01110011 10011111 01111010
01100000 11101011 10010000 01111011 11110011 01000000 00111011 10100100 11000001 00110100
10110110 11011001 10010111 01111101 00001001 00000011 00010010 00000101 01001001 10010010
11011101 11101010 00011110 01111011 00000001 11110100 00100111 10101101 00111000 00010000
00000110 00111001 11001111 10111101 01001011 01010111 01111010 10110001 11011110 11000100
11001011 10011100 11110000 01111000 11111010 11010101 10010100 10010000 10010001 10001101
11010101 01000000 00011110 11000011 10100111 01111010 10011110 00100110 11100000 01110101
11111010 01010110 01001101 01110011 01101100 00001010 01111101 11001011 10001000 01001001
01011100 01100100 11010000 10101100 11000111 11100101 11001111 00010101 00011010 11001000
01000111 01101010 00011010 01000010 10111001 01101101 10100111 00111101 10101010 00111001
01110100 00011011 10111001 00100110 01111011 01101110 00111111 10011101 01011000 01000010
01110001 11110111 10111010 01110111 10101010 01011011 11001001 01100000 00001110 01101010
01010100 01100010 00111011 01110100 11101011 01010011 01101011 11101000 01010101 11001011
01111110 01100110 01111111 00111110 01101010 01001101 11100100 10001111 11111110 10111101
01000001 10010000 01000110 01000101 00110011 01110110 00111000 11101101 11011110 10110010
01101001 10100111 10100000 01101110 01001111 11110011 10110111 00011101 10101001 00110000
01110011 01000111 00111000 10100001 01001111 11110111 10001001 00110101 00101011 01011101
11000111 01110001 10100000 11100100 11110010 01111000 10100111 10110111 00000011 11100100
11100110 10100011 00011100 10001110 01000101 00101010 11111101 11001110 11110100 11110110
01111010 00001010 11100011 11011001 01001101 00100000 00010100 00110001 11111001 01000110
01101000 11100000 11111101 00101000 01111010 11101100 11000001 00000110 00101000 11000001
00100111 10001110 00111101 11101000 01101100 10000000 00001110 00111000 00111111 10100101
00110100 00011111 11000010 10010010 10111000 01011100 00111010 01110110 00010100 00110110
01110111 01111111 10011110 01101001 11011111 10001111 00010100 10111100 01111010 01010011
01101011 01000001 11110101 00011000 11000011 11100100 00100110 10011010 10110001 10110110
01111111 11000010 10100101 10100100 01000110 00111001 00111000 00000011 10011010 00101111
01110111 01110001 00110100 11000110 00111000 11101001 11000111 11010110 10010101 10010100
00000001 11010000 11110011 01001110 01110010 00111010 10011010 00010101 10110010 10000100
01100011 00100010 10000111 00111110 10110110 00011011 11010001 00001101 00001010 00110111
01110011 11111001 11010010 01110101 00100111 10111000 10100001 01110010 00111110 10010100
11110110 01100000 00111101 10000101 00110110 11011011 11010001 10000101 11001000 11011101
00111110 01110001 11000111 01001010 00010101 01111000 11101001 01010010 01111101 11101100
01110001 01001101 01100001 11000111 11001001 01000010 10101000 00111101 01101100 00100000
01010010 10111101 10111010 11010001 10110011 00100011 10100111 00110100 10111001 01101100
00001100 00011111 11001110 10011100 01001001 00100110 10011111 10111010 11111010 10010011
10111000 11000011 00010001 11101000 01000111 10111111 01011010 00011010 00111111 01100010
01110001 01001111 11110011 00111101 10001110 01101001 10111011 10001000 11101101 01000101
11111010 00110000 00010011 00000000 10000001 10010001 01001001 10000010 00111101 11101001
11011110 01100000 11001111 00111001 11001101 00111001 01001000 11011101 11001111 01111010
00011011 10111011 11010000 01111010 10001101 01010101 01100010 00111011 11010010 00111000
11100011 10000000 11111110 11111001 10100111 10110001 11000111 10101101 00110111 00111001
11110101 00010101 01011010 01110101 00001011 00001101 11000110 00000001 00000000 01110010
00101001 01110001 10010100 00011101 01101001 11111001 11100111 10001010 01101011 01110101
00000000 01111110 00110101 00010110 11010100 00110101 00011010 11000011 10001110 01110011
11111001 11010001 10110100 11101110 11001110 01110001 01010010 01100100 01100011 10100111
11010010 10011010 00001000 00111111 10010101 00001110 11010111 10110000 11101110 00011011
01111000 11110110 10101000 11110110 11110110 00011101 01101010 01000010 01111101 00101001
00010100 10001111 11100001 11100110 10101101 11111011 10110110 01110111 00000001 00110110
10011110 00111000 11100110 10010111 00001100 10100011 10100111 01101111 01011010 01010000
11011111 11111101 01101010 01110010 10110110 01001001 11100000 11111011 11010100 01011001
10110111 01100100 00001001 10001101 11100111 01101000 00100100 01010010 00000011 10010011
10000000 00101010 01001110 11011000 00000100 11110001 01000001 11001000 00011001 00100100
11010000 11010100 10101110 00010111 00100010 00101011 10011110 10110100 00000101 11000111
11110001 01100010 10100100 01010010 01110001 01001101 01111110 00000101 00010110 01011101
01000100 10000100 00011100 00001110 10100111 10011010 01000110 11101011 11101011 11101111
01001110 11001111 00111000 11000111 00010100 00000110 00000011 11010100 10001010 00010010
11110111 10110101 00011110 11101100 01101000 11001000 00011100 10000011 10011010 01101011
00000010 01001111 00111001 00000111 11010011 00110101 00110110 01110010 00110011 11010000
11010011 00111010 00010010 01101000 10111011 11011000 00111010 10001001 10110100 10000011
11001000 00110100 11000111 01011110 01000001 00110101 00100111 00100001 00000001 11001001

00111000 10100000 00011100 10011100 11110111 00110100 01000110 11110111 11010100 01010111
11101100 00110011 00011000 11000110 00000111 00010100 10011000 00100000 01100100 11111110
10110101 00101011 11110010 01110011 10011111 11000010 10011010 11011001 10101101 00010011
11010111 01010111 10100000 00001101 11000000 11001000 01011110 01001110 01101001 11000101
01111010 00011100 11110001 01000001 01011111 01111110 10010100 10101110 00000001 00011100
01010010 10010100 10011010 00011011 00011001 11100101 10000011 11001101 00100111 10010110
01001001 11000000 11001111 01001110 11110100 10101000 01110000 10011100 11010011 11010101
10111111 01110110 01001111 00111000 11110101 10100100 11011100 11110111 00001011 00110010
00111100 00110001 11110110 10100001 01100011 00100100 10011110 11111110 10110101 00100010
00110001 11110100 11001101 00101011 00011100 00001110 00000111 00010100 10010100 10011011
01111110 01100001 01110110 10000110 11111001 01100100 00000010 00111011 01010011 00110110
10010001 11011010 10100100 11001001 11111100 11111101 01101001 00110111 01100100 11101101
00111101 01111101 00101001 01011110 11100101 01011111 01001011 10000111 10010110 00001111
00111101 10111101 01101000 11011001 01001010 01111001 00011001 00000100 01111101 00101000
00011000 11000111 01010011 01010101 00011001 01110010 10101011 00010011 10111001 00011100
01101100 01110111 11100111 10011111 01011110 10010100 11111111 00000000 00110000 01101110
00100111 00111001 00000110 10100000 11011010 01001001 11001110 11010011 11001111 10111101
00011110 01011110 00011011 00111011 01111001 11101111 10001110 11110101 01011011 10101011
00100011 00100100 11001001 11010010 01000101 00000111 00100100 01010001 10111001 01000111
00100100 01110000 00111010 00001010 10000101 01110111 00001110 10000000 10001110 01111010
01010011 11110110 10010000 00001111 00011100 00011111 01111110 10010101 10101100 00101001
11011111 10101110 10000011 10111011 00011110 00100100 11101111 10001100 01010010 11100100
10110110 00110001 01010001 11110010 00011100 11100100 11100010 10010101 00110000 00001111
00100111 10000001 01001010 01001011 11111001 01110110 00010010 10111001 00100010 11100111
10011111 11100111 01000011 00011101 11000011 11011110 10100011 00101100 11001000 01111110
01001100 00000001 11111001 11010011 10010100 10110000 00011001 00111110 10110101 00001101
00101011 11111001 10000110 11100010 11110011 10010001 11001101 00101000 11111111 00000000
01011000 01111001 11111010 01100110 10100011 11001001 00110010 00011100 10000000 00010010
10000100 01010010 01011100 10010001 11010011 00111101 01101001 11101010 10011111 00110000
11010110 11011010 00010011 00101001 00111110 10110100 10111001 00100111 10010110 00011100
01010011 00011011 00111110 11000011 11010110 10011010 11011001 00111101 00001001 11100011
10011100 01100110 10110011 01101111 01011011 10010101 11010000 10010111 00000011 10011100
10010010 01101001 01110111 01110011 11101100 01101001 10100000 11110100 00101110 01111110
10011000 10100101 00101011 10001001 00110010 01101001 00111011 00111101 01101110 01001010
01110110 00010011 11001100 11000011 01101101 00011001 11100111 11011010 10011100 10101101
10110100 11110000 00111000 11110101 10100110 11100111 00000111 00111001 11001101 00001010
11011100 00010010 01001111 00010101 10100101 11010100 01110110 00101010 11100011 10011001
10110011 01000111 00111000 11101011 11001001 11101100 01101001 00100001 00011011 10000001
11100111 00010100 00110000 11000001 11111110 10110101 10011101 01001011 01110100 01000100
11011011 10110000 11110110 11001000 00001001 10000011 11000000 11101011 10011010 01010011
11010000 11101101 00011101 11101010 00110000 01111010 11100100 10011010 00010000 10001110
00000110 11100011 10011100 10011110 11010100 00101000 11101001 01100001 01101010 01001000
11000011 10010000 00110011 11001101 00110000 10011100 00010010 00011000 10010000 00001111
01111010 01101011 00010010 00100101 11001000 11001111 11100111 01000110 11011100 11110010
01000001 11001111 10111101 01001100 01010111 01000010 10110101 01000011 10010011 00111000
11000001 00111101 11111010 11100010 10011110 00001001 00110010 01110011 11011010 10100011
01011100 00101000 00000111 00100100 11010010 10010011 11001110 01000111 11101011 01000111
00101010 00011001 00100011 01100111 01111001 11110111 11100110 10011010 11111000 00100000
01010000 00001111 00000100 10010010 01101001 10011001 00011101 01111001 00100100 01010000
10010010 01011010 10100000 01000011 11010101 01110010 00110011 10001010 01101111 01001110
00001111 01111010 01000101 10010011 11111011 10011100 11100110 10000110 11000001 11100111
00011000 00111101 00001000 10101011 01001111 01000000 01111011 10000001 00011011 01111000
00111110 10110100 10101100 01001110 01111011 01111101 00101001 10100111 10110111 01011111
11001010 10010101 11111000 11000001 11101010 01101010 00010010 01101110 11101100 00110110
00011111 11000111 11110111 10101010 00111101 10011001 00100111 10011010 01110110 00000110
00001000 00111101 11001111 11100101 01010001 10000000 01111010 01100111 10100001 10100110
11010101 10110111 00001011 10001110 01001110 10011000 11101010 01101000 01011100 11100100
11111010 01110111 10100110 11100111 00100100 10010001 01001000 01011011 10000000 00001110
01111101 11101001 11110010 00100100 10110101 01100100 11011110 11100011 11011000 10001101
11011011 01101001 10101011 11010000 10010000 10111111 10010101 00100110 11011100 11111101
01111101 00110011 01000011 00101000 11000111 01001110 01101010 10101101 01100010 10000101
01100101 01010010 00110011 11111000 11100110 10010001 00001000 11100111 10110110 00101000
01010000 01000001 11100100 00011100 11010010 11101101 11100011 00111000 11000001 11001111
10100101 01001011 10111011 11010100 01011101 01000000 00001100 10000001 11001111 00011110
10010100 10011011 01000011 01100111 10011110 01111101 11101001 01111111 10001000 11010001
00011010 10110100 10001111 11000111 01001100 11010100 10101001 00110101 10111001 01001100
11011111 11010010 10100010 00010001 11011010 00100111 10100011 10011101 11100010 10110100
01010000 01110110 00111101 00001101 01010110 10000000 00010101 01000000 00001111 01100001
01010110 00110111 01100000 10001100 01110011 01010001 01110111 00110001 11011111 10100001
00111110 00110000 01110001 01001100 01100001 11101101 01000011 00110001 11011111 11001000
11000101 00100011 01001001 10001110 10000011 11101011 10011010 10010110 11100010 10110100
01000000 10011001 00011011 00001111 10010111 00010101 01001110 01100001 10001100 11100000
11010101 10011001 00001110 00000110 01001101 01010010 10011000 10010011 11010010 10101011

10010100 01110111 11010100 10101001 00110000 11011010 00111001 11101011 01010101 11001111
00100011 10011010 10011110 01000000 01011011 10011111 01001010 10000101 11000000 11101100
00001101 01010011 01001001 01101001 10110000 10011011 00101011 10101110 00110000 01101010
00110110 11001000 00011000 00100111 00000010 10101101 00110100 01111100 01010100 01101101
00010110 00000110 01001111 01000011 01011010 01110011 00110101 10101010 00000010 00110001
11001000 11101111 01000011 01110000 01111000 11101011 01000110 00001000 00011000 01100010
01001000 00010100 11100100 11111001 10001110 00000110 01000101 00110100 11010110 10010111
00010000 11011110 00001001 11101111 10011010 01100110 00001111 11100011 01010010 11111001
01100100 00011110 00101001 00011101 01110011 10011111 11110001 10100100 10101100 00100110
10001000 00011011 00011000 11101001 11111001 11010101 01110011 10011100 11010101 10001100
00010001 11101111 01010000 11001010 10111100 11110100 11100110 10101110 00111010 00010010
11011111 01000001 10001100 01110001 11101111 01010001 00010110 11100111 10000110 11000101
00111001 11110010 00000111 11001000 00101010 00100110 00100101 01111000 11000101 01101011
00011001 00001001 10000110 01111001 01111100 11010100 01000100 11101110 11100000 00001010
01110011 11100011 00011110 11011101 11001101 01000101 10010001 10001100 00001110 00101011
01010100 11111101 11010001 00111011 10000001 00111001 00011100 01010010 00110000 11011011
11000000 00011101 01111001 00110100 11011110 11100000 01100111 10001010 01110100 10101101
10011111 01111010 10100111 00101011 11101110 01001010 01001100 01101110 00001110 00111000
11100011 11111001 01010011 01011011 00000011 10100111 00000111 10111101 00101011 10110110
01000111 01001111 11000011 11010010 10100011 11001000 00111001 00011110 11110100 01001001
01000111 01110100 00011110 01000010 11101110 00100100 01110011 11010011 10110101 00110100
00011110 01110001 11111000 11100110 10011011 11001111 01001100 01110001 01000010 10011111
01011010 00100010 11010010 01011010 10001010 11101001 00001001 10010000 01111101 00110011
10011110 00001101 01000000 01001001 11001110 01111011 11111011 11010011 11110011 10000011
10000000 00110010 01101001 00011011 10111001 01101111 11000100 01010110 10110110 01011100
10100110 01101101 11011111 01000100 00110111 10001111 01011100 10010011 11010110 10011111
10001100 01110100 10100100 01011100 00011110 01110001 01001000 01111011 10001010 01101101
11011001 01011101 00001010 11000010 11100100 00010010 01000000 11100000 11100110 10011010
01001111 11001010 01111101 01110011 11000001 10100011 10100111 00100100 01110111 10100111
01110101 11000111 11101010 01101001 01011010 11111010 10000111 01010000 11001111 00100011
00000011 00111110 10111001 10100111 01110110 11001000 00000011 00111101 00101001 00010100
00000110 00000000 11110011 11110101 00011101 10101000 11000001 11101011 11010100 01010010
10110101 11000110 00101010 10011100 00001110 11010100 11101110 10100011 10010001 11000001
11100010 10001110 00110001 11010000 00010001 01001010 01110001 11001001 11000111 11100111
01000100 10000000 00011100 01110111 11001111 10110101 00011101 11000001 11111101 00101001
00010000 00110110 00111111 00011010 00110000 01110010 01111010 11100011 10100101 00111110
01010100 11110110 00011111 01010001 11001000 01110001 00100111 01011100 01110111 10100111
10101111 10100111 01101111 01111010 01100000 00011011 01001001 11001111 11100111 01001111
01011110 01001111 00011100 11010100 01110101 00101010 11101111 10101000 00110111 00100111
00011000 11101011 01000010 01101101 00000100 01111111 10001101 00100011 10000011 10011111
01111110 11010100 00101001 00101010 11100011 10111111 10101101 00001101 01011011 01100000
01100011 10001000 11000001 11100100 11110101 11110111 10100111 01100100 10001110 00111010
00000011 11001110 01101001 10001011 10001001 00000000 11110101 00010101 00100011 00000011
11000000 11111100 11110011 01001010 00111011 10001101 00001000 00000001 11001011 10011110
10011110 10111100 01110100 10101001 00010000 00011100 01100111 11010010 10100011 01100001
10000001 10000000 00111001 10100111 01101110 11110110 11000111 11010110 10010010 01101101
11101010 01010000 11111110 01001111 00001011 11110101 10100111 11100100 11100111 11010111
00111101 11001101 01000110 00110011 11010111 10110001 10100111 00101001 00011000 11100111
10010001 11011010 10100110 11010111 01110111 00010011 10111000 10001000 01011000 01001000
01001000 11000000 00111110 10011111 01011010 10010101 00110011 11000000 00000111 10001110
10010101 00011010 10110111 00011110 10011001 11101100 01101001 11100000 10011111 11001010
10101001 00110101 10101101 10001010 10110001 01100100 00011100 11110001 11111010 11010011
11000110 00001001 00100011 10100001 10101000 11100011 11001111 00011001 01011110 01001111
11100001 01010010 01101101 00011101 01001000 11100110 10111001 10011100 10011100 01110101
00101010 11110111 11011100 01011100 00001110 00110001 11001110 01101000 11110110 11001111
01111010 01110111 01000011 11010111 10000011 11101001 11011110 10000000 00000110 00001001
11101011 01001110 11011101 01000111 10100001 00100010 10111111 11010111 00011110 11110100
11101100 01100100 01100100 00011111 11000110 10100011 00000111 00100011 00111000 11000001
10101001 10100011 01100000 00111010 11100010 10110010 10110010 01111010 10100001 10000010
10010010 10100011 00011110 10110100 10111011 10111100 10110010 00000001 00111101 01101000
01010001 10111001 10010011 10011111 01111010 01111001 11011011 10111011 00011000 00000110
10010011 01001010 11000100 10110010 00111111 10111011 11011111 00111110 11110100 00010011
10000101 11101011 11101111 01001110 11111011 10111100 11110101 00000110 10000110 00011000
11100110 10100111 10011010 11011101 00000000 10001100 00010010 00111010 10011110 00101001
11001010 11000111 10110101 01001001 10001111 10010000 10101001 11101000 01101000 01100010
00111111 11111010 11110101 01101001 10101011 00000110 10111101 01001000 11110000 11011011
01000001 00101101 01001101 00000001 10110001 10011100 11111110 00110101 00100110 01000000
00011100 00001110 10110100 00100001 00011000 11000110 00101010 00011011 01010111 10110010
00101100 01101000 11001110 00111001 00110100 10111000 11000110 00001110 01101000 11000110
00001001 11001110 00111101 10101001 01111010 10001111 01101010 01011011 11110100 00000111
10101110 10100010 01110101 01111100 01110110 11110101 10100111 10101001 01010010 10100111
00011001 11011111 01001100 01010000 00001001 11101011 01001011 10111011 00001111 01001001
00111011 01110100 00010000 01110010 11100111 00111001 11111010 11010000 01110010 00000110

01111010 11111101 00101001 11011100 00000011 11010011 00111001 10100001 01110010 00110010
01000101 01010101 10110101 10111000 11001000 11110010 01001111 01100011 10011010 00000001
11000110 01001001 00010100 10101110 01110011 11010011 00011100 01010010 01110010 01110000
10100111 10100111 01110001 11101011 01000010 10010010 01011101 00000000 01010110 00100100
01110011 11011010 10000001 10010111 01101110 10110100 00110111 01010010 01111011 01010010
01110100 11100100 00010011 10001110 10110101 00101101 00100000 01000010 11100011 10110000
00111001 11000111 01111010 00011001 10000000 11101111 01001001 11010000 01110001 11001001
00110100 00110111 00000011 00100000 01010011 01101011 10100000 00110001 01011000 11100000
10001110 01001111 10101110 00101000 11001111 00111100 01010010 01100111 10111111 00100110
10011011 11100110 01100000 10010011 10001100 11010011 01101001 01011010 11000000 01001101
10001111 01001010 10001100 11110010 01111000 00110100 10101011 10000011 10001111 01001010
01100011 00110000 11001001 11000000 10101010 10110010 11011001 00001100 01111110 11100011
11000000 10100101 01001110 10011000 10100100 01010011 11110010 01100100 11110101 11110110
10100001 01011001 01110001 10010001 11010110 10101001 11000010 11011010 10100000 01100010
11111101 11010011 10001010 01000001 11000011 11111010 11111111 00000000 01011010 00110010
01111001 11110111 11101001 01000111 01001110 00001000 00111001 10101100 10100100 11011011
01110110 00010010 00000111 00011000 11100000 10011110 10011101 10101000 01001111 10010111
11110010 10100100 11100000 01110010 01111011 11110111 10100111 00100001 11100011 10100001
11100110 10001110 01001011 11101011 01110001 11101010 00100100 10000100 11111010 11010001
10000000 10111000 10100000 00011110 01001110 01000111 11100111 01001000 11110010 01110111
00101011 11011111 10001010 01110000 11010011 10100000 10010000 10101100 01110010 11100100
11110110 11111010 01010000 10100100 11110001 01001100 11001110 01111101 01110001 11101101
01001110 11011111 10000001 10001100 01010101 00101101 01000001 11101000 00111001 01001110
11010010 01001111 00000111 11011010 10000101 01101110 11100011 10010000 01111101 01101001
10101010 01001111 00000011 00010100 10111001 00011001 00111100 01010110 01101110 11110110
11010100 10101011 00001010 00011011 00111000 00011110 10110100 10001000 01010100 11110000
01111010 11111010 11010010 00110011 10010000 01111010 01110001 11011010 10011011 11000011
10001110 01111010 01010101 00101011 11101100 10001001 01001011 01010001 11101110 01110001
11001010 00011110 10010100 00101001 11101111 10001110 10110100 11000001 10010000 01111010
01110001 01001110 11001000 11110100 11000000 10100111 00101010 01101101 01101000 00110110
00101111 11100011 01001000 11000011 10110000 10100101 11100111 00000111 10001100 01111010
01010011 00011000 10010001 10011110 00001001 10100110 11011010 11101000 00000011 10000111
00100011 11010011 11010110 10011010 00001000 00100011 10101101 00011011 10110010 00111010
01010010 00011100 10000011 11001101 00010110 10111000 01011101 00001111 11100111 10101101
00101011 00101110 01111001 11001111 00000110 10100011 01011101 11001100 00001111 01000000
00101001 01110010 11011000 11000010 10001010 10010100 10011000 00001110 11110010 11111000
11110101 11110101 00110100 11011100 01100011 11101001 01000111 01100001 11101010 01111011
01010001 11110011 01111010 01110001 01000100 10011010 10111000 11000100 00100011 00000100
00001100 11100111 00110100 11111110 00001000 00000010 10011011 10011100 10011110 01000110
01101001 11001110 01001110 11111100 01101101 00111000 10100001 01011110 11011011 00001011
01011101 10000101 01010001 11011011 10100001 10100100 01010011 11110010 01100100 01100100
11110011 01000110 01001110 01000110 01111101 00101001 10111100 10010011 10010001 11010110
10010010 11101100 10000011 01010001 11001101 11010000 01100011 10001111 10101101 00011100
00010000 00001000 11100111 10110111 11010010 10011000 10100101 10111010 00011100 01100110
10010101 01000011 01110110 11000101 00101011 01011000 00111010 10001110 11100100 10110000
00001011 01001101 11000001 11110101 10100100 00111011 10000111 01101111 11001010 10010100
01101110 11110101 10101011 10010011 01110001 11011000 01001101 00010001 11000110 01001110
00001111 00100111 11110010 11111110 10110100 00101001 01100011 11001110 01110001 11101011
01001101 11011101 11011100 10001111 10100111 11100011 01001010 10101100 00110001 10001111
01001110 11110101 10100011 10010011 01011010 11011000 10001101 00000111 10011100 10010111
00100111 11011010 10000101 11111011 10111111 01111000 10011010 00010101 10000110 01111010
11110110 11101101 01001101 00001100 10100110 10011111 10111100 10110101 00010110 10101100
01111011 10000000 01110000 01111011 00011010 01111110 11010000 11000000 01100011 10001010
01100110 11100011 10001100 00000011 10011010 01011101 10101011 10110111 00101100 10111001
00111110 10111001 10100111 11001011 01100110 11000001 01101010 00111011 00011011 01111000
00110100 10101010 00000110 01111010 11010100 01101010 11011001 00011000 00111001 10100101
00011101 01000101 01100111 00000101 01101001 01011101 10001101 10100001 11100100 00101110
01111011 11010011 11111100 10100001 10000001 10110000 11100110 10100011 11011111 11111100
11111011 11010010 11100101 01001110 00001111 00110101 10101100 10010101 11000000 00001000
00100011 10011100 11110101 11100010 10011110 00000110 00000110 11101111 01011110 10110101
00011011 11100000 00001100 11100011 10011010 01010000 01111101 11111011 01110011 01010001
00001000 00110100 11101100 11000101 01110110 11010000 10101110 00010100 10010000 01000110
01101001 11011001 11000000 11100100 00010010 01001111 11101011 01001101 01111100 00010000
00001000 11111100 01000101 00000000 11100100 00000001 10010011 11000111 01001100 11010110
00001110 01001100 01101011 01010000 01100010 01000110 00000001 01011110 10111101 01000001
10100111 10101111 00011001 11001000 11000101 00100111 00111011 10111110 01111100 01100111
10110101 00001100 00001111 00111111 11100011 01010111 10101011 11010001 11101100 01010010
00011101 11110010 11101101 11111100 01101000 01010010 00110010 01110111 00011100 10001111
01111010 01101010 11111011 00011111 10101111 00110100 11010110 00011000 11101110 00000111
10110111 10101101 00010110 11101000 11001001 10111110 10100100 11100101 10000001 00100000
00000011 11111000 01010001 11010100 11110100 11111001 00101010 00100101 00000000 01110110
11001111 10100101 00101110 01001110 00000000 11101111 11011100 11010010 01101001 00101101
11000011 01010001 11111001 00011101 01111011 01010000 11111101 00111001 11101000 01111101

11101001 10001101 11010011 10010011 01001100 11100101 10000111 11001010 01101000 11100101
11101010 10111010 10000101 11000111 10011100 00000111 11001110 00110010 00101001 11100001
10010100 10011101 10100011 00111110 10111001 10101000 11010011 10000000 01001110 01110011
01000110 11100010 00111001 11001111 01011110 11010100 10101111 01110111 01100110 00010111
00011100 11100111 01110111 00100111 10110111 01010001 10001010 00000001 01011110 01111101
01001111 10110101 01000110 00001001 00111001 11001001 11000110 01101001 00010111 10001110
01110011 01001010 01011010 01101000 11001010 00101100 01111100 10100000 11100000 01111010
01100110 10001101 11011001 01011111 01111010 10000001 10001111 11110001 01110111 00110100
11110100 10010000 01100011 00000111 10101101 00111011 01101011 01100001 11011110 11000010
11100111 11101011 10011010 01101000 01011100 00011111 01011111 10101101 00110101 01001001
00001101 10010001 01001111 00111100 10010001 11001111 11100101 01010101 00011001 00001101
00001010 00001001 00001111 10001100 01100111 11010010 10001100 00110001 11101111 10000001
01001101 01110011 10000110 11001000 00111101 00101001 10101100 01111000 11001001 11111100
11101010 00100110 10110101 11010000 10010111 01100110 00001111 11000111 11010010 10000011
10001100 00001110 11010100 10011001 00011000 11100100 01010010 00110000 11110111 00100100
01010001 11101000 00010110 00011100 11011100 01100011 00110100 00000001 11000111 01010011
11111000 11010010 00110000 00100101 10000111 01010011 11111000 11010010 10010101 11001111
00011000 11101001 01010100 10010101 10111010 10000101 10110101 00001110 01011011 10011100
11111110 00110100 11100110 10010011 00011111 11100011 01001100 01100000 01110000 01110001
11000000 10100001 01000001 11000111 10110111 10111101 00010001 01001011 10111110 10000011
00000111 00111101 11111011 01010100 10110110 01000100 10110101 11010100 01011100 01100100
00010011 11010000 01010100 01000100 10010000 00110011 11000110 00111011 11111011 11010101
10111101 00101100 00011001 00101110 10010011 00100100 10000000 00111101 00101010 01010111
01100000 01000110 11101011 10011100 00001110 00111010 11010101 10011000 11000110 01111001
11110110 10101010 11011000 11001011 01111101 00101010 11000010 11100000 00001010 11100111
10001100 01100101 11010100 10101011 11110110 00010111 10111111 00110100 11010111 01100010
00110011 11000111 00010100 10100111 10010001 11000001 10101000 00011111 10010001 01011010
11000110 00010110 00001011 11011111 01010010 00110111 10010011 00111101 11101010 10110011
10110001 00011001 00000111 10010001 11101011 01010010 00111111 00000011 11111010 01111010
01010101 01101001 10001111 11001010 01110001 10011010 00100101 01100110 11101100 11000111
01110001 10101110 01111000 10101000 01010100 11100101 10111110 10010101 00100111 11011110
11100011 11010010 10010101 01100011 00011011 10111000 11100011 11010110 10000110 10011011
01010111 00011110 11000011 00110110 11100111 10111101 00110101 11010100 10010001 01010110
00110110 11100111 10001010 01100110 00001010 11110010 00111010 01010011 01010010 11010011
01000010 00101110 11101111 10101001 00010010 01000101 10110100 01111011 00011010 00111100
10111100 01110000 00111010 00011010 10011001 10111001 00011100 10001010 01000001 11001101
01011111 11000111 10100101 11000000 10001011 11001011 00100000 01110001 11010111 10110001
10101000 01011110 00100010 10111101 01001101 01011010 11100111 00011100 01111110 01010101
00010100 10011101 00101011 00110111 00011110 01000111 01100100 00100010 10101011 10000000
10111101 11111010 11110110 11110100 10101010 11110010 10000011 10011110 10011001 00011101
01101010 11001100 10000000 11110101 10101010 11110010 10011100 11111010 11100110 10110101
10001111 01110110 00100110 10001000 01001111 11001100 00111010 01010101 01011001 10111110
11110110 00111000 00011111 01010011 01010110 11011100 10000000 00110110 11100011 10011010
10101000 11100011 10010010 00111000 11000111 11010010 10111010 00010011 01001011 01100010
00011010 00100001 01110110 11000000 00000100 01110100 11101001 01010000 10111001 00011110
01100110 01011011 10100111 01001110 00101010 01000111 11100000 00011100 10001110 11010101
00010011 00010011 11000000 00000011 11110011 10101110 10000101 10101010 00100101 00001111
00100100 00000001 11101010 01101010 00110010 01110001 10000010 00101001 11011000 00000100
01110100 11100110 10010001 11111001 10001111 11010011 11101001 01010101 10100011 11101000
00110110 11000110 01100111 01110001 11001110 00111111 01001010 01000110 00111000 11110110
11110101 10100011 00000100 00001100 10010011 11000101 00110000 11110001 10001110 11111101
01111001 10101001 11100101 11101100 01000110 10100011 10011111 00011111 10010101 01000010
11100100 10000110 11000000 11100110 10000011 11000000 11000111 00111100 11010011 01110011
10001010 01110001 00010101 11110100 00000111 00011000 00000111 10010010 01110011 11010111
00010100 11010101 11001110 01000111 10100111 11010110 10011100 10111001 11101101 11001101
00101011 10000001 11000001 00011101 01111011 11010110 10001110 11010110 10111010 00100000
01010001 10001100 11111010 11010011 01110110 10000000 01001111 00111111 01011010 00111111
11100101 10100000 00011101 00110011 01001010 10111001 11100100 10010000 01110010 01101010
00011101 11000011 10101000 10101100 00111000 00000011 00100011 11010111 11110011 10100110
11110010 00000110 00000001 10100111 01100100 00010001 11101110 01111001 10100110 10110110
01000111 01101100 11100011 10101101 01101000 11110110 11010000 10101101 10000101 00111110
11011101 00111011 11010011 11010111 11111101 01011110 01111001 11001101 00110001 01111001
10001111 10000010 01101000 11000001 11000101 01000011 11110011 00000101 10101000 10111011
01110010 01111010 11100000 01010100 10011000 00111111 01010000 01111101 11101001 10110001
10011110 00110011 11001101 00101010 11110101 11000101 00010001 01101001 00010010 00111111
10100000 11100111 10111111 00110100 01101111 11101111 10000001 01001100 11101010 01110001
11001101 00111100 10000011 10000000 00110000 01101001 01110011 11101001 01100010 10000011
00011110 10100100 01110011 11111000 11010010 10101000 00100000 01100100 00011100 01111101
00101001 00110001 11110010 01111100 10111101 01001101 00101110 11001101 10101111 11111000
01111110 00010100 10110100 10110101 11100100 00110000 01011110 11000110 10100100 01010001
10000011 11001111 11100111 01010001 10001111 01011110 11011000 10100101 01010001 10011110
01111101 01101001 01101001 01101101 01000110 00000001 01110010 11111001 00001100 00000101
00111011 00100011 10101011 00010011 10011111 11100111 01001101 00000000 00001010 01111110

00000110 00110000 11011001 11001000 11101110 00111011 11010011 01001010 01001111 01010000
01101001 10001111 11101001 11010110 10011001 11100110 00001100 11111100 11111100 11110001
01001010 01111010 01111010 01111110 00111001 10100100 00010001 11111010 00001110 01111101
11101001 01101000 10010101 10010011 00000111 01110001 11101000 01000110 00110011 11010011
00010100 10111001 01011110 00111101 01000111 01001010 01000101 00000011 00000111 10001010
01010101 01011100 00001110 10011100 11111011 11010010 01010110 10001000 01011001 10010010
00110000 00000111 10011100 11110011 11101111 01000010 10010000 01111001 00011101 01111011
11010010 01110010 00000111 11001100 00111000 11110101 11001101 00101010 10101111 01001101
10100110 10101010 11101010 01001011 11011101 00101000 10010110 00010110 00011011 11111101
01111110 10110101 00110110 11100011 10001110 01000111 00100110 10101011 10101010 10010101
00111001 11001101 01011000 01000001 11001000 01101100 11110101 10101100 00101101 01100111
01100110 01010101 10000101 01100011 10001110 11011001 10100011 01110001 00111101 00010111
11110000 11001101 00101110 11011110 01110011 10011100 00001111 01000001 01000011 00001100
10001110 00101011 00011111 01000010 10101110 00111000 00110001 11000111 01001110 10110100
11100100 00111000 00100011 00110100 11011111 10111100 00000110 00111111 00011100 11010010
10101000 11100011 10011010 01010110 00011001 01100001 01001111 01111010 00110010 00001110
00110010 00101001 10010001 01010100 10001011 11001111 10111101 01100110 11010101 10110111
00000101 10110000 10001100 01110011 10000011 11011010 10010111 00101011 10110000 10011100
11110010 01111101 01101001 00110000 00110111 11100011 11110010 11000101 00001110 10100011
10111001 11100110 10001001 11101010 00001011 01010001 00011110 01001100 00001111 10111011
01001011 10111000 00010001 11001000 11000110 01101001 00111001 11000111 00011111 10011001
00110100 10111000 00000011 00000000 11010001 10100000 11110100 00010101 10110110 10001000
11111001 00000111 11010110 10010000 00110000 00011001 11001000 10100111 10101000 11011100
00111110 01011111 01110001 01001101 11110010 11111100 10110011 10010011 11010111 11101011
01000101 11011101 10101110 01000101 10000110 11100100 11101100 11001001 00011000 00011001
10100001 01011000 11100011 00011011 01110011 11101111 10011100 01010010 10000101 11110111
11100011 00111001 11000101 00101001 00000011 10000010 00101001 11101010 11110110 00101011
01100001 00011001 10110010 01110011 10001100 01100011 11010110 10010001 10001001 11001111
01001111 11001110 10011101 10001100 11100100 11110111 10100100 11000110 01001110 01110011
01010011 11001101 01101111 01010000 10111111 01110000 01100010 11000000 11100111 00000011
00110100 01101110 00100111 10100111 00010100 10101101 11000000 10100011 10000000 01101010
10011011 10110010 10110000 11011011 11101100 00100010 10010011 01000011 01100100 11100100
01100011 11110001 10100111 10110100 01111101 11000001 11100100 11010011 01110001 10110100
01010010 01001001 00100000 11110101 00011010 00110010 00001111 10101101 00101001 11100110
10011111 10000001 11111100 01011000 00010100 01101101 00000011 11011110 10101011 11011101
11011110 11110111 00001101 11110110 00100011 00100100 10101001 11111111 00000000 00001010
00001111 11111010 10111100 01010011 10110000 00110000 00110011 11011110 10011100 01000110
00111000 11101111 11110101 10100010 11101001 01101100 00001110 11100100 01100000 10011100
01100111 00011000 11111010 11010010 10011100 10001110 01010110 10011110 11000001 01001010
11010000 00100011 11000110 01111001 10100010 00101110 11101000 00110100 00100011 00011001
00001101 11101111 01000011 00010010 01011011 10011110 10110100 11101101 10111000 00111001
00011101 11101000 01100100 11001000 11110111 10100101 01110110 10110101 00000001 00110000
01110001 11111101 00101001 00010100 00010000 01110010 00000111 11010110 10100100 01010000
00110000 00001111 11101011 01000000 11000110 01110011 11010010 10010011 10011111 01100000
11110101 00100011 11011100 01001110 01111000 10100101 11000001 11011010 00111000 00111001
11001111 01011010 10010011 10000000 10100111 10011110 01111110 10010100 10000000 11101110
00011100 00011010 10010110 11111001 10011000 00110111 01110001 10011100 10010000 01111011
01111011 11100010 10010111 00000111 01101111 00000111 00000110 10000111 00111100 11100011
00010100 11100110 01101100 00000000 00001101 00111011 10000001 00011011 00010000 11001100
00111000 00111001 00011101 11101001 01011111 10000011 11010011 00111110 11010100 11110101
11000110 11100010 00111101 00111010 11010010 10010000 00111011 01111010 11010011 10001100
10100100 10110101 00010110 11100100 01101011 10010010 01111010 01110110 10100101 11000001
00101001 01001111 11100011 10100001 11101010 00101001 00001000 00000111 10111110 00110001
01000111 00111111 00110011 10110011 00011010 00100011 01011101 11000000 00010010 01111011
10011010 01101110 00001001 01111010 10010000 11110011 10001010 00110001 10010001 11101001
01001110 11110110 11010000 01111011 10001101 00011001 00111111 01111011 10110101 00011011
01001001 11100011 11010110 10011100 00011000 00001110 01101001 11001110 11000011 00111001
11101011 01000010 01101111 10111000 00111101 00001000 01010101 01011000 01110011 01001110
11011010 01000111 00111101 10001101 00111011 11001100 00101101 11110100 00110100 11101001
00011000 10000101 11100011 10110101 01010011 11011110 11001000 00000110 01110011 01000011
01100111 11110001 10100101 00001100 00001000 00011011 00000111 00100010 10010011 00100011
10101111 11110101 10101000 10001010 01110010 11010001 00001001 10110000 11011011 11000101
00100000 11110100 10100111 00011001 00110010 01111001 11001110 00101001 00111000 00111000
00110100 11011010 11010000 00101100 11000011 10011100 11111100 10100010 10010011 10100111
00110100 10111011 10000010 11110011 01001010 11010010 00000011 11110100 11110111 10101000
11011100 01111011 10001101 11100011 00111001 11101110 01101000 00111001 11101101 11111001
11010000 00011000 00000011 11000001 11001110 01101001 11001100 01110000 01110010 00001000
11110111 10101011 10110100 10011011 11011000 00011000 11010000 00001111 11110001 11100110
10010100 11111100 11010100 00101100 10100000 01110000 01000111 11100011 01000010 10010010
00011111 01110110 01111011 11010001 01110111 01110001 00100001 00011001 01000110 01111110
01001100 11111011 10000011 01001101 11011010 11000100 11110001 01010010 00110001 00000100
11100100 11110101 10100100 11011101 10010001 11000101 00100101 10101110 10001001 00000010
00001111 00101111 10001110 01111000 00110100 00000000 00110011 11000101 00100011 11100100

10011100 11100111 10011110 10110100 11000001 00100001 00000111 11101011 01000101 10100100
10110101 10111000 00010011 10010101 00000111 10000000 01111001 11101111 01001101 11011000
10100111 10111101 01000110 10100111 11110010 10100111 11101110 00000111 10100000 00100010
10100010 11011101 10000001 00010101 00110010 01011000 11110100 11100110 10000101 00000100
10101111 10111101 00111001 00110111 00011100 11111010 00001110 11110100 11100110 11111010
01100010 10111010 11010011 01001011 01010011 00110100 01000110 00000110 01001110 01001001
11000001 00111110 11010100 11100000 10111100 01111111 01001010 00011000 11110110 11110101
10100001 01001000 00100011 00011001 11111100 00101000 10010100 10111011 01101100 00111101
10000111 00101010 10011110 01000001 00111000 11001111 01111010 00010001 10011000 11110000
10100011 11011010 10010011 00000100 11100100 11111010 01100010 10100100 11000000 00001001
11011000 00011010 11001101 01011111 10100000 01101000 00110011 00111000 10010000 11110011
10011111 01111010 10010001 01000110 01000111 01011110 11111101 01101001 10101100 01111000
11100011 00011111 10010101 00011100 10010001 10000011 01001110 11011010 11011100 00010000
10111101 11111001 11100100 01010001 10001110 00110000 10011001 11000111 11110010 10100001
10111101 10001110 01111101 01000101 00111101 00011001 01111001 00000100 11111110 00100010
10110101 10110011 10001110 10100101 00001011 10110111 11010110 10011001 10110100 01100100
11100011 10111101 00111010 01010110 01011110 00110001 11111001 01010000 00001001 00111111
01001010 10000111 01010111 10011011 01110010 00010111 01110000 01010000 01000000 11101111
11111110 00010100 11101111 00101111 10001110 10111100 11010011 01110111 00110000 11100011
00000110 10010100 00010011 10001111 01111010 11001110 00001010 11111010 00100110 00111011
10110000 00001001 10111011 10111001 11111100 01001101 00011100 10000001 10001010 01100011
01100000 10100110 00000101 00111000 01110011 00011110 01001101 00110111 11001010 11011110
10100101 00000001 01010010 01000110 01101001 11011000 00011101 00011000 01110100 00011101
11101000 01011100 10000101 11100100 11100110 10000000 01111001 11100010 10100110 01101001
01101101 10110001 00111011 10110000 01000101 01100000 01111001 11000111 10110001 10100111
01100001 10000001 00000110 10000100 01100110 11001111 01011100 10001010 01010101 00100101
10000110 01110001 11000001 00110100 00100110 10100011 00101101 01001010 00010001 10011000
01101111 00100100 10001111 11111110 10110101 00110101 01110011 11010111 11110100 10100100
01110000 11100011 10100110 00111111 00101010 00111010 00000001 10011110 10100010 10100101
11001010 11100000 00001101 10111100 11100000 11110110 11110100 10100111 11100000 11100100
01110111 11110111 11001101 00110111 00100100 10001110 00101001 11101010 01111110 01010010
01111011 01111010 01010101 00101000 11101000 10000010 11000010 00111000 00111001 11100000
11010000 11001010 11001101 10000001 10010000 01111101 00111000 10100000 10011100 01111101
11010001 10000001 11101001 01001010 10000111 10001111 10011100 00001010 00011101 10111001
10001000 10111111 01000010 00111110 01000001 00000011 10101111 10101111 00111101 00101001
11100011 10010000 01001110 00000000 11100110 10010111 00100111 00100101 10111111 00000011
01001000 10101100 00010001 00111010 10001111 11000110 10010011 10001011 01101110 11001000
10111011 00001100 11001001 11110011 00111000 11101101 01001011 10110101 10010111 00111111
00110000 10100111 00101001 11100100 11100111 11111001 01010000 11011000 11001111 00111100
11010000 10010010 01001100 00011011 10111110 11000100 01111000 11100100 01111011 01010010
10101001 11000011 11110010 01101001 11111000 00011011 11110111 00011010 01100011 00011100
10110111 01001110 10110101 10100010 10010100 01101101 10101000 01011100 01000110 11001001
00100000 10001110 10011111 11001110 10011100 00000001 11111011 11011101 00111101 10101001
00010100 10010000 01110001 10011010 01010010 01110010 00001110 11011100 11100111 10111101
01100111 11001100 00011110 01000000 11011100 10100111 10110101 00100000 00011100 01100011
00111100 00000011 11011011 10001010 00000000 11100011 10111111 11100011 01001000 11111001
11011111 11010011 00000011 11010000 01010010 11100110 01111101 00000110 00101110 11011110
10111100 10010010 00101001 00010011 10011100 11110011 01001110 01011110 10011100 00011010
00011111 00001011 10001110 00111010 11010101 01000001 01011011 01010110 01000000 11011110
00001110 01000111 11101010 01101011 01010011 01000001 10001101 10001101 11001001 01100001
10001110 10011000 00111001 10101100 11011100 00001100 01111011 11110111 10101101 10101101
00010001 01001000 10001101 11011011 00011101 01001111 00000111 00110100 10011101 10101101
01110011 01000100 11101110 10110100 00110100 10111100 10111100 01001001 10011110 10100010
10011100 10100000 11100100 11010011 10010000 00110110 00111001 00000000 11010000 11011001
00111100 00001110 10110101 10010011 10010101 11101100 10000010 11100100 01001100 01001111
11110000 11111110 10110101 00010100 10101101 11011011 00010101 01100000 10101001 00000011
10011010 10101010 11100000 01100100 11111010 01110100 10100100 10111001 10010010 10110100
10011000 11011011 01000100 00110011 00011110 11111000 10101010 10101110 11011011 10111000
00011101 01000101 01011000 10010100 11100011 11101001 11010010 10100010 01100000 00001111
01011010 11011001 00101110 11000100 10100110 01000111 10001100 01110011 01001111 11110111
00111111 10010101 00110011 11101011 11010011 10111101 00111101 00111101 00111010 10001010
11001001 11011010 11110110 10110000 11010110 10001100 01010101 11001110 01110010 01110011
01001111 11001000 00011000 11001101 00110011 10110001 00010100 10000011 10111000 00111100
10011111 11001110 10101010 00101001 00100000 10110101 11000101 01101110 10111000 00011111
10101101 01000111 11010011 10011010 01011100 11101101 00111111 11100011 01000011 01001001
10010001 10001010 10100100 10011101 10011101 11000001 10110111 10110001 00010100 10100100
00101111 00111000 11111001 11001111 01111010 01100001 11100111 10101101 00111001 11110001
11011000 11100111 11111010 01010011 00110011 11101111 11010110 10100110 10100010 01110110
01011010 10000001 00000100 10111001 11111100 00101010 00111110 00001000 11000110 00101010
01001001 01111010 00010001 10001100 10001110 11110101 00001011 00011100 00000010 00111111
01011010 01110110 11010010 11100010 00100001 10010111 00000111 11110000 00111101 11101010
10011100 10111101 01110011 01010110 00100100 00111001 00011000 00100100 11010101 00111001
01011011 00111001 11000110 01110001 01011101 00101001 10100111 01100011 00110001 10110010

11110011 11010010 10100001 01010001 10011100 01110010 00111110 10010101 00100001 00100011
10101111 01011010 10001101 11111011 11101100 11100011 11011110 10111010 00101111 01100101
10111001 00111110 10100010 01110100 00100010 10100011 00100111 10101110 01110011 11010110
10001101 11000101 10000001 00000111 10101000 11101111 01000011 00011100 11110110 11101111
01000101 10011011 00010111 01011101 01000110 00110001 11101011 10011100 11111011 01010010
00111111 01011110 00001111 01111110 10000100 01100111 00110100 00110001 00011101 00001111
11100111 01001011 00010010 10000010 01000001 11101101 10011010 10101011 01110010 11101110
00100111 11100100 01000111 10110100 10110111 11001100 01111000 11000101 00011000 11101011
10001110 01101010 11011100 10100011 11010011 10100000 10101010 11011011 01111110 01000011
11001111 00110100 11100000 11011011 00100101 10001101 11100000 10001110 10010100 00101111
00111000 10100001 01000111 00000101 10001111 01000001 11011010 10011101 11110011 00101010
00010010 00111001 10101010 10010010 11101110 00001000 00010100 01110011 10011110 11110100
11010010 10111000 11000110 11001110 01101000 11101100 00111010 10000010 01111011 11010001
10011100 01110011 11101111 01001010 11111101 00101100 01001011 01000010 00101010 11110001
11000111 01011110 10110100 11110110 01101100 10100111 00011101 01111110 10010100 01001010
00001110 00110010 00111111 01001010 00011000 11100101 01000110 00001101 00001110 11100101
00101101 01000110 00000000 01001111 11110001 00000001 10001110 10100000 11110111 10100111
10100110 01001000 00101101 11000111 11010011 00111101 01101001 10011011 10001001 11101011
11000111 11100001 01001010 00110001 10111111 11100111 00111111 01000001 11101011 01010100
10101110 11110111 00000001 11011000 00100001 00110011 10011100 01110011 01001011 11110111
01001000 00111110 10111101 01101000 11001000 00011001 00011001 11101011 01001001 10111000
01101101 00100100 10011110 10011100 01110011 01001010 11011101 10000001 10101101 01001001
00001000 11001000 11111001 01110011 10001111 01001010 01010100 00111111 00110001 11001001
00000000 11111101 01101001 10011001 11100000 00010000 01101001 00011000 11110001 11001111
01111110 11110101 10011011 01001001 10000110 10100100 10011000 00011000 01110010 00001111
11111001 00110100 01100100 10101111 01001111 11010110 10011001 10001101 10100011 11010100
00010001 01000110 01001110 01000111 10100000 10100110 11011010 01100011 00011110 10111100
10010011 11010111 10001110 10100010 10010111 00011100 11100000 01010100 01111011 10110010
01111001 10100111 10000110 00111001 11110011 00001000 00111110 10011000 00011101 00101001
01011011 01011011 00001101 00001010 11000000 10010111 11000110 01111010 01110111 10100111
10000010 00111011 11110111 10100110 01100100 11110110 01101110 10111100 10011111 11000110
10011100 11011100 11111111 00000000 11110101 10101001 10110100 11100011 10100000 01101010
00101111 01111110 00111001 10100111 10101001 01101100 01110100 10101000 11010111 00101011
11000111 01101010 00011100 10110001 11100101 00101010 00010010 10111011 11010000 00101111
11011100 10010011 00111000 00000011 10110111 10101110 00001101 00111011 01101000 00100000
10011010 10001001 00001001 00100100 10011110 00111001 11101101 01001010 00110010 01111001
11011101 10001010 10101011 11000101 10000010 01100100 11001011 10000010 00111000 00011111
10001101 00001011 11000000 11001111 01000011 01001100 11001001 11000111 01101100 01010000
01001001 00100011 00101110 01111110 10000010 10100010 11001010 00111110 01100101 11011100
10010001 01001001 00100111 10010011 10011010 10110001 00011011 01110000 00000110 00111001
11101111 01010100 11010000 11110100 11110101 10101001 11010001 10111110 01111100 00011100
01111011 01010100 11001101 00110110 10101110 00110100 01011001 11101011 10011110 11011110
10010100 01110011 11011000 11010100 01111001 00111000 11111010 10011110 01101001 11111001
00111101 00000101 01000011 01110001 10110000 11101101 01111101 01001001 00010110 01000011
01000110 01110010 01111000 00011001 11000111 01011010 10001100 00101110 00110011 11001001
10100110 11101110 01100000 10111100 01100011 00111110 11110100 01001001 10101001 01101010
00000101 10000010 01110000 00000001 00010101 00111110 11101110 00000111 00011000 10101010
10001011 10010101 01000000 01001001 11001111 10110000 10101001 11010110 01011101 11011101
01111010 01010110 01111011 10111011 01110100 00101011 01010001 11111001 11001001 10100101
01100110 11111001 11110001 11011111 11010110 10100010 01110011 11001110 01000000 11100100
11111110 10110100 11100100 00011100 01100100 10001110 01101010 01111001 01010010 11010001
00000000 11101100 11110101 00010100 10101010 01111011 11010011 00001001 00100100 10000001
10001110 00111101 01101000 11101111 11111101 00101010 00010011 01101001 01011000 10010001
11111001 11100100 00010000 01110001 01000001 00100100 10011100 10011010 01100110 00001111
01010010 01111001 10100011 11100110 11101100 01111000 10101010 11010101 11101110 10001011
00011110 10101101 10011010 00010111 00100111 10110111 00010100 11001110 01000010 11010010
00001100 11110111 00111100 01010010 00001011 00010010 11111010 11010010 00010010 01111010
11110100 10100100 00000111 11100100 11101011 10011110 01111011 11010010 00010001 11001111
00000111 11110011 10100110 11101101 01101111 00110001 01101100 00111001 10001110 11101111
01000001 01000000 01101110 01110001 01001000 01000111 10100101 00110100 10101110 11001100
01110011 11001101 01001101 10010011 00011111 01010001 11101100 01001000 00000111 00000010
10010000 00011100 11100111 10011110 01001111 01101010 00111010 11110101 11111101 01101001
10000001 01000110 11101100 11100111 00000000 11111011 11010110 10001110 11101101 11011010
11000001 10100000 10111000 11001110 00000111 01011010 01111110 01001000 11001111 01110001
01001100 01100001 10001110 01110011 10011111 01001110 01101001 00110010 01111010 11010110
01110110 11010011 01010000 01000011 11110011 10011010 01010111 11001111 11100011 01010001
10101001 11001110 01001000 11101011 01001011 11001001 11101010 01111001 11111010 11010110
10010100 11010010 11010100 00110100 00011100 10111001 11001001 11100110 10000010 01110000
01001111 00111001 00100110 10011000 10111110 10000100 11010000 00001010 10010011 11001001
10101100 01110110 01100011 00010111 01110001 00000111 10001010 01110010 10010110 00011111
00110111 01111010 01100111 11001010 10100111 00111101 01111101 10110011 01000110 01001001
00000011 10110111 00111101 00101011 01010101 00100101 10111101 10000011 01010010 01001111
11000100 11110011 01000010 10011110 11010101 00011010 11110000 00001000 00100000 11100100

00011010 00100101 11100011 10001110 11100110 10000111 00010100 11010101 11001001 00100101
00100111 00011101 11110000 00101001 00110000 00001000 10101000 11110001 11101000 01101001
11101011 11000001 11000101 01000011 01101010 11111010 00000000 01100111 11010100 01010011
10000110 00111100 10111110 10110100 11010011 10000011 11000101 00001101 10010000 10111000
10100010 11001101 00101011 10001110 11111101 11000000 10001100 11110011 10011010 01010101
01100000 00111111 00001110 10110101 00010110 01110111 01110100 10101001 00010011 10000000
01000101 00110100 10011010 11011001 10001101 11101100 00100001 01110011 11111000 11010010
10110100 10000011 01101000 10101000 11010001 01110000 01101001 01001111 01011110 10000111
11011110 10010010 10001010 01011010 10110001 00001010 00001110 01111001 00000111 10011010
00110111 00000011 10011100 10011100 11100011 10101000 10100110 10100010 11110010 01001000
11101111 01001010 01001000 00000000 01110001 11110101 10101011 01110001 10001010 01000011
10111000 10100000 11110010 01001001 00111100 01010001 10111000 00000011 11101101 11011010
10010000 00001110 00110011 11001101 00011000 11101011 11000101 01000010 10110011 01011010
10000101 10000000 00011110 01110010 00000001 11000101 00001100 01110001 11101111 01001001
11010101 01001110 00111000 10100110 10111001 11000010 00001111 01011110 11110101 01001001
11101011 10100011 00010010 01100011 10011011 11101111 11100100 01110001 11101010 00101000
00111000 01101100 11110011 01001101 01001110 01000111 11001000 01000111 11100011 01000001
11001111 01111100 01100011 11011010 10101001 10101101 01110100 00011000 11111100 10000000
00111101 11101001 00111100 11000101 00011101 11110000 01101000 01010011 11000001 00011110
11011101 10101001 10101000 00110001 11001101 00100101 01100000 11010111 10101000 11110110
11000000 00011000 00000111 00100011 00111100 01010000 10011100 11110000 11011100 01010100
01101011 10111011 11001100 11000001 11000110 00111101 01101001 11100000 00010001 11010100
11010011 01110010 10001010 11010010 00101000 00110100 00000110 11101011 10001100 01110011
01000010 11100111 10111001 10100011 10001110 11011001 11001111 11010110 10011011 11001110
00110011 01001010 01001000 01111011 00001111 11101010 01111010 01010010 00110011 01110010
00101001 10100101 10101000 11100011 00011100 01010110 01110110 01101000 01010111 00001100
10010011 11010000 01110111 11101111 01001111 01010010 01010100 11100111 10000011 01001100
01101001 00000000 11100011 10100111 11100011 01001001 10001101 11000111 10101110 00101011
01011010 01101001 11101110 10000010 11100011 11011000 00110111 10101110 00111101 11111101
01101001 10100111 10110001 00111101 10111101 10101001 00001001 11000111 00011101 01111101
00101001 00001011 00010001 11010110 10011100 10111001 01011110 11000011 01111010 10010010
01101110 00000111 10001110 00000001 10100000 00111001 11110100 00000010 10011010 11011000
01100011 11011010 10011011 10111000 11111010 01010010 01010001 01000010 11010101 10001101
11001111 01011110 01111010 11110101 10100100 01100110 11100111 10001110 10111101 11101001
10001101 00100111 01010101 11101011 11101011 01001111 11001000 11011000 00110010 00110001
01011010 00111000 01101001 10101001 10010011 11110011 00010001 01111001 01101100 01100110
10100100 01010101 11100100 10010000 01001110 11001010 01101111 11001011 11000110 00001111
00111101 00101000 11100101 01000110 11011100 11111101 01101010 10010100 01100100 10110111
11011000 00010100 10010010 00011100 10100111 10010000 00000111 11100010 01101000 11001110
01001001 00011001 11001111 11110101 10100101 00111101 01001001 11101111 01000111 10100000
00011101 01111101 01101010 01100100 11111011 00111011 10001101 10100100 00000100 00010001
01001111 01010011 10000001 11110011 10011010 00011100 10011110 01111011 11100011 10001010
01101000 11001001 00011001 11101011 11110101 10101010 01110110 10111000 00001110 01010101
00011011 01111101 01001110 01101001 01011100 01110011 10010001 01010001 10000011 11110011
10001110 11000011 11010010 10100100 01101110 10111001 00000111 11110000 10101000 01101011
01000110 10010010 00000001 00000110 00000001 01000000 00111001 11110101 11001101 01001011
11100101 10101001 00111001 11000111 00111110 10110101 00011001 00000100 00001100 01100011
10001110 10110100 11110100 11000000 10001111 00111001 00100100 10011110 11010101 00001010
11010010 01000001 10110011 00000001 10011110 01111000 11001101 00011100 01110001 11000110
00111111 00011010 00111001 01100100 00000100 01100011 11110011 10100110 00111110 01111111
00001110 11010100 10101001 11111011 10111011 10001010 11011101 10001001 01110110 11110000
01000001 00011100 11111101 01101001 10101100 01111000 00111100 01110100 11110101 10100000
00010110 11000110 01001001 00110100 01100111 00000111 00111100 11111011 00001010 10011110
01101001 00100111 01110100 01011000 11101101 11000000 00101000 11100011 10001010 01000101
11100011 10100000 00000000 01111011 11010010 10001100 01110111 00111000 10100110 10111111
00111101 00111010 01010101 01110011 11101001 10101000 00100110 00000111 00100000 01100000
00011010 01010000 11001100 00000111 01010001 11001111 01100001 01001010 00010100 11110001
11011110 10000101 00011100 10010011 11111000 01100110 10100110 11001110 11110110 11011100
10011011 01011100 01110000 01100010 00100011 00000100 10110000 11001110 01101000 01110010
00111101 01110011 11000111 01011010 01100111 00000111 10101111 01101010 01001001 01010100
00000001 10010001 01000100 01100001 01111101 00010000 00000001 01100110 00000111 00011000
11101011 11011110 10010111 00100100 01110101 01101010 00010111 11101110 01010010 00001100
00111001 11111001 11111000 10101010 10110100 10100000 11010010 00010011 01111101 10000111
00101001 11100111 11100110 00111100 01010011 10010100 01100000 01100100 00011100 11010011
00110010 00000111 10101101 00000011 11101111 11100111 00111111 11111101 01111010 10001011
11011101 10001101 00001111 01011110 00111101 11001001 11101001 01010001 11001010 00001001
00111011 01000001 00011101 00101001 11001100 11000000 10001100 01010011 01110111 00000000
00010000 00111001 00011111 11100011 01010101 00001110 10100101 00001011 10011110 01111001
11001110 01000111 01101010 00011100 10001110 10010100 10001100 01110001 00100001 11001111
00110100 00101110 01110111 11110101 11100011 10110111 00010101 00101110 11100000 10100011
11011000 01101110 11100011 10010001 10111011 00111110 10010100 11111100 11110000 11111101
10111010 01110100 10100011 10011100 10011110 10000100 01110100 10100100 11011111 11101000
00001101 00100101 10101001 00110111 11101000 00110100 11100000 10011100 10100110 01111111

00011010 01111111 01011110 01000111 11100101 01001001 10011111 10010011 00111000 00111001
11110100 10100011 01110000 00101110 00000111 01000011 01001110 11011101 01000111 11010100
00111010 10000001 10000011 01001010 11000100 00011110 10011100 01010001 10000010 00001110
01101001 00110111 00001111 01001111 10100101 01101000 11011010 11100101 10111001 01001100
01011100 11100000 00001100 01110010 01001101 00001101 11010111 11011000 01010000 00011011
00111110 10011111 10010101 00110000 10111001 00011001 00011101 01110011 01010000 10011110
10000100 10111011 01011100 10010001 11000001 01100111 00011101 10111101 01101011 10100110
11010010 10100011 11011011 01101010 10000011 00111100 01100011 00110101 11001011 11000010
01011001 11100101 00000011 11011110 10111011 00101011 01000101 00001011 00010010 00000011
11010111 00010101 10000101 01100100 11101110 10001010 01001111 10101001 00100010 10101111
01111010 01001001 01111001 00011000 00010101 00101011 00001110 00110001 11101001 01010001
10010101 11100000 10010101 11101011 01010101 00010110 11010110 10001000 01011011 10010101
10011000 10110110 11100010 00110011 01010000 00111111 11100011 11110101 10101011 00001100
00110001 01010101 11011100 11100111 10100001 10101000 11110111 10011110 10111011 10100010
11101100 01010111 01110000 01000111 11111001 11101011 01010000 11110011 11101001 11001101
01001101 00101110 00000000 11101011 11001001 10101000 11111110 01100000 01111110 10111101
11101001 11110011 10110101 10101011 00100111 11001000 01000101 11100011 11101011 01000110
01111000 11101001 01001111 01100001 10110100 11010000 01000110 00111110 10011101 11101010
01100011 00100111 01101011 11011100 01110110 00100011 11011100 01110110 10010011 11011111
00011101 10101010 00110110 00100100 10011110 10111111 10010000 10100111 00111000 11000110
01110110 01110111 10100110 11111011 00010011 10001010 10101011 11110101 10010011 00000100
00101001 00100110 01001111 11000000 01100010 10100011 11011100 00000000 10100101 00100100
10001110 10000111 10000011 11010010 10100001 01110010 00001111 00000111 11111001 01010110
10001110 10100011 10110000 10000110 10110011 00010101 10010011 00000111 10111111 01011010
01000010 01001000 00111100 11110011 01001100 10011010 01011100 00001100 10001110 01110011
01010001 10110100 10011100 11110010 01101011 01000110 11011000 00110000 01111111 10111110
01000001 00111100 10011010 10101110 11101111 10000010 01111010 11010011 10100101 10010011
00000100 11100111 10101001 11101111 10001010 10101010 11110010 11110010 01110000 01001110
00111101 01001111 01111010 00100001 01001110 11111010 10110010 00011011 00011011 00110011
00011101 10011001 11101100 01101010 10100011 01001000 01111111 00001010 10010010 01101001
10110011 10001111 01011010 10001111 00111110 10111101 00111011 01010111 01100010 01011010
01101001 10110001 00110111 00010011 10100111 01010001 01010001 10111111 10110001 11100010
10011100 11011110 11011111 10011101 01000100 11100100 11100000 00010001 10000011 11110101
10101011 10000101 10111010 10010010 11101110 00101111 01101110 01111010 11010100 01101100
01111001 11111110 01110100 00010011 10010011 11010000 10010001 11101001 11101011 01001101
00100011 00100111 10001110 00111001 10101101 00010101 10101110 00100111 01111011 00000010
10000010 01001111 01000011 11000101 01011001 01001100 01100011 00011101 00001111 10111111
01111010 00111100 10111100 00000001 10001110 01110011 11111010 01010011 00000110 01000110
01000110 00111010 11110111 10101100 11101110 10110101 01101000 00010111 10011000 11100110
11001000 00111000 11001001 11001111 01111010 10001110 01101000 11111001 11000000 11101010
00101010 01000110 11111011 10100011 11010110 10000110 01010011 11010101 10001000 11100100
01010011 01010001 10010010 01111010 00000001 01010100 11110000 00000000 11001110 00110011
11000110 00101001 10100011 10101000 00011001 00100100 11100011 11010010 10100100 01100101
11110111 11100110 10000010 01001111 00011100 00000001 11101111 01011010 00111001 01101000
01001011 00011000 10100111 00100100 11110010 01000101 00101110 11100001 11010011 00011100
11010010 01100011 10101001 11101100 01101001 00110110 10010011 11011011 00011001 10100111
10111010 11010100 00010000 10111100 10000001 11111101 00101000 00000111 10001111 01001111
11000110 10010001 01000000 01010100 11100100 01110000 00111000 00111001 10100101 01100011
11010011 00000011 11101001 01010011 11010101 01011000 00000000 00000010 01001001 00011001
00011000 11110111 10100101 01010101 11011010 01110010 01111001 00111101 10101001 00011001
10000000 11100011 00010100 10011001 11001001 11110110 11001101 00110110 11011000 10000111
01110100 11111010 10011110 11110100 11101101 11000100 00000001 11000110 01101001 10011101
01111000 11101101 11011010 10011111 11000001 01110001 11011111 11010100 01010000 10011101
10110101 00101000 01010010 00001110 11011110 00001000 10100110 00101011 00000000 00111001
00100011 10011010 01111111 00011000 00100001 01001111 01011010 01000101 00111101 10000000
00011000 11110111 00010101 00110110 00011000 10101001 11010100 10001110 11010100 11110110
00100011 01100001 10100110 00110001 00011000 11100011 10011010 01010000 00110010 00111001
00111111 10011101 01001011 10110010 01111010 00010011 01110000 01010000 01010111 10111110
01111101 01000101 00111101 00110010 00110000 01000111 11100011 10000011 01001100 00100000
10011100 11100110 10001100 10010000 01110011 11010111 11011010 10011101 11110101 10111011
00011000 11110101 01100001 10111000 11110001 11000001 10100000 11100100 01110010 10110101
00011010 10110000 11001111 10100001 11101011 01010010 00110001 11110101 00011100 11010010
10010011 10010011 11011100 10110001 11111001 11001000 11011101 11101001 11011010 10011010
10100100 10011110 10111111 10010101 00110111 11011110 10010101 01111010 11100111 10110000
10100010 00001110 11011010 10010000 10001001 00110011 11011101 01111011 01110101 00010100
10101010 01110000 00111010 11110001 11101111 01010001 10000010 00110011 11101011 11011110
10011100 01001000 00000011 00100000 01100010 10000101 00011011 10101101 00000110 00101111
00000110 10010111 10011100 11110001 01001000 10100111 00110100 10100001 01111001 11000110
00111010 10001010 10000100 11011110 11000001 01110001 11111001 00011111 01001010 01010101
00111100 11100110 10100010 01100000 00000001 11111001 11101001 11100001 10000001 00111000
00000011 00010100 10101110 01011010 00101101 00100011 01100101 01110010 00111111 00111010
10011001 01110001 10001110 00001001 11111100 01101010 10100010 00010011 10111111 10001010
10010011 00100100 01110001 01010000 10100011 11010000 11010010 11011010 00010010 11100111

00000111 10111001 10100100 00100111 00111111 01001010 01000100 11000111 01100011 10001111
01101010 01101011 01100111 00011000 00111111 10011101 00100110 10101101 10111001 00101101
11011000 10010011 01110110 00000101 00111101 01000001 11001111 01011010 10001001 00111001
00000011 10011100 10001010 01010100 11101001 11010111 10000011 01001001 00101011 01101110
01010010 00101100 00101110 00111001 11100110 10010111 01110110 01001111 00010101 00011010
00110000 10100111 00110011 01100000 10000000 00000101 01100100 11000111 10111001 00101110
11100010 00000110 01000001 11111101 00101001 00010101 10000001 11111001 10110001 11001101
01000110 11001100 01000011 10000000 01000111 00110100 11011111 10010111 00111110 10010101
01101110 11101011 01110001 00010011 11100100 11100100 01010011 11110010 10111000 00100010
10100011 11100000 10000001 10000001 11010010 10001101 10100011 00100111 10000011 10001110
10111101 01101011 00100100 10101111 01100100 00001111 01000001 11011001 11100011 10011010
01000010 00000000 00111000 01101100 11110011 11010010 10011000 00111000 00011111 00101110
01111110 10010100 10011001 01100110 00100011 00100011 10100101 00100110 10010110 11101000
01100011 11010100 00010001 11010100 11010010 10110111 01001111 01010010 01111101 01101001
00011011 10010001 11001111 01011110 11010100 11000101 00011101 01111001 10101011 10000100
10010010 01011010 10001001 10101110 10100010 10110011 01111100 10111111 00101111 11101001
01000010 10010110 11100100 11010011 10000000 11100010 10011011 11001001 01001100 10001010
01110111 01001111 01100100 00001011 01010001 11001110 01001111 01010000 00101000 11101011
11001110 01110001 11000111 01111010 01101000 11011101 11001000 11100000 10001010 00011100
10001101 11011000 00110101 00001110 01101110 11100011 11010001 01101000 11000111 00100110
01110011 10001100 01100100 01010010 11100100 00010001 11111000 11010010 01100011 00100011
00100000 11010011 01010001 10110011 11110101 10100110 10010110 10110111 00001101 00000111
01100100 11100000 11101101 10100110 10111001 11111001 11000110 00111001 00111111 11001010
10010011 00100111 00111001 10100101 00111101 01111000 11001000 11001111 10100101 00110111
01110111 10110000 01011010 11111010 10100000 11100100 01110011 11000110 00111010 01010011
11111110 01011110 10000011 10101111 01110011 01001100 01100010 00001000 11011011 10001100
01010000 00110000 00110001 11010111 00000110 10011010 11011011 01100001 11111010 10000111
00000011 11011110 10011101 10011100 10010001 10001110 11011110 10110100 11000000 11000011
00100111 00010100 00000011 10011100 10010000 00101010 00010010 01001111 01010001 01101110
11000111 10010011 10111001 11111001 11000000 11110110 10100011 10100001 11001000 10100110
01101110 00000100 10001100 00011100 10011110 11110100 10101010 01000001 11110101 00100010
10011101 10111010 10001110 11011010 00000010 10011111 01000011 01001111 00011001 11100100
11010100 01111000 00000000 01101110 00011001 11110111 10100100 11101110 00110011 11010011
11010010 10000110 10101101 10110000 10011010 00100100 01011100 10001111 01110011 11101011
01001011 11110111 10010011 10011100 01100111 10101101 00100110 01000000 00111100 11100011
11111010 11010011 01011000 10011111 10101101 00001101 11011101 11101010 00110111 01100001
11001000 01001001 00111101 01110011 01001110 01110001 10010100 11101011 11001000 11101011
01010001 01100100 10000000 00110110 00001110 01111011 11010001 10111000 11100111 00000100
11110010 01101000 10110111 01000100 00100110 01001000 10111001 00100011 00100000 10000000
01111101 11101001 00110010 01001111 01111100 00011110 11111100 11010000 01111000 11000110
00110001 11010110 10011000 01011011 10110110 11010011 10001111 01010001 01000010 01001101
11101010 01000011 10110001 00100010 00110110 00111011 11010010 10101000 00000111 11110101
10101000 01111010 10011110 10011000 00111111 01011010 01011100 01100101 01111000 00011101
01111011 11010000 10010110 10111010 00010110 01001010 10101100 01111010 00000011 10000001
11111100 11101001 10111001 11101011 10011110 00001111 10100101 00110000 10011100 00001110
10011111 01011010 00001001 00000001 00000110 00001111 00110100 11011101 10101100 00111101
10001001 01001001 11101000 00110001 11010110 10011010 00000110 00000101 01000111 10010011
10000001 11101011 01000011 11101110 11101000 00000111 00000111 10111101 01000100 01010101
10011000 10000111 01110010 00001110 01010111 10001010 01001100 11111100 10111100 10011010
00011000 10011110 00110010 00101000 11001111 00011100 10001110 00110011 11010110 10110100
10010100 01011010 01111010 00000101 11000101 00001101 11110010 01110011 11010100 11010010
01110001 11101011 11111001 01010010 01111010 11110001 01001100 11011010 00000001 00011000
11101001 01001111 10010101 10100101 01110110 00000100 10111011 10110001 11000110 00110011
11101011 01001110 01010110 00001101 11101101 01010000 10101100 10000101 01001110 00101001
11011100 10010001 11111111 00000000 11010111 10100011 01001011 01011100 01110110 00010111
01110111 10100111 01000000 01111111 00111010 00001111 00000111 11101011 11111010 01010011
00011001 01000000 00111100 01100100 11010011 11010111 10011100 00010000 01110011 01000100
10101111 10110000 00100111 10101000 10011001 00000000 11110100 11111100 01101001 10101101
10000001 11010100 01110011 11101101 01001110 11001000 11001111 11110011 10100110 10110000
11001001 11000111 10111101 01000111 10011011 00010011 10111101 11000011 01101001 00101001
10010001 11111000 11010010 00110000 01101100 00000001 10001010 10010001 00000001 00011100
01010010 00101001 11101101 10011010 00111001 10011111 01010001 11101000 00110100 01111011
01010011 10011111 10100110 01110000 00101001 10101100 00001111 10111111 00110100 11111100
11100101 00000111 00000110 10101101 00111011 00101101 11000100 00100100 01000011 10000000
01110001 01001011 10001100 11110101 00010100 01101101 00100000 10001111 01011110 11110100
11111101 10100011 10110011 01010010 00001011 11011000 10101010 10001011 00011010 00001110
11111000 00111001 10100001 01001110 00111000 00101100 01001001 11110101 00111101 10000101
00110101 11100101 01001100 00000101 00011101 10111010 01100010 10010111 00100001 01110000
01001010 10011100 10011010 11101000 01110001 01101001 01011110 01001000 11001001 10010011
10100001 11000001 11101001 01001101 01011110 10100100 10011010 10001011 00111100 11110001
11101001 01001011 11001110 00111011 10001111 10100001 10101001 10010100 01111011 10001111
01110010 01011100 00011111 11100000 11000111 10101101 00100010 11100111 00111001 00110101
00011010 11101111 00100111 11100100 11101000 01101010 01000001 11110010 10000010 00011100

```
11111110 00011110 10010101 00001010 10011010 10110110 10000011 00011110 11000100 10000000
00111001 11100100 11010010 10000010 01001010 01100000 01111110 00111001 10101000 11110111
01110100 11100111 11101001 01000000 00111100 11110010 01110001 11110101 10101000 11110111
10010011 01010111 00101011 10100001 00111000 11111011 10011001 00011000 11001111 10111101
00100110 00110000 00111001 11101011 11010110 10100011 00100000 00011100 01110011 11010110
10011010 01001001 00100011 10101111 00010101 01110010 01001101 00111111 01111000 10000110
10011001 00100011 11001000 01110110 10100110 01111010 11010011 11000011 01110100 11101101
01010000 01110010 01111010 01110100 00111101 10111101 00101001 11001100 01110110 11110000
00001111 11001110 01111011 01010100 10101010 01101011 10100001 01011101 00001011 00011011
10110000 01111001 11100010 10011010 01011011 00100011 10100111 00110101 01011111 00100111
00000011 11110111 01100100 10111000 11101111 10011010 01111001 11100100 01100010 10101011
10010010 11011011 00001010 11100100 11101000 11000001 01001110 01001101 00011100 00110111
00011001 11100111 10101001 10101000 01011000 11100111 00000011 10100000 00010100 11110110
00000011 00000111 00011100 00011110 10011100 01010001 01110100 10110100 01100000 10110101
00010111 00000011 00111000 01101110 10011001 11101011 01001110 01010110 01010000 01101010
00001110 10101100 00010111 00111101 00110011 11001101 00101111 00000111 10101111 01011010
11001101 11110010 10110111 10100000 00010011 00111100 10100011 00011001 11000111 01011010
01101010 10001101 11011100 00011010 10001101 10000111 01111110 11110100 10011011 10111000
10100111 01110111 01111101 00001011 01000101 10001100 10000000 00110010 01111101 01111000
10100100 11101001 11011111 10001010 10000001 00001110 01010100 10000011 10011110 01101010
01001000 11001000 11011011 10000010 00001111 11010010 10100101 10110111 01101011 11110100
00010011 01100000 11011100 11110010 00001101 00000100 10001110 00111101 01101001 00000110
00001100 10011000 00011001 00100100 11111011 01010011 01110000 01110111 10001100 00001110
10010100 10010010 10010011 00000101 10101001 00111111 01010001 10010011 01001001 10010000
00000111 00011101 01111101 11101001 10100100 11100111 00000111 11110001 11100010 10000010
00000111 01011100 11010010 10110011 00000100 10101100 00000101 10110000 10000111 00011000
11001111 10111101 00000010 01001110 00110000 01000110 00001001 11101111 01001101 11101001
10011101 11000000 10010011 01001110 01011110 00010011 11111001 11010000 11101111 01100001
11011000 01001100 10010001 11110010 10001110 11111101 11101000 01100011 10000001 11101010
01101001 00110111 01100000 11110100 00111000 11110101 10100011 00111011 10100101 11100000
01100010 10101001 00101011 10101101 10000111 11101000 00011011 10011011 01100001 11000000
11101101 11011110 10010111 01110001 00001010 00000111 01000001 11101101 01001001 11000010
10011100 10010010 01001110 01101001 01110111 00001101 10011101 00101010 01101111 11001010
11000010 11011101 01000101 11011101 11001110 00111011 11111010 11010010 01101110 00100111
10011100 00011110 00111010 01100110 10011110 00110001 10110000 11100111 10111000 10100010
00100110 01010011 10000000 00001101 01010010 01001110 11011101 10001100 11011011 11010100
10001111 00110010 01110100 11110101 10100101 00000101 10110000 01111011 00000011 01000100
10011001 11001001 11110100 11100011 10100101 00101010 10000011 10001100 11100111 00100011
11011111 10110101 01010010 10111011 00101000 01001110 01111011 01010000 00001110 01001000
00111000 11100111 10111101 00011000 00100000 01110101 10100100 01100011 11100101 10001100
11100110 10100110 11010010 01101100 00010011 01000101 11001101 00111010 00111101 11010111
10010001 10101001 11001110 00110011 10010000 01000111 10110101 01110110 00110000 10000001
10001110 01111000 10101110 01011011 01000001 10001100 00011001 11001011 10010001 10011100
01110100 00111101 10101011 10101010 10001001 10000110 11000001 11111010 11010110 00110101
10100011 10101101 10101100 00110111 01100001 11011100 10001010 01100001 11100111 10000000
01111111 00001010 00000011 00011100 01111010 11111010 00011010 01000110 01011111 01111100
00010011 01010001 11010011 01000100 00100100 10001010 11110010 01100001 10010011 11110001
10101010 10101101 10000011 10010010 00101010 11010011 10001100 01100100 01110011 11000001
11101111 01010101 11001000 00011000 11111100 01101001 11110011 10100110 11101100 11001010
01001000 10000001 10000000 01101110 11010100 11001101 10011011 01101010 01100111 00000000
01010100 01100001 10000001 00000111 00111110 10110100 01011011 01011011 00110000 01100100
01101100 01001111 00100011 00010100 00000010 01111010 00011110 01101000 10010100 10010110
11101000 00001110 00101001 10111001 00111001 00100100 10001110 00101010 10010010 01010110
10110000 10101110 00110111 01110111 01011110 00101010 00010110 11000000 10100111 10111011
00010101 11000110 11101110 01111101 01101010 00110011 11001111 01101100 00001110 11111001
10100100 10100010 11000001 00001100 00101101 10000001 11001111 01101010 10101110 11101101
10011100 10110111 10111110 01101001 11110010 11001000 00000111 11011100 00111100 11111111
00000000 00111010 10001001 11111001 01001100 10010011 01010110 10010011 10001010 11010100
01000011 00100101 01101100 11100000 00101111 11100111 01010000 00111011 01111010 01110011
11111000 01010011 10011001 11111101 00101010 10101011 11001000 01000001 00111100 01110001
11101001 11101111 01011011 01000001 11101000 01001011 01101100 01110100 10110010 00001110
10100000 10011111 01111010 10101110 11101100 00000000 11111100 00111011 11010011 00100101
10010000 10001111 10101101 01000000 11111001 00100011 00000100 11110101 00111001 11100110
10111010 01111001 00100101 01101101 01001001 10111111 01100001 11011001 00011101 01111011
11111010 01010011 00111110 01010001 11111100 01011101 01111010 01110001 01000110 00111010
11100100 11100100 11010010 00000000 01111010 10011010 10111101 01111010 10100010 01101110
11000011 00111100 01111010 10001111 01111010 01101001 00000011 10000001 10001100 01110111
11110110 10100111 00100001 11000110 00110010 00111010 11110110 10100110 01001000 11000111
00100100 01110001 11000001 10101001 11011000 01000010 01100111 10010010 00000111 01001111
11100111 01001110 10110101 01011101 11010011 00010010 01111001 00000010 10100011 00011000
11001001 00011111 10010101 01011111 10110101 01011111 00101110 00110001 11000111 01011110
01110011 01010100 11011010 01000101 00100101 01110001 10001110 00001001 11000111 01000000
00000111 10110101 00110110 01001110 00001111 10111001 11110100 10101011 00100100 01110011
```

```
10000011 11010010 10100000 01101100 00000011 10000011 11010110 10110011 01010101 00011010
00011101 10011001 00010010 11110010 01110001 10011111 11001110 10010001 11000001 01011110
01110011 01010010 01101101 00100000 01100111 00011100 00011010 00011000 00011100 11100011
10101101 01101010 10100110 01000011 01010110 00100010 00111001 01100000 01000111 10111111
10101101 01000001 00101000 00100001 11111001 00011100 00001010 10110100 10001010 00000000
00111101 10001001 11110101 10101000 11100101 00011000 00011110 10110100 10010110 11110111
01000010 01100100 00111100 00010011 10001100 00011100 11110110 10100110 01001101 11001001
11000111 01011100 01010011 11111011 01100101 01000111 00010100 11010101 11101000 00110001
11101001 10010010 01101011 01011011 11110101 00010011 01000000 00001111 00000011 11010111
11011111 10111101 00110101 10010100 10101110 01001000 00011001 10101001 01010100 00000111
00000111 11011010 10010000 10001100 11110011 10011110 01111011 01010110 01111010 11110101
00001111 01010010 00111000 10110010 01110011 10111011 10111111 01101010 01011100 01100011
10100111 01111010 01010010 00111000 11000000 10100100 01101100 10001111 10100001 11101010
01101000 01001100 01000010 10111000 11000000 11000110 01110010 00111011 11010000 10000011
00100111 00100011 10100101 00100110 00000110 01001111 00011111 10101101 00101010 00110110
11000000 01110000 10100000 10011010 11010011 01110001 00010010 01100000 00000010 00000001
11101001 11010010 10100011 01011110 01001110 11001100 11100011 10011110 10110100 10010001
10111110 11110110 11001000 00000100 01100011 10000010 00110011 01010010 11101101 11101111
01010000 11011110 10111010 00000010 11110010 00010011 01101110 11010011 10011100 11110011
10001010 01010110 01001110 00000001 00100100 01100010 10001101 10111000 11110111 10100111
00101111 11010011 00011000 10100010 11001001 11101010 01011101 10101100 00011101 00001001
11110111 10100110 01100100 00010011 10000011 11010010 10011111 10000010 11000111 11010111
11010010 10000000 00110111 01111111 11111010 11101000 11010000 00000011 00011000 11101011
11011111 11110101 10100001 10111011 00010011 10011110 10010100 10100111 10000001 11110100
11101000 01101001 00001001 11100011 10011111 11000000 01010000 11010010 01011010 00000010
11010000 01010001 11110100 11001110 01001111 01011010 00110000 00110110 11100011 00111100
11100111 10011010 01010100 00111111 00100111 01101110 01101001 11011011 01001111 01001110
10011100 11100110 10010110 11100000 10000110 10111010 10101010 10001110 00111010 11010000
00001111 00000011 11111010 11010000 11100011 00000111 00000000 01110011 01001110 00000100
01100011 00111000 11001001 11101001 01000010 11011010 11101000 01110111 00010100 00001100
11110110 11100010 10100100 01001100 01100011 00000100 11110000 01101001 10001100 00001111
01011100 01110110 10100111 00000001 10001110 10111110 10011101 01101001 01000101 10111000
11101000 00001000 01101001 01011101 11011001 11110110 10100111 11100011 00011101 01000000
11001101 00100011 00110110 00101001 11001011 11110111 11001111 00011001 11100011 10111101
01000100 11010101 10010101 11010001 01000011 10100011 00100000 10011100 11010100 10111000
00111111 01011100 11010100 01010001 01100000 00110111 01001111 10101101 01011000 01001111
01011110 10100011 00110101 00101001 10100100 11010101 11001010 01001100 00000010 10000010
00001001 00000011 10000000 00111001 11000101 00101010 00000011 11100101 00001101 11100010
10000110 00011001 11001001 00011111 10001110 00101001 11101010 10100100 01100000 11110001
10000011 11101011 01000111 10110100 01010111 10111101 10000011 11010100 01100010 00001110
01001010 11110110 00110100 00100010 01100011 10000010 01101001 11101000 00110000 11000100
10001100 01111010 00011010 00010001 01111001 00111100 01110011 01010001 10100100 10000110
10011011 11101000 00110101 01011011 00011100 01100010 10100110 01010110 00011000 00101101
11011010 10011001 10000011 11100110 00010011 10011110 00110001 01001011 00010111 11011100
11110110 10101100 11100110 11111010 10100000 00011110 11101100 01001110 00000111 01101100
11110110 11101111 01000011 00101000 11001110 00001111 00000110 10100100 01000101 00011101
01000101 00100011 01110010 01110010 01001111 11100111 01010010 11011111 01010110 01010011
01011010 01101000 00011101 00111000 10100001 10110010 01111011 11111110 01010100 10111011
01110010 01000111 10100001 11101101 10011010 00110001 10110100 11110101 11111010 00011010
10111011 10100101 10100110 11000000 11000110 01111111 00001110 00001001 11111100 10101001
11111101 00001001 11001001 11000000 11110110 10100011 11100101 00101011 10010101 10100110
00100001 11001111 01011110 10010101 00011011 00111011 10001011 01010110 00111011 10100001
11001000 00110100 11011100 10000010 01110001 01001111 01010000 00110001 10010000 00111001
10100000 00101000 01101100 10011110 10000110 10001011 11011001 01011100 01110111 11101110
00000000 00001100 00011111 01001010 01100011 01100011 10101111 11100101 01001111 00100000
01101111 00011100 11110001 01001000 11011000 11101100 00001110 00101001 10100110 11000101
01111101 01110100 00011011 10111011 10000000 00101001 00110110 10001111 00110000 00011110
11110101 00100110 11010000 01000110 00101000 11111001 01000011 00011110 00110010 01110001
11011100 01010011 01110100 11101100 00110001 10000100 11110011 01000010 10001110 11111001
11100110 10011110 00001000 00000000 11110000 01110011 11111100 10101001 10011100 01100111
00111001 00111001 11111110 01110100 01101011 01100001 10100001 11011100 10000011 10011100
10000011 01000011 01100001 10111011 11110011 01000011 00001101 11000011 11011000 01010000
10000000 01100111 11110101 11001101 00100111 10100110 10100010 01100011 01111010 11100000
01110111 10100100 01101101 11011000 10101001 00010100 11111010 01110000 01101001 00111001
00111001 11000000 00011111 10011101 01010010 01101110 11001100 00010001 00011110 00001111
00011110 10111101 01101010 01000101 11011100 00111011 01010010 11100011 00000100 10010001
01000001 00100100 01111101 00111101 11101010 01111001 10101110 10111100 11000111 10100101
11001000 11011001 01110000 00001111 00111101 01101000 11000110 00001110 00001001 10100111
10110001 00100111 10001010 01101011 01100111 00111101 00111001 10100110 11011101 11110101
00000110 00000100 01110010 00000111 11100011 01001110 11110010 11111001 11110110 10100110
11100100 11110110 11101011 01010010 00110011 00010000 01110000 00000110 01111101 11000000
10101001 11010101 01101011 11010000 00110101 00011010 10010001 01100100 00111000 11000111
01011110 11110100 11010101 10001100 10101010 01110001 10011100 01111011 10011010 01111111
```

```
10011000 11000100 00010001 10110110 10011111 10111000 10000101 00000000 11010100 11101010
00001110 11100100 01100000 01111011 01110111 11101011 10011010 01010010 10111100 10011100
00011100 10001111 11100111 01001001 10000011 10011110 01001111 11101001 01000110 11101100
00010001 10001010 01101101 10101011 01011000 01111010 00001101 00111001 11011111 10001110
00110001 11011110 10000100 00011001 01111110 00000110 00111101 10101000 01010001 10010010
01001111 00100000 01010011 11110011 10001111 01100011 01001001 01011111 10100000 10011010
01000010 00001000 11111110 01000010 01001111 01011010 01100011 00000110 00011100 01010000
11001100 01001111 00000000 11100110 10010100 11100100 01110001 01011010 01001010 01110110
11011000 00010010 00011011 11100101 10010000 10011111 10101101 00000101 01111010 00011100
11110101 10101001 00110000 11011000 11001110 01111010 01010000 00111101 11111011 11010010
01010110 10111110 10100001 11010100 10000000 11000110 01001011 00001111 01010001 01010010
01111001 01100100 01100100 11101110 00100110 10011110 00000101 00001010 01111010 11110011
11110101 10100101 01111110 11000000 11101100 11000110 11100011 10010001 01001000 11001011
10010011 11010110 10100100 11001110 01001000 11011000 01101001 10001110 00111111 00111100
11010101 00100100 11011111 01010001 11011010 11001111 01010001 00110110 10011101 10100000
00101101 00101010 01000111 11000111 01011110 10010100 00101110 01111010 01010011 10110001
11101011 11001101 01001110 10001001 01110111 00001011 00001100 00101010 01110111 10011111
01011110 10111100 11010010 11111001 01000100 00001110 11011001 11110100 10100111 01100100
01100011 10011110 10010100 00101111 00100100 01110101 10100001 00110101 11010100 00000110
01101101 11110101 10100101 00100011 10001010 00001110 11101110 10010100 01100011 00011100
11100111 10000011 01000011 01110111 11010100 00010111 01100001 10101000 10011000 00000111
10011010 01110110 11001100 00001100 10011010 01000010 00111101 00101001 01000000 00100111
11010111 11110001 10100111 01111001 01011010 11010111 00000000 01001110 11111100 11010010
00111000 00011001 00000111 11011110 10010100 10101111 00111101 01101000 11011100 00001110
00010100 01100110 10010010 01001101 01101110 00110001 11001100 10111101 01001110 11101010
01100011 10010000 00000110 01000111 00110100 11110001 11000001 11111110 01110100 01100000
01110101 00010100 00111110 01011110 10000000 00011011 10110011 11010011 10011010 01101011
00000001 10011110 01101000 11101000 01111110 10110100 11100110 00011011 10001111 11010011
10001010 01101010 01010110 11011100 01010110 11101100 01010011 01010000 00010101 00000001
00111111 01001110 10010100 00001101 11011101 00111000 10100110 10101111 00100100 10011110
10011100 11100100 01010011 01110001 10011001 01110011 10111011 11110010 00010101 11010101
11001010 11100110 11001100 01101101 11011100 01110110 00011000 00011110 01111000 10101001
00011000 10011111 01001110 00111101 00111101 01101010 00111101 10111100 10000000 00111010
01010011 11010100 11110110 11000110 01101010 01100101 01010001 00110110 01010101 10101100
00111111 10010000 01110010 00001111 01101110 10010100 11011101 10111100 11100111 10101110
01101001 10101010 01011011 01111110 11010001 11000010 00001110 11110100 11101100 10010000
01110001 10011110 01101010 01010011 10110011 10111010 00010011 00000001 00010011 01100111
10000011 01001110 01101111 01000010 01111000 10100000 00001100 00011110 01001111 11010110
10010101 01111001 11000111 00000011 10001010 10101101 11110101 01100010 11010100 01010011
11010111 10010011 10001110 11010100 10000000 00000010 00111010 11100100 01110011 01000100
10100000 11100111 10101101 00101100 01100000 01110111 00011100 10011010 01001101 11101110
10000111 01111011 00001110 11011010 00001010 11100111 00111111 11111101 01111010 01101011
01100000 00100110 01111101 01111000 00100111 11010010 10001110 00000001 11011011 10000010
01101000 01001001 00110010 01110001 10000011 10000011 11000101 00101000 00111011 01000111
01110000 10111101 11110110 00001100 10010001 10000001 10001110 10011101 11101001 11001011
11111110 01001101 00110011 00011110 01011111 10100111 00110101 00100010 00000001 11010011
00111000 11111010 11110110 10101011 11010001 01101010 01010010 01111101 00000011 10010110
00100011 10001110 01111101 00101001 01010011 00111100 11100111 10100111 01111010 01110000
01010001 10010001 11000111 11010000 11111010 11010011 00011010 00111100 00011100 00001110
10111001 11101011 10011010 11001011 11100011 10010101 11010000 10111101 00000101 00100000
00001110 10011101 11111011 11010011 01011100 10011100 00011110 01001111 01010001 11010010
10010101 01010100 11100010 10001110 01111011 00001100 11111011 01010100 10110100 11100010
11010011 01000010 10111000 10101100 11000011 10100000 00010100 00000001 10000001 11001001
00000110 10010001 10100010 00111100 00011100 11111101 01001111 10101101 01001000 00111001
01001100 01110001 11110101 10101010 01111100 10110001 01111010 00001100 01001110 01110011
10001110 11110100 11000101 01010110 00001110 01001110 01111111 00011010 01111010 10001100
00010011 10010011 01001011 10011110 00111101 11101001 01011101 00100101 10111000 01101110
00101010 00110001 00011001 11100111 10111101 00110101 10001001 11101011 11011110 10000101
01011101 10100100 10010010 01000000 11001111 00110100 11101100 10000110 11000111 00011111
10011101 01001011 11110111 01000001 10110010 00100100 00100100 10010010 01001001 00011101
01111001 10101001 00000001 11100011 00011100 11110000 01101001 00010100 01000111 11010011
10111000 11101111 11101011 01001110 01100000 00000110 00110010 01101001 01011101 10111101
10000011 01001110 10100010 01101110 11001000 11100000 00011110 00001111 01001010 01100010
10010011 11101000 01101001 11000111 10010000 00110000 01111111 00011010 00010111 10001100
11100011 00111100 11010101 10111000 00101111 10110100 00011110 10000000 00110001 11001110
01111010 11010010 11000111 11000011 01100111 11110011 10100011 00001010 01110000 00111011
11110111 00110100 01100100 01100100 10000000 00001001 11000101 00101011 11011011 01100010
10000101 01100011 11011111 00011110 11011100 11010001 10011110 10000011 10111111 10100101
00001101 00100000 11000110 00101010 00110100 00000000 01111101 11100110 11001001 10100100
10101101 01010011 11100010 11011100 00011011 01110110 00100100 01111100 00000111 11111111
00000000 00111100 11010010 01100100 00001110 11011000 11111010 01010000 01110001 11111000
11110110 10100101 00001010 10100000 00000010 01111010 11010000 11011010 01001111 01010100
01001010 00000010 01001011 01110001 10001010 01001100 00000000 10111100 00011110 10011101
```

10001101 00101111 00000000 10011100 01111111 00111010 00001001 11110110 11001101 00100100
11001010 01000011 01110010 11000011 11010011 00010100 10101101 11000010 01100111 11111010
11010010 10111100 10000000 10001100 01100011 00010100 10001000 00000011 00011100 00000000
01110011 01010101 00011010 10001110 11111010 10010011 01110011 10100001 11110000 11111100
01100011 11001000 00001101 11010111 00110101 10110100 10111100 01111101 01101010 10001101
10000100 01111011 01100010 01000001 11010011 00000011 10011110 00110001 01010110 10001110
00000001 11110111 11001101 01100001 01010001 10110111 00101011 10110010 11011010 00100101
01100011 10000001 11000111 00010100 11001001 00011011 10001110 10111000 00110100 10001100
01110011 01001100 01100011 11111011 11000000 00000111 01011111 01111010 10001001 00111000
11101110 11011110 10000000 01000011 00101011 01100100 10001110 01101010 00110001 10001110
01110000 01111111 00011010 10010001 11000000 11110100 11100110 10100000 01101110 10000101
01101011 00110110 10010011 01101010 11001100 00000100 11000110 01110010 00111111 01011010
10000000 10001100 01110001 01010110 00000000 11100010 10100010 01110101 11000001 00100001
10001111 01011010 10110110 10101100 10110100 00010011 01000011 00110010 01001000 11000111
10101101 01000100 01110011 11010011 00111101 00111111 01011010 10010001 11111000 11101001
11010110 10100001 01010011 10000001 11001000 11100111 11011110 10001011 00111011 01110011
00110001 11011000 10001110 01010110 00101010 00110000 01110001 10000011 01010101 10111100
11000011 11010110 10101100 11001011 10000011 11111110 00010101 01001100 11100100 00010011
10001100 01111110 00110101 01010001 10111011 01010110 10111000 10110111 00011010 11000100
00010000 01000110 01111001 11101001 01010000 11001001 11001111 01011110 10100010 10011101
00100111 11001010 01001001 11101011 11011111 10001110 11110101 00011100 10000111 00111000
00011101 00000001 10101101 11100001 00001110 01100111 01101011 10000101 11001000 00011100
11110010 00000000 11111100 01101010 00101001 01001001 11100100 00000011 11001111 10101101
00111010 01101100 00000011 10011010 10101110 11101101 10111000 01100000 11111110 00000110
10110110 10001010 10001101 11101110 01000011 01101101 10010001 10111001 11001011 10001101
11100011 00000111 00110101 00011011 00011110 01111001 00011100 11110110 10100111 01100000
11100111 11101011 01001100 11011101 10010001 11010011 00000110 10110101 01010111 11011100
10000101 01111110 10100011 00011011 00111100 00011100 11110111 10100001 11011011 11011011
10011111 01011010 00011011 10010011 11001000 10100001 10011000 00011110 11011111 01110010
10110100 10110011 11011101 00010100 11110101 00011011 10010011 10011100 00010110 11101001
01000110 01110010 01111101 00101000 01110001 10011100 10010011 11111000 11010011 00111011
01100100 01110100 00100010 10010011 11010011 11100010 00100000 10010110 00000100 00010010
01001001 10011110 11010101 10100100 01011000 00000001 10001100 01110111 11101101 01010100
11110100 11011000 11110001 10111101 10110011 01011010 00001100 10100011 10001110 00000110
01101011 00111010 10101101 00101011 00101011 10010111 00010010 00110111 11101001 11101010
00101010 00111001 01100011 11011100 00000001 00000111 10110101 01001000 11000000 00010000
01111101 00111010 11010000 10101011 10000111 11000110 01111000 11000000 00110101 00101001
01011001 01101010 00111101 11001010 10011110 01011000 00000011 10101110 00001111 01100011
01000010 10000001 10011110 01001001 11111111 00000000 00011010 01111011 01100011 00100100
11100111 10101001 10100110 00100100 01100000 00011100 11110010 00000000 00110101 10110010
10110011 01011010 00010001 11100100 00001100 00000110 01111111 10100101 00110001 10010100
00010010 00101001 11000100 00001111 00110011 00111110 11111100 01010011 01001011 01101101
00111000 00011001 00100100 10011110 01101001 01011001 00110110 00100110 01000011 00101010
10001110 11011110 10110100 11010110 11000001 11101111 10000001 11101011 01010110 00011100
01100111 00111000 00000111 00100110 10100010 00100000 11101101 11100111 11110010 10100110
10011011 01101110 11000000 11110100 00100011 11100011 10001100 01111110 00010100 01110000
01000110 00111101 11101000 01011100 01101101 00011000 11101101 11101101 01001000 01011100
00000110 11101001 11111010 01110101 10101011 01111110 10100100 11110101 00010101 00110000
01001110 01000001 11100011 10111101 00010010 11100000 10010000 00110001 11001101 00101011
01100001 10110000 00000000 11000101 00110111 01101001 01010010 00000111 00100100 01111011
11010001 00010110 10010000 11101101 01100000 11000110 00111101 11101001 01000110 11011110
01000001 11100010 10010101 00011000 11101110 11000001 11101111 01001110 11101011 10010011
11000101 00111011 01000101 10111011 10100001 01011000 01101011 01100000 00001010 01000101
11000001 11100111 10110111 01101010 01111111 00000011 00011001 00011001 11101111 01001010
11100100 01100000 11100011 10000011 01010001 01100101 01101101 01000101 00010101 10101110
10100010 00010001 11111010 11010001 10111000 11100011 10101111 00011110 10110100 10100000
00000101 11101101 11010111 10101101 00100011 00001100 10010001 11010011 11101011 01001010
00101101 10110111 10100001 01111101 01000101 01010110 11101111 11111001 01010010 00111001
00111011 11001001 11000110 00000101 00101011 01110010 01000000 11000101 00101011 10011100
00010001 11111110 01110011 01000011 01010110 01111010 10001000 01101110 01110010 01000110
00000111 00011110 11110100 11101101 10100001 10110010 00111111 00111010 01111011 00000001
10010001 11101011 11011110 10011000 11100011 10001101 11000011 10100101 00111011 00100100
10110101 01100000 00001000 10100000 00011111 01111010 01110001 00000100 10011111 10010111
11110001 11001101 00110000 00010011 10111100 00011100 01100010 10011110 10100000 11110111
10100011 01010000 00010111 00000100 00001111 11110000 00010100 10101100 01111001 00111000
00010100 10001011 11001000 11100111 10110101 00101110 01111110 01000001 10000001 11001111
01111110 01101010 01010010 10110011 01001101 10010100 10110110 10110000 11101100 10110001
11000000 00110100 11100000 10100100 10011110 10111000 00011101 11111000 10100110 10100000
11100111 00110100 10101110 01000110 01001111 00011111 01011010 01101001 00100100 11110101
00101010 11001000 00011100 01100011 10100001 10100100 01100010 01111000 00110100 10110010
10001110 00000110 00101000 01010000 01110000 00111101 11001101 01100111 00110101 10101000
10011110 10000011 11000011 01100100 10001111 01011111 11100101 01010011 00100110 00001110
01111101 10101010 10111010 11110001 11001111 01011110 01001111 00110100 11110101 01100001

11010000 11010000 10101110 11110100 00011010 10110001 01100011 00100011 00000111 11011110
10010111 00100111 00011100 00011110 10011110 10110100 11010100 01100101 01010011 11010011
00100010 10011101 10010101 00011001 00100100 01110001 01011001 11011001 11000011 01100010
10000001 01000001 11000111 01011100 01010011 10111110 10000110 10001100 10001100 01110011
11000101 00011100 01110100 00010101 01010110 01001110 00110111 01100001 01110000 00000001
01001001 00111011 10111111 00101010 01010101 00100011 00100000 00001100 01100011 10111101
00110000 11101110 11101101 01000011 00101111 00011100 00011110 01001000 11101011 01011000
11101011 01110000 01001010 11000101 10110001 10000010 01110001 11111010 11010001 10000001
10011100 11111011 01010101 01111000 10011000 01100000 10011100 11010101 10000000 01110011
10000001 11011010 10101011 01011111 10001000 10101011 00000111 10010111 10110111 00000100
10011100 10000011 11010010 10000110 00011111 00101000 11100010 10010001 11111000 11100010
10011010 01001110 00111011 11100100 11110111 10101001 01101011 01011111 00100000 01100011
11010101 01010100 01111011 10000011 01000111 11001011 10110111 11101110 11110001 11101100
00101000 01010000 01001111 01000000 01110001 01000001 11001110 01000000 11000111 11100011
01010011 01111001 00100010 01000001 10001111 00111000 11000001 10100101 01011110 10111000
11001111 00111110 11110100 01110011 10001110 01111000 10100110 10101001 11000011 01100111
10110111 01010001 01000010 10001011 01101111 01000110 00011110 10100010 11100100 01110011
11110111 11110010 00101001 00111100 11110101 00101111 10110100 00000011 11111000 11010010
11110010 00111010 10011110 10111101 00101001 00011001 01001111 01000000 00000110 01110011
11010110 10011101 10101101 01101011 10010100 00101001 00100000 00101111 00011001 11001101
00000000 00000010 00111001 10101000 11111001 00000100 00000011 11010111 10111101 00111111
00011101 11111011 01111010 11010011 10111101 11000001 00001101 00100011 10011110 10100100
11100010 10011100 01011000 00011110 11010100 11010001 11010111 00000000 11010001 11010000
01111101 00101010 01110111 00001101 01000011 11001101 00011001 00101000 01000111 00100010
10011100 01001110 00000110 00111101 11101001 10011100 00110111 01000001 11001001 11101111
01000011 01000111 10110100 11110101 00110101 01010010 10110011 01110110 10110000 01011001
01101110 00011001 11100111 10001010 00011001 10001000 11101001 11000001 10100110 01110100
01101100 10000010 01101001 11101001 10011110 10100110 10100110 11101000 00110111 00001111
10011011 11001011 00111100 11100010 10011000 10011011 10001001 11000011 11110010 00101010
01000101 00011001 00111101 01111111 00001010 01110001 11001111 01100011 11001101 00011010
00110101 10100001 01000000 10011000 00000111 00100100 10011100 01010011 10011100 10000011
11010011 10011100 01110011 01010001 11100000 10110111 00000111 00000011 00111101 01110001
01001111 01101000 10001000 00100001 01000001 11000111 10111110 01101011 00110100 11101100
01001000 01100100 11100000 01110001 01000010 10111001 11101000 10111001 11000001 10100100
11011101 11110011 00010101 11100000 10001111 01011010 01010010 11000000 10100000 00011110
11111101 11101010 11011100 10011011 11011100 01100011 00001100 10000011 00100011 01110111
11100111 01001110 11001000 00100010 10010101 01001000 00000001 11110111 00001100 10011100
11010010 10100000 00011101 11111000 00000110 10101010 11110001 10110000 11011011 00100011
01100110 00111110 10110100 11110100 11000111 01110001 11000101 00011000 00000101 11111000
11000000 11000111 11101011 01001001 11000001 01010010 00001001 11101011 11010110 10000111
00001011 00101110 01101110 10000100 10110110 00000100 10000010 01101000 01110000 00001000
11001001 11100111 11010110 10001100 00001111 01001110 10110100 10101100 00000111 01000001
01001010 11101101 00101101 00000111 10100000 10011011 01010101 01000110 11100000 01101001
10111001 00011100 01100100 11110010 01111101 10101001 11100111 00000011 10011100 00001110
00101001 10011111 00101001 11101101 11000101 00110111 00101011 01101100 00000000 11000111
00100000 10011110 01000110 01101000 11111110 01000011 10100101 00111101 00000000 11011001
10011111 01011111 01011010 01100110 01010111 10100001 11001101 01000011 01001101 11101010
00001001 01110110 00011110 00011011 00111100 10010001 11110101 10100001 10001000 00100111
10100111 11100111 01001100 01101100 01111101 01111101 01000101 00011001 00000111 00100100
11100110 10011010 01010110 01000011 01100001 10010000 00011000 11100011 10111101 00111011
11001100 11101001 10001010 01001100 01110001 11000101 00100111 01000011 10010000 00111001
11110111 10100100 10100101 11011101 00000011 11010100 00010100 10000010 00111001 10100100
01110010 00010011 10011101 10100111 00011110 10111001 10100001 10001111 11100010 00001101
00111100 01110010 00110000 01111010 01111010 01010101 00101011 11011000 00101101 11011000
00111110 01010110 00011000 10100110 11110100 11110111 00111110 10100110 10010000 10010000
00001111 10101101 00111111 00100010 10010010 11010000 00111010 10001100 11100111 10000011
01001010 11100001 01100100 00011000 11101111 01000000 11001001 01101110 11011000 11101111
01001110 01101100 00000001 10010001 10010011 10001010 10010110 11011010 01100011 10111000
11001100 00010101 11000111 11100101 01010010 01100100 10000010 00001110 01110011 01010001
10001001 01000001 00111000 01110001 10010001 11011010 10011110 10000111 10001100 00011110
10000110 10110111 10100111 10101110 10000010 01011010 01101100 00101011 00010101 00100011
10000001 11000001 11110101 10100110 00110001 11101001 10001110 00111111 10101101 00011001
00000111 10001010 00011100 01100100 11110011 10011110 00101001 00111101 01000001 10001111
11100111 11010011 11110000 00110100 11000111 11101011 11001111 00010100 11110000 01110001
10001111 01001010 01001001 01000110 01111101 01000101 01100111 01100111 00100000 01100011
01001001 11100100 01110011 01001011 10000011 11101001 01001101 00000100 01101111 00011000
01011010 01011100 10011110 11000000 11100010 10001000 10110110 10010000 10101101 01111101
11001010 00100100 01100100 01100000 00011110 00101001 01010101 01001000 10001111 11011011
11111010 01010011 00010100 10000010 01001101 00111101 10110000 00011000 10000010 00110010
00000000 11001000 10101110 10101000 10100110 10011011 10110110 11000111 00111000 11111110
00111000 00111001 11111100 01101001 01011100 11100011 00111001 00111110 11111001 10101000
10010101 01110111 00010000 00110011 11010111 10011110 01111010 01010010 10100110 00110110
01101101 11101101 11111100 10101001 10100100 10010111 10111100 01010101 11011001 00101110

11100001 11100101 11110011 11111000 10010001 11000101 00100000 00101011 10011110 00110011
01010101 10100101 00000100 01100000 01100111 00100000 10011110 00101010 11000000 11000000
00111000 11100111 00000011 10101001 00011101 11101001 00111011 01101110 10000111 01110010
01010000 00110010 01110001 01001100 00011000 11001111 00000000 00001111 11101011 01001000
10010010 00001110 10100100 10010001 10011111 01001010 01001001 01001001 00110001 10010000
10000111 11101001 01001110 10011011 10110011 11010100 01100100 10001101 00100001 01101110
11011111 10001101 00110101 11011011 00000001 00110001 11010100 11110111 10100111 00100001
00011000 11101001 10010011 11101011 01000001 01000001 10011100 10000101 00000001 11111101
01101010 01011101 01000100 11101111 10100000 00110101 01110001 11011001 01100000 00000110
01000111 01101100 11100110 10000100 00111011 10110011 11010010 10000110 10010000 11000111
10001101 11111101 11000111 01011100 11010100 01111001 00100000 01100101 01111000 11000101
01100111 10111111 10111100 00001010 11000100 11011100 11100111 00111000 10100011 10010011
11000110 01111000 11110101 00110100 11001110 10110001 10000011 10011111 11010110 10001000
10001001 11100100 10011010 10101101 10010010 01101001 00000001 00100001 00100100 00001100
00001110 11010100 10010001 11001000 01011000 10011010 01100100 01100100 10011001 10001000
11001111 00011110 11110100 11110101 01010000 10101110 01110000 01001110 00001111 01101010
01010001 01010111 01001101 11101100 00010111 10110110 10101000 01010000 00001111 11001110
00001001 11111010 00001111 11111110 10111101 01000110 11010010 11101101 10010111 01101111
11110000 01110110 11101111 01001010 11001111 11010111 00011101 10001111 00010101 00010110
11010000 00100100 11001111 11110011 10100010 00001010 11111010 01011000 00110111 11011100
10110001 10111001 10001010 11110011 11001110 01111101 00101001 01010111 00011000 11110100
11111010 01010100 01010001 10001100 00010010 00110010 01110011 01001011 10011110 01111110
01010001 10011010 01110101 00101001 10110100 11101110 11001011 00100100 01010001 10011110
01001111 00110100 01100000 00011110 00110011 11011110 10010011 01110110 11010010 00111000
11000101 00011000 11111001 11110111 01100011 00010101 10010111 11000010 10101110 10001001
01011010 10001011 10010000 00000110 01110011 10011110 01111001 11100110 10011100 10111000
01101110 01000111 01000001 01000001 01010000 11100011 10001010 10000110 00101110 00000111
10100111 11100001 01000011 11010111 01010100 10000110 11011110 10100100 11001001 10110100
10011110 00000110 00101001 01110010 10111101 00011011 10011110 01101010 00110000 01110000
01000110 01101001 11111000 11000110 01110010 01111000 11110101 10101001 01001011 10011011
01110111 01100001 01101000 00111011 10001100 01100011 11110001 11100110 10000110 00100000
10010010 00110001 11000000 00010100 11101100 10101110 01110011 10001110 01110001 11010110
10000001 10000110 11001000 00100111 10010001 01001110 01001111 10100101 11101110 01010110
10000011 00110010 00000001 11000110 01111000 11000101 00101110 11100000 10000000 01010001
10011100 00001110 00110010 00001110 01101000 01101110 01000110 00110001 11000101 00011101
00110101 00100110 11010111 01111010 01101100 00100011 10010001 11000110 00111010 01010000
11001010 00111011 00011010 01010111 00100100 01110011 11010111 11011010 10011100 10100101
01110001 10010000 00111001 00111101 10101001 11000010 00001101 11101010 01010101 11101100
10001000 11000001 11011100 01111000 11101101 01001011 10011110 01001000 11000110 01000001
11100110 10000101 11001000 10010000 10001110 10011110 10010100 00110001 11100011 10100110
00001001 11101111 11101011 01001110 11001101 01011101 10100010 01110111 00011000 11111001
00101010 01110001 01001001 11100110 10001000 11010100 00000010 00111001 11110100 10100111
11110011 10001110 10000010 10001001 00100010 00101101 10000011 11010000 11010110 01001001
10101011 11101010 00001111 01000001 01010000 11110001 10010001 11011110 10101100 11011000
01000111 11100110 01011100 00100111 01011100 01100111 10011100 01010101 01110000 10100000
00000000 01001000 10101101 01101101 00011110 00011100 11001000 01100100 00111001 11000000
00011100 00001111 01011010 00100111 00111110 01000010 11010110 10100110 11101010 01110110
11100010 10010111 00011100 10000011 01001000 10111100 00000001 10011010 01011100 10000011
11000000 10101110 01000111 00100110 11011101 11011000 11101110 00111111 10100001 10100100
00100000 11100011 10001111 01011010 00111010 11110011 10000011 01001011 00101001 00011000
00011110 10110101 00111110 11010001 11001010 01011110 01000011 11010000 10001010 01010000
01001000 10101000 00011111 10101111 00010101 01100001 10001111 01100011 01010000 01001000
01000110 01001110 11010001 11000111 01101010 01110111 10110010 11100110 01000010 10110001
00011100 10011111 11100111 00010101 00010011 10001111 10100101 00111110 01000010 01001000
00000011 00010101 01010101 11011000 11100111 10001010 11011101 01110110 01100010 00000110
01100000 00111110 10110101 00001100 11010010 01111010 10001110 01101001 11010010 10111110
01111101 00101010 10111100 11000100 00011010 01110001 10111110 11110111 00010000 11010111
10010011 10101001 11101011 01010000 01001011 00100111 00110100 00111111 00100000 11111111
00000000 00111010 10001000 11100001 01000000 00000100 11111011 11100110 10011010 10001010
01101111 01000000 10111001 00011011 10110000 00010101 01011110 01101001 00001011 00111110
00000000 11000000 11110101 11001101 00111010 01101111 11110101 10011001 00000111 10101101
01000011 00101001 00100000 01111010 11010111 01000010 10110010 11011011 01110010 01101110
01000110 11000100 11100111 00011000 11100011 10101110 01101010 00010111 00111111 11000010
01111010 01110110 10100111 11101110 00100000 11110001 11111111 00000000 11101011 10101000
10110010 00110010 01001111 01110010 01101011 01111000 00100101 11010100 10011101 01000110
10011100 10000001 10001010 10001101 10001110 11100000 00001111 00111101 01101010 01000111
11001001 00000111 10001010 10001111 10101000 11000000 11101011 01011010 11011001 01011100
01010110 10111000 10011011 10111111 11011001 11001000 11110111 10100110 01100100 01101110
00100111 00000111 11110011 10100111 10001110 10000000 01111010 10011110 10000110 10100011
01100000 00000001 00111001 11101010 00101010 11011100 01111001 00011001 00101100 00011000
01110011 10011111 01101110 01101000 11100011 00111101 01101001 01110000 01011000 11100101
01111000 11100010 10001000 11100011 11111001 11111000 00011101 01101001 00111011 00110111
01110001 01101111 10110001 10100101 01101011 00010110 00100011 00011101 00000111 10101111

00111101 01101010 01100110 00011000 10100111 10100001 01010000 10000011 10110110 00000111
01011010 01000110 01100001 11011000 00011110 01111011 10011010 11100101 10011011 01111011
10011010 10100001 10011000 11100111 00111100 11100110 10000110 00000111 01100001 00111100
01100111 11010010 10010111 10000000 10011101 01111001 00110100 11011110 11100000 10010000
01001111 00110100 10101110 11011011 01010111 00000110 01000001 00101010 11100100 11111011
01010100 01101110 00011011 00000000 00000010 00101010 11011011 00110000 00100000 11100000
01111110 01110101 00001111 00000011 10011111 01010001 10011010 11010001 01001101 11110100
00010101 10101111 10101011 00011010 10011111 01110100 00000010 00111001 00011110 10110100
11000000 00000011 00011110 01000111 00110100 11110110 11001111 01011010 01101001 01101101
10111001 11100011 00100110 10001101 01011010 10111000 00100110 10010000 10000100 11100011
10010010 01110001 01010001 00111000 11001010 01110000 01111001 11101111 01010011 00011101
10100111 10110111 00000000 01110100 00111100 11010011 01110110 11100111 10100000 10101101
01011101 10101111 10111001 00101100 10101001 11100110 01100001 10010000 01100011 10101111
00010100 11110101 10001101 01111011 10001110 01111101 01000101 00101011 01000110 00110011
10010011 11001101 00011001 11100000 11100000 11010001 10100101 11110100 00100010 11010110
00011001 11000110 01001110 01111000 00111111 10100101 00001101 10000010 00111010 01111110
00110100 10001010 10100100 01110010 01000111 01001110 10110100 10111001 01100000 01000000
00000011 10101111 00110100 11101111 11011000 01100000 10100011 01101110 00001101 00111000
10000000 01001110 00000110 00111101 01101001 10111101 00011000 00011110 11110100 10100000
11100100 11110011 01010011 10101000 01011000 01011110 00001010 10001100 00010000 01001111
10100111 00110100 01100100 10010011 10001100 01010011 01001001 11100111 00111101 00000101
00001101 11001011 00001101 10000111 11110011 10101011 11010101 00000111 01000001 11111111
00000000 01111000 00010001 11011011 11011000 11010001 10011111 11000010 10010001 10110010
01000111 00011111 10101101 00110111 00000101 01001000 00111000 11100010 10100101 10110111
01111101 01000001 00001111 00011011 10000001 11001110 01101001 01110111 00000110 00100000
11100011 10100101 00100010 11100010 10010011 00000101 01001111 00011100 11100111 10101101
00001001 10110110 01010011 01011101 01000111 00110111 01001111 11101011 01001110 01100011
10001111 01011100 01111011 01010011 01011000 10110111 10101111 00011101 11101001 00001001
11000000 11000110 01101000 01101001 10101110 10100100 10110010 01000110 00111100 10000010
01101001 01001001 11001000 11101011 11110101 10101000 01110010 00110001 11001110 01101001
11011000 00111110 10111101 10101001 01101111 10101000 11111010 00001111 01010011 11000000
11001101 00101110 01000111 00111110 11011101 11101010 00110110 01011101 10111100 11100100
11100111 00111101 00111101 10101000 11101010 00001001 11000001 11000110 01101010 10111001
10101110 10001010 00011110 00100100 11000000 11111110 10110100 11111101 11000000 10011100
01100011 11011111 00100110 10011010 10111111 01110011 11010100 11010000 11001010 01001000
00011000 00000011 00111101 10101010 01100101 01101011 10000101 10000111 10000010 00110011
11010110 10000110 01100000 00111000 11001111 00000111 10100101 01000110 10011101 01001110
01000111 00011001 00110100 01101110 00000101 01111001 00000011 10101101 00111011 01011111
11100001 00010011 01100100 11101010 01000110 00110001 10001010 00111100 10111100 00011010
10001101 01001000 00101110 01000111 01101010 01010101 11001001 00011100 11110110 00110101
10011110 10101001 11011000 10110010 11011010 01100001 01000111 11001101 01001010 10100100
10000011 11001000 11100100 11110100 10101000 10100010 01100011 10001100 11010100 10011000
00101100 00110010 00111000 11110110 10101001 11100110 01010111 11010100 00000111 01100111
10010001 10110111 11110010 10100001 01011011 00001111 11000111 01111010 01001110 00111010
01110101 10100110 00101010 10010000 00111000 00111100 11100111 10001010 10011111 00100001
11011100 10011011 01110110 00110011 11101001 01001101 11011100 00001100 01111001 11110111
10100100 11101001 10000010 00111010 11110111 10100001 01111001 00011000 00011101 01101010
01010010 11110111 10101100 00010111 10110000 11110000 01111111 00000000 01101010 01011000
11011000 11010101 01100101 00001100 00001001 11001111 11100001 01010010 10101001 11000000
11100100 11010110 10001111 01001000 11011000 00101111 11011100 10010101 11001111 00010100
10001000 01111101 01111010 11010011 00110111 11100111 10011110 11010100 11111100 00011110
00110110 11111110 01110101 10000111 01001011 00110010 10101101 01110001 11111110 01100111
00100011 00011001 10100110 11111001 10000111 00111000 11110101 10100001 10110111 01100011
00100000 01100100 11010000 10100111 00100000 00010010 00111001 00011110 10010101 00111100
10111010 11101000 00110001 00111001 00001111 11010100 11010010 10111001 01101100 10001110
10011000 10100111 00010000 01011011 00000111 11111010 11010011 00010100 10010001 11010010
10011111 00101101 10011110 10100010 00010101 10111001 00000011 10011010 01001100 00011100
10010001 10011100 11111011 11010011 11110001 11000110 01001111 00000110 10001100 00000000
01110000 00111010 11110101 10100001 01011101 00111011 01101110 00110111 11100110 00110000
10010010 00111000 00011100 11110111 10100101 01100110 01100001 11111000 11110111 10100111
00110111 10101110 00110000 01001101 00011111 00101111 11110001 01111110 00010100 11011010
11010100 00011110 10100011 01001001 11011010 01000110 00000111 00011000 11000110 01111101
01101001 00110011 11001110 00110000 01101001 01011100 01110010 00110011 11010011 11010010
10011101 10000101 01010000 01000110 01101011 00111011 00101011 10001010 11110110 00011010
11100000 10001110 01000101 00110101 10000001 00011101 10110011 11011110 10001100 10011100
11100011 00111101 01101001 01110000 11011100 01110011 01011010 10100111 01100000 10111000
00001100 01100110 10011110 10100100 00010001 11000000 11100111 11010010 10011011 10110000
11101110 11101101 11001111 10101101 00111001 11001110 00111010 01010001 11010000 00011010
00011011 10001101 10111001 00111101 11101001 10111100 01100011 00010101 00100111 01011100
01110011 01001101 11000111 00111100 00011010 10100111 10101010 11010000 01101000 01000100
11000000 11100000 01110001 01010010 01110010 11011101 00001110 01001101 01000111 11011011
00000111 10001111 01101010 01010100 10001111 00000111 10010011 01011001 11011010 11111011
10000111 01010000 11100100 00000010 10111001 11100010 10011110 00000111 01001100 01111110

00100110 10011000 10100100 00010010 01000001 00111101 00101001 11100011 00111001 10100001
00100110 00110110 00100011 00000010 00000111 10110101 00110111 01111000 00001001 11010000
01100111 10100110 01101001 11101100 11011000 10100011 11010100 10001100 01100110 10100110
01011010 10110001 00001000 10111101 01111001 11101011 01000010 10001100 00011100 01100111
10001111 01011010 01101111 10111111 01011010 01101011 11110011 10001010 10101011 00111011
11011001 10001100 01111011 01110101 10100111 00101001 11110111 10100110 01100111 00100001
00111101 01000001 10100100 00100111 00011100 01100000 11010100 10100101 01111110 10100000
10010011 00011110 11000111 00110100 00101000 00000111 10001110 10100010 10011011 00011110
01011011 10110110 00000000 11101010 01101000 11011101 10001100 10001100 00010001 11101000
01101011 01001110 01100110 10010110 10000000 00111001 10110010 10101101 11011100 10001010
01100011 11111100 11011100 01010000 10100111 00111100 11100111 00100111 11010010 10010111
01101000 00100000 01100000 01010100 10110111 11011100 01000011 01011000 00000101 11000001
11101111 01010010 01110110 11100111 11110011 10100101 11011011 10000001 11001101 00110001
10000010 10011110 10011111 11001110 10011111 11011001 11010100 01100010 01100001 10001001
11000000 11111101 01101011 10101100 11110000 00000010 01101001 00001100 11010111 10010010
11101011 11010110 11101001 00111101 10110010 00011000 01010011 00101100 11000100 00000100
11011110 11111011 01110111 01110000 01111010 00001100 11010111 00100110 10111011 10000111
00011001 11101001 01010011 00100101 11000100 10001001 01101101 00111100 00010001 11001000
01010010 00111001 11110110 11111001 10001010 01000000 11111001 10110110 10011100 10001111
11010110 10001010 01110010 01001010 01010111 01100010 10010110 10101010 11001000 11110100
01111011 11101111 00000001 11000101 11111101 10110000 11111010 01110010 01111110 11100010
00111011 10011011 11100100 11111011 00111100 11100000 00010110 00101011 00001001 10000110
01100111 00101010 00111001 11110101 10001111 00011111 10000111 10111101 01010010 10111010
11110000 01000110 10010111 01101111 00101010 11000100 11011010 11011000 01011001 01001101
11011010 11011010 10011000 10011011 11001011 00101111 11001011 01101101 11011100 00000010
11001000 01001000 00011001 00111101 00001110 00001110 00110011 10010000 00101011 10011011
00011110 00100111 11010111 00100100 01001011 01000101 01111101 01001010 11100011 00010110
10001100 00011110 00010001 10000101 11111001 00001000 01010010 10111001 11001110 00110010
01111000 00100100 01110011 11101011 01010000 11011111 01101011 11011010 10011101 11101010
10101111 11011010 00101111 00001011 11111100 11100010 01001101 11011110 01011010 00101001
11011100 00001110 01110011 10010000 10100000 11110101 10101101 11011101 01011010 01110010
11010001 00100011 00010100 10100111 11011100 11101100 00011011 11100001 10111011 00101010
11101010 01110000 11111101 10110101 11011010 11110010 11011101 01011010 01001000 00100001
11110010 10000111 11101111 10010000 00000001 10000011 10011100 11110001 10010010 01001000
11111100 00101001 11011010 01000111 11000011 10001000 00101111 10101101 10100110 10111000
10110111 11010100 00100110 10010111 11001011 10111000 10010010 11011111 01100100 01010001
00100001 00111111 00100001 00101010 01001001 11011100 11100000 01110101 00011111 10010001
00010101 11001000 10101111 10001010 10110101 11001111 11101101 00010110 10111110 11111110
11010010 10011011 11101101 01101101 00010111 10010011 11100110 01100001 01111110 11100110
01110011 10001100 01100011 00011101 01101010 00111011 00101101 01111011 01010101 10110001
01001000 11010110 11010010 11101111 11001011 00001000 01001011 00000011 11100101 00100011
00110000 00100100 11100100 10011100 10010101 00100111 10101001 10100001 01111011 00100100
11101111 01100010 10011111 10110101 11101000 11001111 01000000 10110111 11110000 11101110
10011101 10100111 11111000 01100110 01001001 01101110 00101101 11101100 11111110 11010111
00011101 11110001 10110111 01101001 01101111 10111100 11001100 00010101 11011101 10001110
01000100 01000100 11110011 10001110 10011101 10101010 10111111 10001000 00111100 00010111
01100100 11111110 00100001 11010100 01010110 11010110 00011001 11101100 10101100 00101101
01100001 10001101 11011001 10010000 11000110 01010100 01100111 01110110 01011000 10011001
00100100 01011100 00001111 10010111 11111001 11010111 00011101 00001111 10001010 01110101
10111000 11100010 01101000 11010111 01010000 10010000 10101011 01001000 01100101 01100000
11001000 10001101 10010111 00100111 00100100 11110010 00001111 00110100 11001111 11111000
01001010 10110101 11010001 01110001 01110011 00110001 11010100 01100111 00101111 01110000
00010101 01100101 00101100 00010100 10000110 00000011 00111000 00011000 00100011 00011101
11001111 01101110 11110100 11011101 01001010 01011101 10000101 11101100 11101010 01011110
11110111 00111010 11100100 11111000 01110001 00001011 11101011 11101001 01100000 10011010
10001011 01111001 01110010 11011001 00011011 10110101 10010011 11001011 00000100 11110000
11001010 10111000 11100001 10110000 01111110 11110110 01110010 00001101 01010110 10110100
11110000 01010110 10011011 01110111 01100111 10100011 01011101 11000101 10101001 01011110
00001000 10110101 00111001 00001100 01110000 11101110 10110110 01011101 11001010 01111001
00111001 01101111 10011111 10000001 11110010 10011110 10011001 11101101 01011100 11111000
11110001 01100110 10110110 00101110 10000101 11010000 11010100 10100110 11111011 01000010
11000101 11100100 10000111 11011010 10111001 00001001 10010000 01110001 11010011 11010100
00001010 10101011 00010110 10111111 10101010 11011011 11000011 01100001 00001100 00110111
10101110 10110001 01011001 00110110 11101011 01110100 11011010 10111111 00100001 11000001
00011001 11101001 11101110 01101001 01110011 01010010 11011101 00100001 11110010 01010100
10111110 11100100 11010111 01111010 00000100 11110110 11111110 00100100 10010111 01001110
01000010 11110010 01000110 10010111 01000010 11011011 11101101 00011110 01011001 00001010
00001001 00100000 00000010 01111101 00111010 10001110 00110011 01011011 10010111 10011110
00010100 11010011 11101101 11111100 01001111 00011111 10000111 11010110 11111110 11110001
11101111 00100100 01110100 01010011 00100001 10110111 01010001 00011000 00001100 00000001
00111100 11101111 11001111 01001111 01101110 10110101 11001111 11001101 10101111 01101010
11110010 01000011 00110100 00101101 01111101 00110111 10010111 01110011 00110000 10111000
10010100 00000000 10100011 01110100 10000000 10101001 00001101 10010000 00110010 00111110

11100010 11110100 11110100 10101011 00010011 11111000 10100011 01011010 10011010 01100101
10010001 11110101 00001001 01001100 10000001 10010101 10000011 00000100 01000000 11011001
00000111 00100011 10010000 00110011 11011010 10101001 01001110 00001000 01110110 10011100
10001101 11101011 11001111 00000100 01011001 10101101 10010110 10101111 00100101 10101110
10100001 00111001 01111101 00110010 01010101 10001010 01000001 00100100 00001010 10100001
10001001 11000111 11011101 00100001 10001111 01100011 11011100 01010101 11011001 11111110
00011110 11011000 11000111 01111111 01111101 01100100 01110101 00111011 10010011 00110101
10100101 10110000 10111001 01100110 11111011 00111010 11101101 00101010 01110011 11000000
11111001 11110011 10011111 10010100 11010111 00100001 01110011 11100010 10101101 01100110
11101010 00011001 00100000 10111000 11010100 01100100 01111000 10100100 01100000 11001110
10100001 01010001 01110111 10010000 01000001 11100111 00000000 01100111 10100000 10100010
01001111 00010100 01101011 00001111 01110101 01110001 00111011 11101010 00010010 00011011
10001011 10001000 11000100 00110010 00111110 11010101 11001011 00100000 11001111 11001011
11010011 11011100 11010100 11110011 11010011 11101000 10001001 01010001 10101001 11011100
10110111 11100010 10011111 00001110 11000011 10100100 01101001 10011010 01000101 11110101
10011101 11010100 10010011 11000011 10101000 00100001 01110101 01011001 00100010 00001000
11001000 00110000 00001111 00111000 00100100 01110111 11111101 00101011 10011101 11100111
11010110 10101110 01011110 11101010 10010111 10110111 10110110 10110110 10010110 11010111
01010111 00101101 00100100 00010110 10101011 10110010 00010100 00100000 00000000 10000011
00000000 01110110 00011001 11101100 00101010 10000011 01100100 10011100 10001100 01010110
01010101 01110111 11110111 01011001 10110100 01100010 11101101 10101001 11111111 11011001

Thanks to Brent Heeringa and Courtney Wade.

www.bradfarwell.com

www.ingramcontent.com/pod-product-compliance
Lightning Source LLC
Chambersburg PA
CBHW020730180526
45163CB00001B/174
* 9 7 8 0 9 8 8 2 0 9 3 0 5 *